philosophy	*phil*	pejorativo
		filosofia
plural	*pl*	plural
politics	*pol*	política
European Portuguese	*Port*	português de Portugal
past participle	*pp*	particípio passado
prefix	*pref*	prefixo
preposition	*prep*	preposição
present	*pres*	presente
present participle	*pres p*	particípio presente
pronoun	*pron*	pronome
psychology	*psych/psic*	psicologia
past tense	*pt*	pretérito
relative	*rel*	relativo
religion	*relig*	religião
somebody	*sb*	alguém
singular	*sing*	singular
slang	*sl*	gíria
something	*sth*	algo
subjunctive	*subj*	subjuntivo
technology	*techn/tecn*	tecnologia
theatre	*theat/teat*	teatro
television	*TV*	televisão
United Kingdom	*UK*	Reino Unido
United States	*US*	Estados Unidos
university	*univ*	universidade
auxiliary verb	*v aux*	verbo auxiliar
intransitive verb	*vi*	verbo intransitivo
pronominal verb	*vpr*	verbo pronominal
transitive verb	*vt*	verbo transitivo
transitive & intransitive verb	*vt/i*	verbo transitivo e intransitivo

Contents/Índice

Proprietary terms

This dictionary includes some words which are, or are asserted to be, proprietary names or trade marks. Their inclusion does not imply that they have acquired for legal purposes a non-proprietary or general significance, nor is any other judgement implied concerning their legal status. In cases where the editor has some evidence that a word is used as a proprietary name or trade mark this is indicated by the symbol ®, but no judgement concerning the legal status of such words is made or implied thereby.

Nomes comerciais

Este dicionário inclui algumas palavras que são, ou acredita-se ser, nomes comerciais ou marcas registadas. A sua inclusão no dicionário não implica que elas tenham adquirido para fins legais um significado geral ou não-comercial, assim como não afeta em nenhum dos conceitos implícitos o seu status legal. Nos casos em que o editor tenha prova suficiente de que uma palavra seja usada como um nome comercial ou marca registada, este emprego é indicado pelo símbolo ®, mas nenhuma apreciação relativa ao status legal de tais palavras é feita ou sugerida por esta indicação.

Contributors/Colaboradores

Portuguese–English *compiled by John Whitlam*
English–Portuguese *compiled by Lia Correia Raitt*
Revisions for the first and second editions: *Mike Harland, Sarah Bailey*
Revisions for the third edition: *Vanda Meneses Santos, Teresa Barbosa, Daniel Grassi, Helen Newstead, Catarina Fouto, Alison Aiken, Mike Harland, Mariana Cunha, Susana Valdez*

Thanks are due to/Agradecimentos a: Dr John Sykes, Prof. A. W. Raitt, Comandante Virgílio Correia, Marcelo Affonso, Eng. Pedro Carvalho, Eng. Vasco Carvalho, Dr Iva Correia, Dr Ida Reis de Carvalho, Eng. J. Reis de Carvalho, Prof. A. Falcão, Bispo Manuel Falcão, Dr M. Luísa Falcão, Prof. J. Ferraz, Prof. M. de Lourdes Ferraz, Drs Ana e Jorge Fonseca, Mr Robert Howes, Eng. Hugo Pires, Prof. M. Laura Pires, Dr M. Alexandre Pires, Embaixador L. Pazos Alonso, Dr Teresa Pinto Pereira, Dr Isabel Tully, Carlos Wallenstein, e Dr H. Martins e os membros de sua Mesa Lusófona do St Anthony's College, em Oxford.

Introduction

This new edition of the *Oxford Portuguese Mini Dictionary* is designed as a practical reference tool for tourists, students and business people alike, and it includes a host of new features to help the user get the most out of the dictionary.

The wordlist has been updated to include the latest words and meanings in both languages (e.g. *blogger, carbon footprint, social networking; avatar, ciberespeculador, mídia social*), and all the Portuguese text has been revised in line with the latest spelling reform (see also page xv). This new edition also includes notes on life and culture in the United Kingdom and the United States (e.g. *Congress, Edinburgh Festival, gap year*), as well as special treatment of complex grammatical words in both languages, such as *do, have; de, estar*. These expanded entries are presented in boxes to help the user find them more easily, and contain language notes to warn of possible pitfalls. In addition, the *Phrasefinder* offers a list of useful phrases for everyday situations, such as meeting people and booking accommodation.

The dictionary has an easy-to-use, streamlined layout. Bullets separate parts of speech within an entry, and different meanings are signposted using indicators or typical collocates with which the headword frequently occurs. The swung dash (~) is used to replace a headword, or that part of a headword preceding the vertical bar (|).

In both English and Portuguese, only irregular plural forms are given. Plural forms of Portuguese nouns and adjectives ending in a single vowel are formed by adding an s (e.g. *livro*, *livros*). Those ending in *n*, *r*, *s* where the stress falls on the final syllable, and *z*, add *es* (e.g. *mulher*, *mulheres*, *falaz*, *falazes*). Nouns and adjectives ending in *m* change the final *m* to *ns* (e.g. *homem*, *homens*, *bom*, *bons*); those ending in *ol* change their ending to *óis* (e.g. *lençol*, *lençóis*); and nouns ending in *al* change their ending to *ais* (e.g. *casal*, *casais*). Most of those ending in *ão* change their ending to *ões* (e.g. *estação*, *estações*).

Portuguese nouns and adjectives ending in an unstressed *o* form the feminine by changing the *o* to *a* (e.g. *belo*, *bela*). Those ending in *or* become *ora* (e.g. *trabalhador*, *trabalhadora*). All other masculine–feminine changes are shown at the main headword.

English and Portuguese pronunciation is given by means of the International Phonetic Alphabet. It is shown for all headwords, and for those derived words whose pronunciation is not easily deduced from that of a headword.

Portuguese verb tables will be found in the appendix.

Introdução

Esta nova edição do *Oxford Portuguese Mini Dictionary* foi concebida como uma ferramenta de referência prática para turistas, estudantes e profissionais, e inclui uma série de novos recursos para ajudar o utilizador a tirar o máximo proveito do dicionário.

A lista de vocábulos foi atualizada de modo a incluir palavras e significados mais recentes em ambas as línguas (ex. *blogger*, *carbon footprint*, *social networking*; *avatar*, *ciberespeculador*, *mídia social*) e todo o português foi revisto à luz do Acordo Ortográfico. Esta nova edição também inclui notas culturais sobre o Reino Unido e os Estados Unidos (ex. *Congress*, *Edinburgh Festival*, *gap year*), bem como um tratamento especial a palavras gramaticais complexas em português e inglês, tais como *do*, *have*; *de*, *estar*. Estes verbetes mais detalhados encontram-se destacados dentro de caixas, de modo a facilitar a sua identificação, e contêm anotações linguísticas alertando o utilizador para possíveis armadilhas. Além disso, o *Phrasefinder* oferece uma lista de frases úteis para situações do cotidiano, tais como conhecer pessoas e reservas de alojamento.

O dicionário possui uma apresentação visual simplificada e fácil de usar. Em cada verbete, as categorias gramaticais estão separadas por itens e os significados distintos encontram-se sinalizados através de indicadores ou colocações típicas utilizadas no contexto em que a palavra frequentemente ocorre. O sinal (~) é usado para substituir o verbete, ou parte deste precedendo a barra vertical (|).

Tanto em inglês como em português, somente as formas irregulares do plural são dadas. As formas regulares do plural dos substantivos ingleses recebem um s (ex. *teacher*, *teachers*), ou *es* quando terminarem em *ch*, *sh*, *s*, *ss*, *us*, *x* ou *z* (ex. *sash*, *sashes*). Os substantivos terminados em *y* e precedidos por uma consoante, mudam no plural para *ies* (ex. *baby*, *babies*).

O passado e o particípio passado dos verbos regulares ingleses são formados pelo acréscimo de *ed* à forma infinitiva (ex. *last*, *lasted*). Os verbos terminados em *e* recebem *d* (ex. *move*, *moved*). Aqueles terminados em *y* têm o *y* substituído por *ied* (*carry*, *carried*). As formas irregulares dos verbos aparecem no dicionário por ordem alfabética, remetidas à forma infinitiva, e também na lista de verbos no apêndice.

As pronúncias inglesa e portuguesa são dadas em acordo com o Alfabeto Fonético Internacional. A pronúncia é dada para todos os verbetes, assim como para aquelas palavras derivadas cuja pronúncia não seja facilmente deduzida a partir do verbete.

Portuguese Pronunciation

The phonetics shown in this dictionary are for Brazilian Portuguese. The main differences in the pronunciation of European Portuguese are shown at the end of this section.

Vowels and Diphthongs

a, à, á, â	/ã/	chamam, *ambos, antes*	1) before *m* at the end of a word, or before *m* or *n* and another consonant, is nasalized
	/a/	*aba, à, acolá, desânimo*	2) in other positions is like *a* in English *rather*
ã	/ã/	irmã	is nasalized
e	/ẽ/	sem, venda	1) before *m* at the end of a word, or before *m* or *n* and another consonant, is nasalized
	/i/	arte	2) at the end of a word is like *y* in English *happy*
	/e/	menas	3) in other positions is like *e* in English *they*
é	/ɛ/	artéria	is like *e* in English *get*
ê	/e/	fêmur	is like *e* in English *they*
i	/ĩ/	sím, vindo	1) before *m* at the end of a word, or before *m* or *n* and another consonant, is nasalized
	/i/	fíla	2) in other positions is like *ee* in English *see*
o	/õ/	com, sombra, onda	1) before *m* at the end of a word, or before *m* or *n* and another consonant, is nasalized

. . . .

	/u/	muito	2) at the end of a word, unstressed, is like *u* in English *rule*
	/o/	comover	3) in other positions, unstressed, is like *o* in English *pole*
	/o/	bobo	4) stressed, is like *o* in
	/ɔ/	loja	English *pole* or *o* in *shop*
ó	/ɔ/	ópera	is like *o* in English *shop*
ô	/o/	tônica	is like *o* in English *pole*
u, ú		guerra, guisado, que, quilo	1) is usually silent in *gue*, *gui*, *que*, and *qui* but is sometimes pronounced /w/, as in *tranquilo*, *cinquenta*, *unguento*
	/u/	mula, púrpura	2) in other positions is like *u* in English *rule*
ãe	/ãj/	mãe, pães, alemães	is like *y* in English *by*, but nasalized
ai	/aj/	vai, pai, sai, caixa	is like *y* in English *by*
ao, au	/aw/	aos, autodefesa	is like *ow* in English *how*
ão	/ãw/	não	is like *ow* in English *how*, but nasalized
ei	/ej/	lei	is like *ey* in English *they*
eu	/ew/	deus, fleugma	both vowels pronounced separately
õe	/õj/	eleições	is like *oi* in English *coin*, but nasalized
oi	/oj/	noite	is like *oi* in English *coin*
ou	/o/	pouco	is like *o* in English *pole*

Consonants

| b | /b/ | banho | is like *b* in English *ball* |
| c | /s/ | cinza, cem | 1) before *e* or *i* is like *s* in English *sit* |

	/k/	casa	2) in other positions is like *c* in English *cat*
ç	/s/	estação	is like *s* in English *sit*
ch	/ʃ/	chá	is like *sh* in English *shout*
d	/dʒ/	dizer, donde	1) before *i* or final unstressed *e* is like *j* in English *join*
	/d/	dar	2) in other positions is like *d* in English *dog*
f	/f/	falar	is like *f* in English *fall*
g	/ʒ/	agente, giro	1) before *e* or *i* is like *s* in English *vision*
	/g/	gato	2) in other positions is like *g* in English *get*
h		haver	is silent in Portuguese, but see *ch*, *lh*, *nh*
j	/ʒ/	junta	is like *s* in English *vision*
k	/k/	kit	is like *k* in English *key*
l	/w/	falta	1) between a vowel and a consonant, or following a vowel at the end of a word, is like *w* in English *water*
	/l/	lata	2) in other positions is like *l* in English *like*
l	/ʎ/	calhar	is like *lli* in English *million*
m	ambas/ˈãbuʃ/ com/kõ/		1) between a vowel and a consonant, or after a vowel at the end of a word, *m* nasalizes the preceding vowel
	/m/	mato, mão	2) in other positions is like *m* in English *mother*
n	cinza/ˈsĩza/		1) between a vowel and a consonant, *n* nasalizes the preceding vowel

xiii

	/n/	benigno	2) in other positions is like *n* in English *near*
nh	/ɲ/	banho	is like *ni* in English opi*ni*on
p	/p/	paz	is like *p* in English *p*oor
q	/k/	que, inquieto	1) *qu* before *e* or *i* is like English *k*
	/kw/	quase, quórum	2) *qu* before *a* or *o*, or *qü* before *e* or *i*, is like *qu* in English *qu*een
r	/ɾ/	aparato, gordo	1) between two vowels, or between a vowel and a consonant, is trilled
	/x/	rato, garra, melro, genro, Israel	2) at the beginning of a word, or in *rr*, or after *l*, *n*, or *s*, is like *ch* in Scottish lo*ch*
s	/ʃ/	depois	1) at the end of a word is like *sh* in English *sh*oot
	/z/	asa, desde, abismo, Israel	2) between two vowels, or before *b*, *d*, *g*, *l*, *m*, *n*, *r*, *v*, is like *z* in English *z*ebra
	/s/	suave	3) in other positions is like *s* in English *s*it
t	/tʃ/	tio, antes	1) before *i* or final unstressed *e* is like *ch* in English *ch*eese
	/tʃi/	kit	2) at the end of a word is like *chy* in English it*chy*
	/t/	atar	3) in other positions is like *t* in English *t*ap
v	/v/	luva	is like *v* in English *v*ain
w	/u/	watt	is shorter than English *w*
x	/z/	exato, exemplo	1) in the prefix *ex* before a vowel, is pronounced like *z* in *z*ero

	/ʃ/	xícara, baixo, peixe, frouxo	2) at the beginning of a word or after *ai*, *ei* or *ou*, is pronounced like *sh* in *show*
	/s/	explodir, auxiliar	3) is like *s* in English *sit*
	/ks/	axila, fixo	4) is like *x* in English *exit*
			5) in the combination *xce*, *xci*, *x* is not pronounced in Portuguese e.g. *excelente*, *excitar*
z	/s/	falaz	1) at the end of a word, is like *s* in English *sit*
	/z/	dizer	2) in other positions, is like English *z*

European Portuguese Pronunciation

The main differences in pronunciation are:

d	/d/	dar, dizer, balde, donde	1) at the beginning of a word, or after *l*, or *n*, is like *d* in English *dog*
	/ð/	cidade, medroso	2) in other positions is a sound between *d* in English *dog* and *th* in English *this*
e	/ə/	arte	at the end of a word, is like *e* in English *quarrel*
r	/rr/	rato, garra, melro, genro, Israel, guelra, tenro, israelense	at the beginning of a word, or in *rr*, or after *l*, *n*, or *s*, is strongly trilled
s	/ʃ/	depois, asco, raspar, costura	1) at the end of a word, or before *c*, *f*, *p*, *qu*, or *t*, is like English *sh*
	/ʒ/	desde, Islã, abismo, Israel	2) before *b*, *d*, *g*, *l*, *m*, *n*, *r*, or *u* is like *s* in English *vision*
t	/t/	atar, antes, tio	is like *t* in English *tap*
z	/ʃ/	falaz	at the end of a word, is like *sh* in English *shake*

Portuguese spelling reform

Brazil and Portugal are in the process of implementing a new spelling reform, which was agreed between all Portuguese-speaking countries in 1990. The aim of the Portuguese spelling reform is to standardize spellings across all Portuguese-speaking countries, and many of the spelling differences that used to exist between Brazilian and European Portuguese have been eliminated. Brazil and Portugal introduced the new spellings in 2009 and 2008 respectively, but there will be a transition period of four years (in Brazil) and six years (in Portugal) in which both spellings will be accepted.

All the spellings in this dictionary have been updated in line with the new reform. Here follows a summary of the main changes:

– Silent consonants -c- and -p- are omitted in words in which the consonants are not pronounced, e.g.

Pre-spelling reform	Post-spelling reform
Br ator, *Port* actor	ator
Br correto, *Port* correcto	correto
Br ótimo, *Port* óptimo	ótimo

Note, however, that the consonant remains in cases where the pronunciation differs between the two countries, e.g. *Br* fato, *Port* facto; *Br* súdito, *Port* súbdito.

– Accents are suppressed in the diphthongs -éi- and -ói- in penultimate syllables:

Pre-spelling reform	Post-spelling reform
Br/Port bóia	boia
Br idéia, *Port* ideia	ideia

– Words ending in -êem and -ôo lose their accents:

Pre-spelling reform	Post-spelling reform
Br/Port vêem	veem
Br vôo, *Port* voo	voo

– Accents used to differentiate homographs, such as *pára* (verb) and *para* (preposition) have been removed. An important exception is *pôr* (verb) and *por* (preposition), which have not been harmonized.

– The diaeresis is no longer present in -güe-, -güi-, and -qüe-, -qüi-:

Pre-spelling reform	Post-spelling reform
Br agüentar, *Port* aguentar	aguentar
Br cinqüenta, *Port* cinquenta	cinquenta

– Certain hyphenated compounds lose their hyphens:

Pre-spelling reform	Post-spelling reform
Br/Port auto-escola	autoescola
Br/Port mini-saia	minissaia

However, a few differences between European Portuguese and Brazilian spellings still remain, mostly to reflect how the words are pronounced. An important difference to remember is when a written accent is required on *o* or *e* before *m* and *n*, Brazilian Portuguese uses a circumflex, whereas European Portuguese uses an acute accent, e.g. *econômico* (Br), *económico* (Port); *gêmeo* (Br), *gémeo* (Port); *tênis* (Br), *ténis* (Port). Due to the size of the dictionary, it has not been possible to show all European Portuguese spelling variants in the entries. However, the most common European Portuguese lexical variants are included (e.g. *chávena*, *comboio*, *pequeno-almoço*, *telemóvel*).

. . . .

Pronúncia inglesa

. . . .

Vogais e Ditongos

/i:/	*see, tea*	como *i* em g*i*ro
/ɪ/	*sit, happy*	é um som mais breve do que *i* em l*i*
/e/	*set*	como *e* em t*é*pido
/æ/	*hat*	é um som mais breve do que *a* em am*o*r
/ɑ:/	*arm, calm*	como *a* em c*a*rtaz
/ɒ/	*got*	como *o* em ex*ó*tico
/ɔ:/	*saw, more*	como *o* em c*o*rte
/ʊ/	*put, look*	como *u* em m*u*rro
/u:/	*too, due*	como *u* em d*u*ro
/ʌ/	*cup, some*	como *a* em p*a*no
/ɜ:/	*firm, fur*	como *e* em enx*e*rto
/ə/	*ago, weather*	como *e* no português europeu part*e*
/eɪ/	*page, pain, pay*	como *ei* em l*ei*te
/əʊ/	*home, roam*	é um som mais longo do que o *o* em c*o*ma
/aɪ/	*fine, by, guy*	como *ai* em s*ai*
/aɪə/	*fire, tyre*	como *ai* em s*ai* seguido por /ə/
/aʊ/	*now, shout*	como *au* em *au*la
/aʊə/	*hour, flower*	como *au* em *au*la seguido por /ə/
/ɔɪ/	*join, boy*	como *oi* em d*ói*
/ɪə/	*dear, here, beer*	como *ia* em d*ia*
/eə/	*hair, care, bear, there*	como *e* em et*é*reo
/ʊə/	*poor, during*	como *ua* em s*ua*

Consoantes

/p/	*snap*	como *p* em *p*ato
/b/	*bath*	como *b* em *b*ala

. . . .

/t/	tap	como t em tela
/d/	dip	como d em dar
/k/	cat, kite, stomach, pique	como c em casa
/ks/	exercise	como x em axila
/g/	got	como g em gato
/tʃ/	chin	como t em tio
/dʒ/	June, general, judge	como d em dizer
/f/	fall	como f em faca
/v/	vine, of	como v em vaca
/θ/	thin, moth	não tem equivalente, soa como um s entre os dentes
/ð/	this	não tem equivalente, soa com um z entre os dentes
/s/	so, voice	como s em suave
/z/	zoo, rose	como z em fazer
/ʃ/	she, lunch	como ch em chegar
/ʒ/	measure, vision	como j em jamais
/h/	how	h aspirado
/m/	man	como m em mala
/n/	none	como n em nada
/ŋ/	sing	como n em cinto
/l/	leg	como l em luva
/r/	red, write	como r em cara
/j/	yes, yoke	como i em ioga
/w/	weather, switch	como u em égua

' indica a sílaba tônica, e.g. abusar /abu'zar/

Aa

a /a/ ● *artigo*

••••➤ the; **~ casa** the house; **~ Maria ainda não chegou** Maria hasn't arrived yet

! O artigo é omitido em inglês com nomes próprios, ou com parentes: **a vovó já chegou** grandma has arrived; **onde está a joana?** where's Joana?

••••➤ (*com partes do corpo, roupa*) **ela quebrou ~ perna** she broke her leg; **sua camisa está do lado contrário** your shirt is back to front

! Em português, utiliza-se em geral o artigo para se referir a partes do corpo, enquanto no inglês usa-se o pronome possessivo.

● *pron*

••••➤ (*mulher*) her

••••➤ (*coisa*) it

••••➤ (*você*) you

● *prep*

••••➤ (*direção*) to; **vou ~ São Paulo** I am going to São Paulo

••••➤ (*posição*) **à esquerda** on the left; **ao meu lado** by my side

••••➤ (*distância*) **~ dez quilômetros daqui** ten kilometres from here

••••➤ (*frequência*) **uma vez ao ano** once a year; **tenho aulas de dança às sextas** I have dance classes on Fridays

••••➤ (*esporte*) **ganharam de 2 ~ zero** they won 2 nil

••••➤ (*modo, meio*) **ir ~ pé** go on foot; **lavar à mão** handwash; **escrever (ao computador)** type

••••➤ (*com preço, medida*) **cinco libras ~ hora** five pounds an hour; **às centenas** by the hundreds; **vender às dúzias** sell by the dozen

••••➤ (*com tempo, idade, parte do dia*) **às onze** at eleven; **aos cinquenta anos** at (the age of) 50; **à noite** at night

••••➤ (*com velocidade*) **estão ~ 100 quilômetros por hora** they're going at 100 kilometres per hour

••••➤ (*seguido de infinitivo*) **fomos os primeiros ~ chegar** we were the first to arrive

••••➤ (*complemento indireto*) to; **dê isto à sua tia** give this to your aunt

••••➤ (*em expressões*) **provar por ~ mais b** prove beyond doubt

à /a/ **= a** *prep*

aba /'aba/ *f* (*de chapéu*) brim; (*de camisa*) tail; (*de mesa*) flap

abacate /aba'katʃi/ *m* avocado (pear)

abacaxi /abaka'ʃi/ m pineapple; ⓘ (*problema*) pain, headache

aba|de /a'badʒi/ m abbot. **~dia** f abbey

aba|fado /aba'fadu/ a (*tempo*) humid, close; (*quarto*) stuffy. **~far** o (*asfixiar*) stifle; muffle (*som*); smother (*fogo*); suppress (*informação*); cover up (*escândalo, assunto*)

abagunçar /abagũ'sar/ vt mess up

abaixar /aba'ʃar/ vt lower; turn down (*som, rádio*). **~-se** vpr bend down

abaixo /a'baʃu/ adv down; **~ de** below; **mais ~** further down. **~-assinado** m petition

abajur /aba'ʒur/ m (*quebra-luz*) lampshade; (*lâmpada*) (table) lamp

aba|lar /aba'lar/ vt shake; *fig* shock. **~lar-se** vpr be shocked, be shaken. **~lo** m shock

abanar /aba'nar/ vt shake, wave; wag (*rabo*); (*com leque*) fan

abando|nar /abãdo'nar/ vt abandon; (*deixar*) leave. **~no** /o/ m abandonment; (*estado*) neglect

abarcar /abar'kar/ vt comprise, cover

abarro|tado /abaxo'tadu/ a crammed full; (*lotado*) crowded, packed. **~tar** vt cram full, stuff

abastado /abas'tadu/ a wealthy

abaste|cer /abaste'ser/ vt supply; fuel (*motor*); fill up (with petrol) (*carro*); refuel (*avião*). **~cimento** m supply; (*de carro, avião*) refuelling

aba|ter /aba'ter/ vt knock down; cut down, fell (*árvore*); shoot down (*avião, aves*); slaughter (*gado*); knock down, cut (*preço*); **~ter alguém** (*trabalho*) get sb down, wear sb out; (*má notícia*) sadden sb; (*doença*) lay sb low, knock the stuffing out of sb. **~tido** a dispirited, dejected; (*cara*) haggard, worn. **~timento** m dejection; (*de preço*) reduction

abaulado /abaw'ladu/ a convex; (*estrada*) cambered

abcesso /ab'sɛsu/ m Port ▶ ABSCESSO

abdi|cação /abidʒika'sãw/ f abdication. **~car** vt/i abdicate

abdômen /abi'domẽ/ m abdomen

abecedário /abese'dariu/ m alphabet, ABC

abeirar-se /abe'rarsi/ vr draw near

abe|lha /a'beʎa/ f bee. **~lhudo** a inquisitive, nosy

abençoar /abẽso'ar/ vt bless

aber|to /a'bertu/ pp de ▶ ABRIR ● a open; (*céu*) clear; (*gás, torneira*) on; (*sinal*) green. **~tura** f opening; *Foto* aperture; *Pol* liberalization

abeto /a'betu/ m fir (tree)

abis|mado /abiz'madu/ a astonished. **~mo** m abyss

abjeto /abi'ʒetu/ a abject

abóbada /a'bɔbada/ f vault

abobalhado /aboba'ʎadu/ a silly

abóbora /a'bɔbora/ f pumpkin

abobrinha /abo'briɲa/ f courgette, *Amer* zucchini

aboli|ção /aboli'sãw/ f abolition. **~lir** vt abolish

abomi|nação /abomina'sãw/ f abomination. **~nável** (*pl* **~náveis**) a abominable

abo|nar /abo'nar/ vt guarantee (*dívida*); give a bonus to (*empregado*). **~no** /o/ m guarantee; (*no salário*) bonus; (*subsídio*) allowance, benefit; (*reforço*) endorsement

abordar /abor'dar/ vt approach ‹pessoa›; broach, tackle ‹assunto›; Naut board

aborre|cer /aboxe'ser/ vt (irritar) annoy; (entediar) bore. ~**cer-se** vpr get annoyed; get bored. ~**cido** a annoyed; bored. ~**cimento** m annoyance; boredom

abor|tar /abor'tar/ vi miscarry, have a miscarriage ● vt abort. ~**to** /o/ m abortion; (natural) miscarriage

aboto|adura /abotoa'dura/ f cufflink. ~**ar** vt button (up) ● vi bud

abra|çar /abra'sar/ vt hug, embrace; embrace ‹causa›. ~**ço** m hug, embrace

abrandar /abrã'dar/ vt ease ‹dor›; temper ‹calor, frio›; mollify, appease, placate ‹povo›; tone down, smooth over ‹escândalo› ● vi ‹dor› ease; ‹calor, frio› become less extreme; ‹tempestade› die down

abranger /abrã'ʒer/ vt cover; (entender) take in, grasp; ~ **a** extend to

abrasileirar /abrazile'rar/ vt Brazilianize

abre-garrafas /abriga'xafas/ m invar Port bottle opener. ~**latas** m invar Port can opener

abreugrafia /abrewgra'fia/ f X-ray

abrevi|ar /abrevi'ar/ vt abbreviate ‹palavra›; abridge ‹livro›. ~**atura** f abbreviation

abridor /abri'dor/ m ~ **(de lata)** can opener; ~ **de garrafa** bottle opener

abri|gar /abri'gar/ vt shelter; house ‹sem-teto›. ~**gar-se** vpr (take) shelter. ~**go** m shelter

abril /a'briw/ m April

abrir /a'brir/ vt open; (a chave) unlock; turn on ‹gás, torneira›; make ‹buraco, exceção› ● vi open; ‹céu, tempo› clear (up); ‹sinal› turn green. ~**se** vpr open; (desabafar) open up

abrupto /a'bruptu/ a abrupt

abrutalhado /abruta'ʎadu/ a ‹sapato› heavy; ‹pessoa› coarse

abscesso /abi'sesu/ m abscess

absolu|tamente /abisoluta'mẽtʃi/ adv absolutely; (não) not at all. ~**to** a absolute; **em ~to** not at all, absolutely not

absol|ver /abisow'ver/ vt absolve; Jurid acquit. ~**vição** f absolution; Jurid acquittal

absor|ção /abisor'sãw/ f absorption. ~**to** a absorbed. ~**vente** a ‹tecido› absorbent; ‹livro› absorbing. ~**ver** vt absorb. ~**ver-se** vpr get absorbed

abs|têmio /abis'temiu/ a abstemious; (de álcool) teetotal ● m teetotaller. ~**tenção** f abstention. ~**tencionista** a abstaining ● m/f abstainer. ~**ter-se** vpr abstain; ~**ter-se de** refrain from. ~**tinência** f abstinence; **síndrome de ~tinência** withdrawal symptoms pl

abstra|ção /abistra'sãw/ f abstraction; (mental) distraction. ~**ir** vt separate. ~**to** a abstract

absurdo /abi'surdu/ a absurd ● m nonsense

abun|dância /abũ'dãsia/ f abundance. ~**dante** a abundant. ~**dar** vi abound

abu|sar /abu'zar/ vi go too far; ~**sar de** abuse; (aproveitar-se) take advantage of. ~**so** m abuse

abutre /a'butri/ m vulture

acabado | acertar

4

aca|bado /aka'badu/ a finished; (*exausto*) exhausted; (*velho*) decrepit. **~bamento** *m* finish. **~bar** *vt* finish ● *vi* finish, end; (*esgotar-se*) run out; (*abolir, matar*) do away with; split up with ‹*namorado*›; wipe out ‹*adversário*›; **~bou de chegar** he has just arrived; **~bar fazendo** *ou* **por fazer** end up doing. **~bar-se** *vpr* end, be over; (*esgotar-se*) run out

acabrunhado /akabru'nadu/ a dejected

aca|demia /akade'mia/ *f* academy; (*de ginástica etc*) gym. **~dêmico** *a & m* academic

> **Academia Brasileira de Letras** The *Academia Brasileira de Letras* is responsible for promoting Brazilian language and literature, and was founded in Rio de Janeiro in 1897. It was modelled on the French Academy, and comprises 40 life members, known as the *Imortais* (Immortals), including writers, poets, essayists, playwrights and intellectuals.

açafrão /asa'frãw/ *m* saffron

acalentar /akale'tar/ *vt* lull to sleep ‹*bebê*›; cherish ‹*esperanças*›; have in mind ‹*planos*›

acalmar /akaw'mar/ *vt* calm (down) ● *vi* ‹*vento*› drop; ‹*mar*› grow calm. **~se** *vpr* calm down

acam|pamento /akãpa'mẽtu/ *m* camp; (*ato*) camping. **~par** *vi* camp

aca|nhado /aka'nadu/ a shy. **~nhamento** *m* shyness. **~nhar-se** *vpr* be shy

ação /a'sãw/ *f* action; Jurid lawsuit; Com share

acariciar /akarisi'ar/ *vt* (*com a mão*) caress, stroke; (*adular*) make a fuss of; cherish ‹*esperanças*›

acarretar /akaxe'tar/ *vt* bring, cause

acasalar /akaza'lar/ *vt* mate. **~se** *vpr* mate

acaso /a'kazu/ *m* chance; **ao ~** at random; **por ~** by chance

aca|tamento /akata'mẽtu/ *m* respect, deference. **~tar** *vt* respect, defer to ‹*pessoa, opinião*›; obey, abide by ‹*leis, ordens*›; take in ‹*criança*›

acautelar-se /akawte'larsi/ *vpr* be cautious

acei|tação /asejta'sãw/ *f* acceptance. **~tar** *vt* accept. **~tável** (*pl* **~táveis**) a acceptable

acele|ração /aselera'sãw/ *f* acceleration. **~rador** *m* accelerator. **~rar** *vi* accelerate ● *vt* speed up

acenar /ase'nar/ *vi* signal; (*saudando*) wave; **~ com** promise, offer

acender /asẽ'der/ *vt* light ‹*cigarro, fogo, vela*›; switch on ‹*luz*›; heat up ‹*debate*›

aceno /a'senu/ *m* signal; (*de saudação*) wave

acen|to /a'sẽtu/ *m* accent. **~tuar** *vt* accentuate; accent ‹*letra*›

acepção /asep'sãw/ *f* sense

acepipes /ase'pipʃ/ *m pl* Port cocktail snacks

acerca /a'serka/ **~ de** *prep* about, concerning

acercar-se /aser'karsi/ *vpr* **~ de** approach

acertar /aser'tar/ *vt* find ‹(*com o*) *caminho,* (*a*) *casa*›; put right, set ‹*relógio*›; get right ‹*pergunta*›; guess (correctly) ‹*solução*›; hit ‹*alvo*›; make ‹*acordo, negócio*›; fix, arrange ‹*encontro*› • vi (*ter razão*) be right; (*atingir o alvo*) hit the mark; ~ **com** find, happen upon; ~ **em** hit

acervo /a'servu/ m collection; *Jurid* estate

aceso /a'sezu/ *pp de* ▶ ACENDER • a ‹*luz*› on; ‹*fogo*› alight

aces|sar /ase'sar/ vt access. **~sível** (*pl* **~síveis**) a accessible; affordable ‹*preço*›. **~so** (/ ▶ m access; (*de raiva, tosse*) fit; (*de febre*) attack. **~sório** a & m accessory

acetona /ase'tona/ f (*para unhas*) nail varnish remover

achado /a'ʃadu/ m find

achaque /a'ʃaki/ m ailment

achar /a'ʃar/ vt find; (*pensar*) think. **~se** vpr (*estar*) be; (*considerar-se*) think that one is; **acho que sim/não** I think so/I don't think so

achatar /aʃa'tar/ vt flatten; cut ‹*salário*›

aciden|tado /asidẽ'tadu/ a rough ‹*terreno*›; bumpy ‹*estrada*›; eventful ‹*viagem, vida*›; injured ‹*pessoa*›. **~tal** (*pl* **~tais**) a accidental. **~te** m accident

acidez /asi'des/ f acidity

ácido /'asidu/ a & m acid

acima /a'sima/ adv above; ~ **de** above; **mais** ~ higher up

acio|nar /asio'nar/ vt operate; *Jurid* sue. **~nista** m/f shareholder

acirrado /asi'xadu/ a stiff, tough

acla|mação /aklama'sãw/ f acclaim; (*de rei*) acclamation. **~mar** vt acclaim

aclarar /akla'rar/ vt clarify, clear up • vi clear up. **~se** vpr become clear

aclimatar /aklima'tar/ vt acclimatize, *Amer* acclimate. **~se**

vpr get acclimatized, *Amer* get acclimated

aço /'asu/ m steel; ~ **inoxidável** stainless steel

acocorar-se /akoko'rarsi/ vpr squat (down)

acolá /ako'la/ adv over there

acolcho|ado /akowʃo'adu/ m quilt. **~ar** vt quilt; upholster ‹*móveis*›

aco|lhedor /akoʎe'dor/ a welcoming. **~lher** vt welcome ‹*hóspede*›; take in ‹*criança, refugiado*›; accept ‹*decisão, convite*›; respond to ‹*pedido*›. **~lhida** f, **~lhimento** m welcome; (*abrigo*) refuge

acomodar /akomo'dar/ vt accommodate; (*ordenar*) arrange; (*tornar cômodo*) make comfortable. **~se** vpr make o.s. comfortable

acompa|nhamento /akõpaɲa'mẽtu/ m *Mus* accompaniment; (*prato*) side dish; (*comitiva*) escort. **~nhante** m/f companion; *Mus* accompanist. **~nhar** vt accompany, go with; watch ‹*jogo, progresso*›; keep up with ‹*eventos, caso*›; keep up with, follow ‹*aula, conversa*›; share ‹*política, opinião*›; *Mus* accompany; **a estrada ~nha o rio** the road runs alongside the river

aconche|gante /akõʃe'gãtʃi/ a cosy, *Amer* cozy. **~gar** vt (*chegar a si*) cuddle; (*agasalhar*) wrap up; (*na cama*) tuck up; (*tornar cômodo*) make comfortable. **~gar-se** vpr ensconce o.s.; **~gar-se com** snuggle up to. **~go** /e/ m cosiness, *Amer* coziness; (*abraço*) cuddle

acondicionar /akõdʒisio'nar/ vt condition; pack, package ‹*mercadoria*›

aconse|lhar /akõse'ʎar/ vt advise;
~lhar alguém a advise sb to; **~lhar
algo a alguém** recommend sth to
sb. **~lhar-se** vpr consult. **~lhável** (pl
~lháveis) a advisable

aconte|cer /akõte'ser/ vi happen.
~cimento m event

acordar /akor'dar/ vt/i wake up

acorde /a'kɔrdʒi/ m chord

acordeão /akordʒi'ãw/ m
accordion

acordo /a'kordu/ m agreement; **de
~ com** in agreement with <pessoa>;
in accordance with <lei etc>; **estar
de ~** agree

Açores /a'soris/ m pl Azores

açoriano /asori'ano/ a & m
Azorean

acorrentar /akorẽ'tar/ vt chain
(up)

acossar /ako'sar/ vt hound, badger

acos|tamento /akosta'mẽtu/ m
hard shoulder, Amer berm. **~tar-se**
vpr lean back

acostu|mado /akostu'madu/
a usual, customary; **estar ~mado**
a be used to. **~mar** vt accustom;
~mar-se a get used to

acotovelar /akotove'lar/ vt
(empurrar) jostle; (para avisar)
nudge

açou|gue /a'sogi/ m butcher's
(shop). **~gueiro** m butcher

acovardar /akovar'dar/ vt cow,
intimidate

acre /'akri/ a <gosto> bitter;
<aroma> acrid, pungent; <tom>
harsh

acredi|tar /akredʒi'tar/ vt believe;
accredit <representante>; **~tar em**
believe <pessoa, história>; believe in
<Deus, fantasmas>; (ter confiança)
have faith in. **~tável** (pl **~táveis**) a

believable

acre-doce /akri'dosi/ a sweet
and sour

acrescentar /akresẽ'tar/ vt add

acres|cer /akre'ser/ vt (juntar) add;
(aumentar) increase ● vi increase;
~cido de with the addition of; **~ce
que** add to that the fact that

acréscimo /a'krɛsimu/ m
addition; (aumento) increase

acriançado /akriã'sadu/ a childish

acrílico /a'kriliku/ a acrylic

acroba|cia /akroba'sia/ f
acrobatics. **~ta** m/f acrobat

açúcar /a'sukar/ m sugar

açuca|rar /asuka'rar/ vt sweeten;
sugar <café, chá>. **~reiro** m sugar
bowl

açude /a'sudʒi/ m dam

acudir /aku'dʒir/ vt/i **~ (a)** come to
the rescue (of)

acumular /akumu'lar/ vt
accumulate; combine <cargos>

acupuntura /akupũ'tura/ f
acupuncture

acu|sação /akuza'sãw/ f
accusation. **~sar** vt accuse; Jurid
charge; (revelar) reveal, show up;
acknowledge <recebimento>

acústi|ca /a'kustʃika/ f acoustics.
~co a acoustic

adap|tação /adapta'sãw/ f
adaptation. **~tado** a <criança>
well-adjusted. **~tar** vt adapt; (para
encaixar) tailor. **~tar-se** vpr adapt.
~tável (pl **~táveis**) a adaptable

adega /a'dɛga/ f wine cellar

adentro /a'dẽtru/ adv inside; **selva
~** into the jungle

adepto /a'dɛptu/ m follower; Port
(de equipa) supporter

ade|quado /ade'kwadu/ a
appropriate, suitable. **~quar** vt
adapt, tailor
adereços /ade'resus/ m pl props
ade|rente /ade'rētʃi/ m/f follower.
~rir vi ‹cola› stick; join ‹a partido,
causa›; follow ‹a moda›. **~são** f
adhesion; (apoio) support. **~sivo** a
sticky, adhesive ● m sticker
adestrado /ades'tradu/ a skilled.
~trador m trainer. **~trar** vt train;
break in ‹cavalo›
adeus /a'dews/ int goodbye ● m
goodbye, farewell
adian|tado /adʒiã'tadu/ a
advanced; ‹relógio› fast; **chegar
~tado** be early. **~tamento** m
progress; (pagamento) advance.
~tar vt advance ‹dinheiro›; put
forward ‹relógio›; bring forward
‹data, reunião›; get ahead with
‹trabalho› ● vi ‹relógio› gain; (ter
efeito) be of use; **não ~ta (fazer)** it's
no use (doing). **~tar-se** vpr progress,
get ahead. **~te** adv ahead
adi|ar /adʒi'ar/ vt postpone;
adjourn ‹sessão›. **~amento** m
postponement, adjournment
adi|ção /adʒi'sãw/ f addition.
~cionar vt add. **~do** m attaché
adivi|nhação /adʒiviɲa'sãw/ f
guesswork; (por adivinho) fortune
telling. **~nhar** vt guess; tell ‹futuro,
sorte›; read ‹pensamento›. **~nho** m
fortune teller
adjetivo /adʒe'tʃivu/ m adjective
adminis|tração /adʒiministra-
'sãw/ f administration; (de
empresas) management. **~trador**
m administrator; manager. **~trar** vt
administer; manage ‹empresa›
admi|ração /adʒimira'sãw/
f admiration; (assombro)
wonder(ment). **~rado** m admired;

(surpreso) amazed, surprised.
~rador m admirer ● a admiring.
~rar vt admire; (assombrar)
amaze. **~rar-se** vpr be amazed.
~rável (pl **~ráveis**) a admirable;
(assombroso) amazing
admis|são /adʒimi'sãw/ f
admission; (de escola) intake. **~sível**
(pl **~síveis**) a admissible
admitir /adʒimi'tʃir/ vt admit;
(permitir) permit, allow; (contratar)
take on
adoçante /ado'sãtʃi/ m sweetener
adoção /ado'sãw/ f adoption
ado|çar /ado'sar/ vt sweeten.
~cicado a slightly sweet
adoecer /adoe'ser/ vi fall ill ● vt
make ill
adoles|cência /adole'sēsia/
f adolescence. **~cente** a & mf
adolescent
adorar /ado'rar/ vt (amar) adore;
worship ‹deus›, 𝐈 (gostar de) love
adorme|cer /adorme'ser/ vi fall
asleep; ‹perna› go to sleep, go
numb. **~cido** a sleeping; ‹perna›
numb
ador|nar /ador'nar/ vt adorn. **~no**
/o/ m adornment
ado|tar /ado'tar/ vt adopt. **~tivo**
a adopted
adquirir /adʒiki'rir/ vt acquire
adu|bar /adu'bar/ vt fertilize. **~bo**
m fertilizer
adu|lação /adula'sãw/ f flattery;
(do público) adulation. **~lar** vt make
a fuss of; (com palavras) flatter
adulterar /aduwte'rar/ vt
adulterate; cook, doctor ‹contas›
● vi commit adultery
adul|tério /aduw'teriu/ m
adultery. **~to** a & m adult

adúltero /a'duwteru/ *m* adulterer (*f*-ess) ● *a* adulterous

advento /adʒi'vẽtu/ *m* advent

advérbio /adʒi'vɛrbiu/ *m* adverb

adver|sário /adʒiver'sariu/ *m* opponent; (*inimigo*) adversary. **~sidade** *f* adversity. **~so** *a* adverse; (*adversário*) opposed

adver|tência /adʒiver'tẽsia/ *f* warning. **~tir** *vt* warn

advo|cacia /adʒivoka'sia/ *f* legal practice. **~gado** *m* lawyer. **~gar** *vt* advocate; *Jurid* plead ● *vi* practise law

aéreo /a'ɛriu/ *a* air

aeróbica /ae'rɔbika/ *f* aerobics

ae|rodinâmica /aerodʒi'namika/ *f* aerodynamics. **~rodinâmico** *a* aerodynamic. **~ródromo** *m* airfield. **~romoça** /o/ *f* air hostess. **~ronauta** *m* airman (*f*-woman). **~ronáutica** *f* (*força*) air force; (*ciência*) aeronautics. **~ronave** *f* aircraft. **~roporto** /o/ *m* airport

aeros|sol /aero'sɔw/ (*pl* **~sóis**) *m* aerosol

afabilidade /afabili'dadʒi/ *f* friendliness, kindness

afagar /afa'gar/ *vt* stroke

afamado /afa'madu/ *a* renowned, famed

afas|tado /afas'tadu/ *a* remote; ‹*parente*› distant; **~tado de** (far) away from. **~tamento** *m* removal; (*distância*) distance; (*de candidato*) rejection. **~tar** *vt* move away; (*tirar*) remove; ward off ‹*perigo, ameaça*›; put out of one's mind ‹*ideia*›. **~tar-se** *vpr* move away; (*distanciar-se*) distance o.s.; (*de cargo*) step down

afá|vel /a'favew/ (*pl* **~veis**) *a* friendly, genial

afazeres /afa'zeris/ *m pl* business; **~ domésticos** (household) chores

Afeganistão /afeganis'tãw/ *m* Afghanistan

afe|gão /afe'gãw/ *a* & *m* (*f* **~gã**) Afghan

afeição /afej'sãw/ *f* affection, fondness

afeiçoado /afejsu'adu/ *a* (*devoto*) devoted; (*amoroso*) fond

afeminado /afemi'nadu/ *a* effeminate

aferir /afe'rir/ *vt* check, inspect ‹*pesos, medidas*›; (*avaliar*) assess; (*cotejar*) compare

aferrar /afe'xar/ *vt* grasp; **~se a** cling to

afe|tação /afeta'sãw/ *f* affectation. **~tado** *a* affected. **~tar** *vt* affect. **~tivo** *a* (*carinhoso*) affectionate; (*sentimental*) emotional. **~to** /ɛ/ *m* affection. **~tuoso** /o/ *a* affectionate

afi|ado /afi'adu/ *a* sharp; skilled ‹*pessoa*›. **~ar** *vt* sharpen

aficionado /afisio'nadu/ *m* enthusiast

afilhado /afi'ʎadu/ *m* godson (*f*-daughter)

afili|ação /afilia'sãw/ *f* affiliation. **~ada** *a* affiliate. **~ar** *vt* affiliate

afim /a'fĩ/ *a* related, similar

afinado /afi'nadu/ *a* in tune

afinal /afi'naw/ *adv* **~ (de contas)** (*por fim*) in the end; (*pensando bem*) after all

afinar /afi'nar/ *vt* tune ● *vi* taper

afinco /a'fĩku/ *m* perseverance, determination

afinidade /afini'dadʒi/ *f* affinity

afir|mação /afirma'sãw/ *f* assertion. **~mar** *vt* claim, assert. **~mativo** *a* affirmative

afivelar /afive'lar/ vt buckle

afixar /afi'ksar/ vt stick, post

afli|ção /afli'sãw/ f (física) affliction; (cuidado) anxiety. **~gir** vt <doença> afflict; (inquietar) trouble. **~gir-se** vpr worry. **~to** a troubled, worried

afluente /aflu'ẽtʃi/ m tributary

afo|bação /afoba'sãw/ f fluster, flap. **~bado** a in a flap, flustered. **~bar** vt fluster. **~bar-se** vpr get flustered, get in a flap

afo|gado /afo'gadu/ a drowned; morrer **~gado** drown. **~gador** m choke. **~gar** vt/i drown; Auto flood. **~gar-se** vpr (matar-se) drown o.s.

afoito /a'fojtu/ a bold, daring

afora /a'fɔra/ adv pelo mundo **~** throughout the world

afortunado /afortu'nadu/ a fortunate

afresco /a'fresku/ m fresco

África /'afrika/ f Africa; **~ do Sul** South Africa

africano /afri'kanu/ a & m African

afrodisíaco /afrodʒi'ziaku/ a & m aphrodisiac

afron|ta /a'frõta/ f affront, insult. **~tar** vt affront, insult

afrouxar /afro'ʃar/ vt/i loosen; (de rapidez) slow down; (de disciplina) relax

afta /'afta/ f (mouth) ulcer

afugentar /afuʒẽ'tar/ vt drive away; rout <inimigo>

afundar /afũ'dar/ vt sink. **~se** vpr sink

agachar /aga'ʃar/ vi, **~se** vpr bend down

agarrar /aga'xar/ vt grab, snatch. **~se** vpr **~se a** cling to, hold on to

agasa|lhar /agaza'ʎar/ vt, **~lhar-se** vpr wrap up (warmly).

~lho m (casaco) coat; (suéter) sweater

agência /a'ʒẽsia/ f agency; **~ de correio** post office; **~ de viagens** travel agency

agenda /a'ʒẽda/ f diary

agente /a'ʒẽtʃi/ m/f agent

ágil /'aʒiw/ (pl **ágeis**) a <pessoa> agile; <serviço> quick, efficient

agili|dade /aʒili'dadʒi/ f agility; (rapidez) speed. **~zar** vt speed up, streamline

ágio /'aʒiu/ m premium

agiota /aʒi'ɔta/ m/f loan shark

agir /a'ʒir/ vi act

agi|tado /aʒi'tadu/ a agitated; <mar> rough. **~tar** vt wave <braços>; wag <rabo>; shake <garrafa>; (perturbar) agitate. **~tar-se** vpr get agitated; <mar> get rough

aglome|ração /aglomera'sãw/ f collection; (de pessoas) crowd; **~rar** vt collect. **~rar-se** vpr gather

agonia /ago'nia/ f anguish; (da morte) death throes

agora /a'gɔra/ adv now; (há pouco) just now; **~ mesmo** right now; **de ~ em diante** from now on; **até ~** so far, up till now

agosto /a'gostu/ m August

agouro /a'goru/ m omen

agraciar /agrasi'ar/ vt decorate

agra|dar /agra'dar/ vt please; (fazer agrados) be nice to, fuss over ● vi be pleasing, please; (cair no gosto) go down well. **~dável** (pl **~dáveis**) a pleasant

agrade|cer /agrade'ser/ vt **~cer algo a alguém**, **~cer a alguém por algo** thank sb for sth ● vi say thank you. **~cido** a grateful. **~cimento** m gratitude; pl thanks

agrado /a'gradu/ *m* fazer ~s a be nice to, make a fuss of

agra|far /agra'far/ *vt* Port staple. ~fador *m* stapler

agrário /a'grariu/ *a* land, agrarian

agra|vante /agra'vãtʃi/ *a* aggravating ● *f* aggravating circumstance. ~var *vt* aggravate, make worse. ~var-se *vpr* get worse

agredir /agre'dʒir/ *vt* attack

agregado /agre'gadu/ *m* (em casa) lodger

agres|são /agre'sãw/ *f* aggression; (ataque) assault. ~sivo *a* aggressive. ~sor *m* aggressor

agreste /a'grestʃi/ *a* rural

agrião /agri'ãw/ *m* watercress

agrícola /a'grikola/ *a* agricultural

agricul|tor /agrikuw'tor/ *m* farmer. ~tura *f* agriculture, farming

agridoce /agri'dosi/ *a* bittersweet

agropecuá|ria /agropeku'aria/ *f* farming. ~rio *a* agricultural

agru|pamento /agrupa'mẽtu/ *m* grouping. ~par *vt* group. ~par-se *vpr* group (together)

água /'agwa/ *f* water; dar ~ na boca be mouth-watering; ir por ~ abaixo go down the drain; ~ benta holy water; ~ de coco coconut water; ~ doce fresh water; ~ mineral mineral water; ~ salgada salt water; ~ sanitária household bleach

aguaceiro /agwa'seru/ *m* downpour

água-colônia /agwa-ko'lonia/ *f* eau de cologne

aguado /a'gwadu/ *a* watery

aguardar /agwar'dar/ *vt* wait for, await ● *vi* wait

aguardente /agwar'dẽtʃi/ *f* spirit

aguarrás /agwa'xas/ *m* turpentine

água-viva /agwa'viva/ *f* jellyfish

agu|çado /agu'sadu/ *a* pointed; ‹sentidos› acute. ~çar *vt* sharpen. ~deza *f* sharpness; (mental) perceptiveness. ~do *a* sharp; ‹som› shrill; *fig* acute

aguentar /agwẽ'tar/ *vt* stand, put up with; hold ‹peso› ● *vi* ‹pessoa› hold out; ‹suporte› hold

águia /'agia/ *f* eagle

agulha /a'guʎa/ *f* needle

ai /aj/ *m* sigh; (de dor) groan ● *int* ah!; (de dor) ouch!

aí /a'i/ *adv* there; (então) then

aidético /aj'detʃiku/ *a* suffering from Aids ● *m* Aids sufferer

AIDS /'ajdʒis/ *f* Aids; vírus da ~ AIDS virus

ainda /a'ĩda/ *adv* still; melhor ~ even better; não ... ~ not ... yet; ~ assim even so; ~ bem just as well; ~ por cima moreover, in addition; ~ que even if

aipim /aj'pĩ/ *m* cassava

aipo /'ajpu/ *m* celery

ajeitar /aʒej'tar/ *vt* (arrumar) sort out; (arranjar) arrange; (ajustar) adjust. ~se *vpr* adapt; (dar certo) turn out right, work o.s. out

ajoe|lhado /aʒoe'ʎadu/ *a* kneeling (down). ~lhar *vi*, ~lhar-se *vpr* kneel (down)

aju|da /a'ʒuda/ *f* help. ~dante *m*/*f* helper. ~dar *vt* help

ajuizado /aʒui'zadu/ *a* sensible

ajus|tar /aʒus'tar/ *vt* adjust; settle ‹disputa›; take in ‹roupa›. ~tar-se *vpr* conform. ~tável (*pl* ~táveis) *a* adjustable. ~te *m* adjustment; (acordo) settlement

ala /'ala/ *f* wing

ala|gação /alaga'sãw/ f flooding.
~gadiço a marshy ● m marsh. **~gar**
vt flood

alameda /ala'meda/ f avenue

álamo /'alamu/ m poplar (tree)

alarde /a'lardʒi/ m fazer **~ de**
flaunt; make a big thing of ‹notícia›.
~ar vt/i flaunt

alargar /alar'gar/ vt widen; fig
broaden; let out ‹roupa›

alarido /ala'ridu/ m outcry

alar|ma /a'larma/ m alarm.
~mante a alarming. **~mar** vt alarm.
~me m alarm. **~mista** a & m alarmist

alastrar /alas'trar/ vt scatter;
(disseminar) spread ● vi spread

alavanca /ala'vãka/ f lever; **~ de
mudanças** gear lever

alba|nês /awba'nes/ a & m (f
~nesa) Albanian

Albânia /aw'bania/ f Albania

albergue /aw'bergi/ m hostel

álbum /'awbũ/ m album

alça /'awsa/ f handle; (de roupa)
strap; (de fusil) sight

alcachofra /awka'ʃofra/ f artichoke

alçada /aw'sada/ f competence,
power

Alcaida /aw'kaida/ f Port
► AL-QAEDA

álcali /'awkali/ m alkali

alcan|çar /awkã'sar/ vt reach;
(conseguir) attain; (compreender)
understand ● vi reach. **~çável**
(pl **~çáveis**) a reachable; attainable.
~ce m reach; (de tiro) range;
(importância) consequence;
(compreensão) understanding

alcaparra /awka'paxa/ f caper

alcatra /aw'katra/ f rump steak

alcatrão /awka'trãw/ m tar

álcool /'awkɔw/ m alcohol

alcoó|latra /awkɔ'blatra/ m/f
alcoholic. **~lico** a & m alcoholic

alcunha /aw'kuɲa/ f nickname

aldeia /aw'deja/ f village

aleatório /alia'tɔriu/ a random,
arbitrary

alecrim /ale'krĩ/ m rosemary

ale|gação /alega'sãw/ f allegation.
~gar vt allege

ale|goria /alego'ria/ f allegory.
~górico a allegorical

ale|grar /ale'grar/ vt cheer up;
brighten up ‹casa›. **~grar-se** vpr
cheer up. **~gre** /e/ a cheerful;
‹cores› bright. **~gria** f joy

alei|jado /alej'ʒadu/ a crippled ● m
cripple. **~jar** vt cripple

alei|tamento /alejta'mẽtu/ m
breastfeeding. **~tar** vt breastfeed

além /a'lẽj/ adv beyond; **~ de** (ao
lado de lá de) beyond; (mais de) over;
(ademais de) apart from

Alemanha /ale'maɲa/ f Germany

ale|mão /ale'mãw/ a & m (pl **~mães**) a &
m (f **~mã**) German

alen|tador /alẽta'dor/ a
encouraging. **~tar** vt encourage.
~tar-se vpr cheer up. **~to** m
courage; (fôlego) breath

alergia /aler'ʒia/ f allergy

alérgico /a'lerʒiku/ a allergic (a to)

aler|ta /a'lerta/ a & m alert ● adv on
the alert. **~tar** vt alert

alfa|bético /awfa'betʃiku/ a
alphabetical. **~betização** f literacy.
~betizar vt teach to read and write.
~beto m alphabet

alface /aw'fasi/ f lettuce

alfaiate /awfaj'atʃi/ m tailor

al|fândega /aw'fãdʒiga/ f
customs. **~fandegário** a customs
● m customs officer

alfinetada | alojamento

alfine|tada /awfine'tada/ f prick; (dor) stabbing pain; fig dig. **~te** /e/ m pin; **~te de segurança** safety pin

alforreca /alfo'xeka/ f Port jellyfish

alga /'awga/ f seaweed

algarismo /awga'rizmu/ m numeral

algazarra /awga'zaxa/ f uproar, racket

alge|mar /awʒe'mar/ vt handcuff. **~mas** /e/ f pl handcuffs

algibeira /alʒi'bejra/ f Port pocket

algo /'awgu/ pron something; (numa pergunta) anything ● adv somewhat

algodão /awgo'dãw/ m cotton; **~(-doce)** candy floss, Amer cotton candy; **~ (hidrófilo)** cotton wool, Amer absorbent cotton

alguém /aw'gẽj/ pron somebody, someone; (numa pergunta) anybody, anyone

al|gum /aw'gũ/ (f **~guma**) a some; (numa pergunta) any; (nenhum) no, not one ● pron pl some; **~guma coisa** something

algures /aw'guris/ adv somewhere

alheio /a'ʎeju/ a (de outra pessoa) someone else's; (de outras pessoas) other people's; **~ a** foreign to; (impróprio) irrelevant to; (desatento) unaware of; **~ de** removed from

alho /'aʎu/ m garlic. **~poró** m leek

ali /a'li/ adv (over) there

ali|ado /ali'adu/ a allied ● m ally. **~ança** f alliance; (anel) wedding ring. **~ar** vt, **~ar-se** vpr ally

aliás /a'ljaʃ/ adv (além disso) what's more, furthermore; (no entanto) however; (diga-se de passagem) by the way, incidentally; (senão) otherwise

álibi /'alibi/ m alibi

alicate /ali'katʃi/ m pliers; **~ de unhas** nail clippers

alicerce /ali'sersi/ m foundation; fig basis

alie|nado /alie'nadu/ a alienated; (demente) insane. **~nar** vt alienate; transfer ‹bens›. **~nígena** a & m/f alien

alimen|tação /alimẽta'sãw/ f (ato) feeding; (comida) food; Tecn supply. **~tar** a food; ‹hábitos› eating ● vt feed; fig nurture; **~tar-se de** live on. **~tício a** gêneros **~tícios** foodstuffs. **~to** m food

ali|nhado /ali'ɲadu/ a aligned; ‹pessoa› smart, Amer sharp. **~nhar** vt align

alíquota /a'likwota/ f (de imposto) bracket

alisar /ali'zar/ vt smooth (out); straighten ‹cabelo›

alistar /alis'tar/ vt recruit. **~se** vpr enlist

aliviar /alivi'ar/ vt relieve

alívio /a'liviu/ m relief

alma /'awma/ f soul

almanaque /awma'naki/ m yearbook

almejar /awme'ʒar/ vt long for

almirante /awmi'rãtʃi/ m admiral

almo|çar /awmo'sar/ vi have lunch ● vt have for lunch. **~ço** /o/ m lunch

almofada /awmo'fada/ f cushion; Port (de cama) pillow

almôndega /aw'mõdʒiga/ f meatball

almoxarifado /awmoʃari'fadu/ m storeroom

alô /a'lo/ int hallo

alocar /alo'kar/ vt allocate

alo|jamento /aloʒa'mẽtu/ m accommodation, Amer

accommodations; (*habitação*) housing. **~jar** *vt* accommodate; house ‹*sem-teto*›. **~jar-se** *vpr* stay

alongar /alõˈgar/ *vt* lengthen; extend, stretch out ‹*braço*›

alpendre /awˈpẽdri/ *m* shed; (*pórtico*) porch

Alpes /ˈawpis/ *m pl* Alps

alpinis|mo /awpiˈnizmu/ *m* mountaineering. **~ta** *m/f* mountaineer

Al-Qaeda /awˈkaida/ *f BR* Al-Qaeda

alqueire /awˈkeri/ *m*: = 4.84 hectares; (*in São Paulo*) = 2.42 hectares

alquimi|a /awkiˈmia/ *f* alchemy. **~sta** *mf* alchemist

alta /ˈawta/ *f* rise; **dar ~ a** discharge; **ter ~** be discharged

altar /awˈtar/ *m* altar

alterar /awteˈrar/ *vt* alter; (*falsificar*) falsify. **~se** *vpr* change; (*zangar-se*) get angry

alter|nado /awterˈnadu/ *a* alternate. **~nar** *vt/i*, **~nar-se** *vpr* alternate. **~nativa** *f* alternative. **~nativo** *a* alternative; ‹*corrente*› alternating

al|teza /awˈteza/ *f* highness. **~titude** *f* altitude

altifalante /awtʃifaˈlãtʃi/ *m Port* ▶ **ALTO-FALANTE**

alti|vez /awtʃiˈves/ *f* arrogance. **~vo** *a* arrogant; (*elevado*) majestic

alto /ˈawtu/ *a* high; ‹*pessoa*› tall; ‹*barulho*› loud ● *adv* high; ‹*falar*› loud(ly); ‹*ler*› aloud ● *m* top; **os ~s e baixos** the ups and downs ● *int* halt!. **~falante** *m* loudspeaker

altura /awˈtura/ *f* height; (*momento*) moment; **ser à ~ de** be up to

aluci|nação /alusinaˈsãw/ *f* hallucination. **~nante** *a* mind-boggling, crazy

aludir /aluˈdʒir/ *vi* allude (**a** to)

alu|gar /aluˈgar/ *vt* rent ‹*casa*›; hire, rent ‹*carro*›; ‹*locador*› let, rent out, hire out. **~guel**, *Port* **~guer** /ɛ/ *m* rent; (*ato*) renting

alumiar /alumiˈar/ *vt* light (up)

alumínio /aluˈminiu/ *m* aluminium, *Amer* aluminum

aluno /aˈlunu/ *m* pupil

alusão /aluˈzãw/ *f* allusion (**a** to)

alvará /awvaˈra/ *m* permit, licence

alve|jante /awveˈʒãtʃi/ *m* bleach. **~jar** *vt* bleach; (*visar*) aim at

alvenaria /awvenaˈria/ *f* masonry

alvo /ˈawvu/ *m* target

alvorada /awvoˈrada/ *f* dawn

alvoro|çar /awvoroˈsar/ *vt* stir up, agitate; (*entusiasmar*) excite. **~ço** /o/ *m* (*tumulto*) uproar; (*entusiasmo*) excitement

amabilidade /amabiliˈdadʒi/ *f* kindness

amaci|ante /amasiˈãtʃi/ *m* (*de roupa*) (fabric) conditioner. **~ar** *vt* soften; run in ‹*carro*›

amador /amaˈdor/ *a* & *m* amateur. **~ismo** *m* amateurism. **~ístico** *a* amateurish

amadurecer /amadureˈser/ *vt/i* ‹*fruta*› ripen; *fig* mature

âmago /ˈamagu/ *m* heart, core; (*da questão*) crux

amaldiçoar /amawdʒisoˈar/ *vt* curse

amamentar /amamẽˈtar/ *vt* breastfeed

amanhã /amaˈɲã/ *m* & *adv* tomorrow; **depois de ~** the day after tomorrow

amanhecer /amaɲe'ser/ *vi* & *m* dawn

amansar /amã'sar/ *vt* tame; *fig* placate ‹*pessoa*›

a|mante /a'mãtʃi/ *m/f* lover. **~mar** *vt/i* love

amarelo /ama'relu/ *a* & *m* yellow

amar|go /a'margu/ *a* bitter. **~gura** *f* bitterness. **~gurar** *vt* embitter; (*sofrer*) endure

amarrar /ama'xar/ *vt* tie (up); *Naut* moor; **~ a cara** frown, scowl

amarrotar /amaxo'tar/ *vt* crease

amassar /ama'sar/ *vt* crush, squash; screw up ‹*papel*›; crease ‹*roupa*›; dent ‹*carro*›; knead ‹*pão*›; mash ‹*batatas*›

amá|vel /a'mavew/ (*pl* **~veis**) *a* kind

Ama|zonas /ama'zonas/ *m* Amazon. **~zônia** *f* Amazonia

> **Amazônia** The Amazon region is home to the world's largest rainforest, covering 7 million square kilometres, half of which is in Brazilian territory. It is made up of the Amazon Basin, which has the highest flow of river water in the world, and the Amazon Rainforest, and is home to vast biodiversity, including more than sixty thousand types of trees.

âmbar /'ãbar/ *m* amber

ambi|ção /ãbi'sãw/ *f* ambition. **~cionar** *vt* aspire to. **~cioso** /o/ *a* ambitious

ambien|tal /ãbiẽ'taw/ (*pl* **~tais**) *a* environmental. **~tar** *vt* set ‹*filme, livro*›; set up ‹*casa*›. **~tar-se** *vpr* settle in. **~te** *m* environment;

(*atmosfera*) atmosphere

am|biguidade /ãbigwi'dadʒi/ *f* ambiguity. **~biguo** *a* ambiguous

âmbito /'ãbitu/ *m* scope, range

ambos /'ãbus/ *a* & *pron* both

ambu|lância /ãbu'lãsia/ *f* ambulance. **~lante** *a* (*que anda*) walking; ‹*músico*› wandering; ‹*venda*› mobile. **~latório** *m* outpatient clinic

amea|ça /ami'asa/ *f* threat. **~çador** *a* threatening. **~çar** *vt* threaten

ameba /a'mɛba/ *f* amoeba

amedrontar /amedrõ'tar/ *vt* scare. **~se** *vpr* get scared

ameixa /a'meʃa/ *f* plum; (*passa*) prune

amém /a'mẽj/ *int* amen ● *m* agreement; **dizer ~ a** go along with

amêndoa /a'mẽdoa/ *f* almond

amendoim /amẽdo'ĩ/ *m* peanut

ame|nidade /ameni'dadʒi/ *f* pleasantness; pleasantries, small talk. **~nizar** *vt* ease; calm ‹*ânimos*›; settle ‹*disputa*›; tone down ‹*repreensão*›. **~no** /e/ *a* pleasant; mild ‹*clima*›

América /a'mɛrika/ *f* America; **~ do Norte/Sul** North/South America

america|nizar /amerikani'zar/ *vt* Americanize. **~no** *a* & *m* American

amestrar /ames'trar/ *vt* train

ametista /ame'tʃista/ *f* amethyst

amianto /ami'ãtu/ *m* asbestos

ami|gar-se /ami'garsi/ *vpr* make friends. **~gável** (*pl* **~gáveis**) *a* amicable

amígdala /a'migdala/ *f* tonsil

amigdalite /amigda'litʃi/ *f* tonsillitis

amigo /a'migu/ a friendly ● m friend; **~ da onça** false friend

amistoso /amis'tozu/ a & m friendly

amiúde /ami'udʒi/ adv often

amizade /ami'zadʒi/ f friendship

amnésia /ami'nezia/ f amnesia

amnistia /amnis'tia/ f Port
▶ ANISTIA

amo|lação /amola'sãw/ f annoyance. **~lante** a annoying. **~lar** vt annoy, bother; sharpen ‹faca›. **~lar-se** vpr get annoyed

amolecer /amole'ser/ vt/i soften

amol|gadura /amowga'dura/ f dent. **~gar** vt dent

amoníaco /amo'niaku/ m ammonia

amontoar /amõto'ar/ vt pile up; amass ‹riquezas›. **~-se** vpr pile up

amor /a'mor/ m love

amora /a'mɔra/ f ~ **preta**, Port ~ **silvestre** blackberry

amordaçar /amorda'sar/ vt gag

amoroso /amo'rozu/ a loving

amor-perfeito /amorper'fejtu/ m pansy

amor-próprio /amor'propriu/ m self-esteem

amorte|cedor /amortese'dor/ m shock absorber. **~cer** vt deaden; absorb ‹impacto›; break ‹queda› ● vi fade

amostra /a'mɔstra/ f sample

ampa|rar /ãpa'rar/ vt support; fig protect. **~rar-se** vpr lean. **~ro** m (apoio) support; (proteção) protection; (ajuda) aid

ampere /ã'peri/ m amp(ere)

ampli|ação /ãplia'sãw/ f (de foto) enlargement; (de casa) extension. **~ar** vt enlarge ‹foto›; extend ‹casa›; broaden ‹conhecimentos›

amplifi|cador /ãplifika'dor/ m amplifier. **~car** vt amplify

amplo /'ãplu/ a ‹sala› spacious; ‹roupa› full; ‹sentido, conhecimento› broad

ampola /ã'pola/ f ampoule

amputar /ãpu'tar/ vt amputate

Amsterdã /amister'dã/ f, Port **Amsterdão** /amiʃter'dãw/ m Amsterdam

amu|ado /amu'adu/ a in a sulk, sulky. **~ar** vi sulk

amuleto /amu'leto/ m charm

amuo /a'muu/ m sulk

ana|crônico /ana'kroniku/ a anachronistic. **~cronismo** m anachronism

anais /a'najs/ m pl annals

analfabeto /anawfa'betu/ a & m illiterate

analgésico /anaw'ʒeziku/ m painkiller

analisar /anali'zar/ vt analyse

análise /a'nalizi/ f analysis

ana|lista /ana'lista/ m/f analyst. **~lítico** a analytical

analogia /analo'ʒia/ f analogy

análogo /a'nalogu/ a analogous

ananás /ana'naʃ/ m invar Port pineapple

anão /a'nãw/ a & m (f **anã**) dwarf

anarquia /anar'kia/ f anarchy; fig chaos

anárquico /a'narkiku/ a anarchic

anarquista /anar'kista/ m/f anarchist

ana|tomia /anato'mia/ f anatomy. **~tômico** a anatomical

anca /'ãka/ f (de pessoa) hip; (de animal) rump

anchova /ã'ʃova/ f anchovy

ancinho | ano

16

ancinho /ã'siɲu/ *m* rake

âncora /'ãkora/ *f* anchor

anco|radouro /ãkora'doru/ *m* anchorage. **~rar** *vt/i* anchor

andaime /ã'dajmi/ *m* scaffolding

an|damento /ãda'mẽtu/ *m* (*progresso*) progress; (*rumo*) course; **dar ~damento a** set in motion. **~dar** *m* (*jeito de andar*) gait, walk; (*de prédio*) floor; Port (*apartamento*) flat, Amer apartment ● *vi* (*ir a pé*) walk; (*de trem, ônibus*) travel; (*a cavalo, de bicicleta*) ride; (*funcionar, progredir*) go; **ele ~da deprimido** he's been depressed lately

Andes /'ãdʒis/ *m pl* Andes

andorinha /ãdo'riɲa/ *f* swallow

anedota /ane'dɔta/ *f* anecdote

anel /a'nɛw/ (*pl* anéis) *m* ring; (*no cabelo*) curl; **~ viário** ring road

anelado /ane'ladu/ *a* curly

anemia /ane'mia/ *f* anaemia

anêmico /a'nemiku/ *a* anaemic

anes|tesia /aneste'zia/ *f* anaesthesia; (*droga*) anaesthetic. **~tesiar** *vt* anaesthetize. **~tésico** *a & m* anaesthetic. **~tesista** *m/f* anaesthetist

ane|xar /anek'sar/ *vt* annex ‹*terras*›; (*em carta*) enclose; (*juntar*) attach. **~xo** /a'nɛksu/ *a* attached; (*em carta*) enclosed ● *m* annexe; (*em carta*) enclosure ● Comput attachment

anfetamina /ãfeta'mina/ *f* amphetamine

anfíbio /ã'fibiu/ *a* amphibious ● *m* amphibian

anfiteatro /ãfitʃi'atru/ *m* amphitheatre; (*no teatro*) dress circle

anfi|trião /ãfitri'ãw/ *m* (*f* **~triã**) host (*f* -ess)

angariar /ãgari'ar/ *vt* raise ‹*fundos*›; canvass for ‹*votos*›; win ‹*adeptos, simpatia*›

angli|cano /ãgli'kanu/ *a & m* Anglican. **~cismo** *m* Anglicism

anglo-saxônico /ãglusak'soniku/ *a* Anglo-Saxon

Angola /ã'gɔla/ *f* Angola

angolano /ãgo'lanu/ *a & m* Angolan

angra /'ãgra/ *f* inlet, cove

angular /ãgu'lar/ *a* angular

ângulo /'ãgulu/ *m* angle

angústia /ã'gustʃia/ *f* anguish, anxiety

angustiante /ãgustʃi'ãtʃi/ *a* distressing; ‹*momento*› anxious

ani|mado /ani'madu/ *a* (*vivo*) lively; (*alegre*) cheerful; (*entusiasmado*) enthusiastic. **~mador** *a* encouraging ● *m* presenter. **~mal** (*pl* **~mais**) *a & m* animal. **~mar** *vt* encourage; liven up ‹*festa*›. **~mar-se** *vpr* cheer up; ‹*festa*› liven up

ânimo /'animu/ *m* courage, spirit; tempers

animosidade /animozi'dadʒi/ *f* animosity

aniquilar /aniki'lar/ *vt* destroy; (*prostrar*) shatter

anis /a'nis/ *m* aniseed

anistia /anis'tʃia/ *f* amnesty

aniver|sariante /aniversari'ãtʃi/ *m/f* birthday boy (*f* girl). **~sário** *m* birthday; (*de casamento etc*) anniversary

anjo /'ãʒu/ *m* angel

ano /'anu/ *m* year; **fazer ~s** have a birthday; **~ bissexto** leap year; **~ letivo** academic year. **~bom** *m* New Year

anoite|cer /anojte'ser/ *m* nightfall
● *vi* **~ceu** night fell

anomalia /anoma'lia/ *f* anomaly

anonimato /anoni'matu/ *m* anonymity

anônimo /a'nonimu/ *a* anonymous

anorexia /anorek'sia/ *f* anorexia

anoréxico /ano'rɛksiku/ *a* & *m* anorexic

anor|mal /anor'maw/ (*pl* **~mais**) *a* abnormal

ano|tação /anota'sãw/ *f* note. **~tar** *vt* note down, write down

ânsia /'ãsia/ *f* anxiety; (*desejo*) longing; **~s de vômito** nausea

ansi|ar /ãsi'ar/ *vi* **~ por** long for. **~edade** *f* anxiety; (*desejo*) eagerness. **~oso** /o/ *a* anxious

antártico /ã'tartʃiku/ *a* & *m* Antarctic

antebraço /ãtʃi'brasu/ *m* forearm

antece|dência /ãtese'dẽsia/ *f* **com ~dência** in advance. **~dente** *a* preceding. **~dentes** *m pl* record, past

antecessor /ãtese'sor/ *m* (*f* **~a**) predecessor

anteci|pação /ãtʃisipa'sãw/ *f* anticipation; **com ~pação** in advance. **~padamente** *adv* in advance. **~pado** *a* advance. **~par** *vt* anticipate, forestall; (*adiantar*) bring forward. **~par-se** *vpr* be previous

antena /ã'tena/ *f* aerial, *Amer* antenna; (*de inseto*) feeler

anteontem /ãtʃi'õtẽ/ *adv* the day before yesterday

antepassado /ãtʃipa'sadu/ *m* ancestor

anterior /ãteri'or/ *a* previous; (*dianteiro*) front

antes /'ãtʃis/ *adv* before; (*ao contrário*) rather; **~ de/que** before

antessala /ãtʃi'sala/ *f* anteroom

anti|biótico /ãtʃibi'ɔtʃiku/ *a* & *m* antibiotic. **~caspa** *a* anti-dandruff. **~concepcional** (*pl* **~concepcionais**) *a* & *m* contraceptive. **~congelante** *m* antifreeze. **~corpo** *m* antibody

antídoto /ã'tʃidotu/ *m* antidote

antiético /ãtʃi'etʃiku/ *a* unethical

antigamente /ãtʃiga'mẽtʃi/ *adv* formerly

anti|go /ã'tʃigu/ *a* old; (*da antiguidade*) ancient; <*móveis etc*> antique; (*anterior*) former. **~guidade** *f* antiquity; (*numa firma*) seniority; (*monumentos*) antiquities; (*móveis etc*) antiques

anti|higiênico /ãtʃiʒi'eniku/ *a* unhygienic. **~histamínico** *a* & *m* antihistamine. **~horário** *a* anticlockwise

antilhano /ãtʃi'ʎanu/ *a* & *m* West Indian

Antilhas /ã'tʃiʎas/ *f pl* West Indies

anti|patia /ãtʃipa'tʃia/ *f* dislike. **~pático** *a* unpleasant, unfriendly

antiquado /ãtʃi'kwadu/ *a* antiquated, outdated

antis|semitismo /ãtʃisemi'tʃizmu/ *m* anti-Semitism. **~séptico** *a* & *m* antiseptic. **~social** (*pl* **~sociais**) *a* antisocial

antítese /ã'tʃitezi/ *f* antithesis

antologia /ãtolo'ʒia/ *f* anthology

antônimo /ã'tonimu/ *m* antonym

antro /'ãtru/ *m* cavern; (*de animal*) lair; (*de ladrões*) den

antro|pófago /ãtro'pɔfagu/ *a* man-eating. **~pologia** *f* anthropology. **~pólogo** *m* anthropologist

anu|al /anu'aw/ (*pl* ~**ais**) *a* annual, yearly

anu|lação /anula'sãw/ *f* cancellation. ~**lar** *vt* cancel; annul ‹*casamento*›; (*compensar*) cancel out ● *m* ring finger

anunciar /anũsi'ar/ *vt* announce; advertise ‹*produto*›

anúncio /a'nũsiu/ *m* announcement; (*propaganda, classificado*) advert(isement); (*cartaz*) notice

ânus /'anus/ *m invar* anus

an|zol /ã'zɔw/ (*pl* ~**zóis**) *m* fish hook

aonde /a'õdʒi/ *adv* where

apadrinhar /apadri'ɲar/ *vt* be godfather to ‹*afilhado*›; be best man for ‹*noivo*›; (*proteger*) protect; (*patrocinar*) support

apa|gado /apa'gadu/ *a* ‹*fogo*› out; ‹*luz, TV*› off; (*indistinto*) faint; ‹*pessoa*› dull. ~**gar** *vt* put out ‹*cigarro, fogo*›; blow out ‹*vela*›; switch off ‹*luz, TV*›; rub out ‹*erro*›; clean ‹*quadro-negro*›. ~**gar-se** *vpr* ‹*fogo, luz*› go out; ‹*lembrança*› fade; (*desmaiar*) pass out; Ⓣ (*dormir*) nod off

apaixo|nado /apaʃo'nadu/ *a* in love (**por** with). ~**nante** *a* captivating. ~**nar-se** *vpr* fall in love (**por** with)

apalpar /apaw'par/ *vt* touch, feel; ‹*médico*› examine

apanhar /apa'ɲar/ *vt* catch; (*do chão*) pick up; pick ‹*flores, frutas*›; (*ir buscar*) pick up; (*alcançar*) catch up ● *vi* be beaten

aparafusar /aparafu'zar/ *vt* screw

apa|ra-lápis /apara'lapiʃ/ *m invar Port* pencil sharpener. ~**rar** *vt* catch ‹*bola*›; parry ‹*golpe*›; trim ‹*cabelo*›; sharpen ‹*lápis*›

aparato /apa'ratu/ *m* pomp, ceremony

apare|cer /apare'ser/ *vi* appear; ~**çal** do drop in!. ~**cimento** *m* appearance

apare|lhagem /apare'ʎaʒẽ/ *f* equipment. ~**lhar** *vt* equip. ~**lho** /e/ *m* apparatus; (*máquina*) machine; (*de chá*) set, service; (*fone*) phone

aparência /apa'rẽsia/ *f* appearance; **na** ~ apparently

aparen|tado /aparẽ'tadu/ *a* related. ~**tar** *vt* show; (*fingir*) feign. ~**te** *a* apparent

apartado /apar'tadu/ *m Port* PO Box

apar|tamento /aparta'mẽtu/ *m* flat, *Amer* apartment. ~**tar** *vt*, ~**tar-se** *vpr* separate. ~**te** *m* aside

apatia /apa'tʃia/ *f* apathy

apático /a'patʃiku/ *a* apathetic

apavo|rante /apavo'rãtʃi/ *a* terrifying. ~**rar** *vt* terrify. ~**rar-se** *vpr* be terrified

apaziguar /apazi'gwar/ *vt* appease

apear-se /api'arsi/ *vpr* (*de cavalo*) dismount; (*de ônibus*) alight

ape|gar-se /ape'garsi/ *vpr* become attached (**a** to). ~**go** /e/ *m* attachment

ape|lação /apela'sãw/ *f* appeal; *fig* exhibitionism. ~**lar** *vi* appeal (**de** against); ~**lar para** appeal to; *fig* resort to

apeli|dar /apeli'dar/ *vt* nickname. ~**do** *m* nickname

apelo /a'pelu/ *m* appeal

apenas /a'penas/ *adv* only

apêndice /a'pẽdʒisi/ *m* appendix

apendicite /apẽdʒi'sitʃi/ *f* appendicitis

aperceber-se /aperse'bersi/ *vpr* ~
(de) notice, realize

aperfeiçoar /aperfejso'ar/ *vt*
perfect

aperitivo /aperi'tʃivu/ *m* aperitif

aper|tado /aper'tadu/ *a* tight;
(*sem dinheiro*) hard-up. ~**tar** *vt*
(*segurar*) hold tight; tighten ‹*cinto*›;
press ‹*botão*›; squeeze ‹*esponja*›;
take in ‹*vestido*›; fasten ‹*cinto de
segurança*›; step up ‹*vigilância*›;
cut down on ‹*despesas*›; break
‹*coração*›; fig pressurize ‹*pessoa*›;
~**tar a mão de alguém** shake hands
with sb ● *vi* ‹*sapato*› pinch; ‹*chuva,
frio*› get worse; ‹*estrada*› narrow.
~**tar-se** *vpr* (*gastar menos*) tighten
one's belt; (*não ter dinheiro*) feel
the pinch. ~**to** /e/ *m* pressure; (*de
botão*) press; (*dificuldade*) tight spot,
jam; ~**to de mãos** handshake

apesar /ape'zar/ ~ **de** *prep* in
spite of

apeti|te /ape'tʃitʃi/ *m* appetite.
~**toso** /o/ *a* appetizing

apetrechos /ape'treʃus/ *m pl* gear;
(*de pesca*) tackle

apimentado /apimẽ'tadu/ *a*
spicy, hot

apinhar /api'ɲar/ *vt* crowd, pack.
~**se** *vpr* crowd

api|tar /api'tar/ *vi* whistle ● *vt*
referee ‹*jogo*›. ~**to** *m* whistle

aplanar /apla'nar/ *vt* level
‹*terreno*›; fig smooth ‹*caminho*›;
smooth over ‹*problema*›

aplau|dir /aplaw'dʒir/ *vt* applaud.
~**so(s)** *m(pl)* applause

apli|cação /aplika'sãw/
f application; (*de dinheiro*)
investment; (*de lei*) enforcement.
~**car** *vt* apply; invest ‹*dinheiro*›;
enforce ‹*lei*›. ~**car-se** *vpr* apply

(a to); (*ao estudo etc*) apply o.s.
(a to). ~**que** *m* hairpiece

apoderar-se /apode'rarsi/ *vpr*
~ **de** take possession of; ‹*raiva*›
take hold of

apodrecer /apodre'ser/ *vt/i* rot

apoi|ar /apoj'ar/ *vt* lean; *fig*
support; (*basear*) base. ~**ar-se** *vpr*
~**ar-se em** lean on; *fig* be based on,
rest on. ~**o** *m* support

apólice /a'pɔlisi/ *f* policy; (*ação*)
bond

apon|tador /apõta'dor/ *m* pencil
sharpener. ~**tar** *vt* (*com o dedo*)
point at, point to; point out ‹*erro,
caso interessante*›; aim ‹*arma*›;
name ‹*nomes*›; put forward ‹*razão*›
● *vi* ‹*sol, planta*› come up; (*com o
dedo*) point (**para** to)

apoquentar /apokẽ'tar/ *vt* annoy

aporrinhar /apoxi'ɲar/ *vt* annoy

após /a'pɔs/ *adv* after; ‹*loção*›
~**barba** aftershave (lotion)

aposen|tado /apozẽ'tadu/ *a*
retired ● *m* pensioner. ~**tadoria** *f*
retirement; (*pensão*) pension. ~**tar**
vt, ~**tar-se** *vpr* retire. ~**to** *m* room

após-guerra /apɔz'gexa/ *m* post-
war period

apos|ta /a'pɔsta/ *f* bet. ~**tar** *vt* bet
(**em** on); *fig* have faith (**em** in)

apostila /apos'tʃila/ *f* revision aid,
book of key facts

apóstolo /a'pɔstolu/ *m* apostle

apóstrofo /a'pɔstrofu/ *m*
apostrophe

apre|ciação /apresia'sãw/ *f*
appreciation. ~**ciar** *vt* appreciate;
think highly of ‹*pessoa*›. ~**ciativo**
a appreciative. ~**ciável** (*pl* ~**ciáveis**)
a appreciable. ~**ço** /e/ *m* regard

apreen|der /apriẽ'der/ *vt*
seize ‹*contrabando*›; apprehend

apregoar | aquisição

‹*criminoso*›; grasp ‹*sentido*›. **~são**
f apprehension; (*de contrabando*)
seizure; **~sivo** *a* apprehensive

apregoar /aprego'ar/ *vt* proclaim;
cry ‹*mercadoria*›

apren|der /aprẽ'der/ *vt/i* learn.
~diz *m/f* (*de ofício*) apprentice;
(*de direção*) learner; **~dizado**
m, **~dizagem** *f* (*de ofício*)
apprenticeship; (*de profissão*)
training; (*escolar*) learning

apresen|tação /aprezẽta'sãw/
f presentation; (*teatral etc*)
performance; (*de pessoas*)
introduction; **~tador** *m* presenter.
~tar *vt* present; introduce ‹*pessoa*›.
~tar-se *vpr* (*identificar-se*) introduce
o.s.; ‹*ocasião, problema*› present
o.s., arise; **~tar-se a** report to
‹*polícia etc*›; go in for ‹*exame*›;
stand for ‹*eleição*›. **~tável** (*pl*
~táveis) *a* presentable

apres|sado /apre'sadu/ *a* hurried.
~sar *vt* hurry. **~sar-se** *vpr* hurry (up)

aprimorar /aprimo'rar/ *vt*
perfect, refine

aprofundar /aprofũ'dar/ *vt*
deepen; study carefully ‹*questão*›.
~se *vpr* get deeper; **~se em** go
deeper into

aprontar /aprõ'tar/ *vt* get ready;
pick ‹*briga*› ● *vi* act up. **~se** *vpr*
get ready

apropriado /apropri'adu/ *a*
appropriate, suitable

apro|vação /aprova'sãw/ *f*
approval; (*num exame*) pass. **~var**
vt approve of; approve ‹*lei*› ● *vi*
make the grade; **ser ~vado** (*num
exame*) pass

aprovei|tador /aprovejta'dor/
m opportunist. **~tamento** *m*
utilization. **~tar** *vt* take advantage
of; take ‹*ocasião*›; (*utilizar*) use

● *vi* make the most of it; *Port*
(*adiantar*) be of use. **~tar-se** *vpr* take
advantage (**de** of); **~tel** (*divirta-se*)
have a good time!

aproxi|mação /aprosima'sãw/
f (*chegada*) approach; (*estimativa*)
approximation. **~mado** *a* ‹*valor*›
approximate. **~mar** *vt* move nearer;
(*aliar*) bring together. **~mar-se** *vpr*
approach, get nearer (**de** to)

ap|tidão /apt∫i'dãw/ *f* aptitude,
suitability. **~to** *a* suitable

apunhalar /apuɲa'lar/ *vt* stab

apu|rado /apu'radu/ *a* refined.
~rar *vt* (*aprimorar*) refine; (*descobrir*)
ascertain; investigate ‹*caso*›; collect
‹*dinheiro*›; count ‹*votos*›. **~rar-se**
vpr (*com a roupa*) dress smartly. **~ro**
m refinement; (*no vestir*) elegance;
(*dificuldade*) difficulty; *pl* trouble

aquarela /akwa'rela/ *f* watercolour

aquariano /akwari'anu/ *a & m*
Aquarian

aquário /a'kwariu/ *m* aquarium;
Aquário Aquarius

aquartelar /akwarte'lar/ *vt* billet

aquático /a'kwat∫iku/ *a* aquatic,
water

aque|cedor /akese'dor/ *m* heater.
~cer *vt* heat ● *vi*, **~cer-se** *vpr* heat
up. **~cimento** /akesi'mẽtu/ *m*
heating; **~cimento global** global
warming

aqueduto /ake'dutu/ *m* aqueduct

aquele /a'keli/ *a* that; those ● *pron*
that one; those; **~ que** the one that

àquele =A + AQUELE

aqui /a'ki/ *adv* here

aquilo /a'kilu/ *pron* that

àquilo =A + AQUILO

aquisi|ção /akizi'sãw/ *f*
acquisition. **~tivo** **a poder ~tivo**
purchasing power

ar /ar/ m air; (*aspecto*) look, air;
Port (no carro) choke; **ao ~ livre**
in the open air; **no ~** fig up in the
air; TV on air; **~ condicionado** air
conditioning

árabe /'arabi/ a & m Arab; Lang
Arabic

Arábia /a'rabia/ f Arabia; **~ Saudita**
Saudi Arabia

arado /a'radu/ m plough, Amer
plow

aragem /a'raʒẽ/ f breeze

arame /a'rami/ m wire; **~ farpado**
barbed wire

aranha /a'raɲa/ f spider

arar /a'rar/ vt plough, Amer plow

arara /a'rara/ f parrot

arbi|trar /arbi'trar/ vt/i referee
‹*jogo*›; arbitrate ‹*disputa*›. **~trário**
a arbitrary

arbítrio /ar'bitriu/ m judgement;
livre ~ free will

árbitro /'arbitru/ m arbiter ‹*da
moda etc*›; Jurid arbitrator; (*de
futebol*) referee; (*de tênis*) umpire

arborizado /arbori'zadu/ a
wooded, green; (*rua*) tree-lined

arbusto /ar'bustu/ m shrub

ar|ca /'arka/ f **~ca de Noé** Noah's
Ark. **~cada** f (*galeria*) arcade;
(*arco*) arch

arcaico /ar'kajku/ a archaic

arcar /ar'kar/ vt **~ com** deal with

arcebispo /arse'bispu/ m
archbishop

arco /'arku/ m Arquit arch; (*arma,
Mus*) bow; Eletr, Mat arc. **~da-velha**
m coisa do **~da-velha** amazing
thing; **~íris** m invar rainbow

ar|dente /ar'dẽtʃi/ a burning;
fig ardent. **~der** vi burn; ‹*olhos,
ferida*› sting

ardil /ar'dʒiw/ (*pl* **~dis**) m trick,
ruse

ardor /ar'dor/ m heat; fig ardour;
com ~ ardently

árduo /'arduu/ a strenuous,
arduous

área /'aria/ f area; **(grande) ~**
penalty area; **~ (de serviço)** yard

arear /ari'ar/ vt scour ‹*panela*›

areia /a'reja/ f sand

arejar /are'ʒar/ vt air ● vi, **~se**
vpr get some air; (*descansar*) have
a breather

are|na /a'rena/ f arena. **~noso**
/o/ a sandy

arenque /a'rẽki/ m herring

argamassa /arga'masa/ f mortar

Argélia /ar'ʒelia/ f Algeria

argelino /arʒe'linu/ a & m Algerian

Argentina /arʒẽ'tʃina/ f Argentina

argentino /arʒẽ'tʃinu/ a & m
Argentinian

argila /ar'ʒila/ f clay

argola /ar'gɔla/ f ring

arguido /ar'gwidu/ m defendant

argumen|tar /argumẽ'tar/ vt/i
argue. **~to** m argument; (*de filme
etc*) subject matter

ariano /ari'anu/ a & m (*do signo
Aries*) Arian

árido /'aridu/ a arid; barren
‹*deserto*›; fig dull, dry

Áries /'aris/ m Aries

arisco /a'risku/ a timid

aristo|cracia /aristokra'sia/ f
aristocracy. **~crata** m/f aristocrat.
~crático a aristocratic

aritmética /aritʃ'mɛtʃika/ f
arithmetic

arma /'arma/ f weapon; arms; **~ de
fogo** firearm

ar|mação /arma'sãw/ f frame; (de óculos) frames; Naut rigging. **~madilha** f trap. **~madura** f suit of armour; (armação) framework. **~mar** vt (dar armas a) arm; (montar máquina) put up, assemble; set up; set, lay (armadilha); fit out (navio); hatch (plano, complô); cause (briga). **~mar-se** vpr arm o.s.

armarinho /arma'riɲu/ m haberdashery, Amer notions

armário /ar'mariu/ m cupboard; (de roupa) wardrobe

arma|zém /arma'zẽj/ m warehouse; (loja) general store; (depósito) storeroom. **~zenagem** f, **~zenamento** m storage. **~zenar** vt store

Armênia /ar'menia/ f Armenia

armê|nio /ar'meniu/ a & m Armenian

aro /'aru/ m (de roda, óculos) rim; (de porta) frame

aro|ma /a'roma/ m aroma; (perfume) fragrance. **~mático** a aromatic; fragrant

ar|pão /ar'pãw/ m harpoon. **~poar** vt harpoon

arquear /arki'ar/ vt arch. **~se** vpr bend, bow

arque|ologia /arkiolo'ʒia/ f archaeology. **~ológico** a archaeological. **~ólogo** m archaeologist

arquétipo /ar'ketʃipu/ m archetype

arquibancada /arkibã'kada/ f terraces, Amer bleachers

arquipélago /arki'pɛlagu/ m archipelago

arquite|tar /arkite'tar/ vt think up. **~to** /e/ m architect. **~tônico** a architectural. **~tura** f architecture

arqui|var /arki'var/ vt file (papéis); shelve (plano, processo). **~vista** m/f archivist. **~vo** m file; (conjunto) files; (móvel) filing cabinet; (do Estado etc) archives

arran|cada /axã'kada/ f lurch; (de atleta) fig spurt. **~car** vt pull out (cabelo etc); pull off (botão etc); pull up (erva daninha etc); take out (dente); (das mãos de alguém) wrench, snatch; extract (confissão, dinheiro) ● vi (carro) roar off; (pessoa) take off; (dar solavanco) lurch forward. **~car-se** vpr take off. **~co** m pull, tug

arranha-céu /axaɲa'sɛw/ m skyscraper

arra|nhadura /axaɲa'dura/ f scratch. **~nhão** m scratch. **~nhar** vt scratch; have a smattering of (língua)

arran|jar /axã'ʒar/ vt arrange; (achar) get, find; (resolver) settle, sort out. **~jar-se** vpr manage. **~jo** m arrangement

arrasar /axa'zar/ vt devastate; raze, flatten (casa, cidade). **~se** vpr be devastated

arrastar /axas'tar/ vt drag; (corrente, avalancha) sweep away; (atrair) draw ● vi trail. **~se** vpr crawl; (tempo) drag; (processo) drag out

arreba|tador /axebata'dor/ a entrancing; shocking (notícia). **~tar** vt (enlevar) entrance, send; (chocar) shock

arreben|tação /axebẽta'sãw/ f surf. **~tar** vi (bomba) explode; (corda) snap, break; (balão, pessoa) burst; (onda) break; (guerra, incêndio) break out ● vt snap (corda); burst (balão); break down (porta)

arrebitar /axebi'tar/ vt turn up
‹nariz›; prick up ‹orelhas›

arreca|dação /axekada'sãw/
f (dinheiro) tax revenue. **~dar** vt
collect

arredar /axe'dar/ vt **não ~ pé**
stand one's ground

arredio /axe'dʒiu/ a withdrawn

arredondar /axedõ'dar/ vt round
up ‹quantia›; round off ‹ângulo›

arredores /axe'dɔris/ m pl
surroundings; (de cidade) outskirts

arrefecer /axefe'ser/ vt/i cool

arregaçar /axega'sar/ vt roll up

arrega|lado /axega'ladu/ a
‹olhos› wide. **~lar** vt **~lar os olhos**
be wide-eyed with amazement

arreganhar /axega'ɲar/ vt bare
‹dentes›. **~se** vpr grin

arrema|tar /axema'tar/ vt
finish off; (no tricô) cast off. **~te** m
conclusion; (na costura) finishing off;
(no futebol) finishing

arremes|sar /axeme'sar/ vt hurl.
~so /e/ m throw

arrendar /axẽ'dar/ vt rent

arrepen|der-se /axepẽ'dersi/ vpr
be sorry; ‹pecador› repent; **~der-se
de** regret. **~dido** a sorry; ‹pecador›
repentant. **~dimento** m regret; (de
pecado, crime) repentance

arrepi|ado /axepi'adu/ a ‹cabelo›
standing on end; ‹pele, pessoa›
covered in goose pimples. **~ar** vt
(dar calafrios) make shudder; make
stand on end ‹cabelo›; **me ~a
(a pele)** it gives me goose pimples.
~ar-se vpr (estremecer) shudder;
‹cabelo› stand on end; (na pele) get
goose pimples. **~o** m shudder; **me
dá ~os** it makes me shudder

arris|cado /axis'kadu/ a risky.
~car vt risk. **~car-se** vpr take a

risk, risk it

arroba /a'xoba/ m Comput @,
at sign

arro|char /axo'ʃar/ vt tighten up
● vi be tough. **~cho** /o/ m squeeze

arro|gância /axo'gãsia/ f
arrogance. **~gante** a arrogant

arro|jado /axo'ʒadu/ a bold. **~jar**
vt throw

arrombar /axõ'bar/ vt break down
‹porta›; break into ‹casa›; crack
‹cofre›

arro|tar /axo'tar/ vi burp, belch.
~to /o/ m burp

arroz /a'xoz/ m rice; **~ doce** rice
pudding. **~al** (pl **~ais**) m rice field

arrua|ça /axu'asa/ f riot. **~ceiro**
m rioter

arruela /axu'ela/ f washer

arruinar /axui'nar/ vt ruin. **~nar-se**
vpr be ruined

arru|madeira /axuma'dera/ f (de
hotel) chambermaid. **~mar** vt tidy
(up) ‹casa›; sort out ‹papéis, vida›;
pack ‹mala›; (achar) find, get; make
up ‹desculpa›; (vestir) dress up.
~mar-se vpr (aprontar-se) get ready;
(na vida) sort o.s. out

arse|nal /arse'naw/ (pl **~nais**) m
arsenal

arsênio /ar'seniu/ m arsenic

arte /'artʃi/ f art; **fazer ~** ‹criança›
get up to mischief. **~fato** m product,
article

arteiro /ar'teru/ a mischievous

artéria /ar'tɛria/ f artery

artesa|nal /arteza'naw/ (pl **~nais**)
a craft. **~nato** m craftwork

arte|são /arte'zãw/ (pl **~s**) m (f
~sã) artisan, craftsman (f-woman)

ártico /'artʃiku/ a & m arctic

articu|lação /artʃikula'sãw/ f articulation; (Anat, Tecn) joint. **~lar** vt articulate

arti|ficial /artʃifisi'aw/ (pl **~ficiais**) a artificial. **~fício** m trick

artigo /ar'tʃigu/ m article; Com item

arti|lharia /artʃiʎa'ria/ f artillery. **~lheiro** m Mil gunner; (no futebol) striker

artimanha /artʃi'maɲa/ f trick; (método) clever way

ar|tista /ar'tʃista/ m/f artist. **~tístico** a artistic

artrite /ar'tritʃi/ f arthritis

árvore /'arvori/ f tree

arvoredo /arvo'redu/ m grove

ás /as/ m ace

às ▶ A

asa /'aza/ f wing; (de xícara) handle. **~delta** f hang-glider

ascen|dência /asẽ'dẽsia/ f ancestry; (superioridade) ascendancy. **~dente** a rising. **~der** vi rise; ascend ‹ao trono›. **~são** f rise; Relig Ascension; **em ~são** rising; fig up and coming. **~sor** m lift, Amer elevator. **~sorista** m/f lift operator

asco /'asku/ m revulsion, disgust; **dar ~** be revolting

asfalto /as'fawtu/ m asphalt

asfixiar /asfiksi'ar/ vt/i asphyxiate

Ásia /'azia/ f Asia

asiático /azi'atʃiku/ a & m Asian

asilo /a'zilu/ m (refúgio) asylum; (de velhos, crianças) home

as|ma /'azma/ f asthma. **~mático** a & m asthmatic

asneira /az'nera/ f stupidity; (uma) stupid thing

aspargo /as'pargu/ m asparagus

aspas /'aspas/ f pl inverted commas

aspecto /as'pektu/ m appearance, look; (de um problema) aspect

aspereza /aspe'reza/ f roughness; (do clima, de um som) harshness; fig rudeness

áspero /'asperu/ a rough; ‹clima, som› harsh; fig rude

aspi|ração /aspira'sãw/ f aspiration; Med inhalation. **~rador** m vacuum cleaner. **~rar** vt inhale, breathe in ‹ar, fumaça›; suck up ‹líquido›; **~rar a** aspire to

aspirina /aspi'rina/ f aspirin

asqueroso /aske'rozu/ a revolting, disgusting

assa|do /a'sadu/ a & m roast. **~dura** f (na pele) sore patch

assalariado /asalari'adu/ a salaried ● m salaried worker

assal|tante /asaw'tãtʃi/ m/f robber; (na rua) mugger; (de casa) burglar. **~tar** vt rob; burgle, Amer burglarize ‹casa›. **~to** m (roubo) robbery; (a uma casa) burglary; (ataque) assault; (no boxe) round

assanhado /asa'ɲadu/ a worked up; ‹criança› excitable; (erótico) amorous

assar /a'sar/ vt roast

assassi|nar /asasi'nar/ vt murder; Pol assassinate. **~nato** m murder; Pol assassination. **~no** m murderer; Pol assassin

asseado /asi'adu/ a well-groomed

as|sediar /asedʒi'ar/ vt besiege ‹cidade›; fig harass. **~sédio** m siege; fig pestering; **~sédio sexual** sexual harassment

assegurar /asegu'rar/ vt (tornar seguro) secure; (afirmar) guarantee; **~ a alguém algo/que** assure s.o. of sth/that; **~se de/que** make sure of/that

assembleia /ɐsē'bleja/ f *Pol* assembly; *Com* meeting

Assembleia da República *i*
The Portuguese Assembly of the Republic, located in the Palácio de São Bento, Lisbon, is the Portuguese parliament. The Assembly's 230 seats are allocated by proportional representation, and the members collectively represent the country's twenty-two constituencies and the two autonomous regions, Madeira and the Azores.

---

assemelhar /ɐseme'ʎar/ vt liken. **~se** vpr be alike; **~se a** resemble, be like

assen|tar /ɐsē'tar/ vt (*estabelecer*) establish, define; settle <povo>; lay <tijolo>; **~tar com** go with; **~tar a** <roupa> suit ● vi <pó> settle. **~tar-se** vpr settle down. **~to** m seat; fig basis; **tomar ~to** take a seat; <pó> settle

assen|tir /ɐsē'tʃir/ vi agree. **~timento** m agreement

assertivo /ɐser'tʃivu/ a assertive

assessor /ɐse'sor/ m adviser. **~ar** vt advise

assexuado /ɐseksu'adu/ a asexual

assiduidade /ɐsidui'dadʒi/ f (à escola) regular attendance; (diligência) diligence

assíduo /a'siduu/ a (que frequenta) regular; (diligente) assiduous

assim /a'sī/ adv like this, like that; (portanto) therefore; **e ~ por diante** and so on; **~ como** as well as; **~ que** as soon as

assimétrico /ɐsi'metriku/ a asymmetrical

assimilar /ɐsimi'lar/ vt assimilate. **~se** vpr be assimilated

assinalar /ɐsina'lar/ vt (marcar) mark; (distinguir) distinguish; (apontar) point out

assi|nante /ɐsi'nɐ̃tʃi/ m/f subscriber. **~nar** vt/i sign. **~natura** f (nome) signature; (de revista) subscription

assis|tência /ɐsis'tẽsia/ f assistance; (presença) attendance; (público) audience. **~tente** a m/f assistant; **~tente social** social worker. **~tir (a)** vt/i (ver) watch; (presenciar) attend; assist <doente>

assoalho /ɐso'aʎu/ m floor

assoar /ɐso'ar/ vt **~ o nariz**, Port **~se** blow one's nose

assobi|ar /ɐsobi'ar/ vt/i whistle. **~o** m whistle

associ|ação /ɐsosia'sãw/ f association. **~ado** a & m associate. **~ar** vt associate (**a** with). **~ar-se** vpr associate; Com go into partnership (**a** with)

assolar /ɐso'lar/ vt devastate

assom|bração /ɐsõbra'sãw/ f ghost. **~brar** vt astonish, amaze. **~brar-se** vpr be amazed. **~bro** m amazement, astonishment; (coisa) marvel. **~broso** /o/ a astonishing, amazing

assoprar /ɐso'prar/ vi blow ● vt blow; blow out <vela>

assoviar etc ▶ ASSOBIAR etc

assu|mido /ɐsu'midu/ a (confesso) confirmed, self-confessed. **~mir** vt assume, take on; accept, admit <defeito> ● vi take office

assunto /a'sũtu/ m subject; (negócio) matter

assustador | ativa

assus|tador /asusta'dor/ a frightening. **~tar** vt frighten, scare. **~tar-se** vpr get frightened, get scared

asterisco /aste'risku/ m asterisk

as|tral /as'traw/ (pl **~trais**) m 🄴 state of mind. **~tro** m star. **~trologia** f astrology. **~trólogo** m astrologer. **~tronauta** m/f astronaut. **~tronave** f spaceship. **~tronomia** f astronomy. **~tronômico** a astronomical. **~trônomo** m astronomer

as|túcia /as'tusia/ f cunning. **~tuto** a cunning; ‹comerciante› astute

ata /'ata/ f minutes

ataca|dista /ataka'dʒista/ m/f wholesaler. **~do** m por **~do** wholesale

ata|cante /ata'kãtʃi/ a attacking ● m/f attacker. **~car** vt attack; tackle ‹problema›

atadura /ata'dura/ f bandage

ata|lhar /ata'ʎar/ vi take a shortcut. **~lho** m shortcut

ataque /a'taki/ m attack; ‹de raiva, riso› fit; **~ aéreo** air strike

atar /a'tar/ vt tie

atarantado /ataɾã'tadu/ a flustered, in a flap

atarefado /atare'fadu/ a busy

atarracado /ataxa'kadu/ a stocky

atarraxar /ataxa'ʃar/ vt screw

até /a'tɛ/ prep (up) to, as far as; ‹tempo› until ● adv even; **~ logo** goodbye; **~ que** until

ateia /a'teja/ a & f ▶ ATEU

ateliê /ateli'e/ m studio

atemorizar /atemori'zar/ vt frighten

Atenas /a'tenas/ f Athens

aten|ção /atẽ'sãw/ f attention; pl (bondade) thoughtfulness; **com ~ção** attentively. **~cioso** a thoughtful, considerate

aten|der /atẽ'der/ **~der (a)** vt/i answer ‹telefone, porta›; answer to ‹pessoa›; serve ‹freguês›; see ‹paciente, visitante›; grant, meet ‹pedido›; heed ‹conselho›. **~dimento** m service; (de médico etc) consultation

aten|tado /atẽ'tadu/ m murder attempt; Pol assassination attempt; (ataque) attack (contra on). **~tar** vi **~tar contra** make an attempt on

atento /a'tẽtu/ a attentive; **~ a** mindful of

aterrador /atexa'dor/ a terrifying

ater|ragem /ate'xaʒẽ/ f Port landing. **~rar** vi Port land

aterris|sagem /atexi'saʒẽ/ f landing. **~sar** vi land

aterro /a'texu/ m **~ (sanitário)** landfill

ater-se /a'tersi/ vpr **~ a** keep to, go by

ates|tado /ates'tadu/ m certificate. **~tar** vt attest (to)

ateu /a'tew/ a & m (f **ateia**) atheist

atiçar /atʃi'sar/ vt poke ‹fogo›; stir up ‹ódio, discórdia›; arouse ‹pessoa›

atinar /atʃi'nar/ vt work out, guess; **~ com** find; **~ em** notice

atingir /atʃi'ʒir/ vt reach; hit ‹alvo›; (conseguir) attain; (afetar) affect

atirar /atʃi'rar/ vt throw ● vi shoot; **~ em** fire at

atitude /atʃi'tudʒi/ f attitude; **tomar uma ~** take action

ati|va /a'tʃiva/ f active service. **~var** vt activate. **~vidade** f activity. **~vo** a active ● m Com assets

Atlântico /at'lātʃiku/ m Atlantic

atlas /'atlas/ m atlas

at|leta /at'lɛta/ m/f athlete. **~lético** a athletic. **~letismo** m athletics

atmosfera /atʃimos'fera/ f atmosphere

ato /'atu/ m act; (ação) action; **no ~** on the spot

ato|lar /ato'lar/ vt bog down. **~lar-se** vpr get bogged down. **~leiro** m bog; fig fix, spot of trouble

atômico /a'tomiku/ a atomic

atomizador /atomiza'dor/ m atomizer spray

átomo /'atomu/ m atom

atônito /a'tonitu/ a astonished, stunned

ator /a'tor/ m actor

atordoar /atordo'ar/ vt ‹golpe, notícia› stun; ‹som› deafen; (alucinar) bewilder

atormentar /atormẽ'tar/ vt plague, torment

atração /atra'sãw/ f attraction

atracar /atra'kar/ vt/i Naut moor. **~-se** vpr grapple. 🄣 neck

atraente /atra'ẽtʃi/ a attractive

atraiçoar /atrajso'ar/ vt betray

atrair /atra'ir/ vt attract

atrapalhar /atrapa'ʎar/ vt/i (confundir) confuse; (estorvar) hinder; (perturbar) disturb. **~-se** vpr get mixed up

atrás /a'traʃ/ adv behind; (no fundo) at the back; **~** de behind; (depois de, no encalço de) after; **um mês ~** a month ago; **ficar ~** be left behind

atra|sado /atra'zadu/ a late; ‹país, criança› backward; ‹relógio› slow; ‹pagamento› overdue; ‹ideias› old-fashioned. **~sar** vt delay; put back ‹relógio› ● vi be late; ‹relógio›

lose. **~sar-se** vpr be late; (num trabalho) get behind; (no pagar) get into arrears. **~so** m delay; (de país etc) backwardness; pl Com arrears; **com ~so** late

atrativo /atra'tʃivu/ m attraction

através /atra'ves/ **~ de** prep through; (de um lado ao outro) across

atravessado /atrave'sadu/ a ‹espinha› stuck; **estar com alguém ~ na garganta** be fed up with sb

atravessar /atrave'sar/ vt go through; cross ‹rua, rio›

atre|ver-se /atre'versi/ vpr dare; **~ver-se a** dare to. **~vido** a daring; (insolente) impudent. **~vimento** m daring, boldness; (insolência) impudence

atribu|ir /atribu'ir/ vt attribute (a to); confer ‹prêmio, poderes› (a on); attach ‹importância› (a to). **~to** m attribute

atrito /a'tritu/ m friction; (desavença) disagreement

atriz /a'tris/ f actress

atrocidade /atrosi'dadʒi/ f atrocity

atrope|lar /atrope'lar/ vt run over, knock down ‹pedestre›; (empurrar) jostle; mix up ‹palavras›; **~lamento** m (de pedestre) running over. **~lo** /e/ m scramble

atroz /a'tros/ a awful, terrible; heinous ‹crime›; cruel ‹pessoa›

atuação /atua'sãw/ f (ação) action; (desempenho) performance

atu|al /atu'aw/ (pl **~ais**) a current, present; ‹assunto, interesse› topical; ‹pessoa, carro› up-to-date. **~alidade** f (presente) present (time); (de um livro) topicality; pl current affairs. **~alizado** a up-to-date

~alizar vt update. **~alizar-se** vpr bring o.s. up to date. **~almente** adv at present, currently

atum /a'tũ/ m tuna

aturdir /atur'dʒir/ vt ▶ ATORDOAR

audácia /aw'dasia/ f boldness; (insolência) audacity

audi|ção /awdʒi'sãw/ f hearing; (concerto) recital. **~ência** f audience; Jurid hearing

audiovisu|al /awdʒiovizu'aw/ (pl ~ais) a audiovisual

auditório /awdʒi'tɔriu/ m auditorium; programa de ~ variety show

auge /'awʒi/ m peak, height

aula /'awla/ f class, lesson; dar ~ teach

aumen|tar /awmẽ'tar/ vt increase; raise <preço, salário>; extend <casa>; (com lente) magnify; (acrescentar) add ● vi increase; <preço, salário> go up. **~to** m increase; (de salário) rise, Amer raise

au|sência /aw'zẽsia/ f absence. **~sente** a absent ● m/f absentee

aus|pícios /aws'pisius/ m pl auspices. **~picioso** /o/ a auspicious

auste|ridade /awsteri'dadʒi/ f austerity. **~ro** /ɛ/ a austere

Austrália /aws'tralia/ f Australia

australiano /awstrali'anu/ a & m Australian

Áustria /'awstria/ f Austria

austríaco /aws'triaku/ a & m Austrian

autarquia /awtar'kia/ f public authority

autêntico /aw'tẽtʃiku/ a authentic; genuine <pessoa>; true <fato>

autobio|grafia /awtobiogra'fia/ f autobiography. **~gráfico** a autobiographical

autocarro /awto'kaxu/ m Port bus

autocrata /awto'krata/ a autocratic

autodefesa /awtode'feza/ f self-defence

autodidata /awtodʒi'data/ a & m/f self-taught (person)

autódromo /aw'tɔdromu/ m race track

autoescola /awtois'kɔla/ f driving school

autoestrada /awtois'trada/ f motorway, Amer expressway

autógrafo /aw'tɔgrafu/ m autograph

auto|mação /awtoma'sãw/ f automation. **~mático** a automatic. **~matizar** vt automate

auto|mobilismo /awtomobi-'lizmu/ m motoring; (esporte) motor racing. **~móvel** (pl ~móveis) m motor car, Amer automobile

automutilação /awtomutʃila'sãw/ f self-harm

au|tonomia /awtono'mia/ f autonomy. **~tônomo** a autonomous; <trabalhador> self-employed

autopeça /awto'pesa/ f car spare

autópsia /aw'tɔpsia/ f autopsy

autor /aw'tor/ m (f ~a) author; (de crime) perpetrator; Jurid plaintiff

autoria /awto'ria/ f authorship; (de crime) responsibility (de for)

autori|dade /awtori'dadʒi/ f authority. **~zação** f authorization. **~zar** vt authorize

autorretrato /awtoxe'tratu/ *m* self-portrait

autuar /awtu'ar/ *vt* sue

au|xiliar /awsili'ar/ *a* auxiliary ● *m/f* assistant ● *vt* assist. **~xílio** /o/ *m* assistance, aid

aval /a'vaw/ (*pl* **avais**) *m* endorsement; *Com* guarantee

avali|ação /avalia'sãw/ *f* (*de preço*) valuation; *fig* evaluation. **~ar** *vt* value <*quadro etc*> (**em** at); assess <*danos, riscos*>; *fig* evaluate

avan|çar /avã'sar/ *vt* move forward ● *vi* move forward; *Mil fig* advance; **~çar a** (*montar*) amount to. **~ço** *m* advance

avar|eza /ava'reza/ *f* meanness. **~ento** *a* mean

ava|ria /ava'ria/ *f* damage; (*de máquina*) breakdown. **~riado** *a* damaged; <*máquina*> out of order; <*carro*> broken down. **~riar** *vt* damage ● *vi* be damaged; <*máquina*> break down

avatar /ava'tar/ *m* avatar

ave /'avi/ *f* bird; **~ de rapina** bird of prey

aveia /a'veja/ *f* oats

avelã /ave'lã/ *f* hazelnut

avenida /ave'nida/ *f* avenue

aven|tal /avẽ'taw/ (*pl* **~tais**) *m* apron

aventu|ra /avẽ'tura/ *f* adventure; (*amorosa*) fling. **~rar** *vt* venture. **~rar-se** *vpr* venture (**a** to). **~reiro** *a* adventurous ● *m* adventurer

averiguar /averi'gwar/ *vt* check (out)

avermelhado /averme'ʎadu/ *a* reddish

aver|são /aver'sãw/ *f* aversion. **~so** *a* averse (**a** to)

aves|sas /a'vesas/ **às ~sas** the wrong way round; (*de cabeça para baixo*) upside down. **~so** /e/ *m* **ao ~so** inside out

avestruz /aves'trus/ *m* ostrich

avi|ação /avia'sãw/ *f* aviation. **~ão** *m* (aero)plane, *Amer* (air)plane; **~ão a jato** jet

avi|dez /avi'des/ *f* (*cobiça*) greediness

ávido /'avidu/ *a* greedy

avi|sar /avi'zar/ *vt* (*informar*) tell, let know; (*advertir*) warn. **~so** *m* notice; (*advertência*) warning

avistar /avis'tar/ *vt* catch sight of

avo /'avu/ *m* **um doze ~s** one twelfth

avó /a'vɔ/ *f* grandmother. **~s** *m pl* grandparents

avô /a'vo/ *m* grandfather

avoado /avo'adu/ *a* dizzy, scatterbrained

avulso /a'vuwsu/ *a* loose, odd

avultado /avuw'tadu/ *a* bulky

axila /ak'sila/ *f* armpit

azaléia /aza'lɛja/ *f* azalea

azar /a'zar/ *m* bad luck; **ter ~** be unlucky. **~ado, ~ento** *a* unlucky

aze|dar /aze'dar/ *vt* sour ● *vi* go sour. **~do** /e/ *a* sour

azei|te /a'zejtʃi/ *m* oil. **~tona** /o/ *f* olive

azevinho /aze'viɲu/ *m* holly

azia /a'zia/ *f* heartburn

azucrinar /azukri'nar/ *vt* annoy

azul /a'zuw/ (*pl* **azuis**) *a* blue

azulejo /azu'leʒu/ *m* (ceramic) tile

azul-marinho /azuwma'riɲu/ *a invar* navy blue

Bb

babá /ba'ba/ f nanny; **~ eletrônica** baby alarm

ba|bado /ba'badu/ m frill. **~bador** m bib. **~bar** vt/i, **~bar-se** vpr drool (por over); <bebê> dribble. **~beiro** Port m bib

baby-sitter /bejbi'siter/ (pl **~s**) m/f babysitter

bacalhau /baka'ʎaw/ m cod

bacalhau *Bacalhau* is the Portuguese word for 'cod', although it is most commonly used to refer to salt (or dried) cod. Salt cod originated during the time of the Portuguese discoveries, when people needed a way to preserve fish before the advent of refrigeration. It's a hugely popular food, so much so that it's commonly said there are 365 ways to cook *bacalhau*, one for each day of the year, but in reality, there are many more.

bacana /ba'kana/ a 🇧🇷 great

bacha|rel /baʃa'rɛw/ (pl **~réis**) m bachelor. **~relado** m bachelor's degree. **~relar-se** vpr graduate

bacia /ba'sia/ f basin; (da privada) bowl; Anat pelvis

backup /be'kap/ m Port Comput backup

baço /'basu/ m spleen

bacon /bejkõ/ m bacon

bactéria /bak'tɛria/ f bacterium; pl bacteria

bada|lado /bada'ladu/ a 🇧🇷 talked about. **~lar** vt ring <sino> ● vi ring; 🇧🇷 go out and about. **~lativo** a 🇧🇷 fun-loving

badejo /ba'deʒu/ m sea bass

baderna /ba'dɛrna/ f (tumulto) commotion; (desordem) mess

badulaque /badu'laki/ m trinket

bafafá /bafa'fa/ m 🇧🇷 to-do, kerfuffle

ba|fo /'bafu/ m bad breath. **~fômetro** m Breathalyser. **~forada** f puff

bagaço /ba'gasu/ m pulp; Port (aguardente) brandy

baga|geiro /baga'ʒeru/ m (de carro) roof rack; Port (homem) porter. **~gem** f luggage; (cultural etc) baggage

bagatela /baga'tɛla/ f trifle

Bagdá /bagi'da/ f Baghdad

bago /'bagu/ m berry; (de chumbo) pellet

bagulho /ba'guʎu/ m piece of junk; pl junk; **ele é um ~** he's as ugly as sin

bagun|ça /ba'gũsa/ f mess. **~çar** vt mess up. **~ceiro** a messy

baía /ba'ia/ f bay

baiano /ba'janu/ a & m Bahian

baila /'bajla/ f **trazer/vir à ~** bring/come up

bai|lar /baj'lar/ vt/i dance. **~larino** m ballet dancer. **~le** m dance; (de gala) ball

bainha /ba'iɲa/ f (de vestido) hem; (de arma) sheath

baioneta /bajo'neta/ f bayonet

bairro /'bajxu/ m neighbourhood, area

baixa /'baʃa/ f drop, fall; (de guerra) casualty; (dispensa) discharge

~mar f low tide

baixar /baj'far/ vt lower; issue ‹ordem›; pass ‹lei›; Comput download ● vi drop, fall; 🔲 (pintar) turn up

baixaria /baʃa'ria/ f sordidness; (uma) sordid thing

baixela /ba'ʃela/ f set of cutlery

baixeza /ba'ʃeza/ f baseness

baixo /'baʃu/ a low; ‹pessoa› short; ‹som, voz› quiet, soft; ‹cabeça, olhos› lowered; (vil) sordid ● adv low; ‹falar› softly, quietly ● m bass; **em ~** underneath; (em casa) downstairs; **em ~ de** under; **para ~** down; (em casa) downstairs; **por ~ de** under(neath)

baju|lador /baʒula'dor/ a obsequious ● m sycophant. **~lar** vt fawn on

bala /'bala/ f (de revólver) bullet; (doce) sweet

balada /ba'lada/ f ballad

balaio /ba'laju/ m linen basket

balan|ça /ba'lãsa/ f scales; **Balança** (signo) Libra; **~ça de pagamentos** balance of payments. **~çar** vt/i (no ar) swing; (numa cadeira etc) rock; ‹carro, avião› shake; ‹navio› roll. **~çar-se** vpr swing. **~cete** /e/ m trial balance. **~ço** m Com balance sheet; (brinquedo) swing; (movimento no ar) swinging; (de carro, avião) shaking; (de navio) rolling; (de cadeira) rocking; **fazer um ~ço de** fig take stock of

balangandã /balãgã'dã/ m bauble

balão /ba'lãw/ m balloon; **soltar um ~ de ensaio** fig put out feelers

balar /ba'lar/ vi bleat

balbu|ciar /bawbusi'ar/ vt/i babble. **~cio** m babble, babbling

balbúrdia /baw'burdʒia/ f hubbub

bal|cão /baw'kãw/ m (em loja) counter; (de informações, bilhetes) desk; (de cozinha) worktop, Amer counter; (no teatro) circle. **~conista** m/f shop assistant

balde /'bawdʒi/ m bucket

baldeação /bawdʒia'sãw/ f fazer ~ change (trains)

baldio /baw'dʒiu/ a fallow; **terreno ~** (piece of) waste ground

balé /ba'lε/ m ballet

balear /bali'ar/ vt shoot

baleia /ba'leja/ f whale

balido /ba'lidu/ m bleat, bleating

balísti|ca /ba'listʃika/ f ballistics. **~co** a ballistic

bali|za /ba'liza/ f marker; (luminosa) beacon. **~zar** vt mark out

balneário /bawni'ariu/ m seaside resort

balofo /ba'lofu/ a fat, tubby

baloiço, balouço /ba'lojsu, ba'losu/ Port m (de criança) swing

balsa /'bawsa/ f (de madeira etc) raft; (que vai e vem) ferry

bálsamo /'bawsamu/ m balm

báltico /'bawtʃiku/ a & m Baltic

baluarte /balu'artʃi/ m bulwark

bambo /'bãbu/ a loose, slack; ‹pernas› limp; ‹mesa› wobbly

bambo|lê /bãbo'le/ m hula hoop. **~lear** vi ‹pessoa› sway, totter; ‹coisa› wobble

bambu /bã'bu/ m bamboo

ba|nal /ba'naw/ (pl **~nais**) a banal. **~nalidade** f banality

bana|na /ba'nana/ f banana ● m/f 🔲 wimp. **~nada** f banana fudge. **~neira** f banana tree; **plantar ~neira** do a handstand

banca /'bãka/ f (de trabalho) bench; (de jornais) news stand; ~ **examinadora** examining board. ~**da** f Pol bench

bancar /bã'kar/ vt (custear) finance; (fazer papel de) play; (fingir) pretend

bancário /bã'kariu/ a bank ● m bank employee

bancarrota /bãka'xota/ f bankruptcy; **ir à** ~ go bankrupt

banco /'bãku/ m Com bank; (no parque) bench; (na cozinha, num bar) stool; (de bicicleta) saddle; (de carro) seat; ~ **de areia** sandbank; ~ **de dados** database

banda /'bãda/ f band; (lado) side; **de** ~ sideways on; **nestas** ~**s** in these parts; ~ **desenhada** Port cartoon; ~ **larga** broadband

bandeira /bã'dera/ f flag; (divisa) banner; **dar** ~**ra** 🖬 give o.s. away. ~**rante** m/f pioneer ● f girl guide. ~**rinha** m linesman

bandeja /bã'deʒa/ f tray

bandido /bã'dʒidu/ m bandit

bando /'bãdu/ m (de pessoas) band; (de pássaros) flock

bandolim /bãdo'lĩ/ m mandolin

bangalô /bãga'lo/ m bungalow

Bangcoc /bã'koki/ f Bangkok

bangue-bangue /bãgi'bãgi/ m 🖬 western

banguela /bã'gela/ a toothless

banha /'bana/ f lard; pl (no corpo) flab

banhar /ba'nar/ vt (molhar) bathe; (lavar) bathe. ~**se** vpr bathe

banheira /ba'nera/ f bath, Amer bathtub. ~**ro** m bathroom; Port lifeguard

banhista /ba'nista/ m/f bather

banho /'banu/ m bath; (no mar) bathe, dip; **tomar** ~ have a bath; (no chuveiro) have a shower; **tomar um** ~ **de loja/cultura** go on a shopping/cultural spree; ~ **de espuma** bubble bath; ~ **de sol** sunbathing. ~**maria** (pl ~**s-maria**) m bain-marie

ba|nimento /bani'mẽtu/ m banishment. ~**nir** vt banish

banjo /'bãʒu/ m banjo

banqueiro /bã'keru/ m banker

banqueta /bã'keta/ f footstool

banque|te /bã'ketʃi/ m banquet. ~**teiro** m caterer

banzé /bã'ze/ m 🖬 commotion, uproar

baque /'baki/ m thud, crash; (revés) blow. ~**ar** vi topple over ● vt hit hard, knock for six

bar /bar/ m bar

barafunda /bara'fũda/ f jumble; (barulho) racket

baralhada /bara'ʎada/ f jumble. ~**lho** m pack of cards, Amer deck of cards

barão /ba'rãw/ m baron

barata /ba'rata/ f cockroach

baratear /baratʃi'ar/ vt cheapen. ~**teiro** a cheap

baratinar /baratʃi'nar/ vt fluster; (transtornar) rattle, shake up

barato /ba'ratu/ a cheap ● adv cheaply ● m 🖬 um ~ great; **que** ~! that's brilliant!

barba /'barba/ f beard; pl (de gato etc) whiskers; **fazer a** ~ shave. ~**da** f walkover; (cavalo) favourite. ~**do** a bearded

barbante /bar'bãtʃi/ m string

bar|baridade /barbari'dadʒi/ f barbarity; 🖬 (muito dinheiro) fortune. **~bárie** f, **~barismo** m barbarism

bárbaro /'barbaru/ m barbarian
● a barbaric; 🇵 (*forte, bom*) terrific

barbatana /barba'tana/ f fin

bar|beador /barbia'dor/ m shaver. **~bear** vt shave. **~bear-se** vpr shave. **~bearia** f barber's shop. **~beiragem** f 🇵 bit of bad driving. **~beiro** m barber; 🇵 (*motorista*) bad driver

bar|ca /'barka/ f barge; (*balsa*) ferry. **~caça** f barge. **~co** m boat; **~co a motor** motor boat; **~co a remo/vela** rowing/sailing boat, *Amer* rowboat/sailboat

barga|nha /bar'gaɲa/ f bargain. **~nhar** vt/i bargain

barítono /ba'ritonu/ m baritone

barômetro /ba'rometru/ m barometer

baronesa /baro'neza/ f baroness

barra /'baxa/ f bar; (*sinal gráfico*) slash, stroke; 🇵 (*situação*) situation; **segurar a ~** hold out; **forçar a ~** force the issue

barra|ca /ba'xaka/ f (*de acampar*) tent; (*na feira*) stall; (*casinha*) hut; (*guarda-sol*) sunshade. **~cão** m shed. **~co** m shack, shanty

barragem /ba'xaʒẽ/ f (*represa*) dam

barra-pesada /baxape'zada/ a invar 🇵 <*bairro*> rough; <*pessoa*> shady; (*difícil*) tough

bar|rar /ba'xar/ vt bar. **~reira** f barrier; (*em corrida*) hurdle; (*em futebol*) wall

barrento /ba'xẽtu/ a muddy

barricada /baxi'kada/ f barricade

barri|ga /ba'xiga/ f stomach, *Amer* belly; **~ga da perna** calf. **~gudo** a pot-bellied

bar|ril /ba'xiw/ (*pl* **~ris**) m barrel

barro /'baxu/ m (*argila*) clay; (*lama*) mud

barroco /ba'xoku/ a & m baroque

barrote /ba'xɔtʃi/ m beam, joist

baru|lheira /baru'ʎera/ f racket, din. **~lhento** a noisy. **~lho** m noise

base /'bazi/ f base; fig (*fundamento*) basis; **com ~ em** on the basis of; **na ~ de** based on. **~ado** a based; (*firme*) well-founded ● m 🇵 joint. **~ar** vt base; **~ar-se em** be based on

básico /'baziku/ a basic

basquete /bas'ketʃi/ m, **basquetebol** /basketʃi'bɔw/ m basketball

bas|ta /'basta/ m **dar um ~ta em** call a halt to. **~tante** a (*muito*) quite a lot of; (*suficiente*) enough ● adv (*com adjetivo, advérbio*) quite; (*com verbo*) quite a lot; (*suficientemente*) enough

bastão /bas'tãw/ m stick; (*num revezamento, de comando*) baton

bastar /bas'tar/ vi be enough

bastidores /bastʃi'doris/ m pl (*no teatro*) wings; **nos ~** fig behind the scenes

bata /'bata/ f (*de mulher*) smock; (*de médico etc*) overall

bata|lha /ba'taʎa/ f battle. **~lhador** a plucky, feisty ● m fighter. **~lhão** m battalion. **~lhar** vi battle; (*esforçar-se*) fight hard ● vt fight hard to get

batata /ba'tata/ f potato; **~ doce** sweet potato; **~ frita** chips, *Amer* French fries; (*salgadinhos*) crisps, *Amer* potato chips

bate-boca /batʃi'boka/ m row, argument

bate|deira /bate'dera/ f whisk; (*de manteiga*) churn. **~dor** m (*policial* *etc*) outrider; (*no criquete*) batsman; (*no beisebol*) batter; (*de caça*) beater; **~dor de carteiras** pickpocket

batelada /bate'lada/ *f* batch; **~s de heaps of**

batente /ba'tẽtʃi/ *m* (*de porta*) doorway; **para o/no ~** 🔲 (*ao trabalho*) to/at work

bate-papo /batʃi'papu/ *m* chat

bater /ba'ter/ *vt* beat; stamp ‹*pé*›; slam ‹*porta*›; strike ‹*horas*›; take ‹*foto*›; flap ‹*asas*›; (*datilografar*) type; (*lavar*) wash; (*usar muito*) wear a lot ‹*roupa*›; 🔲 pinch ‹*carteira*›; **~ à máquina** type; **~ à ou na porta** knock at the door; **~ em** hit; harp on ‹*assunto*›; **~ com o carro** crash one's car, have a crash; **~ com a cabeça** bang one's head; **ele batia os dentes de frio** his teeth were chattering with cold; **ele não bate bem** 🔲 he's not all there ● *vi* ‹*coração*› beat; ‹*porta*› slam; ‹*janela*› bang; ‹*horas*› strike; ‹*sino*› ring; (*à porta*) knock; (*com o carro*) crash; ‹*luz, sol*› shine on. **~se** *vpr* (*lutar*) fight

bate|ria /bate'ria/ *f* *Eletr* battery; *Mus* drums; **~ria de cozinha** kitchen utensils. **~rista** *m/f* drummer

bati|da /ba'tʃida/ *f* beat; (*à porta*) knock; (*com o carro*) crash; (*policial*) raid; (*bebida*) cocktail of rum, sugar and fruit juice. **~do** *a* beaten; ‹*roupa*› well worn; ‹*assunto*› hackneyed ● *m* **~do de leite** *Port* milkshake

batina /ba'tʃina/ *f* cassock

ba|tismo /ba'tʃizmu/ *m* baptism. **~tizado** *m* christening. **~tizar** *vt* baptize; (*pôr nome*) christen

batom /ba'tõ/ *m* lipstick

batu|cada /batu'kada/ *f* samba percussion group. **~car** *vt/i* drum

in a samba rhythm. **~que** *m* samba rhythm

batuta /ba'tuta/ *f* baton; **sob a ~ de** under the direction of

baú /ba'u/ *m* trunk

baunilha /baw'niʎa/ *f* vanilla

bazar /ba'zar/ *m* bazaar; (*loja*) stationery and haberdashery shop

bê-a-bá /bea'ba/ *m* ABC

bea|titude /beatʃi'tudʒi/ *f* (*felicidade*) bliss; (*devoção*) piety, devoutness. **~to** *a* (*devoto*) pious, devout; (*feliz*) blissful

bêbado /'bebadu/ *a & m* drunk

bebê /be'be/ *m* baby; **~ de proveta** test-tube baby

bebe|deira /bebe'dera/ *f* (*estado*) drunkenness; (*ato*) drinking bout. **~dor** *m* drinker. **~douro** *m* drinking fountain

beber /be'ber/ *vt/i* drink

bebericar /beberi'kar/ *vt/i* sip

bebida /be'bida/ *f* drink

beca /'beka/ *f* gown

beça /'besa/ *f* **a ~** 🔲 (*com substantivo*) loads of; (*com adjetivo*) really; (*com verbo*) a lot

becape /be'kap/ *m* *Comput* backup

beco /'beku/ *m* alley; **~ sem saída** dead end

bedelho /be'deʎu/ *m* **meter o ~ (em)** stick one's oar in(to)

bege /'beʒi/ *a invar* beige

bei|cinho /bej'siɲu/ *m* **fazer ~cinho** pout. **~ço** *m* lip. **~çudo** *a* thick-lipped

beija-flor /bejʒa'flor/ *m* hummingbird

bei|jar /bej'ʒar/ *vt* kiss. **~jo** *m* kiss. **~joca** /ɔ/ *f* peck

bei|ra /'bera/ *f* edge; *fig* (*do desastre etc*) verge, brink; **à ~ra de** at the

edge of; *fig* on the verge of. **~rada**
f edge. **~ra-mar** f seaside. **~rar** *vt*
(*ficar*) border (on); (*andar*) skirt;
fig border on, verge on; **ele está**
~rando os 30 anos he's nearing
thirty

beisebol /bejjsi'bɔw/ *m* baseball

belas-artes /bɛlaʃ'artʃiʃ/ f *pl*
fine arts

beldade /bew'dadʒi/ f, **beleza**
/be'leza/ f beauty

belga /'bɛwga/ a & *m* Belgian

Bélgica /'bɛwʒika/ f Belgium

beliche /be'liʃi/ *m* bunk

bélico /'bɛliku/ a war

belicoso /beli'kozu/ a warlike

belis|cão /belis'kãw/ *m* pinch.
~car *vt* pinch; nibble ‹*comida*›

Belize /be'lizi/ *m* Belize

belo /'bɛlu/ a beautiful

beltrano /bew'tranu/ *m* such-
and-such

bem /bẽj/ *adv* well; (*bastante*) quite;
(*muito*) very ● *m* (*pl* **bens**) good; *pl*
goods, property; **está ~** (it's) fine,
OK; **fazer ~ a** be good for; **tudo ~?**
🔲 how's things?; **se ~ que** even
though; **~ feito (por você)** 🔲 it
serves you right; **muito ~!** well
done!; **de ~ com alguém** on good
terms with sb; **~ como** as well as

bem-apessoado
/bẽjapeso'adu/ a nice-looking.
~comportado a well-behaved;
~disposto a keen, willing; **~estar**
m well-being; **~humorado** a good-
humoured; **~intencionado** a well-
intentioned; **~passado** a ‹*carne*›
well-done; **~sucedido** a successful;
~vindo a welcome; **~visto** a well
thought of

bênção /'bẽsãw/ (*pl* **~s**) f blessing

bendito /bẽ'dʒitu/ a blessed

benefi|cência /benefi'sẽsia/
f (*bondade*) goodness, kindness;
(*caridade*) charity. **~cente** a
‹*associação*› charitable; ‹*concerto,*
feira› charity. **~ciado** *m* beneficiary.
~ciar *vt* benefit. **~ciar-se** *vpr* benefit
(de from)

benefício /bene'fisiu/ *m* benefit;
em ~ de in aid of

benéfico /be'nɛfiku/ a beneficial
(a to)

benevolência /benevo'lẽsia/ f
benevolence

benévolo /be'nɛvolu/ a
benevolent

benfeitor /bẽfej'tor/ *m* benefactor

bengala /bẽ'gala/ f walking stick;
(*pão*) French stick

benigno /be'niginu/ a benign

ben|to /'bẽtu/ a blessed; ‹*água*›
holy. **~zer** *vt* bless. **~zer-se** *vpr*
cross o.s.

berço /'bersu/ *m* (*de embalar*)
cradle; (*caminha*) cot; *fig* birthplace;
ter ~ be from a good family

berimbau /beri'baw/ *m* Brazilian
percussion instrument shaped
like a bow

berinjela /beri'ʒela/ f aubergine,
Amer eggplant

Berlim /ber'lĩ/ f Berlin

berma /'berma/ f *Port* hard
shoulder, *Amer* berm

bermuda /ber'muda/ f Bermuda
shorts

Berna /'berna/ f Berne

ber|rante /be'xãtʃi/ a a loud, flashy.
~rar *vi* ‹*pessoa*› shout; ‹*criança*›
bawl; ‹*boi*› bellow. **~reiro** *m*
(*gritaria*) yelling, shouting; (*choro*)
crying, bawling. **~ro** /ɛ/ *m* yell,
shout; (*de boi*) bellow; **aos ~ros**
shouting

besouro /be'zoru/ m beetle

bes|ta /'bɛʃta/ a (idiota) stupid; (cheio de si) full of o.s.; (pedante) pretentious ● f (pessoa) dimwit, numbskull; **ficar ~ta 🇧🇷** be taken aback. **~teira** f stupidity; (uma) stupid thing; **falar ~teira** talk rubbish. **~tial** (pl **~tiais**) a bestial. **~tificar** vt astound, dumbfound

besuntar /bezũ'tar/ vt coat; (sujar) smear

betão /be'tãw/ Port m concrete

beterraba /bete'xaba/ f beetroot

betoneira /beto'nera/ f cement mixer

bexiga /be'ʃiga/ f bladder

bezerro /be'zeru/ m calf

bibelô /bibe'lo/ m ornament

Bíblia /'biblia/ f Bible

bíblico /'bibliku/ a biblical

biblio|grafia /bibliogra'fia/ f bibliography. **~teca** /e/ f library. **~tecário** m librarian ● a library

bica /'bika/ f tap; Port (cafezinho) espresso; **suar em ~s** drip with sweat

bicama /bi'kama/ f truckle bed

bicar /bi'kar/ vt peck

bíceps /'biseps/ m invar biceps

bicha /'biʃa/ f 🇧🇷 queer, fairy; Port (fila) queue

bicheiro /bi'ʃeru/ m organizer of illegal numbers game, racketeer

bicho /'biʃu/ m animal; (inseto) insect, Amer bug; **que ~ te mordeu?** what's got into you? **~da-seda** (pl **~s-da-seda**) m silkworm; **~ de sete cabeças** m 🇧🇷 big deal, big thing; **~ do mato** 🇧🇷 **~s do mato**) m very shy person

bicho-papão /biʃupa'pãw/ m (pl bichos-papões) bogeyman

bicicleta /bisi'kleta/ f bicycle, bike

bico /'biku/ m (de ave) beak; (de faca) point; (de sapato) toe; (de bule) spout; (de caneta) nib; (do seio) nipple; (de gás) jet; (emprego) odd job, sideline; (boca) mouth

bidê /bi'de/ m bidet

bidimensio|nal /bidʒimẽsio'naw/ (pl **~nais**) a two-dimensional

biela /bi'ɛla/ f connecting rod

Bielo-Rússia /bielo'xusia/ f Byelorussia

bielo-russo /bielo'xusu/ a & m Byelorussian

bie|nal /bie'naw/ (pl **~nais**) a biennial ● f biennial art exhibition

bife /'bifi/ m steak

bifo|cal /bifo'kaw/ (pl **~cais**) a bifocal

bifur|cação /bifurka'sãw/ f fork. **~car-se** vpr fork

bigamia /biga'mia/ f bigamy

bígamo /'bigamu/ a bigamous ● m bigamist

bigo|de /bi'gɔdʒi/ m moustache. **~dudo** a with a big moustache

bigorna /bi'gɔrna/ f anvil

bijuteria /biʒute'ria/ f costume jewellery

bilate|ral /bilate'raw/ (pl **~rais**) a bilateral

bilhão /bi'ʎãw/ m thousand million, Amer billion

bilhar /bi'ʎar/ m pool, billiards

bilhe|te /bi'ʎetʃi/ m ticket; (recado) note; **~te de ida e volta** return ticket, Amer round-trip ticket; **~te de identidade** Port identity card; **o ~te azul** 🇧🇷 the sack. **~teria** f, Port **~teira** f (no cinema, teatro) box office; (na estação) ticket office

bilíngue /bi'līgwi/ a bilingual

bilionário /bilio'nariu/ a & m
billionaire

bilis /'bilis/ f bile

binário /bi'nariu/ a binary

bingo /'bĩgu/ m bingo

binóculo /bi'nɔkulu/ m binoculars

biocombustível
/biokõbus'tʃivew/ m biofuel

biodegradável
/biodegra'davew/ (pl ~veis) a
biodegradable

biodiesel /bio'dʒizew/ m
biodiesel

biodiversidade
/biodʒiversi'dadʒi/ f biodiversity

bio|grafia /biogra'fia/ f biography.
~gráfico a biographical

biógrafo /bi'ɔgrafu/ m biographer

bio|logia /biolo'ʒia/ f biology.
~lógico a biological

biólogo /bi'ɔlogu/ m biologist

biombo /bi'õbu/ m screen

biônico /bi'oniku/ a bionic; Pol
unelected

biópsia /bi'ɔpsia/ f biopsy

bioquími|ca /bio'kimika/ f
biochemistry. ~co a biochemical
● m biochemist

biquíni /bi'kini/ m bikini

birma|nês /birma'nes/ a & m (f
~nesa) Burmese

Birmânia /bir'mania/ f Burma

birô /bi'ro/ m bureau

bir|ra /'bixa/ f wilfulness; fazer ~ra
have a tantrum. ~rento a a wilful

biruta /bi'ruta/ 1 a crazy ● f
windsock

bis /bis/ int encore!, more! ● m invar
encore

bisa|vó /biza'vɔ/ f great-
grandmother. ~vós m pl great-
grandparents. ~vô m great-
grandfather

bisbilho|tar /bizbiʎo'tar/ vt pry
into ● vi pry. ~teiro a a prying ● m
busybody. ~tice f prying

bisca|te /bis'katʃi/ m odd job.
~teiro m odd-job man

biscoito /bis'kojtu/ m biscuit,
Amer cookie

bisnaga /biz'naga/ f (pão) bridge
roll; (tubo) tube

bisne|ta /biz'neta/ f great-
granddaughter. ~to /ɛ/ m great-
grandson; pl great-grandchildren

bis|pado /bis'padu/ m bishopric.
~po m bishop

bissexto /bi'sestu/ a occasional;
ano ~ leap year

bissexu|al /biseksu'aw/ (pl ~ais)
a & m/f bisexual

bisturi /bistu'ri/ m scalpel

bito|la /bi'tɔla/ f gauge. ~lado a
narrow-minded

bizarro /bi'zaxu/ a bizarre

blablablá /blabla'bla/ m 1
chit-chat

black /'blɛki/ m black market. ~tie
m evening dress

blas|femar /blasfe'mar/ vi
blaspheme. ~fêmia f blasphemy.
~femo /e/ a blasphemous ● m
blasphemer

blecaute /ble'kawtʃi/ m power cut

ble|far /ble'far/ vi bluff. ~fe /ɛ/
m bluff

blin|dado /blĩ'dadu/ a armoured.
~dagem f armour plating

blitz /blits/ f invar police spot check
(on vehicles)

blo|co /'blɔku/ m block; Pol bloc; (de papel) pad; (no carnaval) section.

blogar /blo'gar/ vt blog

blogue /'blɔgi/ m blog

blogueiro /blo'gejru/ m, Port **bloguista** /blo'giʃta/ m/f blogger

blo|quear /blo'kjar/ vt block; Mil blockade. **~queio** m blockage; Psic mental block; Mil blockade

blusa /'bluza/ f shirt; (de mulher) blouse; (de lã) sweater

blusão /blu'zãw/ m jacket

boa /'boa/ f de ▶ BOM ● numa ~ I well; (sem problemas) easily; estar numa ~ I be doing fine. **~gente** a invar I nice; **~nova** (pl ~s-novas) f good news. **~pinta** (pl ~s-pintas) a I nice-looking; **~praça** (pl ~s-praças) a I friendly, sociable

boate /bo'atʃi/ f nightclub

boato /bo'atu/ m rumour

boa|-vida /boa'vida/ (pl ~s-vidas) m/f good-for-nothing, waster. **~zinha** a sweet, kind

bo|bagem /bo'baʒẽ/ f silliness; (uma) silly thing. **~beada** f slip-up. **~bear** vi slip up. **~beira** f ▶ BOBAGEM

bobe /'bɔbi/ m curler, roller

bobina /bo'bina/ f reel; Eletr coil

bobo /'bobu/ a silly ● m fool; (da corte) jester. **~ca** /ɔ/ a I stupid ● m/f I twit

bo|ca /'boka/ f mouth; (no fogão) ring; **~ca da noite** nightfall. **~cado** m (na boca) mouthful; (pedaço) piece, bit. **~cal** (pl ~cais) m mouthpiece

boce|jar /bose'ʒar/ vi yawn. **~jo** /e/ m yawn

boche|cha /bo'ʃeʃa/ f cheek. **~char** vi rinse one's mouth. **~cho**

/e/ m mouthwash. **~chudo** a with puffy cheeks

bodas /'bodas/ f pl wedding anniversary; ~ **de prata/ouro** silver/ golden wedding

bode /'bɔdʒi/ m (billy) goat; ~ **expiatório** scapegoat

bodega /bo'dɛga/ f (de bebidas) off-licence, Amer liquor store; (de secos e molhados) grocer's shop, corner shop

boêmio /bo'emiu/ a & m Bohemian

bofe|tada /bofe'tada/ f, **bofetão** /bofe'tãw/ m slap. **~tear** vt slap

boi /boj/ m bullock, Amer steer

bói /bɔj/ m office boy

boia /'bɔja/ f (de balizamento) buoy; (de cortiça, isopor etc) float; (câmara de borracha) rubber ring; (de braço) armband, water wing; (na caixa-d'água) ballcock; I (comida) grub; ~ **salva-vidas** lifebelt. **~fria** (pl ~s-frias) m/f itinerant farm labourer

boiar /bo'jar/ vt/i float; I be lost

boico|tar /bojko'tar/ vt boycott. **~te** /ɔ/ m boycott

boiler /'bojler/ (pl ~s) m boiler

boina /'bojna/ f beret

bo|jo /'boʒu/ m bulge. **~judo** a (cheio) bulging; (arredondado) bulbous

bola /'bɔla/ f ball; dar ~ **para** I give attention to <pessoa>; care about <coisa>; ~ **de gude** marble; ~ **de neve** snowball

bolacha /bo'laʃa/ f (biscoito) biscuit, Amer cookie; (descanso) beer mat; I (tapa) slap

bo|lada /bo'lada/ f large sum of money. **~lar** vt think up, devise

boleia /bo'leja/ f cab; Port (carona) lift

boletim /bole'tʃĩ/ m bulletin; (*escolar*) report

bolha /'boʎa/ f bubble; (*na pele*) blister ● m/f 🔲 pain

boliche /bo'liʃi/ m skittles

Bolívia /bo'livia/ f Bolivia

boliviano /bolivi'anu/ a & m Bolivian

bolo /'bolu/ m cake

bolor /bo'lor/ m mould, mildew. **~lorento** a mouldy

---

bolo rei A ring-shaped fruit 🇮 bread, covered in crystallized fruit and nuts, and eaten at Christmas time. Traditionally, a lucky coin or trinket and a *fava* (bean) would be hidden in the cake. In Portugal, whoever found the *fava* would be entitled to make a wish.

---

bolota /bo'lɔta/ f (*glande*) acorn; (*bolinha*) little ball

bol|sa /'bowsa/ f bag; **~sa (de estudo)** scholarship; **~sa (de valores)** stock exchange. **~sista** m/f, Port **~seiro** m scholarship student. **~so** /o/ m pocket

bom /bõ/ a (f **boa**) good; (*de saúde*) well; (*comida*) nice; **está ~** that's fine

bomba[1] /'bõba/ f (*explosiva*) bomb; (*doce*) eclair; *fig* bombshell; **levar ~** 🔲 fail

bomba[2] /'bõba/ f (*de bombear*) pump; **~ de gasolina** Port petrol pump

Bombaim /bõba'ĩ/ f Bombay

bombar|dear /bõbardʒi'ar/ vt bombard; (*do ar*) bomb. **~deio** m bombardment; (*do ar*) bombing

bomba|-relógio /bõbaxe'lɔʒiu/ (*pl* **~s-relógio**) f time bomb

bom|bear /bõbi'ar/ vt pump. **~beiro** m fireman; (*encanador*) plumber

bombom /bõ'bõ/ m chocolate

bombordo /bõ'bɔrdu/ m port

bondade /bõ'dadʒi/ f goodness

bonde /'bõdʒi/ m tram; (*teleférico*) cable car

bondoso /bõ'dozu/ a good(-hearted)

boné /bo'nɛ/ m cap

bone|ca /bo'nɛka/ f doll. **~co** /ɛ/ m dummy

bonificação /bonifika'sãw/ f bonus

bonito /bo'nitu/ a ‹*mulher*› pretty; ‹*homem*› handsome; ‹*tempo, casa etc*› lovely

bônus /'bonus/ m *invar* bonus

boqui|aberto /bokia'bɛrtu/ a open-mouthed, flabbergasted. **~nha** f snack

borboleta /borbo'leta/ f butterfly; (*roleta*) turnstile

borbotão /borbo'tãw/ m spurt

borbu|lha /bor'buʎa/ f bubble. **~lhar** vi bubble

borda /'bɔrda/ f edge. **~do** a edged; (*à linha*) embroidered ● m embroidery

bordão /bor'dãw/ m (*frase*) catchphrase

bordar /bor'dar/ vt (*à linha*) embroider

bordel /bor'dɛw/ (*pl* **~déis**) m brothel

bordo /'bɔrdu/ m a **~** aboard

borra /'boxa/ f dregs; (*de café*) grounds

borra|cha /boˈxaʃa/ f rubber. **~cheiro** m tyre fitter

bor|rão /boˈxãw/ m (de tinta) blot; (rascunho) rough draft. **~rar** vt (sujar) blot; (riscar) cross out; (pintar) daub

borrasca /boˈxaska/ f squall

borri|far /boxiˈfar/ vt sprinkle. **~fo** m sprinkling

bosque /ˈbɔski/ m wood

bosta /ˈbɔsta/ f (de animal) dung; (chulo) crap

bota /ˈbɔta/ f boot

botâni|ca /boˈtanika/ f botany. **~co** a botanical ● m botanist

bo|tão /boˈtãw/ m button; (de flor) bud; **falar com os seus ~tões** say to o.s.

botar /boˈtar/ vt put; put on ‹roupa›; set ‹mesa, despertador›; lay ‹ovo›; find ‹defeito›

bote[1] /ˈbɔtʃi/ m (barco) dinghy; **~ salva-vidas** lifeboat; (de borracha) life raft

bote[2] /ˈbɔtʃi/ m (de animal etc) lunge

botequim /butʃiˈkĩ/ m bar

botoeira /botoˈera/ f buttonhole

boxe /ˈbɔksi/ m boxing. **~ador** m boxer

brabo /ˈbrabu/ a ‹animal› ferocious; ‹calor, sol› fierce; ‹doença› bad; ‹prova, experiência› tough; (zangado) angry

bra|çada /braˈsada/ f armful; (em natação) stroke. **~cadeira** f (faixa) armband; (ferragem) bracket; (de atleta) sweatband. **~çal** (pl **~cais**) a manual. **~celete** /e/ m bracelet. **~ço** m arm; **~ço direito** fig (pessoa) right-hand man

bra|dar /braˈdar/ vt/i shout. **~do** m shout

braguilha /braˈgiʎa/ f fly, flies

braile /ˈbrajli/ m Braille

bra|mido /braˈmidu/ m roar. **~mir** vi roar

branco /ˈbrãku/ a white ● m (homem) white man; (espaço) blank; **em ~** ‹cheque etc› blank; **noite em ~** sleepless night

bran|do /ˈbrãdu/ a gentle; ‹doença› mild; (indulgente) lenient, soft. **~dura** f gentleness; (indulgência) softness, leniency

brasa /ˈbraza/ f em **~** red-hot; **mandar ~** 🔲 go to town

brasão /braˈzãw/ m coat of arms

braseiro /braˈzeru/ m brazier

Brasil /braˈziw/ m Brazil

brasi|leiro /braziˈleru/ a & m Brazilian. **~liense** a & m/f (person) from Brasilia

bra|vata /braˈvata/ f bravado. **~vio** a wild; ‹mar› rough. **~vo** a (corajoso) brave; (zangado) angry; ‹mar› rough. **~vura** f bravery

breca /ˈbrɛka/ f **levado da ~** very naughty

brecar /breˈkar/ vt stop ‹carro›; fig curb ● vi brake

brecha /ˈbrɛʃa/ f gap; (na lei) loophole

bre|ga /ˈbrega/ a 🔲 tacky, naff. **~guice** f 🔲 tack, tackiness

brejo /ˈbreʒu/ m marsh; **ir para o ~** fig go down the drain

brenha /ˈbreɲa/ f thicket

breque /ˈbreki/ m brake

breu /brew/ m tar, pitch

bre|ve /ˈbrevi/ a short, brief; **em ~** soon, shortly. **~vidade** f shortness, brevity

briga /ˈbriga/ f fight; (bate-boca) argument

briga|da /bri'gada/ f brigade.
~deiro m brigadier; (doce) chocolate
truffle

bri|gão /bri'gãw/ a (f **~gona**)
belligerent; (na fala) argumentative
● m (f **~gona**) troublemaker. **~gar**
vi fight; (com palavras) argue;
‹cores› clash

bri|lhante /bri'ʎãtʃi/ a (reluzente)
shiny; fig brilliant. **~lhar** vi shine.
~lho m (de sapatos etc) shine;
(dos olhos, de metais) gleam; (das
estrelas) brightness; (de uma cor)
brilliance; fig (esplendor) splendour

brin|cadeira /brĩka'dera/ f
(piada) joke; (brinquedo, jogo) game;
de ~cadeira for fun. **~calhão** (f
~calhona) a playful ● m joker. **~car**
vi (divertir-se) play; (gracejar) joke

brinco /'brĩku/ m earring

brin|dar /brĩ'dar/ vt (saudar) toast,
drink to; (presentear) give a gift
to; **~dar alguém com algo** afford
sb sth; (de presente) give sb sth
as a gift. **~de** m (saudação) toast;
(presente) free gift

brinquedo /brĩ'kedu/ m toy

brio /'briu/ m self-esteem,
character. **~so** /o/ a self-confident

brisa /'briza/ f breeze

britadeira /brita'dera/ f
pneumatic drill

britânico /bri'taniku/ a British ● m
Briton; **os ~s** the British

broca /'brɔka/ f drill

broche /'brɔʃi/ m brooch

brochura /bro'ʃura/ f **livro de ~**
paperback

brócolis /'brɔkulis/ m pl, Port
brócolos /'brɔkuluʃ/ m pl broccoli

bron|ca /'brɔka/ f telling-off;
dar uma ~ca em alguém tell sb off.
~co a coarse, rough

bronquite /brõ'kitʃi/ f bronchitis

bronze /'brõzi/ m bronze. **~ado** a
tanned, brown ● m (sun)tan. **~ador**
a tanning ● m suntan lotion.
~amento m tanning. **~ar** vt tan.
~ar-se vpr go brown, tan

bro|tar /bro'tar/ vt sprout ‹folhas,
flores›; spout ‹lágrimas, palavras›
● vi ‹planta› sprout; ‹água› spout;
‹ideias› pop up. **~tinho** m 🄣
youngster. **~to** /o/ m shoot; 🄣
youngster

broxa /'brɔʃa/ f (large) paint brush
● a 🄣 impotent

bruços /'brusus/ **de ~** face down

bruma /'bruma/ f mist. **~moso**
/o/ a misty

brusco /'brusku/ a brusque,
abrupt

bru|tal /bru'taw/ a (pl **~tais**) a brutal.
~talidade f brutality. **~to** a ‹feições›
coarse; ‹homem› brutish; ‹tom,
comentário› aggressive; ‹petróleo›
crude; ‹peso, lucro, salário› gross
● m brute

bruxa /'bruʃa/ f witch; (feia) hag.
~ria f witchcraft

Bruxelas /bru'ʃelas/ f Brussels

bruxo /'bruʃu/ m wizard

bruxulear /bruʃuli'ar/ vi flicker

bucha /'buʃa/ f (tampão) bung;
(para paredes) Rawlplug®; **acertar
na ~** 🄣 hit the nail on the head

bucho /'buʃu/ m gut; **~ de boi** tripe

budis|mo /bu'dʒizmu/ m
Buddhism. **~ta** a & m/f Buddhist

bueiro /bu'eru/ m storm drain

búfalo /'bufalu/ m buffalo

bu|fante /bu'fãtʃi/ a full, puffed.
~far vi snort; (reclamar) grumble,
moan

bufê /bu'fe/ *m (refeição)* buffet; *(serviço)* catering service; *(móvel)* sideboard

bugiganga /buʒi'gãga/ *f* knick-knack

bujão /bu'ʒãw/ *m ~* **de gás** gas cylinder

bula /'bula/ *f (de remédio)* directions; *(do Papa)* bull

bulbo /'buwbu/ *m* bulb

bule /'buli/ *m (de chá)* teapot; *(de café etc)* pot

Bulgária /buw'garia/ *f* Bulgaria

búlgaro /'buwgaru/ *a & m* Bulgarian

bulhufas /bu'ʎufas/ *pron* 🔲 nothing

bulício /bu'lisiu/ *m* bustle

bulimia /buli'mia/ *f* bulimia

bullying /'bolĩʒ/ *m* bullying

bumbum /bũ'bũ/ *m* 🔲 bottom, bum

bunda /'bũda/ *f* bottom

buquê /bu'ke/ *m* bouquet

buraco /bu'raku/ *m* hole; *(de agulha)* eye; *(jogo de cartas)* rummy; *~* **da fechadura** keyhole

burburinho /burbu'riɲu/ *m (de vozes)* hubbub

burca /'burka/ *f* burka

burguês /bur'ges/ *a & m (f ~guesa)* bourgeois. **~guesia** *f* bourgeoisie

burlar /bur'lar/ *vt* get round <*lei*>; get past <*defesas, vigilância*>

buro|cracia /burokra'sia/ *f* bureaucracy. **~crata** *m/f* bureaucrat. **~crático** *a* bureaucratic. **~cratizar** *vt* make bureaucratic

bur|rice /bu'xisi/ *f* stupidity; *(uma)* stupid thing. **~ro** *a* stupid; *(ignorante)* dim ● *m (animal)*

donkey; *(pessoa)* halfwit, dunce; **~ro de carga** *fig* workhorse

bus|ca /'buska/ *f* search; **dar ~ca em** search. **~ca-pé** *m* banger. **~car** *vt* fetch; *(de carro)* pick up; **mandar ~car** send for

bússola /'busola/ *f* compass; *fig* guide

busto /'bustu/ *m* bust

butique /bu'tʃiki/ *f* boutique

buzi|na /bu'zina/ *f* horn. **~nada** *f* toot (of the horn). **~nar** *vi* sound the horn, toot the horn

Cc

cá /ka/ *adv* here; **o lado de ~** this side; **para ~** here; **de ~ para lá** back and forth; **de lá para ~** since then; **~ entre nós** between you and me

ca|bal /ka'baw/ *(pl ~bais)* a complete, full; <*prova*> conclusive

cabana /ka'bana/ *f* hut; *(casinha no campo)* cottage

cabeça /ka'besa/ *f* head; *(de lista)* top; *(inteligência)* mind ● *m/f (chefe)* ringleader; *(pessoa inteligente)* brains; **de ~** off the top of one's head; **de ~ para baixo** upside down; **deu-lhe na ~ de** he took it into his head to; **esquentar a ~** 🔲 get worked up; **fazer a ~ de alguém** convince sb; **quebrar a ~** rack one's brains; **subir à ~** go to sb's head; **ter a ~ no lugar** have one's head screwed on. **~da** *f (no futebol)* header; *(pancada)* head butt; **dar uma ~da no teto** bang one's head on the ceiling.

~ de porco f tenement; **~ de vento** m/f scatterbrain, airhead. **~lho** m heading

cabe|cear /kabesi'ar/ vt head ‹bola›. **~ceira** f head. **~cudo** a pig-headed

cabe|dal /kabe'daw/ (pl **~dais**) m wealth

cabelei|ra /kabe'lera/ f head of hair; (peruca) wig. **~reiro** m hairdresser

cabe|lo /ka'belu/ m hair; **cortar o ~lo** have one's hair cut. **~ludo** a hairy; (difícil) complicated; ‹palavra, piada› dirty

caber /ka'ber/ vi fit; (ter cabimento) be fitting; **~ a** ‹mérito, parte› be due to; ‹tarefa› fall to; **cabe a você** it is up to you to go; **~ em alguém** fit sb

cabide /ka'bidʒi/ m (peça de madeira, arame etc) hanger; (móvel) hat stand; (na parede) coat rack

cabimento /kabi'mẽtu/ m **ter** ~ be fitting, be appropriate; **não ter** ~ be out of the question

cabine /ka'bini/ f cabin; (de avião) cockpit; (de loja) changing room; **~ telefônica** phone box, Amer phone booth

cabisbaixo /kabiz'baʃu/ a crestfallen

cabí|vel /ka'bivew/ (pl **~veis**) a appropriate, fitting

cabo¹ /'kabu/ m (militar) corporal; **ao ~ de** after; **levar a ~** carry out; **~ eleitoral** campaign worker

cabo² /'kabu/ m (fio) cable; (de panela etc) handle; **TV por ~** cable TV; **~ de extensão** extension lead; **~ de força** tug of war

caboclo /ka'boklu/ a & m mestizo

ca|bra /'kabra/ f goat. **~brito** m kid

ca|ça /'kasa/ f (atividade) hunting; (caçada) hunt; (animais) game ● m (avião) fighter; **à ~ça de** in pursuit of; **~ça das bruxas** fig witch hunt. **~çador** m hunter. **~ça-minas** m invar minesweeper; **~ça-níqueis** m invar slot machine. **~çar** vt hunt ‹animais, criminoso etc›; (procurar) hunt for ● vi hunt

cacareco /kaka'rɛku/ m piece of junk; pl junk

cacare|jar /kakare'ʒar/ vi cluck. **~jo** /e/ m clucking

caçarola /kasa'rɔla/ f saucepan

cacau /ka'kaw/ m cocoa

cace|tada /kase'tada/ f blow with a club; fig annoyance. **~te** /e/ m club ● int 🔲 damn

cachaça /ka'ʃasa/ f white rum

> cachaça Also known as *aguardente de cana* (sugar-cane rum), *cachaça* is Brazil's most popular alcoholic drink. It's made by fermenting sugar-cane juice, and is extremely alcoholic. Brazilians refer to the drink informally as *caninha*, *pinga*, or *canha*, and it is mixed with lemon juice and sugar to make *caipirinha*, Brazil's most famous cocktail.   *i*

---

cachê /ka'ʃe/ m fee

cache|col /kaʃe'kɔw/ (pl **~cóis**) m scarf

cachimbo /ka'ʃĩbu/ m pipe

cacho /'kaʃu/ m (de banana, uva) bunch; (de cabelo) lock; (🔲 (caso) affair

cachoeira /kaʃo'era/ f waterfall

cachor|rinho /kaʃoˈxiɲu/ m (nado) doggy paddle. **~ro** /o/ m dog; Port puppy; (pessoa) scoundrel. **~ro-quente** (pl **~ros-quentes**) m hot dog

cacife /kaˈsifi/ m fig pull

caci|que /kaˈsiki/ m (índio) chief; (político) boss. **~quia** f leadership

caco /ˈkaku/ m shard; (pessoa) old crock

cacto /ˈkaktu/ m cactus

caçula /kaˈsula/ m/f youngest child ● a youngest

cada /ˈkada/ a each; **~ duas horas** every two hours; **custam £5 ~ (um)** they cost £5 each; **~ vez mais** more and more; **~ vez mais fácil** easier and easier; **ele fala ~ coisa** 🗓 he says the most amazing things

cadafalso /kadaˈfawsu/ m gallows

cadarço /kaˈdarsu/ m shoelace

cadas|trar /kadasˈtrar/ vt register. **~tro** m register; (ato) registration; (policial, bancário) records, files; (imobiliário) land register

ca|dáver /kaˈdaver/ m (dead) body, corpse. **~davérico** a cadaverous, corpse-like; ‹exame› post-mortem

cadê /kaˈde/ adv 🗓 where is/are...?

cadeado /kadʒiˈadu/ m padlock

cadeia /kaˈdeja/ f (de eventos, lojas etc) chain; (prisão) prison; (rádio, TV) network

cadeira /kaˈdera/ f (móvel) chair; (no teatro) stall; (de político) seat; (função de professor) chair; (matéria) subject; pl Anat hips; **~ de balanço** rocking chair; **~ de rodas** wheelchair; **~ elétrica** electric chair

ca|dência /kaˈdẽsia/ f Mus (da voz) cadence; (compasso) rhythm. **~denciado** a rhythmic; ‹passos› measured

cader|neta /kaderˈneta/ f notebook; (de professor) register; (de banco) passbook; **~neta de poupança** savings account. **~no** /e/ m exercise book; (pequeno) notebook; (no jornal) section

cadete /kaˈdetʃi/ m cadet

cadu|car /kaduˈkar/ vi ‹pessoa› become senile; ‹contrato› lapse. **~co** a ‹pessoa› senile; ‹contrato› lapsed. **~quice** f senility

cafajeste /kafaˈʒestʃi/ m swine

ca|fé /kaˈfe/ m coffee; (estabelecimento) cafe; **~fé da manhã** breakfast; **tomar ~fé** have breakfast. **~fé-com-leite** a invar coffee-coloured, light brown ● a white coffee. **~feeiro** a coffee ● m coffee plant. **~feicultura** f coffee-growing. **~feína** f caffein(e)

cafetã /kafeˈtã/ m caftan

cafetão /kafeˈtãw/ m pimp

cafe|teira /kafeˈtera/ f coffee pot; **~ de pistão** cafetière. **~zal** (pl **~zais**) m coffee plantation. **~zinho** m small black coffee

cafo|na /kaˈfɔna/ a 🗓 naff, tacky. **~nice** f tackiness; (coisa) tacky thing

cágado /ˈkagadu/ m turtle

caiar /kajˈar/ vt whitewash

cãibra /ˈkãjbra/ f cramp

caí|da /kaˈida/ f fall; ▶ QUEDA. **~do** a ‹árvore etc› fallen; ‹beiços etc› drooping; (deprimido) dejected; (apaixonado) smitten

caimento /kajˈmẽtu/ m fall

caipi|ra /kajˈpira/ a ‹pessoa› countrified; ‹festa, música› country; ‹sotaque› rural ● m/f country person; (depreciativo) country bumpkin. **~rinha** f cachaça with limes, sugar and ice

cair /ka'ir/ *vi* fall; *‹dente, cabelo›* fall out; *‹botão etc›* fall off; *‹comércio, trânsito etc›* fall off; *‹tecido, cortina›* hang; ~ **bem/mal** *‹roupa›* go well/ badly; *‹ato, dito›* go down well/ badly; **estou caindo de sono** I'm really sleepy

cais /kajs/ *m* quay; *Port (na estação)* platform

caixa /'kaʃa/ *f* box; *(de loja etc)* cash desk ● *m/f* cashier; ~ **de correio** letter box; ~ **de entrada** *Comput* inbox; ~ **de mudanças**, *Port* ~ **de velocidades** gear box; ~ **postal** post office box, PO Box; ~ **de saída** *Comput* outbox. ~**d'água** (*pl* ~**s-d'água**) *f* water tank; ~**forte** (*pl* ~**s-fortes**) *f* vault

cai|xão /ka'ʃãw/ *m* coffin. ~**xeiro** *m (em loja)* assistant; salesman. ~**xilho** *m* frame. ~**xote** /ɔ/ *m* crate

caju /ka'ʒu/ *m* cashew fruit. ~**eiro** *m* cashew tree

cal /kaw/ *f* lime

calado /ka'ladu/ *a* quiet

calafrio /kala'friu/ *m* shudder, shiver

calami|dade /kalami'dadʒi/ *f* calamity. ~**toso** /o/ *a* calamitous

calar /ka'lar/ *vi* be quiet ● *vt* keep quiet about *‹segredo, sentimento›*; silence *‹pessoa›*. ~**se** *vpr* go quiet

calça /'kawsa/ *f* trousers, *Amer* pants

calça|da /kaw'sada/ *f* pavement, *Amer* sidewalk; *Port (rua)* roadway. ~**dão** *m* pedestrian precinct. ~**deira** *f* shoehorn. ~**do** *a* paved ● *m* shoe; *pl* footwear

calcanhar /kawka'ɲar/ *m* heel

calção /kaw'sãw/ *m* shorts; ~ **de banho** swimming trunks

calcar /kaw'kar/ *vt (pisar)* trample; *(comprimir)* press; ~ **algo em** *fig* base sth on, model sth on

calçar /kaw'sar/ *vt* put on *‹sapatos, luvas›*; take *‹número›*; pave *‹rua›*; *(com calço)* wedge ● *vi ‹sapato›* fit. ~**se** *vpr* put one's shoes on

calcário /kaw'kariu/ *m* limestone ● *a ‹água›* hard

calças /'kawsas/ *f pl* ▶ **CALÇA**

calcinha /kaw'siɲa/ *f* knickers, *Amer* panties

cálcio /'kawsiu/ *m* calcium

calço /'kawsu/ *m* wedge

calcu|ladora /kawkula'dora/ *f* calculator. ~**lar** *vt/i* calculate. ~**lista** *a* calculating ● *m/f* opportunist

cálculo /'kawkulu/ *m* calculation; *(diferencial)* calculus; *Med* stone

cal|da /'kawda/ *f* syrup; *pl* hot springs. ~**deira** *f* boiler. ~**deirão** *m* cauldron. ~**do** *m (sopa)* broth; *(suco)* juice; ~**do de carne/galinha** beef/ chicken stock

calefação /kalefa'sãw/ *f* heating

caleidoscópio /kalejdos'kɔpiu/ *m* kaleidoscope

calejado /kale'ʒadu/ *a ‹mãos›* calloused; *‹pessoa›* experienced

calendário /kalẽ'dariu/ *m* calendar

calha /'kaʎa/ *f (no telhado)* gutter; *(sulco)* gulley

calhamaço /kaʎa'masu/ *m* tome

calhambeque /kaʎã'bɛki/ *m* 🔟 banger

calhar /ka'ʎar/ *vi* **calhou que** it so happened that; **calhou pegarem o mesmo trem** they happened to get the same train; ~ **de** happen to; **vir a** ~ come at the right time

cali|brado /kali'bradu/ a ⟨bêbado⟩ tipsy. **~brar** vt calibrate; check (the pressure of) ⟨pneu⟩. **~bre** m calibre; **coisas desse ~bre** things of this order

cálice /'kalisi/ m (copo) liqueur glass; (na missa) chalice

caligrafia /kaligra'fia/ f (letra) handwriting; (arte) calligraphy

calista /ka'lista/ m/f chiropodist, Amer podiatrist

cal|ma /'kawma/ f calm. **com ~ma** int calm down. **~mante** m tranquilizer. **~mo** a calm

calo /'kalu/ m (na mão) callus; (no pé) corn

calombo /ka'lõbu/ m bump

calor /ka'lor/ m heat; (agradável) fig warmth; **estar com ~** be hot

calo|rento /kalo'rẽtu/ a ⟨pessoa⟩ sensitive to heat; ⟨lugar⟩ hot. **~ria** f calorie. **~roso** /o/ a warm; ⟨protesto⟩ lively

calota /ka'lɔta/ f hubcap

calo|te /ka'lɔtʃi/ m bad debt. **~teiro** m bad risk

calouro /ka'loru/ m (na faculdade) freshman; (em outros ramos) novice

ca|lúnia /ka'lunia/ f slander. **~luniar** vt slander. **~lunioso** /o/ a slanderous

cal|vície /kaw'visi/ f baldness. **~vo** a bald

cama /'kama/ f bed; **~ de casal/ solteiro** double/single bed. **~beliche** (pl **~s-beliches**) f bunk bed

camada /ka'mada/ f layer; (de tinta) coat

câmara /'kamara/ f chamber; (fotográfica) camera; **em ~ lenta** in

slow motion; **~ de ar** inner tube; **~ digital** digital camera; **~ municipal** town council; Port town hall

camarada /kama'rada/ a friendly ● m/f comrade. **~gem** f comradeship; (convivência agradável) camaraderie

camarão /kama'rãw/ m shrimp; (maior) prawn

cama|reira /kama'rera/ f chambermaid. **~rim** m dressing room. **~rote** /ɔ/ m (no teatro) box; (num navio) cabin

cambada /kã'bada/ f gang, horde

cambalacho /kãba'laʃu/ m scam

camba|lear /kãbali'ar/ vi stagger. **~lhota** f somersault

cambi|al /kãbi'aw/ (pl **~ais**) a exchange. **~ante** m shade. **~ar** vt change

câmbio /'kãbiu/ m exchange; (taxa) rate of exchange; **~ oficial/ paralelo** official/black market exchange rate

cambista /kã'bista/ m/f (de entradas) ticket tout, Amer scalper; (de dinheiro) money changer

Camboja /kã'bɔʒa/ m Cambodia

cambojano /kãbo'ʒanu/ a & m Cambodian

camburão /kãbu'rãw/ m police van

camelo /ka'melu/ m camel

camelô /kame'lo/ m street vendor

camião /kami'ãw/ m Port m
  ▶ CAMINHÃO

caminhada /kami'nada/ f walk

caminhão /kami'nãw/ m lorry, Amer truck

cami|nhar /kami'ɲar/ vi walk; fig advance, progress. **~nho** m way;

(*estrada*) road; (*trilho*) path; **a ~nho** on the way; **a meio ~nho** halfway; **~nho de ferro** *Port* railway, *Amer* railroad

caminho|neiro /kamiɲo'neru/ *m* lorry driver, *Amer* truck driver. **~nete** /e/ *m* van

camio|neta /kamio'neta/ *f* van. **~nista** *Port* m/f ▸ CAMINHONEIRO

cami|sa /ka'miza/ *f* shirt. **~sa de força** straitjacket; **~sa de vênus** condom. **~seta** /e/ *f* T-shirt; (*de baixo*) vest. **~sinha** *f* 🄵 condom. **~sola** /ɔ/ *f* nightdress; *Port* sweater

camomila /kamo'mila/ *f* camomile

campainha /kãpa'iɲa/ *f* bell; (*da porta*) doorbell

campanário /kãpa'nariu/ *m* belfry

campanha /kã'paɲa/ *f* campaign

campe|ão /kãpi'ãw/ *m* (*f ~ã*) champion. **~onato** *m* championship

cam|pestre /kã'pɛstri/ *a* rural. **~pina** *f* grassland

camping /'kãpĩ/ *m* camping; (*lugar*) campsite. **~pismo** *Port m* camping

campo /'kãpu/ *m* field; (*interior*) country; (*de futebol*) pitch; (*de golfe*) course; **~ de concentração** concentration camp. **~nês** *m* (*f ~nesa*) peasant

camu|flagem /kamu'flaʒẽ/ *f* camouflage. **~flar** *vt* camouflage

camundongo /kamũ'dõgu/ *m* mouse

cana /'kana/ *f* cane; **~ de açúcar** sugar cane

Canadá /kana'da/ *m* Canada

canadense /kana'dẽsi/ *a & m* Canadian

ca|nal /ka'naw/ (*pl ~nais*) *m* channel; (*hidrovia*) canal; **~ de televisão a cabo** cable channel

canalha /ka'naʎa/ *m/f* scoundrel

canali|zação /kanaliza'sãw/ *f* piping; **~zador** *Port m* plumber. **~zar** *vt* channel ‹*líquido, esforço, recursos*›; canalize ‹*rio*›; pipe for water and drainage ‹*cidade*›

canário /ka'nariu/ *m* canary

canastrão /kanas'trãw/ *m* (*f ~trona*) ham actor, (*f* actress)

canavi|al /kanavi'aw/ (*pl ~ais*) *m* cane field. **~eiro** *a* sugar cane

canção /kã'sãw/ *f* song

cance|lamento /kãsela'mẽtu/ *m* cancellation. **~lar** *vt* cancel; (*riscar*) cross out

câncer /'kãser/ *m* cancer; **C~** (*signo*) Cancer

cance|riano /kãseri'anu/ *a & m* Cancerian. **~rígeno** *a* carcinogenic. **~roso** /o/ *a* cancerous ● *m* person with cancer

cancro /'kãkru/ *m Port* (*câncer*) cancer; *fig* canker

candango /kã'dãgu/ *m* person from Brasília

cande|eiro /kãdʒi'eru/ *m* (*oil*) lamp. **~labro** *m* candelabra

candida|tar-se /kãdʒida'tarsi/ *vpr* (*a vaga*) apply (**a** for); (*à presidência etc*) stand; *Amer* run (**a** for). **~to** *m* candidate (**a** for); (*a vaga*) applicant (**a** for). **~tura** *f* candidature; (*a vaga*) application (**a** for)

cândido /'kãdʒidu/ *a* innocent

candomblé /kãdõ'blɛ/ *m* Afro-Brazilian cult; (*reunião*) candomble meeting

2

candomblé *Candomblé* is
one of the principally
Afro-Brazilian religions that
worship the gods of Western
Africa, known as *orixás*. The
ceremonies take place in *terreiros*
to the sound of percussion, and
can include animal sacrifices and
the consumption of alcoholic
drinks in a bid to 'raise the spirit'.
The main festival is the *Festa de
Iemanjá*, the Queen of the Ocean,
on the 2nd of February.

candura /kã'dura/ f innocence

cane|ca /ka'nɛka/ f mug. **~co** /ɛ/
m tankard

canela¹ /ka'nɛla/ f (*condimento*)
cinnamon

canela² /ka'nɛla/ f (*da perna*) shin.
~da f **dar uma ~da em alguém**
kick sb in the shins; **dar uma ~da
em algo** hit one's shins on sth

cane|ta /ka'neta/ f pen; **~
esferográfica** ballpoint pen.
~ta-tinteiro (*pl* **~tas-tinteiro**) f
fountain pen

cangote /kã'gɔtʃi/ m nape of
the neck

canguru /kãgu'ru/ m kangaroo

canhão /ka'ɲãw/ m (*arma*) cannon;
(*vale*) canyon

canhoto /ka'ɲotu/ a a left-handed
● m (*talão*) stub

cani|bal /kani'baw/ (*pl* **~bais**) m/f
cannibal. **~balismo** m cannibalism

caniço /ka'nisu/ m reed; (*pessoa*)
skinny person

canícula /ka'nikula/ f heat wave

ca|nil /ka'niw/ (*pl* **~nis**) m kennel

canivete /kani'vetʃi/ m penknife

canja /'kãʒa/ f chicken soup; 🔟
piece of cake

canjica /kã'ʒika/ f corn porridge

cano /'kanu/ m pipe; (*de bota*) top;
(*de arma de fogo*) barrel

cano|a /ka'noa/ f canoe. **~agem** f
canoeing. **~ista** m/f canoeist

canonizar /kanoni'zar/ vt
canonize

can|saço /kã'sasu/ m tiredness.
~sado a tired. **~sar** vt tire;
(*aborrecer*) bore ● vi; **~sar-se** vpr get
tired. **~sativo** a tiring; (*aborrecido*)
boring. **~seira** f tiredness; (*lida*) toil

can|tada /kã'tada/ f 🔟 chat-up.
~tar vt/i sing; 🔟 chat up

cântaro /'kãtaru/ m **chover a ~s**
pour down, bucket down

cantarolar /kãtaro'lar/ vt/i hum

cantei|ra /kã'tera/ f quarry. **~ro**
m (*de flores*) flower bed; (*artífice*)
stonemason; **~ro de obras** site office

cantiga /kã'tʃiga/ f ballad

can|til /kã'tʃiw/ (*pl* **~tis**) m canteen.
~tina f canteen

canto¹ /'kãtu/ m (*ângulo*) corner

canto² /'kãtu/ m (*cantar*) singing.
~tor m singer. **~toria** f singing

canudo /ka'nudu/ m (*de beber*)
straw; (*tubo*) tube; 🔟 (*diploma*)
diploma

cão /kãw/ (*pl* **cães**) m dog

caolho /ka'oʎu/ a one-eyed

ca|os /kaws/ m chaos. **~ótico** a
chaotic

capa /'kapa/ f (*de livro, revista*)
cover; (*roupa sem mangas*) cape; **~
de chuva** raincoat

capacete /kapa'setʃi/ m helmet

capacho /ka'paʃu/ m doormat

capaci|dade /kapasi'dadʒi/ f
capacity; (*aptidão*) ability. **~tar** vt
enable; (*convencer*) convince

capataz /kapa'tas/ m foreman

capaz /ka'pas/ a capable (**de** of); **ser ~ de** (poder) be able to; (ser provável) be likely to

cape|la /ka'pɛla/ f chapel. **~lão** (pl **~lães**) m chaplain

capen|ga /ka'pẽga/ a doddery. **~gar** vi dodder

capeta /ka'peta/ m (diabo) devil; (criança) little devil

capilar /kapi'lar/ a hair

ca|pim /ka'pĩ/ m grass. **~pinar** vt/i weed

capi|tal /kapi'taw/ (pl **~tais**) a & m/f capital. **~talismo** m capitalism. **~talista** a & m/f capitalist. **~talizar** vt Com capitalize; (aproveitar) capitalize on

capi|tanear /kapitani'ar/ vt captain ‹navio›; fig lead. **~tania** f captaincy; **~tania do porto** port authority. **~tão** (pl **~tães**) m captain

capitulação /kapitula'sãw/ f capitulation, surrender

capítulo /ka'pitulu/ m chapter; (de telenovela) episode

capô /ka'po/ m bonnet, Amer hood

capoeira /kapo'era/ f Brazilian kick-boxing

---

capoeira Capoeira was created as a form of self-defence by the descendants of African slaves during the colonial period. When the practice was banned by the colonizers, it developed into a gentle and graceful art form, in which participants are not allowed to touch each other. Capoeira originated in the state of Bahia, and is 'played' in pairs to the sound of percussion instruments, such as the berimbau.

---

capo|ta /ka'pɔta/ f roof. **~tar** vi overturn

capote /ka'pɔtʃi/ m overcoat

capri|char /kapri'ʃar/ vi excel o.s. **~cho** m (esmero) care; (desejo) whim; (teimosia) contrariness. **~choso** /o/ a (cheio de caprichos) capricious; (com esmero) painstaking, meticulous

capricorniano /kaprikorni'anu/ a & m Capricorn

Capricórnio /kapri'kɔrniu/ m Capricorn

cápsula /'kapsula/ f capsule

cap|tar /kap'tar/ vt pick up ‹emissão, sinais›; tap ‹água›; catch, grasp ‹sentido›; win ‹simpatia, admiração›. **~tura** f capture. **~turar** vt capture

capuz /ka'pus/ m hood

caquético /ka'kɛtʃiku/ a broken-down, on one's last legs

caqui /ka'ki/ m persimmon

cáqui /'kaki/ a invar & m khaki

cara /'kara/ f face; (aparência) look; (ousadia) cheek ● m 🔢 guy; **a ~** face to face; **de ~** straightaway; **dar de ~ com** run into; **está na ~** it's obvious; **fechar a ~** frown; **~ de pau** cheek ● a cheeky, brazen; **~ de tacho** 🔢 sheepish look

cara|col /kara'kɔw/ (pl **~cóis**) m snail

caracte|re /karak'tɛri/ m character. **~rística** f characteristic, feature. **~rístico** a characteristic. **~rizar** vt characterize. **~rizar-se** vpr be characterized

caramba /ka'rãba/ int (de espanto) wow; (de desagrado) damn

caramelo /kara'mɛlu/ m caramel; (bala) toffee

caramujo /kara'muʒu/ m water snail

caranguejo /karã'geʒu/ m crab

caratê /kara'te/ m karate

caráter /ka'rater/ m character

caravana /kara'vana/ f caravan

car|boidrato /karboi'dratu/ m carbohydrate. **~bono** /kar'bonu/ m carbon; **de ~bono neutro** carbon-neutral ‹produtos, programa›

carbu|rador /karbura'dor/ m carburettor, Amer carburator. **~rante** m fuel

carcaça /kar'kasa/ f carcass; (de navio etc) frame

cárcere /'karseri/ m jail

carcereiro /karse'reru/ m jailer, warder

carcomido /karko'midu/ a worm-eaten; ‹rosto› pockmarked

cardápio /kar'dapiu/ m menu

carde|al /kardʒi'aw/ (pl ~ais) a cardinal

cardíaco /kar'dʒiaku/ a cardiac; **ataque ~** heart attack

cardinal /kardʒi'naw/ a cardinal; **tecla ~** hash key

cardio|lógico /kardʒio'lɔʒiku/ a heart. **~logista** m/f heart specialist, cardiologist

cardume /kar'dumi/ m shoal

careca /ka'rɛka/ a bald • f bald patch

ca|recer /kare'ser/ vt **~ de** lack. **~rência** f lack; (social) deprivation; (afetiva) lack of affection. **~rente** a lacking; (socialmente) deprived; (afetivamente) in need of affection

carestia /kares'tʃia/ f high cost; (geral) high cost of living; (escassez) shortage

careta /ka'reta/ f grimace • a 🆃 straight, square

car|ga /'karga/ f load; (mercadorias) cargo; (elétrica) charge; (de cavalaria) charge; (de caneta) refill; fig burden; **~ga horária** workload. **~go** m (função) post, job; **a ~go de** in the charge of. **~gueiro** m (navio) cargo ship, freighter

cariar /kari'ar/ vi decay

Caribe /ka'ribi/ m Caribbean

caricatu|ra /karika'tura/ f caricature. **~rar** vt caricature. **~rista** m/f caricaturist

carícia /ka'risia/ f (com a mão) stroke, caress; (carinho) affection

cari|dade /kari'dadʒi/ f charity; **obra de ~dade** charity. **~doso** /o/ a charitable

cárie /'kari/ f tooth decay

carim|bar /karĩ'bar/ vt stamp; postmark ‹carta›. **~bo** m stamp; (do correio) postmark

cari|nho /ka'riɲu/ m affection; (um) caress. **~nhoso** /o/ a affectionate

carioca /kari'ɔka/ a from Rio de Janeiro • m/f person from Rio de Janeiro • m Port m weak coffee

caris|ma /ka'rizma/ m charisma. **~mático** a charismatic

carna|val /karna'vaw/ (pl ~vais) m carnival. **~valesco** /e/ a carnival; ‹roupa› over the top, overdone • m carnival organizer

---

Carnaval Carnival is celebrated in Brazil and Portugal in the period just before Lent. The term *Carnaval* ⓘ

originates from the Italian for "to remove meat"; for Roman Catholics, the festivities traditionally preceded a time of abstinence during Lent. The Brazilian carnival is the most famous carnival in the world, and lavish street parties take part across the country for the best part of a week. Carnival is celebrated in Portugal too, mostly on Shrove Tuesday, with street parties and processions throughout the country.

car|ne /'karni/ f (humana etc) flesh; (comida) meat. **~neiro** m sheep; (macho) ram; (como comida) mutton. **~niça** f carrion. **~nificina** f slaughter. **~nívoro** a carnivorous ● m carnivore. **~nudo** a fleshy

caro /'karu/ a expensive; (querido) dear ● adv ‹custar, cobrar› a lot; ‹comprar, vender› at a high price; **pagar ~** pay a high price (for)

caroço /ka'rosu/ m (de pêssego etc) stone; (de maçã) core; (em sopa, molho etc) lump

carona /ka'rona/ f lift

carpete /kar'petʃi/ m fitted carpet

carpin|taria /karpĩta'ria/ f carpentry. **~teiro** m carpenter

carran|ca /ka'xãka/ f scowl. **~cudo** a ‹cara› scowling; ‹pessoa› sullen

carrapato /kaxa'patu/ m (animal) tick; fig hanger-on

carrasco /ka'xasku/ m executioner; fig butcher

carre|gado /kaxe'gadu/ a ‹céu› dark, black; ‹cor› dark; ‹ambiente› tense. **~gador** m /kaxega'dor/ (de celular, computador) charger; (profissão) porter; **~ de pilhas**

battery charger. **~gamento** m loading; (carga) load. **~gar** vt load ‹navio, arma, máquina fotográfica›; (levar) carry; charge ‹bateria, pilha›; **~gar em** overdo; pronounce strongly ‹letra›; Port press

carreira /ka'xera/ f career

carre|tel /kaxe'tɛw/ (pl **~téis**) m reel

car|ril /ka'xiw/ (pl **~ris**) Port m rail

carrinho /ka'xiɲu/ m (para bagagem, compras) trolley; (de criança) pram; **~ de mão** wheelbarrow

carro /'kaxu/ m car; (de bois) cart; **~ alegórico** float; **~ esporte** sports car; **~ fúnebre** hearse. **~ça** /-ɔ/ f cart. **~ceria** f bodywork. **~chefe** (pl **~s-chefes**) m (no carnaval) main float; fig centrepiece; **~forte** (pl **~s-fortes**) m security van

carros|sel /kaxo'sɛw/ (pl **~séis**) m merry-go-round

carruagem /kaxu'aʒẽ/ f carriage

carta /'karta/ f letter; (mapa) chart; (do baralho) card; **~ branca** fig carte blanche; **~ de condução** Port driving licence, Amer driver's license. **~bomba** (pl **~s-bomba**) f letter bomb. **~da** f fig move

cartão /kar'tãw/ m card; Port (papelão) cardboard; **~ de cidadão** Port identity card; **~ de crédito** credit card; **~ de visita** visiting card; **~ magnético** swipe card; **~ prépago** top-up card; **~ SIM** SIM card; **~ telefônico** phonecard. **~postal** (pl **cartões-postais**) m postcard

---

cartão de cidadão All Portuguese citizens above the age of ten are required to carry an identity card. It can be used instead of a passport for travel within the European Union. The older *bilhete de identidade* (identity card) is gradually being phased out in favour of an electronic *cartão de cidadão*, which combines the identity card together with various social security and electoral documents.

car|taz /kar'tas/ *m* poster, *Amer* bill; **em ~** showing, *Amer* playing. **~teira** *f* (*para dinheiro*) wallet; (*cartão*) card; (*mesa*) desk; **~teira de identidade** identity card; **~teira de motorista** driving licence, *Amer* driver's license. **~teiro** *m* postman

carteira de identidade
Carteira de identidade, *cédula de identidade* or *registro geral (RG)* are all names for the identity card that is used throughout Brazil. This contains the holder's name, date of birth, parents' names, signature and the issue date, as well as the bearer's right thumb print.

car|tel /kar'tɛw/ (*pl* **~téis**) *m* cartel
cárter /'karter/ *m* sump
carto|la /kar'tɔla/ *f* top hat ● *m* director. **~lina** *f* card. **~mante** *m/f* tarot reader, fortune teller
cartório /kar'tɔriu/ *m* registry office
cartucho /kar'tuʃu/ *m* cartridge; (*de dinamite*) stick; (*de amendoim etc*) bag
car|tum /kar'tũ/ *m* cartoon. **~tunista** *m/f* cartoonist
caruncho /ka'rũʃu/ *m* woodworm
carvalho /kar'vaʎu/ *m* oak
car|vão /kar'vãw/ *m* coal; (*de desenho*) charcoal. **~voeiro** *a* coal

casa /'kaza/ *f* house; (*comercial*) firm; (*de tabuleiro*) square; (*de botão*) hole; **em ~** at home; **para ~** home; **na ~ dos 30 anos** in one's thirties; **~ da moeda** mint; **~ de banho** *Port* bathroom; **~ de campo** country house; **~ de saúde** private hospital; **~ decimal** decimal place; **~ popular** council house
casaco /ka'zaku/ *m* (*sobretudo*) coat; (*paletó*) jacket; (*de lã*) pullover
ca|sal /ka'zaw/ (*pl* **~sais**) *m* couple. **~samento** *m* marriage; (*cerimônia*) wedding. **~sar** *vt* marry; *fig* combine ● *vi* get married; *fig* go together. **~sar-se** *vpr* get married; *fig* combine; **~sar-se com** marry
casarão /kaza'rãw/ *m* mansion
casca /'kaska/ *f* (*de árvore*) bark; (*de laranja, limão*) peel; (*de banana*) skin; (*de noz, ovo*) shell; (*de milho*) husk; (*de pão*) crust; (*de ferida*) scab
cascalho /kas'kaʎu/ *m* gravel
cascata /kas'kata/ *f* waterfall; 🔟 fib
casca|vel /kaska'vɛw/ (*pl* **~véis**) *f* (*cobra*) rattlesnake; (*mulher*) shrew
casco /'kasku/ *m* (*de cavalo etc*) hoof; (*de navio*) hull; (*garrafa vazia*) empty
ca|sebre /ka'zɛbri/ *m* hovel, shack. **~seiro** *a* ‹comida› home-made; ‹pessoa› home-loving; ‹vida› home ● *m* housekeeper
caserna /ka'zɛrna/ *f* barracks
casmurro /kaz'muxu/ *a* sullen
caso /'kazu/ *m* case; (*amoroso*) affair; (*conto*) story ● *conj* in case; **em todo ou qualquer ~** in any case; **fazer ~ de** take notice of; **vir ao ~** be relevant; **~ contrário** otherwise
casório /ka'zɔriu/ *m* 🔟 wedding

caspa /'kaspa/ f dandruff

casquinha /kas'kiɲa/ f (de sorvete) cone, cornet

cassar /ka'sar/ vt revoke, withdraw ‹direitos, autorização›; ban ‹político›

cassete /ka'setʃi/ m cassette

cassetete /kase'tetʃi/ m truncheon, Amer nightstick

cassino /ka'sinu/ m casino; ~ de oficiais officers' mess

casta|nha /kas'taɲa/ f chestnut; ~nha de caju cashew nut. ~nha-do-pará (pl ~nhas-do-pará) f Brazil nut. ~nheiro m chestnut tree. ~nho a chestnut(-coloured). ~nholas /ɔ/ f pl castanets

castelhano /kaste'ʎanu/ a & m Castilian

castelo /kas'tɛlu/ m castle

casti|çal /kastʃi'saw/ (pl ~çais) m candlestick

cas|tidade /kastʃi'dadʒi/ f chastity. ~tigar vt punish. ~tigo m punishment. ~to a chaste

castor /kas'tor/ m beaver

castrar /kas'trar/ vt castrate

casu|al /kazu'aw/ (pl ~ais) a chance; (fortuito) fortuitous. ~alidade f chance

casulo /ka'zulu/ m (de larva) cocoon

cata /'kata/ f à ~ de in search of

cata|lão /kata'lãw/ (pl ~lães) a & m (f ~lã) Catalan

catalisador /kataliza'dor/ m catalyst; (de carro) catalytic convertor

catalogar /katalo'gar/ vt catalogue

catálogo /ka'talogu/ m catalogue; (de telefones) phone book

Catalunha /kata'luɲa/ f Catalonia

catapora /kata'pɔra/ f chicken pox

catar /ka'tar/ vt (procurar) search for; (recolher) gather; (do chão) pick up; sort ‹arroz, café›

catarata /kata'rata/ f waterfall; (no olho) cataract

catarro /ka'taxu/ m catarrh

catástrofe /ka'tastrofi/ f catastrophe

catastrófico /katas'trɔfiku/ a catastrophic

catecismo /kate'sizmu/ m catechism

cátedra /'katedra/ f chair

cate|dral /kate'draw/ (pl ~drais) f cathedral. ~drático m professor

cate|goria /katego'ria/ f category; (social) class; (qualidade) quality. ~górico a categorical. ~gorizar vt categorize

catinga /ka'tʃiga/ f body odour, stink

cati|vante /katʃi'vãtʃi/ a captivating. ~var vt captivate. ~veiro m captivity. ~vo a & m captive

catolicismo /katoli'sizmu/ m Catholicism

católico /ka'tɔliku/ a & m Catholic

catorze /ka'torzi/ a & m fourteen

cau|da /'kawda/ f tail. ~dal (pl ~dais) m torrent

caule /'kawli/ m stem

cau|sa /'kawza/ f cause; Jurid case; por ~sa de because of; ~sa fraturante divisive issue. ~sar vt cause

caute|la /kaw'tɛla/ f caution; (documento) ticket. ~loso /o/ a cautious, careful

cava /'kava/ f armhole

cava|do /ka'vadu/ a ‹vestido›
low-cut; ‹olhos› deep-set. **~dor** a
hard-working ● m hard worker

cava|laria /kavala'ria/ f cavalry.
~lariça f stable. **~leiro** m horseman;
(na Idade Média) knight

cavalete /kava'letʃi/ m easel

caval|gadura /kavawga'dura/
f mount. **~gar** vt/i ride; sit astride
‹muro, banco›; (saltar) jump

cavalhei|resco /kavaʎe'resku/ a
a gallant, gentlemanly. **~ro** m
gentleman ● a gallant, gentlemanly

cavalo /ka'valu/ m horse; **a ~** on
horseback; **~vapor** (pl **~s-vapor**)
horsepower

cavanhaque /kava'ɲaki/ m
goatee

cavaquinho /kava'kiɲu/ m
ukulele

cavar /ka'var/ vt dig; fig go all out
for ● vi dig; fig go all out; **~ em**
(vasculhar) delve into; **~ a vida**
make a living

caveira /ka'vera/ f skull

caverna /ka'verna/ f cavern

caviar /kavi'ar/ m caviar

cavidade /kavi'dadʒi/ f cavity

cavilha /ka'viʎa/ f peg

cavo /'kavu/ a hollow

cavoucar /kavo'kar/ vt excavate

caxemira /kaʃe'mira/ f cashmere

caxumba /ka'ʃũba/ f mumps

Cc /'sese/ abr (= cópia carbono) Cc

Cco /'seseo/ abr (= com cópia
oculta) Bcc

cear /si'ar/ vt have for supper ● vi
have supper

cebo|la /se'bola/ f onion. **~linha** f
spring onion

ceder /se'der/ vt give up; (dar) give;
(emprestar) lend ● vi (não resistir)

give way; **~ a** yield to

cedilha /se'dʒiʎa/ f cedilla

cedo /'sedu/ adv early; **mais ~ ou
mais tarde** sooner or later

cedro /'sedru/ m cedar

cédula /'sedula/ f (de banco) note,
Amer bill; (eleitoral) ballot paper

ce|gar /se'gar/ vt blind; blunt
‹faca›; **às ~gas** blindly. **~go** /ɛ/ a
blind; ‹faca› blunt ● m blind man

cegonha /se'goɲa/ f stork

cegueira /se'gera/ f blindness

ceia /'seja/ f supper

cei|fa /'sejfa/ f harvest; (massacre)
slaughter. **~far** vt reap; claim
‹vidas›; (matar) mow down

cela /'sela/ f cell

cele|bração /selebra'sãw/ f
celebration. **~brar** vt celebrate

célebre /'sɛlebri/ a celebrated

celebridade /selebri'dadʒi/ f
celebrity

celeiro /se'leru/ m granary

célere /'sɛleri/ a swift, fast

celeste /se'lɛstʃi/ a celestial

celeuma /se'lewma/ f
pandemonium

celibato /seli'batu/ m celibacy

celofane /selo'fani/ m
cellophane®

celta /'sewta/ a Celtic ● m/f Celt ● m
(língua) Celtic

célula /'sɛlula/ f cell; **~ estaminal**
Port stem cell

celu|lar /selu'lar/ a cellular ● m
mobile, Amer cell phone. **~lite** f
cellulite. **~lose** /ɔ/ f cellulose

célula-tronco /'sɛlula'trõku/ f
(pl **células-tronco**) stem cell

cem /sẽj/ a & m hundred

cemitério /semi'teriu/ m cemetery; *fig* graveyard

cena /'sena/ f scene; *(palco)* stage; **em ~** on stage

cenário /se'nariu/ m scenery; *(de crime etc)* scene

cênico /'seniku/ a stage

cenoura /se'nora/ f carrot

cen|so /'sẽsu/ m census. **~sor** m censor. **~sura** f *(de jornais etc)* censorship; *(órgão)* censor(s); *(condenação)* censure. **~surar** vt censor <jornal, filme etc>; *(condenar)* censure

centavo /sẽ'tavu/ m cent

centeio /sẽ'teju/ m rye

centelha /sẽ'teʎa/ f spark; *fig (de gênio etc)* flash

cente|na /sẽ'tena/ f hundred; **uma ~na de** about a hundred; **às ~nas** in their hundreds. **~nário** m centenary

centésimo /sẽ'tezimu/ a hundredth

cen|tígrado /sẽ'tʃigradu/ m centigrade. **~tilitro** m centilitre. **~tímetro** m centimetre

cento /'sẽtu/ a & m hundred; **por ~** per cent

cen|tral /sẽ'traw/ *(pl ~trais)* a central ● f switchboard. **~tralizar** vt centralize. **~trar** vt centre; **~tral eólica** wind farm. **~tro** m centre

cera /'sera/ f wax; **fazer ~** waste time, faff about

cerâmi|ca /se'ramika/ f ceramics, pottery. **~co** a ceramic

cer|ca /'serka/ f fence; **~ca viva** hedge. **~ca de** adv around, about. **~cado** m enclosure; *(para criança)* playpen. **~car** vt surround; *(com muro, cerca)* enclose; *(assediar)* besiege

cercear /sersi'ar/ vt *fig* curtail, restrict

cerco /'serku/ m *Mil* siege; *(policial)* dragnet

cere|al /seri'aw/ *(pl ~ais)* m cereal

cere|bral /sere'braw/ *(pl ~brais)* a cerebral

cérebro /'serebru/ m brain; *(inteligência)* intellect

cere|ja /se'reʒa/ f cherry. **~jeira** f cherry tree

cerimônia /seri'monia/ f ceremony; **sem ~** unceremoniously; **fazer ~** stand on ceremony

cerimoni|al /serimoni'aw/ *(pl ~ais)* a & m ceremonial. **~oso** /o/ a ceremonious

cer|rado /se'xadu/ a <barba, mata> thick; <punho, dentes> clenched ● m scrubland. **~rar** vt close. **~rar-se** vpr close; <noites, trevas> close in

certeiro /ser'teru/ a well-aimed, accurate

certeza /ser'teza/ f certainty; **com ~** certainly; **ter ~ be** sure **(de de que that)**

certidão /sertʃi'dãw/ f certificate; **~ de nascimento** birth certificate

certifi|cado /sertʃifi'kadu/ m certificate; **~car-se de** make sure of. **~car** vt certify

certo /'sertu/ a *(correto)* right; *(seguro)* certain; *(algum)* a certain ● adv right; **dar ~** work

cerveja /ser'veʒa/ f beer. **~ria** f brewery; *(bar)* pub

cervo /'servu/ m deer

cer|zidura /serzi'dura/ f darning. **~zir** vt darn

cesariana /sezari'ana/ f Caesarian

césio /'seziu/ m caesium

cessar /se'sar/ vt/i cease

ces|ta /ˈsɛsta/ f basket; (de comida) hamper; **~to de lixo** waste-paper basket. **~to** /e/ m basket

ceticismo /setʃiˈsizmu/ m scepticism

cético /ˈsɛtʃiku/ a sceptical ● m sceptic

cetim /seˈtʃĩ/ m satin

céu /sɛw/ m sky; (na religião) heaven; **~ da boca** roof of the mouth

cevada /seˈvada/ f barley

chá /ʃa/ m tea; **~ de bar** bachelor party, Amer stag night; **~ de panela** hen night, Amer wedding shower

cha|cal /ʃaˈkaw/ (pl **~cais**) m jackal

chácara /ˈʃakara/ f smallholding; (casa) country cottage

chaci|na /ʃaˈsina/ f slaughter. **~nar** vt slaughter

chafariz /ʃafaˈris/ m fountain

chaga /ˈʃaga/ f sore

chaleira /ʃaˈlera/ f kettle

chama /ˈʃama/ f flame

cha|mada /ʃaˈmada/ f call; (dos presentes) roll call; (dos alunos) register. **~mado** m call ● a (depois do substantivo) called; (antes do substantivo) so-called. **~mar** vt call; (para sair etc) ask, invite; (atrair) ‹atenção› ● vi call; ‹telefone› ring. **~mar-se** vpr be called. **~mariz** m decoy. **~mativo** a showy, flashy

chamejar /ʃameˈʒar/ vi flare

chaminé /ʃamiˈne/ f (de casa, fábrica) chimney; (de navio, trem) funnel

champanhe /ʃãˈpaɲi/ m champagne

champu /ʃãˈpu/ Port m shampoo

chamuscar /ʃamusˈkar/ vt singe, scorch

chance /ˈʃãsi/ f chance

chanceler /ʃãseˈler/ m chancellor

chanchada /ʃãˈʃada/ f (peça) second-rate play; (filme) B movie

chanta|gear /ʃãtaʒiˈar/ vt blackmail. **~gem** f blackmail. **~gista** m/f blackmailer

chão /ʃãw/ (pl **~s**) m ground; (dentro de casa etc) floor

chapa /ˈʃapa/ f sheet; (foto) plate; **~ eleitoral** electoral list; **~ de matrícula** Port number plate, Amer license plate. **~** 🔢 mate

chapéu /ʃaˈpɛw/ m hat

charada /ʃaˈrada/ f riddle

char|ge /ˈʃarʒi/ f (political) cartoon. **~gista** m/f cartoonist

charla|tanismo /ʃarlataˈnizmu/ m charlatanism. **~tão** (pl **~tães**) m (f **~tona**) charlatan

char|me /ˈʃarmi/ m charm; **fazer ~me** turn on the charm. **~moso** /o/ a charming

charneca /ʃarˈnɛka/ f moor

charuto /ʃaˈrutu/ m cigar

chassi /ʃaˈsi/ m chassis

chat /ˈʃat/ m (na internet) chat; **sala de ~** chatroom

chata /ˈʃata/ f (barca) barge

chate|ação /ʃatʃiaˈsãw/ f annoyance. **~ar** vt annoy. **~ar-se** vpr get annoyed

cha|tice /ʃaˈtʃisi/ f nuisance. **~to** a (tedioso) boring; (irritante) annoying; (mal-educado) rude; (plano) flat

chauvinis|mo /ʃoviˈnizmu/ m chauvinism. **~ta** m/f chauvinist ● a chauvinistic

chavão /ʃaˈvãw/ m cliché

cha|ve /ˈʃavi/ f key; (ferramenta) spanner. **~ve de fenda** screwdriver; **~ve inglesa** wrench; **~veiro** m (aro) key ring; (*pessoa*) locksmith

chávena /ˈʃavena/ *f* soup bowl; Port (*xícara*) cup

checar /ʃeˈkar/ *vt* check

check-up /ʃeˈkap/ *m* Med check-up; **fazer um** ~ to have a checkup

che|fe /ˈʃefi/ *m/f* (*patrão*) boss; (*gerente*) manager; (*dirigente*) leader. ~**fia** *f* leadership; (*de empresa*) management; (*sede*) headquarters. ~**fiar** *vt* lead; be in charge of ‹*trabalho*›

chegada /ʃeˈgada/ *f* arrival. ~**gado** *a* ‹*amigo, relação*› close. ~**gar** *vi* arrive; (*deslocar-se*) move up; (*ser suficiente*) be enough ● *vt* bring up ‹*prato, cadeira*›. ~**gar a fazer** go as far as doing; **aonde você quer** ~**gar?** what are you driving at?; ~**gar lá** *fig* make it

cheia /ˈʃeja/ *f* flood

cheio /ˈʃeju/ *a* full; (*farto*) fed up

chei|rar /ʃeˈrar/ *vt/i* smell (**a** of). ~**roso** /o/ *a* scented

cheque /ˈʃɛki/ *m* cheque, Amer check; ~ **de viagem** traveller's cheque; ~ **em branco** blank cheque

chi|ado /ʃiˈadu/ *m* (*de pneus, freios*) screech; (*de porta*) squeak; (*de vapor, numa fita*) hiss. ~**ar** *vi* ‹*porta*› squeak; ‹*pneus, freios*› screech; ‹*vapor, fita*› hiss; ‹*fritura*› sizzle; 🔳 (*reclamar*) grumble, moan

chiclete /ʃiˈklɛtʃi/ *m* chewing gum; ~ **de bola** bubble gum

chico|tada /ʃikoˈtada/ *f* lash. ~**te** /ɔ/ *m* whip. ~**tear** *vt* whip

chi|frar /ʃiˈfrar/ *vt* 🔳 cheat on ‹*marido, esposa*›; two-time ‹*namorado, namorada*›. ~**fre** *m* horn. ~**frudo** *a* horned; 🔳 cuckolded ● *m* cuckold

Chile /ˈʃili/ *m* Chile

chileno /ʃiˈlenu/ *a & m* Chilean

chilique /ʃiˈliki/ 🔳 *m* funny turn

chil|rear /ʃiwxiˈar/ *vi* chirp, twitter. ~**reio** *m* chirping, twittering

chimarrão /ʃimaˈxãw/ *m* unsweetened maté tea

chimpanzé /ʃĩpãˈzɛ/ *m* chimpanzee

China /ˈʃina/ *f* China

chinelo /ʃiˈnɛlu/ *m* slipper

chi|nês /ʃiˈnes/ *a & m* (*f* ~**nesa**) Chinese

chinfrim /ʃĩˈfrĩ/ *a* tatty, shoddy

chio /ˈʃiu/ *m* squeak; (*de pneus*) screech; (*de vapor*) hiss

chique /ˈʃiki/ *a* ‹*pessoa, aparência, roupa*› smart, Amer sharp; ‹*hotel, bairro, loja etc*› smart, upmarket, posh

chiqueiro /ʃiˈkeru/ *m* pigsty

chis|pa /ˈʃispa/ *f* flash. ~**pada** *f* dash. ~**par** *vi* (*soltar chispas*) flash; (*correr*) dash

choca|lhar /ʃokaˈʎar/ *vt/i* rattle. ~**lho** *m* rattle

cho|cante /ʃoˈkãtʃi/ *a* shocking; 🔳 incredible. ~**car** *vt/i* hatch ‹*ovos*›; (*ultrajar*) shock. ~**car-se** *vpr* ‹*carros etc*› crash; ‹*teorias etc*› clash

chocho /ˈʃoʃu/ *a* dull, insipid

chocolate /ʃokoˈlatʃi/ *m* chocolate

chofer /ʃoˈfɛr/ *m* chauffeur

chope /ˈʃopi/ *m* draught lager

choque /ˈʃɔki/ *m* shock; (*colisão*) collision; (*conflito*) clash

cho|radeira /ʃoraˈdera/ *f* fit of crying. ~**ramingar** *vi* whine. ~**ramingas** *m/f invar* whiner. ~**rão** *m* (*salgueiro*) weeping willow ● *a* (*f* ~**rona**) tearful. ~**rar** *vi* cry.

~ro /o/ m crying. **~roso** /o/ a tearful

chouriço /ʃoˈrisu/ m black pudding; *Port* sausage

chover /ʃoˈver/ vt/i rain

chuchu /ʃuˈʃu/ m chayote

chucrute /ʃuˈkrutʃi/ m sauerkraut

chumaço /ʃuˈmasu/ m wad

chum|bado /ʃuˈbadu/ a 🄳 knocked out. **~bar** *Port* vt fill ‹*dente*›; fail ‹*aluno*› ● vi ‹*aluno*› fail. **~bo** m lead; *Port* (*obturação*) filling

chu|par /ʃuˈpar/ vt suck; ‹*esponja*› suck up. **~peta** /e/ f dummy, *Amer* pacifier

churras|caria /ʃuxaskaˈria/ f barbecue restaurant. **~co** m barbecue. **~queira** f barbecue. **~quinho** m kebab

chu|tar /ʃuˈtar/ vt/i kick; 🄳 (*adivinhar*) guess. **~te** m kick. **~teira** f football boot

chu|va /ˈʃuva/ f rain; **~va de pedra** hail. **~varada** f torrential rainstorm. **~veiro** m shower. **~viscar** vi drizzle. **~visco** m drizzle. **~voso** /o/ a rainy

ciberespaço /siberisˈpasu/ m cyberspace

ciberespeculador /siberispekulaˈdor/ m cybersquatter

ciberterrorismo /sibertexoˈrizmu/ m cyberterrorism

cica|triz /sikaˈtris/ f scar. **~trizar** vt scar ● vi ‹*ferida*› heal

ci|clismo /siˈklizmu/ m cycling. **~clista** m/f cyclist. **~clo** m cycle. **~clone** m cyclone. **~clovia** f cycle lane

cida|dania /sidadaˈnia/ f citizenship. **~dão** (*pl* **~dãos**) m (f **~dã**) citizen. **~de** f town; (*grande*) city. **~dela** /ɛ/ f citadel

ciência /siˈẽsia/ f science

cien|te /siˈẽtʃi/ a aware. **~tífico** a scientific. **~tista** m/f scientist

ci|fra /ˈsifra/ f figure; (*código*) cipher. **~frão** m dollar sign. **~frar** vt encode

cigano /siˈganu/ a & m gypsy

cigarra /siˈgaxa/ f cicada; (*dispositivo*) buzzer

cigar|reira /sigaˈxera/ f cigarette case. **~ro** m cigarette

cilada /siˈlada/ f trap; (*estratagema*) trick

cilindrada /siliˈdrada/ f (engine) capacity

cilíndrico /siˈlĩdriku/ a cylindrical

cilindro /siˈlĩdru/ m cylinder; (*rolo*) roller

cílio /ˈsiliu/ m eyelash

cima /ˈsima/ f **em ~** on top; (*na casa*) upstairs; **em ~ de** on, on top of; **para ~** up; (*na casa*) upstairs; **por ~** over the top; **por ~ de** over; **de ~** from above; **ainda por ~** moreover

címbalo /ˈsĩbalu/ m cymbal

cimeira /siˈmera/ f crest; *Port* (*cúpula*) summit

cimen|tar /simẽˈtar/ vt cement. **~to** m cement

cinco /ˈsĩku/ a & m five

cine|asta /siniˈasta/ m/f film-maker. **~ma** /e/ m cinema

cínico /ˈsiniku/ a cynical ● m cynic

cinismo /siˈnizmu/ m cynicism

cinquen|ta /sĩˈkwẽta/ a & m fifty. **~tão** a & m (f **~tona**) fifty-year-old

cinti|lante /sĩtʃiˈlãtʃi/ a glittering. **~lar** vi glitter

cin|to /ˈsĩtu/ m belt; **~to de segurança** seat belt. **~tura** f waist. **~turão** m belt

cin|za /'sĩza/ f ash ● a invar grey. **~zeiro** m ashtray

cin|zel /sĩ'zɛw/ (pl **~zéis**) m chisel. **~zelar** vt carve

cinzento /sĩ'zẽtu/ a grey

ci|pó /si'pɔ/ m vine, liana. **~poal** (pl **~poais**) m jungle

cipreste /si'prɛstʃi/ m cypress

cipriota /sipri'ɔta/ a & m Cypriot

ciranda /si'rãda/ f fig merry-go-round

cir|cense /sir'sẽsi/ a circus. **~co** m circus

circu|ito /sir'kuitu/ m circuit. **~lação** f circulation. **~lar** a & f circular ● vt circulate ● vi <dinheiro, sangue> circulate; <carro> drive; <ônibus> run; <trânsito> move; <pessoa> go round

círculo /'sirkulu/ m circle

circunci|dar /sirkũsi'dar/ vt circumcise. **~são** f circumcision

circun|dar /sirkũ'dar/ vt surround. **~ferência** f circumference. **~flexo** /ɛks/ a & m circumflex. **~scrição** f district; **~scrição eleitoral** constituency. **~specto** /ɛ/ a circumspect. **~stância** f circumstance. **~stanciado** a detailed. **~stancial** (pl **~stanciais**) a circumstantial. **~stante** m/f bystander

cirrose /si'xɔzi/ f cirrhosis

cirur|gia /sirur'ʒia/ f surgery. **~gião** m (f **~giã**) surgeon

cirúrgico /si'rurʒiku/ a surgical

cisão /si'zãw/ f split, division

cisco /'sisku/ m speck

cisma[1] /'sizma/ m schism

cis|ma[2] /'sizma/ f (mania) fixation; (devaneio) imagining, daydream; (prevenção) irrational dislike; (de

criança) whim. **~mar** vt/i be lost in thought; <criança> be insistent; **~mar em** brood over; **~mar de** ou **em fazer** insist on doing; **~mar que** insist on thinking that; **~mar com alguém** take a dislike to sb

cisne /'sizni/ m swan

cistite /sis'tʃitʃi/ f cystitis

ci|tação /sita'sãw/ f quotation; Jurid summons. **~tar** vt quote; Jurid summon

ciúme /si'umi/ m jealousy; **ter ~s de** be jealous of

ciu|meira /siu'mera/ f fit of jealousy. **~mento** a jealous

cívico /'siviku/ a civic

ci|vil /si'viw/ (pl **~vis**) a civil ● m civilian. **~vilidade** f civility

civili|zação /siviliza'sãw/ f civilization. **~zado** a civilized. **~zar** vt civilize

civismo /si'vizmu/ m public spirit

cla|mar /kla'mar/ vt/i cry out, clamour (por for). **~mor** m outcry. **~moroso** /o/ a <protesto> loud, noisy; <erro, injustiça> blatant

clandestino /klãdes'tʃinu/ a clandestine

cla|ra /'klara/ f egg white. **~raboia** f skylight; **~rão** m flash. **~rear** vt brighten; clarify <questão> ● vi brighten up; (fazer-se dia) become light. **~reira** f clearing. **~reza** /e/ f clarity. **~ridade** f brightness; (do dia) daylight

cla|rim /kla'rĩ/ m bugle. **~rinete** /e/ m clarinet

clarividente /klarivi'dẽtʃi/ m/f clairvoyant

claro /'klaru/ a clear; <luz> bright; <cor> light ● adv clearly ● int of course; **~ que sim/não** of course/of course not; **às claras** openly; **noite**

em ~ sleepless night; já é dia ~ it's already daylight

classe /'klasi/ f class; ~ **média** middle class

clássico /'klasiku/ a classical; (famoso, exemplar) classic ● m classic

classifi|cação /klasifika'sãw/ f classification; (numa competição esportiva) placing, place. ~**cado** a classified; ‹candidato› successful; ‹esportista, time› qualified. ~**car** vt classify; (considerar) describe (de as). ~**car-se** vpr ‹candidato, esportista› qualify; (chamar-se) describe o.s. (de as). ~**catório** a qualifying

classudo /kla'sudu/ a 🔲 classy

claustro|fobia /klawstrofo'bia/ f claustrophobia. ~**fóbico** a claustrophobic

cláusula /'klawzula/ f clause

cla|ve /'klavi/ f clef. ~**vícula** f collar bone

cle|mência /kle'mēsia/ f clemency. ~**mente** a ‹pessoa› lenient; ‹tempo› clement

cleptomaníaco /kleptoma'niaku/ m kleptomaniac

clérigo /'klerigu/ m cleric, clergyman

clero /'kleru/ m clergy

clicar /kli'kar/ vi Comput click

clichê /kli'ʃe/ m cliché

clien|te /kli'ẽtʃi/ m/f (de loja) customer; (de advogado, empresa) client. ~**tela** /ɛ/ f (de loja) customers; (de restaurante, empresa) clientele

cli|ma /'klima/ m climate. ~**mático** /kli'matʃiku/ a climatic; **alterações** ~**máticas** climate change

clímax /'klimaks/ m invar climax

clíni|ca /'klinika/ f clinic; ~**ca geral** general practice. ~**co** a clinical ● m ~**co geral** general practitioner, GP

clipe /'klipi/ m clip; (para papéis) paper clip

clonar /klo'nar/ vt clone

clone /'kloni/ m clone

cloro /'klɔru/ m chlorine

close /'klozi/ m close-up

clube /'klubi/ m club

coação /koa'sãw/ f coercion

coadjuvante /koadʒu'vãtʃi/ a ‹ator› supporting ● m/f (em peça, filme) co-star; (em crime) accomplice

coador /koa'dor/ m strainer; (de legumes) colander; (de café) filter bag

coadunar /koadu'nar/ vt combine

coagir /koa'ʒir/ vt compel

coagular /koagu'lar/ vt/i clot. ~**se** vpr clot

coágulo /ko'agulu/ m clot

coalhar /koa'ʎar/ vt/i curdle. ~**se** vpr curdle

coalizão /koali'zãw/ f coalition

coar /ko'ar/ vt strain

coaxar /koa'ʃar/ vi croak ● m croaking

cobaia /ko'baja/ f guinea pig

cober|ta /ko'berta/ f (de cama) bedcover; (de navio) deck. ~**to** /ɛ/ a covered ● pp de ▶ COBRIR. ~**tor** m blanket. ~**tura** f (revestimento) covering; (reportagem) coverage; (seguro) cover; (apartamento) penthouse

cobi|ça /ko'bisa/ f greed, covetousness. ~**çar** vt covet. ~**çoso** /o/ a covetous

cobra /'kɔbra/ f snake

co|brador /kobra'dor/ m (no ônibus) conductor. ~**brança** f *(de dívida)* collection; *(de preço)* charging. **~brança de pênalti/falta** penalty (kick)/free kick. **~brar** vt collect ‹*dívida*›; ask for ‹*coisa prometida*›; take ‹*pênalti*›; **~brar algo a alguém** *(em dinheiro)* charge sb for sth; *fig* make sb pay for sth; **~brar uma falta** *(no futebol)* take a free kick

cobre /'kɔbri/ *m* copper

cobrir /ko'brir/ vt cover. **~se** vpr ‹*pessoa*› cover o.s. up; ‹*coisa*› be covered

cocaína /koka'ina/ f cocaine

coçar /ko'sar/ vt scratch ● vi *(esfregar-se)* scratch; *(comichar)* itch. **~se** vpr scratch o.s.

cócegas /'kɔsegas/ f pl **fazer ~ em** tickle; **sentir ~** be ticklish

coceira /ko'sera/ f itch

cochichar /koʃi'ʃar/ vt/i whisper. **~cho** m whisper

cochilada /koʃi'lada/ f doze. **~lar** vi doze. **~lo** m snooze

coco /'koku/ m coconut

cócoras /'kɔkoras/ f pl de ~ squatting; **ficar de ~** squat

côdea /'kodʒia/ f crust

codificar /kodʒifi'kar/ vt encode ‹*mensagem*›; codify ‹*leis*›

código /'kɔdʒigu/ m code; **~ de barras** bar code

codinome /kodʒi'nomi/ m code name

coeficiente /koefisi'ẽtʃi/ m coefficient; *fig (fator)* factor

coelho /ko'eʎu/ m rabbit

coentro /ko'ẽtru/ m coriander

coerção /koer'sãw/ f coercion

coerência /koe'rẽsia/ f *(lógica)* coherence; *(consequência)* consistency. **~rente** a *(lógico)*

coherent; *(consequente)* consistent

coexistência /koezis'tẽsia/ f coexistence. **~tir** vi coexist

cofre /'kɔfri/ m safe; *(de dinheiro público)* coffer

cogitação /koʒita'sãw/ f contemplation; **fora de ~tação** out of the question. **~tar** vt/i contemplate

cogumelo /kogu'melu/ m mushroom

coibir /koi'bir/ vt restrict; **~se de** keep o.s. from

coice /'kojsi/ m kick

coincidência /koĩsi'dẽsia/ f coincidence. **~dir** vi coincide

coisa /'kojza/ f thing

coitado /koj'tadu/ m poor thing; **~ do pai** poor father

cola /'kɔla/ f glue; *(cópia)* crib

colaboração /kolabora'sãw/ f collaboration; *(de escritor etc)* contribution; **~rador** m collaborator; *(em jornal, livro)* contributor. **~rar** vi collaborate; *(em jornal, livro)* contribute **(em** to)

colagem /ko'laʒẽ/ f collage

colágeno /ko'laʒenu/ m collagen

colapso /ko'lapsu/ m collapse

colar¹ /ko'lar/ m necklace

colar² /ko'lar/ vt *(grudar)* stick; *(copiar)* crib ● vi stick; *(copiar)* crib; ‹*desculpa etc*› stand up, stick

colarinho /kola'riɲu/ m collar; *(de cerveja)* head

colateral /kolate'raw/ *(pl* **~rais**) a **efeito ~ral** side effect

colcha /'kowʃa/ f bedspread. **~chão** m mattress

colchete /kow'ʃetʃi/ m fastener; *(sinal de pontuação)* square bracket; **~ de pressão** press stud, popper

colchonete /kowʃo'nɛtʃi/ *m* (foldaway) mattress

coldre /'kɔwdri/ *m* holster

cole|ção /kole'sãw/ *f* collection. **~cionador** *m* collector. **~cionar** *vt* collect

colega /ko'lɛga/ *m/f* (*amigo*) friend; (*de trabalho*) colleague

colegi|al /koleʒi'aw/ (*pl* **~ais**) *a* school ● *m/f* schoolboy (*f* -girl)

colégio /ko'lɛʒiu/ *m* secondary school, *Amer* high school

coleira /ko'lera/ *f* collar

cólera /'kɔlera/ *f* (*doença*) cholera; (*raiva*) fury

colérico /ko'lɛriku/ *a* (*furioso*) furious ● *m* (*doente*) cholera victim

colesterol /koleste'rɔw/ *m* cholesterol

cole|ta /ko'lɛta/ *f* collection. **~tânea** *f* collection. **~tar** *vt* collect

colete /ko'letʃi/ *m* waistcoat, *Amer* vest; **~ salva-vidas** life jacket, *Amer* life preserver

coletivo /kole'tʃivu/ *a* collective; ‹*transporte*› public ● *m* bus

colheita /ko'ʎejta/ *f* harvest; (*produtos colhidos*) crop

colher[1] /ko'ʎer/ *f* spoon

colher[2] /ko'ʎer/ *vt* pick ‹*flores, frutos*›; gather ‹*informações*›

colherada /koʎe'rada/ *f* spoonful

colibri /koli'bri/ *m* hummingbird

cólica /'kɔlika/ *f* colic

colidir /koli'dʒir/ *vi* collide

coli|gação /koliga'sãw/ *f* Pol coalition. **~gado** *m* Pol coalition partner. **~gar** *vt* bring together. **~gar-se** *vpr* join forces; Pol form a coalition

colina /ko'lina/ *f* hill

colírio /ko'liriu/ *m* eyewash

colisão /koli'zãw/ *f* collision

collant /ko'lã/ (*pl* **~s**) *m* body; (*de ginástica*) leotard

colmeia /kow'meja/ *f* beehive

colo /'kɔlu/ *f* (*regaço*) lap; (*pescoço*) neck

colo|cação /koloka'sãw/ *f* placing; (*emprego*) position; (*exposição de fatos*) statement; (*de aparelho, pneus, carpete etc*) fitting; **~car** put; fit ‹*aparelho, pneus, carpete etc*›; put forward, state ‹*opinião, ideias*›; (*empregar*) get a job for. **~cado** *a* placed; **o primeiro ~cado** (*em ranking*) person in first place. **~cador** *m* fitter

Colômbia /ko'lõbia/ *f* Colombia

colombiano /kolõbi'anu/ *a* & *m* Colombian

cólon /'kɔlõ/ *m* colon

colônia[1] /ko'lonia/ *f* (*colonos*) colony

colônia[2] /ko'lonia/ *f* (*perfume*) cologne

coloni|al /koloni'aw/ (*pl* **~ais**) *a* colonial. **~alismo** *m* colonialism. **~alista** *a* & *m/f* colonialist. **~zar** *vt* colonize

colono /ko'lonu/ *m* settler, colonist; (*lavrador*) tenant farmer

coloqui|al /koloki'aw/ (*pl* **~ais**) *a* colloquial

colóquio /ko'lɔkiu/ *m* (*conversa*) conversation; (*congresso*) conference

colo|rido /kolo'ridu/ *a* colourful ● *m* colouring. **~rir** *vt* colour

coluna /ko'luna/ *f* column; (*vertebral*) spine. **~nável** (*pl* **~náveis**) *a* famous ● *m/f* celebrity. **~nista** *m/f* columnist

com /kõ/ *prep* with; **o comentário foi comigo** the comment was meant for me; **você está ~ a chave?**

have you got the key?; **~ seis anos
de idade** at six years of age
coma /'kɔmɐ/ f coma
comadre /koˈmadri/ f (madrinha)
godmother of one's child; (mãe do
afilhado) mother of one's godchild;
(urinol) bedpan
coman|dante /komɐ̃ˈdãtʃi/ m
commander. **~dar** vt lead; (ordenar)
command; (elevar-se acima de)
dominate. **~do** m command; (grupo)
commando group
comba|te /kõˈbatʃi/ m combat; (a
drogas, doença etc) fight (**a** against).
~ter vt/i fight. **~ter-se** vpr fight
combi|nação /kõbinaˈsɐ̃w/ f
combination; (acordo) arrangement;
(plano) scheme; (roupa) petticoat.
~nar vt (juntar) combine; (ajustar)
arrange ● vi go together, match.
~nar com go with, match; **~nar de
sair** arrange to go out; **~nar-se** vpr
(juntar-se) combine; (harmonizar-se)
go together, match
comboio /kõˈboju/ m convoy; Port
(trem) train
combustí|vel /kõbusˈtʃivew/ (pl
~veis) m fuel
come|çar /komeˈsar/ vt/i start,
begin. **~ço** /e/ m beginning, start
comédia /koˈmɛdʒia/ f comedy
comediante /komedʒiˈãtʃi/ m/f
comedian (f comédienne)
comemo|ração
/komemoraˈsɐ̃w/ f (celebração)
celebration; (lembrança)
commemoration. **~rar** vt (festejar)
celebrate; (lembrar) commemorate
comen|tar /komẽˈtar/ vt comment
on; (falar mal de) make comments
about. **~tário** m comment; (de
texto, na TV etc) commentary; **sem
~tários** no comment. **~tarista** m/f
commentator

comer /koˈmer/ vt eat; (ferrugem
etc) eat away; take (peça de xadrez);
dar de ~ a feed ● vi eat. **~se** vpr (de
raiva etc) be consumed (**de** with)
comerci|al /komersiˈaw/ (pl **~ais**)
a & m commercial. **~alizar** vt market.
~ante m/f trader. **~ar** vi do business,
trade. **~ário** m shopworker
comércio /koˈmɛrsiu/ m
(atividade) trade; (loja etc) business;
(lojas) shops; **~ eletrônico**
e-commerce; **~ justo** fair trade
comes /'kɔmis/ m pl **~ e bebes** 🔲
food and drink. **~tíveis** m pl foods,
food. **~tível** (pl **~tíveis**) a edible
cometa /koˈmeta/ m comet
cometer /komeˈter/ vt commit
(crime); make (erro)
comichão /komiˈʃɐ̃w/ f itch
comício /koˈmisiu/ m rally
cômico /'komiku/ a (de comédia)
comic; (engraçado) comical
comida /koˈmida/ f food; (uma)
meal
comigo = com + mim
comi|lão /komiˈlɐ̃w/ a (f **~lona**)
greedy ● m (f **~lona**) glutton
cominho /koˈmiɲu/ m cummin
comiserar-se /komizeˈrarsi/ vpr
commiserate (**de** with)
comis|são /komiˈsɐ̃w/ f
commission. **~sário** m commissioner;
~sário de bordo (aéreo) steward;
(de navio) purser. **~sionar** vt
commission
comi|tê /komiˈte/ m committee.
~tiva f group; (de uma pessoa)
retinue
como /'komu/ adv (na condição
de) as; (da mesma forma que) like;
(de que maneira) how ● conj as; **~?**
(pedindo repetição) pardon?; **~ se** as
if; **assim ~** as well as

cômoda /'komɐda/ f chest of drawers, *Amer* bureau

como|didade /komodʒi'dadʒi/ f comfort; (*conveniência*) convenience. **~dismo** m complacency. **~dista** a complacent

cômodo /'komodu/ a comfortable; (*conveniente*) convenient ● m (*aposento*) room

como|vente /komo'vẽtʃi/ a moving. **~ver** vt move ● vi be moving. **~ver-se** vpr be moved

compacto /kõ'paktu/ a compact ● m single

compadecer-se /kõpade'sersi/ vpr feel pity for (**de**)

compadre /kõ'padri/ m (*padrinho*) godfather of one's child; (*pai do afilhado*) father of one's godchild

compaixão /kõpaj'ʃãw/ f compassion

companhei|rismo /kõpaɲe'rizmu/ m companionship. **~ro** m (*de viagem etc*) companion; (*amigo*) friend, mate

companhia /kõpa'ɲia/ f company; **fazer ~ a alguém** keep sb company

compa|ração /kõpara'sãw/ f comparison. **~rar** vt compare. **~rativo** a comparative. **~rável** (*pl* **~ráveis**) a comparable

compare|cer /kõpare'ser/ vi appear; **~cer a** attend. **~cimento** m attendance

comparsa /kõ'parsa/ m/f (*ator*) bit player; (*cúmplice*) sidekick

comparti|lhar /kõpartʃi'ʎar/ vt/i share (**de** in). **~mento** m compartment

compassado /kõpa'sadu/ a (*medido*) measured; (*ritmado*) regular

compassivo /kõpa'sivu/ a compassionate

compasso /kõ'pasu/ m *Mus* beat, time; (*instrumento*) compass, pair of compasses

compatí|vel /kõpa'tʃivew/ (*pl* **~veis**) a compatible

compatriota /kõpatri'ɔta/ m/f compatriot, fellow countryman (f -woman)

compelir /kõpe'lir/ vt compel

compene|tração /kõpenetra'sãw/ f conviction. **~trar** vt convince. **~trar-se** vpr convince o.s.

compen|sação /kõpẽsa'sãw/ f compensation; (*de cheques*) clearing; **~sação de carbono** carbon offsetting. **~sar** vt make up for <*defeitos, danos*>; offset <*peso, gastos*>; clear <*cheques*> ● vi <*crime*> pay

compe|tência /kõpe'tẽsia/ f competence. **~tente** a competent

compe|tição /kõpetʃi'sãw/ f competition. **~tidor** m competitor. **~tir** vi compete; **~tir a** be up to. **~tividade** f competitiveness. **~titivo** a competitive

compla|cência /kõpla'sẽsia/ f complaisance. **~cente** a obliging

complemen|tar /kõplemẽ'tar/ vt complement ● a complementary. **~to** m complement

comple|tar /kõple'tar/ vt complete; top up <*copo, tanque etc*>; **~tar 20 anos** turn 20. **~to** /ɛ/ a complete; (*cheio*) full up; **por ~to** completely; **escrever por ~to** write out in full

comple|xado /kõplek'sadu/ a with a complex. **~xidade** f complexity. **~xo** /ɛ/ a & m complex

compli|cação /kõplika'sãw/ f complication. **~cado** a complicated. **~car** vt complicate. **~car-se** vpr get complicated

complô /kõ'plo/ m conspiracy, plot

com|ponente /kõpo'nẽtʃi/ a & m component. **~por** vt/i compose. **~por-se** vpr (controlar-se) compose o.s.; **~por-se de** be composed of

compor|tamento /kõporta'mẽtu/ m behaviour. **~tar** vt hold; bear ‹dor, prejuízo›. **~tar-se** vpr behave

composi|ção /kõpozi'sãw/ f composition; (acordo) conciliation. **~tor** m (de música) composer; (gráfico) compositor

compos|to /kõ'postu/ pp de ► COMPOR ● a compound; ‹pessoa› level-headed ● m compound. **~to de** made up of. **~tura** f composure

compota /kõ'pɔta/ f fruit in syrup

com|pra /'kõpra/ f purchase; pl shopping; **fazer ~pras** go shopping. **~prador** m buyer. **~prar** vt buy; bribe ‹oficial, juiz›; pick ‹briga›

compreen|der /kõpriẽ'der/ vt (conter em si) contain; (estender-se a) cover, take in; (entender) understand. **~são** f understanding. **~sível** (pl **~síveis**) a understandable. **~sivo** a understanding

compres|sa /kõ'prɛsa/ f compress. **~são** f compression. **~sor** m compressor; **rolo ~sor** steamroller

compri|do /kõ'pridu/ a long. **~mento** m length

compri|mido /kõpri'midu/ m pill, tablet ● a ‹ar› compressed. **~mir** vt (apertar) press; (reduzir o volume de) compress

comprome|tedor /kõpromete'dor/ a compromising. **~ter** vt (envolver) involve; (prejudicar) compromise; **~ter alguém a fazer** commit sb to doing. **~ter-se** vpr (obrigar-se) commit o.s.; (prejudicar-se) compromise o.s.. **~tido** a (ocupado) busy; (noivo) spoken for

compromisso /kõpro'misu/ m commitment; (encontro marcado) appointment; **sem ~** without obligation

compro|vação /kõprova'sãw/ f proof. **~vante** m receipt. **~var** vt prove

compul|são /kõpuw'sãw/ f compulsion. **~sivo** a compulsive. **~sório** a compulsory

compu|tação /kõputa'sãw/ f computation; (matéria, ramo) computing; **~ na nuvem** cloud computing. **~tador** m computer. **~tadorizar** vt computerize. **~tar** vt compute

comum /ko'mũ/ a common; (não especial) ordinary; **fora do ~** out of the ordinary; **em ~** ‹trabalho› joint; ‹atuar› jointly; **ter muito em ~** have a lot in common

comungar /komũ'gar/ vi take communion

comunhão /komu'ɲãw/ f communion; Relig (Holy) Communion

comuni|cação /komunika'sãw/ f communication; **~cação social/visual** media studies/ graphic design. **~cado** m notice; Pol communiqué. **~car** vt communicate; (unir) connect ● vi, **~car-se** vpr communicate. **~cativo** a communicative

comu|nidade /komuni'dadʒi/ f community. **~nismo** m communism. **~nista** a & m/f communist. **~nitário** a (da comunidade) community; (para todos juntos) communal

côncavo /'kõkavu/ a concave

conce|ber /kõse'ber/ vt conceive; (imaginar) conceive of ● vi conceive. **~bível** (pl **~bíveis**) a conceivable

conceder /kõse'der/ vt grant; **~ em** accede to

concei|to /kõ'sejtu/ m concept; (opinião) opinion; (fama) reputation. **~tuado** a highly thought of. **~tuar** vt (imaginar) conceptualize; (avaliar) assess

concen|tração /kõsẽtra'sãw/ f concentration; (de jogadores) training camp. **~trar** vt concentrate. **~trar-se** vpr concentrate

concepção /kõsep'sãw/ f conception; (opinião) view

concernir /kõser'nir/ vt **~ a** concern

concerto /kõ'sertu/ m concert

conces|são /kõse'sãw/ f concession. **~sionária** f dealership. **~sionário** m dealer

concha /'kõʃa/ f (de molusco) shell; (colher) ladle

concili|ação /kõsilia'sãw/ f conciliation. **~ador** a conciliatory. **~ar** vt reconcile

concílio /kõ'siliu/ m council

conci|são /kõsi'zãw/ f conciseness. **~so** a concise

conclamar /kõkla'mar/ vt call ‹eleição, greve›; call upon ‹pessoa›

conclu|dente /kõklu'dẽtʃi/ a conclusive. **~ir** vt/i conclude. **~são** f conclusion. **~sivo** a concluding

concor|dância /kõkor'dãsia/ f agreement. **~dante** a consistent.

~dar vi agree (**em** to) ● vt bring into line. **~data** f abrir **~data** go into liquidation

concórdia /kõ'kordʒia/ f concord

concor|rência /kõko'xẽsia/ f competition (a for). **~rente** a competing. **~rer** vi compete (**a** for); **~rer para** contribute to. **~rido** a popular

concre|tizar /kõkretʃi'zar/ vt realize. **~tizar-se** vpr be realized. **~to** /ɛ/ a & m concrete

concurso /kõ'kursu/ m contest; (prova) competition

con|dado /kõ'dadu/ m county. **~de** m count

condeco|ração /kõdekora'sãw/ f decoration. **~rar** vt decorate

conde|nação /kõdena'sãw/ f condemnation; Jurid conviction. **~nar** vt condemn; Jurid convict

conden|sação /kõdẽsa'sãw/ f condensation. **~sar** vt condense. **~sar-se** vpr condense

condescen|dência /kõdesẽ'dẽsia/ f acquiescence. **~dente** a acquiescent. **~der** vi acquiesce; **~der a** comply with ‹pedido, desejo›; **~der a ir** condescend to go

condessa /kõ'desa/ f countess

condi|ção /kõdʒi'sãw/ f condition; (qualidade) capacity; **ter ~ção ou ~ções para** be able to; **em boas ~ções** in good condition. **~cionado** a conditioned. **~cional** (pl **~cionais**) a conditional. **~cionamento** m conditioning

condimen|tar /kõdʒimẽ'tar/ vt season. **~to** m seasoning

condoer-se /kõdo'ersi/ vpr **~ de** feel sorry for

condolência /kõdoˈlẽsia/ f
sympathy; pl condolences

condomínio /kõdoˈminiu/ m
(taxa) service charge

condu|ção /kõduˈsãw/ f (de carro
etc) driving; (transporte) transport.
~cente a conducive (a to). **~ta** f
conduct. **~to** m conduit. **~tor** m (de
carro) driver; Eletr conductor. **~zir** vt
lead; drive <carro>; Eletr conduct ● vi
(de carro) drive; (levar) lead (a to)

cone /ˈkoni/ m cone

conec|tar /konekˈtar/ vt connect.
~tado a connected; Comput online

conectividade
/konektʃiviˈdadʒi/ f connectivity

cone|xão /konekˈsãw/ f
connection. **~xo** /e/ a connected

confec|ção /kõfekˈsãw/ f (roupa)
off-the-peg outfit; (loja) clothes
shop, boutique; (fábrica) clothes
manufacturer. **~cionar** vt make

confederação /kõfederaˈsãw/ f
confederation

confei|tar /kõfejˈtar/ vt ice. **~taria**
f cake shop. **~teiro** m confectioner

confe|rência /kõfeˈrẽsia/ f
conference; (palestra) lecture.
~rencista m/f speaker

conferir /kõfeˈrir/ vt check (com
against); (conceder) confer (a to)
● vi (controlar) check; (estar exato)
tally

confes|sar /kõfeˈsar/ vt/i confess.
~sar-se vpr confess. **~sionário** m
confessional. **~sor** m confessor

confete /kõˈfetʃi/ m confetti

confi|ança /kõfiˈãsa/ f (convicção)
confidence; (fé) trust. **~ante** a
confident (em of). **~ar** vt/i (dar)
entrust; **~ar em** trust. **~ável**
(pl **~áveis**) a reliable. **~dência** f
confidence. **~dencial** (pl **~denciais**)

a confidential. **~denciar** vt tell in
confidence. **~dente** m/f confidant
(f confidante)

configu|ração /kõfiguraˈsãw/ f
configuration. **~rar** vt (representar)
represent; (formar) shape; Comput
configure

con|finar /kõfiˈnar/ vi **~finar com**
border on. **~fins** m pl borders

confir|mação /kõfirmaˈsãw/
f confirmation. **~mar** vt confirm.
~mar-se vpr be confirmed

confis|car /kõfisˈkar/ vt confiscate.
~co m confiscation

confissão /kõfiˈsãw/ f confession

confla|gração /kõflagraˈsãw/ f
conflagration. **~grar** vt set alight; fig
throw into turmoil

confli|tante /kõfliˈtãtʃi/ a
conflicting. **~to** m conflict

confor|mação /kõformaˈsãw/
f resignation. **~mado** a resigned
(com to). **~mar** vt adapt (a to);
~mar-se com conform to <regra,
política>; resign o.s. to, come
to terms with <destino, evento>.
~me /ɔ/ prep according to ● conj
depending on; **~me** it depends.
~midade f conformity. **~mismo**
m conformism. **~mista** a & m/f
conformist

confor|tar /kõforˈtar/ vt comfort.
~tável (pl **~táveis**) a comfortable.
~to /o/ m comfort; **comida de ~to**
comfort eating; **zona de ~to**
comfort zone

confraternizar /kõfraterniˈzar/
vi fraternize

confron|tação /kõfrõtaˈsãw/
f confrontation. **~tar** vt confront;
(comparar) compare. **~to** m
confrontation; (comparação)
comparison

con|fundir /kõfũ'dʒir/ vt confuse.
~fundir-se vpr get confused.
~fusão f confusion; (desordem)
mess; (tumulto) commotion. **~fuso**
a (confundido) confused; (que
confunde) confusing

conge|lador /kõʒela'dor/ m
freezer. **~lamento** m (de preços
etc) freeze. **~lar** vt freeze. **~lar-se**
vpr freeze

congênito /kõ'ʒenitu/ a
congenital

congestão /kõʒes'tãw/ f
congestion

congestio|nado
/kõʒestʃio'nadu/ a ‹rua, cidade›
congested; ‹pessoa, rosto› flushed;
‹olhos› bloodshot. **~namento** m (de
trânsito) traffic jam. **~nar** vt congest.
~nar-se vpr ‹rua› get congested;
‹rosto› flush

conglomerado /kõglome'radu/
m conglomerate

congratular /kõgratu'lar/ vt
congratulate (**por** on)

congre|gação /kõgrega'sãw/ f
(na igreja) congregation; (reunião)
gathering. **~gar** vt bring together.
~gar-se vpr congregate

congresso /kõ'gresu/ m congress

conhaque /ko'ɲaki/ m brandy

conhe|cedor /koɲese'dor/ a
knowing ● m connoisseur. **~cer**
vt know; (ser apresentado a) get
to know; (visitar) go to, visit. **~cido**
a known; (famoso) well-known
● m acquaintance. **~cimento** m
knowledge; **tomar ~cimento de**
learn of; **travar ~cimento com
alguém** make sb's acquaintance,
become acquainted with sb

cônico /'koniku/ a conical

coni|vência /koni'vẽsia/ f
connivance. **~vente** a conniving
(**em** at)

conjetu|ra /kõʒe'tura/ f
conjecture. **~rar** vt/i conjecture

conju|gação /kõʒuga'sãw/ f Ling
conjugation. **~gar** vt conjugate
‹verbo›

cônjuge /'kõʒuʒi/ m/f spouse

conjun|ção /kõʒũ'sãw/
f conjunction. **~tivo** a & m
subjunctive. **~to** a joint ● m set;
(roupa) outfit; (musical) group; o
~to de the body of; **em ~to** jointly.
~tura f state of affairs; (econômica)
state of the economy

conosco = com + nós

cono|tação /konota'sãw/ f
connotation. **~tar** vt connote

conquanto /kõ'kwãtu/ conj
although, even though

conquis|ta /kõ'kista/ f conquest;
(proeza) achievement. **~tador** m
conqueror ● a conquering. **~tar** vt
conquer ‹terra, país›; win ‹riqueza,
independência›; win over ‹pessoa›

consa|gração /kõsagra'sãw/
f (de uma igreja) consecration;
(dedicação) dedication. **~grado**
a ‹artista, expressão› established.
~grar vt consecrate ‹igreja›;
establish ‹artista, estilo›; (dedicar)
dedicate (**a** to); **~grar-se** a dedicate
o.s. to

consci|ência /kõsi'ẽsia/ f
(moralidade) conscience; (sentidos)
consciousness; (no trabalho)
conscientiousness; (de um fato
etc) awareness. **~encioso** /o/ a
conscientious. **~ente** a conscious.
~entizar vt make aware (**de** of).
~entizar-se vpr become aware
(**de** of)

consecutivo /kõseku'tʃivu/ a
consecutive

conse|guinte /kõse'gĩtʃi/ a **por**
~guinte consequently. **~guir** vt
get; **~guir fazer** manage to do ● vi
succeed

conse|lheiro /kõse'ʎeru/ m
counsellor, adviser. **~lho** /e/ m piece
of advice ● pl advice; ⟨órgão⟩ council

consen|so /kõ'sẽsu/ m consensus.
~timento m consent. **~tir** vt allow
● vi consent (**em** to)

conse|quência /kõse'kwẽsia/
f consequence; **por ~quência**
consequently. **~quente** a
consequent; ⟨coerente⟩ consistent

conser|tar /kõser'tar/ vt repair.
~to /e/ m repair

conser|va /kõ'serva/ f ⟨em vidro⟩
preserve; ⟨em lata⟩ tinned food.
~vação f preservation. **~vador**
a & m conservative. **~vadorismo**
m conservatism. **~vante** a & m
preservative. **~var** vt preserve;
⟨manter, guardar⟩ keep. **~var-se** vpr
keep. **~vatório** m conservatory

conside|ração /kõsidera'sãw/
f consideration; ⟨estima⟩ esteem;
levar em ~ração take into
consideration. **~rar** vt consider;
⟨estimar⟩ think highly of ● vi
consider. **~rar-se** vpr consider o.s..
~rável (pl **~ráveis**) a considerable

consig|nação /kõsigna'sãw/ f
consignment. **~nar** vt consign

consigo = **com + si**

consis|tência /kõsis'tẽsia/ f
consistency. **~tente** a firm. **~tir** vi
consist (**em** in)

consoante /kõso'ãtʃi/ f consonant

conso|lação /kõsola'sãw/ f
consolation. **~lador** a consoling. **~lar**
vt console. **~lar-se** vpr console o.s.

consolidar /kõsoli'dar/ vt
consolidate; mend ⟨fratura⟩

consolo /kõ'solu/ m consolation

consórcio /kõ'sɔrsiu/ m
consortium

consorte /kõ'sɔrtʃi/ m/f consort

conspícuo /kõs'pikuu/ a
conspicuous

conspi|ração /kõspira'sãw/
f conspiracy; **teoria da ~ração**
conspiracy theory. **~rador** m
conspirator. **~rar** vi conspire

cons|tância /kõs'tãsia/ f
constancy. **~tante** a & f constant.
~tar vi ⟨em lista etc⟩ appear; **não me**
~ta I am not aware; **~ta que** it is
said that; **~tar de** consist of

consta|tação /kõstata'sãw/ f
observation. **~tar** vt note, notice;
certify ⟨óbito⟩

conste|lação /kõstela'sãw/ f
constellation. **~lado** a star-studded

conster|nação /kõsterna'sãw/ f
consternation. **~nar** vt dismay

consti|pação /kõstʃipa'sãw/
f Port ⟨resfriado⟩ cold. **~pado** a
⟨resfriado⟩ with a cold; ⟨no intestino⟩
constipated. **~par-se** vpr Port
⟨resfriar-se⟩ get a cold

constitu|cional
/kõstʃitusio'naw/ (pl **~cionais**) a
constitutional. **~ição** f constitution.
~inte a constituent ● f **Constituinte**
Constituent Assembly. **~ir** vt form
⟨governo, sociedade⟩; ⟨representar⟩
constitute; ⟨nomear⟩ appoint

constran|gedor /kõstrãʒe'dor/
a embarrassing. **~ger** vt embarrass;
⟨coagir⟩ constrain. **~ger-se** vpr
get embarrassed. **~gimento**
m ⟨embaraço⟩ embarrassment;
⟨coação⟩ constraint

constru|ção /kõstru'sãw/ f
construction; (terreno) building
site. **~ir** vt build ‹casa, prédio›; fig
construct. **~tivo** a constructive.
~tor m builder. **~tora** f building firm

cônsul /'kõsuw/ (pl **~es**) m consul

consulado /kõsu'ladu/ m
consulate

consul|ta /kõ'suwta/ f
consultation. **~tar** vt consult. **~tor**
m consultant. **~toria** f consultancy.
~tório m (médico) surgery, Amer
office

consu|mação /kõsuma'sãw/ f
(taxa) minimum charge. **~mado** a
fato **~mado** fait accompli. **~mar**
vt accomplish ‹projeto›; carry out
‹crime, sacrifício›; consummate
‹casamento›

consu|midor /kõsumi'dor/ a &
m consumer. **~mir** vt consume;
take up ‹tempo›. **~mismo** m
consumerism. **~mista** a & m/f
consumerist. **~mo** m consumption

conta /'kõta/ f (a pagar) bill;
(bancária) account; (contagem)
count; (de vidro etc) bead; pl Com
accounts; **em ~** economical; **por
~ de** on account of; **por ~ própria**
on one's own account; **ajustar ~s**
settle up; **dar ~ de** fig be up to;
dar ~ do recado 🗓 deliver the
goods; **dar-se ~ de** realize; **fazer
de ~** pretend; **ficar por ~ de** be
left to; **levar ou ter em ~** take into
account; **prestar ~s de** account
for; **tomar ~ de** take care of; **~
bancária** bank account; **~
corrente** current account

contabi|lidade /kõtabili'dadʒi/
f accountancy; (contas) accounts;
(seção) accounts department. **~lista**
Port m/f accountant. **~lizar** vt write
up ‹quantia›; fig notch up

contact- Port ▶ **contat-**

conta|dor /kõta'dor/ m (pessoa)
accountant; (de luz etc) meter.
~gem f counting; (de pontos num
jogo) scoring; **~gem regressiva**
countdown

contagi|ante /kõtaʒi'ãtʃi/ a
infectious. **~ar** vt infect. **~ar-se** vpr
become infected

contágio /kõ'taʒiu/ m infection

contagioso /kõtaʒi'ozu/ a
contagious

contami|nação /kõtamina'sãw/
f contamination. **~nar** vt
contaminate

contanto /kõ'tãtu/ adv **~ que**
provided that

contar /kõ'tar/ vt/i count; (narrar)
tell; **~ com** count on

conta|tar /kõta'tar/ vt contact.
~to m contact; **entrar em ~to com**
get in touch with; **tomar ~to com**
come into contact with

contem|plação /kõtẽpla'sãw/ f
contemplation. **~plar** vt (considerar)
contemplate; (dizer respeito a)
concern; **~plar alguém com**
treat sb to ● vi ponder. **~plativo** a
contemplative

contemporâneo /kõtẽpo'raniu/
a & m contemporary

contenção /kõtẽ'sãw/ f
containment

conten|cioso /kõtẽsi'ozu/ a
contentious. **~da** f dispute

conten|tamento /kõtẽta'mẽtu/
m contentment. **~tar** vt satisfy.
~tar-se vpr be content. **~te** a (feliz)
happy; (satisfeito) content. **~to** m a
~to satisfactorily

conter /kõ'ter/ vt contain. **~se** vpr
contain o.s.

conterrâneo /kõteˈxaniu/ m
fellow countryman (f -woman)

contestar /kõtesˈtar/ vt question;
Jurid contest

conteúdo /kõteˈudu/ m (de
recipiente) contents; *fig* (de carta
etc) content

contexto /kõˈtestu/ m context

contigo = com + ti

continência /kõtʃiˈnẽsia/ f Mil
salute

continen|tal /kõtʃinẽˈtaw/
(*pl* ~**tais**) a continental. ~**te** m
continent

contin|gência /kõtʃiˈʒẽsia/ f
contingency. ~**gente** a (*eventual*)
possible; (*incerto*) contingent ● m
contingent

continu|ação /kõtʃinuaˈsãw/ f
continuation. ~**ar** vt/i continue; **eles**
~**am ricos** they are still rich. ~**idade**
f continuity

contínuo /kõˈtʃinuu/ a continuous
● m office junior

con|tista /kõˈtʃista/ m/f (short)
story writer. ~**to** m (short) story;
~**to de fadas** fairy tale; ~**to do
vigário** confidence trick, swindle

contorcer /kõtorˈser/ vt twist.
~**se** vpr (de dor) writhe

contor|nar /kõtorˈnar/ vt go
round; *fig* get round ‹*obstáculo*,
problema›; (*cercar*) surround;
(*delinear*) outline. ~**no** /o/ m outline;
(*da paisagem*) contour

contra /ˈkõtra/ prep against

contra-atacar /kõtrataˈkar/
vt counter-attack. ~**ataque** m
counter-attack

contrabaixo /kõtraˈbaʃu/ m
double bass

contrabalançar /kõtrabalãˈsar/
vt counterbalance

contraban|dear /kõtrabãdʒiˈar/
vt smuggle. ~**dista** m/f smuggler.
~**do** m (ato) smuggling; (*artigos*)
contraband

contração /kõtraˈsãw/ f
contraction

contracenar /kõtraseˈnar/ vi ~
com play up to

contraceptivo /kõtrasepˈtʃivu/
a & m contraceptive

contracheque /kõtraˈʃeki/ m
pay slip

contradi|ção /kõtradʒiˈsãw/
f contradiction. ~**tório** a
contradictory. ~**zer** vt contradict.
~**zer-se** vpr ‹*pessoa*› contradict o.s.;
‹*ideias etc*› be contradictory

contragosto /kõtraˈgostu/ m **a** ~
reluctantly

contrair /kõtraˈir/ vt contract; pick
up ‹*hábito, vício*›. ~**se** vpr contract

contramão /kõtraˈmãw/ f
opposite direction ● a invar one way

contramestre /kõtraˈmestri/ m
supervisor; (*em navio*) bosun

contraofensiva /kõtraofẽˈsiva/ f
counter-offensive

contrapartida /kõtraparˈtʃida/
f *fig* compensation; **em** ~ on the
other hand

contraproducente
/kõtraproduˈsẽtʃi/ a
counterproductive

contrari|ar /kõtrariˈar/ vt go
against, run counter to; (*aborrecer*)
annoy. ~**edade** f adversity;
(*aborrecimento*) annoyance

contrário /kõˈtrariu/ a opposite;
(*desfavorável*) adverse; ~ **a** contrary
to; ‹*pessoa*› opposed to ● m
opposite; **pelo** ou **ao** ~ on the

contrary; **ao ~ de** contrary to; **em ~** to the contrary

contras|tante /kõtras'tãtʃi/ a contrasting. **~tar** vt/i contrast. **~te** m contrast

contratação /kõtrata'sãw/ f (de empregado) recruitment; (de jogador) signing

contra|tante /kõtra'tãtʃi/ m/f contractor. **~tar** vt employ, take on ‹operários›

contra|tempo /kõtra'tẽpu/ m hitch

contra|to /kõ'tratu/ m contract. **~tual** (pl **~tuais**) a contractual

contraven|ção /kõtravẽ'sãw/ f contravention. **~tor** m offender

contribu|ição /kõtribui'sãw/ f contribution. **~inte** m/f contributor; (pagador de impostos) taxpayer. **~ir** vt contribute ● vi contribute; (pagar impostos) pay tax

contrição /kõtri'sãw/ f contrition

contro|lar /kõtro'lar/ vt control; (fiscalizar) check. **~le** /o/, Port **~lo** /o/ m control; (fiscalização) check; **~le de qualidade** quality control

contro|vérsia /kõtro'vɛrsia/ f controversy. **~verso** /ɛ/ a controversial

contudo /kõ'tudu/ conj nevertheless

contundir /kõtũ'dʒir/ vt (dar hematoma em) bruise; injure ‹jogador›. **~se** vpr bruise o.s.; ‹jogador› get injured

conturbado /kõtur'badu/ a troubled

contu|são /kõtu'zãw/ f bruise; (de jogador) injury. **~so** a bruised; ‹jogador› injured

convales|cença /kõvale'sẽsa/ f convalescence. **~cer** vi convalesce

convenção /kõvẽ'sãw/ f convention

conven|cer /kõvẽ'ser/ vt convince. **~cido** a (convicto) convinced; (metido) conceited. **~cimento** m (convicção) conviction; (imodéstia) conceitedness

convencio|nal /kõvẽsio'naw/ (pl **~nais**) a conventional

conveni|ência /kõveni'ẽsia/ f convenience. **~ente** a convenient; (cabível) appropriate

convênio /kõ'veniu/ m agreement

convento /kõ'vẽtu/ m convent

convergir /kõver'ʒir/ vi converge

conver|sa /kõ'vɛrsa/ f conversation; **a ~sa dele** the things he says; **~sa fiada** idle talk. **~sação** f conversation. **~sado** a ‹pessoa› talkative; ‹assunto› talked about. **~sador** a talkative

conversação /kõver'sãw/ f conversion

conversar /kõver'sar/ vi talk

conver|sível /kõver'sivew/ (pl **~síveis**) a & m convertible. **~ter** vt convert. **~ter-se** vpr be converted. **~tido** m convert

con|vés /kõ'vɛs/ (pl **~veses**) m deck

convexo /kõ'veksu/ a convex

convic|ção /kõvik'sãw/ f conviction. **~to** a convinced; (ferrenho) confirmed; ‹criminoso› convicted

convi|dado /kõvi'dadu/ m guest. **~dar** vt invite. **~dativo** a inviting

convincente /kõvĩ'sẽtʃi/ a convincing

convir /kõ'vir/ vi (ficar bem) be appropriate; (concordar) agree (**em** on); **~ a** suit, be convenient for; **convém notar que** one should note that

convite /kõ'vitʃi/ *m* invitation

convi|vência /kõvi'vẽsia/ *f* coexistence; (*relação*) close contact. **~ver** *vi* coexist; (*ter relações*) associate (**com** with)

convívio /kõ'viviu/ *m* association (**com** with)

convocar /kõvo'kar/ *vt* call ‹*eleições, greve*›; call upon ‹*pessoa*› (**a** to); (*ao serviço militar*) call up

convosco = **com** + **vós**

convul|são /kõvuw'sãw/ *f* (*do corpo*) convulsion; (*da sociedade etc*) upheaval. **~sionar** *vt* convulse ‹*corpo*›; *fig* churn up. **~sivo** *a* convulsive

cooper /'kuper/ *m* jogging; **fazer ~** go jogging

coope|ração /koopera'sãw/ *f* cooperation. **~rar** *vi* cooperate. **~rativa** *f* cooperative. **~rativo** *a* cooperative

coorde|nação /koordena'sãw/ *f* coordination. **~nada** *f* coordinate. **~nar** *vt* coordinate

copa /'kɔpa/ *f* (*de árvore*) top; (*aposento*) breakfast room; (*torneio*) cup; *pl* (*naipe*) hearts; **a C~** (*do Mundo*) the World Cup. **~-cozinha** (*pl* **~s-cozinhas**) *f* kitchen-diner

cópia /'kɔpia/ *f* copy

copiar /kopi'ar/ *vt* copy

copiloto /kopi'lotu/ *m* co-pilot

copioso /kopi'ozu/ *a* ample; ‹*refeição*› substantial

copo /'kɔpu/ *m* glass

coque /'kɔki/ *m* (*penteado*) bun

coqueiro /ko'keru/ *m* coconut palm

coqueluche /koke'luʃi/ *f* (*doença*) whooping cough; (*mania*) fad

coque|tel /koke'tɛw/ (*pl* **~téis**) *m* cocktail; (*reunião*) cocktail party

cor¹ /kor/ *m* **de ~** by heart

cor² /kor/ *f* colour; **TV a ~es** colour TV; **pessoa de ~** coloured person

coração /kora'sãw/ *m* heart

cora|gem /ko'raʒẽ/ *f* courage. **~joso** /o/ *a* courageous

co|ral¹ /ko'raw/ (*pl* **~rais**) *m* (*animal*) coral

co|ral² /ko'raw/ (*pl* **~rais**) *m* (*de cantores*) choir ● *a* choral

co|rante /ko'rãtʃi/ *a* & *m* colouring. **~rar** *vt* colour ● *vi* blush

cor|da /'kɔrda/ *f* rope; *Mus* string; (*para roupa lavada*) clothes line; **dar ~da em** wind ‹*relógio*›; **~da bamba** tightrope; **~das vocais** vocal chords. **~dão** *m* cord; (*de sapatos*) lace; (*policial*) cordon

cordeiro /kor'deru/ *m* lamb

cor|del /kor'dɛw/ (*pl* **~déis**) *Port m* string; **literatura de ~del** trash literature

cor-de-rosa /kordʒi'rɔza/ *a invar* pink

cordi|al /kordʒi'aw/ (*pl* **~ais**) *a* & *m* cordial. **~alidade** *f* cordiality

cordilheira /kordʒi'ʎera/ *f* chain of mountains

coreano /kori'anu/ *a* & *m* Korean

Coreia /ko'reja/ *f* Korea

core|ografia /koriogra'fia/ *f* choreography. **~ógrafo** *m* choreographer

coreto /ko'retu/ *m* bandstand

coriza /ko'riza/ *f* runny nose

corja /'kɔrʒa/ *f* pack; (*de pessoas*) rabble

córner /'kɔrner/ *m* corner

coro /'koru/ *m* chorus

coroa /ko'roa/ f crown; (de flores etc) wreath ● **~ação** f coronation. **~ar** vt crown

coronel /koro'nɛw/ (pl **~néis**) m colonel

coronha /ko'roɲa/ f butt

corpete /kor'petʃi/ m bodice

corpo /'korpu/ m body; (físico de mulher) figure; (físico de homem) physique; **~ a ~** m invar pitched battle. **~ de bombeiros** fire brigade; **~ diplomático** diplomatic corps; **~ docente** teaching staff, Amer faculty; **~ral** (pl **~rais**) a physical; ‹pena› corporal

corpulência /korpu'lẽsia/ f stoutness. **~lento** a stout

correção /koxe'sãw/ f correction

corre-corre /kɔxi'kɔxi/ m (debandada) stampede; (correria) rush

corrediço /koxe'dʒisu/ a ‹porta› sliding. **~dor** m (atleta) runner; (passagem) corridor

correia /ko'xeja/ f strap; (peça de máquina) belt; (para cachorro) lead, Amer leash

correio /ko'xeju/ m post, mail; (repartição) post office; **pôr no ~** post, Amer mail; **~ aéreo** air mail; **~ de voz** voicemail; **~ eletrônico** email

correlação /koxela'sãw/ f correlation

correligionário /koxeliʒio'nariu/ m party colleague

corrente /ko'xẽtʃi/ a ‹água› running; ‹mês, conta› current; ‹estilo› fluid; (usual) common ● f (de água, eletricidade) current; (cadeia) chain; **~ de ar** draught. **~za** /e/ f current; (de ar) draught

correr /ko'xer/ vi (à pé) run; (de carro) drive fast, speed; (fazer rápido) rush; ‹água, sangue› flow; ‹tempo› elapse; ‹boato› go round ● vt draw ‹cortina›; run ‹risco›. **~reria** f rush

correspondência /koxespõ'dẽsia/ f correspondence. **~dente** a corresponding ● m/f correspondent; (equivalente) equivalent. **~der** vi **~der a** correspond to; (retribuir) return. **~der-se** vpr correspond (**com** with)

corretivo /koxe'tʃivu/ a corrective ● m punishment. **~to** /ɛ/ a correct

corretor /koxe'tor/ m broker; **~ de imóveis** estate agent, Amer realtor

corrida /ko'xida/ f (prova) race; (ação de correr) run; (de taxi) ride

corrigir /koxi'ʒir/ vt correct

corrimão /koxi'mãw/ (pl **~s**) m handrail; (de escada) banister

corriqueiro /koxi'keru/ a ordinary, run-of-the-mill

corroborar /koxobo'rar/ vt corroborate

corroer /koxo'er/ vt corrode ‹metal›; fig erode. **~-se** vpr corrode; fig erode

corromper /koxõ'per/ vt corrupt. **~-se** vpr be corrupted

corrosão /koxo'zãw/ f (de metal) corrosion; fig erosion. **~sivo** a corrosive

corrupção /koxup'sãw/ f corruption. **~to** a corrupt

cortada /kor'tada/ f (em tênis) smash; (em pessoa) put-down. **~tante** a cutting. **~tar** vt cut; cut off ‹luz, telefone, perna etc›; cut down ‹árvore›; cut out ‹efeito, vício›; take away ‹*prazer*›; (*com o carro*) cut up; (*desprezar*) cut dead; **~tar o cabelo** (*no cabeleireiro*) get one's hair cut ● *vi* cut. **~te**[1] /ɔ/ *m* cut; (*gume*) blade; (*desenho*) cross-section; **sem ~te** ‹*faca*› blunt; **~te de cabelo** haircut

cor|te[2] /'kortʃi/ *f* court. **~tejar** *vt* court. **~tejo** /e/ *m* (*séquito*) retinue; (*fúnebre*) cortège. **~tês** a (*f* **~tesa**) courteous, polite. **~tesão** (*pl* **~tesãos**) *m* courtier. **~tesia** *f* courtesy

corti|ça /kor'tʃisa/ *f* cork. **~ço** *m* (*casa popular*) slum tenement

cortina /kor'tʃina/ *f* curtain

cortisona /kortʃi'zona/ *f* cortisone

coruja /ko'ruʒa/ *f* owl ● a ‹*pai, mãe*› proud, doting

coruscar /korus'kar/ *vi* flash

corvo /'korvu/ *m* crow

cós /kɔs/ *m invar* waistband

coser /ko'zer/ *vt/i* sew

cosmético /koz'mɛtʃiku/ a & *m* cosmetic

cósmico /'kɔzmiku/ a cosmic

cosmo /'kɔzmu/ *m* cosmos. **~nauta** *m/f* cosmonaut. **~polita** a cosmopolitan ● *m/f* globetrotter

costa /'kɔsta/ *f* coast; *pl* (*dorso*) back; **C~ do Marfim** Ivory Coast; **C~ Rica** Costa Rica

costarriquenho /kostaxi'keɲu/ a & *m* Costa Rican

cos|teiro /kos'teru/ a coastal. **~tela** /ɛ/ *f* rib. **~teleta** /e/ *f* chop; *pl* (*suíças*) sideburns. **~telinha** *f* (*de porco*) spare rib

costu|mar /kostu'mar/ *vt* **~ma fazer** he usually does; **~mava fazer** he used to do. **~me** *m* (*uso*) custom; (*traje*) costume; **de ~me** usually; **como de ~me** as usual; **ter**

o **~me de** have a habit of. **~meiro** a customary

costu|ra /kos'tura/ *f* sewing. **~rar** *vt/i* sew. **~reira** *f* (*mulher*) dressmaker; (*caixa*) needlework box

co|ta /'kɔta/ *f* quota. **~tação** *f* (*preço*) rate; (*apreço*) rating. **~tado** a (*ação*) quoted; (*conceituado*) highly rated. **~tar** *vt* rate; quote ‹*ações*›

cote|jar /kote'ʒar/ *vt* compare. **~jo** /e/ *m* comparison

cotidiano /kotʃidʒi'anu/ a everyday ● *m* everyday life

cotonete /koto'netʃi/ *m* cotton bud

cotove|lada /kotove'lada/ *f* (*para abrir caminho*) shove; (*para chamar atenção*) nudge. **~lo** /e/ *m* elbow

coura|ça /ko'rasa/ *f* (*armadura*) breastplate; (*de navio, animal*) armour. **~çado** *Port* *m* battleship

couro /'koru/ *m* leather; **~ cabeludo** scalp

couve /'kovi/ *f* spring greens. **~-de-bruxelas** (*pl* **~s-de-bruxelas**) *f* Brussels sprout; **~-flor** (*pl* **~s-flores**) *f* cauliflower

couvert /ku'vɛr/ (*pl* **~s**) *m* cover charge

cova /'kɔva/ *f* (*buraco*) pit; (*sepultura*) grave

covar|de /ko'vardʒi/ *m/f* coward ● a cowardly. **~dia** *f* cowardice

coveiro /ko'veru/ *m* gravedigger

covil /ko'viw/ (*pl* **~vis**) *m* den, lair

covinha /ko'viɲa/ *f* dimple

co|xa /'koʃa/ *f* thigh. **~xear** *vi* hobble

coxia /ko'ʃia/ *f* aisle

coxo /'koʃu/ a hobbling; **ser ~** hobble

co|zer /ko'zer/ *vt/i* cook. **~zido** *m* stew, casserole

cozi|nha /ko'ziɲa/ *f* (*aposento*) kitchen; (*comida, ação*) cooking; (*arte*) cookery. **~nhar** *vt/i* cook. **~nheiro** *m* cook

crachá /kra'ʃa/ *m* badge, *Amer* button

crânio /'kraniu/ *m* skull; (*pessoa*) genius

crápula /'krapula/ *m/f* scoundrel

craque /'kraki/ *m* (*de futebol*) soccer star; 🔟 expert

crase /'krazi/ *f* contraction; **a com ~ a grave** (à)

crasso /'krasu/ *a* crass

cratera /kra'tera/ *f* crater

cravar /kra'var/ *vt* drive in ‹*prego*›; dig ‹*unha*›; stick ‹*estaca*›; **~ com os olhos** stare at. **~se** *vpr* stick

cravejar /krave'ʒar/ *vt* nail; (*com balas*) spray, riddle

cravo[1] /'kravu/ *m* (*flor*) carnation; (*condimento*) clove

cravo[2] /'kravu/ *m* (*na pele*) blackhead; (*prego*) nail

cravo[3] /'kravu/ *m* (*instrumento*) harpsichord

creche /'krɛʃi/ *f* crèche

credenci|ais /kredẽsi'ajs/ *f pl* credentials. **~ar** *vt* qualify

credi|ário /kredʒi'ariu/ *m* hire purchase agreement, credit plan. **~bilidade** *f* credibility. **~tar** *vt* credit

credifone® /kredʒi'foni/ *m Port* phonecard

crédito /'krɛdʒitu/ *m* credit; **a ~** on credit

cre|do /'krɛdu/ *m* creed ● *int* heavens. **~dor** *m* creditor ● *a* ‹*saldo*› credit

crédulo /'krɛdulu/ *a* gullible

cre|mação /krema'sãw/ *f* cremation. **~mar** *vt* cremate. **~matório** *m* crematorium

cre|me /'krɛmi/ *a invar & m* cream; **~me Chantilly** whipped cream; **~me de leite** (sterilized) cream. **~moso** /o/ *a* creamy

cren|ça /'krẽsa/ *f* belief. **~dice** *f* superstition. **~te** *m* believer; (*protestante*) Protestant ● *a* religious; (*protestante*) Protestant; **estar ~te que** believe that

crepe /'krɛpi/ *m* crepe

crepitar /krepi'tar/ *vi* crackle

crepom /kre'põ/ *m* crepe; **papel ~** tissue paper

crepúsculo /kre'puskulu/ *m* twilight

crer /krer/ *vt/i* believe (**em** in); **creio que** I think (that). **~se** *vpr* believe o.s. to be

cres|cendo /kre'sẽdu/ *m* crescendo. **~cente** *a* growing ● *m* crescent. **~cer** *vi* grow; ‹*bolo*› rise. **~cido** *a* grown. **~cimento** *m* growth

crespo /'krespu/ *a* ‹*cabelo*› frizzy; ‹*mar*› choppy

cretino /kre'tʃinu/ *m* cretin

cria /'kria/ *f* baby; *pl* young

criação /kria'sãw/ *f* creation; (*educação*) upbringing; (*de animais*) raising; (*gado*) livestock

criado /kri'adu/ *m* servant. **~mudo** (*pl* **~s-mudos**) *m* bedside table

criador /kria'dor/ *m* creator; (*de animais*) farmer, breeder

crian|ça /kri'ãsa/ *f* child ● *a* childish. **~çada** *f* kids. **~cice** *f* childishness; (*uma*) childish thing

criar /kri'ar/ *vt* (*fazer*) create; bring up ‹*filhos*›; rear ‹*animais*›; grow ‹*planta*›; pluck up ‹*coragem*›. **~se** *vpr* be brought up, grow up

criati|vidade /kriatʃivi'dadʒi/ f
creativity. **~vo** a creative

criatura /kria'tura/ f creature

crime /'krimi/ m crime

crimi|nal /krimi'naw/ (pl **~nais**) a
criminal. **~nalidade** f crime. **~noso**
m criminal

crina /'krina/ f mane

crioulo /kri'olu/ a & m Creole;
(negro) black

cripta /'kripta/ f crypt

crisálida /kri'zalida/ f chrysalis

crisântemo /kri'zãtemu/ m
chrysanthemum

crise /'krizi/ f crisis

cris|ma /'krizma/ f confirmation.
~mar vt confirm. **~mar-se** vpr get
confirmed

crista /'krista/ f crest

cris|tal /kris'taw/ (pl **~tais**) m
crystal; (vidro) glass. **~talino** a
crystal clear. **~talizar** vt/i crystallize

cris|tandade /kristã'dadʒi/ f
Christendom. **~tão** (pl **~tãos**) a &
m (f **~tã**) Christian. **~tianismo** m
Christianity

Cristo /'kristu/ m Christ

Cristo Redentor Cristo
Redentor (Christ the
Redeemer) is a statue of
Jesus Christ at the peak of the
Corcovado mountain in Rio de
Janeiro. Inaugurated in 1931, the
monument is 38 metres high, and
is situated 710 metres above sea
level. From the statue, you can
see the centre of Rio de Janeiro,
the Pão de Açúcar (Sugarloaf
mountain), the Rodrigo de Freitas
Lagoon, and other tourist
attractions.

---

cri|tério /kri'teriu/ m discretion;
(norma) criterion. **~terioso** a
perceptive, discerning

crítica /'kritʃika/ f criticism;
(análise) critique; (de filme, livro)
review; (críticos) critics

criticar /kritʃi'kar/ vt criticize;
review <filme, livro>

crítico /'kritʃiku/ a critical ● m critic

crivar /kri'var/ vt (furar) riddle

crí|vel /'krivew/ (pl **~veis**) a
credible

crivo /'krivu/ m sieve; fig scrutiny

crocante /kro'kãtʃi/ a crunchy

crochê /kro'ʃe/ m crochet

crocodilo /kroko'dʒilu/ m
crocodile

cromo /'kromu/ m chrome; 🆃
(pessoa) geek 🆃

cromossomo /kromo'somu/ m
chromosome

crôni|ca /'kronika/ f (histórica)
chronicle; (no jornal) feature; (conto)
short story. **~co** a chronic

cronista /kro'nista/ m/f (de jornal)
feature writer; (contista) short story
writer; (historiador) chronicler

crono|grama /krono'grama/ m
schedule. **~logia** f chronology.
~lógico a chronological. **~metrar**
vt time

cronômetro /kro'nometru/ m
stopwatch

croquete /kro'ketʃi/ m savoury
meatball in breadcrumbs

croqui /kro'ki/ m sketch

crosta /'krosta/ f crust; (em ferida)
scab

cru /kru/ a (f **~a**) raw; <luz, tom,
palavra> harsh; <linguagem> crude;
<verdade> unvarnished, plain

cruci|al /krusi'aw/ (pl ~ais) a crucial

crucifi|cação /krusifika'sãw/ f crucifixion. ~car vt crucify. ~xo /ks/ m crucifix

cru|el /kru'ɛw/ (pl ~éis) a cruel. ~eldade f cruelty. ~ento a bloody

crupe /'krupi/ m croup

crustáceos /krus'tasius/ m pl shellfish

cruz /krus/ f cross

cruza|da /kru'zada/ f crusade. ~do¹ /l (soldado) crusader

cru|zado² /kru'zadu/ m (moeda) cruzado. ~zador m cruiser. ~zamento m (de ruas) crossroads, junction, Amer intersection; (de raças) cross. ~zar vt cross ● vi ‹navio› cruise; ~zar com pass. ~zar-se vpr cross; ‹pessoas› pass each other. ~zeiro m (moeda) cruzeiro; (viagem) cruise; (cruz) cross

cu /ku/ m (chulo) arse, Amer ass; ~ de ferro 🚩 swot 🚩

Cuba /'kuba/ f Cuba

cubano /ku'banu/ a & m Cuban

cúbico /'kubiku/ a cubic

cubículo /ku'bikulu/ m cubicle

cubis|mo /ku'bizmu/ m cubism. ~ta a & m/f cubist

cubo /'kubu/ m cube; (de roda) hub

cuca /'kuka/ f 🚩 head

cuco /'kuku/ m cuckoo; (relógio) cuckoo clock

cueca /ku'ɛka/ f underpants; pl Port (de mulher) knickers

cueiro /ku'eru/ m baby wrap

cuia /'kuia/ f gourd

cuidado /kui'dadu/ m care; com ~ carefully; ter ou tomar ~ be careful. ~so /o/ a careful

cuidar /kui'dar/ vi ~ de take care of. ~-se vpr look after o.s.

cujo /'kuʒu/ pron whose

culatra /ku'latra/ f breech; sair pela ~ fig backfire

culi|nária /kuli'naria/ f cookery. ~rio a culinary

culmi|nância /kuwmi'nãsia/ f culmination. ~nante a culminating. ~nar vi culminate (em in)

cul|pa /'kuwpa/ f guilt; foi ~pa minha it was my fault; ter ~pa de be to blame for. ~pabilidade f guilt. ~pado a ● m culprit. ~par vt blame (de for); (na justiça) find guilty (de of). ~par-se vpr take the blame (de for). ~pável (pl ~páveis) a culpable, guilty

culti|var /kuwtʃi'var/ vt cultivate; grow ‹plantas›. ~vo m cultivation; (de plantas) growing

cul|to /'kuwtu/ a cultured ● m cult. ~tura f culture; (de terra) cultivation. ~tural (pl ~turais) a cultural

cumbuca /kũ'buka/ f bowl

cume /'kumi/ m peak

cúmplice /'kuplisi/ m/f accomplice

cumplicidade /kũplisi'dadʒi/ f complicity

cumprimen|tar /kũprimẽ'tar/ vt/i (saudar) greet; (parabenizar) compliment. ~to m (saudação) greeting; (elogio) compliment; (de lei, ordem) compliance (de with); (de promessa, palavra) fulfilment

cumprir /kũ'prir/ vt keep ‹promessa, palavra›; comply with ‹lei, ordem›; do ‹dever›; carry out ‹obrigações›; serve ‹pena›; ~ com keep to ● vi cumpre-nos ir we should go. ~-se vpr be fulfilled

cúmulo /'kumulu/ m height; é o ~l that's the limit!

cunha /'kuɲa/ f wedge; Port (pessoa influente) contact

cunha|da /ku'ɲada/ f sister-in-law. ~do m brother-in-law

cunhar /ku'ɲar/ vt coin ‹palavra, expressão›; mint ‹moedas›

cunho /'kuɲu/ m hallmark

cupim /ku'pĩ/ m termite

cupom /ku'põ/ m coupon

cúpula /'kupula/ f (abóbada) dome; (de abajur) shade; (chefia) leadership; **(reunião de)** ~ summit (meeting)

cura /'kura/ f cure ● m curate, priest

curandeiro /kurã'deru/ m (religioso) faith healer; (índio) medicine man; (charlatão) quack

curar /ku'rar/ vt cure; dress ‹ferida›. ~se vpr be cured

curativo /kura'tʃivu/ m dressing

curá|vel /ku'ravew/ (pl ~veis) a curable

curin|ga /ku'rĩga/ m wild card. ~gão m joker

curio|sidade /kuriozi'dadʒi/ f curiosity. ~so /o/ a curious ● m (espectador) onlooker

cur|ral /ku'xaw/ (pl ~rais) m pen

currículo /ku'xikulu/ m curriculum; (resumo) curriculum vitae, CV

cur|sar /kur'sar/ vt attend ‹escola, aula›; study ‹matéria›. ~so m course. ~sor m cursor

curta|-metragem /kurtame'traʒẽ/ (pl ~s-metragens) m short (film)

cur|tição /kurtʃi'sãw/ f 🅱 enjoyment. ~tir vt 🅱 enjoy; tan ‹couro›

curto /'kurtu/ a short; ‹conhecimento, inteligência› limited. ~-circuito (pl ~s-circuitos) m short circuit

cur|va /'kurva/ f curve; (de estrada, rio) bend; ~va fechada hairpin bend. ~var vt bend; fig bow (a to). ~vo a curved; ‹estrada› winding

cus|parada /kuspa'rada/ f spit. ~pe m spit, spittle. ~pir vt/i spit

cus|ta /'kusta/ f à ~ta de at the expense of. ~tar vt cost ● vi (ser difícil) be hard; ~tar a fazer (ter dificuldade) find it hard to do; (demorar) take a long time to do. ~tear vt finance, fund. ~teio m funding; (relação de despesas) costing. ~to m cost; a ~to with difficulty

custódia /kus'tɔdʒia/ f custody

cutelo /ku'tɛlu/ m cleaver

cutícula /ku'tʃikula/ f cuticle

cútis /'kutʃis/ f invar complexion

cutucar /kutu'kar/ vt (com o cotovelo, joelho) nudge; (com o dedo) poke; (com instrumento) prod

czar /zar/ m tsar

. . . .

Dd

. . . .

da = de + a

dádiva /'dadʒiva/ f gift; (donativo) donation

dado /'dadu/ m (de jogar) die, dice; (informação) fact, piece of information; pl data

dador /da'dor/ m Port donor

daí /da'i/ adv (no espaço) from there; (no tempo) then; **~ por diante** from then on; **e ~?** ⚀ so what?

dali /da'li/ adv from over there

dália /'dalia/ f dahlia

dal|tônico /daw'toniku/ a colour-blind. **~tonismo** m colour blindness

dama /'dama/ f lady; (em jogos) queen; pl (jogo) draughts, Amer checkers; **~ de honra** bridesmaid

da|nado /da'nadu/ a damned; (zangado) angry; (travesso) naughty. **~nar-se** vpr get angry; **~ne-se!** ⚀ who cares?

dan|ça /'dãsa/ f dance. **~çar** vt dance ● vi dance; ⚀ (pessoa) miss out; (coisa) go by the board; (crimonoso) get caught. **~çarino** m dancer. **~ceteria** f discotheque

da|nificar /danifi'kar/ vt damage. **~ninho** a undesirable. **~no** m (pl) damage. **~noso** /o/ a damaging

dantes /'dãtʃis/ adv formerly

daquela(s), daquele(s) = de + aquela(s), aquele(s)

daqui /da'ki/ adv from here; **~ a 2 dias** in 2 days (' time); **~ a pouco** in a minute; **~ em diante** from now on

daquilo = de + aquilo

dar /dar/ vt give; have ‹dormida, lida etc›; do ‹pulo, cambalhota etc›; cause ‹problemas›; produce ‹frutas, leite›; deal ‹cartas›; (lecionar) teach ● vi (ser possível) be possible; (ser suficiente) be enough; **~ com** come across; **~ em** lead to; **ele dá para ator** he'd make a good actor; **~ por** (considerar como) consider to be; (reparar em) notice. **~-se** vpr happen; ‹pessoa› get on

dardo /'dardu/ m dart; (no atletismo) javelin

das = de + as

da|ta /'data/ f date; **de longa ~** long since. **~tar** vt/i date

dati|lografar /datʃilogra'far/ vt/i type. **~lografia** f typing. **~lógrafo** m typist

de /dʒi/ ● prep

••••▶ (matéria, conteúdo, qualidade) of; **um jarro ~ água** a jug of water; **uma mesa ~ madeira** a wooden table; **um livro ~ grande interesse** a book of great interest

••••▶ (em descrições) with; **a mulher ~ cabelo castanho** the woman with brown hair; **o rapaz ~ calças azuis** the boy in blue trousers; **uma camiseta ~ manga curta** a short-sleeved shirt

••••▶ (meio de transporte) by; **~ avião/trem** by plane/train

••••▶ (com números e expressões de tempo) **uma nota ~ 10 reais** a 10-real note; **~ dia** during the day

••••▶ (origem, procedência) from; **eles são ~ São Paulo** they are from São Paulo

••••▶ (posse) **o cachorro da Ana** Ana's dog; **a chave do carro** the car key; **as pernas da mesa** the table legs

••••▶ (série) **~ meia em meia hora** every half hour; **~ de dois em dois metros** every two metres

••••▶ (tema, disciplina) **um livro ~ inglês** an English book; **não entendo nada ~ motores** I don't know a thing about engines

····▸ (indica autor) by; **um livro ~ Machado de Assis** a book by Machado de Assis

····▸ (causa) **morrer ~ fome** die of hunger; **chorar ~ alegria** cry for joy

debaixo /dʒi'baʃu/ adv below; **~ de** under

debalde /dʒi'bawdʒi/ adv in vain

debandada /debã'dada/ f stampede

deba|te /de'batʃi/ m debate; **~te frente a frente** face-to-face debate. **~ter** vt debate. **~ter-se** vpr grapple

debelar /debe'lar/ vt overcome

dé|bil /'dɛbiw/ (pl **~beis**) a feeble; **~bil mental** retarded (person)

debili|dade /debili'dadʒi/ f debility. **~tar** vt debilitate. **~tar-se** vpr become debilitated

debitar /debi'tar/ vt debit

débito /'dɛbitu/ m debit

debo|chado /debo'ʃadu/ a sardonic. **~char** vt mock. **~che** /ɔ/ m jibe

debruar /debru'ar/ vt/i edge

debruçar-se /debru'sarsi/ vpr bend over; **~ sobre** study

debrum /de'brũ/ m edging

debulhar /debu'ʎar/ vt thresh

debu|tante /debu'tãtʃi/ f debutante. **~tar** vi debut, make one's debut

década /'dɛkada/ f decade; **a ~ dos 60** the sixties

deca|dência /deka'dẽsia/ f decadence. **~dente** a decadent

decair /deka'ir/ vi decline; (degringolar) go downhill; ‹planta› wilt

decal|car /dekaw'kar/ vt trace. **~que** m tracing

decapitar /dekapi'tar/ vt decapitate

decatlo /de'katlu/ m decathlon

de|cência /de'sẽsia/ f decency. **~cente** a decent

decepar /dese'par/ vt cut off

decep|ção /desep'sãw/ f disappointment. **~cionar** vt disappoint. **~cionar-se** vpr be disappointed

decerto /dʒi'sɛrtu/ adv certainly

deci|dido /desi'dʒidu/ a ‹pessoa› determined. **~dir** vt/i decide. **~dir-se** vpr make up one's mind; **~dir-se por** decide on

decíduo /de'siduu/ a deciduous

decifrar /desi'frar/ vt decipher

deci|mal /desi'maw/ (pl **~mais**) a & m decimal

décimo /'dɛsimu/ a & m tenth; **~ primeiro** eleventh; **~ segundo** twelfth; **~ terceiro** thirteenth; **~ quarto** fourteenth; **~ quinto** fifteenth; **~ sexto** sixteenth; **~ sétimo** seventeenth; **~ oitavo** eighteenth; **~ nono** nineteenth

deci|são /desi'zãw/ f decision. **~sivo** a decisive

decla|ração /deklara'sãw/ f declaration. **~rado** a ‹inimigo› sworn; ‹crente› avowed; ‹ladrão› self-confessed. **~rar** vt declare

decli|nação /deklina'sãw/ f declension. **~nar** vt **~nar (de)** decline ● vi decline; ‹sol› go down; ‹chão› slope down

declínio /de'kliniu/ m decline

declive /de'klivi/ m (downward) slope, incline

decodificar /dekodʒifi'kar/ vt decode

deco|lagem /deko'laʒẽ/ f take-off. **~lar** vi take off; fig get off the ground

decom|por /dekõ'por/ *vt*
break down; contort ‹feições›.
~por-se *vpr* break down; ‹cadáver›
decompose. **~posição** *f* (*de cadáver*)
decomposition

deco|ração /dekora'sãw/ *f*
decoration; (*aprendizagem*) learning
by heart. **~rar** *vt* (*adornar*) decorate;
(*aprender*) learn by heart, memorize.
~rativo *a* decorative. **~reba** /ɛ/ *f* 🔲
rote learning. **~ro** /o/ *m* decorum.
~roso /o/ *a* decorous

decor|rência /deko'xẽsia/ *f*
consequence. **~rente** *a* resulting
(de from). **~rer** *vi* ‹tempo› elapse;
‹acontecimento› pass off; (*resultar*)
result (de from) ● *m* no ~rer de
in the course of; com o ~rer do
tempo in time, with the passing
of time

deco|tado /deko'tadu/ *a* low-cut.
~te /ɔ/ *m* neckline

decrépito /de'krɛpitu/ *a* decrepit

decres|cente /dekre'sẽtʃi/ *a*
decreasing. **~cer** *vi* decrease

decre|tar /dekre'tar/ *vt* decree;
declare ‹estado de sítio›. **~to** /ɛ/ *m*
decree. **~to-lei** *m* act

decurso /de'kursu/ *m* course

de|dal /de'daw/ (*pl* **~dais**) *m*
thimble. **~dão** *m* (*da mão*) thumb;
(*do pé*) big toe

dedetizar /dedetʃi'zar/ *vt* spray
with insecticide

dedi|cação /dedʒika'sãw/ *f*
dedication. **~car** *vt* dedicate; devote
‹tempo›. **~car-se** *vpr* dedicate o.s.
(a to). **~catória** *f* dedication

dedilhar /dedʒi'ʎar/ *vt* pluck

dedo /'dedu/ *m* finger; (*do pé*) toe;
cheio de ~s all fingers and thumbs;
(*sem graça*) awkward. **~duro**
(*pl* **~s-duros**) *m* sneak; (*político,*

criminoso) informer

dedução /dedu'sãw/ *f* deduction

dedurar /dedu'rar/ *vt* sneak on;
(*à polícia*) inform on

dedu|tivo /dedu'tʃivu/ *a*
deductive. **~zir** *vt* (*descontar*)
deduct; (*concluir*) deduce

defa|sado /defa'zadu/ *a* out of
step. **~sagem** *f* gap, lag

defecar /defe'kar/ *vi* defecate

defei|to /de'fejtu/ *m* defect; botar
~to em find fault with. **~tuoso** /o/
a defective

defen|der /defẽ'der/ *vt* defend.
~der-se *vpr* (*virar-se*) fend for
o.s.; (*contra-atacar*) defend o.s.
(de against). **~siva** *f* na ~siva on
the defensive. **~sor** *m* defender;
(*advogado*) defence counsel

defe|rência /defe'rẽsia/ *f*
deference. **~rente** *a* deferential

defesa /de'feza/ *f* defence ● *m*
defender

defici|ência /defisi'ẽsia/ *f*
deficiency. **~ente** *a* deficient; (*física
ou mentalmente*) handicapped ● *m/f*
handicapped person

déficit /'dɛfisitʃi/ (*pl* **~s**) *m* deficit

deficitário /defisitʃi'ariu/ *a* in
deficit; ‹empresa› loss-making

definhar /defi'ɲar/ *vi* waste away;
‹planta› wither

defi|nição /defini'sãw/ *f*
definition. **~nir** *vt* define. **~nir-se**
vpr (*descrever-se*) define o.s.; (*decidir-se*)
come to a decision; (*explicar-se*)
make one's position clear. **~nitivo**
a definitive. **~nível** (*pl* **~níveis**) *a*
definable

defla|ção /defla'sãw/ *f* deflation.
~cionário *a* deflationary

deflagrar /defla'grar/ *vt* set off
● *vi* break out

defor|mar /defor'mar/ *vt*
misshape; deform *‹corpo›*; distort
‹imagem›. **~midade** *f* deformity

defraudar /defraw'dar/ *vt* defraud
(**de** of)

defron|tar /defrõ'tar/ *vt* **~tar**
com face. **~te** *adv* opposite; **~te**
de opposite

defumar /defu'mar/ *vt* smoke

defunto /de'fũtu/ *a & m* deceased

dege|lar /deʒe'lar/ *vt/i* thaw. **~lo**
/e/ *m* thaw

degeneração /deʒenera'sãw/ *f*
degeneration

degenerar /deʒene'rar/ *vi*
degenerate (**em** into)

degolar /dego'lar/ *vt* cut the
throat of

degra|dação /degrada'sãw/ *f*
degradation. **~dante** *a* degrading.
~dar *vt* degrade

degrau /de'graw/ *m* step

degringolar /degrĩgo'lar/ *vi*
deteriorate, go downhill

degustar /degus'tar/ *vt* taste

dei|tada /dej'tada/ *f* lie-down.
~tado *a* lying down; (*dormindo*)
in bed; 🄸 (*preguiçoso*) idle. **~tar**
vt lay down; (*na cama*) put to bed;
(*pôr*) put; *Port* (*jogar*) throw ● *vi*,
~tar-se *vpr* lie down; (*ir para cama*)
go to bed

dei|xa /'deʃa/ *f* cue. **~xar** *vt* leave;
(*permitir*) let; **~xar de** (*parar*) stop;
(*omitir*) fail; **não pôde ~xar de rir**
he couldn't help laughing; **~xar**
alguém nervoso make sb annoyed;
~xar cair drop; **~xar a desejar**
leave a lot to be desired; **~xa (para**
lá) 🄸 never mind, forget it

dela(s) = **de** + **ela(s)**

delatar /dela'tar/ *vt* report

délavé /dela've/ *a invar* faded

dele(s) = **de** + **ele(s)**

dele|gação /delega'sãw/ *f*
delegation; **~gação de autoridade**
Com empowerment. **~gacia** *f* police
station. **~gado** *m* delegate; **~gado**
de polícia police chief. **~gar** *vt*
delegate

delei|tar /delej'tar/ *vt* delight.
~tar-se *vpr* delight (**com** in). **~te** *m*
delight. **~toso** /o/ *a* delightful

delgado /dew'gadu/ *a* slender

delibe|ração /delibera'sãw/ *f*
deliberation. **~rar** *vt/i* deliberate

delica|deza /delika'deza/ *f*
delicacy; (*cortesia*) politeness. **~do**
a delicate; (*cortês*) polite

delícia /de'lisia/ *f* delight; **ser uma**
~ *‹comida›* be delicious; *‹sol etc›*
be lovely

delici|ar /delisi'ar/ *vt* delight;
~ar-se delight (**com** in). **~oso** /o/ *a*
delightful, lovely; *‹comida›* delicious

deline|ador /delinia'dor/ *m*
eyeliner. **~ar** *vt* outline

delin|quência /delĩ'kwẽsia/
f delinquency. **~quente** *a & m*
delinquent

deli|rante /deli'rãtʃi/ *a* rapturous;
Med delirious. **~rar** *vi* go into
raptures; *‹doente›* be delirious

delírio /de'liriu/ *m* (*febre*) delirium;
(*excitação*) raptures

delito /de'litu/ *m* crime

delonga /de'lõga/ *f* delay

delta /'dewta/ *m* delta

dema|gogia /demago'ʒia/ *f*
demagogy. **~gógico** *a* demagogic.
~gogo /o/ *m* demagogue

demais /dʒi'majs/ *a & adv* (*muito*)
very much; (*em demasia*) too much;
os ~ the rest, the others; **é ~!** 🄸
it's great!

deman|da /de'mãda/ f demand; *Jurid* action. **~dar** vt sue

demão /de'mãw/ f coat

demar|car /demar'kar/ vt demarcate. **~catório** a demarcation

demasia /dema'zia/ f excess; **em ~** too (much, many)

de|mência /de'mēsia/ f insanity; *Med* dementia. **~mente** a insane; *Med* demented

demissão /demi'sãw/ f sacking, dismissal; **pedir ~** resign

demitir /demi'tʃir/ vt sack, dismiss. **~se** vpr resign

demo|cracia /demokra'sia/ f democracy. **~crata** m/f democrat. **~crático** a democratic. **~cratizar** vt democratize. **~grafia** f demography. **~gráfico** a demographic

demo|lição /demoli'sãw/ f demolition. **~lir** vt demolish

demônio /de'moniu/ m demon

demons|tração /demõstra'sãw/ f demonstration. **~trar** vt demonstrate. **~trativo** a demonstrative

demo|ra /de'mɔra/ f delay. **~rado** a lengthy. **~rar** vi (levar) take; (tardar a voltar, terminar etc) be long; (levar muito tempo) take a long time ● vt delay

dendê /dẽ'de/ m (óleo) palm oil

denegrir /dene'grir/ vt denigrate

dengoso /dẽ'gozu/ a coy

dengue /'dẽgi/ m dengue

denomi|nação /denomina'sãw/ f denomination. **~nar** vt name

denotar /deno'tar/ vt denote

den|sidade /dẽsi'dadʒi/ f density. **~so** a dense

den|tado /dẽ'tadu/ a serrated. **~tadura** f (set of) teeth; (postiça) dentures, false teeth. **~tal** (pl **~tais**) a dental. **~tário** a dental. **~te** m tooth; (de alho) clove; **~te do siso** wisdom tooth. **~tição** f teething; (dentadura) teeth. **~tífrico** m toothpaste. **~tista** m/f dentist

dentre =DE + ENTRE

dentro /'dẽtru/ adv inside; **lá ~** in there; **por ~** on the inside; **~ de** inside; (tempo) within

dentu|ça /dẽ'tusa/ f buck teeth. **~ço** a with buck teeth

denúncia /de'nũsia/ f (à polícia etc) report; (na imprensa etc) disclosure

denunciar /denũsi'ar/ vt (à polícia etc) report; (na imprensa etc) denounce

deparar /depa'rar/ vi **~ com** come across

departamento /departa'mẽtu/ m department

depauperar /depawpe'rar/ vt impoverish

depenar /depe'nar/ vt pluck ‹aves›; (roubar) fleece

depen|dência /depẽ'dẽsia/ f dependence; pl premises. **~dente** a dependent (**de** on) ● m/f dependant. **~der** vi depend (**de** on)

depi|lação /depila'sãw/ f depilation. **~lar** vt depilate. **~latório** m depilatory cream

deplo|rar /deplo'rar/ vt deplore. **~rável** (pl **~ráveis**) a deplorable

de|poente /depo'ẽtʃi/ m/f witness. **~poimento** m (à polícia) statement; (na justiça) fig testimony

depois /de'pojs/ adv after(wards). **~ de** after; **~ que** after

depor /de'por/ *vi* (*na polícia*) make a statement; (*na justiça*) give evidence, testify ● *vt* lay down ‹*armas*›; depose ‹*rei, presidente*›

depor|tação /deporta'sãw/ *f* deportation. **~tar** *vt* deport

deposi|tante /depozi'tãtʃi/ *m/f* depositor. **~tar** *vt* deposit; cast ‹*voto*›; place ‹*confiança*›

depósito /de'pɔzitu/ *m* deposit; (*armazém*) warehouse

depra|vação /deprava'sãw/ *f* depravity. **~vado** *a* depraved. **~var** *vt* deprave

depre|ciação /depresia'sãw/ *f* (*perda de valor*) depreciation; (*menosprezo*) deprecation. **~ciar** *vt* (*desvalorizar*) devalue; (*menosprezar*) deprecate. **~ciar-se** *vpr* ‹*bens*› depreciate; ‹*pessoa*› deprecate o.s.. **~ciativo** *a* depreciatory

depre|dação /depreda'sãw/ *f* depredation. **~dar** *vt* wreck

depressa /dʒi'presa/ *adv* fast, quickly

depres|são /depre'sãw/ *f* depression. **~sivo** *a* a depressive

depri|mente /depri'mẽtʃi/ *a* depressing. **~mido** *a* depressed. **~mir** *vt* depress. **~mir-se** *vpr* get depressed

depurar /depu'rar/ *vt* purify

depu|tação /deputa'sãw/ *f* deputation. **~tado** *m* deputy, MP, *Amer* congressman (*f*-woman). **~tar** *vt* delegate

deque /'dɛki/ *m* (sun)deck

deri|va /de'riva/ *f* à **~va** adrift; **andar à ~va** drift. **~vação** *f* derivation. **~var** *vt* derive; (*desviar*) divert ● *vi*, **~var-se** *vpr* derive, be derived (**de** from); ‹*navio*› drift

dermatolo|gia /dermatolo'ʒia/ *f* dermatology. **~gista** *f* dermatologist

derradeiro /dexa'deru/ *a* last, final

derra|mamento /dexama'mẽtu/ *m* spill, spillage. **~mamento de sangue** bloodshed. **~mar** *vt* spill; shed ‹*lágrimas*›. **~mar-se** *vpr* spill. **~me** *m* spill, spillage; **~me cerebral** stroke

derra|pagem /dexa'paʒẽ/ *f* skidding; (*uma*) skid. **~par** *vi* skid

derreter /dexe'ter/ *vt* melt. **~se** *vpr* melt

derro|ta /de'xɔta/ *f* defeat. **~tar** *vt* defeat. **~tismo** *m* defeatism. **~tista** *a* & *m/f* defeatist

derrubar /dexu'bar/ *vt* knock down; bring down ‹*governo*›

desaba|far /dʒizaba'far/ *vi* speak one's mind. **~fo** *m* outburst

desa|bamento /dʒizaba'mẽtu/ *m* collapse. **~bar** *vi* collapse; ‹*chuva*› pour down

desabotoar /dʒizaboto'ar/ *vt* unbutton

desabri|gado /dʒizabri'gadu/ *a* homeless. **~gar** *vt* make homeless

desabrochar /dʒizabro'ʃar/ *vi* blossom, bloom

desaca|tar /dʒizaka'tar/ *vt* defy. **~to** *m* (*de pessoa*) disrespect; (*da lei etc*) disregard

desacerto /dʒiza'sertu/ *m* mistake

desacompanhado /dʒizakõpa'ɲadu/ *a* unaccompanied

desaconse|lhar /dʒizakõse'ʎar/ *vt* advise against. **~lhável** (*pl* **~lháveis**) *a* inadvisable

desacor|dado /dʒizakor'dadu/ *a* unconscious. **~do** /o/ *m* disagreement

desacostu|mado /dʒizakostu'madu/ a unaccustomed. **~mar** vt **~mar alguém de** break sb of the habit of; **~mar-se de** get out of the habit of

desacreditar /dʒizakredʒi'tar/ vt discredit

desafeto /dʒiza'fɛtu/ m disaffection

desafi|ador /dʒizafia'dor/ a ‹tarefa› challenging; ‹pessoa› defiant. **~ar** vt challenge; (fazer face a) defy ‹perigo, morte›

desafi|nado /dʒizafi'nadu/ a out of tune. **~nar** vi (cantando) sing out of tune; (tocando) play out of tune ● vt put out of tune

desafio /dʒiza'fiu/ m challenge

desafivelar /dʒizafive'lar/ vt unbuckle

desafo|gar /dʒizafo'gar/ vt vent; (despertar) relieve. **~gar-se** vpr give vent to one's feelings. **~go** /o/ m (alívio) relief

desafo|rado /dʒizafo'radu/ a cheeky. **~ro** /o/ m cheek; (um) liberty

desafortunado /dʒizafortu'nadu/ a unfortunate

desagra|dar /dʒizagra'dar/ vt displease. **~dável** (pl **~dáveis**) a unpleasant. **~do** m displeasure

desagravo m redress, amends

desagregar /dʒizagre'gar/ vt split up. **~se** vpr split up

desaguar /dʒiza'gwar/ vt drain ● vi ‹rio› flow (em into)

desajeitado /dʒizaʒej'tadu/ a clumsy

desajuizado /dʒizaʒui'zadu/ a foolish

desajus|tado /dʒizaʒus'tadu/ a Psic maladjusted. **~te** m Psic maladjustment

desalen|tar /dʒizalẽ'tar/ vt dishearten. **~tar-se** vpr get disheartened. **~to** m discouragement

desali|nhado /dʒizali'nadu/ a untidy. **~nho** m untidiness

desalojar /dʒizalo'ʒar/ vt turn out ‹inquilino›; flush out ‹inimigo, ladrões›

desamarrar /dʒizama'xar/ vt untie ● vi cast off

desamarrotar /dʒizamaxo'tar/ vt smooth out

desamassar /dʒizama'sar/ vt smooth out

desambientado /dʒizãbiẽ'tadu/ a unsettled

desampa|rar /dʒizãpa'rar/ vt abandon. **~ro** m abandonment

desandar /dʒizã'dar/ vi ‹molho› separate; **~ a** start to

de|sanimar /dʒizani'mar/ vt discourage ● vi ‹pessoa› lose heart; ‹fato› be discouraging. **~sânimo** m discouragement

desapaixonado /dʒizapaʃo'nadu/ a dispassionate

desaparafusar /dʒizaparafu'zar/ vt unscrew

desapare|cer /dʒizapare'ser/ vi disappear. **~cimento** m disappearance

desapego /dʒiza'pegu/ m detachment; (indiferença) indifference

desapercebido /dʒizaperse'bidu/ a unnoticed

desapertar /dʒizaper'tar/ vt loosen

desapon|tamento /dʒizapõta'mẽtu/ m disappointment. **~tar** vt disappoint

desapropriar /dʒizapropriˈar/ vt
expropriate

desapro|vação
/dʒizaprovaˈsãw/ f disapproval.
~var vt disapprove of

desaproveitado /dʒizaprovej-
ˈtadu/ a wasted

desar|mamento
/dʒizarmaˈmẽtu/ m disarmament.
~mar vt disarm; take down
‹barraca›

desarran|jar /dʒizaxãˈʒar/ vt
mess up; upset ‹estômago›. **~jo** m
mess; (do estômago) upset

desarregaçar /dʒizaxegaˈsar/
vt roll down

desarru|mado /dʒizaxuˈmadu/
a untidy. **~mar** vt untidy; unpack
‹mala›

desarticular /dʒizartʃikuˈlar/ vt
dislocate

desarvorado /dʒizarvoˈradu/ a
disoriented, at a loss

desassociar /dʒizasosiˈar/ vt
disassociate. **~se** vpr disassociate
o.s.

desas|trado /dʒizasˈtradu/ a
accident-prone. **~tre** m disaster.
~troso /o/ a disastrous

desatar /dʒizaˈtar/ vt untie; **~ a
chorar** dissolve in tears

desatarraxar /dʒizataxaˈʃar/
vt unscrew

desaten|cioso /dʒizatẽsiˈozu/ a
inattentive. **~to** a oblivious (**a** to)

desati|nar /dʒizatʃiˈnar/ vt
bewilder ● vi not think straight. **~no**
m mental aberration, bewilderment;
(um) folly

desativar /dʒizatʃiˈvar/ vt
deactivate; shut down ‹fábrica›

desatrelar /dʒizatreˈlar/ vt
unhitch

desatualizado /dʒizatualiˈzadu/
a out-of-date

desavença /dʒizaˈvẽsa/ f dispute

desavergonhado
/dʒizavergoˈɲadu/ a shameless

desbancar /dʒizbãˈkar/ vt outdo

desbaratar /dʒizbaraˈtar/ vt
(desperdiçar) waste

desbocado /dʒizboˈkadu/ a
outspoken

desbotar /dʒizboˈtar/ vt/i fade

desbra|vador /dʒizbravaˈdor/ m
explorer. **~var** vt explore

desbun|dante /dʒizbũˈdãtʃi/ a
🄵 mind-blowing. **~dar** vt 🄵 blow
the mind ● vi 🄵 flip, freak out.
~de m 🄵 knockout

descabido /dʒiskaˈbidu/ a
inappropriate

descafeinado /dʒiskafejˈnadu/ a
decaffeinated

descalabro /dʒiskaˈlabru/ m
debacle

descalço /dʒisˈkawsu/ a barefoot

descambar /dʒiskãˈbar/ vi
deteriorate, degenerate

descan|sar /dʒiskãˈsar/ vt/i rest.
~so m rest; (de prato, copo) mat

descapotável /dʒiskapuˈtavɛɫ/
a & m Port convertible

desca|rado /dʒiskaˈradu/ a
blatant. **~ramento** m cheek

descarga /dʒisˈkarga/ f Eletr
discharge; (da privada) flush; **dar ~**
flush (the toilet)

descarregar /dʒiskaxeˈgar/ vt
unload ‹mercadorias›; discharge
‹poluentes›; vent ‹raiva› ● vi
‹bateria› go flat; **~ em cima de
alguém** take it out on sb

descarrilhar /dʒiskaxiˈʎar/
vt/i derail

descar|tar /dʒiskar'tar/ *vt* discard.
~tável (*pl* **~táveis**) *a* disposable

descascar /dʒiskas'kar/ *vt* peel
‹*frutas, batatas*›; shell ‹*nozes*› ● *vi*
‹*pessoa, pele*› peel

descaso /dʒis'kazu/ *m* indifference

descen|dência /deseʹdẽsia/
f descent. **~dente** *a* descended
● *m/f* descendant. **~der** *vi* descend
(**de** from)

descentralizar /dʒisẽtrali'zar/ *vt*
decentralize

des|cer /de'ser/ *vi* go down;
‹*avião*› descend; (*do ônibus, trem*)
get off; (*do carro*) get out ● *vt* go
down ‹*escada, ladeira*›; scroll down
‹*página*›. **~cida** *f* descent

desclassificar /dʒisklasifi'kar/
vt disqualify

desco|berta /dʒisko'bɛrta/ *f*
discovery. **~berto** /ɛ/ *a* uncovered;
‹*conta*› overdrawn; **a ~berto**
overdrawn. **~bridor** *m* discoverer.
~brimento *m* discovery. **~brir** *vt*
discover; (*expor*) uncover

Descobrimentos The term
Descobrimentos refers to
the Age of Discovery in the
15th and 16th centuries, during
which the Portuguese engaged in
extensive maritime travels in
search of new trade routes with
the New World. Significant events
include the route round
Africa to India by Vasco da Gama in
1498, and the discovery of Brazil
by Pedro Álvares Cabral in 1500.

---

descolar /dʒisko'lar/ *vt* unstick;
🄵 (*dar*) give; (*arranjar*) get hold of,
rustle up; Port ‹*avião*› take off

descom|por /dʒisko'por/ *vt*
(*censurar*) scold. **~se** *vpr* ‹*pessoa*›

---

lose one's composure. **~postura**
f (*estado*) loss of composure;
(*censura*) talking-to

descomprometido
/dʒiskõprome'tʃidu/ *a* free

descomu|nal /dʒiskomu'naw/
(*pl* **~nais**) *a* extraordinary; (*grande*)
huge

desconcentrar /dʒiskõse'trar/
vt distract

desconcer|tante
/dʒiskõser'tãtʃi/ *a* disconcerting.
~tar *vt* disconcert

desconexo /dʒisko'nɛksu/ *a*
incoherent

desconfi|ado /dʒiskõfi'adu/ *a*
suspicious. **~ança** *f* mistrust. **~ar**
vi suspect

desconfor|tável
/dʒiskõfor'tavew/ (*pl* **~táveis**)
a uncomfortable. **~to** /o/ *m*
discomfort

descongelar /dʒiskõʒe'lar/ *vt*
defrost ‹*geladeira*›; thaw ‹*comida*›

descongestio|nante
/dʒiskõʒestʃio'nãtʃi/ *a & m*
decongestant. **~nar** *vt* decongest

desconhe|cer /dʒiskoɲe'ser/ *vt*
not know. **~cido** *a* unknown ● *m*
stranger

desconsiderar /dʒiskõside'rar/
vt ignore

desconsolado /dʒiskõso'ladu/ *a*
disconsolate

descontar /dʒiskõ'tar/ *vt* deduct;
(*não levar em conta*) discount

desconten|tamento
/dʒiskõtẽta'mẽtu/ *m* discontent.
~te *a* discontent

descontinuado
/dʒiskõtʃi'nwadu/ *a* discontinued

desconto /dʒis'kõtu/ *m* discount;
dar um ~ *fig* make allowances

descontra|ção /dʒiskõtra'sãw/ f
informality. **~ido** a informal, casual.
~ir vt relax. **~ir-se** vpr relax

descontro|lar-se
/dʒiskõtro'larsi/ vpr ‹pessoa› lose
control; ‹coisa› go out of control.
~le /o/ m lack of control

desconversar /dʒiskõver'sar/ vi
change the subject

descortesia /dʒiskorte'zia/ f
rudeness

descostu|rar /dʒiskostu'rar/ vt
unrip. **~rar-se** vpr come undone

descrédito /dʒis'krɛdʒitu/ m
discredit

descren|ça /dʒis'krẽsa/ f disbelief.
~te a sceptical, disbelieving

des|crever /dʒis'kre'ver/ vt
describe. **~crição** f description.
~critivo a descriptive

descui|dado /dʒiskui'dadu/ a
careless. **~dar** vt neglect. **~do** m
carelessness; (um) oversight

descul|pa /dʒis'kuwpa/ f excuse;
pedir ~pas apologize. **~par** vt
excuse; **~pe!** sorry!. **~par-se** vpr
apologize. **~pável** (pl **~páveis**) a
excusable

---

desde /'dezdʒi/ ● prep

••••➤ since; **moro aqui ~ 2008**
I have lived here since 2008

••••➤ (em expressões) **~ ... até
... from ... to ...; ~ junho até
agosto** from June to August; **a
loja vende tudo, ~ roupas até
livros** the shop sells everything,
from clothes to books; **~ que** as
long as; **~ que você me informe**
as long as you let me know

---

des|dém /dez'dẽj/ m disdain.
~denhar vt disdain. **~denhoso** /o/
a disdainful

desdentado /dʒizdẽ'tadu/ a
toothless

desdita /dʒiz'dʒita/ f unhappiness

desdizer /dʒizdʒi'zer/ vt take
back, withdraw ● vi take back what
one said

desdo|bramento
/dʒizdobra'mẽtu/ m implication.
~brar vt (abrir) unfold; break down
‹dados, contas›. **~brar-se** vpr unfold;
(empenhar-se) go to a lot of trouble,
bend over backwards

dese|jar /deze'ʒar/ vt want;
(apaixonadamente) desire; **~jar algo
a alguém** wish sb sth. **~jável** (pl
~jáveis) a desirable. **~jo** /e/ m wish;
(forte) desire. **~joso** /o/ a desirous

deselegante /dʒizele'gãtʃi/ a
inelegant

desemaranhar /dʒizemara'ɲar/
vt untangle

desembara|çado
/dʒizibara'sadu/ a ‹pessoa›
confident, nonchalant. **~çar-se** vpr
rid o.s. (**de** of). **~ço** m confidence,
ease

desembar|car /dʒizibar'kar/ vt/i
disembark. **~que** m disembarkation;
(seção do aeroporto) arrivals

desembocar /dʒizibo'kar/ vi flow

desembol|sar /dʒizibow'sar/
vt spend, pay out. **~so** /o/ m
expenditure

desembrulhar /dʒizibru'ʎar/
vt unwrap

desembuchar /dʒizibu'ʃar/ vi
🔟 (desabafar) get things off one's
chest; (falar logo) spit it out

desempacotar /dʒizĩpako'tar/
vt unpack

desempatar /dʒizĩpa'tar/ vt
decide ‹jogo›

desempe|nhar /dʒizipe'nar/
vt perform; play ‹papel›. **~nho** m
performance

desempre|gado /dʒizipre'gadu/
a unemployed. **~go** /e/ m
unemployment

desencadear /dʒizikadʒi'ar/ vt
set off, trigger

desencaminhar /dʒizikami'nar/
vt lead astray; embezzle ‹dinheiro›

desencantar /dʒizikã'tar/ vt
disenchant

desencon|trar-se
/dʒizikõ'trarsi/ vpr miss each other,
fail to meet. **~tro** m failure to meet

desencorajar /dʒizikora'ʒar/ vt
discourage

desenferrujar /dʒizifexu'ʒar/
vt derust ‹metal›; stretch ‹pernas›;
brush up ‹língua›

desenfreado /dʒizifri'adu/ a
unbridled

desenganar /dʒiziga'nar/ vt
disabuse; declare incurable ‹doente›

desengonçado /dʒizigõ'sadu/ a
‹pessoa› ungainly

desengre|nado /dʒizigre'nadu/
a ‹carro› in neutral. **~nar** vt put in
neutral ‹carro›; (tecn) disengage

dese|nhar /deze'nar/ vt draw.
~nhista m/f drawer; (industrial)
designer. **~nho** /e/ m drawing

desenlace /dʒizi'lasi/ m
dénouement, outcome

desenrascar-se /dʒizẽxaʃ'karsi/
vpr Port to get by

desenredar /dʒizĩxe'dar/ vt
unravel

desenrolar /dʒizĩxo'lar/ vt unroll
‹rolo›

desenten|der /dʒizĩtẽ'der/ vt
misunderstand. **~der-se** vpr (não se
dar bem) not get on. **~dimento** m

misunderstanding

desenterrar /dʒizĩte'xar/ vt dig
up ‹cadáver›; unearth ‹informação›

desentortar /dʒizĩtor'tar/ vt
straighten out

desentupir /dʒizĩtu'pir/ vt
unblock

desenvol|to /dʒizĩ'vowtu/
a casual, nonchalant. **~tura** f
casualness, nonchalance; com
~tura nonchalantly. **~ver** vt
develop. **~ver-se** vpr develop.
~vimento m development

desequi|librado a unbalanced.
~librar vt unbalance. **~librar-se**
vpr become unbalanced. **~líbrio** m
imbalance

deser|ção /dezer'sãw/ f desertion.
~tar vt/i desert. **~to** /ɛ/ a deserted;
ilha **~ta** desert island ● m desert.
~tor m deserter

desespe|rado /dʒizispe'radu/ a
desperate. **~rador** a hopeless. **~rar**
vt (desesperançar) make despair
● vi, **~rar-se** vpr despair. **~ro** /e/
m despair

desestabilizar /dʒizistabili'zar/
vt destabilize

desestimular /dʒizistʃimu'lar/
vt discourage

desfal|car /dʒisfaw'kar/ vt
embezzle. **~que** m embezzlement

desfa|lecer /dʒisfale'ser/ vt
(desmaiar) faint. **~lecimento** m faint

desfavor /dʒisfa'vor/ m disfavour

desfavo|rável /dʒisfavo'ravew/ a
(pl **~ráveis**) a unfavourable. **~recer**
vt be unfavourable to; treat less
favourably ‹minorias etc›

desfazer /dʒisfa'zer/ vt undo;
unpack ‹mala›; strip ‹cama›; break
‹contrato›; clear up ‹mistério›. **~se**
vpr come undone; ‹casamento›

desfechar | deslocado

break up; ‹sonhos› crumble; ~se
em lágrimas dissolve into tears

desfe|char /dʒisfe'ʃar/ vt throw
‹murro, olhar›. ~cho /e/ m
outcome, dénouement

desfeita /dʒis'fejta/ f slight, insult

desferir /dʒisfe'rir/ vt give
‹pontapé›; launch ‹ataque›; fire
‹flecha›

desfiar /dʒisfi'ar/ vt pick the meat
off ‹frango›. ~se var pick ‹tecido› fray

desfigurar /dʒisfigu'rar/ vt
disfigure; fig distort

desfi|ladeiro /dʒisfila'deru/ m
pass. ~lar vi parade. ~le m parade;
~le de modas fashion show

desflorestamento
/dʒisfloresta'mẽtu/ m deforestation

desforra /dʒis'fɔxa/ f revenge

desfraldar /dʒisfraw'dar/ vt unfurl

desfrutar /dʒisfru'tar/ vt enjoy

desgas|tante /dʒizgas'tãtʃi/ a
wearing, stressful. ~tar vt wear out.
~te m (de máquina etc) wear and
tear; (de pessoa) stress and strain

desgosto /dʒiz'gostu/ m sorrow

desgovernar-se /dʒizgover'narsi/
vpr go out of control

desgraça /dʒiz'grasa/ f
misfortune. ~do a wretched ● m
wretch

desgravar /dʒizgra'var/ vt erase

desgrenhado /dʒizgre'ɲadu/
a unkempt

desgrudar /dʒizgru'dar/ vt
unstick. ~se vpr ‹pessoa› tear
o.s. away

desidra|tação /dʒizidrata'sãw/ f
dehydration. ~tar vt dehydrate

desig|nação /dezigna'sãw/ f
designation. ~nar vt designate

desi|gual /dezi'gwaw/ (pl ~guais)
a unequal; ‹terreno› uneven.
~gualdade f inequality; (de terreno)
unevenness

desilu|dir /dezilu'dʒir/ vt
disillusion. ~são f disillusionment

desinfe|tante /dezĩfe'tãtʃi/ a & m
disinfectant. ~tar vt disinfect

desinibido /dezini'bidu/ a
uninhibited

desintegrar-se /dezĩte'grarsi/
vpr disintegrate

desinteres|sado /dezĩtere'sadu/
a uninterested. ~sante a
uninteresting. ~sar-se vpr lose
interest (de in). ~se /e/ m disinterest

desintoxicação
/dezĩtoksika'sãw/ f rehabilitation;
clínica de ~ rehabilitation centre

desis|tência /dezis'tẽsia/ f giving
up. ~tir vt/i ~tir (de) give up

desle|al /dʒizle'aw/ (pl ~ais) a
disloyal. ~aldade f disloyalty

deslei|xado /dʒizle'ʃadu/ a
sloppy; (no vestir) scruffy. ~xo m
carelessness; (no vestir) scruffiness

desli|gado /dʒizli'gadu/ a ‹luz,
TV› off; ‹pessoa› absent-minded.
~gar vt turn off ‹luz, TV, motor›;
hang up, put down ‹telefone› ● vi
(ao telefonar) hang up, put the
phone down

deslindar /dʒizlĩ'dar/ vt clear
up, solve

desli|zante /dʒizli'zãtʃi/ a
slippery; ‹inflação› creeping. ~zar
vi slip. ~zar-se vpr creep. ~ze m slip;
fig (erro) slip-up

deslo|cado /dʒizlo'kadu/ a
‹membro› dislocated; fig out of
place. ~calizar /dʒizlokali'zar/ vt
Port ‹fábricas, empresas› relocate.
~car /dʒizlo'kar/ vt move;

Med dislocate ‹*fábricas, empresas*› relocate. **~car-se** *vpr* move

deslum|brado /dʒizlũ'bradu/ *a fig* starry-eyed. **~bramento** *m fig* wonderment. **~brante** *a* dazzling. **~brar** *vt* dazzle. **~brar-se** *vpr fig* be dazzled

desmai|ado /dʒizmaj'adu/ *a* unconscious. **~ar** *vi* faint. **~o** *m* faint

desman|cha-prazeres /dʒizmãʃapra'zeris/ *m/f invar* spoilsport. **~char** *vt* break up; break off ‹*noivado*›; shatter ‹*sonhos*›. **~char-se** *vpr* break up; (*no ar, na água, em lágrimas*) dissolve

desmantelar /dʒizmãte'lar/ *vt* dismantle

desmarcar /dʒizmar'kar/ *vt* cancel ‹*encontro*›

desmascarar /dʒizmaske'rar/ *vt* unmask

desma|tamento /dʒizmata'mẽtu/ *m* deforestation. **~tar** *vt* clear (of forest)

desmedido /dʒizme'didu/ *a* excessive

desmemoriado /dʒizmemori'adu/ *a* forgetful

desmen|tido /dʒizmẽ'tʃidu/ *m* denial. **~tir** *vt* deny

desmiolado /dʒizmio'ladu/ *a* brainless

desmontar /dʒizmõ'tar/ *vt* dismantle

desmorali|zante /dʒizmorali'zãtʃi/ *a* demoralizing. **~zar** *vt* demoralize

desmoro|namento /dʒizmorona'mẽtu/ *m* collapse. **~nar** *vt* destroy. **~nar-se** *vpr* collapse

desnatar /dʒizna'tar/ *vi* skim ‹*leite*›

desnecessário /dʒiznese'sariu/ *a* unnecessary

desní|vel /dʒiz'nivew/ (*pl* **~veis**) *m* difference in height

desnortear /dʒiznortʃi'ar/ *vt* disorientate, *Amer* disorient

desnutrição /dʒiznutri'sãw/ *f* malnutrition

desobe|decer /dʒizobede'ser/ *vt/i* **~decer (a)** disobey. **~diência** *f* disobedience. **~diente** *a* disobedient

desobrigar /dʒizobri'gar/ *vt* release (**de** from)

desobstruir /dʒizobistru'ir/ *vt* unblock; empty ‹*casa*›

desocupado /dʒizoku'padu/ *a* unoccupied

desodorante /dʒizodo'rãtʃi/ *m, Port* **desodorizante** /dʒizodori'zãtʃi/ *m* deodorant

deso|lação /dezola'sãw/ *f* desolation. **~lado** *a* ‹*lugar*› desolate; ‹*pessoa*› desolated. **~lar** *vt* desolate

desones|tidade /dʒizonestʃi'dadʒi/ *f* dishonesty. **~to** /ɛ/ *a* dishonest

deson|ra /dʒi'zõxa/ *f* dishonour. **~rar** *vt* dishonour. **~roso** /o/ *a* dishonourable

desor|deiro /dʒizor'deru/ *a* troublemaking. ● *m* troublemaker. **~dem** *f* disorder. **~denado** *a* disorganized; ‹*vida*› disordered. **~denar** *vt* disorganize

desorgani|zação /dʒizorganiza'sãw/ *f* disorganization. **~zar** *vt* disorganize. **~zar-se** *vpr* get disorganized

desorientar /dʒizoriẽ'tar/ *vt* disorientate; *Amer* disorient

desossar /dʒizo'sar/ *vt* bone

deso|va /dʒi'zɔva/ f roe. **~var** vi spawn

despa|chado /dʒispa'ʃadu/ a efficient. **~chante** m/f (de mercadorias) shipping agent; (de documentos) documentation agent. **~char** vt deal with; dispatch, forward ‹mercadorias›. **~cho** m dispatch

desparafusar /dʒisparafu'zar/ vt unscrew

despedaçar /dʒispeda'sar/ vt (rasgar) tear to pieces; (quebrar) smash. **~se** vpr ‹vidro, vaso› smash; ‹papel, tecido› tear

despe|dida /dʒispe'dʒida/ f farewell; **~dida de solteiro** stag night, Amer bachelor party. **~dir** vt dismiss; sack ‹empregado›. **~dir-se** vpr say goodbye (de to)

despedimento /dʒispedi'mẽtu/ m Port dismissal

despe|tado /dʒispej'tadu/ a spiteful. **~to** m spite; **a ~to de** despite, in spite of

despe|jar /dʒispe'ʒar/ vt pour out ‹líquido›; empty ‹recipiente›; evict ‹inquilino›. **~jo** m (de inquilino) eviction

despencar /dʒispẽ'kar/ vi plummet

despender /dʒispẽ'der/ vt spend ‹dinheiro›

despensa /dʒis'pẽsa/ f pantry, larder

despentear /dʒispẽtʃi'ar/ vt mess up ‹cabelo›; mess up the hair of ‹pessoa›

despercebido /dʒisperse'bidu/ a unnoticed

desper|diçar /dʒisperdʒi'sar/ vt waste. **~dício** m waste

desper|tador /dʒisperta'dor/ m alarm clock. **~tar** vt rouse ‹pessoa›; fig arouse ‹interesse, suspeitas etc› ● vi awake

despesa /dʒis'peza/ f expense

des|pido /des'pidu/ a bare, stripped (**de** of). **~pir** vt strip (**de** of); strip off ‹roupa›. **~pir-se** vpr strip (off), get undressed

despo|jar /dʒispo'ʒar/ vt strip (**de** of). **~jar-se** vpr divest o.s. (**de** of). **~jo** /o/ m spoils, booty; **~jos mortais** mortal remains

despontar /dʒispõ'tar/ vi emerge

despor|tista /dʃipur'tiʃta/ Port m/f sportsman (f -woman). **~tivo** m Port a sporting. **~to** /o/ Port m sport; **carro de ~to** sports car

déspota /'dɛspota/ m/f despot

despótico /des'pɔtʃiku/ a despotic

despovoar /dʒispovo'ar/ vt depopulate

desprender /dʒisprẽ'der/ vt detach; (da parede) take down. **~se** vpr come off; fig detach o.s.

despreocupado /dʒisprioku'padu/ a unconcerned

despreparado /dʒisprepa'radu/ a unprepared

desprestigiar /dʒisprestʃiʒi'ar/ vt discredit

despretensioso /dʒispretẽsi'ozu/ a unpretentious

desprevenido /dʒispreve'nidu/ a off one's guard, unprepared; **apanhar ~** catch unawares

despre|zar /dʒispre'zar/ vt despise; (ignorar) ignore. **~zível** (pl **~zíveis**) a despicable. **~zo** /e/ m contempt

desproporção /dʒispropor'sãw/ f disproportion

desproporcio|nado
/dʒispropɔrsjo'nadu/ a
disproportionate. **~nal** (pl **~nais**) a
disproportional

despropositado
/dʒispropozi'tadu/ a (absurdo)
preposterous

desprovido /dʒispro'vidu/ a **~**
de without

desqualificar /dʒiskwalifi'kar/
vt disqualify

desqui|tar-se /dʒiski'tarsi/ vpr
(legally) separate. **~te** m (legal)
separation

desrespei|tar /dʒizxespej'tar/
vt not respect; (ignorar) disregard.
~to m disrespect. **~toso** /o/ a
disrespectful

dessa(s), desse(s) = de +
essa(s), esse(s)

desta = de + esta

desta|camento /dʒistaka'mẽtu/
m detachment. **~car** vt detach;
(ressaltar) bring out, make stand
out. **~car-se** vpr (desprender-se)
come off; (corredor) break away;
(sobressair) stand out (sobre
against). **~cável** (pl **~cáveis**) a
detachable; (caderno) pull-out

destam|pado /dʒista'padu/ a
(panela) uncovered. **~par** vt remove
the lid of

destapar /dʒista'par/ vt uncover

destaque /dʒis'taki/ m
prominence; (coisa, pessoa)
highlight; (do noticiário) headline

destas, deste = de + estas, este

destemido /dʒiste'midu/ a
intrepid, courageous

desterrar /dʒiste'xar/ vt (exilar)
exile

destes = de + estes

destilar /dʒesti'lar/ vt distil. **~ia** f
distillery

desti|nado /dʒestʃi'nadu/ a
(fadado) destined. **~nar** vt intend,
mean (para for). **~natário** m
addressee. **~no** m (de viagem)
destination; (sorte) fate

destituir /dʒestʃitu'ir/ vt remove

desto|ante /dʒisto'ãtʃi/ a (sons)
discordant; (cores) clashing. **~ar** vi
~ar de clash with

destrancar /dʒistrã'kar/ vt unlock

destreza /des'treza/ f skill

destrinchar /dʒistrĩ'ʃar/ vt (expor)
dissect; (resolver) sort out

destro /'destru/ a skilful

destro|çar /dʒistro'sar/ vt wreck.
~ços m pl wreckage

destronar /dʒistro'nar/ vt depose

destroncar /dʒistrõ'kar/ vt rick

destrui|ção /dʒistrui'sãw/ f
destruction. **~idor** a destructive ● m
destroyer. **~ir** vt destroy

desumano /dʒizu'manu/ a
inhuman; (cruel) inhumane

desunião /dʒizuni'ãw/ f disunity

desu|sado /dʒizu'zadu/ a disused.
~so m disuse

desvairado /dʒizvaj'radu/ a
delirious, raving

desvalori|zação
/dʒizvaloriza'sãw/ f devaluation.
~zar vt devalue

desvanta|gem /dʒizvã'taʒẽ/
f disadvantage. **~joso** /o/ a
disadvantageous

desve|lar /dʒizve'lar/ vt unveil;
uncover (segredo). **~lar-se** vpr go to
a lot of trouble. **~lo** /e/ m great care

desvencilhar /dʒizvẽsi'ʎar/ vt
extricate, free

desvendar /dʒizvẽ'dar/ vt reveal ‹segredo›; solve ‹mistério›

desventura /dʒizvẽ'tura/ f misfortune; (infelicidade) unhappiness

desviar /dʒizvi'ar/ vt divert ‹trânsito, rio, atenção, dinheiro›; avert ‹golpe, suspeitas, olhos›. ~se vpr deviate; ‹do tema› digress

desvincular /dʒizvĩku'lar/ vt free

desvio /dʒiz'viu/ m diversion; (do trânsito) diversion, Amer detour; (linha ferroviária) siding

desvirtuar /dʒizvirtu'ar/ vt misrepresent ‹verdade›

deta|lhado /deta'ʎadu/ a detailed. ~lhar vt detail. ~lhe m detail

detec|tar /detek'tar/ vt detect. ~tor m detector

de|tenção /detẽ'sãw/ f (prisão) detention. ~tentor m holder. ~ter vt (ter) hold; (prender) detain

detergente /deter'ʒẽtʃi/ m detergent

deterio|ração /deterjora'sãw/ f deterioration. ~rar vt damage. ~rar-se vpr deteriorate

determi|nação /determina'sãw/ f determination. ~nado a ‹certo› certain; (resoluto) determined. ~nar vt determine

detestar /detes'tar/ vt hate

detetive /dete'tʃivi/ m detective

detido /de'tʃidu/ pp de ▶ DETER ● a thorough ● m detainee

detonar /deto'nar/ vt detonate; 🄸 (criticar) pull to pieces ● vi detonate

detrás /de'traʃ/ adv behind ● prep ~ de behind

detrito /de'tritu/ m detritus

deturpar /detur'par/ vt misrepresent, distort

deus /dews/ m (f **deusa**) god (f goddess). ~dará m ao ~dará at the mercy of chance

devagar /dʒiva'gar/ adv slowly

deva|near /devani'ar/ vi daydream. ~neio m daydream

devas|sar /deva'sar/ vt expose. ~sidão f debauchery. ~so a debauched

devastar /devas'tar/ vt devastate

devedor /deve'dor/ a debit ● m debtor

---

dever /de'ver/ ● vt

••••▶ (seguido de substantivo) owe; **devo R$5/uma explicação para você** I owe you R$5/an explanation (seguido de infinitivo: obrigação) must; **você deve estudar!** you must study!; **ela já deve estar em casa** she must be at home by now; **não deve ser fácil** it can't be easy (seguido de infinitivo: conselho, crítica) should; **você não devia sair assim!** you shouldn't go out like that!; **você deveria ter vindo mais cedo** you should have come earlier

● vpr

••••▶ ~se a algo be due to sth; **isso se deve à falta de recursos** that's due to a lack of funds

● m

••••▶ duty; **cumprir o ~ do** one's duty

••••▶ (em expressões) **como deve ser: uma carta como deve ser** a proper letter; **coma como deve ser** eat properly

---

de|vido /de'vidu/ a due (**a** to); ~voção f devotion

de|volução /devolu'sãw/ f return. **~volver** vt return

devorar /devo'rar/ vt devour

devo|tar /devo'tar/ vt devote. **~tar-se** vpr devote o.s. (**a** to). **~to** /ɔ/ a devout

dez /dɛs/ a & m ten

dezanove /dza'nɔv/ Port a & m nineteen

dezas|seis /dza'sejʃ/ Port a & m sixteen. **~sete** /ɛ/ Port a & m seventeen

dezembro /de'zẽbru/ m December

deze|na /de'zena/ f ten; **uma ~ (de)** about ten. **~nove** /ɔ/ a & m nineteen

dezes|seis /dʒize'sejs/ a & m sixteen. **~sete** /ɛ/ a & m seventeen

dezoito /dʒi'zojtu/ a & m eighteen

dia /'dʒia/ m day; **de ~** by day; **(no) ~ 20 de julho** (on) July 20th; **~ de folga** day off; **~ útil** working day. **o ~ a ~** m everyday life

dia|bete /dʒia'bɛtʃi/ f diabetes. **~bético** a & m diabetic

dia|bo /dʒi'abu/ m devil. **~bólico** a diabolical, devilish. **~brete** /e/ m little devil. **~brura** f (de criança) bit of mischief; pl mischief

diadema /dʒia'dema/ f tiara

diafragma /dʒia'fragima/ m diaphragm

diag|nosticar /dʒiagnostʃi'kar/ vt diagnose. **~nóstico** m diagnosis • a diagnostic

diago|nal /dʒiago'naw/ (pl **~nais**) a & f diagonal

diagra|ma /dʒia'grama/ m diagram. **~mação** f design. **~mador** m designer. **~mar** vt design ‹livro, revista›

dia|lética /dʒia'lɛtʃika/ f dialectics. **~leto** /e/ m dialect

dialogar /dʒialo'gar/ vi talk; Pol hold talks

diálogo /dʒi'alogu/ m dialogue

diamante /dʒia'mãtʃi/ m diamond

diâmetro /dʒi'ametru/ m diameter

dian|te /dʒi'ãtʃi/ adv **de ... em ~te** from ... on(wards); **~te de** (enfrentando) faced with; (perante) before. **~teira** f lead. **~teiro** a front

diapasão /dʒiapa'zãw/ m tuning fork

diapositivo /dʒiapozi'tʃivu/ m transparency

diá|ria /dʒi'aria/ f daily rate. **~rio** a daily

diarista /dʒia'rista/ m/f day labourer; (faxineira) daily (help)

diarreia /dʒia'xeja/ f diarrhoea

dica /'dʒika/ f tip, hint

dicção /dʒik'sãw/ f diction

dicionário /dʒisio'nariu/ m dictionary

didáti|ca /dʒi'datʃika/ f teaching methodology. **~co** a teaching; ‹livro› educational; ‹estilo› didactic

die|ta /dʒi'ɛta/ f diet; **de ~ta** on a diet. **~tista** m/f dietician

difa|mação /dʒifama'sãw/ f defamation. **~mar** vt defame. **~matório** a defamatory

diferen|ça /dʒife'rẽsa/ f difference. **~cial** (pl **~ciais**) a & f differential. **~ciar** vt differentiate. **~ciar-se** vpr differ. **~te** a different

dife|rimento /dʒiferi'mẽtu/ m deferment. **~rir** vt defer • vi differ

difícil /dʒi'fisiw/ (pl **~ceis**) a difficult; (improvável) unlikely

dificilmente /dʒifisiw'mẽtʃi/ adv ~ poderá fazê-lo he's unlikely to be able to do it

dificul|dade /dʒifikuw'dadʒi/ f difficulty. ~tar vt make difficult

difteria /dʒifte'ria/ f diphtheria

difun|dir /dʒifũ'dʒir/ vt spread; (pela rádio) broadcast; diffuse ‹luz, calor›. ~dir-se vpr spread

difu|são /dʒifu'zãw/ f diffusion. ~so a diffuse

dige|rir /dʒiʒe'rir/ vt digest. ~rível (pl ~ríveis) a digestible

diges|tão /dʒiʒes'tãw/ f digestion. ~tivo a digestive

digi|tal /dʒiʒi'taw/ (pl ~tais) a digital; **impressão ~tal** fingerprint. ~tar vt key

dígito /'dʒiʒitu/ m digit

digladiar /dʒigladʒi'ar/ vi do battle

dig|nar-se /dʒig'narsi/ vpr deign (de to). ~nidade f dignity. ~nificar vt dignify. ~no a worthy (de of); (decoroso) dignified

digressão /dʒigra'sãw/ f Port (de concerto, volta de bicicleta) tour

dilace|rante /dʒilase'rãtʃi/ a ‹dor› excruciating. ~rar vt tear to pieces

dilapidar /dʒilapi'dar/ vt squander

dilatar /dʒila'tar/ vt expand; Med dilate. ~se vpr expand; Med dilate

dilema /dʒi'lema/ m dilemma

diletante /dʒile'tãtʃi/ a & m/f dilettante

dili|gência /dʒili'ʒẽsia/ f diligence; (carruagem) stagecoach. ~gente a diligent, hard-working

diluir /dʒilu'ir/ vt dilute

dilúvio /dʒi'luviu/ m deluge

dimen|são /dʒimẽ'sãw/ f dimension. ~sionar vt size up

diminu|ição /dʒiminui'sãw/ f reduction. ~ir vt reduce ● vi lessen; ‹carro, motorista› slow down. ~tivo a & m diminutive. ~to a minute

Dinamarca /dʒina'marka/ f Denmark

dinamar|quês /dʒinamar'kes/ (f ~quesa) a Danish ● m Dane

dinâmi|ca /dʒi'namika/ f dynamics. ~co a dynamic

dina|mismo /dʒina'mizmu/ m dynamism. ~mite f dynamite

dínamo /'dʒinamu/ m dynamo

dinastia /dʒinas'tʃia/ f dynasty

dinda /'dʒĩda/ f 🔲 godmother

dinheiro /dʒi'ɲeru/ m money

dinossauro /dʒino'sawru/ m dinosaur

diocese /dʒio'sezi/ f diocese

dióxido /dʒi'ɔksidu/ m dioxide; ~ **de carbono** carbon dioxide

diplo|ma /dʒi'ploma/ m diploma. ~macia f diplomacy. ~mar-se vpr take one's diploma. ~mata m/f diplomat ● a diplomatic. ~mático a diplomatic

direção /dʒire'sãw/ f (sentido) direction; (de empresa) management; (condução de carro) driving; (manuseio do volante) steering

direi|ta /dʒi'rejta/ f right. ~tinho adv exactly right. ~tista a right-wing ● m/f right-winger, rightist. ~to a right; (ereto) straight ● adv properly ● m right

dire|tas /dʒi'retas/ f pl direct (presidential) elections. ~to a direct ● adv directly. ~tor m director; (de escola) head teacher; (de jornal) editor; ~tor-gerente managing director. **~toria** f (diretores) board of directors; (sala) boardroom. **~tório** m directory. **~triz** f directive

diri|gente /dʒiri'ʒẽtʃi/ a leading ● m/f leader. **~gir** vt direct; manage ‹empresa›; drive ‹carro›. **~gir-se** vpr (ir) make one's way; **~gir-se a** (falar com) address

dis|cagem /dʒis'kaʒẽ/ f dialling; **~cagem rápida** speed dialling. **~car** vt/i dial

discente /dʒi'sẽtʃi/ a **corpo ~** student body

discer|nimento /dʒiserni'mẽtu/ m discernment. **~nir** vt discern

discipli|na /dʒisi'plina/ f discipline. **~nador** a disciplinary. **~nar** vt discipline

discípulo /dʒi'sipulu/ m disciple

disco-jóquei /dʒisk'ʒɔkej/ m disc jockey

disco /'dʒisku/ m disc; (de música) record; (no atletismo) discus ● f [1] disco; **~ flexível/rígido** floppy/hard disk; **~ laser** CD, compact disc; **~ voador** flying saucer

discor|dante /dʒiskor'dãtʃi/ a conflicting. **~dar** vi disagree (de with)

discote|ca /dʒisko'tɛka/ f discotheque. **~cário** m DJ

discre|pância /dʒiskre'pãsia/ f discrepancy. **~pante** a inconsistent. **~par** vi diverge (de from)

dis|creto /dʒis'krɛtu/ a discreet. **~crição** f discretion

discrimi|nação /dʒiskrimina'sãw/ f discrimination; (descrição) description. **~nar** vt discriminate. **~natório** a discriminatory

discur|sar /dʒiskur'sar/ vi speak. **~so** m speech

discussão /dʒisku'sãw/ f discussion; (briga) argument

discu|tir /dʒisku'tʃir/ vt/i discuss; (brigar) argue. **~tível** (pl **~tíveis**) a debatable

disenteria /dʒizẽte'ria/ f dysentery

disfar|çar /dʒisfar'sar/ vt disguise. **~çar-se** vpr disguise o.s.. **~ce** m disguise

dis|lético /dʒiz'lɛtʃiku/ a & m dyslexic. **~lexia** f dyslexia. **~léxico** a & m dyslexic

dispa|rada /dʒispa'rada/ f bolt. **~rado** adv o melhor **~rado** the best by a long way. **~rar** vt fire ‹arma› ● vi (com arma) fire; ‹preços, inflação› shoot up; ‹corredor› surge ahead

disparate /dʒispa'ratʃi/ m piece of nonsense; pl nonsense

dis|pêndio /dʒis'pẽdʒiu/ m expenditure. **~pendioso** /o/ a costly

dispen|sa /dʒis'pẽsa/ f exemption. **~sar** vt (distribuir) dispense; (isentar) exempt (de from); (prescindir de) dispense with. **~sável** (pl **~sáveis**) a dispensable

dispersar /dʒisper'sar/ vt disperse; waste ‹energias› ● vi, **~se** vpr disperse

disperso /dʒis'persu/ a scattered

dispo|nibilidade /dʒisponibili'dadʒi/ f availability. **~nível** (pl **~níveis**) a available

dis|por /dʒis'por/ vt arrange ● vi **~por de** have at one's disposal. **~por-se** vpr form up ● m **ao seu ~por** at your disposal. **~posição** f (vontade) willingness; (arranjo) arrangement; (de espírito) frame of mind; (de testamento etc) provision; **à ~posição de alguém** at sb's

disposal. **~positivo** m device.
~posto a prepared, willing (**a** to)

dispu|ta /dʒis'puta/ f dispute.
~tar vt dispute; (*tentar ganhar*)
compete for

disquete /dʒis'ketʃi/ m diskette,
floppy (disk)

dissabores /dʒisa'boris/ m pl
troubles

disseminar /dʒisemi'nar/ vt
disseminate

dissertação /dʒiserta'sãw/ f
dissertation, lecture

dissi|dência /dʒisi'dẽsia/ f
dissidence. **~dente** a & m dissident

dissídio /dʒi'sidʒiu/ m dispute

dissimular /dʒisimu'lar/ vt hide
● vi dissimulate

dissipar /dʒisi'par/ vt clear
‹*nevoeiro*›; dispel ‹*dúvidas,
suspeitas, ilusões*›; dissipate
‹*fortuna*›. **~-se** vpr ‹*nevoeiro*› clear;
‹*dúvidas etc*› be dispelled

disso = de + isso

dissolu|ção /dʒisolu'sãw/ f
dissolution. **~to** a dissolute

dissolver /dʒisow'ver/ vt dissolve.
~se vpr dissolve

dissuadir /dʒisua'dʒir/ vt dissuade
(**de** from)

distância /dʒis'tãsia/ f distance

distan|ciar /dʒistãsi'ar/ vt
distance. **~ciar-se** vpr distance o.s..
~te a distant

disten|der /dʒistẽ'der/ vt stretch
‹*pernas*›; relax ‹*músculo*›. **~der-se**
vpr relax. **~são** f Med pull; **~são
muscular** pulled muscle

distin|ção /dʒistʃi'sãw/ f
distinction. **~guir** vt distinguish (**de**
from). **~guir-se** vpr distinguish o.s..
~tivo a distinctive ● m badge. **~to** a
distinct; ‹*senhor*› distinguished

disto = de + isto

distor|ção /dʒistor'sãw/ f
distortion. **~cer** vt distort

distra|ção /dʒistra'sãw/ f
distraction. **~ído** a absent-minded.
~ir vt distract; (*divertir*) amuse.
~ir-se vpr be distracted; (*divertir-se*)
amuse o.s.

distribu|ição /dʒistribui'sãw/
f distribution. **~idor** m distributor.
~idora f distributor, distribution
company. **~ir** vt distribute

distrito /dʒis'tritu/ m district

distúrbio /dʒis'turbiu/ m trouble

di|tado /dʒi'tadu/ m dictation;
(*provérbio*) saying. **~tador** m
dictator. **~tadura** f dictatorship.
~tame m dictate. **~tar** vt dictate.
~tatorial (*pl* **~tatoriais**) a dictatorial

dito /'dʒitu/ a ~ **e feito** no sooner
said than done ● m remark

ditongo /dʒi'tõgu/ m diphthong

DIU /'dʒiu/ m IUD, coil

diurno /dʒi'urnu/ a day

divã /dʒi'vã/ m couch

divagar /dʒiva'gar/ vi digress

diver|gência /dʒiver'ʒẽsia/ a
divergence. **~gente** a divergent.
~gir vi diverge (**de** from).
~são f diversion; (*divertimento*)
amusement. **~sidade** f diversity.
~sificar vt/i diversify. **~so** /ɛ/ a
(*diferente*) diverse; (*pl* (*vários*) several.
~tido a (*engraçado*) funny; (*que
se curte*) enjoyable. **~timento** m
enjoyment, fun; (*um*) amusement.
~tir vt amuse. **~tir-se** vpr enjoy o.s.,
have fun

dívida /'dʒivida/ f debt; **~ externa**
foreign debt

divi|dendo /dʒivi'dẽdu/ m
dividend. **~dido** a (*pessoa*) torn.

~dir vt divide; (compartilhar) share. **~dir-se** vpr be divided

divindade /dʒivĩˈdadʒi/ f divinity

divino /dʒiˈvinu/ a divine

divi|sa /dʒiˈviza/ f (lema) motto; (galão) stripes; (fronteira) border; pl foreign currency. **~são** f division. **~sória** f partition

divorci|ado /dʒivorsiˈadu/ a divorced ● m divorcé (f divorcée). **~ar** vt divorce; **~ar-se** vpr get divorced; **~ar-se de** divorce

divórcio /dʒiˈvɔrsiu/ m divorce

divul|gado /dʒivuwˈgadu/ a widespread. **~gar** vt spread; publish <notícia>; divulge <segredo>. **~gar-se** vpr be spread

dizer /dʒiˈzer/ vt say; **~ a alguém que** tell sb that; **~ para alguém fazer** tell sb to do ● vi **~ com** go with. **~se** vpr claim to be ● m saying

dizimar /dʒiziˈmar/ vt decimate

do ▶ DE + o

dó /dɔ/ m pity; **dar ~** be pitiful; **ter ~ de** feel sorry for

do|ação /doaˈsãw/ f donation. **~ador** m donor. **~ar** vt donate

do|bra /ˈdɔbra/ f fold; (de calça) turn-up, Amer cuff. **~bradiça** f hinge. **~bradiço** a pliable. **~brado** a (duplo) double. **~brar** vt (duplicar) double; (fazer dobra em) fold; (curvar) bend; go round <esquina>; ring <sinos>; Port dub <filme> ● vi double; <sinos> ring. **~brar-se** vpr bend. **~bro** m double

doca /ˈdɔka/ f dock

doce /ˈdosi/ a sweet; <água> fresh ● m sweet; **~ de leite** fudge

docente /doˈsẽtʃi/ a teaching; **corpo ~** teaching staff, Amer faculty

dócil /ˈdɔsiw/ a (pl **~ceis**) a docile

documen|tação /dokumẽtaˈsãw/ f documentation. **~tar** vt document. **~tário** a & m documentary. **~to** m document

doçura /doˈsura/ f sweetness

dodói /doˈdɔj/ 🗓 m ter **~** have a pain ● a poorly, ill

doen|ça /doˈẽsa/ f illness; (infecciosa) fig disease; **~ da vaca louca** mad cow disease. **~te** a ill. **~tio** a <criança, aspecto> sickly; <interesse, curiosidade> morbid

doer /doˈer/ vi hurt; <cabeça, músculo> ache

dog|ma /ˈdɔgima/ m dogma. **~mático** a dogmatic

doido /ˈdojdu/ a crazy

dois /dojs/ a & m (f **duas**) two

dólar /ˈdɔlar/ m dollar

dolo|rido /doloˈridu/ a sore. **~roso** /o/ a painful

dom /dõ/ m gift

do|mador /domaˈdor/ m tamer. **~mar** vt tame

doméstica /doˈmɛstʃika/ f housemaid

domesticar /domestʃiˈkar/ vt domesticate

doméstico /doˈmɛstʃiku/ a domestic

domi|ciliar /domisiliˈar/ a home. **~cílio** m home

domi|nação /dominaˈsãw/ f domination. **~nador** a domineering. **~nante** a dominant. **~nar** vt dominate; have a command of <língua>; **~nar-se** vpr control o.s.

domin|go /doˈmĩgu/ m Sunday. **~gueiro** a Sunday

domini|cal /dominiˈkaw/ (pl **~cais**) a Sunday. **~cano** a & m Dominican

domínio /do'miniu/ *m* command

dona /'dona/ *f* owner; **D~** (*com nome*) Miss. **~ de casa** housewife

donativo /dona'tʃivu/ *m* donation

donde /'dõdʒi/ *adv* from where; (*motivo*) from whence

dono /'donu/ *m* owner

donut /'donut/ *m* doughnut

donzela /dõ'zɛla/ *f* maiden

dopar /do'par/ *vt* drug

dor /dor/ *f* pain; (*menos aguda*) ache; **~ de cabeça** headache

dor|mente /dor'mẽtʃi/ *a* numb ● *m* sleeper. **~mida** *f* sleep. **~minhoco** /o/ *m* sleepyhead. **~mir** *vi* sleep. **~mitar** *vi* doze. **~mitório** *m* bedroom; (*comunitário*) dormitory

dorso /'dorsu/ *m* back; (*de livro*) spine

dos = de + os

do|sagem /do'zaʒẽ/ *f* dosage. **~sar** *vt* moderate. **~se** /ɔ/ *f* dose; (*de uísque etc*) shot, measure

dossiê /dosi'e/ *m* file

do|tado /dota'sãw/ *a* gifted; **~tado de** endowed with. **~tar** *vt* endow (**de** with). **~te** /ɔ/ *m* (*de noiva*) dowry; (*dom*) endowment

dou|rado /do'radu/ *a* (*de cor*) golden; (*revestido de ouro*) gilded, gilt ● *m* gilt. **~rar** *vt* gild

dou|to /'dotu/ *a* learned. **~tor** *m* doctor. **~torado** *m* doctorate, PhD. **~trina** *f* doctrine. **~trinar** *vt* indoctrinate

doutoramento /dotora'mẽtu/ *m* PhD

doze /'dozi/ *a* & *m* twelve

dragão /dra'gãw/ *m* dragon

dragar /dra'gar/ *vt* dredge

drágea /'draʒia/ *f* lozenge

dra|ma /'drama/ *m* drama. **~malhão** *m* melodrama. **~mático** *a* dramatic. **~matizar** *vt* dramatize. **~maturgo** *m* dramatist, playwright

drapeado /drapi'adu/ *a* draped

drástico /'drastʃiku/ *a* drastic

dre|nagem /dre'naʒẽ/ *f* drainage. **~nar** *vt* drain. **~no** /ɛ/ *m* drain

driblar /dri'blar/ *vt* (*em futebol*) dribble round, beat; *fig* get round

drinque /'drĩki/ *m* drink

drive /'drajvi/ *m* disk drive

dro|ga /'drɔga/ *f* drug; 🇵🇹 (*coisa sem valor*) dead loss; (*coisa chata*) drag ● *int* damn. **~gado** *a* on drugs ● *m* drug addict. **~gar** *vt* drug. **~gar-se** *vpr* take drugs. **~garia** *f* dispensing chemist's, pharmacy

duas /'duas/, ▶ **DOIS**

dúbio /'dubiu/ *a* dubious

dub|lagem /du'blaʒẽ/ *f* dubbing. **~lar** *vt* dub ‹*filme*›; mime ‹*música*›. **~lê** *m* double

ducentésimo /dusẽ'tezimu/ *a* two-hundredth

ducha /'duʃa/ *f* shower

duche /'duʃe/ *m* Port shower

ducto /'duktu/ *m* duct

duelo /du'ɛlu/ *m* duel

dueto /du'etu/ *m* duet

duna /'duna/ *f* dune

duodécimo /duo'desimu/ *a* twelfth

duodeno /duo'denu/ *m* duodenum

dupla /'dupla/ *f* pair, duo; ‹*no tênis*› doubles

duplex /du'plɛks/ *a invar* two-floor ● *m invar* two-floor apartment, *Amer* duplex

dupli|car /dupli'kar/ *vt/i* double. **~cidade** *f* duplicity. **~cata** *f* duplicate

duplo /'duplu/ *a* double

duque /'duki/ *m* duke. **~sa** /e/ *f* duchess

du|ração /dura'sãw/ *f* duration. **~radouro** *a* lasting. **~rante** *prep* during. **~rar** *vi* last. **~rável** (*pl* **~ráveis**) *a* durable

durex® /du'rɛks/ *m invar* Sellotape®

du|reza /du'reza/ *f* hardness. **~ro** *a* hard; **[2]** (*sem dinheiro*) hard up, broke

dúvida /'duvida/ *f* doubt; (*pergunta*) query

duvi|dar /duvi'dar/ *vt/i* doubt. **~doso** /o/ *a* doubtful

duzentos /du'zẽtus/ *a* & *m* two hundred

dúzia /'duzia/ *f* dozen

DVD /deve'de/ *m* DVD; **gravador de ~** DVD burner; **leitor de ~** DVD player

....

Ee

....

e /i/ *conj* and

ébano /'ɛbanu/ *m* ebony

ébrio /'ɛbriu/ *a* drunk ● *m* drunkard

ebulição /ebuli'sãw/ *f* boiling

eclesiástico /eklezi'astʃiku/ *a* ecclesiastical

eclético /e'klɛtʃiku/ *a* eclectic

eclip|sar /eklip'sar/ *vt* eclipse. **~se** *m* eclipse

eclodir /eklo'dʒir/ *vi* emerge; (*estourar*) break out; <*flor*> open

eco /'ɛku/ *m* echo; **ter ~** have repercussions. **~ar** *vt/i* echo

ecografia /ekogra'fia/ *f* ultrasound (scan)

eco|logia /ekolo'ʒia/ *f* ecology. **~lógico** /eko'lɔʒiku/ *a* ecological; **grupo ~lógico** environmental group. **~logista** *m/f* ecologist

eco|nomia /ekono'mia/ *f* economy; (*ciência*) economics; *pl* (*dinheiro poupado*) savings. **~nômico** *a* economic; (*rentável, barato*) economical. **~nomista** *m/f* economist. **~nomizar** *vt* save ● *vi* economize

ecoponto /eko'põtu/ *m* Port recycling point

ecossistema /ekosiʃ'tema/ *m* ecosystem

écran /ɛ'krã/ Port *m* screen

eczema /ek'zema/ *m* eczema

edição /edʒi'sãw/ *f* edition; (*de filmes*) editing

edificante /edʒifi'kãtʃi/ *a* edifying

edifício /edʒi'fisiu/ *m* building

Edimburgo /edʒĩ'burgu/ *f* Edinburgh

edi|tal /edʒi'taw/ (*pl* **~tais**) *m* announcement. **~tar** *vt* publish; Comput edit. **~to** *m* edict. **~tor** *m* publisher. **~tora** *f* publishing company. **~torial** (*pl* **~toriais**) *a* publishing ● *m* editorial

edredom /edre'dõ/ *m*, Port **edredão** /edre'dãw/ *m* quilt

educa|ção /eduka'sãw/ *f* (*ensino*) education; (*polidez*) good manners; **é falta de ~ção** it's rude. **~cional** (*pl* **~cionais**) *a* education

edu|cado /edu'kadu/ *a* polite. **~car** *vt* educate. **~cativo** *a* educational

EEB /ee'be/ *f* BSE

efeito /e'fejtu/ *m* effect; **fazer ~** have an effect; **para todos os ~s** to all intents and purposes; **~ colateral** side effect; **~ estufa** greenhouse effect

efémero /e'fɛmeru/ *a* ephemeral

efeminado /efemi'nadu/ *a* effeminate

efervescente /eferve'sẽtʃi/ *a* effervescent

efe|tivar /efetʃi'var/ *vt* bring into effect; (*contratar*) make a permanent member of staff. **~tivo** *a* real, effective; ‹*cargo, empregado*› permanent. **~tuar** *vt* carry out, effect

efi|cácia /efi'kasia/ *f* effectiveness. **~caz** *a* effective

efici|ência /efisi'ẽsia/ *f* efficiency. **~ente** *a* efficient

efígie /e'fiʒi/ *f* effigy

Egeu /e'ʒew/ *a & m* Aegean

égide /'ɛʒidʒi/ *f* aegis

egípcio /e'ʒipsiu/ *a & m* Egyptian

Egito /e'ʒitu/ *m* Egypt

ego /'ɛgu/ *m* ego. **~cêntrico** *a* self-centred, egocentric. **~ísmo** *m* selfishness. **~ísta** *a* selfish ● *m/f* egoist ● *m* (*de rádio etc*) earplug

égua /'ɛgwa/ *f* mare

eis /ejs/ *adv* (*aqui está*) here is/are; (*isso é*) that is

eixo /'ejʃu/ *m* axle; *Mat* (*entre cidades*) axis; **pôr nos ~s** set straight

ela /'ɛla/ ● *pron*

••••▸ (*pessoa*) she; **~ e Catarina são primas** she and Catarina are cousins; (*complemento, em comparações*) her; **é para ~** it's for her; **você é mais alto do que**

~ you're taller than her; (*coisa*) it; **~ mesma** (she) herself

elaborar /elabo'rar/ *vt* (*fazer*) make, produce; (*desenvolver*) work out

elasticidade /elastʃisi'dadʒi/ *f* (*de coisa*) elasticity; (*de pessoa*) suppleness

elástico /e'lastʃiku/ *a* elastic ● *m* (*de borracha*) elastic band; (*de calcinha etc*) elastic

ele /'eli/ ● *pron*

••••▸ (*pessoa*) he; **~ e José são primos** he and José are cousins; **~ é um rapaz simpático** he's a nice boy; (*complemento, em comparações*) him; **é para ~** it's for him; **você é mais alto do que ~** you're taller than him; (*coisa*) it; **~ mesmo** (he) himself

elefante /ele'fãtʃi/ *m* elephant

ele|gância /ele'gãsia/ *f* elegance. **~gante** *a* elegant

eleger /ele'ʒer/ *vt* elect. **~-se** *vpr* get elected

elegia /ele'ʒia/ *f* elegy

elei|ção /elej'sãw/ *f* election. **~to** *a* elected, elect; ‹*povo*› chosen. **~tor** *m* voter. **~torado** *m* electorate. **~toral** (*pl* **~torais**) *a* electoral

elemen|tar /elemẽ'tar/ *a* elementary. **~to** *m* element

elenco /e'lẽku/ *m* (*de filme, peça*) cast

eles /'elis/, **elas** /'ɛlas/ ● *pron*

••••▸ (*sujeito*) they; (*complemento, em comparações*) them; **isto é para eles** this is for them

·····► (*em expressões*) **agora é que são elas!** now comes the difficult part!; **elas por elas: o plano do governo deu elas por elas** the government's plan made no difference

eletri|cidade /eletrisi'dadʒi/ f electricity. **~cista** m/f electrician

elétrico /i'lektriku/ *Port* m tram, *Amer* streetcar ● a electric

eletri|ficar /eletrifi'kar/ vt electrify. **~zar** vt electrify

eletro /e'letru/ m ECG. **~cutar** vt electrocute. **~do** /o/ m electrode. **~domésticos** m pl electrical appliances

eletrôni|ca /ele'tronika/ f electronics. **~co** a electronic

ele|vação /eleva'sãw/ f elevation; (*aumento*) rise. **~vado** a high; ‹*sentimento, estilo*› elevated. **~vador** m lift, *Amer* elevator. **~var** vt raise; (*promover*) elevate. **~var-se** vpr rise

elimi|nar /elimi'nar/ vt eliminate. **~natória** f heat. **~natório** a eliminatory

elipse /e'lipsi/ f ellipse

elíptico /e'liptʃiku/ a elliptical

eli|te /e'litʃi/ f elite. **~tismo** m elitism. **~tista** a & m/f elitist

elmo /'ɛwmu/ m helmet

elo /'ɛlu/ m link

elo|giar /eloʒi'ar/ vt praise; **~giar alguém por** compliment sb on. **~gio** m (*louvor*) praise; (*um*) compliment. **~gioso** /o/ a complimentary

elo|quência /elo'kwẽsia/ f eloquence. **~quente** a eloquent

eluci|dar /elusi'dar/ vt elucidate. **~dativo** a elucidatory

em /ẽj/ prep in; (*sobre*) on; **ela está no Eduardo** she's at Eduardo's (house); **de casa ~ casa** from house to house; **aumentar ~ 10%** increase by 10%

emagre|cer /emagre'ser/ vi lose weight, get thinner ● vt make thinner. **~cimento** m slimming

emanar /ema'nar/ vi emanate (**de** from)

emanci|pação /emãsipa'sãw/ f emancipation. **~par** vt emancipate. **~par-se** vpr become emancipated

emara|nhado /emara'ɲadu/ a tangled ● m tangle. **~nhar** vt tangle; (*envolver*) entangle. **~nhar-se** vpr get tangled up; (*envolver-se*) become entangled (**em** in)

embacar /ĩba'sar/, *Port* **embaciar** /ĩbasi'ar/ vt steam up ‹*vidro*› ● vi ‹*vidro*› steam up; ‹*olhos*› grow misty

embainhar /ĩbaj'ɲar/ vt hem ‹*vestido*›

embaixa|da /ĩba'ʃada/ f embassy. **~dor** m ambassador. **~triz** f ambassador; (*esposa*) ambassador's wife

embaixo /ĩ'baʃu/ adv underneath; (*em casa*) downstairs; **~ de** under

emba|lagem /ĩba'laʒẽ/ f packaging

emba|lar /ĩba'lar/ vt pack; (*move back and forth*) rock ‹*criança*›. **~lo** m fig excitement, thrill

embalsamar /ĩbawsa'mar/ vt embalm

embara|çar /ĩbara'sar/ vt embarrass. **~çar-se** vpr get embarrassed (**com** by). **~ço** m embarrassment. **~çoso** /o/ a embarrassing

embaralhar /ĩbara'ʎar/ vt muddle up; shuffle ‹cartas›. **~se** vpr get muddled up

embarcação /ĩbarka'sãw/ f vessel. **~cadouro** m wharf. **~car** vt/i board, embark

embargado /ĩbar'gadu/ a ‹voz› faltering. **~go** m embargo

embarque /ĩ'barki/ m boarding; (seção do aeroporto) departures

embasbacado /ĩbazba'kadu/ a open-mouthed. **~car-se** vpr be left open-mouthed

embate /ĩ'batʃi/ m (de carros etc) crash; fig clash

embebedar /ĩbebe'dar/ vt make drunk. **~se** vpr get drunk

embeber /ĩbe'ber/ vt soak; **~se de** soak up; **~se em** get absorbed in

embelezador /ĩbeleza'dor/ a ‹cirurgia› cosmetic. **~zar** vt embellish; spruce up ‹casa›. **~zar-se** vpr make o.s. beautiful

embevecer /ĩbeve'ser/ vt captivate, engross. **~se** vpr get engrossed, be captivated

emblema /ĩ'blema/ m emblem

embocadura /ĩboka'dura/ f (de instrumento) mouthpiece; (de freio) bit; (de rio) mouth; (de rua) entrance

êmbolo /'ẽbulu/ m piston

embolsar /ĩbow'sar/ vt pocket; (reembolsar) reimburse

embora /ĩ'bɔra/ adv away ● conj although

emborcar /ĩbor'kar/ vi overturn; ‹barco› capsize

emboscada /ĩbos'kada/ f ambush

embraiagem /ĩbraj'aʒẽ/ Port f ▶ EMBREAGEM. **~ar** Port vi ▶ EMBREAR

embreagem /ẽbri'aʒẽ/ f clutch. **~ar** vi let in the clutch

embriagar /ẽbria'gar/ vt intoxicate. **~gar-se** vpr get drunk, become intoxicated. **~guez** /e/ f drunkenness; **~guez no volante** drunken driving

embrião /ẽbri'ãw/ m embryo. **~onário** a embryonic

embromação /ẽbroma'sãw/ f flannel. **~mar** vt flannel, string along; (enganar) con ● vi stall, drag one's feet

embrulhada /ẽbru'ʎada/ f muddle. **~lhar** vt wrap up ‹pacote›; upset ‹estômago›; (confundir) muddle up. **~lhar-se** vpr ‹pessoa› get muddled up. **~lho** m parcel; fig mix-up

emburrado /ĩbu'xadu/ a sulky. **~rar** vi sulk

embuste /ĩ'bustʃi/ m hoax, put-up job

embutido /ĩbu'tʃidu/ a built-in, fitted. **~tir** vt build in, fit

emenda /e'mẽda/ f correction, improvement; (de lei) amendment. **~dar** vt correct; amend ‹lei›. **~dar-se** vpr mend one's ways

ementa /i'mẽta/ Port f menu

emergência /emer'ʒẽsia/ f emergency. **~gente** a emergent. **~gir** vi surface

emigração /emigra'sãw/ f emigration; (de aves etc) migration. **~grado** a & m émigré. **~grante** a & m/f emigrant. **~grar** vi emigrate; ‹aves, animais› migrate

eminência /emi'nẽsia/ f eminence. **~nente** a eminent

emissão /emi'sãw/ f (de ações etc) issue; (na rádio, TV) transmission, broadcast; (de som, gases) emission.

~sário *m* emissary. **~sor** *m* transmitter. **~sora** f (*de rádio*) radio station; (*de TV*) TV station

emitir /emi't∫ir/ *vt* issue ‹ações, selos etc›; emit ‹sons›; (*pela rádio, TV*) transmit, broadcast

emoção /emo'sãw/ f emotion; (*excitação*) excitement

emocio|nal /emosio'naw/ (*pl* ~nais*) a emotional. **~nante** a (*excitante*) exciting; (*comovente*) touching, emotional. **~nar** *vt* (*excitar*) excite; (*comover*) move, touch. **~nar-se** *vpr* get emotional

emoldurar /emowdu'rar/ *vt* frame

emotivo /emo't∫ivu/ a emotional

empacar /ĩpa'kar/ *vi* ‹cavalo› baulk; ‹negociações etc› grind to a halt; ‹orador› dry up

empacotar /ĩpako'tar/ *vt* pack up; (*pôr em pacotes*) packet

empa|da /ĩ'pada/ f pie. **~dão** *m* (large) pie

empalhar /ĩpa'ʎar/ *vt* stuff

empalidecer /ĩpalide'ser/ *vi* turn pale

empanar¹ /ĩpa'nar/ *vt* tarnish, dull

empanar² /ĩpa'nar/ *vt* cook in batter ‹carne etc›

empanturrar /ĩpãtu'xar/ *vt* stuff. **~se** *vpr* stuff o.s. (**de** with)

empapar /ĩpa'par/ *vt* soak

empa|tar /ĩpa'tar/ *vt* draw ‹jogo› ● *vi* ‹times› draw; ‹corredores› tie. **~te** *m* (*em jogo*) draw; (*em corrida, votação*) tie; (*em xadrez*) fig stalemate

empatia /ĩpa't∫ia/ f empathy

empecilho /ĩpe'siʎu/ *m* hindrance

empenar /ĩpe'nar/ *vt/i* warp

empe|nhar /ĩpe'nar/ *vt* (*penhorar*) pawn; (*prometer*) pledge. **~nhar-se** *vpr* do one's utmost (**em** to). **~nho** /e/ *m* (*compromisso*) pledge; (*diligência*) effort, commitment

emperrar /ĩpe'xar/ *vt* make stick ● *vi* stick

emperti|gado /ĩpert∫i'gadu/ a upright. **~gar-se** *vpr* stand up straight

empilhar /ĩpi'ʎar/ *vt* pile up

empi|nado /ĩpi'nadu/ a erect; (*íngreme*) sheer, steep; ‹nariz› turned-up; fig stuck-up. **~nar** *vt* stand upright; fly ‹pipa›; tip up ‹copo›

empírico /ĩ'piriku/ a empirical

emplacar /ĩpla'kar/ *vt* notch up ‹pontos, sucessos, anos›; license ‹carro›

emplastro /ĩ'plastru/ *m* surgical plaster; **~ de nicotina** nicotine patch

empobre|cer /ĩpobre'ser/ *vt* impoverish. **~cimento** *m* impoverishment

empoderamento /ĩpodera'mẽtu/ Port *m* empowerment

empoleirar /ĩpole'rar/ *vt* perch. **~se** *vpr* perch

empol|gação /ĩpowga'sãw/ f fascination. **~gante** a fascinating. **~gar** *vt* fascinate

empossar /ĩpo'sar/ *vt* swear in

empreen|dedor /ĩpriẽde'dor/ a enterprising ● *m* entrepreneur. **~der** *vt* undertake. **~dimento** *m* undertaking

empre|gada /ĩpre'gada/ f (*doméstica*) maid. **~gado** *m* employee. **~gador** *m* employer. **~gar** *vt* employ. **~gar-se** *vpr* get a job. **~gatício** a vínculo **~gatício** contract of employment. **~go** /e/ m (*trabalho*) job; (*uso*) use

emprei|tada /īpreiˈtada/ f commission, contract; (*empreendimento*) venture. **~teira** f contractor, firm of contractors. **~teiro** m contractor

empre|sa /īˈpreza/ f company. **~sa dot.com** dot-com. **~sariado** m business community. **~sarial** (*pl* **~sariais**) a business. **~sário** m businessman; (*de cantor etc*) manager

empres|tado /īpresˈtadu/ a on loan; **pedir ~tado** (ask to) borrow; **tomar ~tado** borrow. **~tar** vt lend

empréstimo /īˈprestʃimu/ m loan

empur|rão /īpuˈxãw/ m push. **~rar** vt push

emular /emuˈlar/ vt emulate

enamorado /enamoˈradu/ a (*apaixonado*) in love

encabeçar /īkabeˈsar/ vt head

encabu|lado /īkabuˈladu/ a shy. **~lar** vt embarrass. **~lar-se** vpr be shy

encadear /īkadeˈar/ vt chain ou link together

encader|nação /īkaderˈnasãw/ f binding. **~nado** a bound; (*com capa dura*) hardback. **~nar** vt bind

encai|xar /īkaˈʃar/ vt/i fit. **~xe** m (*cavidade*) socket; (*juntura*) joint

encalço /īˈkawsu/ m pursuit; **no ~ de** in pursuit of

encalhar /īkaˈʎar/ vi ‹*barco*› run aground; *fig* get bogged down; ‹*mercadoria*› not sell; ☐ (*ficar solteiro*) be left on the shelf

encaminhar /īkamiˈɲar/ vt (*dirigir*) steer, direct; (*remeter*) pass on; set in motion ‹*processo*›. **~se** vpr set out

encana|dor /īkanaˈdor/ m plumber. **~mento** m plumbing

encan|tador /īkãtaˈdor/ a enchanting. **~tamento** m enchantment. **~tar** vt enchant. **~to** m charm

encaraco|lado /īkarakoˈladu/ a curly. **~lar** vt curl. **~lar-se** vpr curl up

encarar /īkaˈrar/ vt confront, face

encarcerar /īkarseˈrar/ vt imprison

encardido /īkarˈdʒidu/ a grimy

encarecidamente /īkaresidaˈmētʃi/ adv insistently

encargo /īˈkargu/ m task, responsibility

encar|nação /īkarnaˈsãw/ f (*do espírito*) incarnation; (*de um personagem*) embodiment. **~nar** vt embody; play ‹*papel*›

encarre|gado /īkaxeˈgadu/ a in charge (**de** of) ● m person in charge; (*de operários*) foreman; **~gado de negócios** chargé d'affaires. **~gar** vt **~gar alguém de** put sb in charge of; **~gar-se de** undertake to

encarte /īˈkartʃi/ m insert

ence|nação /īsenaˈsãw/ f (*de peça*) production; (*fingimento*) play-acting. **~nar** vt put on ● vi put it on

ence|radeira /īseraˈdera/ f floor polisher. **~rar** vt wax

encer|rado /īseˈxadu/ a ‹*assunto*› closed. **~ramento** m close. **~rar** vt close. **~rar-se** vpr close

encharcar /īʃarˈkar/ vt soak

en|chente /ēˈʃẽtʃi/ f flood. **~cher** vt fill; ☐ annoy ● vi ☐ be annoying. **~cher-se** vpr fill up; ☐ (*fartar-se*) get fed up (**de** with)

enciclopédia /ēsikloˈpedʒia/ f encyclopaedia

enco|berto /ĩkoˈbɛrtu/ a ‹céu, tempo› overcast. ~**brir** vt cover up • vi ‹tempo› become overcast

encolher /ĩkoˈʎer/ vt shrug ‹ombros›; pull up ‹pernas›; shrink ‹roupa› • vi ‹roupa› shrink; ~**se** vpr (de medo) shrink; (de frio) huddle; (espremer-se) squeeze up

encomen|da /ĩkoˈmẽda/ f order; **de** ou **sob** ~**da** to order. ~**dar** vt order (a from)

encon|trão /ĩkõˈtrãw/ m bump; (empurrão) shove. ~**trar** vt (achar) find; (ver) meet; ~**trar com** meet. ~**trar-se** vpr (ver-se) meet; (estar) be. ~**tro** m meeting; Mil encounter; **ir ao** ~**tro de** go to meet; fig meet; **ir de** ~**tro a** run into; fig go against

encorajar /ĩkoraˈʒar/ vt encourage

encor|pado /ĩkorˈpadu/ a stocky; ‹vinho› full-bodied. ~**par** vt/i fill out

encos|ta /ĩˈkɔsta/ f slope. ~**tar** vt (apoiar) lean; park ‹carro›; leave on the latch ‹porta›; (pôr de lado) put aside • vi ‹carro› pull in. ~**tar-se** vpr lean. ~**to** /o/ m back

encrava|do /ĩkraˈvadu/ a ‹unha, pelo› ingrowing. ~**var** vt stick

encren|ca /ĩˈkrẽka/ f fix, jam; pl trouble. ~**car** vt get into trouble ‹pessoa›; complicate ‹situação› • vi ‹situação› get complicated; ‹carro› break down. ~**car-se** vpr ‹pessoa› get into trouble. ~**queiro** m troublemaker

encres|pado /ĩkresˈpadu/ a ‹mar› choppy. ~**par** vt frizz ‹cabelo›. ~**par-se** vpr ‹cabelo› go frizzy; ‹mar› get choppy

encruzilhada /ĩkruziˈʎada/ f crossroads

encurralar /ĩkuxaˈlar/ vt hem in

encurtar /ĩkurˈtar/ vt shorten

endere|çar /ĩdereˈsar/ vt address. ~**ço** /e/ m address; Comput ~**ço de e-mail** email address

endinheirado /ĩdʒiɲeˈradu/ a well-off

endireitar /ĩdʒirejˈtar/ vt straighten. ~**se** vpr straighten up

endivi|dado /ĩdʒiviˈdadu/ a in debt. ~**dar** vt put into debt. ~**dar-se** vpr get into debt

endoidecer /ĩdojdeˈser/ vi get mad

endos|sar /ĩdoˈsar/ vt endorse. ~**so** /o/ m endorsement

endurecer /ĩdureˈser/ vt/i harden

ener|gético /enerˈʒɛtʃiku/ a energy. ~**gia** /enerˈʒia/ f energy; ~**gia solar/nuclear/eólica** solar/ nuclear/wind power

enérgico /eˈnɛrʒiku/ a vigorous; ‹remédio, discurso› powerful

enevoado /enevuˈadu/ a (com névoa) misty; (com nuvens) cloudy

enfarte /ĩˈfartʃi/ m heart attack

ênfase /ˈẽfazi/ f emphasis; **dar** ~ a emphasize

enfático /ẽˈfatʃiku/ a emphatic

enfatizar /ẽfatʃiˈzar/ vt emphasize

enfei|tar /ĩfejˈtar/ vt decorate. ~**tar-se** vpr dress up. ~**te** m decoration

enfeitiçar /ĩfejtʃiˈsar/ vt bewitch

enfer|magem /ĩferˈmaʒẽ/ f nursing. ~**maria** f ward. ~**meira** f nurse. ~**meiro** m male nurse. ~**midade** f illness. ~**mo** a sick • m patient

enferru|jado /ĩfexuˈʒadu/ a rusty. ~**jar** vt/i rust

enfezado /ĩfeˈzadu/ a bad-tempered

enfiar /ẽfiˈar/ vt put; slip on ‹roupa›; thread ‹agulha›; string ‹pérolas›

enfileirar /ĩfilejˈrar/ vt line up. **~se** vpr line up

enfim /ẽˈfĩ/ adv (finalmente) finally; (resumindo) anyway

enfo|car /ĩfoˈkar/ vt tackle. **~que** m approach

enfor|camento /ĩforkaˈmẽtu/ m hanging. **~car** vt hang. **~car-se** vpr hang o.s.

enfraquecer /ĩfrakeˈser/ vt/i weaken

enfrentar /ĩfrẽˈtar/ vt face

enfumaçado /ĩfumaˈsadu/ a smoky

enfurecer /ĩfureˈser/ vt infuriate. **~se** vpr get furious

enga|jamento /ĩgaʒaˈmẽtu/ m commitment. **~jado** a committed. **~jar-se** vpr get involved (**em** in)

engalfinhar-se /ĩgawfiˈɲarsi/ vpr grapple

enga|nado /ĩgaˈnadu/ a (errado) mistaken. **~nar** vt deceive; cheat on ‹marido, esposa›; stave off ‹fome›. **~nar-se** vpr be mistaken. **~no** m (erro) mistake; (desonestidade) deception

engarra|famento /ĩgaxafaˈmẽtu/ m traffic jam. **~far** vt bottle ‹vinho etc›; block ‹trânsito›

engas|gar /ĩgazˈgar/ vt choke ● vi choke; ‹motor› backfire. **~go** m choking

engastar /ĩgaʃˈtar/ vt set ‹joias›

engatar /ĩgaˈtar/ vt hitch ‹reboque etc› (**a** to); engage ‹marcha›

engatinhar /ĩgatʃiˈɲar/ vi crawl; fig start out

engave|tamento /ĩgavetaˈmẽtu/ m pile-up. **~tar** vt shelve

engelhar /ĩʒeˈʎar/ vi (pele) wrinkle

enge|nharia /ĩʒeɲaˈria/ f engineering. **~nheiro** /e/ m engineer. **~nho** /e/ m (de pessoa) ingenuity; (de açúcar) sugar mill; (máquina) device. **~nhoca** /ɔ/ f gadget. **~nhoso** a ingenious

engessar /ĩʒeˈsar/ vt put in plaster

engodo /ĩˈgodu/ m lure

engolir /ĩgoˈlir/ vt/i swallow; **~ em seco** gulp

engomar /ĩgoˈmar/ vt press; (com goma) starch

engonhar /ĩgoˈɲar/ vi Port faff about ou around

engordar /ĩgorˈdar/ vt make fat; fatten ‹animais› ● vi ‹pessoa› put on weight; ‹comida› be fattening

engraçado /ĩgraˈsadu/ a funny

engradado /ĩgraˈdadu/ m crate

engravidar /ĩgraviˈdar/ vt make pregnant ● vi get pregnant

engraxar /ĩgraˈʃar/ vt polish

engre|nado /ĩgreˈnadu/ a ‹carro› in gear. **~nagem** f gear; fig mechanism. **~nar** vt put into gear ‹carro›; strike up ‹conversa›. **~nar-se** vpr mesh; fig ‹pessoas› get on

engrossar /ĩgroˈsar/ vt thicken; raise ‹voz› ● vi thicken; ‹pessoa› turn nasty

enguia /ĩˈgia/ f eel

engui|çar /ĩgiˈsar/ vi break down. **~ço** m breakdown

enigma /eˈnigma/ m enigma. **~mático** a enigmatic

enjaular /ĩʒawˈlar/ vt cage

enjo|ar /ĩʒoˈar/ vt sicken ● vi, **~ar-se** vpr get sick (**de** of). **~ativo** a ‹comida› sickly; ‹livro etc› boring

enjoo /ĩˈʒou/ m sickness

enlameado /ĩlami'adu/ a muddy

enlatado /ĩla'tadu/ a tinned, canned. **~s** m pl tinned foods

enle|var /ĩle'var/ vt enthral. **~vo** /e/ m rapture

enlouquecer /ĩloke'ser/ vt drive mad ● vi go mad

enluarado /ĩlua'radu/ a moonlit

enor|me /e'nɔrmi/ a enormous. **~midade** f enormity

enquadrar /ĩkwa'drar/ vt fit ● vi, **~se** vpr fit in

enquanto /ĩ'kwãtu/ conj while; **~ isso** meanwhile; **por ~** for the time being

enquete /ã'ketʃi/ f survey

enraivecer /ĩxajve'ser/ vt enrage

enredo /ĩ'redu/ m plot

enrijecer /ĩxiʒe'ser/ vt stiffen. **~se** vpr stiffen

enrique|cer /ĩxike'ser/ vt (dar dinheiro a) make rich; fig enrich ● vi get rich. **~cimento** m enrichment

enro|lado /ĩxo'ladu/ a complicated. **~lar** vt (envolver) roll up; (complicar) complicate; (enganar) cheat. **~lar-se** vpr (envolver-se) roll up; (confundir-se) get mixed up

enroscar /ĩxos'kar/ vt twist

enrouquecer /ĩxoke'ser/ vi go hoarse

enrugar /ĩxu'gar/ vt wrinkle ‹pele, tecido›; furrow ‹testa›

enrustido /ĩxus'tʃidu/ a repressed

ensaboar /ĩsabo'ar/ vt soap

ensai|ar /ĩsaj'ar/ vt (provar) try out; (repetir) rehearse. **~o** m (prova) test; (repetição) rehearsal; (escrito) essay

ensanguentado /ĩsãgwẽ'tadu/ a bloody, bloodstained

enseada /ĩsi'ada/ f inlet

ensebado /ĩse'badu/ a greasy

ensimesmado /ĩsimez'madu/ a lost in thought

ensi|nar /ĩsi'nar/ vt/i teach (algo a alguém sb sth); **~nar alguém a nadar** teach sb to swim. **~no** m teaching; (em geral) education

ensolarado /ĩsola'radu/ a sunny

enso|pado /ĩso'padu/ a soaked ● m stew. **~par** vt soak

ensurde|cedor /ĩsurdese'dor/ a deafening. **~cer** vt deafen ● vi go deaf

entabular /ĩtabu'lar/ vt open, start

entalar /ĩta'lar/ vt wedge, jam; (em apertos) get. **~se** vpr get wedged, get jammed; (em apertos) get caught up

entalhar /ĩta'ʎar/ vt carve

entanto /ĩ'tãtu/ m no **~** however

---

então /ĩ'tãw/ ● adv

••••▶ (aquela época) desde **~** since then; **fui no casamento do Pedro e não o vejo desde ~** I went to Pedro's wedding and I haven't seen him since

••••▶ (naquele tempo) at that time; **~ era mais magro** I was thinner at that time

••••▶ (por isso) so; **eles não vinham, ~ fui embora** they didn't come, so I left

● int

••••▶ (para animar) **~, anime-se!** come on, cheer up!

••••▶ (para chamar a atenção) **~, o que você pensa que está fazendo?!** hey, what do you think you're doing?!

(em expressões) **e ~?...** (não dar importância) so what?;

(*para saber informação extra*) so, what happened then?

entardecer /ĩtarde'ser/ *m* sunset

ente /'ẽtʃi/ *m* being

entea|da /ẽtʃi'ada/ *f* stepdaughter. **~do** *m* stepson

entedi|ante /ĩtedʒi'ãtʃi/ *a* boring. **~ar** *vt* bore. **~ar-se** *vpr* get bored

enten|der /ĩtẽ'der/ *vt* understand; **dar a ~der** give to understand; **~der de futebol** know about football. **~der-se** *vpr* (*dar-se bem*) get on (**com** with). **~dimento** *m* understanding

enternecedor /ĩternese'dor/ *a* touching

enter|rar /ĩte'xar/ *vt* bury. **~ro** /e/ *m* burial; (*cerimônia*) funeral

entidade /ẽtʃi'dadʒi/ *f* entity; (*órgão*) body

entornar /ĩtor'nar/ *vt* tip over, spill

entorpe|cente /ĩtorpe'sẽtʃi/ *m* drug, narcotic. **~cer** *vt* numb

entortar /ĩtor'tar/ *vt* make crooked

entrada /ẽ'trada/ *f* entry; (*onde se entra*) entrance; (*bilhete*) ticket; (*prato*) starter; (*pagamento*) deposit; *pl* (*no cabelo*) receding hairline; **dar ~ a** enter; **~ proibida** no entry

entranhas /ĩ'traɲas/ *f pl* entrails

entrar /ẽ'trar/ *vi* go/come in; **~ com** enter <*dados*>; put in <*dinheiro*>; **~ em detalhes** go into details; **~ em vigor** come into force

entravar /ẽtra'var/ *vt* hamper

entre /'ẽtri/ *prep* between; (*em meio a*) among

entreaberto /ẽtria'bertu/ *a* half-open

entrecortar /ẽtrikor'tar/ *vt* intersperse; (*cruzar*) intersect

entre|ga /ĩ'trega/ *f* delivery; (*rendição*) surrender; **~ga a domicílio** home delivery. **~gar** *vt* hand over; deliver <*mercadorias, cartas*>; hand in <*caderno, trabalho escolar*>. **~gar-se** *vpr* give o.s. up (**a** to). **~gue** *pp de* ▶ ENTREGAR

entrelaçar /ẽtrela'sar/ *vt* intertwine; clasp <*mãos*>

entrelinhas /ẽtri'liɲas/ *f pl* **ler nas ~** read between the lines

entremear /ẽtrimi'ar/ *vt* intersperse

entreolhar-se /ẽtrio'ʎarsi/ *vpr* look at one another

entretanto /ẽtre'tãtu/ *conj* however

entre|tenimento /ẽtreteni'mẽtu/ *m* entertainment. **~ter** *vt* entertain

entrever /ẽtre'ver/ *vt* glimpse

entrevis|ta /ẽtre'vista/ *f* interview. **~tador** *m* interviewer. **~tar** *vt* interview

entristecer /ĩtriste'ser/ *vt* sadden ● *vi* be saddened (**com** by)

entroncamento /ĩtrõka'mẽtu/ *m* junction

entrosar /ĩtro'zar/ *vt/i* integrate

entu|lhar /ĩtu'ʎar/ *vt* cram (**de** with). **~lho** *m* rubble

entupir /ĩtu'pir/ *vt* block. **~pir-se** *vpr* get blocked; (*de comida*) stuff o.s. (**de** with)

enturmar-se /ĩtur'marsi/ *vpr* mix in, fit in

entusias|mar /ĩtuziaz'mar/ *vt* fill with enthusiasm. **~mar-se** *vpr* get enthusiastic (**com** about). **~mo** *m* enthusiasm. **~ta** *m/f* enthusiast ● *a* enthusiastic

entusiástico /ĩtuzi'astʃiku/ *a* enthusiastic

enumerar /enumeˈrar/ vt
enumerate

envelhecer /ĩveʎeˈser/ vt/i age

envelope /ẽveˈlɔpi/ m envelope

envenenar /ĩveneˈnar/ vt poison;
⚡ soup up ‹carro›

envergadura /ĩvergaˈdura/ f
wingspan; fig scale

envergo|nhado /ĩvergoˈɲadu/
a ashamed; (constrangido)
embarrassed. **~nhar** vt disgrace;
(constranger) embarrass. **~nhar-se**
vpr be ashamed; (acanhar-se) get
embarrassed

envernizar /ĩverniˈzar/ vt varnish

en|viado /ẽviˈadu/ m envoy. **~viar**
vt send. **~vio** m (ato) sending;
(remessa) consignment

envidraçar /ĩvidraˈsar/ vt glaze

enviesado /ĩvieˈzadu/ a (não
vertical) slanting; (torto) crooked

envol|vente /ĩvowˈvẽtʃi/ a
compelling, gripping. **~ver** vt
(embrulhar) wrap; (enredar) involve.
~ver-se vpr (enrolar-se) wrap o.s.;
(enredar-se) get involved. **~vimento**
m involvement

enxada /ẽˈʃada/ f hoe

enxaguar /ẽʃaˈgwar/ vt rinse

enxame /ẽˈʃami/ m swarm

enxaqueca /ẽʃaˈkeka/ f migraine

enxergar /ẽʃerˈgar/ vt/i see

enxer|tar /ẽʃerˈtar/ vt graft. **~to**
/e/ m graft

enxofre /ẽˈʃofri/ m sulphur

enxotar /ẽʃoˈtar/ vt drive away

enxo|val /ẽʃoˈvaw/ (pl **~vais**) m (de
noiva) trousseau; (de bebê) layette

enxugar /ĩʃuˈgar/ vt dry. **~se** vpr
dry o.s.

enxurrada /ĩʃuˈxada/ f torrent;
fig flood

enxuto /ĩˈʃutu/ a dry; ‹corpo›
shapely

enzima /ẽˈzima/ f enzyme

epicentro /epiˈsẽtru/ m epicentre

épico /ˈɛpiku/ a epic

epidemia /epideˈmia/ f epidemic

epi|lepsia /epilepˈsia/ f epilepsy.
~léptico a & m epileptic

epílogo /eˈpilogu/ m epilogue

episódio /epiˈzɔdʒiu/ m episode

epitáfio /epiˈtafiu/ m epitaph

época /ˈɛpoca/ f time; (da história)
age, period; **fazer ~** make history;
móveis da ~ period furniture

epopeia /epoˈpeja/ f epic

equação /ekwaˈsãw/ f equation

equador /ekwaˈdor/ m equator;
o **E~** Ecuador

equatori|al /ekwatoriˈaw/ (pl
~ais) a equatorial. **~ano** a & m
Ecuadorian

equilibrar /ekiliˈbrar/ vt balance.
~se vpr balance

equilíbrio /ekiˈlibriu/ m balance

equipa /eˈkipa/ Port f team

equi|pamento /ekipaˈmẽtu/ m
equipment. **~par** vt equip

equiparar /ekipaˈrar/ vt equate
(com with). **~se** vpr compare
(a with)

equipe /eˈkipi/ f team

equitação /ekitaˈsãw/ f riding

equiva|lência /ekivaˈlẽsia/ f
equivalence. **~lente** a equivalent.
~ler vi be equivalent (a to)

equivo|cado /ekivoˈkadu/
a mistaken. **~car-se** vpr make a
mistake

equívoco /eˈkivoku/ a equivocal.
● m mistake

era /ˈɛra/ f era

erário /e'rariu/ *m* exchequer

ereção /ere'sãw/ *f* erection

eremita /ere'mita/ *m/f* hermit

ereto /e'rɛtu/ *a* erect

erguer /er'ger/ *vt* raise; erect
‹*monumento etc*›. **~-se** *vpr* rise

eri|çado /eri'sadu/ *a* bristling.
~çar-se *vpr* bristle

ermo /'ermu/ *a* deserted ● *m*
wilderness

erosão /ero'zãw/ *f* erosion

erótico /e'rɔtʃiku/ *a* erotic

erotismo /ero'tʃizmu/ *m* eroticism

er|rado /e'xadu/ *a* wrong. **~rante**
a wandering. **~rar** *vt* (*não fazer
certo*) get wrong; miss ‹*alvo*› ● *vi*
(*enganar-se*) be wrong; (*vaguear*)
wander. **~ro** /e/ *m* mistake; **fazer
um ~ro** make a mistake. **~rôneo**
a erroneous

erudi|ção /erudʒi'sãw/ *f* learning.
~to *a* learned; ‹*música*› classical
● *m* scholar

erupção /erup'sãw/ *f* (*vulcânica*)
eruption; (*cutânea*) rash

erva /'ɛrva/ *f* herb. **~ daninha**
weed. **~-doce** *f* aniseed

ervilha /er'viʎa/ *f* pea

esban|jador /izbãʒa'dor/ *a*
extravagant ● *m* spendthrift. **~jar**
vt squander; burst with ‹*saúde,
imaginação, energia etc*›

esbar|rão /izba'xãw/ *m* bump.
~rar *vi* **~rar com ou em** bump
into ‹*pessoa*›; come up against
‹*problema*›

esbelto /iz'bɛwtu/ *a* svelte

esbo|çar /izbo'sar/ *vt* sketch
‹*desenho etc*›; outline ‹*plano etc*›;
~çar um sorriso give a hint of a
smile. **~ço** /o/ *m* (*desenho*) sketch;
(*plano*) outline; (*de um sorriso*) hint

esbofetear /izbofetʃi'ar/ *vt* slap

esborrachar /izboxa'ʃar/ *vt*
squash. **~-se** *vpr* crash

esbravejar /izbrave'ʒar/ *vi*
rant, rail

esbuga|lhado /izbuga'ʎadu/
a ‹*olhos*› bulging. **~lhar-se** *vpr*
‹*olhos*› pop out

esbura|cado /izbura'kadu/ *a* full
of holes. **~car** *vt* make holes in

escabroso /iska'brozu/ *a fig*
difficult, tough

escada /is'kada/ *f* (*dentro de casa*)
stairs; (*na rua*) steps; (*de mão*)
ladder; **~ de incêndio** fire escape;
~ rolante escalator. **~ria** *f* staircase

escafan|drista /iskafã'drista/ *m/f*
diver. **~dro** *m* diving suit

escala /is'kala/ *f* scale; (*de navio*)
port of call; (*de avião*) stopover;
fazer ~ stop over; **sem ~** ‹*voo*›
non-stop

esca|lada /iska'lada/ *f fig*
escalation. **~lão** *m* echelon, level.
~lar *vt* (*subir a*) scale; (*designar*)
select

escaldar /iskaw'dar/ *vt* scald;
blanch ‹*vegetais*›

escalfar /iskaw'far/ *vt* poach

escalonar /iskalo'nar/ *vt* schedule
‹*pagamento*›

escama /is'kama/ *f* scale

escanca|rado /iskãka'radu/ *a*
wide open. **~rar** *vt* open wide

escandalizar /iskãdali'zar/ *vt*
scandalize. **~-se** *vpr* be scandalized

escândalo /is'kãdalu/ *m* (*vexame*)
scandal; (*tumulto*) fuss, uproar;
fazer um ~ make a scene

escandaloso /iskãda'lozu/
a (*chocante*) scandalous;
(*espalhafatoso*) outrageous, loud

Escandinávia /iskãdʒi'navia/ f
Scandinavia

escandinavo /iskãdʒi'navu/
a & m Scandinavian

escanga|lhado /iskãga'ʎadu/ a
broken. ~**lhar** vt break up. ~**lhar-se**
vpr fall to pieces; ~**lhar-se de rir**
split one's sides laughing

escaninho /iska'niɲu/ m
pigeonhole

escanteio /iskã'teju/ m corner

esca|pada /iska'pada/ f (fuga)
escape; (aventura) escapade.
~**pamento** m exhaust. ~**par** vi
~**par a** ou **de** (livrar-se) escape
from; (evitar) escape; ~**pou-lhe a
palavra** the word slipped out; **o
copo ~pou-me das mãos** the glass
slipped out of my hands; **o nome
me ~pa** the name escapes me;
~**par de boa** have a narrow escape.
~**patória** f way out; (desculpa)
pretext. ~**pe** m (escape); (de carro etc)
exhaust. ~**pulir** vi escape (de from)

escaramuça /iskara'musa/ f
skirmish

escaravelho /iskara'veʎu/ m
beetle

escarcéu /iskar'sɛw/ m uproar, fuss

escarlate /iskar'latʃi/ a scarlet

escarnecer /iskarni'ser/ vt mock

escárnio /is'karniu/ m derision

escarpado /iskar'padu/ a steep

escarrado /iska'xadu/ **m ele é
o pai ~** he's the spitting image of
his father

escarro /is'kaxu/ m phlegm

escas|sear /iskasi'ar/ vi run short.
~**sez** f shortage. ~**so** a (raro) scarce;
(ralo) scant

esca|vadeira /iskava'dera/ f
digger. ~**var** vt excavate

esclare|cer /isklare'ser/ vt
explain; enlighten «pessoa».
~**cer-se** vpr «fato» be explained;
«pessoa» find out. ~**cimento** m (de
pessoas) enlightenment; (de fatos)
explanation

esclerosado /isklero'zadu/ a
senile

escoar /isko'ar/ vt/i drain

esco|cês /isko'ses/ a (f ~**cesa**)
Scottish ● m (f ~**cesa**) Scot

Escócia /is'kɔsia/ f Scotland

esco|la /is'kɔla/ f school; ~**la
de samba** samba school; ~**lar** a
school ● m/f schoolchild. ~**laridade**
f schooling

escola de samba *Escolas de
samba* (samba schools) are
local organizations in which
people sing and dance to samba
music, often in competition with
other schools. The samba schools
parade on floats once a year,
during Carnival. The most famous
parades take place in the Rio de
Janeiro Carnival, in the Avenida
Marquês de Sapucaí Sambadrome.

esco|lha /is'koʎa/ f choice. ~**lher**
vt choose

escol|ta /is'kɔwta/ f escort. ~**tar**
vt escort

escombros /is'kõbrus/ m pl debris

escon|de-esconde
/iskõdʒis'kõdʒi/ m hide-and-
seek. ~**der** vt hide. ~**der-se** vpr
hide. ~**derijo** m hiding place; (de
bandidos) hideout. ~**didas** f pl **às
~didas** secretly

esco|ra /is'kɔra/ f prop. ~**rar** vt
prop up. ~**rar-se** vpr «argumento
etc» be based (em on)

escore /is'kɔri/ m score

escória /is'kɔria/ f scum, dross

escori|ação /iskoria'sãw/ f graze, abrasion. **~ar** vt graze

escorpião /iskorpi'ãw/ m scorpion; E~ Scorpio

escorredor /iskoxe'dor/ m drainer

escorrega /isko'xega/ f slide

escorre|gador /iskoxega'dor/ m slide. **~gão** m slip. **~gar** vi slip

escor|rer /isko'xer/ vt drain ● vi trickle. **~rido** a <cabelo> straight

escoteiro /isko'teru/ m boy scout

escotilha /isko'tʃiʎa/ f hatch

esco|va /is'kova/ f brush; **fazer ~va no cabelo** blow-dry one's hair; **~va de dentes** toothbrush. **~var** vt brush. **~vinha** f **cabelo à ~vinha** crew cut

escra|chado /iskra'ʃadu/ a 🇵🇹 outspoken. **~char** vt 🇵🇹 tell off

escra|vatura /iskrava'tura/ f slavery. **~vidão** f slavery. **~vizar** vt enslave. **~vo** m slave

escre|vente /iskre'vẽtʃi/ m/f clerk. **~ver** vt/i write

escri|ta /is'krita/ f writing; **~ta inteligente** Telec predictive text messaging. **~to** pp de ► ESCREVER ● a written; **por ~to** in writing. **~tor** m writer. **~tório** m office; (numa casa) study

escritu|ra /iskri'tura/ f (a Bíblia) scripture; (contrato) deed. **~ração** f bookkeeping. **~rar** vt keep, write up <contas>; draw up <documento>

escri|vaninha /iskriva'niɲa/ f bureau, writing desk. **~vão** m (f **~vã**) registrar

escrúpulo /is'krupulu/ m scruple

escrupuloso /iskrupu'lozu/ a scrupulous

escrutínio /iskru'tʃiniu/ m ballot

escu|dar /isku'dar/ vt shield. **~deria** f team. **~do** m shield; (moeda) escudo

escula|chado /iskula'ʃadu/ a 🇵🇹 sloppy. **~char** vt 🇵🇹 mess up <coisa>; tell off <pessoa>. **~cho** m 🇵🇹 (bagunça) mess; (bronca) telling-off

escul|pir /iskuw'pir/ vt sculpt. **~tor** m sculptor. **~tura** f sculpture. **~tural** (pl **~turais**) a statuesque

escuma /is'kuma/ f scum. **~deira** f skimmer

escuna /is'kuna/ f schooner

escu|ras /is'kuras/ f pl **às ~ras** in the dark. **~recer** vt darken ● vi get dark. **~ridão** f darkness. **~ro** a & m dark

escuso /is'kuzu/ a shady

escu|ta /is'kuta/ f listening; **estar à ~ta** be listening; **~ta telefônica** phone tapping. **~tar** vt (perceber) hear; (prestar atenção a) listen to ● vi (poder ouvir) hear; (prestar atenção) listen

esdrúxulo /iz'druʃulu/ a weird

esfacelar /isfase'lar/ vt wreck

esfalfar /isfaw'far/ vt wear out. **~se** vpr get worn out

esfaquear /isfaki'ar/ vt stab

esfarelar /isfare'lar/ vt crumble. **~se** vpr crumble

esfarrapado /isfaxa'padu/ a ragged; <desculpa> lame

es|fera /is'fera/ f sphere. **~férico** a spherical

esferográfi|co /isfero'grafiku/ a **caneta ~ca** ballpoint pen

esfiapar /isfia'par/ vt fray. **~se** vpr fray

esfinge /is'fiʒi/ f sphinx

esfolar /isfo'lar/ vt skin; fig
overcharge

esfomeado /isfomi'adu/ a
starving, famished

esfor|çar-se /isfor'sarsi/ vpr make
an effort. **~ço** /o/ m effort; **fazer
~ço** make an effort

esfre|gaço /isfre'gasu/ m smear.
~gar vt rub; (para limpar) scrub

esfriar /isfri'ar/ vt cool ● vi cool
(down); (sentir frio) get cold

esfumaçado /isfuma'sadu/ a
smoky

esfuziante /isfuzi'ãtʃi/ a
irrepressible, exuberant

esganar /izga'nar/ vt throttle

esganiçado /izgani'sadu/ a shrill

esgarçar /izgar'sar/ vt/i fray

esgo|tado /izgo'tadu/ a
exhausted; (estoque, lotação) sold
out. **~tamento** m exhaustion;
~tamento nervoso nervous
breakdown. **~tar** vt exhaust;
(gastar) use up. **~tar-se** vpr (pessoa)
become exhausted; (estoque,
lotação) sell out; (recursos,
provisões) run out. **~to** /o/ m drain;
(de detritos) sewer

esgri|ma /iz'grima/ f fencing.
~mir vt brandish ● vi fence. **~mista**
m/f fencer

esgrouvinhado /izgrovi'ɲadu/
a tousled, dishevelled

esgueirar-se /izge'rarsi/ vpr
slip, sneak

esguelha /iz'geʎa/ f **de ~** askew;
(olhar) askance

esgui|char /izgi'ʃar/ vt/i spurt,
squirt. **~cho** /o/ m jet, spurt

esguio /iz'giu/ a slender

eslavo /iz'lavu/ a Slavic ● m Slav

esmaecer /izmaj'ser/ vi fade

esma|gador /izmaga'dor/ a
(vitória, maioria) overwhelming;
(provas) incontrovertible. **~gar**
vt crush

esmalte /iz'mawtʃi/ m enamel; **~
de unhas** nail varnish

esmeralda /izme'rawda/ f
emerald

esme|rar-se /izme'rarsi/ vpr take
great care (**em** over). **~ro** /e/ m
great care

esmigalhar /izmiga'ʎar/ vt
crumble (pão etc); shatter (vidro,
copo). **~se** vpr (pão etc) crumble;
(vidro, copo) shatter

esmiuçar /izmiu'sar/ vt examine
in detail

esmo /'ezmu/ m **a ~** (escolher) at
random; (andar) aimlessly; (falar)
nonsense

esmola /iz'mɔla/ f donation; pl
charity

esmorecer /izmore'ser/ vi flag

esmurrar /izmu'xar/ vt punch

esno|bar /izno'bar/ vt snub ● vi be
snobbish. **~be** /ɛ iz'nɔbi/ a snobbish
● m/f snob. **~bismo** /i/ m snobbishness

esotérico /ezo'teriku/ a esoteric

espa|çar /ispa'sar/ vt space out;
make less frequent (visitas, consultas
etc). **~cial** /p/ (pl ~ciais) a space.
~ço m space; (cultural etc) venue. **~çoso**
/o/ a spacious

espada /is'pada/ f sword; pl (naipe)
spades. **~chim** m swordsman

espádua /is'padua/ f shoulder
blade

espaguete /ispa'getʃi/ m
spaghetti

espairecer /ispajre'ser/ vt amuse
● vi relax; (dar uma volta) go for a
walk. **~cimento** m recreation

espaldar /ispaw'dar/ m back

espalhafato /ispaʌaˈfatu/ *m*
(*barulho*) fuss, uproar; (*de roupa etc*)
extravagance. **~so** /ɔ/ *a* (*barulhento*)
noisy, rowdy; (*ostentoso*)
extravagant

espalhar /ispaˈʌar/ *vt* scatter;
spread ‹*notícia, terror etc*›; shed
‹*luz*›. **~se** *vpr* spread; ‹*pessoas*›
spread out

espa|nador /ispanaˈdor/ *m*
feather duster. **~nar** *vt* dust

espan|camento /ispãkaˈmẽtu/
m beating. **~car** *vt* beat up

Espanha /isˈpaɲa/ *f* Spain

espa|nhol /ispaˈɲɔw/ (*pl* **~nhóis**)
a (*f* **~nhola**) Spanish ● *m* (*f* **~nhola**)
Spaniard; (*língua*) Spanish; **os
~nhóis** the Spanish

espan|talho /ispãˈtaʌu/ *m*
scarecrow. **~tar** *vt* (*admirar*) amaze;
(*assustar*) scare; (*afugentar*) drive
away. **~tar-se** *vpr* (*admirar-se*) be
amazed; (*assustar-se*) get scared.
~to *m* (*susto*) fright; (*admiração*)
amazement. **~toso** /o/ *a* amazing

esparadrapo /isparaˈdrapu/ *m*
sticking plaster

espargo /isˈpargu/ *Port m*
asparagus

esparramar /ispaxaˈmar/ *vt*
scatter. **~se** *vpr* be scattered,
spread

espartano /isparˈtanu/ *a* spartan

espartilho /isparˈtiʌu/ *m* corset

espas|mo /isˈpazmu/ *m* spasm.
~módico *a* spasmodic

espatifar /ispatʃiˈfar/ *vt* smash.
~se *vpr* smash; ‹*carro, avião*› crash

especi|al /ispesiˈaw/ (*pl* **~ais**)
a special. **~alidade** *f* speciality.
~alista *m/f* specialist

especiali|zado /ispesialiˈzadu/
a specialized; ‹*mão de obra*› skilled.

~zar-se *vpr* specialize (**em** in)

especiaria /ispesiaˈria/ *f* spice

espécie /isˈpɛsi/ *f* sort, kind; (*de
animais*) species

especifi|cação /ispesifikaˈsãw/ *f*
specification. **~car** *vt* specify

específico /ispeˈsifiku/ *a* a specific

espécime /isˈpɛsimi/ *m* specimen

espectador /ispektaˈdor/ *m* (*de
TV*) viewer; (*de jogo, espetáculo*)
spectator; (*de acidente etc*) onlooker

espectro /isˈpɛktru/ *m* (*fantasma*)
spectre; (*de cores*) spectrum

especu|lação /ispekulaˈsãw/ *f*
speculation. **~lador** *m* speculator.
~lar *vi* speculate (**sobre** on).
~lativo *a* speculative

espe|lhar /ispeˈʌar/ *vt* mirror.
~lhar-se *vpr* be mirrored. **~lho** /e/
m mirror; **~lho retrovisor** rear-view
mirror

espelunca /ispeˈlũka/ *f* 🔲 dive 🔲

espera /isˈpera/ *f* wait; **à ~ de**
waiting for

esperança /ispeˈrãsa/ *f* hope.
~çoso /o/ *a* hopeful

esperar /ispeˈrar/ *vt* (*aguardar*)
wait for; (*desejar*) hope for; (*contar
com*) expect ● *vi* wait (**por** for);
fazer alguém ~ keep sb waiting;
espero que ele venha I hope (that)
he comes; **espero que sim/não** I
hope so/not

esperma /isˈperma/ *m* sperm

espernear /isperniˈar/ *vi* kick; *fig*
(*reclamar*) kick up

esper|talhão /ispertaˈʌãw/ *m*
(*f* **~talhona**) wise guy. **~teza** /e/ *f*
cleverness; (*uma*) clever move. **~to**
/e/ *a* clever

espes|so /isˈpesu/ *a* thick. **~sura**
f thickness

espe|tacular /ispetaku'lar/ a
spectacular. **~táculo** m (no teatro
etc) show; (cena impressionante)
spectacle. **~taculoso** /o/ a
spectacular

espe|tar /ispe'tar/ vt (cravar) stick;
(furar) skewer. **~tar-se** vpr (cravar-se)
stick; (ferir-se) prick o.s.. **~tinho** m
skewer; (de carne etc) kebab. **~to**
/e/ m spit

espevitado /ispevi'tadu/ a
cheeky

espezinhar /ispezi'ɲar/ vt walk
all over

espi|a /is'pia/ m/f spy. **~ão** m (f **~ã**)
spy. **~ada** f peep. **~ar** vt (observar)
spy on; (aguardar) watch for ● vi
peer, peep

espicaçar /ispika'sar/ vt goad
‹pessoa›; excite ‹imaginação,
curiosidade›

espichar /ispi'ʃar/ vt stretch ● vi
shoot up. **~se** vpr stretch out

espiga /is'piga/ f (de trigo etc) ear;
(de milho) cob

espina|fração /ispinafra'sãw/
f T telling-off. **~frar** vt T tell off.
~fre m spinach

espingarda /ispĩ'garda/ f rifle,
shotgun

espinha /is'piɲa/ f (de peixe) bone;
(na pele) spot; **~ dorsal** spine

espinho /is'piɲu/ m thorn. **~so** /o/
a thorny; fig difficult, tough

espio|nagem /ispio'naʒẽ/ f
espionage, spying. **~nar** vt spy on
● vi spy

espi|ral /ispi'raw/ (pl **~rais**) a & f
spiral

espirita /is'pirita/ a & m/f
spiritualist

espiritismo /ispiri'tʃizmu/ m
spiritualism

espírito /is'piritu/ m spirit;
(graça) wit

espiritu|al /ispiritu'aw/ (pl **~ais**)
a spiritual. **~oso** /o/ a witty

espir|rar /ispi'xar/ vt spurt ● vi
‹pessoa› sneeze; ‹lama, tinta etc›
spatter; ‹fogo, lenha, fritura etc›
spit. **~ro** m sneeze

esplêndido /is'plẽdʒidu/ a
splendid

esplendor /isplẽ'dor/ m splendour

espoleta /ispo'leta/ f fuse

espoliar /ispoli'ar/ vt plunder,
pillage

espólio /is'pɔliu/ m (herdado)
estate; (roubado) spoils

espon|ja /is'põʒa/ f sponge. **~joso**
/o/ a spongy

espon|taneidade
/ispõtanej'dadʒi/ f spontaneity.
~tâneo a spontaneous

espora /is'pɔra/ f spur

esporádico /ispo'radʒiku/ a
sporadic

esporear /ispori'ar/ vt spur on

espor|te /is'pɔrtʃi/ m sport ● a
invar ‹roupa› casual; carro **~te**
sports car. **~tista** m/f sportsman (f
-woman). **~tiva** f sense of humour.
~tivo a sporting

espo|sa /is'poza/ f wife. **~so** m
husband

espregui|cadeira
/ispregisa'dera/ f (tipo cadeira)
deckchair; (tipo cama) sun lounger.
~car-se vpr stretch

esprei|ta /is'prejta/ f ficar à **~ta**
lie in wait. **~tar** vt stalk ‹caça,
vítima›; spy on ‹vizinhos, inimigos
etc›; look out for ‹ocasião› ● vi
peep, spy

espre|medor /ispreme'dor/ m
squeezer. **~mer** vt squeeze; wring

out <*roupa*>; squash <*pessoa*>.
~mer-se *vpr* squeeze up

espu|ma /is'puma/ *f* foam; **~ma de borracha** foam rubber. **~mante** *a* <*vinho*> sparkling. **~mar** *vi* foam, froth

espúrio /is'puriu/ *a* spurious

esqua|dra /is'kwadra/ *f* squad; **~dra de polícia** Port police station. **~drão** *m* squadron. **~dria** *f* doors and windows. **~drinhar** *vt* explore. **~dro** *m* set square

esqualidez /iskwali'des/ *f* squalor

esquálido /is'kwalidu/ *a* squalid

esquartejar /iskwarte'ʒar/ *vt* chop up

esque|cer /iske'ser/ *vt/i* forget; **~cer-se de** forget. **~cido** *a* forgotten; (*com memória fraca*) forgetful. **~cimento** *m* oblivion; (*memória fraca*) forgetfulness

esque|lético /iske'letʃiku/ *a* skinny, skeleton-like. **~leto** /e/ *m* skeleton

esque|ma /is'kema/ *m* outline, draft; (*operação*) scheme; **~ma de segurança** security operation. **~mático** *a* schematic

esquentar /iskẽ'tar/ *vt* warm up; **~ a cabeça** 🔲 get worked up ● *vi* warm up; <*roupa*> be warm. **~se** *vpr* get annoyed

esquer|da /is'kerda/ *f* left; **à ~da** (*posição*) on the left; (*direção*) to the left. **~dista** *a* left-wing ● *m/f* left-winger. **~do** /e/ *a* left

esqui /is'ki/ *m* ski; (*esporte*) skiing; **~ aquático** water skiing. **~ador** *m* skier. **~ar** *vi* ski

esquilo /is'kilu/ *m* squirrel

esquina /is'kina/ *f* corner

esquisi|tice /iskizi'tʃisi/ *f* strangeness; (*uma*) strange thing.

~to *a* strange

esqui|var-se /iski'varsi/ *vpr* dodge out of the way; **~var-se de** dodge. **~vo** *a* elusive; <*pessoa*> aloof, antisocial

esquizo|frenia /iskizofre'nia/ *f* schizophrenia. **~frênico** *a* & *m* schizophrenic

es|sa /'esa/ *pron* that (one); **~sa é boa** that's a good one; **~sa não** come off it; **por ~sas e outras** for these and other reasons. **~se** /e/ *a* that; *pl* those; 🔲 (*este*) this; *pl* those ● *pron* that one; *pl* those; 🔲 (*este*) this one; *pl* these

essência /e'sẽsia/ *f* essence

essenci|al /esẽsi'aw/ (*pl* **~ais**) *a* essential; **o ~al** what is essential

estabele|cer /istabele'ser/ *vt* establish. **~cer-se** *vpr* establish o.s.. **~cimento** *m* establishment

estabili|dade /istabili'dadʒi/ *f* stability. **~zar** *vt* stabilize. **~zar-se** *vpr* stabilize

estábulo /is'tabulu/ *m* cowshed

estaca /is'taka/ *f* stake; (*de barraca*) peg; **voltar à ~ zero** go back to square one

estação /ista'sãw/ *f* (*do ano*) season; (*ferroviária etc*) station; **~ balneária** seaside resort

estacar /ista'kar/ *vi* stop short

estacio|namento /istasiona'mẽtu/ *m* (*ação*) parking; (*lugar*) car park, *Amer* parking lot. **~nar** *vt/i* park

estada /is'tada/ *f*, **estadia** /ista'dʒia/ *f* stay

estádio /is'tadʒiu/ *m* stadium

esta|dista /ista'dʒista/ *m/f* statesman (*f*-woman). **~do** *m* state; **~do civil** marital status; **~do de espírito** state of mind; **Estados**

Unidos da América United States of America. **Estado-Maior** m Staff. **~dual** (pl **~duais**) a state

esta|fa /isˈtafa/ f exhaustion. **~fante** a exhausting. **~far** vt tire out. **~far-se** vpr get tired out

estagi|ar /istaʒiˈar/ vi do a traineeship. **~ário** m trainee

estágio /isˈtaʒiu/ m traineeship

estag|nado /istagiˈnadu/ a stagnant. **~nar** vi stagnate

estalagem /istaˈlaʒẽ/ f inn

estalar /istaˈlar/ vt (quebrar) crack; (fazer barulho com) click ● vi crack

estaleiro /istaˈleru/ m shipyard

estalo /isˈtalu/ m crack; (de dedos, língua) click; **me deu um ~** it clicked (in my mind)

estam|pa /isˈtãpa/ f print. **~pado** a <tecido> patterned ● m (desenho) pattern; (tecido) print. **~par** vt print

estampido /istãˈpidu/ m bang

estancar /istãˈkar/ vt staunch. **~se** vpr dry up

estância /isˈtãsia/ f **~ hidromineral** spa

estandarte /istãˈdartʃi/ m banner

estanho /isˈtaɲu/ m tin

estanque /isˈtãki/ a watertight

estante /isˈtãtʃi/ f bookcase

estapafúrdio /istapaˈfurdʒiu/ a weird, odd

estar /isˈtar/ ● vi

····▶ (com lugar) be; **a Lúcia está em casa** is Lúcia at home?

····▶ (achar-se) **doente/ cansado** be ill/tired

····▶ (aparência) look; **você está muito bonita!** you look very pretty!

····▶ **~ em** (consistir em) lie in; **o êxito do grupo está na sua originalidade** the group's success lies in their originality

····▶ **~ a** Port (seguido de infinitivo) **estavam a jogar** they were playing

● v aux

····▶ (com gerúndio) **eles estão brincando** they're playing; **está fazendo 40ºC em São Paulo** it's 40ºC in São Paulo

····▶ (com particípio) **o arroz está cozido** the rice is cooked; **está aberto** it's open

● v imp

····▶ (com temperatura) **está frio/calor** it's cold/hot

····▶ (em expressões) **está bem?** (de acordo?) OK?; **você me empresta, está bem?** you'll lend it to me, won't you?; **~ a** Port (com data) **estamos a dois de junho** it's the second of June; (com preço) **a quanto está a banana?** how much are the bananas?; **~ com** (apoiar) be rooting for; **força, estou contigo!** go for it! I'm rooting for you; (doença) have; **estou com gripe** I've got the flu; **~ de partida** be leaving soon; **estou de partida para Londres** I'm leaving for London soon; **~ em** (com data) **estamos em três de abril** it's the third of April; **~ numa de** be into; **ultimamente ela está numa de ouvir rock** she's been into rock music lately; **estar sem: estou sem dinheiro** I haven't got any money; **está sem comer há três dias** she hasn't eaten for three days; **estoul, está lá!** Port (ao telefone) hello!; **não ~**

para not to be in the mood for; **não estou para brincadeiras** I'm not in the mood for jokes

❗ Quando o verbo **estar** é parte integrante de uma frase como por exemplo **estar acostumado**, **estar com pressa**, **estar de acordo**, **estar de pé**, pesquise pelo adjetivo ou substantivo que o acompanha.

estardalhaço /istarda'ʎasu/ m (barulho) fuss; (ostentação) extravagance

estarre|cedor /istaxese'dor/ a horrifying. **~cer** vt horrify. **~cer-se** vpr be horrified

esta|tal /ista'taw/ (pl **~tais**) a state-owned ● f state company

estate|lado /istate'ladu/ a sprawling. **~lar** vt knock down. **~lar-se** vpr go sprawling

estático /is'tatʃiku/ a static

estatísti|ca /ista'tʃistʃika/ f statistics. **~co** a statistical

estati|zação /istatʃiza'sãw/ f nationalization. **~zar** vt nationalize

estátua /is'tatua/ f statue

estatueta /istatu'eta/ f statuette

estatura /ista'tura/ f stature

estatuto /ista'tutu/ m statute

está|vel /is'tavew/ (pl **~veis**) a stable

este[1] /'estʃi/ a invar & m east

este[2] /'estʃi/ a this; pl these ● pron this one; pl these; (mencionado por último) the latter

esteio /is'teju/ m prop; fig mainstay

esteira /is'tera/ f (tapete) mat; (rastro) wake

estelionato /istelio'natu/ m fraud

estender /istẽ'der/ vt (desdobrar) spread out; (alongar) stretch; (ampliar) extend; hold out ‹mão›;

hang out ‹roupa›; roll out ‹massa›; draw out ‹conversa›. **~se** vpr (deitar-se) stretch out; (ir longe) stretch, extend; **~se sobre** dwell on

esteno|datilógrafo /istenodatʃi'lɔgrafu/ m shorthand typist. **~grafia** f shorthand

estepe /is'tɛpi/ m spare wheel

esterco /is'terku/ m dung

estéreo /is'teriu/ a invar stereo

estere|otipado /isteriotʃi'padu/ a stereotypical. **~ótipo** m stereotype

esté|ril /is'tɛriw/ (pl **~reis**) a sterile

esterili|dade /isterili'dadʒi/ f sterility. **~zar** vt sterilize

esterli|no /ister'linu/ a libra **~na** pound sterling

esteroide /iste'rɔjdʒi/ m steroid

estética /is'tɛtʃika/ f aesthetics

esteticista /istetʃi'sista/ m/f beautician

estético /is'tɛtʃiku/ a aesthetic

estetoscópio /istetos'kɔpiu/ m stethoscope

estiagem /istʃi'aʒẽ/ f dry spell

estibordo /istʃi'bɔrdu/ m starboard

esti|cada /istʃi'kada/ f **dar uma ~cada** go on. **~car** vt stretch ● vi 🄸 go on. **~car-se** vpr stretch out

estigma /is'tʃigima/ m stigma. **~tizar** vt brand (**de** as)

estilha|çar /istʃiʎa'sar/ vt shatter. **~çar-se** vpr shatter. **~ço** m shard, fragment

estilingue /istʃi'lĩgi/ m catapult

estilis|mo /istʃi'lizmu/ m fashion design. **~ta** m/f fashion designer

esti|lístico /istʃi'listʃiku/ a stylistic. **~lizar** vt stylize. **~lo** m style; **~lo de vida** lifestyle

esti|ma /es'tʃima/ f esteem. **~mação** f estimation; **cachorro de ~mação** pet dog. **~mado** a esteemed; **Estimado Senhor** Dear Sir. **~mar** vt value ‹bens, joias etc› **(em** at); estimate ‹valor, preço etc› **(em** at); think highly of ‹pessoa›. **~mativa** f estimate

estimu|lante /istʃimu'lãtʃi/ a stimulating ● m stimulant. **~lar** vt stimulate; (incentivar) encourage

estímulo /is'tʃimulu/ m stimulus; (incentivo) incentive

estio /is'tʃiu/ m summer

estipu|lação /istʃipula'sãw/ f stipulation. **~lar** vt stipulate

estirar /istʃi'rar/ vt stretch. **~se** vpr stretch

estirpe /is'tʃirpi/ f stock, line

estivador /istʃiva'dor/ m docker

estocada /isto'kada/ f thrust

estocar /isto'kar/ vt stock ● vi stock up

Estocolmo /isto'kɔwmu/ f Stockholm

esto|far /isto'far/ vt upholster ‹móveis›. **~fo** /o/ m upholstery

estoico /is'tɔjku/ a & m stoic

estojo /is'toʒu/ m case

estômago /is'tomagu/ m stomach

Estônia /is'tonia/ f Estonia

estonte|ante /istõtʃi'ãtʃi/ a stunning, mind-boggling. **~ar** vt stun

estopim /isto'pĩ/ m fuse; fig flashpoint

estoque /is'tɔki/ m stock

estore /is'tɔri/ m blind

estória /is'tɔria/ f story

estor|var /istor'var/ vt hinder; obstruct ‹entrada, trânsito›. **~vo** /o/ m hindrance

estou|rado /isto'radu/ a ‹pessoa› explosive. **~rar** vi ‹bomba, escândalo, pessoa› blow up; ‹pneu› burst; ‹guerra› break out; ‹moda, cantor etc› make it big. **~ro** m (de bomba, moda etc) explosion; (de pessoa) outburst; (de pneu) blowout; (de guerra) outbreak

estrábico /is'trabiku/ a ‹olhos› squinty; ‹pessoa› squint-eyed

estrabismo /istra'bizmu/ m squint

estraçalhar /istrasa'ʎar/ vt tear to pieces

estrada /is'trada/ f road; **~ de ferro** railway, Amer railroad; **~ de rodagem** highway; **~ de terra** dirt road

estrado /is'tradu/ m podium; (de cama) base

estragão /istra'gãw/ m tarragon

estraga-prazeres /istragapra'zeris/ m/f invar spoilsport

estra|gar /istra'gar/ vt (tornar desagradável) spoil; (acabar com) ruin ● vi (quebrar) break; (apodrecer) go off. **~go** m damage; pl damage; (da guerra, do tempo) ravages

estrangeiro /istrã'ʒeru/ a foreign ● m foreigner; **do ~** from abroad; **para o/no ~** abroad

estrangular /istrãgu'lar/ vt strangle

estra|nhar /istra'ɲar/ vt (achar estranho) find strange; (não se adaptar a) find it hard to get used to; (não se sentir à vontade com) be shy with; **~nhar que** find it strange that; **estou te ~nhando** that's not like you; **não é de se ~nhar** it's not surprising. **~nheza** /e/ f (esquisitice) strangeness; (surpresa) surprise. **~nho** a strange ● m stranger

estratagema /istrata'ʒema/ m stratagem

estraté|gia /istra'tɛʒia/ f strategy. **~gico** a strategic

estrato /is'tratu/ m (camada) stratum; (nuvem) stratus. **~sfera** f stratosphere

estre|ante /istri'ãtʃi/ a new ● m/f newcomer. **~ar** vt premiere ‹peça, filme›; embark on ‹carreira›; wear for the first time ‹roupa› ● vi ‹pessoa› make one's debut; ‹filme, peça› open

estrebaria /istreba'ria/ f stable

estreia /is'treja/ f (de pessoa) debut; (de filme, peça) premiere

estrei|tar /istrej'tar/ vt narrow; take in ‹vestido›; make closer ‹relações, laços› ● vi narrow. **~tar-se** vpr ‹relações› become closer. **~to** a narrow; ‹relações, laços› close; ‹saia› straight ● m strait

estre|la /is'trela/ f star. **~lado** a ‹céu› starry; ‹ovo› fried; **~lado por** ‹filme etc› starring. **~la-do-mar** (pl **~las-do-mar**) f starfish. **~lar** vt fry ‹ovo›; star in ‹filme, peça›. **~lato** m stardom. **~lismo** m star quality

estreme|cer /istreme'ser/ vt shake; strain ‹relações, amizade› ● vi shudder; ‹relações, amizade› become strained. **~cimento** m shudder; (de relações, amizade) strain

estrepar-se /istre'parsi/ vpr 🄴 come a cropper

estrépito /is'trepitu/ m noise; **com ~** noisily

estrepitoso /istrepi'tozu/ a noisy; ‹sucesso etc› resounding

estres|sante /istre'sãtʃi/ a stressful. **~sar** vt stress. **~se** /ɛ/ m stress

estria /is'tria/ f streak; (no corpo) stretch mark

estribeira /istri'bera/ f stirrup; **perder as ~s** lose control

estribilho /istri'biʎu/ m chorus

estribo /is'tribu/ m stirrup

estridente /istri'dẽtʃi/ a strident

estripulia /istripu'lia/ f antic

estrito /is'tritu/ a strict

estrofe /is'trɔfi/ f stanza, verse

estrógeno /is'trɔʒenu/ m oestrogen

estroganofe /istrogo'nɔfi/ m stroganoff

estron|do /is'trõdu/ m crash. **~doso** /o/ a loud; ‹aplausos› thunderous; ‹sucesso, fracasso› resounding

estropiar /istropi'ar/ vt cripple ‹pessoa›; mangle ‹palavras›

estrume /is'trumi/ m manure

estrutu|ra /istru'tura/ f structure. **~ral** (pl **~rais**) a structural. **~rar** vt structure

estuário /istu'ariu/ m estuary

estudan|te /istu'dãtʃi/ m/f student. **~til** (pl **~tis**) a student

estudar /istu'dar/ vt/i study

estúdio /is'tudʒiu/ m studio

estu|dioso /istudʒi'ozu/ a studious ● m scholar. **~do** m study

estufa /is'tufa/ f (para plantas) greenhouse; (de aquecimento) stove. **~do** m stew

estupefato /istupe'fatu/ a dumbfounded

estupendo /iste'pẽdu/ a stupendous

estupidez /istupi'des/ f (grosseria) rudeness; (uma) rude thing; (burrice) stupidity; (uma) stupid thing

estúpido /is'tupɪdu/ a (grosso)
rude, coarse; (burro) stupid ● m lout

estupor /istu'por/ m stupor

estu|prador /istupra'dor/ m
rapist. **~prar** vt rape. **~pro** m rape

esturricar /istuxi'kar/ vt parch

esvair-se /izva'irsi/ vpr fade; **~ em
sangue** bleed to death

esvaziar /izvazi'ar/ vt empty. **~se**
vpr empty

esverdeado /izverdʒi'adu/ a
greenish

esvoa|çante /izvoa'sãtʃi/ a
‹cabelo› flyaway. **~çar** vi flutter

eta /'eta/ int what a

etapa /e'tapa/ f stage; (de corrida,
turnê etc) leg

etário /e'tariu/ a age

éter /'eter/ m ether

etéreo /e'teriu/ a ethereal

eter|nidade /eterni'dadʒi/ f
eternity. **~no** /e/ a eternal

éti|ca /'etʃika/ f ethics. **~co** a ethical

etimo|logia /etʃimolo'ʒia/ f
etymology. **~lógico** a etymological

etíope /e'tʃiopi/ a & m/f Ethiopian

Etiópia /etʃi'ɔpia/ f Ethiopia

etique|ta /etʃi'keta/ f (rótulo)
label; (bons modos) etiquette. **~tar**
vt label

étnico /'etʃniku/ a ethnic

eu /ew/ pron I ● m self; **mais alto do
que ~** taller than me; **sou ~** it's me

EUA m pl USA

eucalipto /ewka'liptu/ m
eucalyptus

eufemismo /ewfe'mizmu/ m
euphemism

euforia /ewfo'ria/ f euphoria

euro /'ewru/ m euro

Europa /ew'rɔpa/ f Europe

euro|peu /ewro'pew/ a & m
(f ~**peia**) European

eutanásia /ewta'nazia/ f
euthanasia

evacu|ação /evakua'sãw/ f
evacuation. **~ar** vt evacuate

evadir /eva'dʒir/ vt evade. **~se** vpr
escape (de from)

evan|gelho /evã'ʒeλu/ m gospel

evaporar /evapo'rar/ vt evaporate.
~se vpr evaporate

eva|são /eva'zãw/ f escape; (fiscal
etc) evasion; **~ fiscal** tax evasion;
~são escolar truancy. **~siva** f
excuse. **~sivo** a evasive

even|to /e'vẽtu/ m event. **~tual**
(pl **~tuais**) a possible. **~tualidade** f
eventuality

evidência /evi'dẽsia/ f evidence

eviden|ciar /evidẽsi'ar/ vt show
up. **~ciar-se** vpr show up. **~te** a
obvious, evident

evi|tar /evi'tar/ vt avoid; **~tar de
beber** avoid drinking. **~tável** (pl
~táveis) a avoidable

evocar /evo'kar/ vt call to mind,
evoke ‹passado etc›; call up
‹espíritos etc›

evolu|ção /evolu'sãw/ f evolution.
~ir vi evolve

exacerbar /ezaser'bar/ vt
exacerbate

exage|rado /ezaʒe'radu/ a over
the top. **~rar** vt (atribuir proporções
irreais a) exaggerate; (fazer em
excesso) overdo ● vi (ao falar)
exaggerate; (exceder-se) overdo it.
~ro /e/ m exaggeration

exa|lação /ezala'sãw/ f fume;
(agradável) scent. **~lar** vt give off
‹perfume etc›

exal|tação /ezawta'sãw/
f (excitação) agitation;

(*engrandecimento*) exaltation.
~tar *vt* (*excitar*) agitate; (*enfurecer*)
infuriate; (*louvar*) exalt. **~tar-se**
vpr (*excitar-se*) get agitated;
(*enfurecer-se*) get furious

exa|me /e'zami/ *m* examination;
(*na escola*) exam(ination); **~me
de sangue** blood test. **~minar** *vt*
examine

exaspe|ração /ezaspera'sãw/ *f*
exasperation. **~rar** *vt* exasperate.
~rar-se *vpr* get exasperated

exa|tidão /ezatʃi'dãw/ *f* exactness.
~to *a* exact

exaurir /ezaw'rir/ *vt* exhaust. **~se**
vpr become exhausted

exaus|tivo /ezaws'tʃivu/ *a*
‹*estudo*› exhaustive; ‹*trabalho*›
exhausting. **~to** *a* exhausted

exceção /ese'sãw/ *f* exception;
abrir ~ make an exception; **com ~
de** with the exception of

exce|dente /ese'dẽtʃi/ *a & m*
excess, surplus. **~der** *vt* exceed.
~der-se *vpr* overdo it

exce|lência /ese'lẽsia/ *f*
excellence; (*tratamento*) excellency.
~lente *a* excellent

excentricidade /esẽtrisi'dadʒi/
f eccentricity

excêntrico /e'sẽtriku/ *a & m*
eccentric

excep|cional /esepsjo'naw/ (*pl*
~cionais) *a* exceptional; (*deficiente*)
handicapped

exces|sivo /ese'sivu/ *a* excessive.
~so /ɛ/ *m* excess; **~so de bagagem**
excess baggage; **~so de velocidade**
speeding

exce|to /e'sɛtu/ *prep* except. **~tuar**
vt except

exci|tação /esita'sãw/ *f*
excitement. **~tante** *a* exciting. **~tar**
vt excite. **~tar-se** *vpr* get excited

excla|mação /isklama'sãw/ *f*
exclamation. **~mar** *vt/i* exclaim

exclu|ir /isklu'ir/ *vt* exclude. **~são**
f exclusion; **com ~são de** with the
exclusion of. **~sividade** *f* exclusive
rights; **com ~sividade** exclusively.
~sivo *a* exclusive. **~so** *a* excluded

excomungar /iskomũ'gar/ *vt*
excommunicate

excremento /iskre'mẽtu/ *m*
excrement

excur|são /iskur'sãw/ *f* excursion;
(*a pé*) hike, walk. **~sionista** *m/f* day
tripper; (*a pé*) hiker, walker

execu|ção /ezeku'sãw/ *f*
execution. **~tante** *m/f* performer.
~tar *vt* carry out ‹*ordem, plano etc*›;
perform ‹*papel, música*›; execute
‹*preso, criminoso etc*›. **~tivo** *a & m*
executive

exem|plar /ezẽ'plar/ *a* exemplary
● *m* (*de espécie*) example; (*de
livro, jornal etc*) copy. **~plificar** *vt*
exemplify

exemplo /e'zẽplu/ *m* example; **a ~
de** following the example of; **por ~**
for example; **dar o ~** set an example

exequí|vel /eze'kwivew/ (*pl
~veis*) *a* feasible

exer|cer /ezer'ser/ *vt* exercise;
exert ‹*pressão, influência*›; carry
on ‹*profissão*›. **~cício** *m* exercise;
Mil drill; (*de profissão*) practice;
(*financeiro*) financial year. **~citar** *vt*
exercise; practise ‹*ofício*›. **~citar-se**
vpr train

exército /e'zɛrsitu/ *m* army

exibição /ezibi'sãw/ *f* (*de filme,
passaporte etc*) showing; (*de talento,
força, ostentação*) show

exibicionis|mo /ezibisio'nizmu/ m exhibitionism. **~ta** a & m/f exhibitionist

exi|bido /ezi'bidu/ a ‹pessoa› pretentious ● m show-off. **~bir** vt show; (ostentar) show off. **~bir-se** vpr (ostentar-se) show off

exi|gência /ezi'ʒēsia/ f demand. **~gente** a demanding. **~gir** vt demand

exíguo /e'zigwu/ a (muito pequeno) tiny; (escasso) minimal

exi|lado /ezi'ladu/ a exiled ● m exile. **~lar** vt exile. **~lar-se** vpr go into exile

exílio /e'ziliu/ m exile

exímio /e'zimiu/ a distinguished

eximir /ezi'mir/ vt exempt (de from); **~se de** get out of

exis|tência /ezis'tēsia/ f existence. **~tencial** (pl **~tenciais**) a existential. **~tente** a existing. **~tir** vi exist

êxito /'ezitu/ m success; (música, filme etc) hit; **ter ~** succeed

êxodo /'ezodu/ m exodus

exonerar /ezone'rar/ vt (de cargo) dismiss, sack. **~se** vpr resign

exorbitante /ezorbi'tãtʃi/ a exorbitant

exor|cismo /ezor'sizmu/ m exorcism. **~cista** m/f exorcist. **~cizar** vt exorcize

exótico /e'zɔtʃiku/ a exotic

expan|dir /ispã'dʒir/ vt spread. **~dir-se** vpr spread; ‹pessoa› open up; **~dir-se sobre** expand upon. **~são** f expansion. **~sivo** a expansive, open

expatri|ado /ispatri'adu/ a & m expatriate. **~ar-se** vpr leave one's country

expectativa /ispekta'tʃiva/ f expectation; **na ~ de** expecting; **estar na ~** wait to see what happens; **~ de vida** life expectancy

expedição /espedʒi'sãw/ f (de encomendas, cartas) dispatch; (de passaporte, diploma etc) issue; (viagem) expedition

expediente /ispedʒi'ẽtʃi/ a ‹pessoa› resourceful ● m (horário) working hours; (meios) expedient; **meio ~** part-time

expe|dir /ispe'dʒir/ vt dispatch ‹encomendas, cartas›; issue ‹passaporte, diploma›. **~dito** a prompt, quick

expelir /ispe'lir/ vt expel

experi|ência /isperi'ẽsia/ f experience; (teste, tentativa) experiment. **~ente** a experienced

experimen|tação /isperimẽta'sãw/ f experimentation. **~tado** a experienced. **~tar** vt (provar) try out; try on ‹roupa›; try ‹comida›; (sentir, viver) experience. **~to** m experiment

expi|ar /espi'ar/ vt atone for. **~atório** a **bode ~atório** scapegoat

expi|ração /espira'sãw/ f (vencimento) expiry; (de ar) exhalation. **~rar** vt exhale ● vi (morrer, vencer) expire; (expelir ar) breath out, exhale

expli|cação /isplika'sãw/ f explanation. **~car** vt explain. **~car-se** vpr explain o.s.. **~cável** (pl **~cáveis**) a explainable

explicitar /isplisi'tar/ vt set out

explícito /is'plisitu/ a explicit

explodir /isplo'dʒir/ vt explode ● vi explode; ‹ator etc› make it big

explo|ração /isplora'sãw/ f (uso, abuso) exploitation; (pesquisa) exploration. **~rar** *vt* (*tirar proveito de*) exploit; (*esquadrinhar*) explore

explo|são /isplo'zãw/ *f* explosion. **~sivo** *a* & *m* explosive

expor /es'por/ *vt* (*sujeitar, arriscar*) expose (**a** to); (*exibir*) display ‹*mercadorias*›; exhibit ‹*obras de arte*›; (*explicar*) expound; **~ a vida** risk one's life. **~-se** *vpr* expose o.s. (**a** to)

expor|tação /isporta'sãw/ *f* export. **~tador** *a* exporting ● *m* exporter. **~tadora** *f* export company. **~tar** *vt* export

exposi|ção /ispozi'sãw/ *f* (*de arte etc*) exhibition; (*de mercadorias*) display; (*de filme fotográfico*) exposure; (*explicação*) exposition. **~tor** *m* exhibitor

exposto /is'postu/ *a* exposed (**a** to); ‹*mercadoria, obra de arte*› on display

expres|são /ispre'sãw/ *f* expression. **~sar** *vt* express. **~sar-se** *vpr* express o.s.. **~sivo** *a* expressive; ‹*número, quantia*› significant. **~so** /ε/ *a* & *m* express

exprimir /ispri'mir/ *vt* express. **~se** *vpr* express o.s.

expropriar /ispropri'ar/ *vt* expropriate

expul|são /ispuw'sãw/ *f* expulsion; (*de jogador*) sending off. **~sar** *vt* (*de escola, partido, país etc*) expel; (*de clube, bar, festa etc*) throw out; (*de jogo*) send off. **~so** *pp de* ▶ EXPULSAR

expur|gar /ispur'gar/ *vt* purge; expurgate ‹*livro*›. **~go** *m* purge

êxtase /'estazi/ *f* ecstasy

extasiado /istazi'adu/ *a* ecstatic

exten|são /istẽ'sãw/ *f* extension; (*tamanho, alcance, duração*) extent; (*de terreno*) expanse; **~são** (de

arquivo) *Comput* (file) extension. **~sivo** *a* extensive. **~so** *a* extensive; **por ~so** in full

extenu|ante /istenu'ãtʃi/ *a* wearing, tiring. **~ar** *vt* tire out. **~ar-se** *vpr* tire o.s. out

exterior /isteri'or/ *a* outside, exterior; ‹*aparência*› outward; ‹*relações, comércio etc*› foreign ● *m* outside, exterior; (*de pessoa*) exterior; **o ~** (*outros países*) abroad; **para o/no ~** abroad

exter|minar /istermi'nar/ *vt* exterminate. **~mínio** *m* extermination

exter|nar /ister'nar/ *vt* show. **~na** /ε/ *f* location shot. **~no** /ε/ *a* external; ‹*dívida etc*› foreign ● *m* day pupil

extin|ção /istʃi'sãw/ *f* extinction. **~guir** *vt* extinguish ‹*fogo*›; wipe out ‹*dívida, animal, povo*›. **~guir-se** *vpr* ‹*fogo, luz*› go out; ‹*animal, planta*› become extinct. **~to** *a* extinct; ‹*organização, pessoa*› defunct. **~tor** *m* fire extinguisher

extirpar /istʃir'par/ *vt* remove ‹*tumor etc*›; uproot ‹*ervas daninhas*›; eradicate ‹*abusos*›

extor|quir /istor'kir/ *vt* extort. **~são** *f* extortion

extra /'estra/ *a* & *m/f* extra; **horas ~s** overtime

extração /istra'sãw/ *f* extraction; (*da loteria*) draw

extraconju|gal /estrakõʒu'gaw/ (*pl* **~gais**) *a* extramarital

extracurricular /estrakuxiku'lar/ *a* extracurricular

extradi|ção /istradʒi'sãw/ *f* extradition. **~tar** *vt* extradite

extrair /istra'ir/ *vt* extract; draw ‹*números da loteria*›

extrajudici|al /estraʒudʒisi'aw/
(pl **~ais**) a out-of-court. **~almente**
adv out of court

extraordinário /istraordʒi'nariu/
a extraordinary

extrapolar /istrapo'lar/ vt
(exceder) overstep; (calcular)
extrapolate ● vi overstep the mark,
go too far

extrasensori|al /estrasẽsori'aw/
(pl **~ais**) a extrasensory

extraterrestre /estrate'xestri/
a & m extraterrestrial

extrato /is'trato/ m extract; (de
conta) statement

extrava|gância /istrava'gãsia/ f
extravagance. **~gante** a extravagant

extravasar /istrava'zar/ vt release,
let out <emoções, sentimentos> ● vi
overflow

extra|viado /istravi'adu/ a lost.
~viar vt lose, mislay <papéis, carta>;
lead astray <pessoa>; embezzle
<dinheiro>. **~viar-se** vpr go astray;
<carta> get lost. **~vio** m (perda)
misplacement; (de dinheiro)
embezzlement

extre|midade /estremi'dadʒi/ f
end; (do corpo) extremity. **~mismo**
m extremism. **~mista** a & m/f
extremist. **~mo** /e/ a & m extreme;
o Extremo Oriente the Far East.
~moso /o/ a doting

extrovertido /istrover'tʃido/
a & m extrovert

exube|rância /ezube'rãsia/ f
exuberance. **~rante** a exuberant

exultar /ezuw'tar/ vi exult

exumar /ezu'mar/ vt exhume
<cadáver>; dig up <documentos etc>

Ff

fã /fã/ m/f fan

fábrica /'fabrika/ f factory

fabri|cação /fabrika'sãw/
f manufacture. **~cante** m/f
manufacturer. **~car** vt manufacture;
(inventar) fabricate

fábula /'fabula/ f fable; 🅣
(dinheirão) fortune

fabuloso /fabu'lozu/ a fabulous

faca /'faka/ f knife. **~da** f knife blow;
dar uma **~da em** fig get some
money off

façanha /fa'saɲa/ f feat

facção /fak'sãw/ f faction

face /'fasi/ f face; (do rosto) cheek.
~ta /e/ f facet

fachada /fa'ʃada/ f facade

facho /'faʃu/ m beam

faci|al /fasi'aw/ (pl **~ais**) a facial

fácil /'fasiw/ (pl **~ceis**) a easy;
(pessoa) easy-going

facili|dade /fasili'dadʒi/ f ease;
(talento) facility. **~tar** vt facilitate

facilitismo /facili'tiʒmu/ m o
~ na educação falling education
standards

fã-clube /fã'klubi/ m fan club

fac-símile /fak'simili/ m facsimile;
(fax) fax

fact- Port ▶ **fat-**

facul|dade /fakuw'dadʒi/
f (mental etc) faculty; (escola)
university, Amer college; fazer
~dade go to university. **~tativo**
a optional

fada /'fada/ f fairy. **~do** a destined, doomed. **~madrinha** (pl **~s-madrinhas**) f fairy godmother

fadiga /fa'dʒiga/ f fatigue

fa|dista /fa'dʒista/ m/f fado singer. **~do** m fado

> *i* **fado** *Fado, literally meaning 'fate', is a traditional Portuguese style of song dating back to the early 19th century. The songs have a melancholy, plaintive style, and are associated with the Portuguese concept of* saudade *(longing). There are two types of* fado: *Lisbon* fado *is traditionally sung by a woman accompanied by two or three guitarists, whereas Coimbra* fado *is performed by a male soloist.*

fagote /fa'gɔtʃi/ m bassoon

fagulha /fa'guʎa/ f spark

faia /'faja/ f beech

faisão /faj'zãw/ m pheasant

faísca /fa'iska/ f spark

fais|cante /fajs'kãtʃi/ a sparkling. **~car** vi spark; (cintilar) sparkle

faixa /'fajʃa/ f strip; (cinto) sash; (em karatê, judô) belt; (da estrada) lane; (de ônibus) lane; (para pedestres) zebra crossing, Amer crosswalk; (atadura) bandage; (de disco) track; **~ etária** age group

fajuto /fa'ʒutu/ a 🔲 fake

fala /'fala/ f speech

fala-barato /'fala'baratu/ m/f invar Port ▶ **TAGARELA**

falácia /fa'lasia/ f fallacy

fa|lado /fa'ladu/ a ‹língua› spoken; ‹caso, pessoa› talked about. **~lante** a talkative. **~lar** vt/i speak; (dizer)

say; **~lar com** talk to; **~lar de** ou **em** talk about; **por ~lar em** speaking of; **sem ~lar em** not to mention; **~lou!** 🔲 OK!. **~latório** m (boatos) talk; (som de vozes) talking

falaz /fa'las/ a fallacious

falcão /faw'kãw/ m falcon

falcatrua /fawka'trua/ f swindle

fale|cer /fale'ser/ vi die, pass away. **~cido** a & m deceased. **~cimento** m death

falência /fa'lẽsia/ f bankruptcy; **ir à ~** go bankrupt

falésia /fa'lɛzia/ f cliff

fa|lha /'faʎa/ f fault; (omissão) failure. **~lhar** vi fail. **~lho** a faulty

fálico /'faliku/ a phallic

fa|lido /fa'lidu/ a & m bankrupt. **~lir** vi go bankrupt. **~lível** (pl **~líveis**) a fallible

falo /'falu/ m phallus

fal|sário /faw'sariu/ m forger. **~sear** vt falsify. **~sete** m falsetto. **~sidade** f falseness; (mentira) falsehood

falsifi|cação /fawsifika'sãw/ f forgery. **~cador** m forger. **~car** vt falsify; forge ‹documentos, notas›

falso /'fawsu/ a false

fal|ta /'fawta/ f lack; (em futebol) foul; **em ~ta** at fault; **por ~ta de** for lack of; **sem ~ta** without fail; **fazer ~ta** be needed; **sentir a ~ta de** miss. **~tar** vi be missing; ‹aluno› be absent; **~tam dois dias para** it's two days until; **me ~ta ...** I don't have ...; **~tar a** miss ‹aula etc›; break ‹palavra, promessa›. **~to a** short (**de** of)

fa|ma /'fama/ f reputation; (celebridade) fame. **~migerado** a notorious

família /fa'milia/ f family

famili|ar /famili'ar/ a familiar; (de família) family. ~aridade f familiarity. ~arizar vt familiarize. ~arizar-se vpr familiarize o.s.

faminto /fa'mĩtu/ a starving

famoso /fa'mozu/ a famous

fanático /fa'natʃiku/ a fanatical ● m fanatic

fanatismo /fana'tʃizmu/ m fanaticism

fanfarrão /fãfa'xãw/ m braggart

fanhoso /fa'ɲozu/ a nasal; **ser ~** talk through one's nose

fanta|sia /fãta'zia/ f (faculdade) imagination; (devaneio) fantasy; (roupa) fancy dress. ~siar vt dream up ● vi fantasize. ~siar-se vpr dress up (de as). ~sioso /o/ a fanciful; ‹pessoa› imaginative. ~sista a imaginative

fantasma /fã'tazma/ m ghost. ~górico a ghostly

fantástico /fã'tastʃiku/ a fantastic

fantoche /fã'tɔʃi/ m puppet

faqueiro /fa'keru/ m canteen of cutlery

fara|ó /fara'ɔ/ m pharaoh. ~ônico a fig of epic proportions

farda /'farda/ f uniform. ~do a uniformed

fardo /'fardu/ m fig burden

fare|jador /fareʒa'dor/ a cão ~jador sniffer dog. ~jar vt sniff out ● vi sniff

farelo /fa'rɛlu/ m bran; (de pão) crumb; (de madeira) sawdust

farfalhar /farfa'ʎar/ vi rustle

farináceo /fari'nasiu/ a starchy. ~s m pl starchy foods

farin|ge /fa'rĩʒi/ f pharynx. ~gite f pharyngitis

farinha /fa'riɲa/ f flour; **~ de rosca** breadcrumbs

far|macêutico /farma'sewtʃiku/ a pharmaceutical ● m (pessoa) pharmacist. ~mácia f (loja) chemist's, Amer pharmacy; (ciência) pharmacy

faro /'faru/ f sense of smell; fig nose

faroeste /faro'estʃi/ m (filme) western; (região) wild west

faro|fa /fa'rɔfa/ f fried manioc flour. ~feiro m 🄃 day tripper

fa|rol /fa'rɔw/ m (pl ~róis) m (de carro) headlight; (de trânsito) traffic light; (à beira-mar) lighthouse; ~rol alto full beam; ~rol baixo dipped beam. ~roleiro a boastful ● m big-head. ~rolete /e/ m, Port ~rolim m sidelight; (traseiro) tail light

farpa /'farpa/ f splinter; (de metal) fig barb. ~do a arame ~do barbed wire

farra /'faxa/ f 🄃 partying; **cair na ~** go out and party

farrapo /fa'xapu/ m rag

far|rear /faxi'ar/ vi 🄃 party. ~rista m/f 🄃 raver 🄃

far|sa /'farsa/ f (peça) farce; (fingimento) pretence. ~sante m/f (brincalhão) joker; (pessoa sem seriedade) unreliable character

far|tar /far'tar/ vt satiate. ~tar-se vpr (saciar-se) gorge o.s. (de with); (cansar) tire (de of). ~to a (abundante) plentiful; (cansado) fed up (de with). ~tura f abundance

fascículo /fa'sikulu/ m instalment

fasci|nação /fasina'sãw/ f fascination. ~nante a fascinating. ~nar vt fascinate

fascínio /fa'siniu/ m fascination

fas|cismo /fa'sizmu/ m fascism. ~cista a & m/f fascist

fase /'fazi/ f phase

fa|tal /fa'taw/ (pl **~tais**) a fatal. **~talismo** m fatalism. **~talista** a fatalistic ● m/f fatalist. **~talmente** adv inevitably

fatia /fa'tʃia/ f slice

fatídico /fa'tʃidʒiku/ a fateful

fati|gante /fatʃi'gãtʃi/ a tiring. **~gar** vt tire, fatigue

> **Fátima** Fátima is a town in central Portugal famous for its Marian shrine, the Basilica of Our Lady of Fátima. The shrine was built to commemorate the reported apparition of the Virgin Mary to three shepherds in 1917, and it attracts millions of Catholic pilgrims every year. *i*

fato¹ /'fatu/ m fact; **de ~** as a matter of fact, in fact; **~ consumado** fait accompli

fato² /'fatu/ Port m suit

fator /fa'tor/ m factor

fátuo /'fatuu/ a fatuous

fatu|ra /fa'tura/ f invoice. **~ramento** m turnover. **~rar** vt invoice for ‹encomenda›; make ‹dinheiro›; fig ‹emplacar› notch up ● vi 🔢 rake it in 🔢

fauna /'fawna/ f fauna

fava /'fava/ f broad bean; **mandar alguém a ~s** tell sb where to get off

favela /fa'vɛla/ f shanty town. **~do** m shanty-dweller

> **favela** Favelas are Brazilian shanty towns, characterized by precarious housing, very little infrastructure and a lack of official recognition. The houses in the *favelas* are known as *barracos*, and many have no running water or sanitation. The most famous shanty towns in Brazil are in Rio de Janeiro, such as the *Favela da Rocinha*, which is home to sixty thousand people. *i*

favo /'favu/ m honeycomb

favor /fa'vor/ m favour; **a ~ de** in favour of; **por ~** please; **faça ~** please

favo|rável /favo'ravew/ (pl **~ráveis**) a favourable. **~recer** vt favour. **~ritismo** m favouritism. **~rito** a & m favourite

faxi|na /fa'ʃina/ f clean-up. **~neiro** m cleaner

fazen|da /fa'zẽda/ f (de café, gado etc) farm; (tecido) fabric, material; (pública) treasury. **~deiro** m farmer

> **fazer** /fa'zer/ ● vt
>
> ┄┄► (produzir, preparar) make; **~ uma blusa** make a blouse; **~ muito ruído** make a lot of noise; **~ um café** make a coffee; **~ uma pergunta** ask a question
>
> ┄┄► (realizar) to do; **~ um exame/lição de casa** do an exam/some homework
>
> ┄┄► (praticar) do; **~ ginástica / judô** do gymnastics/judo
>
> ┄┄► (favor) do; **você me faria um favor?** can you do me a favour?
>
> ┄┄► (comentário, promessa, esforço) make; **você precisa ~ um esforço** you have to make an effort
>
> ┄┄► (amor) make; **faça amor, não faça guerra** make love not war

····➤ (*anos*) be; **ela faz 20 anos em março** she'll be 20 in March

····➤ (*profissão*) do; **o que você faz? Sou piloto** what do you do? I'm a pilot

····➤ (*obrigar*) make; **~ alguém rir** make sb laugh; **você me faz vir aqui todos os dias** you make me come here everyday

● *vi*

····➤ (*com tempo atmosférico*) **faz frio/calor** it's cold/hot

····➤ (*em expressões*) **~ bem/mal** (*ao agir*) be right/wrong; (*à saúde*) **fumar faz mal à saúde** smoking is bad for you; **o exercício faz bem** exercise is good for you; **~ de conta que** pretend; **ela fez de conta que não me viu** she pretended she hadn't seen me; **não faz mal** (*não importa*) it doesn't matter

● *vpr*

····➤ **~-se de** (*fingir*) pretend; **ele se fez de burro** he pretended not to understand

faz-tudo /fas'tudu/ *m/f invar* jack of all trades

fé /fɛ/ *f* faith

fe|bre /'fɛbri/ *f* fever; **~bre amarela** yellow fever; **~bre do feno** hay fever. **~bril** (*pl* **~bris**) *a* feverish

fe|chado /fe'ʃadu/ *a* closed; ‹*curva*› sharp; ‹*sinal*› red; ‹*torneira*› off; ‹*tempo*› overcast; ‹*cara*› stern; ‹*pessoa*› reserved. **~chadura** *f* lock. **~chamento** *m* closure. **~char** *vt* close, shut; turn off ‹*torneira*›; do up ‹*calça, casaco*›; close ‹*negócio*› ● *vi* close, shut; ‹*sinal*› go red; ‹*tempo*› cloud over; **~char à chave** lock; **~char a cara** frown. **~cho** /e/

m fastener; **~cho** ecler zip

fécula /'fɛkula/ *f* starch

fecun|dar /fekũ'dar/ *vt* fertilize. **~do** *a* fertile

feder /fe'der/ *vi* stink

fede|ração /federa'sãw/ *f* federation. **~ral** (*pl* **~rais**) *a* federal; 🇧 huge. **~rativo** *a* federal

fedor /fe'dor/ *m* stink, stench. **~ento** *a* stinking

feérico /feeriku/ *a* magical

feições /fej'sõjs/ *f pl* features

fei|jão /fe'ʒãw/ *m* bean; (*coletivo*) beans. **~joada** *f* bean stew. **~joeiro** *m* bean plant

feijoada Feijoada is Brazil's most typical dish, and is traditionally made with black beans, pork meat and pork trimmings, such as the ear, feet, and tail. It is often served with sautéed greens, orange and farofa, toasted manioc flour. The dish dates back to the colonial period when African slaves had to make use of the parts of the pig that had been discarded by their owners. Portugal also has its own version of feijoada, made with pork, kidney beans, chouriço (cured sausage) and cabbage.

feio /'feju/ *a* ugly; ‹*palavra, situação, tempo*› nasty; ‹*olhar*› dirty. **~so** /o/ *a* plain

fei|ra /'fera/ *f* market; (*industrial*) trade fair. **~rante** *m/f* market trader

feiti|çaria /fejtʃi'sera/ *f* magic. **~ceira** *f* witch. **~ceiro** *m* wizard ● *a* bewitching. **~ço** *m* spell

fei|tio /fej'tʃiu/ *m* (*de pessoa*) make-up. **~to** *pp de* ▶ FAZER ● *m* (*ato*) deed; (*proeza*) feat ● *conj* like;

bem **~to por ele** (it) serves him right. **~tura** f making

feiura /fej'ura/ f ugliness

feixe /'fejʃi/ m bundle

fel /fɛw/ m gall; fig bitterness

felicidade /felisi'dadʒi/ f happiness

felici|tações /felisita'sõjs/ f pl congratulations. **~tar** vt congratulate (**por** on)

felino /fe'linu/ a feline

feliz /fe'lis/ a happy. **~ardo** a lucky. **~mente** adv fortunately

fel|pa /'fewpa/ f (de pano) nap; (penugem) down, fluff. **~pudo** a fluffy

feltro /'fewtru/ m felt

fêmea /'femia/ a & f female

femi|nil /femi'niw/ (pl **~nis**) a feminine. **~nilidade** f femininity. **~nino** a female; <palavra> feminine. **~nismo** f feminism. **~nista** a & m/f feminist

fêmur /'femur/ m femur

fen|da /'fẽda/ f crack. **~der** vt/i split, crack

feno /'fenu/ m hay

fenome|nal /fenome'naw/ (pl **~nais**) a phenomenal

fenômeno /fe'nomenu/ m phenomenon

fera /'fera/ f wild beast; **ficar uma ~** get really angry; **ser ~ em** 🔠 be brilliant at

féretro /'feretru/ m coffin

feriado /feri'adu/ m public holiday

férias /'fɛrias/ f pl holiday(s), Amer vacation; **de ~** on holiday; **tirar ~** take a holiday

feri|da /fe'rida/ f injury; (com arma) wound. **~do** a injured; Mil wounded ● m injured person; **os ~dos** the injured; Mil the wounded.

~r vt injure; (com arma) wound; (magoar) hurt

fermen|tar /fermẽ'tar/ vt/i ferment. **~to** m yeast; fig ferment; **~to em pó** baking powder

fe|rocidade /ferosi'dadʒi/ f ferocity. **~roz** a ferocious

fer|rado /fe'xadu/ a **estou ~rado** 🔠 I've had it 🔠; **~rado no sono** fast asleep. **~radura** f horseshoe. **~ragem** f ironwork; pl hardware. **~ramenta** f tool; (coletivo) tools. **~rão** m (de abelha) sting. **~rar** vt brand <gado>; shoe <cavalo>. **~rar-se** vpr 🔠 come a cropper. **~reiro** m blacksmith. **~renho** a <partidário etc> staunch; <vontade> iron

férreo /'fɛxiu/ a iron

ferro /'fexu/ m iron. **~lho** /o/ m bolt. **~velho** (pl **~s-velhos**) m (pessoa) scrap-metal dealer; (lugar) scrap-metal yard. **~via** f railway, Amer railroad. **~viário** a railway ● m railway worker

ferrugem /fe'xuʒẽ/ f rust

fér|til /'fɛrtʃiw/ (pl **~teis**) a fertile

fertili|dade /fertʃili'dadʒi/ f fertility. **~zante** m fertilizer. **~zar** vt fertilize

fer|vente /fer'vẽtʃi/ a boiling. **~ver** vi boil; (de raiva) seethe. **~vilhar** vi bubble; **~vilhar de** swarm with. **~vor** m fervour. **~vura** f boiling

fes|ta /'festa/ f party; (religiosa) festival. **~tejar** vt/i celebrate; (acolher) fete. **~tejo** /e/ m celebration. **~tim** m feast. **~tival** (pl **~tivais**) m festival. **~tividade** f festivity. **~tivo** a festive

festa Every town in Portugal has its own patron saint, and festivals, called *festas*, are held nationwide during the summer months to celebrate the local saint's day. The festivals consist of colourful processions through the town, coupled with music, street food and much revelry. One of the most famous festivals is the *Festa de Santo António* in Lisbon during which a mass wedding is held at Lisbon Cathedral in honour of St Anthony, the saint of marriages.

festas juninas *Festas juninas* are festivals that take place in Brazil over the month of June in honour of various saints: St Anthony on the 13th, St John on the 24th, and St Peter and St Paul on the 29th. During these festivals, various typical dishes are served, such as roasted sweet potato, popcorn, rice pudding, corn bread, and *quentão*, a hot drink made with wine, sugar, cloves and cinnamon. The festivities often include lighting bonfires, releasing hot-air balloons and dancing to *música caipira*, Brazilian country music.

feti|che /feˈtiʃi/ *m* fetish. **~chismo** *m* fetishism. **~chista** *m/f* fetishist ● *a* fetishistic

fétido /ˈfɛtʃidu/ *a* fetid

feto[1] /ˈfɛtu/ *m* (no útero) foetus

feto[2] /ˈfɛtu/ *Port m* (planta) fern

feu|dal /few'daw/ (*pl* **~dais**) *a* feudal. **~dalismo** *m* feudalism

fevereiro /feveˈreru/ *m* February

fezes /ˈfɛzis/ *f pl* faeces

fia|ção /fiaˈsãw/ *f Eletr* wiring; (*fábrica*) mill

fia|do /fiˈadu/ *a* ‹conversa› idle ● *adv* ‹comprar› on credit. **~dor** *m* guarantor

fiambre /fiˈãbri/ *m* cooked ham

fiança /fiˈãsa/ *f* surety; *Jurid* bail

fiapo /fiˈapu/ *m* thread

fiar /fiˈar/ *vt* spin ‹lã etc›

fiasco /fiˈasku/ *m* fiasco

fibra /ˈfibra/ *f* fibre

ficar /fiˈkar/ ● *vi*

••••▸ (estar situado) be; **onde fica a casa deles?** where is their home?

••••▸ (permanecer) stay; **~ em casa** stay at home

••••▸ (restar) be left (over); **~am apenas 3 concorrentes** there were just 3 contestants left

••••▸ (tornar-se) **~ rico/doente/velho/gordo** get rich/ill/old/fat; **~ careca/cego** go bald/blind

••••▸ **~ com** (guardar) **~ com o troco** keep the change

••••▸ **~ de** (prometer) **ele ficou de me ajudar** he promised to help me; (concordar) **ficamos de nos encontrar na terça-feira** we agreed to meet on Tuesday

••••▸ **~ por** (custar) **este vestido ficou por R$30** this dress cost me R$30

••••▸ **~ sem** (perder) lose; **ela ficou sem o emprego** she lost her job; (esgotar-se) run out of; **fiquei sem açúcar** I ran out of sugar

••••▸ (em expressões) **~ bem/mal**: ‹roupa› **a camisa fica bem em você** the shirt suits you; **~ para trás: ande, não fique para trás** come on, don't get left behind

fic|ção /fik'sãw/ f fiction; **~ção científica** science fiction. **~cionista** m/f fiction writer

fi|cha /'fiʃa/ f (de telefone) token; (de jogo) chip; (da caixa) ticket; (de fichário) file card; (na polícia) record; Port (tomada) plug. **~chário** m, Port **~cheiro** m file; (móvel) filing cabinet

fictício /fik'tʃisiu/ a fictitious

fidalgo /fi'dalgu/ m nobleman

fide|digno /fide'dʒignu/ a trustworthy. **~lidade** f fidelity

fiduciário /fidusi'ariu/ a fiduciary ● m trustee

fi|el /fi'ɛw/ (pl **~éis**) a faithful ● m os **~éis** (na igreja) the congregation

figa /'figa/ f talisman

fígado /'figadu/ m liver

fi|go /'figu/ m fig. **~gueira** f fig tree

figu|ra /fi'gura/ f figure; (carta de jogo) face card; **E** (pessoa) character; **fazer (má) ~ra** make a (bad) impression. **~rado** a figurative. **~rante** m/f extra. **~rão** m big shot. **~rar** vi appear, figure. **~rativo** a figurative. **~rinha** f sticker. **~rino** m fashion plate; (de filme, peça) costume design; fig model; **como manda o ~rino** as it should be

fila /'fila/ f line; (de espera) queue, Amer line; (fileira) row; **fazer ~** queue up, Amer stand in line; **~ indiana** single file

filamento /fila'mẽtu/ m filament

filante /fi'lãtʃi/ m/f **E** sponger

filan|tropia /filãtro'pia/ f philanthropy. **~trópico** a philanthropic. **~tropo** /o/ m philanthropist

filão /fi'lãw/ m (de ouro) seam; fig money-spinner

filar /fi'lar/ vt **E** sponge **E**, cadge **E**

filar|mónica /filar'monika/ f philharmonic (orchestra). **~mónico** a philharmonic

filate|lia /filate'lia/ f philately. **~lista** m/f philatelist

filé /fi'lɛ/ m fillet

fileira /fi'lera/ f row

filete /fi'letʃi/ m fillet

fi|lha /'fiʎa/ f daughter. **~lho** m son; **~lho da puta** (vulg) bastard, Amer son of a bitch; **~lho de criação** foster child; **~lho único** only child ● pl (crianças) children. **~lhote** m (de cão) pup; (de lobo etc) cub; pl young

fili|ação /filia'sãw/ f affiliation. **~al** (pl **~ais**) a filial ● f branch

Filipinas /fili'pinas/ f pl Philippines

filipino /fili'pinu/ a & m Filipino

fil|madora /fiwma'dora/ f camcorder. **~magem** f filming. **~mar** vt/i film. **~me** m film

fi|lologia /filolo'ʒia/ f philology. **~lólogo** m philologist

filo|sofar /filozo'far/ vi philosophize. **~sofia** f philosophy. **~sófico** a philosophical

filósofo /fi'lɔzofu/ m philosopher

fil|trar /fiw'trar/ vt filter. **~tro** m filter

fim /fĩ/ m end; **a ~ de** (para) in order to; **estar a ~ de** fancy; **por ~** finally; **sem ~** endless; **ter ~** come to an end; **~ de semana** weekend

fi|nado /fi'nadu/ a & m deceased, departed. **~nal** (pl **~nais**) a final ● m end ● f final. **~nalista** m/f finalist. **~nalizar** vt/i finish

finan|ças /fi'nãsas/ f pl finances. **~ceiro** a financial ● m financier. **~ciamento** m financing; (um) loan. **~ciar** vt finance. **~cista** m financier

fincar /fĩ'kar/ vt plant; **~ o pé** dig one's heels in

findar /fiˈdar/ vt/i end

fineza /fiˈneza/ f finesse; (favor) kindness

fin|gido /fiˈʒidu/ a feigned; ‹pessoa› insincere. **~gimento** m pretence. **~gir** vt pretend; feign ‹doença etc› ● vi pretend; **~gir-se de** pretend to be

fi|ninho /fiˈniɲu/ adv **sair de ~ninho** slip away. **~no** a (não grosso) thin; ‹areia, pó etc› fine; (refinado) refined. **~nório** a crafty. **~nura** f thinness; fineness

finito /fiˈnitu/ a finite

finlan|dês /fĩlɐˈdes/ a (f **~desa**) Finnish ● m (f **~desa**) Finn; (língua) Finnish

Finlândia /fĩˈlɐdʒia/ f Finland

fio /ˈfiu/ m thread; (elétrico) wire; (de sangue, água) trickle; (de luz, esperança) glimmer; (de navalha etc) edge; **horas a ~** hours on end

fir|ma /ˈfirma/ f firm; (assinatura) signature. **~mamento** m firmament. **~mar** vt fix; (basear) base ● vi settle. **~mar-se** vpr be based (em on). **~me** a firm; ‹tempo› settled ● adv firmly. **~meza** f firmness

fis|cal /fisˈkaw/ (pl **~cais**) m inspector. **~calização** f inspection. **~calizar** vt inspect. **~co** m inland revenue, Amer internal revenue service

fis|gada /fizˈgada/ f stabbing pain. **~gar** vt hook

físi|ca /ˈfizika/ f physics. **~co** a physical ● m (de pessoa) physicist; (corpo) physique

fisio|nomia /fiziˈonoˈmia/ f face. **~nomista** m/f **ser ~nomista** have a good memory for faces. **~terapeuta** m/f physiotherapist. **~terapia** f physiotherapy

fissura /fiˈsura/ f fissure; 🅸 craving. **~do** a **~do em** 🅸 mad about

fita /ˈfita/ f tape; 🅸 (encenação) play-acting; **fazer ~** 🅸 put on an act; **~ adesiva** Port adhesive tape; **~ métrica** tape measure

fitar /fiˈtar/ vt stare at

FIV abr f (= fertilização in vitro) IVF

fivela /fiˈvɛla/ f buckle

fi|xador /fiksaˈdor/ m (de cabelo) setting lotion; (de fotos) fixative. **~xar** vt fix; stick up ‹cartaz›. **~xo** a fixed

flácido /ˈflasidu/ a flabby

flagelo /flaˈʒelu/ m scourge

fla|grante /flaˈgrɐtʃi/ a flagrant; **apanhar em ~grante (delito)** catch in the act. **~grar** vt catch

flame|jante /flameˈʒɐtʃi/ a blazing. **~jar** vi blaze

flamengo /flaˈmẽgu/ a Flemish ● m Fleming; (língua) Flemish

flamingo /flaˈmĩgu/ m flamingo

flâmula /ˈflamula/ f pennant

flanco /ˈflɐku/ m flank

flanela /flaˈnɛla/ f flannel

flanquear /flɐkiˈar/ vt flank

flash /flɛʃ/ m invar flash

flau|ta /ˈflawta/ f flute. **~tista** m/f flautist

flecha /ˈflɛʃa/ f arrow

fler|tar /flerˈtar/ vi flirt. **~te** m flirtation

fleuma /ˈflewma/ f phlegm

flex /flɛks/ m invar ‹carro› flexible-fuel car (car designed to run on petrol and ethanol)

fle|xão /flekˈsɐw/ f press-up, Amer push-up; Ling inflection. **~xibilidade** f flexibility. **~xionar** vt/i flex ‹perna, braço›; Ling inflect. **~xível** (pl

~xíveis) a flexible

fliperama /flipe'rama/ m pinball machine

floco /'flɔku/ m flake

flor /flor/ f flower; **a fina ~** the cream; **à ~ da pele** fig on edge

flo|ra /'flɔra/ f flora. **~reado** a full of flowers; ⟨fala⟩ florid. **~reio** m clever turn of phrase. **~rescer** vi flower. **~resta** /ɛ/ f forest. **~restal** (pl **~restais**) a forest. **~rido** a in flower; fig florid. **~rir** vi flower

flotilha /flo'tʃiʎa/ f flotilla

flu|ência /flu'ẽsia/ f fluency. **~ente** a fluent

flui|dez /flui'des/ f fluidity. **~do** a & m fluid

fluir /flu'ir/ vi flow

fluminense /flumi'nẽsi/ a & m (person) from Rio de Janeiro state

fluorescente /fluore'sẽtʃi/ a fluorescent

flutu|ação /flutua'sãw/ f fluctuation. **~ante** a floating. **~ar** vi float; ⟨bandeira⟩ flutter; (hesitar) waver

fluvi|al /fluvi'aw/ (pl **~ais**) a a river

fluxo /'fluksu/ m flow. **~grama** m flow chart

fobia /fo'bia/ f phobia

foca /'fɔka/ f seal

focalizar /fokali'zar/ vt focus on

focinho /fo'siɲu/ m snout

foco /'fɔku/ m focus; fig centre

fofo /'fofu/ a soft; ⟨pessoa⟩ cuddly

fofo|ca /fo'fɔka/ f piece of gossip; pl gossip. **~car** vi gossip. **~queiro** m gossip ● a gossipy

fo|gão /fo'gãw/ m stove; (de cozinhar) cooker. **~go** /o/ m fire; **tem ~go?** have you got a light?; **ser ~go** ⛒ (ser chato) be a pain in the

neck; (ser incrível) be amazing; **~gos de artifício** fireworks. **~goso** /o/ a fiery. **~gueira** f bonfire. **~guete** /e/ m rocket

foice /'fojsi/ f scythe

fol|clore /fow'klɔri/ m folklore. **~clórico** a folk

fole /'fɔli/ m bellows

fôlego /'folegu/ m breath; fig stamina

fol|ga /'fɔwga/ f rest, break; ⛒ (cara de pau) cheek. **~gado** a ⟨roupa⟩ full, loose; ⟨vida⟩ leisurely; ⛒ (atrevido) cheeky. **~gar** vt loosen ● vi have time off

fo|lha /'foʎa/ f leaf; (de papel) sheet; **novo em ~lha** brand new; **~lha de pagamento** payroll. **~lhagem** f foliage. **~lhear** vt leaf through. **~lheto** /e/ m pamphlet. **~lhinha** f tear-off calendar. **~lhudo** a leafy

folhado /fo'ʎadu/ m (massa) puff pastry

foli|a /fo'lia/ f revelry. **~ão** m (f **~ona**) reveller

folículo /fo'likulu/ m follicle

fome /'fɔmi/ f hunger; **estar com ~** be hungry

fomentar /fomẽ'tar/ vt foment

fone /'fɔni/ m (do telefone) receiver; (de rádio etc) headphones

fonema /fo'nema/ m phoneme

fonéti|ca /fo'nɛtʃika/ f phonetics. **~co** a phonetic

fonologia /fonolo'ʒia/ f phonology

fonte /'fõtʃi/ f (de água) spring; fig source

fora /'fɔra/ adv outside; (não em casa) out; (viajando) away ● prep except; **dar um ~** drop a clanger; **dar um ~ em alguém** cut sb dead; chuck ⟨namorado⟩; **por ~** on the outside. **~ de lei** m/f invar outlaw

foragido /fora'ʒidu/ *a* at large, on the run ● *m* fugitive

forasteiro /foras'teru/ *m* outsider

forca /'fɔrka/ *f* gallows

for|ça /'fɔrsa/ *f* (*vigor*) strength; (*violência*) force; (*elétrica*) power; **dar uma ~ça a alguém** help sb out; **fazer ~ça** make an effort; **~ças armadas** armed forces. **~çar** *vt* force. **~ça-tarefa** (*pl* **~ças-tarefa**) *f* task force

fórceps /'fɔrseps/ *m invar* forceps

forçoso /for'sozu/ *a* forced

for|ja /'fɔrʒa/ *f* forge. **~jar** *vt* forge

forma¹ /'fɔrma/ *f* form; (*contorno*) shape; (*maneira*) way; **de qualquer ~** anyway; **manter a ~** keep fit

forma² /'fɔrma/ *f* mould; (*de cozinha*) baking tin

for|mação /forma'sãw/ *f* formation; (*educação*) education; (*profissionalizante*) training. **~mado** *m* graduate. **~mal** (*pl* **~mais**) *a* formal. **~malidade** *f* formality. **~malizar** *vt* formalize. **~mar** *vt* form; (*educar*) educate; **~mar-se** *vpr* be formed; (*estudante*) graduate. **~mato** *m* format. **~matura** *f* graduation

formatar /forma'tar/ *vt* Comput format

formidá|vel /formi'davew/ (*pl* **~veis**) *a* formidable; (*muito bom*) tremendous

formi|ga /for'miga/ *f* ant. **~gamento** *m* pins and needles. **~gar** *vi* swarm (**de** with); (*perna, mão etc*) tingle. **~gueiro** *m* ants' nest

formosura /formo'zura/ *f* beauty

fórmula /'fɔrmula/ *f* formula

formu|lação /formula'sãw/ *f* formulation. **~lar** *vt* formulate.

~lário *m* form

fornalha /for'naʎa/ *f* furnace

forne|cedor /forne'dor/ *m* supplier. **~cer** *vt* supply; **~cer algo a alguém** supply sb with sth. **~cimento** *m* supply

forno /'fornu/ *m* oven; (*para louça etc*) kiln

foro /'foru/ *m* forum

forra /'fɔxa/ *f* **ir à ~** get one's own back

for|ragem /fo'xaʒẽ/ *f* fodder. **~rar** *vt* line ‹roupa, caixa etc›; cover ‹sofá etc›; carpet ‹assoalho, sala etc›. **~ro** /o/ *m* (*de roupa, caixa etc*) lining; (*de sofá etc*) cover; (*carpete*) (fitted) carpet

forró /fo'xɔ/ *m* type of Brazilian dance

fortale|cer /fortale'ser/ *vt* strengthen. **~cimento** *m* strengthening. **~za** /e/ *f* fortress

for|te /'fɔrtʃi/ *a* strong; ‹golpe› hard; ‹chuva› heavy; (*físico*) muscular ● *adv* strongly; ‹bater, chover› hard ● *m* (*militar*) fort; (*habilidade*) strong point, forte. **~tificação** *f* fortification. **~tificar** *vt* fortify

fortu|ito /for'tuitu/ *a* chance. **~na** *f* fortune

fosco /'fosku/ *a* dull; ‹vidro› frosted

fosfato /fos'fatu/ *m* phosphate

fósforo /'fɔsforu/ *m* match; (*elemento químico*) phosphor

fossa /'fɔsa/ *f* pit; **na ~** *fig* miserable, depressed

fós|sil /'fɔsiw/ (*pl* **~seis**) *m* fossil

fosso /'fosu/ *m* ditch; (*de castelo*) moat

foto /'fɔtu/ *f* photo. **~cópia** *f* photocopy. **~copiadora** *f* photocopier. **~copiar** *vt* photocopy.

139

~gênico a photogenic. **~grafar** vt photograph. **~grafia** f photography. **~gráfico** a photographic

fotógrafo /fo'tɔgrafu/ m photographer

foz /fɔs/ f mouth

fração /fra'sãw/ f fraction

fracas|sado /fraka'sadu/ a failed ● m failure. **~sar** vi fail. **~so** m failure

fracionar /frasio'nar/ vt break up

fraco /'fraku/ a weak; ‹luz, som› faint; ‹medíocre› poor ● m weakness, weak spot

frade /'fradʒi/ m friar

fragata /fra'gata/ f frigate

frá|gil /'fraʒiw/ (pl **~geis**) a fragile; ‹pessoa› frail

fragilidade /fraʒili'dadʒi/ f fragility; (de pessoa) frailty

fragmen|tar /fragmē'tar/ vt fragment. **~tar-se** vpr fragment. **~to** m fragment

fra|grância /fra'grãsia/ f fragrance. **~grante** a fragrant

fralda /'frawda/ f nappy, Amer diaper

framboesa /frãbo'eza/ f raspberry

França /'frãsa/ f France

fran|cês /frã'ses/ a (f **~cesa**) French ● m (f **~cesa**) Frenchman (f-woman); (língua) French; **os ~ceses** the French

franco /'frãku/ a (honesto) frank; (óbvio) clear; (gratuito) free ● m franc. **~atirador** (pl **~atiradores**) m sniper; fig maverick

frangalho /frã'gaʎu/ m tatter

frango /'frãgu/ m chicken

franja /'frãʒa/ f fringe; (do cabelo) fringe, Amer bangs

fran|quear /frãki'ar/ vt frank ‹carta›. **~queza** /e/ f frankness.

~quia f (de cartas) franking; Jurid franchise

fran|zino /frã'zinu/ a skinny. **~zir** vt gather ‹tecido›; wrinkle ‹testa›

fraque /'fraki/ m morning suit

fraqueza /fra'keza/ f weakness; (de luz, som) faintness

frasco /'frasku/ m bottle

frase /'frazi/ f (oração) sentence; (locução) phrase. **~ado** m phrasing

frasqueira /fras'kera/ f vanity case

frater|nal /frater'naw/ (pl **~nais**) a fraternal. **~nidade** f fraternity. **~nizar** vi fraternize. **~no** a fraternal

fratu|ra /fra'tura/ f fracture. **~rar** vt fracture. **~rar-se** vpr fracture

frau|dar /fraw'dar/ vt defraud. **~dulento** a fraudulent

frear /fri'ar/ vt/i brake

freezer /'frizer/ m freezer

fre|guês /fre'ges/ m (f **~guesa**) customer. **~guesia** f (de loja etc) clientele; (paróquia) parish

frei /frej/ m brother

freio /'freju/ m brake; (de cavalo) bit

freira /'frera/ f nun

freixo /'frefu/ m ash

fremir /fre'mir/ vi shake

frêmito /'fremitu/ m wave

frenesi /frene'zi/ m frenzy

frenético /fre'netʃiku/ a frantic

frente /'frētʃi/ f front; **em ~ a** ou de in front of; **para a ~** forward; **pela ~** ahead; **fazer ~ a** face

frequência /fre'kwẽsia/ f frequency; (assiduidade) attendance; **com muita ~** often

frequen|tador /frekwẽta'dor/ m regular visitor (**de** to). **~tar** vt frequent; (cursar) attend. **~te** a frequent

fres|cão /freʃ'kãw/ m air-conditioned coach. **~co** /e/ a ‹comida etc› fresh; ‹vento, água, quarto› cool; 🅃 (afetado) affected; (exigente) fussy. **~cobol** m kind of racquetball. **~cor** m freshness. **~cura** f 🅃 (afetação) affectation; (ser exigente) fussiness; (coisa sem importância) trifle

fresta /'frɛsta/ f slit

fre|tar /fre'tar/ vt charter ‹avião›; hire ‹caminhão›. **~te** /e/ m freight; (aluguel de avião) charter; (de caminhão) hire

frevo /'frevu/ m type of Brazilian dance

fria /'fria/ f 🅃 difficult situation, spot. **~gem** f chill

fric|ção /frik'sãw/ f friction. **~cionar** vt rub

fri|eira /fri'era/ f chilblain. **~eza** /e/ f coldness

frigideira /friʒi'dera/ f frying pan

frígido /'friʒidu/ a frigid

frigorífico /frigo'rifiku/ m cold store, refrigerator, fridge

frincha /'frĩʃa/ f chink

frio /'friu/ a & m cold; **estar com ~** be cold. **~rento** a sensitive to the cold

frisar /fri'zar/ vt (enfatizar) stress; crimp ‹cabelo›

friso /'frizu/ m frieze

fri|tada /fri'tada/ f fry-up. **~tar** vt fry. **~tas** f pl chips, Amer French fries. **~to** a fried; **está ~to** 🅃 he's had it 🅃. **~tura** f fried food

frivolidade /frivoli'dadʒi/ f frivolity. **frívolo** a frivolous

fronha /'froɲa/ f pillowcase

fronte /'frõtʃi/ f forehead, brow

frontei|ra /frõ'tera/ f border. **~riço** a border

frota /'frɔta/ f fleet

frou|xidão /froʃi'dãw/ f looseness; (moral) laxity. **~xo** a loose; ‹regulamento› lax; ‹pessoa› lackadaisical

fru|gal /fru'gaw/ (pl **~gais**) a frugal. **~galidade** f frugality

frus|tração /frustra'sãw/ f frustration. **~trante** a frustrating. **~trar** vt frustrate

fru|ta /'fruta/ f fruit. **~ta-do-conde** (pl **~tas-do-conde**) f sweetsop; **~ta-pão** (pl **~tas-pão**) f breadfruit. **~teira** f fruit bowl. **~tífero** a fig fruitful. **~to** m fruit

fubá /fu'ba/ m maize flour

fu|çar /fu'sar/ vi nose around. **~ças** f pl 🅃 face, chops 🅃

fu|ga /'fuga/ f escape. **~gaz** a fleeting. **~gida** f escape. **~gir** vi run away; (soltar-se) escape; **~gir a** avoid. **~gitivo** a & m fugitive

fulano /fu'lanu/ m whatever his name is

fuleiro /fu'leru/ a downmarket, cheap and cheerful

fulgor /fuw'gor/ m brightness; fig splendour

fuligem /fu'liʒẽ/ f soot

fulmi|nante /fuwmi'nãtʃi/ a devastating. **~nar** vt strike down; fig devastate; **~nado por um raio** struck by lightning ● vi (criticar) rail

fulo /'fulu/ a Port furious

fu|maça /fu'masa/ f smoke. **~maceira** f cloud of smoke. **~mante**, Port **~mador** m smoker. **~mar** vt/i smoke. **~mê** a invar smoked. **~megar** vi smoke. **~mo** /'fumu/ m (tabaco) tobacco; Port (fumaça) smoke; (fumar) smoking; **~mo**

passivo passive smoking

função /fũ'sãw/ f function; **em ~ de** as a result of; **fazer as funções de** function as

funcho /'fũʃu/ m fennel

funcio|nal /fũsio'naw/ (*pl* **~nais**) a functional. **~nalismo** m civil service. **~namento** m working. **~nar** vi work. **~nário** m employee; **~nário público** civil servant

fun|dação /fũda'sãw/ f foundation. **~dador** m founder ● a founding

fundamen|tal /fũdamẽ'taw/ (*pl* **~tais**) a fundamental. **~tar** vt (*basear*) base; (*justificar*) substantiate. **~to** m foundation

fun|dar /fũ'dar/ vt (*criar*) found; (*basear*) base. **~dar-se** vpr be based (**em** on). **~dear** vi drop anchor, anchor. **~dilho** m seat

fundir /fũ'dʒir/ vt melt *‹ouro, ferro›*; cast *‹sino, estátua›*; (*juntar*) merge. **~se** vpr *‹ouro, ferro›* melt; (*juntar-se*) merge

fundo /'fũdu/ a deep ● m (*parte de baixo*) bottom; (*parte de trás*) back; (*de quadro, foto*) background; (*de dinheiro*) fund; **no ~** basically. **~s** m pl (*da casa etc*) back; (*recursos*) funds

fúnebre /'funebri/ a funereal

funerário /fune'rariu/ a funeral

funesto /fu'nestu/ a fatal

fungar /fũ'gar/ vt/i sniff

fungo /'fũgu/ m fungus

fu|nil /fu'niw/ (*pl* **~nis**) m funnel. **~nilaria** f panel beating; (*oficina*) body shop

furacão /fura'kãw/ m hurricane

furado /fu'radu/ a **papo ~** 🗉 hot air

furão /fu'rãw/ m (*animal*) ferret

furar /fu'rar/ vt pierce *‹orelha etc›*; puncture *‹pneu›*; make a

hole in *‹roupa etc›*; jump *‹fila›*; break *‹greve›* ● vi *‹roupa etc›* go into a hole; *‹pneu›* puncture; 🗉 *‹programa›* fall through

fur|gão /fur'gãw/ m van. **~goneta** /e/ *Port* f van

fúria /'furia/ f fury

furioso /furi'ozu/ a furious

furo /'furu/ m hole; (*de pneu*) puncture; (*jornalístico*) scoop; 🗉 (*gafe*) blunder, faux pas; **dar um ~** put one's foot in it

furor /fu'ror/ m furore

fur|ta-cor /furta'kor/ a invar iridescent. **~tar** vt steal. **~tivo** a furtive. **~to** m theft

furúnculo /fu'rũkulu/ m boil

fusão /fu'zãw/ f fusion; (*de empresas*) merger

fusca /'fuska/ f VW beetle

fuselagem /fuze'laʒẽ/ f fuselage

fusível /fu'zivew/ (*pl* **~veis**) m fuse

fuso /'fuzu/ m spindle; **~ horário** time zone

fustigar /fustʃi'gar/ vt lash; *fig* (*com palavras*) lash out at

futebol /futʃi'bɔw/ m football. **~ístico** a football

fútil /'futʃiw/ (*pl* **~teis**) a frivolous, inane

futilidade /futʃili'dadʒi/ f frivolity, inanity; (*uma*) frivolous thing

futu|rismo /futu'rizmu/ m futurism. **~rista** a & m futurist. **~rístico** a futuristic. **~ro** a & m future

fu|zil /fu'ziw/ (*pl* **~zis**) m rifle. **~zilamento** m shooting. **~zilar** vt shoot ● vi flash. **~zileiro** m rifleman; **~zileiro naval** marine

fuzuê /fuzu'e/ m commotion

Gg

gabarito /gaba'ritu/ *m* calibre

gabar-se /ga'barsi/ *vpr* boast (de of)

gabinete /gabi'netʃi/ *m* (*em casa*) study; (*escritório*) office; (*ministros*) cabinet

gado /'gadu/ *m* livestock; (*bovino*) cattle

gaélico /ga'eliku/ *a & m* Gaelic

gafanhoto /gafa'ɲotu/ *m* (*pequeno*) grasshopper; (*grande*) locust

gafe /'gafi/ *f* faux pas, gaffe

gafieira /gafi'era/ *f* dance; (*salão*) dance hall

gagá /ga'ga/ *a* 🅘 senile

ga|go /'gagu/ *a* stuttering ● *m* stutterer. **~gueira** *f* stutter. **~guejar** *vi* stutter

gaiato /gaj'atu/ *a* funny

gaiola /gaj'ɔla/ *f* cage

gaita /'gajta/ *f* **~ de foles** bagpipes

gaivota /gaj'vɔta/ *f* seagull

gajo /'gaʒu/ *m Port* guy, bloke

gala /'gala/ *f* **festa de ~** gala; **roupa de ~** formal dress

galã /ga'lã/ *m* leading man

galan|tear /galãtʃi'ar/ *vt* woo. **~teio** *m* wooing; (*um*) courtesy

galão /ga'lãw/ *m* (*enfeite*) braid; *Mil* stripe; (*medida*) gallon; *Port* (*café*) white coffee

galáxia /ga'laksia/ *f* galaxy

galé /ga'lɛ/ *f* galley

galego /ga'legu/ *a & m* Galician

galera /ga'lɛra/ *f* 🅘 crowd

galeria /gale'ria/ *f* gallery

Gales /'galis/ *m* **País de G~** Wales

ga|lês /ga'les/ *a* (*f* **~lesa**) Welsh ● *m* (*f* **~lesa**) Welshman (*f*-woman); (*língua*) Welsh

galeto /ga'letu/ *m* spring chicken

galgar /gaw'gar/ *vt* (*transpor*) jump over; climb ‹*escada*›

galgo /'gawgu/ *m* greyhound

galheteiro /gaʎe'teru/ *m* cruet stand

galho /'gaʎu/ *m* branch; **quebrar um ~** 🅘 help out

galináceos /gali'nasius/ *m pl* poultry

gali|nha /ga'liɲa/ *f* chicken. **~nheiro** *m* chicken coop

galo /'galu/ *m* cock; (*inchação*) bump

galocha /ga'lɔʃa/ *f* Wellington boot

galo|pante /galo'pãtʃi/ *a* galloping. **~par** *vi* gallop. **~pe** /ɔ/ *m* gallop

galpão /gaw'pãw/ *m* shed

galvanizar /gawvani'zar/ *vt* galvanize

gama /'gama/ *f* (*musical*) scale; *fig* range

gamado /ga'madu/ *a* besotted (por with)

gamão /ga'mãw/ *m* backgammon

gamar /ga'mar/ *vi* fall in love (por with)

gana /'gana/ *f* desire

ganância /ga'nãsia/ *f* greed

ganancioso /ganãsi'ozu/ *a* greedy

gancho /'gãʃu/ *m* hook

gangorra /gã'goxa/ *f* see-saw

gangrena /gã'grena/ *f* gangrene

gangue /'gãgi/ *m* gang

ga|nhador /gaɲa'dor/ *m* winner
● *a* winning. **~nhar** *vt* win ‹*corrida, prêmio*›; earn ‹*salário*›; get ‹*presente*›; gain ‹*vantagem, tempo, amigo*› ● *vi* win; **~nhar a vida** earn a living. **~nha-pão** *m* livelihood. **~nho** *m* gain; *pl* (*no jogo*) winnings

ga|nido *m* squeal; (*de cachorro*) yelp. **~nir** *vi* squeal; ‹*cachorro*› yelp

ganso /'gãsu/ *m* goose

gara|gem /ga'raʒẽ/ *f* garage.
~gista *m/f* garage attendant

garanhão /gara'ɲãw/ *m* stallion

garan|tia /garã'tʃia/ *f* guarantee.
~tir *vt* guarantee

garatujar /garatu'ʒar/ *vt* scribble

gar|bo /'garbu/ *m* grace. **~boso** *a* graceful

garça /'garsa/ *f* heron

gar|çom /gar'sõ/ *m* waiter.
~conete /ɛ/ *f* waitress

gar|fada /gar'fada/ *f* forkful. **~fo** *m* fork

gargalhada /garga'ʎada/ *f* gale of laughter; **rir às ~s** roar with laughter

gargalo /gar'galu/ *m* bottleneck;
tomar no ~ drink out of the bottle

garganta /gar'gãta/ *f* throat

gargare|jar /gargare'ʒar/ *vi* gargle. **~jo** /e/ *m* gargle

gari /ga'ri/ *m/f* (*lixeiro*) dustman, *Amer* garbage collector; (*varredor de rua*) roadsweeper, *Amer* streetsweeper

garim|par /garĩ'par/ *vi* prospect.
~peiro *m* prospector. **~po** *m* mine

garo|a /ga'roa/ *f* drizzle. **~ar** *vi* drizzle

garo|ta /ga'rota/ *f* girl. **~to** /o/ *m* boy; *Port* (*café*) coffee with milk

garoupa /ga'ropa/ *f* grouper

garra /'gaxa/ *f* claw; *fig* drive, determination; *pl* (*poder*) clutches

garra|fa /ga'xafa/ *f* bottle. **~fada** *f* blow with a bottle. **~fão** *m* flagon

garrancho /ga'xãʃu/ *m* scrawl

garrido /ga'xidu/ *a* (*alegre*) lively

garupa /ga'rupa/ *f* (*de animal*) rump; (*de moto*) pillion seat

gás /gas/ *m* gas; *pl* (*intestinais*) wind, *Amer* gas; **~ lacrimogêneo** tear gas

gasóleo /ga'zɔliu/ *m* diesel oil

gasolina /gazo'lina/ *f* petrol

gaso|sa /ga'zɔza/ *f* fizzy lemonade, *Amer* soda. **~so** *a* gaseous; ‹*bebida*› fizzy

gáspea /'gaspia/ *f* upper

gas|tador /gasta'dor/ *a & m* spendthrift. **~tar** *vt* spend ‹*dinheiro, tempo*›; use up ‹*energia*›; wear out ‹*roupa, sapatos*›. **~to** *m* expense; *pl* spending, expenditure; **dar para o ~to** do

gastrenterite /gastrẽte'ritʃi/ *f* gastroenteritis

gástrico /'gastriku/ *a* gastric

gastrite /gas'tritʃi/ *f* gastritis

gastronomia /gastrono'mia/ *f* gastronomy

ga|ta /'gata/ *f* cat; 🄵 sexy woman.
~tão *m* 🄼 hunk 🄼

gatilho /ga'tʃiʎu/ *m* trigger

ga|tinha /ga'tʃina/ *f* 🄵 sexy woman. **~to** *m* cat; 🄼 hunk 🄼;
fazer alguém de ~to-sapato treat sb like a doormat

gatuno /ga'tunu/ *m* crook ● *a* crooked

gaúcho /ga'uʃu/ *a & m* (person) from Rio Grande do Sul

gaveta /ga'veta/ *f* drawer

gavião /gavi'ãw/ *m* hawk

gaze /'gazi/ f gauze

gazela /ga'zɛla/ f gazelle

gazeta /ga'zeta/ f gazette

geada /ʒi'ada/ f frost

ge|ladeira /ʒela'dera/ f fridge.
~lado a frozen; (muito frio) freezing
● m Port ice cream. **~lar** vt/i freeze

gelati|na /ʒela'tʃina/ f (sobremesa)
jelly; (pó) gelatine. **~noso** /o/ a
gooey

geleia /ʒe'lɛja/ f jam

ge|leira /ʒe'lera/ f glacier. **~lo**
/e/ m ice

gema /'ʒema/ f (de ovo) yolk;
(pedra) gem; **carioca da ~** carioca
born and bred. **~da** f egg yolk
whisked with sugar

gêmeo /'ʒemiu/ a & m twin;
Gêmeos (signo) Gemini

ge|mer /ʒe'mer/ vi moan, groan.
~mido /e/ m moan, groan

gene /'ʒeni/ m gene. **~alogia** f
genealogy. **~alógico** a genealogical;
árvore ~alógica family tree

Genebra /ʒe'nebra/ f Geneva

gene|ral /ʒene'raw/ (pl ~rais) m
general. **~ralidade** f generality.
~ralização f generalization.
~ralizar vt/i generalize. **~ralizar-se**
vpr become generalized

genérico /ʒe'nɛriku/ a generic

gênero /'ʒeneru/ m type, kind;
(gramatical) gender; (literário)
genre; **~s** goods; **~s alimentícios**
foodstuffs; **ela não faz o meu ~**
she's not my type

gene|rosidade /ʒenerozi'dadʒi/
f generosity. **~roso** /o/ a generous

genéti|ca /ʒe'netʃika/ f genetics.
~co a genetic

gengibre /ʒẽ'ʒibri/ m ginger

gengiva /ʒẽ'ʒiva/ f gum

geni|al /ʒeni'aw/ (pl ~ais) a brilliant

gênio /'ʒeniu/ m genius;
(temperamento) temperament

genioso /ʒeni'ozu/ a
temperamental

geni|tal /ʒeni'taw/ (pl ~tais) a
genital

genitivo /ʒeni'tʃivu/ a & m genitive

genocídio /ʒeno'sidʒiu/ m
genocide

genro /'ʒẽxu/ m son-in-law

gente /'ʒẽtʃi/ f people; 🗓 folks;
a ~ (sujeito) we; (objeto) us ● interj
🗓 gosh

gen|til /ʒẽ'tʃiw/ (pl ~tis) a kind.
~tileza /e/ f kindness

genuíno /ʒenu'inu/ a genuine

geo|grafia /ʒeogra'fia/ f
geography. **~gráfico** a geographical

geógrafo /ʒe'ɔgrafu/ m
geographer

geo|logia /ʒeolo'ʒia/ f geology.
~lógico a geological

geólogo /ʒe'ɔlogu/ m geologist

geo|metria /ʒeome'tria/ f
geometry. **~métrico** a geometrical.
~político a geopolitical

Geórgia /ʒi'ɔrʒia/ f Georgia

georgiano /ʒiorʒi'anu/ a & m
Georgian

gera|ção /ʒera'sãw/ f generation.
~dor m generator

ge|ral /ʒe'raw/ (pl ~rais) a general
● f (limpeza) spring clean; **em ~ral**
in general

gerânio /ʒe'raniu/ m geranium

gerar /ʒe'rar/ vt create; generate
‹eletricidade›

gerência /ʒe'rẽsia/ f management

gerenci|ador /ʒerẽsia'dor/
m manager. **~al** (pl ~ais) a
management. **~ar** vt manage

gerente /ʒeˈrẽtʃi/ *m* manager ● *a* managing

gergelim /ʒerʒeˈlĩ/ *m* sesame

geri|atria /ʒeriaˈtria/ *f* geriatrics. **~átrico** *a* geriatric

geringonça /ʒerĩˈgõsa/ *f* contraption

gerir /ʒeˈrir/ *vt* manage

germânico /ʒerˈmaniku/ *a* Germanic

ger|me /ˈʒermi/ *m* germ; **~me de trigo** wheatgerm. **~minar** *vi* germinate

gerúndio /ʒeˈrũdʒiu/ *m* gerund

gesso /ˈʒesu/ *m* plaster

ges|tação /ʒestaˈsãw/ *f* gestation. **~tante** *a f* pregnant woman

gestão /ʒesˈtãw/ *f* management

ges|ticular /ʒestʃikuˈlar/ *vi* gesticulate. **~to** *m* gesture

gibi /ʒiˈbi/ *m* 🄁 comic

Gibraltar /ʒibrawˈtar/ *f* Gibraltar

gigan|te /ʒiˈgãtʃi/ *a & m* giant. **~tesco** /e/ *a* gigantic

gilete /ʒiˈletʃi/ *f* razor blade ● *a & m/f* 🄁 bisexual

gim /ʒĩ/ *m* gin

ginásio /ʒiˈnaziu/ *m* (*escola*) secondary school; (*de ginástica*) gymnasium

ginasta /ʒiˈnasta/ *m/f* gymnast

ginásti|ca /ʒiˈnastʃika/ *f* gymnastics; (*aeróbica*) aerobics. **~co** *a* gymnastic

ginecolo|gia /ʒinekoloˈʒia/ *f* gynaecology. **~gista** *m/f* gynaecologist

gingar /ʒĩˈgar/ *vi* sway

gira-discos /ʒiraˈdiʃkuʃ/ *m invar* Port record player

girafa /ʒiˈrafa/ *f* giraffe

gi|rar /ʒiˈrar/ *vt/i* spin, revolve. **~rassol** (*pl* **~rassóis**) *m* sunflower. **~ratório** *a* revolving

gíria /ˈʒiria/ *f* slang; (*uma ~*) slang expression

giro /ˈʒiru/ *m* spin, turn ● *a* Port 🄁 nice, cute

giz /ʒiʃ/ *m* chalk

gla|cê /glaˈse/ *m* icing. **~cial** (*pl* **~ciais**) *a* icy

glamour /glaˈmur/ *m* glamour. **~oso** /o/ *a* glamorous

glândula /ˈglãdula/ *f* gland

glandular /glãduˈlar/ *a* glandular

glicerina /gliseˈrina/ *f* glycerine

glicose /gliˈkɔzi/ *f* glucose

glo|bal /gloˈbaw/ (*pl* **~bais**) *a* (*mundial*) global; ‹*preço etc*› overall. **~bo** /o/ *m* globe; **~bo ocular** eyeball

globalização /globalizaˈsãw/ *f* globalization

globalizar /globaliˈzar/ *vt* globalize

glóbulo /ˈglɔbulu/ *m* globule; (*do sangue*) corpuscle

glória /ˈglɔria/ *f* glory

glorifi|car /glorifiˈkar/ *vt* glorify. **~oso** /o/ *a* glorious

glossário /gloˈsariu/ *m* glossary

glu|tão /gluˈtãw/ *m* (*f* **~tona**) glutton ● *a* (*f* **~tona**) greedy

gnomo /giˈnomu/ *m* gnome

godê /goˈde/ *a* flared

goela /goˈela/ *f* gullet

gogó /goˈgɔ/ *m* 🄁 Adam's apple

goia|ba /goˈaba/ *f* guava. **~bada** *f* guava jelly. **~beira** *f* guava tree

gol /ˈgow/ (*pl* **~s**) *m* goal

gola /ˈgɔla/ *f* collar

gole /ˈgɔli/ *m* mouthful

go|lear /goli'ar/ vt thrash. **~leiro** m
goalkeeper

golfe /'gowfi/ m golf

golfinho /gow'fiɲu/ m dolphin

golfista /gow'fista/ m/f golfer

golo /'golu/ m Port goal

golpe /'gɔwpi/ m blow; (manobra)
trick; **~ (de estado)** coup (d'état);
~ de mestre masterstroke; **~ de
vento** gust of wind; **~ de vista**
glance. **~ar** vt hit

goma /'goma/ f gum; (para roupa)
starch

gomo /'gomu/ m segment

gôndola /'gõdola/ f rack

gongo /'gõgu/ m gong

gonorreia /gono'xeja/ f
gonorrhea

gonzo /'gõzu/ m hinge

googar /gu'gar/ vt google

gorar /go'rar/ vi go wrong, fail

gor|do /'gordu/ a fat. **~ducho**
a plump

gordu|ra /gor'dura/ f fat. **~rento**
a greasy. **~roso** /u/ a fatty; ‹pele›
greasy, oily

gorgolejar /gorgole'ʒar/ vi gurgle

gorila /go'rila/ m gorilla

gor|jear /gorʒi'ar/ vi twitter. **~jeio**
m twittering

gorjeta /gor'ʒeta/ f tip

gorro /'goxu/ m hat

gos|ma /'gɔzma/ f slime. **~mento**
a slimy

gos|tar /gos'tar/ vi **~tar de** like.
~to /o/ m taste; (prazer) pleasure;
para o meu ~to for my taste;
ter ~to de taste of. **~toso** a nice;
‹comida› nice, tasty; ⚏ ‹pessoa›
gorgeous

go|ta /'gota/ f drop; (que cai) drip;
(doença) gout; **foi a ~ta d'água**

fig it was the last straw. **~teira** f
(buraco) leak; (cano) gutter. **~tejar**
vi drip; ‹telhado› leak ● vt drip

gótico /'gɔtʃiku/ a Gothic

gotícula /go'tʃikula/ f droplet

gourmet /gur'me/ a gourmet;
loja ~ delicatessen

gover|nador /governa'dor/
m governor. **~namental** (pl
~namentais) a governmental.
~nanta f housekeeper. **~nante**
a ruling ● m/f ruler. **~nar** vt govern.
~nista a government ● m/f
government supporter. **~no** /e/ m
government

go|zação /goza'sãw/ f joking;
(uma) send-up. **~zado** a funny. **~zar**
vt **~zar (de)** enjoy; ⚏ (zombar de)
make fun of ● vi (ter orgasmo) come.
~zo m (prazer) enjoyment; (posse)
possession; (orgasmo) orgasm; **ser
um ~zo** be funny

Grã-Bretanha /grãbre'taɲa/ f
Great Britain

graça /'grasa/ f grace; (piada)
joke; (humor) humour, funny side;
Jurid pardon; **de ~** for nothing;
sem ~ (enfadonho) dull; (não
engraçado) unfunny; (envergonhado)
embarrassed; **ter ~** be lovely;
ter ~ be funny; **não tem ~ sair
sozinho** it's no fun to go out alone;
~s a thanks to

grace|jar /grase'ʒar/ vi joke. **~jo**
/e/ m joke

graci|nha /gra'siɲa/ f **ser uma
~nha** be sweet. **~oso** /o/ a gracious

grada|ção /grada'sãw/ f
gradation. **~tivo** a gradual

grade /'gradʒi/ f grille, grating;
(cerca) railings; **atrás das ~s** behind
bars. **~ado** a ‹janela› barred

grado /'gradu/ m **de bom/mau ~**
willingly/unwillingly

gradu|ação /gradua'sãw/ f graduation; *Mil* rank; (*variação*) gradation. **~ado** a ‹*escala*› graduated; ‹*estudante*› graduate; ‹*militar*› high-ranking; (*eminente*) respected. **~al** (*pl* **~ais**) a gradual. **~ar** *vt* graduate ‹*escala*›; (*ordenar*) grade; (*regular*) regulate. **~ar-se** *vpr* ‹*estudante*› graduate

grafia /gra'fia/ f spelling

gráfi|ca /'grafika/ f (*arte*) graphics; (*oficina*) print shop. **~co** a graphic ● *m* (*pessoa*) printer; (*diagrama*) graph; *pl* (*de computador*) graphics

grã-fino /grã'finu/ 🔢 a posh, upper-class ● *m* posh person

grafite /gra'fitʃi/ f (*mineral*) graphite; (*de lápis*) lead; (*pichação*) piece of graffiti

grafiteiro /grafi'teru/ m graffitist

grafiti /gra'fiti/ *m Port* ▶ **grafite**

gra|fologia /grafolo'ʒia/ f graphology. **~fólogo** m graphologist

grama[^1] /'grama/ m gramme

grama[^2] /'grama/ f grass. **~do** m lawn; (*campo de futebol*) field

gramática /gra'matʃika/ f grammar

gramati|cal /gramatʃi'kaw/ (*pl* **~cais**) a grammatical

gram|peador /grãpia'dor/ m stapler. **~pear** *vt* staple ‹*papéis etc*›; tap ‹*telefone*›. **~po** m (*de cabelo*) hair clip; (*para papéis etc*) staple; (*ferramenta*) clamp

grana /'grana/ f 🔢 cash

granada /gra'nada/ f (*projétil*) grenade; (*pedra*) garnet

gran|dalhão /grãda'ʎãw/ a (f **~dalhona**) enormous. **~dão** a (f **~dona**) huge. **~de** a big; *fig* ‹*escritor, amor etc*› great. **~deza** /e/

f greatness; (*tamanho*) magnitude. **~dioso** /o/ a grand

granel /gra'nɛw/ m a **~** in bulk

granito /gra'nitu/ m granite

granizo /gra'nizu/ m hail

gran|ja /'grãʒa/ f farm. **~jear** *vt* win, gain

granulado /granu'ladu/ a granulated

grânulo /'granulu/ m granule

grão /grãw/ (*pl* **~s**) m grain; (*de café*) bean. **~-de-bico** (*pl* **~s-de-bico**) m chickpea

grasnar /graz'nar/ *vi* ‹*pato*› quack; ‹*rã*› croak; ‹*corvo*› caw

grati|dão /gratʃi'dãw/ f gratitude. **~ficação** f (*dinheiro a mais*) gratuity; (*recompensa*) gratification. **~ficante** a gratifying. **~ficar** *vt* (*dar dinheiro a*) give a gratuity to; (*recompensar*) gratify

gratinado /gratʃi'nadu/ a & m gratin

grátis /'gratʃis/ *adv* free

grato /'gratu/ a grateful

gratuito /gra'tuito/ a (*de graça*) free; (*sem motivo*) gratuitous

grau /graw/ m degree; **escola de 1°/2°** **~** primary/secondary school

graúdo /gra'udu/ a big; (*importante*) important

gra|vação /grava'sãw/ f (*de som*) recording; (*de desenhos etc*) engraving. **~vador** m (*pessoa*) engraver; (*máquina*) tape recorder. **~vadora** f record company. **~var** *vt* record ‹*música, disco*›; (*fixar na memória*) memorize; (*estampar*) engrave

gravata /gra'vata/ f tie; (*golpe*) stranglehold; **~ borboleta** bow tie

grave /'gravi/ a serious; ‹*voz, som*› deep; ‹*acento*› grave

grávida /'gravida/ a pregnant

gravidade /gravi'dadʒi/ f gravity

gravidez /gravi'des/ f pregnancy

gravura /gra'vura/ f engraving; (em livro) illustration

graxa /'graʃa/ f (de sapatos) polish; (de lubrificar) grease

Grécia /'grɛsia/ f Greece

grego /'gregu/ a & m Greek

grei /grej/ f flock

gre|lha /'grɛʎa/ f grill. **~lhado** a grilled ● m grill. **~lhar** vt grill

grêmio /'gremiu/ m guild, association

grená /gre'na/ a & m dark red

gre|ta /'greta/ f crack. **~tar** vt/i crack

gre|ve /'grevi/ f strike; **entrar em ~ve** go on strike; **~ve de fome** hunger strike. **~vista** m/f striker

gri|fado /gri'fadu/ a in italics. **~far** vt italicize

griffe /'grifi/ f label, line

gri|lado /gri'ladu/ a 🄐 hung up. **~lar** vt 🄐 hang up. **~lar-se** vpr 🄐 get hung up (**com** about)

grilhão /gri'ʎãw/ m fetter

grilo /'grilu/ m (bicho) cricket; 🄐 (preocupação) hang-up; (problema) hassle; (barulho) squeak

grinalda /gri'nawda/ f garland

gringo /'grĩgu/ 🄐 a foreign ● m foreigner

gri|pado /gri'padu/ a **estar/ficar ~pado** have/get the flu. **~par-se** vpr get the flu. **~pe** /'gripi/ f flu, influenza; **~pe das aves** bird flu; **~pe suína** swine flu

grisalho /gri'zaʎu/ a grey

gri|tante /gri'tãtʃi/ a ‹erro› glaring, gross; ‹cor› loud, garish. **~tar** vt/i shout; (de medo) scream.

~taria f shouting. **~to** m shout; (de medo) scream; **aos ~tos** in a loud voice; **no ~to** 🄐 by force

grogue /'grɔgi/ a groggy

grosa /'grɔza/ f gross

groselha /gro'zeʎa/ f (vermelha) redcurrant; (espinhosa) gooseberry; **~ negra** blackcurrant

gros|seiro /gro'seru/ a rude; (tosco, malfeito) rough. **~seria** f rudeness; (uma) rude thing. **~so** /o/ a thick; ‹voz› deep; 🄐 ‹pessoa, atitude› rude. **~sura** f thickness; 🄐 (grosseria) rudeness

grotesco /gro'tesku/ a grotesque

grua /'grua/ f crane

gru|dado /gru'dadu/ a stuck; fig very attached (**em** to). **~dar** vt/i stick. **~de** m glue. **~dento** a sticky

gru|nhido /gru'nidu/ m grunt. **~nhir** vi grunt

grupo /'grupu/ m group

gruta /'gruta/ f cave

guaraná /gwara'na/ m guarana

> *i*
> **guaraná** *Guaraná* is a common plant native to the Amazon Basin. The term is used to refer to the small fruit of the *guaraná* plant, but also to soft drinks made with guaraná extract, which are very popular in Brazil. *Guaraná* is also used as a stimulant in herbal supplements due to its high caffeine content.

guarani /gwara'ni/ a & m/f Guarani

guarda /'gwarda/ f guard ● m/f guard; (policial) policeman (f -woman); **~** costeira coastguard. **~chuva** m umbrella; **~costas** m invar bodyguard; **~florestal** (pl **~s-florestais**) m/f forest ranger;

~louça m china cupboard; **~noturno** (pl **~s-noturnos**) m night watchman. **~dor** m parking attendant. **~napo** m napkin, serviette

guardar /gwar'dar/ vt (pôr no lugar) put away; (conservar) keep; (vigiar) guard; (não esquecer) remember; **~se de** guard against

guarda|-redes /'gwarda-'xedʃ/ m invar Port goalkeeper. **~roupa** m wardrobe; **~sol** (pl **~sóis**) m sunshade

guardi|ão /gwardʒi'ãw/ (pl **~ães** ou **~ões**) m (f **~ã**) guardian

guarita /gwa'rita/ f sentry box

guar|necer /gwarne'ser/ vt (fortificar) garrison; (munir) equip; (enfeitar) garnish. **~nição** f Mil garrison; (enfeite) garnish

Guatemala /gwate'mala/ f Guatemala

guatemalteco /gwatemal'tɛku/ a & m Guatemalan

gude /'gudʒi/ m **bola de ~** marble

guelra /'gɛwxa/ f gill

guer|ra /'gɛxa/ f war. **~reiro** m warrior ● a warlike. **~rilha** f guerrilla war. **~rilheiro** a & m guerrilla

gueto /'getu/ m ghetto

gugar /gu'gar/ vt ▶ googar

guia /'gia/ m/f guide ● m guide(book) ● f delivery note

Guiana /gi'ana/ f Guyana

guianense /gia'nẽsi/ a & m/f Guyanan

guiar /gi'ar/ vt guide; drive ‹veículo› ● vi drive. **~se** vpr be guided

guichê /gi'ʃe/ m window

guidom /gi'dõ/, Port **guidão** /gi'dãw/ m handlebars

guilhotina /giʎo'tʃina/ f guillotine

guimba /'gĩba/ f butt

guinada /gi'nada/ f change of direction; **dar uma ~** change direction

guinchar¹ /gĩ'ʃar/ vi squeal; ‹freios› screech

guinchar² /gĩ'ʃar/ vt tow ‹carro›; (içar) winch

guincho¹ /'gĩʃu/ m squeal; (de freios) screech

guincho² /'gĩʃu/ m (máquina) winch; (veículo) tow truck

guin|dar /gĩ'dar/ vt hoist. **~daste** m crane

Guiné /gi'nɛ/ f Guinea

gui|sado /gi'zadu/ m stew. **~sar** vt stew

guitar|ra /gi'taxa/ f (electric) guitar. **~rista** m/f guitarist

guizo /'gizu/ m bell

gu|la /'gula/ f greed. **~lodice** f greed. **~loseima** f delicacy. **~loso** /o/ a greedy

gume /'gumi/ m cutting edge

guri /gu'ri/ m boy. **~a** f girl

guru /gu'ru/ m guru

gutu|ral /gutu'raw/ (pl **~rais**) a guttural

· ·

Hh

· ·

há|bil /'abiw/ (pl **~beis**) a clever, skilful

habili|dade /abili'dadʒi/ f skill; **ter ~dade com** be good with. **~doso** /o/ a skilful. **~tação** f qualification. **~tar** vt qualify

habi|tação /abita'sãw/ f housing; (casa) dwelling. **~tacional** (pl

~tacionais) *a* housing. **~tante** *m/f* inhabitant. **~tar** *vt* inhabit ● *vi* live. **~tável** (*pl* **~táveis**) *a* habitable

hábito /'abitu/ *m* habit

habitu|al /abitu'aw/ (*pl* **~ais**) *a* habitual. **~ar** *vt* accustom (**a** to). **~ar-se** *vpr* get accustomed (**a** to)

hacker /'aker/ *m/f BR* hacker

hacking *m BR* hacking

hadoque /a'dɔki/ *m* haddock

Haia /'aja/ *f* the Hague

Haiti /aj'tʃi/ *m* Haiti

haitiano /ajtʃi'anu/ *a* & *m* Haitian

hálito /'alitu/ *m* breath

halitose /ali'tɔzi/ *f* halitosis

hall /xɔw/ (*pl* **~s**) *m* hall; (*de hotel*) foyer

halogênio /alo'ʒenju/ *m* halogen

halte|re /aw'teri/ *m* dumb-bell. **~rofilismo** *m* weightlifting. **~rofilista** *m/f* weightlifter

hambúrguer /ã'burger/ *m* hamburger

hangar /ã'gar/ *m* hangar

haras /'aras/ *m invar* stud farm

hardware /'xarduer/ *m* hardware

harmo|nia /armo'nia/ *f* harmony. **~nioso** /o/ *a* harmonious. **~nizar** *vt* harmonize; (*conciliar*) reconcile. **~nizar-se** *vpr* (*combinar*) tone in; (*concordar*) coincide

har|pa /'arpa/ *f* harp. **~pista** *m/f* harpist

haste /'astʃi/ *m* pole; (*de planta*) stem, stalk. **~ar** *vt* hoist, raise

Havaí /ava'i/ *m* Hawaii

havaiano /avaj'anu/ *a* & *m* Hawaiian

haver /a'ver/ *m* credit; *pl* possessions ● *vt auxiliar* **havia sido** it had been; (*impessoal*) **há** there is/ are; **ele trabalha aqui há anos** he's

been working here for years; **ela morreu há vinte anos (atrás)** she died twenty years ago

haxixe /a'ʃiʃi/ *m* hashish

he|braico /e'brajku/ *a* & *m* Hebrew. **~breu** *a* & *m* (*f* **~breia**) Hebrew

hectare /ek'tari/ *m* hectare

hediondo /edʒi'õdu/ *a* hideous

hein /ẽj/ *int* eh

hélice /'elisi/ *f* propeller

helicóptero /eli'kɔpteru/ *m* helicopter

hélio /'eliu/ *m* helium

heliporto /eli'portu/ *m* heliport

hem /ẽj/ *int* eh

hematoma /ema'toma/ *m* bruise

hemisfério /emis'feriu/ *m* hemisphere; **Hemisfério Norte/Sul** Northern/Southern Hemisphere

hemo|filia /emofi'lia/ *f* haemophilia. **~fílico** *a* & *m* haemophiliac. **~globina** *f* haemoglobin. **~grama** *m* blood count

hemor|ragia /emoxa'ʒia/ *f* haemorrhage. **~roidas** *f pl* haemorrhoids

henê /e'ne/ *m* henna

hepatite /epa'tʃitʃi/ *f* hepatitis

hera /'era/ *f* ivy

heráldi|ca /e'rawdʒika/ *f* heraldry. **~co** *a* heraldic

herança /e'rãsa/ *f* inheritance; (*de um povo etc*) heritage

her|bicida /erbi'sida/ *m* weedkiller. **~bívoro** *a* herbivorous ● *m* herbivore

her|dar /er'dar/ *vt* inherit. **~deiro** *m* heir

hereditário /eredʒi'tariu/ *a* hereditary

here|ge /e'rɛʒi/ *m/f* heretic. **~sia**
f heresy

herético /e'rɛtʃiku/ *a* heretical

hermético /er'mɛtʃiku/ *a* airtight;
fig obscure

hérnia /'ɛrnia/ *f* hernia

her|ói /e'rɔj/ *m* hero. **~oico** *a* heroic

hero|ína /ero'ina/ *f* (*mulher*)
heroine; (*droga*) heroin. **~ísmo** *m*
heroism

herpes /'ɛrpis/ *m invar* herpes.
~zoster *m* shingles

hesi|tação /ezita'sãw/ *f* hesitation.
~tante *a* hesitant. **~tar** *vi* hesitate

hetero|doxo /etero'dɔksu/
a unorthodox. **~gêneo** *a*
heterogeneous

heterossexu|al /eteroseksu'aw/
(*pl* **~ais**) *a & m* heterosexual

hexago|nal /eksago'naw/
(*pl* **~nais**) *a* hexagonal

hexágono /ek'sagonu/ *m*
hexagon

hiato /i'atu/ *m* hiatus

hiber|nação /iberna'sãw/ *f*
hibernation. **~nar** *vi* hibernate

híbrido /'ibridu/ *a* hybrid;
carro ~ hybrid car

hidrante /i'drãtʃi/ *m* fire hydrant

hidra|tante /idra'tãtʃi/ *a*
moisturising ● *m* moisturizer. **~tar**
vt moisturize <*pele*>. **~to** *m* **~to de
carbono** carbohydrate

hidráuli|ca /i'drawlika/ *f*
hydraulics. **~co** *a* hydraulic

hidrelétri|ca /idre'lɛtrika/ *f*
hydroelectric power station. **~co** *a*
hydroelectric

hidro|avião /idroavi'ãw/ *m*
seaplane. **~carboneto** /e/ *m*
hydrocarbon

hidrófilo /i'drɔfilu/ *a* absorbent;
algodão ~ cotton wool, *Amer*
absorbent cotton

hidrofobia /idrofo'bia/ *f* rabies

hidro|gênio /idro'ʒeniu/ *m*
hydrogen. **~massagem** *f* **banheira
de ~massagem** jacuzzi. **~via** *f*
waterway

hiena /i'ena/ *f* hyena

hierarquia /ierar'kia/ *f* hierarchy

hieróglifo /ie'rɔglifu/ *m*
hieroglyphic

hífen /'ifẽ/ *m* hyphen

higi|ene /iʒi'eni/ *f* hygiene. **~ênico**
a hygienic

hilari|ante /ilari'ãtʃi/ *a* hilarious.
~dade *f* hilarity

Himalaia /ima'laja/ *m* Himalayas

hin|di /ĩ'dʒi/ *m* Hindi. **~du** *a &
m/f* Hindu. **~duísmo** *m* Hinduism.
~duísta *a & m/f* Hindu

hino /'inu/ *m* hymn; **~ nacional**
national anthem

hipermercado /ipermer'kadu/
m hypermarket

hipersensí|vel /ipersẽ'sivew/
(*pl* **~veis**) *a* hypersensitive

hipertensão /ipertẽ'sãw/ *f*
hypertension

hípico /'ipiku/ *a* horse riding

hipismo /i'pizmu/ *m* horse riding;
(*corridas*) horse racing

hip|nose /ipi'nɔzi/ *f* hypnosis.
~nótico *a* hypnotic. **~notismo**
m hypnotism. **~notizador** *m*
hypnotist. **~notizar** *vt* hypnotize

hipnoterapia /ipnotera'pia/ *f*
hypnotherapy

hipocondríaco /ipokõ'driaku/
a & m hypochondriac

hipocrisia /ipokri'zia/ *f* hypocrisy

hipócrita /i'pɔkrita/ *m/f* hypocrite
● *a* hypocritical

hipódromo /i'pɔdromu/ *m* race
course, *Amer* race track

hipopótamo /ipo'pɔtamu/ *m*
hippopotamus

hipote|ca /ipo'tɛka/ *f* mortgage.
~car *vt* mortgage. **~cário** *a*
mortgage

hipotermia /ipoter'mia/ *f*
hypothermia

hipótese /i'pɔtezi/ *f* hypothesis;
na ~ de in the event of; **na pior das
~s** at worst

hipotético /ipo'tɛtʃiku/ *a*
hypothetical

hirto /'irtu/ *a* rigid, stiff

hispânico /is'paniku/ *a* Hispanic

histamina /ista'mina/ *f* histamine

his|terectomia /isterekto'mia/
f hysterectomy. **~teria** *f* hysteria.
~térico *a* hysterical. **~terismo** *m*
hysteria

his|tória /is'tɔria/ *f (do passado)*
history; *(conto)* story; *pl (amolação)*
trouble. **~toriador** *m* historian.
~tórico *a* historical; *(marcante)*
historic ● *m* history

hoje /'oʒi/ *adv* today; **~ em dia**
nowadays; **~ de manhã** this
morning; **~ à noite** tonight

Holanda /o'lãda/ *f* Holland

holan|dês /olã'des/ *a* (f **~desa**)
Dutch ● *m* (f **~desa**) Dutchman
(f-woman); *(língua)* Dutch; **os
~deses** the Dutch

holding /'xɔwdʒ/ (*pl* **~s**) *f* holding
company

holerite /ole'ritʃi/ *m* pay slip

holo|causto /olo'kawstu/ *m*
holocaust. **~fote** /ɔ/ *m* spotlight.
~grama *m* hologram

homem /'omẽ/ *m* man; **~ de
negócios** businessman. **~rã**
(*pl* **homens-rã**) *m* frogman

homena|gear /omenaʒi'ar/ *vt*
pay tribute to. **~gem** *f* tribute; **em
~gem a** in honour of

homeo|pata /omio'pata/
m/f homoeopath. **~patia**
f homoeopathy. **~pático** *a*
homoeopathic

homérico /o'mɛriku/
a (estrondoso) booming;
(extraordinário) phenomenal

homi|cida /omi'sida/ *a* homicidal
● *m/f* murderer. **~cídio** *m* homicide;
~cídio involuntário manslaughter

homo|geneizado
/omoʒenej'zadu/ *a <leite>*
homogenized. **~gêneo** *a*
homogeneous

homologar /omolo'gar/ *vt* ratify

homólogo /o'mɔlogu/ *m* opposite
number ● *a* equivalent

homônimo /o'monimu/ *m (xará)*
namesake; *(vocábulo)* homonym

homossexu|al /omoseksu'aw/
(*pl* **~ais**) *a* & *m* homosexual. **~alismo**
m homosexuality

Honduras /õ'duras/ *f* Honduras

hondurenho /õdu'reɲu/ *a* & *m*
Honduran

hones|tidade /onestʃi'dadʒi/ *f*
honesty. **~to** /ɛ/ *a* honest

hono|rário /ono'rariu/ *a*
honorary. **~rários** *m pl* fees. **~rífico**
a honorific

hon|ra /'õxa/ *f* honour. **~radez**
f honesty, integrity. **~rado** *a*
honourable. **~rar** *vt* honour. **~roso**
/o/ *a* honourable

hóquei /'ɔkej/ *m* (field) hockey;
~ sobre gelo ice hockey; **~ sobre
patins** roller hockey

hora /'ɔra/ f (*unidade de tempo*) hour; (*ocasião*) time; **que ~s são?** what's the time?; **a que ~s?** at what time?; **às três ~s** at three o'clock; **dizer as ~s** tell the time; **tem ~s?** do you have the time?; **em cima da ~** at the last minute; **na ~** (*naquele momento*) at the time; (*no ato*) on the spot; (*a tempo*) on time; **está na ~ de ir** it's time to go; **na ~ H** (*no momento certo*) at just the right moment; (*no momento crítico*) at the crucial moment; **meia ~** half an hour; **toda ~** all the time; **fazer ~** kill time; **marcar ~** make an appointment; **perder a ~** lose track of time; **não tenho ~** my time is my own; **não vejo a ~ de ir** I can't wait to go; **~s extras** overtime; **~s vagas** spare time

horário /o'rariu/ a hourly; **km ~s** km per hour ● m (*hora*) time; (*tabela*) timetable; (*de trabalho etc*) hours; **~ nobre** prime time

horda /'ɔrda/ f horde

horista /o'rista/ a paid by the hour ● m/f worker paid by the hour

horizon|tal /orizõ'taw/ (*pl* ~**tais**) a & f horizontal. ~**te** m horizon

hor|monal /ormo'naw/ (*pl* ~**monais**) a hormonal. ~**mônio** m hormone

horóscopo /o'rɔskopu/ m horoscope

horrendo /o'xẽdu/ a horrid

horripi|lante /oxipi'lãtʃi/ a horrifying. ~**lar** vt horrify

horrí|vel /o'xivew/ (*pl* ~**veis**) a horrible, awful

horror /o'xor/ m horror (**a** of); (*coisa horrorosa*) horrible thing; **ser um ~** be awful; **que ~!** how awful!

horro|rizar /oxori'zar/ vt/i horrify. ~**rizar-se** vpr be horrified. ~**roso** /o/

a horrible

horta /'ɔrta/ f vegetable plot; **~ comercial** market garden, *Amer* truck farm. ~**liça** f vegetable

hortelã /orte'lã/ f mint; ~**pimenta** peppermint

horti|cultor /ortʃikuw'tor/ m horticulturalist. ~**cultura** f horticulture. ~**frutigranjeiros** m pl fruit and vegetables. ~**granjeiros** m pl vegetables

horto /'ɔrtu/ m market garden; (*viveiro*) nursery

hospe|dagem /ospe'daʒẽ/ f accommodation. ~**dar** vt put up. ~**dar-se** vpr stay

hóspede /'ɔspidʒi/ m/f guest

hospedei|ra /ospe'dera/ f landlady; ~**ra de bordo** *Port* flight attendant. ~**ro** m landlord

hospício /os'pisiu/ m (*de loucos*) asylum

hospi|tal /ospi'taw/ (*pl* ~**tais**) m hospital. ~**talar** a hospital. ~**taleiro** a hospitable. ~**talidade** f hospitality. ~**talizar** vt hospitalize

hóstia /'ɔstʃia/ f Host, Communion wafer

hos|til /os'tʃiw/ (*pl* ~**tis**) a hostile. ~**tilidade** f hostility. ~**tilizar** vt antagonize

ho|tel /o'tew/ (*pl* ~**téis**) m hotel. ~**teleiro** a hotel ● m hotelier

huma|nidade /umani'dadʒi/ f humanity. ~**nismo** m humanism. ~**nista** a & m/f humanist. ~**nitário** a & m humanitarian. ~**nizar** vt humanize. ~**no** a human; (*compassivo*) humane. ~**nos** m pl humans

húmido /'umidu/ a *Port* humid

humil|dade /umiw'dadʒi/ f humility. ~**de** a humble

humi|lhação /umiʎaˈsãw/ f
humiliation. **~lhante** a humiliating.
~lhar vt humiliate

humor /uˈmor/ m humour;
(disposição do espírito) mood; **de
bom/mau ~** in a good/bad mood

humo|rismo /umoˈrizmu/
m humour. **~rista** m/f (no palco)
comedian; (escritor) humorist.
~rístico a humorous

húngaro /ˈũgaru/ a & m Hungarian

Hungria /ũˈgria/ f Hungary

hurra /ˈuxa/ int hurrah ● m cheer

. . . .

I i

. . . .

ia|te /iˈatʃi/ m yacht. **~tismo** m
yachting. **~tista** m/f yachtsman
(f-woman)

ibérico /iˈberiku/ a & m Iberian

ibope /iˈbɔpi/ m **dar ~** 🆒 be
popular

içar /iˈsar/ vt hoist

iceberg /ajsˈbergi/ (pl **~s**) m
iceberg

ícone /ˈikoni/ m icon

iconoclasta /ikonoˈklasta/ m/f
iconoclast ● a iconoclastic

icterícia /ikteˈrisia/ f jaundice

ida /ˈida/ f going; **na ~** on the
way there; **~ e volta** return, Amer
round trip

idade /iˈdadʒi/ f age; **meia ~** middle
age; **homem de meia ~** middle-
aged man; **senhor de ~** elderly
man; **Idade Média** Middle Ages

ide|al /ideˈaw/ (pl **~ais**) a & m ideal.
~alismo m idealism. **~alista** m/f

idealist ● a idealistic. **~alizar** vt
(criar) devise; (sublimar) idealize.
~ar vt devise. **~ário** m ideas

ideia /iˈdeja/ f idea; **mudar de ~**
change one's mind

idem /ˈidẽ/ adv ditto

idêntico /iˈdẽtʃiku/ a identical

identi|dade /idẽtʃiˈdadʒi/ f
identity. **~ficar** vt identify. **~ficar-se**
vpr identify (**com** with)

ideo|logia /ideoloˈʒia/ f ideology.
~lógico a ideological

idílico /iˈdʒiliku/ a idyllic

idílio /iˈdʒiliu/ m idyll

idio|ma /idʒiˈoma/ m language.
~mático a idiomatic

idio|ta /idʒiˈɔta/ m/f idiot ● a
idiotic. **~tice** f stupidity; (uma)
stupid thing

idola|trar /idolaˈtrar/ vt idolize.
~tria f idolatry

ídolo /ˈidulu/ m idol

idôneo /iˈdoniu/ a suitable

idoso /iˈdozu/ a elderly

Iêmen /iˈemẽ/ m Yemen

iemenita /iemeˈnita/ a & m/f
Yemeni

iene /iˈeni/ m yen

iglu /iˈglu/ m igloo

ignição /igniˈsãw/ f ignition

ignomínia /ignoˈminia/ f
ignominy

igno|rância /ignoˈrãsia/ f
ignorance. **~rante** a ignorant.
~rar vt (desconsiderar) ignore;
(desconhecer) not know

igreja /iˈgreʒa/ f church

igu|al /iˈgwaw/ (pl **~ais**) a equal;
(em aparência) identical; (liso) even
● m/f equal; **por ~** equally. **~alar**
vt equal; level ‹terreno›; **~alar(-se)**
a be equal to. **~aldade** f equality.

~alitário a egalitarian. **~almente** adv equally; (*como resposta*) the same to you. **~alzinho** a exactly the same (**a as**)

iguaria /igwaˈria/ f delicacy

iídiche /iˈidiʃi/ m Yiddish

ile|gal /ileˈgaw/ (*pl* **~gais**) a illegal. **~galidade** f illegality

ilegítimo /ileˈʒitʃimu/ a illegitimate

ilegí|vel /ileˈʒivew/ (*pl* **~veis**) a illegible

ileso /iˈlezu/ a unhurt

iletrado /ileˈtradu/ a & m illiterate

ilha /ˈiʎa/ f island

ilharga /iˈʎarga/ f side

ilhéu /iˈʎew/ m (f **ilhoa**) islander

ilhós /iˈʎɔs/ m invar eyelet

ilhota /iˈʎɔta/ f small island

ilícito /iˈlisitu/ a illicit

ilimitado /ilimiˈtadu/ a unlimited

ilógico /iˈlɔʒiku/ a illogical

iludir /iluˈdʒir/ vt delude. **~se** vpr delude o.s.

ilumi|nação /iluminaˈsãw/ f lighting; (*inspiração*) enlightenment. **~nar** vt light up, illuminate; (*inspirar*) enlighten

ilu|são /iluˈzãw/ f illusion; (*sonho*) delusion. **~sionista** m/f illusionist. **~sório** a illusory

ilus|tração /ilustraˈsãw/ f illustration; (*erudição*) learning. **~trador** m illustrator. **~trar** vt illustrate. **~trativo** a illustrative. **~tre** a illustrious; **~tríssimo senhor** Dear Sir

ímã /ˈimã/ m magnet

imaculado /imakuˈladu/ a immaculate

imagem /iˈmaʒẽ/ f image; (*da TV*) picture

imagi|nação /imaʒinaˈsãw/ f imagination. **~nar** vt imagine. **~nário** a imaginary. **~nativo** a imaginative. **~nável** (*pl* **~náveis**) a imaginable. **~noso** /o/ a imaginative

imatu|ridade /imaturiˈdadʒi/ f immaturity. **~ro** a immature

imbati|vel /ibaˈtʃivew/ (*pl* **~veis**) a unbeatable

imbe|cil /ibeˈsiw/ (*pl* **~cis**) a stupid ● m/f imbecile

imberbe /iˈberbi/ a (*sem barba*) beardless

imbricar /ibriˈkar/ vt overlap. **~se** vpr overlap

imedia|ções /imedʒiaˈsõjs/ f pl vicinity. **~tamente** adv immediately. **~to** a immediate

imemori|al /imemoriˈaw/ (*pl* **~ais**) a immemorial

imen|sidão /imẽsiˈdãw/ f vastness. **~so** a immense

imergir /imerˈʒir/ vt immerse

imi|gração /imigraˈsãw/ f immigration. **~grante** a & m/f immigrant. **~grar** vi immigrate

imi|nência /imiˈnẽsia/ f imminence. **~nente** a imminent

imiscuir-se /imiskuˈirsi/ vpr interfere

imi|tação /imitaˈsãw/ f imitation. **~tador** m imitator. **~tar** vt imitate

imobili|ária /imobiliˈaria/ f estate agent's, *Amer* realtor. **~ário** a property. **~dade** f immobility. **~zar** vt immobilize

imo|ral /imoˈraw/ (*pl* **~rais**) a immoral. **~ralidade** f immorality

imor|tal /imorˈtaw/ (*pl* **~tais**) a immortal ● m/f member of the Brazilian Academy of Letters.

~talidade f immortality. **~talizar** vt immortalize

imó|vel /i'mɔvew/ (pl **~veis**) a motionless, immobile ● m building, property; pl property, Amer real estate

impaci|ência /ĩpasi'ẽsia/ f impatience. **~entar-se** vpr get impatient. **~ente** a impatient

impacto /ĩ'paktu/, Port **impacte** /ĩ'paktʃi/ m impact

impagá|vel /ĩpa'gavew/ (pl **~veis**) a priceless

ímpar /'ĩpar/ a unique; ‹número› odd

imparci|al /ĩparsi'aw/ (pl **~ais**) a impartial. **~alidade** f impartiality

impasse /ĩ'pasi/ m impasse

impassí|vel /ĩpa'sivew/ (pl **~veis**) a impassive

impecá|vel /ĩpe'kavew/ (pl **~veis**) a impeccable

impe|dido /ĩpe'dʒidu/ a ‹rua› blocked; Port ‹ocupado› engaged, Amer busy; (no futebol) offside. **~dimento** m prevention; (estorvo) obstruction; (no futebol) offside position. **~dir** vt stop; (estorvar) hinder; block ‹rua›; **~dir alguém de ir** ou **que alguém vá** stop sb going

impelir /ĩpe'lir/ vt drive

impenetrá|vel /ĩpene'travew/ (pl **~veis**) a impenetrable

impensá|vel /ĩpẽ'savew/ (pl **~veis**) a unthinkable

impe|rador /ĩpera'dor/ m emperor. **~rar** vi reign, rule. **~rativo** a & m imperative. **~ratriz** f empress

impercepti|vel /ĩpersep'tʃivew/ (pl **~veis**) a imperceptible

imperdí|vel /ĩper'dʒivew/ (pl **~veis**) a unmissable

imperdoá|vel /ĩperdo'avew/ (pl **~veis**) a unforgivable

imperfei|ção /ĩperfej'sãw/ f imperfection. **~to** a & m imperfect

imperi|al /ĩperi'aw/ (pl **~ais**) a imperial ● f Port (de cerveja) glass of draught beer. **~alismo** m imperialism. **~alista** a & m/f imperialist

império /ĩ'periu/ m empire

imperioso /ĩperi'ozu/ a imperious; ‹necessidade› pressing

imperme|abilizar /ĩpermiabili'zar/ vt waterproof. **~ável** (pl **~áveis**) a waterproof; fig impervious (**a** to) ● m raincoat

imperti|nência /ĩpertʃi'nẽsia/ f impertinence. **~nente** a impertinent

impesso|al /ĩpeso'aw/ (pl **~ais**) a impersonal

ímpeto /'ĩpetu/ m (vontade) urge, impulse; (de emoção) surge; (movimento) start; (na física) impetus

impetuo|sidade /ĩpetuozi'dadʒi/ f impetuosity. **~so** /o/ a impetuous

impiedoso /ĩpie'dozu/ a merciless

impingir /ĩpĩ'ʒir/ vt foist (**a** on)

implacá|vel /ĩpla'kavew/ (pl **~veis**) a implacable

implan|tar /ĩplã'tar/ vt introduce; (no corpo) implant. **~te** m implant

implemen|tar /ĩplemẽ'tar/ vt implement. **~to** m implement

impli|cação /ĩplika'sãw/ f implication; f (ato) harassment; (antipatia) grudge; **estar de ~cância com** have it in for. **~cante** a troublesome ● m/f troublemaker. **~car** vt (comprometer) implicate; **~car (em)**

(*dar a entender*) imply; (*acarretar, exigir*) involve; **~car com** (*provocar*) pick on; (*antipatizar*) not get on with

implícito /i'plisitu/ *a* implicit

implorar /iplo'rar/ *vt* plead for (a from)

imponente /ĩpo'nẽtʃi/ *a* imposing

impopular /ĩpopu'lar/ *a* unpopular

impor /ĩ'por/ *vt* impose (**a** on); command <respeito>. **~se** *vpr* assert o.s.

impor|tação /ĩporta'sãw/ *f* import. **~tador** *m* importer. **~tadora** *f* import company. **~tados** *m pl* imported goods. **~tância** *f* importance; (*quantia*) amount; **ter ~tância** be important. **~tante** *a* important. **~tar** *vt* import <mercadorias>; **~tar em** (*montar a*) amount to; (*resultar em*) lead to ● *vi* matter; **~tar-se (com)** mind

importu|nar /ĩportu'nar/ *vt* bother. **~no** *a* annoying

imposição /ĩpozi'sãw/ *f* imposition

impossibili|dade /ĩposibili'dadʒi/ *f* impossibility. **~tar** *vt* make impossible; **~tar alguém de ir, ~tar a alguém ir** prevent sb from going, make it impossible for sb to go

impossí|vel /ĩpo'sivew/ (*pl* **~veis**) *a* impossible

impos|to /ĩ'postu/ *m* tax; **~to de renda** income tax; **~to sobre o valor acrescentado** *Port* VAT. **~tor** *m* impostor. **~tura** *f* deception

impo|tência /ĩpo'tẽsia/ *f* impotence. **~tente** *a* impotent

impreci|são /ĩpresi'zãw/ *f* imprecision. **~so** *a* imprecise

impregnar /ĩpreg'nar/ *vt* impregnate

imprensa /ĩ'prẽsa/ *f* press; **~ marrom** gutter press

imprescindí|vel /ĩpresĩ'dʒivew/ (*pl* **~veis**) *a* essential

impres|são /ĩpre'sãw/ *f* impression; (*no prelo*) printing; **~são digital** fingerprint. **~sionante** *a* (*imponente*) impressive; (*comovente*) striking. **~sionar** *vt* (*causar admiração*) impress; (*comover*) make an impression on. **~sionar-se** *vpr* be impressed (**com** by). **~sionável** (*pl* **~sionáveis**) *a* impressionable. **~sionismo** *m* Impressionism. **~sionista** *a & m/f* Impressionist. **~so** *a* printed ● *m* printed sheet; *pl* printed matter. **~sor** *m* printer. **~sora** *f* printer

imprestá|vel /ĩpres'tavew/ (*pl* **~veis**) *a* useless

impre|visível /ĩprevi'zivew/ (*pl* **~visíveis**) *a* unpredictable. **~visto** *a* unforeseen ● *m* unforeseen circumstance

imprimir /ĩpri'mir/ *vt* print

impropério /ĩpro'periu/ *m* term of abuse; *pl* abuse

impróprio /ĩ'prɔpriu/ *a* improper; (*inadequado*) unsuitable (**para** for)

imprová|vel /ĩpro'vavew/ (*pl* **~veis**) *a* unlikely

improvi|sação /ĩproviza'sãw/ *f* improvisation. **~sar** *vt/i* improvise. **~so** *m* **de ~so** on the spur of the moment

impru|dência /ĩpru'dẽsia/ *f* recklessness. **~dente** *a* reckless

impul|sionar /ĩpuwsio'nar/ *vt* drive. **~sivo** *a* impulsive. **~so** *m* impulse

impu|ne /i'puni/ a unpunished. **~nidade** f impunity

impu|reza /ipu'reza/ f impurity. **~ro** a impure

imun|dície /imũ'dʒisi/ f filth. **~do** a filthy

imu|ne /i'muni/ a immune (**a** to). **~nidade** f immunity. **~nizar** vt immunize

inabalá|vel /inaba'lavew/ (pl **~veis**) a unshakeable

iná|bil /i'nabiw/ (pl **~beis**) a (desafeitado) clumsy

inabitado /inaba'badu/ a uninhabited

inacabado /inaka'badu/ a unfinished

inaceitá|vel /inasej'tavew/ (pl **~veis**) a unacceptable

inacessí|vel /inase'sivew/ (pl **~veis**) a inaccessible

inacreditá|vel /inakredʒi'tavew/ (pl **~veis**) a unbelievable

inadequado /inade'kwadu/ a unsuitable

inadmissí|vel /inadʒimi'sivew/ (pl **~veis**) a inadmissible

inadvertência /inadʒiver'tẽsia/ f oversight

inalar /ina'lar/ vt inhale

inalcançá|vel /inawkã'savew/ (pl **~veis**) a unattainable

inalterá|vel /inawte'ravew/ (pl **~veis**) a unchangeable

inanição /inani'sãw/ f starvation

inanimado /inani'madu/ a inanimate

inapto /i'naptu/ a (incapaz) unfit

inati|vidade /inatʃivi'dadʒi/ f inactivity. **~vo** a inactive

inato /i'natu/ a innate

inaudito /inaw'dʒitu/ a unheard of

inaugu|ração /inawgura'sãw/ f inauguration. **~ral** (pl **~rais**) a inaugural. **~rar** vt inaugurate

incabí|vel /ĩka'bivew/ (pl **~veis**) a inappropriate

incalculá|vel /ĩkawku'lavew/ (pl **~veis**) a incalculable

incandescente /ĩkãde'sẽtʃi/ a red-hot

incansá|vel /ĩkã'savew/ (pl **~veis**) a tireless

incapaci|tado /ĩkapasi'tadu/ a ‹pessoa› disabled. **~tar** vt incapacitate

incauto /ĩ'kawtu/ a reckless

incendi|ar /ĩsẽdʒi'ar/ vt set alight. **~ar-se** vpr catch fire. **~ário** a incendiary; fig ‹discurso› inflammatory ● m arsonist; fig agitator

incêndio /ĩ'sẽdʒiu/ m fire

incenso /ĩ'sẽsu/ m incense

incenti|var /ĩsẽtʃi'var/ vt encourage. **~vo** m incentive

incer|teza /ĩser'teza/ f uncertainty. **~to** /ɛ/ a uncertain

inces|to /ĩ'sɛstu/ m incest. **~tuoso** /o/ a incestuous

in|chação /ĩʃa'sãw/ f swelling. **~char** vt/i swell

inci|dência /ĩsi'dẽsia/ f incidence. **~dente** m incident. **~dir** vi **~dir em** ‹luz› shine on; ‹imposto› be payable on

incineradora /ĩsinera'dora/ f incinerator

incinerar /ĩsine'rar/ vt incinerate

inci|são /ĩsi'zãw/ f incision. **~sivo** a incisive

incitar /ĩsi'tar/ vt incite

incli|nação /ĩklinaˈsãw/ f (do chão) incline; (da cabeça) nod; (propensão) inclination. **~nado** a ‹chão› sloping; ‹edifício› leaning; (propenso) inclined (**a** to). **~nar** vt tilt; nod ‹cabeça› ● vi ‹chão› slope; ‹edifício› lean; (tender) incline (**para** towards). **~nar-se** vpr lean

inclu|ir /ĩkluˈir/ vt include. **~são** f inclusion. **~sive** prep including ● adv inclusive; (até) even. **~so** a included

incoe|rência /ĩkoeˈrẽsia/ f (falta de nexo) incoherence; (inconsequência) inconsistency. **~rente** a (sem nexo) incoherent; (inconsequente) inconsistent

incógni|ta /ĩˈkɔgnita/ f unknown. **~to** adv incognito

incolor /ĩkoˈlor/ a colourless

incólume /ĩˈkɔlumi/ a unscathed

incomodar /ĩkomoˈdar/ vt bother ● vi be a nuisance. **~se** vpr (dar-se ao trabalho) bother (**em** to); **~se** (**com**) be bothered (by), mind

incômodo /ĩˈkomodu/ a (desagradável) tiresome; (sem conforto) uncomfortable ● m nuisance

incompa|rável /ĩkõpaˈravew/ (pl **~ráveis**) a incomparable. **~tível** (pl **~tíveis**) a incompatible

incompe|tência /ĩkõpeˈtẽsia/ f incompetence. **~tente** a incompetent

incompleto /ĩkõˈpletu/ a incomplete

incompreensí|vel /ĩkõprieˈsivew/ (pl **~veis**) a incomprehensible

inconcebí|vel /ĩkõseˈbivew/ (pl **~veis**) a inconceivable

incondicio|nal /ĩkõdʒisioˈnaw/ (pl **~nais**) a unconditional; ‹fã,

partidário› firm

inconformado /ĩkõforˈmadu/ a unreconciled (**com** to)

inconfundí|vel /ĩkõfũˈdʒivew/ (pl **~veis**) a unmistakeable

inconsciente /ĩkõsiˈẽtʃi/ a & m unconscious

inconsequente /ĩkõseˈkwẽtʃi/ a inconsistent

incons|tância /ĩkõsˈtãsia/ f changeability. **~tante** a changeable

inconstitucio|nal /ĩkõstʃitusioˈnaw/ (pl **~nais**) a unconstitutional

incontestá|vel /ĩkõtesˈtavew/ (pl **~veis**) a indisputable

incontorná|vel /ĩkõtorˈnavew/ a unavoidable

inconveniente /ĩkõveniˈẽtʃi/ a (difícil) inconvenient; (desagradável) annoying, tiresome; (indecente) unseemly ● m drawback

incorporar /ĩkorpoˈrar/ vt incorporate

incorrer /ĩkoˈxer/ vi **~ em** ‹multa etc› incur

incorrigí|vel /ĩkoxiˈʒivew/ (pl **~veis**) a incorrigible

incrédulo /ĩˈkredulu/ a incredulous

incremen|tado /ĩkremẽˈtadu/ a 🔲 stylish. **~tar** vt build up; 🔲 jazz up. **~to** m development, growth

incriminar /ĩkrimiˈnar/ vt incriminate

incrí|vel /ĩˈkrivew/ (pl **~veis**) a incredible

incu|bação /ĩkubaˈsãw/ f incubation. **~badora** f incubator. **~bar** vt/i incubate

inculto /ĩˈkuwtu/ a ‹pessoa› uneducated; ‹terreno› uncultivated

incum|bência /ĩkũˈbẽsia/ f task. **~bir** vt ‹bir alguém de algo/de ir assign sb sth/to go ● vi **~bir a** be up to; **~bir-se de** take on

incurá|vel /ĩkuˈravew/ (pl **~veis**) a incurable

incursão /ĩkurˈsãw/ f incursion

incutir /ĩkuˈtʃir/ vt instil (**em** in)

indagar /ĩdaˈgar/ vt inquire (into)

inde|cência /ĩdeˈsẽsia/ f indecency. **~cente** a indecent

indecifrá|vel /ĩdesiˈfravew/ (pl **~veis**) a indecipherable

indeciso /ĩdeˈsizu/ a undecided

indecoroso /ĩdekoˈrozu/ a indecorous

indefi|nido /ĩdefiˈnidu/ a indefinite. **~nível** (pl **~níveis**) a indefinable

indelé|vel /ĩdeˈlεvew/ (pl **~veis**) a indelible

indelica|deza /ĩdelikaˈdeza/ f impoliteness; (uma) impolite thing. **~do** a impolite

indeni|zação /ĩdenizaˈsãw/ f compensation. **~zar** vt compensate

indepen|dência /ĩdepẽˈdẽsia/ f independence. **~dente** a independent

indescriti|vel /ĩdʒiskriˈtʃivew/ (pl **~veis**) a indescribable

indesculpá|vel /ĩdʒiskuwˈpavew/ (pl **~veis**) a inexcusable

indesejá|vel /ĩdezeˈʒavew/ (pl **~veis**) a undesirable

indestruti|vel /ĩdʒistruˈtʃivew/ (pl **~veis**) a indestructible

indeterminado /ĩdetermiˈnadu/ a indeterminate

indevido /ĩdeˈvidu/ a undue

indexar /ĩdekˈsar/ vt index; index-link ‹salário, preços›

Índia /ˈĩdʒia/ f India

indiano /ĩdʒiˈanu/ a & m Indian

indi|cação /ĩdʒikaˈsãw/ f indication; (do caminho) directions; (nomeação) nomination; (recomendação) recommendation. **~cador** m indicator; (dedo) index finger ● a indicative (**de** of). **~car** vt indicate; (para cargo, prêmio) nominate (**para** for); (recomendar) recommend. **~cativo** a & m indicative

índice /ˈĩdʒisi/ m (taxa) rate; (em livro etc) index; **~ de audiência** ratings

indiciar /ĩdʒisiˈar/ vt charge

indício /ĩˈdʒisiu/ m sign, indication; (de crime) clue

indife|rença /ĩdʒifeˈrẽsa/ f indifference. **~rente** a indifferent

indígena /ĩˈdʒiʒena/ a indigenous, native ● m/f native

indiges|tão /ĩdʒiʒesˈtãw/ f indigestion. **~to** a indigestible; fig heavy going

indig|nação /ĩdʒignaˈsãw/ f indignation. **~nado** a indignant. **~nar** vt make indignant. **~nar-se** vpr get indignant (**com** about)

indig|nidade /ĩdʒigniˈdadʒi/ f indignity. **~no** a ‹pessoa› unworthy; ‹ato› despicable

índio /ˈĩdʒiu/ a & m Indian

indire|ta /ĩdʒiˈreta/ f hint. **~to** /ε/ a indirect

indis|creto /ĩdʒisˈkretu/ a indiscreet. **~crição** f indiscretion

indiscriminado /ĩdʒiskrimi-ˈnadu/ a indiscriminate

indiscuti|vel /ĩdʒiskuˈtʃivew/ (pl **~veis**) a unquestionable

indispensá|vel /ĩdʒispẽ'savew/
(pl ~**veis**) a indispensable

indisponi|vel /ĩdʒispo'nivew/
(pl ~**veis**) a unavailable

indis|por /ĩdʒis'por/ vt upset;
~**por alguém contra** turn sb
against. ~**por-se** vpr fall out (**com**
with). ~**posição** f indisposition.
~**posto** a (doente) indisposed

indistinto /ĩdʒis'tʃĩtu/ a indistinct

individu|al /ĩdʒividu'aw/ (pl ~**ais**)
a individual. ~**alidade** f individuality.
~**alismo** m individualism. ~**alista**
a & m/f individualist

indivíduo /ĩdʒi'viduu/ m
individual

indizí|vel /ĩdʒi'zivew/ (pl ~**veis**) a
unspeakable

índole /'ĩdoli/ f nature

indo|lência /ĩdo'lẽsia/ f indolence.
~**lente** a indolent

indolor /ĩdo'lor/ a painless

Indonésia /ĩdo'nɛzia/ f Indonesia

indonésio /ĩdo'nɛziu/ a & m
Indonesian

indubitá|vel /ĩdubi'tavew/
(pl ~**veis**) a undoubted

indul|gência /ĩduw'ʒẽsia/ f
indulgence. ~**gente** a indulgent

indulto /ĩ'duwtu/ m pardon

indumentária /ĩdumẽ'taria/
f outfit

indústria /ĩ'dustria/ f industry

industri|al /ĩdustri'aw/ (pl ~**ais**)
a industrial ● m/f industrialist.
~**alizado** a (país) industrialized;
‹mercadoria› manufactured;
‹comida› processed. ~**alizar** vt
industrialize ‹país, agricultura etc›;
process ‹comida, lixo etc›. ~**oso** /o/
a industrious

induzir /ĩdu'zir/ vt (persuadir)
induce; (inferir) infer (**de** from);
~ **em erro** lead astray, mislead sb

inebriante /inebri'ãtʃi/ a
intoxicating

inédito /i'nɛdʒitu/ a unheard-of,
unprecedented; (não publicado)
unpublished

ineficaz /inefi'kas/ a ineffective

inefici|ência /inefisi'ẽsia/ f
inefficiency. ~**ente** a inefficient

inegá|vel /ine'gavew/ (pl ~**veis**) a
undeniable

inépcia /i'nɛpsia/ f ineptitude

inepto /i'nɛptu/ a inept

inequívoco /ine'kivoku/ a
unmistakeable

inércia /i'nɛrsia/ f inertia

inerente /ine'rẽtʃi/ a inherent
(**a** in)

inerte /i'nɛrtʃi/ a inert

inesgotá|vel /inezgo'tavew/
(pl ~**veis**) a inexhaustible

inesperado /inespe'radu/ a
unexpected

inesquecí|vel /ineske'sivew/
(pl ~**veis**) a unforgettable

inevitá|vel /inevi'tavew/
(pl ~**veis**) a inevitable

inexato /ine'zatu/ a inaccurate

inexis|tência /inezis'tẽsia/ f lack.
~**tente** a non-existent

inexperi|ência /inisperi'ẽsia/ f
inexperience. ~**ente** a inexperienced

inexpressivo /inespre'sivu/ a
expressionless

infalí|vel /ĩfa'livew/ (pl ~**veis**) a
infallible

infame /ĩ'fami/ a despicable;
(péssimo) dreadful

infâmia /ĩ'famia/ f disgrace

infância /ĩ'fãsia/ f childhood

infantaria /ĩfãta'ria/ f infantry

infan|til /ĩfã'tʃiw/ a <roupa, livro> children's; (bobo) childish. **~tilidade** f childishness; (uma) childish thing

infarto /ĩ'fartu/ m heart attack

infec|ção /ĩfek'sãw/ f infection. **~cionar** vt infect. **~cioso** a infectious

infeliz /ĩfe'lis/ a (não contente) unhappy; (inconveniente) unfortunate; (desgraçado) wretched ● m (desgraçado) wretch. **~mente** adv unfortunately

inferi|or /ĩferi'or/ a lower; (em qualidade) inferior (a to). **~oridade** f inferiority

inferir /ĩfe'rir/ vt infer

infer|nal /ĩfer'naw/ (pl **~nais**) a infernal. **~nizar** vt **~nizar a vida dele** make his life hell. **~no** /ɛ/ m hell

infér|til /ĩ'fɛrtʃiw/ (pl **~teis**) a infertile

infertilidade /ĩfertʃili'dadʒi/ f infertility

infestar /ĩfes'tar/ vt infest

infetar /ĩfe'tar/ vt infect

infidelidade /ĩfideli'dadʒi/ f infidelity

infi|el /ĩfi'ɛw/ (pl **~éis**) a unfaithful

infiltrar /ĩfiw'trar/ vt infiltrate; **~se em** infiltrate

ínfimo /'ĩfimu/ a lowest; (muito pequeno) tiny

infindá|vel /ĩfĩ'davew/ (pl **~veis**) a unending

infinidade /ĩfini'dadʒi/ f infinity; **uma ~** de an infinite number of

infini|tesimal /ĩfinitezi'maw/ (pl **~tesimais**) a infinitesimal. **~tivo** a & m infinitive. **~to** a infinite ● m infinity

infla|ção /ĩfla'sãw/ f inflation. **~cionar** vt inflate. **~cionário** a inflationary. **~cionista** a & m/f inflationist

infla|mação /ĩflama'sãw/ f inflammation. **~mar** vt inflame. **~mar-se** vpr become inflamed. **~matório** a inflammatory. **~mável** (pl **~máveis**) a inflammable

in|flar /ĩ'flar/ vt inflate. **~flar-se** vpr inflate. **~flável** (pl **~fláveis**) a inflatable

infle|xibilidade /ĩfleksibili'dadʒi/ f inflexibility. **~xível** (pl **~xíveis**) a inflexible

infligir /ĩfli'ʒir/ vt inflict (a on)

influência /ĩflu'ẽsia/ f influence

influen|ciar /ĩfluẽsi'ar/ vt **~ciar (em)** influence. **~ciar-se** be influenced. **~ciável** (pl **~ciáveis**) a open to influence. **~te** a influential

influir /ĩflu'ir/ vi **~ em** ou **sobre** influence

informação /ĩforma'sãw/ f information; (uma) a piece of information; Mil intelligence; pl information

infor|mal /ĩfor'maw/ (pl **~mais**) a informal. **~malidade** f informality

infor|mar /ĩfor'mar/ vt inform. **~mar-se** vpr find out (de about). **~mática** /ĩfoʁ'matʃika/ f information technology; **especialista em ~mática** IT specialist. **~mativo** a informative. **~matizar** vt computerize. **~me** m Mil piece of intelligence

informático /ĩfor'matʃiku/ a computer ● m Port IT specialist

informatização /ĩformatʃiza'sãw/ f computerization

infortúnio /ĩfor'tuniu/ m misfortune

infração /ifra'sãw/ f infringement

infraestrutura /ifraistru'tura/ f infrastructure

infrator /ifra'tor/ m offender

infravermelho /ifraver'meʎu/ a infrared

infringir /ifrĩ'ʒir/ vt infringe

infrutífero /ifru'tʃiferu/ a fruitless

infundado /ifũ'dadu/ a unfounded

infundir /ifũ'dʒir/ vt (insuflar) infuse; (incutir) instil

infusão /ifu'zãw/ f infusion

ingenuidade /iʒenui'dadʒi/ f naivety

ingênuo /i'ʒenuu/ a naive

ingerir /iʒe'rir/ vt ingest; (engolir) swallow

Inglaterra /igla'tɛra/ f England

in|glês /i'gles/ a (f ~**glesa**) English ● m (f ~**glesa**) Englishman (f -woman); (língua) English; **os ~gleses** the English

ingra|tidão /igratʃi'dãw/ f ingratitude. ~**to** a ungrateful

ingrediente /igredʒi'ẽtʃi/ m ingredient

íngreme /'igrimi/ a steep

ingres|sar /igre'sar/ vi ~**sar em** join. ~**so** m entry; (bilhete) ticket

inhame /i'ɲami/ m yam

ini|bição /inibi'sãw/ f inhibition. ~**bir** vt inhibit

inici|ado /inisi'adu/ m initiate. ~**al** (pl ~**ais**) a & f initial. ~**ar** vt (começar) begin; (em ciência, seita etc) initiate (em into) ● vi begin. ~**ativa** f initiative

início /i'nisiu/ m beginning

inigualá|vel /inigwa'lavew/ (pl ~**veis**) a unparalleled

inimaginá|vel /inimaʒi'navew/ (pl ~**veis**) a unimaginable

inimi|go /ini'migu/ a & m enemy. ~**zade** f enmity

ininterrupto /inĩte'xuptu/ a continuous

inje|ção /iʒe'sãw/ f injection. ~**tado** a (olhos) bloodshot. ~**tar** vt inject. ~**tável** (pl ~**táveis**) a ‹droga› intravenous

injúria /i'ʒuria/ f insult

injuriar /iʒuri'ar/ vt insult

injus|tiça /iʒus'tʃisa/ f injustice. ~**tiçado** a wronged. ~**to** a unfair, unjust

ino|cência /ino'sẽsia/ f innocence. ~**centar** vt clear (de of). ~**cente** a innocent

inocular /inoku'lar/ vt inoculate

inócuo /i'nɔkuu/ a harmless

inodoro /ino'dɔru/ a odourless

inofensivo /inofẽ'sivu/ a harmless

inoportuno /inopor'tunu/ a inopportune

inorgânico /inor'ganiku/ a inorganic

inóspito /i'nɔspitu/ a inhospitable

ino|vação /inova'sãw/ f innovation. ~**var** vt/i innovate

inoxidá|vel /inoksi'davew/ (pl ~**veis**) a ‹aço› stainless

inquérito /i'keritu/ m inquiry

inquie|tação /ikieta'sãw/ f concern. ~**tador**, ~**tante** a worrying. ~**tar** vt worry. ~**tar-se** vpr worry. ~**to** /ɛ/ a uneasy

inquili|nato /ikili'natu/ m tenancy. ~**no** m tenant

inquirir /iki'rir/ vt cross-examine ‹testemunha›

Inquisição /ĩkizi'sãw/ f a ~ the Inquisition

insaciá|vel /ĩsasi'avew/ (pl ~veis) a insatiable

insalubre /ĩsa'lubri/ a unhealthy

insatis|fação /ĩsatʃisfa'sãw/ f dissatisfaction. ~fatório a unsatisfactory. ~feito a dissatisfied

ins|crever /ĩskre'ver/ vt (registrar) register; (gravar) inscribe. ~crever-se vpr register; (em escola etc) enrol. ~crição f (registro) registration; (em clube, escola) enrolment; (em monumento etc) inscription

insegu|rança /ĩsegu'rãsa/ f insecurity. ~ro a insecure

insemi|nação /ĩsemina'sãw/ f insemination. ~nar vt inseminate

insen|satez /ĩsẽsa'tes/ f folly. ~sato a foolish. ~sibilidade f insensitivity. ~sível (pl ~síveis) a insensitive

insepará|vel /ĩsepa'ravew/ (pl ~veis) a inseparable

inserção /ĩser'sãw/ f insertion

inserir /ĩse'rir/ vt insert; enter ‹dados›

inse|ticida /ĩsetʃi'sida/ m insecticide. ~to /ɛ/ m insect

insígnia /ĩ'signia/ f insignia

insignifi|cância /ĩsignifi'kãsia/ f insignificance. ~cante a insignificant

insincero /ĩsĩ'seru/ a insincere

insinu|ante /ĩsinu'ãtʃi/ a suggestive. ~ar vt/i insinuate

insípido /ĩ'sipidu/ a insipid

insis|tência /ĩsis'tẽsia/ f insistence. ~tente a insistent. ~tir vt/i insist (em on)

insolação /ĩsola'sãw/ f sunstroke

inso|lência /ĩso'lẽsia/ f insolence. ~lente a insolent

insólito /ĩ'sɔlitu/ a unusual

insolú|vel /ĩso'luvew/ (pl ~veis) a insoluble

insone /ĩ'sɔni/ a ‹noite› sleepless; ‹pessoa› insomniac ● m/f insomniac

insônia /ĩ'sonia/ f insomnia

insosso /ĩ'sosu/ a bland; (sem sabor) tasteless; (sem sal) unsalted

inspe|ção /ĩspe'sãw/ f inspection. ~cionar vt inspect. ~tor m inspector

inspi|ração /ĩspira'sãw/ f inspiration. ~rar vt inspire. ~rar-se vpr take inspiration (em from)

instabilidade /ĩstabili'dadʒi/ f instability

insta|lação /ĩstala'sãw/ f installation. ~lar vt install. ~lar-se vpr install o.s.

instan|tâneo /ĩstã'taniu/ a instant. ~te m instant

instaurar /ĩstaw'rar/ vt set up

instá|vel /ĩ'stavew/ (pl ~veis) a unstable; ‹tempo› unsettled

insti|gação /ĩstʃiga'sãw/ f instigation. ~gante a stimulating. ~gar vt incite

instin|tivo /ĩstʃĩ'tʃivu/ a instinctive. ~to m instinct

institu|cional /ĩstʃitusio'naw/ (pl ~cionais) a institutional. ~ição f institution. ~ir vt set up; set ‹prazo›. ~to m institute

instru|ção /ĩstru'sãw/ f instruction. ~ir vt instruct; train ‹recrutas›; (informar) advise (sobre of)

instrumen|tal /ĩstrumẽ'taw/ (pl ~tais) a instrumental. ~tista m instrumentalist. ~to m instrument

instru|tivo /ĩstru'tʃivu/ a
instructive. **~tor** m instructor

insubstitui|vel /ĩsubistʃitu'ivew/
(pl **~veis**) a irreplaceable

insucesso /ĩsu'sesu/ m failure

insufici|ência /ĩsufisi'ẽsia/ f
insufficiency; (dos órgãos) failure.
~ente a insufficient

insulina /ĩsu'lina/ f insulin

insul|tar /ĩsuw'tar/ vt insult. **~to**
m insult

insuperá|vel /ĩsupe'ravew/
(pl **~veis**) a ‹problema›
insurmountable; ‹qualidade›
unsurpassed

insuportá|vel /ĩsupor'tavew/
(pl **~veis**) a unbearable

insur|gente /ĩsur'ʒẽtʃi/ a & m/f
insurgent. **~gir-se** vpr rise up, revolt.
~reição f insurrection

intato /ĩ'tatu/ a intact

íntegra /'ĩtegra/ f full text; **na**
~ in full

inte|gração /ĩtegra'sãw/ f
integration. **~gral** (pl **~grais**) a
whole; **arroz/pão ~gral** brown
rice/bread. **~grante** a integral ● m/f
member. **~grar** vt make up, form;
~grar-se em become a part of.
~gridade f integrity

íntegro /'ĩtegru/ a honest

intei|ramente /ĩtera'mẽtʃi/ adv
completely. **~rar** vt (informar) fill in,
inform (de about). **~rar-se** vpr find
out (de about). **~riço** a in one piece.
~ro a whole

intelec|to /ĩte'lektu/ m intellect.
~tual (pl **~tuais**) a & m/f intellectual

inteli|gência /ĩteli'ʒẽsia/
f intelligence. **~gente** a clever,
intelligent. **~gível** (pl **~gíveis**)
a intelligible

intem|périe /ĩtẽ'peri/ f bad
weather. **~pestivo** a ill-timed

inten|ção /ĩtẽ'sãw/ f intention;
segundas ~ções ulterior motives

intencio|nado /ĩtẽsio'nadu/ a
bem ~nado well-meaning. **~nal** (pl
~nais) a intentional. **~nar** vt intend

inten|sidade /ĩtẽsi'dadʒi/ f
intensity. **~sificar** vt intensify.
~sificar-se vpr intensify. **~sivo** a
intensive. **~so** a intense

intento /ĩ'tẽtu/ m intention

intera|ção /ĩtera'sãw/ f
interaction. **~gir** vi interact. **~tivo**
a interactive

inter|calar /ĩterka'lar/ vt insert.
~câmbio m exchange. **~ceptar** vt
intercept

intercontinen|tal
/ĩterkõtʃinẽ'taw/ (pl **~tais**) a
intercontinental

interdepen|dência
/ĩterdepẽ'dẽsia/ f interdependence.
~dente a interdependent

interdi|ção /ĩterdʒi'sãw/ f closure;
Jurid injunction. **~tar** vt close ‹rua
etc›; (proibir) ban

interes|sante /ĩtere'sãtʃi/ a
interesting. **~sar** vt interest ● vi be
relevant. **~sar-se** vpr be interested
(**em** ou **por** in). **~se** /e/ m interest;
(próprio) self-interest. **~seiro** a
self-seeking

interestadu|al /ĩterestadu'aw/
(pl **~ais**) a interstate

interface /ĩter'fasi/ f interface

interfe|rência /ĩterfe'rẽsia/ f
interference. **~rir** vi interfere

interfone /ĩter'fɔni/ m intercom

ínterim /'ĩteri/ m interim; **nesse** ~
in the interim

interino /ĩte'rinu/ a temporary

interior /ĩteri'or/ a inner; (dentro do país) internal, domestic ● m inside; (do país) country, interior

inter|jeição /ĩterʒej'sãw/ f interjection. **~ligar** vt interconnect. **~locutor** m interlocutor. **~mediário** a & m intermediary

intermédio /ĩter'mɛdʒiu/ m por ~ de through

intermináível /ĩtermi'navew/ (pl ~veis) a interminable

internacional /ĩternasio'naw/ (pl ~nais) a international

inter|nar /ĩter'nar/ vt intern <preso>; admit to hospital <doente>. **~nato** m boarding school

internauta /ĩter'nawta/ m/f Comput netsurfer

Internet /ĩter'nɛt/ f Internet

interno /i'tɛrnu/ a internal

interpelar /ĩterpe'lar/ vt question

interpor /ĩter'por/ vt interpose. **~se** vpr intervene

interpre|tação /ĩterpreta'sãw/ f interpretation. **~tar** vt interpret; perform <papel, música>. **intérprete** m/f (de línguas) interpreter; (de teatro etc) performer

interro|gação /ĩtexoga'sãw/ f interrogation. **~gar** vt interrogate, question. **~gativo** a interrogative. **~gatório** m interrogation

inter|romper /ĩtexõ'per/ vt interrupt. **~rupção** f interruption. **~ruptor** m switch

interurbano /ĩterur'banu/ a long-distance ● m trunk call

intervalo /ĩter'valu/ m interval

inter|venção /ĩterve'sãw/ f intervention. **~vir** vi intervene

intestiinal /ĩtestʃi'naw/ (pl ~nais) a intestinal. **~no** m intestine

inti|mação /ĩtʃima'sãw/ f (da justiça) summons. **~mar** vt order; (à justiça) summon

intimidade /ĩtʃimi'dadʒi/ f intimacy; (entre amigos) closeness; (vida íntima) private life; **ter ~ com** be close to

intimidar /ĩtʃimi'dar/ vt intimidate. **~se** vpr be intimidated

íntimo /'ĩtʃimu/ a intimate; <amigo> close; <vida> private ● m close friend

intitular /ĩtʃitu'lar/ vt entitle

intocáível /ĩto'kavew/ (pl ~veis) a untouchable

intole|rância /ĩtole'rãsia/ f intolerance. **~rável** (pl ~ráveis) a intolerable

intoxi|cação /ĩtoksika'sãw/ f poisoning; **~cação alimentar** food poisoning. **~car** vt poison

intragáível /ĩtra'gavew/ (pl ~veis) a <comida> inedible; <pessoa> unbearable

intransigente /ĩtrãzi'ʒẽtʃi/ a uncompromising

intransiítável /ĩtrãzi'tavew/ (pl ~táveis) a impassable. **~tivo** a intransitive

intratáível /ĩtra'tavew/ (pl ~veis) a <pessoa> difficult

intrauterino /ĩtrawte'rinu/ a **dispositivo ~** intrauterine device, IUD

intrépido /ĩ'trɛpidu/ a intrepid

intri|ga /ĩ'triga/ f intrigue; (enredo) plot. **~gante** a intriguing. **~gar** vt intrigue

intrincado /ĩtrĩ'kadu/ a intricate

intrínseco /ĩ'trĩsiku/ a intrinsic

introduição /ĩtrodu'sãw/ f introduction. **~tório** a introductory. **~zir** vt introduce

introme|ter-se /ĩtrome'tersi/
vpr interfere. **~tido** *a* interfering ● *m* busybody

introspec|ção /ĩtrospek'sãw/ *f* introspection. **~tivo** *a* introspective

introvertido /ĩtrover'tʃidu/ *a* introverted ● *m* introvert

intruso /ĩ'truzu/ *a* intrusive ● *m* intruder

intu|ição /ĩtui'sãw/ *f* intuition. **~ir** *vt* intuit. **~itivo** *a* intuitive. **~ito** *m* purpose

inumano /inu'manu/ *a* inhuman

inumerá|vel /inume'ravew/ (*pl* **~veis**) *a* innumerable

inúmero /i'numeru/ *a* countless

inun|dação /inũda'sãw/ *f* flood. **~dar** *vt/i* flood

inusitado /inuzi'tadu/ *a* unusual

inú|til /i'nutʃiw/ (*pl* **~teis**) *a* useless

inutilizar /inutʃili'zar/ *vt* render useless; damage ‹*aparelho*›; thwart ‹*esforços*›

inutilmente /inutʃiw'mẽtʃi/ *adv* in vain

invadir /ĩva'dʒir/ *vt* invade

invali|dar /ĩvali'dar/ *vt* invalidate; disable ‹*pessoa*›. **~dez** /e/ *f* disability

inválido /ĩ'validu/ *a* & *m* invalid

invariá|vel /ĩvari'avew/ (*pl* **~veis**) *a* invariable

inva|são /ĩva'zãw/ *f* invasion. **~sor** *m* invader ● *a* invading

inve|ja /ĩ'vɛʒa/ *f* envy. **~jar** *vt* envy. **~jável** (*pl* **~jáveis**) *a* enviable. **~joso** /o/ *a* envious

inven|ção /ĩvẽ'sãw/ *f* invention. **~tar** *vt* invent. **~tário** *m* inventory. **~tivo** *a* inventive. **~tor** *m* inventor

inver|nar /ĩver'nar/ *vi* winter, spend the winter. **~no** /ɛ/ *m* winter

inverossí|mil /ivero'simiw/ (*pl* **~meis**) *a* improbable

inver|são /ĩver'sãw/ *f* inversion. **~so** *a* inverse; ‹*ordem*› reverse ● *m* reverse. **~ter** *vt* reverse; ‹*colocar de cabeça para baixo*› invert

invertebrado /ĩverte'bradu/ *a* & *m* invertebrate

invés /ĩ'ves/ *m* **ao ~ de** instead of

investida /ĩves'tʃida/ *f* attack

investidura /ĩvestʃi'dura/ *f* investiture

investi|gação /ĩvestʃiga'sãw/ *f* investigation. **~gar** *vt* investigate

inves|timento /ĩvestʃi'mẽtu/ *m* investment. **~tir** *vt/i* invest; **~tir contra** attack

inveterado /ĩvete'radu/ *a* inveterate

inviá|vel /ĩvi'avew/ (*pl* **~veis**) *a* impracticable

invicto /ĩ'viktu/ *a* unbeaten

invisí|vel /ĩvi'zivew/ (*pl* **~veis**) *a* invisible

invocar /ĩvo'kar/ *vt* invoke; ⚠ pester

invólucro /ĩ'vɔlukru/ *m* covering

involuntário /ĩvolũ'tariu/ *a* involuntary

invulnerá|vel /ĩvuwne'ravew/ (*pl* **~veis**) *a* invulnerable

iodo /i'odu/ *m* iodine

ioga /i'ɔga/ *f* yoga

iogurte /io'gurtʃi/ *m* yoghurt

---

ir /ir/ ● *vi*

••••> (*deslocar-se*) go; **vamos para Paris** we are going to Paris; **~ de carro/trem...** go by car/train...; **como vão as coisas em casa?** how are things at home?

····› *(estar)* be; **~ bem vestido** be well dressed

····› *(começar)* **vai fazendo sua lição de casa** start doing your homework

····› *(em expressões)* **~ com** *(combinar roupa)* go with; **essa camisa não vai com o casaco** that shirt doesn't go with that coat; **~ dar em** *(ruas)* lead to; **esta rua vai dar no banco** this street leads to the bank; **~ de:** *(vestido)* **ele foi de palhaço/de azul** he was dressed as a clown, in blue; **~ para:** *(profissão ou área de estudos)* **ele vai para medicina** he is going to study medicine; **~ indo, como vai a sua mãe? Vai indo** how's your mother? Not so bad; **já vou!** coming!; **vamos...?** shall we...?

● *v aux*

····› *(seguido de infinitivo)* **vamos vender a casa** we are going to sell our house; **você vai gostar** you're going to like it; *(em ordens)* **vai pôr a mesa!** go and lay the table!; **vai falar com o seu pai!** go and talk to your father!

● *vpr*

····› **~-se** *(partir)* go; **fui-me embora** I left; *(morrer)* **ele se foi** he died

ira /'ira/ *f* wrath

Irã /i'rã/ *m* Iran

iraniano /irani'anu/ *a & m* Iranian

Irão /i'rãw/ *m* Port Iran

Iraque /i'raki/ *m* Iraq

iraquiano /iraki'anu/ *a & m* Iraqi

Irlanda /ir'lãda/ *f* Ireland

irlan|dês /irlã'des/ *a* (*f* **~desa**) Irish ● *m* (*f* **~desa**) Irishman (*f* -woman);

(língua) Irish; **os ~deses** the Irish

irmã /ir'mã/ *f* sister

irmandade /irmã'dadʒi/ *f* *(associação)* brotherhood

irmão /ir'mãw/ *(pl* **~s**) *m* brother

ironia /iro'nia/ *f* irony

irônico /i'roniku/ *a* ironic

IRPF *abr m* (= **Imposto de Renda de Pessoa Física**) income tax

irracio|nal /ixasio'naw/ *(pl* **~nais**) *a* irrational

irradiar /ixadʒi'ar/ *vt* radiate; *(pelo rádio)* broadcast ● *vi* shine. **~-se** *vpr* spread, radiate

irre|al /ixe'aw/ *(pl* **~ais**) *a* unreal

irreconhecí|vel /ixekoɲe'sivew/ *(pl* **~veis**) *a* unrecognizable

irrecuperá|vel /ixekupe'ravew/ *(pl* **~veis**) *a* irretrievable

irrefletido /ixefle'tʃidu/ *a* rash

irregu|lar /ixegu'lar/ *a* irregular; *(inconstante)* erratic. **~laridade** *f* irregularity

irrelevante /ixele'vãtʃi/ *a* irrelevant

irrepará|vel /ixepa'ravew/ *(pl* **~veis**) *a* irreparable

irrepreensí|vel /ixeprie'sivew/ *(pl* **~veis**) *a* irreproachable

irrequieto /ixeki'etu/ *a* restless

irresistí|vel /ixezis'tʃivew/ *(pl* **~veis**) *a* irresistible

irresoluto /ixezo'lutu/ *a* *‹questão›* unresolved; *‹pessoa›* indecisive

irresponsá|vel /ixespõ'savew/ *(pl* **~veis**) *a* irresponsible

irreverente /ixeve'rẽtʃi/ *a* irreverent

irri|gação /ixiga'sãw/ *f* irrigation. **~gar** *vt* irrigate

irrisório /ixi'zɔriu/ *a* derisory

irri|tação /ixita'sãw/ f irritation. **~tadiço** a irritable. **~tante** a irritating. **~tar** vt irritate. **~tar-se** vpr get irritated

irromper /ixõ'per/ vi ~ **em** burst into

IRS /ir'jes/ abr m (Port = Imposto sobre o Rendimento das Pessoas Singulares) income tax

isca /'iska/ f bait

isen|ção /izẽ'sãw/ f exemption. **~tar** vt exempt. **~to** a exempt

Islã /iz'lã/ m Islam

islâmico /iz'lamiku/ a Islamic

isla|mismo /izla'mizmu/ m Islam. **~mita** a & m/f Muslim

islan|dês /izlã'des/ a (f **~desa**) Icelandic ● m (f **~desa**) Icelander; (língua) Icelandic

Islândia /iz'lãdʒia/ f Iceland

iso|lamento /izola'mẽtu/ m isolation; Eletr insulation. **~lante** a insulating. **~lar** vt isolate; Eletr insulate ● vi (contra azar) touch wood, Amer knock on wood

isopor /izo'por/ m polystyrene

isqueiro /is'keru/ m lighter

Israel /izxa'ɛw/ m Israel

israe|lense /izraj'lẽsi/ a & m/f Israeli. **~lita** a & m/f Israelite

---

isso /'isu/ ● pron

••••▶ that; **o que é ~?** what's that?

••••▶ (em expressões) **~!** (aprovação) Well done!; **nem por ~** not really; **para ~** in order to; **quer passar? Para ~ você terá que estudar** do you want to pass? You'll have to study in order to do that; **por ~** so; **ganhei na loteria, por ~ vou**

---

viajar muito I won the lottery, so I am going to travel a lot

isto /'istu/ pron this; ~ **é** that is

Itália /i'talia/ f Italy

italiano /itali'anu/ a & m Italian

itálico /i'taliku/ a & m italic

item /'itẽ/ m item

itine|rante /itʃine'rãtʃi/ a itinerant. **~rário** m itinerary

lugoslávia /iugoz'lavia/ f Yugoslavia

iugoslavo /iugoz'lavu/ a & m Yugoslavian

IVA /'iva/ abr m VAT

••••••••••••••••••••••••••••••••

Jj

já /ʒa/ adv already; (agora) right away ● conj on the other hand; **desde ~** from now on; ~ **não** no longer; ~ **que** since; ~, ~ in no time

jabuticaba /ʒabutʃi'kaba/ f jaboticaba

jaca /'ʒaka/ f jack fruit

jacaré /ʒaka'rɛ/ m alligator

jacinto /ʒa'sĩtu/ m hyacinth

jactância /ʒak'tãsia/ f boasting

jade /'ʒadʒi/ m jade

jaguar /ʒagu'ar/ m jaguar

jagunço /ʒa'gũsu/ m hired gunman

Jamaica /ʒa'majka/ f Jamaica

jamaicano /ʒamaj'kanu/ a & m Jamaican

jamais /ʒa'majs/ adv never

jamanta /ʒa'mãta/ f juggernaut

janeiro /ʒa'neru/ m January

janela /ʒa'nɛla/ f window; **~ de oportunidade** window of opportunity

jangada /ʒã'gada/ f (fishing) raft

janta /'ʒãta/ f 🗓 dinner

jantar /ʒã'tar/ m dinner ● vi have dinner ● vt have for dinner

Japão /ʒa'pãw/ m Japan

japo|na /ʒa'pɔna/ f pea jacket ● m/f 🗓 Japanese. **~nês** a & m (f **~nesa**) Japanese

jaqueira /ʒa'kera/ f jackfruit tree

jaqueta /ʒa'keta/ f jacket

jarda /'ʒarda/ f yard

jar|dim /ʒar'dʒĩ/ m garden. **~dim de infância** (pl **~dins de infância**) f kindergarten

jardim-escola /ʒardʒĩ'kɔla/ m (pl **jardins-escola**) Port nursery school

jardi|nagem /ʒardʒi'naʒẽ/ f gardening. **~nar** vi garden. **~neira** f (calça) dungarees; (vestido) pinafore dress, Amer jumper; (ônibus) open-sided bus; (para flores) flower stand. **~neiro** m gardener

jargão /ʒar'gãw/ m jargon

jar|ra /'ʒaxa/ f pot. **~ro** m jug

jasmim /ʒaz'mĩ/ m jasmine

jato /'ʒatu/ m jet

jaula /'ʒawla/ f cage

ja|zer /ʒa'zer/ vi lie. **~zida** f deposit. **~zigo** m family grave

jazz /dʒaz/ m jazz. **~ista** m/f jazz artist. **~ístico** a jazzy

jeans /dʒĩ:z/ m pl jeans

jeca /'ʒɛka/ m/f country bumpkin ● a countrified; (cafona) tacky. **~tatu** m/f country bumpkin

jei|tão /ʒej'tãw/ m 🗓 individual style. **~tinho** m knack. **~to** m way;

(de pessoa) manner; (habilidade) skill; **de qualquer ~to** anyway; **de ~to nenhum** no way; **pelo ~to** by the looks of things; **sem ~to** awkward; **dar um ~to** find a way; **dar um ~to em** (arrumar) tidy up; (consertar) fix; (torcer) twist ‹pé etc›; **ter ~to** to look like; **ter** ou **levar ~to para** be good at; **tomar ~to** pull one's socks up. **~toso** /o/ a skilful; (de aparência) elegant

je|juar /ʒeʒu'ar/ vi fast. **~jum** m fast

Jeová /ʒio'va/ m **testemunha de ~** Jehovah's witness

jérsei /'ʒersej/ m jersey

jesuíta /ʒezu'ita/ a & m/f Jesuit

Jesus /ʒe'zus/ m Jesus

jiboia /ʒi'bɔja/ f boa constrictor

jiboiar /ʒiboj'ar/ vi have a rest to let one's dinner go down

jiló /ʒi'lɔ/ m okra

jipe /'ʒipi/ m jeep

jiu-jítsu /ʒiu'ʒitsu/ m jiu-jitsu

joa|lheiro /ʒoa'ʎeru/ m jeweller. **~lheria** f jeweller's (shop)

joaninha /ʒoa'niɲa/ f ladybird, Amer ladybug; (alfinete) safety pin

João-ninguém /ʒoãwnĩ'gẽj/ (pl **joões-ninguém**) m nobody

jocoso /ʒo'kozu/ a jocular

joe|lhada /ʒoe'ʎada/ f blow with the knee. **~lheira** f kneepad. **~lho** /e/ m knee; **de ~lhos** kneeling

jo|gada /ʒo'gada/ f move. **~gado** a ‹pessoa› flat out; ‹papéis, roupa etc› lying around. **~gador** m player; (no cassino etc) gambler. **~gar** vt play; (atirar) throw; (arriscar no jogo) gamble ● vi play; (no cassino etc) gamble; (balançar) toss. **~gar fora** throw away. **~gatina** f gambling

jogging /'ʒɔgĩ/ m (cooper) jogging; (roupa) track suit

jogo /'ʒogu/ m (*partida*) game; (*ação de jogar*) play; (*jogatina*) gambling; (*conjunto*) set; **em ~** at stake; **~ de cintura** *fig* flexibility, room to manoeuvre; **~ de luz** lighting effects; **~ do bicho** illegal numbers game; **Jogos Olímpicos** Olympic Games. **~ da velha** m noughts and crosses

joguete /ʒo'getʃi/ m plaything

joia /'ʒɔja/ f jewel; (*propina*) entry fee ● a 🔟 great

joio /'ʒoju/ m chaff; **separar o ~ do trigo** separate the wheat from the chaff

jóquei /'ʒɔkej/ m (*pessoa*) jockey; (*lugar*) race course

Jordânia /ʒor'dania/ f Jordan

jordaniano /ʒordani'anu/ a & m Jordanian

jornada /ʒor'nada/ f (*viagem*) journey; **~nada de trabalho** working day. **~leiro** m (*vendedor*) newsagent, *Amer* newsdealer; (*entregador*) paper boy. **~lismo** m journalism. **~lista** m/f journalist. **~lístico** a journalistic

jornal /ʒor'naw/ m newspaper; (*na TV*) news

jornaleco /ʒorna'leku/ m rag, scandal sheet. **~leiro** m (*vendedor*) newsagent, *Amer* newsdealer; (*entregador*) paper boy. **~lismo** m journalism. **~lista** m/f journalist. **~lístico** a journalistic

jorrar /ʒo'xar/ vi gush, spurt. **~ro** /'ʒoxu/ m spurt

jota /'ʒɔta/ m (letter) J

jovem /'ʒovẽ/ a young; (*criado por jovens*) youth ● m/f young man (f -woman); pl young people

jovial /ʒovi'aw/ a (pl **~ais**) a jovial

juba /'ʒuba/ f mane

jubileu /ʒubi'lew/ m jubilee

júbilo /'ʒubilu/ m joy

judaico /ʒu'dajku/ a Jewish. **~daísmo** m Judaism. **~deu** a (f **~dia**) Jewish ● m (f **~dia**) Jew. **~diação** f

ill-treatment; (*uma*) terrible thing. **~diar** vi **~diar de** ill-treat

judicial /ʒudʒisi'aw/ (pl **~ais**) a judicial. **~ário** a judicial ● m judiciary. **~oso** /o/ a judicious

judô /ʒu'do/ m judo

judoca /ʒu'dɔka/ m/f judo player

jugo /'ʒugu/ m yoke

juiz /ʒu'is/ m (f **juíza**) judge; (*em jogos*) referee

juizado /ʒui'zadu/ m court

juízo /ʒu'izu/ m judgement; (*tino*) sense; (*tribunal*) court; **perder o ~** lose one's head; **ter ~** be sensible; **tomar** ou **criar ~** come to one's senses

jujuba /ʒu'ʒuba/ f (*bala*) fruit jelly

julgamento /ʒuwga'mẽtu/ m judgement. **~gar** vt judge; pass judgement on ‹*réu*›; (*imaginar*) think. **~gar-se** vpr consider o.s.

julho /'ʒuʎu/ m July

jumento /ʒu'mẽtu/ m donkey

junção /ʒũ'sãw/ f join; (*ação*) joining

junco /'ʒũku/ m reed

junho /'ʒuɲu/ m June

junino /ʒu'ninu/ a **festa ~na** St John's Day festival

júnior /'ʒunior/ a & m junior

junta /'ʒũta/ f board; *Pol* junta. **~tar** vt (*acrescentar*) add; (*uma coisa a outra*) join; (*uma coisa com outra*) combine; save up ‹*dinheiro*›; gather up ‹*papéis, lixo etc*› ● vi gather. **~tar-se** vpr join together; ‹*multidão*› gather; ‹*casal*› live together; **~tar-se a** join. **~to a** together ● adv together; **~to a** next to; **~to com** together with

jura /'ʒura/ f vow. **~rado** m juror. **~ramentado** a accredited.

~ramento m oath. **~rar** vt/i swear; **~ra?** 🔊 really?

júri /ˈʒuri/ m jury

jurídico /ʒuˈridʒiku/ a legal

juris|consulto /ʒuriskõˈsuwtu/ m legal advisor. **~dição** f jurisdiction. **~prudência** f jurisprudence. **~ta** m/f jurist

juros /ˈʒurus/ m pl interest

jus /ʒus/ m fazer **~** a live up to

jusante /ʒuˈzãtʃi/ f a **~** downstream

justamente /ʒustaˈmẽtʃi/ adv exactly; (com justiça) fairly

justapor /ʒustaˈpor/ vt juxtapose

justi|ça /ʒusˈtʃisa/ f (perante a lei) justice; (para com outros) fairness; (tribunal) court. **~ceiro** a fair-minded ● m vigilante

justifi|cação /ʒustʃifikaˈsãw/ f justification. **~car** vt justify. **~cativa** f justification. **~cável** (pl **~cáveis**) a justifiable

justo /ˈʒustu/ a fair; (apertado) tight ● adv just

juve|nil /ʒuveˈniw/ (pl **~nis**) a youthful; (para jovens) for young people; ‹time, torneio› junior ● m junior championship

juventude /ʒuvẽˈtudʒi/ f youth

Kk

karaokê /karaoˈke/ m karaoke

karatê /karaˈte/ m karate

karateca /karaˈtɛka/ m/f karate expert

kart /ˈkartʃi/ (pl **~s**) m go-kart

ketchup /keˈtʃupi/ m ketchup

kickboxing /kikbɔksĩŋ/ m kickboxing

kilowatt /kiloˈwɔt/ m kilowatt

kispo® /ˈkiʃpu/ m Port anorak

kit /ˈkitʃi/ (pl **~s**) m kit

kitchenette /kitʃeˈnetʃi/ f bedsitter

kiwi /kiˈvi/ m kiwi

Kuwait /kuˈwajtʃi/ m Kuwait

kuwaitiano /kuwajtʃiˈanu/ a & m Kuwaiti

Ll

lá /la/ ● adv

‥‥▸ there; **até ~** ‹ir› there; ‹esperar etc› until then; **por ~** (naquela direção) that way; (naquele lugar) around there; **~ fora** outside; **sei ~** how should I know?

lã /lã/ f wool

labareda /labaˈreda/ f flame

lábia /ˈlabia/ f flannel; **ter ~** have the gift of the gab

lábio /ˈlabiu/ m lip

labirinto /labiˈritu/ m labyrinth

laboral /laboˈraw/ a Port labour; **horário ~** working hours

laboratório /laboraˈtɔriu/ m laboratory

laborioso /laboriˈozu/ a hard-working

labu|ta /laˈbuta/ f drudgery. **~tar** vi slog

laca /'laka/ f lacquer

laçada /la'sada/ f slip knot

lacaio /la'kaju/ m lackey

la|çar /la'sar/ vt lasso ‹boi›. **~ço** m bow; (de vaqueiro) lasso; ‹vínculo› tie

lacônico /la'koniku/ a laconic

lacraia /la'kraja/ f centipede

la|crar /la'krar/ vt seal. **~cre** m (substância) sealing wax; (fechamento) seal

lacri|mejar /lakrime'ʒar/ vi water. **~mogêneo** a ‹gás› tear; ‹filme› tear-jerking. **~moso** /o/ a tearful

lácteo /'laktʃiu/ a milk; **Via Láctea** Milky Way

laticínio /laktʃi'siniu/ m
▶ **LATICÍNIO**

lacuna /la'kuna/ f gap

ladainha /lada'iɲa/ f litany

la|dear /ladʒi'ar/ vt flank; sidestep ‹dificuldade›. **~deira** f slope

lado /'ladu/ m side; **o ~ de cá/lá** this/that side; **ao ~ de** beside; **~ a ~** side by side; **para este ~** this way; **por outro ~** on the other hand

la|drão /la'drãw/ m (f **~dra**) thief; (tubo) overflow pipe ● a thieving

ladrar /la'drar/ vi bark

ladri|lhar /ladri'ʎar/ vt tile. **~lho** m tile

ladroagem /ladro'aʒẽ/ f stealing

lagar|ta /la'garta/ f caterpillar; (numa roda) caterpillar track. **~tear** vi bask in the sun. **~tixa** f gecko. **~to** m lizard

lago /'lagu/ m lake

lagoa /la'goa/ f lagoon

lagos|ta /la'gosta/ f lobster. **~tim** m crayfish, Amer crawfish

lágrima /'lagrima/ f tear

laia /'laja/ f kind

laico /'lajku/ adj ‹pessoa› lay; ‹ensino› secular

laivos /'lajvus/ m pl traces

laje /'laʒi/ m flagstone. **~ar** vt pave

lajota /la'ʒɔta/ f small paving stone

lama /'lama/ f mud. **~çal** (pl **~çais**) m bog. **~cento** a muddy

lamba|da /lã'bada/ f lambada. **~teria** f lambada club

lam|ber /lã'ber/ vt lick. **~bida** f lick

lambreta /lã'breta/ f moped

lambris /lã'bris/ m pl panelling

lambuzar /lãbu'zar/ vt smear. **~se** vpr get sticky

lamen|tar /lamẽ'tar/ vt (lastimar) lament; (sentir) be sorry; **~tar-se de** lament. **~tável** (pl **~táveis**) a lamentable. **~to** m lament

lâmina /'lamina/ f blade; (de persiana) slat

laminar /lami'nar/ vt laminate

lâmpada /'lãpada/ f light bulb; (abajur) lamp; **~ compacta** energy-saving lightbulb

lampe|jar /lãpe'ʒar/ vi flash. **~jo** /e/ m flash

lampião /lãpi'ãw/ m lantern

lamúria /la'muria/ f moaning

lamuriar-se /lamuri'arsi/ vpr moan (de about)

lan|ça /'lãsa/ f spear. **~çamento** m (de navio, foguete, produto) launch; (de filme, disco) release; (novo produto) new line; (novo filme, disco) release; (novo livro) new title; (em livro comercial) entry. **~çar** vt (atirar) throw; launch ‹navio, foguete, novo produto, livro›; release ‹filme, disco›; (em livro comercial) enter; (em leilão) bid; **~çar mão de** make use of. **~ce** m (num filme, jogo) bit, moment; (episódio) episode; (questão) matter;

(*jogada*) move; (*em leilão*) bid; (*de escada*) flight; (*de casas*) row

lancha /ˈlãʃa/ f launch

lan|char /lãˈʃar/ vi have a snack ● vt have a snack of. **~che** m snack. **~chonete** /e/ f snack bar

lancinante /lãsiˈnãtʃi/ a <*dor*> shooting; <*grito*> piercing

lânguido /ˈlãgidu/ a languid

lan house m internet cafe

lantejoula /lãteˈʒola/ f sequin

lanter|na /lãˈtɛrna/ f lantern; (*de bolso*) torch, *Amer* flashlight. **~nagem** f panel beating; (*oficina*) body shop. **~ninha** m/f usher; (f usherette)

lanugem /laˈnuʒẽ/ f down

lapela /laˈpɛla/ f lapel

lapidar /lapiˈdar/ vt cut <*pedra preciosa*>; fig polish

lápide /ˈlapidʒi/ f tombstone

lápis /ˈlapis/ m invar pencil

lapiseira /lapiˈzera/ f propelling pencil; (*caixa*) pencil box

Lapônia /laˈponia/ f Lapland

lapso /ˈlapsu/ m lapse

laptop /lapˈtɔp/ m laptop

la|quê /laˈke/ m lacquer. **~quear** vt lacquer

lar /lar/ m home

laran|ja /laˈrãʒa/ f orange ● a invar orange. **~jada** f orangeade. **~jeira** f orange tree

lareira /laˈrera/ f hearth, fireplace

lar|gada /larˈgada/ f start; dar a **~gada** start off. **~gar** vt (*soltar*) let go of; give up <*estudos, emprego etc*>; **~gar de fumar** give up smoking. **~go** a wide; <*roupa*> loose ● m (*praça*) square; ao **~go** (*no alto-mar*) out at sea. **~gura** f width

larin|ge /laˈrĩʒi/ f larynx. **~gite** f laryngitis

larva /ˈlarva/ f larva

lasanha /laˈzaɲa/ f lasagne

las|ca /ˈlaska/ f chip. **~car** vt/i chip; **de ~car** 🅣 awful

lástima /ˈlastʃima/ f shame

lastro /ˈlastru/ m ballast

la|ta /ˈlata/ f (*material*) tin; (*recipiente*) tin, *Amer* can; **~ta de lixo** dustbin, *Amer* trash can. **~tão** m brass

late|jante /lateˈʒãtʃi/ a throbbing. **~jar** vi throb

latente /laˈtẽtʃi/ a latent

late|ral /lateˈraw/ (*pl* **~rais**) a side, lateral

laticínio /latʃiˈsiniu/ m dairy product

latido /laˈtʃidu/ m bark

lati|fundiário /latʃifũdʒiˈariu/ a landowning ● m landowner. **~fúndio** m estate

latim /laˈtʃĩ/ m Latin

latino /laˈtʃinu/ a & m Latin. **~-americano** a & m Latin American

latir /laˈtʃir/ vi bark

latitude /latʃiˈtudʒi/ f latitude

lauda /ˈlawda/ f side

laudo /ˈlawdu/ m report, findings

lava /ˈlava/ f lava

lava|bo /laˈvabu/ m toilet. **~dora** f washing machine. **~gem** f washing; **~gem a seco** dry cleaning; **~gem cerebral** brainwashing

lavanda /laˈvãda/ f lavender

lavanderia /lavãdeˈria/ f laundry

lavar /laˈvar/ vt wash; **~ a seco** dry-clean. **~-se** vpr wash

lavatório /lavaˈtɔriu/ m *Port* washbasin

lavoura /laˈvora/ f (*agricultura*) farming; (*terreno*) field

lav|rador /lavra'dor/ *m* farmhand. **~rar** *vt* work; draw up ‹documento›

laxante /la'ʃãtʃi/ *a* & *m* laxative

lazer /la'zer/ *m* leisure

le|al /le'aw/ (*pl* **~ais**) *a* loyal. **~aldade** *f* loyalty

leão /le'ãw/ *m* lion; **Leão** (*signo*) Leo. **~ de chácara** (*pl* **leões de chácara**) *m* bouncer

lebre /'lɛbri/ *f* hare

lecionar /lesio'nar/ *vt/i* teach

le|gação /lega'sãw/ *f* legation. **~gado** *m* (*pessoa*) legate; (*herança*) legacy

le|gal /le'gaw/ (*pl* **~gais**) *a* legal; 🇧 good; ‹pessoa› nice; **tá ~gal** OK. **~galidade** *f* legality. **~galizar** *vt* legalize

legar /le'gar/ *vt* bequeath

legenda /le'ʒẽda/ *f* (*de quadro*) caption; (*de filme*) subtitle; (*inscrição*) inscription

legi|ão /leʒi'ãw/ *f* legion. **~onário** *m* (*romano*) legionary; (*da legião estrangeira*) legionnaire

legis|lação /leʒizla'sãw/ *f* legislation. **~lador** *m* legislator. **~lar** *vi* legislate. **~lativo** *a* legislative ● *m* legislature. **~latura** *f* legislature. **~ta** *m/f* legal expert

légua /'lɛgwa/ *f* league

legume /le'gumi/ *m* vegetable

lei /lej/ *f* law

leigo /'lejgu/ *a* lay ● *m* layman

lei|lão /lej'lãw/ *m* auction. **~loar** *vt* auction. **~loeiro** *m* auctioneer

leitão /lej'tãw/ *m* sucking pig

lei|te /'lejtʃi/ *m* milk; **~te condensado/desnatado** condensed/skimmed milk. **~teira** *f* (*jarro*) milk jug; (*panela*) milk saucepan. **~teiro** *m* milkman ● *a* ‹vaca› dairy

leito /'lejtu/ *m* bed

leitor /lej'tor/ *m* reader

leitoso /lej'tozu/ *a* milky

leitura /lej'tura/ *f* (*ação*) reading; (*material*) reading matter

lema /'lema/ *m* motto

lem|brança /lẽ'brãsa/ *f* memory; (*presente*) souvenir. **~brar** *vt/i* remember; **~brar-se de** remember; **~brar algo a alguém** remind sb of sth. **~brete** /e/ *m* reminder

leme /'lemi/ *m* rudder

len|ço /'lẽsu/ (*pl* **lenços**) *m* (*para o nariz*) handkerchief; (*para vestir*) scarf. **~çol** /ɔ/ *m* sheet

len|da /'lẽda/ *f* legend. **~dário** *a* legendary

lenha /'leɲa/ *f* firewood; (*uma*) log. **~dor** *m* woodcutter

lente /'lẽtʃi/ *f* lens; **~ de contato** contact lens

lentidão /lẽtʃi'dãw/ *f* slowness

lentilha /lẽ'tʃiʎa/ *f* lentil

lento /'lẽtu/ *a* slow

leoa /le'oa/ *f* lioness

leopardo /lio'pardu/ *m* leopard

le|pra /'lɛpra/ *f* leprosy. **~proso** /o/ *a* leprous ● *m* leper

leque /'lɛki/ *m* fan; *fig* array

ler /ler/ *vt/i* read

LER *abr f* (= **lesão por esforço repetitivo**) RSI

ler|deza /ler'deza/ *f* sluggishness. **~do** /e/ *a* sluggish

le|são /le'zãw/ *f* lesion, injury; **~são por esforço repetitivo** repetitive strain injury. **~sar** *vt* damage

lésbi|ca /'lɛzbika/ f lesbian. **~co** a lesbian

lesionado /lezio'nadu/ a injured

lesionar /lezio'nar/ vt injure

lesma /'lezma/ f slug

leste /'lɛstʃi/ m east

le|tal /le'taw/ (pl **~tais**) a lethal

le|tão /le'tãw/ a & m (f **~tã**) Latvian

letargia /letar'ʒia/ f lethargy

letivo /le'tʃivu/ a **ano ~** academic year

Letônia /le'tonia/ f Latvia

letra /'letra/ f letter; (de música) lyrics, words; (caligrafia) writing; **Letras** Modern Languages; **ao pé da ~** literally; **com todas as ~s** in no uncertain terms; **tirar de ~** take in one's stride; **~ de forma** block letter

letreiro /le'treru/ m sign

leucemia /lewse'mia/ f leukaemia

leva /ɛ/ f batch

levado /le'vadu/ a naughty

levan|tamento /levãta'mẽtu/ m (enquete) survey; (rebelião) uprising; **~tamento de pesos** weightlifting. **~tar** vt raise; lift ‹peso› ● vi get up. **~tar-se** vpr get up; (revoltar-se) rise up

levante /le'vãtʃi/ m east

levar /le'var/ vt take; lead ‹vida›; get ‹tapa, susto etc› ● vi lead (a to)

leve /'levi/ a light; (não grave) slight; **de ~** lightly

levedura /leve'dura/ f yeast

leveza /le'veza/ f lightness

levi|andade /levia'dadʒi/ f frivolity. **~ano** a frivolous

levitar /levi'tar/ vi levitate

lexi|cal /leksi'kaw/ (pl **~cais**) a lexical

lêxico /'lɛksiku/ m lexicon

lhe /ʎi/ pron (a ele) to him; (a ela) to her; (a você) to you. **~s** pron to them; (a vocês) to you

liba|nês /liba'nes/ a & m (f **~nesa**) Lebanese

Líbano /'libanu/ m Lebanon

libélula /li'bɛlula/ f dragonfly

libe|ração /libera'sãw/ f release. **~ral** (pl **~rais**) a & m liberal. **~ralismo** m liberalism. **~ralizar** vt liberalize. **~rar** vt release

liberdade /liber'dadʒi/ f freedom; **pôr em ~** set free; **~ condicional** probation

libero /'liberu/ m sweeper

liber|tação /liberta'sãw/ f liberation. **~tar** vt free

Líbia /'libia/ f Libya

libi|dinoso /libidʒi'nozu/ a lecherous. **~do** f libido

líbio /'libiu/ a & m Libyan

li|bra /'libra/ f pound; **Libra** (signo) Libra. **~briano** a & m Libran

lição /li'sãw/ f lesson

licen|ça /li'sẽsa/ f leave; (documento) licence; **com ~ça** excuse me; **de ~ça** on leave; **sob ~ça** under licence. **~ciar** vt (autorizar) license; (dar férias a) give leave to. **~ciar-se** vpr (tirar férias) take leave; (formar-se) graduate. **~ciatura** f degree. **~cioso** /o/ a licentious

licenciado /lisẽsi'adu/ m graduate

liceu /li'sew/ m Port secondary school, Amer high school

licor /li'kor/ m liqueur

lida /'lida/ f slog, grind; (leitura) read

lidar /li'dar/ vt/i **~ com** deal with

lide /'lidʒi/ f (trabalho) work

líder /'lider/ m/f leader

lide|rança /lide'rãsa/ f (de partido etc) leadership; (em corrida, jogo etc) lead. **~rar** vt lead

lido /'lidu/ a well-read

liga /'liga/ f (aliança) league; (tira) garter; (presilha) suspender; (de metais) alloy

li|gação /liga'sãw/ f connection; (telefônica) call; (amorosa) liaison. **~gada** f call, ring. **~gado** a ‹luz, TV› on; **~gado em** attached to ‹pessoa›; hooked on ‹droga›. **~gamento** m ligament. **~gar** vt join, connect; switch on ‹luz, TV etc›; start up ‹carro›; bind ‹amigos› ● vi ring up, call; **~gar para** (telefonar) ring, call; (dar importância) care about; (dar atenção) pay attention to. **~gar-se** vpr join

ligeiro /li'ʒeru/ a light; ‹ferida, melhora› slight; ‹ágil› nimble

lilás /li'las/ m lilac ● a invar mauve

lima¹ /'lima/ f (ferramenta) file

lima² /'lima/ f (fruta) lime

limão /li'mãw/ m lime; (amarelo) lemon

limar /li'mar/ vt file

limeira /li'mera/ f lime tree

limiar /limi'ar/ m threshold

limi|tação /limita'sãw/ f limitation. **~tar** vt limit. **~tar-se** vpr limit o.s.; **~tar(-se) com** border on. **~te** m limit; (de terreno) boundary; **passar dos ~tes** go too far; **~te de velocidade** speed limit

limo|eiro /limo'eiru/ m lemon tree. **~nada** f lemonade

lim|pador /lĩpa'dor/ m **~pador de para-brisas** windscreen wiper. **~par** vt clean; wipe ‹lágrimas, suor›; fig clean up ‹cidade, organização›.

~peza /e/ f (ato) cleaning; (qualidade) cleanness; fig clean-up; **~peza pública** sanitation. **~po** a clean; ‹céu, consciência› clear; ‹lucro› net, clear; fig pure; **passar a ~po** write up ‹trabalho›; fig sort a ~po get to the bottom of ‹caso›

limusine /limu'zini/ f limousine

lince /'lĩsi/ m lynx

lindo /'lĩdu/ a beautiful

linear /lini'ar/ a linear

lingote /lĩ'gɔtʃi/ m ingot

língua /'lĩgwa/ f (na boca) tongue; (idioma) language; **~ materna** mother tongue

linguado /lĩ'gwadu/ m sole

lingua|gem /lĩ'gwaʒẽ/ f language. **~jar** m speech, dialect

lingueta /lĩ'gweta/ f bolt

linguiça /lĩ'gwisa/ f pork sausage

lin|guista /lĩ'gwiʃta/ m/f linguist. **~guística** f linguistics. **~guístico** a linguistic

linha /'liɲa/ f line; (fio) thread; **perder a ~** lose one's cool; **~ aérea** airline; **~ de fogo** firing line; **~ de montagem** assembly line. **~gem** f lineage

linho /'liɲu/ m linen; (planta) flax

link /lĩk/ m Comput link, hyperlink

linóleo /li'nɔliu/ m lino(leum)

lipoaspiração /lipoaspira'sãw/ f liposuction

liqui|dação /likida'sãw/ f liquidation; (de loja) clearance sale; (de conta) settlement. **~dar** vt liquidate; settle ‹conta›; pay off ‹dívida›; sell off, clear ‹mercadorias›

liquidificador /likwidʒifika'dor/ m liquidizer

líquido /'likidu/ a liquid; ‹lucro, salário› net ● m liquid

líri|ca /'lirika/ f Mus lyrics; (poesia) lyric poetry. **~co** a lyrical; ‹poesia› lyric

lírio /'liriu/ m lily

Lisboa /liz'boa/ f Lisbon

Lisboa – O Grande Terremoto The 1755 Lisbon earthquake, also known as the Great Lisbon Earthquake, took place on Saturday 1 November 1755. The earthquake was followed by fires and a tsunami, which caused near-total destruction of Lisbon and adjoining areas. Estimates place the death toll in Lisbon alone between 10,000 and 100,000 people, making it one of the deadliest earthquakes in history.

---

lisboeta /lizbo'eta/ a & m/f (person) from Lisbon

liso /'lizu/ a smooth; (sem desenho) plain; ‹cabelo› straight; ⚠ (duro) broke

lison|ja /li'zõʒa/ f flattery. **~jear** vt flatter

lista /'lista/ f list; (listra) stripe; **~ telefônica** telephone directory

listra /'listra/ f stripe. **~do** a striped, stripey

lite|ral /lite'raw/ (pl **~rais**) a literal. **~rário** a literary. **~ratura** f literature

litígio /li'tʃiʒiu/ m dispute; Jurid lawsuit

lito|ral /lito'raw/ (pl **~rais**) m coastline. **~râneo** a coastal

litro /'litru/ m litre

Lituânia /litu'ania/ f Lithuania

lituano /litu'anu/ a & m Lithuanian

living /'livĩ/ (pl **~s**) m living room

livrar /li'vrar/ vt free; (salvar) save. **~se** vpr escape; **~se de** get rid of

livraria /livra'ria/ f bookshop

livre /'livri/ a free; **~ de impostos** tax-free. **~arbítrio** m free will

liv|reiro /li'vreru/ m bookseller. **~ro** m book; **~ro de consulta** reference book; **~ro de cozinha** cookery book; **~ro de texto** textbook; **~ro eletrônico** e-book

li|xa /'liʃa/ f (de unhas) emery board; (para madeira etc) sandpaper. **~xar** vt sand ‹madeira›; file ‹unhas›; **estou me ~xando** ⚠ I couldn't care less

li|xeira /li'ʃeira/ f dustbin, Amer garbage can. **~xeiro** m dustman, Amer garbage collector. **~xo** m rubbish, Amer garbage; (atômico) waste

lobisomem /lobi'zomẽ/ m werewolf

lobo /'lobu/ m wolf. **~marinho** (pl **~s-marinhos**) m sea lion

lóbulo /'lɔbulu/ m lobe

lo|cação /loka'sãw/ f (de imóvel) lease; (de carro) rental. **~cador** (de casa) landlord. **~cadora** f rental company; (de vídeos) video shop

lo|cal /lo'kaw/ (pl **~cais**) a local ● m site; (de um acidente etc) scene. **~calidade** f locality. **~calização** f location. **~calizar** vt locate. **~calizar-se** vpr (orientar-se) get one's bearings

loção /lo'sãw/ f lotion; **~ após-barba** aftershave lotion

locatário /loka'tariu/ m (de imóvel) tenant; (de carro etc) hirer

locomo|tiva /lokomo'tʃiva/ f locomotive. **~ver-se** vpr get around

locu|ção /loku'sãw/ f phrase. **~tor** m announcer

lodo /'lodu/ m mud. **~so** /o/ a muddy

logaritmo /loga'ritʃimu/ m logarithm

lógi|ca /'lɔʒika/ f logic. **~co** a logical

logo /'lɔgu/ adv (em seguida) straightaway; (em breve) soon; (justamente) just; **~ mais** later; **~ antes/depois** just before/straight after; **~ que** as soon as; **até ~** goodbye

logotipo /logo'tʃipu/ m logo

logradouro /logra'doru/ m public place

loiro /'lojru/ a ▶ LOURO

lo|ja /'lɔja/ f shop, Amer store; **~ja de departamentos** department store; **~ja maçônica** Masonic lodge. **~jista** m/f shopkeeper

lom|bada /lõ'bada/ f (de livro) spine; (na rua) speed bump. **~binho** m tenderloin. **~bo** m back; (carne) loin

lona /'lona/ f canvas

Londres /'lõdris/ f London

londrino /lõ'drinu/ a London ● m Londoner

longa-metragem /lõga me'traʒẽ/ (pl **longas-metragens**) a feature film

longe /'lõʒi/ adv far, a long way; **de ~** from a distance; (por muito) by far; **~ disso** far from it

longevidade /lõʒevi'dadʒi/ f longevity

longínquo /lõ'ʒĩkwu/ a distant

longitude /lõʒi'tudʒi/ f longitude

longo /'lõgu/ a long ● m long dress; **ao ~ de** along; (durante)

through, over

lontra /'lõtra/ f otter

lorde /'lɔrdʒi/ m lord

lorota /lo'rɔta/ f 🆒 fib

losango /lo'zãgu/ m diamond

lo|tação /lota'sãw/ f capacity; (ônibus) bus; **~tação esgotada** full house. **~tado** a crowded; (teatro, ônibus) full. **~tar** vt fill ● vi fill up

lote /'lɔtʃi/ m (quinhão) portion; (de terreno) plot, Amer lot; (em leilão) lot; (porção de coisas) batch

loteria /lote'ria/ f lottery

louça /'losa/ f china; (pratos etc) crockery; **lavar a ~** wash up, Amer do the dishes

lou|co /'loku/ a mad, crazy ● m madman; **estou ~co para ir** 🆒 I'm dying to go. **~cura** f madness; (uma) crazy thing

louro /'loru/ a blond ● m laurel; (condimento) bay leaf

lou|var /lo'var/ vt praise. **~vável** (pl **~váveis**) a praiseworthy. **~vor** /o/ m praise

lua /'lua/ f moon. **~ de mel** f honeymoon

lu|ar /lu'ar/ m moonlight. **~arento** a moonlit

lubrifi|cação /lubrifika'sãw/ f lubrication. **~cante** a lubricating ● m lubricant. **~car** vt lubricate

lucidez /lusi'des/ f lucidity

lúcido /'lusidu/ a lucid

lu|crar /lu'krar/ vi profit (**com** by). **~cratividade** f profitability. **~crativo** a profitable, lucrative. **~cro** m profit

ludibriar /ludʒibri'ar/ vt cheat

lúdico /'ludʒiku/ a playful

lugar /lu'gar/ m place; (espaço) room; **em ~ de** in place of; **em**

primeiro ~ in the first place; **em algum** ~ somewhere; **em todo** ~ everywhere; **dar** ~ **a** give rise to; **ter** ~ take place

lugarejo /luga'reʒu/ m village

lúgubre /'lugubri/ a gloomy, dismal

lula /'lula/ f squid

lume /'lumi/ m fire

luminária /lumi'naria/ f light, lamp; pl illuminations

luminoso /lumi'nozu/ a luminous; ‹ideia› brilliant

lunar /lu'nar/ a lunar ● m mole

lupa /'lupa/ f magnifying glass

lusco-fusco /lusku'fusku/ m twilight

lusitano /luzi'tanu/, **luso** /'luzu/ a & m Portuguese

lus|trar /lus'trar/ vt shine, polish. **~tre** m shine; fig lustre; (luminária) light, lamp. **~troso** /o/ a shiny

luto /'lutu/ m mourning

luva /'luva/ f glove

luxação /luʃa'sãw/ f dislocation

Luxemburgo /luʃẽ'burgu/ m Luxembourg

luxembur|guês /luʃebur'ges/ a (f **~guesa**) Luxembourg ● m (f **~guesa**) Luxembourger; (língua) Luxembourgish

luxo /'luʃu/ m luxury; **hotel de** ~ luxury hotel; **cheio de** ~ 🔢 fussy

luxuoso /luʃu'ozu/ a luxurious

luxúria /lu'ʃuria/ f lust

luxuriante /luʃuri'ãtʃi/ a lush

luz /lus/ f light; **à** ~ **de** by the light of ‹velas etc›; in the light of ‹fatos

etc›; **dar à** ~ give birth to

luzidio /luzi'dʒio/ a shiny

luzir /lu'zir/ vi shine

·····························

Mm

·····························

maca /'maka/ f stretcher

maçã /ma'sã/ f apple

macabro /ma'kabru/ a macabre

maca|cão /maka'kãw/ m (de trabalho) overalls, Amer coveralls; (tipo de calça) dungarees; (roupa inteiriça) jumpsuit; (para bebê) romper suit. **~co** m monkey; (aparelho) jack

maçada /ma'sada/ f bore

maçaneta /masa'neta/ f doorknob

maçante /ma'sãtʃi/ a boring

macar|rão /maka'xãw/ m pasta; (espaguete) spaghetti. **~ronada** f pasta with tomato sauce and cheese

macarrônico /maka'xoniku/ a broken

macete /ma'setʃi/ m trick

machado /ma'ʃadu/ m axe

ma|chão /ma'ʃãw/ a tough ● m tough guy. **~chismo** m machismo. **~chista** a chauvinistic ● m male chauvinist. **~cho** a male; ‹homem› macho ● m male

machu|cado /maʃu'kadu/ m injury; (na pele) sore patch. **~car** vt/i hurt. **~car-se** vpr hurt o.s.

maciço /ma'sisu/ a solid; ‹dose etc› massive ● m massif

macieira /masi'era/ f apple tree

maciez /masi'es/ f softness

macilento /masi'lẽtu/ a haggard

macio /ma'siu/ a soft; ‹carne›
tender

maço /'masu/ m (de cigarros)
packet; (de notas) bundle

ma|çom /ma'sõ/ m freemason.
~çonaria f freemasonry

maconha /ma'koɲa/ f marijuana

maçônico /ma'soniku/ a Masonic

má-criação /makria'sãw/ f
rudeness

macrobiótico /makrobi'ɔtʃiku/
a macrobiotic

macum|ba /ma'kũba/ f Afro-
Brazilian cult; (uma) spell. **~beiro**
m follower of macumba ● a macumba

madame /ma'dami/ f lady

madeira /ma'dera/ f wood ● m
(vinho) Madeira; **~ de lei** hardwood

Madeira /ma'dera/ f Madeira

madeirense /made'rẽsi/ a & m
Madeiran

madeixa /ma'deʃa/ f lock

madrasta /ma'drasta/ f
stepmother

madrepérola /madre'pɛrola/ f
mother of pearl

madressilva /madre'siwva/ f
honeysuckle

Madri /ma'dri/ f Madrid

madrinha /ma'driɲa/ f (de
batismo) godmother; (de casamento)
bridesmaid

madru|gada /madru'gada/ f
early morning. **~gador** m early riser.
~gar vi get up early

maduro /ma'duru/ a ‹fruta› ripe;
‹pessoa› mature

mãe /mãj/ f mother. **~ de santo** (pl
~s de santo) f macumba priestess

maes|tria /majs'tria/ f expertise.
~tro m conductor

máfia /'mafia/ f mafia

magazine /maga'zini/ m
department store

magia /ma'ʒia/ f magic

mági|ca /'maʒika/ f magic; (uma)
magic trick. **~co** a magic ● m
magician

magis|tério /maʒis'teriu/ m
teaching; (professores) teachers.
~trado m magistrate

magnânimo /mag'nanimu/ a
magnanimous

magnata /mag'nata/ m magnate

magnésio /mag'neziu/ m
magnesium

mag|nético /mag'netʃiku/ a
magnetic. **~netismo** m magnetism.
~netizar vt magnetize; fig
mesmerize

mag|nificência /magnifi'sẽsia/ f
magnificence. **~nifico** a magnificent

magnitude /magni'tudʒi/ f
magnitude

mago /'magu/ m magician; **os reis
~s** the Three Wise Men

mágoa /'magoa/ f sorrow

magoar /mago'ar/ vt/i hurt. **~-se**
vpr be hurt

ma|gricela /magri'sɛla/ a skinny.
~gro a thin; ‹leite› skimmed;
‹carne› lean; fig meagre

maio /'maju/ m May

maiô /ma'jo/ m swimsuit

maionese /majo'nezi/ f
mayonnaise

maior /ma'jɔr/ a bigger; ‹escritor,
amor etc› greater; **o ~ carro** the
greatest car; **o ~ escritor** the
greatest writer; **~ de idade** of age

Maiorca /ma'jɔrka/ f Majorca

maio|ria /majo'ria/ f majority;
a ~ria dos brasileiros most

mais | majoritário

182

Brazilians. **~ridade** *f* majority, adulthood

mais /majs/ ● *adv*

••••➤ *(uso comparativo: com adjetivos)* more; **~ fácil** easier; **~ inteligente** more intelligent; **é ~ alta/elegante que eu** she's taller/slimmer than me

❗ Os adjetivos de uma sílaba formam o comparativo com o acréscimo *–er*: **mais devagar** *slower*, **mais rico** *richer*. Para formar o comparativo da maioria de adjetivos de duas ou mais sílabas, usa-se *more* + adjetivo: **mais caro** *more expensive*.

••••➤ *(uso comparativo com verbos)* **durar ~** last longer; **trabalhar ~** work harder; **~ de** more than; **você viajou ~ do que eu** you've travelled more than me; **~ de 2 semanas** more than 2 weeks; **gosto ~ de peixe** I like fish better

••••➤ *(uso superlativo)* most; **a cidade ~ bonita do mundo** the most beautiful city in the world; **o ~ simpático de todos** the nicest of all; **a loja que vendeu ~ livros** the shop that sold most books

❗ Os adjetivos de uma sílaba formam o superlativo com o acréscimo *–est*: **a cidade mais fria** *the coldest city*, **a mulher mais rica** *the richest woman*. Para formar o superlativo da maioria de adjetivos de duas ou mais sílabas, usa-se *most* + adjetivo: **o mais inteligente** *the most intelligent*.

••••➤ *(com pronomes)* else; **você tem ~ alguma coisa para me**

dizer? have you got anything else to tell me?; **~ alguém?** anyone else?; **~ nada** nothing else; **~ ninguém** nobody else

••••➤ *(em exclamações)* **que paisagem ~ bonita!** what lovely scenery!

••••➤ *(em negativas)* **não sabemos ~ do que disseram no rádio** we only know what it said on the radio; **não foi ~ que uma coincidência** it was just a coincidence

● *prep*

••••➤ *Mat* plus; **5 ~ 5 são 10** 5 plus 5 makes ten

••••➤ *(em expressões)* **a ~** *(para além do necessário)* too much, too many; **há 2 cadeiras a ~** there are 2 chairs too many; *(de sobra)* spare; **eu tenho uma caneta a ~** I've got a spare pen; **~ nada** nothing else; **não tenho ~ nada para lhe dizer** I've got nothing else to tell you; **~ ou menos** more or less; **ela ganha ~ ou menos R$200 por dia** she earns around R$200 a day; **~ dia menos dia** one of these days; **ela vai emigrar, ~ dia menos dia** she's going to emigrate one of these days; **além do ~** what's more

maisena /maj'zena/ *f* cornflour, *Amer* cornstarch

maître /mɛtr/ *m* head waiter

maiúscula /ma'juskula/ *f* capital letter

majes|tade /maʒes'tadʒi/ *f* majesty. **~toso** *a* majestic

major /ma'ʒɔr/ *m* major

majoritário /maʒori'tariu/ *a* majority

mal /maw/ ● *adv*

····▸ (*imperfeitamente*) badly; **portar-se ~/falar ~** behave/ speak badly; **cheirar ~** smell; **ela ouve muito ~** her hearing is very bad

····▸ (*erradamente*) wrong; **você escolheu ~** you made the wrong choice

····▸ (*quase não*) hardly; **eles ~ se falaram** they hardly spoke; (*quase nunca*) hardly ever; **~ os vemos** we hardly ever see them

····▸ (*doente*) **estar ~** be quite ill; **sentir-se ~** feel ill

● *m*

····▸ (*dano*) harm; **não lhe desejo nenhum ~** I don't wish you any harm

····▸ (*maldade*) **o bem e o ~** good and evil

····▸ (*doença*) illness; **tem um ~ incurável** he has an incurable illness

····▸ (*problema*) **esse foi um ~ menor** that was the least of my troubles

● *conj*

····▸ (*logo que*) as soon as; **~ chegaram** as soon as they arrived

····▸ (*em expressões*) **estar ~ de** (*dinheiro*) be short of; **não fazer por ~** mean no harm; **ele não faz por ~** he doesn't mean any harm

mala /'mala/ *f* suitcase; (*do carro*) boot, *Amer* trunk; **~ aérea** air courier

malabaris|mo /malaba'rizmu/ *m* juggling act. **~ta** *m/f* juggler

mal-agradecido /malagrade'sidu/ *a* ungrateful

malagueta /mala'geta/ *f* chilli pepper

malaio /ma'laju/ *a* & *m* Malay

Malaísia /mala'izia/ *f* Malaysia

malaísio /mala'iziu/ *a* & *m* Malaysian

malan|dragem /malã'draʒẽ/ *f* hustling; (*uma*) clever trick. **~dro** *a* cunning ● *m* hustler

malária /ma'laria/ *f* malaria

mal-assombrado /malasõ'bradu/ *a* haunted

Malavi /mala'vi/ *m* Malawi

malcriado /mawkri'adu/ *a* rude

mal|dade /maw'dadʒi/ *f* wickedness; (*uma*) wicked thing; **por ~dade** out of spite. **~dição** *f* curse. **~dito** *a* cursed, damned. **~doso** /o/ *a* wicked

maleá|vel /mali'avew/ (*pl* **~veis**) *a* malleable

maledicência /maledi'sẽsia/ *f* malicious gossip

maléfico /ma'lɛfiku/ *a* evil; (*prejudicial*) harmful

mal-encarado /malĩka'radu/ *a* shady, dubious ● *m* shady character

mal-entendido /malĩtẽ'dʒidu/ *m* misunderstanding

mal-estar /malis'tar/ *m* (*doença*) ailment; (*constrangimento*) discomfort

maleta /ma'leta/ *f* overnight bag

malévolo /ma'lɛvolu/ *a* malevolent

malfei|to /maw'fejtu/ *a* badly done; ‹*roupa etc*› badly made; *fig* wrongful. **~tor** *m* wrongdoer. **~toria** *f* wrongdoing

ma|lha /'maʎa/ *f* (*ponto*) stitch; (*tricô*) knitting; (*tecido*) jersey; (*casaco*) jumper, *Amer* sweater;

(*para ginástica*) leotard; (*de rede*) mesh; **fazer ~lha** knit. **~lhado** *a* ⟨*animal*⟩ dappled; ⟨*roque*⟩ heavy. **~lhar** *vt* beat; thresh ⟨*trigo etc*⟩ ● *vi* 🄓 work out

mal-humorado /malumo'radu/ *a* in a bad mood, grumpy

malícia /ma'lisia/ *f* (*má índole*) malice; (*astúcia*) guile; (*humor*) innuendo

malicioso /malisi'ozu/ *a* (*mau*) malicious; (*astuto*) crafty; (*que põe malícia*) dirty-minded

maligno /ma'liginu/ *a* malignant

malmequer /mawme'ker/ *m* marigold

malnutrido /mawnu'tridu/ *a* malnourished

maloca /ma'lɔka/ *f* Indian village

malo|grar-se /malo'grarsi/ *vpr* go wrong, fail. **~gro** /o/ *m* failure

malpassado /mawpa'sadu/ *a* ⟨*carne*⟩ rare

Malta /'mawta/ *f* Malta

malte /'mawtʃi/ *m* malt

maltrapilho /mawtra'piʎu/ *a* scruffy

maltratar /mawtra'tar/ *vt* ill-treat, mistreat

malu|co /ma'luku/ *a* 🄓 mad, crazy 🄓 ● *m* madman. **~quice** *f* madness; (*uma*) crazy thing

malvado /maw'vadu/ *a* wicked

malver|sação /mawversa'sãw/ *f* mismanagement; (*de fundos*) misappropriation. **~sar** *vt* mismanage; misappropriate ⟨*dinheiro*⟩

Malvinas /maw'vinas/ *f pl* Falklands

mamadeira /mama'dera/ *f* (baby's) bottle

mamãe /ma'mãj/ *f* mum

mamão /ma'mãw/ *m* papaya

ma|mar /ma'mar/ *vi* suckle. **~mata** *f* 🄓 fiddle

mamífero /ma'miferu/ *m* mammal

mamilo /ma'milu/ *m* nipple

mamoeiro /mamo'eru/ *m* papaya tree

mamografia /mamogra'fia/ *f* mammography

mamoplastia /mamoplaʃ'tʃia/ *f* breast surgery, mammoplasty

manada /ma'nada/ *f* herd

manan|cial /manãsi'aw/ (*pl* **~ais**) *m* spring; *fig* rich source

man|cada /mã'kada/ *f* blunder. **~car** *vi* limp. **~car-se** *vpr* 🄓 take the hint, get the message

man|cha /'mãʃa/ *f* stain; (*na pele*) mark. **~char** *vt* stain

Mancha /'mãʃa/ *f* **o canal da ~** the English Channel

manchete /mã'ʃetʃi/ *f* headline

manco /'mãku/ *a* lame ● *m* cripple

mandachuva /mãda'ʃuva/ *m* 🄓 bigwig; (*chefe*) boss

man|dado /mã'dadu/ *m* order; **~dado de busca** search warrant; **~dado de prisão** arrest warrant. **~damento** *m* commandment. **~dante** *m/f* person in charge. **~dão** *a* (*f* **~dona**) bossy. **~dar-se** *vpr* 🄓 take off. **~dato** *m* mandate

---

mandar /mã'dar/ ● *vt*

⟶ (*ordenar*) tell; **faça o que eu lhe mando** do what I tell you

⟶ (*enviar*) send; **mande a carta para mim pelo correio** send the letter to me by mail

····➤ (atirar) throw; **mande a bola** throw the ball

····➤ (em expressões) **~ fazer algo** have sth done; **vou ~ consertar o carro** I'm going to have the car repaired; **~ buscar/ chamar alguém** send for sb; **mandei buscar o cozinheiro** I sent for the chef; **~ dizer** send word; **~ alguém às favas** tell sb to get lost

● vi

····➤ (ser o chefe) be in charge; **quem manda aqui?** who's in charge here?. **~dar-se**

● vpr

····➤ 🔲 take off

mandíbula /mã'dʒibula/ f (lower) jaw

mandioca /mãdʒi'ɔka/ f manioc

maneira /ma'nera/ f way; pl (boas) manners; **desta ~** in this way; **de qualquer ~** anyway

mane|jar /mane'ʒar/ vt handle; operate <máquina>. **~jável** (pl **~jáveis**) a manageable. **~jo** /e/ m handling

manequim /mane'kĩ/ m (boneco) dummy; (medida) size ● m/f mannequin, model

maneta /ma'neta/ a one-armed ● m/f person with one arm

manga[1] /'mãga/ f (de roupa) sleeve

manga[2] /'mãga/ f (fruta) mango

manganês /mãga'nes/ m manganese

mangue /'mãgi/ m mangrove swamp

mangueira[1] /mã'gera/ f (tubo) hose

mangueira[2] /mã'gera/ f (árvore) mango tree

manha /'maɲa/ f tantrum

manhã /ma'ɲã/ f morning; **de ~** in the morning

manhoso /ma'ɲozu/ a wilful

mania /ma'nia/ f (moda) craze; (doença) mania

maníaco /ma'niaku/ a manic ● m maniac. **~depressivo** a & m manic depressive

manicômio /mani'komiu/ m lunatic asylum

manicura /mani'kura/ f manicure; (pessoa) manicurist

manifes|tação /manifesta'sãw/ f manifestation; (passeata) demonstration. **~tante** m/f demonstrator. **~tar** vt manifest, demonstrate. **~tar-se** vpr (revelar-se) manifest o.s.; (exprimir-se) express an opinion. **~to** /e/ a manifest, clear ● m manifesto

manipular /manipu'lar/ vt manipulate

manjedoura /mãʒe'dora/ f manger

manjericão /mãʒeri'kãw/ m basil

mano|bra /ma'nɔbra/ f manoeuvre. **~brar** vt manoeuvre. **~brista** m/f parking valet

mansão /mã'sãw/ f mansion

man|sidão /mãsi'dãw/ f gentleness; (do mar) calm. **~sinho** adv de **~sinho** (devagar) slowly; (de leve) gently; (de fininho) stealthily. **~so** a gentle; <mar> calm; <animal> tame

manta /'mãta/ f blanket; (casaco) cloak

mantei|ga /mã'tejga/ f butter. **~gueira** f butter dish

manter /mã'ter/ vt keep. **~-se** vpr keep; (sustentar-se) keep o.s.

mantimentos /mãtʃi'mẽtus/ m pl provisions

manto /ˈmãtu/ m mantle

manu|al /manuˈaw/ (pl ~**ais**) a & m manual. ~**fatura** f manufacture; (fábrica) factory. ~**faturar** vt manufacture

manuscrito /manusˈkritu/ a handwritten ● m manuscript

manu|sear /manuziˈar/ vt handle. ~**seio** m handling

manutenção /manuˈtẽsãw/ f maintenance; (de prédio) upkeep

mão /mãw/ (pl ~**s**) f hand; (do trânsito) direction; (de tinta) coat; **abrir ~ de** give up; **aguentar a ~** hang on; **dar a ~ a alguém** hold sb's hand; (cumprimentando) shake sb's hand; **deixar alguém na ~** let sb down; **enfiar ou meter a ~ em** hit, slap; **lançar ~ de** make use of; **escrito à ~** written by hand; **ter à ~** have to hand; **de ~s dadas** hand in hand; **em segunda ~** second-hand; **fora de ~** out of the way; **~ única** one way. ~**-de-obra** f labour

mapa /ˈmapa/ m map

maquete /maˈketʃi/ f model

maqui|agem /makiˈaʒẽ/ f make-up. ~**ar** vt make up. ~**ar-se** vpr put on make-up

maquiavélico /makiaˈveliku/ a Machiavellian

maqui|lagem, ~**lar**, Port ~**lhagem**, ~**lhar** ▶ MAQUIAGEM

máquina /ˈmakina/ f machine; (ferroviária) engine; **escrever à ~** type; **~ de costura** sewing machine; **~ de escrever** typewriter; **~ de lavar (roupa)** washing machine; **~ de lavar pratos** dishwasher; **~ fotográfica** camera

maqui|nação /makinaˈsãw/ f machination. ~**nal** (pl ~**nais**) a

mechanical. ~**nar** vt/i plot. ~**nária** f machinery. ~**nista** m/f (ferroviário) engine driver; (de navio) engineer

mar /mar/ m sea

maracu|já /marakuˈʒa/ m passion fruit. ~**jazeiro** m passion fruit plant

marasmo /maˈrazmu/ f stagnation

marato|na /maraˈtona/ f marathon. ~**nista** m/f marathon runner

maravi|lha /maraˈviʎa/ f marvel; **às mil ~lhas** wonderfully. ~**lhar** vt amaze. ~**lhar-se** vpr marvel (**de** at). ~**lhoso** /o/ a marvellous

mar|ca /ˈmarka/ f (sinal) mark; (de carro, máquina) make; (de cigarro, sabão etc) brand; ~**ca registrada** registered trademark. ~**cação** /markaˈsãw/ f marking; Port (discagem) dialling; **~ rápida** Port Telec speed dialling. ~**cador** m marker; (em livro) bookmark; (placar) scoreboard; (jogador) scorer. ~**cante** a outstanding. ~**ca-passo** m pacemaker. ~**car** vt mark; arrange ‹hora, encontro, jantar etc›; score ‹gol, ponto›; Port (discar) dial; ‹relógio, termômetro› show; brand ‹gado›; (observar) keep a close eye on; (impressionar) leave one's mark on; ~**car época** make history; ~**car hora** make an appointment; ~**car o compasso** beat time; ~**car os pontos** keep the score ● vi make one's mark

marce|naria /marsenaˈria/ f cabinetmaking; (oficina) cabinet maker's workshop. ~**neiro** m cabinetmaker

mar|cha /ˈmarʃa/ f march; (de carro) gear; **pôr-se em ~cha** get going; ~**cha à ré**, Port ~**cha atrás** reverse. ~**char** vi march

marci|al /marsi'aw/ (pl ~**ais**) a martial. ~**ano** a & m Martian

marco[1] /'marku/ m (sinal) landmark

marco[2] /'marku/ m (moeda) mark

março /'marsu/ m March

maré /ma'rɛ/ f tide

mare|chal /mare'ʃaw/ (pl ~**chais**) m marshal

maresia /mare'zia/ f smell of the sea

marfim /mar'fĩ/ m ivory

margarida /marga'rida/ f daisy; (para impressora) daisy wheel

margarina /marga'rina/ f margarine

mar|gem /'marʒẽ/ f (de rio) bank; (de lago) shore; (parte em branco) fig margin. ~**ginal** (pl ~**ginais**) a marginal; (delinquente) delinquent ● m/f delinquent ● f (rua) riverside road. ~**ginalidade** f delinquency. ~**ginalizar** vt marginalize

marido /ma'ridu/ m husband

marimbondo /marĩ'bõdu/ m hornet

marina /ma'rina/ f marina

mari|nha /ma'riɲa/ f navy; ~**nha mercante** merchant navy. ~**nheiro** m sailor. ~**nho** a marine

marionete /mario'netʃi/ f puppet

mariposa /mari'poza/ f moth

mariscos /ma'riskus/ m seafood

mari|tal /mari'taw/ (pl ~**tais**) a marital

marítimo /ma'ritʃimu/ a sea; ‹cidade› seaside

marmanjo /mar'mãʒu/ m grown-up

marme|lada /marme'lada/ f ⚊ fix. ~**lo** /ɛ/ m quince

marmita /mar'mita/ f (de soldado) mess tin; (de trabalhador) lunch box

mármore /'marmori/ m marble

marmóreo /mar'mɔriu/ a marble

marquise /mar'kizi/ f awning

marreco /ma'xeku/ m wild duck

Marrocos /ma'xɔkus/ m Morocco

marrom /ma'xõ/ a & m brown

marroquino /maxo'kinu/ a & m Moroccan

Marte /'martʃi/ m Mars

marte|lada /marte'lada/ f hammer blow. ~**lar** vt/i hammer; ~**lar em** fig go on and on about. ~**lo** /ɛ/ m hammer

mártir /'martʃir/ m/f martyr

mar|tírio /mar'tʃiriu/ m martyrdom; fig torture. ~**tirizar** vt martyr; fig torture

marujo /ma'ruʒu/ m sailor

mar|xismo /mark'sizmu/ m Marxism. ~**xista** a & m/f Marxist

mas /mas/ conj but

mascar /mas'kar/ vt chew

máscara /'maskara/ f mask; (tratamento facial) face pack

mascarar /maska'rar/ vt mask

mascate /mas'katʃi/ m street vendor

mascavo /mas'kavu/ a **açúcar** ~ brown sugar

mascote /mas'kɔtʃi/ f mascot

masculino /masku'linu/ a male; (para homens) men's; ‹palavra› masculine ● m masculine

másculo /'maskulu/ a masculine

masmorra /maz'moxa/ f dungeon

masoquis|mo /mazo'kizmu/ m masochism. ~**ta** m/f masochist ● a masochistic

massa /'masa/ f mass; (de pão) dough; (de torta, empada) pastry; (macarrão etc) pasta; **cultura de ~** mass culture; **em ~** en masse; **as ~s** the masses

massa|crante /masa'krãtʃi/ a gruelling. **~crar** vt massacre; fig (maçar) wear out. **~cre** m massacre

massa|gear /masaʒi'ar/ vt massage. **~gem** f massage. **~gista** m/f masseur (f masseuse)

mastigar /mastʃi'gar/ vt chew; (ponderar) chew over

mastro /'mastru/ m mast; (de bandeira) flagpole

mastur|bação /masturba'sãw/ f masturbation. **~bar-se** vpr masturbate

mata /'mata/ f forest

mata-borrão /matabo'xãw/ m blotting paper

matadouro /mata'doru/ m slaughterhouse

mata|gal /mata'gaw/ (pl ~gais) m thicket

mata-moscas /mata'moskas/ m invar fly spray

ma|tança /ma'tãsa/ f slaughter. **~tar** vt kill; satisfy ‹fome›; quench ‹sede›; guess ‹charada›; (fazer nas coxas) dash off; T skive off ‹aula, serviço› ● vi kill

mata-ratos /mata'xatus/ m invar rat poison

mate[1] /'matʃi/ m (chá) maté

mate[2] /'matʃi/ a invar matt

matemáti|ca /mate'matʃika/ f mathematics. **~co** a mathematical ● m mathematician

matéria /ma'teria/ f (assunto, disciplina) subject; (no jornal) article; (substância) matter; (usada para

fazer algo) material; **em ~ de** in the way of

materi|al /materi'aw/ (pl ~ais) m materials ● a material. **~alismo** m materialism. **~alista** a materialistic ● m/f materialist. **~alizar-se** vpr materialize

matéria-prima /materia'prima/ (pl matérias-primas) f raw material

mater|nal /mater'naw/ (pl ~nais) a maternal. **~nidade** f maternity; (clínica) maternity hospital. **~no** /ɛ/ a maternal; **língua ~na** mother tongue

mati|nal /matʃi'naw/ (pl ~nais) a morning. **~nê** f matinee

matiz /ma'tʃis/ m shade; (político) colouring; (pontinha) (de ironia etc) tinge

matizar /matʃi'zar/ vt tinge (**de** with)

mato /'matu/ m scrubland, bush

matraca /ma'traka/ f rattle; (tagarela) chatterbox

matreiro /ma'treru/ a cunning

matriar|ca /matri'arka/ f matriarch. **~cal** (pl ~cais) a matriarchal

matrícula /ma'trikula/ f enrolment; (taxa) enrolment fee; Port (de carro) number plate, Amer license plate

matricular /matriku'lar/ vt enrol. **~-se** vpr enrol

matri|monial /matrimoni'aw/ (pl ~moniais) a marriage. **~mônio** m marriage

matriz /ma'tris/ f matrix; (útero) womb; (sede) head office

maturidade /maturi'dadʒi/ f maturity

matutino /matu'tʃinu/ a morning ● m morning paper

matuto /maˈtutu/ a countrified
● m country bumpkin

mau /maw/ a (f **má**) bad. **~caráter**
m invar bad lot ● a invar no-good;
~olhado m evil eye

mausoléu /mawzoˈlɛw/ m
mausoleum

maus-tratos /mawsˈtratus/ m pl
ill-treatment

maxilar /maksiˈlar/ m jaw

máxima /ˈmasima/ f maxim

maximizar /masimiˈzar/ vt
maximize; (exagerar) play up

máximo /ˈmasimu/ a (antes do
substantivo) utmost, greatest;
(depois do substantivo) maximum
● m maximum; **o ~** 🆃 (o melhor)
really something; **ao ~** to the
maximum; **no ~** at most

maxixe /maˈʃiʃi/ m gherkin

me /mi/ pron me; (indireto) (to) me;
(reflexivo) myself

meada /miˈada/ f skein; **perder o
fio da ~** lose one's thread

meados /miˈadus/ m pl **~ de maio**
mid-May

meandro /miˈãdru/ f meander; pl
fig twists and turns

mecânica /meˈkanika/ f
mechanics. **~co** a mechanical ● m
mechanic

mecanismo /mekaˈnizmu/ m
mechanism. **~nizar** vt mechanize

mecenas /meˈsenas/ m invar patron

mecha /ˈmeʃa/ f (de vela) wick; (de
bomba) fuse; (porção de cabelos)
lock; (cabelo tingido) highlight. **~do**
a highlighted

medalha /meˈdaʎa/ f medal.
~lhão m medallion; (joia) locket

média /ˈmɛdʒia/ f average; (café)
white coffee; **em ~** on average

mediação /medʒiaˈsãw/ f
mediation. **~ador** m mediator.
~ante prep through, by. **~ar** vi
mediate

medicação /medʒikaˈsãw/ f
medication. **~mento** m medicine

medição /medʒiˈsãw/ f
measurement

medicar /medʒiˈkar/ vt treat ● vi
practise medicine. **~se** vpr dose
o.s. up

medicina /medʒiˈsina/ f
medicine; **~na legal** forensic
medicine. **~nal** (pl **~nais**) a
medicinal

médico /ˈmɛdʒiku/ m doctor ● a
medical. **~legal** (pl **~legais**) a
forensic; **~legista** (pl **~s-legistas**)
m/f forensic scientist

medida /meˈdʒida/ f measure;
(dimensão) measurement; **à ~da
que** as; **sob ~da** made to measure;
tirar as ~das de alguém take sb's
measurements. **~dor** m meter

medieval /medʒieˈvaw/ (pl
~vais) a medieval

médio /ˈmɛdʒiu/ a (típico) average;
‹tamanho, prazo› medium; ‹classe,
dedo› middle

mediocre /meˈdʒiokri/ a
mediocre

mediocridade
/medʒiokriˈdadʒi/ f mediocrity

medir /meˈdʒir/ vt measure; weigh
‹palavras› ● vi measure. **~se** vpr
measure o.s.; **quanto você mede?**
how tall are you?

meditação /medʒitaˈsãw/ f
meditation. **~tar** vi meditate

mediterrâneo /medʒiteˈxaniu/
a Mediterranean ● m o
Mediterrâneo the Mediterranean

médium /ˈmɛdʒiũ/ m/f medium

medo /'medu/ *m* fear; **ter ~ de** be afraid of; **com ~** afraid. **~nho** /o/ *a* frightful

medroso /me'drozu/ *a* fearful, timid

medula /me'dula/ *f* marrow

megalomania /megaloma'nia/ *f* megalomania

meia /'meja/ *f* (*comprida*) stocking; (*curta*) sock; (*seis*) six. **~calça** (*pl* **~s-calças**) *f* tights, *Amer* pantihose; **~idade** *f* middle age; **~noite** *f* midnight; **~volta** (*pl* **~s-voltas**) *f* about-turn

mei|go /'mejgu/ *a* sweet. **~guice** *f* sweetness

meio /'meju/ *a* half ● *adv* rather ● *m* (*centro*) middle; (*ambiente*) environment; (*recurso*) means; **~ litro** half a litre; **dois meses e ~** two and a half months; **em ~ a** amid; **por ~ de** through; **o ~ ambiente** the environment; **os ~s de comunicação** the media; **~s de comunicação social** *Port* social media. **~dia** *m* midday; **~fio** *m* kerb; **~termo** (*acordo*) compromise

mel /mew/ *m* honey

mela|ço /me'lasu/ *m* molasses. **~do** *a* sticky ● *m* treacle

melancia /melã'sia/ *f* watermelon

melan|colia /melãko'lia/ *f* melancholy. **~cólico** *a* melancholic

melão /me'lãw/ *m* melon

melar /me'lar/ *vt* make sticky

melhor /me'ʎɔr/ *a & adv* better; **o ~** the best

melho|ra /me'ʎɔra/ *f* improvement; **~ras!** get well soon! **~ramento** *m* improvement. **~rar** *vt* improve ● *vi* improve; ‹*doente*› get better

melin|drar /meli'drar/ *vt* hurt. **~drar-se** *vpr* be hurt. **~droso** /o/ *a* delicate; ‹*pessoa*› sensitive

melodi|a /melo'dʒia/ *f* melody. **~oso** /o/ *a* melodious

melodra|ma /melo'drama/ *m* melodrama. **~mático** *a* melodramatic

meloso /me'lozu/ *a* sickly sweet

melro /'mewxu/ *m* blackbird

membrana /mẽ'brana/ *f* membrane

membro /'mẽbru/ *m* member; (*braço, perna*) limb

memo|rando /memo'rãdu/ *m* memo. **~rável** (*pl* **~ráveis**) *a* memorable

memória /me'mɔria/ *f* memory; *pl* (*autobiografia*) memoirs

men|ção /mẽ'sãw/ *f* mention; **fazer ~ção de** mention. **~cionar** *vt* mention

mendi|cância /mẽdʒi'kãsia/ *f* begging. **~gar** *vi* beg. **~go** *m* beggar

menina /me'nina/ *f* girl; **a ~ dos olhos de alguém** the apple of sb's eye

meningite /menĩ'ʒitʃi/ *f* meningitis

meni|nice /meni'nisi/ *f* (*idade*) childhood. **~no** *m* boy

menopausa /meno'pawza/ *f* menopause

menor /me'nɔr/ *a* smaller ● *m/f* minor; **o/a ~** the smallest; (*mínimo*) the slightest, the least

menos /'menos/ *adv & pron* less ● *prep* except; **dois dias a ~** two days less; **a ~ que** unless; **ao ou pelo ~** at least; **o ~ bonito** the least pretty. **~prezar** *vt* look down upon. **~prezo** /e/ *m* disdain

mensa|geiro /mēsaˈʒeru/ *m* messenger. **~gem** /mēˈsaʒẽ ʃ/ *f* message; **~gem instantânea** *Telec* instant messaging. **~gem escrita** (*telec*) text message

men|sal /mēˈsaw/ (*pl* **~sais**) *a* monthly. **~salidade** *f* monthly payment. **~salmente** *adv* monthly

menstru|ação /mēstruaˈsãw/ *f* menstruation. **~ada** *a* **estar ~ada** be having one's period. **~al** (*pl* **~ais**) *a* menstrual. **~ar** *vi* menstruate

menta /ˈmēta/ *f* mint

men|tal /mēˈtaw/ (*pl* **~tais**) *a* mental. **~talidade** *f* mentality. **~te** *f* mind

men|tir /mēˈtʃir/ *vi* lie. **~tira** *f* lie. **~tiroso** /o/ *a* lying ● *m* liar

mentor /mēˈtor/ *m* mentor

mercado /merˈkadu/ *m* market. **~ria** *f* commodity; *pl* goods

mercan|te /merˈkãtʃi/ *a* merchant. **~til** (*pl* **~tis**) *a* mercantile

mercê /merˈse/ *f* **à ~ de** at the mercy of

merce|aria /mersiaˈria/ *f* grocer's. **~eiro** *m* grocer

mercenário /merseˈnariu/ *a & m* mercenary

mercúrio /merˈkuriu/ *m* mercury; **Mercúrio** Mercury

merda /ˈmerda/ *f* (*vulgar*) shit

mere|cedor /mereseˈdor/ *a* deserving. **~cer** *vt* deserve ● *vi* be deserving. **~cimento** *m* merit

merenda /meˈrēda/ *f* packed lunch; **~ escolar** school dinner

mere|trício /mereˈtrisiu/ *m* prostitution. **~triz** *f* prostitute

mergu|lhador /merguʎaˈdor/ *m* diver. **~lhar** *vt* dip (**em** into) ● *vi* (*na água*) dive; (*no trabalho*) bury o.s..

~lho *m* dive; (*esporte*) diving; (*banho de mar*) dip

meridi|ano /meridʒiˈanu/ *m* meridian. **~onal** (*pl* **~onais**) *a* southern

mérito /ˈmeritu/ *m* merit

merluza /merˈluza/ *f* hake

mero /ˈmeru/ *a* mere

mês /mes/ (*pl* **meses**) *m* month

mesa /ˈmeza/ *f* table; (*de trabalho*) desk; **~ de centro** coffee table; **~ de jantar** dining table; **~ telefônica** switchboard

mesada /meˈzada/ *f* monthly allowance

mescla /ˈmeskla/ *f* mixture, blend

mesmice /mezˈmisi/ *f* sameness

mesmo /ˈmezmu/ *a* same ● *adv* (*até*) even; (*justamente*) right; (*de verdade*) really; **você ~** you yourself; **hoje ~** this very day; **~ assim** even so; **~ que** even if; **dá no ~** it comes to the same thing; **fiquei na mesma** I'm none the wiser

mesqui|nharia /meskiɲaˈria/ *f* meanness; (*uma*) mean thing. **~nho** *a* mean

mesquita /mesˈkita/ *f* mosque

Messias /meˈsias/ *m* Messiah

mesti|çagem /mestʃiˈsaʒẽ/ *f* interbreeding. **~ço** *a* ⟨*pessoa*⟩ of mixed race; ⟨*animal*⟩ cross-bred ● *m* (*pessoa*) person of mixed race; (*animal*) mongrel

mes|trado /mesˈtradu/ *m* master's degree. **~tre** /ε/ *m* (*f* **~tra**) master; mistress; (*de escola*) teacher ● *a* main; ⟨*chave*⟩ master. **~tre de obras** (*pl* **~tres de obras**) *m* foreman; **~tre-sala** (*pl* **~tres-salas**) *m* master of ceremonies (in carnival procession). **~tria** *f* expertise

meta /'mɛta/ f (de corrida) finishing post; (gol) fig goal

meta|bólico /meta'bɔliku/ a metabolic. **~bolismo** m metabolism

metade /me'tadʒi/ f half; **pela ~** halfway

metafísi|ca /meta'fizika/ f metaphysics. **~co** a metaphysical

metáfora /me'tafora/ f metaphor

metafórico /meta'fɔriku/ a metaphorical

me|tal /me'taw/ (pl **~tais**) m metal; pl (numa orquestra) brass. **~tálico** a metallic

meta|lurgia /metalur'ʒia/ f metallurgy. **~lúrgica** f metal works. **~lúrgico** a metallurgical ● m metalworker

metamorfose /metamor'fɔzi/ f metamorphosis

metano /me'tanu/ m methane

meteórico /mete'ɔriku/ a meteoric

meteoro /mete'ɔru/ m meteor. **~logia** f meteorology. **~lógico** a meteorological. **~logista** m/f (cientista) meteorologist; (na TV) weather forecaster

meter /me'ter/ vt put; **~ medo** be frightening. **~-se** vpr (envolver-se) get (em into); (intrometer-se) meddle (em in)

meticuloso /metʃiku'lozu/ a meticulous

metido /me'tʃidu/ a snobbish; **ele é ~ a perito** he thinks he's an expert

metódico /me'tɔdʒiku/ a methodical

metodista /meto'dʒista/ a & m/f Methodist

método /'mɛtodu/ m method

metra|lhadora /metraʎa'dora/ f machine gun. **~lhar** vt machine-gun

métri|co /'mɛtriku/ a metric; **fita ~ca** tape measure

metro[1] /'mɛtru/ m metre

metro[2] /'mɛtru/ m Port (metropolitano) underground, Amer subway

metrô /me'tro/ m underground, Amer subway

metrópole /me'trɔpoli/ f metropolis

metropolitano /metropoli'tanu/ a metropolitan ● m Port underground, Amer subway

meu /mew/ a (f **minha**) my ● pron (f **minha**) mine; **um amigo ~** a friend of mine; **fico na minha** 🆒 I keep myself to myself

mexer /me'ʃer/ vt move; (com colher etc) stir ● vi move; **~ com** (comover) affect, get to; (brincar com) tease; (trabalhar com) work with; **~ em** touch. **~-se** vpr move; (apressar-se) get a move on

mexeri|ca /meʃe'rika/ f tangerine. **~car** vi gossip. **~co** m piece of gossip; pl gossip. **~queiro** a gossiping ● m gossip

mexicano /meʃi'kanu/ a & m Mexican

México /'mɛʃiku/ m Mexico

mexido /me'ʃidu/ a **ovos ~s** scrambled eggs

mexilhão /meʃi'ʎãw/ m mussel

mi|ado /mi'adu/ m miaow. **~ar** vi miaow

micreiro /mi'krejru/ m PC hacker

micróbio /mi'krɔbiu/ m microbe

micro|cosmo /mikro'kɔzmu/ m microcosm. **~empresa** /e/ f small business. **~empresário** m small businessman. **~filme** m microfilm.

~fone *m* microphone. **~onda** *f*
microwave. **(forno de) ~ondas**
m microwave (oven). **~ônibus** *m*
invar minibus. **~processador** *m*
microprocessor

microrganismo
/mikrorga'nizmu/ *m* microorganism

microscó|pico /mikros'kɔpiku/
a microscopic. **~pio** *m* microscope

mídia /'midʒia/ *f* media; **~ social**
social media

migalha /mi'gaʎa/ *f* crumb

mi|gração /migra'sãw/ *f*
migration. **~grar** *vi* migrate

mijar /mi'ʒar/ *vi* 🔲 pee. **~jar-se** *vpr*
wet o.s.. **~jo** *m* 🔲 pee

mil /miw/ *a* & *m invar* thousand;
estar a ~ be on top form

mila|gre /mi'lagri/ *m* miracle.
~groso /o/ *a* miraculous

milênio /mi'leniu/ *m* millennium

milésimo /mi'lɛzimu/ *a*
thousandth

milha /'miʎa/ *f* mile

milhão /mi'ʎãw/ *m* million; **um ~**
de dólares a million dollars

milhar /mi'ʎar/ *m* thousand; **~es**
de vezes thousands of times; **aos**
~es in their thousands

milho /'miʎo/ *m* maize, *Amer* corn

milico /mi'liku/ *m* 🔲 military man;
os ~s the military

mili|grama /mili'grama/ *m*
milligram. **~litro** *m* millilitre.
milímetro /e/ *m* millimetre

milionário /milio'nariu/ *a* & *m*
millionaire

mili|tante /mili'tãtʃi/ *a* & *m*
militant. **~tar** *a* military ● *m* soldier

mim /mĩ/ *pron* me

mimar /mi'mar/ *vt* spoil

mímica /'mimika/ *f* mime;
(*brincadeira*) charades

mi|na /'mina/ *f* mine. **~nar** *vt* mine;
fig (*prejudicar*) undermine

mindinho /mĩ'dʒiɲu/ *m* little
finger, *Amer* pinkie

mineiro /mi'neru/ *a* mining; (*de*
MG) from Minas Gerais ● *m* miner;
(*de MG*) person from Minas Gerais

mine|ração /minera'sãw/
f mining. **~ral** (*pl* **~rais**) *a* & *m*
mineral. **~rar** *vt/i* mine

minério /mi'nɛriu/ *m* ore

mingau /mĩ'gaw/ *m* porridge

míngua /'mĩgwa/ *f* lack

minguante /mĩ'gwãtʃi/ *a* quarto
~ last quarter

minguar /mĩ'gwar/ *vi* dwindle

minha /'miɲa/ *a* & *pron* ▶ **MEU**

minhoca /mi'ɲɔka/ *f* worm

miniatura /minia'tura/ *f*
miniature

mini|malista /minima'lista/ *a* &
m/f minimalist. **~mizar** *vt* minimize;
(*subestimar*) play down

mínimo /'minimu/ *a* (*muito*
pequeno) tiny; (*mais baixo*)
minimum ● *m* minimum; **a mínima**
ideia the slightest idea; **no ~** at
least

minissaia /mini'saja/ *f* miniskirt

minis|terial /ministeri'aw/
(*pl* **~teriais**) *a* ministerial. **~tério**
m ministry; **Ministério do Interior**
Home Office, *Amer* Department of
the Interior

minis|trar /minis'trar/ *vt*
administer. **~tro** *m* minister;
primeiro ~tro prime minister

Minorca /mi'nɔrka/ *f* Menorca

mino|ritário /minori'tariu/ *a*
minority. **~ria** *f* minority

minúcia /mi'nusia/ f detail

minucioso /minusi'ozu/ a thorough

minúscu|la /mi'nuskula/ f small letter. ~**lo** a ⟨letra⟩ small; (muito pequeno) minuscule

minuta /mi'nuta/ f (rascunho) rough draft

minuto /mi'nutu/ m minute

miolo /mi'olu/ f (de fruta) flesh; (de pão) crumb; pl brains

míope /'miopi/ a short-sighted

miopia /mio'pia/ f myopia

mira /'mira/ f sight; **ter em** ~ have one's sights on

mirabolante /mirabo'lãtʃi/ a amazing; ⟨ideias, plano⟩ grandiose

mi|ragem /mi'raʒẽ/ f mirage. ~**rante** m lookout. ~**rar** vt look at. ~**rar-se** vpr look at o.s.

mirim /mi'ri/ a little

miscelânea /mise'lania/ f miscellany

miscigenação /misiʒena'sãw/ f interbreeding

miserá|vel /mize'ravew/ (pl ~**veis**) a miserable

miséria /mi'zeria/ f misery; (pobreza) poverty; **uma** ~ (pouco dinheiro) a pittance; **chorar** ~ claim poverty

miseri|córdia /mizeri'kɔrdʒia/ f mercy. ~**cordioso** a merciful

misógino /mi'zɔʒinu/ m misogynist ● a misogynistic

miss /'misi/ f beauty queen

missa /'misa/ f mass

missão /mi'sãw/ f mission

mis|sil /'misiw/ (pl ~**seis**) m missile; ~**sil de longo alcance** long-range missile

missionário /misio'nariu/ m missionary

missiva /mi'siva/ f missive

mis|tério /mis'teriu/ m mystery. ~**terioso** /o/ a mysterious. ~**ticismo** m mysticism

místico /'mistʃiku/ m mystic ● a mystical

misto /'mistu/ a mixed ● m mix; ~ **quente** toasted ham and cheese sandwich

mistu|ra /mis'tura/ f mixture. ~**rar** vt mix; (confundir) mix up. ~**rar-se** vpr mix (**com**) with

mítico /'mitʃiku/ a mythical

mito /'mitu/ m myth. ~**logia** f mythology. ~**lógico** a mythological

miudezas /miu'dezas/ f pl odds and ends

miúdo /mi'udu/ a tiny, minute; ⟨chuva⟩ fine; ⟨despesas⟩ minor ● m ⟨criança⟩ child, little one; pl (de galinha) giblets; **trocar em** ~**s** go into detail

mixaria /miʃa'ria/ f ① (soma irrisória) pittance

mixórdia /mi'ʃɔrdʒia/ f muddle

MMS abr m (= Serviço de Mensagens Multimédia) MMS

mnemônico /ne'moniku/ a mnemonic

mobilar /mobi'lar/ vt Port furnish

mobília /mo'bilia/ f furniture

mobili|ar /mobili'ar/ vt furnish. ~**ário** m furniture

mobili|dade /mobili'dadʒi/ f mobility. ~**zar** vt mobilize

moça /'mosa/ f girl

moçambicano /mosãbi'kanu/ a & m Mozambican

Moçambique /mosã'biki/ m Mozambique

moção /mo'sãw/ f motion

mochila /mo'ʃila/ f rucksack

moço /'mosu/ a young ● m boy, lad

moda /'mɔda/ f fashion; **na ~** fashionable

modalidade /modali'dadʒi/ f (*esporte*) event

mode|lagem /mode'laʒẽ/ f modelling. **~lar** vt model (**a** on). **~lar-se** vpr model o.s. (**a** on). **~lo** /e/ a model ● m model

mode|ração /modera'sãw/ f moderation. **~rado** a moderate. **~rar** vt moderate; reduce ‹velocidade, despesas›. **~rar-se** vpr restrain oneself

moder|nidade /moderni'dadʒi/ f modernity. **~nismo** m modernism. **~nista** a & m/f modernist. **~nizar** vt modernize. **~no** /ɛ/ a modern

modess™ /'mɔdʒis/ m invar ™sanitary towel

modéstia /mo'destʃia/ f modesty

modesto /mo'destu/ a modest

módico /'mɔdʒiku/ a modest

modifi|cação /modʒifika'sãw/ f modification. **~car** vt modify

mo|dismo /mo'dʒizmu/ m idiom. **~dista** f dressmaker

modo /'mɔdu/ m way; Ling mood; pl (*maneiras*) manners

modular /modu'lar/ vt modulate ● a modular

módulo /'mɔdʒiku/ m module

moeda /mo'ɛda/ f (*peça de metal*) coin; (*dinheiro*) currency

mo|edor /moe'dor/ m **~edor de café** coffee grinder; **~edor de carne** mincer. **~er** vt grind ‹café, trigo›; squeeze ‹cana›; mince ‹carne›; (*bater*) beat

mo|fado /mo'fadu/ a mouldy. **~far** vi moulder. **~fo** /o/ m mould

mogno /'mɔgnu/ m mahogany

moinho /mo'iɲu/ m mill; **~ de vento** windmill

moisés /moj'zɛs/ m invar carrycot

moita /'mojta/ f bush

mola /'mɔla/ f spring

mol|dar /mow'dar/ vt mould; cast ‹metal›. **~de** /ɔ/ m mould; (*para costura etc*) pattern

moldu|ra /mow'dura/ f frame. **~rar** vt frame

mole /'mɔli/ a soft; ‹pessoa› listless; Ⓘ (*fácil*) easy ● adv easily; **é ~?** Ⓘ can you believe it?

molécula /mo'lɛkula/ f molecule

moleque /mo'lɛki/ m (*menino*) lad; (*de rua*) urchin; (*homem*) scoundrel

molestar /moles'tar/ vt molest

moléstia /mo'lestʃia/ f disease

moletom /mole'tõ/ m (*tecido*) knitted cotton; (*blusa*) sweatshirt

moleza /mo'leza/ f softness; (*de pessoa*) laziness; **viver na ~** lead a cushy life; **ser ~** be easy

mo|lhado /mo'ʎadu/ a wet. **~lhar** vt wet. **~lhar-se** vpr get wet

molho[1] /'mɔʎu/ m (*de chaves*) bunch; (*de palha*) sheaf

molho[2] /'moʎu/ m sauce; (*para salada*) dressing; **deixar de ~** leave in soak ‹roupa›; **~ inglês** Worcester sauce

molusco /mo'lusku/ m mollusc

momen|tâneo /momẽ'taniu/ a momentary. **~to** m moment; (*força*) momentum

Mônaco /'monaku/ m Monaco

monar|ca /mo'narka/ m/f monarch. **~quia** f monarchy. **~quista** a & m/f monarchist

monástico /mo'nastʃiku/ a monastic

monção /mõ'sãw/ f monsoon

mone|tário /mone'tariu/ a monetary. **~tarismo** m monetarism. **~tarista** a & m/f monetarist

monge /'mõʒi/ m monk

monitor /moni'tor/ m monitor; **~ de vídeo** VDU

monitorar /monito'rar/ vt monitor

mono|cromo /mono'krɔmu/ a monochrome. **~gamia** f monogamy

monógamo /mo'nɔgamu/ a monogamous

monograma /mono'grama/ m monogram

monólogo /mo'nɔlogu/ m monologue

mononucleose /mononukli'ɔzi/ f glandular fever

mono|pólio /mono'pɔliu/ m monopoly. **~polizar** vt monopolize

monossílabo /mono'silabu/ a monosyllabic ● m monosyllable

monotonia /monoto'nia/ f monotony

monótono /mo'nɔtonu/ a monotonous

monóxido /mo'nɔksidu/ m **~ de carbono** carbon monoxide

mons|tro /'mõstru/ m monster. **~truosidade** f monstrosity. **~truoso** /o/ a monstrous

monta|dor /mõta'dor/ m (de cinema) editor. **~dora** f assembly company. **~gem** f assembly; (de filme) editing; (de peça teatral) production

montanha /mõ'taɲa/ f mountain. **~nha-russa** (pl **~nhas-russas**) f roller coaster. **~nhismo**

m mountaineering. **~nhoso** /o/ a mountainous

mon|tante /mõ'tãtʃi/ m amount ● a rising; **a ~tante** upstream. **~tão** m heap. **~tar** vt ride ‹cavalo, bicicleta›; assemble ‹peças, máquina›; put up ‹barraca›; set up ‹empresa, escritório›; mount ‹guarda, diamante›; put on ‹espetáculo, peça›; edit ‹filme›; **~tar a** amount to; **~tar em** (subir em) mount ● vi ride. **~taria** f mount. **~te** /o/ heap; **um ~te de coisas** 🗉 loads of things; **o Monte Branco** Mont Blanc

Montevidéu /mõtʃivi'dew/ f Montevideo

montra /'mõtra/ f Port shop window

monumen|tal /monumē'taw/ (pl **~tais**) a monumental. **~to** m monument

mo|rada /mo'rada/ f dwelling; Port address. **~dia** f dwelling. **~dor** m resident

mo|ral /mo'raw/ (pl **~rais**) a moral ● f (ética) morals; (de uma história) moral ● m (ânimo) morale; (de pessoa) moral sense. **~ralidade** f morality. **~ralista** a moralistic ● m/f moralist. **~ralizar** vt moralize

morango /mo'rãgu/ m strawberry

morar /mo'rar/ vi live

moratória /mora'tɔria/ f moratorium

mórbido /'mɔrbidu/ a morbid

morcego /mor'segu/ m bat

mor|daça /mor'dasa/ f gag; (para cão) muzzle. **~daz** a scathing. **~der** vt/i bite. **~dida** f bite

mordo|mia /mordo'mia/ f (no emprego) perk; (de casa etc) comfort. **~mo** /o/ m butler

more|na /moˈrena/ f brunette. **~no** a dark; (*bronzeado*) brown ● *m* dark person

morfina /morˈfina/ f morphine

moribundo /moriˈbũdu/ a dying

moringa /moˈrĩga/ f water jug

morma|cento /mormaˈsẽtu/ a sultry. **~ço** *m* sultry weather

morno /ˈmornu/ a lukewarm

moro|sidade /moroziˈdadʒi/ f slowness. **~so** /o/ a slow

morrer /moˈxer/ *vi* die; ‹*luz, dia, ardor, esperança etc*› fade; ‹*carro*› stall

morro /ˈmoxu/ *m* hill; fig ‹*favela*› slum

mortadela /mortaˈdɛla/ f mortadella, salami

mor|tal /morˈtaw/ (*pl* **~tais**) a & *m* mortal. **~talha** f shroud. **~talidade** f mortality. **~tandade** f slaughter. **~te** /ɔ/ f death. **~tífero** a deadly. **~tificar** *vt* mortify. **~to** /o/ a dead

mosaico /moˈzajku/ *m* mosaic

mosca /ˈmoska/ f fly

Moscou /mosˈku/, *Port* **Moscovo** /moʃˈkovu/ f Moscow

mosquito /mosˈkitu/ *m* mosquito

mostarda /mosˈtarda/ f mustard

mosteiro /mosˈteru/ *m* monastery

mos|tra /ˈmɔstra/ f display; **dar ~tras de** show signs of; **pôr à ~tra** show up. **~trador** *m* face, dial. **~trar** *vt* show. **~trar-se** *vpr* (*revelar-se*) show o.s. to be; (*exibir-se*) show off. **~truário** *m* display case

mo|tel /moˈtew/ (*pl* **~téis**) *m* motel

motim /moˈtʃĩ/ *m* riot; (*na marinha*) mutiny

moti|vação /motʃivaˈsãw/ f motivation. **~var** *vt* (*incentivar*) motivate; (*provocar*) cause. **~vo** *m*

(*razão*) reason; (*estímulo*) motive; (*na arte, música*) motif; **dar ~vo de** give cause for

moto /ˈmɔtu/ f motorbike. **~ca** /mɔˈtɔka/ f ⚠ motorbike

motoci|cleta /motosiˈkleta/ f motorcycle. **~clismo** *m* motorcycling. **~clista** *m/f* motorcyclist

motoqueiro /motoˈkeru/ *m* ⚠ biker

motor /moˈtor/ *m* (*de carro, avião etc*) engine; (*elétrico*) motor ● a (f **motriz**) ‹*força*› driving; Anat motor; **~ de arranque** starter motor; **~ de popa** outboard motor

moto|rista /motoˈrista/ *m/f* driver. **~rizado** a motorized. **~rizar** *vt* motorize

mouse *m* Comput mouse

mousepad *m* Comput mousemat

movedi|ço /moveˈdʒisu/ a unstable, moving; **areia ~ça** quicksand

mó|vel /ˈmɔvew/ (*pl* **~veis**) a ‹*peça, parte*› moving; ‹*tropas*› mobile; ‹*festa*› movable ● *m* piece of furniture; *pl* furniture

mo|ver /moˈver/ *vt* move; (*impulsionar*) fig drive. **~ver-se** *vpr* move. **~vido** a driven; **~vido a álcool** alcohol-powered

movimen|tação /movimẽtaˈsãw/ f bustle. **~tado** a ‹*rua, loja*› busy; ‹*música*› upbeat, lively; ‹*pessoa, sessão*› lively. **~tar** *vt* liven up. **~tar-se** *vpr* move. **~to** *m* movement; Tecn motion; (*na rua etc*) activity

MP3 *m* MP3 player

muam|ba /muˈãba/ f contraband. **~beiro** *m* smuggler

muco /ˈmuku/ *m* mucus

muçulmano /musuw'manu/ a & m Muslim

mu|da /'muda/ f (planta) seedling; **~da de roupa** change of clothes. **~dança** f change; (de casa) move; (de carro) transmission. **~dar** vt/i change; **~dar de assunto** change the subject; **~dar (de casa)** move (house); **~dar de cor** change colour; **~dar de ideia** change one's mind; **~dar de lugar** change places; **~dar de roupa** change (clothes). **~dar-se** vpr move

mu|dez /mu'des/ f silence. **~do** a silent; (deficiente) dumb; <telefone> dead ● m mute

mu|gido /mu'ʒidu/ m moo. **~gir** vi moo

muito /'mũitu/ a a lot of; pl many ● pron a lot ● adv (com adjetivo, advérbio) very; (com verbo) a lot; **~ maior** much bigger; **~ tempo** a long time

mula /'mula/ f mule

mulato /mu'latu/ a & m mulatto

muleta /mu'leta/ f crutch

mulher /mu'ʎɛr/ f woman; (esposa) wife

mulherengo /muʎe'rẽgu/ a womanizing ● m womanizer, ladies' man

mul|ta /'muwta/ f fine. **~tar** vt fine

multicolor /muwtʃiko'lor/ a multicoloured

multidão /muwtʃi'dãw/ f crowd

multinacio|nal /muwtʃinasio'naw/ (pl **~nais**) a & f multinational

multipli|cação /muwtʃiplika'sãw/ f multiplication. **~car** vt multiply. **~car-se** vpr multiply. **~cidade** f multiplicity

múltiplo /'muwtʃiplu/ a & m multiple

multirraci|al /muwtʃixasi'aw/ (pl **~ais**) a multiracial

múmia /'mumia/ f mummy

mun|dano /mũ'danu/ a <prazeres etc> worldly; <vida, mulher> society. **~dial** (pl **~diais**) a world ● m world championship. **~do** m world; **todo (o) ~do** everybody

munição /muni'sãw/ f ammunition

muni|cipal /munisi'paw/ (pl **~cipais**) a municipal. **~cípio** m (lugar) borough, community; (prédio) town hall; (autoridade) local authority

munir /mu'nir/ vt provide (de with). **~se** vpr equip o.s. (de with)

mu|ral /mu'raw/ (pl **~rais**) a & m mural. **~ralha** f wall

mur|char /mur'ʃar/ vi <planta> wither, wilt; <salada> go limp; <beleza> fade ● vt wither, wilt <planta>. **~cho** a <planta> wilting; <pessoa> broken

mur|murar /murmu'rar/ vi murmur; (queixar-se) mutter ● vt murmur. **~múrio** m murmur

muro /'muru/ m wall

murro /'muxu/ m punch

musa /'muza/ f muse

muscu|lação /muskula'sãw/ f weight training. **~lar** a muscular. **~latura** f musculature

músculo /'muskulu/ m muscle

musculoso /musku'lozu/ a muscular

museu /mu'zew/ m museum

musgo /'muzgu/ m moss

música /'muzika/ f music; (uma) song; **~ de câmara** chamber music;

~ de fundo background music; **~ clássica** ou **erudita** classical music

musi|cal /muzi'kaw/ (*pl* **~cais**) *a* & *m* musical. **~car** *vt* set to music

músico /'muziku/ *m* musician ● *a* musical

musse /'musi/ *f* mousse

mutilar /mutʃi'lar/ *vt* mutilate; maim ‹*pessoa*›

mutirão /mutʃi'rãw/ *m* joint effort

mútuo /'mutuu/ *a* mutual

muxoxo /mu'ʃoʃu/ *m* **fazer ~** tut

....

Nn

na = **em** + **a**

nabo /'nabu/ *m* turnip

nação /na'sãw/ *f* nation

nacio|nal /nasio'naw/ (*pl* **~nais**) *a* national; (*brasileiro*) home-produced. **~nalidade** *f* nationality. **~nalismo** *m* nationalism. **~nalista** *a* & *m/f* nationalist. **~nalizar** *vt* nationalize

naco /'naku/ *m* chunk

nada /'nada/ *pron* nothing ● *adv* not at all; **de ~** (*não há de quê*) don't mention it; **que ~!**, **~ disso!** no way!

na|dadeira /nada'dera/ *f* (*de peixe*) fin; (*de mergulhador*) flipper. **~dador** *m* swimmer. **~dar** *vi* swim

nadador-salvador /nada'dorsawva'dor/ *m* (*pl* **nadadores-salvadores**) Port lifeguard

nádegas /'nadegas/ *f pl* buttocks

nado /'nadu/ *m* **~ borboleta** butterfly stroke; **~ de costas** backstroke; **~ de peito** breaststroke; **atravessar a ~** swim across

náilon /'najlõ/ *m* nylon

naipe /'najpi/ *m* (*em jogo de cartas*) suit

namo|rada /namo'rada/ *f* girlfriend. **~rado** *m* boyfriend. **~rador** *a* amorous ● *m* ladies' man. **~rar** *vt* (*ter relação com*) go out with; (*cobiçar*) eye up ● *vi* ‹*casal*› (*ter relação*) go out together; (*beijar-se etc*) kiss and cuddle; ‹*homem*› have a girlfriend; ‹*mulher*› have a boyfriend. **~ro** /o/ *m* relationship

nanar /na'nar/ *vi* (*col*) sleep

nanico /na'niku/ *a* tiny

nanotecnologia /ˌnãnoteknolo'ʒia/ *f* nanotechnology

não /nãw/ *adv* not; (*resposta*) no ● *m* no. **~ alinhado** *a* non-aligned; **~ conformista** *a* & *m/f* nonconformist

naquela, naquele, naquilo = **em** + **aquela, aquele, aquilo**

narci|sismo /narsi'zizmu/ *m* narcissism. **~sista** *m/f* narcissist ● *a* narcissistic. **~so** *m* narcissus

narcótico /nar'kɔtʃiku/ *a* & *m* narcotic

narcotraficante /ˌnarkotrafi'kãntʃi/ *m/f* drug dealer

narcotráfico /narko'trafiku/ *m* drug trafficking

nari|gudo /nari'gudu/ *a* with a big nose; **ser ~gudo** have a big nose. **~na** *f* nostril

nariz /na'ris/ *m* nose

nar|ração /naxa'sãw/ *f* narration. **~rador** *m* narrator. **~rar** *vt* narrate

~rativa f narrative. **~rativo** a narrative

nas = em + as

na|sal /na'zaw/ (pl **~sais**) a nasal. **~salizar** vt nasalize

nas|cença /na'sēsa/ f birth. **~cente** a nascent ● f source. **~cer** vi be born; <dente, espinha> grow; <planta> sprout; <sol, lua> rise; <dia> dawn; fig <empresa, projeto etc> come into being ● m o **~cer do sol** sunrise. **~cimento** m birth

nata /'nata/ f cream

natação /nata'sāw/ f swimming

na|tal /na'taw/ (pl **~tais**) a <país, terra> native

Natal /na'taw/ m Christmas

nata|lício /nata'lisiu/ a & m birthday. **~lidade** f índice de **~lidade** birth rate. **~lino** a Christmas

nati|vidade /natʃivi'dadʒi/ f nativity. **~vo** a & m native

nato /'natu/ a born

natu|ral /natu'raw/ (pl **~rais**) a natural; (oriundo) originating (de from) ● m native (de of)

natura|lidade /naturali'dadʒi/ f naturalness; **com ~lidade** matter-of-factly; **de ~lidade carioca** born in Rio de Janeiro. **~lismo** m naturalism. **~lista** a & m/f naturalist. **~lizar** vt naturalize. **~lizar-se** vpr become naturalized

natureza /natu'reza/ f nature; **~ morta** still life

naturis|mo /natu'rizmu/ m naturism. **~ta** m/f naturist

nau|fragar /nawfra'gar/ vi <navio> be wrecked; <tripulação> be shipwrecked; fig <plano, casamento etc> founder. **~frágio** m shipwreck; fig failure

náufrago /'nawfragu/ m castaway

náusea /'nawzia/ f nausea

nauseabundo /nawzia'bũdu/ a nauseating
~co a nautical

náuti|ca /'nawtʃika/ f navigation. **~co** a nautical

na|val /na'vaw/ (pl **~vais**) a naval; **construção ~val** shipbuilding

navalha /na'vaʎa/ f razor. **~da** f cut with a razor

nave /'navi/ f nave; **~ espacial** spaceship

nave|gação /navega'sāw/ f navigation; (tráfego) shipping. **~gador** m navigator; Comput browser. **~gante** m/f seafarer. **~gar** vt navigate; sail <mar> ● vi sail; (traçar o rumo) navigate. **~gável** (pl **~gáveis**) a navigable

navio /na'viu/ m ship; **~ cargueiro** cargo ship; **~ de guerra** warship; **~ petroleiro** oil tanker

nazista /na'zista/, Port **nazi** /na'zi/ a & m/f Nazi

neblina /ne'blina/ f mist

nebulo|sa /nebu'lɔza/ f nebula. **~sidade** f cloud. **~so** /o/ a cloudy; fig obscure

neces|saire /nese'sɛr/ m toilet bag. **~sário** a necessary. **~sidade** f necessity; (que se impõe) need; (pobreza) need. **~sitado** a needy ● m person in need. **~sitar** vt require; (tornar necessário) necessitate. **~sitar de** need

necro|lógio /nekro'lɔʒiu/ m obituary column. **~tério** m mortuary, Amer morgue

nectarina /nekta'rina/ f nectarine

nefasto /ne'fastu/ a fatal

ne|gação /nega'sāw/ f denial; Ling negation; **ser uma ~gação em** be hopeless at. **~gar** vt deny; **~gar-se**

a refuse to. **~gativa** f refusal; *Ling* negative. **~gativo** a & m negative

negli|gência /negli'ʒẽsia/ f negligence. **~genciar** vt neglect. **~gente** a negligent

negoci|ação /negosia'sãw/ f negotiation. **~ador** m negotiator. **~ante** m/f dealer (de in). **~ar** vt/i negotiate; **~ar em** deal in. **~ata** f shady deal. **~ável** (pl **~áveis**) a negotiable

negócio /ne'gɔsiu/ m deal; ⚀ (coisa) thing; pl business; **a** ou **de ~s** on business

negocista /nego'sista/ m wheeler-dealer ● a wheeler-dealing

ne|grito /ne'gritu/ m bold. **~gro** /e/ a & m black; (de raça) Negro

nela, nele = em + ela, ele

nem /nẽj/ adv not even ● conj **~** ... **~** ... neither ... nor ...; **~ sempre** not always; **~ todos** not all; **~ que** not even if; **que ~** like; **~ eu** nor do I

nenê /ne'ne/, **neném** /ne'nẽj/ m baby

nenhum /ne'nũ/ a (f **nenhuma**) no ● pron (f **nenhuma**) not one; **~ dos dois** neither of them; **~ erro** no mistakes; **erro ~** no mistakes at all, not a single mistake; **~ lugar** nowhere

nenúfar /ne'nufar/ m water lily

neoconservador /neokõserva'dor/ a a neoconservative

neologismo /neolo'ʒizmu/ m neologism

néon /'nɛõ/ m neon

neozelan|dês /neozelã'des/ a (f **~desa**) New Zealand ● m (f **~desa**) New Zealander

Nepal /ne'paw/ m Nepal

nervo /'nervu/ m nerve. **~sismo** m (chateação) annoyance; (medo)

nervousness. **~so** /o/ a ‹sistema, doença› nervous; (chateado) annoyed; (medroso) nervous; **deixar alguém ~so** get on sb's nerves

nessa(s), nesse(s) = em + essa(s), esse(s)

nesta(s), neste(s) = em + esta(s), este(s)

ne|ta /'neta/ f granddaughter. **~to** /e/ m grandson; pl grandchildren

neuro|logia /newrolo'ʒia/ f neurology. **~lógico** a neurological. **~logista** m/f neurologist

neu|rose /new'rɔzi/ f neurosis. **~rótico** a neurotic

neutrali|dade /newtrali'dadʒi/ f neutrality. **~zar** vt neutralize

neutrão /new'trãw/ m Port
▶ **NÊUTRON**

neutro /'newtru/ a neutral

nêutron /'newtrõ/ m neutron

ne|vada /ne'vada/ f snowfall. **~vado** a snow-covered. **~var** vi snow. **~vasca** f snowstorm. **~ve** /e/ f snow

névoa /'nɛvoa/ f haze

nevoeiro /nevo'eru/ m fog

nexo /'neksu/ m connection; **sem ~** incoherent

Nicarágua /nika'ragwa/ f Nicaragua

nicaraguense /nikara'gwẽsi/ a & m/f Nicaraguan

nicho /'niʃu/ m niche

nicotina /niko'tʃina/ f nicotine

Níger /'niʒer/ m Niger

Nigéria /ni'ʒeria/ f Nigeria

nigeriano /niʒeri'anu/ a & m Nigerian

Nilo /'nilu/ m Nile

ninar /ni'nar/ vt lull to sleep

ninfa /'nĩfa/ f nymph

ninguém /niˈgẽj/ pron no one, nobody

ninhada /niˈɲada/ f brood

ninharia /niɲaˈria/ f trifle

ninho /ˈniɲu/ m nest

níquel /ˈnikew/ m nickel

nisei /niˈsej/ a & m/f Japanese Brazilian

nisso = em + isso

nisto = em + isto

nitidez /nitʃiˈdes/ f (de imagem etc) sharpness

nítido /ˈnitʃidu/ a ‹imagem, foto› sharp; ‹diferença, melhora› distinct, clear

nitrogênio /nitroˈʒeniu/ m nitrogen

ní|vel /ˈnivew/ (pl ~veis) m level; a ~vel de in terms of

nivelamento /nivelaˈmẽtu/ m levelling

nivelar /niveˈlar/ vt level

no = em + o

nó /nɔ/ m knot; **dar um ~** tie a knot; **~ dos dedos** knuckle; **um ~ na garganta** a lump in one's throat

nobre /ˈnɔbri/ a noble; ‹bairro› exclusive ● m/f noble. **~za** /e/ f nobility

noção /noˈsãw/ f notion; pl (rudimentos) elements

nocaute /noˈkawtʃi/ m knockout; **pôr alguém ~** knock sb out. **~ar** vt knock out

nocivo /noˈsivu/ a harmful

nódoa /ˈnɔdoa/ f Port stain

nogueira /noˈgera/ f (árvore) walnut tree

noi|tada /nojˈtada/ f night. **~te** f night; (antes de dormir) evening; **à** ou **de ~te** at night; (antes de dormir) in the evening; **hoje à ~te**

tonight; **ontem à ~te** last night; **boa ~te** (ao chegar) good evening; (ao despedir-se) good night; **~te em branco** ou **claro** sleepless night

noi|vado /nojˈvadu/ m engagement. **~va** f fiancée; (no casamento) bride. **~vo** m fiancé; (no casamento) bridegroom; **os ~vos** the engaged couple; (no casamento) the bride and groom; **ficar ~vo** get engaged

no|jento /noˈʒẽtu/ a disgusting. **~jo** /o/ m disgust

nômade /ˈnomadʒi/ m/f nomad ● a nomadic

nome /ˈnomi/ m name; **de ~** by name; **em ~ de** in the name of; **~ comercial** trade name; **~ de batismo** Christian name; **~ de guerra** professional name

nome|ação /nomiaˈsãw/ f appointment. **~ar** vt (para cargo) appoint; (chamar pelo nome) name

nomi|nal /nomiˈnaw/ (pl ~nais) a nominal

nonagésimo /nonaˈʒɛzimu/ a ninetieth

nono /ˈnonu/ a & m ninth

nora /ˈnɔra/ f daughter-in-law

nordes|te /norˈdestʃi/ m north-east. **~tino** a north-eastern ● m person from the north-east (of Brazil)

nórdico /ˈnɔrdʒiku/ a Nordic

nor|ma /ˈnɔrma/ f norm. **~mal** (pl ~mais) a normal

normali|dade /normaliˈdadʒi/ f normality. **~zar** vt bring back to normal; normalize ‹relações diplomáticas›. **~zar-se** vpr return to normal

noroeste /noroˈestʃi/ a & m north-west

norte /'nɔrtʃi/ a & m north. **~africano** a & m North African; **~americano** a & m North American; **~coreano** a & m North Korean

nortista /nor'tʃista/ a Northern ● m/f Northerner

Noruega /noru'ega/ f Norway

norue|guês /norue'ges/ a & m (f **~guesa**) Norwegian

nos¹ = **em** + **os**

nos² /nus/ pron us; (indireto) (to) us; (reflexivo) ourselves

nós /nɔs/ pron we; (depois de preposição) us

nos|sa /'nɔsa/ int gosh. **~so** /ɔ/ a our ● pron ours

nos|talgia /nostaw'ʒia/ f nostalgia. **~tálgico** a nostalgic

nota /'nɔta/ f note; (na escola etc) mark; (conta) bill; **custar uma ~ (preta)** Ⓣ cost a bomb; **tomar ~** take note (**de** of); **~ fiscal** receipt

no|tação /nota'sãw/ f notation. **~tar** vt notice, note; **fazer ~tar** point out. **~tável** (pl **~táveis**) a & m/f notable

notícia /no'tʃisia/ f piece of news; pl news

notici|ar /notʃi'sjar/ vt report. **~ário** m (na TV) news; (em jornal) news section. **~arista** m/f (na TV) newsreader; (em jornal) news reporter. **~oso** /o/ a **agência ~osa** news agency

notifi|cação /notʃifika'sãw/ f notification. **~car** vt notify

notívago /no'tʃivagu/ a nocturnal ● m night person

notório /no'tɔriu/ a well-known

noturno /no'turnu/ a night; ‹animal› nocturnal

nova /'nɔva/ f piece of news. **~mente** adv again

novato /no'vatu/ m novice

nove /'nɔvi/ a & m nine. **~centos** a & m nine hundred

novela /no'vela/ f (na TV) soap opera; (livro) novella

novembro /no'vẽbru/ m November

noventa /no'vẽta/ a & m ninety

noviço /no'visu/ m novice

novidade /novi'dadʒi/ f novelty; (notícia) piece of news; pl (notícias) news

novilho /no'viλu/ m calf

novo /'novu/ a new; (jovem) young; **de ~** again; **~ em folha** brand new

noz /nɔs/ f walnut; **~ moscada** nutmeg

nu /nu/ a (f **~a**) ‹corpo, pessoa› naked; ‹braço, parede, quarto› bare ● m nude; **~ em pelo** stark naked; **a verdade ~a e crua** the plain truth

nuança /nu'ãsa/ f nuance

nu|blado /nu'bladu/ a cloudy. **~blar** vt cloud. **~blar-se** vpr cloud over

nuca /'nuka/ f nape of the neck

nuclear /nukli'ar/ a nuclear

núcleo /'nukliu/ m nucleus

nu|dez /nu'des/ f nakedness; (na TV etc) nudity; (da parede etc) bareness. **~dismo** m nudism. **~dista** m/f nudist

nulo /'nulu/ a void

num, numa(s) = **em** + **um, uma(s)**

nume|ral /nume'raw/ (pl **~rais**) a & m numeral. **~rar** vt number

numérico /nu'mɛriku/ a numerical

número /'numeru/ m number; (de jornal, revista) issue; (de sapatos) size; (espetáculo) act; **fazer ~** make up the numbers

numeroso /nume'rozu/ a numerous

nunca /'nũka/ adv never; **~ mais** never again

nuns = em + uns

nupci|al /nupsi'aw/ (pl **~ais**) a bridal

núpcias /'nupsias/ f pl marriage

nu|trição /nutri'sãw/ f nutrition. **~trir** vt nourish; fig harbour ‹ódio, esperança›. **~tritivo** a nourishing; ‹valor› nutritional

nuvem /'nuvẽ/ f cloud

....

Oo

....

o /u/ ● artigo

····➤ the; **~ trem** the train; **~ vizinho ao lado** the next-door neighbour; **~ João está em casa** João is at home

❗ O artigo é omitido em inglês com nomes próprios, ou com parentes: **o João já chegou** granddad has arrived; **onde está o Carlos?** where's Carlos?

····➤ (com partes do corpo, roupa) **lavei ~ cabelo** I washed my hair; **~ sapato está desamarrado** your shoe is undone

❗ Em português, utiliza-se em geral o artigo para se referir a partes do corpo, enquanto no inglês usa-se o pronome possessivo.

····➤ (com adjetivo) **~ interessante...** what's interesting...; **~ difícil é...** the difficult thing is...

····➤ (com substantivo abstrato) **~ amor** love; **~ sucesso** success; **~ conhecimento** knowledge

····➤ (com substantivo usado em sentido geral) **na prisão** in jail; **no hospital** in hospital

❗ Observe que o artigo não é traduzido com substantivos abstratos ou substantivos usados em sentido geral: **ele está no hospital** he's in hospital.

● pron

····➤ (ele) him; **eu ~ vi no sábado à tarde** I saw him on Saturday afternoon

····➤ (coisa) it; **onde é que você ~ guarda** where do you keep it?

····➤ (você) you; **eu ~ avisei?** I told you so!

····➤ **~ de** (com características, procedência) the one with/from; **~ de barba** the one with the beard; **~ do Rio** the one from Rio; **~ que** (pessoa) the one; **~ que eu vi era mais alto** the one I saw was taller; (quem quer que) whoever; **~ que chegar primeiro faz o café** whoever gets there first has to make the coffee; **~ que** (como) what; **nem imagina ~ que foi aquilo** you can't imagine what it was like; **~ que** (referindo-se a toda a frase anterior) which; **ele disse que era professor, ~ que não é verdade** he said he was a teacher, which isn't true

ó /ɔ/ int 🗓 look

ô /o/ int oh

oásis /oˈazis/ *m invar* oasis

oba /ˈoba/ *int* great

obcecar /obiseˈkar/ *vt* obsess

obe|decer /obedeˈser/ *vt* **~decer a** obey. **~diência** *f* obedience. **~diente** *a* obedient

obe|sidade /obeziˈdadʒi/ *f* obesity. **~so** /e/ *a* obese

óbito /ˈɔbitu/ *m* death

obituário /obituˈariu/ *m* obituary

obje|ção /obiʒeˈsãw/ *f* objection. **~tar** *vt/i* object (**a** to)

objeti|va /obiʒeˈtʃiva/ *f* lens. **~vidade** *f* objectivity. **~vo** *a & m* objective

objeto /obiˈʒɛtu/ *m* object

objetor /obiʒeˈtor/ *m* objector; **~ de consciência** conscientious objector

oblíquo /oˈblikwu/ *a* oblique; ‹olhar› sidelong

obliterar /obliteˈrar/ *vt* obliterate

oblongo /oˈblõgu/ *a* oblong

obo|é /oboˈɛ/ *m* oboe. **~ísta** *m/f* oboist

obra /ˈɔbra/ *f* work; **em ~s** being renovated; **~ de arte** work of art; **~ de caridade** charity. **~prima** (*pl* **~s-primas**) *f* masterpiece

obri|gação /obrigaˈsãw/ *f* obligation; (*título*) bond. **~gado** *int* thank you; (*não querendo*) no thank you. **~gar** *vt* force, oblige (**a** to). **~gar-se** *vpr* undertake (**a** to). **~gatório** *a* obligatory, compulsory

obsce|nidade /obiseniˈdadʒi/ *f* obscenity. **~no** /e/ *a* obscene

obscu|ridade /obiskuriˈdadʒi/ *f* obscurity. **~ro** *a* obscure

obséquio /obiˈsɛkiu/ *m* favour

obsequioso /obisekiˈozu/ *a* obsequious

obser|vação /obiservaˈsãw/ *f* observation. **~vador** *a* observant ● *m* observer. **~vância** *f* observance. **~var** *vt* observe. **~vatório** *m* observatory

obses|são /obiseˈsãw/ *f* obsession. **~sivo** *a* obsessive

obsoleto /obisoˈletu/ *a* obsolete

obstáculo /obisˈtakulu/ *m* obstacle

obstar /obisˈtar/ *vt* stand in the way (**a** of)

obs|tetra /obisˈtɛtra/ *m/f* obstetrician. **~tetrícia** *f* obstetrics. **~tétrico** *a* obstetric

obsti|nação /obistinaˈsãw/ *f* obstinacy. **~nado** *a* obstinate. **~nar-se** *vpr* insist (**em** on)

obstru|ção /obistruˈsãw/ *f* obstruction. **~ir** *vt* obstruct

ob|tenção /obitẽˈsãw/ *f* obtaining. **~ter** *vt* obtain

obtu|ração /obituraˈsãw/ *f* filling. **~rador** *m* shutter. **~rar** *vt* fill ‹dente›

obtuso /obiˈtuzu/ *a* obtuse

óbvio /ˈɔbviu/ *a* obvious

ocasi|ão /okaziˈãw/ *f* occasion; (*oportunidade*) opportunity; (*compra*) bargain. **~onal** (*pl* **~onais**) *a* chance. **~onar** *vt* cause

Oceania /osiaˈnia/ *f* Oceania

oce|ânico /osiˈaniku/ *a* ocean. **~ano** *m* ocean

ociden|tal /osidẽˈtaw/ (*pl* **~tais**) *a* western ● *m/f* Westerner. **~te** *m* West

ócio /ˈɔsiu/ *m* (*lazer*) leisure; (*falta de trabalho*) idleness

ocioso /osiˈozu/ *a* idle ● *m* idler

oco /ˈoku/ *a* hollow; ‹cabeça› empty

ocor|rência /okoˈxẽsia/ *f* occurrence. **~rer** *vi* occur (**a** to)

ocu|lar /oku'lar/ a testemunha ~lar eye witness. ~lista m/f optician

óculos /'ɔkulus/ m pl glasses; ~ de sol sunglasses

ocul|tar /okuw'tar/ vt conceal. ~to a hidden; (sobrenatural) occult

ocu|pação /okupa'sãw/ f occupation. ~pado a <pessoa> busy; <cadeira> taken; <telefone> engaged, Amer busy. ~par vt occupy; take up <tempo, espaço>; hold <cargo>. ~par-se vpr keep busy; ~par-se com ou de be involved with <política, literatura etc>; take care of <cliente, doente, problema>; occupy one's time with <leitura, palavras cruzadas etc>

ocupacional /okupasio'naw/ a occupational; **terapia** ~ occupational therapy

odiar /odʒi'ar/ vt hate

ódio /'ɔdʒiu/ m hatred, hate; (raiva) anger

odioso /odʒi'ozu/ a hateful

odontologia /odõtolo'ʒia/ f dentistry

odor /o'dor/ m odour

oeste /o'estʃi/ a & m west

ofe|gante /ofe'gãtʃi/ a panting. ~gar vi pant

ofen|der /ofẽ'der/ vt offend. ~der-se vpr take offence. ~sa f insult. ~siva f offensive. ~sivo a offensive

ofere|cer /ofere'ser/ vt offer. ~cer-se vpr <pessoa> offer o.s. (como as); <ocasião> arise; ~cer-se para ajudar offer to help. ~cimento m offer

oferenda /ofe'rẽda/ f offering

oferta /o'ferta/ f offer; **em** ~ on offer; **a** ~ **e a demanda** supply and demand

offline /of'lajni/ a & adv Comput offline

ofici|al /ofisi'aw/ (pl ~ais) a official ● m officer. ~alizar vt make official. ~ar vi officiate

oficina /ofi'sina/ f workshop; (para carros) garage, Amer shop

ofício /o'fisiu/ m (profissão) trade; (na igreja) service

oficioso /ofisi'ozu/ a unofficial

ofus|cante /ofus'kãtʃi/ a dazzling. ~car vt dazzle <pessoa>; obscure <sol etc>; fig (eclipsar) outshine

OGM /oʒe'ẽ/ m Biol GMO

oi /oj/ int (cumprimento) hi; (resposta) yes?

oi|tavo /oi'tavu/ a & m eighth. ~tenta a & m eighty. ~to a & m eight. ~tocentos a & m eight hundred

olá /o'la/ int hello

olaria /ola'ria/ f pottery

óleo /'ɔliu/ m oil

oleo|duto /oliu'dutu/ m oil pipeline. ~so /o/ a oily

olfato /ow'fatu/ m sense of smell

olhada /o'ʎada/ f look; **dar uma** ~ have a look

olhar /o'ʎar/ vt look at; (assistir) watch ● vi look ● m look; ~ **para** look at; ~ **por** look after; **e olhe lá** 🄳 and that's pushing it

olheiras /o'ʎeras/ f pl dark rings under one's eyes

olho /'oʎu/ m eye; **a** ~ **nu** with the naked eye; **custar os** ~**s da cara** cost a fortune; **ficar de** ~ keep an eye out; **ficar de** ~ **em** keep an eye on; **pôr alguém no** ~ **da rua** throw sb out; **não pregar o** ~ not sleep a wink; ~ **gordo** ou **grande** envy; ~ **mágico** peephole; ~ **roxo** black eye

Olimpíada /oli'piada/ f Olympic Games

olímpico /o'lĩpiku/ a ‹jogos, vila› Olympic; fig blithe

oliveira /oli'vera/ f olive tree

olmo /'owmu/ m elm

om|breira /õ'brera/ f (para roupa) shoulder pad; **~bro** m shoulder; **dar de ~bros** shrug one's shoulders

omelete /ome'letʃi/, Port **omeleta** /ome'leta/ f omelette

omis|são /omi'sãw/ f omission. **~so** a negligent, remiss

omitir /omi'tʃir/ vt omit

omni- Port ▶ **oni-**

omoplata /omo'plata/ f shoulder blade

onça¹ /'õsa/ f (peso) ounce

onça² /'õsa/ f (animal) jaguar

onda /'õda/ f wave. **pegar ~** 🄸 surf

onde /'õdʒi/ adv where; **por ~?** which way?; **~ quer que** wherever

ondu|lação /õdula'sãw/ f undulation; (do cabelo) wave. **~lado** a wavy. **~lante** a undulating. **~lar** vt wave ‹cabelo› ● vi undulate

onerar /one'rar/ vt burden

ONG /'õgi/ abr f (= Organização Não Governamental) NGO

ônibus /'õnibus/ m invar bus; **~ espacial** space shuttle

onipotente /onipo'tẽtʃi/ a omnipotent

onírico /o'niriku/ a dreamlike

onisciente /onisi'ẽtʃi/ a omniscient

online /õ'lajni/ a & adv Comput online

onomatopeia /onomato'peja/ f onomatopoeia

ontem /'õtẽ/ adv yesterday

onze /'õzi/ a & m eleven

opaco /o'paku/ a opaque

opala /o'pala/ f opal

opção /opi'sãw/ f option

ópera /'ɔpera/ f opera

ope|ração /opera'sãw/ f operation; (bancária etc) transaction. **~rador** m operator. **~rar** vt operate; operate on ‹doente›; work ‹milagre› ● vi operate. **~rar-se** vpr (acontecer) come about; (fazer operação) have an operation. **~rário** a working ● m worker

opereta /ope'reta/ f operetta

opinar /opi'nar/ vt think ● vi express one's opinion

opinião /opini'ãw/ f opinion; **na minha ~** in my opinion; **~ pública** public opinion

ópio /'ɔpiu/ m opium

opor /o'por/ vt put up ‹resistência, argumento›; (pôr em contraste) contrast (a with); **~se a** (não aprovar) oppose; (ser diferente) contrast with

oportu|nidade /oportuni'dadʒi/ f opportunity. **~nista** a & m/f opportunist. **~no** a opportune

oposi|ção /opozi'sãw/ f opposition (a to). **~cionista** a opposition ● m/f opposition politician

oposto /o'postu/ a & m opposite

opres|são /opre'sãw/ f oppression; (no peito) tightness. **~sivo** a oppressive. **~sor** m oppressor

oprimir /opri'mir/ vt oppress; (com trabalho) weigh down ● vi be oppressive

optar /opi'tar/ vi opt (por for); **~ por ir** opt to go

óptica, óptico ▶ **ÓTICA, ÓTICO**

opu|lência /opu'lẽsia/ f opulence. **~lento** a opulent

ora /ˈɔra/ adv & conj now ● int come; **~ essa!** come now! **~ ..., ~ ...** first ..., then...

oração /oraˈsãw/ f (prece) prayer; (discurso) oration; (frase) clause

oráculo /oˈrakulu/ m oracle

orador /oraˈdor/ m orator

oral /oˈraw/ (pl **orais**) a & f oral

orar /oˈrar/ vi pray

órbita /ˈɔrbita/ f orbit; (do olho) socket

orçamen|tário /orsamẽˈtariu/ a budgetary. **~to** m (plano financeiro) budget; (previsão dos custos) estimate

orçar /orˈsar/ vt estimate (**em** at)

ordeiro /orˈderu/ a orderly

ordem /ˈɔrdẽ/ f order; **por ~ alfabética** in alphabetical order; **~ de pagamento** banker's draft; **~ do dia** agenda

orde|nação /ordenaˈsãw/ f ordering; (de padre) ordination. **~nado** a ordered ● m wages. **~nar** vt order; put in order <papéis, livros etc>; ordain <padre>

ordenhar /ordeˈɲar/ vt milk

ordinário /ordʒiˈnariu/ a (normal) ordinary; (grosseiro) vulgar; (de má qualidade) inferior; (sem caráter) rough

ore|lha /oˈreʎa/ f ear. **~lhão** m phone booth. **~lhudo** a with big ears; **ser ~lhudo** have big ears

orfanato /orfaˈnatu/ m orphanage

ór|fão /ˈɔrfãw/ (pl **~fãos**) a & m (f **~fã**) orphan

orgânico /orˈganiku/ a organic

orga|nismo /orgaˈnizmu/ m organism; (do Estado etc) institution; **~ geneticamente modificado** GMO. **~nista** m/f organist

organi|zação /organizaˈsãw/ f organization. **~zador** a organizing ● m organizer. **~zar** vt organize

órgão /ˈɔrgãw/ (pl **~s**) m organ; (do Estado etc) body

orgasmo /orˈgazmu/ m orgasm

orgia /orˈʒia/ f orgy

orgu|lhar /orguˈʎar/ vt make proud. **~lhar-se** vpr be proud (**de** of). **~lho** m pride. **~lhoso** /o/ a proud

orien|tação /oriẽtaˈsãw/ f orientation; (direção) direction; (vocacional etc) guidance. **~tador** m advisor. **~tal** (pl **~tais**) a eastern; (da Ásia) oriental. **~tar** vt direct; (aconselhar) advise; (situar) position. **~tar-se** vpr get one's bearings; **~tar-se por** be guided by. **~te** m east; **Oriente Médio** Middle East; **Extremo Oriente** Far East

orifício /oriˈfisiu/ m opening; (no corpo) orifice

origem /oˈriʒẽ/ f origin; **dar ~ a** give rise to; **ter ~** originate

origi|nal /oriʒiˈnaw/ (pl **~nais**) a & m original. **~nalidade** f originality. **~nar** vt give rise to. **~nar-se** vpr originate. **~nário** a <planta, animal> native (**de** to); <pessoa> originating (**de** from)

oriundo /oˈrjũdu/ a originating (**de** from)

orla /ˈɔrla/ f border; **~ marítima** seafront

ornamen|tação /ornamẽtaˈsãw/ f ornamentation. **~tal** (pl **~tais**) a ornamental. **~tar** vt decorate. **~to** m ornament

orques|tra /orˈkestra/ f orchestra. **~tra sinfônica** symphony orchestra. **~tral** (pl **~trais**) a orchestral. **~trar** vt orchestrate

orquídea /or'kidʒia/ f orchid

ortodoxo /orto'dɔksu/ a orthodox

orto|grafia /ortogra'fia/ f spelling, orthography. **~gráfico** a orthographic

orto|pedia /ortope'dʒia/ f orthopaedics. **~pédico** a orthopaedic. **~pedista** m/f orthopaedic surgeon

orvalho /or'vaʎu/ m dew

---

os /us/, **as** /as/ ● *artigo*

····▸ the; **os livros que comprei ontem** the books I bought yesterday

● *pron*

····▸ them; **eu os/as vi no cinema** I saw them at the cinema; **os/as de** (*características, procedência*) the ones with/from; **os de branco** the ones in white; **as de Salvador** the ones from Salvador; **os da minha avó** my grandmother's ▸ **o**

---

oscilar /osi'lar/ vi oscillate

ósseo /'ɔsiu/ a bone

os|so /'osu/ m bone. **~sudo** a bony

ostensivo /ostẽ'sivu/ a ostensible

osten|tação /ostẽta'sãw/ f ostentation. **~tar** vt show off. **~toso** a showy, ostentatious

osteopata /ostʃo'pata/ m/f osteopath

ostra /'ostra/ f oyster

ostracismo /ostra'sizmu/ m ostracism

otário /o'tariu/ m 🇧 fool

óti|ca /'ɔtʃika/ f (*ciência*) optics; (*loja*) optician's; (*ponto de vista*) viewpoint. **~co** a optical

otimis|mo /otʃi'mizmu/ m optimism. **~ta** m/f optimist ● a optimistic

otimizar /otʃimi'zar/ vt optimize

ótimo /'otʃimu/ a excellent

otorrino /oto'xinu/ m ear, nose and throat specialist

ou /o/ conj or; **~ ... ~ ...** either ... or ...; **~ seja** in other words

ouriço /o'risu/ m hedgehog. **~do-mar** (pl **~s-do-mar**) m sea urchin

ouri|ves /o'rivis/ m/f invar jeweller. **~vesaria** f (*loja*) jeweller's

ouro /'oru/ m gold; pl (*naipe*) diamonds; **de ~** golden

ou|sadia /oza'dʒia/ f daring; (*uma*) daring step. **~sado** a daring. **~sar** vt/i dare

outdoor /'awtdor/ (pl **~s**) m billboard

outo|nal /oto'naw/ (pl **~nais**) a autumnal. **~no** /o/ m autumn, Amer fall

outorgar /otor'gar/ vt grant

ou|trem /o'trẽj/ pron (*outro*) someone else; (*outros*) others. **~tro** a other ● pron (*um*) another (one); others; **~tra coisa** something else; **~tro dia** the other day; **no ~tro dia** the next day; **~tra vez** again. **~tro copo** another glass. **~trora** adv once upon a time. **~trossim** adv equally

outubro /o'tubru/ m October

ou|vido /o'vidu/ m ear; **de ~vido** by ear; **dar ~vidos a** listen to. **~vinte** m/f listener. **~vir** vt hear; (*atentamente*) listen to ● vi hear; **~vir dizer que** hear that; **~vir falar de** hear of

ovação /ova'sãw/ f ovation

oval /o'vaw/ (pl **ovais**) a & f oval

ovário /o'variu/ m ovary

ovelha /o'veʎa/ f sheep

overdose /over'dɔzi/ f overdose

óvni /'ɔvni/ m UFO

ovo /'ovu/ m egg; **~ cozido/ frito/mexido/pochê** boiled/fried/ scrambled/poached egg

oxi|genar /oksiʒe'nar/ vt bleach ‹cabelo›. **~gênio** m oxygen

ozônio /o'zoniu/ m ozone; **camada de ~** ozone layer

ozono /o'zonu/ m Port ▶ **ozônio** /o'zonju/

....

Pp

....

pá /pa/ f spade; (de hélice) blade; (de moinho) sail ● m Port 🆃 mate

pacato /pa'katu/ a quiet

pachorra /pa'ʃoxa/ f Port 🆃 patience; **não tenho ~** I can't be bothered

paci|ência /pasi'ẽsia/ f patience. **~ente** a & m/f patient

pacificar /pasifi'kar/ vt pacify

pacífico /pa'sifiku/ a peaceful; **Oceano Pacífico** Pacific Ocean; **ponto ~** undisputed point

pacifis|mo /pasi'fizmu/ m pacifism. **~ta** a & m/f pacifist

paço /'pasu/ m palace

pacote /pa'kɔtʃi/ m (de biscoitos etc) packet; (mandado pelo correio) parcel; (econômico, turístico, software) package

pacto /'paktu/ m pact

pactuar /paktu'ar/ vi **~ com** collude with

padaria /pada'ria/ f baker's (shop), bakery

padecer /pade'ser/ vt/i suffer

padeiro /pa'deru/ m baker

padiola /padʒi'ɔla/ f stretcher

padrão /pa'drãw/ m standard; (desenho) pattern

padrasto /pa'drastu/ m stepfather

padre /'padri/ m priest

padrinho /pa'driɲu/ m (de batismo) godfather; (de casamento) best man

padroeiro /padro'eru/ m patron saint

padronizar /padroni'zar/ vt standardize

paga /'paga/ f pay. **~mento** m payment

pa|gão /pa'gãw/ (pl **~gãos**) a & m (f **~gã**) pagan

pagar /pa'gar/ vt pay for ‹compra, erro etc›; pay ‹dívida, conta, empregado etc›; pay back ‹empréstimo›; repay ‹gentileza etc› ● vi pay; **pode pagar para ver** I'll believe it when I see it

página /'paʒina/ f page; **~ web** web page

pago /'pagu/ a paid ● pp de ▶ **PAGAR**

pagode /pa'gɔdʒi/ m (torre) pagoda; 🆃 singalong

pai /paj/ m father; pl (pai e mãe) parents. **~ de santo** (pl **~s-de-santo**) m macumba priest

pai|nel /paj'nɛw/ (pl **~néis**) m panel; (de carro) dashboard

paio /'paju/ m pork sausage

pairar /paj'rar/ vi hover

país /pa'is/ m country; **P~ de Gales** Wales; **P~es Baixos** Netherlands

paisa|gem /paj'zaʒẽ/ f landscape. **~gista** m/f landscape gardener

paisana /paj'zana/ f à ~ <policial> in plain clothes; <soldado> in civilian clothes

paixão /pa'ʃãw/ f passion

pala /'pala/ f (de boné) peak; (de automóvel) sun visor

palácio /pa'lasiu/ m palace

Palácio do Planalto The *Palácio do Planalto* is the main working office of the President of Brazil. It is the seat of the government and the President's official residence, and it also houses important government offices, such as the *Casa Civil* (Chief of Staff) and the *Gabinete de Segurança Institucional* (Office for Institutional Security).

---

paladar /pala'dar/ m palate, taste

palanque /pa'lãki/ m stand

palavra /pa'lavra/ f word; **pedir a ~** ask to speak; **ter ~** be reliable; **tomar a ~** start to speak; **sem ~** <pessoa> unreliable; **~ de ordem** watchword; **~s cruzadas** crossword

palavra-chave /palavra'ʃavi/ f (pl **palavras-chave**) password

palavrão /pala'vrãw/ m swear word

palco /'pawku/ m stage

palestino /pales'tʃinu/ a & m Palestinian

palestra /pa'lɛstra/ f lecture

paleta /pa'leta/ f palette

paletó /pale'tɔ/ m jacket

palha /'paʎa/ f straw

palha|çada /paʎa'sada/ f joke. **~ço** m clown

palhinha /pa'ʎiɲa/ f Port (para bebidas) straw

paliativo /palia'tʃivu/ a & m palliative

palidez /pali'des/ f paleness

pálido /'palidu/ a pale

pali|tar /pali'tar/ vt pick ● vi pick one's teeth. **~teiro** m toothpick holder. **~to** m (para dentes) toothpick; (de fósforo) matchstick; (pessoa magra) beanpole

pal|ma /'pawma/ f palm; pl (aplauso) clapping; **bater ~mas** clap. **~meira** f palm tree. **~mito** m palm heart. **~mo** m span; **~mo a ~mo** inch by inch

palpá|vel /paw'pavew/ (pl **~veis**) a palpable

pálpebra /'pawpebra/ f eyelid

palpi|tação /pawpita'sãw/ f palpitation. **~tante** a fig thrilling. **~tar** vi <coração> flutter; <pessoa> tremble; (dar palpite) stick one's oar in. **~te** m (pressentimento) hunch; (no jogo etc) tip; **dar ~te** stick one's oar in

panaceia /pana'seja/ f panacea

panaché /pana'ʃɛ/ m Port (bebida) shandy

Panamá /pana'ma/ m Panama

panamenho /pana'meɲu/ a & m Panamanian

pan-americano /panameri'kanu/ a Pan-American

pança /'pãsa/ f paunch

pancada /pã'kada/ f blow; **~ d'água** downpour. **~ria** f fight, punch-up

pâncreas /'pãkrias/ m invar pancreas

pançudo /pã'sudu/ a paunchy

panda /'pãda/ m panda

pandarecos /pãda'rɛkus/ m pl **aos** ou **em ~** battered

pandeiro /pã'deru/ *m* tambourine
pandemônio /pãde'moniu/ *m* pandemonium
pane /'pani/ *f* breakdown
panela /pa'nɛla/ *f* saucepan; ~ **de pressão** pressure cooker
panfleto /pã'fletu/ *m* pamphlet
pânico /'paniku/ *m* panic; **em** ~ in a panic; **entrar em** ~ panic
panifica|ção /panifika'sãw/ *f* bakery. **~dora** *f* bakery
pano /'panu/ *m* cloth; ~ **de fundo** backdrop; ~ **de pó** duster; ~ **de pratos** tea towel
pano|rama /pano'rama/ *m* panorama. **~râmico** *a* panoramic
panqueca /pã'kɛka/ *f* pancake
panta|nal /pãta'naw/ (*pl* **~nais**) *m* marshland

>
> **Pantanal** The *Pantanal* is a tropical wetland located within the states of Mato Gross and Mato Grosso do Sul, covering an area of 250 thousand square kilometres. Much of the floodplains are submerged during the rainy season, forming a unique ecosystem which has been designated a UNESCO World Heritage Site, and one of Brazil's most important sites of national heritage. The area is home to hundreds of species of mammals, fish, birds and reptiles, including caimans, capybaras, and piranhas.

pântano /'pãtanu/ *m* marsh
pantanoso /pãta'nozu/ *a* marshy
pantera /pã'tɛra/ *f* panther
pantufa /pã'tufa/ *f* slipper
pão /pãw/ (*pl* **pães**) *m* bread; ~ **de forma** sliced loaf; ~ **integral** brown bread. ~ **de ló** *m* sponge cake; **~duro** (*pl* **pães-duros**) 🄱 *a* stingy, tight-fisted ● *m/f* skinflint. **~zinho** *m* bread roll

>
> **Pão de Açúcar** The *Pão de Açúcar* is a mountain situated at the mouth of Guanabara Bay in Rio de Janeiro. The summit stands at 395 meters above sea level, and is one of the city's most famous landmarks. A cable car (*Bondinho do Pão de Açúcar*) runs tourists up to the top, from which they can view Botafogo Bay, Leme Beach and the vast Atlantic Ocean.

papa /'papa/ *f* (*de nenem*) food; (*arroz etc*) mush
Papa /'papa/ *m* Pope
papagaio /papa'gaju/ *m* parrot
papai /pa'paj/ *m* dad, daddy; **Papai Noel** Father Christmas
papão /pa'pãw/ *m Port* bogeyman
papar /pa'par/ *vt/i* 🄱 eat
papari|car /papari'kar/ *vt* pamper. **~cos** *m pl* pampering
pa|pel /pa'pɛw/ (*pl* **~péis**) *m* (*de escrever etc*) paper; (*um*) piece of paper; (*numa peça, filme*) part; *fig* (*função*) role; **de** **~pel passado** officially; **~pel de alumínio** aluminium foil; **~pel higiênico** toilet paper. **~pelada** *f* paperwork. **~pelão** *m* cardboard. **~pelaria** *f* stationer's (shop). **~pelzinho** *m* scrap of paper
papo /'papu/ *f* 🄱 (*conversa*) talk; (*do rosto*) double chin; **bater um** ~ 🄱 have a chat; ~ **furado** idle talk
papoula /pa'pola/ *f* poppy
páprica /'paprika/ *f* paprika

paque|ra /pa'kera/ f 🅇 pick-up. **~rador** a flirtatious ● m flirt. **~rar** vt flirt with ‹pessoa›; eye up ‹vestido, carro etc› ● vi flirt

paquista|nês /pakista'nes/ a & m (f ~**nesa**) Pakistani

Paquistão /pakis'tãw/ m Pakistan

par /par/ a even ● m pair; (parceiro) partner; **a ~ de** up to date with ‹notícias etc›; **sem ~** unequalled

para /'para/ ● prep

••••▶ (uso, finalidade) for; **é ~ você** it's for you; **muito útil ~ a chuva** very useful for the rain; **muito complicado ~ mim** too complicated for me; **~ que você quer?** what do you want it for?; **detergente ~ máquina** machine detergent

••••▶ (direção) **~ sul/norte** towards south/north; **foi ~ a cama** she went to bed; **vai ~ casa!** go home!

••••▶ (com destino a) **~ São Paulo** to São Paulo; **o voo ~ Salvador** the flight to Salvador

••••▶ (seguido de infinitivo) **vieram ~ ficar** they've come to stay

••••▶ (tempo futuro) **~ a próxima semana** for next week; **preciso disto ~ segunda** I need it for Monday; **são cinco ~ as dez** it's five to ten

••••▶ (lugar impreciso) **estava (lá) ~ Recife** he was somewhere in Recife

••••▶ (em expressões) **~ com** to; **foi muito simpático ~ com ela** he was very nice to her; **~ isso: foi ~ isso que você me chamou?** you called me here

just for that?; **~ mim** (opinião) for me; **~ mim, ele é o melhor jogador** he is the best player for me; **~ que** so (that); **ela trabalhou muito ~ que ficasse tudo pronto na hora** she worked hard so (that) everything would be ready in time; **~ si** to yourself; **dizer algo ~ si próprio** say sth to o.s.

para|benizar /parabeni'zar/ vt congratulate (**por** on). **~béns** m pl congratulations

parábola /pa'rabola/ f (conto) parable; (curva) parabola

parabóli|co /para'bɔliku/ a **antena ~ca** satellite dish

para|brisa /para'briza/ m windscreen, Amer windshield. **~choque** m bumper

para|da /pa'rada/ f stop; (interrupção) stoppage; (militar) parade; 🅇 (coisa difícil) ordeal, challenge; **~da cardíaca** cardiac arrest. **~deiro** m whereabouts

paradisíaco /paradʒi'ziaku/ a idyllic

parado /pa'radu/ a ‹trânsito, carro› at a standstill, stopped; fig ‹pessoa› dull; **ficar ~** ‹pessoa› stand still; ‹trânsito› stop; (deixar de trabalhar) stop work

parado|xal /paradok'saw/ (pl ~**xais**) a paradoxical. **~xo** /ɔ/ m paradox

parafina /para'fina/ f paraffin

paráfrase /pa'rafrazi/ f paraphrase

parafrasear /parafrazi'ar/ vt paraphrase

parafuso /para'fuzu/ f screw; **entrar em ~** get into a state

para|gem /pa'raʒẽ/ f Port (parada) stop; **nestas ~gens** in these parts

parágrafo /pa'ragrafu/ m paragraph

Paraguai /para'gwaj/ m Paraguay

paraguaio /para'gwaju/ a & m Paraguayan

paraíso /para'izu/ m paradise

para-lama /para'lama/ m (de carro) wing, Amer fender; (de bicicleta) mudguard

parale|la /para'lɛla/ f parallel; pl (aparelho) parallel bars. **~lepípedo** m paving stone. **~lo** /ɛ/ a & m parallel

para|lisar /parali'zar/ vt paralyse; bring to a halt ‹fábrica, produção›. **~lisar-se** vpr become paralysed; ‹fábrica, produção› grind to a halt. **~lisia** f paralysis. **~lítico** a & m paralytic. **~médico** m paramedic

paranoi|a /para'nɔja/ f paranoia. **~co** a paranoid

parapeito /para'pejtu/ m (muro) parapet; (da janela) window sill

paraque|das /para'kedas/ m invar parachute. **~dista** m/f parachutist; (militar) paratrooper

parar /pa'rar/ vt/i stop; **~ de fumar** stop smoking; **ir ~** end up

para-raios /para'xajus/ m invar lightning conductor

parasita /para'zita/ a & m/f parasite

parceiro /par'seru/ m partner

parce|la /par'sela/ f (de terreno) plot; (prestação) instalment. **~lar** vt spread ‹pagamento›

parceria /parse'ria/ f partnership

parci|al /parsi'aw/ (pl **~ais**) a partial; (partidário) biased. **~alidade** f bias

parco /'parku/ a frugal; ‹recursos› scant

par|dal /par'daw/ (pl **~dais**) m sparrow. **~do** ‹papel› brown;

‹pessoa› mulatto

pare|cer /pare'ser/ vi (ter aparência de) seem; (ter semelhança com) be like; **~cer-se com** look like, resemble ● m opinion. **~cido** a similar (com to)

parede /pa'redʒi/ f wall

paren|te /pa'rẽtʃi/ m/f relative, relation. **~tesco** /e/ m relationship

parêntese /pa'rẽtʃizi/ f parenthesis; pl (sinais) brackets, parentheses

paridade /pari'dadʒi/ f parity

parir /pa'rir/ vt give birth to ● vi give birth

parlamen|tar /parlamẽ'tar/ a parliamentary ● m/f member of parliament. **~tarismo** m parliamentary system. **~to** m parliament

parmesão /parme'zãw/ a & m (queijo) ~ Parmesan (cheese)

paródia /pa'rɔdʒia/ f parody

parodiar /parodʒi'ar/ vt parody

paróquia /pa'rɔkia/ f parish

parque /'parki/ m park. **~ temático** m theme park

parquímetro /par'kimetru/ m parking meter

parte /'partʃi/ f part; (quinhão) share; (num litígio, contrato) party; **a maior ~** de most of; **à ~** (de lado) aside; (separadamente) separately; **um erro da sua ~** a mistake on your part; **em ~** in part; **em alguma ~** somewhere; **por toda ~** everywhere; **por ~ do pai** on one's father's side; **fazer ~ de** be part of; **tomar ~ em** take part in

parteira /par'tera/ f midwife

partici|pação /partʃisipa'sãw/ f participation; (numa empresa, nos lucros) share. **~pante** a participating

● *m/f* participant. **~par** *vi* take part (**de** ou **em** in)

particípio /partʃiˈsipiu/ *m* participle

particula /parˈtʃikula/ *f* particle

particu|lar /partʃikuˈlar/ *a* private; (*especial*) unusual ● *m* (*pessoa*) private individual; *pl* (*detalhes*) particulars; **em ~lar** (*especialmente*) in particular; (*a sós*) in private. **~laridade** *f* peculiarity

partida /parˈtʃida/ *f* (*saída*) departure; (*de corrida*) start; (*de futebol, xadrez etc*) match; **dar ~ em** start up

par|tidário /partʃiˈdariu/ *a* partisan ● *m* supporter. **~tido** *a* broken ● *m* (*político*) party; (*casamento, par*) match; **tirar ~tido de** benefit from; **tomar o ~tido de** side with. **~tilha** *f* division. **~tir** *vi* (*sair*) depart; (*corredor*) start; **a ~tir de ...** from ... onwards; **~tir para** ⚀ resort to; **~tir para outra** do something different, change direction ● *vt* break. **~tir-se** *vpr* break. **~titura** *f* score

partilhar /partʃiˈʎar/ *vt/i* Port share

parto /ˈpartu/ *m* birth

parvo /ˈparvu/ *a* Port stupid

Páscoa /ˈpaskoa/ *f* Easter

pas|mar /pazˈmar/ *vt* amaze. **~mar-se** *vi* be amazed (**com** at). **~mo** *a* amazed ● *m* amazement

passa /ˈpasa/ *f* raisin

pas|sada /paˈsada/ *f* **dar uma ~sada em** call in at. **~sadeira** *f* (*mulher*) woman who irons; Port (*faixa*) zebra crossing, Amer crosswalk. **~sado** *a* ‹*ano, mês, semana*› last; ‹*tempo, particípio etc*› past; ‹*fruta, comida*› off; **são duas horas ~sadas** it's gone two o'clock; **bem/mal ~sado** well done/

rare ● *m* past

passa|geiro /pasaˈʒeri/ *m* passenger ● *a* passing. **~gem** *f* passage; (*bilhete*) ticket; **de ~gem** in passing; **estar de ~gem** be passing through; **~gem de ida e volta** return ticket, Amer round trip ticket

passaporte /pasaˈpɔrtʃi/ *m* passport

passar /paˈsar/ *vt* pass; spend ‹*tempo*›; cross ‹*ponte, rio*›; (*a ferro*) iron ‹*roupa etc*›; (*aplicar*) put on ‹*creme, batom etc*› ● *vi* pass; (*dor, medo, chuva etc*) go; (*ser aceitável*) be passable; **passou a beber muito** he started to drink a lot; **passei dos 30 anos** I'm over thirty; **não passa de um boato** it's nothing more than a rumour; **~ sem** do without; **~ por** go through; go along ‹*rua*›; (*ser considerado*) be taken for; **fazer-se ~ por** pass o.s. off as; **~ por cima de** *fig* overlook ● *m* passing. **~se** *vpr* happen

passarela /pasaˈrɛla/ *f* (*sobre rua*) footbridge; (*para desfile de moda*) catwalk

pássaro /ˈpasaru/ *m* bird

passatempo /pasaˈtẽpu/ *m* pastime

passe /ˈpasi/ *m* pass

pas|sear /pasiˈar/ *vi* go out and about; (*viajar*) travel around ● *vt* take for a walk. **~seata** *f* protest march. **~seio** *m* outing; (*volta a pé*) walk; (*volta de carro*) drive; **dar um ~seio** (*a pé*) go for a walk; (*de carro*) go for a drive

passio|nal /pasioˈnaw/ (*pl* **~nais**) *a* crime of passion. **~nal** crime of passion

passista /paˈsista/ *m/f* dancer

passí|vel /paˈsivew/ (*pl* **~veis**) *a* **~vel de** subject to

passi|vidade /pasivi'dadʒi/ f
passivity. **~vo** a passive ● m Com
liabilities; Ling passive

passo /'pasu/ m step; (velocidade)
pace; (barulho) footstep; **~ a ~**
step by step; **a dois ~s de** a stone's
throw from; **dar um ~** take a step

pasta /'pasta/ f (matéria) paste;
(bolsa) briefcase; (fichário) folder;
ministro sem ~ minister without
portfolio; **~ de dentes** toothpaste

pas|tagem /pas'taʒẽ/ f pasture.
~tar vi graze

pas|tel /pas'tɛw/ (pl **~téis**) m
(para comer) samosa; Port (doce)
pastry; Port (pastéis) pastries; (para
desenhar) pastel. **~telão** m (comédia)
slapstick. **~telaria** f (loja) samosa
vendor; Port pastry shop

> **pastelaria** You can't go
> very far in Portugal without
> coming across a *pastelaria*.
> These are shops or cafes serving a
> huge variety of cakes and pastries,
> many of which originated in
> Portuguese convents. The fillings
> are often rich in egg yolk, left over
> after the nuns had used the whites
> to starch their habits.   *i*

pasteurizado /pastewri'zadu/ a
pasteurized

pastilha /pas'tʃiʎa/ f pastille

pas|to /'pastu/ m (erva) fodder,
feed; (lugar) pasture. **~tor** m (de
gado) shepherd; (clérigo) vicar; **~tor
alemão** (cachorro) Alsatian. **~toral**
(pl **~torais**) a pastoral

pata /'pata/ f paw. **~da** f kick

patamar /pata'mar/ m landing;
fig level

patê /pa'te/ m pâté

patente /pa'tẽtʃi/ a obvious ● f Mil
rank; (de invenção) patent. **~ar** vt
patent ‹produto, invenção›

pater|nal /pater'naw/ (pl **~nais**) a
paternal. **~nidade** f paternity. **~no**
/ɛ/ a paternal

pate|ta /pa'teta/ a daft, silly ● m/f
fool. **~tice** f stupidity; (uma) silly
thing

patético /pa'tɛtʃiku/ a pathetic

patíbulo /pa'tʃibulu/ m gallows

pati|faria /patʃifa'ria/ f
roguishness; (uma) dirty trick. **~fe**
m scoundrel

patim /pa'tʃĩ/ m skate; **~ de rodas**
roller skate

pati|nação /patʃina'sãw/ f
skating; (rinque) skating rink.
~nador m skater. **~nar** vi
skate; ‹carro› skid. **~nete** /ɛ/ m
skateboard

pátio /'patʃiu/ m courtyard; (de
escola) playground

pato /'patu/ m duck

pato|logia /patolo'ʒia/ f
pathology. **~lógico** a pathological.
~logista m/f pathologist

patrão /pa'trãw/ m boss

pátria /'patria/ f homeland

patriar|ca /patri'arka/ m patriarch.
~cal (pl **~cais**) a patriarchal

patrimônio /patri'moniu/ m
(bens) estate, property; fig (herança)
heritage

patri|ota /patri'ɔta/ m/f patriot.
~ótico a patriotic. **~otismo** m
patriotism

patroa /pa'troa/ f boss; Ⅱ (esposa)
missus, wife

patro|cinador /patrosina'dor/ m
sponsor. **~cinar** vt sponsor. **~cínio**
m sponsorship

patru|lha /pa'truʎa/ f patrol.
~lhar vt/i patrol.

pau /paw/ m stick; 🇧 (cruzeiro)
cruzeiro; (chulo) (pênis) prick; pl
(naipe) clubs; **a meio ~** at half
mast; **rachar ~** 🇧 (brigar) row,
fight like cat and dog. **~lada** f blow
with a stick

paulista /paw'lista/ a & m/f
(person) from (the state of) São
Paulo. **~no** a & m (person) from (the
city of) São Paulo

pausa /'pawza/ f pause. **~do** a slow

pauta /'pawta/ f (em papel) lines;
(de música) stave; fig (de discussão
etc) agenda. **~do** a (papel) lined

pavão /pa'vãw/ m peacock

pavilhão /pavi'ʎãw/ m pavilion;
(no jardim) summer house

pavimen|tar /pavimẽ'tar/ vt
pave. **~to** m floor; (de rua etc)
surface

pavio /pa'viu/ m wick

pavor /pa'vor/ m terror; **ter ~ de**
be terrified of. **~oso** /o/ a dreadful

paz /pas/ f peace; **fazer as ~s**
make up

pé /pɛ/ m foot; (planta) plant; (de
móvel) leg; **a ~** on foot; **ao ~ da
letra** literally; **estar de ~** <festa etc>
be on; **ficar de ~** stand up; **em ~**
standing (up); **em ~ de igualdade**
on an equal footing; **~ de atleta**
athlete's foot; **~ de meia** nest egg;
~ de pato flipper; **~ de vento** gust
of wind

peão /pi'ãw/ m Port (pedestre)
pedestrian; (no xadrez) pawn

peça /'pɛsa/ f piece; (de máquina,
carro etc) part; (teatral) play;
pregar uma ~ em play a trick on;
~ de reposição spare part; **~ de**

vestuário item of clothing

pe|cado /pe'kadu/ m sin. **~cador** m
sinner. **~caminoso** /o/ a sinful. **~car**
vi (contra a religião) sin; fig fall down

pechin|cha /pe'ʃĩʃa/ f bargain.
~char vi bargain, haggle

peçonhento /peso'ɲẽtu/ a
animais **~s** vermin

pecu|ária /peku'aria/ f livestock
farming. **~ário** a livestock. **~arista**
m/f livestock farmer

peculi|ar /pekuli'ar/ a peculiar.
~aridade f peculiarity

pecúlio /pe'kuliu/ m savings

pedaço /pe'dasu/ m piece; **aos ~s**
in pieces; **cair aos ~s** fall to pieces

pedágio /pe'daʒiu/ m toll; (cabine)
tollbooth

peda|gogia /pedago'ʒia/ f
education. **~gógico** a educational.
~gogo /o/ m educationalist

pe|dal /pe'daw/ (pl **~dais**) m pedal.
~dalar vt/i pedal

pedante /pe'dãtʃi/ a pretentious
● m/f pseud

pederneira /peder'nera/ f flint

pedes|tal /pedes'taw/ (pl **~tais**)
m pedestal

pedestre /pe'destri/ a & m/f
pedestrian

pedia|tra /pedʒi'atra/ m/f
paediatrician. **~tria** f paediatrics

pedicuro /pedʒi'kuru/ m
chiropodist, Amer podiatrist

pe|dido /pe'dʒidu/ m request;
(encomenda) order; **a ~dido de** at
the request of; **~dido de demissão**
resignation; **~dido de desculpa**
apology. **~dir** vt ask for; (num
restaurante etc) order; **~dir algo
a alguém** ask sb for sth; **~dir**

para algém ir ask sb to go; **~dir desculpa** apologize; **~dir em casamento** propose to ● *vi* ask; (*num restaurante etc*) order

pedinte /pe'dʒitʃi/ *m/f* beggar

pedra /'pedra/ stone; **~ de gelo** ice cube; **chuva de ~** hail; **~ pomes** pumice stone

pedregoso /pedre'gozu/ *a* stony

pedreiro /pe'dreru/ *m* builder

pegada /pe'gada/ *f* footprint; (*de goleiro*) save; **~ ecológica** carbon footprint

pegajoso /pega'ʒozu/ *a* sticky

pegar /pe'gar/ *vt* get; catch ‹*bola, doença, ladrão, ônibus*›; (*segurar*) get hold of; pick up ‹*emissora, hábito, mania*›; **~ bem/mal** go down well/badly; **~ fogo** catch fire; **pega essa rua** take that street; **~ em grab**; **~ no sono** get to sleep ● *vi* (*aderir*) stick; ‹*doença*› be catching; ‹*moda*› catch on; ‹*carro, motor*› start; ‹*mentira, desculpa*› stick. **~se** *vpr* come to blows

pego /'pegu/; *pp de* ▶ PEGAR

pei|dar /pej'dar/ *vi* (*chulo*) fart. **~do** *m* (*chulo*) fart

pei|to /'pejtu/ *m* chest; (*seio*) breast; *fig* (*coragem*) guts. **~toril** (*pl* **~toris**) *m* window sill. **~tudo** *a* ‹*mulher*› busty; *fig* (*corajoso*) gutsy

pei|xaria /pe'ʃaria/ *f* fishmonger's. **~xe** *m* fish; **Peixes** (*signo*) Pisces. **~xeiro** *m* fishmonger

pela = **por** + **a**

pelado /pe'ladu/ *a* (*nu*) naked, in the nude

pelan|ca /pe'lãka/ *f* roll of fat; *pl* flab. **~cudo** *a* flabby

pelar /pe'lar/ *vt* peel ‹*fruta, batata*›; skin ‹*animal*›; Ⓣ (*tomar dinheiro de*) fleece

pelas = **por** + **as**

pele /'peli/ *f* skin; (*como roupa*) fur. **~teiro** *m* furrier. **~teria** *f* furrier's

pelica /pe'lika/ *f* **luvas de ~** kid gloves

pelicano /peli'kanu/ *m* pelican

película /pe'likula/ *f* skin

pelo /'pelu/ *m* hair; (*de animal*) coat; **nu em ~** stark naked; **montar em ~** ride bareback

pelo² = **por** + **o**

pelos = **por** + **os**

pelotão /pelo'tãw/ *m* platoon

pelúcia /pe'lusia/ *f* **bicho de ~** soft toy, fluffy animal

peludo /pe'ludu/ *a* hairy

pen /'pɛn/ *f* Port memory stick

pena¹ /'pena/ *f* (*de ave*) feather; (*de caneta*) nib

pena² /'pena/ *f* (*castigo*) penalty; (*de amor etc*) pang; **é uma ~ que** it's a pity that; **que ~!** what a pity! **dar ~** be upsetting; **estar com** ou **ter ~ de** feel sorry for; **(não) vale a ~** it's (not) worth it; **vale a ~ tentar** it's worth trying; **~ de morte** death penalty

penada /pe'nada/ *f* stroke of the pen

pe|nal /pe'naw/ (*pl* **~nais**) *a* penal. **~nalidade** *f* penalty. **~nalizar** *vt* penalize

pênalti /'pɛnawtʃi/ *m* penalty

penar /pe'nar/ *vi* suffer

pen|dente /pẽ'dẽtʃi/ *a* hanging; *fig* (*causa*) pending. **~der** *vi* hang; (*inclinar-se*) slope; (*tender*) be inclined (**a** to). **~dor** *m* inclination

pen drive *m* memory stick

pêndulo /'pẽdulu/ *m* pendulum

pendu|rado /pẽdu'radu/ *a* hanging; Ⓣ (*por fazer, pagar*)

outstanding. **~rar** *vt* hang (up); 🔲
put on the slate *<compra>* ● *vi* 🔲
pay later. **~ricalho** *m* pendant

penedo /pe'nedu/ *m* rock

penei|ra /pe'nera/ *f* sieve. **~rar** *vt*
sieve, sift ● *vi* drizzle

pene|tra /pe'nɛtra/ *m/f* 🔲
gatecrasher. **~tração** *f* penetration;
fig perspicacity. **~trante** *a* *<som,
olhar>* piercing; *<dor>* sharp;
<ferida> deep; *<frio>* biting; *<análise,
espírito>* incisive, perceptive. **~trar**
vt penetrate ● *vi* **~trar em** enter
<casa>; *fig* penetrate

penhasco /pe'nasku/ *m* cliff

penhoar /peno'ar/ *m* dressing
gown

penhor /pe'ɲor/ *m* pledge; **casa de
~es** pawnshop

penicilina /penisi'lina/ *f* penicillin

penico /pe'niku/ *m* potty

península /pe'nĩsula/ *f* peninsula

pênis /'penis/ *m invar* penis

penitência /peni'tẽsia/ *f*
(arrependimento) penitence;
(expiação) penance

penitenciá|ria /penitẽsi'aria/ *f*
prison. **~rio** *a* prison ● *m* prisoner

penoso /pe'nozu/ *a* *<experiência,
tarefa, assunto>* painful; *<trabalho,
viagem>* hard, difficult

pensa|dor /pẽsa'dor/ *m* thinker.
~mento *m* thought

pensão /pẽ'sãw/ *f (renda)* pension;
(hotel) guest house; **~ (alimentícia)**
(paga por ex-marido) alimony; **~
completa** full board

pen|sar /pẽ'sar/ *vt/i* think (**em** of
ou about). **~sativo** *a* thoughtful,
pensive

pên|sil /'pẽsiw/ *(pl* **~seis)** **a ponte
~sil** suspension bridge

penso /'pẽsu/ *m (curativo)* dressing

pentágono /pẽ'tagonu/ *m*
pentagon

pentatlo /pẽ'tatlu/ *m* pentathlon

pente /'pẽtʃi/ *m* comb. **~adeira** *f*
dressing table. **~ado** *m* hairstyle,
hairdo. **~ar** *vt* comb. **~ar-se** *vpr*
do one's hair; *(com pente)* comb
one's hair

Pentecostes /pẽte'kɔstʃis/ *m*
Whitsun

pente-fino /pẽtʃi'finu/ *m* **passar a
~** go over with a fine-tooth comb

pente|lhar /pẽte'ʎar/ *vt* 🔲 bother.
~lho /e/ *m* pubic hair; 🔲 *(pessoa
inconveniente)* pain (in the neck)

penugem /pe'nuʒe/ *f* down

penúltimo /pe'nuwtʃimu/ *a* last
but one, penultimate

penumbra /pe'nũbra/ *f* half-light

penúria /pe'nuria/ *f* penury,
extreme poverty

pepino /pe'pinu/ *m* cucumber

pepita /pe'pita/ *f* nugget

peque|nez /peke'nes/ *f* smallness;
fig pettiness. **~nininho** *a* tiny. **~no**
/e/ *a* small; *(mesquinho)* petty

pequeno-almoço
/pikenaw'mosu/ *m (pl* **pequenos-
almoços)** *Port* breakfast

Pequim /pe'kĩ/ *f* Peking, Beijing

pequinês /peki'nes/ *m* Pekinese

pera /'pera/ *f* pear

perambular /perãbu'lar/ *vi*
wander

perante /pe'rãtʃi/ *prep* before

percalço /per'kawsu/ *m* pitfall

perceber /perse'ber/ *vt* realize;
Port (entender) understand; *(psíqu)*
perceive

percen|tagem /persẽ'taʒe/ *f*
percentage. **~tual** *(pl* **~tuais)** *a & m*
percentage

percep|ção /persep'sãw/ f
perception. **~tível** (pl **~tíveis**) a
perceptible

percevejo /perse'veʒu/ m (bicho)
bedbug; (tachinha) drawing pin,
Amer thumbtack

per|correr /perko'xer/ vt cross;
cover ‹distância›; (viajar por) travel
through. **~curso** m journey

percus|são /perku'sãw/
f percussion. **~sionista** m/f
percussionist

percutir /perku'tʃir/ vt strike

perda /'perda/ f loss; **~ de tempo**
waste of time

perdão /per'dãw/ f pardon

perder /per'der/ vt lose; (não
chegar a ver, pegar) miss ‹ônibus,
programa na TV etc›; waste
‹tempo›; **~ algo de vista** lose sight
of sth ● vi lose. **~se** vpr get lost;
~se de alguém lose sb

perdiz /per'dʒis/ f partridge

perdoar /perdo'ar/ vt forgive (algo
a alguém sb for sth)

perdulário /perdu'lariu/ a & m
spendthrift

perdurar /perdu'rar/ vi endure;
‹coisa ruim› persist

pere|cer /pere'ser/ vi perish. **~cível**
(pl **~cíveis**) a perishable

peregri|nação /peregrina'sãw/ f
peregrination; (romaria) pilgrimage.
~nar vi roam; (por motivos religiosos)
go on a pilgrimage. **~no** m pilgrim

pereira /pe'rera/ f pear tree

peremptório /perẽp'tɔriu/ a
peremptory

perene /pe'reni/ a perennial

perereca /pere'reka/ f tree frog

perfazer /perfa'zer/ vt make up

perfeccionis|mo
/perfeksio'nizmu/ m perfectionism.
~ta a & m/f perfectionist

perfei|ção /perfej'sãw/ f
perfection. **~to** a & m perfect

per|fil /per'fiw/ (pl **~fis**) m profile.
~filar vt line up. **~filar-se** vpr line up

perfu|mado /perfu'madu/ a ‹flor,
ar› fragrant; ‹sabonete etc› scented;
‹pessoa› with perfume on. **~mar** vt
perfume. **~mar-se** vpr put perfume
on. **~maria** f perfumery; [T]
trimmings, frills. **~me** m perfume

perfu|rador /perfura'dor/
m punch. **~rar** vt punch ‹papel,
bilhete›; drill through ‹chão›;
perforate ‹úlcera, pulmão etc›.
~ratriz f drill

pergaminho /perga'miɲu/ m
parchment

pergun|ta /per'gũta/ f question;
fazer uma ~ta ask a question. **~tar**
vt/i ask; **~tar algo a alguém** ask sb
sth; **~tar por** ask after

perícia /pe'risia/ f (mestria)
expertise; (inspeção) investigation;
(peritos) experts

perici|al /perisi'aw/ (pl **~ais**) a
expert

pericli|tante /perikli'tãtʃi/ a
precarious. **~tar** vi be at risk

peri|feria /perife'ria/ f periphery;
(da cidade) outskirts. **~férico** a & m
peripheral

perigo /pe'rigu/ m danger. **~so** /o/
a dangerous

perímetro /pe'rimetru/ m
perimeter

periódico /peri'ɔdʒiku/ a periodic
● m periodical

período /pe'riodu/ m period;
trabalhar meio ~ work part-time

peripécias /peri'pesias/ f pl ups and downs, vicissitudes

periquito /peri'kitu/ m parakeet; (de estimação) budgerigar

periscópio /peris'kopiu/ m periscope

perito /pe'ritu/ a & m expert (em at)

per|jurar /perʒu'rar/ vi commit perjury. **~júrio** m perjury. **~juro** m perjurer

perma|necer /permane'ser/ vi remain. **~nência** f permanence; (estadia) stay. **~nente** a permanent ● f perm

permeá|vel /permi'avew/ (pl **~veis**) a permeable

permis|são /permi'sãw/ f permission. **~sível** (pl **~síveis**) a permissible. **~sivo** a permissive

permitir /permi'tʃir/ vt allow, permit; **~ a alguém ir** allow sb to go

permutar /permu'tar/ vt exchange

perna /'pɛrna/ f leg

pernicioso /pernisi'ozu/ a pernicious

per|nil /per'niw/ (pl **~nis**) m leg

pernilongo /perni'lõgu/ m (large) mosquito

pernoi|tar /pernoj'tar/ vi spend the night. **~te** m overnight stay

pérola /'pɛrola/ f pearl

perpendicular /perpẽdʒiku'lar/ a perpendicular

perpetrar /perpe'trar/ vt perpetrate

perpetu|ar /perpetu'ar/ vt perpetuate. **~idade** f perpetuity

perpétu|o /per'pɛtuu/ a perpetual; **prisão ~a** life imprisonment

perple|xidade /perpleksi'dadʒi/ f puzzlement. **~xo** /ɛ/ a puzzled

persa /'pɛrsa/ a & m/f Persian

perse|guição /persegi'sãw/ f pursuit; (de minorias etc) persecution. **~guidor** m pursuer; (de minorias etc) persecutor. **~guir** vt pursue; persecute ‹minoria, seita etc›

perseve|rança /perseve'rãsa/ f perseverance. **~rante** a persevering. **~rar** vi persevere

persiana /persi'ana/ f blind

pérsico /'pɛrsiku/ a **Golfo Pérsico** Persian Gulf

persignar-se /persig'narsi/ vt cross o.s.

persis|tência /persis'tẽsia/ f persistence. **~tente** a persistent. **~tir** vi persist

perso|nagem /perso'naʒẽ/ m/f (pessoa famosa) personality; (em livro, filme etc) character. **~nalidade** f personality. **~nalizar** vt personalize. **~nificar** vt personify

perspectiva /perspek'tʃiva/ f (na arte, ponto de vista) perspective; (possibilidade) prospect

perspi|cácia /perspi'kasia/ f insight, perceptiveness. **~caz** a perceptive

persua|dir /persua'dʒir/ vt persuade (**alguém a** s.o. to). **~são** f persuasion. **~sivo** a persuasive

perten|cente /pertẽ'sẽtʃi/ a belonging (**a** to); (que tem a ver com) pertaining (**a** to). **~cer** vi belong (a to); (referir-se) pertain (**a** to). **~ces** m pl belongings

perto /'pɛrtu/ adv near (**de** to); **aqui ~** near here, nearby; **de ~** closely; ‹ver› close up

pertur|bação /perturba'sãw/ f
disturbance; (do espírito) anxiety.
~bado a ⟨pessoa⟩ unsettled,
troubled. **~bar** vt disturb. **~bar-se**
vpr get upset, be perturbed

peru /pe'ru/ m turkey

Peru /pe'ru/ m Peru

perua /pe'rua/ f (carro grande)
estate car, Amer station wagon;
(caminhonete) van; (para escolares
etc) minibus; ⟦!⟧ (mulher) brassy
woman

peruano /peru'ano/ a & m
Peruvian

peruca /pe'ruka/ f wig

perver|são /perver'sãw/ f
perversion. **~so** a perverse. **~ter**
vt pervert

pesadelo /peza'delu/ m nightmare

pesado /pe'zadu/ a heavy; ⟨estilo,
livro⟩ heavy going ● adv heavily

pêsames /'pezamis/ m pl
condolences

pesar¹ /pe'zar/ vt weigh; fig (avaliar)
weigh up ● vi weigh; (influir) carry
weight; **~ sobre** ⟨ameaça etc⟩ hang
over. **~se** vpr weigh o.s.

pesar² /pe'zar/ m sorrow. **~oso** /o/
a sorry, sorrowful

pes|ca /'peska/ f fishing; **ir à ~ca** go
fishing. **~cador** m fisherman. **~car**
vt catch; (retirar da água) fish out
● vi fish; ⟦!⟧ (entender) understand;
(cochilar) nod off; **~car de** ⟦!⟧ know
all about

pescoço /pes'kosu/ m neck

peseta /pe'zeta/ f peseta

peso /'pezu/ m weight; **de ~**
fig ⟨pessoa⟩ influential; ⟨livro,
argumento⟩ authoritative

pesqueiro /pes'keru/ a fishing

pesqui|sa /pes'kiza/ f research;
(uma) study; pl research; **~sa de**
mercado market research. **~sador**
m researcher. **~sar** vt/i research

pêssego /'pesigu/ m peach

pessegueiro /pesi'geru/ m
peach tree

pessimis|mo /pesi'mizmu/ m
pessimism. **~ta** a pessimistic ● m/f
pessimist

péssimo /'pesimu/ a terrible, awful

pesso|a /pe'soa/ f person; pl
people; **em ~a** in person. **~al** (pl
~ais) a personal ● m staff; ⟦!⟧ folks

pesta|na /pes'tana/ f eyelash; **tirar
uma ~na** ⟦!⟧ have a nap. **~nejar**
vi blink; **sem ~nejar** fig without
batting an eyelid

pes|te /'pestʃi/ f (doença) plague;
(criança etc) pest. **~ticida** m
pesticide

pétala /'petala/ f petal

peteca /pe'tɛka/ f kind of
shuttlecock; (jogo) kind of
badminton played with the hand

peteleco /pete'lɛku/ m flick

petição /petʃi'sãw/ f petition

petisco /pe'tʃisku/ m savoury, titbit

petrifi|car /petrifi'kar/ vt petrify;
(de surpresa) stun. **~se** vpr be
petrified; (de surpresa) be stunned

petroleiro /petro'leru/ a oil ● m
oil tanker

petróleo /pe'trɔliu/ m oil,
petroleum; **~ bruto** crude oil

petrolífero /petro'liferu/ a
oil-producing

petroquími|ca /petro'kimika/
f petrochemicals. **~co** a
petrochemical

petu|lância /petu'lãsia/ f cheek.
~lante a cheeky

peúga /pi'uga/ f Port sock

pevide /pe'vidʒi/ f Port pip

pia /'pia/ f (*do banheiro*) washbasin; (*da cozinha*) sink; ~ **batismal** font

piada /pi'ada/ f joke

pia|nista /pia'nista/ m/f pianist. ~**no** m piano; ~**no de cauda** grand piano

piar /pi'ar/ vi ⟨*pinto*⟩ cheep; ⟨*coruja*⟩ hoot

picada /pi'kada/ f (*de agulha, alfinete etc*) prick; (*de abelha, vespa*) sting; (*de mosquito, cobra*) bite; (*de heroína*) shot; (*de avião*) nosedive; **o fim da** ~ fig the limit

picadeiro /pika'deru/ m ring

picante /pi'kãtʃi/ a ⟨*comida*⟩ hot, spicy; ⟨*piada*⟩ risqué; ⟨*filme, livro*⟩ raunchy

pica-pau /pika'paw/ m woodpecker

picar /pi'kar/ vt (*com agulha, alfinete etc*) prick; ⟨*abelha, vespa, urtiga*⟩ sting; ⟨*mosquito, cobra*⟩ bite; ⟨*pássaro*⟩ peck; chop ⟨*carne, alho etc*⟩; shred ⟨*papel*⟩ ● vi ⟨*peixe*⟩ bite; ⟨*lã, cobertor*⟩ prickle

picareta /pika'reta/ f pickaxe

pi|chação /piʃa'sãw/ f piece of graffiti, pl graffiti. ~**char** vt spray with graffiti ⟨*muro, prédio*⟩; spray ⟨*grafite, desenho*⟩. ~**che** m pitch

picles /'piklis/ m pl pickles

pico /'piku/ m peak; **20 anos e** ~ Port just over 20

picolé /piko'lɛ/ m ice lolly

pico|tar /piko'tar/ vt perforate. ~**te** /ɔ/ m perforations

pie|dade /pie'dadʒi/ f (*religiosidade*) piety; (*compaixão*) pity. ~**doso** /o/ a merciful, compassionate

pie|gas /pi'egas/ a invar ⟨*filme, livro*⟩ sentimental, schmaltzy; ⟨*pessoa*⟩ soppy. ~**guice** f sentimentality

piercing m piercing

pifar /pi'far/ vi 🔲 break down, go wrong

pigar|rear /pigaxi'ar/ vi clear one's throat. ~**ro** m frog in the throat

pigmento /pig'mẽtu/ m pigment

pig|meu /pig'mew/ a & m (f ~**meia**) pygmy

pijama /pi'ʒama/ m pyjamas

pilantra /pi'lãtra/ m/f 🔲 crook

pilão /pi'lãw/ m (*na cozinha*) pestle; (*na construção*) ram

pilar /pi'lar/ m pillar

pilastra /pi'lastra/ f pillar

pileque /pi'lɛki/ m drinking session; **tomar um** ~ get drunk

pilha /'piʎa/ f (*monte*) pile; (*elétrica*) battery

pilhar /pi'ʎar/ vt pillage

pilhéria /pi'ʎɛria/ f joke

pilotar /pilo'tar/ vt fly, pilot ⟨*avião*⟩; drive ⟨*carro*⟩

pilotis /pilo'tʃis/ m pl pillars

piloto /pi'lotu/ m pilot; (*de carro*) driver; (*de gás*) pilot light ● a invar pilot

pílula /'pilula/ f pill

pimen|ta /pi'mẽta/ f pepper; ~**ta-de-Caiena** cayenne pepper. ~**ta-do-reino** f black pepper; ~**ta-malagueta** /e/ f ~**tas-malagueta**/ f chilli pepper. ~**tão** m (bell) pepper. ~**teira** f pepper pot

PIN /'pin/ m PIN (number)

pinacoteca /pinako'tɛka/ f art gallery

pin|ça /'pĩsa/ (*para tirar pelos*) tweezers; (*para segurar*) tongs; (*de siri etc*) pincer. ~**çar** vt pluck ⟨*sobrancelhas*⟩

pin|cel /pĩ'sɛw/ (pl ~**céis**) m brush. ~**celada** f brush stroke. ~**celar** vt paint

pin|ga /'pĩga/ f Brazilian rum. ~**gado** a ‹café› with a dash of milk. ~**gar** vi drip; (começar a chover) spit (with rain) ● vt drip. ~**gente** m pendant. ~**go** m drop; (no i) dot

pingue-pongue /pĩgi'põgi/ m table tennis

pinguim /pĩ'gwĩ/ m penguin

pi|nha /'piɲa/ f pine cone. ~**nheiro** f pine tree. ~**nho** m pine

pino /'pinu/ m pin; (para trancar carro) lock; a ~ upright; **bater** ~ ‹carro› knock

pin|ta /'pĩta/ f (sinal) mole; 🅵 (aparência) look. ~**tar** vt paint; dye ‹cabelo›; make-up on ‹rosto, olhos› ● vi paint; 🅵 ‹pessoa› show up; ‹problema, oportunidade› crop up. ~**tar-se** vpr put on make-up

pintarroxo /pĩta'xoʃu/ m robin

pinto /'pĩtu/ m chick

pin|tor /pĩ'tor/ m painter. ~**tura** f painting

pio¹ /'piu/ m (de pinto) cheep; (de coruja) hoot

pio² /'piu/ a pious

piolho /pi'oʎu/ m louse

pioneiro /pio'neru/ m pioneer ● a pioneering

pior /pi'ɔr/ a & adv worse; **o** ~ the worst

pio|ra /pi'ɔra/ f worsening. ~**rar** vt make worse, worsen ● vi get worse, worsen

pipa /'pipa/ f (que voa) kite; (de vinho) cask

pipilar /pipi'lar/ vi chirp

pipo|ca /pi'pɔka/ f popcorn. ~**car** vi spring up. ~**queiro** m popcorn seller

pique /'piki/ m (disposição) energy; **a** ~ vertically; **ir a** ~ ‹navio› sink

piquenique /piki'niki/ m picnic

pique|te /pi'ketʃi/ m picket. ~**teiro** m picket

pirado /pi'radu/ a 🅵 crazy

pirâmide /pi'ramidʒi/ f pyramid

piranha /pi'raɲa/ f piranha; 🅵 (mulher) maneater

pirar /pi'rar/ vi 🅵 flip out 🅵, go mad 🅵

pirata /pi'rata/ a & m/f pirate; ~ **informático** Port hacker. ~**ria** f piracy; ~**ria informática** Port hacking

pírcingue /'pirsĩge/ m Port piercing; ~ **de corpo** body piercing

pires /'piris/ m invar saucer

pirilampo /piri'lãpu/ m glow-worm

Pirineus /piri'news/ m pl Pyrenees

pirra|ça /pi'xasa/ f spiteful act; **fazer** ~**ça** be spiteful. ~**cento** a spiteful

pirueta /piru'eta/ f pirouette

pirulito /piru'litu/ m lollipop

pi|sada /pi'zada/ f step; (rastro) footprint. ~**sar** vt tread on; tread ‹uvas, palco›; (esmagar) trample on ● vi step; ~**sar em** step on; (entrar) set foot in

pis|cadela /piska'dɛla/ f wink. ~**ca-pisca** m indicator. ~**car** vi (com o olho) wink; (pestanejar) blink; ‹estrela, luz› twinkle; ‹motorista› indicate ● m num ~**car de olhos** in a flash

piscicultura /pisikuw'tura/ f fish farming; (lugar) fish farm

piscina /pi'sina/ f swimming pool

piso /'pizu/ m floor

pisotear /pizotʃi'ar/ vt trample

pista /'pista/ f track; (*da estrada*) carriageway; (*para aviões*) runway; (*de circo*) ring; (*dica*) clue; **~ de dança** dance floor

pistache /pis'tafi/ m, **pistacho** /pis'tafu/ m pistachio (nut)

pisto|la /pis'tɔla/ f pistol; (*para pintar*) spray gun. **~lão** m influential contact. **~leiro** m gunman

pitada /pi'tada/ f pinch

piteira /pi'tera/ f cigarette holder

pitoresco /pito'resku/ a picturesque

pitu /pi'tu/ m crayfish

pivete /pi'vetfi/ m/f child thief

pivô /pi'vo/ m pivot

pixaim /pifa'i/ a frizzy

pizza /'pitsa/ f pizza. **~ria** f pizzeria

placa /'plaka/ f plate; (*de carro*) number plate, *Amer* license plate; (*comemorativa*) plaque; (*em computador*) board; **~ de sinalização** road sign

placar /pla'kar/ m scoreboard; (*escore*) scoreline

plácido /'plasidu/ a placid

plagi|ário /plaʒi'ariu/ m plagiarist. **~ar** vt plagiarize

plágio /'plaʒiu/ m plagiarism

plaina /'plajna/ f plane

planador /plana'dor/ m glider

planalto /pla'nawtu/ m plateau

planar /pla'nar/ vi glide

planeamento, planear *Port* ▶ PLANEJAMENTO

plane|jamento /planeʒa'mẽtu/ m planning; **~jamento familiar** family planning. **~jar** vt plan

planeta /pla'neta/ m planet

planície /pla'nisi/ f plain

planificar /planifi'kar/ vt (*programar*) plan (out)

planilha /pla'niʎa/ f spreadsheet

plano /'planu/ a flat ● m plan; (*superfície, nível*) plane; **primeiro ~** foreground

planta /'plãta/ f plant; (*do pé*) sole; (*de edifício*) ground plan. **~ção** f (*ato*) planting; (*terreno*) plantation. **~do** a **deixar alguém ~do** 🛈 keep sb waiting around

plantão /plã'tãw/ m duty; (*noturno*) night duty; **estar de ~** be on duty

plantar /plã'tar/ vt plant

plas|ma /'plazma/ m plasma. **~mar** vt mould, shape

plásti|ca /'plastfika/ f facelift. **~co** a & m plastic

plataforma /plata'fɔrma/ f platform

plátano /'platanu/ m plane tree

plateia /pla'teja/ f audience; (*parte do teatro*) stalls, *Amer* orchestra

platina /pla'tfina/ f platinum. **~dos** m pl points

platônico /pla'toniku/ a platonic

plausí|vel /plaw'zivew/ (*pl* **~veis**) a plausible

ple|be /'plɛbi/ f common people. **~beu** a (f **~beia**) plebeian ● m (f **~beia**) commoner. **~biscito** m plebiscite

plei|tear /plejtfi'ar/ vt contest. **~to** m (*litígio*) case; (*eleitoral*) contest

ple|namente /plena'mẽtfi/ adv fully. **~nário** a plenary ● m plenary assembly. **~no** /e/ a full; **em ~no verão** in the middle of summer

plissado /pli'sadu/ a pleated

pluma /'pluma/ f feather. **~gem** f plumage

plu|ral /plu'raw/ (*pl* **~rais**) a & m plural

plutónio /plu'toniu/ m plutonium

pluvi|al /pluvi'aw/ (pl ~ais) a rain

pneu /pi'new/ m tyre. ~mático a pneumatic ● m tyre

pneumonia /pineumo'nia/ f pneumonia

pó /pɔ/ m powder; (poeira) dust; **leite em ~** powdered milk; **~ de arroz** (face) powder

pobre /'pɔbri/ a poor ● m/f poor man (f woman); **os ~s** the poor. **~za** /e/ f poverty

poça /'posa/ f pool; (deixada pela chuva) puddle

poção /po'sãw/ f potion

pocilga /po'siwga/ f pigsty

poço /'posu/ f (de água, petróleo) well; (de mina, elevador) shaft

podar /po'dar/ vt prune

podcast m podcast

----

poder /po'der/ ● v aux

····▶ (capacidade) can, to be able to; **posso escolher São Paulo ou Porto Alegre** I can choose São Paulo or Porto Alegre; **não podia acreditar** I couldn't believe it; **desde então, ele não pode andar** he hasn't been able to walk since then

····▶ (permissão) can, may; **posso sair?** can ou may I go out?

❗ Há duas traduções possíveis de **poder** quando se pede permissão para fazer algo: may e can. No entanto, observe que may é mais formal do que can: **posso entrar?** may I come in?, can I come in? (probabilidade) may, could, might; **isso pode ou não ser verdade** that may or may not be true

----

❗ **could** e **might** exprimem uma probabilidade menor do que may

● m

····▶ power; **tomar o ~** seize power; **~ de compra** purchasing power; **~ executivo/legislativo** executive/legislative power; **plenos ~es** full authority

····▶ (em expressões) **não ~ com alguém** dislike sb; **não posso com ele!** I can't stand him!; **não ~ mais** be exhausted; **querer é ~** where there's a will, there's a way

pode|rio /pode'riu/ m might. **~roso** /o/ a powerful

pódio /'pɔdʒiu/ m podium

podre /'podri/ a rotten; 🆃 (cansado) exhausted; (doente) grotty; **~ de rico** filthy rich. **~s** m pl faults

poei|ra /po'era/ f dust. **~rento** a dusty

poe|ma /po'ema/ m poem. **~sia** f (arte) poetry; (poema) poem. **~ta** m poet

poético /po'etʃiku/ a poetic

poetisa /poe'tʃiza/ f poetess

pois /pojs/ conj as, since; **~ é** that's right; **~ não** of course; **~ não?** can I help you?; **~ sim** certainly not

polaco /pu'laku/ Port a Polish ● m Pole; (língua) Polish

polar /po'lar/ a polar

polarizar /polari'zar/ vt polarize. **~-se** vpr polarize

pole|gada /pole'gada/ f inch. **~gar** m thumb

poleiro /po'leru/ m perch

polêmi|ca /po'lemika/ f
controversy, debate. **~co** a
controversial

pólen /'pɔlẽ/ m pollen

policia /po'lisia/ f police ● m/f
policeman (f-woman)

polici|al /polisi'aw/ (pl **~ais**)
a <carro, inquérito etc> police;
<romance, filme> detective ● m/f
policeman (f-woman). **~amento** m
policing. **~ar** vt police

poli|dez /poli'des/ f politeness.
~do a polite

poli|gamia /poliga'mia/ f
polygamy. **~glota** a & m/f polyglot

Polinésia /poli'nezia/ f Polynesia

polinésio /poli'neziu/ a & m
Polynesian

pólio /'pɔliu/ f polio

polir /po'lir/ vt polish

polissílabo /poli'silabu/ m
polysyllable

políti|ca /po'litʃika/ f politics;
(uma) policy. **~co** a political ● m
politician

polo[1] /'pɔlu/ m pole

polo[2] /'pɔlu/ m (jogo) polo; **~**
aquático water polo

polo|nês /polo'nes/ a (f **~nesa**)
Polish ● m (f **~nesa**) Pole; (língua)
Polish

Polônia /po'lonia/ f Poland

polpa /'powpa/ f pulp

poltrona /pow'trona/ f armchair

polu|ente /polu'ẽtʃi/ a & m
pollutant. **~ição** f pollution. **~ir**
vt pollute

polvilhar /powvi'ʎar/ vt sprinkle

polvo /'powvu/ m octopus

pólvora /'pɔwvora/ f gunpowder

polvorosa /powvo'rɔza/ f uproar;
em ~ in uproar; <pessoa> in a flap

pomada /po'mada/ f ointment

pomar /po'mar/ m orchard

pom|ba /'põba/ f dove. **~bo** m
pigeon

pomo de Adão /pomudʒia'dãw/
m Adam's apple

pom|pa /'põpa/ f pomp. **~poso** /o/
a pompous

ponche /'põʃi/ m punch

ponderar /põde'rar/ vt/i ponder

pônei /'ponej/ m pony

ponta /'põta/ f end; (de faca, prego)
point; (de nariz, dedo, língua) tip; (de
sapato) toe; Cine, Teat (papel curto)
walk-on part; (no campo de futebol)
wing; (jogador) winger; **na ~ dos**
pés on tiptoe; **uma ~ de** a touch of
<ironia etc>; **aguentar as ~s** 🛈 hold
on. **~cabeça** /e/ f de **~cabeça**
upside down

pontada /põ'tada/ f (dor) twinge

pontapé /põta'pɛ/ m kick; **~ inicial**
kick-off

pontaria /põta'ria/ f aim; **fazer**
~ take aim

ponte /'põtʃi/ f bridge; **~ aérea**
shuttle; (em tempo de guerra) airlift;
~ de safena heart bypass; **~ pênsil**
suspension bridge

> ⓘ **ponte** If a public holiday
> falls on a Thursday or a
> Tuesday, it's common for
> people in Portugal or Brazil to take
> a day off in between. In Portugal, this
> practice is called *fazer ponte*
> (literally "make a bridge") between
> the holiday and the weekend,
> and is a very common way of
> extending holiday celebrations.

ponteiro /põ'teru/ m pointer; (de
relógio) hand

pontiagudo /pŏtʃiaˈgudu/ a sharp

pontilhado /pŏtʃiˈʎadu/ a dotted

ponto /ˈpõtu/ m point; (de costura, tricô) stitch; (no final de uma frase) full stop, Amer period; (sinalzinho, no i) dot; (de ônibus) stop; (no teatro) prompter; **a ~ de** on the point of; **ao ~** <carne> medium; **até certo ~** to a certain extent; **às duas em ~** at exactly two o'clock; **dormir no ~** 🛈 miss the boat; **entregar os ~s** 🛈 give up; **fazer ~** 🛈 hang out; **dois ~s** colon; **~ de exclamação/interrogação** exclamation/question mark; **~ de reciclagem** recycling point; **~ de táxi** taxi rank, Amer taxi stand; **~ de vista** point of view; **~ morto** neutral. **~ e vírgula** m semicolon

pontu|ação /põtuaˈsãw/ f punctuation. **~al** (pl **~ais**) a punctual. **~alidade** f punctuality. **~ar** vt punctuate

pontudo /põˈtudu/ a pointed

popa /ˈpopa/ f stern

popu|lação /populaˈsãw/ f population. **~lacional** (pl **~lacionais**) a population. **~lar** a popular. **~laridade** f popularity. **~larizar** vt popularize. **~larizar-se** vpr become popular

pôquer /ˈpoker/ m poker

por /por/ ● prep

••••➤ (lugar) circular pela direita drive on the right; passar pelo centro de Brasília go through the centre of Brasília; viajar pelo Brasil travel round Brazil; você passa ~ uma farmácia? are you going past a chemist's?; passo pela sua casa amanhã I'll drop in tomorrow

••••➤ (durante) for; só ~ uns dias only for a few days; (tempo aproximado) about; ~ volta de 8 horas about 8

••••➤ (causa) foi despedido ~ ser preguiçoso he was sacked for being lazy; ~ inveja/ciúme/hábito out of jealousy/envy/habit; faria qualquer coisa ~ você I'll do anything for you; trabalhar ~ dinheiro work for money

••••➤ (agente) by; assinado/escrito/pintado ~ signed/written/painted by

••••➤ (para com) for; sentir carinho ~ alguém to feel affection for sb

••••➤ (não feito) ~ lavar not yet washed; tive de deixar o trabalho ~ acabar I had to leave the work unfinished

••••➤ (substituição) ela irá ~ mim she'll go instead of me

••••➤ (preço) for; comprei ~ mil euros I bought it for a thousand euros

••••➤ (com verbos como agarrar, pegar) by; segurei-o pelo braço I grabbed him by the arm

••••➤ (em expressões) ~ isso so; ~ mim (no que me diz respeito) as far as I'm concerned; ~ mais que however much

pôr /por/ vt put; put on <roupa, chapéu, óculos>; (a <mesa, ovos> ● m o ~ do sol sunset. **~-se** vpr <sol> set; **~-se a** start to; **~-se a caminho** set off

porão /poˈrãw/ m (de prédio) basement; (de casa) cellar; (de navio) hold

porca /ˈpɔrka/ f (de parafuso) nut; (animal) sow

porção /porˈsãw/ f portion; **uma ~ de** (muitos) a lot of

porcaria /porkaˈria/ f (sujeira) filth; (coisa malfeita) piece of trash; pl trash

porcelana /porseˈlana/ f china

porcentagem /porsẽˈtaʒẽ/ f percentage

porco /ˈporku/ a filthy ● m (animal) pig; (carne) pork. **~espinho** (pl **~s-espinhos**) m porcupine

porém /poˈrẽj/ conj however

pormenor /pormeˈnɔr/ m detail

por|nô /porˈno/ a porn ● m porn film. **~nografia** f pornography. **~nográfico** a pornographic

poro /ˈpɔru/ m pore. **~so** /o/ a porous

por|quanto /porˈkwãtu/ conj since. **~que** /porˈki/ conj because; Port (por quê?) why. **~quê** /porˈke/ adv Port why ● m reason why

porquinho-da-índia /porkiɲuuadˈiˈdʒia/ (pl **~s-da-índia**) m guinea pig

porrada /poˈxada/ f 🔢 beating

porre /ˈpɔxi/ m 🔢 drinking session, booze-up 🔢; **de ~** drunk; **tomar um ~** get drunk

porta /ˈpɔrta/ f door

porta-aviões /pɔrtaviˈõjs/ m invar aircraft carrier

porta-bagagens /pɔrtabaˈgaʒãjʃ/ m Port ▶ PORTA-MALAS

porta-chaves /pɔrtaˈʃaviʃ/ m invar keyholder ou key-ring. **~joias** m invar jewellery box; **~lápis** m invar pencil holder; **~luvas** m invar glove compartment; **~malas** m invar boot, Amer trunk; **~níqueis** m invar purse

portador /portaˈdor/ m bearer

portagem /porˈtaʒẽ/ f Port toll

portanto /porˈtãtu/ conj therefore

portão /porˈtãw/ m gate

portar /porˈtar/ vt carry. **~-se** vpr behave

porta-retrato /pɔrtaxeˈtratu/ m photo frame. **~revistas** m invar magazine rack

portaria /portaˈria/ f (entrada) entrance; (decreto) decree

portátil /porˈtatʃiu/ m Port laptop

porta-toalhas /pɔrtatoˈaʎas/ m invar towel rail. **~voz** m/f spokesman (f-woman)

porte /ˈpɔrtʃi/ m (frete) carriage; (de cartas etc) postage; (de pessoa) bearing; (dimensão) scale; **de grande/pequeno ~** large-/small-scale

porteiro /porˈteru/ m doorman; **~ eletrônico** entryphone

porto /ˈportu/ m port; **o P~** Oporto. **~ de escala** m port of call; **P~ Rico** m Puerto Rico; **~riquenho** /e/ a & m Puerto Rican; **~ USB** m USB port

portuário /portuˈariu/ a port ● m dock worker, docker

portuense /portuˈẽsi/ a & m/f (person) from Oporto

Portugal /portuˈgaw/ m Portugal

portu|guês /portuˈges/ a & m (f **~guesa**) Portuguese

Português With over 250 million speakers, Portuguese is the sixth most widely spoken language in the world. The CPLP (Comunidade dos Países de Língua Portuguesa) comprises eight countries that have Portuguese as an official language: Angola, Brazil, Cape Verde, East Timor, Guinea-Bissau, Mozambique, Portugal, and São Tomé and Príncipe. African Portuguese-speaking countries are referred to as the PALOP (*Países Africanos de Língua Oficial Portuguesa*).

po|sar /po'zar/ *vi* pose. **~se** /o/ *f* pose; (*de filme*) exposure

pós-datar /pɔzda'tar/ *vt* post-date

pós-escrito /pɔzis'kritu/ *m* postscript

pós-gradua|ção /pɔzgradua'sãw/ *f* postgraduation. **~do** *a* & *m* postgraduate

pós-guerra /pɔz'gɛxa/ *m* post-war period; **a Europa do ~** post-war Europe

posi|ção /pozi'sãw/ *f* position. **~cionar** *vt* position. **~tivo** *a* & *m* positive

posologia /pozolo'ʒia/ *f* dosage

pos|sante /po'sãtʃi/ *a* powerful. **~se** /ɔ/ *f* (*de casa etc*) possession, ownership; (*do presidente etc*) swearing in; *pl* (*pertences*) possessions; **tomar ~se** take office; **tomar ~se de** take possession of

posses|são /pose'sãw/ *f* possession. **~sivo** *a* possessive. **~so** /ɛ/ *a* possessed; (*com raiva*) furious

possibili|dade /posibili'dadʒi/ *f* possibility. **~tar** *vt* make possible

possí|vel /po'sivew/ (*pl* **~veis**) *a* possible; **fazer todo o ~vel** do one's best

possuir /posu'ir/ *vt* possess; (*ser dono de*) own

posta /'pɔsta/ *f* (*de peixe*) steak

pos|tal /pos'taw/ (*pl* **~tais**) *a* postal ● *m* postcard

postar /pos'tar/ *vt* place. **~se** *vpr* position o.s.

poste /'pɔstʃi/ *m* post

pôster /'poster/ *m* poster

posteri|dade /posteri'dadʒi/ *f* posterity. **~or** *a* (*no tempo*) subsequent, later; (*no espaço*) rear. **~ormente** *adv* subsequently

postiço /pos'tʃisu/ *a* false

posto /'postu/ *m* post; **~ de gasolina**; petrol station, *Amer* gas station; **~ de saúde** health centre ● *pp de* ▶ **PÔR**. **~ que** although

póstumo /'pɔstumu/ *a* posthumous

postura /pos'tura/ *f* posture

potá|vel /po'tavew/ (*pl* **~veis**) *a* **água ~vel** drinking water

pote /'pɔtʃi/ *m* pot; (*de vidro*) jar

potência /po'tẽsia/ *f* power

poten|cial /potẽsi'aw/ (*pl* **~ciais**) *a* & *m* potential. **~te** *a* potent

potencializar /potẽsiali'zar/ *vt* ‹*vendas, crescimento*› boost

potenciar /putẽsi'ar/ *vt Port* ▶ **POTENCIALIZAR**

potro /'potru/ *m* foal

pouco /'poku/ *a* & *pron* little ● *adv* not much ● *m* **um ~** a little; **~ a ~** little by little; **aos ~s** gradually; **daqui a ~** shortly; **por ~** almost; **~ tempo** a short time

pou|pança /po'pãsa/ *f* saving; (*conta*) savings account. **~par** *vt* save; spare ‹*vida*›

pouquinho /po'kiɲu/ *m* **um ~ (de)** a little

pou|sada /po'zada/ *f inn*. **~sar** /a/ *vi* land. **~so** *m* landing

pousada In the 1940s, the *i* Portuguese government decided to create a series of hotels, called *pousadas*, in buildings of historic interest, such as convents, monasteries and castles. Although privately owned now, Portuguese *pousadas* still offer high-quality accommodation in very unique settings. In Brazil, a *pousada* is usually a guest house or a budget hotel.

po|vão /po'vãw/ *m* common people. **~vo** /o/ *m* people

povo|ação /povoa'sãw/ *f* settlement. **~ar** *vt* populate

poxa /'poʃa/ *int* gosh

pra /pra/ *prep* 🔃 ► **PARA**

praça /'prasa/ *f* (*largo*) square; (*mercado*) market ● *m* (*soldado*) private

prado /'pradu/ *m* meadow

pra-frente /pra'frẽtʃi/ *a invar* 🔃 with it 🔃, modern

praga /'praga/ *f* curse; (*inseto, doença, pessoa*) pest

prag|mático /prag'matʃiku/ *a* pragmatic. **~matismo** *m* pragmatism

praguejar /prage'ʒar/ *vt/i* curse

praia /'praja/ *f* beach

pran|cha /'prãʃa/ *f* plank; (*de surfe*) board. **~cheta** /e/ *f* drawing board

pranto /'prãtu/ *m* weeping

pra|ta /'prata/ *f* silver. **~taria** *f* (*coisas de prata*) silverware. **~teado** *a* silver-plated; (*cor*) silver

prateleira /prate'lera/ *f* shelf

prática /'pratʃika/ *f* practice; **na ~** in practice

prati|cante /pratʃi'kãtʃi/ *a* practising ● *m/f* apprentice; (*de esporte etc*) player. **~car** *vt* practise; (*cometer, executar*) carry out ● *vi* practise. **~cável** (*pl* **~cáveis**) *a* practicable

prático /'pratʃiku/ *a* practical

prato /'pratu/ *m* (*objeto*) plate; (*comida*) dish; (*parte de uma refeição*) course; (*do toca-discos*) turntable; *pl* (*instrumento*) cymbals; **~ fundo** dish; **~ principal** main course

praxe /'praʃi/ *f* normal practice; **de ~** usually

praxe The *código da praxe* *i* refers to a set of rules and traditions to be followed by students at Portuguese universities. Thought to have originated at Portugal's oldest university in Coimbra, the traditions start in freshers' week in which the *caloiros* (freshers) are subjected to various initiation rites and practical jokes, such as being made to walk around town with cans attached to their feet.

prazer /pra'zer/ *m* pleasure; **muito ~ (em conhecê-lo)** pleased to meet you. **~oso** /o/ *a* pleasurable

prazo /'prazu/ *m* term, time; **a ~** <*compra etc*> on credit; **a curto/ longo ~** in the short/long term; **último ~** deadline

preâmbulo /pri'ãbulu/ *m* preamble

precário /pre'kariu/ *a* precarious

precaução /prekaw'sãw/ *f* precaution

preca|ver-se /preka'versi/ *vpr* take precautions (**de** against). **~vido** *a* cautious

prece /'prɛsi/ f prayer

prece|dência /prɛse'dēsia/ f
precedence. **~dente** a preceding
● m precedent. **~der** vt/i precede

preceito /pre'sejtu/ m precept

precioso /presi'ozu/ a precious

precipício /presi'pisiu/ m
precipice

precipi|tação /presipita'sãw/
f haste; (chuva etc) precipitation.
~tado a ‹fuga› headlong;
‹decisão, ato› hasty, rash. **~tar** vt
(lançar) throw; (antecipar) hasten.
~tar-se vpr (lançar-se) throw o.s.;
(apressar-se) rush; (agir sem pensar)
act rashly

precisamente /presiza'mētʃi/
adv precisely

precisão /presi'zãw/ f precision,
accuracy

preci|sar /presi'zar/ vt (necessitar)
need; (indicar com exatidão) specify
● vi be necessary; **~sar de** need;
~so ir I have to go; **~sa-se** wanted.
~so a (exato) precise; (necessário)
necessary

preço /'presu/ m price; **~ de custo**
cost price; **~ fixo** set price

precoce /pre'kɔsi/ a ‹fruto› early;
‹velhice, calvície etc› premature;
‹criança› precocious

precon|cebido /prekõse'bidu/ a
preconceived. **~ceito** m prejudice.
~ceituoso a prejudiced

preconizar /prekoni'zar/ vt
advocate

precursor /prekur'sor/ m
forerunner

preda|dor /preda'dor/ m predator.
~tório a predatory

predecessor /predese'sor/ m
predecessor

predestinar /predestʃi'nar/ vt
predestine

predeterminar
/predetermi'nar/ vt predetermine

predição /predʒi'sãw/ f prediction

predile|ção /predʒile'sãw/ f
preference. **~to** /ɛ/ a favourite

prédio /'prɛdʒiu/ m building

predis|por /predʒis'por/ vt
prepare (para for); (tornar parcial)
prejudice (contra against).
~por-se vpr prepare o.s.. **~posto** a
predisposed; (contra) prejudiced

predizer /predʒi'zer/ vt predict,
foretell

predomi|nância
/predomi'nãsia/ f predominance.
~nante a predominant. **~nar** vi
predominate

predomínio /predo'miniu/ m
predominance

preencher /priē'ʃer/ vt fill; fill in,
Amer fill out ‹formulário›; meet
‹requisitos›

pré-escola /preis'kɔla/ f infant
school, Amer preschool. **~escolar**
a preschool; **~estreia** f preview;
~fabricado a prefabricated

prefácio /pre'fasiu/ m preface

prefei|to /pre'fejtu/ m mayor.
~tura f prefecture; (prédio) town
hall

prefe|rência /prefe'rēsia/ f
preference; (direito no trânsito)
right of way; **de ~rência**
preferably. **~rencial** (pl **~renciais**)
a preferential; ‹rua› main. **~rido** a
favourite. **~rir** vt prefer (a to). **~rível**
(pl **~ríveis**) a preferable

prefixo /pre'fiksu/ m prefix

prega /'prega/ f pleat

pregador¹ /prega'dor/ m (de
roupa) peg

pre|gador² /prega'dor/ *m* (*quem prega*) preacher. **~gão** *m* (*de vendedor*) cry; **o ~gão** (*na bolsa de valores*) trading; (*em leilão*) bidding

pregar¹ /pre'gar/ *vt* fix; (*com prego*) nail; sew on ‹botão›; **não ~ olho** not sleep a wink; **~ uma peça em** play a trick on; **~ um susto em alguém** give sb a fright

pregar² /pre'gar/ *vt/i* preach

prego /'pregu/ *m* nail

pregui|ça /pre'gisa/ *f* laziness; (*bicho*) sloth; **estou com ~ça de ir** I can't be bothered to go. **~çoso** *a* lazy

pré-histórico /prejs'tɔriku/ *a* prehistoric

preia-mar /preja'mar/ *f* high tide

prejudi|car /preʒudʒi'kar/ *vt* harm; damage ‹saúde›. **~car-se** *vpr* harm o.s.. **~cial** (*pl* **~ciais**) *a* harmful, damaging (**a** to)

prejuízo /preʒu'izu/ *m* damage; (*financeiro*) loss; **em ~ de** to the detriment of

prejulgar /preʒuw'gar/ *vt* prejudge

preliminar /prelimi'nar/ *a & m/f* preliminary

prelo /'prelu/ *m* printing press; **no ~** being printed

prelúdio /pre'ludʒiu/ *m* prelude

prematuro /prema'turu/ *a* premature

premeditar /premedʒi'tar/ *vt* premeditate

premente /pre'mẽtʃi/ *a* pressing

premi|ado /premi'adu/ *a* ‹romance, atleta etc› prizewinning; ‹bilhete, número etc› winning ● *m* prizewinner. **~ar** *vt* award a prize to ‹romance, atleta etc›; reward ‹honestidade, mérito›

prêmio /'premiu/ *m* prize; (*de seguro*) premium; **Grande Prêmio** (*de F1*) Grand Prix

premir /pre'mir/ *vt Port* press ‹tecla›

premissa /pre'misa/ *f* premiss

premonição /premoni'sãw/ *f* premonition

pré-na|tal /prena'taw/ (*pl* **~tais**) *a* antenatal, *Amer* prenatal

prenda /'prẽda/ *f Port* present; **~s domésticas** household chores. **~do** *a* domesticated

pren|dedor /prẽde'dor/ *m* clip; **~dedor de roupa** clothes peg. **~der** *vt* (*pregar*) fix; (*capturar*) arrest; (*atar*) tie up ‹cachorro›; tie back ‹cabelo›; (*restringir*) restrict; (*ligar afetivamente*) bind; **~der** (**a atenção de**) **alguém** grab sb ('s attention)

prenhe /'preɲi/ *a* pregnant

prenome /pre'nomi/ *m* first name

pren|sa /'prẽsa/ *f* press. **~sar** *vt* press

preocu|pação /preokupa'sãw/ *f* concern. **~pante** *a* worrying. **~par** *vt* worry. **~par-se** *vpr* worry (**com** about)

prepa|ração /prepara'sãw/ *f* preparation. **~rado** *m* preparation. **~rar** *vt* prepare. **~rar-se** *vpr* prepare, get ready. **~rativos** *m pl* preparations. **~ro** *m* preparation; (*competência*) knowledge; **~ro físico** physical fitness

preponderar /prepõde'rar/ *vi* prevail (**sobre** over)

preposição /prepozi'sãw/ *f* preposition

prerrogativa /prexoga'tʃiva/ *f* prerogative

presa /'preza/ *f* (*de caça*) prey; (*de cobra*) fang; (*de elefante*) tusk; **~ de guerra** spoils of war

prescin|dir /presi'dʒir/ vi ~dir de dispense with. ~dível (pl ~díveis) a dispensable

pres|crever /preskre'ver/ vt prescribe. ~crição f prescription; (norma) rule

presen|ça /pre'zẽsa/ f presence; ~ça de espírito presence of mind. ~ciar vt (estar presente a) be present at; (testemunhar) witness. ~te a & m present. ~tear vt ~tear alguém (com algo) give sb (sth as) a present

presépio /pre'zɛpiu/ m crib

preser|vação /prezerva'sãw/ f preservation. ~var vt preserve, protect. ~vativo m (em comida) preservative; (camisinha) condom

presi|dência /prezi'dẽsia/ f presidency; (de uma reunião) chair. ~dencial (pl ~denciais) a presidential. ~dencialismo m presidential system. ~dente (f ~denta) president; (de uma reunião) chairperson

presidiário /prezidʒi'ariu/ m convict

presídio /pre'zidʒiu/ m prison

presidir /prezi'dʒir/ vi preside (a over)

presilha /pre'ziʎa/ f fastener; (de cabelo) slide

preso /'prezu/ pp de ▶ PRENDER ● m prisoner; ficar ~ get stuck; ‹saia, corda etc› get caught

pressa /'presa/ f hurry; às ~s in a hurry, hurriedly; estar com ou ter ~ be in a hurry

presságio /pre'saʒiu/ m omen

pressão /pre'sãw/ f pressure; fazer ~ sobre put pressure on; ~ arterial blood pressure

pressen|timento /presẽtʃi'mẽtu/ m premonition, feeling. ~tir vt sense

pressionar /presio'nar/ vt press ‹botão›; pressure ‹pessoa›

pressupor /presu'por/ vt ‹pessoa› presume; ‹coisa› presuppose

pressurizado /presuri'zadu/ a pressurized

pres|tação /presta'sãw/ f repayment, instalment. ~tar vt render ‹contas, serviço›; não ~ta he/it is no good; ~tar atenção pay attention; ~tar juramento take an oath ● vi be of use. ~tativo a helpful. ~tável (pl ~táveis) a serviceable

prestes /'prestʃis/ a invar ~ a about to

prestidigita|ção /prestʃidʒiʒita-'sãw/ f conjuring. ~dor m conjurer

pres|tigiar /prestʃiʒi'ar/ vt give prestige to. ~tígio m prestige. ~tigioso /o/ a prestigious

préstimo /'prestʃimu/ m merit

presumir /prezu'mir/ vt presume

presun|ção /prezũ'sãw/ f presumption. ~çoso /o/ a presumptuous

presunto /pre'zũtu/ m ham

pretendente /pretẽ'dẽtʃi/ m/f (candidato) candidate, applicant

preten|der /pretẽ'der/ vt intend. ~são f pretension. ~sioso /o/ a pretentious

preterir /prete'rir/ vt disregard

pretérito /pre'teritu/ m preterite

pretexto /pre'testu/ m pretext

preto /'pretu/ a & m black. ~ e branco a invar black and white

prevalecer /prevale'ser/ vi prevail

prevenção /preve'sãw/ f (impedimento) prevention; (parcialidade) bias

prevenir /preve'nir/ vt (evitar) prevent; (avisar) warn. **~-se** vpr take precautions

preventivo /prevẽ'tʃivu/ a preventive

prever /pre'ver/ vt foresee, predict

previdência /previ'dẽsia/ f foresight; **~ social** social security

prévio /'previu/ a prior

previ|são /previ'zãw/ f prediction, forecast; **~são do tempo** weather forecast. **~sível** (pl **~síveis**) a predictable

pre|zado /pre'zadu/ a esteemed; **Prezado Senhor** Dear Sir. **~zar** vt think highly of. **~zar-se** vpr have self-respect

prima /'prima/ f cousin

primário /pri'mariu/ a primary; (fundamental) basic

primata /pri'mata/ m primate

primave|ra /prima'vera/ f spring; (flor) primrose. **~ril** (pl **~ris**) a spring

primazia /prima'zia/ f primacy

primei|ra /pri'mera/ f (marcha) first (gear); **de ~ra** first-rate; ‹carne› prime. **~ra-dama** (pl **~ras-damas**) f first lady. **~ranista** m/f first-year (student). **~ro** a & adv first; **no dia ~ro de maio** on the first of May; **em ~ro lugar** (para começar) in the first place; (numa corrida, competição) in first place; **~ro de tudo** first of all; **~ros socorros** first aid. **~ro-ministro** (pl **~ros-ministros**) m (f **~ra-ministra**) prime-minister

primitivo /primi'tʃivu/ a primitive

primo /'primu/ m cousin ● a **número ~** prime number. **~-gênito**

a & m firstborn

primor /pri'mor/ m perfection

primordi|al /primordʒi'aw/ (pl **~ais**) a (primitivo) primordial; (fundamental) fundamental

primoroso /primo'rozu/ a exquisite

princesa /pri'seza/ f princess

princi|pado /prisipi'adu/ m principality. **~pal** (pl **~pais**) a main ● m principal

príncipe /'prisipi/ m prince

principiante /prisipi'ãtʃi/ m/f beginner

princípio /pri'sipiu/ m (início) beginning; (regra) principle; **em ~** in principle; **por ~** on principle

priori|dade /priori'dadʒi/ f priority. **~tário** a priority

prisão /pri'zãw/ f (ato de prender) arrest; (cadeia) prison; (encarceramento) imprisonment; **~ perpétua** life imprisonment; **~ de ventre** constipation

prisioneiro /prizio'neru/ m prisoner

prisma /'prizma/ m prism

privação /priva'sãw/ f deprivation

privacidade /privasi'dadʒi/ f privacy

pri|vada /pri'vada/ f toilet. **~vado** a private; **~vado de** deprived of. **~var** vt deprive (de of). **~var-se** vpr deprive o.s. (de of)

privati|vo /priva'tʃivu/ a private. **~zar** vt privatize

privi|legiado /privileʒi'adu/ a privileged; ‹tratamento› preferential. **~legiar** vt favour. **~légio** m privilege

pro Ⓘ = **para + o**

pró /prɔ/ adv for ● m os ~s e os contras the pros and cons

proa /'proa/ f bow, prow

proativo /prɔa'tivu/ a proactive

probabilidade /probabili'dadʒi/ f probability

proble|ma /pro'blema/ m problem. ~mático a problematic

proce|dência /prose'dẽsia/ f origin. ~dente a logical; ~dente de coming from. ~der vi proceed; (comportar-se) behave; (na justiça) take legal action; ~der de come from. ~dimento m procedure; (comportamento) behaviour; (na justiça) proceedings

proces|sador /prosesa'dor/ m processor. ~sador de texto word processor. ~samento m processing; (na justiça) prosecution; ~samento de dados data processing. ~sar vt process; (por crime) prosecute; (por causa civil) sue. ~so /ɛ/ m process; (criminal) trial; (civil) lawsuit

procla|mação /proklama'sãw/ f proclamation. ~mar vt proclaim

procri|ação /prokria'sãw/ f procreation. ~ar vt/i procreate

procu|ra /pro'kura/ f search; (de produto) demand; à ~ra de in search of. ~ração f power of attorney. ~rado a sought after, in demand; ~rado pela polícia wanted by the police. ~rador m (mandatário) proxy; (advogado) public prosecutor. ~rar vt look for; (contatar) get in touch with; (ir visitar) look up; ~rar saber try to find out

prodígio /pro'dʒiʒiu/ m wonder; (pessoa) prodigy

prodigioso /prodʒiʒi'ozu/ a prodigious

pródigo /'prɔdigu/ a lavish, extravagant

produ|ção /produ'sãw/ f production. ~tividade f productivity. ~tivo a productive. ~to m product; (renda) proceeds; ~to nacional bruto gross national product; ~tos agrícolas agricultural produce. ~tor m producer ● a país ~tor de trigo wheat-producing country. ~zido a 🛈 (arrumado) done up. ~zir vt produce

proeminente /proemi'nẽtʃi/ a prominent

proeza /pro'eza/ f achievement

profa|nar /profa'nar/ vt desecrate. ~no a profane

profecia /profe'sia/ f prophecy

proferir /profe'rir/ vt utter; give ‹discurso, palestra›; pass ‹sentença›

profes|sar /profe'sar/ vt profess. ~so /ɛ/ a professed; ‹político etc› seasoned. ~sor m teacher; ~sor catedrático professor

pro|feta /pro'fɛta/ m prophet. ~fético a prophetic. ~fetizar vt prophesy

profissão /profi'sãw/ f profession

profissio|nal /profisio'naw/ (pl ~nais) a & m/f professional. ~nalismo m professionalism. ~nalizante a vocational. ~nalizar-se vpr ‹esportista etc› turn professional

profun|didade /profũdʒi'dadʒi/ f depth. ~do a deep; ‹sentimento etc› profound

profusão /profu'zãw/ f profusion

prog|nosticar /prognostʃi'kar/ vt forecast. ~nóstico m forecast; Med prognosis

progra|ma /pro'grama/ m programme; (de computador)

program; (*diversão*) thing to do.
~mação f programming. **~mador**
m programmer. **~mar** vt plan;
program ‹*computador etc*›. **~mável**
(*pl* **~máveis**) a programmable
progredir /progre'dʒir/ vi
progress
progres|são /progre'sãw/
f progression. **~sista** a & m/f
progressive. **~sivo** a progressive.
~so /ε/ m progress
proi|bição /proibi'sãw/ f ban
(**de** on). **~bido** a forbidden. **~bir**
vt forbid (**alguém de** sb to); ban
‹*livro, importações etc*›. **~bitivo** a
prohibitive
proje|ção /proʒe'sãw/ f
projection. **~tar** vt plan ‹*viagem,
estrada etc*›; design ‹*casa, carro etc*›;
project ‹*filme, luz*›
projé|til /pro'ʒεtʃiw/ (*pl* **~teis**) m
projectile
proje|tista /proʒe'tʃista/ m/f
designer. **~to** /ε/ m project; (*de casa,
carro*) design; **~to de lei** bill. **~tor**
m projector
prol /prɔw/ m **em** ~ **de** on behalf of
prole /'prɔli/ f offspring. **~tariado**
m proletariat. **~tário** a & m
proletarian
promessa /pro'mεsa/ f promise
prome|tedor /promete'dor/
a promising. **~ter** vt promise ● vi

(*dar esperança*) show promise; **~ter**
voltar promise to return
promíscuo /pro'miskuu/ a
promiscuous
promis|sor /promi'sor/ a
promising. **~sória** f promissory note
promoção /promo'sãw/ f
promotion
promontório /promõ'tɔriu/ m
promontory
promo|tor /promo'tor/ m
promoter; (*advogado*) prosecutor.
~ver vt promote
promulgar /promuw'gar/ vt
promulgate
prono|me /pro'nomi/ m pronoun.
~minal /e/ m ~minais) a pronominal
pron|tidão /prõtʃi'dãw/ f
readiness; **com ~tidão** promptly;
estar de ~tidão be at the ready.
~tificar vt get ready. **~tificar-se**
vpr volunteer (**a** to **para** for). **~to**
a ready; (*rápido*) prompt ● int
that's that. **~to-socorro** (*pl* **~tos-
socorros**) m casualty department;
Port (*reboque*) tow truck. **~tuário**
m (*manual*) manual, handbook;
(*médico*) notes; (*policial*) record, file
pronto-a-comer
/prõtwaku'mer/ m invar Port take-
away, Amer take-out
pronúncia /pro'nũsia/ f
pronunciation
pronunci|ado /pronũsi'adu/
a pronounced. **~amento** m
pronouncement. **~ar** vt pronounce
propagar /propa'gar/ vt
propagate ‹*espécie*›; spread
‹*notícia, ideia, fé*›. **~se** vpr spread;
‹*espécie*› propagate
propen|são /propẽ'sãw/ f
propensity. **~so** a inclined (**a** to)

pro|piciar /propisi'ar/ vt provide.
~pício a propitious

propina /pro'pina/ f bribe; Port
(escolar) fee

propor /pro'por/ vt propose.
~se vpr set o.s. <objetivo>; **~se a
estudar** set out to study

proporção /propor'sãw/ f
proportion

proporcio|nado
/proporsio'nadu/ a proportionate
(a to); **bem~nado** well
proportioned. **~nal** (pl **~nais**) a
proportional. **~nar** vt provide

proposi|ção /propozi'sãw/ f
proposition. **~tado** a, **~tal** (pl **~tais**)
a intentional

propósito /pro'pɔzitu/ m
intention; **a ~** by the way; **a ~ de** on
the subject of; **chegar a ~** arrive at
the right time; **de ~** on purpose

proposta /pro'pɔsta/ f proposal

propriamente /propria'mẽtʃi/
adv strictly; **a casa ~ dita** the house
proper

proprie|dade /proprie'dadʒi/
f property; (direito sobre bens)
ownership. **~tário** m owner; (de casa
alugada) landlord

próprio /'prɔpriu/ a (de si) own;
<sentido> literal; <nome> proper;
meu ~ carro my own car; **um carro
~** a car of my own; **o ~ rei** the king
himself; **~ a** peculiar to; **~ para**
suited to

prorro|gação /proxoga'sãw/ f
extension; (de dívida) deferment;
(em futebol etc) extra time. **~gar** vt
extend <prazo>; defer <pagamento>

pro|sa /'prɔza/ f prose. **~sador** m
prose writer. **~saico** a prosaic

proscrever /proskre'ver/ vt
proscribe

prospecto /pros'pektu/ m (livro)
brochure; (folheto) leaflet

prospe|rar /prospe'rar/ vi prosper.
~ridade f prosperity

próspero /'prɔsperu/ a prosperous

prosse|guimento
/prosegi'mẽtu/ m continuation.
~guir vt continue ● vi proceed,
go on

prostitu|ição /prostʃitui'sãw/ f
prostitution. **~ta** f prostitute

pros|tração /prostra'sãw/ f
debility. **~trado** a prostrate. **~trar**
vt prostrate; (enfraquecer) debilitate.
~trar-se vpr prostrate o.s.

protago|nista /protago'nista/
m/f protagonist. **~nizar** vt be at the
centre of <acontecimento>; feature
in <peça, filme>

prote|ção /prote'sãw/ f
protection. **~cionismo** m
protectionism. **~cionista** a & m/f
protectionist. **~ger** vt protect.
~gido m protégé

proteína /prote'ina/ f protein

protelar /prote'lar/ vt put off

protes|tante /protes'tãtʃi/ a & m/f
Protestant. **~tar** vt/i protest. **~to**
/ɛ/ m protest

protetor /prote'tor/ m protector
● a protective

protocolo /proto'kɔlu/ m
protocol; (registro) register

protótipo /pro'tɔtʃipu/ m
prototype

protuberância /protube'rãsia/
f bulge

pro|va /'prɔva/ f (que comprova)
proof; (teste) trial; (exame) exam;
(esportiva) competition; (de livro etc)

proof; pl (*na justiça*) evidence; **à ~va de bala** bulletproof; **pôr à ~va** put to the test. **~vado** a proven. **~var** vt try <*comida*>; try on <*roupa*>; try out <*carro, novo sistema etc*>; (*comprovar*) prove

prová|vel /proˈvavew/ (pl **~veis**) a probable

proveito /proˈvejtu/ m profit, advantage; **tirar ~ de** (*beneficiar-se*) profit from; (*explorar*) take advantage of. **~so** /o/ a useful

proveni|ência /proveniˈẽsia/ f origin. **~ente** a originating (**de** from)

proventos /proˈvẽtus/ m pl proceeds

prover /proˈver/ vt provide (**de** with)

provérbio /proˈverbiu/ m proverb

proveta /proˈveta/ f test tube; **bebê de ~** test-tube baby

provi|dência /proviˈdẽsia/ f (*medida*) measure, step; (*divina*) providence; **tomar ~dências** take steps, take action. **~denciar** vt (*prover*) get hold of, provide; (*resolver*) see to, take care of ● vi take action

província /proˈvĩsia/ f province; (*longe da cidade*) provinces

provinci|al /provĩsiˈaw/ (pl **~ais**) a provincial. **~ano** a & m provincial

provir /proˈvir/ vi come (**de** from); (*resultar*) be due (**de** to)

provi|são /proviˈzãw/ f provision. **~sório** a provisional

provo|cação /provokaˈsãw/ f provocation. **~cador, ~cante** a provocative. **~car** vt provoke; (*ocasionar*) cause

proximidade /prosimiˈdadʒi/ f closeness; pl (*imediações*) vicinity

próximo /ˈprɔsimu/ a (*no tempo*) next; (*perto*) near, close (**de** to); <*parente*> close; <*futuro*> near ● m neighbour, fellow man

pru|dência /pruˈdẽsia/ f prudence. **~dente** a prudent

prumo /ˈprumu/ m plumb line; **a ~** vertically

prurido /pruˈridu/ m itch

pseudônimo /psewˈdonimu/ m pseudonym

psica|nálise /psikaˈnalizi/ f psychoanalysis. **~nalista** m/f psychoanalyst

psi|cologia /psikoloˈʒia/ f psychology. **~cológico** a psychological. **~cólogo** m psychologist

psico|pata /psikoˈpata/ m/f psychopath. **~se** /ɔ/ f psychosis. **~terapeuta** m/f psychotherapist. **~terapia** f psychotherapy

psicótico /psiˈkɔtʃiku/ a & m psychotic

psique /ˈpsiki/ f psyche

psiqui|atra /psikiˈatra/ m/f psychiatrist. **~atria** f psychiatry. **~átrico** a psychiatric

psíquico /ˈpsikiku/ a psychic

pua /ˈpua/ f bit

puberdade /puberˈdadʒi/ f puberty

publi|cação /publikaˈsãw/ f publication. **~car** vt publish

publici|dade /publisiˈdadʒi/ f publicity; (*reclame*) advertising. **~tário** a publicity; (*de reclame*) advertising ● m advertising executive

público /'publiku/ a public ● m
public; (*plateia*) audience; **em ~**
in public; **o grande ~** the general
public

pudera /pu'dɛra/ int no wonder!

pudico /pu'dʒiku/ a prudish

pudim /pu'dʒĩ/ m pudding

pudor /pu'dor/ m modesty, shame

puelril /pue'riw/ (*pl* **~ris**) a puerile

pugilis|mo /puʒi'lizmu/ m
boxing. **~ta** m boxer

pu|ído /pu'idu/ a worn through.
~ir vt wear through

pujan|ça /pu'ʒãsa/ f power. **~te** a
powerful; (*de saúde*) robust

pular /pu'lar/ vt jump (over);
(*omitir*) skip ● vi jump; **~ de
contente** jump for joy; **~ carnaval**
celebrate Carnival; **~ corda** skip

pulga /'puwga/ f flea

pulmão /puw'mãw/ m lung

pulo /'pulu/ m jump; **dar um ~ em**
drop by; **dar ~s** jump up and down

pulôver /pu'lover/ m pullover

púlpito /'puwpitu/ m pulpit

pul|sar /puw'sar/ vi pulsate. **~seira**
f bracelet. **~so** m (*do braço*) wrist;
(*batimento arterial*) pulse

pulular /pulu'lar/ vi swarm (**de**
with)

pulveri|zador /puwveriza'dor/
m spray. **~zar** vt spray (*líquido*);
(*reduzir a pó*) fig pulverize

pun|gente /pũ'ʒẽtʃi/ a
consuming. **~gir** vt afflict

pu|nhado /pu'ɲadu/ m handful.
~nhal (*pl* **~nhais**) m dagger.
~nhalada f stab wound. **~nho**
m fist; (*de camisa etc*) cuff; (*de
espada*) hilt

pu|nição /puni'sãw/ f punishment.
~nir vt punish. **~nitivo** a punitive

pupila /pu'pila/ f pupil

purê /pu're/ m purée; **~ de batata**
mashed potato

pureza /pu'reza/ f purity

pur|gante /pur'gãtʃi/ a & m
purgative. **~gar** vt purge. **~gatório**
m purgatory

purificar /purifi'kar/ vt purify

puritano /puri'tanu/ a & m puritan

puro /'puru/ a pure; (*aguardente*)
neat; **~ e simples** pure and simple.
~sangue (*pl* **~s-sangues**) a & m
thoroughbred

púrpura /'purpura/ a purple

purpurina /purpu'rina/ f glitter

purulento /puru'lẽtu/ a festering

pus /pus/ m pus

pusilânime /puzi'lanimi/ a
faint-hearted

pústula /'pustula/ f pimple

puta /'puta/ f whore ● a ihvar 🅣 **um
~ carro** one hell of a car; **filho da
~** (*vulg*) bastard; **~ que (o) pariu!**
(*chulo*) fucking hell!

puto /'putu/ a 🅣 furious

putrefazer /putrefa'zer/ vi
putrefy

puxa /'puʃa/ int gosh

pu|xado /pu'ʃadu/ a 🅣 (*exame*)
tough; (*trabalho*) hard; (*aluguel,
preço*) steep. **~xador** m handle.
~xão m pull, tug. **~xa-puxa** m
toffee. **~xar** vt pull; strike up
(*conversa*); bring up (*assunto*);
~xar de uma perna limp; **~xar
para** (*parecer com*) take after; **~xar
por** (*exigir muito de*) push (hard).
~xa-saco m 🅣 creep

Qq

QI /ke i/ *m* IQ

quadra /'kwadra/ *f (de tênis etc)*
court; *(quarteirão)* block. **~do** *a* & *m*
a fortieth

quadragésimo /kwadra'ʒezimu/
a fortieth

qua|dril /kwa'driw/ *(pl **~dris**)*
m hip

quadrilha /kwa'driʎa/ *f (bando)*
gang; *(dança)* square dance

quadrinho /kwa'driɲu/ *m* frame;
história em ~s comic strip

quadro /'kwadru/ *m* picture;
(pintado) painting; *(tabela)* table;
(pessoal) staff; *(equipe)* team; *(de
uma peça)* scene; **~ interativo**
interactive whiteboard. **~-negro**
*(pl **~s-negros**)* *m* blackboard

quadruplicar /kwadrupli'kar/
vt/i quadruple

quádruplo /'kwadruplu/ *a*
quadruple. **~s** *m pl (crianças)* quads

qual /kwaw/ *pron* which
(one); o/a **~** *(coisa)* that, which;
(pessoa) that, who; **~ é o seu
nome?** what's your name?; **seja ~
for** a decisão whatever the decision
may be

qualidade /kwali'dadʒi/ *f* quality;
na ~ de in one's capacity as, as

qualifi|cação /kwalifika'sãw/
f qualification. **~car** *vt* qualify;
(descrever) describe **(de** as). **~car-se**
vpr qualify

qualitativo /kwalita'tʃivu/ *a*
qualitative

qualquer /kwaw'kɛr/ • *a* & *pron*

····▸ *(não importa qual)* any;
**pegue ~ ônibus que vai para o
centro** catch any bus that goes
downtown; **em ~ caso** in any
case; **em ~ momento** at any
time; **~ coisa/pessoa** anything/
any one; **~ uma serve** any of
them will do; **~ um** *(qualquer
pessoa)* **~ um pode se enganar**
anyone can make a mistake;
~ um sabe isso everybody
knows that; *(entre dois)* either
one; **qual dos dois livros devo
levar? ~ um** which of the two
books should I take?_either one

····▸ *(em expressões)* **~ dia** one
of these days

quando /'kwãdu/ *adv & conj* when;
~ quer que whenever; **~ de** at the
time of; **~ muito** at most

quantia /kwã'tʃia/ *f* amount

quanti|dade /kwãtʃi'dadʒi/ *f*
quantity; **uma ~dade de** a lot of;
em ~dade in large amounts. **~ficar**
vt quantify. **~tativo** *a* quantitative

quanto /'kwãtu/ *adv & pron* how
much; *pl* how many; **~ tempo?** how
long?; **~ mais barato melhor** the
cheaper the better; **tão alto ~ eu** as
tall as me; **~ ri!** how I laughed!; **~ a**
as for; **~ antes** as soon as possible

quaren|ta /kwa'rẽta/ *a* & *m* forty.
~tão *a* & *m (f* **~tona)** forty-year-old.
~tena /e/ *f* quarantine

quaresma /kwa'rɛzma/ *f* Lent

quarta /'kwarta/ *f (dia)*
Wednesday; *(marcha)* fourth
(gear). **~ de final** *(pl* **~s de final)** *f*
quarter final; **~-feira** *(pl* **~s-feiras)** *f*
Wednesday

quartanista /kwarta'nista/ *m/f*
fourth-year (student)

quarteirão /kwarte'rãw/ *m* block

quar|tel /kwar'tɛw/ (*pl* ~**téis**) *m*
barracks. ~**tel-general** (*pl* ~**téis-
generais**) *m* headquarters

quarteto /kwar'tetu/ *m* quartet;
~ **de cordas** string quartet

quarto /'kwartu/ *a* fourth
● *m* (*parte*) quarter; (*aposento*)
bedroom; (*guarda*) watch; **são três
e/menos um** ~ *Port* it's quarter
past/to three; ~ **de banho** *Port*
bathroom; ~ **de hora** quarter of an
hour; ~ **de hóspedes** guest room

quartzo /'kwartzu/ *m* quartz

quase /'kwazi/ *adv* almost, nearly;
~ **nada/nunca** hardly anything/ever

quatro /'kwatru/ *a* & *m* four; **de**
~ (*no chão*) on all fours; ~ **por** ‹*carro*› four-by-four. ~**centos** *a* & *m*
four hundred

que /ki/ ● *pron rel*
····▸ (*pessoas, sujeito*) who,
that; **o homem** ~ **esteve aqui
ontem** the man who came here
yesterday; (*pessoas, complemento*)
whom, that; **o rapaz** ~ **você
conheceu** the boy (whom) you
met; (*coisas*) that, which; **o carro**
~ **está estacionado na praça** the
car that is parked in the square

! quando *que* é complemento,
é frequentemente omitido:
**a revista que lhe emprestei
ontem** the magazine (that/which)
I lent you yesterday

● *conj*
····▸ (*integrante*) that; **disse** ~
viria esta semana he said (that)
he would come this week; (*em
ordens*) **quero** ~ **me deixem em**
paz! I want to be left alone!; (*em
comparações*) than; **o meu irmão
é mais alto do** ~ **eu** my brother
is taller than me; (*resultado*) that;
estava tão cansada ~ **adormeci**
I was so tired (that) I fell asleep;
(*causa*) **não saias** ~ **está a
chover muito** don't go out
because it's pouring

● *pron*
····▸ (*interrogativo*) what; ~
horas são? what time is it?; **em**
~ **andar você mora?** what floor
do you live on?; (*com escolha
limitada*) which; **com** ~ **carro
vamos hoje? o seu ou o meu?**
which car shall we take today?
yours or mine?; (*exclamação*)
what; ~ **casas tão bonitas!** what
lovely houses!; ~ **vida!** what a
life!; ~ **horror!** how dreadful!; ~
aborrecimento! how annoying!

····▸ (*em expressões*) ~ **tal?:
que tal foi o filme?** how was the
film?; ~ **tal um café?** how about
a coffee?

quê /ke/ *pron* what ● *m* **um** ~
something; **não tem de** ~ don't
mention it

quebra /'kɛbra/ *f* break; (*de
empresa, banco*) crash; (*de força*)
cut; **de** ~ in addition. ~**cabeça** *m*
jigsaw (puzzle); *fig* puzzle. ~**diço** *a*
breakable. ~**do** *a* broken; ‹*carro*›
broken down. ~**dos** *m pl* small
change. ~**galho** *m* **I** stopgap;
~**mar** *m* breakwater; ~**molas**
m invar speed bump; ~**nozes** *m
invar* nutcrackers; ~**pau** *m* **I** row;
~**quebra** *m* riot

quebrar /ke'brar/ *vt* break ● *vi*
break; ‹*carro etc*› break down;
‹*banco, empresa etc*› crash, go bust.
~**se** *vpr* break

queda /'kɛda/ f fall; **ter uma ~ por** have a soft spot for. **~ de braço** f arm wrestling

queijeira /ke'ʒera/ f cheese dish. **~jo** m cheese; **~jo prato** Cheddar. **~jo de minas** m Cheshire cheese

queima /'kejma/ f burning. **~da** f forest fire. **~do** a burnt; (*bronzeado*) tanned, brown; **cheiro de ~do** smell of burning

queimar /kej'mar/ vt burn; (*bronzear*) tan ● vi burn; <*lâmpada*> go; <*fusível*> blow. **~se** vpr burn o.s.; (*bronzear-se*) go brown

queima-roupa /kejma'xopa/ f **à ~** point-blank

quei|**xa** /'keʃa/ f complaint. **~xar-se** vpr complain (**de** about)

queixo /'keʃu/ m chin; **bater o ~** shiver

queixoso /ke'ʃozu/ a plaintive ● m plaintiff

quem /kẽj/ pron who; (*a pessoa que*) anyone who, he who; **de ~ é este livro?** whose is this book?; **~ quer que** whoever; **seja ~ for** whoever it is; **~ falou isso fui eu** it was me who said that; **~ me dera (que) ...** I wish ..., if only ...

Quênia /'kenia/ m Kenya

queniano /keni'anu/ a & m Kenyan

quen|**tão** /kẽ'tãw/ m mulled wine. **~te** a hot; (*com calor agradável*) warm. **~tura** f heat

quepe /'kɛpi/ m cap

quer /kɛr/ conj **~ ... ~ ...** whether ... or ...

querer /ke'rer/ vt/i want; **quero ir** I want to go; **quero que você vá** I want you to go; **eu queria falar com o Sr X** I'd like to speak to Mr X;

vai ~ vir amanhã? do you want to come tomorrow?; **vou ~ um cafezinho** I'd like a coffee; **se você quiser** if you want; **queira sentar** do sit down; **~ dizer** mean; **quer dizer** (*isto é*) that is to say, I mean

querido /ke'ridu/ a dear ● m darling

quermesse /ker'mesi/ f fête, fair

querosene /kero'zeni/ m kerosene

questão /kes'tãw/ m question; (*assunto*) matter; **em ~** in question; **fazer ~** de really want to; **não faço ~ de ir** I don't mind not going

questio|**nar** /kestʃio'nar/ vt/i question. **~nário** m questionnaire. **~nável** (*pl* **~náveis**) a questionable

quiabo /ki'abu/ m okra

quibe /'kibi/ m savoury meatball

quicar /ki'kar/ vt/i bounce

quiche /'kiʃi/ f quiche

quie|**to** /ki'etu/ a (*calado*) quiet; (*imóvel*) still. **~tude** f quiet

quilate /ki'latʃi/ m carat; fig calibre

quilha /'kiʎa/ f keel

quilo /'kilo/ m kilo. **~grama** m kilogram. **~metragem** f mileage. **~métrico** a mile-long

quilômetro /ki'lometru/ m kilometre

quimbanda /kĩ'bãda/ m Afro-Brazilian cult

qui|**mera** /ki'mera/ f fantasy. **~mérico** a fanciful

quími|**ca** /'kimika/ f chemistry. **~co** a chemical ● m chemist

quimioterapia /kimiotera'pia/ f chemotherapy

quimono /ki'mɔnu/ m kimono

quina /'kina/ f **de ~** edgeways

quindim /kĩ'dʒĩ/ *m* sweet made of coconut, sugar and egg yolks

quinhão /ki'ɲãw/ *m* share

quinhentos /ki'ɲẽtuʃ/ *a* & *m* five hundred

quinina /ki'nina/ *f* quinine

quinquagésimo /kwĩkwa'ʒezimu/ *a* fiftieth

quinquilharias /kĩkiʎa'riaʃ/ *f pl* knick-knacks

quinta[1] /'kĩta/ *f* (*fazenda*) farm

quinta[2] /'kĩta/ *f* (*dia*) fifth. **~-feira** (*pl* **~s-feiras**) *f* Thursday

quin|tal /kĩ'taw/ (*pl* **~tais**) *m* back yard

quinteiro /kĩ'tajru/ *m* Port farmer

quinteto /kĩ'tetu/ *m* quintet

quin|to /'kĩtu/ *a* & *m* fifth. **quintuplo** a fivefold. **quintuplos** *m pl* (*crianças*) quins

quinze /'kĩzi/ *a* & *m* fifteen; **às dez e ~** at quarter past ten; **são ~ para as dez** it's quarter to ten. **~na** /e/ *f* fortnight. **~nal** (*pl* **~nais**) a fortnightly. **~nalmente** adv fortnightly

quiosque /ki'ɔski/ *m* (*banca*) kiosk; (*no jardim*) gazebo

quiro|mância /kiro'mãsia/ *f* palmistry. **~mante** *m/f* palmist

quisto /'kistu/ *m* cyst

quitan|da /ki'tãda/ *f* grocer's (shop). **~deiro** *m* grocer

qui|tar /ki'tar/ *vt* pay off <*dívida*>. **~te a estar ~te** be quits

quociente /kwosi'ẽtʃi/ *m* quotient

quórum /'kwɔrũ/ *m* quorum

Rr

rã /xã/ *f* frog

rabanete /xaba'netʃi/ *m* radish

rabear /xabi'ar/ *vi* <*caminhão*> jack-knife

rabino /xa'binu/ *m* rabbi

rabis|car /xabiʃ'kar/ *vt* scribble
● *vi* (*escrever mal*) scribble; (*fazer desenhos*) doodle. **~co** *m* doodle

rabo /'xabu/ *m* (*de animal*) tail; **com o ~ do olho** out of the corner of one's eye. **~ de cavalo** (*pl* **~s de cavalo**) *m* pony tail

rabugento /xabu'ʒẽtu/ *a* grumpy

raça /'xasa/ *f* (*de homens*) race; (*de animais*) breed

ração /xa'sãw/ *f* (*de comida*) ration; (*para animal*) food

racha /'xaʃa/ *f* crack. **~dura** *f* crack

rachar /xa'ʃar/ *vt* (*dividir*) split; (*abrir fendas em*) crack; chop <*lenha*>; split <*despesas*> ● *vi* (*dividir-se*) split; (*apresentar fendas*) crack; (*ao pagar*) split the cost

raci|al /xasi'aw/ (*pl* **~ais**) *a* racial

racio|cinar /xasiosi'nar/ *vi* reason. **~cínio** *m* reasoning. **~nal** (*pl* **~nais**) a rational. **~nalizar** *vt* rationalize

racio|namento /xasiona'mẽtu/ *m* rationing. **~nar** *vt* ration

racis|mo /xa'sizmu/ *m* racism. **~ta** a & *m/f* racist

radar /xa'dar/ *m* radar; (*na estrada*) speed camera

radia|ção /xadʒia'sãw/ *f* radiation. **~dor** *m* radiator

radialista /radʒia'lista/ *m/f* radio announcer

radiante /xadʒi'ãtʃi/ *a* (*de alegria*) overjoyed

radi|**cal** /xadʒi'kaw/ (*pl* ~**cais**) *a & m* radical. ~**car-se** *vpr* settle

rádio[1] /'xadʒiu/ *m* radio ● *f* radio station

rádio[2] /'xadʒiu/ *m* (*elemento*) radium

radioati|**vidade** /xadioatʃivi'dadʒi/ *f* radioactivity. ~**vo** *a* radioactive

radiodifusão /xadʒiodʒifu'zãw/ *f* broadcasting

radiogra|**far** /xadʒiogra'far/ *vt* X-ray ‹*pulmões, osso etc*›; radio ‹*mensagem*›. ~**fia** *f* X-ray

radiolo|**gia** /xadʒiolo'ʒia/ *f* radiology. ~**gista** *m/f* radiologist

radio|**novela** /xadʒiono'vɛla/ *f* radio serial. ~**patrulha** *f* patrol car. ~**táxi** *m* radio taxi. ~**terapia** *f* radiotherapy, ray treatment

raia /'xaja/ *f* (*em corrida*) lane; (*peixe*) ray

rainha /xa'iɲa/ *f* queen. ~**-mãe** *f* queen mother

raio /'xaju/ *m* (*de luz etc*) ray; (*de círculo*) radius; (*de roda*) spoke; (*relâmpago*) bolt of lightning; ~ **de ação** range

rai|**va** /'xajva/ *f* rage; (*doença*) rabies; **estar com** ~**va** be furious (**de** with); **ter** ~**va de alguém** have it in for sb. ~**voso** *a* furious; ‹*cachorro*› rabid

raiz /xa'iz/ *f* root; ~ **quadrada/ cúbica** square/cube root

rajada /xa'ʒada/ *f* (*de vento*) gust; (*de tiros*) burst

ra|**lador** /xala'dor/ *m* grater. ~**lar** *vt* grate

ralé /xa'lɛ/ *f* rabble

ralhar /xa'ʎar/ *vi* scold

ralo[1] /'xalu/ *m* (*ralador*) grater; (*de escoamento*) drain

ralo[2] /'xalu/ *a* ‹*cabelo*› thinning; ‹*sopa, tecido*› thin; ‹*vegetação*› sparse; ‹*café*› weak

ra|**mal** /xa'maw/ (*pl* ~**mais**) *m* (*telefone*) extension; (*de ferrovia*) branch line

ramalhete /xama'ʎetʃi/ *m* posy, bouquet

ramifi|**cação** /xamifika'sãw/ *f* branch. ~**car-se** *vi* branch off

ramo /'xamu/ *m* branch; (*profissional etc*) field; (*buquê*) bunch; **Domingo de Ramos** Palm Sunday

rampa /'xãpa/ *f* ramp

rancor /xã'kor/ *m* resentment. ~**oso** /o/ *a* resentful

rançoso /xã'sozu/ *a* rancid

ran|**ger** /xã'ʒer/ *vt* grind ‹*dentes*› ● *vi* creak. ~**gido** *m* creak

ranhura /xa'ɲura/ *f* groove; (*para moedas*) slot

ranzinza /xã'zĩza/ *a* cantankerous

rapariga /xapa'riga/ *f Port* girl

rapaz /xa'pas/ *m* boy

rapé /xa'pɛ/ *m* snuff

rapel /ra'pɛw/ *m* abseiling

rapidez /xapi'des/ *f* speed

rápido /'xapidu/ *a* fast ● *adv* ‹*fazer*› quickly; ‹*andar*› fast

rapina /xa'pina/ *f* **ave de** ~ bird of prey

rapo|**sa** /xa'poza/ *f* vixen. ~**so** *m* fox

rapsódia /xap'sɔdʒia/ *f* rhapsody

rap|**tar** /xap'tar/ *vt* abduct, kidnap ‹*criança*›. ~**to** *m* abduction, kidnapping (*de criança*)

raquete /xa'ketʃi/ f, Port **raqueta** /xa'keta/ f racquet

raquítico /xa'kitʃiku/ a puny

ra|ramente /xara'mētʃi/ adv rarely. **~ridade** f rarity. **~ro** a rare ● adv rarely

rascunho /xas'kuɲu/ m rough version, draft

ras|gado /xaz'gadu/ a torn; fig <elogios etc> effusive. **~gão** m tear. **~gar** vt tear; (em pedaços) tear up ● vi, **~gar-se** vpr tear. **~go** m tear; fig burst

raso /'xazu/ a <água> shallow; <sapato> flat; <colher etc> level

ras|pão /xas'pãw/ m graze; **atingir de ~pão** graze. **~par** vt shave <cabeça, pelos>; plane <madeira>; (para limpar) scrape; (tocar de leve) graze; **~par em** scrape

rasteiro /xas'teru/ a <planta> creeping; <animal> crawling. **~tejante** a crawling; <voz> slurred. **~tejar** vi crawl

rasto /'xastu/ m ▶ RASTRO

ras|trear /xastri'ar/ vt track <satélite etc>; scan <céu, corpo etc>. **~tro** m trail

rasura /xa'zura/ f crossing-out

rasurar /xazu'rar/ vt to cross out

ratear¹ /xatʃi'ar/ vi <motor> miss

ra|tear² /xatʃi'ar/ vt share. **~teio** m sharing

ratifi|cação /xatʃifika'sãw/ f ratification. **~car** vt ratify

rato /'xatu/ m rat; (camundongo) mouse; Port Comput mouse. **~eira** f mousetrap

ravina /xa'vina/ f ravine

razão /xa'zãw/ f reason; (proporção) ratio ● m ledger; **à ~ de** at the rate of; **em ~ de** on account of; **ter ~** be right; **não ter ~** be wrong

razoá|vel /xazo'avew/ (pl **~veis**) a reasonable

ré¹ /xɛ/ f (na justiça) defendant

ré² /xɛ/ f (marcha) reverse; **dar ~** reverse

reabastecer /xeabaste'ser/ vt/i refuel

reabilitar /xeabili'tar/ vt rehabilitate

rea|ção /xea'sãw/ f reaction. **~ção em cadeia** chain reaction. **~cionário** a & m reactionary

readmitir /xeadʒimi'tʃir/ vt reinstate <funcionário>

reagir /xea'ʒir/ vi react; <doente> respond

reajus|tar /xeaʒus'tar/ vt readjust. **~te** m adjustment

re|al /xe'aw/ (pl **~ais**) a <verdadeiro> real; (da realeza) royal

real|çar /xeaw'sar/ vt highlight. **~ce** m prominence

realejo /xea'leʒu/ m barrel organ

realeza /xea'leza/ f royalty

realidade /xeali'dadʒi/ f reality

realimentação /xealimēta'sãw/ f feedback

realis|mo /xea'lizmu/ m realism. **~ta** a realistic ● m/f realist

realiza|ção /xealiza'sãw/ f (de projeto) implementation; (de sonho, objetivo) fulfilment; Cine direction

reali|zado /xeali'zadu/ a <pessoa> fulfilled. **~zar** vt (fazer) carry out; (tornar real) realize <sonho, capital>. **~zar-se** vpr <sonho> come true; <pessoa> fulfil o.s.; <casamento, reunião etc> take place

realizador /xializa'dor/ m Port Cine director

realmente /xeaw'mētʃi/ adv really

reaparecer /xeapare'ser/ vi
reappear

reativar /xeatʃi'var/ vt reactivate

reaver /xea'ver/ vt get back

reavivar /xeavi'var/ vt revive

rebaixar /xeba'ʃar/ vt lower
‹preço›; fig demean ● vi ‹preços›
drop. **~se** vpr demean o.s.

rebanho /xe'baɲu/ m herd; ‹fiéis›
flock

reba|te /xe'batʃi/ m alarm. **~ter** vt
return ‹bola›; refute ‹acusação›;
(ao computador) retype

rebelar-se /xebe'larsi/ vpr rebel

rebel|de /xe'bewdʒi/ a rebellious
● m/f rebel. **~dia** f rebelliousness

rebelião /xebeli'ãw/ f rebellion

reben|tar /xebẽ'tar/ vt/i
▶ ARREBENTAR. **~to** m (de planta)
shoot; (descendente) offspring

rebite /xe'bitʃi/ m rivet

rebobinar /xebobi'nar/ vt rewind

rebo|cador /xeboka'dor/ m tug.
~car vt (tirar) tow; (cobrir com
reboco) plaster. **~co** /o/ m plaster

rebolar /xebo'lar/ vi swing one's
hips

reboque /xe'bɔki/ m towing;
(veículo a ~) trailer; (com guindaste)
towtruck; **a ~** on tow

rebote /xe'bɔtʃi/ m (esporte)
rebound

rebuçado /xebu'sadu/ m Port
sweet, Amer candy

rebuliço /xebu'lisu/ m commotion

rebuscado /xebus'kadu/ a
recherché

recado /xe'kadu/ m message

reca|ída /xeka'ida/ f relapse. **~ir** vi
relapse; ‹acento, culpa› fall

recal|cado /xekaw'kadu/ a
repressed. **~car** vt repress

recanto /xe'kãtu/ m nook, recess

recapitular /xekapitu'lar/ vt
review ● vi recap

recarga /xe'karga/ f (de caneta)
refill

recarregar /xekare'gar/ vt
recharge ‹bateria›; top up ‹crédito›

reca|tado /xeka'tadu/ a reserved,
withdrawn. **~to** m reserve

recear /xesi'ar/ vt/i fear (por for)

rece|ber /xese'ber/ vt receive;
entertain ‹convidados› ● vi (~ber
salário) get paid; (~ber convidados)
entertain. **~bimento** m receipt

receio /xe'seju/ m fear

recei|ta /xe'sejta/ f (de cozinha)
recipe; (médica) prescription;
(dinheiro) revenue. **~tar** vt prescribe

recém-casados /xesẽjka'zadus/
m pl newly-weds. **~chegado** m
newcomer; **~nascido** a newborn
● m newborn child, baby

recenseamento /xesẽsja'mẽtu/
m Port ▶ CENSO

recente /xe'sẽtʃi/ a recent.
~mente adv recently

receoso /xese'ozu/ a (apreensivo)
afraid

recep|ção /xesep'sãw/ f reception;
Port (de carta) receipt; **~ção de
sinal** Telec reception. **~cionar** vt
receive. **~cionista** f receptionist.
~táculo m receptacle. **~tivo** a
receptive. **~tor** m receiver

reces|são /xese'sãw/ f recession.
~so /ɛ/ m recess

re|chear /xeʃi'ar/ vt stuff ‹frango,
assado›; fill ‹empada›. **~cheio**
m (para frango etc) stuffing; (de
empada etc) filling

rechonchudo /xeʃõ'ʃudu/ a
plump

recibo /xe'sibu/ m receipt

reciclagem /xesi'klaʒẽj/ f
recycling

reciclar /xesik'lar/ vt recycle

recife /xe'sifi/ m reef

recinto /xe'sĩtu/ m enclosure

recipiente /xesipi'ẽtʃi/ m
container

reciprocar /xesipro'kar/ vt
reciprocate

recíproco /xe'siproku/ a
reciprocal; ‹sentimento› mutual

reci|tal /xesi'taw/ (pl ~tais) m
recital. **~tar** vt recite

recla|mação /xeklama'sãw/ f
complaint; (no seguro) claim. **~mar**
vt claim ● vi complain (de about);
(no seguro) claim. **~me** m, Port **~mo**
m advertising

reclinar-se /xekli'narsi/ vpr
recline

recluso /xe'kluzu/ a reclusive ● m
recluse

recobrar /xeko'brar/ vt recover.
~se vpr recover

recolher /xeko'ʎer/ vt collect;
(retirar) withdraw. **~se** vpr retire

recomeçar /xekome'sar/ vt/i
start again

recomen|dação /xekomẽda'sãw/
f recommendation. **~dar** vt
recommend. **~dável** (pl **~dáveis**)
a advisable

recompen|sa /xekõ'pẽsa/ f
reward. **~sar** vt reward

reconcili|ação /xekõsilia'sãw/
f reconciliation. **~ar** vt reconcile.
~ar-se vpr be reconciled

reconhe|cer /xekoɲe'ser/ vt
recognize; (admitir) acknowledge;
Mil reconnoitre; identify ‹corpo›.
~cimento m recognition; (gratidão)
gratitude; Mil reconnaissance;

(de corpo) identification. **~cível**
(pl **~cíveis**) a recognizable

reconsiderar /xekõside'rar/ vt/i
reconsider

reconstituinte /xekõstʃitu'ĩtʃi/
m tonic

reconstituir /xekõstʃitu'ir/ vt
reform; reconstruct ‹crime, cena›

reconstruir /xekõstru'ir/ vt
rebuild

recor|dação /xekorda'sãw/ f
recollection; (objeto) memento.
~dar vt recollect; **~dar-se (de)**
recall

recor|de /xe'kɔrdʒi/ a invar & m
record. **~dista** a record-breaking
● m/f record holder

recorrer /xeko'xer/ vi **~ a** turn
to ‹médico, amigo›; resort to
‹violência, tática›; **~ de** appeal
against

recor|tar /xekor'tar/ vt cut out.
~te /ɔ/ m cutting, Amer clipping

recostar /xekos'tar/ vt lean back.
~se vpr lean back

recreio /xe'kreju/ m recreation;
(na escola) break

recriar /xekri'ar/ vt recreate

recriminação /xekrimina'sãw/ f
recrimination

recrudescer /xekrude'ser/ vi
intensify

recru|ta /xe'kruta/ m/f recruit.
~tamento m recruitment. **~tar**
vt recruit

recu|ar /xeku'ar/ vi move back;
‹tropas› retreat; (no tempo) go
back; (ceder) back down; (não
cumprir) back out (de of) ● vt move
back. **~o** m retreat; fig (de intento)
climbdown

recupe|ração /xekupera'sãw/ f
recovery. **~rar** vt recover; make up

‹atraso, tempo perdido›. **~rar-se** vpr recover (**de** from)

recurso /xe'kursu/ m resort; (coisa útil) resource; (na justiça) appeal; pl resources

recu|sa /xe'kuza/ f refusal. **~sar** vt refuse; turn down ‹convite, oferta›. **~sar-se** vpr refuse (**a** to)

reda|ção /xeda'sãw/ f (de livro, contrato) draft; (pessoal) editorial staff; (seção) editorial department; (na escola) composition. **~tor** m editor

rede /'xedʒi/ f net; (para deitar) hammock; fig (sistema) network; **~ social** social network. **~ corporativa** Comput intranet

rédea /'xedʒia/ f rein

redemoinho /xedemo'iɲu/ m ▶ RODAMOINHO

reden|ção /xedẽ'sãw/ f redemption. **~tor** a redeeming ● m redeemer

redigir /xedʒi'ʒir/ vt draw up ‹contrato›; write ‹artigo›; edit ‹dicionário›

redimir /xedʒi'mir/ vt redeem

redobrar /xedo'brar/ vt redouble

redon|deza /xedõ'deza/ f roundness; pl vicinity. **~do** a round

redor /xe'dɔr/ m ao ou em **~ de** around

redução /xedu'sãw/ f reduction

redun|dante /xedũ'dãtʃi/ a redundant. **~dar** vi **~dar em** develop into

redu|zido /xedu'zidu/ a limited; (pequeno) small. **~zir** vt reduce. **~zir-se** vpr (ficar reduzido) be reduced (**a** to); (resumir-se) come down (**a** to)

reeleger /xeele'ʒer/ vt re-elect

reeleição /xeelej'sãw/ f re-election

reembol|sar /xeẽbow'sar/ vt reimburse ‹pessoa›; refund ‹dinheiro›. **~so** /o/ m refund; **~so postal** cash on delivery

reencarnação /xeẽkarna'sãw/ f reincarnation

reentrância /xeẽ'trãsia/ f recess

reescalonar /xeeskalo'nar/ vt reschedule

reescrever /xeeskre'ver/ vt rewrite

refastelar-se /xefaste'larsi/ vpr stretch out

refazer /xefa'zer/ vt redo; rebuild ‹vida›. **~se** vpr recover (**de** from)

refei|ção /xefej'sãw/ f meal. **~tório** m dining hall

refém /xe'fẽj/ m hostage

referência /xefe'rẽsia/ f reference; **com ~** a with reference to

referendum /xefe'rẽdũ/ m referendum

refe|rente /xefe'rẽtʃi/ a **~rente** regarding. **~rir** vt report. **~rir-se** vpr refer (**a** to)

refestelar-se /xefeste'larsi/ vpr Port ▶ REFASTELAR-SE

re|fil /xe'fiw/ (pl **~fis**) m refill

refi|nado /xefi'nadu/ a refined. **~namento** m refinement. **~nar** vt refine. **~naria** f refinery

refle|tido /xefle'tʃidu/ a ‹decisão› well-thought-out; ‹pessoa› thoughtful. **~tir** vt/i reflect. **~tir-se** vpr be reflected. **~xão** /ks/ f reflection. **~xivo** /ks/ a reflexive. **~xo** /eks/ a ‹luz› reflected; ‹ação› reflex ● m (de luz etc) reflection; (físico) reflex; (no cabelo) streak

refluxo /xe'fluksu/ m ebb

refo|gado /xefo'gadu/ m lightly fried mixture of onions and garlic. **~gar** vt fry lightly

reforçar /xefor'sar/ vt reinforce. **~ço** /o/ m reinforcement

reforma /xe'fɔrma/ f (da lei etc) reform; (na casa etc) renovation; (de militar) discharge; (pensão) pension; **~ma ministerial** cabinet reshuffle. **~mado** a reformed; Port (aposentado) retired ● m Port pensioner. **~mar** vt reform ‹lei, sistema etc›; renovate ‹casa, prédio›; Port (aposentar) retire. **~mar-se** vpr Port (aposentar-se) retire; ‹criminoso› reform. **~matório** m reform school. **~mista** a & m/f reformist

refrão /xe'frãw/ m chorus

refratário /xefra'tariu/ a ‹tigela etc› ovenproof, heatproof

refrear /xefri'ar/ vt rein in ‹cavalo›; fig curb, keep in check ‹paixões etc›. **~se** vpr restrain o.s.

refrega /xe'frega/ f clash, fight

refrescante /xefres'kãtʃi/ a refreshing. **~car** vt freshen, cool ‹ar›; refresh ‹pessoa, memória etc› ● vi get cooler. **~car-se** vpr refresh o.s.. **~co** /e/ m (bebida) soft drink; pl refreshments

refrigerado /xefriʒe'radu/ a cooled; ‹casa etc› air-conditioned; (na geladeira) refrigerated. **~rador** m refrigerator. **~rante** m soft drink. **~rar** vt keep cool; (na geladeira) refrigerate

refugiado /xefuʒi'adu/ m refugee. **~ar-se** vpr take refuge

refúgio /xe'fuʒiu/ m refuge

refugo /xe'fugu/ m waste, refuse

refutar /xefu'tar/ vt refute

regaço /xe'gasu/ m lap

regador /xega'dor/ m watering can

regalia /xega'lia/ f privilege

regar /xe'gar/ vt water

regata /xe'gata/ f regatta

regatear /xegatʃi'ar/ vi bargain, haggle

regência /xe'ʒẽsia/ f (de verbo etc) government. **~gente** m/f (de orquestra) conductor. **~ger** vt govern ● vi rule

regenerar /xeʒene'rar/ vt regenerate

região /xeʒi'ãw/ f region; (de cidade etc) area

regime /xe'ʒimi/ m regime; (dieta) diet; **fazer ~me** diet. **~mento** m (militar) regiment; (regulamento) regulations

régio /'xɛʒiu/ a regal

> **Regiões Autónomas (de Portugal)** The autonomous regions of Portugal are the archipelagos of Madeira and the Azores. Together with mainland Portugal, these make up the Portuguese Republic. Each autonomous region has its own government and legislative assembly.

regional /xeʒio'naw/ (pl **~nais**) a regional

registar /xeʒiʃ'tar/ vt Port ▶ **registrar** /xeʒiʃ'trar/

registo /xe'ʒiʃtu/ m Port ▶ **registro** /xe'ʒiʃtru/

registrador /xeʒiʃtra'dor/ **caixa ~tradora** cash register. **~trar** vt register; (anotar) record. **~tro** m (lista) register; (de um fato, em banco de dados) record; (ato de ~trar) registration

rego /'xegu/ m (de arado) furrow; (de roda) rut; (para escoamento) ditch

regozi|jar /xegozi'ʒar/ vt delight.
~jar-se vpr be delighted. **~jo** m
delight

regra /'xɛgra/ f rule; pl
(menstruações) periods; **em ~** as
a rule

regres|sar /xegre'sar/ vi return.
~sivo a regressive; contagem **~siva**
countdown. **~so** /e/ m return

régua /'xɛgwa/ f ruler

regu|lagem /xegu'laʒẽ/ f
(de carro) tuning. **~lamento**
m regulations. **~lar** a regular;
‹estatura, qualidade etc› average
● vt regulate; tune ‹carro, motor›;
set ‹relógio›; **~lar-se por** go by, be
guided by ● vi work. **~laridade** f
regularity. **~larizar** vt regularize

regurgitar /xegurʒi'tar/ vt
bring up

rei /xej/ m king. **~nado** m reign

reincidir /xeĩsi'dʒir/ vi ‹criminoso›
reoffend

reino /'xejnu/ m kingdom; fig (da
fantasia etc) realm; **Reino Unido**
United Kingdom

reiterar /xejte'rar/ vt reiterate

reitor /xej'tor/ m chancellor, Amer
president

reivindi|cação /xejvĩdʒika'sãw/ f
demand. **~car** vt claim, demand

reje|ção /xeʒe'sãw/ f rejection.
~tar vt reject

rejuvenescer /xeʒuvene'ser/ vt
rejuvenate ● vi be rejuvenated

rela|ção /xela'sãw/ f relationship;
(relatório) account; (lista) list; pl
relations; **com** ou **em ~** a in relation
to, regarding

relacio|namento /xelasiona-
'mẽtu/ m relationship. **~nar** vt relate
(com to); (listar) list. **~nar-se** vpr
relate (com to)

relações-públicas
/xelasõjs'publikas/ m/f invar public
relations person

relâmpago /xe'lãpagu/ m flash of
lightning; pl lightning ● a lightning;
num ~ in a flash

relampejar /xelãpe'ʒar/ vi flash;
relampejou there was a flash of
lightning

relance /xe'lãsi/ m glance; **olhar
de ~** glance (at)

rela|tar /xela'tar/ vt relate. **~tivo**
a relative. **~to m** account. **~tório**
m report

rela|xado /xela'ʃadu/ a relaxed;
‹disciplina› lax; ‹pessoa› lazy,
complacent. **~xamento** m (físico)
relaxation; (de pessoa) complacency.
~xante a relaxing ● m tranquillizer.
~xar vt relax ● vi (descansar) relax;
(tornar-se omisso) get complacent.
~xar-se vpr relax. **~xe** m relaxation

reles /'xɛlis/ a invar ‹gente›
common; ‹ação› despicable

rele|vância /xele'vãsia/ f
relevance. **~vante** a relevant. **~var**
vt emphasize. **~vo** /e/ m relief;
(importância) prominence

religi|ão /xeliʒi'ãw/ f religion.
~oso /o/ a religious

relin|char /xelĩ'ʃar/ vi neigh.
~cho m neighing

relíquia /xe'likia/ f relic

relógio /xe'lɔʒiu/ m clock; (de
pulso) watch

relu|tância /xelu'tãsia/ f
reluctance. **~tante** a reluctant.
~tar vi be reluctant (**em** to)

reluzente /xelu'zẽtʃi/ a shining,
gleaming

relva /'xɛwva/ f grass. **~do** m lawn

remador /xema'dor/ m rower

remanescente /xemane'sɛtʃi/ a remaining ● m remainder

remar /xe'mar/ vt/i row

rema|tar /xema'tar/ vt finish off. **~te** m finish; (adorno) finishing touch; (de piada) punch line

remediar /xemedʒi'ar/ vt remedy

remédio /xe'mɛdʒiu/ m (contra doença) medicine, drug; (a problema etc) remedy

remelento /xeme'lẽtu/ a bleary

remen|dar /xemẽ'dar/ vt mend; (com pedaço de pano) patch. **~do** m mend; (pedaço de pano) patch

remessa /xe'mesa/ f (de mercadorias) shipment; (de dinheiro) remittance

reme|tente /xeme'tẽtʃi/ m/f sender. **~ter** vt send <mercadorias, dinheiro etc>; refer <leitor> (a to)

remexer /xeme'ʃer/ vt shuffle <papéis>; stir up <poeira, lama>; wave <braços> ● vi rummage. **~se** vpr move around

reminiscência /xemini'sẽsia/ f reminiscence

remir /xe'mir/ vt redeem. **~se** vpr redeem o.s.

remissão /xemi'sãw/ f (de pecados) redemption; (de doença, pena) remission; (num livro) cross reference

remo /'xemu/ m oar; (esporte) rowing

remoção /xemo'sãw/ f removal

remoinho /xemo'iɲu/ m Port
▶ RODAMOINHO

remontar /xemõ'tar/ vi **~ a** <coisa> date back to; <pessoa> think back to

remorso /xe'mɔrsu/ m remorse

remo|to /xe'mɔtu/ a remote. **~ver** vt remove

remune|ração /xemunera'sãw/ f payment. **~rador** a profitable. **~rar** vt pay

rena /'xena/ f reindeer

re|nal /xe'naw/ (pl **~nais**) a renal, kidney

Renascença /xena'sẽsa/ f Renaissance

renas|cer /xena'ser/ vi be reborn. **~cimento** m rebirth

renda¹ /'xẽda/ f (tecido) lace

ren|da² /'xẽda/ f income; Port (aluguel) rent; **~der** bring in, yield <lucro>; earn <juros>; fetch <preço>; bring <resultado> ● vi <investimento, trabalho, ação> pay off; <comida> go a long way; <produto comprado> give value for money. **~der-se** vpr surrender. **~dição** f surrender. **~dimento** m (renda) income; (de investimento, terreno) yield; (de motor etc) output; (de produto comprado) value for money. **~doso** /o/ a profitable

rene|gado /xene'gadu/ a & m renegade. **~gar** vt renounce

renhido /xe'ɲidu/ a hard-fought

Reno /'xenu/ m Rhine

reno|mado /xeno'madu/ a renowned. **~me** /o/ m renown

reno|vação /xenova'sãw/ f renewal. **~var** vt renew

renque /'xẽki/ m row

ren|tabilidade /xẽtabili'dadʒi/ f profitability. **~tável** (pl **~táveis**) a profitable

rente /'xẽtʃi/ adv **~ a** close to ● a <cabelo> cropped

renúncia /xe'nũsia/ f renunciation (a of); (a cargo) resignation (a from)

renunciar /xenũsi'ar/ *vi*
‹presidente etc› resign; ~ **a** give up;
waive ‹direito›

reorganizar /xeorgani'zar/ *vt*
reorganize

repa|ração /xepara'sãw/ *f*
reparation; (conserto) repair. ~**rar**
vt (consertar) repair; make up for
‹ofensa, injustiça, erro›; make good
‹danos, prejuízo› ● *vi* ~**rar (em)**
notice. ~**ro** *m* (conserto) repair

repar|tição /xeparti'sãw/
f division; (seção do governo)
department. ~**tir** *vt* divide up

repassar /xepa'sar/ *vt* revise
‹matéria, lição›

repatriar /xepatri'ar/ *vt* repatriate

repe|lente /xepe'lẽtʃi/ *a & m*
repellent. ~**lir** *vt* repel; reject ‹ideia,
proposta etc›

repensar /xepẽ'sar/ *vt/i* rethink

repen|te /xe'pẽtʃi/ *m* **de** ~**te**
suddenly; 🇧 (talvez) maybe. ~**tino**
a sudden

reper|cussão /xeperku'sãw/
f repercussion. ~**cutir** *vi* ‹som›
reverberate; *fig* (ter efeito) have
repercussions

repertório /xeper'tɔriu/ *m*
(músico etc) repertoire; (lista) list

repe|tição /xepetʃi'sãw/ *f*
repetition. ~**tido** *a* repeated; ~**tidas
vezes** repeatedly. ~**tir** *vt* repeat ● *vi*
(ao comer) have seconds. ~**tir-se**
vpr ‹pessoa› repeat o.s.; ‹fato,
acontecimento› recur. ~**titivo** *a*
repetitive

repi|car /xepi'kar/ *vt/i* ring. ~**que**
m ring

replay /xe'plej/ (*pl* ~**s**) *m* action
replay

repleto /xe'plɛtu/ *a* full up

réplica /'xɛplika/ *f* reply; (cópia)
replica

replicar /xepli'kar/ *vt* answer
● *vi* reply

repolho /xe'poλu/ *m* cabbage

repor /xe'por/ *vt* (num lugar) put
back; (substituir) replace

reportagem /xepor'taʒẽ/ *f* (uma)
report; (ato) reporting

repórter /xe'porter/ *m/f* reporter

reposição /xepozi'sãw/ *f*
replacement

repou|sar /xepo'sar/ *vt/i* rest.
~**so** *m* rest

repreen|der /xeprié'der/ *vt*
rebuke, reprimand. ~**são** *f* rebuke,
reprimand. ~**sível** (*pl* ~**síveis**) *a*
reprehensible

represa /xe'preza/ *f* dam

represália /xepre'zalia/ *f* reprisal

represen|tação /xeprezẽta'sãw/
f representation; (espetáculo)
performance; (ofício de ator) acting.
~**tante** *m/f* representative. ~**tar**
vt represent; (no teatro) perform
‹peça›; play ‹papel, personagem›
● *vi* ‹ator› act. ~**tativo** *a*
representative

repres|são /xepre'sãw/ *f*
repression. ~**sivo** *a* repressive

repri|mido /xepri'midu/ *a*
repressed. ~**mir** *vt* repress

reprise /xe'prizi/ *f* (na TV) repeat;
(de filme) rerun

reprodu|ção /xeprodu'sãw/ *f*
reproduction. ~**zir** *vt* reproduce.
~**zir-se** *vpr* (multiplicar-se)
reproduce; (repetir-se) recur

repro|vação /xeprova'sãw/ *f*
disapproval; (em exame) failure.
~**var** *vt* (rejeitar) disapprove of; (em
exame) fail; **ser** ~**vado** ‹aluno› fail

rép|til /'xɛptʃiw/ (*pl* ~**teis**) *m* reptile

república /xe'publika/ f republic; (de estudantes) hall of residence

republicano /xepubli'kanu/ a & m republican

repudiar /xepudʒi'ar/ vt disown; repudiate ‹esposa›

repug|nância /xepug'nãsia/ f repugnance. ~nante a repugnant

repul|sa /xe'puwsa/ f repulsion; (recusa) rejection. ~sivo a repulsive

reputação /xeputa'sãw/ f reputation

requebrar /xeke'brar/ vt swing. ~se vpr sway

requeijão /xeke'ʒãw/ m cheese spread, cottage cheese

reque|rer /xeke'rer/ vt (pedir) apply for; (exigir) require. ~rimento m application

requin|tado /xekĩ'tadu/ a refined. ~tar vt refine. ~te m refinement

requisi|ção /xekizi'sãw/ f requisition. ~tar vt requisition. ~to m requirement

rês /xes/ (pl reses) m head of cattle; pl cattle

rescindir /xesĩ'dʒir/ vt rescind

rés do chão /xezdu'ʒãw/ m invar Port ground floor, Amer first floor

rese|nha /xe'zeɲa/ f review. ~nhar vt review

reser|va /xe'zɛrva/ f reserve; (em hotel, avião etc, ressalva) reservation. ~var vt reserve. ~vatório m reservoir. ~vista m/f reservist

resfri|ado /xesfri'adu/ a estar ~ado have a cold ● m cold. ~ar vt cool ● vi get cold; (tornar-se morno) cool down. ~ar-se vpr catch a cold

resga|tar /xezga'tar/ vt (salvar) rescue; (remir) redeem. ~te m (salvamento) rescue; (pago

por refém) ransom; (remissão) redemption

resguardar /xezgwar'dar/ vt protect. ~se vpr protect o.s. (de from)

residência /xezi'dẽsia/ f residence

residen|cial /xezidẽsi'aw/ (pl ~ciais) a ‹bairro› residential; ‹telefone etc› home. ~te a & m/f resident

residir /xezi'dʒir/ vi reside

resíduo /xe'ziduu/ m residue

resig|nação /xezigna'sãw/ f resignation. ~nado a resigned. ~nar-se vpr resign o.s. (com to)

resiliente /xezili'ẽtʃi/ a resilient

resina /xe'zina/ f resin

resis|tência /xezis'tẽsia/ f resistance; (de atleta, mental) endurance; (de material, objeto) toughness. ~tente a strong, tough; ‹tecido, roupa› hard-wearing; ‹planta› hardy; ~tente a resistant to. ~tir vi (opor ~tência) resist; (aguentar) ‹pessoa› hold out; ‹objeto› hold; ~tir a (combater) resist; (aguentar) withstand; ~tir ao tempo stand the test of time

resmun|gar /xezmũ'gar/ vi grumble. ~go m grumbling

resolu|ção /xezolu'sãw/ f resolution; (firmeza) resolve; (de problema) solution. ~to a resolute; ~to a resolved to

resolver /xezow'ver/ vt (esclarecer) sort out; solve ‹problema, enigma›; (decidir) decide. ~se vpr make up one's mind (a to)

respaldo /xes'pawdu/ m (de cadeira) back; fig (apoio) backing

respetivo /xespe'tʃivu/ a respective

respei|tabilidade
/xespejtabili'dadʒi/ f respectability.
~tador a respectful. **~tar** vt
respect. **~tável** (pl **~táveis**) a
respectable. **~to** m respect (por
for); **a ~to de** about; **a este ~to** in
this respect; **com ~to a** with regard
to; **dizer ~to a** concern. **~toso** /o/
a respectful

respin|gar /xespĩ'gar/ vt/i splash.
~go m splash

respi|ração /xespira'sãw/ f
breathing. **~rador** m respirator.
~rar vt/i breathe. **~ratório**
a respiratory. **~ro** m breath;
(descanso) break, breather

resplande|cente /xesplãde'sẽtʃi/
a resplendent. **~cer** vi shine

resplendor /xesplẽ'dor/ m
brilliance; fig glory

respon|dão /xespõ'dãw/ a
(f **~dona**) cheeky. **~der** vt/i answer;
(com insolência) answer back; **~der**
a answer; **~der por** answer for, take
responsibility for

responsabili|dade
/xespõsabili'dadʒi/ f responsibility.
~zar vt hold responsible (por for).
~zar-se vpr take responsibility
(por for)

responsá|vel /xespõ'savew/ a
(pl **~veis**) a responsible (por for)

resposta /xes'pɔsta/ f answer

resquício /xes'kisiu/ m vestige,
remnant

ressabiado /xesabi'adu/ a wary,
suspicious

ressaca /xe'saka/ f (depois de beber)
hangover; (do mar) undertow

ressaltar /xesaw'tar/ vt emphasize
● vi stand out

ressalva /xe'sawva/ f reservation,
proviso; (proteção) safeguard

ressarcir /xesar'sir/ vt refund

resse|cado /xese'kadu/ a ‹terra›
parched; ‹pele› dry. **~car** vt/i dry up

ressen|tido /xesẽ'tʃidu/ a
resentful. **~timento** m resentment.
~tir-se vpr **~tir-se de** (ofender-se)
resent; (ser influenciado) show the
effects of

ressequido /xese'kidu/ a
▶ RESSECADO

resso|ar /xeso'ar/ vi resound.
~nância f resonance. **~nante** a
resonant. **~nar** vi Port snore

ressurgimento /xesurʒi'mẽtu/
m resurgence

ressurreição /xesuxej'sãw/ f
resurrection

ressuscitar /xesusi'tar/ vt revive

restabele|cer /xestabele'ser/ vt
restore; restore to health ‹doente›.
~cer-se vpr recover. **~cimento** m
restoration; (de doente) recovery

res|tante /xes'tãtʃi/ a remaining
● m remainder. **~tar** vi remain;
~ta-me dizer que ... it remains for
me to say that

restau|ração /xestawra'sãw/ f
restoration. **~rante** m restaurant.
~rar vt restore

restitu|ição /xestʃitui'sãw/ f
return, restitution. **~ir** vt (devolver)
return; restore ‹forma, força etc›;
reinstate ‹funcionário›

resto /'xestu/ m rest; pl (de comida)
leftovers; (de cadáver) remains; **de ~**
besides

restrição /xestri'sãw/ f restriction

restringir /xestrĩ'ʒir/ vt restrict

restrito /xes'tritu/ a restricted

resul|tado /xezuw'tadu/ m result.
~tante a resulting (de from). **~tar** vi
result (de from em in)

resu|mir /xezu'mir/ vt (abreviar) summarize; (conter em poucas palavras) sum up. **~mir-se** vpr (ser expresso em poucas palavras) be summed up; **~mir-se em** (ser apenas) come down to. **~mo** m summary; **em ~mo** briefly

resvalar /xezva'lar/ vi (sem querer) slip; (deslizar) slide

reta /'xɛta/ f (linha) straight line; (de pista etc) straight; **~ final** home straight

retaguarda /xeta'gwarda/ f rearguard

retalho /xe'taʎu/ m scrap; **a ~** Port retail

retaliação /xetalia'sãw/ f retaliation

retangular /xetãgu'lar/ a rectangular

retângulo /xe'tãgulu/ m rectangle

retar|dado /xetar'dadu/ a retarded ● m retard. **~dar** vt delay. **~datário** m latecomer

retenção /xetẽ'sãw/ f retention

reter /xe'ter/ vt keep <pessoa>; hold back <águas, riso, lágrimas>; (na memória) retain. **~se** vpr restrain o.s.

rete|sado /xete'zadu/ a taut. **~sar** vt pull taut

reticência /xetʃi'sẽsia/ f reticence

reti|dão /xetʃi'dãw/ f rectitude. **~ficar** vt rectify

reti|rada /xetʃi'rada/ f (de tropas) retreat; (de dinheiro) withdrawal. **~rado** a secluded. **~rar** vt withdraw; (afastar) move away. **~rar-se** vpr <tropas> retreat; (afastar-se) withdraw; (de uma atividade) retire. **~ro** m retreat

reto /'xɛtu/ a <linha etc> straight; <pessoa> honest

retocar /xeto'kar/ vt touch up <desenho, maquiagem etc>; alter <texto>

reto|mada /xeto'mada/ f (continuação) resumption; (reconquista) retaking. **~mar** vt (continuar com) resume; (conquistar de novo) retake

retoque /xe'tɔki/ m finishing touch

retorcer /xetor'ser/ vt twist. **~se** vpr writhe

retóri|ca /xe'tɔrika/ f rhetoric. **~co** a rhetorical

retor|nar /xetor'nar/ vi return. **~no** m return; (na estrada) turning place; **dar ~no** do a U-turn

retrair /xetra'ir/ vt retract, withdraw. **~se** vpr (recuar) withdraw; (encolher-se) retract

retrasa|do /xetra'zadu/ a **a semana ~da** the week before last

retratar¹ /xetra'tar/ vt (desdizer) retract

retra|tar² /xetra'tar/ vt (em quadro, livro) portray, depict. **~to** m portrait; (foto) photo; (representação) portrayal; **~to falado** identikit

retribuir /xetribu'ir/ vt return <favor, visita>; repay <gentileza>

retroativo /xetroa'tʃivu/ a retroactive; <pagamento> backdated

retro|ceder /xetrose'der/ vi retreat; (desistir) back down. **~cesso** /ɛ/ m retreat; (ao passado) regression

retrógrado /xe'trɔgradu/ a retrograde

retrospe|tiva /xetrospe'tʃiva/ f retrospective. **~tivo** a retrospective. **~to** /ɛ/ m look back; **em ~to** in retrospect

retrovisor /xetrovi'zor/ a & m
(espelho) ~ rear-view mirror

retrucar /xetru'kar/ vt/i retort

retum|bante /xetũ'bãtʃi/ a
resounding. **~bar** vi resound

réu /'xɛw/ m (f ré) defendant

reumatismo /xewma'tʃizmu/ m
rheumatism

reu|nião /xeuni'ãw/ f meeting;
(descontraída) get-together; (de
família) reunion; **~nião de cúpula**
summit meeting. **~nir** vt bring
together ‹pessoas›; combine
‹qualidades›. **~nir-se** vpr meet;
‹amigos, familiares› get together;
~nir-se a join

revanche /xe'vãʃi/ f revenge;
(jogo) return match

reveillon /xeve'jõ/ (pl **~s**) m New
Year's Eve

reve|lação /xevela'sãw/ f
revelation; (de fotos) developing;
(novo talento) promising newcomer.
~lar vt reveal; develop ‹filme, fotos›.
~lar-se vpr (vir a ser) turn out to be

revelia /xeve'lia/ f **à ~** by default;
à ~ de without the knowledge of

reven|dedor /xevẽde'dor/ m
dealer. **~der** vt resell

rever /xe'ver/ vt (ver de novo) see
again; (revisar) revise; (examinar)
check

reve|rência /xeve'resia/ f
reverence; (movimento do busto)
bow; (dobrando os joelhos) curtsey.
~rente a reverent

reverso /xe'vɛrsu/ m reverse; **o
~ da medalha** the other side of
the coin

revés /xe'vɛs/ (pl reveses) m
setback

reves|timento /xevestʃi'mẽtu/ m
covering. **~tir** vt cover

reve|zamento /xeveza'mẽtu/
m alternation. **~zar** vt/i alternate.
~zar-se vpr alternate

revi|dar /xevi'dar/ vt return ‹golpe,
insulto›; refute ‹crítica›; (retrucar)
retort ● vi hit back. **~de** m response

revigorar /xevigo'rar/ vt
strengthen ● vi. **~se** vpr regain
one's strength

revi|rar /xevi'rar/ vt turn out
‹bolsos, gavetas›; turn over ‹terra›;
turn inside out ‹roupa›; roll ‹olhos›.
~rar-se vpr toss and turn. **~ravolta**
/ɔ/ f (na política etc) about-face,
about-turn; (da situação) turnabout,
dramatic change

revi|são /xevi'zãw/ f (de lições
etc) revision; (de máquina, motor)
overhaul; (de carro) service; **~são de
provas** proofreading. **~sar** vt revise
‹provas, lições›; service ‹carro›.
~sor m (de bilhetes) ticket inspector;
~sor de provas proofreader

revista /xe'vista/ f (para ler)
magazine; (teatral) revue; (de tropas
etc) review; **passar ~ta a** review.
~tar vt search

reviver /xevi'ver/ vt relive ● vi
revive

revogar /xevo'gar/ vt revoke ‹lei›;
cancel ‹ordem›

revol|ta /xe'vɔwta/ f (rebelião)
revolt; (indignação) disgust. **~tante**
a disgusting. **~tar** vt disgust.
~tar-se vpr (rebelar-se) revolt;
(indignar-se) be disgusted. **~to**
/o/ a ‹casa, gaveta› upside down;
‹cabelo› dishevelled; ‹mar› rough;
‹mundo, região› troubled; ‹anos›
turbulent

revolu|ção /xevolu'sãw/ f
revolution. **~cionar** vt revolutionize.
~cionário a & m revolutionary

revolver /xevow'ver/ *vt* turn over
‹*terra*›; roll ‹*olhos*›; go through
‹*gavetas, arquivos*›

revólver /xe'vɔwver/ *m* revolver

re|za /'xeza/ *f* prayer. **~zar** *vi* pray
● *vt* say ‹*missa, oração*›; (*dizer*) state

riacho /xi'aʃu/ *m* stream

ribalta /xi'bawta/ *f* footlights

ribanceira /xibã'sera/ *f*
embankment

ribombar /xibõ'bar/ *vi* rumble

rico /'xiku/ *a* rich ● *m* rich man; **os
~s** the rich

ricochete /xiko'ʃetʃi/ *m* ricochet.
~ar *vi* ricochet

ricota /xi'kɔta/ *f* curd cheese,
ricotta

ridicularizar /xidʒikulari'zar/
vt ridicule

ridículo /xi'dʒikulu/ *a* ridiculous

ri|fa /'xifa/ *f* raffle. **~far** *vt* raffle

rifão /xi'fãw/ *m* saying

rifle /'xifli/ *m* rifle

rigidez /xiʒi'des/ *f* rigidity

rígido /'xiʒidu/ *a* rigid

rigor /xi'gor/ *m* severity;
(*meticulosidade*) rigour; **vestido a ~**
evening dress; **de ~** essential

rigoroso /xigo'rozu/ *a* strict;
‹*inverno, pena*› severe, harsh;
‹*lógica, estudo*› rigorous

rijo /'xiʒu/ *a* stiff; ‹*músculos*› firm

rim /xĩ/ *m* kidney; *pl* (*parte das
costas*) small of the back

ri|ma /'xima/ *f* rhyme. **~mar** *vt/i*
rhyme

rí|mel /'ximew/ (*pl* **~meis**) *m*
mascara

ringue /'xĩgi/ *m* ring

rinoceronte /xinose'rõtʃi/ *m*
rhinoceros

rinque /'xĩki/ *m* rink

rio /'xio/ *m* river

riqueza /xi'keza/ *f* wealth;
(*qualidade*) richness; *pl* riches

rir /xir/ *vi* laugh (**de** at)

risada /xi'zada/ *f* laugh, laughter;
dar ~ laugh

ris|ca /'xiska/ *f* stroke; (*listra*) stripe;
(*do cabelo*) parting; **à ~ca** to the
letter. **~car** *vt* (*apagar*) cross out
‹*erro*›; strike ‹*fósforo*›; scratch
‹*mesa, carro etc*›; write off ‹*amigo*›

risco[1] /'xisku/ *m* (*na parede etc*)
scratch; (*no papel*) line; (*esboço*) sketch

risco *m* risk

riso /'xizu/ *m* laugh. **~nho** /o/ *a*
smiling

ríspido /'xispidu/ *a* harsh

rítmico /'xitʃmiku/ *a* rhythmic

ritmo /'xitʃimu/ *m* rhythm

rito /'xitu/ *m* rite

ritu|al /xitu'aw/ (*pl* **~ais**) *a* & *m*
ritual

ri|val /xi'vaw/ (*pl* **~vais**) *a* & *m/f*
rival. **~validade** *f* rivalry. **~valizar** *vt*
rival ● *vi* vie (**com** with)

rixa /'xiʃa/ *f* fight

roaming /'xõming/ *m* *Telec*
roaming

robô /xo'bo/ *m* robot

robusto /xo'bustu/ *a* robust

roça /'xɔsa/ *f* (*campo*) country

rocambole /xokã'bɔli/ *m* roll

roçar /xo'sar/ *vt* graze; **~ em** brush
against

ro|cha /'xɔʃa/ *f* rock. **~chedo** /e/
m cliff

roda /'xɔda/ *f* (*de carro etc*) wheel;
(*de amigos etc*) circle; **~ dentada**
cog. **~da** *f* round. **~do a saia ~da**
full skirt. **~~gigante** (*pl* **~s-gigantes**)
f big wheel, *Amer* Ferris wheel.

~moinho m (de vento) whirlwind; (na água) whirlpool; fig whirl, swirl. **~pé** m skirting board, Amer baseboard

rodar /xo'dar/ vt (fazer girar) spin; (viajar por) go round; do ‹quilometragem›; shoot ‹filme›; run ‹programa› ● vi (girar) spin; (de carro) drive round

rodear /xodʒi'ar/ vt (circundar) surround; (andar ao redor de) go round

rodeio /xo'deju/ m (ao falar) circumlocution; (de gado) round-up; **falar sem ~s** talk straight

rodela /xo'dɛla/ f (de limão etc) slice; (peça de metal) washer

rodízio /xo'dʒiziu/ m rota

rodo /'xodu/ m rake

rodopiar /xodopi'ar/ vi spin round

rodovi|a /xodo'via/ f highway. **~ária** f bus station; **polícia ~ária** traffic police. **~ário** a road

ro|edor /xoe'dor/ m rodent. **~er** vt gnaw; bite ‹unhas›; fig eat away

rogar /xo'gar/ vi request

rojão /xo'ʒãw/ m rocket

rol /xɔw/ (pl róis) m roll

rolar /xo'lar/ vt roll ● vi roll; ▣ (acontecer) happen

roldana /xow'dana/ f pulley

roleta /xo'leta/ f (jogo) roulette; (borboleta) turnstile

rolha /'xoʎa/ f cork

roliço /xo'lisu/ a ‹objeto› cylindrical; ‹pessoa› plump

rolo /'xolu/ m (de filme, tecido etc) roll; (máquina, de cabelo) roller; **~ compressor** steamroller; **~ de massa** rolling pin

Roma /'xoma/ f Rome

romã /xo'mã/ f pomegranate

roman|ce /xo'mãsi/ m (livro) novel; (caso) romance. **~cista** m/f novelist

romano /xo'manu/ a & m Roman

romântico /xo'mãtʃiku/ a romantic

romantismo /xomã'tʃizmu/ m (amor) romance; (idealismo) romanticism

romaria /xoma'ria/ f pilgrimage

rombo /'xõbu/ m hole

Romênia /xo'menia/ f Romania

romeno /xo'menu/ a & m Romanian

rom|per /xõ'per/ vt break; break off ‹relações› ● vi ‹dia› break; ‹sol› rise; **~per com** break up with. **~pimento** m break; (de relações) breaking off

ron|car /xõ'kar/ vi (ao dormir) snore; ‹estômago› rumble. **~co** m snoring; (um) snore; (de motor) roar

ron|da /'xõda/ f round, patrol. **~dar** vt (patrulhar) patrol; (espreitar) prowl around ● vi ‹vigia etc› patrol; ‹animal, ladrão› prowl around

ronronar /xõxo'nar/ vi purr

roque[1] /'xɔki/ m (em xadrez) rook

ro|que[2] /'xɔki/ m (música) rock. **~queiro** m rock musician

rosa /'xɔza/ f rose ● a invar pink. **~do** a rosy; ‹vinho› rosé

rosário /xo'zariu/ m rosary

rosbife /xoz'bifi/ m roast beef

rosca /'xoska/ f (de parafuso) thread; (biscoito) rusk; **farinha de ~** breadcrumbs

roseira /xo'zera/ f rose bush

roseta /xo'zeta/ f rosette

rosnar /xoz'nar/ vi ‹cachorro› growl; ‹pessoa› snarl

rosto /'xostu/ m face

rota /'xɔta/ f route

rota|ção /xota'sãw/ f rotation. **~tividade** f turnround. **~tivo** a rotating

rotei|rista /xote'rista/ m/f scriptwriter. **~ro** m (de viagem) itinerary; (de filme, peça) script; (de discussão etc) outline

roti|na /xo'tʃina/ f routine. **~neiro** a routine

rótula /'xɔtula/ f kneecap

rotular /xotu'lar/ vt label (de as)

rótulo /'xɔtulu/ m label

rou|bar /xo'bar/ vt steal ‹dinheiro, carro etc›; rob ‹pessoa, loja etc› ● vi steal; (em jogo) cheat. **~bo** m theft, robbery

rouco /'xoku/ a hoarse; ‹voz› gravelly

rou|pa /'xopa/ f clothes; (uma) outfit; **~pa de baixo** underwear; **~pa de cama** bedclothes. **~pão** m dressing gown

rouquidão /xoki'dãw/ f hoarseness

rouxi|nol /xoʃi'nɔw/ (pl **~nóis**) m nightingale

roxo /'xoʃu/ a purple

rua /'xua/ f street

rubéola /xu'bɛola/ f German measles

rubi /xu'bi/ m ruby

rude /'xudʒi/ a rude

rudimentos /xudʒi'mẽtus/ m pl rudiments, basics

ruela /xu'ɛla/ f backstreet

rufar /xu'far/ vi ‹tambor› roll ● m roll

ruga /'xuga/ f (na pele) wrinkle; (na roupa) crease

ru|gido /xu'ʒidu/ m roar. **~gir** vi roar

ruibarbo /xui'barbu/ m rhubarb

ruído /xu'idu/ m noise

ruidoso /xui'dozu/ a noisy

ruim /xu'ĩ/ a bad

ruína /xu'ina/ f ruin

ruivo /'xuivu/ a ‹cabelo› red; ‹pessoa› red-haired ● m redhead

rulê /xu'le/ a **gola ~** roll-neck

rum /xũ/ m rum

ru|mar /xu'mar/ vi head (para for). **~mo** m course; **~mo a** a heading for; **sem ~mo** ‹vida› aimless; ‹andar› aimlessly

rumor /xu'mor/ m (da rua, de vozes) hum; (do trânsito) rumble; (boato) rumour

ru|ral /xu'raw/ (pl **~rais**) a rural

rusga /'xuzga/ f quarrel, disagreement

rush /xaʃ/ m rush hour

Rússia /'xusia/ f Russia

russo /'xusu/ a & m Russian

rústico /'xustʃiku/ a rustic

Ss

Saara /saa'ra/ m Sahara

sábado /'sabadu/ m Saturday

sabão /sa'bãw/ m soap; **~ em pó** soap powder

sabatina /saba'tʃina/ f test

sabedoria /sabedo'ria/ f wisdom

saber /sa'ber/ vt/i know (de about); (descobrir) find out (de about) ● m knowledge; **eu sei cantar** I know how to sing, I can sing; **sei lá** I've no idea; **que eu saiba** as far as I know

sabiá /sabi'a/ m thrush

sabi|chão /sabi'ʃãw/ a & m (f ~**chona**) know-it-all

sábio /'sabiu/ a wise ● m wise man

sabone|te /sabo'netʃi/ m bar of soap. ~**teira** f soap dish

sabor /sa'bor/ m flavour; **ao ~ de** at the mercy of

sabo|rear /sabori'ar/ vt savour. ~**roso** a tasty

sabo|tador /sabota'dor/ m saboteur. ~**tagem** f sabotage. ~**tar** vt sabotage

saca /'saka/ f sack

sacada /sa'kada/ f balcony

sa|cal /sa'kaw/ (pl ~**cais**) a 🄱 boring

saca|na /sa'kana/ 🄱 a (desonesto) devious; (lascivo) dirty-minded, naughty ● m/f rogue. ~**nagem** f 🄱 (esperteza) trickery; (sexo) sex; (uma) dirty trick. ~**near** vt 🄱 (enganar) do the dirty on; (amolar) take the mickey out of

sacar /sa'kar/ vt/i withdraw ‹dinheiro›; draw ‹arma›; (em tênis, vôlei etc) serve; 🄱 (entender) understand

saçaricar /sasari'kar/ vi play around

sacarina /saka'rina/ f saccharine

saca-rolhas /saka'xoʎas/ m invar corkscrew

sacer|dócio /saser'dɔsiu/ m priesthood. ~**dote** /ɔ/ m priest. ~**dotisa** f priestess

sachê /sa'ʃe/ m sachet

saciar /sasi'ar/ vt satisfy

saco /'saku/ m bag; **que ~!** 🄱 what a pain! **estar de ~ cheio (de)** 🄱 be fed up (with), be sick (of); **encher o ~ de alguém** 🄱 get on sb's nerves;

puxar o ~ de alguém 🄱 suck up to sb; **~ de dormir** sleeping bag. ~**la** /ɔ/ f bag. ~**lão** m wholesale fruit and vegetable market. ~**lejar** vt shake

sacramento /sakra'mẽtu/ m sacrament

sacri|ficar /sakrifi'kar/ vt sacrifice; have put down ‹cachorro etc›. ~**fício** m sacrifice. ~**légio** m sacrilege

sacrílego /sa'krilegu/ a sacrilegious

sacro /'sakru/ a ‹música› religious

sacrossanto /sakro'sãtu/ a sacrosanct

sacu|dida /saku'dʒida/ f shake. ~**dir** vt shake

sádico /'sadʒiku/ a sadistic ● m sadist

sadio /sa'dʒiu/ a healthy

sadismo /sa'dʒizmu/ m sadism

safa|deza /safa'deza/ f (desonestidade) deviousness; (libertinagem) indecency; (uma) dirty trick. ~**do** a (desonesto) devious; (lascivo) dirty-minded; (esperto) quick; ‹criança› naughty

safena /sa'fena/ f **ponte de ~** heart bypass. ~**do** m bypass patient

safira /sa'fira/ f sapphire

safra /'safra/ f crop

sagitariano /saʒitari'anu/ a & m Sagittarian

Sagitário /saʒi'tariu/ m Sagittarius

sagrado /sa'gradu/ a sacred

saguão /sa'gwãw/ m (de teatro, hotel) foyer, Amer lobby; (de estação, aeroporto) concourse

saia /'saja/ f skirt. ~**calça** (pl ~**s-calças**) f culottes

saída /sa'ida/ f (partida) departure; (porta) fig way out; **de ~** at the outset; **estar de** ~ be on one's way out

sair /sa'ir/ vi (de dentro) go/come out; (partir) leave; (desprender-se) come off; (resultar) turn out; ~ **mais barato** work out cheaper. ~**se** vpr fare; ~**se com** (dizer) come out with

sal /saw/ (pl **sais**) m salt; ~ **de frutas** Epsom salts

sala /'sala/ f (numa casa) lounge; (num lugar público) hall; (classe) class; **fazer ~ a** entertain; ~ (de **aula**) classroom; ~ **de embarque** departure lounge; ~ **de espera** waiting room; ~ **de jantar** dining room; ~ **de operação** operating theatre

sala|da /sa'lada/ f salad; fig jumble, mishmash; ~**da de frutas** fruit salad. ~**deira** f salad bowl

sala e quarto /sali'kwartu/ m two-room flat

sala|me /sa'lami/ m salami. ~**minho** m pepperoni

salão /sa'lãw/ m hall; (de cabeleireiro) salon; (de carros) show; ~ **de beleza** beauty salon

salari|al /salari'aw/ (pl ~**ais**) a wage

salário /sa'lariu/ m salary

sal|dar /saw'dar/ vt settle. ~**do** m balance

saleiro /sa'leru/ m salt cellar

sal|gadinhos /sawga'dʒiɲus/ m pl snacks. ~**gado** a salty; ‹preço› exorbitant. ~**gar** vt salt

salgueiro /saw'geru/ m willow; ~ **chorão** weeping willow

saliência /sali'ẽsia/ f projection

salien|tar /saliẽ'tar/ vt (deixar claro) point out; (acentuar) highlight. ~**tar-se** vpr distinguish

o.s.. ~**te** a prominent

saliva /sa'liva/ f saliva

salmão /saw'mãw/ m salmon

salmo /'sawmu/ m psalm

salmonela /sawmo'nela/ f salmonella

salmoura /saw'mora/ f brine

salpicar /sawpi'kar/ vt sprinkle; (sem querer) spatter

salsa /'sawsa/ f parsley

salsicha /saw'sifa/ f sausage

saltar /saw'tar/ vt (pular) jump; (omitir) skip ● vi jump; ~ **à vista** be obvious; ~ **do ônibus** get off the bus

saltear /sawtʃi'ar/ vt sauté ‹batatas etc›

saltitar /sawtʃi'tar/ vi hop

salto /'sawtu/ m (pulo) jump; (de sapato) heel; ~ **com vara** pole vault; ~ **em altura** high jump; ~ **em distância** long jump. ~**mortal** (pl ~**s-mortais**) m somersault

salu|bre /sa'lubri/ a healthy. ~**tar** a salutary

salva[1] /'sawva/ f (de canhões) salvo; (bandeja) salver; ~ **de palmas** round of applause

salva[2] /'sawva/ f (erva) sage

salva|ção /sawva'sãw/ f salvation. ~**dor** m saviour

salvaguar|da /sawva'gwarda/ f safeguard. ~**dar** vt safeguard

sal|vamento /sawva'mẽtu/ m rescue; (de navio) salvage. ~**var** vt save. ~**var-se** vpr escape. ~**va-vidas** m invar (bóia) lifebelt ● m/f (pessoa) lifeguard ● a barco ~**va-vidas** lifeboat. ~**vo** a safe ● prep save; **a ~vo** safe

samambaia /samã'baja/ f fern

sam|ba /'sãba/ *m* samba.
~ba-canção (*pl* **~bas-canção**) *m* slow
samba ● *a invar* **cueca ~ba-canção**
boxer shorts; **~ba-enredo** (*pl*
~bas-enredo) *m* samba story. **~bar**
vi samba. **~bista** *m/f* (*dançarino*)
samba dancer; (*compositor*)
composer of sambas. **~bódromo** *m*
Carnival parade ground

samovar /samo'var/ *m* tea urn

sanar /sa'nar/ *vt* cure

san|ção /sã'sãw/ *f* sanction.
~cionar *vt* sanction

sandália /sã'dalia/ *f* sandal

sandes /'sãdʒiʃ/ *f invar* Port sandwich

sanduíche /sãdu'iʃi/ *m* sandwich

sane|amento /sania'mẽtu/ *m*
(*esgotos*) sanitation; (*de finanças*)
rehabilitation. **~ar** *vt* set straight
⟨*finanças*⟩

sanfona /sã'fona/ *f* (*instrumento*)
accordion; (*tricô*) ribbing. **~do** *a*
⟨*porta*⟩ folding; ⟨*pulôver*⟩ ribbed

san|grar /sã'grar/ *vt/i* bleed.
~grento *a* bloody; ⟨*carne*⟩ rare.
~gria *f* bloodshed; (*de dinheiro*)
extortion

sangue /'sãgi/ *m* blood; **~ pisado**
bruise. **~-frio** *m* cool, coolness

sanguessuga /sãgi'suga/ *f* leech

sanguinário /sãgi'nariu/ *a*
bloodthirsty

sanguíneo /sã'giniu/ *a* blood

sanidade /sani'dadʒi/ *f* sanity

sanitário /sani'tariu/ *a* sanitary.
~s *m pl* toilets

san|tidade /sãtʃi'dadʒi/ *f* sanctity.
~tificar *vt* sanctify. **~to** *a* holy;
todo ~to dia every single day ● *m*
saint. **~tuário** *m* sanctuary

são /sãw/ (*pl* **~s**) *a* (*f* **sã**) healthy;
(*mentalmente*) sane; ⟨*conselho*⟩
sound

São /sãw/ *a* Saint

sapataria /sapata'ria/ *f* shoe shop

sapate|ado /sapatʃi'adu/ *m* tap
dancing. **~ador** *m* tap dancer. **~ar** *vi*
tap one's feet; (*dançar*) tap-dance

sapa|teiro /sapa'teru/ *m*
shoemaker. **~tilha** *f* pump; **~tilha
de balé** ballet shoe

sapato /sa'patu/ *m* shoe

sapeca /sa'pɛka/ *a* saucy

sa|pinho /sa'piɲu/ *m* thrush. **~po**
m toad

saque[1] /'saki/ *m* (*do banco*)
withdrawal; (*em tênis, vôlei etc*) serve

saque[2] /'saki/ *m* (*de loja etc*)
looting. **~ar** *vt* loot

saraiva /sa'rajva/ *f* hail. **~da** *f*
hailstorm; **uma ~da de** a hail of

sarampo /sa'rãpu/ *m* measles

sarar /sa'rar/ *vt* cure ● *vi* get better;
⟨*ferida*⟩ heal

sar|casmo /sar'kazmu/ *m*
sarcasm. **~cástico** *a* sarcastic

sarda /'sarda/ *f* freckle

Sardenha /sar'deɲa/ *f* Sardinia

sardento /sar'dẽtu/ *a* freckled

sardinha /sar'dʒiɲa/ *f* sardine

sardônico /sar'doniku/ *a* sardonic

sargento /sar'ʒẽtu/ *m* sergeant

sarjeta /sar'ʒeta/ *f* gutter

Satanás /sata'nas/ *m* Satan

satânico /sa'taniku/ *a* satanic

satélite /sa'tɛlitʃi/ *a & m* satellite

sátira /'satʃira/ *f* satire

satírico /sa'tʃiriku/ *a* satirical

satirizar /satʃiri'zar/ *vt* satirize

satisfa|ção /satʃiʃfa'sãw/ *f*
satisfaction; **dar ~ções** a answer
to. **~tório** *a* satisfactory. **~zer** *vt*
~zer (a) satisfy ● *vi* be satisfactory.
~zer-se *vpr* be satisfied

satisfeito /satʃiˈfejtu/ a satisfied; (*contente*) content; (*de comida*) full

saturar /satuˈrar/ vt saturate

Saturno /saˈturnu/ m Saturn

saudação /sawdaˈsãw/ f greeting

saudade /sawˈdadʒi/ f longing; (*lembrança*) nostalgia; **estar com ~s de** miss; **matar ~s** catch up

saudar /sawˈdar/ vt greet

saudá|vel /sawˈdavew/ (*pl* **~veis**) a healthy

saúde /saˈudʒi/ f health ● *int* (*ao beber*) cheers; (*ao espirrar*) bless you

saudo|sismo /sawdoˈzizmu/ m nostalgia. **~so** /o/ a longing; **estar ~so de** miss; **o nosso ~so amigo** our much-missed friend

sauna /ˈsawna/ f sauna

saxofo|ne /saksoˈfoni/ m saxophone. **~nista** m/f saxophonist

sazo|nado /sazoˈnadu/ a seasoned. **~nal** (*pl* **~nais**) a seasonal

---

se /si/ ● *conj*

····▸ (*causa*) if; **~ chover, não vamos** if it rains, we won't go; **~ fosse rico, comprava uma moto** if I were rich, I'd buy a motorbike

❗ É mais correto dizer if I/he/she/it **were**, mas coloquialmente usa-se frequentemente **was**. (*dúvida*) whether; **não sei se vou ou se fico** I don't know whether to stay or go

❗ usa-se **whether** e não **if** antes de infinitivo e depois de preposições. (*desejo*) if; **se ao menos você tivesse me dito!** if only you had told me!

● *pron*

····▸ (*reflexo*) (ele) himself, (ela) herself; (*coisa*) itself; (*você*)

yourself; (*vocês*) yourselves; (*eles, elas*) themselves; **ela ~ cortou** she's cut herself; **vocês ~ magoaram** you've hurt yourselves; **eles ~ lavaram** they've washed themselves; (*recíproco*) each other, one another; **eles ~ amam** they love each other; **eles ~ telefonam todos os dias** they phone each other every day

····▸ (*passivo*) **registaram-~ três mortos** three deaths were recorded (*sujeito indeterminado*) **fala-~ alemão** German is spoken

····▸ (*em expressões*) **bem que** although

sebo /ˈsebu/ m (*sujeira*) grease; (*livraria*) second-hand bookshop. **~so** /o/ a greasy; ‹*pessoa*› slimy

seca /ˈseka/ f drought. **~dor m ~dor de cabelo** hairdryer. **~dora** f tumble dryer

seção /seˈsãw/ f section; (*de loja*) department

secar /seˈkar/ vt/i dry

sec|ção /sekˈsãw/ f ▶ **SEÇÃO**. **~cionar** vt split up

seco /ˈseku/ a dry; ‹*resposta, tom*› curt; ‹*pessoa, caráter*› cold; ‹*barulho, pancada*› dull; **estar ~ por** I'm dying for

secretaria /sekretaˈria/ f (*de empresa*) general office; (*ministério*) department

secretá|ria /sekreˈtaria/ f secretary; **~ria eletrônica** ansaphone. **~rio** m secretary

secreto /seˈkretu/ a secret

secular /sekuˈlar/ a (*não religioso*) secular; (*antigo*) age-old

século /ˈsekulu/ m century; *pl* (*muito tempo*) ages

secundário /sekuˈdariu/ a
secondary

secura /seˈkura/ f dryness; **estar
com uma ~ de** be longing for/to

seda /ˈseda/ f silk

sedativo /sedaˈtʃivu/ a & m
sedative

sede¹ /ˈsɛdʒi/ f headquarters; (*local
do governo*) seat

sede² /ˈsedʒi/ f thirst (**de** for); **estar
com ~** be thirsty

sedentário /sedẽˈtariu/ a
sedentary

sedento /seˈdẽtu/ a thirsty (**de** for)

sediar /sedʒiˈar/ vt host

sedimen|tar /sedʒimẽˈtar/ vt
consolidate. **~to** m sediment

sedoso /seˈdozu/ a silky

sedu|ção /seduˈsãw/ f seduction.
~tor a seductive. **~zir** vt seduce

segmento /segˈmẽtu/ m segment

segredo /seˈgredu/ m secret; (*de
cofre etc*) combination

segregar /segreˈgar/ vt segregate

segui|da /seˈgida/ f **em ~da**
(*imediatamente*) straight away;
(*depois*) next; **cinco horas ~das**
five hours running. **~do** a followed
(**de** by). **~dor** m follower. **~mento**
m continuation; **dar ~mento a** go
on with

se|guinte /seˈgĩtʃi/ a following;
‹*dia, semana etc*› next. **~guir** vt/i
follow; (*continuar*) continue; **~guir
em frente** (*ir embora*) go; (*indicação
na rua*) go straight ahead. **~guir-se**
vpr follow

segun|da /seˈgũda/ f (*dia*) Monday;
(*marcha*) second; **de ~da** second-
rate; **~das intenções** ulterior
motives; **de ~da mão** second-hand.
~da-feira (*pl* **~das-feiras**) f Monday.
~do a & m second ● adv secondly

● prep according to ● conj according
to what

segu|rança /seguˈrãsa/ f security;
(*estado de seguro*) safety; (*certeza*)
assurance ● m/f security guard. **~rar**
vt hold. **~rar-se** vpr (*controlar-se*)
control o.s.; **~rar-se em** hold on to;
fazer ~ro de insure. **~ro** a secure;
(*fora de perigo*) safe; (*com certeza*)
sure ● m insurance; **estar no ~ro**
be insured. **~ro-desemprego** m
unemployment benefit

seio /ˈseju/ m breast, bosom; **no ~
de** within

seis /sejs/ a & m six. **~centos** a & m
six hundred

seita /ˈsejta/ f sect

seixo /ˈsejʃu/ m pebble

sela /ˈsɛla/ f saddle

selar¹ /seˈlar/ vt saddle ‹*cavalo*›

selar² /seˈlar/ vt seal; (*franquear*)
stamp

sele|ção /seleˈsãw/ f selection;
(*time*) team. **~cionar** vt select. **~to**
/ɛ/ a select

selim /seˈlĩ/ m saddle

selo /ˈselu/ m seal; (*postal*) stamp;
(*de discos*) label

selva /ˈsɛwva/ f jungle. **~gem** a
wild. **~geria** f savagery

sem /sẽj/ prep without; **~ eu saber**
without me knowing; **ficar ~
dinheiro** run out of money

semáforo /seˈmaforu/ m (*na rua*)
traffic lights; (*de ferrovia*) signal

sema|na /seˈmana/ f week. **~nal**
(*pl* **~nais**) a weekly. **~nalmente** adv
weekly. **~nário** m weekly

semear /semiˈar/ vt sow

semelhan|ça /semeˈʎãsa/ f
similarity. **~te** a similar; (*tal*) such

sêmen /ˈsemẽ/ m semen

semente /se'mẽtʃi/ f seed; (em fruta) pip

semestre /se'mɛstri/ m six months; (da faculdade etc) term, Amer semester

semi|círculo /semi'sirkulu/ m semicircle. **~final** (pl **~finais**) f semi-final

seminário /semi'nariu/ m (aula) seminar; (colégio religioso) seminary

sem-número /sẽ'numeru/ m um **~ de** innumerable

sempre /'sẽpri/ adv always; **como ~** as usual; **para ~** for ever; **~ que** whenever

sem-terra /sẽ'texa/ m/f invar landless labourer. **~teto** a homeless ● m/f homeless person; **~vergonha** a invar brazen ● m/f invar scoundrel

sena|do /se'nadu/ m senate. **~dor** m senator

senão /si'nãw/ conj otherwise; (mas antes) but rather ● m snag

senda /'sẽda/ f path

senha /'seɲa/ f (palavra) password; (número) code; (sinal) signal

senhor /se'ɲor/ m gentleman; (homem idoso) older man; (tratamento) sir ● a (f **~a**) mighty; **Senhor** (com nome) Mr; (Deus) Lord; **o ~** (você) you

senho|ra /se'ɲɔra/ f lady; (mulher idosa) older woman; (tratamento) madam; **Senhora** (com nome) Mrs; **a ~a** (você) you; **nossa ~a!** 🛇 gosh. **~ria** f Vossa Senhoria you. **~rita** f young lady; (tratamento) miss; **Senhorita** (com nome) Miss

se|nil (pl **~nis**) a senile. **~nilidade** f senility

sensação /sẽsa'sãw/ f sensation

sensacio|nal /sẽsasio'naw/ (pl **~nais**) a sensational. **~nalismo**

m sensationalism. **~nalista** a sensationalist

sen|sato /sẽ'satu/ a sensible. **~sibilidade** f sensitivity. **~sível** (pl **~síveis**) a sensitive; (que se pode sentir) noticeable. **~so** m sense. **~sual** (pl **~suais**) a sensual

sen|tado /sẽ'tadu/ a sitting. **~tar** vt/i sit. **~tar-se** vpr sit down

sentença /sẽ'tẽsa/ f sentence

sentido /sẽ'tʃidu/ m sense; (direção) direction ● a hurt; **fazer** ou **ter ~** make sense

sentimen|tal /sẽtʃimẽ'taw/ (pl **~tais**) a sentimental; **vida ~tal** love life. **~to** m feeling

sentinela /sẽtʃi'nɛla/ f sentry

sentir /sẽ'tʃir/ vt feel; (notar) sense; smell ‹cheiro›; taste ‹gosto›; tell ‹diferença›; (ficar magoado por) be hurt by ● vi feel. **~se** vpr feel; **sinto muito** I'm very sorry

sepa|ração /separa'sãw/ f separation. **~rado** a separate; ‹casal› separated. **~rar** vt separate. **~rar-se** vpr separate

séptico /'sɛptʃiku/ a septic

sepul|tar /sepuw'tar/ vt bury. **~tura** f grave

sequência /se'kwẽsia/ f sequence

sequer /se'ker/ adv **nem ~** not even

seques|trador /sekwestra'dor/ m kidnapper; (de avião) hijacker. **~trar** vt kidnap ‹pessoa›; hijack ‹avião›; sequestrate ‹bens›. **~tro** /ɛ/ m (de pessoa) kidnapping; (de avião) hijack; (de bens) sequestration

ser /ser/ ● vi
····▶ be; **é alta** she's tall; **sou de Porto Alegre** I'm from Porto Alegre; **2 e 2 são 4** two and two are four; **são três reais** it's three

reais; **o banco é na praça** the bank is in the square; *(com as horas)* **são sete horas** it's seven o'clock; **~ de** *(material)* be made of; **é de alumínio** it's made of aluminium; *(lugar)* be from; **ele é do Brasil** he's from Brazil; *(grupo esportivo)* support; **é do Flamengo** she is a Flamengo supporter

● *v aux*

····▶ *(passiva)* to be; **ele será julgado segunda-feira** he will be tried on Monday

● *nm*

····▶ being; **um ~ humano** a human being; **um ~ vivo** a living being

····▶ *(em expressões)* **é que:** *(ênfase)* **é que não me apetece** I just don't feel like it; **seja como for, seja o que for, seja quem for** no matter how/what/who; **sou eu/é você etc** it's me/you etc

sereia /se'reja/ *f* mermaid
serenata /sere'nata/ *f* serenade
sereno /se'renu/ *a* serene; *‹tempo›* fine
série /'sɛri/ *f* series; *(na escola)* grade; **fora de ~** 🄸 incredible
seriedade /serie'dadʒi/ *f* seriousness
serin|ga /se'rĩga/ *f* syringe. **~gueiro** *m* rubber tapper
sério /'sɛriu/ *a* serious; *(responsável)* responsible; **~?** really?; **falar ~** be serious; **levar a ~** take seriously
sermão /ser'mãw/ *m* sermon
seropositivo /sɛropuzi'tivu/ *a* Port ▶ **soropositivo** /soropozi'tʃivu/
serpen|te /ser'pẽtʃi/ *f* serpent. **~tear** *vi* wind. **~tina** *f* streamer

serra[1] /'sɛxa/ *f (montanhas)* mountain range
serra[2] /'sɛxa/ *f (de serrar)* saw. **~gem** *f* sawdust. **~lheiro** *m* locksmith
serrano /se'xanu/ *a* mountain
serrar /se'xar/ *vt* saw
ser|tanejo /serta'neʒu/ *a* from the backwoods ● *m* backwoodsman. **~tão** *m* backwoods
servente /ser'vẽtʃi/ *m/f* labourer
Sérvia /'sɛrvia/ *f* Serbia
servi|çal /servi'saw/ *(pl* **~çais)** *a* helpful ● *m/f* servant. **~ço** *m* service; *(trabalho)* work; *(tarefa)* job; **estar de ~ço** be on duty. **~dor** *m* servant; Comput server. **~dor público** *m* civil servant
ser|vil /ser'viw/ *(pl* **~vis)** *a* servile
sérvio /'sɛrviu/ *a* & *m* Serbian
servir /ser'vir/ *vt* serve; serve as ● *vi* serve; *(ser adequado)* do; *(ser útil)* be of use; *‹roupa, sapato etc›* fit; **~ como** ou **de** serve as; **para que serve isso?** what is this (used) for?. **~se** *vpr (ao comer etc)* help o.s. *(de* to); **~se de** make use of
sessão /se'sãw/ *f* session; *(no cinema)* showing, performance
sessenta /se'sẽta/ *a* & *m* sixty
seta /'sɛta/ *f* arrow; *(de carro)* indicator
sete /'sɛtʃi/ *a* & *m* seven. **~centos** *a* & *m* seven hundred
setembro /se'tẽbru/ *m* September
setenta /se'tẽta/ *a* & *m* seventy
sétimo /'sɛtʃimu/ *a* seventh
setor /se'tor/ *m* sector
setuagésimo /setua'ʒɛzimu/ *a* seventieth
seu /sew/ *a (f* **sua)** *(dele)* his; *(dela)* her; *(de coisa)* its; *(deles)* their;

(de você, de vocês) your ● *pron* (dele)
his; (dela) hers; (deles) theirs; (de
você, de vocês) yours; ~ **idiota!** you
idiot!; **seu João** Mr John

seve|ridade /severi'dadʒi/ f
severity. ~**ro** /ɛ/ a severe

sexagésimo /seksa'ʒezimu/ a
sixtieth

sexo /'seksu/ m sex; **fazer** ~ have
sex; **do mesmo** ~ ‹casais, pessoas›
same-sex

sex|ta /'sesta/ f Friday. ~**ta-feira**
(pl ~**tas-feiras**) f Friday; **Sexta-feira
Santa** Good Friday. ~**to** /e/ a &
m sixth

sexu|al /seksu'aw/ (pl ~**ais**) a
sexual; **vida** ~**al** sex life

sexy /'seksi/ a invar sexy

shopping /'ʃɔpi/ (pl ~**s**) m
shopping centre, Amer mall

short /'ʃɔrtʃi/ m (pl ~**s**) shorts; **um**
~ a pair of shorts

show /'ʃou/ (pl ~**s**) m show; (de
música) concert

si /si/ pron (ele) himself; (ela) herself;
(coisa) itself; (você) yourself; (eles)
themselves; (vocês) yourselves;
(qualquer pessoa) oneself; **em** ~ in
itself; **fora de** ~ beside o.s.; **cheio
de** ~ full of o.s.; **voltar a** ~ come
round

sibilar /sibi'lar/ vi hiss

SIDA /'sida/ f Port ▶ AIDS

side|ral /side'raw/ (pl ~**rais**) a
espaço ~**ral** outer space

siderurgia /siderur'ʒia/ f iron and
steel industry

siderúrgi|ca /side'rurʒika/ f
steelworks. ~**co** a iron and steel ● m
steelworker

sifão /si'fãw/ m syphon

sífilis /'sifilis/ f syphilis

sigilo /si'ʒilu/ m secrecy. ~**so** /o/
a secret

sigla /'sigla/ f acronym

signatário /signa'tariu/ m
signatory

signifi|cação /signifika'sãw/ f
significance. ~**cado** m meaning.
~**car** vt mean. ~**cativo** a significant

signo /'signu/ m sign

sílaba /'silaba/ f syllable

silenciar /silẽsi'ar/ vt silence

silêncio /si'lẽsiu/ m silence

silencioso /silẽsi'ozu/ a silent ● m
silencer, Amer muffler

silhueta /siʎu'eta/ f silhouette

silício /si'lisiu/ m silicon

silicone /sili'kɔni/ m silicone

silo /'silu/ m silo

silvar /siw'var/ vi hiss

sil|vestre /siw'vestri/ a wild.
~**vicultura** f forestry

sim /sĩ/ adv yes; **acho que** ~
I think so

simbólico /sĩ'bɔliku/ a symbolic

simbo|lismo /sĩbo'lizmu/ m
symbolism. ~**lizar** vt symbolize

símbolo /'sĩbolu/ m symbol

si|metria /sime'tria/ f symmetry.
~**métrico** a symmetrical

similar /simi'lar/ a similar

sim|patia /sĩpa'tʃia/ f (qualidade)
pleasantness; (afeto) fondness
(**por** for); (compreensão, apoio)
sympathy; pl sympathies; **ter** ~**patia
por** be fond of. ~**pático** a nice

simpati|zante /sĩpatʃi'zãtʃi/
a sympathetic ● m/f sympathizer.
~**zar** vi ~**zar com** take a liking to
‹pessoa›; sympathize with ‹ideias,
partido etc›

simples /'sĩplis/ a invar simple;
(único) single ● f (no tênis etc)

singles. **~mente** *adv* simply

simpli|cidade /sīplisiˈdadʒi/ f simplicity. **~ficar** *vt* simplify

simplório /sīˈplɔriu/ *a* simple

simpósio /sīˈpɔziu/ *m* symposium

simu|lação /simulaˈsãw/ f simulation. **~lar** *vt* simulate

simultâneo /simuwˈtaniu/ *a* simultaneous

sina /ˈsina/ f fate

sinagoga /sinaˈgɔga/ f synagogue

si|nal /siˈnaw/ (*pl* **~nais**) *m* sign; (*aviso, de rádio etc*) signal; (*de trânsito*) traffic light; (*no telefone*) tone; (*dinheiro*) deposit; (*na pele*) mole; **por ~nal**, as a matter of fact; **~nal de pontuação** punctuation mark. **~naleira** f traffic lights. **~nalização** f (*na rua*) road signs. **~nalizar** *vt* signal; signpost ‹*rua, cidade*›

since|ridade /sīseriˈdadʒi/ f sincerity. **~ro** /e/ *a* sincere

sincro|nia /sīkroˈnia/ f synchronization. **~nizar** *vt* synchronize

sindi|cal /sīdʒiˈkaw/ (*pl* **~cais**) *a* trade union. **~calismo** *m* trade unionism. **~calista** *m/f* trade unionist. **~calizar** *vt* unionize. **~cato** *m* trade union

síndico /ˈsīdʒiku/ *m* house manager

síndrome /ˈsīdromi/ f syndrome

sinergia /sinerˈʒia/ f synergy

sineta /siˈneta/ f bell

sin|fonia /sīfoˈnia/ f symphony. **~fônica** f symphony orchestra

Singapura /sīgaˈpura/ f Singapore

singe|leza /sīʒeˈleza/ f simplicity. **~lo** /e/ *a* simple

singu|lar /sīguˈlar/ *a* singular; (*estranho*) peculiar. **~larizar** *vt* single out

sinis|trado /sinisˈtradu/ *a* damaged. **~tro** *a* sinister ● *m* accident

sino /ˈsinu/ *m* bell

sinônimo /siˈnonimu/ *a* synonymous ● *m* synonym

sintaxe /sīˈtaksi/ f syntax

síntese /ˈsītezi/ f synthesis

sin|tético /sīˈtɛtʃiku/ *a* (*artificial*) synthetic; (*resumido*) concise. **~tetizar** *vt* summarize

sinto|ma /sīˈtoma/ *m* symptom. **~mático** *a* symptomatic

sintoni|zador /sītonizaˈdor/ *m* tuner. **~zar** *vt* tune ‹*rádio, TV*›; tune in to ‹*emissora*› ● *vi* be in tune (**com** with)

sinuca /siˈnuka/ f snooker

sinuoso /sinuˈozu/ *a* winding

sinusite /sinuˈzitʃi/ f sinusitis

siri /siˈri/ *m* crab

Síria /ˈsiria/ f Syria

sírio /ˈsiriu/ *a* & *m* Syrian

siso /ˈsizu/ *m* good sense

siste|ma /sisˈtema/ *m* system. **~mático** *a* systematic

sisudo /siˈzudu/ *a* serious

site /sajt/ *m* Comput website

sítio /ˈsitʃiu/ *m* (*chácara*) farm; *Port* (*local*) place; **estado de ~** state of siege

situ|ação /situaˈsãw/ f situation; (*no governo*) party in power. **~ar** *vt* situate. **~ar-se** *vpr* be situated; ‹*pessoa*› position o.s.

smoking /izˈmokĩ/ (*pl* **~s**) *m* dinner jacket, *Amer* tuxedo

só /sɔ/ *a* alone; (*sentindo solidão*) lonely ● *adv* only; **um ~ voto** one single vote; **~ um carro** only one car; **~s** alone; **imagina ~** just imagine; **~ que** except (that)

soalho /so'aʎu/ *m* floor

soar /so'ar/ *vt/i* sound

sob /'sobi/ *prep* under

sobera|nia /sobera'nia/ *f* sovereignty. **~no** *a & m* sovereign

soberbo /so'berbu/ *a* <pessoa> haughty; (*magnífico*) splendid

sobra /'sɔbra/ *f* surplus; *pl* leftovers; **tempo de ~** (*muito*) plenty of time; **ficar de ~** be left over; **ter algo de ~** (*sobrando*) have sth left over

sobraçar /sobra'sar/ *vt* carry under one's arm

sobrado /so'bradu/ *m* (*casa*) house; (*andar*) upper floor

sobrancelha /sobrã'seʎa/ *f* eyebrow

so|brar /so'brar/ *vi* be left; **~bram-me dois** I have two left

sobre /'sobri/ *prep* (*em cima de*) on; (*por cima de, acima de*) over; (*acerca de*) about

sobreaviso /sobria'vizu/ *m* **estar de ~** be on one's guard

sobrecapa /sobri'kapa/ *f* dust jacket

sobrecarregar /sobrikaxe'gar/ *vt* overload

sobreloja /sobri'lɔʒa/ *f* mezzanine

sobremesa /sobri'meza/ *f* dessert

sobrenatu|ral /sobrinatu'raw/ (*pl* **~rais**) *a* supernatural

sobrenome /sobri'nomi/ *m* surname

sobrepor /sobri'por/ *vt* superimpose

sobrepujar /sobripu'ʒar/ *vt* (*em altura*) tower over; (*em valor, número etc*) surpass; overwhelm

<adversário>; overcome <problemas>

sobrescritar /sobriskri'tar/ *vt* address

sobressair /sobrisa'ir/ *vi* stand out. **~se** *vpr* stand out

sobressalente /sobrisa'lẽtʃi/ *a* spare

sobressal|tar /sobrisaw'tar/ *vt* startle. **~tar-se** *vpr* be startled. **~to** *m* (*movimento*) start; (*susto*) fright

sobretaxa /sobri'taʃa/ *f* surcharge

sobretudo /sobri'tudu/ *adv* above all ● *m* overcoat

sobrevir /sobri'vir/ *vi* happen suddenly; (*seguir*) ensue; **~ a** follow

sobrevi|vência /sobrivi'vẽsia/ *f* survival. **~vente** *a* m/f surviving ● m/f survivor. **~ver** *vt/i* **~ver (a)** survive

sobrevoar /sobrivo'ar/ *vt* fly over

sobri|nha /so'briɲa/ *f* niece. **~nho** *m* nephew

sóbrio /'sɔbriu/ *a* sober

socar /so'kar/ *vt* (*esmurrar*) punch; (*amassar*) crush

soci|al /sosi'aw/ (*pl* **~ais**) *a* social; **camisa ~al** dress shirt. **~alismo** *m* socialism. **~alista** *a & m/f* socialist. **~alite** /-a'lajtʃi/ *m/f* socialite. **~ável** (*pl* **~áveis**) *a* sociable

sociedade /sosie'dadʒi/ *f* society; (*parceria*) partnership; **~ anônima** limited company

sócio /'sɔsiu/ *m* (*de empresa*) partner; (*de clube*) member

socioeconômico /sosioeko'nomiku/ *a* socio-economic

soci|ologia /sosiolo'ʒia/ *f* sociology. **~ológico** *a* sociological. **~ólogo** *m* sociologist

soco /'soku/ *m* punch; **dar um ~ em** punch

socor|rer /soko'xer/ *vt* help. **~ro**
m aid; **primeiros ~ros** first aid
● *int* help

soda /'sɔda/ *f (água)* soda water;
~ cáustica caustic soda

sódio /'sɔdʒiu/ *m* sodium

sofá /so'fa/ *m* sofa. **~-cama**
(pl **~s-camas)** *m* sofa bed

sofisticado /sofistʃi'kadu/ *a*
sophisticated

so|fredor /sofre'dor/ *a* martyred.
~frer *vt* suffer *‹dor, derrota, danos
etc›*; have *‹acidente›*; undergo
‹operação, mudança etc› ● *vi* suffer;
~frer de suffer from *‹doença›*;
have trouble with *‹coração etc›*.
~frido *a* long-suffering. **~frimento**
m suffering. **~frível** *(pl* **~fríveis)** *a*
passable

soft /'sɔftʃi/ *(pl* **~s)** *m* software
package. **~ware** *m* software; *(um)*
software package

so|gra /'sɔgra/ *f* mother-in-law.
~gro /o/ *m* father-in-law. **~gros** /ɔ/
m pl in-laws

soja /'sɔʒa/ *f* soya, *Amer* soy

sol /sɔw/ *(pl* **sóis)** *m* sun; **faz ~** it's
sunny

sola /'sɔla/ *f* sole. **~do a** *‹bolo›* flat

solapar /sola'par/ *vt* undermine

solar¹ /so'lar/ *a* solar

solar² /so'lar/ *vt* sole *‹sapato›* ● *vi*
‹bolo› go flat

solavanco /sola'vãku/ *m* jolt;
dar ~s jolt

soldado /sow'dadu/ *m* soldier

sol|dadura /sowda'dura/ *f* weld.
~dar *vt* weld

soldo /'sowdu/ *m* pay

soleira /so'lera/ *f* doorstep

sole|ne /so'leni/ *a* solemn.
~nidade *f (cerimônia)* ceremony;

(qualidade) solemnity

soletrar /sole'trar/ *vt* spell

solici|tação /solisita'sãw/
f request *(de* for); *(por escrito)*
application *(de* for). **~tante** *m/f*
applicant. **~tar** *vt* request; *(por
escrito)* apply for

solícito /so'lisitu/ *a* helpful

solidão /soli'dãw/ *f* loneliness

solida|riedade /solidarie'dadʒi/
f solidarity. **~dário** *a* supportive
(com of)

soli|dez /soli'des/ *f* solidity.
~dificar *vt* solidify. **~dificar-se** *vpr*
solidify

sólido /'sɔlidu/ *a & m* solid

solista /so'lista/ *m/f* soloist

solitá|ria /soli'taria/ *f (verme)*
tapeworm; *(cela)* solitary
confinement. **~rio** *a* solitary

solo¹ /'sɔlu/ *m (terra)* soil; *(chão)*
ground

solo² /'sɔlu/ *m* solo

soltar /sow'tar/ *vt* let go
‹prisioneiros, animal etc›; let loose
‹cães›; *(deixar de segurar)* let go
of; loosen *‹gravata, corda etc›*; let
down *‹cabelo›*; let out *‹grito, suspiro
etc›*; let off *‹foguetes›*; tell *‹piada›*;
take off *‹freio›*. **~se** *vpr ‹peça,
parafuso›* come loose; *‹pessoa›*
let o.s. go

soltei|ra /sow'tera/ *f* single
woman. **~rão** *m* bachelor. **~ro**
a single ● *m* single man. **~rona** *f*
spinster

solto /'sowtu/ *a (livre)* free; *‹cães›*
loose; *‹cabelo›* down; *‹arroz›* fluffy;
(frouxo) loose; *(à vontade)* relaxed;
(abandonado) abandoned; **correr
~** run wild

solução /solu'sãw/ *f* solution

soluçar /solu'sar/ vi (ao chorar) sob; (engasgar) hiccup

solucionar /solusio'nar/ vt solve

soluço /so'lusu/ m (ao chorar) sob; (engasgo) hiccup; **estar com ~s** have the hiccups

solúvel /so'luvew/ (pl ~veis) a soluble

solvente /sow'vẽtʃi/ a & m solvent

som /sõ/ m sound; (aparelho) stereo; **um ~** 🔲 (música) a bit of music

soma /'soma/ f sum. **~mar** vt add up ‹números etc›; (ter como soma) add up to

sombra /'sõbra/ f shadow; (área abrigada do sol) shade; **à ~ de** in the shade of; **sem ~ de dúvida** without a shadow of a doubt

sombre|ado /sõbri'adu/ a shady ● m shading. **~ar** vt shade

sombrinha /sõ'briɲa/ f parasol

sombrio /sõ'briu/ a gloomy

somente /so'mẽtʃi/ adv only

sonâmbulo /so'nãbulu/ m sleepwalker

sonante /so'nãtʃi/ a **moeda ~** hard cash

sonata /so'nata/ f sonata

son|da /'sõda/ f probe. **~dagem** f (no mar) sounding; (de terreno) survey; **~dagem de opinião** opinion poll. **~dar** vt probe; sound ‹profundeza›; fig sound out ‹pessoas, opiniões etc›

soneca /so'nɛka/ f nap; **tirar uma ~** have a nap

sone|gação /sonega'sãw/ f (de impostos) tax evasion. **~gador** m tax dodger. **~gar** vt withhold

soneto /so'netu/ m sonnet

sonhador /soɲa'dor/ a dreamy ● m dreamer. **~nhar** vt/i dream (com about). **~nho** /'soɲu/ m dream; (doce) doughnut

sono /'sonu/ m sleep; **estar com ~** be sleepy; **pegar no ~** get to sleep. **~lento** a sleepy

sono|plastia /sonoplas'tʃia/ f sound effects. **~ridade** f sound quality. **~ro** /ɔ/ a sound; ‹voz› sonorous; ‹consoante› voiced

sonso /'sõsu/ a devious

sopa /'sopa/ f soup

sopapo /so'papu/ m slap; **dar um ~ em** slap

sopé /so'pɛ/ m foot

sopeira /so'pera/ f soup tureen

soprano /so'pranu/ m/f soprano

so|prar /so'prar/ vt blow ‹folhas etc›; blow up ‹balão›; blow out ‹vela› ● vi blow. **~pro** m blow; (de vento) puff; **instrumento de ~pro** wind instrument

soquete[1] /so'ketʃi/ f ankle sock

soquete[2] /so'ketʃi/ m socket

sordidez /sordʒi'des/ f sordidness; (imundície) squalor

sórdido /'sɔrdʒidu/ a (reles) sordid; (imundo) squalid

soro /'soru/ m (remédio) serum; (de leite) whey

soropositivo /soropozi'tʃivu/ a HIV-positive

sorrateiro /soxa'teru/ a crafty

sor|ridente /soxi'dẽtʃi/ a smiling. **~rir** vi smile. **~riso** m smile

sorte /'sɔrtʃi/ f luck; (destino) fate; **pessoa de ~** lucky person; **por ~** luckily; **ter ou dar ~** be lucky; **tive a ~ de conhecê-lo** I was lucky enough to meet him; **tirar a ~** draw lots; **trazer ~** bring good luck

sor|tear /sortʃi'ar/ vt draw for ‹prêmio›; select in a draw ‹pessoa›. **~teio** m draw

sorti|do /sor'tʃidu/ a assorted. **~mento** m assortment

sorumbático /sorū'batʃiku/ a sombre, gloomy

sorver /sor'ver/ vt sip ‹bebida›

sósia /'sɔzia/ m/f double

soslaio /soz'laju/ m **de ~** sideways; ‹olhar› askance

sosse|gado /sose'gadu/ a ‹vida› quiet; **ficar ~gado** ‹pessoa› rest assured. **~gar** vt reassure ● vi rest. **~go** /e/ m peace

sótão /'sɔtãw/ (pl **~s**) m attic, loft

sotaque /so'taki/ m accent

soterrar /sote'xar/ vt bury

soutien /suti'ã/ (pl **~s**) m Port bra

sova|co /so'vaku/ m armpit. **~queira** f BO, body odour

soviético /sovi'etʃiku/ a & m Soviet

sovi|na /so'vina/ a stingy, mean, Amer cheap ● m/f cheapskate. **~nice** f stinginess, meanness, Amer cheapness

sozinho /so'ziɲu/ a (sem ninguém) alone, on one's own; (por si próprio) by o.s.; **falar ~** talk to o.s.

spam m (em correio eletrônico) spam

spray /is'prej/ (pl **~s**) m spray

squash /is'kwɛʃ/ m squash

stand /is'tãdʒi/ (pl **~s**) m stand

status /is'tatus/ m status

stripper /is'triper/ (pl **~s**) m/f stripper

striptease /istripi'tʃizi/ m striptease

sua /'sua/ a & pron ▶ **SEU**

su|ado /su'adu/ a ‹pessoa, roupa› sweaty; fig hard-earned. **~ar** vt/i sweat; **~ar por/para** fig work hard

for/to; **~ar frio** come out in a cold sweat

sua|ve /su'avi/ a ‹toque, subida› gentle; ‹gosto, cheiro, dor, inverno› mild; ‹música, voz› soft; ‹vinho› smooth; ‹trabalho› light; ‹prestações› easy. **~vidade** f gentleness; mildness; softness; smoothness; ▶ **SUAVE**. **~vizar** vt soften; soothe ‹dor, pessoa›

subalterno /subaw'tɛrnu/ a & m subordinate

subconsciente /subikõsi'ẽtʃi/ a & m subconscious

subdesenvolvido /subidʒizĩvow-'vidu/ a underdeveloped

súbdito /'subditu/ m Port ▶ **SÚDITO**

subdividir /subidʒivi'dʒir/ vt subdivide

subemprego /subĩ'pregu/ m menial job

subemprei|tar /subĩprej'tar/ vt subcontract. **~teiro** m subcontractor

subenten|der /subĩtẽ'der/ vt infer. **~dido** a implied ● m insinuation

subestimar /subestʃi'mar/ vt underestimate

su|bida /su'bida/ f (ação) ascent; (ladeira) incline; (de preços etc) fig rise. **~bir** vi go up; ‹rio, águas› rise ● vt go up, climb; **~bir em** climb ‹árvore›; get up onto ‹mesa›; get on ‹ônibus›

súbito /'subitu/ a sudden; **(de) ~** suddenly

subjacente /subiʒa'sẽtʃi/ a underlying

subjeti|vidade /subiʒetʃivi'dadʒi/ f subjectivity. **~vo** a subjective

subjugar /subiʒu'gar/ vt subjugate

subjuntivo /subiʒũ'tʃivu/ a & m subjunctive

sublevar-se /suble'varsi/ vpr rise up

sublime /su'blimi/ a sublime

subli|nhado /subli'nadu/ m underlining. **~nhar** vt underline

sublocar /sublo'kar/ vt/i sublet

submarino /subima'rinu/ a underwater ● m submarine

submer|gir /submer'ʒir/ vt submerge. **~gir-se** vpr submerge. **~so** a submerged

submeter /subime'ter/ vt subject (a to); put down, subdue ‹povo, rebeldes etc›; submit ‹projeto›. **~se** vpr (render-se) submit; **~se a** (sofrer) undergo

submis|são /submi'sãw/ f submission. **~so** a submissive

submundo /subi'mũdu/ m underworld

subnutrição /subinutri'sãw/ f malnutrition

subordi|nado /subordʒi'nadu/ a & m subordinate. **~nar** vt subordinate (a to)

subor|nar /subor'nar/ vt bribe. **~no** /o/ m bribe

subproduto /subipro'dutu/ m by-product

subs|crever /subiskre'ver/ vt sign ‹carta etc›; subscribe to ‹opinião›; subscribe ‹dinheiro› (para to). **~crever-se** vpr sign one's name. **~crição** f subscription. **~crito** pp de ▶ SUBSCREVER

subsequente /subise'kwẽtʃi/ a subsequent

subserviente /subiservi'ẽtʃi/ a subservient

subsidiar /subsidʒi'ar/ vt subsidize

subsidiá|ria /subisidʒi'aria/ f subsidiary. **~rio** a subsidiary

subsídio /subi'sidʒiu/ m subsidy

subsistência /subisis'tẽsia/ f subsistence

subsolo /subi'sɔlu/ m (porão) basement

substância /subis'tãsia/ f substance

substan|cial /subistãsi'aw/ (pl **~ciais**) a substantial. **~tivo** m noun

substitu|ição /subistʃitui'sãw/ f replacement; substitution. **~ir** vt (pôr B no lugar de A) replace (A por B A with B); (usar B em vez de A) substitute (A por B B for A). **~to** a & m substitute

subterfúgio /subiter'fuʒiu/ m subterfuge

subterrâneo /subite'xaniu/ a underground

sub|til /sub'til/ (pl **~tis**) a Port ▶ SUTIL

subtra|ção /subitra'sãw/ f subtraction. **~ir** vt subtract ‹números›; (roubar) steal

suburbano /subur'banu/ a suburban

subúrbio /su'burbiu/ m suburbs

subven|ção /subivẽ'sãw/ f grant, subsidy. **~cionar** vt subsidize

subver|são /subiver'sãw/ f subversion. **~sivo** a & m subversive

suca|ta /su'kata/ f scrap metal. **~tear** vt scrap

sucção /suk'sãw/ f suction

suce|der /suse'der/ vi (acontecer) happen ● vt **~der a** succeed ‹rei etc›; (vir depois) follow. **~der-se** vpr follow on from one another. **~dido** a bem-~dido successful

suces|são /suse'sãw/ f succession. **~sivo** a successive. **~so** /ε/ m success; (música) hit; **fazer ~so** be successful; **~sor** m successor

sucinto /su'sĩtu/ a succinct

suco /'suku/ m juice

suculento /suku'lẽtu/ a juicy

sucumbir /sukũ'bir/ vi succumb (a to)

sucur|sal /sukur'saw/ (pl **~sais**) f branch

Sudão /su'dãw/ m Sudan

sudário /su'dariu/ m shroud

sudeste /su'dεstʃi/ a & m southeast; **o Sudeste Asiático** South East Asia

súdito /'sudʒitu/ m subject

sudoeste /sudo'εstʃi/ a & m southwest

Suécia /su'εsia/ f Sweden

sueco /su'εku/ a & m Swedish

suéter /su'eter/ m/f sweater

sufici|ência /sufisi'ẽsia/ f sufficiency. **~ente** a enough, sufficient; **o ~ente** enough

sufixo /su'fiksu/ m suffix

suflê /su'fle/ m soufflé

sufo|cante /sufo'kãtʃi/ a stifling. **~car** vt (asfixiar) suffocate; fig stifle ● vi suffocate; **~co** /o/ m hassle; **estar num ~co** be having a tough time

sufrágio /su'fraʒiu/ m suffrage

sugar /su'gar/ vt suck

sugerir /suʒe'rir/ vt suggest

suges|tão /suʒes'tãw/ f suggestion; **dar uma ~tão** make a suggestion. **~tivo** a suggestive

Suíça /su'isa/ f Switzerland

suíças /su'isas/ f pl sideburns

sui|cida /sui'sida/ a suicidal; **ataque ~** suicide bombing; **bombardeador ~** suicide bomber ● m/f suicide (victim). **~cidar-se** vpr commit suicide. **~cídio** m suicide

suíço /su'isu/ a & m Swiss

suíno /su'inu/ a & m pig

suíte /su'itʃi/ f suite

su|jar /su'ʒar/ vt dirty; fig sully ‹reputação etc› ● vi, **~se** vpr get dirty; **~jar-se com alguém** queer one's pitch with sb. **~jeira** f dirt; (uma) dirty trick

sujei|tar /suʒei'tar/ vt subject (a to). **~tar-se** vpr subject o.s. (a to). **~to** a subject (a to) ● m (de oração) subject; (pessoa) person

su|jidade /suʒi'dadʒi/ f Port dirt. **~jo** a dirty

sul /suw/ a invar & m south. **~africano** a & m South African; **~americano** a & m South American; **~coreano** a & m South Korean

sul|car /suw'kar/ vt furrow ‹testa›. **~co** m furrow

sulfúrico /suw'furiku/ a sulphuric

sulista /su'lista/ a southern ● m/f southerner

sultão /suw'tãw/ m sultan

sumário /su'mariu/ a ‹justiça› summary; ‹roupa› skimpy, brief

su|miço /su'misu/ m disappearance; **dar ~miço em** spirit away; **tomar chá de ~miço** disappear. **~mido** a ‹cor, voz› faint. **~mir** vi disappear; **ele anda ~mido** he's disappeared

sumo /'sumu/ m Port juice

sumptuoso /sũtu'ozu/ a Port
▶ SUNTUOSO

sunga /'sũga/ f swimming trunks

suntuoso /sũtu'ozu/ a sumptuous

suor /su'or/ m sweat

superar /supe'rar/ vt overcome
⟨dificuldade etc⟩; surpass
⟨expetativa, pessoa⟩

superá|vel /supe'ravew/ (pl
~veis) a surmountable. **~vit** (pl
~vits) m surplus

superestimar /superestʃi'mar/ vt
overestimate

superestrutura
/superistru'tura/ f superstructure

superfici|al /superfisi'aw/ (pl
~ais) a superficial

superfície /super'fisi/ f surface;
(medida) area

supérfluo /su'perfluu/ a
superfluous

superintendência /superĩtē-
'dēsia/ f bureau

superi|or /superi'or/ a (de cima)
upper; ⟨ensino⟩ higher; ⟨número,
temperatura etc⟩ greater (a than);
(melhor) superior (a to) ● m
superior. **~oridade** f superiority

superlativo /superla'tʃivu/ a & m
superlative

superlota|ção /superlota'sãw/ f
overcrowding. **~do** a overcrowded

supermercado /supermer'kadu/
m supermarket

superpotência /superpo'tēsia/
f superpower

superpovoado /superpovo'adu/
a overpopulated

supersecreto /superse'kretu/ a
top secret

supersensí|vel /supersē'sivew/
(pl ~veis) a oversensitive

supersônico /super'soniku/ a
supersonic

supersti|ção /superstʃi'sãw/
f superstition. **~cioso** /o/ a
superstitious

supervi|são /supervi'zãw/ f
supervision. **~sionar** vt supervise.
~sor m supervisor

supetão /supe'tãw/ m **de ~** all of
a sudden

suplantar /suplã'tar/ vt supplant

suplemen|tar /suplemē'tar/ a
supplementary ● vt supplement.
~to m supplement

suplente /su'plētʃi/ a & m/f
substitute

supletivo /suple'tʃivu/ a
supplementary; **ensino ~** adult
education

súplica /'suplika/ f plea; **tom de ~**
pleading tone

suplicar /supli'kar/ vt plead for;
(em juízo) petition for

suplício /su'plisiu/ m torture; fig
(aflição) torment

supor /su'por/ vt suppose

supor|tar /supor'tar/ vt (sustentar)
support; (tolerar) stand, bear.
~tável (pl ~táveis) a bearable. **~te**
/ɔ/ m support

suposição /supozi'sãw/ f
supposition

supositório /supozi'tɔriu/ m
suppository

supos|tamente /suposta'mētʃi/
adv supposedly. **~to** /o/ a supposed;
~to que supposing that

supre|macia /suprema'sia/ f
supremacy. **~mo** /e/ a supreme

supressão /supre'sãw/ f ‹de lei, cargo, privilégio› abolition; ‹de jornal, informação, nomes› suppression; ‹de palavras, cláusula› deletion

suprimento /supri'mẽtu/ m supply

suprimir /supri'mir/ vt abolish ‹lei, cargo, privilégio›; suppress ‹jornal, informação, nomes›; delete ‹palavras, cláusula›

suprir /su'prir/ vt provide for ‹família, necessidades›; make up for ‹falta›; make up ‹quantia›; supply ‹o que falta›; (substituir) take the place of; ~ alguém de provide sb with; ~ A por B substitute B for A

supurar /supu'rar/ vi turn septic

surdez /sur'des/ f deafness. ~do a deaf; ‹consoante› voiceless ● m deaf person; os ~dos the deaf. ~do-mudo (pl ~dos-mudos) a deaf and dumb ● m deaf mute

surfe /'surfi/ m surfing. ~fista m/f surfer

surgimento /surʒi'mẽtu/ m appearance. ~gir vi arise; ~gir à mente spring to mind

Suriname /suri'nami/ m Surinam

surpreendente /surprič'dẽtʃi/ a surprising. ~der vt surprise ● vi be surprising. ~der-se vpr be surprised (de at)

surpresa /sur'preza/ f surprise; de ~sa by surprise. ~so /e/ a surprised

surra /'suxa/ f thrashing. ~rado a ‹roupa› worn-out. ~rar vt thrash ‹pessoa›; wear out ‹roupa›

surrealismo /suxea'lizmu/ m surrealism. ~ta a & m/f surrealist

surtir /sur'tʃir/ vt produce; ~ efeito be effective

surto /'surtu/ m outbreak

suscetibilidade /susetʃibili-'dadʒi/ f ‹de pessoa› sensitivity. ~tível (pl ~tíveis) a ‹pessoa› touchy, sensitive; ~tível de open to

suscitar /susi'tar/ vt cause; raise ‹dúvida, suspeita›

suspeita /sus'pejta/ f suspicion. ~tar vt/i ~tar (de) suspect. ~to a suspicious; (duvidoso) suspect ● m suspect. ~toso /o/ a suspicious

suspender /suspẽ'der/ vt suspend. ~são f suspension. ~se m suspense. ~so a suspended. ~sórios m pl braces, Amer suspenders

suspirar /suspi'rar/ vi sigh; ~rar por long for. ~ro m sigh; (doce) meringue

sussurrar /susu'xar/ vt/i whisper. ~ro m whisper

sustar /sus'tar/ vt/i stop

sustenido /suste'nidu/ a Mús sharp; tecla ~ hash key

sustentabilidade /suʃtẽtabili'dadʒi/ f sustainability

sustentáculo /suʃtẽ'takulu/ m mainstay. ~tar vt support; (afirmar) maintain. ~to m support; (ganha-pão) livelihood

sustentável /suʃtẽ'tavew/ a sustainable

susto /'sustu/ m fright

sutiã /sutʃi'ã/ m bra

sutil /su'tʃiw/ (pl ~tis) a subtle. ~tileza f subtlety

sutura /su'tura/ f suture. ~rar vt suture

SUV m (carro) SUV

sweatshirt /swet'farte/ f Port sweatshirt

Tt

tá /ta/ *int* 🔲 OK; ▶ ESTAR

taba|caria /tabaka'ria/ *f* tobacconist's. **~co** *m* tobacco

tabefe /ta'bɛfi/ *m* slap

tabe|la /ta'bɛla/ *f* table. **~lar** *vt* tabulate

tablado /ta'bladu/ *m* platform

tabu /ta'bu/ *a & m* taboo

tábua /'tabua/ *f* board; **~ de passar roupa** ironing board

tabuleiro /tabu'leru/ *m* (*de xadrez etc*) board

tabuleta /tabu'leta/ *f* (*letreiro*) sign

taça /'tasa/ *f* (*prêmio*) cup; (*de champanhe etc*) glass

ta|cada /ta'kada/ *f* shot; **de uma ~cada** in one go. **~car** *vt* hit ‹*bola*›; 🔲 throw

tacha /'taʃa/ *f* tack

tachar /ta'ʃar/ *vt* brand (**de as**)

tachinha /ta'ʃiɲa/ *f* drawing pin, *Amer* thumbtack

tácito /'tasitu/ *a* tacit

taciturno /tasi'turnu/ *a* taciturn

taco /'taku/ *m* (*de golfe*) club; (*de bilhar*) cue; (*de hóquei*) stick

tagare|la /taga'rɛla/ *a* chatty, talkative ● *m/f* chatterbox. **~lar** *vi* chatter

tailan|dês /tajlã'des/ *a & m* (*f* **~desa**) Thai

Tailândia /taj'lãdʒia/ *f* Thailand

tailleur /ta'jɛr/ (*pl* **~s**) *m* suit

Taiti /taj'tʃi/ *m* Tahiti

tal /taw/ (*pl* **tais**) *a* such; **que ~?** what do you think?; *Port* how are you?; **que ~ uma cerveja?** how about a beer?; **~ como** such as; **~ qual** just like; **um ~ de João** someone called John; **e ~** and so on

tala /'tala/ *f* splint

talão /ta'lãw/ *m* stub; **~ de cheques** chequebook

talco /'tawku/ *m* talc

talen|to /ta'lẽtu/ *m* talent. **~toso** /o/ *a* talented

talhar /ta'ʎar/ *vt* slice ‹*dedo, carne*›; carve ‹*pedra, imagem*›

talharim /taʎa'rĩ/ *m* tagliatelle

talher /ta'ʎer/ *m* set of cutlery; *pl* cutlery

talho /'taʎu/ *m Port* butcher's

talismã /taliz'mã/ *m* charm, talisman

talo /'talu/ *m* stalk

talvez /taw'ves/ *adv* perhaps; **~ ele venha amanhã** he may come tomorrow

tamanco /ta'mãku/ *m* clog

tamanho /ta'maɲu/ *m* size ● *adj* such

tâmara /'tamara/ *f* date

tamarindo /tama'rĩdu/ *m* tamarind

também /tã'bẽj/ *adv* also; **~ não** not ... either, neither

tam|bor /tã'bor/ *m* drum. **~borilar** *vi* ‹*dedos*› drum; ‹*chuva*› patter. **~borim** *m* tambourine

Tâmisa /'tamiza/ *m* Thames

tam|pa /'tãpa/ *f* lid. **~pão** *m* (*vaginal*) tampon. **~par** *vt* put the lid on ‹*recipiente*›; (*tapar*) cover. **~pinha** *f* top ● *m/f* 🔲 shorthouse

tampouco /tã'poku/ *adv* nor, neither

tanga /'tãga/ f G-string; (*avental*) loincloth

tangente /tã'ʒẽtʃi/ f tangent; **pela ~** *fig* narrowly

tangerina /tãʒe'rina/ f tangerine

tango /'tãgu/ m tango

tanque /'tãki/ m tank; (*para lavar roupa*) sink

tanto /'tãtu/ a & *pron* so much; *pl* so many ● *adv* so much; **~ ... como ...** both ... and ...; **~ (...) quanto** as much (...) as; **~ melhor** so much the better; **~ tempo** so long; **vinte e ~ anos** twenty odd years; **nem ~** not as much; **um ~ difícil** somewhat difficult; **~ que** to the extent that

Tanzânia /tã'zania/ f Tanzania

tão /tãw/ *adv* so; **~ grande quanto** as big as. **~ somente** *adv* solely

tapa /'tapa/ m ou f slap; **dar um ~ em** slap

tapar /ta'par/ *vt* (*cobrir*) cover; block ‹*luz, vista*›; cork ‹*garrafa*›

tapeçaria /tapesa'ria/ f (*pano*) tapestry; (*loja*) carpet shop

tape|tar /tape'tar/ *vt* carpet. **~te** /e/ m carpet; **~te de rato** Port (*comput*) mousemat

tapioca /tapi'ɔka/ f tapioca

tapume /ta'pumi/ m fence

taquicardia /takikar'dʒia/ f palpitations

taquigra|far /takigra'far/ *vt/i* write in shorthand. **~fia** f shorthand

tara /'tara/ f fetish. **~do** a sex-crazed; **ser ~do por** be crazy about ● *m* sex maniac

tar|dar /tar'dar/ *vi* (*atrasar*) be late; (*demorar muito*) be long ● *vt* delay; **~dar a responder** take a long time to answer, be a long time answering; **o mais ~dar** at the latest; **sem mais ~dar** without

further delay. **~de** *adv* late; **~de da noite** late at night ● f afternoon; **hoje à ~de** this afternoon. **~dinha** f late afternoon. **~dio** a late

tarefa /ta'refa/ f task, job

tarifa /ta'rifa/ f tariff; **~ de embarque** airport tax

tarimbado /tarĩ'badu/ a experienced

tarja /'tarʒa/ f strip

ta|rô /ta'ro/ m tarot. **~rólogo** m tarot reader

tartamu|dear /tartamudʒi'ar/ *vi* stammer. **~do** a stammering ● m stammerer

tártaro /'tartaru/ m tartar

tartaruga /tarta'ruga/ f (*bicho*) turtle; (*material*) tortoiseshell

tatear /tatʃi'ar/ *vt* feel ● *vi* feel one's way

táti|ca /'tatʃika/ f tactics. **~co** a tactical

tá|til /'tatʃiw/ (*pl* **~teis**) a tactile

tato /'tatu/ m (*sentido*) touch; (*diplomacia*) tact

tatu /ta'tu/ m armadillo

tatu|ador /tatua'dor/ m tattooist. **~agem** f tattoo. **~ar** *vt* tattoo

tauromaquia /tawroma'kia/ f bullfighting

taxa /'taʃa/ f (a *pagar*) charge; (*índice*) rate; **~ de câmbio** exchange rate; **~ de juros** interest rate; **~ rodoviária** road tax

taxar /ta'ʃar/ *vt* tax

taxativo /taʃa'tʃivu/ a firm, categorical

táxi /'taksi/ m taxi

taxiar /taksi'ar/ *vi* taxi

taxímetro /tak'simetru/ m taxi meter

taxista /tak'sista/ m/f taxi driver

tchã /tʃã/ m Ⅱ special something

tchau /tʃaw/ int goodbye, bye

tcheco /'tʃɛku/ a & m Czech

Tchecoslováquia
/tʃekoslo'vakia/ f Czechoslovakia

te /tʃi/ pron you; (a ti) to you

tear /tʃi'ar/ m loom

tea|tral /tʃia'traw/ (pl ~trais) a
theatrical; ‹grupo› theatre. ~tro m
theatre. ~trólogo m playwright

tece|lagem /tese'laʒẽ/ f (trabalho)
weaving; (fábrica) textile factory.
~lão m (f ~lã) weaver

te|cer /te'ser/ vt/i weave. ~cido m
cloth; (no corpo) tissue

te|cla /'tɛkla/ f key. ~cladista
m/f (músico) keyboard player; (de
computador) keyboard operator.
~clado m keyboard. ~clar vt key (in)

técni|ca /'tɛknika/ f technique.
~co a technical ● m specialist; (de
time) manager; (que mexe com
máquinas) technician

tecno|crata /tekno'krata/ m/f
technocrat. ~logia f technology.
~lógico a technological

teco-teco /tɛku'tɛku/ m light
aircraft

tédio /'tɛdʒiu/ m boredom

tedioso /tedʒi'ozu/ a boring,
tedious

Teerã /tee'rã/ f Teheran

teia /'teja/ f web

tei|ma /'tejma/ f persistence. ~mar
vi insist; ~mar em ir insist on going.
~mosia f stubbornness. ~moso /o/
a stubborn; ‹ruído› insistent

teixo /'tejʃu/ m yew

Tejo /'teʒu/ m Tagus

tela /'tɛla/ f (de cinema, TV etc)
screen; (tecido, pintura) canvas.
~ plana f flat screen

telecoman|dado
/telekomã'dadu/ a remote-
controlled. ~do m remote control

telecomunicação
/telekomunika'sãw/ f
telecommunication

teleférico /tele'fɛriku/ m cable car

telefo|nar /telefo'nar/ vi
telephone; ~nar para alguém
phone sb. ~ne /o/ m telephone;
(número) phone number; ~ne
celular cell phone; ~ne sem fio
cordless phone. ~nema /e/ m phone
call. ~nia f telephone technology

telefôni|co /tele'foniku/ a
telephone; cabine f phone box,
Amer phone booth; mesa ~ca
switchboard

telefonista /telefo'nista/ m/f (da
companhia telefônica) operator;
(dentro de empresa etc) telephonist

tele|grafar /telegra'far/ vt/i
telegraph. ~gráfico a telegraphic

telégrafo /te'lɛgrafu/ m telegraph

tele|grama /tele'grama/ m
telegram. ~guiado a remote-
controlled

telejor|nal /teleʒor'naw/
(pl ~nais) m television news

telemóvel /tele'mɔvew/ m Port
mobile phone, Amer cell phone

tele|novela /teleno'vɛla/ f TV
soap opera. ~objetiva f telephoto
lens

tele|patia /telepa'tʃia/ f telepathy.
~pático a telepathic

telescó|pico /teles'kɔpiku/ a
telescopic. ~pio m telescope

telespectador /telespekta'dor/
m television viewer ● a viewing

teletrabalho /teletra'baʎu/ m
teleworking

televi|são /televiˈzɐ̃w/ f television; **~são a cabo** cable television; **~são digital** digital television. **~sionar** vt televise. **~sivo** a television. **~sor** m television set

telex /teˈlɛks/ m invar telex

telha /ˈteʎa/ f tile. **~do** m roof

te|ma /ˈtema/ m theme. **~mático** a thematic

temer /teˈmer/ vt fear ● vi be afraid; **~ por** fear for

teme|rário /temeˈrariu/ a reckless. **~ridade** f recklessness. **~roso** /o/ a fearful

te|mido /teˈmidu/ a feared. **~mível** (pl **~míveis**) a fearsome. **~mor** m fear

tempão /tẽˈpɐ̃w/ m **um ~** a long time

temperado /tẽpeˈradu/ a ‹clima› temperate ● pp de ▶ TEMPERAR

temperamen|tal /tẽperamẽˈtaw/ (pl **~tais**) a temperamental. **~to** m temperament

temperar /tẽpeˈrar/ vt season ‹comida›; temper ‹aço›

temperatura /tẽperaˈtura/ f temperature

tempero /tẽˈperu/ m seasoning

tempestade /tẽpesˈtadʒi/ f storm

templo /ˈtẽplu/ m temple

tempo /ˈtẽpu/ m (período) time; (atmosférico) weather; (do verbo) tense; (de jogo) half; **ao mesmo ~** at the same time; **nesse meio ~** in the meantime; **o ~ todo** all the time; **de todos os ~s** of all time; **quanto ~** how long; **muito/pouco ~** a long/short time; **~ integral** full time

tempo|rada /tẽpoˈrada/ f (sazão) season; (tempo) while. **~ral** (pl

~rais) a temporal ● m storm. **~rário** a temporary

te|nacidade /tenasiˈdadʒi/ f tenacity. **~naz** a tenacious ● f tongs

tenção /tẽˈsɐ̃w/ f intention

tencionar /tẽsioˈnar/ vt intend

tenda /ˈtẽda/ f tent

tendão /tẽˈdɐ̃w/ m tendon; **~ de Aquiles** Achilles tendon

tendência /tẽˈdẽsia/ f (moda) trend; (propensão) tendency

tendencioso /tẽdẽsiˈozu/ a tendentious

ten|der /tẽˈder/ vi tend (**para** towards); **~de a engordar** he tends to get fat; **o tempo ~de a ficar bom** the weather is improving

tenebroso /teneˈbrozu/ a dark; fig (terrível) dreadful

tenente /teˈnẽtʃi/ m/f lieutenant

tênis /ˈtenis/ m invar (jogo) tennis; (sapato) trainer; **um ~** (par) a pair of trainers; **~ de mesa** table tennis

tenista /teˈnista/ m/f tennis player

tenor /teˈnor/ m tenor

tenro /ˈtẽxu/ a tender

ten|são /tẽˈsɐ̃w/ f tension; **~são (arterial)** blood pressure. **~so** a tense

tentação /tẽtaˈsɐ̃w/ f temptation

tentáculo /tẽˈtakulu/ m tentacle

ten|tador /tẽtaˈdor/ a tempting. **~tar** vt try; (seduzir) tempt ● vi try. **~tativa** f attempt. **~tativo** a tentative

tênue /ˈtenui/ a faint

teo|logia /teoloˈʒia/ f theology. **~lógico** a theological

teólogo /teˈɔlogu/ m theologian

teor /teˈor/ m (de gordura etc) content; (de carta, discurso) drift

teo|rema /teo'rema/ *m* theorem.
~ria *f* theory

teórico /te'ɔriku/ *a* theoretical

teorizar /teori'zar/ *vt* theorize

tépido /'tɛpidu/ *a* tepid

---

ter /ter/ ● *vt*

⋯▶ *(posse)* have got, have;
você tem irmãos? have you got
any brothers or sisters?, do you
have any brothers or sisters?; **ele
não tem dinheiro nenhum** he
doesn't have any money

! **ter** pode ser traduzido como
have ou *have got*, mas observe
que *have got* é muito mais
comum em inglês britânico.

⋯▶ *(idade, tamanho)* be; **a
minha filha tem 10 anos** my
daughter is ten; **tem três metros
de comprimento** it's three
metres long

⋯▶ *(doença, dor)* have; **~ dor
de dente/pneumonia/febre** to
have toothache/pneumonia/a
temperature

⋯▶ *(sentir)* **~ medo** be scared;
~ frio be cold; **~ ciúmes** be
jealous

! Observe que **ter + substantivo**
em geral é traduzido como *to
be* + *adjetivo* quando significa
'sentir': **tenho medo** I'm scared.

⋯▶ *(dar à luz)* **~ um bebê**
have a baby

● *v aux*

⋯▶ *(estar obrigado a)* **~ que**
ou **de fazer algo** have to do
sth; **tiveram que ir embora
imediatamente** they had to
leave straight away; **você tem de
dizer a ele** you must tell him

⋯▶ *(seguido de particípio)*
tenho dito muitas vezes...
I have often said...

⋯▶ *(em expressões)* **ir ~ com**
(encontrar-se) meet up with;
fiquei de ir ~ com ele logo
I arranged to meet up with
him later

---

tera|peuta /tera'pewta/ *m/f*
therapist. **~pêutico** *a* therapeutic.
~pia *f* therapy

terça /'tersa/ *f* Tuesday. **~feira**
(pl **~s-feiras)** *f* Tuesday; **Terça-Feira
Gorda** Shrove Tuesday

tercei|ra /ter'sera/ *f (marcha)* third.
~ranista *m/f* third-year. **~ro** *a* third
● *m* third party

terço /'tersu/ *m* third

ter|çol *(pl* **~çóis)** *m* stye

tergal /ter'gaw/ *m* Terylene

térmi|co /'tɛrmiku/ *a* thermal;
garrafa ~ca Thermos® flask

termi|nal /termi'naw/ *(pl* **~nais)**
a & m terminal; **~nal de vídeo** VDU.
~nante *a* definite. **~nar** *vt* finish ● *vi*
‹*pessoa, coisa*› finish; ‹*coisa*› end;
~nar com alguém *(cortar relação)*
break up with sb

ter|minologia /terminolo'ʒia/
f terminology. **~mo** [1] /'termu/ *m*
term; **pôr ~mo a** put an end to;
meio ~mo compromise

termo [2] /'termu/ *m* Port Thermos®
(flask)

ter|mômetro /ter'mometru/
m thermometer. **~mostato** *m*
thermostat

terno [1] /'ternu/ *m* suit

ter|no [2] /'ternu/ *a* tender. **~nura** *f*
tenderness

terra /'tɛxa/ *f* land; *(solo, elétrico)*
earth; *(chão)* ground; **a Terra** Earth;

por ~ on the ground; ~ **natal** homeland

terraço /te'xasu/ *m* terrace

terra|cota /texa'kɔta/ *f* terracotta. **~moto** /texa'mɔtu/ *m* Port earthquake. **~plenagem** *f* earth moving

terreiro /te'xeru/ *m* meeting place for Afro-Brazilian cults

terremoto /texe'mɔtu/ *m* earthquake

terreno /te'xenu/ *a* earthly ● *m* ground; *Geog* terrain; (*um*) piece of land; ~ **baldio** piece of waste ground

térreo /'texiu/ *a* ground-floor; (**andar**) ~ ground-floor, *Amer* first-floor

terrestre /te'xɛstri/ *a* ‹animal, batalha, forças› land; (*da Terra*) of the Earth, the Earth's; ‹alegrias etc› earthly

terrificante /texifi'kãtʃi/ *a* terrifying

terrina /te'xina/ *f* tureen

territori|al /texitori'aw/ (*pl* ~**ais**) *a* territorial

território /texi'tɔriu/ *m* territory

terrí|vel /te'xivew/ (*pl* ~**veis**) *a* terrible

terror /te'xor/ *m* terror; **filme de** ~ horror film

terroris|mo /texo'rizmu/ *m* terrorism. **~ta** *a* & *m/f* terrorist

tese /'tɛzi/ *f* theory; (*escrita*) thesis

teso /'tezu/ *a* (*apertado*) taut; (*rígido*) stiff

tesoura /te'zora/ *f* scissors; **uma** ~ a pair of scissors

tesou|reiro /tezo'reru/ *m* treasurer. **~ro** *m* treasure; (*do Estado*) treasury

testa /'tɛsta/ *f* forehead. ~ **de ferro** (*pl* ~**s-de-ferro**) *m* frontman

testamento /testa'mẽtu/ *m* will; (*na Bíblia*) testament

tes|tar /tes'tar/ *vt* test. ~**te** /ɛ/ *m* test

testemu|nha /teste'muɲa/ *f* witness; **~nha ocular** eye witness. **~nhar** *vt* bear witness to ● *vi* testify. **~nho** *m* evidence, testimony

testículo /tes'tʃikulu/ *m* testicle

teta /'teta/ *f* teat

tétano /'tɛtanu/ *m* tetanus

teto /'tetu/ *m* ceiling; ~ **solar** sun roof

tétrico /'tɛtriku/ *a* (*triste*) dismal; (*medonho*) horrible

teu /tew/ (*f* **tua**) *a* your ● *pron* yours

têx|til /'testʃiw/ (*pl* ~**teis**) *m* textile

tex|to /'testu/ *m* text. ~**tura** /u/ *f* texture

texugo /te'ʃugu/ *m* badger

tez /tes/ *f* complexion

ti /tʃi/ *pron* you

tia /'tʃia/ *f* aunt. ~**avó** (*pl* ~**s-avós**) *f* great aunt

tiara /tʃi'ara/ *f* tiara

tíbia /'tʃibia/ *f* shin bone

ticar /tʃi'kar/ *vt* tick

tico /'tʃiku/ *m* **um** ~ **de** a little bit of

tiete /tʃi'etʃi/ *m/f* fan

tifo /'tʃifu/ *m* typhoid

tigela /tʃi'ʒɛla/ *f* bowl; **de meia** ~ small-time

tigre /'tʃigri/ *m* tiger. ~**sa** /e/ *f* tigress

tijolo /tʃi'ʒolu/ *m* brick

til /tʃiw/ (*pl* **tis**) *m* tilde

tilintar /tʃilĩ'tar/ *vi* jingle ● *m* jingling

timão /tʃi'mãw/ *m* tiller

timbre /'tʃibri/ m (insígnia) crest; (em papel) heading; (de som) tone; (de vogal) quality

time /'tʃimi/ m team

timidez /tʃimi'des/ f shyness

tímido /'tʃimidu/ a shy

tímpano /'tʃipanu/ m (tambor) kettledrum; (no ouvido) eardrum

tina /'tʃina/ f vat

tingir /tʃi'ʒir/ vt dye ‹tecido, cabelo›; fig tinge

ti|nido /tʃi'nidu/ m tinkling. **~nir** vi tinkle; ‹ouvidos› ring; (tremer) tremble; **estar ~nindo** fig be in peak condition

tino /'tʃinu/ m sense, judgement; **ter ~ para** have a flair for

tin|ta /'tʃita/ f (para pintar) paint; (para escrever) ink; (para tingir) dye. **~teiro** m inkwell

tintim /tʃi'tʃi/ m **contar ~ por ~** give a blow-by-blow account of

tin|to /'tʃitu/ a dyed; ‹vinho› red. **~tura** f dye; fig tinge. **~turaria** f dry cleaner's

tio /'tʃiu/ m uncle; pl (e tia) uncle and aunt. **~avô** (pl **~s-avôs**) m great uncle

típico /'tʃipiku/ a typical

tipo /'tʃipu/ m type

tipoia /tʃi'pɔja/ f sling

tique /'tʃiki/ m (sinal) tick; (do rosto etc) twitch

tíquete /'tʃiketʃi/ m ticket

tiquinho /tʃi'kiɲu/ m **um ~ de** a tiny bit of

tira /'tʃira/ f strip • m/f 🔳 copper, Amer cop

tiracolo /tʃira'kɔlu/ m **a ~** ‹bolsa› over one's shoulder; ‹pessoa› in tow

tiragem /tʃi'raʒẽ/ f (de jornal) circulation

tira|-gosto /tʃira'gostu/ m snack. **~manchas** m invar stain remover

ti|rania /tʃira'nia/ f tyranny. **~rânico** a tyrannical. **~rano** m tyrant

tirar /tʃi'rar/ vt (afastar) take away; (de dentro) take out; take off ‹roupa, sapato, tampa›; take ‹foto, cópia, férias›; clear ‹mesa›; get ‹nota, diploma,'salário›; get out ‹mancha›

tiritar /tʃiri'tar/ vi shiver

tiro /'tʃiru/ m shot; **~ ao alvo** shooting; **é ~ e queda** 🔳 it can't fail. **~teio** m shoot-out

titânio /tʃi'taniu/ m titanium

títere /'tʃiteri/ m puppet

ti|tia /tʃi'tʃia/ f auntie. **~tio** m uncle

titití /tʃitʃi'tʃi/ m 🔳 talk

titubear /tʃitubi'ar/ vi stagger, totter; fig (hesitar) waver

titular /tʃitu'lar/ m/f title holder; (de time) captain • vt title

título /'tʃitulu/ m title; (obrigação) bond; **a ~ de** on the basis of; **a ~ pessoal** on a personal basis; **~ eleitoral** electoral register

toa /'toa/ f **à ~** (sem rumo) aimlessly; (ao acaso) at random; (sem motivo) without reason; (em vão) for nothing; (desocupado) at a loose end; (de repente) out of the blue

toada /to'ada/ f melody

toalete /toa'letʃi/ m toilet

toalha /to'aʎa/ f towel; **~ de mesa** tablecloth

tobogã /tobo'gã/ m (rampa) slide; (trenó) toboggan

toca /'tɔka/ f burrow

toca|-discos /toka'dʒiskus/ m invar record player. **~fitas** m invar tape player

tocaia /to'kaja/ f ambush

tocante /to'kãtʃi/ a (enternecedor) moving

tocar /to'kar/ vt touch; play ‹piano, música, disco etc›; ring ‹campainha› ● vi touch; ‹pianista, música, disco etc› play; ~ a (dizer respeito) concern; ~ em touch; touch on ‹assunto›; ‹campainha, telefone, sino› ring. ~se vpr touch; (mancar-se) take the hint

tocha /'tɔʃa/ f torch

toco /'toku/ m (de árvore) stump; (de cigarro) butt

toda /'toda/ f a ~ at full speed

todavia /toda'via/ conj however

todo /'todu/ a all; (cada) every; pl all; ~ o dinheiro all the money; ~ dia, ~s os dias every day; ~s os alunos all the pupils; o dia ~ all day; em ~ lugar everywhere; ~ mundo, ~s everyone; ~s nós all of us; ao ~ in all. ~poderoso a almighty

todo-o-terreno /todutʃe'xenu/ a & m Port Auto four-by-four

tofe /'tɔfi/ m toffee

toga /'tɔga/ f gown; (de romano) toga

toicinho /toj'siɲu/ m bacon

toldo /'towdu/ m awning

tole|rância /tole'rãsia/ f tolerance. ~rante a tolerant. ~rar vt tolerate. ~rável (pl ~ráveis) a tolerable

to|lice /to'lisi/ f foolishness; (uma) foolish thing. ~lo /o/ a foolish ● m fool

tom /tõ/ m tone; ~ de toque Telec ringtone

to|mada /to'mada/ f (conquista) capture; (elétrica) plughole; (de filme) shot. ~mar vt take; (beber) drink; ~mar café have breakfast

tomara /to'mara/ int I hope so; ~ que let's hope that. ~que caia a invar ‹vestido› strapless

tomate /to'matʃi/ m tomato

tom|bar /tõ'bar/ vt (derrubar) knock down; list ‹edifício› ● vi fall over. ~bo m fall; levar um ~bo have a fall

tomilho /to'miλu/ m thyme

tomo /'tomu/ m volume

tona /'tona/ f trazer à ~ bring up; vir à ~ emerge

tonalidade /tonali'dadʒi/ f (de música) key; (de cor) shade

to|nel /to'nɛw/ (pl ~néis) m cask. ~nelada f tonne

tôni|ca /'tonika/ f tonic; fig (assunto) keynote. ~co a & m tonic

tonificar /tonifi'kar/ vt tone up

ton|tear /tõtʃi'ar/ vt ~tear alguém make sb's head spin. ~teira f dizziness. ~to a (zonzo) dizzy; (bobo) stupid; ~to a (atrapalhado) flustered. ~tura f dizziness

to|pada /to'pada/ f trip; dar uma ~pada em stub one's toe on. ~par vt agree to, accept; ~par com bump into ‹pessoa›; come across ‹coisa›

topázio /to'paziu/ m topaz

topete /to'petʃi/ m quiff

tópico /'tɔpiku/ a topical ● m topic

topless /topi'lɛs/ a invar & adv topless

topo /'topu/ m top

topografia /topogra'fia/ f topography

topônimo /to'ponimu/ m place name

toque /'tɔki/ m touch; (da campainha, do telefone) ring; (de instrumento) playing; dar um ~ em 🔢 have a word with

Tóquio /'tɔkiu/ f Tokyo

tora /'tɔra/ f log

toranja /to'rãʒa/ f grapefruit

tórax /'tɔraks/ m invar thorax

tor|ção /tor'sãw/ f (do braço etc) sprain. ~**cedor** m supporter. ~**cer** vt twist; (machucar) sprain; (espremer) wring ‹roupa›; (centrifugar) spin ‹roupa› ● vi (gritar) cheer (por for); (desejar sucesso) keep one's fingers crossed (**por** for **para que** that). ~**cer-se** vpr twist about. ~**cicolo** /ɔ/ m stiff neck. ~**cida** f (torção) twist; (torcedores) supporters; (gritaria) cheering

tormen|ta /tor'mẽta/ f storm. ~**to** m torment. ~**toso** /o/ a stormy

tornado /tor'nadu/ m tornado

tornar /tor'nar/ vt make. ~**se** vpr become

torne|ado /torni'adu/ a bem ~**ado** shapely. ~**ar** vt turn

torneio /tor'neju/ m tournament

torneira /tor'nera/ f tap, Amer faucet

torniquete /torni'ketʃi/ m (para ferido) tourniquet; Port (de entrada) turnstile

torno /'tornu/ m lathe; (de ceramista) wheel; **em ~ de** around

tornozelo /torno'zelu/ m ankle

toró /to'rɔ/ m downpour

torpe /'tɔrpi/ a dirty

torpe|dear /torpedʒi'ar/ vt torpedo. ~**do** /e/ m torpedo

torpor /tor'por/ m torpor

torra|da /to'xada/ f piece of toast; pl toast. ~**deira** f toaster

torrão /to'xãw/ m (de terra) turf; (de açúcar) lump

torrar /to'xar/ vt toast ‹pão›; roast ‹café›; blow ‹dinheiro›; sell off

‹mercadorias›

torre /'toxi/ f tower; (em xadrez) rook; ~ **de controle** control tower. ~**ão** m turret

torrefação /toxefa'sãw/ f (ação) roasting; (fábrica) coffee-roasting plant

torren|cial /toxẽsi'aw/ (pl ~**ciais**) a torrential. ~**te** f torrent

torresmo /to'xezmu/ m crackling

tórrido /'tɔxidu/ a torrid

torrone /to'xoni/ m nougat

torso /'torsu/ m torso

torta /'tɔrta/ f pie, tart

tor|to /'tortu/ a crooked; **a ~ e a direito** left, right and centre. ~**tuoso** a winding

tortu|ra /tor'tura/ f torture. ~**rador** m torturer. ~**rar** vt torture

to|sa /'tɔza/ f (de cachorro) clipping; (de ovelhas) shearing. ~**são** m fleece. ~**sar** vt clip ‹cachorro›; shear ‹ovelhas›; crop ‹cabelo›

tosco /'tosku/ a rough, coarse

tosquiar /toski'ar/ vt shear ‹ovelha›

tos|se /'tɔsi/ f cough; ~**se de cachorro** whooping cough. ~**sir** vi cough

tostão /tos'tãw/ m penny

tostar /tos'tar/ vt brown ‹carne›; tan ‹pele, pessoa›. ~**se** vpr (ao sol) go brown

to|tal /to'taw/ (pl ~**tais**) a & m total

totali|dade /totali'dadʒi/ f entirety. ~**tário** a totalitarian. ~**zar** vt total

touca /'toka/ f bonnet; (de freira) wimple; ~ **de banho** bathing cap. ~**dor** m dressing table

toupeira /to'pera/ f mole

tou|rada /to'rada/ f bullfight.
~reiro m bullfighter. **~ro** m bull;
Touro (signo) Taurus

tóxico /'tɔksiku/ a toxic ● m toxic
substance

toxicômano /toksi'komanu/ m
drug addict

toxina /tok'sina/ f toxin

traba|lhador /trabaʎa'dor/ a
‹pessoa› hard-working; ‹classe›
working ● m worker. **~lhar** vt work
● vi work; (numa peça, filme) act.
~lheira f big job. **~lhista** a labour.
~lho m work; (um) job; (na escola)
assignment; **dar-se o ~lho de** go
to the trouble of; **~lho de parto**
labour; **~lhos forçados** hard labour.
~lhoso a laborious

traça /'trasa/ f moth

tração /tra'sãw/ f traction

tra|çar /tra'sar/ vt draw; draw up
‹plano›; set out ‹ordens›. **~ço** m
stroke; (entre frases) dash; (vestígio)
trace; (característica) trait; pl (do
rosto) features

tradi|ção /tradʒi'sãw/ f tradition.
~cional (pl **~cionais**) a traditional

tradu|ção /tradu'sãw/ f
translation. **~tor** m translator. **~zir**
vt/i translate (**de** from **para** into)

trafe|gar /trafe'gar/ vi run. **~gável**
(pl **~gáveis**) a open to traffic

tráfego /'trafegu/ m traffic

trafi|cância /trafi'kãsia/ f
trafficking. **~cante** /trafi'kãtʃi/ m/f
trafficker; **~cante de droga** drug
dealer; **~cante sexual** sex trafficker.
~car vt/i traffic (**com** in)

tráfico /'trafiku/ m traffic

tra|gada /tra'gada/ f (de bebida)
swallow; (de cigarro) drag. **~gar** vt
swallow; inhale ‹fumaça›

tragédia /tra'ʒedʒia/ f tragedy

trágico /'traʒiku/ a tragic

trago /'tragu/ m (de bebida)
swallow; (de cigarro) drag; **de um
~** in one go

trai|ção /traj'sãw/ f (ato) betrayal;
(deslealdade) treachery; (da pátria)
treason. **~çoeiro** a treacherous.
~dor a treacherous ● m traitor

trailer /'trejler/ (pl **~s**) m (de filme
etc) trailer; (casa móvel) caravan,
Amer trailer

traineira /traj'nera/ f trawler

training /'trejnĩ/ (pl **~s**) m track
suit

trair /tra'ir/ vt betray; be unfaithful
to ‹marido, mulher›. **~se** vpr give
o.s. away

tra|jar /tra'ʒar/ vt wear. **~jar-se** vpr
dress (**de** in). **~je** m outfit; **~je a
rigor** evening dress; **~je espacial**
space suit

traje|to /tra'ʒetu/ m (percurso)
journey; (caminho) route. **~tória** f
trajectory; fig course

tralha /'traʎa/ f (trastes) junk

tra|ma /'trama/ f plot. **~mar**
vt/i plot

trambi|que /trã'biki/ m ⊡ con.
~queiro m ⊡ con artist

tramitar /trami'tar/ vi be
processed

trâmites /'tramitʃis/ m pl channels

tramoia /tra'mɔja/ f scheme

trampolim /trãpo'lĩ/ m (de
ginástica) trampoline; (de piscina) fig
springboard

tranca /'trãka/ f bolt; (em carro)
lock

trança /'trãsa/ f (de cabelo) plait

tran|cafiar /trãkafi'ar/ vt lock up.
~car vt lock; cancel ‹matrícula›

trançar /trã'sar/ vt plait ‹cabelo›; weave ‹palha etc›

tranco /'trãku/ m jolt; **aos ~s e barrancos** in fits and starts

tranqueira /trã'kera/ f junk

tranqui|lidade /trãkwili'dadʒi/ f tranquillity. **~lizador** a reassuring. **~lizante** m tranquillizer ● a reassuring. **~lizar** vt reassure. **~lizar-se** vpr be reassured. **~lo** a ‹bairro, sono› peaceful; ‹pessoa, voz, mar› calm; ‹consciência› clear; ‹sucesso, lucro› sure-fire ● adv with no trouble

transa /'trãza/ f ⊞ ‹negócio› deal; ‹caso› affair. **~ção** f transaction. **~do** a ⊞ ‹roupa, pessoa, casa› stylish; ‹relação› healthy

Transamazônica /tranzama'zonika/ f trans-Amazonian highway

transar /trã'zar/ ⊞ vt set up; do ‹drogas› ● vi ‹negociar› deal; ‹fazer sexo› have sex

transatlântico /trãzat'lãtʃiku/ a transatlantic ● m liner

transbordar /trãzbor'dar/ vi overflow

transcen|dental /trãsẽdẽ'taw/ (pl **~dentais**) a transcendental. **~der** vt/i **~der (a)** transcend

trans|crever /trãskre'ver/ vt transcribe. **~crição** f transcription. **~crito** a transcribed ● m transcript

transe /'trãzi/ m trance

transeunte /trãzi'ũtʃi/ m/f passer-by

transfe|rência /trãsfe'rẽsia/ f transfer. **~ridor** m protractor. **~rir** vt transfer. **~rir-se** vpr transfer

transfor|mação /trãsforma'sãw/ f transformation. **~mador** m transformer. **~mar** vt transform.

~mar-se vpr be transformed

trânsfuga /'trãsfuga/ m/f deserter; ‹de um país› defector

transfusão /trãsfu'zãw/ f transfusion

trans|gredir /trãzgre'dʒir/ vt infringe. **~gressão** f infringement

transi|ção /trãzi'sãw/ f transition. **~cional** (pl **~cionais**) a transitional

transi|gente /trãzi'ʒẽtʃi/ a open to compromise. **~gir** vi compromise

transis|tor /trãzis'tor/ m transistor. **~torizado** a transistorized

transi|tar /trãzi'tar/ vi pass. **~tável** (pl **~táveis**) a passable. **~tivo** a transitive

trânsito /'trãzitu/ m traffic; **em ~** in transit

transitório /trãzi'tɔriu/ a transitory

translúcido /trãz'lusidu/ a translucent

transmis|são /trãzmi'sãw/ f transmission. **~sor** m transmitter

transmitir /trãzmi'tʃir/ vt transmit ‹programa, calor, doença›; convey ‹notícia, ordens›; transfer ‹herança, direito›. **~se** vpr ‹doença› be transmitted

transpa|recer /trãspare'ser/ vi be visible; fig ‹emoção, verdade› come out. **~rência** f transparency. **~rente** a transparent

transpi|ração /trãspira'sãw/ f perspiration. **~rar** vi exude ● vi ‹suar› perspire; ‹notícia› trickle through; ‹verdade› come out

transplan|tar /trãsplã'tar/ vt transplant. **~te** m transplant

transpor /trãs'por/ vt cross ‹rio, fronteira›; get over ‹obstáculo, *dificuldade*>; transpose ‹*letras, música*›

transpor|tadora /trãsporta'dora/ f transport company. **~tar** vt transport; (*em contas*) carry forward. **~te** m transport; **~te coletivo** public transport

transposto /trãs'postu/ pp de ▶ TRANSPOR

transtor|nar /trãstor'nar/ vt mess up ‹*papéis, casa*›; disrupt ‹*rotina, ambiente*›; disturb, upset ‹*pessoa*›. **~nar-se** vpr ‹*pessoa*› be rattled. **~no** /o/ m (*de casa, rotina*) disruption; (*de pessoa*) disturbance; (*contratempo*) upset; **~no obsessivo compulsivo** Psic obsessive-compulsive disorder

transver|sal /trãzver'saw/ (*pl* **~sais**) a (*rua*) **~sal** cross street. **~so** /ɛ/ a transverse

transvi|ado /trãzvi'adu/ a wayward. **~ar** vt lead astray

trapa|ça /tra'pasa/ f swindle. **~cear** vi cheat. **~ceiro** a crooked ● m cheat

trapa|lhada /trapa'ʎada/ f bungle. **~lhão** a (f **~lhona**) f bungling ● m (f **~lhona**) bungler

trapézio /tra'pɛziu/ m trapeze

trapezista /trape'zista/ m/f trapeze artist

trapo /'trapu/ m rag

traqueia /tra'keja/ f windpipe, trachea

traquejo /tra'keʒu/ m knack

traquinas /tra'kinas/ a invar mischievous

trás /tras/ adv **de ~** from behind; **a roda de ~** the back wheel; **de ~ para frente** back to front; **para ~** backwards; **deixar para ~** leave behind; **por ~ de** behind

traseiro /tra'zeru/ a rear, back ● m bottom

trasladar /trazla'dar/ vt transport

traspas|sado /traspa'sadu/ a ‹*paletó*› double-breasted. **~sar** vt pierce

traste /'trastʃi/ m (*pessoa*) pain; (*coisa*) piece of junk

tra|tado /tra'tadu/ m (*pacto*) treaty; (*estudo*) treatise. **~tamento** m treatment; (*título*) title. **~tar** vt treat; negotiate ‹*preço, venda*› ● vi (*manter relações*) have dealings (**com** with); (*combinar*) negotiate (**com** with); **~tar de** deal with; **~tar alguém de** ou **por** address sb. as; **~tar de voltar** (*tentar*) seek to return; (*resolver*) decide to return; **~tar-se de** be a matter of. **~tável** (*pl* **~táveis**) a ‹*doença*› treatable; ‹*pessoa*› accommodating. **~tos** m pl **maus~tos** ill-treatment

trator /tra'tor/ m tractor

trauma /'trawma/ m trauma. **~tizante** a traumatic. **~tizar** vt traumatize

tra|vão /tra'vãw/ m Port brake. **~var** vt lock ‹*rodas, músculos*›; stop ‹*carro*›; block ‹*passagem*›; strike up ‹*amizade, conversa*›; wage ‹*luta, combate*› ● vi Port brake

trave /'travi/ f beam, joist; (*do gol*) crossbar

traves|sa /tra'vesa/ f (*trave*) crossbar; (*rua*) side street; (*prato*) dish; (*pente*) slide. **~são** m dash. **~seiro** m pillow. **~sia** f crossing. **~so** /ɛ/ a ‹*criança*› naughty. **~sura** f prank; pl mischief

travesti /traves'tʃi/ m transvestite; (*artista*) drag artist. **~do** a in a drag

trazer /tra'zer/ vt bring; bear ‹*nome, ferida*›; wear ‹*barba, chapéu, cabelo curto*›

trecho /ˈtreʃu/ m (de livro etc) passage; (de rua etc) stretch

treco /ˈtreku/ m 🇧🇷 (coisa) thing; (ataque) turn

trégua /ˈtregwa/ f truce; fig respite

trei|nador /trejnaˈdor/ m trainer. **~namento** m training. **~nar** vt train ‹atleta, animal›; practise ‹língua etc› ● vi ‹atleta› train; ‹pianista, principiante› practise. **~no** m training; (um) training session

trejeito /treˈʒejtu/ m grimace

trela /ˈtrɛla/ f lead, Amer leash

treliça /treˈlisa/ f trellis

trem /trẽj/ m train; **~ de aterrissagem** undercarriage; **~ de carga** goods train, Amer freight train

trema /ˈtrema/ m dieresis

treme|deira /tremeˈdera/ f shiver. **~licar** vi tremble. **~luzir** vi glimmer, flicker

tremendo /treˈmẽdu/ a tremendous

tre|mer /treˈmer/ vi tremble; ‹terra› shake. **~mor** m tremor; (tremedeira) shiver. **~mular** vi ‹bandeira› flutter; ‹luz, estrela› glimmer, flicker

trêmulo /ˈtremulu/ a trembling; ‹luz› flickering

trena /ˈtrena/ f tape measure

trenó /treˈnɔ/ m sledge, Amer sled; (puxado a cavalos etc) sleigh

tre|padeira /trepaˈdera/ f climbing plant. **~par** vt climb ● vi climb; (chulo) fuck

três /tres/ a & m three

tresloucado /trezloˈkadu/ a deranged

trevas /ˈtrevas/ f pl darkness

trevo /ˈtrevu/ m (planta) clover; (rodoviário) interchange

treze /ˈtrezi/ a & m thirteen

trezentos /treˈzẽtus/ a & m three hundred

triagem /triˈaʒẽ/ f (escolha) selection; (separação) sorting; **fazer uma ~ de** sort

tri|angular /triãɡuˈlar/ a triangular. **~ângulo** m triangle

tri|bal /triˈbaw/ (pl **~bais**) a tribal. **~bo** f tribe

tribu|na /triˈbuna/ f rostrum. **~nal** (pl **~nais**) m court

tribu|tação /tributaˈsãw/ f taxation. **~tar** vt tax. **~tário** a tax ● m tributary. **~to** m tribute

tri|cô /triˈko/ m knitting; **artigos de ~cô** knitwear. **~cotar** vt/i knit

tridimensio|nal /tridʒimẽsioˈnaw/ (pl **~nais**) a three-dimensional

trigêmeo /triˈʒemiu/ m triplet

trigésimo /triˈʒezimu/ a thirtieth

tri|go /ˈtrigu/ m wheat. **~gueiro** a dark

trilha /ˈtriʎa/ f path; (pista, de disco) track; **~ sonora** soundtrack

trilhão /triˈʎãw/ m billion, Amer trillion

trilho /ˈtriʎu/ m track

trilogia /triloˈʒia/ f trilogy

trimes|tral /trimesˈtraw/ (pl **~trais**) a quarterly. **~tre** /ɛ/ m quarter; (do ano letivo) term

trincar /trĩˈkar/ vt/i crack

trincheira /trĩˈʃera/ f trench

trinco /ˈtrĩku/ m latch

trindade /trĩˈdadʒi/ f trinity

trinta /ˈtrĩta/ a & m thirty

trio /ˈtriu/ m trio; **~ elétrico** music float

tripa /ˈtripa/ f gut

tripé /triˈpɛ/ m tripod

tripli|car /tripli'kar/ *vt/i*, **~se** *vpr* treble. **~cata** f triplicate

triplo /'triplu/ *a & m* triple

tripu|lação /tripula'sãw/ f crew. **~lante** *m/f* crew member. **~lar** *vt* man

triste /'tristʃi/ *a* sad. **~za** /e/ f sadness; **é uma ~za** 🖪 it's pathetic

tritu|rador /tritura'dor/ *m* (*de papel*) shredder; **~rador de lixo** waste disposal unit. **~rar** *vt* shred <*legumes, papel*>; grind up <*lixo*>

triun|fal /triũ'faw/ (*pl* **~fais**) *a* triumphal. **~fante** *a* triumphant. **~far** *vi* triumph. **~fo** *m* triumph

trivi|al /trivi'aw/ (*pl* **~ais**) *a* trivial. **~alidade** f triviality; *pl* trivia

triz /tris/ *m* **por um ~** narrowly, by a hair's breadth; **não foi atropelado por um ~** he narrowly missed being knocked down

tro|ca /'trɔka/ f exchange; **em ~ca de** in exchange for. **~cadilho** *m* pun. **~cado** *m* change. **~cador** *m* conductor. **~car** *vt* (*dar e receber*) exchange (**por** for); change <*dinheiro, lençóis, lâmpada, lugares etc*>; (*transpor*) change round; (*confundir*) mix up; **~car de roupa/trem/lugar** change clothes/trains/places. **~car-se** *vpr* change. **~ca-troca** *m* swap. **~co** /o/ *m* change; **a ~co de quê?** what for?; **dar o ~co em alguém** 🖪 pay sb back

troço /'trɔsu/ *m* 🖪 (*coisa*) thing; (*ataque*) turn; **me deu um ~** I had a funny turn

troféu /tro'few/ *m* trophy

trólebus /'trɔlebus/ *m invar* trolley bus

trom|ba /'trõba/ f (*de elefante*) trunk; (*cara amarrada*) long face. **~bada** f crash. **~ba-d'água**

(*pl* **~bas-d'água**) f downpour. **~badinha** *m* bag snatcher. **~bar** *vi* **~bar com** crash into <*poste, carro*>; bump into <*pessoa*>

trombo|ne /trõ'bɔni/ *m* trombone. **~nista** *m/f* trombonist

trompa /'trõpa/ f French horn; **~ de Falópio** fallopian tube

trompe|te /trõ'petʃi/ *m* trumpet. **~tista** *m/f* trumpeter

tron|co /'trõku/ *m* trunk. **~cudo** *a* stocky

trono /'trɔnu/ *m* throne

tropa /'trɔpa/ f troop; (*exército*) army; *pl* troops; **~ de choque** riot police

trope|ção /trope'sãw/ *m* trip; (*erro*) slip-up. **~çar** *vi* trip; (*errar*) slip up. **~ço** /e/ *m* stumbling block

trôpego /'tropegu/ *a* unsteady

tropi|cal /tropi'kaw/ (*pl* **~cais**) *a* tropical

trópico /'trɔpiku/ *m* tropic

tro|tar /tro'tar/ *vi* trot. **~te** /ɔ/ *m* (*de cavalo*) trot; (*de estudantes*) practical joke; (*mentira*) hoax

trouxa /'troʃa/ f (*de roupa etc*) bundle ● *m/f* 🖪 sucker 🖪 ● *a* 🖪 gullible

tro|vão /tro'vãw/ *m* clap of thunder; *pl* thunder. **~vejar** *vi* thunder. **~voada** f thunderstorm. **~voar** *vi* thunder

trucidar /trusi'dar/ *vt* slaughter

trucu|lência /truku'lẽsia/ f barbarity. **~lento** *a* (*cruel*) barbaric; (*brigão*) belligerent

trufa /'trufa/ f truffle

trunfo /'trũfu/ *m* trump; *fig* trump card

truque /'truki/ *m* trick

truta /'truta/ f trout

tu /tu/ *pron* you

tua /'tua/ ▶ **TEU**

tuba /'tuba/ *f* tuba

tubarão /tuba'rãw/ *m* shark

tubá|rio /tu'bariu/ *a* **gravidez ~ria** ectopic pregnancy

tuberculose /tubercu'lɔzi/ *f* tuberculosis

tubo /'tubu/ *m* tube; (*no corpo*) duct

tubulação /tubula'sãw/ *f* ducting

tucano /tu'kanu/ *m* toucan

---

tudo /'tudu/ ● *pron*

····▶ all; **é ~ por hoje** that's all for today; (*todas as coisas*) everything; **~ tinha ido** everything had gone

····▶ (*em expressões*) **dar/fazer ~ por ~** give one's all; **no fim de ~** after all; **por ~ e por nada** over the slightest thing; **dar ~ por** ou **para algo** (*desejar muito*) give one's all for sth

---

tufão /tu'fãw/ *m* typhoon

tulipa /tu'lipa/ *f* tulip

tumba /'tũba/ *f* tomb

tumor /tu'mor/ *m* tumour; **~ cerebral** brain tumour

túmulo /'tumulu/ *m* grave

tumul|to /tu'muwtu/ *m* commotion; (*motim*) riot. **~tuado** *a* disorderly, rowdy. **~tuar** *vt* disrupt ● *vi* cause a commotion. **~tuoso** *a* tumultuous

tú|nel /'tunew/ (*pl* **~neis**) *m* tunnel

túnica /'tunika/ *f* tunic

Tunísia /tu'nizia/ *f* Tunisia

tupiniquim /tupini'kĩ/ *a* Brazilian

turbante /tur'bãtʃi/ *m* turban

turbilhão /turbi'ʎãw/ *m* whirlwind

turbina /tur'bina/ *f* turbine

turbu|lência /turbu'lẽsia/ *f* turbulence. **~lento** *a* turbulent

turco /'turku/ *a* & *m* Turkish

turfa /'turfa/ *f* peat

turfe /'turfe/ *m* horse racing

turis|mo /tu'rizmu/ *m* tourism; **fazer ~mo** go sightseeing. **~ta** *m/f* tourist

turístico /tu'ristʃiku/ *a* ‹*ponto, indústria*› tourist; ‹*viagem*› sightseeing

turma /'turma/ *f* group; (*na escola*) class

turnê /tur'ne/ *f* tour

turno /'turnu/ *m* (*de trabalho*) shift; (*de competição, eleição*) round

turquesa /tur'keza/ *m/f* & *a invar* turquoise

Turquia /tur'kia/ *f* Turkey

turra /'tuxa/ *f* **às ~s com** at loggerheads with

tur|var /tur'var/ *vt* cloud. **~vo** *a* cloudy

tutano /tu'tanu/ *m* marrow

tutela /tu'tɛla/ *f* guardianship

tutor /tu'tor/ *m* guardian

tutu /tu'tu/ *m* (*vestido*) tutu; (*prato*) beans with bacon and manioc flour

TV /te've/ *f* TV

Uu

ubíquo /u'bikwu/ *a* ubiquitous

Ucrânia /u'krania/ *f* Ukraine

ucraniano /ukrani'anu/ *a* & *m* Ukrainian

ué /u'ɛ/ *int* hang on

ufa /ˈufa/ *int* phew

ufanis|mo /ufaˈnizmu/ *m* chauvinism. **~ta** *a* & *m/f* chauvinist

Uganda /uˈgãda/ *m* Uganda

ui /uj/ *int* (*de dor*) ouch; (*de nojo*) ugh; (*de espanto*) oh

uísque /uˈiski/ *m* whisky

ui|var /ujˈvar/ *vi* howl. **~vo** *m* howl

úlcera /ˈuwsera/ *f* ulcer

ulterior /uwteriˈor/ *a* further

ulti|mamente /uwtʃimaˈmẽtʃi/ *adv* recently. **~mar** *vt* finalize. **~mato** *m* ultimatum

último /ˈuwtʃimu/ *a* last; ‹*moda, notícia etc*› latest; **em ~ caso** as a last resort; **nos ~s anos** in recent years; **por ~** last

ultra|jante /uwtraˈʒãtʃi/ *a* offensive. **~jar** *vt* offend. **~je** *m* outrage

ultraleve /uwtraˈlɛvi/ *m* microlite

ultra|mar /uwtraˈmar/ *m* overseas. **~marino** *a* overseas

ultrapas|sado /uwtrapaˈsadu/ *a* outdated. **~sagem** *f* overtaking, *Amer* passing. **~sar** *vt* (*de carro*) overtake, *Amer* pass; (*ser superior a*) surpass; (*exceder*) exceed; (*extrapolar*) go beyond ● *vi* overtake, *Amer* pass

ultrassonografia /uwtrasonograˈfia/ *f* ultrasound scan

ultravioleta /uwtravioˈleta/ *a* ultraviolet

ulu|lante /uluˈlãtʃi/ *a fig* blatant. **~lar** *vi* wail

um /ũ/ (*f* **uma**, *pl* **uns**, *f pl* **umas**) ● *artigo*

┅┅▸ a, an (*antes de som vocálico*); **~ carro** a car; **uma maçã** an apple

ufa *a* forma **an** emprega-se antes de uma vogal ou som vocálico; **uma árvore** *a tree*; **um braço** *an arm*. **uns, umas** some; **preciso de uns sapatos novos** I need some new shoes; **já que você vai lá, compre umas bananas** get some bananas while you're there

● *a*

┅┅▸ (*numeral*) one; **disse ~ quilo, não dois** I said one kilo, not two; (*aproximadamente*) about; **uns quinze dias** about a fortnight

● *pron*

┅┅▸ one; (*plural*) some; **como não tinha gravata, emprestei-lhe uma** he didn't have a tie so I lent him one; **uns gostam, outros não** some like it, some don't

┅┅▸ (*em expressões*) **~ ao outro, uma à outra** *etc* each other; **ajudaram-se uns aos outros** they helped each other; **~ a ~, ~ por ~** one by one; **verifiquei os itens da lista ~ a ~** I went through the things on the list one by one

umbanda /ũˈbãda/ *m* Afro-Brazilian cult

umbigo /ũˈbigu/ *m* navel

umbili|cal /ũbiliˈkaw/ (*pl* **~cais**) *a* umbilical

umedecer /umedeˈser/ *vt* moisten. **~se** *vpr* moisten

umidade /umiˈdadʒi/ *f* moisture; (*desagradável*) damp; (*do ar*) humidity

úmido /ˈumidu/ *a* moist; ‹*parede, roupa etc*› damp; ‹*ar, clima*› humid

unânime /uˈnanimi/ *a* unanimous

unanimidade /unanimiˈdadʒi/ *f* unanimity

undécimo /ũ'dɛsimu/ a eleventh

unguento /ũ'gwẽtu/ m ointment

unha /'uɲa/ f nail; (de animal, utensílio) claw

união /uni'ãw/ f union; (concórdia) unity; (ato de unir) joining; ~ **civil** (entre pessoas do mesmo sexo) civil partnership; **União Européia** European Union, EU

unicamente /unika'mẽtʃi/ adv only

único /'uniku/ a only; (ímpar) unique

uni|dade /uni'dadʒi/ f unit. ~**do** a united; ⟨família⟩ close

unifi|cação /unifika'sãw/ f unification. ~**car** vt unify

unifor|me /uni'fɔrmi/ a uniform; ⟨superfície⟩ even ● m uniform. ~**midade** f uniformity. ~**mizado** a ⟨policial etc⟩ uniformed; (padronizado) standardized. ~**zar** vt (padronizar) standardize

unilate|ral /unilate'raw/ (pl ~**rais**) a unilateral

unir /u'nir/ vt unite ⟨povo, nações, família etc⟩; (ligar, casar) join; (combinar) combine (**a** ou **com** with). ~**se** vpr (aliar-se) unite (**a** with); (juntar-se) join together; (combinar-se) combine (**a** ou **com** with)

unissex /uni'sɛks/ a invar unisex

uníssono /u'nisonu/ m **em** ~ in unison

univer|sal /univer'saw/ (pl ~**sais**) a universal

universi|dade /universi'dadʒi/ f university. ~**tário** a university ● m university student

universo /uni'vɛrsu/ m universe

untar /ũ'tar/ vt grease ⟨fôrma⟩; spread ⟨pão⟩; smear ⟨corpo⟩

upa /'upa/ int (incentivando) ups-a-daisy; (ao cair algo etc) whoops

urânio /u'raniu/ m uranium

Urano /u'ranu/ m Uranus

urbanis|mo /urba'nizmu/ m town planning. ~**ta** a/f town planner

urbani|zado /urbani'zadu/ a built-up. ~**zar** vt urbanize

urbano /ur'banu/ a (da cidade) urban; (refinado) urbane

urdir /ur'dʒir/ vt weave; (maquinar) hatch

urdu /ur'du/ m Urdu

ur|gência /ur'ʒẽsia/ f urgency. ~**gente** a urgent. ~**gir** vi be urgent; ⟨tempo⟩ press; ~**gir irmos** we must go urgently

uri|na /u'rina/ f urine. ~**nar** vt pass ● vi urinate. ~**nol** (pl ~**nóis**) m (penico) chamber pot; (em banheiro) urinal

urna /'urna/ f (para cinzas) urn; (para votos) ballot box; pl fig polls

ur|rar /u'xar/ vt/i roar. ~**ro** m roar

urso /'ursu/ m bear. ~**-branco** (pl ~**s-brancos**) m polar bear

urti|cária /urtʃi'karia/ f nettle rash. ~**ga** f nettle

urubu /uru'bu/ m black vulture

Uruguai /uru'gwaj/ m Uruguay

uruguaio /uru'gwaju/ a & m Uruguayan

urze /'urzi/ f heather

usado /u'zadu/ a used; ⟨roupa⟩ worn; ⟨palavra⟩ common

usar /u'zar/ vt wear ⟨roupa, óculos, barba etc⟩; ~ **(de)** (utilizar) use

USB a & m USB; **porta** ~ USB port

usina /u'zina/ f plant; ~ **termonuclear** nuclear power station

uso /'uzu/ m use; (de palavras, linguagem) usage; (praxe) practice

usual /uzu'aw/ (pl **~ais**) a common. **~ário** m user. **~fruir** vt enjoy ‹coisas boas›; have the use of ‹prédio, jardim etc›. **~fruto** m use

usuário /uzu'arju/ m Comput user; **nome do ~** username

usurário /uzu'rariu/ a money-grubbing ● m moneylender

usurpar /uzur'par/ vt usurp

utensílio /utẽ'siliu/ m utensil. **~te** m/f Port user

útero /'uteru/ m uterus, womb

UTI /ute'i/ f intensive care unit

útil /'utʃiw/ (pl **úteis**) a useful; **dia ~** workday

utili|dade /utʃili'dadʒi/ f usefulness; (uma) utility. **~tário** a utilitarian. **~zar** vt (empregar) use; (tornar útil) utilize. **~zável** (pl **~záveis**) a usable

utilizador /utʃiliza'dor/ m Port ▶ USUÁRIO

utopia /uto'pia/ f Utopia

utópico /u'tɔpiku/ a Utopian

uva /'uva/ f grape

úvula /'uvula/ f uvula

. . . .

Vv

vaca /'vaka/ f cow

vaci|lante /vasi'lãtʃi/ a wavering ‹luz› flickering. **~lar** vi waver; ‹luz› flicker; Ⅱ (bobear) slip up

vaci|na /va'sina/ f vaccine. **~nação** f vaccination. **~nar** vt vaccinate

vácuo /'vakuu/ m vacuum

va|diar /vadʒi'ar/ vi (viver ocioso) laze around; (fazer cera) mess about. **~dio** a idle ● m idler

vaga /'vaga/ f (posto) vacancy; (para estacionar) parking place

vagabun|dear /vagabũdʒi'ar/ vi (perambular) roam; (vadiar) laze around. **~do** a ‹pessoa, vida› idle; ‹produto, objeto› shoddy ● m tramp; (pessoa vadia) bum

vaga-lume /vaga'lumi/ m glow-worm

va|gão /va'gãw/ m (de passageiros) carriage, Amer car; (de carga) wagon. **~gão-leito** (pl **~gões-leitos**) m sleeping car; **~gão-restaurante** (pl **~gões-restaurantes**) m dining car

vagar¹ /va'gar/ vi ‹pessoa› wander about; ‹barco› drift

vagar² /va'gar/ vi ‹cargo, apartamento› become vacant

vagaroso /vaga'rozu/ a slow

vagem /'vaʒẽ/ f green bean

vagi|na /va'ʒina/ f vagina. **~nal** (pl **~nais**) a vaginal

vago¹ /'vagu/ a (indefinido) vague

vago² /'vagu/ a (desocupado) vacant; ‹tempo› spare

vaguear /vagi'ar/ vi roam

vai|a /'vaja/ f boo. **~ar** vi boo

vai|dade /vaj'dadʒi/ f vanity. **~doso** a vain

vaivém /vaj'vẽj/ m comings and goings, toing and froing

vala /'vala/ f ditch; **~ comum** mass grave

vale¹ /'vali/ m (de rio etc) valley

vale² /'vali/ m (ficha) voucher; **~ postal** postal order

valen|tão /valẽ'tãw/ a (f**~tona**) tough ● m tough guy. **~te** a brave. **~tia** f bravery; (uma) feat

valer /va'ler/ vt be worth ● vi be valid; ~ **algo a alguém** earn sb sth; ~**-se** de avail o.s. of; ~ **a pena** be worth it; **vale a pena tentar** it's worth trying; **mais vale desistir** it's better to give up; **vale tudo** anything goes; **fazer** ~ enforce ‹*lei*›; stand up for ‹*direitos*›; **para** ~ (a sério) for real; (muito) really

vale|-refeição /valirefej'sãw/ (pl ~**s-refeição**) m luncheon voucher

valeta /va'leta/ f gutter

valete /va'letʃi/ m jack

valia /va'lia/ f value

validar /vali'dar/ vt validate

válido /'validu/ a valid

valioso /vali'ozu/ a valuable

valise /va'lizi/ f travelling bag

valor /va'lor/ m value; (valentia) valour; pl (títulos) securities; **no** ~ **de** to the value of; **sem** ~ worthless; **objetos de** ~ valuables; ~ **nominal** face value

valori|zação /valoriza'sãw/ f (apreciação) valuing; (aumento no valor) increase in value. ~**zado** a highly valued. ~**zar** vt (apreciar) value; (aumentar o valor de) increase the value of. ~**zar-se** vt ‹coisa› increase in value; ‹pessoa› value o.s.

val|sa /'vawsa/ f waltz. ~**sar** vi waltz

válvula /'vawvula/ f valve

vampiro /vã'piru/ m vampire

vandalismo /vãda'lizmu/ m vandalism

vândalo /'vãdalu/ m vandal

vangloriar-se /vãglori'arsi/ vpr brag (de about)

vanguarda /vã'gwarda/ f vanguard; (de arte) avant-garde

vanta|gem /vã'taʒẽ/ f advantage; **contar** ~**gem** boast; **levar** ~**gem**

have the advantage (**a** over); **tirar** ~**gem de** take advantage of. ~**joso** /o/ a advantageous

vão /vãw/ (pl ~**s**) a (f **vã**) vain; **em** ~ in vain ● m gap

vapor /va'por/ m (fumaça) steam; (gás) vapour; (barco) steamer; **máquina a** ~ steam engine; **a todo** ~ at full blast

vaporizar /vapori'zar/ vt vaporize; (com spray) spray

vaqueiro /va'keru/ m cowboy

vaquinha /va'kiɲa/ f collection, whip-round

vara /'vara/ f rod; ~ **civil** civil district; ~ **mágica** ou **de condão** magic wand

va|ral /va'raw/ (pl ~**rais**) m washing line

varanda /va'rãda/ f veranda

varão /va'rãw/ m male

varar /va'rar/ vt (furar) pierce; (passar por) sweep through

varejão /vare'ʒãw/ m wholesale store

varejeira /vare'ʒera/ f bluebottle

vare|jista /vare'ʒista/ a retail ● m/f retailer. ~**jo** /e/ m retail trade; **vender a** ~**jo** sell retail

vari|ação /varia'sãw/ f variation. ~**ado** a varied. ~**ante** a & f variant. ~**ar** vt/i vary; **para** ~**ar** for a change. ~**ável** (pl ~**áveis**) a variable; ‹tempo› changeable

varicela /vari'sela/ f chickenpox

variedade /varie'dadʒi/ f variety

varinha /va'riɲa/ f ~ **de condão** magic wand; ~ **mágica** Port (utensílio culinário) hand mixer

varíola /va'riola/ f smallpox

vários /'varius/ a pl several

variz /va'ris/ f varicose vein

varo|nil /varo'niw/ (pl **~nis**) a manly

var|rer /va'xer/ vt sweep; fig sweep away. **~rido a um doido** ~rido a raving lunatic

Varsóvia /var'sɔvia/ f Warsaw

vasculhar /vasku'ʎar/ vt search through

vasectomia /vazekto'mia/ f vasectomy

vaselina /vaze'lina/ f vaseline

vasilha /va'ziʎa/ f jug

vaso /'vazu/ m pot; (para flores) vase; **~ sanguíneo** blood vessel

vassoura /va'sora/ f broom

vas|tidão /vastʃi'dãw/ f vastness. **~to a** vast

vatapá /vata'pa/ m spicy North-Eastern dish

Vaticano /vatʃi'kanu/ m Vatican

vati|cinar /vatʃisi'nar/ vt prophesy. **~cínio** m prophecy

va|zamento /vaza'mẽtu/ m leak. **~zante** f ebb tide. **~zão** m outflow; **dar ~zão a** fig give vent to. **~zar** vt/i leak

vazio /va'ziu/ a empty ● m emptiness; (um) void

veado /vi'adu/ m deer

ve|dação /veda'sãw/ f (de casa, janela) insulation; (em motor etc) gasket. **~dar** vt seal ‹recipiente, abertura›; stanch ‹sangue›; seal off ‹saída, área›; **~dar algo (a alguém)** prohibit sth (for s.o.)

vedete /ve'dete/ f star

vee|mência /vee'mẽsia/ f vehemence. **~mente** a vehement

vege|tação /veʒeta'sãw/ f vegetation. **~tal** (pl **~tais**) a & m vegetable. **~tar** vi vegetate. **~tariano** a & m vegetarian

veia /'veja/ f vein

veicular /veiku'lar/ vt convey; place ‹anúncios›

veículo /ve'ikulu/ m vehicle; **~ utilitário desportivo** sports utility vehicle, SUV; (de comunicação etc) medium

vela[1] /'vɛla/ f (de barco) sail; (esporte) sailing

vela[2] /'vɛla/ f candle; (em motor) spark plug; **segurar a ~** 🔲 play gooseberry

velar[1] /ve'lar/ vt (cobrir) veil

velar[2] /ve'lar/ vt watch over ● vi keep vigil

veleidade /velej'dadʒi/ f whim

ve|leiro /ve'leru/ m sailing boat. **~lejar** vi sail

velhaco /ve'ʎaku/ a crooked ● m crook

ve|lharia /veʎa'ria/ f old thing. **~lhice** f old age. **~lho** /ɛ/ a old ● m old man. **~lhote** /ɔ/ m old man

velocidade /velosi'dadʒi/ f speed; Port (marcha) gear; **a toda ~** at full speed; **~ máxima** speed limit

velocímetro /velo'simetru/ m speedometer

velocista /velo'sista/ m/f sprinter

velório /ve'lɔriu/ m wake

veloz /ve'los/ a fast

veludo /ve'ludu/ m velvet; **~ cotelê** corduroy

ven|cedor /vẽse'dor/ a winning ● m winner. **~cer** vt win over ‹adversário etc›; win ‹partida, corrida, batalha› ● vi (triunfar) win; ‹prestação, aluguel, dívida› fall due; ‹contrato, passaporte, prazo› expire; ‹apólice› mature. **~cido a dar-se por ~cido** give in. **~cimento** m (de dívida, aluguel) due date; (de contrato, prazo) expiry date; (de *alimento, remédio etc*) best before date; (*salário*) payment; *pl*, earnings

venda¹ /'vẽda/ *f* sale; (*loja*) general store; **à ~** on sale; **pôr à ~** put up for sale

ven|da² /'vẽda/ *f* blindfold. **~dar** *vt* blindfold

venda|val /vẽda'vaw/ (*pl* **~vais**) *m* gale, storm

ven|dável /vẽ'davew/ (*pl* **~dáveis**) *a* saleable. **~dedor** *m* (*de loja*) shop assistant; (*em geral*) seller. **~der** *vt/i* sell; **estar ~dendo saúde** be bursting with health

vendeta /vẽ'deta/ *f* vendetta

veneno /ve'nenu/ *m* poison; (*de cobra etc, malignidade*) venom. **~so** /o/ *a* poisonous; (*maldoso*) venomous

vene|ração /venera'sãw/ *f* reverence; (*de Deus etc*) worship. **~rar** *vt* revere; worship ‹*Deus etc*›

vené|reo /ve'nεriu/ *a* **doença ~rea** venereal disease

Veneza /ve'neza/ *f* Venice

veneziana /venezi'ana/ *f* shutter

Venezuela /venezu'εla/ *f* Venezuela

venezuelano /venezue'lanu/ *a* & *m* Venezuelan

venta /'vẽta/ *f* nostril

ven|tania /vẽta'nia/ *f* gale. **~tar** *vi* be windy. **~tarola** /ɔ/ *f* fan

venti|lação /vẽtʃila'sãw/ *f* ventilation. **~lador** *m* fan. **~lar** *vt* ventilate; air ‹*sala, roupa*›

ven|to /'vẽtu/ *m* wind; **de ~to em popa** smoothly. **~toinha** *f* (*cata-vento*) weather vane; *Port* (*ventilador*) fan. **~tosa** /ɔ/ *f* sucker. **~toso** /o/ *a* windy

ven|tre /'vẽtri/ *m* belly. **~tríloquo** *m* ventriloquist

Vênus /'venus/ *f* Venus

ver /ver/ *vt* see; watch ‹*televisão*›; (*resolver*) see to ● *vi* see; **ter a ~ com** have to do with; **vai ~ que ela não sabe** 🄑 I bet she doesn't know; **vê se você não volta tarde** see you don't get back late; **viu?** 🄑 right? ● *m* **a meu ~** in my view. **~se** *vpr* (*no espelho etc*) see o.s.; (*em estado, condição*) find o.s.; (*um ao outro*) see each other

veracidade /verasi'dadʒi/ *f* truthfulness

vera|near /verani'ar/ *vi* spend the summer. **~neio** *m* summer holiday, *Amer* summer vacation. **~nista** *m/f* holidaymaker, *Amer* vacationer

verão /ve'rãw/ *m* summer

veraz /ve'ras/ *a* truthful

ver|bal /ver'baw/ (*pl* **~bais**) *a* verbal. **~bete** /e/ *m* entry. **~bo** *m* verb. **~borragia** *f* waffle. **~boso** /o/ *a* verbose

verbas /'verbas/ *f pl* funds

verda|de /ver'dadʒi/ *f* truth; **de ~de** ‹*coisa*› real; ‹*fazer*› really; **na ~de** actually; **para falar a ~de** to tell the truth. **~deiro** *a* ‹*declaração, pessoa*› truthful; (*real*) true

verde /'verdʒi/ *a* & *m* green; **jogar ~ para colher maduro** fish for information. **~abacate** *a invar* avocado; **~amarelo** *a* yellow and green; (*brasileiro*) Brazilian; (*nacionalista*) nationalistic; **~esmeralda** *a invar* emerald green. **~jar** *vi* turn green

verdu|ra /ver'dura/ *f* (*para comer*) greens; (*da natureza*) greenery. **~reiro** *m* greengrocer, *Amer* produce dealer

vereador /veria'dor/ *m* councillor

vereda /ve'reda/ *f* path

veredito /vere'dʒitu/ *m* verdict

vergar /ver'gar/ *vt/i* bend

vergo|nha /ver'goɲa/ *f (pudor)* shame; *(constrangimento)* embarrassment; *(timidez)* shyness; *(uma)* disgrace; **ter ~nha** be ashamed; be embarrassed; be shy; **cria** ou **tome ~nha na cara!** you should be ashamed of yourself!. **~nhoso** *a* shameful

verídico /ve'ridʒiku/ *a* true

verificar /verifi'kar/ *vt* check, verify *‹fatos, dados etc›*; **~ que** ascertain that; **~ se** check that. **~-se** *vpr ‹previsão etc›* come true; *‹acidente etc›* happen

verme /'vermi/ *m* worm

verme|lhidão /vermeʎi'dãw/ *f* redness. **~lho** /e/ *a & m* red; **no ~lho** *(endividado)* in the red

vernáculo /ver'nakulu/ *a & m* vernacular

verniz /ver'nis/ *f* varnish; *(couro)* patent leather

veros|símil /vero'simiw/ *(pl* **~símeis)** *a* plausible. **~similhança** *f* plausibility

verruga /ve'xuga/ *f* wart

ver|sado /ver'sadu/ *a* well-versed (em in). **~são** *f* version. **~sar** *vi* **~sar sobre** concern. **~sátil** *(pl* **~sáteis)** *a* versatile. **~satilidade** *f* versatility. **~sículo** *m (da Bíblia)* verse. **~so** [1] /e/ *m* verse

verso[2] /ε/ *m (de página)* reverse, other side; **vide ~** see over

vértebra /'vertebra/ *f* vertebra

verte|brado /verte'bradu/ *a & m* vertebrate. **~bral** *(pl* **~brais)** *a* spinal

ver|tente /ver'tẽtʃi/ *f* slope. **~ter** *vt (derramar)* pour; shed *‹lágrimas, sangue›*; *(traduzir)* render **(para** into)

verti|cal /vertʃi'kaw/ *(pl* **~cais)** *a & f* vertical. **~gem** *f* dizziness. **~ginoso** /o/ *a* dizzy

vesgo /'vezgu/ *a* cross-eyed

vesícula /ve'zikula/ *f* gall bladder

vespa /'vespa/ *f* wasp

véspera /'vespera/ *f* **a ~** the day before; **a ~ de** the eve of; **a ~ de Natal** Christmas Eve; **nas ~s de** on the eve of

vespertino /vesper'tʃinu/ *a* evening

ves|te /'vestʃi/ *f* robe. **~tiário** *m (para se trocar)* changing room; *(para guardar roupa)* cloakroom

vestibular /vestʃibu'lar/ *m* university entrance exam

> **vestibular** The *vestibular* is a highly competitive exam that is taken by any student wishing to apply to university in Brazil. Candidates are tested on various subjects, such as Portuguese Language, History, Geography, Maths, etc. The most popular courses, such as Medicine, Dentistry, and Engineering, have as many as 70 applicants per place, and students are selected for admission based on their overall *vestibular* grade.

vestíbulo /ves'tʃibulu/ *m* hall(way); *(do teatro)* foyer

vestido /ves'tʃidu/ *m* dress ● *a* dressed **(de** in)

vestígio /ves'tʃiʒiu/ *m* trace

ves|timenta /vestʃi'mẽta/ *f (de sacerdote)* vestments. **~tir** *vt (pôr)* put on; *(usar)* wear; *(pôr roupa em)* dress; *(dar roupa a)* clothe. **~tir-se** *vpr* dress; **~tir-se de branco/de**

padre dress in white/as a priest. **~tuário** m clothing

vetar /ve'tar/ vt veto

veterano /vete'ranu/ a & m veteran

veterinário /veteri'nariu/ a veterinary ● m vet

veto /'vetu/ m veto

véu /vɛw/ m veil

vexa|me /ve'ʃami/ m disgrace; **dar um ~me** make a fool of o.s.. **~minoso** /o/ a disgraceful

vexar /ve'ʃar/ vt shame. **~se** vpr be ashamed (**de** of)

vez /ves/ f (ocasião) time; (turno) turn; **às ~es** sometimes; **cada ~ mais** more and more; **de ~** for good; **desta ~** this time; **de ~ em quando** now and again, from time to time; **de uma ~** (ao mesmo tempo) at once; (de um golpe) in one go; **de uma ~ por todas** once and for all; **duas ~es** twice; **em ~ de** instead of; **fazer as ~es de** take the place of; **mais uma ~, outra ~** again; **muitas ~es** (com muita frequência) often; (repetidamente) many times; **raras ~es** seldom; **repetidas ~es** repeatedly; **uma ~** once; **uma ~ que** since

via /'via/ f (estrada) road; (rumo, meio) way; (exemplar) copy; pl (trâmites) channels ● prep via; **em ~s de** on the point of; **por ~ aérea/marítima** by air/sea; **por ~ das dúvidas** just in case; **por ~ de regra** as a rule; **Via Láctea** Milky Way

viabili|dade /viabili'dadʒi/ f feasibility. **~zar** vt make feasible

viação /via'sãw/ f (transporte) road transport; (estradas) road network; (companhia) bus company

viaduto /via'dutu/ m viaduct; (rodoviário) flyover, Amer overpass

via|gem /vi'aʒē/ f (uma) trip, journey; (em geral) travelling; pl (de uma pessoa) travels; (em geral) travel; **boa ~gem!** have a good trip! **~gem de negócios** business trip. **~jado** a well-travelled. **~jante** a travelling ● m/f traveller. **~jar** vi travel; **estar ~jando** 🗊 (com o pensamento longe) be miles away

viário /vi'ariu/ a road; **anel ~** ring road

viatura /via'tura/ f vehicle

viá|vel /vi'avew/ (pl **~veis**) a feasible

víbora /'vibora/ f viper

vi|bração /vibra'sãw/ f vibration; fig thrill. **~brante** a vibrant. **~brar** vt shake ● vi vibrate; fig be thrilled (**com** by)

vice /'visi/ m/f deputy

vice-cam|peão /visikãpi'ãw/ m (f **~peã**) runner-up

vicejar /vise'ʒar/ vi flourish

vice-presiden|te /visiprezi'dētʃi/ m (f **~ta**) vice-president

vice-rei /visi'xej/ m viceroy

vice-versa /visi'vɛrsa/ adv vice versa

vici|ado /visi'adu/ a addicted (**em** to) ● m addict; **um ~ado em drogas** a drug addict. **~ar** vt (falsificar) tamper with; (estragar) ruin ● vi (droga) be addictive. **~ar-se** vpr get addicted (**em** to)

vício /'visiu/ m vice

vicioso /visi'ozu/ a círculo **~** vicious circle

vicissitudes /visisi'tudʒis/ f pl ups and downs

viço /'visu/ m (de plantas) exuberance; (de pessoa, pele) freshness. **~so** /o/ a ‹planta› lush;

‹pele, pessoa› fresh

vida /ˈvida/ f life; **sem ~** lifeless; **dar ~ a** liven up

videira /viˈdera/ f vine

vidente /viˈdẽtʃi/ m/f clairvoyant

vídeo /ˈvidʒiu/ m video; (tela) screen

video|cassete /vidʒiukaˈsɛtʃi/ m (fita) video tape; (aparelho) video, Amer VCR. **~clipe** m video. **~clube** m video club. **~game** m video game. **~teipe** m video tape

vidra|ça /viˈdrasa/ f window pane. **~çaria** f (fábrica) glassworks; (vidraças) glazing. **~ceiro** m glazier

vi|drado /viˈdradu/ a glazed; **estar ~drado em** ou **por** [I] love. **~drar** vt glaze ● vi [I] fall in love (**em** ou **por** with). **~dro** m (material) glass; (pote) jar; (janela) window; **~dro fumê** tinted glass

viela /viˈɛla/ f alley

Viena /viˈena/ f Vienna

Vietnã /vietʃiˈnã/ m, Port **Vietname** /vietˈnam/ m Vietnam

vietnamita /vietnaˈmita/ a & m/f Vietnamese

viga /ˈviga/ f joist

vigarice /vigaˈrisi/ f swindle

vigário /viˈgariu/ m vicar

vigarista /vigaˈrista/ m/f swindler, con artist

vi|gência /viˈʒẽsia/ f (qualidade) force; (tempo) period in force. **~gente** a in force

vigésimo /viˈʒɛzimu/ a twentieth

vigi|a /viˈʒia/ f (guarda) watch; (em navio) porthole ● m night watchman. **~ar** vt (observar) watch; (cuidar de) watch over; (como sentinela) guard ● vi keep watch

vigi|lância /viʒiˈlãsia/ f vigilance. **~lante** a vigilant

vigília /viˈʒilia/ f vigil

vigor /viˈgor/ m vigour; **em ~** in force

vigo|rar /vigoˈrar/ vi be in force. **~roso** a vigorous

VIH /veiaˈga/ abr m (= Vírus da Imunodeficiência Humana) HIV

vil /viw/ a (pl **vis**) base, despicable

vila /ˈvila/ f (cidadezinha) small town; (casa elegante) villa; (conjunto de casas) housing estate; **~ olímpica** Olympic village

vi|lania /vilaˈnia/ f villainy. **~lão** m (f **~lã**) villain

vilarejo /vilaˈreʒu/ m village

vilipendiar /vilipẽdʒiˈar/ vt disparage

vime /ˈvimi/ m wicker

vina|gre /viˈnagri/ m vinegar. **~grete** /ɛ/ m vinaigrette

vin|car /vĩˈkar/ vt crease; line ‹rosto›. **~co** m crease; (no rosto) line

vincular /vĩkuˈlar/ vt bond, tie

vínculo /ˈvĩkulu/ m link, bond; **~ empregatício** contract of employment

vinda /ˈvĩda/ f coming; **dar as boas ~s a** welcome

vindicar /vĩdʒiˈkar/ vt vindicate

vindima /vĩˈdʒima/ f vintage

vin|do /ˈvĩdu/ pp e pres de **vir**. **~douro** a coming

vin|gança /vĩˈgãsa/ f vengeance, revenge. **~gar** vt avenge ● vi ‹flores› thrive; ‹criança› survive; ‹plano, empreendimento› be successful. **~gar-se** vpr take one's revenge (**de** for **em** on). **~gativo** a vindictive

vinha /ˈviɲa/ f vineyard

vinhedo /vi'ɲedu/ *m* vineyard

vinheta /vi'ɲeta/ *f* (*na TV etc*) sequence

vinho /'viɲu/ *m* wine ● *a invar* maroon; **~ do Porto** port

---

vinho verde *Vinho verde* (literally 'green wine') is a light, slightly sparkling Portuguese wine originating from the Minho area in the north of the country. The 'green' in its name refers to its young age rather than to its colour, and it is available in white, red and rosé varieties.

---

vinícola /vi'nikola/ *a* wine-growing

vinicul|tor /vinikuw'tor/ *m* wine grower. **~tura** *f* wine growing

vinil /vi'niw/ *m* vinyl

vinte /'vĩtʃi/ *a & m* twenty. **~na** /e/ *f* score

viola /vi'ɔla/ *f* viola

violação /viola'sãw/ *f* violation

violão /vio'lãw/ *m* guitar

violar /vio'lar/ *vt* violate

vio|lência /vio'lẽsia/ *f* violence; (*uma*) act of violence. **~lentar** *vt* rape <*mulher*>. **~lento** *a* violent

violeta /vio'leta/ *f* violet ● *a invar* violet

violi|nista /violi'nista/ *m/f* violinist. **~no** *m* violin

violonce|lista /violõse'lista/ *m/f* cellist. **~lo** /ɛ/ *m* cello

vir /vir/ *vi* come; **o ano que vem** next year; **venho lendo os jornais** I have been reading the papers; **vem cá** come here; **ⓘ** listen; **isso não vem ao caso** that's irrelevant; **~ a ser** turn out to be; **~ com** give

<*argumento etc*>

virabrequim /virabre'kĩ/ *m* crankshaft

viração /vira'sãw/ *f* breeze

vira-casaca /viraka'zaka/ *m/f* turncoat

vira|da /vi'rada/ *f* turn. **~do** *a* <*roupa*> inside out; (*de cabeça para baixo*) upside down; **~do para** facing

vira-lata /vira'lata/ *m* mongrel

virar /vi'rar/ *vt* turn; turn over <*disco, barco etc*>; turn inside out <*roupa*>; turn out <*bolsos*>; tip <*balde, água etc*> ● *vi* turn; <*barco*> turn over; (*tornar-se*) become; **vira e mexe** every so often. **~se** *vpr* turn round; (*na vida*) get by, cope; **~se para** turn to

viravolta /vira'vɔwta/ *f* about-turn

virgem /'virʒẽ/ *a* <*fita*> blank; <*floresta, noiva etc*> virgin ● *f* virgin; **Virgem** (*signo*) Virgo

virgindade /virʒĩ'dadʒi/ *f* virginity

vírgula /'virgula/ *f* comma; (*decimal*) point

vi|ril /vi'riw/ (*pl* **~ris**) *a* virile

virilha /vi'riʎa/ *f* groin

virilidade /virili'dadʒi/ *f* virility

virtu|al /virtu'aw/ (*pl* **~ais**) *a* virtual

virtude /vir'tudʒi/ *f* virtue

virtuo|sismo /virtuo'zizmu/ *m* virtuosity. **~so** /o/ *a* virtuous ● *m* virtuoso

virulento /viru'lẽtu/ *a* virulent

vírus /'virus/ *m invar* virus

visão /vi'zãw/ *f* vision; (*aspeto, ponto de vista*) view

visar /viˈzar/ *vt* aim at ‹*caça, alvo*›; ~ (a) aim for ‹*objetivo*›; ‹*medida, ação*› be aimed at

vísceras /ˈviseras/ *f pl* innards

viscon|de /visˈkõdʒi/ *m* viscount. ~dessa /e/ *f* viscountess

viscoso /visˈkozu/ *a* viscous

viseira /viˈzera/ *f* visor

visibilidade /vizibiliˈdadʒi/ *f* visibility

visionário /vizioˈnariu/ *a* & *m* visionary

visi|ta /viˈzita/ *f* visit; (*visitante*) visitor; **fazer uma ~ta a alguém** pay s.o. a visit. ~tante *a* visiting ● *m/f* visitor. ~tar *vt* visit

visí|vel /viˈzivew/ (*pl* ~veis) *a* visible

vislum|brar /vizlũˈbrar/ *vt* (*entrever*) glimpse; (*imaginar*) envisage. ~bre *m* glimpse

visom /viˈzõ/ *m* mink

visor /viˈzor/ *m* viewfinder

vis|ta /ˈvista/ *f* sight; (*dos olhos*) eyesight; (*panorama*) view; **à ~ta** (*visível*) in view; (*em dinheiro*) in cash; **à primeira ~ta** at first sight; **pôr à ~ta** put on show; **de ~ta** ‹*conhecer*› by sight; **em ~ta de** in view of; **ter em ~ta** have in view; **dar na ~ta** attract attention; **fazer ~ta** look nice; **fazer ~ta grossa** turn a blind eye (a to); **perder de ~ta** lose sight of; **a perder de ~ta** as far as the eye can see; **uma ~ta de olhos** a quick look. ~**to** *a* seen ● *m* visa; (*de peixes*) by the looks of things; ~**to que** seeing that

visto|ria /vistoˈria/ *f* inspection. ~**riar** *vt* inspect

vistoso /visˈtozu/ *a* eye-catching

visu|al /vizuˈaw/ (*pl* ~**ais**) *a* visual ● *m* look. ~**alizar** *vt* visualize

vi|tal /viˈtaw/ (*pl* ~**tais**) *a* vital. ~**talício** *a* for life. ~**talidade** *f* vitality

vita|mina /vitaˈmina/ *f* vitamin; (*bebida*) liquidized fruit drink. ~**minado** *a* with added vitamins. ~**mínico** *a* vitamin

vitela /viˈtela/ *f* (*carne*) veal

viticultura /vitʃikuwˈtura/ *f* viticulture

vítima /ˈvitʃima/ *f* victim

viti|mar /vitʃiˈmar/ *vt* (*matar*) claim the life of; **ser ~mado por** fall victim to

vitória /viˈtɔria/ *f* victory

vitorioso /vitoriˈozu/ *a* victorious

vi|tral /viˈtraw/ (*pl* ~**trais**) *m* stained glass window

vitrine /viˈtrini/ *f* shop window

vitrola /viˈtrɔla/ *f* jukebox

viú|va /viˈuva/ *f* widow. ~**vo** *a* widowed ● *m* widower

viva /ˈviva/ *f* cheer ● *int* hurray; ~ **a rainha** long live the queen

vivacidade /vivasiˈdadʒi/ *f* vivacity

vivalma /viˈvawma/ *f* **não há ~ lá fora** there's not a soul outside

vivar /viˈvar/ *vt/i* cheer

vivaz /viˈvas/ *a* a lively, vivacious; ‹*planta*› hardy

viveiro /viˈveru/ *m* (*de plantas*) nursery; (*de peixes*) fishpond; (*de aves*) aviary; *fig* breeding ground

vivência /viˈvẽsia/ *f* experience

vivenda /viˈvẽda/ *f* *Port* detached house

viver /vi'ver/ vt/i live (**de** on);
ele vive reclamando he's always
complaining ● m life

víveres /'viveris/ m pl provisions

vívido /'vividu/ a vivid

vivissecção /vivisek'sãw/ f
vivisection

vivo /'vivu/ a (que vive) living;
(animado) lively; ‹cor› bright ● m os
~s the living; **ao** ~ live; **estar** ~ be
alive; **dinheiro** ~ cash

vizi|nhança /vizi'ñãsa/
f neighbourhood. **~nho** a
neighbouring ● m neighbour

vo|ador /voa'dor/ a flying. **~ar** vi
fly; (explodir) blow up; **sair ~ando**
rush off

vocabulário /vokabu'lariu/ m
vocabulary

vocábulo /vo'kabulu/ m word

voca|ção /voka'sãw/ f vocation.
~cional (pl **~cionais**) a vocational;
orientação ~cional careers
guidance

vo|cal /vo'kaw/ (pl **~cais**) a vocal

você /vo'se/ pron you. **~s** pron you

vociferar /vosife'rar/ vi shout
abuse

vodca /'vɔdʒka/ f vodka

voga /'vɔga/ f (moda) vogue

vo|gal /vo'gaw/ (pl **~gais**) f vowel

volante /vo'lãtʃi/ m (de carro)
steering wheel

volá|til /vo'latʃiw/ (pl **~teis**) a
volatile

vôlei /'volej/ m, **voleibol**
/'volejbɔl/ m volleyball

volt /'vɔwtʃ/ (pl **~s**) m volt

volta /'vɔwta/ f (retorno) return;
(da pista) lap; (resposta) response;
às ~s com tied up with; **de** ~ back;

em ~ **de** around; **na** ~ on the way
back; **na** ~ **do correio** by return of
post; **por** ~ **de** around; **dar a** ~ **ao
mundo** go round the world; **dar a**
~ **por cima** make a comeback; **dar
meia** ~ turn round; **dar uma** ~ (a
pé) go for a walk; (de carro) go for
a drive; **dar uma** ~ **em** turn round;
dar ~s spin round; **ter** ~ get a
response; ~ **e meia** every so often.
~**do a** ~**do para** geared towards

voltagem /vow'taʒẽ/ f voltage

voltar /vow'tar/ vi go/come back,
return; ~ **a si** come to; ~ **a fazer** do
again; ~ **atrás** backtrack ● vt rewind
‹fita›. ~**-se** vpr turn round; ~**-se
para/contra** turn to/against

volu|me /vo'lumi/ m volume.
~**moso** a sizeable; ‹som› loud

voluntário /volũ'tariu/ a & m
volunteer

volúpia /vo'lupia/ f sensuality, lust

voluptuoso /voluptu'ozu/ a
sensual; ‹mulher› voluptuous

volú|vel /vo'luvew/ (pl **~veis**)
a fickle

vomitar /vomi'tar/ vt/i vomit

vômito /'vomitu/ m vomit; pl
vomiting

vontade /võ'tadʒi/ f will; **à** ~
(bem) at ease; (quanto quiser) as
much as one likes; **fique à** ~ make
yourself at home; **tem comida à** ~
there's plenty of food; **estar com** ~
de feel like; **isso me dá** ~ **de chorar**
it makes me feel like crying; **fazer a**
~ **de alguém** do what sb wants

voo /'vou/ m flight; **levantar** ~ take
off; ~ **livre** hang-gliding

voraz /vo'ras/ a voracious

vos /vus/ pron you; (a vocês) to you

vós /vɔs/ pron you

vosso /'vosu/ *a* your ● *pron* yours

vo|tação /vota'sãw/ *f* vote. **~tante**
m/f voter. **~tar** *vt* vote on ‹*lei etc*›;
(*dedicar*) devote; (*prometer*) vow ● *vi*
vote (**em** for)

voto /'vɔtu/ *m* (*em votação*) vote;
(*promessa*) vow; *pl* (*desejos*) wishes

vo|vó /vo'vɔ/ *f* grandma. **~vô** *m*
grandpa

voz /vɔs/ *f* voice; **dar ~ de** prisão a
alguém place s.o. under arrest

vozerio /voze'riu/ *m* shouting

vul|cânico /vuw'kaniku/ *a*
volcanic. **~cão** *m* volcano

vul|gar /vuw'gar/ *a* ordinary;
(*baixo*) vulgar. **~garizar** *vt*
popularize; (*tornar baixo*) vulgarize.
~go *adv* commonly known as

vulne|rabilidade
/vuwnerabili'dadʒi/ *f* vulnerability.
~rável (*pl* **~ráveis**) *a* vulnerable

vul|to /'vuwtu/ *m* (*figura*) figure;
(*tamanho*) bulk; (*importância*)
importance; **de ~to** important.
~toso /o/ *a* bulky

Ww

walkie-talkie /uɔki'tɔki/ (*pl* **~s**)
m walkie-talkie

Walkman® /uɔk'mɛn/ *m invar*
Walkman®

WAP /uap/ *a* (*telec*) WAP

watt /u'tʃi/ (*pl* **~s**) *m* watt

web /ueb/ *m* web, WWW

windsur|fe /uĩ'surfi/ *m*
windsurfing. **~fista** *m/f* windsurfer

Xx

xadrez /ʃa'dres/ *m* (*jogo*) chess;
(*desenho*) check; 🔲 (*prisão*) prison
● *a invar* check

xaile /'ʃajle/ *m* ▶ xale

xale /'ʃali/ *m* shawl

xampu /ʃã'pu/ *m* shampoo

xará /ʃa'ra/ *m/f* namesake

xarope /ʃa'rɔpi/ *m* syrup

xaxim /ʃa'ʃĩ/ *m* plant fibre

xenofobia /ʃenofo'bia/ *f*
xenophobia

xenófobo /ʃe'nɔfobu/ *a*
xenophobic ● *m* xenophobe

xepa /'ʃepa/ *f* scraps

xeque¹ /'ʃeki/ *m* (*árabe*) sheikh

xeque² /'ʃeki/ *m* (*no xadrez*) check.
~mate *m* checkmate

xere|ta /ʃe'reta/ 🔲 *a* nosy ● *m/f*
nosy parker. **~tar** *vi* 🔲 nose around

xerez /ʃe'res/ *m* sherry

xerife /ʃe'rifi/ *m* sheriff

xerocar /ʃero'kar/ *vt* photocopy

xerox /ʃe'rɔks/ *m invar* photocopy

xexelento /ʃeʃe'lẽtu/ 🔲 *a* scruffy
● *m* scruff

xícara /'ʃikara/ *f* cup

xiita /ʃi'ita/ *a* & *m/f* Shiite

xilofone /ʃilo'foni/ *m* xylophone

xingar /ʃĩ'gar/ *vt* swear at ● *vi* swear

xis /ʃis/ *m invar* letter X; **o ~ do
problema** the crux of the problem

xixi /ʃi'ʃi/ *m* 🔲 wee; **fazer ~** do a
wee 🔲

xô /ʃo/ *int* shoo

xucro /'ʃukru/ *a* ignorant

Zz

zagueiro /za'geru/ *m* full back

Zaire /'zajri/ *m* Zaire

Zâmbia /'zãbia/ *f* Zambia

zan|gado /zã'gadu/ *a* cross, annoyed. **~gar** *vt* annoy. **~gar-se** *vpr* get cross, get annoyed (**com** with)

zanzar /zã'zar/ *vi* wander

zarpar /zar'par/ *vi* set off; (*de navio*) set sail

zebra /'zebra/ *f* zebra; (*pessoa*) fool; (*resultado*) upset

ze|lador /zela'dor/ *m* caretaker, *Amer* janitor. **~lar** *vt* **~lar (por)** take care of. **~lo** /e/ *m* zeal; **~lo por** devotion to. **~loso** /o/ *a* zealous

zé-ninguém /zɛnĩ'gẽ/ *m* **ser um ~** to be a nobody

zero /'zeru/ *m* zero; (*em escores*) nil. **~quilômetro** *a invar* brand new

ziguezague /zigi'zagi/ *m* zigzag. **~ar** *vi* zigzag

Zimbábue /zĩ'babui/ *m* Zimbabwe

zinco /'zĩku/ *m* zinc

zíper /'ziper/ *m* zip, zipper

zodíaco /zo'dʒiaku/ *m* zodiac

zoeira /zo'era/ *f* din

zom|bador /zõba'dor/ *a* mocking. **~bar** *vi* **~bar (de)** mock. **~baria** *f* mockery

zona /'zona/ *f* (*área*) zone; (*de cidade*) district; (*desordem*) mess; (*tumulto*) commotion; (*bairro do meretrício*) red-light district

zonzo /'zõzu/ *a* dizzy

zoo /'zou/ *m* zoo

zoo|logia /zoolo'ʒia/ *f* zoology. **~lógico** *a* zoological

zoólogo /zo'ɔlogu/ *m* zoologist

zulu /zu'lu/ *a* & *m/f* Zulu

zum /zũ/ *m* zoom lens

zumbi /zũ'bi/ *m* zombie

zum|bido /zũ'bidu/ *m* buzz; (*no ouvido*) ringing. **~bir** *vi* buzz

zu|nido /zu'nidu/ *m* (*de vento, bala*) whistle; (*de inseto*) buzz. **~nir** *vi* ‹*vento, bala*› whistle; ‹*inseto*› buzz

zunzum /zũ'zũ/ *m* rumour

Zurique /zu'riki/ *f* Zurich

zurrar /zu'xar/ *vi* bray

Phrasefinder

Useful phrases

Frases úteis

yes, please//no, thank you
sorry
excuse me
I'm sorry, I don't understand

sim, por favor//não, obrigado/a
desculpe, perdão
com licença
perdão, não entendo

Meeting people

Conhecendo/encontrando pessoas

good morning/afternoon/evening
hello/goodbye
how are you?
nice to meet you

bom dia/boa tarde/boa noite
olá/até logo
como está?
prazer lhe conhecer

Asking questions

Fazendo perguntas

do you speak English/Portuguese?
what's your name?
where are you from?
how much is it?
where is ...?
would you like ...?

fala inglês/português?
como se chama?
você é de onde?
quanto é?/qual é o preço?
onde é/onde fica ...?
(você) queria/aceita ...?

Statements about yourself

Informações pessoais

my name is ...
I'm American//English
I don't speak Portuguese/English
I live near Salvador/Chester
I'm a student
I work in an office

meu nome é .../eu me chamo ...
sou americano/a//inglês/inglesa
não falo português/inglês
moro perto de Salvador/Chester
sou estudante
trabalho num escritório

Emergencies

Emergências

can you help me, please?
I'm lost
I'm ill/feeling ill
call an ambulance

poderia me ajudar, por favor
estou perdido/a
estou doente/estou passando mal
chame a ambulância

Reading signs

Lendo as placas

no entry
no smoking
fire exit
for sale

não entrar
não fumar
saída de emergência
à venda/vende-se

❶ Going Places

On the road	Na estrada
where's the nearest service station?	onde fica o posto de gasolina mais perto?
what's the best way to get there?	qual é o melhor caminho para chegar lá?
I've got a puncture	furou o pneu
I'd like to hire a bike/car	eu queria alugar uma bicicleta/um carro
there's been an accident	houve um acidente
my car's broken down	meu carro quebrou/(Port) avariou
the car won't start	meu carro não liga

By rail	De trem, (Port) comboio
where can I buy a ticket?	onde fica a bilheteria?
what time is the next train to York/Porto?	qual é o horário do próximo trem para York?/comboio para Porto?
do I have to change?	é preciso mudar?
can I take my bike on the train?	posso levar a minha bicicleta no trem/comboio?
which platform for the train to Salvador?	qual é a plataforma do trem/comboio para Salvador ?
there's a train to Porto at 10 o'clock	há um trem/comboio para Porto às 10h/22h
a single/return to ..., please	um bilhete para ..., por favor
a return ticket to ..., please	uma ida e volta para ..., por favor
I'd like an all-day ticket	eu queria um passe para o dia todo
I'd like to reserve a ticket for ...	eu queria reservar um bilhete para ...

At the airport	No aeroporto
when's the next flight to Rome?	quando sai o próximo voo para Roma?
where do I check in?	onde é o check-in?
I'd like to confirm my flight	eu gostaria de confirmar meu voo
I'd like a window seat/an aisle seat	eu queria uma janela/corredor
I want to change/cancel my reservation	quero mudar/cancelar a minha reserva

Getting there	Chegando
could you tell me the way to the castle?	podia me indicar o caminho para o castelo?
how long will it take to get there?	quanto tempo leva para chegar lá?
how far is it from here?	a que distância fica?
which bus do I take for the cathedral?	qual é o ônibus/(Port) autocarro que eu pego para a catedral?
can you tell me where to get off?	podia me dizer onde devo descer?
what time is the last bus?	a que horas sai o último ônibus/(Port) autocarro?
how do I get to the airport?	como se vai para o aeroporto?
where's the nearest underground station, (US) subway station?	onde é a estação de metrô/(Port) metro mais perto?
I'll take a taxi	vou pegar um taxi
can you call me a taxi?	podia chamar um taxi para mim?
take the first turning on the right	pegue a primeira entrada à direita
turn left at the traffic lights	vire à esquerda no semáforo

❷ Keeping in touch

On the phone	No telefone
may I use your phone?	poderia usar seu telefone?
do you have a mobile, (US) cell phone?	você tem um celular/(Port) telemóvel?
what is the code for São Paulo/Cardiff?	qual é o código para São Paulo/ Cardiff ?
I want to make a phone call	quero fazer um telefonema
I'd like to reverse the charges, (US) call collect	quero ligar a cobrar
I need to top up my mobile, (US) cell phone	preciso colocar crédito no meu celular, (Port) telemóvel
the line's busy	a linha está ocupada
there's no answer	ninguém atende
hello, this is Natalia	alô, fala Natália
is João there, please?	João está?
who's calling?	quem fala/está falando?
sorry, wrong number	desculpe, foi engano
just a moment, please	um momento, por favor
would you like to hold?	poderia aguardar?
please tell him/her I called	por favor diga a ele/ela que telefonei
I'd like to leave a message for him/her	eu queria deixar uma mensagem para ele/ela
... I'll try again later	... vou tentar mais tarde
tell him/her that Maria called	diga a ele/ela que Maria telefonou
can he/she ring me back?	ele/ela poderia me retornar?
my home number is ...	meu telefone de casa é ...
my business number is ...	meu telefone do trabalho é ...
my mobile, (US) cell phone number is ...	meu (número de) celular/(Port) telemóvel é ...
we were cut off	caiu a linha

Writing

what's your address?

where is the nearest post office?

could I have a stamp for Angola, please?

I'd like to send a parcel/a fax

Escrevendo

qual é seu endereço?

onde fica o correio mais próximo?

podia me dar um selo para Angola por favor?

eu gostaria de enviar um pacote/fax

On line

are you on the Internet?

what's your e-mail address?

we could send it by e-mail

I'll e-mail it to you on Tuesday

I looked it up on the Internet

the information is on their website

Online

está conectado/a à Internet?

qual é seu e-mail?

poderíamos enviar por e-mail

eu lhe enviarei por e-mail na terça feira

pesquisei na Internet

as informações estão no site deles

Meeting up

what shall we do this evening?

where shall we meet?

I'll be outside the café at 6 o'clock

see you later

I can't today, I'm busy

Encontrando

o que vamos fazer hoje à noite?

onde vamos nos encontrar?

estarei na frente do café às 18 horas

até mais tarde

hoje não posso, estou ocupado/a

❸ Food and Drink

Reservations / Reservas

can you recommend a good restaurant?	podia indicar-me um bom restaurante?
I'd like to reserve a table for four	eu queria reservar uma mesa para quatro
a reservation for tomorrow at eight o'clock	uma reserva para amanhã às 20 horas

Ordering / Fazendo o pedido

the menu/wine list, please?	o cardápio/(Port) menu, por favor?
do you have a children's menu?	tem menu para crianças?
as a starter ... and to follow ...	como entrada ... e a seguir
could we have some more bread/rice?	poderia nos trazer mais pão/arroz, por favor?
what would you recommend?	o que me sugere?
I'd like a	eu queria um
... white coffee, (US) coffee with cream	... café com leite/creme
... black coffee	... café/cafezinho/expresso
... a decaffeinated coffee	... um descafeinado
... a liqueur	... um licor
could I have the bill, (US) check?	a conta, por favor?

You will hear / Escutará

já está pronto/a para pedir?	are you ready to order?
deseja (sing) um aperitivo?	would you like an aperitif?
desejam (pl) uma entrada?	would you like a starter?
o que gostaria como prato principal?	what will you have for the main course?
queriam café/licores?	would you like coffee/liqueurs?
alguma coisa mais?	anything else?
bom apetite!	enjoy your meal!
o serviço não está incluído	service is not included.

The menu | O cardápio/(Port) menu

starters/entradas

hors d'oeuvres	tira-gostos
omelette	omelete
soup	sopa

fish/peixe

bass	labro
cod	bacalhau
eel	enguia
hake	merluza
herring	arenque
monk fish	peixe-sapo
mussels	mexilhões
oyster	ostra
prawns	camarões
red mullet	saramunete
salmon	salmão
sardines	sardinhas
shrimps	camarões
sole	linguado
squid	lula
trout	truta
tuna	atum
turbot	rodavalho

meat/carne

beef	carne (de vaca, bovina)
chicken	galinha
duck	pato
goose	ganso
guinea fowl	guiné
hare	lebre
ham	presunto
kidneys	rins
lamb	carneiro
liver	fígado
pork	carne de porco
rabbit	coelho

entradas/starters

omelete	omelette
sopa	soup
tira-gostos	hors d'oeuvres

peixe/fish

arenque	herring
atum	tuna
bacalhau	cod
camarões	prawns, shrimps
enguia	eel
labro	bass
linguado	sole
lula	squid
merluza	hake
mexilhões	mussels
ostra	oyster
peixe-sapo	monk fish
rodavalho	turbot
salmão	salmon
saramunete	red mullet
sardinhas	sardines
truta	trout

carne/meat

bife, filé	steak
carne (de vaca, bovina)	beef
carne de porco	pork
carne de veado	venison
carne de vitela	veal
carneiro	lamb
coelho	rabbit
fígado	liver
galinha	chicken
ganso	goose
guiné	guinea fowl
javali	wild boar

❸ Food and Drink

steak	bife, filé	lebre	hare
turkey	peru	pato	duck
veal	carne de vitela	peru	turkey
venison	carne de veado	presunto	ham
wild boar	javali	rins	kidneys

vegetables/verduras		**verduras/vegetables**	
artichoke	alcachofra	abobrinha	zucchini
asparagus	aspargo	alcachofra	artichoke
aubergine	berinjela	alface	lettuce
beans	feijão, fava	aspargo	asparagus
carrots	cenoura	aipo	celery
cabbage	couve, repolho	batata doce	sweet potato
celery	aipo	batata inglesa	potato
endive	endívia	berinjela	aubergine
lettuce	alface	cebola	onion
mushrooms	cogumelo, champignon	cenoura	carrot
		cogumelo, champignon	mushroom
peas	ervilha		
pepper	pimentão	couve, repolho	cabbage
potatoes	batata inglesa	couveflor	cauliflower
runner bean	vagem	ervilha	peas
tomato	tomate	fava	broad bean
sweet potato	batata doce	feijão	beans
salad	salada	pimenta	chilli
zucchini	abobrinha	pimentão verde/ vermelho	green/red pepper
		vagem	runner bean

the way it's cooked/como se prepara		**como se prepara/the way it's cooked**	
boiled	cozido-da, fervido-da	assado-da	roast
		bem passado-da	well done
fried	frito-ta	cozido-da, fervido-da	boiled
griddled	na chapa		
grilled	grelhado-da	ensopado-da	stewed
pureed	puré de	frito-ta	fried
rare	malpassado-da	grelhado-da	grilled
roast	assado-da	guisado-da	stewed
stewed	ensopado-da, guisado-da	malpassado	rare
		na chapa	griddled
well done	bem passado-da	puré de	pureed

desserts/sobremesas

ice cream	sorvete
fruits	fruta
pie	torta, pastel (Port)

other/outros

bread	pão
butter	manteiga
cheese	queijo
cheeseboard	mesa de queijos
garlic	alho
mayonnaise	maionese
mustard	mostarda
olive oil	azeite de oliva
pepper (black)	pimenta do reino
rice	arroz
salt	sal
sauce	molho
seasoning	tempero, condimento
vinegar	vinagre

drinks/bebidas

beer	cerveja
bottle	garrafa
carbonated	com gás
half-bottle	meia garrafa
liqueur	licor
mineral water	água mineral
red wine	vinho tinto
rosé	vinho rosado
soft drink	bebida não alcoólica
still	sem gás
house wine	vinho da casa
table wine	vinho de mesa
white wine	vinho branco
wine	vinho

sobremesas/desserts

fruta	fruit
sorvete	ice cream
torta, pastel (Port)	tart, pie

outros/other

azeite de oliva	olive oil
alho	garlic
arroz	rice
condimento	seasoning
manteiga	butter
maionese	mayonnaise
mesa de queijos	cheeseboard
molho	sauce
mostarda	mustard
pão	bread
pimenta do reino	(black) pepper
queijo	cheese
sal	salt
tempero	seasoning
vinagre	vinegar

bebidas/drinks

agua mineral	mineral water
bebida não alcoólica	soft drink
cerveja	beer
com gás	carbonated
garrafa	bottle
meia garrafa	half-bottle
licor	liqueur
sem gás	still
vinho	wine
vinho branco	white wine
vinho da casa	house wine
vinho de mesa	table wine
vinho rosado	rosé
vinho tinto	red wine

❹ Places to stay

Camping	**Camping**
can we pitch our tent here?	poderíamos armar nossa barraca aqui?
can we park our caravan here?	poderíamos estacionar nosso trailer/(Port) nossa roulotte aqui?
what are the facilities like?	quais são as infraestruturas?
how much is it per night?	quanto custa por noite?
where do we park the car?	onde podemos estacionar?
we're looking for a campsite	estamos procurando um *camping*
this is a list of local campsites	aqui tem/isto é um lista de locais para acampar
we go on a camping holiday every year	nós costumamos acampar todo ano

At the hotel	**No hotel**
I'd like a single/double room with bath	eu queria um quarto para uma pessoa/duplo com banheiro/(Port) com casa de banho
we have a reservation in the name of Morris	temos uma reserva no nome de Morris
we'll be staying three nights	queremos passar três noites
how much does the room cost?	quanto custa o quarto?
I'd like to see the room	eu gostaria de ver o quarto
what time is breakfast?	qual é o horário do café da manhã/(Port) pequeno almoço
can I leave this in your safe?	eu poderia deixar isto no seu cofre?
bed and breakfast	pernoite com café da manhã/(Port) dormida com pequeno almoço
we'd like to stay another night	gostaríamos de ficar outra noite
please call me at 7:30	por favor me chame às 7:30
are there any messages for me?	tem algum recado para mim?

Hostels

could you tell me where the youth hostel is?

what time does the hostel close?

I'll be staying in a hostel

the hostel we're staying in is great value

I know a really good hostel in Dublin

I'd like to go backpacking in Australia

Albergues

a senhora/o senhor poderia me informar onde fica o albergue?

a que horas fecha o albergue?

vou ficar num albergue

o albergue onde estamos hospedados é muito razoável

conheço um albergue ótimo em Dublin

eu queria viajar de mochila na Austrália

Rooms to rent

I'm looking for a room with a reasonable rent

I'd like to rent an apartment for a few weeks

where do I find out about rooms to rent?

what's the weekly rent?

I'm staying with friends at the moment

I rent an apartment on the outskirts of town

the room's fine – I'll take it

is there a larger room/that has a sea view?

the deposit is one month's rent in advance

Aluga-se quartos/quartos para alugar

estou procurando um quarto com aluguel razoável

eu gostaria de alugar um apartamento por algumas semanas

onde posso me informar sobre quartos para alugar?

quanto é o aluguel por semana?

estou hospedado(a) com amigos no momento

alugo um apartamento nos arredores da cidade

o quarto está bom – vou querê-lo

há outro quarto maior/com vista para o mar?

há um depósito de um mês adiantado

❺ Shopping and money

banking	No banco
I'd like to change some money	eu gostaria de trocar dinheiro
I want to change some dollars into euros	quero cambiar uns dólares por euros
do you need identification?	precisa de algum documento de identificação?
what's the exchange rate today?	qual é o câmbio de hoje?
do you accept traveller's cheques, (US) traveler's checks?	aceita *traveler*/cheque de viagem?
I'd like to transfer some money from my account	eu gostaria de fazer uma transferência da minha conta
where is there an ATM?	aonde tem um banco 24 horas?
I'd like high value notes, (US) bills	eu queria notas de valores mais altos
I'm with another bank	sou cliente de outro banco

Finding the right shop	Encontrando a loja certa
where's the main shopping district?	onde é a área comercial principal?
where can I buy batteries/postcards?	onde posso comprar pilhas/cartões postais?
where's the nearest pharmacy/bookshop?	onde fica a farmácia/livraria mais próxima?
is there a good food shop around here?	onde poderia comprar alimentos por aqui?
what time do the shops open/close?	qual é o horário de funcionamento das lojas/do comércio?
where did you get that/these shoes?	onde comprou isso/estes sapatos?
I'm looking for presents for my family	estou buscando lembranças para minha família
we'll do our shopping on Saturday	faremos nossas compras sábado
I love shopping	adoro fazer compras

Are you being served?	**Já foi atendido/a?**
how much does that cost?	quanto custa aquilo?
can I try it on?	posso experimentar?
could you wrap it for me, please?	pode embrulhar (para presente) para mim por favor?
can I pay by credit card?	posso pagar com cartão (de crédito)?
do you have this in another colour, (US) color?	tem isto em outra cor?
could I have a bag, please?	poderia me dar um sacola, por favor?
I'm just looking	só estou olhando
I'll think about it	vou pensar
I'd like a receipt, please	poderia me dar um recibo, por favor
I need a bigger/smaller size	preciso de um tamanho maior/menor
I take a size 10/a S/M/Large	uso tamanho 10/Pequeno/Médio/Grande
it doesn't suit me	não ficou bem em mim
I'm sorry, I don't have any change	lamento, mas não tenho trocado
that's all, thank you	é só isto, obrigado/obrigada

Changing things	**Trocando compras**
I'd like to change this shirt, please	eu queria trocar esta camisa, por favor
I bought this here yesterday	comprei isto aqui ontem
can I have a refund?	eu poderia ter um reembolso?
can you mend it for me?	poderia consertar isto para mim?
it doesn't work	não funciona
can I speak to the manager?	eu poderia falar com o gerente?

❻ Sport and leisure

Keeping fit	Mantendo a forma
where can we play football/squash?	onde podemos jogar futebol/squash?
where is the sports centre, (US) center?	onde fica o centro de esportes/desportos?
what's the charge per day?	quanto custa a diária?
is there a reduction for children/students?	tem desconto para crianças/estudantes?
I'm looking for a swimming pool	estou procurando uma piscina
you have to be a member	tem de ser sócio
I play tennis on Mondays	jogo tênis/(Port) ténis nas segundas (feiras)
I would like to go fishing/riding	gostaria de pescar/andar a cavalo
I want to do aerobics	quero fazer aeróbica
I love swimming/rollerblading/walking	adoro nadar/patinar/caminhar
we want to hire skis/snowboards	queremos alugar esquis/snowboards

Watching sport	Assistir esportes/(Port) desportos
is there a football match on Saturday?	tem jogo de futebol no sábado?
which teams are playing?	quais times/(Port) clubes estão jogando
where can I get tickets?	onde posso comprar ingressos/(Port) bilhetes?
I'd like to see a rugby/football match	eu queria ver um jogo de rúgby/futebol
my favourite, (US) favorite team is ...	meu time/(Port) clube predileto é ...
let's watch the game on TV	vamos assistir o jogo na TV

Going to the cinema/theatre/club	**Indo ao cinema/teátro/boate …**
what film/show is on?	qual é o filme/o show que está passando?
when does the box office open/close?	a que horas abre/fecha a bilheteria?
what time does the concert/performance start?	a que horas começa o concerto/espetáculo?
when does it finish?	a que horas termina?
are there any seats left for tonight?	ainda tem lugares para hoje à noite?
how much are the tickets?	quanto custam os ingressos/(Port) bilhetes?
where can I get a programme, (US) program?	onde tem programas?
I want tickets for tonight's performance	quero fazer uma reserva para o espetáculo de hoje à noite
I'll book seats in the circle	vou reservar lugares no balcão
I'd rather have seats in the stalls	prefiro poltronas na plateia, no térreo
a seat in the middle, but not too far back	um lugar no meio, mas não muito para trás
four, please	quatro, por favor
for Saturday	para sábado
we'd like to go to a club	gostaríamos de ir para uma boate
I go clubbing every weekend	vou para uma boate todo final de semana

Hobbies	**Passatempos prediletos**
what do you do at the weekend?	o que você faz nos finais de semana?
I like yoga/listening to music	eu gosto de ioga/escutar música
I spend a lot of time surfing the Net	passo muito tempo surfando/(Port) a navegar na Internet
I read a lot	leio muito
I collect instruments	coleciono instrumentos musicais

❼ Good timing

Telling the time	Vendo a hora
what time is it?	que horas são?
it's 2 o'clock	são duas horas
at about 8 o'clock (am/pm)	às oito/vinte horas aproximada-mente
from 10 o'clock onwards	a partir das dez horas
at 5 o'clock in the morning/afternoon	às cinco da manhã/tarde
it's five past/quarter past one	é uma e cinco/quinze/(Port) um quarto
it's half past one	é uma e meia
it's twenty to/quarter to three	são vinte/quinze para as três/(Port) são três menos vinte/um quarto
in a quarter/three quarters of an hour	em quinze/quarenta e cinco minutos

Days and dates	Dias e datas
Sunday, Monday, Tuesday, Wednesday, Thursday, Friday, Saturday	domingo, segunda-feira, terça-feira, quarta-feira, quinta-feira, sexta-feira, sábado
January, February, March, April, May, June, July, August, September, October, November, December	janeiro, fevereiro, março, abril, maio, junho, julho, agosto, setembro, outubro, novembro, dezembro
what's the date?	qual é a data?
it's the second of June	é dois de junho
we meet up every Monday	nós nos encontramos toda segunda-feira
we're going away in August	vamos viajar em agosto
on November 8th	no dia oito de novembro

Public holidays and special days	Feriados e dias especiais
Bank holiday (UK)	feriado nacional
New Year's Day (Jan 1)	Dia de Ano Novo
Epiphany (Jan 6)	Dia de Reis
St Valentine's Day (Feb 14)	Dia de São Valentino (= Dia dos Namorados)
Shrove Tuesday	Terça-feira de carnaval
Ash Wednesday	Quarta-feira de Cinzas
St Anthony's Day (June 13) *(similar to Valentines Day)*	Dia de Santo Antônio/(Port) António/ Dia dos Namorados
Independence Day (July 4, US)	Dia da Independência
Good Friday	Sexta-feira da Paixão
May Day (May 1)	Dia do Trabalhador
Brazilian Independence Day (Sept 7)	Dia da Independência do Brasil
Portuguese Republic Day (Oct 5)	Dia da República
Halloween (Oct 31)	Noite das Bruxas
All Saints' Day	Dia de Todos os Santos
All Souls' Day	Dia de Finados, Dia dos Mortos
Bonfire Night (Nov 5) (UK)	*tentativa de incendiar o parlamento inglês em 1605*
Thanksgiving (Nov, US)	*primeiros colonos ingleses na América do Norte*
Remembrance Sunday (Nov, UK)	*os mortos nas guerras*
Immaculate Conception (Dec 8)	Imaculada Conceição
Christmas Eve (Dec 24)	Véspera de Natal
Christmas Day (Dec 25)	Dia de Natal
New Year's Eve (Dec 31)	Véspera de Ano Novo, Reveillon

❽ Weights & measures/Pesos e medidas

Length/Comprimento

inches/polegadas	0.39	3.9	7.8	11.7	15.6	19.7	39
cm/centímetros	1	10	20	30	40	50	100

Distance/Distância

miles/milhas	0.62	6.2	12.4	18.6	24.9	31	62
km/quilómetros/ (Port) quilómetros	1	10	20	30	40	50	100

Weight/Peso

pounds/libras	2.2	22	44	66	88	110	220
kilos/quilos	1	10	20	30	40	50	100

Capacity/Capacidade

US gallons/galões	0.26	2.64	5.28	7.92	10.56	13.2	26.4
litres/litros	1	10	20	30	40	50	100

Temperature/Temperatura

°C	0	5	10	15	20	25	30	37	38	40
°F	32	41	50	59	68	77	86	98.4	100	104

Clothing and shoe sizes/Roupas e número calçado

Women's clothing sizes/Tamanhos de roupa feminina

UK	8	10	12	14	16	18
US	6	8	10	12	14	16
Europa	36	38	40	42	44	46

Men's clothing sizes/Tamanhos de roupa masculina

UK/US	36	38	40	42	44	46
Europa	46	48	50	52	54	56

Men's and women's shoes/Sapatos masculinos e femininos

UK women	4	5	6	7	7.5	8				
UK men				6	7	8	9	10	11
US	6.5	7.5	8.5	9.5	10.5	11.5	12.5	13.5	14.5
Europa	37	38	39	40	41	42	43	44	45

Aa

a /ə/ emphatic /eɪ/ ●

! before vowel or mute h **an**
/ən/ emphatic /æn/ ● *indefinite
article*

····▸ um(a); ~ **pencil** um lápis;
~ **pen** uma caneta

! When talking about what
people do, **a** is not translated
into Portuguese **she's a doctor**
ela é médica

! **a** is not translated into
Portuguese in the numbers
a hundred and **a thousand: a
hundred years ago** *há cem anos;*
**there were a thousand people
there** *havia mil pessoas lá*

····▸ per; **two pounds ~ metre**
duas libras o metro; **sixty miles
~n hour** sessenta milhas por
hora, (P) à hora; **once ~ year**
uma vez por ano; **twice ~ year**
duas vezes por ano

aback /ə'bæk/ *adv* **taken ~**
desconcertado, (P) surpreendido
abandon /ə'bændən/ *vt*
abandonar ● *n* abandono *m.* ~**ed**
a abandonado; ‹*behaviour*› livre,
dissoluto
abate /ə'beɪt/ *vt/i* abater, abrandar,
diminuir
abattoir /'æbətwɑː(r)/ *n*
matadouro *m*
abbey /'æbɪ/ *n* abadia *f*, mosteiro *m*
abbreviat|e /ə'briːvɪeɪt/ *vt*
abreviar. ~**ion** /-'eɪʃn/ *n* abreviação *f*;

(*short form*) abreviatura *f*
abdicat|e /'æbdɪkeɪt/ *vt/i* abdicar.
~**ion** /-'keɪʃn/ *n* abdicação *f*
abdom|en /'æbdəmən/ *n*
abdómen *m*, (P) abdómen *m*. ~**inal**
/-'dɒmɪnl/ *a* abdominal
abduct /æb'dʌkt/ *vt* raptar. ~**ion**
/-ʃn/ *n* rapto *m*
aberration /æbə'reɪʃn/ *n*
aberração *f*
abeyance /ə'beɪəns/ *n* **in ~**
‹*matter*› em suspenso; ‹*custom*›
em desuso
abhor /əb'hɔː(r)/ *vt* (*pt* **abhorred**)
abominar, ter horror a. ~**rence**
/-'hɒrəns/ *n* horror *m*. ~**rent**
/-'hɒrənt/ *a* abominável, execrável
abide /ə'baɪd/ *vt* (*pt* **abided**)
suportar, tolerar; ~ **by** ‹*promise*›
manter; ‹*rules*› acatar
ability /ə'bɪlətɪ/ *n* capacidade *f*
(**to do** para or de fazer); (*cleverness*)
habilidade *f*, esperteza *f*
abject /'æbdʒekt/ *a* abjeto, (P)
abjecto
ablaze /ə'bleɪz/ *a* em chamas; *fig*
aceso, (P) excitado
abl|e /'eɪbl/ *a* (**er, est**) capaz (**to** de);
be ~e to (*have power, opportunity*)
ser capaz de, poder; (*know how
to*) ser capaz de, saber. ~**y** *adv*
habilmente
abnormal /æb'nɔːml/ *a*
anormal. ~**ity** /-'mælətɪ/ *n*
anormalidade *f*. ~**ly** *adv* (*unusually*)
excepcionalmente

aboard /ə'bɔːd/ adv a bordo ● prep a bordo de

abolish /ə'bɒlɪʃ/ vt abolir, extinguir. **~tion** /æbə'lɪʃn/ n abolição f, extinção f

abominable /ə'bɒmɪnəbl/ a abominável, detestável

abort /ə'bɔːt/ vt/i (fazer) abortar. **~ive** a ‹attempt etc› abortado, malogrado

abortion /ə'bɔːʃn/ n aborto m; **have an ~** fazer um aborto, ter um aborto

abound /ə'baʊnd/ vi abundar (in em)

about /ə'baʊt/ adv (approximately) aproximadamente, cerca de; (here and there) aqui e ali; (all round) por todos os lados, em roda, em volta; (in existence) por aí; **~ here** por aqui; **be ~ to** estar prestes a; **he was ~ to eat** ia comer; **how or what ~ leaving?** e se nós fôssemos embora?; **know/talk ~** saber/falar sobre ● prep acerca de, sobre; (round) em torno de; (somewhere in) em, por. **~-face**, **~-turn** ns reviravolta f

above /ə'bʌv/ adv acima, por cima ● prep sobre; **he's not ~ lying** ele não é de mentir; **~ all** sobretudo. **~ board** a franco, honesto ● adv com lisura; **~-mentioned** a acima, supracitado

abrasive /ə'breɪsɪv/ a abrasivo; fig agressivo ● n abrasivo m

abreast /ə'brest/ adv lado a lado; **keep ~ of** manter-se a par de

abridge /ə'brɪdʒ/ vt abreviar

abroad /ə'brɔːd/ adv no estrangeiro; (far and wide) por todo o lado; **go ~** ir para o estrangeiro

abrupt /ə'brʌpt/ a (sudden, curt) brusco; (steep) abrupto

abscess /'æbsɪs/ n abscesso m, (P) abcesso m

abscond /əb'skɒnd/ vi evadir-se, andar fugido

absent[1] /'æbsənt/ a ausente; ‹look etc› distraído. **~ce** n ausência f; (lack) falta f. **~t-minded** a distraído; **~t-mindedness** n distração f, (P) distracção f

absent[2] /əb'sent/ v refl **~ o.s.** ausentar-se

absentee /æbsen'tiː/ n ausente mf, (P) absentista mf

absolute /'æbsəluːt/ a absoluto; ⊤ ‹coward etc› autêntico, (P) verdadeiro. **~ly** adv absolutamente

absor|b /əb'zɔːb/ vt absorver. **~ption** n absorção f

absorbent /əb'zɔːbənt/ a absorvente; **~ cotton** Amer algodão hidrófilo m

abst|ain /əb'steɪn/ vi abster-se (from de). **~ention** /-'stenʃn/ n abstenção f

abstemious /əb'stiːmɪəs/ a abstêmio, (P) abstémio, sóbrio

abstinen|ce /'æbstɪnəns/ n abstinência f

abstract[1] /'æbstrækt/ a abstrato

abstract[2] /əb'strækt/ vt (take out) extrair; (separate) abstrair

absurd /əb'sɜːd/ a absurdo. **~ity** n absurdo m

abundan|t /ə'bʌndənt/ a abundante. **~ce** n abundância f

abuse[1] /ə'bjuːz/ vt (misuse) abusar de; (ill-treat) maltratar; (insult) injuriar, insultar

abus|e[2] /ə'bjuːs/ n (wrong use) abuso m (of de); (insults) insultos mpl. **~ive** a injurioso, ofensivo

abysmal /ə'bɪzməl/ a abismal; ☐ (bad) abissal

abyss /ə'bɪs/ n abismo m

academic /ækə'demɪk/ a acadêmico, (P) académico, universitário; (scholarly) intelectual; pej acadêmico; (P) teórico ● n universitário

academy /ə'kædəmɪ/ n academia f

accelerat|e /ək'seləreɪt/ vt acelerar ● vi acelerar-se; Auto acelerar. **~ion** /-'reɪʃn/ n aceleração f

accelerator /ək'seləreɪtə(r)/ n Auto acelerador m

accent[1] /'æksənt/ n acento m; (local pronunciation) sotaque m

accent[2] /æk'sent/ vt acentuar

accept /ək'sept/ vt aceitar. **~able** a aceitável. **~ance** n aceitação f; (approval) aprovação f

access /'ækses/ n acesso m (to a). **~ible** /ək'sesəbl/ a acessível

accessory /ək'sesərɪ/ a acessório ● n acessório m; Jur (person) cúmplice mf

accident /'æksɪdənt/ n acidente m, desastre m; (chance) acaso m. **~al** /-'dentl/ a acidental, fortuito. **~ally** /-'dentəlɪ/ adv acidentalmente, por acaso

acclaim /ə'kleɪm/ vt aclamar ● n aplauso m, aclamações fpl

acclimatiz|e /ə'klaɪmətaɪz/ vt/i aclimatar(-se)

accommodat|e /ə'kɒmədeɪt/ vt acomodar; (lodge) alojar; (adapt) adaptar; (supply) fornecer; (oblige) fazer a vontade de. **~ing** a obsequioso, amigo de fazer vontades. **~ion** /-'deɪʃn/ n acomodação f; (rooms) alojamento m, quarto m

accompan|y /ə'kʌmpənɪ/ vt acompanhar. **~iment** n acompanhamento m

accomplice /ə'kʌmplɪs/ n cúmplice mf

accomplish /ə'kʌmplɪʃ/ vt (perform) executar, realizar; (achieve) realizar, conseguir fazer. **~ed** a acabado. **~ment** n realização f; (ability) talento m, dote m

accord /ə'kɔːd/ vi concordar ● vt conceder ● n acordo m; **of one's own ~** por vontade própria, espontaneamente. **~ance** n **in ~ance with** em conformidade com, de acordo com

according /ə'kɔːdɪŋ/ adv **~ to** conforme. **~ly** adv (therefore) por conseguinte, por consequência; (appropriately) conformemente

accordion /ə'kɔːdɪən/ n acordeão m

accost /ə'kɒst/ vt abordar, abeirar-se de

account /ə'kaʊnt/ n Comm conta f; (description) relato m; (importance) importância f ● vt considerar; **~ for** dar contas de, explicar; **on ~ of** por causa de; **on no ~** em caso algum; **take into ~** ter or levar em conta. **~ number** n número f da conta, (P) número m de conta. **~able** /-əbl/ a responsável (for por)

accountant /ə'kaʊntənt/ n contador(a) m/f, (P) contabilista mf

accumulat|e /ə'kjuːmjʊleɪt/ vt/i acumular(-se). **~ion** /-'leɪʃn/ n acumulação f, acréscimo m

accura|te /'ækjərət/ a exato, preciso. **~cy** n exatidão f, precisão f

accus|e /ə'kjuːz/ vt acusar; **the ~ed** o acusado. **~ation** /ækjuː'zeɪʃn/ n acusação f

accustom /əˈkʌstəm/ vt acostumar, habituar; **get ~ed to** acostumar-se a, habituar-se a. **~ed** a acostumado, habituado

ace /eɪs/ n ás m

ache /eɪk/ n dor f ● vi doer; **my leg ~s** dói-me a perna, tenho dores na perna

achieve /əˈtʃiːv/ vt realizar, efetuar; ‹success› alcançar. **~ment** n realização f; ‹feat› feito m, façanha f, sucesso m

acid /ˈæsɪd/ a ácido; ‹wine› azedo; ‹words› áspero ● n ácido m. **~ity** /əˈsɪdətɪ/ n acidez f

acknowledge /əkˈnɒlɪdʒ/ vt reconhecer; **~ (receipt of)** acusar a recepção de. **~ment** n reconhecimento m; (letter etc) acusação f de recebimento, (P) aviso m de recepção

acne /ˈæknɪ/ n acne mf

acorn /ˈeɪkɔːn/ n bolota f, glande f

acoustic /əˈkuːstɪk/ a acústico. **~s** npl acústica f

acquaint /əˈkweɪnt/ vt **~ sb with sth** pôr alguém a par de algo; **be ~ed with** ‹person, fact› conhecer. **~ance** n (knowledge, person) conhecimento m; (person) conhecido m

acquire /əˈkwaɪə(r)/ vt adquirir. **~sition** /ækwɪˈzɪʃn/ n aquisição f

acquit /əˈkwɪt/ vt (pt acquitted) absolver; **~ o.s. well** sair-se bem. **~tal** n absolvição f

acrid /ˈækrɪd/ a acre

acrimonious /ækrɪˈməʊnɪəs/ a acrimonioso

acrobat /ˈækrəbæt/ n acrobata mf. **~ic** /-ˈbætɪk/ a acrobático. **~ics** /-ˈbætɪks/ npl acrobacia f

acronym /ˈækrənɪm/ n sigla f

across /əˈkrɒs/ adv & prep (side to side) de lado a lado (de), de um lado para o outro (de); (on the other side) do outro lado (de); (crosswise) através (de), de través; **~ a** atravessar; **swim ~** atravessar a nado

act /ækt/ n (deed) Theatr ato m; (in variety show) número m; (decree) lei f ● vi agir, atuar; Theatr representar; (function) funcionar; (pretend) fingir ● vt ‹part, role› desempenhar; **~ as** servir de. **~ing** a interino ● n Theatr desempenho m

action /ˈækʃn/ n ação f; Mil combate m; **out of ~** fora de combate; Techn avariado; **take ~** agir, atuar

active /ˈæktɪv/ a ativo; ‹interest› vivo; ‹volcano› em atividade. **~ity** /-ˈtɪvətɪ/ n atividade f

actor /ˈæktə(r)/ n ator m. **~tress** n atriz f

actual /ˈæktʃʊəl/ a real, verdadeiro; ‹example› concreto; **the ~ pen which** a própria caneta que. **~ly** adv (in fact) na realidade

acupuncture /ˈækjʊpʌŋktʃə(r)/ n acupuntura f, (P) acupuntura f. **~ist** n acupunturador m, (P) acupunturista mf

acute /əˈkjuːt/ a agudo; ‹mind› perspicaz; ‹emotion› intenso, vivo; ‹shortage› grande. **~ly** adv vivamente

ad /æd/ n 🔢 anúncio m

AD abbr dC

adamant /ˈædəmənt/ a inflexível

adapt /əˈdæpt/ vt/i adaptar(-se). **~ation** /ædæpˈteɪʃn/ n adaptação f

adaptable /əˈdæptəbl/ a adaptável

add /æd/ *vt/i* acrescentar; ~ **(up)** somar; ~ **up to** (*total*) elevar-se a

adder /ˈædə(r)/ *n* víbora *f*

addict /ˈædɪkt/ *n* viciado *m*; **drug** ~ viciado em droga, viciado da droga, (P) toxicodependente *mf*

addict|ed /əˈdɪktɪd/ *a* **be** ~**ed to** ‹*drink, drugs*› *also fig* ter o vício de. ~**ion** /-ʃn/ *n* Med dependência *f*; *fig* vício *m*. ~**ive** *a* que produz dependência

addition /əˈdɪʃn/ *n* adição *f*; **in** ~ além disso; **in** ~ **to** além de. ~**al** /-ʃənl/ *a* adicional, suplementar

address /əˈdres/ *n* endereço *m*; (*speech*) discurso *m* ● *vt* endereçar; (*speak to*) dirigir-se a

adequa|te /ˈædɪkwət/ *a* adequado; (*satisfactory*) satisfatório

adhere /ədˈhɪə(r)/ *vi* aderir (**to** a)

adhesive /ədˈhiːsɪv/ *a* & *n* adesivo *m*; ~ **plaster** esparadrapo *m*, (P) adesivo *m*

adjacent /əˈdʒeɪsnt/ *a* adjacente, contíguo (**to** a)

adjective /ˈædʒɪktɪv/ *n* adjetivo *m*

adjoin /əˈdʒɔɪn/ *vt* confinar com, ficar contíguo a

adjourn /əˈdʒɜːn/ *vt* adiar ● *vi* suspender a sessão; ~ **to** (*go*) passar a, ir para

adjudicate /əˈdʒuːdɪkeɪt/ *vt/i* julgar; (*award*) adjudicar

adjust /əˈdʒʌst/ *vt/i* (*alter*) ajustar, regular; (*arrange*) arranjar; ~ **(o.s.) to** adaptar-se a. ~**able** *a* regulável. ~**ment** *n* Techn regulação *f*, afinação *f*; (*of person*) adaptação *f*

ad lib /ædˈlɪb/ *vi* (*pt* **ad libbed**) Ⅰ improvisar ● *adv* à vontade

administer /ədˈmɪnɪstə(r)/ *vt* administrar

administrat|e /ədˈmɪnɪstreɪt/ *vt* administrar, gerir. ~**ion** /-ˈstreɪʃn/ *n* administração *f*. ~**or** *n* administrador *m*

admirable /ˈædmərəbl/ *a* admirável

admiral /ˈædmərəl/ *n* almirante *m*

admir|e /ədˈmaɪə(r)/ *vt* admirar. ~**ation** /-mɪˈreɪʃn/ *n* admiração *f*. ~**er** /-ˈmaɪərə(r)/ *n* admirador *m*

admission /ədˈmɪʃn/ *n* admissão *f*; (*to museum, theatre, etc*) ingresso *m*, (P) entrada *f*; (*confession*) confissão *f*

admit /ədˈmɪt/ *vt* (*pt* **admitted**) (*let in*) admitir, permitir a entrada a; (*acknowledge*) reconhecer, admitir; ~ **to** confessar. ~**tance** *n* admissão *f*

admoni|sh /ədˈmɒnɪʃ/ *vt* admoestar

adolescen|t /ædəˈlesnt/ *a* & *n* adolescente *mf*. ~**ce** *n* adolescência *f*

adopt /əˈdɒpt/ *vt* adotar; ~**ed child** filho adotivo. ~**ion** /-ʃn/ *n* adoção *f*

ador|e /əˈdɔː(r)/ *vt* adorar. ~**able** *a* adorável. ~**ation** /ædəˈreɪʃn/ *n* adoração *f*

adorn /əˈdɔːn/ *vt* adornar, enfeitar

adrenalin /əˈdrenəlɪn/ *n* adrenalina *f*

adrift /əˈdrɪft/ *a* & *adv* à deriva

adult /ˈædʌlt/ *a* & *n* adulto *m*. ~**hood** *n* idade *f* adulta, (P) maioridade *f*

adulterat|e /əˈdʌltəreɪt/ *vt* adulterar

adulter|y /əˈdʌltərɪ/ *n* adultério *m*. ~**er**, ~**ess** *ns* adúlter/o, -a *mf*. ~**ous** *a* adúltero

advance /ədˈvɑːns/ *vt/i* avançar ● *n* avanço *m*; (*payment*) adiantamento *m* ● *a* ‹*payment, booking*› adiantado; **in** ~ com antecedência. ~**d** *a* avançado. ~**ment** *n* promoção *f*, ascensão *f*

advantage /əd'vɑ:ntɪdʒ/ n
vantagem f; **take ~ of** aproveitar-se
de, tirar partido de; (*person*)
explorar. **~ous** /ædvən'teɪdʒəs/ a
vantajoso

adventur|e /əd'ventʃə(r)/ n
aventura f. **~er** n aventureiro m,
explorador m. **~ous** a aventuroso

adverb /'ædvɜ:b/ n advérbio m

adversary /'ædvəsərɪ/ n
adversário m, antagonista mf

advers|e /'ædvɜ:s/ a (*contrary*)
adverso; (*unfavourable*)
desfavorável. **~ity** /əd'vɜ:sətɪ/ n
adversidade f

advert /'ædvɜ:t/ n 🔲 anúncio m

advertise /'ædvətaɪz/ vt/i anunciar,
fazer publicidade (de); (*sell*) pôr um
anúncio (para); **~r** /-ə(r)/ n anunciante mf

advertisement /əd'vɜ:tɪsmənt/
n anúncio m; (*advertising*)
publicidade f

advice /əd'vaɪs/ n conselho(s) mpl;
Comm aviso m

advis|e /əd'vaɪz/ vt aconselhar;
(*inform*) avisar, informar; **~e
against** desaconselhar. **~able** a
aconselhável. **~er** n conselheiro m;
(*in business*) consultor m. **~ory** a
consultivo

advocate[1] /'ædvəkət/ n *Jur*
advogado m; (*supporter*) defensor(a)
mf

advocate[2] /'ædvəkeɪt/ vt advogar,
defender

aerial /'eərɪəl/ a aéreo ● n antena f

aerobics /eə'rəʊbɪks/ n ginástica
f aeróbica

aeroplane /'eərəpleɪn/ n avião m

aerosol /'eərəsɒl/ n aerossol m

aesthetic /i:s'θetɪk/ a estético

affair /ə'feə(r)/ n (*business*) negócio
m; (*romance*) ligação f, aventura f;
(*matter*) assunto m; **love ~** paixão f

affect /ə'fekt/ vt afetar. **~ation**
/æfek'teɪʃn/ n afetação f. **~ed** a
afetado, pretencioso

affection /ə'fekʃn/ n afeição f,
afeto m

affectionate /ə'fekʃənət/ a
afetuoso, carinhoso

affiliat|e /ə'fɪliɛɪt/ vt afiliar; **~ed
company** filial f. **~ion** /-'eɪʃn/ n
afiliação f

affirm /ə'fɜ:m/ vt afirmar. **~ation**
/æfə'meɪʃn/ n afirmação f

affirmative /ə'fɜ:mətɪv/ a
afirmativo ● n afirmativa f

afflict /ə'flɪkt/ vt afligir. **~ion** /-ʃn/
n aflição f

affluen|t /'æfluənt/ a rico,
afluente. **~ce** n riqueza f, afluência f

afford /ə'fɔ:d/ vt (*have money for*)
permitir-se, ter meios (para); **can
you ~ the time?** você teria tempo?;
I can't ~ a car eu não posso
comprar um carro; **we can't ~ to
lose** não podemos perder

affront /ə'frʌnt/ n afronta f ● vt
insultar

afloat /ə'fləʊt/ adv & a à tona, a
flutuar; (*at sea*) no mar; ‹business›
lançado, (P) sem dívidas

afraid /ə'freɪd/ a **be ~** ter medo
(**of, to** de **that** que); (*be sorry*)
lamentar, ter muita pena; **I'm ~
(that)** (*regret to say*) lamento or
tenho muita pena de dizer que

Africa /'æfrɪkə/ n África f. **~n** a & n
africano m

after /'ɑ:ftə(r)/ adv depois ● prep
depois de ● conj depois que; **~ all**
afinal de contas; **~ doing** depois
de fazer; **be ~** (*seek*) querer,

pretender. **~effect** n sequela f, efeito m retardado; (of drug) efeito m secundário

aftermath /ˈɑːftəmæθ/ n consequências fpl

afternoon /ɑːftəˈnuːn/ n tarde f

aftershave /ˈɑːftəʃeɪv/ n loção f pós-barba, (P) loção f para a barba

afterthought /ˈɑːftəθɔːt/ n reflexão f posterior; **as an ~** pensando melhor

afterwards /ˈɑːftəwədz/ adv depois, mais tarde

again /əˈgen/ adv de novo, outra vez; (on the other hand) por outro lado; **then ~** além disso

against /əˈgenst/ prep contra

age /eɪdʒ/ n idade f; (period) época f, idade f; **~s** 🔢 (very long time) há séculos mpl; **of ~** Jur maior; **ten years of ~** cerca de dez anos; **under ~** menor ● vt/i (pres p **ageing**) envelhecer. **~ group** n faixa etária f. **~less** a sempre jovem

aged[1] /ˈeɪdʒd/ a **~ six** de seis anos de idade

aged[2] /ˈeɪdʒɪd/ a idoso, velho

agen|cy /ˈeɪdʒənsɪ/ n agência f; (means) intermédio m. **~t** n agente m/f

agenda /əˈdʒendə/ n ordem f do dia

aggravat|e /ˈægrəveɪt/ vt agravar; 🔢 (annoy) irritar. **~ion** /-ˈveɪʃn/ n (worsening) agravamento m; (exasperation) irritação f, 🔢 (trouble) aborrecimentos mpl

aggregate /ˈægrɪgeɪt/ vt/i agregar(-se) ● /ˈægrɪgət/ a total, global ● n (total, mass, materials) agregado m; **in the ~** no todo

aggress|ive /əˈgresɪv/ a agressivo; (weapons) ofensivo. **~ion** /-ʃn/ n agressão f. **~or** n agressor m

agil|e /ˈædʒaɪl/ a ágil. **~ity** /əˈdʒɪlətɪ/ n agilidade f

agitat|e /ˈædʒɪteɪt/ vt agitar. **~ion** /-ˈteɪʃn/ n agitação f

agnostic /ægˈnɒstɪk/ a & n agnóstico m

ago /əˈgəʊ/ adv há; **a month ~** há um mês; **long ~** há muito tempo

agon|y /ˈægənɪ/ n agonia f; (mental) angústia f. **~ize** vi atormentar-se, torturar-se

agree /əˈɡriː/ vt/i concordar; (of figures) acertar; **~ that** reconhecer que; **~ to** do concordar em or aceitar fazer; **~ to sth** concordar com alguma coisa; **seafood doesn't ~ with me** não me dou bem com mariscos. **~d** a ‹time, place› combinado; **be ~d** estar de acordo

agreeable /əˈɡriːəbl/ a agradável; **be ~** to estar de acordo com a

agreement /əˈɡriːmənt/ n acordo m; Gramm concordância f; (contract) contrato m; **in ~** de acordo

agricultur|e /ˈægrɪkʌltʃə(r)/ n agricultura f. **~al** /-ˈkʌltʃərəl/ a agrícola

aground /əˈɡraʊnd/ adv **run ~** (of ship) encalhar

ahead /əˈhed/ adv à frente, adiante; (in advance) adiantado; **~ of sb** diante de alguém, à frente de alguém; **~ of time** antes da hora, adiantado; **straight ~** sempre em frente

aid /eɪd/ vt ajudar; **~ and abet** ser cúmplice de ● n ajuda f; **in ~ of** em auxílio de, a favor de

AIDS /eɪdz/ n Med AIDS f, (P) sida m. **~ awareness** n conscientização f sobre a AIDS, (P) consciencialização f sobre a SIDA; **~ virus** n vírus m da AIDS, (P) vírus m da SIDA

aim /eɪm/ vt ‹gun› apontar; ‹efforts› dirigir; (send) atirar (at para) ● vi visar ● n alvo m; ~ at visar; ~ to aspirar a, tencionar; take ~ fazer pontaria. **~less** a, **~lessly** adv sem objetivo

air /eə(r)/ n ar m; in the ~ ‹rumour› espalhado; ‹plans› no ar; on the ~ Radio no ar ● vt arejar; ‹views› expor ● a ‹base etc› aéreo; ~ force Força f Aérea; ~ hostess aeromoça f, (P) hospedeira f de bordo; ~ raid ataque m aéreo. **~-conditioned** a com ar condicionado; **~ conditioning** n condicionamento m do ar, (P) ar m condicionado; **~ strike** n ataque m aéreo

aircraft /ˈeəkrɑːft/ n (pl invar) avião m. **~ carrier** n porta-aviões m

airfield /ˈeəfiːld/ n campo m de aviação

airgun /ˈeəgʌn/ n espingarda f de pressão

airlift /ˈeəlɪft/ n ponte f aérea ● vt transportar em ponte aérea

airline /ˈeəlaɪn/ n linha f aérea

airmail /ˈeəmeɪl/ n correio m aéreo; by ~ por avião

airport /ˈeəpɔːt/ n aeroporto m

airtight /ˈeətaɪt/ a hermético

airy /ˈeərɪ/ a (-ier, -iest) arejado; ‹manner› desenvolto

aisle /aɪl/ n (of church) nave f lateral; (gangway) coxia f

ajar /əˈdʒɑː(r)/ adv & a entreaberto

à la carte /ɑːlɑːˈkɑːt/ adv & a à la carte, (P) à lista

alarm /əˈlɑːm/ n alarme m; (clock) campainha f ● vt alarmar. **~ clock** n despertador m. **~ing** a alarmante

alas /əˈlæs/ int ai ai de mim!

album /ˈælbəm/ n álbum m

alcohol /ˈælkəhɒl/ n álcool m. **~ic** /-ˈhɒlɪk/ a ‹person, drink› alcoólico ● n alcoólico m. **~ism** n alcoolismo m

alcove /ˈælkəʊv/ n recesso m, alcova f

ale /eɪl/ n cerveja f inglesa

alert /əˈlɜːt/ a (lively) vivo; (watchful) vigilante ● n alerta m; be on the ~ estar alerta ● vt alertar

algebra /ˈældʒɪbrə/ n álgebra f

Algeria /ælˈdʒɪərɪə/ n Argélia f

alias /ˈeɪlɪəs/ n (pl -ases) outro nome m, nome falso m, (P) pseudónimo m ● adv aliás

alibi /ˈælɪbaɪ/ n (pl -is) álibi m, (P) álibi m

alien /ˈeɪlɪən/ n & a estrangeiro m; ~ to (contrary) contrário a; (differing) alheio a, estranho a

alienat|**e** /ˈeɪlɪəneɪt/ vt alienar

alight¹ /əˈlaɪt/ vi descer; (bird) pousar

alight² /əˈlaɪt/ a (on fire) em chamas; (lit up) aceso

align /əˈlaɪn/ vt alinhar. **~ment** n alinhamento m

alike /əˈlaɪk/ a semelhante, parecido ● adv da mesma maneira; **look** or **be** ~ parecer-se

alimony /ˈælɪmənɪ/ n pensão f alimentar, (P) de alimentos

alive /əˈlaɪv/ a vivo; ~ to sensível a; ~ with fervilhando de, (P) a fervilhar de

alkali /ˈælkəlaɪ/ n (pl -is) álcali m, (P) alcali m

---

all /ɔːl/ ● a

••••> (with singular noun) todo, toda; ~ **the wine** o vinho todo; ~ **my money** todo o meu dinheiro

····▸ (*with plural noun*) todos, todas; ~ **the men** todos os homens; ~ **the women** todas as mulheres

● *pron*

····▸ (*plural*) todos, todas; ~ **are here** todos estão aqui; **are we going?** vamos todos?

····▸ (*everything*) tudo; ~ **she said was...** tudo o que ela disse foi...; **I ate ~ of it** Eu comi tudo

····▸ (*in phrases*) ~ **in** de modo geral; **in** ~ (*in total*) no total; **not at** ~ (*in no way*) de modo algum; **it was not at ~ expensive** não foi nem um pouco caro; (*answer to 'thank you'*) de nada

● *adv*

····▸ (*completely*) completamente; ~ **by myself** completamente só; ~ **in white** todo de branco; (*in scores*) **two** ~ dois a dois

····▸ (*in phrases*) ~ **along** todo o tempo; ~ **but** quase, todos menos; ~ **in** (*exhausted*) esgotado; ~ **over** (*in all parts of*) por todo; **I ache** ~ **over** dói-me o corpo inteiro; ~ **the better/less/ more/worse** *etc* tanto melhor/ menos/mais/pior *etc*; ~ **right** bem; (*in phrases*) está bem.

~**in** *a* tudo incluído; ~**out** *a* ‹*effort*› máximo; ~**round** *a* completo

allegation /ælɪˈɡeɪʃn/ *n* alegação *f*

allege /əˈledʒ/ *vt* alegar

allegiance /əˈliːdʒəns/ *n* fidelidade *f*, lealdade *f*

allerg|y /ˈælədʒɪ/ *n* alergia *f*. ~**ic** /əˈlɜːdʒɪk/ *a* alérgico

alleviate /əˈliːvɪeɪt/ *vt* aliviar

alley /ˈælɪ/ *n* (*pl* -**eys**) (*street*) viela *f*; (*for bowling*) pista *f*

alliance /əˈlaɪəns/ *n* aliança *f*

allied /ˈælaɪd/ *a* aliado

alligator /ˈælɪɡeɪtə(r)/ *n* jacaré *m*

allocat|e /ˈæləkeɪt/ *vt* (*share out*) distribuir; (*assign*) destinar. ~**ion** /-ˈkeɪʃn/ *n* atribuição *f*

allot /əˈlɒt/ *vt* (*pt* **allotted**) atribuir. ~**ment** *n* atribuição *f*; (*share*) distribuição *f*; (*land*) horta *f* alugada

allow /əˈlaʊ/ *vt* permitir; (*grant*) conceder, dar; (*reckon on*) contar com; (*agree*) admitir, reconhecer; ~ **sb to** permitir a alguém (+ *inf*) or que (+ *subj*); ~ **for** levar em conta

allowance /əˈlaʊəns/ *n* (*for employees*) ajudas *fpl* de custo; (*monthly, for wife, child*) benefício *m*; (*tax*) desconto *m*; **make** ~**s for** (*person*) levar em consideração, ser indulgente para com; (*take into account*) atender a, levar em consideração

alloy /ˈælɔɪ/ *n* liga *f*

allude /əˈluːd/ *vi* ~ **to** aludir a

allure /əˈlʊə(r)/ *vt* seduzir, atrair

allusion /əˈluːʒn/ *n* alusão *f*

ally[1] /ˈælaɪ/ *n* (*pl* -**lies**) aliado *m*

ally[2] /əˈlaɪ/ *vt* aliar; ~ **oneself with/ to** aliar-se com/a

almighty /ɔːlˈmaɪtɪ/ *a* todo-poderoso; 🅵 grande; formidável

almond /ˈɑːmənd/ *n* amêndoa *f*; ~ **paste** maçapão *m*

almost /ˈɔːlməʊst/ *adv* quase

alone /əˈləʊn/ *a* & *adv* só; **leave** ~ (*abstain from interfering with*) deixar em paz; **let** ~ (*without considering*) sem or para não falar de

along /əˈlɒŋ/ *prep* ao longo de ● *adv* (*onward*) para diante; **all** ~ durante todo o tempo; ~ **with** com; **move ~,** please ande, por favor

alongside /əlɒŋ'saɪd/ adv Naut atracado; **come ~** acostar ● prep ao lado de

aloof /ə'luːf/ adv à parte ● a distante

aloud /ə'laʊd/ adv em voz alta

alphabet /'ælfəbet/ n alfabeto m. **~ical** /-'betɪkl/ a alfabético

alpine /'ælpaɪn/ a alpino, alpestre

Alps /ælps/ npl **the ~** os Alpes mpl

Al-Qaeda /ælkæ'iːdə/ pr n Al-Qaeda f, (P) Alcaida f

already /ɔːl'redɪ/ adv já

also /'ɔːlsəʊ/ adv também

altar /'ɔːltə(r)/ n altar m

alter /'ɔːltə(r)/ vt/i alterar(-se), modificar(-se). **~ation** /-'reɪʃn/ n alteração f, (to garment) modificação f

alternate¹ /ɔːl'tɜːnət/ a alternado

alternat|e² /'ɔːltəneɪt/ vt/i alternar(-se); **~ing current** Electr corrente f alterna

alternative /ɔːl'tɜːnətɪv/ a alternativo ● n alternativa f. **~ly** adv em alternativa; **or ~ly** ou então

although /ɔːl'ðəʊ/ conj embora, conquanto

altitude /'æltɪtjuːd/ n altitude f

altogether /ɔːltə'geðə(r)/ adv (completely) completamente; (in total) ao todo; (on the whole) de modo geral

aluminium /ælju'mɪnɪəm/ n Amer **aluminum** /ə'luːmɪnəm/ n alumínio m

always /'ɔːlweɪz/ adv sempre

am /æm/ ▸ BE

a.m. /eɪ'em/ adv da manhã

amass /ə'mæs/ vt amontoar, juntar

amateur /'æmətə(r)/ n & a amador m. **~ish** a pej de amador, (P) amadorístico

amaz|e /ə'meɪz/ vt assombrar, espantar. **~ed** a assombrado. **~ement** n assombro m

Amazon /'æməzən/ n **the ~** o Amazonas

ambassador /æm'bæsədə(r)/ n embaixador m

amber /'æmbə(r)/ n âmbar m; (traffic light) luz f amarela

ambigu|ous /æm'bɪgjʊəs/ a ambíguo. **~ity** /-'gjuːətɪ/ n ambiguidade f

ambiti|on /æm'bɪʃn/ n ambição f. **~ous** a ambicioso

ambivalen|t /æm'bɪvələnt/ a ambivalente

amble /'æmbl/ vi caminhar sem pressa

ambulance /'æmbjʊləns/ n ambulância f

ambush /'æmbʊʃ/ n emboscada f ● vt fazer uma emboscada para, (P) fazer uma emboscada a

amend /ə'mend/ vt emendar, corrigir. **~ment** n (to rule) emenda f. **~s** n **make ~s for** reparar, compensar

amenities /ə'miːnətɪz/ npl (pleasant features) atrativos mpl; (facilities) confortos mpl, comodidades fpl

America /ə'merɪkə/ n América f. **~n** a & n americano m. **~nism** /-nɪzm/ n americanismo m

American dream O conceito de "sonho americano" baseia-se na ideia de que qualquer pessoa que vive nos Estados Unidos pode alcançar o

sucesso se trabalhar arduamente. Para os imigrantes e para as minorias, o conceito inclui também liberdade e igualdade de direitos.

amiable /ˈeɪmɪəbl/ *a* amável

amicable /ˈæmɪkəbl/ *a* amigável, amigo

amid(st) /əˈmɪd(st)/ *prep* entre, no meio de

amiss /əˈmɪs/ *a* & *adv* mal; **sth** ~ qq coisa que não está bem; **take sth** ~ levar qq coisa a mal

ammonia /əˈməʊnɪə/ *n* amoníaco *m*

ammunition /æmjʊˈnɪʃn/ *n* munições *fpl*

amnesia /æmˈniːzɪə/ *n* amnésia *f*

amnesty /ˈæmnəstɪ/ *n* anistia *f*, (P) amnistia *f*

among(st) /əˈmʌŋ(st)/ *prep* entre, no meio de; ~ **ourselves** (aqui) entre nós

amoral /eɪˈmɒrəl/ *a* amoral

amorous /ˈæmərəs/ *a* amoroso

amount /əˈmaʊnt/ *n* quantidade *f*; (*total*) montante *m*; (*sum of money*) quantia *f* ● *vi* ~ **to** elevar-se a; *fig* equivaler a

amp /æmp/ *n* 🔲 ampere *m*

amphibian /æmˈfɪbɪən/ *n* anfíbio *m*. ~**ous** *a* anfíbio

ample /ˈæmpl/ *a* (-**er**, -**est**) (*large*, *roomy*) amplo; (*enough*) suficiente, bastante

amplify /ˈæmplɪfaɪ/ *vt* ampliar, amplificar. ~**ier** *n* amplificador *m*

amputate /ˈæmpjʊteɪt/ *vt* amputar. ~**ion** /-ˈteɪʃn/ *n* amputação *f*

amuse /əˈmjuːz/ *vt* divertir. ~**ment** *n* divertimento *m*. ~**ing** *a* divertido

an /ən, æn/ ▶ A

anaemia /əˈniːmɪə/ *n* anemia *f*. ~**ic** *a* anêmico, (P) anémico

anaesthetic /ænɪsˈθetɪk/ *n* anestético *m*, (P) anestésico *m*; **give an** ~ **to** anestesiar

anaesthetist /əˈniːsθətɪst/ *n* anestesista *mf*

anagram /ˈænəgræm/ *n* anagrama *m*

analogue /ˈænəlɒg/ *a* análogo

analogy /əˈnælədʒɪ/ *n* analogia *f*

analyse /ˈænəlaɪz/ *vt* analisar. ~**t** /-ɪst/ *n* analista *mf*

analysis /əˈnæləsɪs/ *n* (*pl* -**yses** /-əsiːz/) análise *f*

analytic(al) /ænəˈlɪtɪk(l)/ *a* analítico

anarchy /ˈænəkɪ/ *n* anarquia *f*. ~**ist** *n* anarquista *mf*

anatomy /əˈnætəmɪ/ *n* anatomia *f*. ~**ical** /ænəˈtɒmɪkl/ *a* anatômico, (P) anatómico

ancestor /ˈænsestə(r)/ *n* antepassado *m*

ancestry /ˈænsestrɪ/ *n* ascendência *f*, estirpe *f*

anchor /ˈæŋkə(r)/ *n* âncora *f* ● *vt/i* ancorar

ancient /ˈeɪnʃənt/ *a* antigo

and /ənd emphatic ænd/ *conj* e; **go** ~ **see** vá ver; **better** ~ **better** / **less** ~ **less** *etc* cada vez melhor/ menos *etc*

anecdote /ˈænɪkdəʊt/ *n* anedota *f*

angel /ˈeɪndʒl/ *n* anjo *m*. ~**ic** /ænˈdʒelɪk/ *a* angélico, angelical

anger /ˈæŋgə(r)/ *n* cólera *f*, zanga *f* ● *vt* irritar

angle[1] /ˈæŋgl/ *n* ângulo *m*

angle[2] /ˈæŋgl/ *vi* (*fish*) pescar (à linha); ~ **for** *fig* *compliments,* *information*⟩ andar à procura de. **~r** /-ə(r)/ n pescador m

Anglo-Saxon /ˈæŋgləʊˈsæksn/ a & n anglo-saxão m

angr|y /ˈæŋgrɪ/ a (**-ier, -iest**) zangado; **get ~y** zangar-se (**with** com)

anguish /ˈæŋgwɪʃ/ n angústia f

angular /ˈæŋgjʊlə(r)/ a angular; ⟨*features*⟩ anguloso

animal /ˈænɪml/ a & n animal m

animate¹ /ˈænɪmət/ a animado

animat|e² /ˈænɪmeɪt/ vt animar; **~ed cartoon** filme m de bonecos animados or (P) de desenhos animados. **~ion** /-ˈmeɪʃn/ n animação f

animosity /ænɪˈmɒsətɪ/ n animosidade f

aniseed /ˈænɪsiːd/ n semente f de anis

ankle /ˈæŋkl/ n tornozelo m; **~ sock** meia f soquete

annex /əˈneks/ vt anexar

annexe /ˈæneks/ n anexo m

annihilate /əˈnaɪəleɪt/ vt aniquilar

anniversary /ænɪˈvɜːsərɪ/ n aniversário m

announce /əˈnaʊns/ vt anunciar. **~ment** n anúncio m. **~r** /-ə(r)/ n *Radio, TV* locutor m

annoy /əˈnɔɪ/ vt irritar, aborrecer. **~ance** n aborrecimento m. **~ed** a aborrecido (**with** com); **get ~ed** aborrecer-se. **~ing** a irritante

annual /ˈænjʊəl/ a anual ● n *Bot* planta f anual; (*book*) anuário m

annul /əˈnʌl/ vt (*pt* **annulled**) anular

anomaly /əˈnɒmalɪ/ n anomalia f

anonym|ous /əˈnɒnɪməs/ a anônimo, (P) anónimo

anorak /ˈænəræk/ n anoraque m, anorak m

another /əˈnʌðə(r)/ a & *pron* (um) outro; **~ ten minutes** mais dez minutos; **to one ~** um ao outro, uns aos outros

answer /ˈɑːnsə(r)/ n resposta f; (*solution*) solução f ● vt responder a; ⟨*prayer*⟩ atender a ● vi responder; **~ the door** atender à porta; **~ back** retrucar, (P) responder torto; **~ for** responder por. **~ing machine** n secretária f eletrônica, (P) atendedor m de chamadas

ant /ænt/ n formiga f

antagonis|m /ænˈtægənɪzəm/ n antagonismo m. **~tic** /-ˈnɪstɪk/ a antagônico, (P) antagónico, hostil

antagonize /ænˈtægənaɪz/ vt antagonizar, hostilizar

Antarctic /ænˈtɑːktɪk/ n Antártico, (P) Antárctico ● a antártico, (P) antárctico

antelope /ˈæntɪləʊp/ n antílope m

antenatal /ˈæntɪˈneɪtl/ a pré-natal

antenna /ænˈtenə/ n (*pl* **-ae** /-iː/) antena f

anthem /ˈænθəm/ n cântico m; **national ~** hino m nacional

anthology /ænˈθɒlədʒɪ/ n antologia f

anthropolog|y /ænθrəˈpɒlədʒɪ/ n antropologia f. **~ist** n antropólogo m

anti- /ænti/ *pref* anti-

antibiotic /æntɪbaɪˈɒtɪk/ n antibiótico m

antibody /ˈæntɪbɒdɪ/ n anticorpo m

anticipat|e /ænˈtɪsɪpeɪt/ vt (*foresee, expect*) prever; (*forestall*) antecipar-se a. **~ion** /-ˈpeɪʃn/ n antecipação f; (*expectation*) expectativa f; **in ~ion of** na previsão or expectativa de

anticlimax /ˌæntɪˈklaɪmæks/ n
anticlímax m; **it was an ~** não correspondeu à expectativa

anticlockwise /ˌæntɪˈklɒkwaɪz/
adv & a no sentido contrário ao dos
ponteiros do relógio

antics /ˈæntɪks/ npl (of clown)
palhaçadas fpl; (behaviour)
comportamento m bizarro

antidote /ˈæntɪdəʊt/ n antídoto m

antifreeze /ˈæntɪfriːz/ n
anticongelante m

antipathy /ænˈtɪpəθɪ/ n antipatia f

antiquated /ˈæntɪkweɪtɪd/ a
antiquado

antique /ænˈtiːk/ a antigo ● n
antiguidade f; **~ dealer** antiquário
m; **~ shop** loja f de antiguidades, (P)
antiquário m

antiquity /ænˈtɪkwɪtɪ/ n
antiguidade f

antiseptic /ˌæntɪˈseptɪk/ a & n
antisséptico m

antisocial /ˌæntɪˈsəʊʃl/ a
antissocial; (unsociable) insociável

antlers /ˈæntləz/ npl chifres mpl,
esgalhos mpl

antonym /ˈæntənɪm/ n antônimo
m, (P) antónimo m

anus /ˈeɪnəs/ n ânus m

anvil /ˈænvɪl/ n bigorna f

anxiety /æŋˈzaɪətɪ/ n ansiedade f;
(eagerness) ânsia f

anxious /ˈæŋkʃəs/ a (worried,
eager) ansioso (**to** de, por)

any /ˈenɪ/ a & pron qualquer,
quaisquer; (in neg and interr sentences)
algum, alguns; (in neg sentences)
nenhum, nenhuns; (every) todo; **at
~ moment** a qualquer momento;
at ~ rate de qualquer modo, em

todo o caso; **in ~ case** em todo o
caso; **have you ~ money/friends?**
você tem (algum) dinheiro/(alguns)
amigos?; **I don't have ~ time** não
tenho nenhum tempo or tempo
nenhum or tempo algum; **has she
~?** ela tem algum?; **she doesn't
have ~** ela não tem nenhum ● adv
(at all) de modo algum or nenhum;
(a little) um pouco; **~ the less/the
worse** etc menos/pior etc

anybody /ˈenɪbɒdɪ/ pron qualquer
pessoa; (somebody) alguém; (after
negative) ninguém; **he didn't see ~**
ele não viu ninguém

anyhow /ˈenɪhaʊ/ adv (no matter
how) de qualquer modo; (badly) de
qualquer maneira, ao acaso; (in any
case) em todo o caso; **you can try,
~** em todo o caso, você pode tentar

anyone /ˈenɪwʌn/ pron = ANYBODY

anything /ˈenɪθɪŋ/ pron
(something) alguma coisa; (no
matter what) qualquer coisa; (after
negative) nada; **~ you do** tudo o
que você fizer; **he didn't say ~** não
disse nada; **it is ~ but cheap** é tudo
menos barato

anyway /ˈenɪweɪ/ adv de qualquer
modo; (in any case) em todo o caso

anywhere /ˈenɪweə(r)/ adv
(somewhere) em qualquer parte;
(after negative) em parte alguma/
nenhuma; **~ else** em qualquer
outro lado; **~ you go** onde quer que
você vá; **he doesn't go ~** ele não
vai a lado nenhum

apart /əˈpɑːt/ adv à parte,
(separated) separado; (into pieces)
aos bocados; **~ from** à parte,
além de; **ten metres ~** a dez
metros de distância entre si; **come
~** desfazer-se; **keep ~** manter
separado; **take ~** desmontar

apartment /ə'pɑːtmənt/ n Amer apartamento m; **~s** aposentos mpl

apath|y /'æpəθɪ/ n apatia f

ape /eɪp/ n macaco m ● vt macaquear

aperitif /ə'perətɪf/ n aperitivo m

apex /'eɪpeks/ n ápice m, cume m

apologetic /əpɒlə'dʒetɪk/ a <tone etc> apologético, de desculpas; **be ~** desculpar-se

apologize /ə'pɒlədʒaɪz/ vi desculpar-se (**for** de, por to junto de, perante) pedir desculpa (**for** por)

apology /ə'pɒlədʒɪ/ n desculpa f; (defence of belief) apologia f

apostle /ə'pɒsl/ n apóstolo m

apostrophe /ə'pɒstrəfɪ/ n apóstrofe f

appal /ə'pɔːl/ vt (pt -**led**) estarrecer. **~ling** a estarrecedor

apparatus /æpə'reɪtəs/ n aparelho m

apparent /ə'pærənt/ a aparente. **~ly** adv aparentemente

apparition /æpə'rɪʃn/ n aparição f

appeal /ə'piːl/ vi Jur apelar (**to** para); (attract) atrair (**to** a); (for funds) angariar ● n apelo m; (attractiveness) atrativo m; (for funds) angariação f; **~ to sb for sth** pedir algo a alguém. **~ing** a (attractive) atraente

appear /ə'pɪə(r)/ vi aparecer; (seem) parecer; (in court, theatre) apresentar-se. **~ance** n aparição f; (aspect) aparência f; (in court) comparecimento m, (P) comparência f

appease /ə'piːz/ vt apaziguar

appendicitis /əpendɪ'saɪtɪs/ n apendicite f

appendix /ə'pendɪks/ n (pl -ices /-siːz/) (of book) apêndice m; (pl -ixes /-ksɪz/) Anat apêndice m

appetite /'æpɪtaɪt/ n apetite m

appetizer /'æpɪtaɪzə(r)/ n (snack) tira-gosto m, (P) aperitivo m; (drink) aperitivo m

appetizing /'æpɪtaɪzɪŋ/ a apetitoso

applau|d /ə'plɔːd/ vt/i aplaudir. **~se** n aplauso(s) m(pl)

apple /'æpl/ n maçã f; **~ tree** macieira f

appliance /ə'plaɪəns/ n aparelho m, instrumento m, utensílio m; **household ~s** utensílios mpl domésticos

applicable /'æplɪkəbl/ a aplicável

applicant /'æplɪkənt/ n candidato m (**for** a)

application /æplɪ'keɪʃn/ n aplicação f; (request) pedido m; (form) formulário m; (for job) candidatura f

appl|y /ə'plaɪ/ vt aplicar ● vi **~y to** (refer) aplicar-se a; (ask) dirigir-se a; **~y for** <job, grant> candidatar-se a; **~y o.s. to** aplicar-se a. **~ied** a aplicado

appoint /ə'pɔɪnt/ vt (to post) nomear; <time, date> marcar. **well-~ed** a bem equipado, bem provido. **~ment** n nomeação f; (meeting) entrevista f; (with friends) encontro m; (with doctor etc) consulta f, (P) marcação f; (job) posto m

apprais|e /ə'preɪz/ vt avaliar. **~al** n avaliação f

appreciable /ə'priːʃəbl/ a apreciável

appreciat|e /ə'priːʃɪeɪt/ vt (value) apreciar; (understand) compreender; (be grateful for)

estar/ficar grato por ● vi encarecer.
~ion /-'eɪʃn/ n apreciação f;
(*rise in value*) encarecimento m;
(*gratitude*) reconhecimento m. **~ive**
/ə'priːʃɪətɪv/ a apreciador; (*grateful*)
reconhecido

apprehen|d /æprɪ'hend/ vt (*seize,
understand*) apreender; (*dread*)
recear. **~sion** n apreensão f

apprehensive /æprɪ'hensɪv/ a
apreensivo

apprentice /ə'prentɪs/ n aprendiz,
-a mf ● vt pôr como aprendiz (**to** de).
~ship n aprendizagem f

approach /ə'prəʊtʃ/ vt aproximar;
(*with request or offer*) abordar ● vi
aproximar-se n aproximação
f; **~ to** (*problem*) abordagem f
de; (*place*) acesso m a; (*person*)
diligência junto de. **~able** a
acessível

appropriate[1] /ə'prəʊprɪət/ a
apropriado, próprio

appropriate[2] /ə'prəʊprɪeɪt/ vt
apropriar-se de

approval /ə'pruːvl/ n aprovação
f; **on ~** Comm sob condição, à
aprovação

approv|e /ə'pruːv/ vt/i aprovar; **~e
of** aprovar

approximate[1] /ə'prɒksɪmət/
a aproximado. **~ly** adv
aproximadamente

approximat|e[2] /ə'prɒksɪmeɪt/ vt/i
aproximar(-se) de. **~ion** /-'meɪʃn/ n
aproximação f

apricot /'eɪprɪkɒt/ n damasco m

April /'eɪprəl/ n Abril m; **~ Fool's
Day** o primeiro de Abril, o dia das
mentiras; **make an ~ fool of** pregar
uma mentira em, (P) pregar uma
mentira a

apron /'eɪprən/ n avental m

apt /æpt/ a apto; (*pupil*) dotado; **be
~ to** ser propenso a

aptitude /'æptɪtjuːd/ n aptidão f,
(P) aptidão f

aqualung /'ækwəlʌŋ/ n
escafandro autônomo, (P)
autónomo m

aquarium /ə'kweərɪəm/ n (pl
-ums) aquário m

Aquarius /ə'kweərɪəs/ n Astr
Aquário m

aquatic /ə'kwætɪk/ a aquático;
(*sport*) náutico, aquático

Arab /'ærəb/ a & n árabe mf. **~ic**
a & n Lang árabe m, arábico m; **~ic
numerals** algarismos mpl árabes
or arábicos

Arabian /ə'reɪbɪən/ a árabe

arable /'ærəbl/ a arável

arbitrary /'ɑːbɪtrərɪ/ a arbitrário

arbitrat|e /'ɑːbɪtreɪt/ vi arbitrar.
~ion /-'treɪʃn/ n arbitragem f

arc /ɑːk/ n arco m; **~ lamp** lâmpada
f de arco; **~ welding** soldadura
f a arco

arcade /ɑː'keɪd/ n (*shop*) arcada f;
amusement ~ fliperama m

arch /ɑːtʃ/ n arco m; (*vault*) abóbada
f ● vt/i arquear(-se)

arch- /ɑːtʃ/ pref arqui-

archaeolog|y /ɑːkɪ'ɒlədʒɪ/ n
arqueologia f. **~ical** /-'lɒdʒɪkl/ a
arqueológico. **~ist** n arqueólogo m

archaic /ɑː'keɪɪk/ a arcaico

archbishop /ɑːtʃ'bɪʃəp/ n
arcebispo m

archer /'ɑːtʃə(r)/ n arqueiro m. **~y** n
tiro m ao arco

archetype /'ɑːkɪtaɪp/ n
arquétipo m

architect /'ɑːkɪtekt/ n arquiteto m

architectur|e /'ɑːkɪtektʃə(r)/ n arquitetura f. **~al** /-'tektʃərəl/ a arquitetônico, (P) arquitetónico

archiv|es /'ɑːkaɪvz/ npl arquivo m

archway /'ɑːtʃweɪ/ n arcada f

Arctic /'ɑːktɪk/ n ártico ● a ártico; **~ weather** tempo m glacial

ardent /'ɑːdnt/ a ardente

ardour /'ɑːdə(r)/ n ardor m

arduous /'ɑːdjʊəs/ a árduo

are /ə(r)/ emphatic ɑː(r)/ ▶ BE

area /'eərɪə/ n área f

arena /ə'riːnə/ n arena f

Argentin|a /ɑːdʒən'tiːnə/ n Argentina f. **~ian** /-'tɪnɪən/ a & n argentino m

argu|e /'ɑːgjuː/ vi discutir; (reason) argumentar, arguir ● vt (debate) discutir; **~e that** alegar que

argument /'ɑːgjʊmənt/ n (dispute) disputa f; (reasoning) argumento m. **~ative** /-'mentətɪv/ a que gosta de discutir, argumentativo

arid /'ærɪd/ a árido

Aries /'eəriːz/ n Astr áries m, Carneiro m

arise /ə'raɪz/ vi (pt arose, pp arisen) surgir; **~ from** resultar de

aristocracy /ærɪ'stɒkrəsɪ/ n aristocracia f

aristocrat /'ærɪstəkræt/ n aristocrata mf. **~ic** /-'krætɪk/ a aristocrático

arithmetic /ə'rɪθmətɪk/ n aritmética f

arm[1] /ɑːm/ n braço m; **~ in ~** de braço dado

arm[2] /ɑːm/ vt armar; **~ed robbery** assalto à mão armada m ● n Mil arma f

armament /'ɑːməmənt/ n armamento m

armchair /'ɑːmtʃeə(r)/ n cadeira f de braços, poltrona f

armour /'ɑːmə(r)/ n armadura f; (on tanks etc) blindagem f. **~ed** a blindado

armpit /'ɑːmpɪt/ n axila f, sovaco m

arms /ɑːmz/ npl armas fpl; **coat of ~** brasão m

army /'ɑːmɪ/ n exército m

aroma /ə'rəʊmə/ n aroma m. **~tic** /ærə'mætɪk/ a aromático

arose /ə'rəʊz/ ▶ ARISE

around /ə'raʊnd/ adv em redor, em volta; (here and there) por aí ● prep em redor de, em torno de, em volta de; (approximately) aproximadamente; **~ here** por aqui

arouse /ə'raʊz/ vt despertar; (excite) excitar

arrange /ə'reɪndʒ/ vt arranjar; ‹time, date› combinar; **~ to do sth** combinar fazer algo. **~ment** n arranjo m; (agreement) acordo m; **make ~ments (for)** ‹plans› tomar disposições (para); ‹preparations› fazer preparativos (para)

arrears /ə'rɪəz/ npl dívidas fpl em atraso, atrasos mpl; **in ~** em atraso

arrest /ə'rest/ vt (by law) deter, prender; ‹process, movement› deter ● n captura f; **under ~** sob prisão

arrival /ə'raɪvl/ n chegada f; **new ~** recém-chegado m

arrive /ə'raɪv/ vi chegar

arrogan|t /'ærəgənt/ a arrogante. **~ce** n arrogância f

arrow /'ærəʊ/ n flecha f, seta f

arson /'ɑːsn/ n fogo m posto. **~ist** n incendiário m

art¹ /ɑːt/ n arte f; **the ~s** Univ letras fpl; **fine ~s** belas-artes fpl; **~ gallery** museu m (de arte); (private) galeria f de arte

artery /'ɑːtərɪ/ n artéria f

arthritis /ɑː'θraɪtɪs/ n artrite f

artichoke /'ɑːtɪtʃəʊk/ n alcachofra f; **Jerusalem ~** topinambo m

article /'ɑːtɪkl/ n artigo m

articulate¹ /ɑː'tɪkjʊlət/ a que se exprime com clareza; <speech> bem articulado

articulat|e² /ɑː'tɪkjʊleɪt/ vt/i articular; **~ed lorry** camião m articulado

artificial /ɑːtɪ'fɪʃl/ a artificial

artillery /ɑː'tɪlərɪ/ n artilharia f

artisan /ɑːtɪ'zæn/ n artífice mf, artesão m, artesã f

artist /'ɑːtɪst/ n artista mf. **~ic** /-'tɪstɪk/ a artístico

artiste /ɑː'tiːst/ n artista mf

as /əz emphatic æz/ adv & conj como; (while) enquanto; (when) quando; **~ a gift** de presente; (P) **~ tall ~** tão alto quanto, (P) tão alto como; **~ if** como se; **~ much** tanto, tantos; **~ many** quanto, quantos; **~ soon ~** logo que; **~ well** (also) também; **~ well ~** (in addition to) assim como; **~ for, ~** to quanto a; **~ from** a partir de ● pron que; **I ate the same ~ him** comi o mesmo que ele

asbestos /æz'bestəs/ n asbesto m, amianto m

ASBO, Asbo /'æzbəʊ/ abbr (pl ASBOs, Asbos) Ordem f de Comportamento Antissocial

ascend /ə'send/ vt/i subir; **~ the throne** ascender or subir ao trono

ascent /ə'sent/ n ascensão f; (slope) subida f, rampa f

ascertain /æsə'teɪn/ vt certificar-se de; **~ that** certificar-se de que

ash¹ /æʃ/ n **~(-tree)** freixo m

ash² /æʃ/ n cinza f. **A~ Wednesday** Quarta-feira f de Cinzas

ashamed /ə'ʃeɪmd/ a **be ~** ter vergonha, ficar envergonhado (**of** de, por)

ashore /ə'ʃɔː(r)/ adv em terra; **go ~** desembarcar

ashtray /'æʃtreɪ/ n cinzeiro m

Asia /'eɪʃə/ n Ásia f. **~n** a & n asiático m

aside /ə'saɪd/ adv de lado, de parte ● n Theat aparte m; **~ from** Amer à parte

ask /ɑːsk/ vt/i pedir; <a question> perguntar; (invite) convidar; **~ sb sth** pedir algo a alguém; **~ about** informar-se de; **~ after sb** pedir notícias de alguém, perguntar por alguém; **~ for** pedir; **~ sb in** mandar entrar alguém; **~ sb to do sth** pedir a alguém para fazer algo

askew /ə'skjuː/ adv & a de través, de esguelha

asleep /ə'sliːp/ adv & a adormecido; (numb) dormente; **fall ~** adormecer

asparagus /ə'spærəgəs/ n (plant) espargo m, (P) espargo m; Culin aspargos mpl, (P) espargo m

aspect /'æspekt/ n aspecto m; (direction) exposição f

asphalt /'æsfælt/ n asfalto m ● vt asfaltar

asphyxiat|e /əs'fɪksɪeɪt/ vt/i asfixiar. **~ion** /-'ion/ n asfixia f

aspir|e /ə'spaɪə(r)/ vi **~e to** aspirar a. **~ation** /æspə'reɪʃn/ n aspiração f

aspirin /'æsprɪn/ n aspirina f

ass /æs/ n burro m; **make an ~ of o.s.** fazer papel de palhaço, (P) fazer figura de parvo

assail /əˈseɪl/ vt assaltar, agredir. **~ant** n assaltante mf, agressor m

assassin /əˈsæsɪn/ n assassino m

assassinat|e /əˈsæsɪneɪt/ vt assassinar. **~ion** /-ˈeɪʃn/ n assassinato m

assault /əˈsɔːlt/ n assalto m ● vt assaltar, atacar

assemble /əˈsembl/ vt ‹people› reunir; ‹fit together› montar ● vi reunir-se

assembly /əˈsemblɪ/ n assembleia f; **~ line** linha f de montagem

assent /əˈsent/ n assentimento m ● vi **~ to** consentir em

assert /əˈsɜːt/ vt afirmar; ‹one's rights› reivindicar; **~ o.s.** impor-se. **~ion** /-ʃn/ n asserção f. **~ive** a dogmático, peremptório

assess /əˈses/ vt avaliar; ‹payment› estabelecer o montante de. **~ment** n avaliação f

asset /ˈæset/ n ‹advantage› vantagem f; **~s** Comm ativo m; ‹possessions› bens mpl

assign /əˈsaɪn/ vt atribuir, destinar; Jur transmitir; **~ sb to** designar alguém para

assignment /əˈsaɪnmənt/ n tarefa f, missão f; Jur transmissão f

assimilat|e /əˈsɪmɪleɪt/ vt/i assimilar(-se)

assist /əˈsɪst/ vt/i ajudar. **~ance** n ajuda f, assistência f

assistant /əˈsɪstənt/ n ‹helper› assistente mf, auxiliar mf; ‹in shop› ajudante mf, empregado m ● a adjunto

associat|e¹ /əˈsəʊʃɪeɪt/ vt associar ● vi **~ with** conviver com. **~ion** /-ˈeɪʃn/ n associação f

associate² /əˈsəʊʃɪət/ a & n associado m

assort|ed /əˈsɔːtɪd/ a variados; ‹foods› sortidos. **~ment** n sortimento m, (P) sortido m

assume /əˈsjuːm/ vt assumir; (presume) supor, presumir

assumption /əˈsʌmpʃn/ n suposição f

assurance /əˈʃʊərəns/ n certeza f, garantia f; (insurance) seguro m; (self-confidence) segurança f, confiança f

assure /əˈʃʊə(r)/ vt assegurar. **~d** a certo, garantido; **rest ~d that** ficar certo que

asterisk /ˈæstərɪsk/ n asterisco m

asthma /ˈæsmə/ n asma f

astonish /əˈstɒnɪʃ/ vt espantar. **~ment** n espanto m

astound /əˈstaʊnd/ vt assombrar

astray /əˈstreɪ/ adv & a **go ~** perder-se, extraviar-se; **lead ~** desencaminhar

astride /əˈstraɪd/ adv & prep escarranchado (em)

astrolog|y /əˈstrɒlədʒɪ/ n astrologia f. **~er** n astrólogo m

astronaut /ˈæstrənɔːt/ n astronauta mf

astronom|y /əˈstrɒnəmɪ/ n astronomia f. **~er** n astrônomo m, (P) astrónomo m. **~ical** /æstrəˈnɒmɪkl/ a astronômico, (P) astronómico

astute /əˈstjuːt/ a astuto, astucioso

asylum /əˈsaɪləm/ n asilo m

---

at /ət emphatic æt/ ● prep

┅┅➤ (position) em; (at home) em casa; (at school) na escola; (at sea) no mar; (at the door) à porta

! The preposition em often contracts with definite and indefinite articles o, a and um,

uma to form *no*, *na* and *num*,
numa

····▶ (*at someone's house*) na
casa de; ~ Peter's na casa do
Pedro; (*at someone's business*)
em; ~ **the doctor's** no médico

····▶ (*time*) ~ **two o'clock** às
duas horas; ~ **three years of age**
aos três anos ; ~ **night** à noite;
~ **Christmas/Easter** no Natal/
na Páscoa

····▶ (*price*) a; ~ **£2.20 each** a
duas libras e vinte cada

····▶ (*speed*) ~ **50 mph** a
cinquenta milhas por hora

····▶ (*in email addresses*=@)
arroba

····▶ (*in phrases*) ~ **once**
imediatamente; ~ **the same
time** ao mesmo tempo; ~ **times**
às vezes; **be good/bad** ~ **sth**
ser bom/ruim em aco; **two** ~ **a
time** dois de cada vez; **be angry/
surprised** ~ **sb** estar brabo/
surpreendido com alguém

ate /et/ ▶ EAT

atheis|t /'eɪθɪɪst/ *n* ateu *m*. ~**m**
/-zəm/ *n* ateísmo *m*

athlet|e /'æθliːt/ *n* atleta *mf*. ~**ic**
/-'letɪk/ *a* atlético. ~**ics** /-'letɪks/ *n*(*pl*)
atletismo *m*

Atlantic /ət'læntɪk/ *a* atlântico ● *n*
~ (**Ocean**) Atlântico *m*

atlas /'ætləs/ *n* atlas *m*

atmospher|e /'ætməsfɪə(r)/ *n*
atmosfera *f*

atom /'ætəm/ *n* átomo *m*. ~**ic**
/ə'tɒmɪk/ *a*, (P) atómico;
~(**ic**) **bomb** bomba *f* atômica, (P)
atómica

atone /ə'təʊn/ *vi* ~ **for** expiar

atrocious /ə'trəʊʃəs/ *a* atroz

atrocity /ə'trɒsətɪ/ *n* atrocidade *f*

attach /ə'tætʃ/ *vt/i* (*affix*) ligar(-se),
prender(-se); (*join*) juntar(-se). ~**ed**
a <*document*> junto, anexo; **be** ~**ed
to** (*like*) estar apegado a. ~**ment**
n ligação *f*; (*affection*) apego *m*;
(*accessory*) acessório *m*; (*in email*)
anexo *m*

attack /ə'tæk/ *n* ataque *m* ● *vt/i*
atacar. ~**er** *n* atacante *mf*

attain /ə'teɪn/ *vt* atingir. ~**able** *a*
atingível

attempt /ə'tempt/ *vt* tentar ● *n*
tentativa *f*

attend /ə'tend/ *vt/i* atender (**to** a);
(*escort*) acompanhar; (*look after*)
tratar; <*meeting*> comparecer
a; <*school*> frequentar. ~**ance**
n comparecimento *m*; (*times present*)
frequência *f*; (*people*) assistência *f*

attendant /ə'tendənt/ *a*
concomitante, que acompanha ● *n*
empregado *m*; (*servant*) servidor *m*

attention /ə'tenʃn/ *n* atenção *f*; ~**!**
Mil sentido! **pay** ~ prestar atenção
(**to** a)

attentive /ə'tentɪv/ *a* atento;
(*considerate*) atencioso

attic /'ætɪk/ *n* sótão *m*, água-
furtada *f*

attitude /'ætɪtjuːd/ *n* atitude *f*

attorney /ə'tɜːnɪ/ *n* (*pl* -**eys**)
procurador *m*; *Amer* advogado *m*

attract /ə'trækt/ *vt* atrair. ~**ion**
/-ʃn/ *n* atração *f*; (*charm*) atrativo *m*

attractive /ə'træktɪv/ *a* atraente

attribute[1] /ə'trɪbjuːt/ *vt* ~ **to**
atribuir a

attribute[2] /'ætrɪbjuːt/ *n* atributo *m*

aubergine /'əʊbəʒiːn/ *n* berinjela *f*

auburn /'ɔːbən/ *a* cor de acaju,
castanho-avermelhado

auction /'ɔːkʃn/ n leilão m ● vt leiloar. **~eer** /-ə'nɪə(r)/ n leiloeiro m, (P) pregoeiro m

audaci|ous /ɔː'deɪʃəs/ a audacioso, audaz. **~ty** /-æsətɪ/ n audácia f

audible /'ɔːdəbl/ a audível

audience /'ɔːdɪəns/ n auditório m; Theat, Radio (interview) audiência f

audiovisual /ɔːdɪəʊ'vɪʒʊəl/ a audiovisual

audit /'ɔːdɪt/ n auditoria f ● vt fazer uma auditoria

audition /ɔː'dɪʃn/ n audição f ● vt dar/fazer uma audição

auditor /'ɔːdɪtə(r)/ n perito-contador m, (P) perito-contabilista m

auditorium /ɔːdɪ'tɔːrɪəm/ n auditório m

augment /ɔːg'ment/ vt/i aumentar(-se)

August /'ɔːgəst/ n agosto m

aunt /ɑːnt/ n tia f

au pair /əʊ'peə(r)/ n au pair f

aura /'ɔːrə/ n aura f, emanação f

auspicious /ɔː'spɪʃəs/ a auspicioso

auster|e /ɔː'stɪə(r)/ a austero. **~ity** /-erətɪ/ n austeridade f

Australia /ɒ'streɪlɪə/ n Austrália f. **~n** a & n australiano m

Austria /'ɒstrɪə/ n Áustria f. **~n** a & n austríaco m

authentic /ɔː'θentɪk/ a autêntico. **~ity** /-ən'tɪsətɪ/ n autenticidade f

authenticate /ɔː'θentɪkeɪt/ vt autenticar

author /'ɔːθə(r)/ n autor m, autora f

authoritarian /ɔːθɒrɪ'teərɪən/ a autoritário

authorit|y /ɔː'θɒrətɪ/ n autoridade f, (permission) autorização f. **~ative** /-ɪtətɪv/ a (trusted) autorizado;

(manner) autoritário

authoriz|e /'ɔːθəraɪz/ vt autorizar. **~ation** /-'zeɪʃn/ n autorização f

autistic /ɔː'tɪstɪk/ a autista, autístico

autobiography /ɔːtə'baɪəgrəfɪ/ n autobiografia f

autograph /'ɔːtəgrɑːf/ n autógrafo m ● vt autografar

automat|e /'ɔːtəment/ vt automatizar. **~ion** /-tə'meɪʃn/ n automação f

automatic /ɔːtə'mætɪk/ a automático ● n (car) automático m. **~ally** /-klɪ/ adv automaticamente

automobile /'ɔːtəməbiːl/ n Amer automóvel m

autonom|y /ɔː'tɒnəmɪ/ n autonomia f. **~ous** a autônomo, (P) autónomo

autopsy /'ɔːtɒpsɪ/ n autópsia f

autumn /'ɔːtəm/ n outono m. **~al** /-'tʌmnəl/ a outonal

auxiliary /ɔːg'zɪlɪərɪ/ a & n auxiliar mf; **~ verb** verbo m auxiliar

avail /ə'veɪl/ vt **~ o.s. of** servir-se de ● vi (be of use) valer ● n of no **~** inútil; **to no ~** sem resultado, em vão

availab|le /ə'veɪləbl/ a disponível. **~ility** /-'bɪlətɪ/ n disponibilidade f

avalanche /'ævəlɑːnʃ/ n avalanche f

avarice /'ævərɪs/ n avareza f

avatar /'ævətɑː(r)/ n avatar m

avenge /ə'vendʒ/ vt vingar

avenue /'ævənjuː/ n avenida f; fig (line of approach) via f

average /'ævərɪdʒ/ n média f; ● a médio ● vt tirar a média de; (produce, do) fazer em média ● vi **~ out at** dar de média, dar uma média de; **on** ~ em média

avers|e /əˈvɜːs/ a **be** ~**e to** ser avesso a. ~**ion** /-ʃn/ n aversão f, repugnância f

avert /əˈvɜːt/ vt (turn away) desviar; (ward off) evitar

aviary /ˈeɪvɪərɪ/ n aviário m

aviation /eɪvɪˈeɪʃn/ n aviação f

avid /ˈævɪd/ a ávido

avocado /ævəˈkɑːdəʊ/ n (pl -s) abacate m

avoid /əˈvɔɪd/ vt evitar. ~**able** a que se pode evitar, evitável. ~**ance** n evitação f

await /əˈweɪt/ vt aguardar

awake /əˈweɪk/ vt/i (pt awoke, pp awoken) acordar ● a **be** ~ estar acordado

awaken /əˈweɪkən/ vt/i despertar. ~**ing** n despertar m

award /əˈwɔːd/ vt atribuir, conferir; Jur adjudicar ● n recompensa f, prêmio m, (P) prémio m; ‹scholarship› bolsa f

aware /əˈweə(r)/ a ciente, cônscio; **be** ~ **of** estar consciente de or ter consciência de; **become** ~ **of** tomar consciência de; **make sb** ~ **of** sensibilizar alguém para. ~**ness** n consciência f

away /əˈweɪ/ adv (at a distance) longe; (to a distance) para longe; (absent) fora; (persistently) sem parar; (entirely) completamente; **eight miles** ~ a oito milhas (de distância); **four days** ~ daí a quatro dias ● a & n ~ (**match**) jogo m fora de casa

awe /ɔː/ n assombro m, admiração f reverente, terror m respeitoso. ~**some** a assombroso

awful /ˈɔːfl/ a terrível. ~**ly** adv muito, terrivelmente

awkward /ˈɔːkwəd/ a difícil; (clumsy, difficult to use) desajeitado, maljeitoso; (inconvenient) inconveniente; (embarrassing) embaraçoso; (embarrassed) embaraçado; **an** ~ **customer** ⟦I⟧ um freguês perigoso or intratável

awning /ˈɔːnɪŋ/ n toldo m

awoke, **awoken** /əˈwəʊk, əˈwəʊkən/ ▶ AWAKE

awry /əˈraɪ/ adv torto; **go** ~ dar errado; **be** ~ estar torto

axe /æks/ n machado m ● vt (pres p axing) (reduce) cortar; (dismiss) despedir

axis /ˈæksɪs/ n (pl axes /-iːz/) eixo m

axle /ˈæksl/ n eixo (de roda) m

Azores /əˈzɔːz/ n Açores mpl

Bb

BA abbr (= Bachelor of Arts)
▶ BACHELOR

baboon /bəˈbuːn/ n babuíno m

baby /ˈbeɪbɪ/ n bebê m, (P) bebé m; ~ **carriage** Amer carrinho m de bebê, (P) bebé. ~**sit** vi tomar conta de crianças; ~**sitter** n baby-sitter mf, babá f

babyish /ˈbeɪbɪʃ/ a infantil

bachelor /ˈbætʃələ(r)/ n solteiro m; B~ **of Arts/Science** Bacharel m em Letras/Ciências

back /bæk/ n (of person, hand, chair) costas fpl; (of animal) dorso m; (of car, train) parte f traseira; (of house, room) fundo m; (of coin) reverso m; (of page) verso m; Football beque m;

backache | baffle

zagueiro *m*, (*P*) defesa *m*; **at the ~ of beyond** em casa do diabo, no fim do mundo ● *a* traseiro, posterior; ‹*taxes*› em atraso; **~ number** número *m* atrasado ● *adv* atrás, para trás; (*returned*) de volta ● *vt* (*support*) apoiar; ‹*horse*› apostar em; ‹*car*› (fazer) recuar ● *vi* recuar; **~ down** desistir (**from** de); **~ out** (*of an undertaking etc*) fugir (ao combinado *etc*); **~ up** *Auto* fazer marcha à ré, (*P*) dar marcha atrás; *Comput* tirar um back-up de. **~up** *n* apoio *m*; *Comput* back-up *m*; *Amer* (*traffic jam*) engarrafamento *m* ● *a* de reserva; *Comput* backup

backache /ˈbækeɪk/ *n* dor *f* nas costas

backbiting /ˈbækbaɪtɪŋ/ *n* maledicência *f*

backbone /ˈbækbəʊn/ *n* espinha *f* dorsal

backdate /bækˈdeɪt/ *vt* antedatar

backer /ˈbækə(r)/ *n* (*of horse*) apostador *m*; (*of cause*) partidário *m*, apoiante *mf*; *Comm* patrocinador *m*, financiador *m*

backfire /bækˈfaɪə(r)/ *vi Auto* dar explosões no tubo de escape; *fig* sair o tiro pela culatra

background /ˈbækɡraʊnd/ *n* (*of picture*) fundo *m*, segundo-plano *m*; (*context*) contexto *m*; (*environment*) meio *m*; (*experience*) formação *f*

backhand /ˈbækhænd/ *n Tennis* esquerda *f*. **~ed** *a* com as costas da mão; **~ed compliment** cumprimento *m* ambíguo

backing /ˈbækɪŋ/ *n* apoio *m*; *Comm* patrocínio *m*

backlash /ˈbæklæʃ/ *n fig* reação *f* violenta; repercussões *fpl*

backlog /ˈbæklɒɡ/ *n* acumulação *m* (de trabalho *etc*)

backside /ˈbæksaɪd/ *n* ① (*buttocks*) traseiro *m*

backstage /bækˈsteɪdʒ/ *a & adv* por detrás dos bastidores

backstroke /ˈbækstrəʊk/ *n* nado *m* de costas

backtrack /ˈbæktræk/ *vi fig* voltar atrás

backward /ˈbækwəd/ *a* retrógrado; (*retarded*) atrasado; ‹*step, look, etc*› para trás

backwards /ˈbækwədz/ *adv* para trás; (*walk*) para trás; (*fall*) de costas, para trás; (*in reverse order*) de trás para diante, às avessas; **go ~ and forwards** ir e vir, andar para trás e para a frente; **know sth ~** saber algo de trás para a frente

backwater /ˈbækwɔːtə(r)/ *n pej* (*place*) lugar *m* atrasado

bacon /ˈbeɪkən/ *n* toucinho *m* defumado; (*in rashers*) bacon *m*

bacteria /bækˈtɪərɪə/ *npl* bactérias *fpl*

bad /bæd/ *a* (**worse, worst**) mau; ‹*accident*› grave; ‹*food*› estragado; (*ill*) doente; **feel ~** sentir-se mal; **~ language** palavrões *mpl*. **~-mannered** *a* mal-educado; **~-tempered** *a* mal-humorado. **~ly** *adv* mal; (*seriously*) gravemente; **want ~ly** (*desire*) desejar imensamente, ter muita vontade de; (*need*) precisar muito de

badge /bædʒ/ *n* emblema *m*; (*policeman's*) crachá *m*, (*P*) distintivo *m*

badger /ˈbædʒə(r)/ *n* texugo *m* ● *vt* atormentar; (*pester*) importunar

badminton /ˈbædmɪntən/ *n* badminton *m*

baffle /ˈbæfl/ *vt* atrapalhar, desconcertar

bag /bæg/ n saco m; (handbag) bolsa f, carteira f. **~s** (luggage) malas fpl ● vt (pt bagged) ensacar; 🄸 (take) embolsar

baggage /'bægɪdʒ/ n bagagem f

baggy /'bægɪ/ a <clothes> muito largo, bufante

bagpipes /'bægpaɪps/ npl gaita f de foles

Bahamas /bə'hɑːməz/ npl the ~ as Bahamas fpl

bail¹ /beɪl/ n fiança f ● vt pôr em liberdade sob fiança; **be out on ~** estar solto sob fiança

bail² /beɪl/ vt **~ (out)** Naut esgotar, tirar água de

bailiff /'beɪlɪf/ n (officer) oficial m de diligências; (of estate) feitor m

bait /beɪt/ n isca f ● vt pôr isca; fig atormentar (com insultos); atazanar

bak|e /beɪk/ vt/i cozer (no forno); <bread, cakes, etc> assar; (in the sun) torrar. **~er** n padeiro m; (of cakes) doceiro m. **~ing** n cozedura f; (batch) fornada f; **~ing tin** forma f. **~ing powder** n fermento m em pó

bakery /'beɪkərɪ/ n padaria f; (cakes) confeitaria f

balance /'bæləns/ n equilíbrio m; (scales) balança f; (sum) saldo m; Comm balanço m; **~ of power** equilíbrio m político; **~ of trade** balança f comercial ● vt equilibrar; (weigh up) pesar; <budget> equilibrar ● vi equilibrar-se. **~ sheet** n balanço m. **~d** a equilibrado

balcony /'bælkənɪ/ n balcão m; (in a house) varanda f

bald /bɔːld/ a (-er, -est) calvo, careca; <tyre> careca. **~ing** a be **~ing** ficar calvo. **~ly** adv a nu e cru, (P) secamente. **~ness** n calvície f

bale¹ /beɪl/ n (of straw) fardo m; (of cotton) balote m ● vt enfardar

bale² /beɪl/ vi **~ out** saltar de paraquedas

balk /bɔːk/ vt frustrar, contrariar ● vi **~ at** assustar-se com, recuar perante

ball¹ /bɔːl/ n bola f

ball² /bɔːl/ n (dance) baile m

ballad /'bæləd/ n balada f

ballerina /bælə'riːnə/ n bailarina f

ballet /'bæleɪ/ n balé m, (P) ballet m, bailado m

balloon /bə'luːn/ n balão m

ballot /'bælət/ n escrutínio m ● vt (members) consultar por voto secreto ● vi Pol votar. **~ (paper)** n cédula f eleitoral, (P) boletim m de voto; **~ box** n urna f

ballroom /'bɔːlruːm/ n salão m de baile

balm /bɑːm/ n bálsamo m. **~y** a balsâmico; (mild) suave

bamboo /bæm'buː/ n bambu m

ban /bæn/ vt (pt banned) banir; **~ from** proibir de ● n proibição f

banal /bə'nɑːl/ a banal. **~ity** /-ælətɪ/ n banalidade f

banana /bə'nɑːnə/ n banana f

band /bænd/ n (for fastening) cinta f, faixa f; (strip) tira f, banda f; Mus, Mil banda f; Mus (dance, jazz) conjunto m; (group) bando m ● vi **~ together** juntar-se

bandage /'bændɪdʒ/ n atadura f, (P) ligadura f ● vt ligar

bandit /'bændɪt/ n bandido m

bandstand /'bændstænd/ n coreto m

bandwagon /'bændwægən/ n **climb on the ~** fig apanhar o trem, (P) o comboio

bang /bæŋ/ n (blow) pancada f; (loud noise) estouro m, estrondo m; (of gun) detonação f ● vt/i (hit, shut) bater ● vi explodir ● int pum; ~ **in the middle** jogar no meio; **shut the door with a** ~ bater (com) a porta

banger /'bæŋə(r)/ n (firework) bomba f; ⊠ (sausage) salsicha f; (old) ~ ⊠ (car) calhambeque m ⊡

bangle /'bæŋgl/ n pulseira f, bracelete m

banish /'bænɪʃ/ vt banir, desterrar

banisters /'bænɪstəz/ npl corrimão m

banjo /'bændʒəʊ/ n (pl -os) banjo m

bank¹ /bæŋk/ n (of river) margem f; (of earth) talude m; (of sand) banco m ● vt amontoar ● vi Aviat inclinar-se numa curva

bank² /bæŋk/ n Comm banco m; ~ **account** conta f bancária; ~ **holiday** feriado m nacional; ~ **rate** taxa f bancária ● vt depositar no banco; ~ **on** contar com; ~ **with** ter conta em

bank|er /'bæŋkə(r)/ n banqueiro m. ~**ing** /-ɪŋ/ n operações fpl bancárias; (career) carreira f bancária, banca f

banknote /'bæŋknəʊt/ n nota f de banco

bankrupt /'bæŋkrʌpt/ a & n falido m; **go** ~ falir ● vt levar à falência. ~**cy** n falência f, bancarrota f

banner /'bænə(r)/ n bandeira f, estandarte m

banquet /'bæŋkwɪt/ n banquete m

banter /'bæntə(r)/ n gracejo m, brincadeira f ● vi gracejar, brincar

baptism /'bæptɪzəm/ n batismo m

Baptist /'bæptɪst/ n batista mf

baptize /bæp'taɪz/ vt batizar

bar /ba:(r)/ n (of chocolate) tablette f, barra f; (of metal, soap, sand etc) barra f; (of door, window) tranca f;

(in pub) bar m; (counter) balcão m, bar m; Mus barra f de compasso; fig (obstacle) barreira f; (in law court) teia f; **the B~** a advocacia f; ~ **code** código m de barra; **behind** ~s na cadeia ● vt (pt barred) (obstruct) barrar; (prohibit) proibir (from de); (exclude) excluir; ‹door, window› trancar ● prep salvo, exceto; ~ **none** sem exceção

Barbados /ba:'beɪdɒs/ n Barbados mpl

barbarian /ba:'beərɪən/ n bárbaro m

barbari|c /ba:'bærɪk/ a bárbaro. ~**ty** /-ətɪ/ n barbaridade f

barbarous /'ba:bərəs/ a bárbaro

barbecue /'ba:bɪkju:/ n (grill) churrasqueira f; (occasion, food) churrasco m ● vt assar

barbed /ba:bd/ a ~ **wire** arame m farpado

barber /'ba:bə(r)/ n barbeiro m

bare /beə(r)/ a (-er, -est) nu; ‹room› vazio; (mere) mero ● vt pôr à mostra, pôr a nu, descobrir

bareback /'beəbæk/ adv em pelo

barefaced /'beəfeɪst/ a descarado

barefoot /'beəfʊt/ adv descalço

barely /'beəlɪ/ adv apenas, mal

bargain /'ba:gɪn/ n (deal) negócio m; (good buy) pechincha f ● vi negociar; (haggle) regatear; ~ **for** esperar

barge /ba:dʒ/ n barcaça f ● vi ~ **in** interromper (despropositadamente); (into room) irromper

bark¹ /ba:k/ n (of tree) casca f

bark² /ba:k/ n (of dog) latido m ● vi latir; **his** ~ **is worse than his bite** cão que ladra não morde

barley /'ba:lɪ/ n cevada f

barmaid /'bɑːmeɪd/ n empregada f de bar

barman /'bɑːmən/ n (pl **-men**) barman m, empregado m de bar

barmy /'bɑːmɪ/ a ⊠ maluco ⚡

barn /bɑːn/ n celeiro m

barometer /bə'rɒmɪtə(r)/ n barômetro m, (P) barómetro m

baron /'bærən/ n barão m. **~ess** n baronesa f

barracks /'bærəks/ n quartel m, caserna f

barrage /'bærɑːʒ/ n barragem f; fig enxurrada f; Mil fogo m de barragem

barrel /'bærəl/ n (of oil, wine) barril m; (of gun) cano m

barren /'bærən/ a estéril; ‹soil› árido, estéril

barricade /bærɪ'keɪd/ n barricada f ● vt barricar

barrier /'bærɪə(r)/ n barreira f; (hindrance) entrave m, barreira f

barrister /'bærɪstə(r)/ n advogado m

barrow /'bærəʊ/ n carrinho m de mão

barter /'bɑːtə(r)/ n troca f ● vt trocar

base /beɪs/ n base f ● vt basear (on em) ● a baixo, ignóbil. **~less** a infundado

baseball /'beɪsbɔːl/ n beisebol m

basement /'beɪsmənt/ n porão m, (P) cave f

bash /bæʃ/ vt bater com violência ● n pancada f forte; **have a ~ at** experimentar

bashful /'bæʃfl/ a tímido

basic /'beɪsɪk/ a básico, elementar, fundamental. **~ally** adv basicamente, no fundo

basin /'beɪsn/ n bacia f; (for food) tigela f; Naut ante-doca f; (for washing) pia f

basis /'beɪsɪs/ n (pl **bases** /-siːz/) base f

bask /bɑːsk/ vi **~ in the sun** apanhar sol

basket /'bɑːskɪt/ n cesto m

basketball /'bɑːskɪtbɔːl/ n basquete(bol) m

Basque /bɑːsk/ a & n basco m

bass[1] /bæs/ n (pl **bass**) (fish) perca f

bass[2] /beɪs/ a Mus grave ● n (pl **basses**) Mus baixo m

bassoon /bə'suːn/ n fagote m

bastard /'bɑːstəd/ n (illegitimate child) bastardo m; ⊠ pej safado m ⊠; ⊠ not pej cara m ⚡

bat[1] /bæt/ n Cricket pá f; Baseball bastão m; Table Tennis rafuete f ● vt/i (pt **batted**) bater (em); **without ~ting an eyelid** sem pestanejar

bat[2] /bæt/ n Zool morcego m

batch /bætʃ/ n (loaves) fornada f; (people) monte m; (goods) remessa f; (papers, letters etc) batelada f, monte m

bath /bɑːθ/ n (pl **-s** /bɑːðz/) banho m; (tub) banheira f. **~s** (washing) banho m público; (swimming) piscina f ● vt dar banho a ● vi tomar banho

bathe /beɪð/ vt dar banho em; ‹wound› limpar ● vi tomar banho (de mar) ● n banho m (de mar). **~r** /-ə(r)/ n banhista mf

bathing /'beɪðɪŋ/ n banho m de mar. **~ costume/suit** n traje m de banho, (P) fato m de banho

bathrobe /'bɑːθrəʊb/ n Amer roupão m

bathroom /'bɑːθruːm/ n banheiro m, (P) casa f de banho

battalion /bə'tælɪən/ n batalhão m

batter /'bætə(r)/ vt bater, espancar, maltratar ● n Culin (for cakes) massa f de bolos; Culin (for frying) massa f de empanar. **~ed** a ‹car, pan› amassado; ‹child, wife› maltratado, espancado

battery /'bætərɪ/ n Mil, Auto bateria f; Electr pilha f

battle /'bætl/ n batalha f; fig luta f ● vi combater, batalhar, lutar

battlefield /'bætlfiːld/ n campo m de batalha

battleship /'bætlʃɪp/ n couraçado m

baulk /bɔːlk/ vt/i = BALK

bawl /bɔːl/ vt/i berrar

bay¹ /beɪ/ n Bot loureiro m

bay² /beɪ/ n Geog baía f; **~ window** janela f saliente

bay³ /beɪ/ n (bark) latido m ● vi latir; **at ~** (animal; also fig) cercado, (P) em apuros; **keep at ~** manter à distância

bayonet /'beɪənɪt/ n baioneta f

bazaar /bə'zɑː(r)/ n bazar m

BC abbr (= before Christ) a C

bcc abbr (= blind carbon copy) Cco Com cópia oculta

be /biː/ ● vi (pres am, are, is, pt was, were, pp been);

❗ Portuguese has two verbs meaning be: ser and estar. As a general rule, ser is used to describe a permanent state or inherent characteristic, e.g. **I'm Brazilian** sou brasileiro, whereas estar is used to describe temporary states, e.g. **I'm tired** estou cansado.

····➤ (identity or characteristic) ser; **I'm Portuguese** sou português; **it's yellow** é amarelo

····➤ (temporary state) estar; **I'm angry/bored** estou brabo/entediado

····➤ (situation) ficar; **where's the town centre?** onde é que fica o centro?; **it's 10 minutes away** fica a 10 minutos

····➤ (cost) ser; **how much is it?** quanto é?; **it's £15** são 15 libras

····➤ (feelings) estar com; **I'm hungry/thirsty/sleepy** estou com fome/sede/sono; **I'm cold** estou com frio

····➤ (health) estar; **how are you?** como está?; **he's ill** ele está doente

····➤ (age) ter; **he's twenty** ele tem vinte anos

····➤ (weather) estar; **it's hot/cold** está calor/frio; **it's 30 degrees today** hoje estão 30 graus

····➤ (become) ficar; **he was disappointed** ficou desapontado

● vaux

····➤ (in continuous tense) **I am working** estou trabalhando, (P) estou a trabalhar; **She is leaving next week** ela vai embora na próxima semana

····➤ (in passives) **he was killed** ele foi morto; **the window has been fixed** a janela foi consertada

····➤ (in tag questions) **their house is lovely, isn't it?** a casa deles é linda, não é?

⋯▸ (*in short answers*) **are you a doctor? yes, I am** é médico? sim, sou.

⋯▸ (*with infinitive*) **she is to go immediately** ela tem que ir imediatamente; **they are to be married in August** eles vão casar em agosto

beach /biːtʃ/ n praia f

beacon /ˈbiːkən/ n farol m; (*marker*) baliza f

bead /biːd/ n conta f; **~ of sweat** gota f de suor

beak /biːk/ n bico m

beam /biːm/ n (*of wood*) trave f, viga f; (*of light*) raio m; (*of torch*) feixe m de luz ● vt/i (*radiate*) irradiar; *fig* sorrir radiante. **~ing** a radiante

bean /biːn/ n feijão m; **broad ~** fava f; **coffee ~s** café m em grão; **runner ~** feijão m verde

bear¹ /beə(r)/ n urso m

bear² /beə(r)/ vt/i (*pt* **bore**, *pp* **borne**) sustentar, suportar; (*endure*) aguentar, suportar; (*child*) dar à luz; **~ in mind** ter em mente, lembrar; **~ left** virar à esquerda; **~ on** relacionar-se com, ter a ver com; **~ out** confirmar; **~ up!** coragem!. **~able** a tolerável, suportável. **~er** n portador m

beard /bɪəd/ n barba f. **~ed** a barbado, com barba

bearing /ˈbeərɪŋ/ n (*manner*) porte m; (*relevance*) relação f; *Naut* marcação f; **get one's ~s** orientar-se

beast /biːst/ n (*animal, person*) besta f, animal m; (*in fables*) fera f; **~ of burden** besta f de carga

beat /biːt/ vt/i (*pt* **beat**, *pp* **beaten**) bater; **~ about the bush** estar com rodeios; **~ a retreat** bater em retirada; **~ it** 🅇 (*go away*) pôr-se

a andar; **it ~s me** 🅇 não consigo entender; **~ up** espancar ● n *Med* batimento m; *Mus* compasso m, ritmo m; (*of drum*) toque m; (*of policeman*) ronda f, (*P*) giro m. **~ing** n sova f

beautician /bjuːˈtɪʃn/ n esteticista mf

beautiful /ˈbjuːtɪfl/ a belo, lindo

beautify /ˈbjuːtɪfaɪ/ vt embelezar

beauty /ˈbjuːtɪ/ n beleza f; **~ parlour** instituto m de beleza; **~ spot** sinal m no rosto, mosca f; (*place*) local m pitoresco

beaver /ˈbiːvə(r)/ n castor m

became /bɪˈkeɪm/ ▶ BECOME

because /bɪˈkɒz/ conj porque ● adv **~ of** por causa de

beckon /ˈbekən/ vt/i **~ (to)** fazer sinal (para)

become /bɪˈkʌm/ vt/i (*pt* **became**, *pp* **become**) tornar-se; (*befit*) ficar bem a; **what has ~ of her?** que é feito dela?

becoming /bɪˈkʌmɪŋ/ a que fica bem, apropriado

bed /bed/ n cama f; (*layer*) camada f; (*of sea*) fundo m; (*of river*) leito m; (*of flowers*) canteiro m; **~ and breakfast (b & b)** quarto m com café da manhã, (*P*) com pequeno-almoço ● vt/i (*pt* **bedded**) **~ down** ir deitar-se; **~ in** plantar. **~sit(ter)** n 🅇 misto m de quarto e sala; **go to ~** ir para cama; **in ~** na cama. **~ding** n roupa f de cama

---

> *i*
>
> **bed and breakfast** Os *bed and breakfast*, ou *B&B*, são casas particulares ou pequenos hotéis que oferecem alojamento e café da manhã aos hóspedes a preços normalmente baixos.

bedclothes /'bedkləʊðz/ n roupa f de cama

bedroom /'bedru:m/ n quarto m de dormir

bedside /'bedsaɪd/ n cabeceira f; **~ manner** (*doctor's*) modos mpl que inspiram confiança

bedspread /'bedspred/ n colcha f

bedtime /'bedtaɪm/ n hora f de deitar, hora f de ir para a cama

bee /bi:/ n abelha f; **make a ~line for** ir direto a

beech /bi:tʃ/ n faia f

beef /bi:f/ n carne f de vaca

beefburger /'bi:fbɜːgə(r)/ n hambúrguer m

beehive /'bi:haɪv/ n colmeia f

been /bi:n/ ▶ BE

beer /bɪə(r)/ n cerveja f

beet /bi:t/ n beterraba f

beetle /'bi:tl/ n escaravelho m

beetroot /'bi:tru:t/ n (raiz de) beterraba f

before /bɪ'fɔː(r)/ prep (*time*) antes de; (*place*) em frente de • adv antes; (*already*) já • conj antes que; **~ leaving** antes de partir; **~ he leaves** antes que ele parta, antes de ele partir

beforehand /bɪ'fɔːhænd/ adv de antemão, antecipadamente

befriend /bɪ'frend/ vt tornar-se amigo de; (*be helpful to*) auxiliar

beg /beg/ vt/i (pt **begged**) mendigar; (*entreat*) suplicar; **~ sb's pardon** pedir desculpa a alguém; **~ the question** fazer uma petição de princípio; **it's going ~ging** está sobrando, (P) a sobrar

began /bɪ'gæn/ ▶ BEGIN

beggar /'begə(r)/ n mendigo m, pedinte mf; 🔟 (*person*) cara m 🔟

begin /bɪ'gɪn/ vt/i (pt **began**, pp **begun**, pres p **beginning**) começar, principiar. **~ner** n principiante mf. **~ning** n começo m, princípio m

begrudge /bɪ'grʌdʒ/ vt ter inveja de; (*give*) dar de má vontade; **~ doing** fazer de má vontade or a contragosto

beguile /bɪ'gaɪl/ vt enganar

begun /bɪ'gʌn/ ▶ BEGIN

behalf /bɪ'hɑːf/ n on **~** of em nome de; (*in the interest of*) em favor de

behave /bɪ'heɪv/ vi portar-se; **~ (o.s.)** portar-se bem

behaviour /bɪ'heɪvjə(r)/ n conduta f, comportamento m

behead /bɪ'hed/ vt decapitar

behind /bɪ'haɪnd/ prep atrás de • adv atrás; (*late*) com atraso • n 🔟 (*buttocks*) traseiro m 🔟; **~ the times** antiquado, retrógrado; **leave ~** deixar para trás

beige /beɪʒ/ a & n bege m, (P) beige m

being /'bi:ɪŋ/ n ser m; **bring into ~** criar; **come into ~** nascer, originar-se

belated /bɪ'leɪtɪd/ a tardio, atrasado

belch /beltʃ/ vi arrotar • vt **~ out** (*smoke*) vomitar, lançar • n arroto m

belfry /'belfrɪ/ n campanário m

Belgi|um /'beldʒəm/ n Bélgica f. **~an** a & n belga mf

belief /bɪ'li:f/ n crença f; (*trust*) confiança f; (*opinion*) convicção f

believ|e /bɪ'li:v/ vt/i acreditar; **~e in** acreditar em. **~able** a crível. **~er** /-ə(r)/ n crente mf

belittle /bɪ'lɪtl/ vt depreciar

bell /bel/ n sino m; (small) sineta f; (on door, of phone) campainha f; (on cat, toy) guizo m

bellow /'beləʊ/ vt/i berrar, bramir; ~ **out** rugir

belly /'belɪ/ n barriga f, ventre m

belong /bɪ'lɒŋ/ vi ~ **(to)** pertencer (a); ‹club› ser sócio (de)

belongings /bɪ'lɒŋɪŋz/ npl pertences mpl; **personal** ~ objetos mpl de uso pessoal

beloved /bɪ'lʌvɪd/ a & n amado m

below /bɪ'ləʊ/ prep abaixo de, debaixo de ● adv abaixo, em baixo; (on page) abaixo

belt /belt/ n cinto m; Techn correia f; fig zona f ● vt ⊠ (hit) zurzir ● vi ⊠ (rush) safar-se

bemused /bɪ'mju:zd/ a estonteado, confuso; (thoughtful) pensativo

bench /bentʃ/ n banco m; (seat, working-table) bancada f; **the** ~ Jur os magistrados (no tribunal)

bend /bend/ vt/i (pt, pp **bent**) curvar(-se); ‹arm, leg› dobrar; (road, river) fazer uma curva, virar ● n curva f; ~ **over** debruçar-se ou inclinar-se sobre

beneath /bɪ'ni:θ/ prep abaixo de, debaixo de; fig abaixo de ● adv debaixo, em baixo

benefactor /'benɪfæktə(r)/ n benfeitor m

beneficial /benɪ'fɪʃl/ a benéfico, proveitoso

beneficiary /benɪ'fɪʃərɪ/ n beneficiário m

benefit /'benɪfɪt/ n (advantage, performance) benefício m; (profit) proveito m; (allowance) subsídio m ● vt/i (pt **benefited**, pres p **benefiting**) (be useful to) beneficiar

(by de); (do good to) beneficiar, fazer bem a; (receive benefit) lucrar; ganhar (**by**, **from** com)

benevolen|t /bɪ'nevələnt/ a benevolente. ~**ce** n benevolência f

bent /bent/ ▶ BEND n (skill) aptidão f; jeito m (**for** para); (liking) queda f (**for** para) ● a curvado; (twisted) torcido; ⊠ (dishonest) desonesto; ~ **on** decidido a

bequeath /bɪ'kwi:ð/ vt legar

bereave|d /bɪ'ri:vd/ a **the** ~**d wife**/etc a esposa/etc do falecido; **the** ~**d family** a família enlutada. ~**ment** n luto m

beret /'bereɪ/ n boina f

Bermuda /bə'mju:də/ n Bermudas fpl

berry /'berɪ/ n baga f

berth /bɜ:θ/ n (in ship) beliche m; (in train) couchette f; (anchorage) ancoradouro m ● vi atracar; **give a wide** ~ **to** passar ao largo, (P) de largo

beside /bɪ'saɪd/ prep ao lado de, junto de; ~ **o.s.** fora de si; **be** ~ **the point** não vir a ter com o assunto, não vir ao caso

besides /bɪ'saɪdz/ prep além de; (except) fora, salvo ● adv além disso

besiege /bɪ'si:dʒ/ vt sitiar, cercar; ~ **with** assediar

best /best/ a & n (**the**) ~ (o/a) melhor mf ● adv melhor; ~ **man** padrinho m de casamento; **at** (**the**) ~ na melhor das hipóteses; **do one's** ~ fazer o (melhor) que se pode; **make the** ~ **of** tirar o melhor partido de; **the** ~ **part of** a maior parte de; **to the** ~ **of my knowledge** que eu saiba

bestseller /best'selə(r)/ n bestseller m

bet /bet/ n aposta f ● vt/i (pt bet or betted) apostar (on em)

betray /bɪ'treɪ/ vt trair. ~al n traição f

better /'betə(r)/ a & adv melhor; **all the ~** tanto melhor; **~ off** (richer) mais rico; **he's ~ off at home** é melhor para ele ficar em casa; **I'd ~ go** é melhor ir-me embora; **get ~** melhorar ● vt melhorar ● vr our **~s** os nossos superiores mpl; **the ~ part of it** a maior parte disso; **get the ~ of sb** levar a melhor em relação a alguém

between /bɪ'twi:n/ prep entre ● adv in ~ no meio, no intervalo; ~ **you and me** aqui entre nós

beverage /'bevərɪdʒ/ n bebida f

beware /bɪ'weə(r)/ vi acautelar-se (of com) tomar cuidado (of com)

bewilder /bɪ'wɪldə(r)/ vt desorientar. **~ment** n desorientação f, confusão f

bewitch /bɪ'wɪtʃ/ vt encantar, cativar

beyond /bɪ'jɒnd/ prep além de (doubt, reach) fora de ● adv além; **it's ~ me** isso ultrapassa-me; **he lives ~ his means** ele vive acima dos seus meios

bias /'baɪəs/ n parcialidade f; pej (prejudice) preconceito m; Sewing viés m ● vt (pt biased) influenciar; **~ed against** de prevenção contra, (P) de pé atrás contra. **~ed** a parcial

bib /bɪb/ n babeiro m, babette m

Bible /'baɪbl/ n Bíblia f

biblical /'bɪblɪkl/ a bíblico

bibliography /bɪblɪ'ɒɡrəfɪ/ n bibliografia f

biceps /'baɪseps/ n bíceps m

bicker /'bɪkə(r)/ vi questionar, discutir

bicycle /'baɪsɪkl/ n bicicleta f ● vi andar de bicicleta

bid /bɪd/ n oferta f, lance m; (attempt) tentativa f ● vt/i (pt bid, pres p bidding) fazer uma oferta, lançar, oferecer como lance. **~der** n licitante mf; **the highest ~der** quem dá or oferece mais

bide /baɪd/ vt **one's time** esperar pelo bom momento

big /bɪɡ/ a (bigger, biggest) grande; ▣ (generous) generoso; ~ **shot** ▣ mandachuva m ● adv ▣ em grande; **talk ~** gabar-se ▣; **think ~** ▣ ter grandes planos. **~headed** a pretensioso, convencido

bigam|y /'bɪɡəmɪ/ n bigamia f. **~ist** n bígamo m. **~ous** a bígamo

bigot /'bɪɡət/ n fanático m, intolerante mf. **~ed** a fanático, intolerante. **~ry** n fanatismo m, intolerância f

bigwig /'bɪɡwɪɡ/ n ▣ mandachuva m

bike /baɪk/ n ▣ bicicleta f

bikini /bɪ'ki:nɪ/ n (pl -is) biquíni m

bile /baɪl/ n bílis f

bilingual /baɪ'lɪŋɡwəl/ a bilíngue

bilious /'bɪlɪəs/ a bilioso

bill¹ /bɪl/ n (invoice) fatura f; (in restaurant) conta f; Pol projeto m de lei; Amer (banknote) nota f de banco; (poster) cartaz m; ~ **of exchange** letra f de câmbio ● vt faturar; Theatr anunciar, pôr no programa; ~ **sb for** apresentar a alguém a conta de

bill² /bɪl/ n (of bird) bico m

billiards /'bɪlɪədz/ n bilhar m

billion /'bɪlɪən/ n (10⁹) mil milhões; (10¹²) um milhão de milhões

bin /bɪn/ n (for storage) caixa f, lata f; (for rubbish) lata f do lixo,

(P) caixote m

bind /baɪnd/ vt (pt bound) (tie) atar;
‹book› encadernar; fur obrigar;
(cover the edge of) debruar ● n ⓧ
(bore) chatice f ⓧ; **be ~ing on** ser
obrigatório para

binding /ˈbaɪndɪŋ/ n
encadernação f; (braid) debrum m

binge /bɪndʒ/ n ⓧ **go on a ~** cair
na farra; (overeat) empanturrar-se.
~ drinking n: consumo excessivo de
álcool em pouco tempo

bingo /ˈbɪŋgəʊ/ n bingo m ● int
acertei!

binoculars /bɪˈnɒkjʊləz/ npl
binóculo m

biochemistry /baɪəʊˈkemɪstrɪ/ n
bioquímica f

biodegradable
/baɪəʊdɪˈgreɪdəbl/ a biodegradável

biodiesel /ˈbaɪəʊdiːzl/ n
biodiesel m

biograph|y /baɪˈɒgrəfɪ/ n
biografia f. **~er** n biógrafo m

biolog|y /baɪˈɒlədʒɪ/ n biologia f.
~ical /-əˈlɒdʒɪkl/ a biológico. **~ist**
n biólogo m

birch /bɜːtʃ/ n (tree) bétula f

bird /bɜːd/ n ave f, pássaro m; ⓧ
(girl) garota f ⓧ; **~ sanctuary**
refúgio m ornitológico. **~ flu** n
gripe f aviária, (P) gripe f das aves;
~watcher n ornitófilo m

Biro® /ˈbaɪərəʊ/ n (pl -os) (caneta)
esferográfica f, Bic® f

birth /bɜːθ/ n nascimento
m; **~ certificate** certidão f de
nascimento; **~ control|rate**
controle m índice m de natalidade;
give ~ to dar à luz. **~place** n lugar m
de nascimento

birthday /ˈbɜːθdeɪ/ n aniversário
m, (P) dia m de anos; **his ~ is on 9**

July ele faz anos no dia 9 de julho

birthmark /ˈbɜːθmɑːk/ n sinal m

biscuit /ˈbɪskɪt/ n biscoito m,
bolacha f

bishop /ˈbɪʃəp/ n bispo m

bit¹ /bɪt/ n (small piece, short time)
pedaço m, bocado m; (of bridle) freio
m; (of tool) boca f. **a ~** um pouco

bit² /bɪt/ ▶ BITE

bitch /bɪtʃ/ n cadela f; ⓧ (woman)
peste f; fig cadela f ⓧ ● vt/i ⓧ
(criticize) malhar, (P) cortar (em)
ⓧ; ⓧ (grumble) resmungar. **~y** a
ⓧ maldoso

bite /baɪt/ vt/i (pt bit, pp bitten)
morder; (insect) picar ● n mordida
f; (sting) picada f; **have a ~ (to eat)**
comer qualquer coisa

biting /ˈbaɪtɪŋ/ a cortante

bitter /ˈbɪtə(r)/ a amargo; (weather)
glacial. **~ly** adv amargamente; **it's
~ly cold** está um frio de rachar.
~ness n amargura f; (resentment)
ressentimento m

bizarre /bɪˈzɑː(r)/ a bizarro

black /blæk/ a (-er, -est) negro,
preto; **~ and blue** coberto de
nódoas negras; **~ coffee** café m
(sem leite); **~ eye** olho m negro;
~ ice gelo m negro sobre o asfalto;
~ market mercado m negro ● n
negro m, preto m; **a ~** (person) um
preto, um negro ● vt enegrecer;
(goods) boicotar

blackberry /ˈblækbərɪ/ n amora
f silvestre

blackbird /ˈblækbɜːd/ n melro m

blackboard /ˈblækbɔːd/ n quadro
m preto

blackcurrant /ˈblækkʌrənt/ n
groselha f negra

blacken /ˈblækən/ vt/i escurecer;
~ sb's name difamar, denigrir

blacklist /'blæklɪst/ n lista f negra
● vt pôr na lista negra

blackmail /'blækmeɪl/ n
chantagem f ● vt fazer chantagem.
~er n chantagista mf

blackout /'blækaʊt/ n (wartime)
blecaute m, (P) blackout m; Med
desmaio m; Electr falta f de corrente;
Theatr apagar m de luzes

bladder /'blædə(r)/ n bexiga f

blade /bleɪd/ n lâmina f; (of oar,
propeller) pá f; (of grass) ervinha f,
folhinha f de erva

blame /bleɪm/ vt culpar ● n culpa
f; **be to ~** ser o culpado. **~less** a
irrepreensível; (innocent) inocente

bland /blænd/ a (-er, -est) (of
manner) suave; (mild) brando;
(insipid) insípido

blank /blæŋk/ a <space, cheque>
em branco; <look> vago; <wall> nu
● n espaço m em branco; <cartridge>
cartucho m sem bala

blanket /'blæŋkɪt/ n cobertor
m; fig manto m ● vt (pt blanketed)
cobrir com cobertor; (cover
thickly) encobrir, recobrir; **wet ~**
desmancha-prazeres mf

blare /bleə(r)/ vt/i ressoar, atroar
● n clangor m; (of horn) buzinar m

blasé /'blɑːzeɪ/ a blasé

blasphem|y /'blæsfəmɪ/ n
blasfêmia f, blasfémia f

blast /blɑːst/ n (gust) rajada f;
(sound) som m; (explosion) explosão
f ● vt dinamitar; **~!** drogа!, (P) raios!.
~ed a maldito.

blatant /'bleɪtnt/ a flagrante;
(shameless) descarado

blaze /bleɪz/ n chamas fpl; (light)
clarão m; (outburst) explosão f
● vi arder; (shine) resplandecer,
brilhar; **~ a trail** abrir o caminho,

ser pioneiro

blazer /'bleɪzə(r)/ n blazer m

bleach /bliːtʃ/ n descolorante,
descorante m; (household) água f
sanitária, (P) lixívia f ● vt/i branquear;
<hair> oxigenar

bleak /bliːk/ a (-er, -est)
<place> desolado; (chilly) frio; fig
desanimador

bleary-eyed /'blɪərɪaɪd/ a com
olhos injetados

bleat /bliːt/ n balido m ● vi balir

bleed /bliːd/ vt/i (pt bled) sangrar

bleep /bliːp/ n bip m. **~er** n bip m

blemish /'blemɪʃ/ n defeito m; (on
reputation) mancha f ● vt manchar

blend /blend/ vt/i misturar(-se);
(go well together) combinar-se ● n
mistura f. **~er** n Culin liquidificador m

bless /bles/ vt abençoar; **be ~ed
with** ter a felicidade de ter. **~ing**
n bênção f; (thing one is glad of)
felicidade f; **it's a ~ing in disguise**
há males que vêm para bem

blessed /'blesɪd/ a bem-
aventurado; [!] (cursed) maldito

blew /bluː/ ▶ BLOW[1]

blight /blaɪt/ n doença f de plantas;
fig influência f maligna ● vt arruinar,
frustrar

blind /blaɪnd/ a cego; **~ alley**
(also fig) beco m sem saída; **~
man/woman** cego m /cega f ● vt
cegar ● n (on window) persiana f;
(deception) ardil m; **be ~ to** não
ver; **turn a ~ eye to** fingir não ver,
fechar os olhos a. **~ly** adv às cegas.
~ness n cegueira f

blindfold /'blaɪndfəʊld/ a & adv
de olhos vendados ● n venda f ● vt
vendar os olhos a

bling /blɪŋ/, **bling bling** /'blɪŋ
blɪŋ/ ns [!] bling-bling m, estilo

adotado principalmente por
rappers, que se caracteriza pelo uso
de muitas joias

blink /blɪŋk/ vi piscar

bliss /blɪs/ n felicidade f, beatitude f.
~ful a felicíssimo

blister /'blɪstə(r)/ n bolha f, empola
f ● vi empolar

blizzard /'blɪzəd/ n tempestade f
de neve, nevasca f

bloated /'bləʊtɪd/ a inchado

blob /blɒb/ n pingo m grosso;
(stain) mancha f

block /blɒk/ n bloco m; (buildings)
quarteirão m; (in pipe) entupimento
m; ~ (of flats) prédio m (de andares)
m; ~ letters maiúsculas fpl ● vt
bloquear, obstruir; <pipe> entupir.
~age n obstrução f

blockade /blɒ'keɪd/ n bloqueio m
● vt bloquear

blog /blɒg/ n blogue m, (P) blog m
● vi blogar

blogger /'blɒgə(r)/ n blogueiro m,
(P) bloguista m

bloke /bləʊk/ n 🔲 sujeito m 🔲;
cara m 🔲

blond /blɒnd/ a & n louro m

blonde /blɒnd/ a & n loura f

blood /blʌd/ n sangue m ● a <bank,
donor, transfusion, etc> de sangue;
<poisoning> do sangue; <group,
vessel> sanguíneo; ~ pressure
tensão f arterial; ~ test exame m de
sangue. ~curdling a horrendo

bloodhound /'blʌdhaʊnd/ n
sabujo m

bloodshed /'blʌdʃed/ n
derramamento m de sangue,
carnificina f

bloodshot /'blʌdʃɒt/ a injetado
de sangue

bloodstream /'blʌdstriːm/ n
sangue m, fluxo m sanguíneo

bloodthirsty /'blʌdθɜːstɪ/ a
sanguinário

bloody /'blʌdɪ/ a (-ier, -iest)
ensanguentado; (with much
bloodshed) sangrento; 🔲 grande;
maldito ● adv 🔲 pra burro.
~-minded a 🔲 do contra 🔲;
chato 🔲

bloom /bluːm/ n flor f; (beauty)
frescura f, viço m; **in** ~ em flor ● vi
florir; fig vicejar

blossom /'blɒsəm/ n flor f, **in** ~ em
flor ● vi (flower) florir, desabrochar;
(develop, flourish) florescer,
desabrochar

blot /blɒt/ n mancha f ● vt (pt
blotted) manchar; (dry) secar;
~ out apagar; (hide) tapar, toldar

blotch /blɒtʃ/ n mancha f. ~y a
manchado

blouse /blaʊz/ n blusa f; (in
uniform) blusão m

blow[1] /bləʊ/ vt/i (pt blew, pp blown)
soprar; (fuse) fundir-se, queimar; 🔲
(squander) esbanjar; <trumpet etc>
tocar; ~ a whistle apitar; ~ one's
nose assoar o nariz; ~ out <candle>
apagar, soprar; ~ over passar ▢ ~
away, ~ off vt levar, soprar ● vi
voar, ir pelos ares (fora) ▢ ~ up vt
(explode) explodir; <tyre> encher;
<photograph> ampliar ● vi (explode)
explodir. ~-dry vt <hair> fazer um
brushing ● n brushing m

blow[2] /bləʊ/ n pancada f; (slap)
bofetada f; (punch) murro m; fig
golpe m

blowlamp /'bləʊlæmp/ n
maçarico m

blown /bləʊn/ ▶ BLOW[1]

blue /bluː/ a (-er, -est) azul; (indecent) indecente ● n azul m; **come out of the ~** ser inesperado. **~s** n Mus blues; **have the ~s** 🆃 estar deprimido

bluebell /'bluːbel/ n jacinto m dos bosques

bluebottle /'bluːbɒtl/ n mosca f varejeira

blueprint /'bluːprɪnt/ n cópia f fotográfica de planta; fig projeto m

bluff /blʌf/ vi blefar, (P) fazer bluff ● vt enganar (fingindo), blefar ● n blefe m, (P) bluff m

blunder /'blʌndə(r)/ vi cometer um erro crasso; (move) avançar às cegas or tateando ● n erro m crasso, (P) bronca f

blunt /blʌnt/ a (-er, -est) embotado; <person> direto ● vt embotar. **~ly** adv sem rodeios

blur /blɜː(r)/ n mancha f ● vt (pt blurred) (smear) manchar; (make indistinct) toldar

blurb /blɜːb/ n contracapa f, sinopse f de um livro

blurt /blɜːt/ vt **~ out** deixar escapar

blush /blʌʃ/ vi corar ● n rubor m, vermelhidão f

bluster /'blʌstə(r)/ vi (wind) soprar em rajadas; (swagger) andar com ar fanfarrão. **~y** a borrascoso

boar /bɔː(r)/ n varrão m; **wild ~** javali m

board /bɔːd/ n tábua f; (for notices) quadro m, (P) placard m; (food) pensão f; Admin conselho m ● vt/i cobrir com tábuas; <aircraft, ship, train> embarcar (em); <bus, train> subir (em); **full ~** pensão f completa; **half ~** meia-pensão f; **on ~** a bordo; **~ up** entaipar; **~ with** ser pensionista em casa de. **~er** n

pensionista mf; (at school) interno m. **~ing card** n cartão m de embarque; **~ing school** n internato m

boast /bəʊst/ vi gabar-se ● vt orgulhar-se de ● n gabarolice f. **~ful** a vaidoso

boat /bəʊt/ n barco m; **in the same ~** nas mesmas circunstâncias

bob /bɒb/ vt/i (pt bobbed) (curtsy) inclinar-se; (hair) cortar pelos ombros, (P) cortar à Joãozinho; **~ (up and down)** andar para cima e para baixo

bobsleigh /'bɒbsleɪ/ n trenó m

bodily /'bɒdɪlɪ/ a corporal, físico ● adv (in person) fisicamente, em pessoa; (lift) em peso

body /'bɒdɪ/ n corpo m; (organization) organismo m; **in a ~** em massa; **the main ~ of** o grosso de. **~(work)** n (of car) carroçaria f. **~building** n body building m; **~ piercing** n piercing m no corpo, (P) pírcingue m de corpo

bodyguard /'bɒdɪgɑːd/ n guarda-costas m; (escort) escolta f

bog /bɒg/ n pântano m ● vt **get ~ged down** atolar-se; fig ficar emperrado

bogus /'bəʊgəs/ a falso

boil[1] /bɔɪl/ n Med furúnculo m

boil[2] /bɔɪl/ vt/i ferver; **come to the ~** ferver; **~ down to** resumir-se a; **~ over** transbordar, (P) a ferver. **~ing hot** fervendo; **~ing point** ponto m de ebulição

boiler /'bɔɪlə(r)/ n caldeira f; **~ suit** macacão m, (P) fato m de macaco

boisterous /'bɔɪstərəs/ a turbulento; (noisy and cheerful) animado

bold /bəʊld/ a (-er, -est) ousado; (of colours) vivo. **~ness** n ousadia f

Bolivia /bə'lɪvɪə/ n Bolívia f. **~n a &** n boliviano m

bolster /'bəʊlstə(r)/ n travesseiro m ● vt sustentar; ajudar; **~ one's spirits** levantar o moral

bolt /bəʊlt/ n (on door etc) ferrolho m; (for nut) parafuso m; (lightning) relâmpago m; **~ upright** reto or (P) direito como um fuso ● vt aferrolhar; ‹food› engolir ● vi fugir, disparar

bomb /bɒm/ n bomba f ● vt bombardear. **~er** n (aircraft) bombardeiro m; (person) bombista mf

bombard /bɒm'bɑːd/ vt bombardear

bombastic /bɒm'bæstɪk/ a bombástico

bombshell /'bɒmʃel/ n granada f; fig bomba f

bond /bɒnd/ n (agreement) compromisso m; (link) laço m, vínculo m; Comm obrigação f; **in ~** em depósito na alfândega

bondage /'bɒndɪdʒ/ n escravidão f, servidão f

bone /bəʊn/ n osso m; (of fish) espinha f; **~ idle** preguiçoso ● vt desossar. **~ dry** a completamente seco, ressecado

bonfire /'bɒnfaɪə(r)/ n fogueira f

bonnet /'bɒnɪt/ n chapéu m; Auto capô m do motor, (P) capot m

bonus /'bəʊnəs/ n bônus m, (P) bónus m

bony /'bəʊnɪ/ a (-ier, -iest) ossudo; ‹meat, fish› cheio de ossos/de espinhas

boo /buː/ int fora ● vt/i vaiar ● n vaia f

boob /buːb/ n 🗵 (mistake) asneira f; disparate m ● vi 🗵 fazer asneira(s)

booby /'buːbɪ/ n **~ prize** prêmio or (P) prémio m de consolação; **~ trap** bomba f armadilhada

book /bʊk/ n livro m; **~s** Comm contas fpl, escrita f; **~ of matches** carteira f de fósforos; **~ of tickets** (bus, tube) caderneta f de módulos; **~ing office** bilheteria f, (P) bilheteira f ● vt (enter) averbar, registrar; Comm escriturar; (reserve) marcar, reservar; **be fully ~ed** ter a lotação esgotada

bookcase /'bʊkkeɪs/ n estante f

bookkeep|er /'bʊkkiːpə(r)/ n guarda-livros m. **~ing** n contabilidade f, escrituração f

booklet /'bʊklɪt/ n brochura f

bookmaker /'bʊkmeɪkə(r)/ n book (maker) m

bookmark /'bʊkmɑːk/ n marca f de livro, marcador m de página

bookseller /'bʊkselə(r)/ n livreiro m

bookshop /'bʊkʃɒp/ n livraria f

bookstall /'bʊkstɔːl/ n quiosque m

boom /buːm/ vi ribombar; (of trade) prosperar ● n (sound) ribombo m; Comm boom m, prosperidade f

boon /buːn/ n bênção f, vantagem f

boost /buːst/ vt desenvolver, promover; ‹morale› levantar; ‹price› aumentar ● n força f 🗓. **~er** n Med dose suplementar f; (vaccine) revacinação f, (P) reforço m

boot /buːt/ n bota f; Auto portamala f, bagageira f ● vt **~ (up)** Comput dar carga em; **to ~** (in addition) ainda por cima

booth /buːð/ n barraca f; (telephone, voting) cabine f

booty /'buːtɪ/ n saque m, pilhagem f

booze /buːz/ vi 🔢 embebedar-se
🔢; encharcar-se 🔢 ● n 🔢 pinga f 🔢

border /ˈbɔːdə(r)/ n borda f,
margem f; (frontier) fronteira f;
(garden bed) canteiro m ● vi ~ on
confinar com; (be almost the same
as) atingir as raias de

borderline /ˈbɔːdəlaɪn/ n linha f
divisória; ~ case caso m limite

bore[1] /bɔː(r)/ ▶ BEAR[2]

bore[2] /bɔː(r)/ vt/i Techn furar,
perfurar ● n (of gun barrel) calibre m

bore[3] /bɔː(r)/ vt aborrecer, entediar
● n maçante m; (thing) chatice f; **be
~d** aborrecer-se, maçar-se. **~dom** n
tédio m. **boring** a tedioso, maçante

born /bɔːn/ a nascido; **be ~** nascer

borne /bɔːn/ ▶ BEAR[2]

borough /ˈbʌrə/ n município m

borrow /ˈbɒrəʊ/ vt pedir
emprestado (**from** a)

bosom /ˈbʊzəm/ n peito m;
(woman's; also fig) (midst) seio m;
~ **friend** amigo íntimo m

boss /bɒs/ n 🔢 patrão m; patroa f;
mandachuva m 🔢 ● vt mandar; ~ **sb
about** 🔢 mandar em alguém

bossy /ˈbɒsɪ/ a mandão, autoritário

botan|y /ˈbɒtənɪ/ n botânica f.
~ical /bəˈtænɪkl/ a botânico. **~ist**
/-ɪst/ n botânico m

botch /bɒtʃ/ vt aborrecer; (spoil)
estragar, escangalhar

both /bəʊθ/ a & pron ambos, os
dois; ~ **of us** nós dois; ~ **the
books** ambos os livros ● adv ~ ... **and** não
só ... mas também, tanto ... como

bother /ˈbɒðə(r)/ vt/i
incomodar(-se) ● n (inconvenience)
incômodo m, (P) incómodo m;
trabalho m; (effort) custo m, trabalho
m; (worry) preocupação f; **don't ~**
não se incomode; **I can't be ~ed**

não posso me dar o trabalho

bottle /ˈbɒtl/ n garrafa f; (small)
frasco m; (for baby) mamadeira f,
(P) biberão m ● vt engarrafar; ~ **up**
reprimir. **~ opener** n saca-rolhas m

bottleneck /ˈbɒtlnek/ n
(obstruction) entrave m; (traffic jam)
engarrafamento m

bottom /ˈbɒtəm/ n fundo m; (of
hill) sopé m; (buttocks) traseiro m ● a
inferior; (last) último; **from top to ~**
de alto a baixo

bough /baʊ/ n ramo m

bought /bɔːt/ ▶ BUY

boulder /ˈbəʊldə(r)/ n
pedregulho m

bounce /baʊns/ vi saltar; (of
person) pular, dar pulos; 🔢 (of
cheque) ser devolvido ● vt fazer
saltar ● n (of ball) salto m, (P)
ressalto m

bound[1] /baʊnd/ vi pular; (move by
jumping) ir aos pulos ● n pulo m

bound[2] /baʊnd/ ▶ BIND ● **be ~
for** ir com destino a, ir para; **be ~
to** (obliged) ser obrigado a; (certain)
haver de; **she's ~ to like it** ela há de
gostar disso

boundary /ˈbaʊndrɪ/ n limite m

bound|s /baʊndz/ npl limites mpl;
out of ~s interdito; **~ed by** limitado
por. **~less** a sem limites

bouquet /bʊˈkeɪ/ n ramo m de
flores; (wine) aroma m

bout /baʊt/ n período m; Med
ataque m; Boxing combate m

boutique /buːˈtiːk/ n boutique f

bow[1] /bəʊ/ n (weapon) Mus arco
m; (knot) laço m. ~ **tie** n gravata
borboleta f, (P) laço m

bow[2] /baʊ/ n vênia f, (P) vénia f ● vt/i
inclinar(-se), curvar-se

bow[3] /baʊ/ n Naut proa f

bowels /'baʊəlz/ npl intestinos mpl; fig entranhas fpl

bowl[1] /bəʊl/ n (basin) bacia f; (for food) tigela f; (of pipe) fornilho m

bowl[2] /bəʊl/ n (ball) boliche m, (P) bola f de madeira ● vt Cricket lançar; ~ **over** siderar, varar. ~**ing** n boliche m, (P) bowling m. ~s npl boliche m, (P) jogo m com bolas de madeira: ~**ing alley** n pista f

bowler[1] /'bəʊlə(r)/ n Cricket lançador m

bowler[2] /'bəʊlə(r)/ n ~ **(hat)** (chapéu de) coco m

box[1] /bɒks/ n caixa f; Theatr camarote m; B~**ing Day** feriado m no primeiro dia útil depois do Natal ● vt pôr dentro duma caixa; ~ **in** fechar. ~ **office** n bilheteira f, (P) bilheteira f

box[2] /bɒks/ vt/i Sport lutar boxe; ~ **the ears of** esbofetear. ~**er** n pugilista m, boxeur m. ~**ing** n boxe m, pugilismo m

boy /bɔɪ/ n rapaz m. ~**friend** n namorado m. ~**ish** a de menino

boycott /'bɔɪkɒt/ vt boicotar ● n boicote m

bra /brɑː/ n soutien m

brace /breɪs/ n braçadeira f; (dental) aparelho m; (tool) berbequim m; (of birds) par m ● vt apoiar, firmar; ~ **o.s.** concentrar as energias, fazer força; (for blow) preparar-se. ~**s** npl (for trousers) suspensórios mpl

bracelet /'breɪslɪt/ n bracelete m, pulseira f

bracing /'breɪsɪŋ/ a tonificante, estimulante

bracket /'brækɪt/ n suporte m; (group) grupo m; **age/income** ~ faixa f etária/salarial; **round**

~**s** parênteses mpl; **square** ~**s** parênteses mpl, colchetes mpl (pt bracketed) pôr entre parênteses; (put together) pôr em pé de igualdade, agrupar

brag /bræg/ vi (pt bragged) gabar-se (**about** de)

braid /breɪd/ n galão m; (of hair) trança f

Braille /breɪl/ n braile m

brain /breɪn/ n cérebro m; miolos mpl 🔢; fig inteligência f; ~**s** Culin miolos mpl. ~**less** a estúpido

brainwash /'breɪnwɒʃ/ vt fazer uma lavagem cerebral

brainwave /'breɪnweɪv/ n ideia f genial

brainy /'breɪnɪ/ a (-ier, -iest) inteligente, esperto

braise /breɪz/ vt Culin estufar

brake /breɪk/ n travão m ● vt/i travar; ~ **light** farol m do freio, (P) luz f de travagem

branch /brɑːntʃ/ n ramo m; (of road) ramificação f; (of railway line) ramal m; Comm sucursal f; (of bank) balcão m ● vi ~ **(off)** bifurcar-se, ramificar-se

brand /brænd/ n marca f; ~ **name** marca f de fábrica ● vt marcar; ~ **sb as** tachar alguém de, (P) rotular alguém de. ~**new** a novo em folha

brandish /'brændɪʃ/ vt brandir

brandy /'brændɪ/ n aguardente f, conhaque m

brass /brɑːs/ n latão m; **the** ~ Mus os metais mpl; **top** ~ 🔲 os chefões 🔢 ● a de cobre, de latão; **get down to** ~ **tacks** tratar das coisas sérias

brassiere /'bræsɪə(r)/ n soutien m

brat /bræt/ n pej fedelho m

bravado /brə'vɑːdəʊ/ n bravata f

brave /breɪv/ a (-er, -est) bravo, valente ● vt arrostar. **~ry** /-əɪɪ/ n bravura f

brawl /brɔːl/ n briga f, rixa f, desordem f ● vi brigar

brawn /brɔːn/ n força f muscular, músculo m. **~y** a musculoso

bray /breɪ/ n zurro m ● vi zurrar

brazen /ˈbreɪzn/ a descarado

Brazil /brəˈzɪl/ n Brasil m; **~ nut** castanha f do Pará. **~ian** a & n brasileiro m

breach /briːtʃ/ n quebra f, (gap) brecha f ● vt abrir uma brecha em; **~ of contract** quebra f de contrato; **~ of the peace** perturbação f da ordem pública; **~ of trust** abuso m de confiança

bread /bred/ n pão m. **~winner** n ganha-pão m

breadcrumbs /ˈbredkrʌmz/ npl migalhas fpl; Culin farinha f de rosca

breadth /bredθ/ n largura f; (of mind, view) abertura f

break /breɪk/ vt (pt broke, pp broken) partir, quebrar; ⟨vow, silence, etc⟩ quebrar; ⟨law⟩ transgredir; ⟨journey⟩ interromper; ⟨news⟩ dar; ⟨a record⟩ bater; **~ one's arm/leg** quebrar or (P) partir o braço/a perna ● vi partir-se, quebrar-se; ⟨voice, weather⟩ mudar; **~ in** forçar uma entrada; **~ out** rebentar ● n quebra f, ruptura f, (interval) intervalo m; 🄰 (opportunity) oportunidade f, chance f ☐ **~ down** vt analisar ● vi (of person) ir-se abaixo; (of machine) avariar-se. **~ off** vt quebrar ● vi desligar-se. **~ up** vt/i terminar ● vi (of schools) entrar em férias. **~able** a quebrável. **~age** n quebra f

breakdown /ˈbreɪkdaʊn/ n Techn avaria f, pane f; Med esgotamento

m nervoso; (of figures) análise f ● a Auto de pronto-socorro; **~ van** pronto-socorro m

breaker /ˈbreɪkə(r)/ n vaga f de rebentação

breakfast /ˈbrekfəst/ n café m da manhã, (P) pequeno-almoço

breakthrough /ˈbreɪkθruː/ n descoberta f decisiva, avanço m

breakwater /ˈbreɪkwɔːtə(r)/ n quebra-mar m

breast /brest/ n peito m. **~feed** vt amamentar; **~stroke** n estilo m bruços

breath /breθ/ n respiração f; **bad ~** mau hálito m; **out of ~** sem fôlego; **under one's ~** num murmúrio, baixo. **~less** a ofegante

breathe /briːð/ vt/i respirar; **~ in** inspirar; **~ out** expirar. **~ing** n respiração f. **~ing space** n pausa f

breather /ˈbriːðə(r)/ n pausa f de descanso, momento m para respirar

breathtaking /ˈbreθteɪkɪŋ/ a assombroso, arrebatador

bred /bred/ ▶ BREED

breed /briːd/ vt (pt bred) criar ● vi reproduzir-se ● n raça f. **~er** n criador m. **~ing** n criação f; fig educação f

breez|e /briːz/ n brisa f. **~y** a fresco

brevity /ˈbrevətɪ/ n brevidade f

brew /bruː/ vt ⟨beer⟩ fabricar; ⟨tea⟩ fazer; fig armar; tramar ● vi fermentar; ⟨tea⟩ preparar; fig armar-se; preparar-se ● n decocção f, (tea) infusão f. **~er** n cervejeiro m. **~ery** n cervejaria f

bribe /braɪb/ n suborno m ● vt subornar. **~ry** /-ərɪ/ n suborno m, corrupção f

brick /brɪk/ n tijolo m

bricklayer /ˈbrɪkleɪə(r)/ n pedreiro m

bridal /ˈbraɪdl/ a nupcial

bride /braɪd/ n noiva f

bridegroom /ˈbraɪdɡrʊm/ n noivo m

bridesmaid /ˈbraɪdzmeɪd/ n dama f de honra, (P) de honor

bridge[1] /brɪdʒ/ n ponte f; (of nose) cana f ● vt ~ **a gap** preencher uma lacuna

bridge[2] /brɪdʒ/ n Cards bridge m

bridle /ˈbraɪdl/ n cabeçada f, freio m ● vt refrear

brief[1] /briːf/ a (-er, -est) breve. ~**s** npl (men's) cueca f, (P) slip m; (women's) calcinhas fpl, (P) cuecas fpl. ~**ly** adv brevemente

brief[2] /briːf/ n Jur sumário m; (case) causa f; (instructions) instruções fpl ● vt dar instruções a

briefcase /ˈbriːfkeɪs/ n pasta f

brigade /brɪˈɡeɪd/ n brigada f

bright /braɪt/ a (-er, -est) brilhante; (of colour) vivo; (of light) forte; (room) claro; (cheerful) alegre; (clever) inteligente. ~**ness** n (sheen) brilho m; (clarity) claridade f; (intelligence) inteligência f

brighten /ˈbraɪtn/ vt alegrar ● vi (of weather) clarear; (of face) animar-se, iluminar-se

brilliant /ˈbrɪljənt/ a brilhante. ~**ce** n brilho m

brim /brɪm/ n borda f; (of hat) aba f ● vi (pt brimmed) ~ **over** transbordar, cair por fora

bring /brɪŋ/ vt (pt brought) trazer; ~ **about** causar; ~ **back** trazer (de volta); (call to mind) relembrar; ~ **down** trazer para baixo; (bird, plane) abater; (prices) baixar; ~ **forward** adiantar, apresentar; ~ **it**

off ser bem sucedido (em alguém coisa); ~ **out** (take out) tirar; (show) revelar; (book) publicar; ~ **round** or to reanimar, fazer voltar a si; ~ **to bear** (pressure etc) exercer; ~ **up** educar; Med vomitar; (question) levantar

brink /brɪŋk/ n beira f, borda f

brisk /brɪsk/ a (-er, -est) (pace, movement) vivo, rápido; (business, demand) grande

bristl|e /ˈbrɪsl/ n pelo m

Britain /ˈbrɪtn/ n Grã-Bretanha f

British /ˈbrɪtɪʃ/ a britânico; **the** ~ o povo m britânico, os britânicos mpl

brittle /ˈbrɪtl/ a frágil

broach /brəʊtʃ/ vt abordar, entabular, encetar

broad /brɔːd/ a (-er, -est) largo; (daylight) pleno; ~**band** banda f larga; ~**bean** fava f. ~**minded** a tolerante, liberal. ~**ly** adv de modo geral

broadband /ˈbrɔːdbænd/ n banda larga f

broadcast /ˈbrɔːdkɑːst/ vt/i (pt broadcast) transmitir, fazer uma transmissão; (person) cantar, falar etc na rádio or na TV ● n emissão f. ~**ing** a & n (de) rádiodifusão f

broaden /ˈbrɔːdn/ vt/i alargar(-se)

broccoli /ˈbrɒkəli/ n inv brócolis mpl, (P) brócolos mpl

brochure /ˈbrəʊʃə(r)/ n brochura f

broke /brəʊk/ ▶ BREAK a 🅇 depenado 🅇 liso, (P) 🅇 teso 🅇

broken /ˈbrəʊkən/ a ~ **English** inglês m estropeado. ~**hearted** a com o coração despedaçado

broker /ˈbrəʊkə(r)/ n corretor m, broker m

bronchitis /brɒŋˈkaɪtɪs/ n bronquite f

bronze /brɒnz/ n bronze m

brooch /brəʊtʃ/ n broche m

brood /bru:d/ n ninhada f • vi chocar; fig cismar. **~y** a (hen) choca; fig sorumbático

brook /brʊk/ n regato m, ribeiro m

broom /bru:m/ n vassoura f; Bot giesta f

broth /brɒθ/ n caldo m

brothel /ˈbrɒθl/ n bordel m

brother /ˈbrʌðə(r)/ n irmão m. **~-in-law** (pl **~s-in-law**) cunhado m. **~hood** n irmandade f; fraternidade f. **~ly** a fraternal

brought /brɔːt/ ▶ BRING

brow /braʊ/ n (forehead) testa f; (of hill) cume m; (eyebrow) sobrancelha f

brown /braʊn/ a (-er, -est) castanho • n castanho m • vt/i acastanhar; (in the sun) bronzear, tostar; ‹meat› alourar

browse /braʊz/ vi (through book) folhear; (of animal) pastar; (in a shop) olhar sem comprar. **~r** n Comput navegador m

bruise /bru:z/ n hematoma m, contusão f • vt causar um hematoma. **~d** a coberto de hematomas, contuso; ‹fruit› machucado, (P) pisado

brunette /bru:ˈnet/ n morena f

brunt /brʌnt/ n the **~ of** o maior peso de, o pior de

brush /brʌʃ/ n escova f; (painter's) pincel m; (skirmish) escaramuça f; **~ against** roçar; **~ aside** não fazer caso de; **~ off** (reject) mandar passear ⊡; **~ up (on)** aperfeiçoar

brusque /bru:sk/ a brusco

Brussels /ˈbrʌslz/ n Bruxelas f; **~ sprouts** couve-de-Bruxelas f

brutal /ˈbru:tl/ a brutal. **~ity** /-ˈtælətɪ/ n brutalidade f

brute /bru:t/ n & a (animal, person) bruto m; **by ~ force** por força bruta

BSc abbr (= Bachelor of Science)
▶ BACHELOR

BSE /ˈbiːɛsˈiː/ n EEB, encefalopatia espongiforme bovina

btw abbr (= by the way) a propósito; **Thursday, ~, is also the day that our new kitchen gets delivered** a propósito, quinta-feira é também o dia em que nos entregam a nova cozinha

bubble /ˈbʌbl/ n bolha f; (of soap) bola f de sabão • vi borbulhar; **~ over** transbordar. **~le gum** n chiclete m, (P) pastilha f elástica. **~ly** a efervescente

buck[1] /bʌk/ n macho m • vi dar galões, (P) corcovear ⊡ **~ up** vt/i animar(-se); ⊠ (rush) apressar-se; despachar-se

buck[2] /bʌk/ n Amer ⊠ dólar m

buck[3] /bʌk/ n **pass the ~** ⊠ fazer o jogo do empurra ⊡

bucket /ˈbʌkɪt/ n balde m

buckle /ˈbʌkl/ n fivela f • vt/i afivelar(-se); (bend) torcer(-se), vergar; **~ down to** empenhar-se

bud /bʌd/ n botão m, rebento m • vi (pt budded) rebentar; **in ~** em botão

Buddhist /ˈbʊdɪst/ a & n budista mf. **~m** /-zəm/ n budismo m

budding /ˈbʌdɪŋ/ a nascente, em botão, incipiente

budge /bʌdʒ/ vt/i mexer(-se)

budget /ˈbʌdʒɪt/ n orçamento m • vi (pt budgeted) **~ for** prever no orçamento m

buff /bʌf/ n (colour) cor f de camurça; ⊡ fanático m; entusiasta *mf* ● *vt* polir

buffalo /ˈbʌfələʊ/ *n* (*pl* **-oes**) búfalo *m*; *Amer* bisão *m*

buffer /ˈbʌfə(r)/ *n* para-choque *m*

buffet[1] /ˈbʊfeɪ/ *n* (*meal, counter*) bufê *m*, (*P*) bufete *m*

buffet[2] /ˈbʌfɪt/ *vt* (*pt* **buffeted**) esbofetear

bug /bʌg/ *n* (*insect*) bicho *m*; (*bedbug*) percevejo *m*; ⊠ (*germ*) vírus *m*; ⊠ (*device*) microfone *m* de escuta; ⊠ (*defect*) defeito *m* ● *vt* (*pt* **bugged**) grampear; *Amer* ⊠ (*annoy*) chatear ⊠

buggy /ˈbʌgɪ/ *n* (*for baby*) carrinho *m*

bugle /ˈbjuːgl/ *n* clarim *m*

build /bɪld/ *vt/i* (*pt* **built**) construir, edificar ● *n* físico *m*, compleição *f* □ **~ up** *vt/i* criar; (*increase*) aumentar; (*accumulate*) acumular(-se). **~up** *n* acumulação *f*, *fig* publicidade *f*. **~er** *n* construtor *m*, empreiteiro *m*; (*workman*) operário *m*

building /ˈbɪldɪŋ/ *n* edifício *m*, prédio *m*; **~ site** canteiro *m* de obras; **~ society** sociedade *f* de investimentos imobiliários

built /bɪlt/ ▸ BUILD. **~-in** *a* incorporado; **~-in wardrobe** armário *m* embutido na parede; **~-up** *a* urbanizado

bulb /bʌlb/ *n* bolbo *m*; *Electr* lâmpada *f*. **~ous** *a* bolboso

Bulgaria /bʌlˈgeərɪə/ *n* Bulgária *f*

bulge /bʌldʒ/ *n* bojo *m*, saliência *f* ● *vi* inchar; (*jut out*) fazer uma saliência. **~ing** *a* inchado; ‹*pocket etc*› cheio

bulk /bʌlk/ *n* quantidade *f*, volume *m*; **in ~** por grosso; (*loose*) a granel; **the ~ of** a maior parte de. **~y** *a*

volumoso

bull /bʊl/ *n* touro *m*. **~seye** *n* (*of target*) centro *m* do alvo, mosca *f*

bulldog /ˈbʊldɒg/ *n* buldogue *m*

bulldoze /ˈbʊldəʊz/ *vt* terraplanar. **~r** /-ə(r)/ *n* bulldozer *m*

bullet /ˈbʊlɪt/ *n* bala *f*. **~proof** *a* à prova de balas; ‹*vehicle*› blindado

bulletin /ˈbʊlətɪn/ *n* boletim *m*

bullfight /ˈbʊlfaɪt/ *n* tourada *f*, corrida *f* de touros. **~er** *n* toureiro *m*. **~ing** *n* tauromaquia *f*

bullring /ˈbʊlrɪŋ/ *n* arena *f*, (*P*) praça *f* de touros

bully /ˈbʊlɪ/ *n* mandão *m*, pessoa *f* prepotente; *Schol* terror *m*, o mau ● *vt* intimidar; (*treat badly*) atormentar; (*coerce*) forçar (**into** a)

bum[1] /bʌm/ *n* ⊠ (*buttocks*) traseiro *m*; bunda *f* ⊠

bum[2] /bʌm/ *n* *Amer* ⊠ vagabundo *m*

bump /bʌmp/ *n* choque *m*, embate *m*; (*swelling*) inchaço *m*; (*on head*) galo *m* ● *vt/i* bater, chocar; **~ into** bater em, chocar com; (*meet*) esbarrar com, encontrar. **~y** *a* ‹*surface*› irregular; ‹*ride*› aos solavancos

bumper /ˈbʌmpə(r)/ *n* para-choques *m inv* ● *a* excepcional

bun /bʌn/ *n* pãozinho *m* doce com passas; (*hair*) coque *m*

bunch /bʌntʃ/ *n* (*of flowers*) ramo *m*; (*of keys*) molho *m*; (*of people*) grupo *m*; (*of grapes*) cacho *m*

bundle /ˈbʌndl/ *n* molho *m* ● *vt* atar num molho; (*push*) despachar

bung /bʌŋ/ *n* batoque *m*, rolha *f* ● *vt* rolhar; ⊠ (*throw*) atirar; deitar; **~ up** entupir

bungalow /ˈbʌŋgələʊ/ *n* chalé *m*; (*outside Europe*) bungalô *m*, (*P*) bungalow *m*

bungle /ˈbʌŋgl/ vt fazer malfeito, estragar

bunion /ˈbʌnjən/ n Med joanete m

bunk /bʌŋk/ n (in train) couchette f; (in ship) beliche m. **~ beds** npl beliches mpl

bunker /ˈbʌŋkə(r)/ n Mil abrigo m, casamata f, bunker m; Golf obstáculo m em cova de areia

buoy /bɔɪ/ n boia f • vt **~ up** animar

buoyan|t /ˈbɔɪənt/ a flutuante; fig alegre. **~cy** n fig alegria f; exuberância f

burden /ˈbɜːdn/ n fardo m • vt carregar, sobrecarregar

bureau /ˈbjʊərəʊ/ n (pl **-eaux** /-əʊz/) (desk) secretária f; (office) seção f, (P) secção f

bureaucracy /bjʊəˈrɒkrəsɪ/ n burocracia f

bureaucrat /ˈbjʊərəkræt/ n burocrata mf. **~ic** /-ˈkrætɪk/ a burocrático

burger /ˈbɜːgə(r)/ n hambúrguer m

burglar /ˈbɜːglə(r)/ n ladrão m, assaltante mf. **~ alarm** n alarme m contra ladrões. **~ize** vt Amer assaltar. **~y** n assalto m

burgle /ˈbɜːgl/ vt assaltar

burial /ˈberɪəl/ n enterro m

burka, burkha /ˈbɜːkə, ˈbʊrkə/ n burca f

burly /ˈbɜːlɪ/ a (**-ier, -iest**) robusto e corpulento, forte

Burm|a /ˈbɜːmə/ n Birmânia f. **~ese** /-ˈmiːz/ a & n birmanês m

burn /bɜːn/ vt (pt **burned** or **burnt**) queimar • vi queimar(-se), arder • n queimadura f; **~ down** reduzir a cinzas. **~er** n (of stove) bico m de gás

burnt /bɜːnt/ ▶ BURN

burp /bɜːp/ n 🔢 arroto m • vi 🔢 arrotar

burrow /ˈbʌrəʊ/ n toca f • vi cavar, fazer uma toca

burst /bɜːst/ vt/i (pt **burst**) arrebentar; **~ into** ‹flames, room etc› irromper em; **~ into tears** desatar num choro, desfazer-se em lágrimas; **~ out laughing** desatar a rir • n estouro m, rebentar m; (of anger, laughter) explosão f; (of firing) rajada f; (of energy) acesso m

bury /ˈberɪ/ vt sepultar, enterrar; (hide) esconder; (engross, thrust) mergulhar

bus /bʌs/ n (pl **buses**) ônibus m, (P) autocarro m; **~ lane** faixa f de ônibus, (P) de autocarro. **~ stop** n paragem f

bush /bʊʃ/ n arbusto m; (land) mato m. **~y** a espesso

business /ˈbɪznɪs/ n (trade, shop, affair) negócio m; (task) função f; (occupation) ocupação f; **have no ~ to** não ter o direito de; **it's no of yours** não é da sua conta; **mind your own ~** cuide da sua vida; **that's my ~** isso é meu problema. **~like** a eficiente, sistemático. **~man** n homem m de negócios, comerciante m

busker /ˈbʌskə(r)/ n músico m ambulante

bust[1] /bʌst/ n busto m

bust[2] /bʌst/ vt/i (pt **busted** or **bust**) 🔢 BURST, ▶ BREAK • a falido; **go ~** falir. **~-up** n 🔢 discussão f, (P) bulha f

bustl|e /ˈbʌsl/ vi andar numa azáfama; (hurry) apressar-se • n azáfama f. **~ing** a animado, movimentado

bus|y /ˈbɪzɪ/ a (**-ier, -iest**) ocupado; ‹street› movimentado; ‹day› atarefado ● vt **~y o.s. with** ocupar-se com. **~ily** adv ativamente, atarefadamente

busybody /'bɪzɪbɒdɪ/ n intrometido m, pessoa f abelhuda

but /bʌt/ conj mas ● prep exceto, (P) excepto, senão ● adv apenas, só; **all ~** todos menos; (nearly) quase, por pouco não; **~ for** sem, se não fosse; **last ~ one/two** penúltimo/ antepenúltimo; **nobody ~** ninguém a não ser

butcher /'bʊtʃə(r)/ n açougueiro m, (P) homem m do talho; fig carrasco m; **the ~'s** açougue m, (P) talho m ● vt chacinar

butler /'bʌtlə(r)/ n mordomo m

butt /bʌt/ n (of gun) coronha f; (of cigarette) ponta f; (target) alvo m de troça, de ridículo etc; (cask) barril m ● vt/i dar cabeçada em; **~ in** interromper

butter /'bʌtə(r)/ n manteiga f ● vt pôr manteiga em

buttercup /'bʌtəkʌp/ n botão-de-ouro m

butterfly /'bʌtəflaɪ/ n borboleta f

buttock /'bʌtək/ n nádega f

button /'bʌtn/ n botão m ● vt/i abotoar(-se)

buttonhole /'bʌtnhəʊl/ n casa f de botão; (in lapel) botoeira f ● vt fig obrigar a ouvir

buttress /'bʌtrɪs/ n contraforte m; fig esteio m ● vt sustentar

buy /baɪ/ vt (pt **bought**) comprar (**from** a); ✗ (believe) engolir 🔢 n compra f. **~er** n comprador m

buzz /bʌz/ n zumbido m ● vi zumbir; **~ off** pôr-se a andar. **~er** n campainha f

by /baɪ/ prep (near) junto de, perto de; (along, past, means) por;

(according to) conforme; (before) antes de; **~ accident/mistake** sem querer; **~ bike/car** etc de bicicleta/ carro etc; **~ day/night** de dia/noite; **~ the kilo** por quilo; **~ land/sea/ air** por terra/mar/ar; **~ now** a esta hora; **~ oneself** sozinho ● adv (near) perto; **~ and ~** muito em breve; **~ and large** no conjunto. **~-election** n eleição f suplementar; **~-product** n derivado m

bye(-bye) /'baɪ(baɪ)/ int 🔢 adeus; adeusinho

bypass /'baɪpɑːs/ n (estrada) secundária f, desvio m; Med by-pass m, ponte f de safena ● vt fazer um desvio; fig contornar

bystander /'baɪstændə(r)/ n circunstante mf, espectador m

byte /baɪt/ n byte m

Cc

cab /kæb/ n táxi m; (of lorry, train) cabina f, cabine f

cabaret /'kæbareɪ/ n variedades fpl, cabaré m

cabbage /'kæbɪdʒ/ n couve f, repolho m

cabin /'kæbɪn/ n cabana f; (in plane) cabina f; (in ship) camarote m

cabinet /'kæbɪnɪt/ n armário m; **C~** Pol gabinete m

cable /'keɪbl/ n cabo m ● n funicular m, teleférico m; **~ railway** funicular m; **~ television** televisão f a cabo. **~ channel** n canal de tevê a cabo f, (P) canal de televisão por cabo m

cache | campsite

cache /kæʃ/ n (esconderijo m de) tesouro m, armas fpl, provisões fpl

cackle /'kækl/ n cacarejo m ● vi cacarejar

cactus /'kæktəs/ n (pl es or cacti /-taɪ/) cacto m

caddie /'kædɪ/ n Golf caddie m

caddy /'kædɪ/ n lata f para o chá

cadet /kə'det/ n cadete m

cadge /kædʒ/ vt/i filar, (P) cravar

Caesarean /sɪ'zeərɪən/ a ~ (section) cesariana f

cafe /'kæfeɪ/ n café m

cafeteria /kæfɪ'tɪərɪə/ n cafeteria f, restaurante m self-service

cafetière /kæfə'tjeə(r)/ n cafeteira de pistão f

caffeine /'kæfiːn/ n cafeína f

cage /keɪdʒ/ n gaiola f

cagey /'keɪdʒɪ/ a (secretive) misterioso; reservado

cake /keɪk/ n bolo m; **a piece of ~** 🔲 canja f 🔲. ● a empastado; **his shoes were ~d with mud** tinha os sapatos cobertos de lama

calamity /kə'læmətɪ/ n calamidade f

calcium /'kælsɪəm/ n cálcio m

calculat|e /'kælkjʊleɪt/ vt/i calcular; Amer (suppose) supor. **~ed** a ‹action› deliberado, calculado. **~ing** a calculista. **~ion** /-'leɪʃn/ n cálculo m. **~or** n calculador m, (P) máquina f de calcular

calendar /'kælɪndə(r)/ n calendário m

calf[1] /kɑːf/ n (pl calves) (young cow or bull) vitelo m, bezerro m; (of other animals) cria f

calf[2] /kɑːf/ n (pl calves) (of leg) barriga f da perna

calibre /'kælɪbə(r)/ n calibre m

call /kɔːl/ vt/i chamar; (summon) convocar; (phone) telefonar; **~ (in or round)** (visit) passar por casa de; **be ~ed** (named) chamar-se; **~ back** (phone) tornar a telefonar; (visit) voltar; **~ for** (demand) pedir, requerer; (fetch) ir buscar; **~ off** cancelar; **~ on** (visit) visitar; (phone) telefonar a; **~ out (to)** chamar; **~ up** Mil mobilizar, recrutar; (phone) telefonar ● n chamada f; (bird's cry) canto m; (shout) brado m, grito m; **be on ~** estar de serviço. **~ centre** n central f telefónica, (P) telefónica. **~er** n visitante f, visita f; (phone) chamador m, (P) pessoa f que faz a chamada. **~ing** n vocação f

callous /'kæləs/ a insensível

calm /kɑːm/ a (-er, -est) calmo ● n calma f ● vt/i **~ (down)** acalmar(-se). **~ness** n calma f

calorie /'kælərɪ/ n caloria f

camcorder /'kæmkɔːdə(r)/ n câmera f or (P) câmara f de filmar

came /keɪm/ ▶ COME

camel /'kæml/ n camelo m

camera /'kæmərə/ n máquina f fotográfica; Cine, TV câmera f, (P) câmara. **~man** a (pl -men) operador m; **~phone** n celular com câmera m, (P) telemóvel com câmara m

camouflage /'kæməflɑːʒ/ n camuflagem f ● vt camuflar

camp[1] /kæmp/ n acampamento m ● vi acampar. **~ bed** n cama f de campanha. **~er** n campista mf; (car) autocaravana f. **~ing** n campismo m

camp[2] /kæmp/ a afetado, efeminado

campaign /kæm'peɪn/ n campanha f ● vi fazer campanha

campsite /'kæmpsaɪt/ n área f de camping, (P) parque m de campismo

campus /'kæmpəs/ n (pl -puses /-pəsɪz/) campus m, (P) cidade f universitária

can¹ /kæn/ n vasilha f de lata; (for food) lata f (de conserva) ● vt (pt **canned**) enlatar; **~ned music** música f em fita para locais públicos. **~ opener** n abridor m de latas, (P) abrelatas m

can² /kæn unstressed kən /(pres can, pt **could**) ● vaux

‥‥➤ (be able to) poder, conseguir; **I ~'t do it** não consigo fazer isso; **I could if I had time** poderia se tivesse tempo; **she ~ help you** ela pode ajudá-lo

‥‥➤ (know how to) saber; **I ~ speak English** sei falar inglês; **he ~ drive** ele sabe dirigir

‥‥➤ (be allowed to) poder, ser permitido; **you ~'t park here** não é permitido estacionar aqui; **nobody ~ take pictures** ninguém pode tirar fotografias

‥‥➤ (in requests) poder; **I ~ have a glass of water, please?** podia me dar um copo de água, por favor?; **could you ring me tomorrow?** podia me telefonar amanhã?

‥‥➤ (with verbs of perception); **I ~ hear you** eu consigo ouvir você; **~ they see us?** eles conseguem nos ver?

‥‥➤ could (possibility); **we could have won** podíamos ter ganhado; **I could phone her now, if you want** poderia telefonar para ela agora, se você quiser

Canad|a /'kænədə/ n Canadá m. **~ian** /kə'neɪdɪən/ a & n canadense

mf, (P) canadiano m

canal /kə'næl/ n canal m

canary /kə'neərɪ/ n canário m. **C~ Islands** npl as (Ilhas) Canárias

cancel /'kænsl/ vt (pt **cancelled**) cancelar; (cross out) riscar; ‹stamps› inutilizar □ **~ out** vi/t fig neutralizar-se mutuamente. **~lation** /-'leɪʃn/ n cancelamento m

cancer /'kænsə(r)/ n câncer m, cancro m; **C~** Astrol Caranguejo m, Câncer m. **~ous** a canceroso

candid /'kændɪd/ a franco

candida|te /'kændɪdeɪt/ n candidato m

candle /'kændl/ n vela f; (in church) vela f, círio m

candlestick /'kændlstɪk/ n castiçal m

candy /'kændɪ/ n bala f, (P) açúcar cândi; Amer (sweet, sweets) doce(s) m. **~ floss** n algodão-doce m

cane /keɪn/ n cana f; (walking stick) bengala f; (for baskets) verga f; Schol (for punishment) vergasta f ● vt vergastar

canine /'keɪnaɪn/ a & n canino m

cannabis /'kænəbɪs/ n cânhamo m, maconha f

cannibal /'kænɪbl/ n canibal mf. **~ism** /-zəm/ n canibalismo m

cannon /'kænən/ n inv canhão m

cannot /'kænət/ (= can not) ▶ CAN²

canny /'kænɪ/ a (-ier, -iest) astuto, manhoso

canoe /kə'nuː/ n canoa f ● vi andar de canoa

canon /'kænən/ n cônego m, (P) cónego m; (rule) cânone m

can't /kɑːnt/ (= can not) ▶ CAN²

canteen /kæn'tiːn/ n cantina f;
(*flask*) cantil m; (*for cutlery*) estojo m

canter /'kæntə(r)/ n meio galope m,
cânter m ● vi andar a meio galope

canvas /'kænvəs/ n lona f; (*for
painting or tapestry*) tela f

canvass /'kænvəs/ vt/i angariar
votos or fregueses

canyon /'kænjən/ n canhão m, (P)
desfiladeiro m

cap /kæp/ n (*with peak*) boné m;
(*without peak*) barrete m; (*of nurse*)
touca f; (*of bottle, pen, tube, etc*)
tampa f; Mech tampa f, tampão m
● vt (*pt* **capped**) <*bottle, pen, tube,
etc*> tapar, tampar; (*rates*) impôr
um limite a; (*outdo*) suplantar; Sport
seleccionar, (P) seleccionar; **~ped
with** encimado de, coroado de

capab|le /'keɪpəbl/ a <*person*>
capaz (**of** de); <*things, situations*>
susceptível (**of** de). **~ility** /-'bɪlətɪ/ n
capacidade f

capacity /kə'pæsətɪ/ n capacidade
f; **in one's ~ as** na (sua) qualidade
de

cape¹ /keɪp/ n (*cloak*) capa f

cape² /keɪp/ n Geog cabo m

caper¹ /'keɪpə(r)/ vi andar aos
pinotes

caper² /'keɪpə(r)/ n Culin alcaparra f

capital /'kæpɪtl/ a capital; **~
(letter)** maiúscula f ● n (*town*)
capital f; (*money*) capital m; **~
punishment** pena f de morte

capitalis|t /'kæpɪtəlɪst/ a &
n capitalista mf. **~m** /-zəm/ n
capitalismo m

Capitol O Capitólio, como
é conhecida a sede do
Congresso (*Congress*) dos
Estados Unidos, é situado em
Washington DC. Como está
situado em *Capitol Hill*, a imprensa
utiliza com frequência este termo
para se referir ao Congresso dos
Estados Unidos.

Capricorn /'kæprɪkɔːn/ n Astrol
Capricórnio m

capsicum /'kæpsɪkəm/ n
pimento m

capsize /kæp'saɪz/ vt/i virar(-se)

capsule /'kæpsjuːl/ n cápsula f

captain /'kæptɪn/ n capitão m;
Navy capitão-de-mar-e-guerra m ● vt
capitanear, comandar

caption /'kæpʃn/ n legenda f;
(*heading*) título m

captivate /'kæptɪveɪt/ vt cativar

captiv|e /'kæptɪv/ a & n cativo
m, prisioneiro m. **~ity** /-'tɪvətɪ/ n
cativeiro m

captor /'kæptə(r)/ n captor m

capture /'kæptʃə(r)/ vt capturar;
<*attention*> prender ● n captura f

car /kɑː(r)/ n carro m; **~ ferry** barca
f para carros; **~ phone** telefone
m de carro. **~ park** (parque m de
estacionamento m; **~ wash** n
estação f de lavagem

carafe /kə'ræf/ n garrafa f para água
ou vinho

caramel /'kærəmel/ n caramelo m

carat /'kærət/ n quilate f

caravan /'kærəvæn/ n caravana f,
reboque m

carbohydrate /kɑːbəʊ'haɪdreɪt/
n hidrato m de carbono

carbon /'kɑːbən/ n carbono m;
~ copy cópia f em papel carbono,
(P) químico; **~ monoxide** óxido
m de carbono; **~ paper** papel m
carbono, (P) químico. **~ footprint**
n pegada f de carbono, (P)

pegada f ecológica ; ~ **neutral** a
carbono m neutro ; ~ **offsetting** n
compensação f de carbono

carburettor /ˌkɑːbjʊˈretə(r)/ n
carburador m

carcass /ˈkɑːkəs/ n carcaça f

card /kɑːd/ n cartão m; (postcard)
postal m; (playing card) carta f. ~
game(s) n(pl) jogo(s) m(pl) de cartas;
~ **index** n fichário m, (P) ficheiro m

cardboard /ˈkɑːdbɔːd/ n cartão
m, papelão m

cardigan /ˈkɑːdɪɡən/ n casaco
m de lã

cardinal /ˈkɑːdɪnl/ a cardeal,
principal; ~ **number** numeral m
cardinal n Relig cardeal m

care /keə(r)/ n cuidado m; (concern)
interesse m ● vi ~ **about** (be
interested) estar interessado por;
(be worried) estar preocupado com;
~ **for** (like) gostar de; (look after)
tomar conta de; **take** ~ tomar
cuidado; **take** ~ **of** cuidar de; (deal
with) tratar de; **he couldn't** ~ **less**
ele está pouco ligando, ele não dá
a menor 🗓

career /kəˈrɪə(r)/ n carreira f ● vi ir a
toda a velocidade, ir numa carreira

carefree /ˈkeəfriː/ a
despreocupado

careful /ˈkeəfl/ a cuidadoso;
(cautious) cauteloso; ~**!** cuidado!

careless /ˈkeəlɪs/ a descuidado
(about com). ~**ness** n descuido m,
negligência f

caress /kəˈres/ n carícia f ● vt
acariciar

caretaker /ˈkeəteɪkə(r)/ n zelador
m duma casa vazia; (janitor) zelador
m, (P) porteiro m

cargo /ˈkɑːɡəʊ/ n (pl -**oes**)
carregamento m, carga f

Caribbean /ˌkærɪˈbiːən/ a caraíba;
the ~ **as** Caraíbas fpl

caricature /ˈkærɪkətʃʊə(r)/ n
caricatura f ● vt caricaturar

caring /ˈkeərɪŋ/ a carinhoso,
afetuoso

carnage /ˈkɑːnɪdʒ/ n carnificina f

carnation /kɑːˈneɪʃn/ n cravo m

carnival /ˈkɑːnɪvl/ n carnaval m

carol /ˈkærəl/ n cântico or canto m
de Natal m

carp[1] /kɑːp/ n inv carpa f

carp[2] /kɑːp/ vi ~ **(at)** criticar

carpent|er /ˈkɑːpɪntə(r)/ n
carpinteiro m. ~**ry** n carpintaria f

carpet /ˈkɑːpɪt/ n tapete m; **with
fitted** ~ (estar) atapetado; **be on
the** ~ 🗓 ser chamado à ordem ● vt
(pt **carpeted**) atapetar

carriage /ˈkærɪdʒ/ n carruagem
f; (of goods) frete m, transporte m;
(cost, bearing) porte m

carrier /ˈkærɪə(r)/ n transportador
m; (company) transportadora f;
Med portador m; ~ **(bag)** saco m
de plástico

carrot /ˈkærət/ n cenoura f

carry /ˈkæri/ vt/i levar; ⟨goods⟩
transportar; (involve) acarretar;
(have for sale) ter à venda; **be
carried away** entusiasmar-se,
deixar-se levar; ~ **off** levar à força;
⟨prize⟩ incluir; ~ **it off** sair-se bem
(de); ~ **on** continuar; 🗓 (flirt)
flertar; 🗓 (behave) portar-se (mal);
~ **out** executar; ⟨duty⟩ cumprir;
~ **through** levar a cabo

cart /kɑːt/ n carroça f; carro m ● vt
acarretar; 🗓 carregar com

carton /ˈkɑːtn/ n embalagem f de
cartão or de plástico; (of yogurt)
embalagem f, pote m; (of milk)
pacote m

cartoon /kɑːˈtuːn/ n desenho m humorístico, caricatura f; (strip) estória f em quadrinhos, (P) banda f desenhada; (film) desenhos mpl animados. **~ist** n caricaturista mf; (of strip, film) desenhador f

cartridge /ˈkɑːtrɪdʒ/ n cartucho m

carv|e /kɑːv/ vt esculpir, talhar; ‹meat› trinchar; **~ing knife** faca f de trinchar, trinchante m. **~ing** n obra f de talha; (on tree trunk) incisão f

case¹ /keɪs/ n caso m; Jur causa f, processo m; Phil argumentos mpl; **in any ~** em todo caso; **in ~ (of)** no caso (de); **in that ~** nesse caso

case² /keɪs/ n caixa f; (crate) caixa f, caixote m; (for camera, jewels, spectacles, etc) estojo m; (suitcase) mala f; (for cigarettes) cigarreira f

cash /kæʃ/ n dinheiro m, numerário m, cash m; **be short of ~** ter pouco dinheiro; **in ~** em dinheiro; **pay ~** pagar em dinheiro; **~ desk** caixa f; **~ dispenser** caixa f electrónica, (P) multibanco m; **~ register** caixa f registadora, (P) registadora f ● vt (obtain money for) cobrar, receber; (give money for) pagar; **~ a cheque** (receive/give) cobrar/ descontar um cheque; **~ in** receber; **~ in (on)** aproveitar-se de. **~ flow** n cash-flow m

cashback /ˈkæʃbæk/ n cashback m possibilidade que o cliente tem de pagar acima do valor da compra com cartão de crédito e receber 'troco'

cashew /ˈkæʃuː/ n caju m

cashier /kæˈʃɪə(r)/ n caixa mf

cashmere /kæʃˈmɪə(r)/ n caxemira f

casino /kəˈsiːnəʊ/ n (pl -os) casino m

casserole /ˈkæsərəʊl/ n caçarola f; (stew) estufado m

cassette /kəˈset/ n cassette f; **~ player** gravador m. **~ recorder** n gravador m

cast /kɑːst/ vt (pt cast) lançar, arremessar; (shed) despojar-se de; (vote) dar; ‹metal› fundir; ‹shadow› projetar ● n Theatr elenco m; (mould) molde m; Med aparelho m de gesso. **~-iron** n de ferro fundido; fig muito forte; **~-offs** npl roupa f velha

castanets /kæstəˈnets/ npl castanholas fpl

castaway /ˈkɑːstəweɪ/ n náufrago m

caste /kɑːst/ n casta f

castigate /ˈkæstɪgeɪt/ vt castigar

castle /ˈkɑːsl/ n castelo m; Chess torre f

castor /ˈkɑːstə(r)/ n roda f de pé de móvel; **~ sugar** açúcar m em pó

casual /ˈkæʒʊəl/ a (chance) ‹meeting› casual; (careless, unmethodical) descuidado; (informal) informal; **~ clothes** roupa f prática or de lazer; **~ work** trabalho m ocasional

casualty /ˈkæʒʊəltɪ/ n (dead) morto m; (death) morte f; (injured) ferido m; (victim) vítima f; Mil baixa f

cat /kæt/ n gato m. **~seyes®** npl reflectores mpl

catalogue /ˈkætəlɒg/ n catálogo m ● vt catalogar

Catalonia /kætəˈləʊnɪə/ n Catalunha f

catalyst /ˈkætəlɪst/ n catalisador m

catapult /ˈkætəpʌlt/ n (child's) atiradeira f, (P) fisga f ● vt catapultar

cataract /ˈkætərækt/ f (waterfall & Med) catarata f

catarrh /kəˈtɑː(r)/ n catarro m

catastroph|e /kə'tæstrəfi/ n catástrofe f. **~ic** /kætə'strɒfik/ a catastrófico

catch /kætʃ/ vt (pt caught) apanhar; (grasp) agarrar; (hear) perceber; **~ sb's eye** atrair a atenção de alguém; **~ sight of** avistar ● vi prender-se (in em); (get stuck) ficar preso; **~ fire** pegar fogo, (P) incendiar-se; **~ on** 🄴 pegar, tornar-se popular; **~ up (with)** pôr-se a par (com); «work» pôr em dia ● n apanha f; (of fish) pesca f; (trick) ratoeira f; (snag) problema m; (on door) trinco m; (fastener) fecho m. **~phrase** n clichê m

catching /'kætʃɪŋ/ a contagioso, infeccioso

catchy /'kætʃɪ/ a que pega fácil

categorical /kætɪ'gɒrɪkl/ a categórico

category /'kætɪgəri/ n categoria f

cater /'keɪtə(r)/ vi fornecer comida (para clubes, casamentos, etc); **~ for** (pander to) satisfazer; «consumers» dirigir-se a. **~er** n fornecedor m. **~ing** n catering m

caterpillar /'kætəpɪlə(r)/ n lagarta f

cathedral /kə'θiːdrəl/ n catedral f

catholic /'kæθəlɪk/ a universal; (eclectic) eclético. **C~** a & n católico m. **~ism** /kə'θɒlɪsɪzəm/ n catolicismo m

cattle /'kætl/ npl gado m

catty /'kæti/ a (dissimuladamente) maldoso, com perfídia

caught /kɔːt/ ▸ CATCH

cauliflower /'kɒlɪflaʊə(r)/ n couve-flor f

cause /kɔːz/ n causa f ● vt causar; **~ sth to grow/move** etc fazer algo crescer/mexer etc

cauti|on /'kɔːʃn/ n cautela f; (warning) aviso m ● vt avisar. **~ous** /'kɔːʃəs/ a cauteloso

cavalry /'kævəlrɪ/ n cavalaria f

cave /keɪv/ n caverna f, gruta f ● vi **~ in** desabar, dar de si

caveman /'keɪvmæn/ n (pl -men) troglodita m, homem m das cavernas; fig (tipo) primário m

cavern /'kævən/ n caverna f

caviare /'kævɪɑː(r)/ n caviar m

cavity /'kævətɪ/ n cavidade f

cc abbr (= carbon copy) cópia f com papel carbono, (P) cópia f carbono

CD /siː'diː/ ▸ COMPACT DISC

cease /siːs/ vt/i cessar. **~fire** n cessar-fogo m. **~less** a incessante

cedar /'siːdə(r)/ n cedro m

cedilla /sɪ'dɪlə/ n cedilha f

ceiling /'siːlɪŋ/ n lit & fig teto m

celebrat|e /'selɪbreɪt/ vt/i celebrar, festejar. **~ion** /-'breɪʃn/ n celebração f, festejo m

celebrated /'selɪbreɪtɪd/ a célebre

celebrity /sɪ'lebrətɪ/ n celebridade f

celery /'seləri/ n aipo m

celiba|te /'selɪbət/ a celibatário. **~cy** n celibato m

cell /sel/ n (of prison, convent) cela f; Biol, Pol, Electr célula f; **~ phone** celular m, (P) telemóvel

cellar /'selə(r)/ n porão m, cave f; (for wine) adega f, cave f

cell|o /'tʃeləʊ/ n (pl -os) violoncelo m. **~ist** n violoncelista mf

cellphone /'selfəʊn/ n celular m, (P) telemóvel m

cellular /'seljʊlə(r)/ a celular

Celt /kelt/ n celta mf. **~ic** a celta, céltico

cement /sɪ'ment/ n cimento m ● vt cimentar

cemetery /'semətrɪ/ n cemitério m

censor /'sensə(r)/ n censor m ● vt censurar. **~ship** n censura f

censure /'senʃə(r)/ n censura f, crítica f ● vt censurar, criticar

census /'sensəs/ n recenseamento m, censo m

cent /sent/ n cêntimo m

centenary /sen'ti:nərɪ/ n centenário m

centigrade /'sentɪɡreɪd/ a centígrado

centimetre /'sentɪmi:tə(r)/ n centímetro m

central /'sentrəl/ a central; **~ heating** aquecimento m central. **~ize** vt centralizar

centre /'sentə(r)/ n centro m ● vt (pt centred) centrar ● vi **~ on** concentrar-se em, fixar-se em

century /'sentʃərɪ/ n século m

ceramic /sɪ'ræmɪk/ a ⟨object⟩ em cerâmica. **~s** n cerâmica f

cereal /'sɪərɪəl/ n cereal m

ceremonial /serɪ'məʊnɪəl/ a de cerimónia ● n cerimonial m

ceremon|y /'serɪmənɪ/ n cerimónia f, (P) cerimónia f. **~ious** /-'məʊnɪəs/ a cerimonioso

certain /'sɜːtn/ a certo; **be ~** ter a certeza; **for ~** com certeza, ao certo; **make ~** confirmar, verificar. **~ly** adv com certeza, certamente. **~ty** n certeza f

certificate /sə'tɪfɪkət/ n certificado m; ⟨birth, marriage⟩ certidão f; ⟨health⟩ atestado m

certif|y /'sɜːtɪfaɪ/ vt/i certificar

chafe /tʃeɪf/ vt/i esfregar; ⟨make/ become sore⟩ esfolar/ficar esfolado;

fig irritar(-se)

chaffinch /'tʃæfɪntʃ/ n tentilhão m

chain /tʃeɪn/ n corrente f, cadeia f; ⟨series⟩ cadeia f; **~ store** loja f pertencente a uma cadeia ● vt acorrentar; **~ reaction** reação f em cadeia. **~-smoke** vi fumar cigarros um atrás do outro

chair /tʃeə(r)/ n cadeira f; ⟨position of chairman⟩ presidência f; Univ cátedra f ● vt presidir

chairman /'tʃeəmən/ n (pl -men) presidente mf

chalet /'ʃæleɪ/ n chalé m

chalk /tʃɔːk/ n greda f, cal f; ⟨for writing⟩ giz m ● vt traçar com giz

challeng|e /'tʃælɪndʒ/ n desafio m; ⟨by sentry⟩ interpelação f ● vt desafiar; ⟨question the truth of⟩ contestar. **~er** n Sport pretendente (ao título) mf. **~ing** a estimulante, que constitui um desafio

chamber /'tʃeɪmbə(r)/ n old use aposento m; **~ music** música f de câmara; **C~ of Commerce** Câmara f de Comércio. **~maid** n arrumadeira f, (P) criada f

chamois /'ʃæmɪ/ n **~(-leather)** camurça f

champagne /ʃæm'peɪn/ n champanhe m

champion /'tʃæmpɪən/ n campeão m, campeã f ● vt defender. **~ship** n campeonato m

chance /tʃɑːns/ n acaso m; ⟨luck⟩ sorte f; ⟨opportunity⟩ oportunidade f, chance f; ⟨likelihood⟩ hipótese f, probabilidade f; ⟨risk⟩ risco m ● a casual, fortuito ● vi calhar ● vt arriscar; **by ~** por acaso

chancellor /'tʃɑːnsələ(r)/ n chanceler m; **C~ of the Exchequer** Ministro m das Finanças

chancy /'tʃɑːnsɪ/ a arriscado

chandelier /ʃændə'lɪə(r)/ n lustre m

change /tʃeɪndʒ/ vt mudar; (exchange) trocar ‹clothes, house, trains, etc› mudar de; ~ hands (ownership) mudar de dono; ~ one's mind mudar de ideia(s) ● vi mudar; (~ clothes) mudar-se, mudar de roupa; ~ into ‹a butterfly etc› transformar-se em; ‹evening dress etc› pôr; ~ over passar, mudar (to para) ● n mudança f; (money) troco m; a ~ of clothes uma muda de roupa. ~able a variável

channel /'tʃænl/ n canal m ● vt (pt **channelled**) canalizar; **the C~ Islands** as Ilhas do Canal da Mancha; **the (English) C~** o Canal da Mancha

chant /tʃɑːnt/ n cântico m ● vt/i cantar, entoar

chao|s /'keɪɒs/ n caos m. ~tic /-'ɒtɪk/ a caótico

chap /tʃæp/ n 🔲 sujeito m; cara m 🔲, (P) tipo m

chapel /'tʃæpl/ n capela f

chaplain /'tʃæplɪn/ n capelão m

chapter /'tʃæptə(r)/ n capítulo m

character /'kærəktə(r)/ n caráter m, (P) carácter m; (in novel, play) personagem m; (reputation) fama f; (eccentric person) excêntrico m; (letter) caractere m, (P) carácter m. ~ize vt caracterizar

characteristic /kærəktə'rɪstɪk/ a característico ● n característica f

charade /ʃə'rɑːd/ n charada f

charcoal /'tʃɑːkəʊl/ n carvão m de lenha

charge /tʃɑːdʒ/ n preço m; Electr, Mil carga f; Jur acusação f; (task, custody) cargo m ● vt/i ‹price› cobrar; ‹enemy› atacar; Jur

incriminar; **be in ~ of** ter a cargo; **take ~ of** encarregar-se de

chariot /'tʃærɪət/ n carro m de guerra or triunfal

charisma /kə'rɪzmə/ n carisma m. ~tic /kærɪz'mætɪk/ a carismático

charit|y /'tʃærətɪ/ n caridade f; (society) instituição f de caridade. ~able a caridoso

charm /tʃɑːm/ n encanto m, charme m; (spell) feitiço m; (talisman) amuleto m ● vt encantar. ~ing a encantador

chart /tʃɑːt/ n Naut carta f; (table) mapa m, gráfico m, tabela f ● vt fazer o mapa de

charter /'tʃɑːtə(r)/ n carta f; ~ (flight) (voo) charter m ● vt fretar

chase /tʃeɪs/ vt perseguir ● vi 🔲 correr (after atrás de) ● n caça f, perseguição f; ~ away or off afugentar, expulsar

chasm /'kæzm/ n abismo m

chassis /'ʃæsɪ/ n chassi m

chaste /tʃeɪst/ a casto

chastise /tʃæs'taɪz/ vt castigar

chastity /'tʃæstɪtɪ/ n castidade f

chat /tʃæt/ n conversa f; **have a ~** bater um papo, (P) dar dois dedos de conversa ● vi (pt **chatted**) conversar, cavaquear. ~room n sala f de chat. ~ty a conversador

chatter /'tʃætə(r)/ vi tagarelar; **his teeth are ~ing** seus dentes estão tiritando ● n tagarelice f

chauffeur /'ʃəʊfə(r)/ n motorista m, chofer (particular) m, chauffeur m

chauvinis|t /'ʃəʊvɪnɪst/ n chauvinista mf; **male ~t** pej machista m. ~m /-zəm/ n chauvinismo m

cheap /tʃiːp/ a (-er, -est) barato; ‹fare, rate› reduzido

cheapen /'tʃiːpən/ vt depreciar

cheat /tʃiːt/ vt enganar, trapacear ● vi (at games) roubar, (P) fazer batota; (in exams) copiar ● n intrujão m; (at games) trapaceiro m, (P) batoteiro m

check¹ /tʃek/ vt/i (examine) verificar; ‹tickets› revisar; (restrain) controlar, refrear; ~ **in** assinar o registro or (P) registo; (at airport) fazer o check-in; ~ **out** pagar a conta ● n verificação f; ‹tickets› controle m; (curb) freio m; Chess xeque m; Amer (bill) conta f; Amer (cheque) cheque m. ~ **in** n check-in m; ~**out** n caixa f; ~**up** n exame m médico, check-up m

check² /tʃek/ n (pattern) xadrez m. ~**ed** a de xadrez

cheek /tʃiːk/ n face f; fig descaramento m. ~**y** a descarado

cheer /tʃɪə(r)/ n alegria f; (shout) viva m ● vt/i aclamar, aplaudir; ~**s!** à sua!, (P) vossa (saúde)!; (thank you) obrigado; ~ **(up)** animar(-se). ~**ful** a bem disposto; alegre

cheerio /tʃɪərɪˈəʊ/ int 🄳 até logo, (P) adeusinho 🄳

cheese /tʃiːz/ n queijo m

cheetah /ˈtʃiːtə/ n chita f, lobo-tigre m

chef /ʃef/ n cozinheiro-chefe m

chemical /ˈkemɪkl/ a químico ● n produto m químico

chemist /ˈkemɪst/ n farmacêutico m; (scientist) químico m. ~**'s (shop)** n farmácia f. ~**ry** n química f

cheque /tʃek/ n cheque m. ~**book** n talão m de cheques, (P) livro m de cheques; ~ **card** n cartão m de banco

cherish /ˈtʃerɪʃ/ vt estimar, querer; ‹hope› acalentar

cherry /ˈtʃerɪ/ n cereja f

chess /tʃes/ n jogo m de xadrez. ~**board** n tabuleiro m de xadrez

chest /tʃest/ n peito m; (for money, jewels) cofre m; ~ **of drawers** cômoda f, (P) cómoda f

chestnut /ˈtʃesnʌt/ n castanha f

chew /tʃuː/ vt mastigar. ~**ing gum** n chiclete m, (P) pastilha f elástica

chic /ʃiːk/ a chique

chick /tʃɪk/ n pinto m

chicken /ˈtʃɪkɪn/ n galinha f ● vi ~ **out** 🅇 acovardar-se. ~**pox** n catapora f, (P) varicela f

chief /tʃiːf/ n chefe m ● a principal. ~**ly** adv principalmente

child /tʃaɪld/ n (pl **children** /ˈtʃɪldrən/) criança f; (son) filho m; (daughter) filha f. ~**hood** n infância f, meninice f. ~**ish** a infantil; (immature) acriançado, pueril. ~**less** a sem filhos. ~**like** a infantil. ~**minder** n babá f que cuida de crianças em sua própria casa, (P) ama

childbirth /ˈtʃaɪldbɜːθ/ n parto m

Chile /ˈtʃɪlɪ/ n Chile m. ~**an** a & n chileno m

chill /tʃɪl/ n frio m; Med resfriado m, (P) constipação f ● vt/i arrefecer; Culin refrigerar. ~**y** a frio; **be** or **feel** ~**y** ter frio

chilli /ˈtʃɪlɪ/ n (pl -**ies**) malagueta f

chime /tʃaɪm/ n carrilhão m; (sound) música f de carrilhão ● vt/i tocar

chimney /ˈtʃɪmnɪ/ n (pl -**eys**) chaminé f

chimpanzee /tʃɪmpænˈziː/ n chimpanzé m

chin /tʃɪn/ n queixo m

china /ˈtʃaɪnə/ n porcelana f; (crockery) louça f

Chin|a /ˈtʃaɪnə/ n China f. **~ese** /-ˈniːz/ a & n chinês m

chink¹ /tʃɪŋk/ n (*crack*) fenda f, fresta f

chink² /tʃɪŋk/ n tinir m ● vt/i (*fazer*) tinir

chip /tʃɪp/ n (*broken piece*) bocado m; Culin batata f frita em palitos; (*gambling*) ficha f; (*electronic*) chip m, circuito m integrado ● vt/i (*pt* chipped) lascar(-se)

chiropodist /kɪˈrɒpədɪst/ n calista mf

chirp /tʃɜːp/ n pipilar m; (*of cricket*) cricri m ● vi pipilar; <cricket> cantar, fazer cricri

chivalr|y /ˈʃɪvlrɪ/ n cavalheirismo m. **~ous** a cavalheiresco

chive /tʃaɪv/ n cebolinho m

chlorine /ˈklɔːriːn/ n cloro m

chocolate /ˈtʃɒklɪt/ n chocolate m

choice /tʃɔɪs/ n escolha f ● a escolhido, seleto, (P) selecionado

choir /ˈkwaɪə(r)/ n coro m

choirboy /ˈkwaɪəbɔɪ/ n menino m de coro, corista m, (P) coralista m

choke /tʃəʊk/ vt/i sufocar; (*on food*) engasgar(-se) ● n Auto afogador m, (P) botão m do ar ⊞

cholesterol /kəˈlestərɒl/ n colesterol m

choose /tʃuːz/ vt/i (*pt* chose, *pp* chosen) escolher; (*prefer*) preferir; **~ to do** decidir fazer

choosy /ˈtʃuːzɪ/ a ⊞ exigente; difícil de contentar

chop /tʃɒp/ vt/i (*pt* chopped) cortar ● n <wood> machadada f; Culin costeleta f. **~ down** abater. **~per** n cutelo m; ⊠ (*helicopter*) helicóptero m

choppy /ˈtʃɒpɪ/ a <sea> picado

chopstick /ˈtʃɒpstɪk/ n fachis m, pauzinho m

choral /ˈkɔːrəl/ a coral

chord /kɔːd/ n Mus acorde m

chore /tʃɔː(r)/ n trabalho m; (*unpleasant task*) tarefa f maçante; **household ~s** afazeres mpl domésticos

choreograph|er /kɒrɪˈɒɡrəfə(r)/ n coreógrafo m. **~y** n coreografia f

chorus /ˈkɔːrəs/ n coro m; (*of song*) refrão m, estribilho m

chose, chosen /tʃəʊz, ˈtʃəʊzn/ ▶ CHOOSE

Christ /kraɪst/ n Cristo m

christen /ˈkrɪsn/ vt batizar. **~ing** n batismo m

Christian /ˈkrɪstʃən/ a & n cristão m; **~ name** nome m de batismo. **~ity** /-strˈænɪtɪ/ n cristandade f

Christmas /ˈkrɪsməs/ n Natal m ● a do Natal; **~ card** cartão m de Boas Festas; **~ Day/Eve** dia m /véspera f de Natal; **~ tree** árvore f de Natal

chrome /krəʊm/ n cromo m

chromosome /ˈkrəʊməsəʊm/ n cromossoma m

chronic /ˈkrɒnɪk/ a crônico, (P) crónico

chronicle /ˈkrɒnɪkl/ n crônica f, (P) crónica f

chronological /krɒnəˈlɒdʒɪkl/ a cronológico

chrysanthemum /krɪˈsænθəməm/ n crisântemo m

chubby /ˈtʃʌbɪ/ a (**-ier, -iest**) gorducho, rechonchudo

chuck /tʃʌk/ vt ⊞ deitar; atirar; **~ out** <person> expulsar; <thing> jogar fora, (P) deitar fora

chuckle /ˈtʃʌkl/ n riso m abafado ● vi rir sozinho

chum /tʃʌm/ n 🔢 amigo m íntimo, camarada mf. **~my** a amigável

chunk /tʃʌŋk/ n (grande) bocado m, naco m

church /tʃɜ:tʃ/ n igreja f

churchyard /'tʃɜ:tʃjɑ:d/ n cemitério m

churlish /'tʃɜ:lɪʃ/ a grosseiro, indelicado

churn /tʃɜ:n/ n batedeira f; (milk can) vasilha f de leite ● vt bater; **~ out** produzir em série

chutney /'tʃʌtnɪ/ n (pl -eys) chutney m

cider /'saɪdə(r)/ n sidra f, (P) cidra f

cigar /sɪ'gɑ:(r)/ n charuto m

cigarette /sɪgə'ret/ n cigarro m

cinema /'sɪnəmə/ n cinema m

cinnamon /'sɪnəmən/ n canela f

circle /'sɜ:kl/ n círculo m; Theat balcão m ● vt dar a volta a ● vi descrever círculos, voltear

circuit /'sɜ:kɪt/ n circuito m

circuitous /sɜ:'kju:ɪtəs/ a indireto, tortuoso

circular /'sɜ:kjʊlə(r)/ a circular

circulat|e /'sɜ:kjʊleɪt/ vt/i (fazer) circular. **~ion** /-'leɪʃn/ n circulação f; (sales of newspaper) tiragem f

circumcis|e /'sɜ:kəmsaɪz/ vt circuncidar. **~ion** /-'sɪʒn/ n circuncisão f

circumference /sə'kʌmfərəns/ n circunferência f

circumflex /'sɜ:kəmfleks/ n circunflexo m

circumstance /'sɜ:kəmstəns/ n circunstância f; **~s** (means) situação f económica, (P) económica

circus /'sɜ:kəs/ n circo m

cistern /'sɪstən/ n reservatório m; (of WC) autoclismo m

cit|e /saɪt/ vt citar. **~ation** /-'teɪʃn/ n citação f

citizen /'sɪtɪzn/ n cidadão m, cidadã f; (of town) habitante mf. **~ship** n cidadania f

citrus /'sɪtrəs/ n **~ fruit** citrino m

city /'sɪtɪ/ n cidade f

> **The City** Área situada dentro dos limites da antiga cidade de Londres. Atualmente, é o centro financeiro da capital, na qual muitas instituições financeiras têm as suas sedes centrais. Muitas vezes, quando se fala de *The City*, está se referindo a essas sedes e não à área da cidade propriamente dita. ⓘ

civic /'sɪvɪk/ a cívico

civil /'sɪvl/ a civil; ‹rights› cívico; (polite) delicado; **~ servant** funcionário m público; **C~ Service** Administração f Pública; **~ war** guerra f civil. **~ partnership** n união m civil entre homossexuais, (P) união f de facto entre pessoas do mesmo sexo. **~ity** /-'vɪlətɪ/ n civilidade f, cortesia f

civilian /sɪ'vɪlɪən/ a & n civil mf, paisano m

civiliz|e /'sɪvəlaɪz/ vt civilizar. **~ation** /-'zeɪʃn/ n civilização f

claim /kleɪm/ vt reclamar; (assert) pretender ● vi (from insurance) reclamar ● n reivindicação f; (assertion) afirmação f; (right) direito m; (from insurance) reclamação f

clairvoyant /kleə'vɔɪənt/ n vidente mf ● a clarividente

clam /klæm/ n molusco m

clamber /'klæmbə(r)/ vi trepar

clammy /'klæmɪ/ a (-ier, -iest) úmido, (P) húmido e pegajoso

clamour /'klæmə(r)/ n clamor m, vociferação f ● vi ~ **for** exigir aos gritos

clamp /klæmp/ n grampo m; (for car) bloqueador m ● vt prender com grampo; ‹a car› bloquear; ~ **down on** apertar, suprimir; ⊞ cair em cima de ⊞

clan /klæn/ n clã m

clang /klæŋ/ n tinir m

clap /klæp/ vt/i (pt **clapped**) aplaudir; (put) meter ● n aplauso m; (of thunder) ribombo m; ~ **one's hands** bater palmas

claret /'klærət/ n clarete m

clarify /'klærɪfaɪ/ vt esclarecer. ~**ication** /-ɪ'keɪʃn/ n esclarecimento m

clarinet /klærɪ'net/ n clarinete m

clarity /'klærətɪ/ n claridade f

clash /klæʃ/ n choque m; (sound) estridor m; fig conflito m ● vt/i entrechocar(-se); (of colours) destoar

clasp /klɑːsp/ n (fastener) fecho m; (hold, grip) aperto m de mão ● vt apertar, serrar

class /klɑːs/ n classe f ● vt classificar

classic /'klæsɪk/ a & n clássico m. ~**s** npl letras fpl clássicas, (P) estudos mpl clássicos. ~**al** a clássico

classify /'klæsɪfaɪ/ vt classificar; ~**ied advertisement** anúncio m classificado. ~**ication** /-ɪ'keɪʃn/ n classificação f

classroom /'klɑːsruːm/ n sala f de aulas

clatter /'klætə(r)/ n estardalhaço m ● vi fazer barulho

clause /klɔːz/ n cláusula f; Gram oração f

claustrophobia /klɔːstrə'fəʊbɪə/ n claustrofobia f. ~**ic** a claustrofóbico

claw /klɔː/ n garra f; (of lobster) tenaz f, pinça f ● vt (seize) agarrar; (scratch) arranhar; (tear) rasgar

clay /kleɪ/ n argila f, barro m

clean /kliːn/ a (-er, -est) limpo ● adv completamente ● vt limpar ● vi ~ **up** fazer a limpeza. ~**er** n faxineira f, (P) mulher f da limpeza; (of clothes) empregado m da tinturaria

cleanse /klenz/ vt limpar; fig purificar; ~**ing cream** creme m de limpeza

clear /klɪə(r)/ a (-er, -est) claro; ‹glass› transparente; (without obstacles) livre; ‹profit› líquido; ‹sky› limpo; ~ **of** (away from) afastado de ● adv claramente ● vt ‹snow, one's name, etc› limpar; ‹the table› tirar; ‹jump› transpor; ‹debt› saldar; Jur absolver; (through customs) despachar; ~ **out** (clean) fazer a limpeza; ~ **up** (tidy) arrumar; ‹mystery› desvendar ● vi ‹fog› dissipar-se; ‹sky› limpar; ~ **off** or **out** ⊞ sair andando, zarpar; ~ **up** (of weather) clarear, limpar

clearance /'klɪərəns/ n autorização f; (for ship) despacho m; (space) espaço m livre; ~ **sale** liquidação f, saldos mpl

clearing /'klɪərɪŋ/ n clareira f

cleaver /'kliːvə(r)/ n cutelo m

clench /klentʃ/ vt ‹teeth, fists› cerrar; (grasp) agarrar

clergy /'klɜːdʒɪ/ n clero m. ~**man** (pl -**men**) n clérigo m, sacerdote m

cleric /'klerɪk/ n clérigo m. ~**al** a Relig clerical; (of clerks) de escritório

clerk /klɑːk/ n auxiliar m de escritório

clever /'klevə(r)/ a (-er, -est)
esperto, inteligente; (skilful) hábil,
habilidoso

cliché /'kli:ʃeɪ/ n chavão m, lugar-
comum m, clichê m

click /klɪk/ n estalido m, clique m
● vi dar um estalido; Comput clicar

client /'klaɪənt/ n cliente mf

cliff /klɪf/ n penhasco m. ~s npl
falésia f

climat|e /'klaɪmɪt/ n clima m. ~
change n alterações f climáticas

climax /'klaɪmæks/ n clímax m,
ponto m culminante

climb /klaɪm/ vt <stairs> subir;
<tree, wall> subir em, trepar em, (P)
subir, trepar; <mountain> escalar ● vi
subir, trepar ● n subida f; (mountain)
escalada f; ~ down descer; fig dar
a mão à palmatória fig. ~er n Sport
alpinista mf; (plant) trepadeira f

cling /klɪŋ/ vi (pt clung) ~ (to)
agarrar-se (a); (stick) colar-se (a)

clinic /'klɪnɪk/ n clínica f

clinical /'klɪnɪkl/ a clínico

clink /klɪŋk/ n tinido m ● vt/i (fazer)
tilintar

clip[1] /klɪp/ n (for paper) clipe m; (for
hair) grampo m, (P) gancho m; (for
tube) braçadeira f ● vt (pt clipped)
prender

clip[2] /klɪp/ vt (pt clipped) cortar;
(trim) aparar ● n tosquia f; ▣ (blow)
murro m. ~ping n recorte m

cloak /kləʊk/ n capa f, manto m

cloakroom /'kləʊkruːm/ n
vestiário m; (toilet) toalete m, (P)
lavabo m

clock /klɒk/ n relógio m ● vi ~ in/
out marcar o ponto (à entrada/a
saída); ~ up ▣ <miles etc> fazer

clockwise /'klɒkwaɪz/ a & adv no
sentido dos ponteiros do relógio

clockwork /'klɒkwɜːk/ n
mecanismo m; go like ~ ir às mil
maravilhas

clog /klɒg/ n tamanco m, soco m
● vt/i (pt clogged) entupir(-se)

cloister /'klɔɪstə(r)/ n claustro m

close[1] /kləʊs/ a (-er, -est) próximo
(to de); <link, collaboration> estreito;
<friend> íntimo; <weather> abafado;
have a ~ shave fig escapar por um
triz ● adv perto; ~ at hand, ~ by
muito perto; ~ together (crowded)
espremido. ~up n grande plano m.
~ly adv de perto

close[2] /kləʊz/ vt/i fechar(-se); (end)
terminar; (of shop etc) fechar ● n fim
m; ~d shop organização f que só
admite trabalhadores sindicalizados

closet /'klɒzɪt/ n armário m

closure /'kləʊʒə(r)/ n
encerramento m

clot /klɒt/ n coágulo m ● vi (pt
clotted) coagular

cloth /klɒθ/ n pano m; (tablecloth)
toalha f de mesa

cloth|e /kləʊð/ vt vestir. ~ing n
vestuário m, roupa f

clothes /kləʊðz/ npl roupa f,
vestuário m. ~ line n varal m para
roupa

cloud /klaʊd/ n nuvem f ● vt/i
toldar(-se). ~ computing n
computação f na nuvem. ~y a
nublado, toldado; <liquid> turvo

clout /klaʊt/ n cascudo m, (P) carolo
m; ▣ (power) poder m efectivo ● vt
▣ bater

clove /kləʊv/ n cravo m; ~ of garlic
dente m de alho

clover /'kləʊvə(r)/ n trevo m

clown /klaʊn/ n palhaço m ● vi
fazer palhaçadas

club /klʌb/ n clube m; (*weapon*) cacete m; **~s** *Cards* paus mpl ● vt/i (*pt* **clubbed**) dar bordoadas or cacetadas (em); **~ together** (*share costs*) cotizar-se

clue /kluː/ n indício m, pista f; (*in crossword*) definição f; **not have a ~** 🔲 não fazer a menor ideia

clump /klʌmp/ n maciço m, tufo m

clumsy /ˈklʌmzɪ/ a (-ier, -iest) desajeitado

clung /klʌŋ/ ▶ CLING

cluster /ˈklʌstə(r)/ n (*pequeno*) grupo m; *Bot* cacho m ● vt/i agrupar(-se)

clutch /klʌtʃ/ vt agarrar (em), apertar ● vi agarrar-se (**at** a) ● n *Auto* embreagem f, (P) embraiagem f. **~es** npl garras fpl

clutter /ˈklʌtə(r)/ n barafunda f, desordem f ● vt atravancar

coach /kəʊtʃ/ n ônibus m, (P) autocarro m, camioneta f; (*of train*) carruagem f; *Sport* treinador m ● vt (*tutor*) dar aulas a; *Sport* treinar

coal /kəʊl/ n carvão m

coalition /kəʊəˈlɪʃn/ n coligação f

coarse /kɔːs/ a (-er, -est) grosseiro

coast /kəʊst/ n costa f ● vi costear; (*cycle*) descer em roda-livre; (*car*) ir em ponto morto

coastguard /ˈkəʊstɡɑːd/ n polícia f marítima

coastline /ˈkəʊstlaɪn/ n litoral m

coat /kəʊt/ n casaco m; (*of animal*) pelo m; (*of paint*) camada f, demão f; **~ of arms** brasão m ● vt cobrir. **~ing** n camada f

coax /kəʊks/ vt levar com afagos ou lisonjas, convencer

cobble /ˈkɒbl/ n **~(-stone)** pedra de f calçada

cobweb /ˈkɒbweb/ n teia f de aranha

cocaine /kəʊˈkeɪn/ n cocaína f

cock /kɒk/ n (*male bird*) macho m; (*rooster*) galo m ● vt ‹*gun*› engatilhar; ‹*ears*› fitar

cockerel /ˈkɒkərəl/ n frango m, galo m novo

cockney /ˈkɒknɪ/ n (*pl* -eys) (*person*) londrino m; (*dialect*) dialeto m do leste de Londres

cockpit /ˈkɒkpɪt/ n cabine f

cockroach /ˈkɒkrəʊtʃ/ n barata f

cocktail /ˈkɒkteɪl/ n cocktail m, coquetel m; **fruit ~** salada f de fruta

cocky /ˈkɒkɪ/ a (-ier, -iest) convencido 🔲

cocoa /ˈkəʊkəʊ/ n cacau m

coconut /ˈkəʊkənʌt/ n coco m

cod /kɒd/ n (*pl invar*) bacalhau m; **~liver oil** óleo m de fígado de bacalhau

code /kəʊd/ n código m ● vt codificar

coerc|e /kəʊˈɜːs/ vt coagir. **~ion** /-ʃn/ n coação f

coexist /kəʊɪɡˈzɪst/ vi coexistir. **~ence** n coexistência f

coffee /ˈkɒfɪ/ n café m; **~ bar** café m. **~ table** n mesa f baixa

coffin /ˈkɒfɪn/ n caixão m

cogent /ˈkəʊdʒənt/ a convincente; (*relevant*) pertinente

cognac /ˈkɒnjæk/ n conhaque m

cohabit /kəʊˈhæbɪt/ vi coabitar

coherent /kəʊˈhɪərənt/ a coerente

coil /kɔɪl/ vt/i enrolar(-se) ● n rolo m; *Electr* bobina f; (*one ring*) espiral f; (*contraceptive*) dispositivo m intrauterino, DIU

coin /kɔɪn/ n moeda f ● vt cunhar

coincide /kəʊɪnˈsaɪd/ vi coincidir

coinciden|ce /kəʊ'ɪnsɪdəns/ *n* coincidência *f*. **~tal** /-'dentl/ *a* que acontece por coincidência

colander /'kʌləndə(r)/ *n* peneira *f*, (*P*) coador *m*

cold /kəʊld/ *a* (**-er**, **-est**) frio; **be** or **feel ~** estar com frio; **it's ~** está frio; **~ cream** creme *m* para a pele ● *n* frio *m*; *Med* resfriado *m*, constipação *f*. **~-blooded** *a* ‹*person*› insensível; ‹*deed*› a sangue frio. **~ness** *n* frio *m*; (*of feeling*) frieza *f*

coleslaw /'kəʊlslɔ:/ *n* salada *f* de repolho cru

colic /'kɒlɪk/ *n* cólica(s) *f*(*pl*)

collaborat|e /kə'læbəreɪt/ *vi* colaborar. **~ion** /-'reɪʃn/ *n* colaboração *f*. **~or** *n* colaborador *m*

collapse /kə'læps/ *vi* desabar; *Med* ter um colapso ● *n* colapso *m*

collapsible /kə'læpsəbl/ *a* desmontável, dobrável

collar /'kɒlə(r)/ *n* gola *f*; (*of shirt*) colarinho *m*; (*of dog*) coleira *f* ● *vt* [I] pôr a mão a. **~bone** *n* clavícula *f*

colleague /'kɒli:g/ *n* colega *mf*

collect /kə'lekt/ *vt* (*gather*) juntar; (*fetch*) ir/vir buscar; ‹*money, rent*› cobrar; (*as hobby*) colecionar ● *vi* juntar-se; **call ~** *Amer* chamar a cobrar. **~ion** /-ʃn/ *n* coleção *f*, (*in church*) coleta *f*, (*of mail*) tiragem *f*; coleta *f*, (*P*) abertura *f*. **~or** *n* (*as hobby*) colecionador *m*

college /'kɒlɪdʒ/ *n* colégio *m*

collide /kə'laɪd/ *vi* colidir

colliery /'kɒlɪərɪ/ *n* mina *f* de carvão

collision /kə'lɪʒn/ *n* colisão *f*, choque *m*; *fig* conflito *m*

colloquial /kə'ləʊkwɪəl/ *a* coloquial

colon /'kəʊlən/ *n Gram* dois pontos *mpl*; *Anat* cólon *m*

colonel /'kɜ:nl/ *n* coronel *m*

colonize /'kɒlənaɪz/ *vt* colonizar

colon|y /'kɒlənɪ/ *n* colônia *f*, (*P*) colónia *f*. **~ial** /kə'ləʊnɪəl/ *a & n* colonial *mf*

colossal /kə'lɒsl/ *a* colossal

colour /'kʌlə(r)/ *n* cor *f* ● *a* ‹*photo, TV, etc*› a cores; ‹*film*› colorido ● *vt* colorir, dar cor a ● *vi* (*blush*) corar. **~-blind** *a* daltônico, (*P*) daltónico. **~ful** *a* colorido. **~ing** *n* (*of skin*) cor *f*; (*in food*) corante *m*. **~less** *a* descolorido

coloured /'kʌləd/ *a* ‹*pencil, person*› de cor ● *n* pessoa *f* de cor

column /'kɒləm/ *n* coluna *f*

columnist /'kɒləmnɪst/ *n* colunista *mf*

coma /'kəʊmə/ *n* coma *m*

comb /kəʊm/ *n* pente *m* ● *vt* pentear; (*search*) vasculhar; **~ one's hair** pentear-se

combat /'kɒmbæt/ *n* combate *m* ● *vt* (*pt* **combated**) combater

combination /kɒmbɪ'neɪʃn/ *n* combinação *f*

combine /kəm'baɪn/ *vt/i* combinar(-se), juntar(-se), reunir(-se)

combustion /kəm'bʌstʃən/ *n* combustão *f*

come /kʌm/ *vi* (*pt* **came**, *pp* **come**) vir; (*arrive*) chegar; (*occur*) suceder; **~ about** acontecer; **~ across** encontrar, dar com; **~ away** or **off** soltar-se; **~ back** voltar; **~ by** obter; **~ down** descer; ‹*price*› baixar; **~ from** vir de; **~ in** entrar; **~ into** ‹*money*› herdar; **~ off** (*succeed*) ter êxito; (*fare*) sair-se; ~ **on!** vamos!; ~ **out** sair; ~ **round** (*after fainting*) voltar a si; (*be converted*) deixar-se convencer; ~ **to** (*amount to*) montar a; ~ **up** subir; (*seeds*) despontar; *fig* surgir; ~ **up with** (*idea*) ter, vir com, propor. **~back** *n* regresso *m*; (*retort*) réplica *f*; **~down** *n* humilhação *f*

comedian /kəˈmiːdɪən/ *n* comediante *mf*

comedy /ˈkɒmədɪ/ *n* comédia *f*

comet /ˈkɒmɪt/ *n* cometa *m*

comfort /ˈkʌmfət/ *n* conforto *m* ● *vt* confortar, consolar. ~ **food** *n* comida *f* de conforto; ~ **zone** *n* zona *f* de conforto; **to be in/out of one's ~ zone** estar dentro/fora da sua zona de conforto. **~able** *a* confortável

comic /ˈkɒmɪk/ *a* cómico, (*P*) cómico ● *n* cómico *m*, (*P*) cómico *m*; (*periodical*) estórias *fpl* em quadrinhos, (*P*) revista *f* de banda desenhada; ~ **strip** estória *f* em quadrinhos, (*P*) banda *f* desenhada

coming /ˈkʌmɪŋ/ *n* vinda *f*; ~**s and goings** idas e vindas *fpl* ● *a* próximo

comma /ˈkɒmə/ *n* vírgula *f*

command /kəˈmɑːnd/ *n* *Mil* comando *m*; (*order*) ordem *f*; (*mastery*) domínio *m* ● *vt* comandar; (*respect*) inspirar, impor. **~er** *n* comandante *m*

commemorat|e /kəˈmeməreɪt/ *vt* comemorar. **~ion** /-ˈreɪʃn/ *n* comemoração *f*. **~ive** *a* comemorativo

commence /kəˈmens/ *vt/i* começar

commend /kəˈmend/ *vt* louvar; (*entrust*) confiar. **~able** *a* louvável. **~ation** /kɒmenˈdeɪʃn/ *n* louvor *m*

comment /ˈkɒment/ *n* comentário *m* ● *vi* comentar; ~ **on** comentar, fazer comentários

commentary /ˈkɒməntrɪ/ *n* comentário *m*; *Radio, TV* relato *m*

commentat|e /ˈkɒmənteɪt/ *vi* fazer um relato. **~or** *n* *Radio, TV* comentarista *mf*, (*P*) comentador *m*

commerce /ˈkɒmɜːs/ *n* comércio *m*

commercial /kəˈmɜːʃl/ *a* comercial ● *n* publicidade (comercial) *f*. **~ize** *vt* comercializar

commiserat|e /kəˈmɪzəreɪt/ *vi* ~ **with** compadecer-se de. **~ion** /-ˈreɪʃn/ *n* comiseração *f*, pesar *m*

commission /kəˈmɪʃn/ *n* comissão *f*; (*order for work*) encomenda *f* ● *vt* encomendar; *Mil* nomear; ~ **to do** encarregar de fazer; **out of** ~ fora de serviço ativo. **~er** *n* comissário *m*; *Police* chefe *m*

commit /kəˈmɪt/ *vt* (*pt* **committed**) cometer; (*entrust*) confiar; ~ **o.s.** comprometer-se, empenhar-se; ~ **suicide** suicidar-se; ~ **to memory** decorar. **~ment** *n* compromisso *m*

committee /kəˈmɪtɪ/ *n* comissão *f*, comité *m*, (*P*) comité *m*

commodity /kəˈmɒdətɪ/ *n* artigo *m*, mercadoria *f*

common /ˈkɒmən/ *a* (**-er, -est**) comum; (*usual*) usual, corrente, *pej* (*ill-bred*) ordinário; ~ **law** direito *m* consuetudinário; **C~ Market** Mercado *m* Comum; ~ **sense** bom senso *m*, senso *m* comum ● *n* prado *m* público, (*P*) baldio *m*; **House of C~s** Câmara *f* dos Comuns; **in** ~ em comum. ~ **room** *n* sala *f* comum. **~ly** *adv* mais comum

commoner /ˈkɒmənə(r)/ *n* plebeu *m*

commonplace /'kɒmənpleɪs/ a banal ● n lugar-comum m

> **Commonwealth** A associação das antigas colônias e territórios que formavam o Império Britânico. De dois em dois anos, celebra-se um encontro de cúpula dos respectivos chefes de governo. Entre os países-membros existem inúmeros vínculos culturais, educativos e desportivos. Nos Estados Unidos, o termo *Commonwealth* emprega-se oficialmente quando se refere ao conjunto de quatro estados: Kentucky, Massachusetts, Pensilvânia e Virgínia.

commotion /kə'məʊʃn/ n agitação f, confusão f, barulheira f

communal /'kɒmjunl/ a (of a commune) comunal; (shared) comum

commune /'kɒmjuːn/ n comuna f

communicat|e /kə'mjuːnɪkeɪt/ vt/i comunicar. **~ion** /-'keɪʃn/ n comunicação f. **~ion cord** sinal m de alarme. **~ive** /-ətɪv/ a comunicativo

communion /kə'mjuːnɪən/ n comunhão f

communis|t /'kɒmjunɪst/ n comunista mf ● a comunista. **~m** /-zəm/ n comunismo m

community /kə'mjuːnətɪ/ n comunidade f; **~ centre** centro m comunitário

commute /kə'mjuːt/ vi viajar diariamente para o trabalho. **~r** /-ə(r)/ n pessoa f que viaja diariamente para o trabalho

compact¹ /kəm'pækt/ a compacto. **~ disc** n cd m

compact² /'kɒmpækt/ n estojo m de pó-de-arroz; (P) caixa f

companion /kəm'pænɪən/ n companheiro m. **~ship** n companhia f, convívio m

company /'kʌmpənɪ/ n companhia f; (guests) visitas fpl; **keep sb ~** fazer companhia a alguém

comparable /'kɒmpərəbl/ a comparável

compar|e /kəm'peə(r)/ vt/i comparar(-se) (**to, with** com). **~ative** /-'pærətɪv/ a comparativo; ‹comfort etc› relativo

comparison /kəm'pærɪsn/ n comparação f

compartment /kəm'pɑːtmənt/ n compartimento m

compass /'kʌmpəs/ n bússola f; **~es** compasso m

compassion /kəm'pæʃn/ n compaixão f. **~ate** a compassivo

compatib|le /kəm'pætəbl/ a compatível. **~ility** /-'bɪlətɪ/ n compatibilidade f

compel /kəm'pel/ vt (pt compelled) compelir, forçar. **~ling** a irresistível, convincente

compensat|e /'kɒmpənseɪt/ vt/i compensar. **~ion** /-'seɪʃn/ n compensação f; (financial) indenização f, (P) indemnização f

compete /kəm'piːt/ vi competir; **~ with** rivalizar com

competen|t /'kɒmpɪtənt/ a competente. **~ce** n competência f

competition /kɒmpə'tɪʃn/ n competição f; Comm concorrência f

competitive /kəm'petɪtɪv/ a ‹sport, prices› competitivo; **~ examination** concurso m

competitor /kəm'petɪtə(r)/ n competidor m, concorrente mf

compile /kəm'paɪl/ vt compilar, coligir. **~r** /-ə(r)/ n compilador m

complacen|t /kəm'pleɪsnt/ a satisfeito consigo mesmo, (P) complacente. **~cy** n (auto-)satisfação f, (P) complacência f

complain /kəm'pleɪn/ vi queixar-se (**about**)

complaint /kəm'pleɪnt/ n queixa f, (in shop) reclamação f; Med doença f, achaque m

complement /'kɒmplɪmənt/ n complemento m ● vt completar, complementar. **~ary** /-'mentrɪ/ a complementar

complet|e /kəm'pliːt/ a completo; (finished) acabado; (downright) perfeito ● vt completar; «a form» preencher. **~ely** adv completamente. **~ion** /-ʃn/ n conclusão f, feitura f, realização f

complex /'kɒmpleks/ a complexo ● n complexo m. **~ity** /kəm'pleksətɪ/ n complexidade f

complexion /kəm'plekʃn/ n cor f da tez, tez f; fig caráter m, (P) carácter m, aspecto m

compliance /kəm'plaɪəns/ n docilidade f; (agreement) conformidade f; **in ~ with** em conformidade com

complicat|e /'kɒmplɪkeɪt/ vt complicar. **~ed** a complicado. **~ion** /-'keɪʃn/ n complicação f

compliment /'kɒmplɪmənt/ n cumprimento m, elogio m ● vt /'kɒmplɪment/ cumprimentar, elogiar

complimentary /kɒmplɪ'mentrɪ/ a amável, elogioso; **~ copy** oferta f; **~ ticket** bilhete m grátis

comply /kəm'plaɪ/ vi **~ with** agir em conformidade com

component /kəm'pəʊnənt/ n componente m; (of machine) peça f ● a componente, constituinte

compose /kəm'pəʊz/ vt compor; **~ o.s.** acalmar-se, dominar-se. **~d** a calmo, senhor de si. **~r** /-ə(r)/ n compositor m

composition /kɒmpə'zɪʃn/ n composição f

compost /'kɒmpɒst/ n húmus m, adubo m

composure /kəm'pəʊʒə(r)/ n calma f, domínio m de si mesmo

compound /'kɒmpaʊnd/ n composto m; (enclosure) cercado m, recinto m ● a composto; **~ fracture** fratura f exposta

comprehen|d /kɒmprɪ'hend/ vt compreender. **~sion** /-ʃn/ n compreensão f

comprehensive /kɒmprɪ'hensɪv/ a compreensivo, vasto; (insurance) contra todos os riscos; **~ school** escola f de ensino secundário técnico e académico or (P) acadêmico

compress /kəm'pres/ vt comprimir. **~ion** /-ʃn/ n compressão f

comprise /kəm'praɪz/ vt compreender, abranger

compromise /'kɒmprəmaɪz/ n compromisso m ● vt comprometer ● vi chegar a um meio-termo

compulsion /kəm'pʌlʃn/ n (constraint) coação f; Psych desejo m irresistível, compulsão f

compulsive /kəm'pʌlsɪv/ a Psych compulsivo; «liar, smoker etc» inveterado

compulsory /kəm'pʌlsərɪ/ a obrigatório, compulsório

computer /kəm'pju:tə(r)/
n computador m; ~ **science**
informática f. **~ize** vt computerizar

comrade /'kɒmreɪd/ n camarada mf

con[1] /kɒn/ vt (pt **conned**) ⊠
enganar ● n ⊠ intrujice f; vigarice
f; burla f; ~ **man** ⊠ intrujão m,
vigarista m, burlão m

con[2] /kɒn/ ▸ **PRO**[1]

concave /kɒn'keɪv/ a côncavo

conceal /kən'si:l/ vt ocultar,
esconder

concede /kən'si:d/ vt conceder,
admitir; (in a game etc) ceder, dar-se
por vencido

conceit /kən'si:t/ n presunção
f. **~ed** a presunçoso, presumido,
cheio de si

conceivabl|e /kən'si:vəbl/ a
concebível

conceive /kən'si:v/ vt/i conceber

concentrat|e /'kɒnsntreɪt/ vt/i
concentrar(-se). **~ion** /-'treɪʃn/ n
concentração f

concept /'kɒnsept/ n conceito m

conception /kən'sepʃn/ n
concepção f

concern /kən'sɜːn/ n (worry)
preocupação f; (business) negócio
m ● vt dizer respeito a, respeitar; ~
o.s. with, be ~ed with interessar-se
por, ocupar-se de; (regard) dizer
respeito a; **it's no ~ of mine** não
me diz respeito. **~ing** prep sobre,
respeitante a

concerned /kən'sɜːnd/ a inquieto;
preocupado (**about** com)

concert /'kɒnsət/ n concerto m

concession /kən'seʃn/ n
concessão f

conclu|de /kən'klu:d/ vt concluir
● vi terminar. **~sion** n conclusão f

conclusive /kən'klu:sɪv/ a
conclusivo

concoct /kən'kɒkt/ vt preparar
por mistura; fig (invent) fabricar.
~ion /-ʃn/ n mistura f; fig invenção
f; mentira f

concrete /'kɒŋkri:t/ n concreto
m, (P) cimento m ● a concreto ● vt
concretar, (P) cimentar

concur /kən'kɜː(r)/ vi (pt
concurred) concordar; (of
circumstances) concorrer

concussion /kən'kʌʃn/ n
comoção f cerebral

condemn /kən'dem/ vt condenar.
~ation /kɒndem'neɪʃn/ n
condenação f

condens|e /kən'dens/
vt/i condensar(-se). **~ation**
/kɒnden'seɪʃn/ n condensação f

condescend /kɒndɪ'send/
vi condescender; (lower o.s.)
rebaixar-se

condition /kən'dɪʃn/ n condição
f; **on ~ that** com a condição de que
● vt condicionar. **~al** a condicional.
~er n (for hair) condicionador m,
creme m rinse

condolences /kən'dəʊlənsɪz/
npl condolências fpl, pêsames mpl,
sentimentos mpl

condom /'kɒndəm/ n
preservativo m

condone /kən'dəʊn/ vt desculpar,
fechar os olhos a

conducive /kən'dju:sɪv/ a be ~ **to**
contribuir para, ser propício a

conduct[1] /kən'dʌkt/ vt conduzir,
dirigir; ‹orchestra› reger

conduct[2] /'kɒndʌkt/ n conduta f

conductor /kən'dʌktə(r)/ n
maestro m; Electr (of bus) condutor m

cone /kəʊn/ n cone m; Bot pinha f; (for ice cream) casquinha f, (P) cone m

confectioner /kənˈfekʃnə(r)/ n confeiteiro m, (P) pasteleiro m. **~y** n confeitaria f, (P) pastelaria f

conference /ˈkɒnfərəns/ n conferência f; **in** ~ em reunião f

confess /kənˈfes/ vt/i confessar; Relig confessar(-se). **~ion** /-ʃn/ n confissão f

confetti /kənˈfeti/ n confetes mpl, (P) confetti mpl

confide /kənˈfaɪd/ vt confiar ● vi **in** confiar em

confiden|t /ˈkɒnfɪdənt/ a confiante, confiado. **~ce** n confiança f; (boldness) confiança f em si; (secret) confidência f. **~ce trick** vigarice f. **in** ~**ce** em confidência

confidential /kɒnfɪˈdenʃl/ a confidencial

confine /kənˈfaɪn/ vt fechar; (limit) limitar (**to** a). **~ment** n detenção f; Med parto m

confirm /kənˈfɜːm/ vt confirmar. **~ation** /kɒnfəˈmeɪʃn/ n confirmação f. **~ed** a (bachelor) inveterado

confiscat|e /ˈkɒnfɪskeɪt/ vt confiscar. **~ion** /-ˈkeɪʃn/ n confiscação f

conflict[1] /ˈkɒnflɪkt/ n conflito m

conflict[2] /kənˈflɪkt/ vi estar em contradição. **~ing** a contraditório

conform /kənˈfɔːm/ vt/i conformar(-se)

confront /kənˈfrʌnt/ vt confrontar, defrontar, enfrentar; ~ **with** confrontar-se com. **~ation** /kɒnfrʌnˈteɪʃn/ n confrontação f

confus|e /kənˈfjuːz/ vt confundir. **~ed** a confuso. **~ing** a que faz

confusão. **~ion** /-ʒn/ n confusão f

congeal /kənˈdʒiːl/ vt/i congelar, solidificar

congenial /kənˈdʒiːnɪəl/ a (agreeable) simpático

congest|ed /kənˈdʒestɪd/ a congestionado. **~ion** /-tʃn/ n (traffic) congestionamento m; Med congestão f

congratulat|e /kənˈgrætjʊleɪt/ vt felicitar; dar os parabéns (**on** por). **~ions** /-ˈleɪʃnz/ npl felicitações fpl, parabéns mpl

congregat|e /ˈkɒŋgrɪgeɪt/ vi reunir-se. **~ion** /-ˈgeɪʃn/ n (in church) congregação f, fiéis mpl

congress /ˈkɒŋgres/ n congresso m; C~ Amer Congresso m

> **Congress** O Congresso é
> o órgão legislativo dos
> Estados Unidos. Reúne-se no
> Capitólio (Capitol) e é composto
> por duas câmaras: o Senado e a
> Câmara de Representantes. O
> Congresso é renovado de dois em
> dois anos, e a sua função é
> elaborar leis que devem ser
> aprovadas, primeiro pelas duas
> câmaras e posteriormente pelo
> Presidente.

---

conjecture /kənˈdʒektʃə(r)/ n conjetura f, (P) conjetura f ● vt/i conjeturar, (P) conjeturar

conjugat|e /ˈkɒndʒʊgeɪt/ vt conjugar. **~ion** /-ˈgeɪʃn/ n conjugação f

conjunction /kənˈdʒʌŋkʃn/ n conjunção f

conjur|e /ˈkʌndʒə(r)/ vi fazer truques mágicos ● vt **~e up** fazer aparecer. **~or** n mágico m, prestidigitador m

connect /kə'nekt/ vt/i ligar(-se); (of train) fazer ligação. **~ed** a ligado; **be ~ed with** estar relacionado com

connection /kə'nekʃn/ n relação f; Rail (phone call) ligação f; Electr contacto m

connectivity /kɒnek'tɪvəti/ n conectividade f

connoisseur /kɒnə'sɜː(r)/ n conhecedor m, apreciador m

conquer /'kɒŋkə(r)/ vt vencer; ‹country› conquistar. **~or** n conquistador m

conquest /'kɒŋkwest/ n conquista f

conscience /'kɒnʃəns/ n consciência f

conscientious /kɒnʃi'enʃəs/ a consciencioso

conscious /'kɒnʃəs/ a consciente. **~ness** n consciência f

conscript¹ /kən'skrɪpt/ vt recrutar. **~ion** /-ʃn/ n serviço m militar obrigatório

conscript² /'kɒnskrɪpt/ n recruta m

consecrate /'kɒnsɪkreɪt/ vt consagrar

consecutive /kən'sekjʊtɪv/ a consecutivo, seguido

consensus /kən'sensəs/ n consenso m

consent /kən'sent/ vi consentir (to em) ● n consentimento m

consequence /'kɒnsɪkwəns/ n consequência f

consequent /'kɒnsɪkwənt/ a resultante (on, upon de). **~ly** adv por consequência, por conseguinte

conservation /kɒnsə'veɪʃn/ n conservação f

conservative /kən'sɜːvətɪv/ a conservador; (estimate) moderado. ● **C~** a & n conservador m

conservatory /kən'sɜːvətrɪ/ n (greenhouse) estufa f; (house extension) jardim m de inverno

conserve /kən'sɜːv/ vt conservar

consider /kən'sɪdə(r)/ vt considerar; (allow for) levar em consideração. **~ation** /-'reɪʃn/ n consideração f. **~ing** prep em vista de, tendo em conta

considerabl|e /kən'sɪdərəbl/ a considerável; (much) muito

considerate /kən'sɪdərət/ a atencioso, delicado

consign /kən'saɪn/ vt consignar. **~ment** n consignação f

consist /kən'sɪst/ vi consistir (of, em)

consisten|t /kən'sɪstənt/ a (unchanging) constante; (not contradictory) coerente; **~t with** conforme com. **~cy** n consistência f; fig coerência f. **~tly** adv regularmente

consol|e /kən'səʊl/ vt consolar. **~ation** /kɒnsə'leɪʃn/ n consolação f; **~ation prize** prêmio m or (P) prémio m de consolação

consolidat|e /kən'sɒlɪdeɪt/ vt/i consolidar(-se). **~ion** /-'deɪʃn/ n consolidação f

consonant /'kɒnsənənt/ n consoante f

conspicuous /kən'spɪkjʊəs/ a conspícuo, visível; (striking) notável; **make o.s. ~** fazer-se notar, chamar a atenção

conspira|cy /kən'spɪrəsɪ/ n conspiração f. **~cy theory** n teoria f da conspiração

conspire /kən'spaɪə(r)/ vi conspirar

constable /'kʌnstəbl/ n polícia m

constant /'kɒnstənt/ a constante.
~ly adv constantemente

constellation /kɒnstə'leɪʃn/ n
constelação f

constipation /kɒnstɪ'peɪʃn/ n
prisão f de ventre

constituency /kən'stɪtjʊənsɪ/ n
(pl -cies) círculo m eleitoral

constituent /kən'stɪtjʊənt/ a & n
constituinte m

constitut|e /'kɒnstɪtjuːt/
vt constituir. **~ion** /-'tjuːʃn/ n
constituição f. **~ional** /-'tjuːʃənl/ a
constitucional

constrain /kən'streɪn/ vt
constranger

constraint /kən'streɪnt/ n
constrangimento m

constrict /kən'strɪkt/ vt
constringir, apertar

construct /kən'strʌkt/ vt
construir. **~ion** /-ʃn/ n construção f;
under ~ion em construção

constructive /kən'strʌktɪv/ a
construtivo

consul /'kɒnsl/ n cônsul m

consulate /'kɒnsjʊlət/ n
consulado m

consult /kən'sʌlt/ vt consultar.
~ation /kɒnsl'teɪʃn/ n consulta f

consultant /kən'sʌltənt/ n
consultor m; Med especialista mf

consume /kən'sjuːm/ vt consumir.
~r /-ə(r)/ n consumidor m

consumption /kən'sʌmpʃn/ n
consumo m

contact /'kɒntækt/ n contato m,
(P) contacto m; <person> relação f;
~ lenses lentes fpl de contato or (P)
contacto ● vt contactar

contagious /kən'teɪdʒəs/ a
contagioso

contain /kən'teɪn/ vt conter; **~ o.s.**
conter-se. **~er** n recipiente m; (for
transport) contentor m

contaminat|e /kən'tæmɪneɪt/
vt contaminar. **~ion** /-'neɪʃn/ n
contaminação f

contemplat|e /'kɒntempleɪt/ vt
contemplar; (intend) ter em vista;
(consider) esperar, pensar em. **~ion**
/-'pleɪʃn/ n contemplação f

contemporary /kən'temprərɪ/
a & n contemporâneo m

contempt /kən'tempt/ n desprezo
m. **~ible** a desprezível. **~uous**
/-tʃʊəs/ a desdenhoso

contend /kən'tend/ vt afirmar,
sustentar ● vi **~ with** lutar contra.
~er n adversário m, contendor m

content¹ /kən'tent/ a satisfeito,
contente ● vt contentar. **~ed** a
satisfeito, contente. **~ment** n
contentamento m, satisfação f

content² /'kɒntent/ n conteúdo m;
(table of) ~s índice m

contention /kən'tenʃn/ n
disputa f, contenda f; (assertion)
argumento m

contest¹ /'kɒntest/ n competição f;
(struggle) luta f

contest² /kən'test/ vt contestar.
(compete for) disputar. **~ant** n
concorrente mf

context /'kɒntekst/ n contexto m

continent /'kɒntɪnənt/ n
continente m; **the C~** a Europa
(continental) f. **~al** /-'nentl/ a
continental; (of mainland Europe)
europeu; **~al breakfast** café m da
manhã europeu, (P) pequeno-
almoço m europeu; **~al quilt**
edredom m, (P) edredão m

contingen|t /kənˈtɪndʒənt/ *a & n*
contingente *m*. **~cy** *n* contingência *f*;
~cy plan plano *m* de emergência

continual /kənˈtɪnjʊəl/ *a*
contínuo. **~ly** *adv* continuamente

continu|e /kənˈtɪnju:/ *vt/i*
continuar. **~ation** /-tɪnjʊˈeɪʃn/ *n*
continuação *f*

continuity /kɒntɪˈnju:ətɪ/ *n*
continuidade *f*

continuous /kənˈtɪnjʊəs/ *a*
contínuo. **~ly** *adv* continuamente

contort /kənˈtɔ:t/ *vt* contorcer; *fig*
distorcer. **~ion** /-ʃn/ *n* contorção *f*

contour /ˈkɒntʊə(r)/ *n* contorno *m*

contraband /ˈkɒntrəbænd/ *n*
contrabando *m*

contraception /kɒntrəˈsepʃn/ *n*
contracepção *f*

contraceptive /kɒntrəˈseptɪv/
a & n contraceptivo *m*

contract¹ /ˈkɒntrækt/ *n* contrato *m*

contract² /kənˈtrækt/ *vt/i*
contrair(-se); (*make a contract*)
contratar. **~ion** /-ʃn/ *n* contração *f*

contractor /kənˈtræktə(r)/
n empreiteiro *m*; (*firm*) firma
f empreiteira de serviços, (P)
recrutadora *f* de mão-de-obra
temporária

contradict /kɒntrəˈdɪkt/
vt contradizer. **~ion** /-ʃn/ *n*
contradição *f*. **~ory** *a* contraditório

contrary¹ /ˈkɒntrərɪ/ *a & n*
(*opposite*) contrário *m* ● *adv* **~ to**
contrariamente a; **on the ~** ao or
pelo contrário

contrary² /kənˈtreərɪ/ *a* (*perverse*)
do contra, embirrento

contrast¹ /ˈkɒntrɑːst/ *n* contraste *m*

contrast² /kənˈtrɑːst/ *vt/i*
contrastar. **~ing** *a* contrastante

contraven|e /kɒntrəˈviːn/
vt infringir. **~tion** /-ˈvenʃn/ *n*
contravenção *f*

contribut|e /kənˈtrɪbjuːt/ *vt/i*
contribuir (**to** para); (*to newspaper
etc*) colaborar (**to** em). **~ion**
/kɒntrɪˈbjuːʃn/ *n* contribuição *f*. **~or**
/-ˈtrɪbjutə(r)/ *n* contribuinte *mf*; (*to
newspaper*) colaborador *m*

contrivance /kənˈtraɪvəns/ *n*
(*invention*) engenho *m*; (*device*)
engenhoca *f*; (*trick*) maquinação *f*

control /kənˈtrəʊl/ *vt* (*pt
controlled*) (*check, restrain*)
controlar; ‹*firm etc*› dirigir ● *n*
controle *m*; (*management*) direção
f; **~s** (*of car, plane*) comandos *mpl*;
(*knobs*) botões *mpl*; **be in ~ of**
dirigir; **under ~** sob controle

controversial /kɒntrəˈvɜ:ʃl/ *a*
controverso, discutível

controversy /ˈkɒntrəvɜ:sɪ/ *n*
controvérsia *f*

convalesce /kɒnvəˈles/ *vi*
convalescer. **~nce** *n* convalescença *f*

convene /kənˈviːn/ *vt* convocar
● *vi* reunir-se

convenience /kənˈviːnɪəns/
n conveniência *f*; **~s** (*appliances*)
comodidades *fpl*; (*lavatory*) privada
f, (P) casa *f* de banho; **at your ~**
quando (e como) lhe convier;
~ foods alimentos *mpl* semiprontos

convenient /kənˈviːnɪənt/ *a*
conveniente; **be ~ for** convir a. **~ly**
adv sem inconveniente; (*situated*)
bem; (*arrive*) a propósito

convent /ˈkɒnvənt/ *n* convento *m*;
~ school colégio *m* de freiras

convention /kənˈvenʃn/ *n*
convenção *f*; (*custom*) uso *m*,
costume *m*. **~al** *a* convencional

converge /kənˈvɜ:dʒ/ *vi* convergir

conversation /kɒnvəˈseɪʃn/ n conversa f. **~al** a de conversa, coloquial

converse[1] /kənˈvɜːs/ vi conversar

converse[2] /ˈkɒnvɜːs/ a & n inverso m. **~ly** /-ˈvɜːsɪlɪ/ adv ao invés, inversamente

conver|t[1] /kənˈvɜːt/ vt converter; (house) transformar. **~sion** /-ʃn/ n conversão f; (house) transformação f. **~tible** a convertível, conversível ● n Auto conversível m

convert[2] /ˈkɒnvɜːt/ n convertido m, converso m

convex /ˈkɒnveks/ a convexo

convey /kənˈveɪ/ vt transmitir; (goods) transportar; (idea, feeling) comunicar; **~or belt** tapete m rolante, correia f transportadora

convict[1] /kənˈvɪkt/ vt declarar culpado. **~ion** /-ʃn/ n condenação f; (opinion) convicção f

convict[2] /ˈkɒnvɪkt/ n condenado m

convinc|e /kənˈvɪns/ vt convencer. **~ing** a convincente

convoy /ˈkɒnvɔɪ/ n escolta f

convuls|e /kənˈvʌls/ vt convulsionar; fig abalar; **be ~ed with laughter** torcer-se de riso

coo /kuː/ vi (pt cooed) arrulhar ● n arrulho m

cook /kʊk/ vt/i cozinhar; **~ up** 🄓 cozinhar fig, fabricar ● n cozinheira f, cozinheiro m

cooker /ˈkʊkə(r)/ n fogão m

cookery /ˈkʊkərɪ/ n cozinha f; **~ book** livro m de culinária

cookie /ˈkʊkɪ/ n Amer biscoito m

cool /kuːl/ a (-er, -est) fresco; (calm) calmo; (unfriendly) frio ● n frescura f; 🄓 (composure) sangue-frio m ● vt/i arrefecer. **~ box** n geladeira f portátil. **in the ~** no

fresco. **~ly** /ˈkuːllɪ/ adv calmamente; fig friamente. **~ness** n frescura f; fig frieza f

coop /kuːp/ n galinheiro m ● vt **~ up** engaiolar, fechar

co-operat|e /kəʊˈɒpəreɪt/ vi cooperar. **~ion** /-ˈreɪʃn/ n cooperação f

cooperative /kəʊˈɒpərətɪv/ a cooperativo ● n cooperativa f

coordinat|e /kəʊˈɔːdɪneɪt/ vt coordenar. **~ion** /-ˈneɪʃn/ n coordenação f

cop /kɒp/ n 🅰 porco m 🅰, (P) chui m 🅰

cope /kəʊp/ vi aguentar-se, arranjar-se; **~ with** poder com, dar conta de

copious /ˈkəʊpɪəs/ a copioso

copper[1] /ˈkɒpə(r)/ n cobre m ● a de cobre

copper[2] /ˈkɒpə(r)/ n 🅰 porco m 🅰, (P) chui m 🅰

coppice /ˈkɒpɪs/, **copse** /kɒps/ ns mata f de corte

copulat|e /ˈkɒpjʊleɪt/ vi copular

copy /ˈkɒpɪ/ n cópia f; (of book) exemplar m; (of newspaper) número m ● vt/i copiar

copyright /ˈkɒpɪraɪt/ n direitos mpl autorais, (P) direitos npl de autor

coral /ˈkɒrəl/ n coral m

cord /kɔːd/ n cordão m; Electr fio m

cordial /ˈkɔːdɪəl/ a & n cordial m

cordon /ˈkɔːdn/ n cordão m ● vt **~ off** fechar (com um cordão de isolamento)

corduroy /ˈkɔːdərɔɪ/ n veludo m cotelé

core /kɔː(r)/ n âmago m; (of apple, pear) coração m

cork /kɔːk/ n cortiça f; (for bottle) rolha f ● vt rolhar

corkscrew /'kɔːkskruː/ n saca-rolhas m

corn[1] /kɔːn/ n trigo m; Amer (maize) milho m; (seed) grão m; ~ **on the cob** espiga f de milho, cozinhada inteira

corn[2] /kɔːn/ n (hard skin) calo m

corner /'kɔːnə(r)/ n canto m; (of street) esquina f; (bend in road) curva f ● vt encurralar; (market) monopolizar ● vi dar uma curva, virar

cornet /'kɔːnɪt/ n Mus cornetim m; (for ice cream) casquinha f, (P) cone m

cornflakes /'kɔːnfleɪks/ npl cornflakes mpl, cereais mpl

cornflour /'kɔːnflaʊə(r)/ n fécula f de milho, maisena f

corny /'kɔːnɪ/ a 🄸 batido, (P) estafado

coronation /kɒrə'neɪʃn/ n coroação f

coroner /'kɒrənə(r)/ n magistrado m que investiga os casos de morte suspeita

corporal[1] /'kɔːpərəl/ n Mil cabo m

corporal[2] /'kɔːpərəl/ a ~ **punishment** castigo m corporal

corporate /'kɔːpərət/ a coletivo; (body) corporativo

corporation /kɔːpə'reɪʃn/ n corporação f; (of town) municipalidade f

corps /kɔː(r)/ n (pl corps /kɔːz/) corpo m

corpse /kɔːps/ n cadáver m

correct /kə'rekt/ a correto; **the ~ time** a hora certa; **you are ~** você tem razão ● vt corrigir. **~ion** /-ʃn/ n correção f, emenda f

correlat|e /'kɒrəleɪt/ vt/i correlacionar(-se). **~ion** /-'leɪʃn/ n correlação f

correspond /kɒrɪ'spɒnd/ vi corresponder (**to, with** a). **~ence** n correspondência f. **~ent** n correspondente mf. **~ing** a correspondente

corridor /'kɒrɪdɔː(r)/ n corredor m

corro|de /kə'rəʊd/ vt/i corroer(-se). **~sion** n corrosão f

corrugated /'kɒrəgeɪtɪd/ a corrugado; ~ **cardboard** cartão m canelado; ~ **iron** chapa f ondulada

corrupt /kə'rʌpt/ a corrupto ● vt corromper. **~ion** /-ʃn/ n corrupção f

corset /'kɔːsɪt/ n espartilho m; (elasticated) cinta f elástica

Corsica /'kɔːsɪkə/ n Córsega f

cosmetic /kɒz'metɪk/ n cosmético m ● a cosmético; fig superficial

cosmonaut /'kɒzmənɔːt/ n cosmonauta mf

cosmopolitan /kɒzmə'pɒlɪtən/ a & n cosmopolita mf

cosset /'kɒsɪt/ vt (pt cosseted) proteger

cost /kɒst/ vt (pt cost) custar; (pt costed) fixar o preço de ● n custo m; ~**s** Jur custos mpl; **at all** ~**s** custe o que custar; **to one's** ~ à sua custa; ~ **of living** custo m de vida

costly /'kɒstlɪ/ a (-ier, -iest) caro ● a caro; (valuable) precioso

costume /'kɒstjuːm/ n traje m

cos|y /'kəʊzɪ/ a (-ier, -iest) confortável, íntimo ● n abafador m (do bule do chá)

cot /kɒt/ n cama f de bebê, (P) de bebé, berço m

cottage /'kɒtɪdʒ/ n pequena casa f de campo; ~ **cheese** requeijão m, ricota f; ~ **industry** artesanato m;

~ pie empada f de carne picada

cotton /'kɒtn/ n algodão m; (thread) fio m, linha f; **~ wool** algodão m hidrófilo

couch /kautʃ/ n divã m

couchette /ku:'ʃet/ n couchette f

cough /kɒf/ vi tossir ● n tosse f

could /kud, kəd/ pt of ▶ **CAN²**

council /'kaunsl/ n conselho m; **~ house** casa f de bairro popular

councillor /'kaunsələ(r)/ n vereador m

counsel /'ka.unsl/ n conselho m; (pl invar) Jur advogado m. **~lor** n conselheiro m

count¹ /kaunt/ vt/i contar; **~ on** contar com ● n conta f. **~down** n (rocket) contagem f regressiva or (P) decrescente

count² /kaunt/ n (nobleman) conde m

counter¹ /'kauntə(r)/ n (in shop) balcão m; (in game) ficha f, (P) tento m

counter² /'kauntə(r)/ adv **~ to** contrário a; **~ to** (in the opposite direction) em sentido contrário a ● a oposto ● vt opor; <blow> aparar ● vi ripostar

counter- /'kauntə(r)/ pref contra-

counteract /kauntər'ækt/ vt neutralizar, frustrar

counter-attack /'kauntərətæk/ n contra-ataque m ● vt/i contra-atacar

counterbalance /'kauntəbæləns/ n contrapeso m ● vt contrabalançar

counterfeit /'kauntəfit/ a falsificado, falso ● n falsificação f ● vt falsificar

counterfoil /'kauntəfɔil/ n talão m, canhoto m

counterpart /'kauntəpɑ:t/ n equivalente m; (person) homólogo m

counterproductive /'kauntəprədʌktiv/ a contraproducente

countersign /'kauntəsain/ vt subscrever documento já assinado; <cheque> contrassinar

countess /'kauntis/ n condessa f

countless /'kauntlis/ a sem conta, incontável, inúmero

country /'kʌntri/ n país m; (homeland) pátria f; (countryside) campo m

countryside /'kʌntrisaid/ n campo m

county /'kaunti/ n condado m

coup /ku:/ n **~ (d'état)** golpe m (de estado)

couple /'kʌpl/ n par m, casal m; **a ~ of** um par de ● vt/i unir(-se), ligar(-se); Techn acoplar

coupon /'ku:pɒn/ n cupão m

courage /'kʌridʒ/ n coragem f. **~ous** /kə'reidʒəs/ a corajoso

courgette /kuə'ʒet/ n abobrinha f

courier /'kuriə(r)/ n correio m; (for tourists) guia mf; (for parcels, mail) estafeta m

course /kɔ:s/ n curso m; (series) série f; Culin prato m; (for golf) campo m; fig caminho m; **in due ~** na altura devida, oportunamente; **in the ~ of** durante; **of ~** está claro, com certeza

court /kɔ:t/ n (of monarch) corte f; (courtyard) pátio m; Tennis court m; quadra f, (P) campo m; Jur tribunal m ● vt cortejar; (danger) provocar; **~ martial** (pl **courts martial**) conselho m de guerra

courteous /'kɜ:tiəs/ a cortês, delicado

courtesy /ˈkɜːtəsɪ/ n cortesia f

courtyard /ˈkɔːtjɑːd/ n pátio m

cousin /ˈkʌzn/ n primo m; **first/ second ~** primo m em primeiro/ segundo grau

cove /kəʊv/ n angra f, enseada f

cover /ˈkʌvə(r)/ vt/i cobrir; **~ up** tapar; fig encobrir ● n cobertura f; (for bed) colcha f, (for book, furniture) capa f, (lid) tampa f; (shelter) abrigo m; **~ charge** serviço m; **take ~** abrigar-se; **under separate ~** em separado. **~ing** n cobertura f; **~ing letter** carta (que acompanha um documento) f. **~up** n fig encobrimento m

coverage /ˈkʌvərɪdʒ/ n (of events) reportagem f, cobertura f

covet /ˈkʌvɪt/ vt cobiçar

cow /kaʊ/ n vaca f

coward /ˈkaʊəd/ n covarde mf. **~ly** a covarde

cowardice /ˈkaʊədɪs/ n covardia f

cowboy /ˈkaʊbɔɪ/ n cowboy m, vaqueiro m

cower /ˈkaʊə(r)/ vi encolher-se (de medo)

cowshed /ˈkaʊʃed/ n estábulo m

coy /kɔɪ/ a (-er, -est) (falsamente) tímido

crab /kræb/ n caranguejo m

crack /kræk/ n fenda f, (in glass) rachadura f, (noise) estalo m; ⊠ (joke) piada f, (drug) crack m ● ⊠ de elite ● vt/i estalar; ‹nut› quebrar, (P) partir; ‹problem› resolver; ‹voice› mudar; **~ down on** ⊠ cair em cima de, arrochar; **get ~ing** ⊠ pôr mãos à obra

cracker /ˈkrækə(r)/ n busca-pé m, bomba f de estalo; Culin bolacha f de água e sal

crackers /ˈkrækəz/ a ⊠ desmiolado; maluco 🇬🇧

crackle /ˈkrækl/ vi crepitar ● n crepitação f

cradle /ˈkreɪdl/ n berço m ● vt embalar

craft¹ /krɑːft/ n ofício m; (technique) arte f, (cunning) manha f, astúcia f

craft² /krɑːft/ n (invar) (boat) embarcação f

craftsman /ˈkrɑːftsmən/ n (pl -men) artífice mf. **~ship** n arte f

crafty /ˈkrɑːftɪ/ a (-ier, -iest) manhoso, astucioso

crag /kræg/ n penhasco m. **~gy** a escarpado, íngreme

cram /kræm/ vt (pt crammed) ~ **(for an exam)** decorar, (P) empinar; ~ **into/with** entulhar com

cramp /kræmp/ n cãibra f ● vt restringir, tolher. **~ed** a apertado

crane /kreɪn/ n grua f, (bird) grou m ● vt ‹neck› esticar

crank¹ /kræŋk/ n Techn manivela f. **~shaft** n Techn cambota f

crank² /kræŋk/ n excêntrico m. **~y** a excêntrico

crash /kræʃ/ n acidente m; (noise) estrondo m; Comm falência f, (financial) colapso m, crash m ● vt/i (fall/strike) cair/bater com estrondo; ‹two cars› chocar, bater; Comm abrir falência; ‹plane› cair; ~ **out** 🇬🇧 (go to sleep) apagar, (P) apagar-se; (be out of competition, race) ser eliminado, (P) cair de sono ● a ‹course, programme› intensivo. ~ **helmet** n capacete m; **~land** vi fazer uma aterrissagem forçada, (P) uma aterragem forçada

crate /kreɪt/ n engradado m

crater /ˈkreɪtə(r)/ n cratera f

crav|e /kreɪv/ vt/i **~e (for)** ansiar por. **~ing** n desejo m irresistível, ânsia f

crawl /krɔːl/ vi rastejar; (of baby) engatinhar, (P) andar de gatas; (of car) mover-se lentamente ● n rasteja m; (swimming) crawl m; **be ~ing with** fervilhar de, estar cheio de

crayfish /ˈkreɪfɪʃ/ n (pl invar) lagostim m

crayon /ˈkreɪən/ n crayon m, lápis m de pastel

craze /kreɪz/ n moda f, febre f

craz|y /ˈkreɪzɪ/ a (-ier, -iest) doido; louco (**about** por). **~iness** n loucura f

creak /kriːk/ n rangido m ● vi ranger

cream /kriːm/ n (milk fat; also fig) nata f, (cosmetic) Culin creme m ● a creme invar ● vt desnatar; **~ cheese** queijo-creme m. **~y** a cremoso

crease /kriːs/ n vinco m ● vt/i amarrotar(-se)

creat|e /kriːˈeɪt/ vt criar. **~ion** /-ʃn/ n criação f. **~ive** a criador, criativo. **~or** n criador m

creature /ˈkriːtʃə(r)/ n criatura f

crèche /kreɪʃ/ n creche f

credentials /krɪˈdenʃlz/ npl credenciais fpl; (of competence etc) referências fpl

credib|le /ˈkredəbl/ a crível, verossímil. **~ility** /-ˈbɪlətɪ/ n credibilidade f

credit /ˈkredɪt/ n crédito m; (honour) honra f, **~s** (cinema) créditos mpl; **~ card** cartão m de crédito ● vt (pt credited) acreditar em; Comm creditar; **~ sb with** atribuir a alguém. **~or** n credor m

creditable /ˈkredɪtəbl/ a louvável, honroso

creed /kriːd/ n credo m

creek /kriːk/ n enseada f estreita; **be up the ~** ✕ estar frito ✕

creep /kriːp/ vi (pt crept) rastejar; (move stealthily) mover-se furtivamente ● n ✕ cara m nojento, (P) tipo m nojento; **give sb the ~s** dar arrepios a alguém. **~er** n (planta f) trepadeira f. **~y** a arrepiante

cremat|e /krɪˈmeɪt/ vt cremar. **~ion** /-ʃn/ n cremação f

crematorium /kreməˈtɔːriəm/ n (pl -ia) crematório m

crêpe /kreɪp/ n crepe m; **~ paper** papel m crepom, (P) plissado

crept /krept/ ▶ CREEP

crescent /ˈkresnt/ n crescente m; (street) rua f em semicírculo

cress /kres/ n agrião m

crest /krest/ n (of bird, hill) crista f, (on coat of arms) timbre m

crevasse /krɪˈvæs/ n fenda(em geleira) f

crevice /ˈkrevɪs/ n racha f, fenda f

crew¹ /kruː/ ▶ CROW

crew² /kruː/ n tripulação f, (gang) bando m. **~ cut** n corte m à escovinha; **~ neck** n gola f redonda e um pouco subida, meia gola

crib¹ /krɪb/ n berço m; (Christmas) presépio m

crib² /krɪb/ vt/i (pt cribbed) 🎓 colar, (P) ✕ cabular ● n cópia f, plágio m; (translation) burro m ✕

cricket¹ /ˈkrɪkɪt/ n críquete m. **~er** n jogador m de críquete

cricket² /ˈkrɪkɪt/ n (insect) grilo m

crime /kraɪm/ n crime m; (minor) delito m; (collectively) criminalidade f

criminal /'krɪmɪnl/ a & n
criminoso m

crimson /'krɪmzn/ a & n
carmesim m

cring|e /krɪndʒ/ vi encolher-se

crinkle /'krɪŋkl/ vt/i enrugar(-se)
● n vinco m, ruga f

cripple /'krɪpl/ n aleijado m, coxo m
● vt estropiar; fig paralisar

crisis /'kraɪsɪs/ n (pl crises /-siːz/)
crise f

crisp /krɪsp/ a (-er, est) Culin
crocante; ⟨air⟩ fresco; ⟨manners,
reply⟩ decidido. ~s npl batatas fpl
fritas redondas

criterion /kraɪ'tɪərɪən/ n (pl -ia)
critério m

critic /'krɪtɪk/ n crítico m. ~al a
crítico. ~ally adv de forma crítica;
(ill) gravemente

criticism /'krɪtɪsɪzəm/ n crítica f

criticize /'krɪtɪsaɪz/ vt/i criticar

croak /krəʊk/ n (frog) coaxar m;
(raven) crocitar m, crocito m ● vi
(frog) coaxar; (raven) crocitar

crochet /'krəʊʃeɪ/ n crochê m ● vt
fazer em crochê

crockery /'krɒkərɪ/ n louça f

crocodile /'krɒkədaɪl/ n
crocodilo m

crocus /'krəʊkəs/ n (pl -uses /-sɪz/)
croco m

crony /'krəʊnɪ/ n camarada mf,
amigão m, parceiro m

crook /krʊk/ n 🗓 (criminal)
vigarista mf; (stick) cajado m

crooked /'krʊkɪd/ a torcido;
(winding) tortuoso; (askew) torto; 🗓
(dishonest) desonesto

crop /krɒp/ n colheita f; fig
quantidade f; (haircut) corte m rente
● vt (pt cropped) cortar ● vi ~ up

aparecer, surgir

croquet /'krəʊkeɪ/ n croquet m,
croqué m

cross /krɒs/ n cruz f ● vt/i cruzar;
⟨cheque⟩ cruzar, (P) barrar;
(oppose) contrariar; (of paths)
cruzar-se ● a zangado; ~ off or
out riscar; ~ o.s. benzer-se; ~
sb's mind passar pela cabeça or
pelo espírito de alguém, ocorrer a
alguém; talk at ~ purposes falar
sem se entender. ~-country a &
adv a corta-mato; ~-examine vt
fazer o contrainterrogatório (de
testemunhas); ~-eyed a vesgo,
estrábico; ~-fire n fogo m cruzado;
~-section n corte m transversal; fig
grupo or sector m representativo m

crossbar /'krɒsbɑː(r)/ n barra
f transversal f; (of bicycle) travessão m

crossing /'krɒsɪŋ/ n cruzamento
m; (by boat) travessia f; (on road)
passagem f

crossroads /'krɒsrəʊdz/ n
encruzilhada f, cruzamento m

crossword /'krɒswɜːd/ n palavras
fpl cruzadas

crotch /krɒtʃ/ n entrepernas fpl

crouch /kraʊtʃ/ vi agachar-se

crow /krəʊ/ n corvo m; as the ~
flies em linha reta ● vi (cock) cantar;
cantar; fig rejubilar-se (over com)

crowbar /'krəʊbɑː(r)/ n alavanca f,
pé-de-cabra m

crowd /kraʊd/ n multidão f ● vi
afluir ● vt encher; ~ into apinhar-se
em. ~ed a cheio, apinhado

crown /kraʊn/ n coroa f; (of hill)
topo m, cume m ● vt coroar; ⟨tooth⟩
pôr uma coroa em

crucial /'kruːʃl/ a crucial

crucifix /'kruːsɪfɪks/ n crucifixo m

crucif|y /'kru:sɪfaɪ/ vt crucificar. **~ixion** /-'fɪkʃn/ n crucificação f

crude /kru:d/ a (**-er, -est**) (raw) bruto; (rough, vulgar) grosseiro; **~ oil** petróleo m bruto

cruel /krʊəl/ a (**crueller, cruellest**) cruel. **~ty** n crueldade f

cruis|e /kru:z/ n cruzeiro m ● vi cruzar; (of tourists) fazer um cruzeiro; (of car) ir a velocidade de cruzeiro; **~ing speed** velocidade f de cruzeiro. **~er** n cruzador m

crumb /krʌm/ n migalha f, farelo m

crumble /'krʌmbl/ vt/i desfazer(-se); ‹bread› esmigalhar(-se); (collapse) desmoronar-se

crumple /'krʌmpl/ vt/i amarrotar(-se)

crunch /krʌntʃ/ vt trincar; (under one's feet) fazer ranger

crusade /kru:'seɪd/ n cruzada f. **~r** /-ə(r)/ n cruzado m; fig militante m

crush /krʌʃ/ vt esmagar; ‹clothes, papers› amassar, amarrotar ● n aperto m; **a ~ on** 🄴 uma paixonite or (P) paixoneta por

crust /krʌst/ n côdea f, crosta f. **~y** a crocante

crutch /krʌtʃ/ n muleta f; (crotch) entrepernas fpl

crux /krʌks/ n (pl **cruxes**) o ponto crucial

cry /kraɪ/ n grito m; **a far ~ from** muito diferente de ● vi (weep) chorar; (call out) gritar

crypt /krɪpt/ n cripta f

cryptic /'krɪptɪk/ a críptico, enigmático

crystal /'krɪstl/ n cristal m. **~lize** vt/i cristalizar(-se)

cub /kʌb/ n cria f, filhote m; **C~** (Scout) lobito m

Cuba /'kju:bə/ n Cuba f

cubbyhole /'kʌbɪhəʊl/ n cochicho m; (snug place) cantinho m

cub|e /kju:b/ n cubo m. **~ic** a cúbico

cubicle /'kju:bɪkl/ n cubículo m, compartimento m; (at swimming pool) cabine f

cuckoo /'kʊku:/ n cuco m

cucumber /'kju:kʌmbə(r)/ n pepino m

cuddl|e /'kʌdl/ vt/i abraçar com carinho; (nestle) aninhar(-se) ● n abracinho m, festinha f. **~y** a fofo, aconchegante

cue¹ /kju:/ n Theat deixa f; (hint) sugestão f, sinal m

cue² /kju:/ n (billiards) taco m

cuff /kʌf/ n punho m; (blow) sopapo m; **off the ~** de improviso ● vt dar um sopapo. **~link** n botão m de punho

cul-de-sac /'kʌldəsæk/ n (pl **culs-de-sac**) beco m sem saída

culinary /'kʌlɪnərɪ/ a culinário

cull /kʌl/ vt (select) escolher; (kill) abater seletivamente ● n abate m

culminat|e /'kʌlmɪneɪt/ vi **~e in** acabar em. **~ion** /-'neɪʃn/ n auge m, ponto m culminante

culprit /'kʌlprɪt/ n culpado m

cult /kʌlt/ n culto m

cultivat|e /'kʌltɪveɪt/ vt cultivar. **~ion** /-'veɪʃn/ n cultivo m, cultivação f

cultural /'kʌltʃərəl/ a cultural

culture /'kʌltʃə(r)/ n cultura f. **~d** a culto

cumbersome /'kʌmbəsəm/ a (unwieldy) pesado; incômodo, (P) incómodo

cumulative /'kju:mjʊlətɪv/ a cumulativo

cunning /'kʌnɪŋ/ a astuto, manhoso ● n astúcia f, manha f

cup /kʌp/ n xícara f, (P) chávena f; (prize) taça f, C~ **Final** Final de Campeonato f

cupboard /'kʌbəd/ n armário m

curable /'kjʊərəbl/ a curável

curator /kjʊə'reɪtə(r)/ n (museum) conservador m; Jur curador m

curb /kɜːb/ n freio m ● vt refrear; (price increase etc) sustar

curdle /'kɜːdl/ vt/i coalhar

cure /kjʊə(r)/ vt curar ● n cura f

curfew /'kɜːfjuː/ n toque m de recolher, recolher m obrigatório

curio /'kjʊərɪəʊ/ n (pl -os) curiosidade f

curious /'kjʊərɪəs/ a curioso. ~osity /-'ɒsətɪ/ n curiosidade f

curl /kɜːl/ vt/i encaracolar(-se) ● n caracol m; ~ **up** enroscar(-se)

curler /'kɜːlə(r)/ n rolo m

curly /'kɜːlɪ/ a (-ier, -iest) encaracolado, crespo

currant /'kʌrənt/ n passa f de Corinto

currency /'kʌrənsɪ/ n moeda f corrente; (general use) circulação f; **foreign** ~ moeda f estrangeira

current /'kʌrənt/ a (common) corrente; ‹event, price, etc› atual; ~ **account** conta f corrente; ~ **affairs** atualidades fpl ● n corrente f. ~**ly** adv atualmente

curriculum /kə'rɪkjʊləm/ n (pl -la) currículo m, programa m de estudos. ~ **vitae** n curriculum vitae m

curry[1] /'kʌrɪ/ n caril m

curry[2] /'kʌrɪ/ vt ~ **favour with** procurar agradar a

curse /kɜːs/ n maldição f, praga f; (bad language) palavrão m ● vt amaldiçoar, praguejar contra ● vi praguejar; (swear) dizer palavrões

cursor /'kɜːsə(r)/ n cursor m

cursory /'kɜːsərɪ/ a apressado, superficial; **a ~ look** uma olhada superficial

curt /kɜːt/ a brusco

curtail /kɜː'teɪl/ vt abreviar; ‹expenses etc› reduzir

curtain /'kɜːtn/ n cortina f; Theat pano m

curtsy /'kɜːtsɪ/ n reverência f ● vi fazer uma reverência

curve /kɜːv/ n curva f ● vt/i curvar(-se); (of road) fazer uma curva

cushion /'kʊʃn/ n almofada f ● vt ‹a blow› amortecer; fig proteger

cushy /'kʊʃɪ/ a (-ier, -iest) 🆃 fácil; agradável; ~ **job** sinecura f, tacho m fig

custard /'kʌstəd/ n creme m

custodian /kʌ'stəʊdɪən/ n guarda m

custody /'kʌstədɪ/ n (safe keeping) custódia f; Jur detenção f; (of child) tutela f

custom /'kʌstəm/ n costume m; Comm freguesia f, clientela f. ~**ary** a habitual

customer /'kʌstəmə(r)/ n freguês m, cliente mf

customs /'kʌstəmz/ npl alfândega f ● a alfandegário; ~ **clearance** desembaraço m alfandegário; ~ **officer** funcionário m da alfândega

cut /kʌt/ vt/i (pt **cut**, pres p **cutting**) cortar; ‹prices etc› reduzir; ~ **back** or **down (on)** reduzir; ~ **in** intrometer-se; Auto cortar; ~ **off** cortar; fig isolar; ~ **out** recortar; (leave out) suprimir; ~ **short** encurtar, (P) atalhar ● n corte m, golpe m; (of clothes, hair) corte m; (piece) pedaço m; (prices etc) redução f, corte m; ⊠ (share) comissão f, (P) talhada f ⊠. ~back n corte m; ~out n figura f para recortar; ~price a a preço(s) reduzido(s)

cute /kjuːt/ a (-er, -est) 🗉 (clever) esperto; (attractive) bonito, (P) giro 🗉

cutlery /ˈkʌtlərɪ/ n talheres mpl

cutlet /ˈkʌtlɪt/ n costeleta f

cutting /ˈkʌtɪŋ/ a cortante ● n (from newspaper) recorte m; (plant) estaca f; ~ **edge** gume m

CV abbr ▶ CURRICULUM VITAE

cybercafe /ˈsaɪbəkæfeɪ/ n lan house f, (P) cibercafé m

cyberspace /ˈsaɪbəspeɪs/ n ciberespaço m

cybersquatter /ˈsaɪbəskwɒtə(r)/ n: pessoa que compra nome de domínio de marca famosa para vendê-lo depois com lucro; (P) ciberespeculador/a mf

cyberterrorism /ˈsaɪbəterərɪzəm/ n terrorismo m cibernético, (P) ciberterrorismo m

cycl|e /ˈsaɪkl/ n ciclo m; (bicycle) bicicleta f ● vi andar de bicicleta; ~ **lane** ciclovia f. ~**ing** n ciclismo m. ~**ist** n ciclista mf

cyclone /ˈsaɪkləʊn/ n ciclone m

cylind|er /ˈsɪlɪndə(r)/ n cilindro m. ~**rical** a cilíndrico

cymbals /ˈsɪmblz/ npl Mus pratos mpl

cynic /ˈsɪnɪk/ n cínico m. ~**al** a cínico. ~**ism** /-sɪzəm/ n cinismo m

Cypr|us /ˈsaɪprəs/ n Chipre m. ~**iot** /ˈsɪprɪət/ a & n cipriota mf

cyst /sɪst/ n quisto m

Czech /tʃek/ a & n tcheco m, (P) checo m

Dd

dab /dæb/ vt (pt **dabbed**) aplicar levemente ● n a ~ of uma aplicaçãozinha de; ~ **sth on** aplicar qq coisa em gestos leves

dabble /ˈdæbl/ vi ~ **in** interessar-se por, fazer um pouco de (como amador)

dad /dæd/ n 🗉 paizinho m 🗉. ~**dy** n (children's use) papai m, (P) papá m. ~**dy-long-legs** n pernilongo m

daffodil /ˈdæfədɪl/ n narciso m

daft /dɑːft/ a (-er, -est) doido, maluco

dagger /ˈdægə(r)/ n punhal m; at ~**s drawn** prestes a lutar (**with** com)

> **Dáil Éireann** É o nome da câmara baixa do Parlamento da República da Irlanda. Pronuncia-se /ˈeːrl(ə)n, ˈeːrlʲən/ e é formada por 166 representantes ou deputados, normalmente conhecidos por TDs, que representam 41 circunscrições. São eleitos através do sistema de representação proporcional. De acordo com a Constituição, deve haver um deputado para cada 20.000 ou 30.000 pessoas.

---

daily /ˈdeɪlɪ/ a diário, cotidiano, quotidiano ● adv diariamente, todos os dias ● n (newspaper) diário m; 🗉 (charwoman) faxineira f, (P) mulher f a dias

dainty /ˈdeɪntɪ/ a (-ier, -iest) delicado; (pretty, neat) gracioso

dairy /'deərɪ/ n leiteria f, (P) leitaria; **~ products** laticínios mpl

daisy /'deɪzɪ/ n margarida f

dam /dæm/ n barragem f, represa f ● vt (pt **dammed**) represar

damag|e /'dæmɪdʒ/ n estrago(s) mpl; **~es** Jur perdas fpl e danos mpl ● vt estragar, danificar

dame /deɪm/ n old use dama f; Amer 🇺🇸 mulher f

damn /dæm/ vt Relig condenar ao inferno; (swear at) amaldiçoar, maldizer; fig (condemn) condenar; **I'll be ~ed** if que um raio me atinja se ● int raios!, bolas! ● n **not care a ~** 🇺🇸 estar pouco ligando 🇺🇸, (P) estar-se marimbando 🇵🇹 ● a 🇺🇸 do diabo 🇺🇸, danado ● adv 🇺🇸 muitíssimo. **~ation** /-'neɪʃn/ n danação f, condenação f

damp /dæmp/ n umidade f, (P) humidade f ● a (-er, -est) úmido, (P) húmido ● vt umedecer, (P) humedecer. **~en** vt = DAMP. **~ness** n umidade f, (P) humidade f

dance /dɑːns/ vt/i dançar ● n dança f; **~ hall** sala f de baile. **~r** /-ə(r)/ n dançarino m; (professional) bailarino m

dandelion /'dændɪlaɪən/ n dente-de-leão m

dandruff /'dændrʌf/ n caspa f

Dane /deɪn/ n dinamarquês m

danger /'deɪndʒə(r)/ n perigo m; **be in ~ of** correr o risco de. **~ous** a perigoso

dangle /'dæŋgl/ vi oscilar, pender ● vt ter ou trazer dependurado; (hold) balançar; fig <hopes, etc> acenar com

Danish /'deɪnɪʃ/ a dinamarquês ● n Lang dinamarquês m

dare /deə(r)/ vt **~ to do** ousar fazer; **~ sb to do** desafiar alguém a fazer; **I ~ say** creio ● n desafio m

daredevil /'deədevl/ n louco m, temerário m

daring /'deərɪŋ/ a audacioso ● n audácia f

dark /dɑːk/ a (-er, -est) escuro, sombrio; (gloomy) sombrio; (of colour) escuro; (of skin) moreno; **~ horse** concorrente mf que é uma incógnita ● n escuridão f, escuro m; (nightfall) anoitecer m, cair m da noite; **be in the ~ about** fig ignorar. **~room** n câmara f escura. **~ness** n escuridão f

darken /'dɑːkən/ vt/i escurecer

darling /'dɑːlɪŋ/ a & n querido m

darn /dɑːn/ vt serzir, remendar

dart /dɑːt/ n dardo m, flecha f; **~s** (game) jogo m de dardos ● vi lançar-se

dartboard /'dɑːtbɔːd/ n alvo m

dash /dæʃ/ vi precipitar-se; **~ off** partir a toda velocidade; (letter) escrever à pressa ● vt arremessar; <hopes> destruir ● n corrida f; (stroke) travessão m; (Morse) traço m; **a ~ of** um pouco de

dashboard /'dæʃbɔːd/ n painel m de instrumentos, quadro m de bordo

data /'deɪtə/ npl dados mpl; **~ capture** aquisição f de informações, recolha f de dados; **~ processing** processamento m or tratamento m de dados. **~base** n base f de dados

date¹ /deɪt/ n data f; 🇺🇸 encontro m marcado; vt/i datar; 🇺🇸 andar com; **out of ~** desatualizado; **to ~** até à data; **up to ~** <style> moderno; <information etc> em dia. **~d** a antiquado

date² /deɪt/ n (fruit) tâmara f

383

daub | decay

daub /dɔːb/ vt borrar, pintar toscamente

daughter /'dɔːtə(r)/ n filha f.
~-in-law n (pl **~s-in-law**) nora f

daunt /dɔːnt/ vt assustar, intimidar, desencorajar

dawdle /'dɔːdl/ vi perder tempo

dawn /dɔːn/ n madrugada f ● vi madrugar, amanhecer; **~ on** fig fazer-se luz no espírito de, começar a perceber

day /deɪ/ n dia m; (period) época f, tempo m; **the ~ before** a véspera. **~dream** n devaneio m ● vi devanear

daybreak /'deɪbreɪk/ n romper m do dia, aurora f, amanhecer m

daylight /'deɪlaɪt/ n luz f do dia; **~ robbery** roubar descaradamente

daytime /'deɪtaɪm/ n dia m, dia m claro

daze /deɪz/ vt aturdir ● n **in a ~** aturdido

dazzle /'dæzl/ vt deslumbrar; (with headlights) ofuscar

dead /ded/ a morto; (numb) dormente; **~ end** beco m sem saída; **in the ~ centre** bem no meio ● adv completamente, de todo; **stop ~** estacar ● n **the ~** os mortos; **in the ~ of the night** a horas mortas, na calada da noite. **~pan** a inexpressivo

deaden /'dedn/ vt ‹sound, blow› amortecer; ‹pain› aliviar

deadline /'dedlaɪn/ n prazo m final

deadlock /'dedlɒk/ n impasse m

deadly /'dedlɪ/ a (-ier, -iest) mortal; ‹weapon› mortífero

deaf /def/ a (-er, -est) surdo; **turn a ~ ear** fingir que não ouve; **~ mute** surdo-mudo m. **~ness** n surdez f

deafen /'defn/ vt ensurdecer. **~ing** a ensurdecedor

deal /diːl/ vt (pt dealt) distribuir; ‹a blow, cards› dar ● vi negociar ● n negócio m; Cards vez de dar f; **a great ~** muito (of de); **~ in** negociar em; **~ with** ‹person› tratar (com); ‹affair› tratar de. **~er** n comerciante m; (agent) concessionário m; representante m

dealt /delt/ ▶ DEAL

dean /diːn/ n decano m

dear /dɪə(r)/ a (-er, -est) (cherished) caro, querido; (expensive) caro ● n amor m ● adv caro ● int **oh ~!** meu Deus!. **~ly** adv (very much) muito; ‹pay› caro

dearth /dɜːθ/ n escassez f

death /deθ/ n morte f; **~ certificate** certidão f de óbito; **~ penalty** pena f de morte; **~ rate** taxa f de mortalidade; **~ trap** lugar m perigoso, ratoeira f. **~ly** a de morte, mortal

debase /dɪ'beɪs/ vt degradar

debat|e /dɪ'beɪt/ n debate m ● vt debater. **~able** a discutível

debauchery /dɪ'bɔːtʃərɪ/ n deboche m, devassidão f

debit /'debɪt/ n débito m ● vt (pt debited) debitar

debris /'debriː/ n destroços mpl

debt /det/ n dívida f; **in ~** endividado. **~or** n devedor m

debut /'deɪbjuː/ n (of actor, play etc) estreia f

decade /'dekeɪd/ n década f

decaden|t /'dekədənt/ a decadente. **~ce** n decadência f

decaffeinated /diː'kæfɪneɪtɪd/ a sem cafeína

decapitate /dɪ'kæpɪteɪt/ vt decapitar

decay /dɪ'keɪ/ vi apodrecer, estragar-se; ‹food› fig deteriorar-se;

(*building*) degradar-se ● *n* apodrecimento *m*; (*of tooth*) cárie *f*; *fig* declínio *m*; decadência *f*

deceased /dɪ'si:st/ *a* & *n* falecido *m*, defunto *m*

deceit /dɪ'si:t/ *n* engano *m*. ~ful *a* enganador

deceive /dɪ'si:v/ *vt* enganar, iludir

December /dɪ'sembə(r)/ *n* dezembro *m*

decen|t /'di:snt/ *a* decente; ⊞ (*good*) (bastante) bom; ⊞ (*likeable*) simpático. ~cy *n* decência *f*

decentralize /di:'sentrəlaɪz/ *vt* descentralizar

decept|ive /dɪ'septɪv/ *a* enganador, ilusório. ~ion /-ʃn/ *n* engano *m*

decide /dɪ'saɪd/ *vt/i* decidir; ~ on decidir-se por; ~ to do decidir fazer. ~d /-ɪd/ *a* decidido; (*clear*) definido, nítido. ~dly /-ɪdlɪ/ *adv* decididamente

decimal /'desɪml/ *a* decimal ● *n* (*fração f,*) decimal *m*; ~ **point** vírgula *f* decimal

decipher /dɪ'saɪfə(r)/ *vt* decifrar

decision /dɪ'sɪʒn/ *n* decisão *f*

decisive /dɪ'saɪsɪv/ *a* decisivo; ‹*manner*› decidido

deck /dek/ *n* convés *m*; (*of cards*) baralho *m*. ~**chair** *n* espreguiçadeira *f*

declar|e /dɪ'kleə(r)/ *vt* declarar. ~ation /deklə'reɪʃn/ *n* declaração *f*

decline /dɪ'klaɪn/ *vt* (*refuse*) declinar, recusar delicadamente; *Gram* declinar ● *vi* (*deteriorate*) declinar; (*fall*) baixar ● *n* declínio *m*; (*fall*) abaixamento *m*

decode /di:'kəʊd/ *vt* descodificar

decompos|e /di:kəm'pəʊz/ *vt/i* decompor(-se). ~ition /-ɒmpə'zɪʃn/ *n* decomposição *f*

décor /'deɪkɔ:(r)/ *n* decoração *f*

decorat|e /'dekəreɪt/ *vt* decorar, enfeitar; (*paint*) pintar; (*paper*) pôr papel em. ~ion /-'reɪʃn/ *n* decoração *f*; (*medal etc*) condecoração *f*. ~ive /-ətɪv/ *a* decorativo

decoy[1] /'di:kɔɪ/ *n* chamariz *m*, engodo *m*; (*trap*) armadilha *f*

decoy[2] /dɪ'kɔɪ/ *vt* atrair, apanhar

decrease[1] /dɪ'kri:s/ *vt/i* diminuir

decrease[2] /'di:kri:s/ *n* diminuição *f*

decrepit /dɪ'krepɪt/ *a* decrépito

dedicat|e /'dedɪkeɪt/ *vt* dedicar. ~ed *a* dedicado. ~ion /-'keɪʃn/ *n* dedicação *f*; (*in book*) dedicatória *f*

deduce /dɪ'dju:s/ *vt* deduzir

deduct /dɪ'dʌkt/ *vt* deduzir; (*from pay*) descontar

deduction /dɪ'dʌkʃn/ *n* dedução *f*; (*from pay*) desconto *m*

deed /di:d/ *n* ato *m*; *Jur* contrato *m*

deep /di:p/ *a* (*-er, -est*) profundo; take a ~ **breath** respirar fundo ● *adv* profundamente. ~ **freeze** *n* congelador *m* ● ~**freeze** *vt* congelar

deepen /'di:pən/ *vt/i* aprofundar(-se); ‹*mystery, night*› adensar-se

deer /dɪə(r)/ *n* (*pl invar*) veado *m*

deface /dɪ'feɪs/ *vt* danificar, degradar

default /dɪ'fɔ:lt/ *vi* faltar ● *n* by ~ à revelia; **win by** ~ *Sport* ganhar por não comparecimento, (*P*) comparência ● *n* *Comput* default *m*

defeat /dɪ'fi:t/ *vt* derrotar; (*thwart*) malograr ● *n* derrota *f*; (*of plan, etc*) malogro *m*

defect[1] /'di:fekt/ *n* defeito *m*. ~ive /dɪ'fektɪv/ *a* defeituoso

defect[2] /dɪˈfekt/ vi desertar. **~ion** n defecção m. **~or** n trânsfuga mf, dissidente mf; (*political*) asilado m político

defence /dɪˈfens/ n defesa f. **~less** a indefeso

defend /dɪˈfend/ vt defender. **~ant** n Jur réu m, acusado m. **~er** n advogado m de defesa, defensor m

defensive /dɪˈfensɪv/ a defensivo ● n on the **~** na defensiva f; <*person, sport*> na retranca f 🄸

defer /dɪˈfɜː(r)/ vi (*pt* deferred) adiar, diferir ● vi **~ to** ceder, deferir

deferen|ce /ˈdefərəns/ n deferência f. **~tial** /-ˈrenʃl/ a deferente

defian|ce /dɪˈfaɪəns/ n desafio m; in **~ of** sem respeito por. **~t** a de desafio

deficien|t /dɪˈfɪʃnt/ a deficiente; be **~ in** ter falta de. **~cy** n deficiência f

deficit /ˈdefɪsɪt/ n déficit m

define /dɪˈfaɪn/ vt definir

definite /ˈdefɪnɪt/ a definido; (*clear*) categórico, claro; (*certain*) certo; **~ly** decididamente, (*clearly*) claramente

definition /defɪˈnɪʃn/ n definição f

definitive /dɪˈfɪnətɪv/ a definitivo

deflat|e /dɪˈfleɪt/ vt esvaziar; (*person*) desempoar, desinchar. **~ion** /-ʃn/ n esvaziamento m; Econ deflação f

deflect /dɪˈflekt/ vt/i desviar(-se)

deform /dɪˈfɔːm/ vt deformar. **~ed** a deformado, disforme. **~ity** n deformidade f

defraud /dɪˈfrɔːd/ vt defraudar

defrost /diːˈfrɒst/ vt descongelar

deft /deft/ a (**-er, -est**) hábil

defuse /diːˈfjuːz/ vt <*a bomb*> desativar; <*a situation*> acalmar

defy /dɪˈfaɪ/ vt desafiar; (*attempts*) resistir a; (*the law*) desobedecer a; (*public opinion*) opor-se a

degrade /dɪˈgreɪd/ vt degradar

degree /dɪˈgriː/ n grau m; Univ diploma m; **to a ~** ao mais alto grau, muito

dehydrate /diːˈhaɪdreɪt/ vt/i desidratar(-se)

de-ice /diːˈaɪs/ vt descongelar, degelar; (*windscreen*) tirar o gelo de

deign /deɪn/ vt **~ to do** dignar-se (a) fazer

deity /ˈdiːɪtɪ/ n divindade f

dejected /dɪˈdʒektɪd/ a abatido

delay /dɪˈleɪ/ vt atrasar; (*postpone*) retardar ● vi atrasar-se ● n atraso m, demora f

delegate[1] /ˈdelɪgət/ n delegado m

delegat|e[2] /ˈdelɪgeɪt/ vt delegar. **~ion** /-ˈgeɪʃn/ n delegação f

delet|e /dɪˈliːt/ vt riscar. **~ion** /-ʃn/ n rasura f

deliberate[1] /dɪˈlɪbərət/ a deliberado; (*steps etc*) compassado

deliberate[2] /dɪˈlɪbəreɪt/ vt/i deliberar

delica|te /ˈdelɪkət/ a delicado. **~cy** n delicadeza f; <*food*> guloseima f, iguaria f, (*P*) acepipe m

delicatessen /delɪkəˈtesn/ n (*shop*) mercearias fpl finas

delicious /dɪˈlɪʃəs/ a delicioso

delight /dɪˈlaɪt/ n grande prazer m, delícia f; (*thing*) delícia f, encanto m ● vt deliciar ● vi **~ in** deliciar-se com. **~ed** a deliciado, encantado. **~ful** a delicioso, encantador

delinquen|t /dɪˈlɪŋkwənt/ a & n delinquente mf

deliri|ous /dɪˈlɪrɪəs/ a delirante; **be ~ous** delirar. **~um** /-əm/ n delírio m

deliver /dɪˈlɪvə(r)/ vt entregar; ‹letters› distribuir; ‹free› libertar; Med fazer o parto. **~y** n entrega f; ‹letters› distribuição f; Med parto m

delu|de /dɪˈluːd/ vt enganar; **~de o.s.** ter ilusões. **~sion** /-ʒn/ n ilusão f

deluge /ˈdeljuːdʒ/ n dilúvio m ● vt inundar

de luxe /dɪˈlʌks/ a de luxo

delve /delv/ vi **~ into** pesquisar, rebuscar

demand /dɪˈmɑːnd/ vt exigir; (ask to be told) perguntar ● n exigência f; Comm procura f; ‹claim› reivindicação f; **in ~** procurado. **~ing** a exigente; ‹work› puxado, custoso

demeanour /dɪˈmiːnə(r)/ n comportamento m, conduta f

demented /dɪˈmentɪd/ a louco, demente; **become ~** enlouquecer

demo /ˈdeməʊ/ n (pl -os) 🆃 manifestação f, (P) manif f

democracy /dɪˈmɒkrəsɪ/ n democracia f

democrat /ˈdeməkræt/ n democrata mf. **~ic** /-ˈkrætɪk/ a democrático

demoli|sh /dɪˈmɒlɪʃ/ vt demolir. **~tion** /deməˈlɪʃn/ n demolição f

demon /ˈdiːmən/ n demônio m, (P) demónio m

demonstrat|e /ˈdemənstreɪt/ vt demonstrar ● vi Pol fazer uma manifestação, manifestar-se. **~ion** /-ˈstreɪʃn/ n demonstração f; Pol manifestação f. **~or** n Pol manifestante mf

demonstrative /dɪˈmɒnstrətɪv/ a demonstrativo

demoralize /dɪˈmɒrəlaɪz/ vt desmoralizar

demote /dɪˈməʊt/ vt fazer baixar de posto, despromover, rebaixar

demure /dɪˈmjʊə(r)/ a recatado, modesto

den /den/ n antro m, covil m; (room) cantinho m, recanto m

denial /dɪˈnaɪəl/ n negação f; (refusal) recusa f; (statement) desmentido m

denim /ˈdenɪm/ n brim m; **~s** (jeans) jeans mpl, (P) calças f de ganga

Denmark /ˈdenmɑːk/ n Dinamarca f

denomination /dɪnɒmɪˈneɪʃn/ n denominação f; Relig confissão f, seita f; (money) valor m

denote /dɪˈnəʊt/ vt denotar

denounce /dɪˈnaʊns/ vt denunciar

dens|e /dens/ a (-er, -est) denso; 🆃 ‹person› obtuso. **~ity** n densidade f

dent /dent/ n mossa f, depressão f ● vt dentear

dental /ˈdentl/ a dentário, dental

dentist /ˈdentɪst/ n dentista mf. **~ry** n odontologia f

denture /ˈdentʃə(r)/ n dentadura (postiça) f

deny /dɪˈnaɪ/ vt negar; ‹rumour› desmentir; (disown) renegar; (refuse) recusar

deodorant /diːˈəʊdərənt/ n & a desodorante m, (P) desodorizante m

depart /dɪˈpɑːt/ vi partir; **~ from** (deviate) afastar-se de, desviar-se de

department /dɪˈpɑːtmənt/ n departamento m; (in shop, office) seção f, (P) secção f; (government) repartição f; **~ store** loja f de departamentos, (P) grande armazém m

departure /dɪˈpɑːtʃə(r)/ n partida f; **a ~ from** ‹custom, diet etc› uma mudança de; **a new ~** uma nova orientação

depend /dɪˈpend/ vi **~ on** depender de; (trust) contar com. **~able** a de confiança. **~ence** n dependência f. **~ent (on)** a dependente (de)

dependant /dɪˈpendənt/ n dependente mf

depict /dɪˈpɪkt/ vt descrever; (in pictures) representar

deplor|e /dɪˈplɔː(r)/ vt deplorar. **~able** a deplorável

deport /dɪˈpɔːt/ vt deportar. **~ation** /diːpɔːˈteɪʃn/ n deportação f

depose /dɪˈpəʊz/ vt depor

deposit /dɪˈpɒzɪt/ vt (pt deposited) depositar ● n depósito m; **~ account** conta f de depósito a prazo

depot /ˈdepəʊ/ n Mil depósito m; (buses) garagem f; Amer (station) rodoviária f; estação f de trem, (P) de comboio

deprav|e /dɪˈpreɪv/ vt depravar

depreciat|e /dɪˈpriːʃieɪt/ vt/i depreciar(-se). **~ion** /-ˈeɪʃn/ n depreciação f

depress /dɪˈpres/ vt deprimir; (press down) carregar em. **~ion** /-ʃn/ n depressão f

deprivation /deprɪˈveɪʃn/ n privação f

deprive /dɪˈpraɪv/ vt **~ of** privar de. **~d** a privado; (underprivileged) deserdado (da sorte), destituído; ‹child› carente

depth /depθ/ n profundidade f; **be out of one's ~** perder pé, (P) não ter pé; fig ficar desnorteado, estar

perdido; **in the ~(s) of** no mais fundo de, nas profundezas de

deputy /ˈdepjʊti/ n (pl **-ies**) delegado m ● a adjunto; **~ chairman** vice-presidente m

derail /dɪˈreɪl/ vt descarrilhar; **be ~ed** descarrilhar. **~ment** n descarrilhamento m

deranged /dɪˈreɪndʒd/ a ‹mind› transtornado, louco

derelict /ˈderəlɪkt/ a abandonado

derivative /dɪˈrɪvətɪv/ a derivado; ‹work› pouco original ● n derivado m

deriv|e /dɪˈraɪv/ vt **~e from** tirar de ● vi **~e from** derivar de. **~ation** /derɪˈveɪʃn/ n derivação f

derogatory /dɪˈrɒgətrɪ/ a pejorativo; ‹remark› depreciativo

derv /dɜːv/ n gasóleo m

descend /dɪˈsend/ vt/i descer, descender; **be ~ed from** descender de. **~ant** n descendente mf

descent /dɪˈsent/ n descida f; (lineage) descendência f, origem f

descri|be /dɪsˈkraɪb/ vt descrever. **~ption** /-ˈkrɪpʃn/ n descrição f. **~ptive** /-ˈkrɪptɪv/ a descritivo

desecrat|e /ˈdesɪkreɪt/ vt profanar

desert[1] /ˈdezət/ a & n deserto m; **~ island** ilha f deserta

desert[2] /dɪˈzɜːt/ vt/i desertar. **~ed** a abandonado. **~er** n desertor m. **~ion** /-ʃn/ n deserção f

deserve /dɪˈzɜːv/ vt merecer. **~edly** /dɪˈzɜːvɪdlɪ/ adv merecidamente, a justo título. **~ing** a ‹person› merecedor; ‹action› meritório

design /dɪˈzaɪn/ n desenho m; (artistic) design m; (style of dress) modelo m; (pattern) padrão m, motivo m ● vt desenhar; (devise) conceber. **~er** n desenhador m; (of *dresses)* costureiro *m; (of machine)* inventor *m*

designat|e /'dezɪgneɪt/ *vt* designar. **~ion** /-'neɪʃn/ *n* designação *f*

desir|e /dɪ'zaɪə(r)/ *n* desejo *m* ● *vt* desejar. **~able** *a* desejável, atraente

desk /desk/ *n* secretária *f; (of pupil)* carteira *f; (in hotel)* recepção *f; (in bank)* caixa *f*

desolat|e /'desələt/ *a* desolado. **~ion** /-'leɪʃn/ *n* desolação *f*

despair /dɪ'speə(r)/ *n* desespero *m* ● *vi* desesperar (**of** de)

desperate /'despərət/ *a* desesperado; *(criminal)* capaz de tudo; **be ~ for** ter uma vontade doida de

desperation /despə'reɪʃn/ *n* desespero *m*

despicable /dɪ'spɪkəbl/ *a* desprezível

despise /dɪ'spaɪz/ *vt* desprezar

despite /dɪ'spaɪt/ *prep* apesar de, a despeito de, mau grado

desponden|t /dɪ'spɒndənt/ *a* desanimado

dessert /dɪ'zɜːt/ *n* sobremesa *f.* **~ spoon** *n* colher *f* de sobremesa

destination /destɪ'neɪʃn/ *n* destino *m*, destinação *f*

destiny /'destɪnɪ/ *n* destino *m*

destitute /'destɪtjuːt/ *a* destituído, indigente

destr|oy /dɪ'strɔɪ/ *vt* destruir. **~uction** /-'strʌkʃn/ *n* destruição *f.* **~uctive** *a* destruidor, destruidor

detach /dɪ'tætʃ/ *vt* separar, arrancar. **~able** *a* separável; *‹lining etc›* solto. **~ed** *a* separado; *(impartial)* imparcial; *(unemotional)* desprendido; **~ed house** casa *f* sem parede-meia com outra

detachment /dɪ'tætʃmənt/ *n* separação *f; (indifference)* desprendimento *m; Mil* destacamento *m; (impartiality)* imparcialidade *f*

detail /'diːteɪl/ *n* pormenor *m*, detalhe *m* ● *vt* detalhar; *‹troops›* destacar. **~ed** *a* detalhado

detain /dɪ'teɪn/ *vt* reter; *(in prison)* deter. **~ee** /diːteɪ'niː/ *n* detido *m*

detect /dɪ'tekt/ *vt* detectar. **~ion** /-ʃn/ *n* detecção *f*

detective /dɪ'tektɪv/ *n* detetive *m;* **~ story** romance *m* policial

detention /dɪ'tenʃn/ *n* detenção *f;* **be given a ~** *(school)* ficar de castigo na escola

deter /dɪ'tɜː(r)/ *vt* (*pt* **deterred**) dissuadir; *(hinder)* impedir

detergent /dɪ'tɜːdʒənt/ *a & n* detergente *m*

deteriorat|e /dɪ'tɪərɪəreɪt/ *vi* deteriorar(-se). **~ion** /-'reɪʃn/ *n* deterioração *f*

determin|e /dɪ'tɜːmɪn/ *vt* determinar; **~e to do** decidir fazer. **~ation** /-'neɪʃn/ *n* determinação *f.* **~ed** *a* determinado; **~ed to do** decidido a fazer

deterrent /dɪ'terənt/ *n* dissuasivo *m*

detest /dɪ'test/ *vt* detestar. **~able** *a* detestável

detonat|e /'detəneɪt/ *vt/i* detonar. **~or** *n* espoleta *f*, detonador *m*

detour /'diːtʊə(r)/ *n* desvio *m*

detract /dɪ'trækt/ *vi* **~ from** depreciar, menosprezar

detriment /'detrɪmənt/ *n* detrimento *m.* **~al** /-'mentl/ *a* prejudicial

devalu|e /diː'væljuː/ *vt* desvalorizar. **~ation** /-'eɪʃn/ *n* desvalorização f

devastat|e /'devəsteɪt/ vi devastar; fig (overwhelm) arrasar. **~ing** a devastador; (criticism) de arrasar

develop /dɪ'veləp/ vt/i (pt developed) desenvolver(-se); (get) contrair; (build on) urbanizar; (film) revelar; **~ into** tornar-se; **~ing country** país m em vias de desenvolvimento. **~ment** n desenvolvimento m; (film) revelação f; (of land) urbanização f

deviat|e /'diːvɪeɪt/ vi desviar-se. **~ion** /-'eɪʃn/ n desvio m

device /dɪ'vaɪs/ n dispositivo m; (scheme) processo m; **left to one's own ~s** entregue a si mesmo

devil /'devl/ n diabo m

devious /'diːvɪəs/ a tortuoso; fig ⟨means⟩ escuso; fig ⟨person⟩ pouco franco

devise /dɪ'vaɪz/ vt imaginar, inventar

devoid /dɪ'vɔɪd/ a **~ of** desprovido de, destituído de

devot|e /dɪ'vəʊt/ vt dedicar, devotar. **~ed** a dedicado, devotado. **~ion** /-ʃn/ n devoção f

devotee /devə'tiː/ n **~ of** adepto m de, entusiasta mf de

devour /dɪ'vaʊə(r)/ vt devorar

devout /dɪ'vaʊt/ a devota, ⟨prayers⟩ fervoroso

dew /djuː/ n orvalho m

dext|erity /dek'sterətɪ/ n destreza f, jeito m. **~rous** /'dekstrəs/ a destro, hábil

diabet|es /daɪə'biːtiːz/ n diabetes f. **~ic** /-'betɪk/ a diabético

diabolical /daɪə'bɒlɪkl/ a diabólico

diagnose /'daɪəgnəʊz/ vt diagnosticar

diagnosis /daɪəg'nəʊsɪs/ n (pl **-oses** /-siːz/) diagnóstico m

diagonal /daɪ'ægənl/ a & n diagonal f

diagram /'daɪəgræm/ n diagrama m, esquema m

dial /'daɪəl/ n mostrador m ● vt (pt dialled) ⟨number⟩ marcar, discar; **~ling code** código m de discagem; **~ling tone** sinal m de discar

dialect /'daɪəlekt/ n dialeto m

dialogue /'daɪəlɒg/ n diálogo m

diameter /daɪ'æmɪtə(r)/ n diâmetro m

diamond /'daɪəmənd/ n diamante m, brilhante m; (shape) losango m; **~s** Cards ouros mpl

diaper /'daɪəpə(r)/ n Amer fralda f

diarrhoea /daɪə'rɪə/ n diarreia f

diary /'daɪərɪ/ n agenda f; (record) diário m

dice /daɪs/ n (pl invar) dado m

dictat|e /dɪk'teɪt/ vt/i ditar. **~ion** /-ʃn/ n ditado m

dictator /dɪk'teɪtə(r)/ n ditador m. **~ship** n ditadura f

dictionary /'dɪkʃənrɪ/ n dicionário m

did /dɪd/ ▶ DO

diddle /'dɪdl/ vt 🛈 trapacear; enganar

didn't /'dɪdnt/ (= did not) ▶ DO

die /daɪ/ vi (pres p dying) morrer; **be dying to** estar doido para; **~ down** diminuir, baixar; **~ out** desaparecer, extinguir-se

diesel /'diːzl/ n diesel m; **~ engine** motor m a diesel

diet /'daɪət/ n dieta f ● vi fazer dieta, estar de dieta

differ /'dɪfə(r)/ vi diferir; (disagree) discordar

differen|t /ˈdɪfrənt/ a diferente. ~ce n diferença f; (disagreement) desacordo m. ~ly adv diferentemente

differentiate /dɪfəˈrenʃɪeɪt/ vt/i diferençar(-se), diferenciar(-se)

difficult /ˈdɪfɪkəlt/ a difícil. ~y n dificuldade f

diffiden|t /ˈdɪfɪdənt/ a acanhado, inseguro. ~ce n acanhamento m, insegurança f

diffuse[1] /dɪˈfjuːs/ a difuso

diffus|e[2] /dɪˈfjuːz/ vt difundir

dig /dɪg/ vt/i (pt dug, pres p digging) cavar; (thrust) espetar ● n (with elbow) cotovelada f; (with finger) cutucada f, (P) espetadela f; (remark) ferroada f; Archaeol escavação f; ~s 🔢 quarto m alugado; ~ up desenterrar

digest /dɪˈdʒest/ vt/i digerir. ~ible a digerível, digestível. ~ion /-ʃn/ n digestão f

digit /ˈdɪdʒɪt/ n dígito m

digital /ˈdɪdʒɪtl/ a digital; ~ clock relógio m digital. ~ camera n câmera f digital, (P) câmara f digital; ~ television n televisão f ou TV digital

dignif|y /ˈdɪgnɪfaɪ/ vt dignificar. ~ied a digno

dignitary /ˈdɪgnɪtərɪ/ n dignitário m

dignity /ˈdɪgnətɪ/ n dignidade f

digress /daɪˈgres/ vi digressar, divagar; ~ from desviar-se de. ~ion /-ʃn/ n digressão f

dilapidated /dɪˈlæpɪdeɪtɪd/ a <house> arruinado, degradado; <car> estragado

dilat|e /daɪˈleɪt/ vt/i dilatar(-se)

dilemma /dɪˈlemə/ n dilema m

diligen|t /ˈdɪlɪdʒənt/ a diligente, aplicado. ~ce n diligência f, aplicação f

dilute /daɪˈljuːt/ vt diluir ● a diluído

dim /dɪm/ a (dimmer, dimmest) (weak) fraco; (dark) sombrio; (indistinct) vago; 🔢 (stupid) burro ● vt/i (pt dimmed) <light> baixar. ~ly adv (shine) fracamente; (remember) vagamente

dime /daɪm/ n Amer moeda f de dez centavos

dimension /daɪˈmenʃn/ n dimensão f

diminish /dɪˈmɪnɪʃ/ vt/i diminuir

diminutive /dɪˈmɪnjʊtɪv/ a diminuto ● n diminutivo m

dimple /ˈdɪmpl/ n covinha f

din /dɪn/ n barulheira f, (P) chinfrim m

dine /daɪn/ vi jantar. ~r /-ə(r)/ n (person) comensal m; Rail vagão-restaurante m; Amer (restaurant) lanchonete f

dinghy /ˈdɪŋgɪ/ n (pl -ghies) bote m; (inflatable) bote m de borracha, (P) barco m de borracha

dingy /ˈdɪndʒɪ/ a (-ier, -iest) com ar sujo, esquálido

dining room /ˈdaɪnɪŋruːm/ n sala f de jantar

dinner /ˈdɪnə(r)/ n jantar m; (lunch) almoço m. ~ jacket n smoking m

dinosaur /ˈdaɪnəsɔː(r)/ n dinossauro m

dip /dɪp/ vt/i (pt dipped) mergulhar; (lower) baixar ● n mergulho m; (bathe) banho m rápido, mergulho m; (slope) descida f; Culin molho m; ~ into <book> folhear; ~ one's headlights baixar para médios

diploma /dɪˈpləʊmə/ n diploma m

diplomacy /dɪˈpləʊməsɪ/ n
diplomacia f

diplomat /ˈdɪpləmæt/ n diplomata
mf. **~ic** /-ˈmætɪk/ a diplomático

dire /daɪə(r)/ a (-er, -est) terrível;
‹need, poverty› extremo

direct /dɪˈrekt/ a direto ● adv
diretamente ● vt dirigir; **~ sb to**
indicar a alguém o caminho para

direction /dɪˈrekʃn/ n direção f,
sentido m; **~s** instruções fpl; **~s for
use** modo m de emprego

directly /dɪˈrektlɪ/ adv
diretamente; (at once)
imediatamente, logo

director /dɪˈrektə(r)/ n diretor m

directory /dɪˈrektərɪ/ n
(telephone) **~** lista f telefônica or
(P) telefónica

dirt /dɜːt/ n sujeira, sujidade f;
~ cheap 🄸 baratíssimo

dirty /ˈdɜːtɪ/ a (-ier, -iest) sujo;
‹word› obsceno ● vt/i sujar(-se);
~ trick golpe m baixo, (P) baixa
partida f

disability /dɪsəˈbɪlətɪ/ n
deficiência f

disable /dɪsˈeɪbl/ vt incapacitar. **~d**
a inválido, deficiente

disadvantage /dɪsədˈvɑːntɪdʒ/ n
desvantagem f

disagree /dɪsəˈɡriː/ vi discordar
(with de); **~ with** ‹food, climate›
não fazer bem. **~ment** n desacordo
m; (quarrel) desentendimento m

disagreeable /dɪsəˈɡriːəbl/ a
desagradável

disappear /dɪsəˈpɪə(r)/
vi desaparecer. **~ance** n
desaparecimento m

disappoint /dɪsəˈpɔɪnt/ vt
desapontar, decepcionar. **~ment** n
desapontamento m, decepção f

disapprov|e /dɪsəˈpruːv/ vi **~e (of)**
desaprovar. **~al** n desaprovação f

disarm /dɪsˈɑːm/ vt/i desarmar.
~ament n desarmamento m

disast|er /dɪˈzɑːstə(r)/ n desastre
m. **~rous** a desastroso

disband /dɪsˈbænd/ vt/i debandar;
‹troops› dispersar

disbelief /dɪsbrˈliːf/ n
incredulidade f

disc /dɪsk/ n disco m; **~ jockey**
disc(o) jockey m

discard /dɪsˈkɑːd/ vt pôr de lado,
descartar(-se) de; ‹old clothes etc›
desfazer-se de

discern /dɪˈsɜːn/ vt discernir. **~ible**
a perceptível. **~ing** a perspicaz.
~ment n discernimento m,
perspicácia f

discharge[1] /dɪsˈtʃɑːdʒ/ vt
descarregar; (dismiss) despedir,
mandar embora; ‹duty› cumprir;
‹liquid› vazar, (P) deitar; ‹patient›
dar alta a; ‹prisoner› absolver,
pôr em liberdade; ‹pus› purgar,
(P) deitar

discharge[2] /ˈdɪstʃɑːdʒ/ n descarga
f; (dismissal) despedimento m;
(of patient) alta f; (of prisoner)
absolvição f; Med secreção f

disciple /dɪˈsaɪpl/ n discípulo m

disciplin|e /ˈdɪsɪplɪn/ n disciplina
f ● vt disciplinar; (punish) castigar.
~ary a disciplinar

disclaim /dɪsˈkleɪm/ vt Jur repudiar;
(deny) negar. **~er** n desmentido m

disclos|e /dɪsˈkləʊz/ vt revelar.
~ure /-ʒə(r)/ n revelação f

disco /ˈdɪskəʊ/ n (pl -os) 🄸
discoteca f

discolour /dɪsˈkʌlə(r)/ vt/i
descolorir(-se); (in sunlight)
desbotar(-se)

discomfort /dɪsˈkʌmfət/ n mal-estar m; (lack of comfort) desconforto m

disconcert /dɪskənˈsɜːt/ vt desconcertar. **~ing** a desconcertante

disconnect /dɪskəˈnekt/ vt desligar

discontent /dɪskənˈtent/ n descontentamento m. **~ed** a descontente

discontinue /dɪskənˈtɪnjuː/ vt descontinuar, suspender

discord /ˈdɪskɔːd/ n discórdia f

discount[1] /ˈdɪskaʊnt/ n desconto m

discount[2] /dɪsˈkaʊnt/ vt descontar; (disregard) dar o desconto a

discourage /dɪsˈkʌrɪdʒ/ vt desencorajar

discourteous /dɪsˈkɜːtɪəs/ a indelicado

discover /dɪsˈkʌvə(r)/ vt descobrir. **~y** n descoberta f; (of island etc) descobrimento m

discredit /dɪsˈkredɪt/ vt (pt discredited) desacreditar ● n descrédito m

discreet /dɪˈskriːt/ a discreto

discrepancy /dɪˈskrepənsɪ/ n discrepância f

discretion /dɪˈskreʃn/ n discrição f; (prudence) prudência f

discriminat|e /dɪsˈkrɪmɪneɪt/ vt/i discriminar; **~e against** tomar partido contra, fazer discriminação contra. **~ing** a discriminador; (having good taste) com discernimento. **~ion** /-ˈneɪʃn/ n discernimento m; (bias) discriminação f

discus /ˈdɪskəs/ n disco m

discuss /dɪˈskʌs/ vt discutir. **~ion** /-ʃn/ n discussão f

disdain /dɪsˈdeɪn/ n desdém m ● vt desdenhar. **~ful** a desdenhoso

disease /dɪˈziːz/ n doença f. a <plant> atacado por doença; <person, animal> doente

disembark /dɪsɪmˈbɑːk/ vt/i desembarcar

disenchant /dɪsɪnˈtʃɑːnt/ vt desencantar. **~ment** n desencantamento m

disengage /dɪsɪnˈgeɪdʒ/ vt desprender, soltar; Mech desengatar

disentangle /dɪsɪnˈtæŋgl/ vt desembaraçar, desenredar

disfigure /dɪsˈfɪgə(r)/ vt desfigurar

disgrace /dɪsˈgreɪs/ n vergonha f; (disfavour) desgraça f ● vt desonrar. **~ful** a vergonhoso

disgruntled /dɪsˈgrʌntld/ a descontente

disguise /dɪsˈgaɪz/ vt disfarçar ● n disfarce m; **in ~** disfarçado

disgust /dɪsˈgʌst/ n repugnância f ● vt repugnar. **~ing** a repugnante

dish /dɪʃ/ n prato m ● vt **~ out** 🗊 distribuir; **~ up** servir; **the ~es** (crockery) a louça f

dishcloth /ˈdɪʃklɒθ/ n pano m de prato

dishearten /dɪsˈhɑːtn/ vt desencorajar, desalentar

dishonest /dɪsˈɒnɪst/ a desonesto. **~y** n desonestidade f

dishonour /dɪsˈɒnə(r)/ n desonra f ● vt desonrar. **~able** a desonroso

dishwasher /ˈdɪʃwɒʃə(r)/ n lavadora f de pratos, (P) máquina f de lavar a louça

disillusion /dɪsɪˈluːʒn/ vt desiludir. **~ment** n desilusão f

disinfect /dɪsɪn'fekt/ vt desinfetar, (P) desinfectar. **~ant** n desinfetante m, (P) desinfectante m

disinherit /dɪsɪn'herɪt/ vt deserdar

disintegrate /dɪs'ɪntɪɡreɪt/ vt/i desintegrar(-se)

disinterested /dɪs'ɪntrəstɪd/ a desinteressado

disjointed /dɪs'dʒɔɪntɪd/ a ‹talk› descosido, desconexo

disk /dɪsk/ n Comput disco m Amer ▶ DISC; **~ drive** unidade f de disco

dislike /dɪs'laɪk/ n aversão f, antipatia f ● vt não gostar de, antipatizar com

dislocat|e /'dɪsləkeɪt/ vt ‹limb› deslocar

dislodge /dɪs'lɒdʒ/ vt desalojar

disloyal /dɪs'lɔɪəl/ a desleal. **~ty** n deslealdade f

dismal /'dɪzməl/ a tristonho

dismantle /dɪs'mæntl/ vt desmantelar

dismay /dɪs'meɪ/ n consternação f ● vt consternar

dismiss /dɪs'mɪs/ vt despedir; (from mind) afastar, pôr de lado. **~al** n despedimento m

dismount /dɪs'maʊnt/ vi desmontar

disobedien|t /dɪsə'biːdɪənt/ a desobediente. **~ce** n desobediência f

disobey /dɪsə'beɪ/ vt/i desobedecer (a)

disorder /dɪs'ɔːdə(r)/ n desordem f; Med perturbações fpl, disfunção f. **~ly** a desordenado; (riotous) desordeiro

disown /dɪs'əʊn/ vt repudiar

disparaging /dɪ'spærɪdʒɪŋ/ a depreciativo

dispatch /dɪ'spætʃ/ vt despachar ● n despacho m

dispel /dɪ'spel/ vt (pt dispelled) dissipar

dispensary /dɪ'spensərɪ/ n dispensário m, farmácia f

dispense /dɪ'spens/ vt dispensar ● vi ~ with dispensar, passar sem. **~r** /-ə(r)/ n (container) distribuidor m

dispers|e /dɪ'spɜːs/ vt/i dispersar(-se)

dispirited /dɪ'spɪrɪtɪd/ a desanimado

display /dɪ'spleɪ/ vt exibir, mostrar; ‹feeling› manifestar, dar mostras de ● n exposição f; (of computer) apresentação f visual; Comm objetos mpl expostos

displeas|e /dɪs'pliːz/ vt desagradar a; **~ed with** descontente com. **~ure** /-'pleʒə(r)/ n desagrado m

disposable /dɪ'spəʊzəbl/ a descartável

dispos|e /dɪ'spəʊz/ vt dispor ● vi **~e of** desfazer-se de; **well ~ed towards** bem disposto para com. **~al** n (of waste) eliminação f; **at sb's ~al** à disposição de alguém

disposition /dɪspə'zɪʃn/ n disposição f; (character) índole f

disproportionate /dɪsprə'pɔːʃənət/ a desproporcionado

disprove /dɪs'pruːv/ vt refutar

dispute /dɪ'spjuːt/ vt contestar; (fight for, quarrel) disputar ● n disputa f; (industrial) Pol conflito m; **in ~** em questão

disqualif|y /dɪs'kwɒlɪfaɪ/ vt tornar inapto; Sport desqualificar; **~y from driving** apreender a carteira de motorista, (P) a carta de condução. **~ication** /-ɪ'keɪʃn/ n desqualificação f

disregard /dɪsrɪ'gɑːd/ vt não fazer caso de ● n indiferença f (**for** por)

disrepair /dɪsrɪ'peə(r)/ n mau estado m, abandono m, degradação f

disreputable /dɪs'repjʊtəbl/ a pouco recomendável; (in appearance) com mau aspecto; (in reputation) vergonhoso, de má fama

disrepute /dɪsrɪ'pjuːt/ n descrédito m

disrespect /dɪsrɪ'spekt/ n falta f de respeito. **~ful** a desrespeitoso, irreverente

disrupt /dɪs'rʌpt/ vt perturbar; ‹plans› transtornar; (break up) dividir. **~ion** /-ʃn/ n perturbação f. **~ive** a perturbador

dissatisf|ied /dɪ'sætɪsfaɪd/ a descontente. **~action** /dɪsætɪs'fækʃn/ n descontentamento m

dissect /dɪ'sekt/ vt dissecar. **~ion** /-ʃn/ n dissecação f

dissent /dɪ'sent/ vi dissentir, discordar ● n dissensão f, desacordo m

dissertation /dɪsə'teɪʃn/ n dissertação f

disservice /dɪs'sɜːvɪs/ n **do sb a ~** prejudicar alguém

dissident /'dɪsɪdənt/ a & n dissidente mf

dissimilar /dɪ'sɪmɪlə(r)/ a diferente

dissociate /dɪ'səʊʃɪeɪt/ vt dissociar, desassociar

dissolve /dɪ'zɒlv/ vt/i dissolver(-se)

dissuade /dɪ'sweɪd/ vt dissuadir

distance /'dɪstəns/ n distância f; **from a ~** de longe; **in the ~** ao longe, à distância

distant /'dɪstənt/ a distante; ‹relative› afastado

distil /dɪ'stɪl/ vt (pt distilled) destilar

distillery /dɪ'stɪlərɪ/ n destilaria f

distinct /dɪ'stɪŋkt/ a distinto; (marked) claro, nítido. **~ion** /-ʃn/ n distinção f. **~ive** a distintivo, característico. **~ly** adv distintamente; (markedly) claramente

distinguish /dɪ'stɪŋgwɪʃ/ vt/i distinguir. **~ed** a distinto

distort /dɪ'stɔːt/ vt distorcer; (misrepresent) deturpar. **~ion** /-ʃn/ n distorção f; (misrepresentation) deturpação f

distract /dɪ'strækt/ vt distrair. **~ed** a (distraught) desesperado, fora de si. **~ing** a enlouquecedor. **~ion** /-ʃn/ n distração f

distraught /dɪ'strɔːt/ a desesperado, fora de si

distress /dɪ'stres/ n (physical) dor f; (anguish) aflição f; (poverty) miséria f; (danger) perigo m ● vt afligir. **~ing** a aflitivo, doloroso

distribut|e /dɪ'strɪbjuːt/ vt distribuir. **~ion** /-'bjuːʃn/ n distribuição f. **~or** n distribuidor m

district /'dɪstrɪkt/ n região f; (of town) zona f

distrust /dɪs'trʌst/ n desconfiança f ● vt desconfiar de

disturb /dɪ'stɜːb/ vt perturbar; (move) desarrumar; (bother) incomodar. **~ance** n (noise, disorder) distúrbio m. **~ed** a perturbado. **~ing** a perturbador

disused /dɪs'juːzd/ a fora de uso, desusado, em desuso

ditch /dɪtʃ/ n fosso m ● vt 🔲 (abandon) abandonar; largar

dither /'dɪðə(r)/ vi hesitar

ditto /'dɪtəʊ/ *adv* idem

div|e /daɪv/ *vi* mergulhar; *(rush)* precipitar-se ● *n* mergulho *m*; *(of plane)* picada *f*; ✕ *(place)* espelunca *f*. ∼**er** *n* mergulhador *m*. ∼**ing board** *n* prancha *f* de saltos

diverge /daɪ'vɜːdʒ/ *vi* divergir

diverse /daɪ'vɜːs/ *a* diverso

diversify /daɪ'vɜːsɪfaɪ/ *vt* diversificar

diversity /daɪ'vɜːsəti/ *n* diversidade *f*

diver|t /daɪ'vɜːt/ *vt* desviar; *(entertain)* divertir. ∼**sion** /-ʃn/ *n* diversão *f*; *(traffic)* desvio *m*

divide /dɪ'vaɪd/ *vt/i* dividir(-se). ∼ **in two** *(branch, river, road)* bifurcar-se

dividend /'dɪvɪdend/ *n* dividendo *m*

divine /dɪ'vaɪn/ *a* divino

divinity /dɪ'vɪnəti/ *n* divindade *f*; *Theology* teologia *f*

division /dɪ'vɪʒn/ *n* divisão *f*

divorce /dɪ'vɔːs/ *n* divórcio *m* ● *vt/i* divorciar(-se) de. ∼**d** *a* divorciado

divorcee /dɪvɔː'siː/ *n* divorciado *m*

divulge /daɪ'vʌldʒ/ *vt* divulgar

DIY *abbr* ▶ **DO-IT-YOURSELF**

dizz|y /'dɪzɪ/ *a* (-**ier**, -**iest**) tonto; **be** or **feel** ∼**y** ter tonturas, sentir-se tonto. ∼**iness** *n* tontura *f*, vertigem *f*

do /duː/ *unstressed* də/ *(pres* do, *3rd person sing.* **does**, *pt* **did**, *pp* **done**) ● *vt*

┅┅▶ *(carry out)* fazer; **she's** ∼**ing her homework** ela está fazendo os deveres; **what are you** ∼**ing?** o que você está fazendo?; ∼ **something!** faça alguma coisa!;

∼ **the washing-up** lavar a louça; ∼ **the cleaning** fazer a faxina

┅┅▶ *(as job)* **what does she** ∼**?** o que ela faz?

┅┅▶ *(arrange)* ∼ **one's hair** pentear-se; ∼ **one's make-up** maquiar-se

┅┅▶ *(cheat)* enganar; **this isn't a genuine antique, you've been done** esta antiguidade é falsa, você foi enganado

● *vi*

┅┅▶ *(get on)* ir; **how are they** ∼**ing at school?** como eles vão na escola?; **how are you** ∼**ing?** como vai?

┅┅▶ *(with as or adverb)* fazer; ∼ **as they** ∼ faça como eles; **he can** ∼ **as he likes** ele pode fazer do jeito que gosta; **you did well** você fez bem

┅┅▶ *(be suitable)* servir; **this will** ∼ isso serve

┅┅▶ *(be sufficient)* bastar; **one bottle of water will** ∼ uma garrafa de água basta; **will £20** ∼**?** £20 chegam?

┅┅▶ *(in phrases)* **that does it!** chega!; **well done!** muito bem!

● *v aux*

┅┅▶ *(in questions and negatives)* ∼ **you see?** vê?; **I** ∼ **not smoke** não fumo; **Mary didn't phone** a Mary não telefonou; **Don't** ∼ **that!** não faça isso!

┅┅▶ *(in tag questions)* **you like chocolate, don't you?** você gosta de chocolate, não gosta?; **he lives in London, doesn't he?** ele mora em Londres, não mora?

┅┅▶ *(as verb substitute)* **you speak Portuguese better than**

I ~ você fala português melhor do que eu

••••▸ (*in short answers*) does he work there? yes, he does/no, he doesn't ele trabalha ali? sim, trabalha/não, não trabalha

••••▸ (*for emphasis*) **I** ~ like her gosto mesmo dela

● *n* (*pl* dos, *or* do's)

••••▸ festa *f; npl* dos and don'ts regras a seguir

□ ~ away with ● *vt* eliminar. ~ in ● *vt* (*kill* ✕), matar, liquidar. ~ up ● *vt* (*fasten*) <*shoelaces*> amarrar; <*buttons, coat, zip*> fechar; <*house*> renovar. ~ without ● *vt* passar sem. ~ with: ● *vt* (*need*) **I** could ~ with a cup of tea me cairia bem uma xícara de chá; **it** could ~ with a wash precisa de uma lavagem; (*connected with*) **it's** to ~ with tem a ver com; **it's** nothing to ~ with não tem nada a ver com

docile /'dəʊsaɪl/ *a* dócil

dock[1] /dɒk/ *n* doca *f* ● *vt* levar à doca ● *vi* entrar na doca. ~er *n* estivador *m*

dock[2] /dɒk/ *n* Jur banco *m* dos réus

dockyard /'dɒkjɑːd/ *n* estaleiro *m*

doctor /'dɒktə(r)/ *n* médico *m*, doutor *m*; Univ doutor *m* ● *vt* (*cat*) capar; *fig* adulterar; falsificar

doctorate /'dɒktərət/ *n* doutorado *m*, (*P*) doutoramento *m*

doctrine /'dɒktrɪn/ *n* doutrina *f*

document /'dɒkjʊmənt/ *n* documento *m* ● *vt* documentar. ~ary /-'mentrɪ/ *a* documental ● *n* documentário *m*

dodge /dɒdʒ/ *vt/i* esquivar(-se), furtar(-se) a ● *n* ▣ truque *m*

dodgy /'dɒdʒɪ/ *a* (-ier, -iest) ▣ delicado; difícil; embaraçoso; arriscado

does /dʌz/ ▸ DO

doesn't /'dʌznt/ (= does not) ▸ DO

dog /dɒg/ *n* cão *m* ● *vt* (*pt* dogged) ir no encalço de, perseguir. ~-eared *a* com os cantos dobrados

dogged /'dɒgɪd/ *a* obstinado, persistente

dogma /'dɒgmə/ *n* dogma *m*. ~tic /-'mætɪk/ *a* dogmático

dogsbody /'dɒgzbɒdɪ/ *n* ▣ pau-para-toda-obra *m* ▣; factótum *m*

do-it-yourself *a* faça-você-mesmo

doldrums /'dɒldrəmz/ *npl* be in the ~ estar com a neura; <*business*> estar parado

dole /dəʊl/ *vt* ~ out distribuir ● *n* ▣ auxílio *m* de desemprego; on the ~ ▣ desempregado (titular de auxílio)

doll /dɒl/ *n* boneca *f* ● *vt/i* ~ up ▣ embonecar(-se)

dollar /'dɒlə(r)/ *n* dólar *m*

dolphin /'dɒlfɪn/ *n* golfinho *m*

domain /dəʊ'meɪn/ *n* domínio *m*

dome /dəʊm/ *n* cúpula *f*; (*vault*) abóbada *f*

domestic /də'mestɪk/ *a* (*of home, animal, flights*) doméstico; <*trade*> interno; <*news*> nacional. ~ated /-keɪtɪd/ *a* <*animal*> domesticado; <*person*> que gosta de trabalhos caseiros

dominant /'dɒmɪnənt/ *a* dominante

dominat|e /'dɒmɪneɪt/ *vt/i* dominar. ~ion /-'neɪʃn/ *n* dominação *f*, domínio *m*

domineer /dɒmɪ'nɪə(r)/ *vi* ~ **over** mandar (em), ser autocrático (para com). **~ing** *a* mandão, autocrático

domino /'dɒmɪnəʊ/ *n* (*pl* -oes) dominó *m*

donat|e /dəʊ'neɪt/ *vt* fazer doação de, doar, dar. **~ion** /-ʃn/ *n* donativo *m*

done /dʌn/ ▶ DO

donkey /'dɒŋkɪ/ *n* burro *m*

donor /'dəʊnə(r)/ *n* (*of blood*) doador *m*, (P) dador *m*

don't /dəʊnt/ (= do not) ▶ DO

doodle /'duːdl/ *vi* rabiscar

doom /duːm/ *n* ruína *f*; (*fate*) destino *m*; **be ~ed to** ser/estar condenado a; **~ed (to failure)** condenado ao fracasso

door /dɔː(r)/ *n* porta *f*

doorman /'dɔːmən/ *n* (*pl* -men) porteiro *m*

doormat /'dɔːmæt/ *n* capacho *m*

doorstep /'dɔːstep/ *n* degrau *m* da porta

doorway /'dɔːweɪ/ *n* vão *m* da porta, (P) entrada *f*

dope /dəʊp/ *n* 🅛 droga *f*; 🅧 (*idiot*) imbecil *mf* ● *vt* dopar, drogar

dormant /'dɔːmənt/ *a* dormente; (*inactive*) inativo; (*latent*) latente

dormitory /'dɔːmɪtrɪ/ *n* dormitório *m*; *Amer Univ* residência *f*

dos|e /dəʊs/ *n* dose *f* ● *vt* medicar. **~age** *n* dosagem *f*; (*on label*) posologia *f*

dot /dɒt/ *n* ponto *m*; **on the ~** no momento preciso ● *vt* **be ~ted with** estar pejado *de*; **~ted line** linha *f* pontilhada

dot-com /dɒt'kɒm/ *n* empresa *f* dot.com

dote /dəʊt/ *vi* ~ **on** ser louco por

double /'dʌbl/ *a* duplo; (*room, bed*) de casal; ~ **chin** papada *f*; ~ **Dutch** algaraviada *f*, fala *f* incompreensível; ~ **glazing** (janela *f* de) vidro *m* duplo ● *adv* duas vezes mais ● *n* dobro *m*; ~**s** *Tennis* dupla *f*, (P) pares *mpl*; **at the** ~ a passo acelerado ● *vt/i* dobrar, duplicar; (*fold*) dobrar em dois. ~ **bass** *n* contrabaixo *m*; ~**cross** *vt* enganar; ~**decker** *n* ônibus *m*, (P) autocarro *m* de dois andares. **doubly** *adv* duplamente

doubt /daʊt/ *n* dúvida *f* ● *vt* duvidar de; ~ **if** or **that** duvidar que. ~**ful** *a* duvidoso; (*hesitant*) que tem dúvidas. ~**less** *adv* sem dúvida, indubitavelmente

dough /dəʊ/ *n* massa *f*

doughnut /'dəʊnʌt/ *n* sonho *m*, (P) bola *f* de Berlim

dove /dʌv/ *n* pomba *f*

dowdy /'daʊdɪ/ *a* (**-ier, -iest**) sem graça, sem gosto

down¹ /daʊn/ *n* (*feathers, hair*) penugem *f*

down² /daʊn/ *adv* (*to lower place*) abaixo, para baixo; (*in lower place*) em baixo; **be** ~ ‹*level, price*› descer; ‹*sun*› estar posto; **come** or **go** ~ descer; ~ **under** na Austrália; ~ **with** abaixo ● *prep* por (+*n*) (*n*+) abaixo; ~ **the hill/street** *etc* pelo monte/pela rua *etc* abaixo ● *vt* 🅛 (*knock down*) jogar or (P) atirar abaixo; 🅛 (*drink*) esvaziar. ~**-and-out** *n* marginal *m*; ~**hearted** *a* desencorajado, desanimado; ~**to-earth** *a* terra-a-terra *invar*

downcast /'daʊnkɑːst/ *a* abatido, deprimido, desmoralizado

downfall /ˈdaʊnfɔːl/ n queda f, ruína f

downhill /daʊnˈhɪl/ adv go ~ descer; fig ir abaixo ● a /ˈdaʊnhɪl/ a descer, descendente

> **Downing Street** É uma rua no bairro londrino de Westminster. O número 10 é a residência oficial do Primeiro-Ministro, e o número 11, a do *Chancellor of the Exchequer* (Ministro da Economia e Finanças). Os jornalistas costumam utilizar as expressões *Downing Street* ou *Number 10* para se referir ao Primeiro-Ministro e ao Governo.

download /daʊnˈləʊd/ vt Comput baixar

downpour /ˈdaʊnpɔː(r)/ n aguaceiro m forte, (P) chuvada f

downright /ˈdaʊnraɪt/ a franco; (utter) autêntico, verdadeiro ● adv positivamente

downstairs /daʊnˈsteəz/ adv (at/to) em/para baixo, no/para o andar de baixo ● /ˈdaʊnsteəz/ a (flat etc) de baixo, do andar de baixo

downstream /ˈdaʊnstriːm/ adv rio abaixo

downtown /ˈdaʊntaʊn/ n & adv (de, em, para) o centro da cidade; ~ Boston o centro de Boston

downtrodden /ˈdaʊntrɒdn/ a espezinhado, oprimido

downward /ˈdaʊnwəd/ a descendente ● ~(s) adv para baixo

dowry /ˈdaʊərɪ/ n dote m

doze /dəʊz/ vi dormitar; ~ off cochilar ● n soneca f, cochilo m

dozen /ˈdʌzn/ n dúzia f; ~s of 1 dezenas de, dúzias de

Dr abbr (= Doctor) Dr

drab /dræb/ a insípido; (of colour) morto, apagado

draft¹ /drɑːft/ n rascunho m; Comm ordem f de pagamento ● vt fazer o rascunho de; (draw up) redigir; **the ~** Amer Mil recrutamento m

draft² /drɑːft/ n Amer = DRAUGHT

drag /dræg/ vt/i (pt dragged) arrastar(-se); (river) dragar; (pull away) arrancar ● n 1 (task) chatice f 🇽; 1 (person) estorvo m; 🇽 (clothes) travesti m

dragon /ˈdrægən/ n dragão m

dragonfly /ˈdrægənflaɪ/ n libélula f

drain /dreɪn/ vt drenar; (vegetables) escorrer; (glass, tank) esvaziar; (use up) esgotar ● vi ~ (off) escoar-se ● n cano m; ~(pipe) cano m de esgoto. ~s npl (sewers) esgotos mpl. ~age n drenagem f. ~ing board n escorredouro m

drama /ˈdrɑːmə/ n arte f dramática; (play, event) drama m. ~tic /drəˈmætɪk/ a dramático. ~tist /ˈdræmətɪst/ n dramaturgo m. ~tize /ˈdræmətaɪz/ vt dramatizar

drank /dræŋk/ ► DRINK

drape /dreɪp/ vt ~ round/over dispor (tecido) em pregas à volta de ou sobre. ~s npl Amer cortinas fpl

drastic /ˈdræstɪk/ a drástico, violento

draught /drɑːft/ n corrente f de ar; Naut calado m; ~s (game) (jogo m das) damas fpl; ~ beer chope m, (P) cerveja à caneca, imperial f 1. ~y a com correntes de ar, ventoso

draw /drɔː/ vt (pt drew, pp drawn) puxar; (attract) atrair; (picture) desenhar; (in lottery) tirar à sorte; (line) traçar; (open curtains) abrir; (close curtains) fechar ● vi desenhar;

Sport empatar; *(come)* vir ● *n Sport* empate *m*; *(lottery)* sorteio *m*; ~ **back** recuar; ~ **in** *(of days)* diminuir; ~ **near** aproximar-se; ~ **out** ‹*money*› levantar; ~ **up** deter-se, parar; ‹*document*› redigir; ‹*chair*› aproximar, chegar

drawback /'drɔːbæk/ *n* inconveniente *m*, desvantagem *f*

drawer /drɔː(r)/ *n* gaveta *f*

drawing /'drɔːɪŋ/ *n* desenho *m*. ~ **board** *n* prancheta *f*; ~ **pin** *n* percevejo *m*

drawl /drɔːl/ *n* fala *f* arrastada

drawn /drɔːn/ ▶ DRAW

dread /dred/ *n* terror *m* ● *vt* temer

dreadful /'dredfl/ *a* medonho, terrível

dream /driːm/ *n* sonho *m* ● *vt/i* (*pt* **dreamed**, *or* **dreamt**) sonhar (**of** com) ● *a* (*ideal*) dos seus sonhos; ~ **up** imaginar. ~**er** *n* sonhador *m*. ~**y** *a* sonhador; ‹*music*› romântico

dreary /'drɪərɪ/ *a* (**-ier, -iest**) tristonho; *(boring)* aborrecido

dredge /dredʒ/ *n* draga *f* ● *vt/i* dragar. ~**r** /-ə(r)/ *n* draga *f*; *(for sugar)* polvilhador *m*

dregs /dregz/ *npl* depósito *m*, sedimento *m*; *fig* escória *f*

drench /drentʃ/ *vt* encharcar

dress /dres/ *n* vestido *m*; *(clothing)* roupa *f* ● *vt/i* vestir(-se); ‹*food*› temperar; ‹*wound*› fazer curativo, *(P)* tratar, *(P)* pensar; ~ **up as** fantasiar-se de; ~ **up as** fantasiar-se de; **get** ~**ed** vestir-se

dresser /'dresə(r)/ *n* *(furniture)* guarda-louça *f*

dressing /'dresɪŋ/ *n* *(sauce)* tempero *m*; *(bandage)* curativo *m*, *(P)* penso *m*. ~ **gown** *n* roupão *m*;

~ **room** *n Sport* vestiário *m*; *Theat* camarim *m*; ~**table** *n* toucador *m*

dressmak|er /'dresmeɪkə(r)/ *n* costureira *f*, modista *f*. ~**ing** *n* costura *f*

dressy /'dresɪ/ *a* (**-ier, -iest**) elegante, chique *invar*

drew /druː/ ▶ DRAW

dribble /'drɪbl/ *vi* pingar; ‹*person*› babar-se; ‹*football*› driblar

dried /draɪd/ *a* ‹*fruit etc*› seco

drier /'draɪə(r)/ *n* secador *m*

drift /drɪft/ *vi* ir à deriva; *(pile up)* amontoar-se ● *n* força *f* da corrente; *(pile)* monte *m*; *(of events)* rumo *m*; *(meaning)* sentido *m*. ~**er** *n* pessoa *f* sem rumo

drill /drɪl/ *n* *(tool)* broca *f*; *(training)* exercício *m*, treino *m*; *(routine procedure)* exercícios *mpl* ● *vt* furar, perfurar; *(train)* treinar; ‹*tooth*› abrir ● *vi* treinar-se

drink /drɪŋk/ *vt/i* (*pt* **drank**, *pp* **drunk**) beber ● *n* bebida *f*; **a ~ of water** um copo de água; ~**ing water** água *f* potável. ~**able** *a* potável; *(palatable)* bebível. ~**er** *n* bebedor *m*

drip /drɪp/ *vi* (*pt* **dripped**) pingar ● *n* pingar *m*; 🗵 *(person)* banana *mf* 🔢. ~**-dry** *vt* deixar escorrer ● *a* que não precisa passar

drive /draɪv/ *vt* (*pt* **drove**, *pp* **driven** /'drɪvn/) empurrar, impelir, levar; ‹*car, animal*› dirigir, conduzir, *(P)* guiar; ‹*machine*› acionar; ~ **at** chegar a; ~ **in** *(force in)* enterrar; ~ **mad** (fazer) enlouquecer, pôr fora de si ● *vi* dirigir, conduzir, *(P)* guiar; ~ **away** ‹*car*› partir ● *n* passeio *m* de carro; *(private road)* entrada *f* para veículos; *fig* energia *f*; *Psych* drive *m*, compulsão *f*, impulso *m*; *(campaign)* campanha f. **~-in** <bank, cinema etc> banco m, cinema etc em que se é atendido no carro, drive-in m

drivel /'drɪvl/ n baboseira f, bobagem f

driver /'draɪvə(r)/ n condutor m; (of taxi, bus) chofer m, motorista mf

driving /'draɪvɪŋ/ n condução f. **~ licence** n carteira f de motorista, (P) carta f de condução; **~ school** n auto-escola f, (P) escola f de condução; **~ test** n exame m de motorista or (P) de condução

drizzle /'drɪzl/ n chuvisco m ● vi chuviscar

drone /drəʊn/ n zumbido m; (male bee) zângão m ● vi zumbir; fig falar monotonamente

drool /druːl/ vi babar(-se)

droop /druːp/ vi pender, curvar-se

drop /drɒp/ n gota f, (fall) queda f; (distance) altura f de queda ● vt/i (pt dropped) cair; (fall, lower) baixar; **~ (off)** (person from car) deixar, largar; **~ a line** escrever duas linhas (**to** a); **~** in passar por (on em casa de); **~ off** (doze) adormecer; **~ out** (withdraw) retirar-se; (of student) abandonar. **~out** n marginal mf, marginalizado m

droppings /'drɒpɪŋz/ npl excrementos mpl de animal; (of birds) cocó, (P) cocó m 🔲; porcaria f 🔳

drought /draʊt/ n seca f

drove /drəʊv/ ▶ DRIVE

drown /draʊn/ vt/i afogar(-se)

drowsy /'draʊzɪ/ a sonolento; **be** or **feel ~** ter vontade de dormir

drudge /drʌdʒ/ n mouro m de trabalho. **~ry** /-ərɪ/ n trabalho m penoso e monótono, estafa f

drug /drʌg/ n droga f; Med medicamento m, remédio m ● vt (pt

drugged) drogar; **~ addict** drogado m, tóxico-dependente m

drugstore /'drʌgstɔː(r)/ n Amer farmácia f que vende também sorvetes etc, (P) drogaria f

drum /drʌm/ n Mus tambor m; (for oil) barril m, tambor m; **~s** Mus bateria f ● vi (pt drummed) tocar tambor; (with one's fingers) tamborilar ● vt **~ into sb** fazer entrar na cabeça de alguém; **~ up** (support) conseguir obter; (business) criar. **~mer** n tambor m; (in pop group etc) baterista m, (P) bateria m

drunk /drʌŋk/ ▶ DRINK a embriagado, bêbedo; **get ~** embebedar-se, embriagar-se ● n bêbedo m. **~ard** n alcoólico m, bêbedo m. **~en** a embriagado, bêbedo; (habitually) bêbedo

dry /draɪ/ a (drier, driest) seco; (day) sem chuva; **be** or **feel ~** ter sede ● vt/i secar; **~** (dishes) secar a louça; (of supplies) esgotar-se. **~clean** vt limpar a seco; **~cleaner's** n (loja de) lavagem f a seco, lavanderia f. **~ness** n secura f

dual /'djuːəl/ a duplo; **~ carriageway** estrada f dividida por faixa central

dub /dʌb/ vt (pt dubbed) <film> dobrar; <nickname> apelidar de

dubious /'djuːbɪəs/ a duvidoso; <character, compliment> dúbio; **feel ~ about** ter dúvidas quanto a

duchess /'dʌtʃɪs/ n duquesa f

duck /dʌk/ n pato m ● vi abaixar-se rapidamente ● vt <head> baixar; <person> batizar, pregar uma amona em. **~ling** n patinho m

duct /dʌkt/ n canal m, tubo m

dud /dʌd/ a 🔳 (thing) que não presta ou não funciona; 🔳 (coin)

falso; ⊠ (*cheque*) sem fundos, (P)
careca ⊠

due /dju:/ *a* devido; (*expected*)
esperado; **~ to** devido a, por causa
de; **in ~ course** no tempo devido
● *adv* **~ east** /*etc* exatamente, /*etc*
● *n* devido *m*; **~s** direitos *mpl*; (*of
club*) cota *f*

duel /'dju:əl/ *n* duelo *m*

duet /dju:'et/ *n* dueto *m*

dug /dʌg/ ▶ DIG

duke /dju:k/ *n* duque *m*

dull /dʌl/ *a* (-**er**, -**est**) (*boring*)
enfadonho; ‹*colour*› morto;
‹*mirror*› embaçado; ‹*weather*›
encoberto; ‹*sound*› surdo; (*stupid*)
burro

duly /'dju:lɪ/ *adv* devidamente; (*in
due time*) no tempo devido

dumb /dʌm/ *a* (-**er**, -**est**) mudo; ▯
(*stupid*) bronco ▯; burro ▯

dumbfound /dʌm'faʊnd/ *vt*
pasmar

dummy /'dʌmɪ/ *n* imitação *f*, coisa
f simulada; (*of tailor*) manequim *m*;
(*of baby*) chupeta *f*

dump /dʌmp/ *vt* ‹*rubbish*› jogar
fora; (*put down*) deixar cair; ▯
(*abandon*) largar ● *n* monte *m* de
lixo; (*tip*) lixeira *f*; Mil depósito *m*;
▯ buraco *m*

dunce /dʌns/ *n* burro *m*; **~'s cap**
orelhas *fpl* de burro

dune /dju:n/ *n* duna *f*

dung /dʌŋ/ *n* esterco *m*; (*manure*)
estrume *m*

dungarees /dʌŋgə'ri:z/ *npl*
macacão *m*, (P) fato *m* de macaco

dungeon /'dʌndʒən/ *n* calabouço
m, masmorra *f*

dupe /dju:p/ *vt* enganar ● *n*
trouxa *m*

duplicate[1] /'dju:plɪkət/ *n*
duplicado *m* ● *a* idêntico

duplicate[2] /'dju:plɪkeɪt/ *vt*
duplicar, fazer em duplicado; (*on
machine*) fotocopiar

duplicity /dju:'plɪsətɪ/ *n*
duplicidade *f*

durable /'djʊərəbl/ *a* resistente;
(*enduring*) duradouro, durável

duration /djʊ'reɪʃn/ *n* duração *f*

duress /djʊ'res/ *n* **under ~** sob
coação *f*

during /'djʊərɪŋ/ *prep* durante

dusk /dʌsk/ *n* crepúsculo *m*,
anoitecer *m*

dust /dʌst/ *n* pó *m*, poeira *f* ● *vt*
limpar o pó de; (*sprinkle*) polvilhar

dustbin /'dʌstbɪn/ *n* lata *f* do lixo,
(P) caixote *m*

duster /'dʌstə(r)/ *n* pano *m* do pó

dustman /'dʌstmən/ *n* (*pl* -**men**)
lixeiro *m*, (P) homem *m* do lixo

dusty /'dʌstɪ/ *a* (-**ier**, -**iest**)
poeirento, empoeirado

Dutch /dʌtʃ/ *a* holandês; **go ~**
pagar cada um a sua despesa
● *n Lang* holandês *m*. **~man** *n*
holandês *m*

dutiful /'dju:tɪfl/ *a* cumpridor;
(*showing respect*) respeitador

dut|y /'dju:tɪ/ *n* dever *m*; (*tax*)
impostos *mpl*; **~ies** (*of official etc*)
funções *fpl*; **off ~y** de folga; **on ~y**
de serviço. **~y-free** *a* isento de
impostos; **~y-free shop** free shop *m*

duvet /'dju:veɪ/ *n* edredom *m*, (P)
edredão *m* de penas

DVD *abbr* (= Digital Versatile Disc)
DVD *m*. **~ burner** *n* gravador *m* de
DVD; **~ player** *n* leitor *m* de DVD

dwarf /dwɔ:f/ *n* (*pl* -**fs**) anão *m*

dwell /dwel/ vi (pt **dwelt**) morar; ~ **on** alongar-se sobre. ~**ing** n habitação f

dwindle /'dwɪndl/ vi diminuir, reduzir-se

dye /daɪ/ vt (pres p **dyeing**) tingir ● n tinta f

dying /'daɪɪŋ/ ▶ DIE

dynamic /daɪ'næmɪk/ a dinâmico

dynamite /'daɪnəmaɪt/ n dinamite f ● vt dinamitar

dynamo /'daɪnəməʊ/ n (pl -**os**) dínamo m

dysentery /'dɪsəntrɪ/ n disenteria f

dyslex|ia /dɪs'leksɪə/ n dislexia f. ~**ic** a disléxico

....

Ee

....

each /iːtʃ/ a & pron cada; ~ **one** cada um; ~ **other** um ao outro, uns aos outros; **they like** ~ **other** gostam um do outro/uns dos outros; **know/ love/** etc ~ **other** conhecer-se/ amar-se/ etc

eager /'iːgə(r)/ a ansioso (**to** por) desejoso (**for** de); ‹supporter› entusiástico; **be** ~ **to** ter vontade de. ~**ly** adv com impaciência, ansiosamente; ‹keenly› com entusiasmo. ~**ness** n ansiedade f, desejo m; ‹keenness› entusiasmo m

eagle /'iːgl/ n águia f

ear /ɪə(r)/ n ouvido m; ‹external part› orelha f. ~**drum** n tímpano m; ~**ring** n brinco m

earache /'ɪəreɪk/ n dor f de ouvidos

earl /ɜːl/ n conde m

early /'ɜːlɪ/ (-**ier**, -**iest**) adv cedo ● a primeiro; ‹hour› matinal; ‹fruit› temporão; ‹retirement› antecipado; **have an** ~ **dinner** jantar cedo; **in** ~ **summer** no princípio do verão

earmark /'ɪəmɑːk/ vt destinar; reservar (**for** para)

earn /ɜːn/ vt ganhar; ‹deserve› merecer

earnest /'ɜːnɪst/ a sério; **in** ~ a sério

earnings /'ɜːnɪŋz/ npl salário m; ‹profits› ganhos mpl, lucros mpl

earshot /'ɪəʃɒt/ n **within** ~ ao alcance da voz

earth /ɜːθ/ n terra f ● vt Electr ligar à terra; **why on** ~? por que diabo?, porque cargas d'água?. ~**ly** a terrestre, terreno

earthenware /'ɜːθənweə(r)/ n louça f de barro, faiança f

earthquake /'ɜːθkweɪk/ n tremor m de terra, terremoto m, (P) terramoto m

earthy /'ɜːθɪ/ a terroso, térreo; ‹coarse› grosseiro

ease /iːz/ n facilidade f; ‹comfort› bem-estar m; **at** ~ à vontade; Mil descansar; **ill at** ~ pouco à vontade; **with** ~ facilmente ● vt/i ‹from pain, anxiety› acalmar(-se); ‹slow down› afrouxar; ‹slide› deslizar; ~ **in/out** fazer entrar/sair com cuidado

easel /'iːzl/ n cavalete m

east /iːst/ n este m, leste m, oriente m; **the E**~ o Oriente ● a este, (de) leste, Oriental ● adv a/para leste; ~ **of** para o leste de. ~**erly** a oriental, leste, a leste. ~**ward** a, ~**ward(s)** adv para leste

Easter /'iːstə(r)/ n Páscoa f; ~ **egg** ovo m de Páscoa

eastern /'iːstən/ a oriental, leste

easy /'iːzɪ/ a (-ier, -iest) fácil; (relaxed) natural, descontraído; **take it ~** levar as coisas com calma; **~ chair** poltrona f. **~going** a bonacheirão. **easily** adv facilmente

eat /iːt/ vt/i (pt **ate**, pp **eaten**) comer; **~ into** corroer. **~able** a comestível

eaves /iːvz/ npl beiral m

eavesdrop /'iːvzdrɒp/ vi (pt -dropped) escutar por detrás da porta

ebb /eb/ n vazante f, baixa-mar m ● vi vazar; fig declinar

e-book /'iːbʊk/ n livro m eletrônico, (P) eletrónico

EC /iː'siː/ abbr (= European Commission) CE f

eccentric /ɪk'sentrɪk/ a & n excêntrico m. **~ity** /eksen'trɪsətɪ/ n excentricidade f

ecclesiastical /ɪkliːzɪ'æstɪkl/ a eclesiástico

echo /'ekəʊ/ n (pl -oes) eco m ● vt/i (pt echoed, pres p echoing) ecoar; fig repetir

eclipse /ɪ'klɪps/ n eclipse m ● vt eclipsar

ecology /ɪ'kɒlədʒɪ/ n ecologia f. **~ical** /iːkə'lɒdʒɪkl/ a ecológico

e-commerce /'iːkɒmɜːs/ n comércio m eletrônico or (P) eletrónico

economic /iːkə'nɒmɪk/ a econômico, (P) económico; (profitable) rentável. **~al** a econômico, (P) económico. **~s** n economia f política

economist /ɪ'kɒnəmɪst/ n economista mf

economy /ɪ'kɒnəmɪ/ n economia f. **~ize** vt/i economizar

ecstasy /'ekstəsɪ/ n êxtase m

ecstatic /ɪk'stætɪk/ a extático

eczema /'eksɪmə/ n eczema m

edge /edʒ/ n borda f, beira f; (of town) periferia f, limite m; (of knife) fio m ● vt debruar ● vi (move) avançar pouco a pouco

edgy /'edʒɪ/ a irritadiço, nervoso

edible /'edɪbl/ a comestível

edifice /'edɪfɪs/ n edifício m

Edinburgh Festival É o evento cultural mais importante da Grã-Bretanha, que se celebra em agosto, na capital da Escócia desde 1947. O festival atrai um grande número de visitantes e um aspecto muito relevante do evento são os espetáculos que não formam parte do programa oficial, e aos quais se dá o nome de the Fringe.

edit /'edɪt/ vt (pt edited) ‹newspaper› dirigir; ‹text› editar

edition /ɪ'dɪʃn/ n edição f

editor /'edɪtə(r)/ n (of newspaper) diretor m; (P) diretor m; (of text) organizador m de texto; **the ~ (in chief)** redator-chefe m. **~ial** /edɪ'tɔːrɪəl/ a & n editorial m

educate /'edʒʊkeɪt/ vt educar; ‹mind, public› educar. **~ed** a instruído; educado. **~ion** /-'keɪʃn/ n educação f; (schooling) ensino m. **~ional** /-'keɪʃənl/ a educativo, pedagógico

eel /iːl/ n enguia f

eerie /'ɪərɪ/ a (-ier, -iest) arrepiante, misterioso

effect /ɪ'fekt/ n efeito m ● vt efetuar; **come into ~** entrar em vigor; **in ~** na realidade; **take ~** ter efeito

effective /ɪˈfektɪv/ a eficaz, eficiente; (striking) sensacional; (actual) efetivo. **~ly** adv (efficiently) eficazmente; (strikingly) de forma sensacional; (actually) efetivamente. **~ness** n eficácia f

effeminate /ɪˈfemɪnət/ a efeminado, afeminado

effervescent /efəˈvesnt/ a efervescente

efficien|t /ɪˈfɪʃnt/ a eficiente, eficaz. **~cy** n eficiência f. **~tly** adv eficientemente

effort /ˈefət/ n esforço m. **~less** a fácil, sem esforço

e.g. /iːˈdʒiː/ abbr por ex

egg¹ /eg/ n ovo m. **~plant** n beringela f

egg² /eg/ vt **~ on** 🔲 incitar

eggshell /ˈegʃel/ n casca f de ovo

ego /ˈegəʊ/ n (pl -os) ego m, eu m. **~ism** n egoísmo m. **~ist** n egoísta mf. **~tism** n egotismo m. **~tist** n egotista mf

Egypt /ˈiːdʒɪpt/ n Egito m. **~ian** /ɪˈdʒɪpʃn/ a & n egípcio m

eh /eɪ/ int 🔲 hã?

eiderdown /ˈaɪdədaʊn/ n edredão m, edredom m

eight /eɪt/ a & n oito m. **~h** a & n oitavo m

eighteen /eɪˈtiːn/ a & n dezoito m. **~th** a & n décimo oitavo m

eight|y /ˈeɪti/ a & n oitenta m. **~ieth** a & n octogésimo m

either /ˈaɪðə(r)/ a & pron um e outro; (with negative) nem um nem outro; (each) cada ● adv também não ● conj **~ ... or** ou ... ou; (with negative) nem ... nem

ejaculate /ɪˈdʒækjʊleɪt/ vt/i ejacular; (exclaim) exclamar

eject /ɪˈdʒekt/ vt expelir; (expel) expulsar, despejar, ejetar

elaborate¹ /ɪˈlæbərət/ a elaborado, rebuscado, minucioso

elaborate² /ɪˈlæbəreɪt/ vt elaborar ● vi entrar em pormenores; **~ on** estender-se sobre

elapse /ɪˈlæps/ vi decorrer

elastic /ɪˈlæstɪk/ a & n elástico m; **~ band** elástico m

elat|ed /ɪˈleɪtɪd/ a radiante, exultante. **~ion** n exultação f

elbow /ˈelbəʊ/ n cotovelo m

elder¹ /ˈeldə(r)/ a mais velho. **~s** npl pessoas fpl mais velhas

elder² /ˈeldə(r)/ n (tree) sabugueiro m

elderly /ˈeldəlɪ/ a idoso; **the ~** as pessoas de idade

eldest /ˈeldɪst/ a & n o mais velho m

elect /ɪˈlekt/ vt eleger ● a eleito. **~ion** /-kʃn/ n eleição f

electric /ɪˈlektrɪk/ a elétrico

electrician /ɪlekˈtrɪʃn/ n eletricista m

electricity /ɪlekˈtrɪsətɪ/ n eletricidade f

electrify /ɪˈlektrɪfaɪ/ vt eletrificar; fig (excite) eletrizar

electrocute /ɪˈlektrəkjuːt/ vt eletrocutar

electronic /ɪlekˈtrɒnɪk/ a eletrônico, (P) electrónico. **~s** n eletrônica f, (P) eletrónica f

elegan|t /ˈelɪgənt/ a elegante. **~ce** n elegância f

element /ˈelɪmənt/ n elemento m; (of heater etc) resistência f. **~ary** /-ˈmentrɪ/ a elementar; (school) primário

elephant /ˈelɪfənt/ n elefante m

elevat|e /'elɪveɪt/ vt elevar. **~ion** /-'veɪʃn/ n elevação f

elevator /'elɪveɪtə(r)/ n Amer (lift) elevador m; ascensor m

eleven /ɪ'levn/ a & n onze m. **~th** a & n décimo primeiro m; **at the ~th hour** à última hora

eligible /'elɪdʒəbl/ a (for office) idóneo, (P) idóneo (for para); (desirable) aceitável; **be ~ for** (entitled to) ter direito a

eliminat|e /ɪ'lɪmɪneɪt/ vt eliminar

elite /eɪ'liːt/ n elite f

elm /elm/ n olmo m, ulmeiro m

elocution /elə'kjuːʃn/ n elocução f

elope /ɪ'ləʊp/ vi fugir

eloquen|t /'eləkwənt/ a eloquente. **~ce** n eloquência f

else /els/ adv mais; **everybody ~** todos os outros; **nobody ~** mais ninguém; **nothing ~** nada mais; **or ~** ou então, senão; **somewhere ~** noutro lado qualquer. **~where** adv noutro lado

elusive /ɪ'luːsɪv/ a (person) esquivo, difícil de apanhar; (answer) evasivo

emaciated /ɪ'meɪʃɪeɪtɪd/ a emaciado, macilento

email /'iːmeɪl/ n correio m eletrónico, (P) electrónico, e-mail m; **~ address** endereço m de e-mail

embankment /ɪm'bæŋkmənt/ n (of river) dique m; (P) (of railway) terrapleno m; talude m, (P) aterro m

embargo /ɪm'bɑːgəʊ/ n (pl -oes) embargo m

embark /ɪm'bɑːk/ vt/i embarcar; **~ on** (business etc) embarcar em, meter-se em 🆒; (journey) começar

embarrass /ɪm'bærəs/ vt embaraçar, confundir. **~ment** n embaraço m, atrapalhação f

embassy /'embəsɪ/ n embaixada f

embellish /ɪm'belɪʃ/ vt embelezar, enfeitar

embezzle /ɪm'bezl/ vt desviar (fundos). **~ment** n desfalque m

emblem /'embləm/ n emblema m

embod|y /ɪm'bɒdɪ/ vt encarnar; (include) incorporar, incluir. **~iment** n personificação f

embrace /ɪm'breɪs/ vt/i abraçar(-se); (offer, opportunity) acolher ● n abraço m

embroider /ɪm'brɔɪdə(r)/ vt bordar. **~y** n bordado m

embryo /'embrɪəʊ/ n (pl -os) embrião m

emerald /'emərəld/ n esmeralda f

emerge /ɪ'mɜːdʒ/ vi emergir, surgir

emergency /ɪ'mɜːdʒənsɪ/ n emergência f; (urgent case) urgência f; **~ exit** saída f de emergência; **in an ~** em caso de urgência

emigrant /'emɪgrənt/ n emigrante mf

emigrat|e /'emɪgreɪt/ vi emigrar. **~ion** /-'greɪʃn/ n emigração f

eminen|t /'emɪnənt/ a eminente

emi|t /ɪ'mɪt/ vt (pt emitted) emitir. **~ssion** /-ʃn/ n emissão f

emotion /ɪ'məʊʃn/ n emoção f. **~al** a (person, shock) emotivo; (speech, scene) emocionante

emperor /'empərə(r)/ n imperador m

emphasis /'emfəsɪs/ n ênfase f; **lay ~ on** pôr em relevo

emphasize /'emfəsaɪz/ vt enfatizar, sublinhar; (syllable, word) acentuar

emphatic /ɪm'fætɪk/ a enfático; (manner) enérgico

empire /'empaɪə(r)/ n império m

employ /ɪmˈplɔɪ/ vt empregar. **~ee** /emplɔɪˈiː/ n empregado m. **~er** n patrão m. **~ment** n emprego m; **~ment agency** agência f de emprego

empower /ɪmˈpaʊə(r)/ vt autorizar (**to do** a fazer)

empress /ˈemprɪs/ n imperatriz f

empt|y /ˈemptɪ/ a vazio; <promise> falso; **on an ~y stomach** com o estômago vazio, em jejum ● vt/i esvaziar(-se). **~iness** n vazio m

emulsion /ɪˈmʌlʃn/ n emulsão f

enable /ɪˈneɪbl/ vt ~ **sb to do** permitir a alguém fazer

enact /ɪˈnækt/ vt Jur decretar; Theat representar

enamel /ɪˈnæml/ n esmalte m ● vt (pt **enamelled**) esmaltar

enchant /ɪnˈtʃɑːnt/ vt encantar. **~ing** a encantador. **~ment** n encantamento m

encircle /ɪnˈsɜːkl/ vt cercar, rodear

enclose /ɪnˈkləʊz/ vt (land) cercar; (with letter) enviar incluso/junto. **~d** a <space> fechado; (with letter) anexo, incluso, junto

enclosure /ɪnˈkləʊʒə(r)/ n cercado m, recinto m; (with letter) documento m anexo

encore /ɒŋˈkɔː(r)/ int & n bis m

encounter /ɪnˈkaʊntə(r)/ vt encontrar, deparar com ● n encontro m

encourage /ɪnˈkʌrɪdʒ/ vt encorajar. **~ment** n encorajamento m

encroach /ɪnˈkrəʊtʃ/ vi ~ **on** <land> invadir; <time> abusar de

encyclopedd|ia /ɪnsaɪkləˈpiːdɪə/ n enciclopédia f. **~ic** a enciclopédico

end /end/ n fim m; (farthest part) extremo m, ponta f; **in the ~** por fim; **no ~ of** 🔢 muito, enorme,

imenso; **on ~** (upright) em pé; (consecutive) a fio, de seguida ● vt/i acabar, terminar; **~ up** (arrive finally) ir parar (**in** a/em); **~ up doing** acabar por fazer

endanger /ɪnˈdeɪndʒə(r)/ vt pôr em perigo

endeavour /ɪnˈdevə(r)/ n esforço m ● vi esforçar-se (**to** por)

ending /ˈendɪŋ/ n fim m; (of word) terminação f

endless /ˈendlɪs/ a interminável; <times> sem conta; <patience> infinito

endorse /ɪnˈdɔːs/ vt <document> endossar; <action> aprovar. **~ment** n Auto averbamento m

endow /ɪnˈdaʊ/ vt doar. **~ment** n doação f

endur|e /ɪnˈdjʊə(r)/ vt suportar ● vi durar. **~ance** n resistência f

enemy /ˈenəmɪ/ n & a inimigo m

energetic /enəˈdʒetɪk/ a enérgico

energy /ˈenədʒɪ/ n energia f

enforce /ɪnˈfɔːs/ vt aplicar

engage /ɪnˈɡeɪdʒ/ vt (staff) contratar; Mech engrenar ● vi ~ **in** envolver-se em, lançar-se em. **~d** a noivo; (busy) ocupado. **~ment** n noivado m; (undertaking, appointment) compromisso m; Mil combate m

engine /ˈendʒɪn/ n motor m; (of train) locomotiva f

engineer /endʒɪˈnɪə(r)/ n engenheiro m ● vt engenhar. **~ing** n engenharia f

England /ˈɪŋɡlənd/ n Inglaterra f

English /ˈɪŋɡlɪʃ/ a inglês ● n Lang inglês m; **the ~** os ingleses mpl. **~man** n inglês m. **~woman** n inglesa f

engrav|e /ɪnˈɡreɪv/ vt gravar. **~ing** n gravura f

engrossed /ɪnˈɡrəʊst/ a absorto (**in** em)

engulf /ɪnˈɡʌlf/ vt engolfar, tragar

enhance /ɪnˈhɑːns/ vt aumentar; (heighten) realçar

enigma /ɪˈnɪɡmə/ n enigma m. **~tic** /enɪɡˈmætɪk/ a enigmático

enjoy /ɪnˈdʒɔɪ/ vt gostar de; (benefit from) gozar de; **~ o.s.** divertir-se. **~able** a agradável. **~ment** n prazer m

enlarge /ɪnˈlɑːdʒ/ vt/i aumentar; **~ upon** alargar-se sobre. **~ment** n ampliação f

enlighten /ɪnˈlaɪtn/ vt esclarecer. **~ment** n esclarecimento m, elucidação f

enlist /ɪnˈlɪst/ vt recrutar; fig aliciar; granjear ● vi alistar-se

enliven /ɪnˈlaɪvn/ vt animar

enmity /ˈenmətɪ/ n inimizade f

enormous /ɪˈnɔːməs/ a enorme

enough /ɪˈnʌf/ a bastante m, suficiente m ● adv & n bastante m, suficiente m ● int basta!, chega!

enquir|e /ɪnˈkwaɪə(r)/ vt/i perguntar, indagar; **~e about** informar-se de, pedir informações sobre. **~y** n pedido m de informações

enrage /ɪnˈreɪdʒ/ vt enfurecer, enraivecer

enrich /ɪnˈrɪtʃ/ vt enriquecer

enrol /ɪnˈrəʊl/ vt/i (pt **enrolled**) inscrever(-se); School matricular(-se). **~ment** n inscrição f; School matrícula f

ensemble /ɒnˈsɒmbl/ n conjunto m

ensu|e /ɪnˈsjuː/ vi seguir-se. **~ing** a decorrente

ensure /ɪnˈʃʊə(r)/ vt assegurar; **~ that** assegurar-se de que

entail /ɪnˈteɪl/ vt acarretar

entangle /ɪnˈtæŋɡl/ vt emaranhar, enredar

enter /ˈentə(r)/ vt ‹room, club etc› entrar em; (register) registar; ‹data› entrar com ● vi entrar (**into** em); **~ for** inscrever-se em

enterprise /ˈentəpraɪz/ n empresa f, empreendimento m; fig iniciativa f

enterprising /ˈentəpraɪzɪŋ/ a empreendedor

entertain /entəˈteɪn/ vt entreter; ‹guests› receber; ‹ideas› alimentar, nutrir. **~er** n artista mf. **~ment** n entretenimento m; (performance) espetáculo m

enthral /ɪnˈθrɔːl/ vt (pt **enthralled**) fascinar

enthuse /ɪnˈθjuːz/ vi **~ over** entusiasmar-se por

enthusias|m /ɪnˈθjuːzɪæzm/ n entusiasmo m. **~t** n entusiasta mf. **~tic** /-ˈæstɪk/ a entusiástico

entice /ɪnˈtaɪs/ vt atrair; **~ to do** induzir a fazer. **~ment** n tentação f, engodo m

entire /ɪnˈtaɪə(r)/ a inteiro. **~ly** adv inteiramente

entirety /ɪnˈtaɪərətɪ/ n **in its ~** por inteiro, na (sua) totalidade

entitle /ɪnˈtaɪtl/ vt dar direito. **~d** a ‹book› intitulado; **be ~d to sth** ter direito a algo. **~ment** n direito m

entrance /ˈentrəns/ n entrada f (**to** para); (right to enter) admissão f

entrant /ˈentrənt/ n Sport concorrente mf; (in exam) candidato m

entreat /ɪnˈtriːt/ vt rogar, suplicar. ~y n rogo m, súplica f

entrust /ɪnˈtrʌst/ vt confiar

entry /ˈentrɪ/ n entrada f; (on list) item m; (in dictionary) verbete m; ~ form ficha f de inscrição, (P) boletim m de inscrição; **no ~** entrada proibida

envelop /ɪnˈveləp/ vt (pt enveloped) envolver

envelope /ˈenvələʊp/ n envelope m, sobrescrito m

enviable /ˈenvɪəbl/ a invejável

envious /ˈenvɪəs/ a invejoso; **be ~** of ter inveja de

environment /ɪnˈvaɪərənmənt/ n meio m; (ecological) meio ambiente m. ~al /-ˈmentl/ a do meio; (ecological) do ambiente

envisage /ɪnˈvɪzɪdʒ/ vt encarar; (foresee) prever

envoy /ˈenvɔɪ/ n enviado m

envy /ˈenvɪ/ n inveja f ● vt invejar, ter inveja de

epic /ˈepɪk/ n epopeia f ● a épico

epidemic /epɪˈdemɪk/ n epidemia f

epilep|sy /ˈepɪlepsɪ/ n epilepsia f. ~tic /-ˈleptɪk/ a & n epiléptico m, (P) epilético m

episode /ˈepɪsəʊd/ n episódio m

epitom|e /ɪˈpɪtəmɪ/ n (summary) epítome m; (embodiment) modelo m. ~ize vt fig representar; encarnar; (summarize) resumir

epoch /ˈiːpɒk/ n época f. ~-making a que marca uma época

equal /ˈiːkwəl/ a & n igual m; ~ **to** (task) à altura de ● vt (pt equalled) igualar, ser igual a. ~ity /iːˈkwɒlətɪ/ n igualdade f. ~ly adv igualmente; (similarly) de igual modo

equalize /ˈiːkwəlaɪz/ vt/i igualar; Sport empatar

equate /ɪˈkweɪt/ vt equacionar (**with** com); (treat as equal) equiparar (**with** a)

equation /ɪˈkweɪʒn/ n equação f

equator /ɪˈkweɪtə(r)/ n equador m

equilibrium /iːkwɪˈlɪbrɪəm/ n equilíbrio m

equip /ɪˈkwɪp/ vt (pt equipped) equipar (**with** com); munir (**with** de). ~ment n equipamento m

equitable /ˈekwɪtəbl/ a equitativo

equity /ˈekwətɪ/ n equidade f

equivalent /ɪˈkwɪvələnt/ a & n equivalente m

era /ˈɪərə/ n era f, época f

eradicate /ɪˈrædɪkeɪt/ vt erradicar, suprimir

erase /ɪˈreɪz/ vt apagar. ~r /-ə(r)/ n borracha (de apagar) f

erect /ɪˈrekt/ a ereto ● vt erigir. ~ion /-ʃn/ n ereção f; (building) construção f, edifício m

ero|de /ɪˈrəʊd/ vt corroer. ~sion /ɪˈrəʊʒn/ n erosão f

erotic /ɪˈrɒtɪk/ a erótico

err /ɜː(r)/ vi (pt erred) errar

errand /ˈerənd/ n recado m

erratic /ɪˈrætɪk/ a errático, irregular; (person) variável, imprevisível

erroneous /ɪˈrəʊnɪəs/ a errôneo, (P) erróneo, errado

error /ˈerə(r)/ n erro m

erupt /ɪˈrʌpt/ vi (war, fire) irromper; (volcano) entrar em erupção. ~ion /-ʃn/ n erupção f

escalat|e /ˈeskəleɪt/ vt/i intensificar(-se); (of prices) subir em espiral

escalator /ˈeskəleɪtə(r)/ n escada f rolante

escape /ɪˈskeɪp/ vi escapar-se ● vt escapar a ● n fuga f; (of prisoner) evasão f, fuga f; **~ from sb** escapar de alguém; **~ to** fugir para; **have a lucky** or **narrow ~** escapar por um triz

escapism /ɪˈskeɪpɪzəm/ n escapismo m

escort¹ /ˈeskɔːt/ n escolta f; (of woman) cavalheiro m, acompanhante m

escort² /ɪˈskɔːt/ vt escoltar; (accompany) acompanhar

Eskimo /ˈeskɪməʊ/ n (pl -os) esquimó mf

especial /ɪˈspeʃl/ a especial. **~ly** adv especialmente

espionage /ˈespɪənɑːʒ/ n espionagem f

espresso /eˈspresəʊ/ n (pl -os) (coffee) expresso m, (P) bica f

essay /ˈeseɪ/ n ensaio m; Schol redação f

essence /ˈesns/ n essência f

essential /ɪˈsenʃl/ a essencial ● n the **~s** o essencial m. **~ly** adv essencialmente

establish /ɪˈstæblɪʃ/ vt estabelecer; ‹business, state› fundar; (prove) provar, apurar. **~ment** n estabelecimento m; (institution) instituição f; **the E~ment** o Establishment m, a classe f dirigente

estate /ɪˈsteɪt/ n propriedade f; (possessions) bens mpl; (inheritance) herança f; **~ agent** agente m imobiliário; **(housing) ~** conjunto m habitacional; **~ car** perua f, (P) carrinha f

esteem /ɪˈstiːm/ vt estimar ● n estima f

estimate¹ /ˈestɪmət/ n cálculo m, avaliação f; Comm orçamento m, estimativa f

estimat|e² /ˈestɪmeɪt/ vt calcular, estimar. **~ion** /-ˈmeɪʃn/ n opinião f

estuary /ˈestʃʊərɪ/ n estuário m

etc abbr (= et cetera) etc

eternal /ɪˈtɜːnl/ a eterno

eternity /ɪˈtɜːnətɪ/ n eternidade f

ethic /ˈeθɪk/ n ética f; **~s** ética f. **~al** a ético

ethnic /ˈeθnɪk/ a étnico

etiquette /ˈetɪket/ n etiqueta f

eulogy /ˈjuːlədʒɪ/ n elogio m (fúnebre)

euphemism /ˈjuːfəmɪzəm/ n eufemismo m

euro /ˈjʊərəʊ/ n euro m

Europe /ˈjʊərəp/ n Europa f. **E~an** /-ˈpɪən/ a & n europeu m; **E~an Union** União Europeia

evacuat|e /ɪˈvækjʊeɪt/ vt evacuar. **~ion** /-ˈeɪʃn/ n evacuação f

evade /ɪˈveɪd/ vt evadir

evaluate /ɪˈvæljʊeɪt/ vt avaliar

evangelical /iːvænˈdʒelɪkl/ a evangélico

evaporat|e /ɪˈvæpəreɪt/ vt/i evaporar(-se); **~ed milk** leite m evaporado. **~ion** /-ˈreɪʃn/ n evaporação f

evasion /ɪˈveɪʒn/ n evasão f

evasive /ɪˈveɪsɪv/ a evasivo

eve /iːv/ n véspera f

even /ˈiːvn/ a regular; ‹surface› liso, plano; ‹amounts› igual; ‹number› par; **get ~ with** ajustar contas com ● vt/i **~ up** igualar(-se), acertar ● adv mesmo; **~ better** ainda melhor. **~ly** adv uniformemente

evening /ˈiːvnɪŋ/ n entardecer m, anoitecer m; (whole evening) serão m;

~ **class** aula f à noite (para adultos); ~ **dress** traje *m* de cerimónia or (*P*) cerimónia or de rigor; (*woman's*) vestido *m* de noite

event /ɪ'vent/ *n* acontecimento *m*; **in the ~ of** no caso de. **~ful** *a* movimentado, memorável

eventual /ɪ'ventʃʊəl/ *a* final. **~ly** *adv* por fim; (*in future*) eventualmente

ever /'evə(r)/ *adv* jamais; (*at all times*) sempre; **do you ~ go?** você já foi alguma vez?, costuma ir?; **the best I ~ saw** o melhor que já vi; **~ so** ⚆ muitíssimo, tão; **hardly ~** quase nunca. **~ since** *adv* desde então ● *prep* desde ● *conj* desde que

evergreen /'evəgriːn/ *n* sempre-verde f, planta f de folhas persistentes ● *a* persistente

everlasting /'evəlɑːstɪŋ/ *a* eterno

every /'evrɪ/ *a* cada; **~ now and then** de vez em quando, volta e meia; **~ one** cada um; **~ other day** dia sim dia não, de dois em dois dias; **~ three days** de três em três dias

everybody /'evrɪbɒdɪ/ *pron* todo o mundo, todos

everyday /'evrɪdeɪ/ *a* cotidiano, (*P*) quotidiano, diário; (*common*) do dia a dia, vulgar

everyone /'evrɪwʌn/ *pron* todo o mundo, todos

everything /'evrɪθɪŋ/ *pron* tudo

everywhere /'evrɪweə(r)/ *adv* (*position*) em todo lugar, em toda parte; (*direction*) a todo lugar, a toda parte

evict /ɪ'vɪkt/ *vt* expulsar, despejar. **~ion** /-ʃn/ *n* despejo *m*

evidence /'evɪdəns/ *n* evidência f; (*proof*) prova f; (*testimony*) testemunho *m*, depoimento *m*; ~ **of** sinal de; **give ~** testemunhar; **in ~** em evidência

evident /'evɪdənt/ *a* evidente. **~ly** *adv* evidentemente

evil /'iːvl/ *a* mau ● *n* mal *m*

evo|ke /ɪ'vəʊk/ *vt* evocar. **~cative** /ɪ'vɒkətɪv/ *a* evocativo

evolution /iːvə'luːʃn/ *n* evolução f

evolve /ɪ'vɒlv/ *vi* evolucionar, evoluir ● *vt* desenvolver, produzir

ex- /eks/ *pref* ex-

exact /ɪg'zækt/ *a* exato ● *vt* exigir (from de). **~ing** *a* exigente; ‹*task*› difícil. **~ly** *adv* exatamente

exaggerat|e /ɪg'zædʒəreɪt/ *vt/i* exagerar. **~ion** /-'reɪʃn/ *n* exagero *m*

exam /ɪg'zæm/ *n* 🄸 exame *m*

examination /ɪgzæmɪ'neɪʃn/ *n* exame *m*; *Jur* interrogatório *m*

examine /ɪg'zæmɪn/ *vt* examinar; ‹*witness etc*› interrogar. **~r** /-ə(r)/ *n* examinador *m*

example /ɪg'zɑːmpl/ *n* exemplo *m*; **for ~** por exemplo; **make an ~ of** castigar para servir de exemplo

exasperat|e /ɪg'zæspəreɪt/ *vt* exasperar. **~ion** /-'reɪʃn/ *n* exaspero *m*

excavat|e /'ekskəveɪt/ *vt* escavar; (*uncover*) desenterrar. **~ion** /-'veɪʃn/ *n* escavação f

exceed /ɪk'siːd/ *vt* exceder; ‹*speed limit*› ultrapassar, exceder

excel /ɪk'sel/ *vi* (*pt* **excelled**) distinguir-se ● *vt* superar, ultrapassar

excellen|t /'eksələnt/ *a* excelente. **~ce** *n* excelência f

except /ɪk'sept/ *prep* exceto, fora; ~ **for** a não ser, menos, salvo ● *vt*. excetuar. **~ion** /-ʃn/ *n* exceção f; **take ~ion to** (*object to*) achar

inaceitável; (*be offended by*) achar
ofensivo

exceptional /ɪk'sepʃənl/ a
excepcional, (P) excecional

excerpt /'eksɜ:pt/ n trecho m,
excerto m

excess[1] /ɪk'ses/ n excesso m

excess[2] /'ekses/ a excedente,
em excesso; **~ fare** excesso m,
suplemento m; **~ luggage** excesso
m de peso

excessive /ɪk'sesɪv/ a excessivo

exchange /ɪks'tʃeɪndʒ/ vt trocar
● n troca f; (*of currency*) câmbio m;
(telephone) **~** central f telefónica,
(P) telefónica; **~ rate** taxa f de
câmbio

excit|e /ɪk'saɪt/ vt excitar; (*rouse*)
despertar; (*enthuse*) entusiasmar.
~able a excitável. **~ed** a excitado;
get ~ed excitar-se, entusiasmar-se.
~ement n excitação f. **~ing** a
excitante, emocionante

exclaim /ɪk'skleɪm/ vi exclamar

exclamation /eksklə'meɪʃn/ n
exclamação f; **~ mark** ponto m de
exclamação

exclu|de /ɪk'sklu:d/ vt excluir.
~ding prep excluído. **~sion**
/ɪk'sklu:ʒn/ n exclusão f

exclusive /ɪk'sklu:sɪv/ a (*rights
etc*) exclusivo; (*club etc*) seleto;
(*news item*) (em) exclusivo; **~ of**
sem incluir. **~ly** adv exclusivamente

excruciating /ɪk'skru:ʃɪeɪtɪŋ/ a
excruciante, atroz

excursion /ɪk'skɜ:ʃn/ n excursão f

excus|e[1] /ɪk'skju:z/ vt desculpar;
~e me! desculpe!, com licença! **~e
from** (*exempt*) dispensar de. **~able**
a desculpável

excuse[2] /ɪk'skju:s/ n desculpa f

ex-directory /eksdɪ'rektərɪ/
a que não vem no anuário or (P)
na lista

execute /'eksɪkju:t/ vt executar

execution /eksɪ'kju:ʃn/ n
execução f

executive /ɪg'zekjʊtɪv/ a & n
executivo m

exemplary /ɪg'zemplərɪ/ a
exemplar

exemplify /ɪg'zemplɪfaɪ/ vt
exemplificar, ilustrar

exempt /ɪg'zempt/ a isento (**from**
de) ● vt dispensar, eximir. **~ion** /-ʃn/
n isenção f

exercise /'eksəsaɪz/ n exercício m
● vt (*powers, restraint etc*) exercer;
(*dog*) levar para passear ● vi fazer
exercício; **~ book** caderno m (de
exercícios)

exert /ɪg'zɜ:t/ vt empregar, exercer;
~ o.s. esforçar-se, fazer um esforço.
~ion /-ʃn/ n esforço m

exhaust /ɪg'zɔ:st/ vt esgotar ● n
Auto (tubo de) escape m. **~ed** a
esgotado, exausto. **~ion** /-stʃən/ n
esgotamento m, exaustão f

exhaustive /ɪg'zɔ:stɪv/ a
exaustivo, completo

exhibit /ɪg'zɪbɪt/ vt exibir, mostrar;
(*thing, collection*) expor ● n objeto
m, exposto

exhibition /eksɪ'bɪʃn/ n exposição
f; (*act of showing*) demonstração f

exhilarat|e /ɪg'zɪləreɪt/ vt
regozijar; (*invigorate*) animar,
estimular. **~ion** /-'reɪʃn/ n animação
f, alegria f

exile /'eksaɪl/ n exílio m; (*person*)
exilado m ● vt exilar, desterrar

exist /ɪg'zɪst/ vi existir. **~ence** n
existência f; **be in ~ence** existir

exit /'eksɪt/ n saída f

exorbitant /ɪg'zɔːbɪtənt/ a exorbitante

exotic /ɪg'zɒtɪk/ a exótico

expan|d /ɪk'spænd/ vt/i expandir(-se); (extend) estender(-se), alargar(-se); ‹gas, liquid, metal› dilatar(-se). **~sion** n expansão f; (extension) alargamento m; (of gas etc) dilatação f

expanse /ɪk'spæns/ n extensão f

expatriate /eks'pætrɪət/ a & n expatriado m

expect /ɪk'spekt/ vt esperar; (suppose) crer, supor; (require) contar com, esperar; ‹baby› esperar; **~ to do** contar fazer. **~ation** /ekspek'teɪʃn/ n expectativa f

expectan|t /ɪk'spektənt/ a **~t mother** gestante f. **~cy** n expectativa f

expedient /ɪk'spiːdɪənt/ a oportuno ● n expediente m

expedition /ekspɪ'dɪʃn/ n expedição f

expel /ɪk'spel/ vt (pt expelled) expulsar; ‹gas, poison etc› expelir

expend /ɪk'spend/ vt despender

expenditure /ɪk'spendɪtʃə(r)/ n despesa f, gasto m

expense /ɪk'spens/ n despesa f; (cost) custo m; **at sb's ~** à custa de alguém; **at the ~ of** fig à custa de

expensive /ɪk'spensɪv/ a caro, dispendioso; ‹tastes, habits› de luxo

experience /ɪk'spɪərɪəns/ n experiência f ● vt experimentar; (feel) sentir. **~d** a experiente

experiment /ɪk'sperɪmənt/ n experiência f ● vi /ɪk'sperɪment/ fazer uma experiência. **~al** /-'mentl/ a experimental

expert /'ekspɜːt/ a & n perito m

expertise /ekspɜː'tiːz/ n perícia f, competência f

expir|e /ɪk'spaɪə(r)/ vi expirar. **~y** n fim m de prazo, expiração f

expl|ain /ɪk'spleɪn/ vt explicar. **~anation** /eksplə'neɪʃn/ n explicação f. **~anatory** /ɪk'splæ-nətrɪ/ a explicativo

explicit /ɪk'splɪsɪt/ a explícito

explo|de /ɪk'spləʊd/ vt/i (fazer) explodir. **~sion** /ɪk'spləʊʒn/ n explosão f. **~sive** a & n explosivo m

exploit¹ /'eksplɔɪt/ n façanha f

exploit² /ɪk'splɔɪt/ vt explorar. **~ation** /eksplɔɪ'teɪʃn/ n exploração f

explor|e /ɪk'splɔː(r)/ vt explorar; fig examinar. **~ation** /eksplə'reɪʃn/ n exploração f. **~er** n explorador m

export¹ /ɪk'spɔːt/ vt exportar. **~er** n exportador m

export² /'ekspɔːt/ n exportação f

expos|e /ɪk'spəʊz/ vt expor; (disclose) revelar; (unmask) desmascarar. **~ure** /-ʒə(r)/ n exposição f; (cold) frio m

express¹ /ɪk'spres/ a expresso, categórico ● adv (por) expresso ● n (train) rápido m, expresso m. **~ly** adv expressamente

express² /ɪk'spres/ vt exprimir. **~ion** /-ʃn/ n expressão f. **~ive** a expressivo

expulsion /ɪk'spʌlʃn/ n expulsão f

exquisite /'ekskwɪzɪt/ a requintado

exten|d /ɪk'stend/ vt (stretch) estender; (enlarge) aumentar, ampliar; (prolong) prolongar; (grant) oferecer ● vi (stretch) estender-se; (in time) prolongar-se. **~sion** /ɪk'stenʃn/ n (incl phone) extensão f; (of deadline) prorrogação f; (building) anexo m

extensive /ɪk'stensɪv/ a extenso; ‹damage, study› vasto. **~ly** adv muito

extent /ɪk'stent/ n extensão f; (degree) medida f; **to some ~** até certo ponto, em certa medida; **to such an ~ that** a tal ponto que

exterior /ɪk'stɪərɪə(r)/ a & n exterior m

exterminat|e /ɪk'stɜːmɪneɪt/ vt exterminar. **~ion** /-'neɪʃn/ n exterminação f, extermínio m

external /ɪk'stɜːnl/ a externo. **~ly** adv exteriormente

extinct /ɪk'stɪŋkt/ a extinto. **~ion** /-ʃn/ n extinção f

extinguish /ɪk'stɪŋgwɪʃ/ vt extinguir, apagar. **~er** n extintor m

extort /ɪk'stɔːt/ vt extorquir (from a). **~ion** /-ʃn/ n extorsão f

extortionate /ɪk'stɔːʃənət/ a exorbitante

extra /'ekstrə/ a extra, adicional; **~ strong** extra-forte; **~ time** Football prorrogação f, (P) prolongamento m ● adv extra, excepcionalmente, (P) excecionalmente ● n extra m; Cine, Theat extra m, figurante mf

extra- /'ekstrə/ pref extra-

extract[1] /ɪk'strækt/ vt extrair; ‹promise, tooth› arrancar; fig obter. **~ion** /-ʃn/ n extração f; (descent) origem f

extract[2] /'ekstrækt/ n extrato m

extraordinary /ɪk'strɔːdnrɪ/ a extraordinário

extravagan|t /ɪk'strævəgənt/ a extravagante; (wasteful) esbanjador. **~ce** n extravagância f; (wastefulness) esbanjamento m

extrem|e /ɪk'striːm/ a & n extremo m. **~ely** adv extremamente. **~ist** n extremista mf

extricate /'ekstrɪkeɪt/ vt desembaraçar, livrar

extrovert /'ekstrəvɜːt/ n extrovertido m

exuberan|t /ɪg'zjuːbərənt/ a exuberante

exude /ɪg'zjuːd/ vt ‹charm etc› destilar; ressumar, (P) transpirar

exult /ɪg'zʌlt/ vi exultar

eye /aɪ/ n olho m ● vt (pt eyed, pres p eyeing) olhar; **keep an ~ on** vigiar; **see ~ to** concordar inteiramente. **~opener** n revelação f; **~shadow** n sombra f

eyeball /'aɪbɔːl/ n globo m ocular

eyebrow /'aɪbraʊ/ n sobrancelha f

eyelash /'aɪlæʃ/ n pestana f

eyelid /'aɪlɪd/ n pálpebra f

eyesight /'aɪsaɪt/ n vista f

eyesore /'aɪsɔː(r)/ n monstruosidade f, horror m

eyewitness /'aɪwɪtnɪs/ n testemunha f ocular

. . . .

Ff

. . . .

fable /'feɪbl/ n fábula f

fabric /'fæbrɪk/ n tecido m; (structure) edifício m

fabricat|e /'fæbrɪkeɪt/ vt fabricar; (invent) urdir, inventar. **~ion** /-'keɪʃn/ n fabrico m; (invention) invenção f

fabulous /'fæbjʊləs/ a fabuloso

face /feɪs/ n face f, cara f, rosto m; (expression) face f; (grimace) careta f; (of clock) mostrador m; **~ to ~** cara a cara, frente a frente; **in the**

~ of em vista de; **on the** ~ **of it**
a julgar pelas aparências; **pull** ~**s**
fazer caretas ● *vt* (*look towards*)
encarar; (*confront*) enfrentar ● *vi* (*be
opposite*) estar de frente para; ~ **up
to** enfrentar. ~**cloth** *n* toalha *f* de
rosto; ~**lift** *n* cirurgia *f* plástica do
rosto; ~ **pack** *n* máscara *f* de beleza *f*

faceless /'feɪslɪs/ *a fig* anônimo,
(P) anónimo

facet /'fæsɪt/ *n* faceta *f*

facetious /fə'siːʃəs/ *a* faceto; *pej* 🇬🇧
engraçadinho 🇬🇧 *pej*

facial /'feɪʃl/ *a* facial

facile /'fæsaɪl/ *a* fácil; (*superficial*)
superficial

facilitate /fə'sɪlɪteɪt/ *vt* facilitar

facilit|y /fə'sɪlətɪ/ *n* facilidade
f; ~**ies** (*means*) facilidades *fpl*;
(*installations*) instalações *fpl*

facsimile /fæk'sɪməlɪ/ *n* facsímile *m*

fact /fækt/ *n* fato *m*, (P) facto *m*; **in**
~**, as a matter of** ~ na realidade

faction /'fækʃn/ *n* facção *f*, (P)
facção *f*

factor /'fæktə(r)/ *n* fator *m*

factory /'fæktərɪ/ *n* fábrica *f*

factual /'fæktʃʊəl/ *a* concreto, real

faculty /'fækl|tɪ/ *n* faculdade *f*

fad /fæd/ *n* capricho *m*, mania *f*;
(*craze*) moda *f*

fade /feɪd/ *vt/i* ‹*colour*› desbotar;
‹*sound*› diminuir; (*disappear*)
apagar(-se)

faff /fæf/ *vi* enrolar 'ele ficou
enrolando o dia todo', (P) engonhar
'esteve aí só a engonhar o dia todo'

fag /fæg/ *n* 🇬🇧 (*chore*) estafa *f*; 🇺🇸
(*cigarette*) cigarro *m*

fail /feɪl/ *vt/i* falhar; (*in an
examination*) reprovar; (*omit,
neglect*) deixar de; *Comm* falir ● *n*

without ~ sem falta

failing /'feɪlɪŋ/ *n* deficiência *f* ● *prep*
na falta de, à falta de

failure /'feɪljə(r)/ *n* fracasso *m*,
(P) falhanço *m*; (*of engine*) falha
f; (*of electricity*) falta *f*; (*person*)
fracassado *m*

faint /feɪnt/ *a* (**-er, -est**) (*indistinct*)
apagado; (*weak*) fraco; (*giddy*)
tonto ● *vi* desmaiar ● *n* desmaio *m*.
~**ness** *n* debilidade *f*, (*indistinctness*)
apagado *m*

fair[1] /feə(r)/ *n* feira *f*. ~**ground** *n*
parque *m* de diversões, (P) largo
m de feira

fair[2] /feə(r)/ *a* (**-er, -est**) ‹*hair*›
louro; ‹*weather*› bom; (*of moderate
quality*) razoável; (*just*) justo; ~ **play**
jogo *m* limpo, fair play *m*. ~**ly** *adv*
razoavelmente. ~**ness** *n* justiça *f*.
~ **trade** *n* comércio *m* justo

fairy /'feərɪ/ *n* fada *f*; ~ **story,** ~
tale conto *m* de fadas

faith /feɪθ/ *n* fé *f*; (*religion*) religião
f; (*loyalty*) lealdade *f*; **in good** ~
de boa fé

faithful /'feɪθfl/ *a* fiel
● *adv* fielmente; **yours** ~**ly**
atenciosamente. ~**ness** *n* fidelidade *f*

fake /feɪk/ *n* ‹*thing*› imitação *f*;
‹*person*› impostor *m* ● *a* falsificado
● *vt* falsificar; (*pretend*) simular,
fingir

falcon /'fɔːlkən/ *n* falcão *m*

fall /fɔːl/ *vi* (*pt* **fell,** *pp* **fallen**) cair;
~ **back** bater em retirada; ~ **back
on** recorrer a; ~ **behind** atrasar-se
(**with** em); ~ **down** or **off** cair; ~
flat falhar, não resultar; ~ **flat on
one's face** estatelar-se; ~ **for** ‹*a
trick*› cair em, deixar-se levar por;
🇬🇧 ‹*a person*› apaixonar-se por, ficar
caído por 🇬🇧; ~ **in** ‹*roof*› ruir; *Mil*
alinhar-se, pôr-se em forma; ~ **out**

brigar, (P) zangar-se (**with** com); ~
through (of plans) falhar ● n quedas
f, Amer (autumn) outono m. **~s** npl
(waterfall) queda-d'água f, cataratas
fpl. **~out** n poeira f radioativa

fallac|y /ˈfæləsɪ/ n falácia f,
engano m

fallen /ˈfɔːlən/ ▶ FALL

fallible /ˈfæləbl/ a falível

false /fɔːls/ a falso; ~ **teeth**
dentadura f. **~ly** adv falsamente

falsehood /ˈfɔːlshʊd/ n falsidade
f, mentira f

falsify /ˈfɔːlsɪfaɪ/ vt (pt **-fied**)
falsificar; (a story) deturpar

falter /ˈfɔːltə(r)/ vi vacilar; (of the
voice) hesitar

fame /feɪm/ n fama f

familiar /fəˈmɪlɪə(r)/ a familiar;
(intimate) íntimo; **be ~ with** estar
familiarizado com

familiarity /fəmɪlɪˈærɪtɪ/ n
familiaridade f

familiarize /fəˈmɪlɪəraɪz/ vt
familiarizar (**with/to** com); (make
well known) tornar conhecido

family /ˈfæmɪlɪ/ n família f; ~
doctor médico m da família; ~ **tree**
árvore f genealógica

famine /ˈfæmɪn/ n fome f

famished /ˈfæmɪʃt/ a esfomeado,
faminto; **be ~** 🔲 estar morrendo de
fome, (P) estar a morrer de fome

famous /ˈfeɪməs/ a famoso

fan¹ /fæn/ n (in the hand) leque
m; (mechanical) ventilador m, (P)
ventoinha f ● vt (pt **fanned**) abanar;
(a fire) also fig atiçar ● vi ~ **out**
abrir-se em leque; ~ **belt** correia f
da ventoinha

fan² /fæn/ n 🔲 fã mf; ~ **mail** correio
m de fãs

fanatic /fəˈnætɪk/ n fanático m.
~al a fanático. **~ism** /-sɪzəm/ n
fanatismo m

fanciful /ˈfænsɪfl/ a fantasioso,
fantasista

fancy /ˈfænsɪ/ n fantasia f; (liking)
gosto m; **it took my** ~ gostei disso,
(P) deu-me no gosto; **a passing** ~
um entusiasmo passageiro; ~ **dress**
traje m fantasia ● a extravagante,
de fantasia; (of buttons etc)
fantástico; (of prices) exorbitante ● vt
imaginar; 🔲 (like) gostar de;
(want) apetecer

fanfare /ˈfænfeə(r)/ n fanfarra f

fang /fæŋ/ n presa f, dente m canino

fantastic /fænˈtæstɪk/ a fantástico

fantas|y /ˈfæntəsɪ/ n fantasia f.
~ize vt fantasiar, imaginar

far /fɑː(r)/ adv longe; (much, very)
muito ● a distante, longínquo; (end,
side) outro; ~ **away**, ~ **off** ao longe;
as ~ **as** (up to) até; **as** ~ **as I know**
tanto quanto saiba; **the F~ East**
o Extremo-Oriente m. **~fetched**
a forçado; (unconvincing) pouco
plausível; **~reaching** a de grande
alcance

farc|e /fɑːs/ n farsa f. **~ical** a de
farsa; ridículo

fare /feə(r)/ n preço m da passagem;
(in taxi) tarifa f, preço m da corrida;
(passenger) passageiro m; (food)
comida f ● vi (get on) dar-se

farewell /feəˈwel/ int & n adeus m

farm /fɑːm/ n quinta f, fazenda f
● vt cultivar ● vi ser fazendeiro, (P)
lavrador; ~ **out** (of work) delegar
a tarefeiros. **~er** n fazendeiro m,
(P) lavrador m. **~ing** n agricultura
f, lavoura f

farmhouse /ˈfɑːmhaʊs/ n casa f
da fazenda, (P) quinta

farmyard /'fɑːmjɑːd/ n quintal de fazenda m, (P) pátio de quinta

farth|er /'fɑːðə(r)/ adv mais longe ● a mais distante. **~est** adv mais longe ● a o mais distante

fascinat|e /'fæsɪneɪt/ vt fascinar. **~ion** /-'neɪʃn/ n fascínio m, fascinação f

fascis|t /'fæʃɪst/ n fascista mf. **~m** /-zəm/ n fascismo m

fashion /'fæʃn/ n moda f; (manner) maneira f ● vt amoldar, (P) moldar. **~able** a na moda

fast¹ /fɑːst/ a (-er, -est) rápido; (colour) fixo, que não desbota ● adv depressa; (firmly) firmemente, **be ~** (of clock) adiantar-se, estar adiantado; **~ asleep** profundamente adormecido, ferrado no sono. **~ food** n fast-food f

fast² /fɑːst/ vi jejuar ● n jejum m

fasten /'fɑːsn/ vt/i prender; <door, window> fechar(-se); <seat-belt> apertar. **~er**, **~ing** ns fecho m

fastidious /fə'stɪdɪəs/ a exigente

fat /fæt/ n gordura f ● a (fatter, fattest) gordo

fatal /'feɪtl/ a fatal; **~ injuries** ferimentos mpl mortais. **~ity** /fə'tælətɪ/ n fatalidade f. **~ly** adv fatalmente, mortalmente

fate /feɪt/ n (destiny) destino m; (one's lot) destino m, sorte f. **~ful** a fatídico

father /'fɑːðə(r)/ n pai m ● vt gerar. **~-in-law** n (pl **~s-in-law**) sogro m. **~ly** a paternal

fathom /'fæðəm/ n braça f ● vt **~ (out)** (comprehend) compreender

fatigue /fə'tiːg/ n fadiga f ● vt fatigar

fatten /'fætn/ vt/i engordar. **~ing** a que engorda

fatty /'fætɪ/ a (-ier, -iest) gorduroso; (tissue) adiposo

fault /fɔːlt/ n defeito m, falha f; (blame) falta f, culpa f; Geol falha f; **at ~** culpado; **it's your ~** é culpa sua. **~less** a impecável. **~y** a defeituoso

favour /'feɪvə(r)/ n favor m ● vt favorecer; (prefer) preferir; **do sb a ~** fazer um favor a alguém. **~able** a favorável

favourit|e /'feɪvərɪt/ a & n favorito m. **~ism** /-ɪzəm/ n favoritismo m

fawn¹ /fɔːn/ n cervo m novo ● a (colour) castanho claro

fawn² /fɔːn/ vi **~ on** adular, bajular

fax /fæks/ n fax m, fac-símile m; **~ machine** fax m ● vt mandar um fax

fear /fɪə(r)/ n medo m, receio m, temor m; (likelihood) perigo m ● vt recear, ter medo de. **for ~ of/that** com medo de/que. **~ful** a (terrible) medonho; (timid) medroso, receoso. **~less** a destemido, intrépido

feasib|le /'fiːzəbl/ a factível, praticável; (likely) plausível. **~ility** /-'bɪlətɪ/ n possibilidade f; (plausibility) plausibilidade f

feast /fiːst/ n festim m; Relig also fig festa f ● vt/i festejar; (eat and drink) banquetear-se; **~ on** regalar-se com

feat /fiːt/ n feito m, façanha f

feather /'feðə(r)/ n pena f, pluma f

feature /'fiːtʃə(r)/ n feição f, traço m; (quality) característica f; (film) longa-metragem f, (article) artigo m em destaque ● vt representar; <film> ter como protagonista ● vi figurar

February /'febru:ərɪ/ n fevereiro m

fed /fed/ ▶ FEED ● a **be ~ up** estar farto Ⓘ (**with** de)

federa|l /'fedərəl/ a federal. **~tion** /-'reɪʃn/ n federação f

fee /fiː/ n preço m; ~(s) (of
doctor, lawyer etc) honorários mpl;
(member's subscription) quota f;
(P) Univ propinas fpl; (enrolment/
registration) matrícula f; **school** ~s
mensalidades fpl escolares

feeble /ˈfiːbl/ a (-er, -est) débil,
fraco

feed /fiːd/ vt (pt fed) alimentar,
dar de comer a; (suckle) alimentar;
(supply) alimentar, abastecer
● vi alimentar-se ● n comida f;
(breastfeeding) amamentação f;
Mech alimentação f

feedback /ˈfiːdbæk/ n reação f;
Electr regeneração f, (P) feedback m

feel /fiːl/ vt (pt felt) sentir; (touch)
apalpar, tatear ● vi (tired, lonely etc)
sentir-se; ~ **hot/thirsty** ter calor/
sede; ~ **as if** ter a impressão (de)
que; ~ **like** ter vontade de

feeling /ˈfiːlɪŋ/ n sentimento m;
(physical) sensação f

feet /fiːt/ ▶ FOOT

feign /feɪn/ vt fingir

feline /ˈfiːlaɪn/ a felino

fell[1] /fel/ vt abater, derrubar

fell[2] /fel/ ▶ FALL

fellow /ˈfeləʊ/ n companheiro m,
camarada m; (of society, college)
membro m; 🄸 cara m, (P) tipo m 🄸

felt[1] /felt/ n feltro m

felt[2] /felt/ ▶ FEEL

female /ˈfiːmeɪl/ a ‹animal etc›
fêmea f, ‹voice, sex etc› feminino ● n
mulher f; (animal) fêmea f

feminine /ˈfemənɪn/ a & n
feminino m. ~**ity** /-ˈnɪnətɪ/ n
feminilidade f

feminist /ˈfemɪnɪst/ n feminista f

fenc|e /fens/ n tapume m, cerca
f ● vt cercar ● vi esgrimir. ~**er** n
esgrimista mf. ~**ing** n esgrima f;

(fences) tapume m

fend /fend/ vi ~ **for o.s.**
defender-se, virar-se 🄸, governar-se
● vt ~ **off** defender-se de

fender /ˈfendə(r)/ n guarda-fogo m;
Amer (mudguard) para-lama m, (P)
guarda-lamas m

fennel /ˈfenl/ n (herb) funcho m,
erva-doce f

ferment[1] /fəˈment/ vt/i fermentar;
(excite) excitar

ferment[2] /ˈfɜːment/ n fermento m;
fig efervescência f

fern /fɜːn/ n feto m

feroc|ious /fəˈrəʊʃəs/ a feroz. ~**ity**
/-ˈrɒsətɪ/ n ferocidade f

ferry /ˈferɪ/ n barco m de travessia,
ferry(-boat) m ● vt transportar

fertil|e /ˈfɜːtaɪl/ a fértil, fecundo.
~**ity** /fəˈtɪlətɪ/ n fertilidade f,
fecundidade f. ~**ize** /-əlaɪz/ vt
fertilizar, fecundar

fertilizer /ˈfɜːtəlaɪzə(r)/ n adubo
m, fertilizante m

fervent /ˈfɜːvənt/ a fervoroso

fervour /ˈfɜːvə(r)/ n fervor m,
ardor m

fester /ˈfestə(r)/ vt/i infectar; fig
envenenar

festival /ˈfestɪvl/ n festival m;
Relig festa f

festiv|e /ˈfestɪv/ a festivo; ~**e
season** período m das festas. ~**ity**
/feˈstɪvətɪ/ n festividade f, regozijo
m; ~**ities** festas fpl, festividades fpl

festoon /feˈstuːn/ vt engrinaldar
(with de or com)

fetch /fetʃ/ vt (go for) ir buscar;
(bring) trazer; (be sold for) vender-se
por, render

fetching /ˈfetʃɪŋ/ a atraente

fête /feɪt/ n festa or feira f de
caridade ao ar livre f ● vt festejar

fetish /ˈfetɪʃ/ n fetiche m, ídolo m;
(obsession) mania f

feud /fjuːd/ n discórdia f, inimizade
f. **~al** a feudal

fever /ˈfiːvə(r)/ n febre f. **~ish**
a febril

few /fjuː/ a & n poucos mpl; ~ **books**
poucos livros; **they are ~** são
poucos. **a ~** a & n alguns mpl; **a good
~, quite a ~** bastantes

fiancé /fɪˈɒnseɪ/ n noivo m. **~e** n
noiva f

fiasco /fɪˈæskəʊ/ n (pl -os) fiasco m

fib /fɪb/ n lorota f, cascata f, peta f,
mentira f ● vi (pt fibbed) mentir

fibre /ˈfaɪbə(r)/ n fibra f

fibreglass /ˈfaɪbəɡlɑːs/ n fibra f
de vidro

fickle /ˈfɪkl/ a leviano, inconstante

fiction /ˈfɪkʃn/ n ficção f; **(works
of)** ~ romances mpl, obras fpl de
ficção. **~al** a de ficção, fictício

fictitious /fɪkˈtɪʃəs/ a fictício

fiddle /ˈfɪdl/ n 🎻 violino m; 🗵
(swindle) trapaça f, (P) aldrabice f
● vi 🗵 trapacear 🗵, (P) aldrabar ●
vt (falsify) falsificar, cozinhar 🗵; ~
with 🎻 brincar com, remexer em,
(P) estar a brincar com, estar a (re)
mexer em

fidelity /fɪˈdelətɪ/ n fidelidade f

fidget /ˈfɪdʒɪt/ vi (pt fidgeted)
estar irrequieto, remexer-se; ~
with remexer em. **~y** a irrequieto;
(impatient) impaciente

field /fiːld/ n campo m; **F~ Marshal**
marechal de campo m ● vt/i Cricket
(estar pronto para) apanhar ou
interceptar or (P) interceptar a bola

fieldwork /ˈfiːldwɜːk/ n trabalho
m de campo; Mil fortificação f de

campanha

fiend /fiːnd/ n diabo m, demônio m,
(P) demónio m. **~ish** a diabólico

fierce /fɪəs/ a (-er, -est) feroz;
‹storm, attack› violento; ‹heat›
intenso, abrasador. **~ness** n
ferocidade f; (of storm, attack)
violência f; (of heat) intensidade f

fiery /ˈfaɪərɪ/ a (-ier, -iest) ardente;
‹temper, speech› inflamado

fifteen /fɪfˈtiːn/ a & n quinze m. **~th**
a & n décimo quinto m

fifth /fɪfθ/ a & n quinto m

fift|y /ˈfɪftɪ/ a & n cinquenta
m. **~y~y** a meias. **~ieth** a & n
quinquagésimo m

fig /fɪɡ/ n figo m

fight /faɪt/ vi (pt fought) lutar,
combater; ~ **over sth** lutar por algo;
~ **shy of** esquivar-se de, fugir de ● vt
lutar contra, combater ● n luta f;
(quarrel, brawl) briga f. **~er** n lutador
m; Mil combatente mf; (plane) caça
m. **~ing** n combate m

figurative /ˈfɪɡjərətɪv/ a figurado

figure /ˈfɪɡə(r)/ n (number)
algarismo m; (diagram, body)
figura f; ~ **of speech** figura f de
retórica ● vt imaginar, supor; ~ **out**
compreender ● vi (appear) figurar
(in em). **~head** n figura f de proa;
pej (person) testa de ferro m; chefe
m nominal

file[1] /faɪl/ n (tool) lixa f, lima f ● vt
lixar, limar

file[2] /faɪl/ n fichário m, (P) dossier m;
(box, drawer) fichário m, (P) ficheiro
m; Comput arquivo m; (line) fila f;
(in) single ~e (em) fila indiana ● vt
arquivar ● vi ~ (past) desfilar,
marchar em fila; **~ing cabinet** fichário m,
(P) ficheiro m. ~ **extension** n Comput
extensão f de arquivo justo

fill /fɪl/ vt/i encher(-se); ‹vacancy› preencher ● n eat one's ~ comer o que quiser; **have one's ~** estar farto; ~ **in** ‹form› preencher; ~ **out** (get fat) engordar; ~ **up** encher até cima; Auto encher o tanque, (P) atestar o depósito

fillet /ˈfɪlɪt/ n (meat, fish) filé m, (P) filete m ● vt (pt **filleted**) ‹meat, fish› cortar em filés, (P) filetes

filling /ˈfɪlɪŋ/ n recheio m; (of tooth) obturação f, (P) chumbo m; ~ **station** posto m de gasolina

film /fɪlm/ n filme m; ~ **star** estrela or vedete f de cinema, astro m ● vt/i filmar

filter /ˈfɪltə(r)/ n filtro m; ~ **coffee** café m de filtro ● vt/i filtrar(-se)

filth /fɪlθ/ n imundície f; fig obscenidade f. ~**y** a imundo; fig obsceno

fin /fɪn/ n barbatana f

final /ˈfaɪnl/ a final; (conclusive) decisivo ● n Sport final f. ~**s** npl (exams) finais fpl. ~**ist** n finalista mf. ~**ly** adv finalmente, por fim; (once and for all) definitivamente

finale /fɪˈnɑːlɪ/ n final m

finalize /ˈfaɪnəlaɪz/ vt finalizar

financ|e /ˈfaɪnæns/ n finança(s) f ● a financeiro ● vt financiar

financial /faɪˈnænʃl/ a financeiro

find /faɪnd/ vt (pt **found**) ‹sth lost› achar, encontrar; (think) achar; (discover) descobrir; Jur declarar ● n achado m □ ~ **out** vt apurar, descobrir ● vi informar-se (**about** sobre)

fine[1] /faɪn/ n multa f ● vt multar

fine[2] /faɪn/ a (-**er**, -**est**) fino; (splendid) belo, lindo; ~ **arts** belas artes fpl; ~ **weather** bom tempo

● adv (muito) bem; (small) fino, fininho

finesse /fɪˈnes/ n finura f, sutileza f, (P) subtileza f

finger /ˈfɪŋɡə(r)/ n dedo m ● vt apalpar. ~**nail** n unha f

fingerprint /ˈfɪŋɡəprɪnt/ n impressão f digital

fingertip /ˈfɪŋɡətɪp/ n ponta f do dedo

finicky /ˈfɪnɪkɪ/ a meticuloso, miudinho

finish /ˈfɪnɪʃ/ vt/i acabar, terminar ● n fim m; (of race) chegada f; (on wood, clothes) acabamento m; ~ **doing** acabar de fazer; ~ **up doing** acabar por fazer; ~ **up in** ir parar a, acabar em

finite /ˈfaɪnaɪt/ a finito

Fin|land /ˈfɪnlənd/ n Finlândia f. ~**n** n finlandês m. ~**nish** a & n Lang finlandês m

fir /fɜː(r)/ n abeto m

fire /ˈfaɪə(r)/ n fogo m; (conflagration) incêndio m; (heater) aquecedor m; **on** ~ em chamas; **set** ~ **to** pôr fogo a/em; ~ **brigade** bombeiros mpl; ~ **station** quartel m dos bombeiros ~ **alarm** n alarme m de incêndio; ~ **engine** n carro m de bombeiro; ~ **escape** n saída f de incêndio; ~ **extinguisher** n extintor m de incêndio ● vt ‹bullet, gun, etc› disparar; (dismiss) despedir; fig (stimulate) inflamar ● vi atirar; fazer fogo (**at** sobre)

firearm /ˈfaɪərɑːm/ n arma f de fogo

fireman /ˈfaɪəmən/ n (pl -**men**) bombeiro m

fireplace /ˈfaɪəpleɪs/ n chaminé f, lareira f

firewood | flame

firewood /ˈfaɪəwʊd/ n lenha f

firework /ˈfaɪəwɜːk/ n fogo m de artifício

firing squad /ˈfaɪərɪŋskwɒd/ n pelotão m de execução

firm[1] /fɜːm/ n firma f comercial

firm[2] /fɜːm/ a (-er, -est) firme; (belief) firme, inabalável

first /fɜːst/ a & n primeiro m; Auto primeira f; ~ name nome m próprio; **for the ~ time** pela primeira vez; ~ **aid** primeiros socorros mpl ● adv primeiro, em primeiro lugar; **at ~** a princípio, no início; ~ **of all** antes de mais nada. ~**class** a de primeira classe; ~**rate** a excelente. ~**ly** adv primeiramente, em primeiro lugar

fish /fɪʃ/ n (pl usually invar) peixe m ● vt/i pescar; ~ **out** 🄘 tirar. ~**ing** n pesca f; **go** ~**ing** ir pescar, (P) ir à pesca. ~**y** a de peixe; fig (dubious) suspeito

fisherman /ˈfɪʃəmən/ n (pl -men) pescador m

fishmonger /ˈfɪʃmʌŋɡə(r)/ n dono m /empregado m de peixaria; ~'**s** (**shop**) peixaria f

fission /ˈfɪʃn/ n fissão f, cisão f

fist /fɪst/ n punho m, mão f fechada, (P) punho m

fit[1] /fɪt/ n acesso m, ataque m; (of generosity) rasgo m

fit[2] /fɪt/ a (fitter, fittest) de boa saúde, em forma; (proper) próprio; (good enough) em condições; (able) capaz ● vt/i (pt fitted) assentar, ficar bem (a); (into space) caber; (match) ajustar-se (a); (install) instalar; ~ **out** equipar; ~**ted carpet** carpete m, (P) alcatifa f ● n **be a good** ~ assentar bem; **be a tight** ~ estar justo. ~**ness** n saúde f, (P) condição f física

fitting /ˈfɪtɪŋ/ a apropriado ● n (clothes) prova f; ~**s** (fixtures) instalações fpl, (fitments) mobiliário m; ~ **room** cabine f (de provas)

five /faɪv/ a & n cinco m

fix /fɪks/ vt fixar; (mend, prepare) arranjar ● n **in a** ~ em apuros, (P) numa alhada; ~ **sb up with sth** conseguir algo para alguém. ~**ed** a fixo

fixation /fɪkˈseɪʃn/ n fixação f; (obsession) obsessão f

fixture /ˈfɪkstʃə(r)/ n equipamento m, instalação f; Sport (data f marcada para) competição f

fizz /fɪz/ vi efervescer, borbulhar ● n efervescência f. ~**y** a gasoso

fizzle /ˈfɪzl/ vi ~ **out** (plan etc) acabar em nada or (P) em águas de bacalhau 🄘

flab /flæb/ n 🄘 gordura f, banha f 🄘. ~**by** a flácido

flabbergasted /ˈflæbəɡɑːstɪd/ a 🄘 espantado; pasmado 🄘

flag[1] /flæɡ/ n bandeira f ● vt (pt flagged) fazer sinal; ~ **down** fazer sinal para parar. ~**pole** n mastro m (de bandeira)

flag[2] /flæɡ/ vi (pt flagged) (droop) cair, pender, tombar; (of person) esmorecer

flagrant /ˈfleɪɡrənt/ a flagrante

flagstone /ˈflæɡstəʊn/ n laje f

flair /fleə(r)/ n jeito m, habilidade f

flak|e /fleɪk/ n floco m; (paint) lasca f ● vi descamar-se, lascar-se. ~**y** a (paint) descamado, lascado

flamboyant /flæmˈbɔɪənt/ a flamejante; (showy) flamante, vistoso; (of manner) extravagante

flame /fleɪm/ n chama f, labareda f ● vi flamejar; **burst into** ~**s** incendiar-se

flamingo /fləˈmɪŋgəʊ/ n (pl -os) flamingo m

flammable /ˈflæməbl/ a inflamável

flan /flæn/ n torta f, (P) tarte f

flank /flæŋk/ n flanco m ● vt flanquear

flannel /ˈflænl/ n flanela f; (for face) toalha f de rosto

flap /flæp/ vi (pt flapped) bater ● vt ~ its wings bater as asas ● n (of table, pocket) aba f; ▣ (panic) pânico m

flare /fleə(r)/ vi ~ up irromper em chamas; (of war) rebentar; fig (of person) enfurecer-se ● n chamejar m; (dazzling light) clarão m; (signal) foguete m de sinalização. ~d a <skirt> evasê

flash /flæʃ/ vi brilhar subitamente; (on and off) piscar; Auto fazer sinal com o pisca-pisca; ~ past passar como uma bala, (P) passar como uma bala ● vt fazer brilhar; (send) lançar, dardejar; (flaunt) fazer alarde de, ostentar ● n clarão m, lampejo m; Photo flash m

flashback /ˈflæʃbæk/ n cena f retrospectiva or (P) retrospetiva, flashback m

flashlight /ˈflæʃlaɪt/ n lanterna f elétrica

flashy /ˈflæʃɪ/ a espalhafatoso, que dá nas vistas

flask /flɑːsk/ n frasco m; (vacuum flask) garrafa f térmica, (P) termo m

flat /flæt/ a (flatter, flattest) plano, chato; <tyre> arriado, vazio, furado; (battery) fraco; <refusal> categórico; <fare, rate> fixo; (monotonous) monótono; Mus bemol; (out of tune) desafinado; ~ out (drive) em alta velocidade; (work) a dar tudo por

tudo ● n apartamento m; ▣ (tyre) furo m no pneu; Mus bemol m. ~ly adv categoricamente

flatter /ˈflætə(r)/ vt lisonjear, adular. ~ing a lisonjeiro, adulador. ~y n lisonja f

flaunt /flɔːnt/ vt/i pavonear(-se), ostentar

flavour /ˈfleɪvə(r)/ n sabor m (of a) ● vt dar sabor a, temperar. ~ing n aroma m sintético; (seasoning) tempero m

flaw /flɔː/ n falha f, imperfeição f. ~less a perfeito

flea /fliː/ n pulga f

fled /fled/ ▶ FLEE

flee /fliː/ vi (pt fled) fugir ● vt fugir de

fleece /fliːs/ n lã f de carneiro, velo m ● vt fig esfolar; roubar

fleet /fliːt/ n (of warships) esquadra f; (of merchant ships, vehicles) frota f

fleeting /ˈfliːtɪŋ/ a curto, fugaz

Flemish /ˈflemɪʃ/ a & n Lang flamengo m

flesh /fleʃ/ n carne f; (of fruit) polpa f

flew /fluː/ ▶ FLY²

flex¹ /fleks/ vt flexionar

flex² /fleks/ n Electr fio f flexível

flexib|le /ˈfleksəbl/ a flexível. ~ility /-ˈbɪlətɪ/ n flexibilidade f

flick /flɪk/ n (light blow) safanão m; (with fingertip) piparote m ● vt dar um safanão em; (with fingertip) dar um piparote a; ~ through folhear

flicker /ˈflɪkə(r)/ vi vacilar, oscilar, tremular ● n oscilação f, tremular m; (light) luz f trémula

flier /ˈflaɪə(r)/ n = FLYER

flight¹ /flaɪt/ n (flying) voo m; ~ of stairs lance m de escada

flight² /flaɪt/ n (fleeing) fuga f; **put to ~** pôr em fuga; **take ~** pôr-se em fuga

flimsy /ˈflɪmzɪ/ a (-ier, -iest) (material) fino; (object) frágil; ‹excuse etc› fraco, esfarrapado

flinch /flɪntʃ/ vi (wince) retrair-se; (draw back) recuar; (hesitate) hesitar

fling /flɪŋ/ vt/i (pt flung) atirar(-se), arremessar(-se); (rush) precipitar-se

flint /flɪnt/ n sílex m; (for lighter) pedra f

flip /flɪp/ vt (pt flipped) fazer girar com o dedo e o polegar ● n pancadinha f; **~ through** folhear

flippant /ˈflɪpənt/ a irreverente, petulante

flirt /flɜːt/ vt namoriscar, flertar, (P) flartar ● n namorador m, namoradeira f. **~ation** /-ˈteɪʃn/ n namorico m, flerte m, (P) flirt m. **~atious** a namorador m, namoradeira f

flit /flɪt/ vi (pt flitted) esvoaçar

float /fləʊt/ vt/i (fazer) flutuar; (company) lançar ● n boia f; (low cart) carro m alegórico

flock /flɒk/ n (of sheep; congregation) rebanho m; (of birds) bando m; (crowd) multidão f ● vi afluir, juntar-se

flog /flɒg/ vt (pt flogged) açoitar; ⚔ (sell) vender

flood /flʌd/ n inundação f, cheia f; (of tears) dilúvio m, rio m ● vt inundar, alagar ● vi estar inundado; ‹river› transbordar; fig ‹people› afluir

floodlight /ˈflʌdlaɪt/ n projetor m, holofote m ● vt (pt floodlit) iluminar

floor /flɔː(r)/ n chão m, soalho m; (for dancing) pista f; (storey) andar m

● vt assoalhar; (baffle) desconcertar, embatucar

flop /flɒp/ vi (pt flopped) (drop) (deixar-se) cair; (move helplessly) debater-se; ⚔ (fail) ser um fiasco ● n ⚔ fiasco m. **~py** a mole, tombado; **~py (disk)** disquete m

floral /ˈflɔːrəl/ a floral

florid /ˈflɒrɪd/ a florido

florist /ˈflɒrɪst/ n florista m

flounder /ˈflaʊndə(r)/ vi esbracejar, debater-se; fig meter os pés pelas mãos

flour /ˈflaʊə(r)/ n farinha f

flourish /ˈflʌrɪʃ/ vi florescer, prosperar ● vt brandir ● n floreado m; (movement) gesto m elegante

flout /flaʊt/ vt escarnecer (de)

flow /fləʊ/ vi correr, fluir; (traffic) mover-se; (hang loosely) flutuar; (gush) jorrar ● n corrente f; (of tide; also fig) enchente f; **~ into** (of river) desaguar em; **~ chart** organograma m

flower /ˈflaʊə(r)/ n flor f ● vi florir, florescer. **~ bed** n canteiro m. **~y** a florido

flown /fləʊn/ ▶ FLY²

flu /fluː/ n 🔲 gripe f

fluctuat|e /ˈflʌktʃʊeɪt/ vi flutuar, oscilar. **~ion** /-ˈeɪʃn/ n flutuação f, oscilação f

fluen|t /ˈfluːənt/ a fluente; **be ~t (in a language)** falar correntemente (uma língua). **~cy** n fluência f. **~tly** adv fluentemente

fluff /flʌf/ n cotão m; (down) penugem f ● vt 🔲 (bungle) estender-se em ⚔; executar mal. **~y** a penugento, fofo

fluid /ˈfluːɪd/ a & n fluido m

fluke /fluːk/ n bambúrrio m 🔲; golpe m de sorte

flung /flʌŋ/ ▶ FLING

flunk /flʌŋk/ vt/i Amer 🇹 levar pau 🇹,(P) chumbar 🇹

fluorescent /fluə'resnt/ a fluorescente

fluoride /'fluəraɪd/ n flúor m

flush[1] /flʌʃ/ vi corar, ruborizar-se ● vt lavar com água, (P) lavar a jorros de água; ~ **the toilet** dar descarga, (P) puxar o autoclismo ● n rubor m, vermelhidão f; fig excitação f; (of water) jorro m ● a ~ **with** ao nível de, rente a

flush[2] /flʌʃ/ vt ~ **out** desalojar

fluster /'flʌstə(r)/ vt atarantar, perturbar, enervar

flute /fluːt/ n flauta f

flutter /'flʌtə(r)/ vi esvoaçar; <wings> bater; <heart> palpitar ● vt bater; ~ **one's eyelashes** pestanejar ● n (of wings) batimento m; fig agitação f

flux /flʌks/ n **in a state of** ~ em mudança f contínua

fly[1] /flaɪ/ n mosca f

fly[2] /flaɪ/ vi (pt flew, pp flown) voar; <passengers> ir de/viajar de avião; (rush) correr ● vt pilotar; <passengers, goods> transportar por avião; <flag> hastear, (P) arvorar ● n (of trousers) braguilha f

flyer /'flaɪə(r)/ n aviador m; Amer (circular) prospecto m, (P) prospeto m

flying /'flaɪɪŋ/ a voador; **with** ~ **colours** com grande êxito, esplendidamente; ~ **saucer** disco m voador; ~ **start** bom arranque m; ~ **visit** visita f de médico

flyover /'flaɪəʊvə(r)/ n viaduto m

foal /fəʊl/ n potro m

foam /fəʊm/ n espuma f ● vi espumar

fob /fɒb/ vt (pt fobbed) ~ **off** iludir, entreter com artifícios; ~ **off on** impingir a

focus /'fəʊkəs/ n (pl -cuses or -ci) /-saɪ/ foco m; **in** ~ focado, em foco; **out of** ~ desfocado ● vt/i (pt focused) focar

fodder /'fɒdə(r)/ n forragem f

foetus /'fiːtəs/ n (pl -tuses) feto m

fog /fɒg/ n nevoeiro m ● vt/i (pt fogged) enevoar(-se). ~**horn** n sereia f de nevoeiro. ~**gy** a enevoado, brumoso; **it is** ~**gy** está nevoento or (P) de nevoeiro

foible /'fɔɪbl/ n fraqueza f, ponto m fraco

foil[1] /fɔɪl/ n papel m de alumínio; fig contraste m

foil[2] /fɔɪl/ vt frustrar

fold /fəʊld/ vt/i dobrar(-se); <arms> cruzar; 🇹 (fail) falir m dobra f. ~**er** n pasta f; (leaflet) prospecto m or (P) prospeto m (desdobrável) m. ~**ing** a dobrável, dobradiço

foliage /'fəʊlɪɪdʒ/ n folhagem f

folk /fəʊk/ n povo m; ~**s** (family, people) gente f 🇹, pessoal m 🇹 ● a folclórico, popular. ~**lore** n folclore m

follow /'fɒləʊ/ vt/i seguir; **it** ~**s that** quer dizer que; ~ **suit** <cards> servir o naipe jogado; fig seguir o exemplo, fazer o mesmo; ~ **up** (letter etc) dar seguimento a. ~**er** n partidário m, seguidor m. ~**ing** n partidários mpl ● a seguinte ● prep em seguimento a

folly /'fɒlɪ/ n loucura f

fond /fɒnd/ a (-er, -est) carinhoso; (hope) caro; **be** ~ **of** gostar de, ser amigo de. ~**ness** n (for people) afeição f; (for thing) gosto m

fondle /'fɒndl/ vt acariciar

font /fɒnt/ n pia f batismal

food /fuːd/ n alimentação f, comida f; (nutrient) alimento m ● a alimentar; **~ poisoning** envenenamento m alimentar

fool /fuːl/ n idiota mf, parvo m ● vt enganar ● vi **~ around** andar sem fazer nada

foolhardy /ˈfuːlhɑːdɪ/ a imprudente, atrevido

foolish /ˈfuːlɪʃ/ a idiota, parvo. **~ness** n idiotice f, parvoíce f

foolproof /ˈfuːlpruːf/ a infalível

foot /fʊt/ n (pl feet) (of person, bed, stairs) pé m; (of animal) pata f; (measure) pé m (= 30,48 cm); on **~** a pé; **on** or **to one's feet** de pé; **put one's ~ in it** cometer uma gafe; **to be under sb's feet** atrapalhar alguém ● vt **~ the bill** pagar a conta. **~bridge** n passarela f

football /ˈfʊtbɔːl/ n bola f de futebol; (game) futebol m; **~ pools** loteria f esportiva, (P) totobola m. **~er** n futebolista mf, jogador m de futebol

foothills /ˈfʊthɪlz/ npl contrafortes mpl

foothold /ˈfʊthəʊld/ n ponto f de apoio

footing /ˈfʊtɪŋ/ n firm **~** apoio m seguro; **on an equal ~** em pé de igualdade

footlights /ˈfʊtlaɪts/ npl ribalta f

footnote /ˈfʊtnəʊt/ n nota f de rodapé

footpath /ˈfʊtpɑːθ/ n (pavement) calçada f, (P) passeio m; (in open country) atalho m, caminho m

footprint /ˈfʊtprɪnt/ n pegada f

footstep /ˈfʊtstep/ n passo m

footwear /ˈfʊtweə(r)/ n calçado m

for unstressed /fə(r)/ emphatic fɔː(r)/ ● prep

····▸ (expressing purpose) para; **~ me** para mim; **music ~ dancing** música para dançar; **what is it ~?** para que serve isto?; **what have you got ~ a cold?** o que tem para a gripe?

····▸ (on behalf of, in place of) por; **I did it ~ you** fiz isso por si; **I took her classes ~ her** fiquei com as turmas dela; **I'm speaking ~ everyone in this department** falo por todos neste departamento

····▸ (expressing worth) no valor de; **a check/bill ~ ten euros** um cheque/uma conta no valor de dez euros

····▸ (expressing reason) por; **famous ~ its wine** famoso pelo seu vinho; **he was sentenced to death ~ murder** ele foi condenado à morte por homicídio; **~ fear/love of** por medo/amor de

▌ the preposition por often contracts with the definite articles o and a to form pelo, pela

····▸ (expressing direction) para; **the train ~ Oxford** o trem para Oxford

····▸ (with a time period that is still continuing) há; **I've been waiting ~ two hours** estou esperando há duas horas; **I haven't seen him ~ ten years** há dez anos que não o vejo; (with a time period that has ended) durante; **I waited ~ two hours** esperei durante duas horas; (with a future time period) durante; **I'm going to Paris ~ six weeks** vou para Paris por seis semanas; **he'll be away ~ a few weeks** ele vai ficar fora durante algumas semanas

····▶ (with distances) durante; **I drove ~ 50 kilometres** dirigi durante 50 quilômetros

● conj

····▶ porque, visto que; **he's not coming, ~ he has no money** ele não vem, porque não tem dinheiro

forbade /fə'bæd/ ▶ FORBID

forbid /fə'bɪd/ vt (pt **forbade**, pp **forbidden**) proibir; **you are ~den to smoke** você está proibido de fumar, (P) estás proibido de fumar. **~ding** a severo, intimidante

force /fɔːs/ n força f; **come into ~** entrar em vigor; **the ~s** as Forças Armadas ● vt forçar; **~ into** fazer entrar à força; **~ on** impor a. **~d** a forçado. **~ful** a enérgico

force-feed /'fɔːsfiːd/ vt (pt **-fed**) alimentar à força

forceps /'fɔːseps/ n ; pl invar fórceps m

forcibl|e /'fɔːsəbl/ a convincente; (done by force) à força. **~y** adv à força

ford /fɔːd/ n vau m ● vt passar a vau, vadear

fore /fɔː(r)/ a dianteiro ● n **to the ~** em evidência

forearm /'fɔːrɑːm/ n antebraço m

forecast /'fɔːkɑːst/ vt (pt **forecast**) prever ● n previsão f; **weather ~** boletim m meteorológico, previsão f do tempo

forefinger /'fɔːfɪŋɡə(r)/ n (dedo) indicador m

foregone /'fɔːɡɒn/ a **~ conclusion** resultado m previsto

foreground /'fɔːɡraʊnd/ n primeiro plano m

forehead /'fɒrɪd/ n testa f

foreign /'fɒrən/ a estrangeiro; ‹trade› externo; ‹travel› ao estrangeiro; **F~ Office** Ministério m dos Negócios Estrangeiros. **~er** n estrangeiro m

foreman /'fɔːmən/ n (pl **foremen**) contramestre m; (of jury) primeiro jurado m

foremost /'fɔːməʊst/ a principal, primeiro ● adv **first and ~** antes de mais nada, em primeiro lugar

forename /'fɔːneɪm/ n prenome m

forerunner /'fɔːrʌnə(r)/ n precursor m

foresee /fɔː'siː/ vt (pt **-saw**, pp **-seen**) prever. **~able** a previsível

foresight /'fɔːsaɪt/ n previsão f, previdência f

forest /'fɒrɪst/ n floresta f

forestry /'fɒrɪstrɪ/ n silvicultura f

forever /fə'revə(r)/ adv (endlessly) constantemente, para sempre

foreword /'fɔːwɜːd/ n prefácio m

forfeit /'fɔːfɪt/ n penalidade f, preço m; (in game) prenda f ● vt perder

forgave /fə'ɡeɪv/ ▶ FORGIVE

forge¹ /fɔːdʒ/ vi **~ ahead** tomar a dianteira, avançar

forge² /fɔːdʒ/ n forja f ● vt ‹metal, friendship› forjar; (counterfeit) falsificar, forjar. **~r** /-ə(r)/ n falsificador m, forjador m. **~ry** /-ərɪ/ n falsificação f

forget /fə'ɡet/ vt/i (pt **forgot**, pp **forgotten**) esquecer; **~ o.s.** portar-se com menos dignidade, esquecer-se de quem é. **~me-not** n miosótis m, (P) ~. **~ful** a esquecido. **~fulness** n esquecimento m

forgive | found

forgive /fə'gɪv/ vt (pt **forgave**, pp **forgiven**) perdoar (**sb for sth** algo a alguém). **~ness** n perdão m

forgo /fɔː'gəʊ/ vt (pt **forwent**, pp **forgone**) renunciar a

fork /fɔːk/ n garfo m; (for digging etc) forquilha f; (in road) bifurcação f • vi bifurcar; **~ out** 🄣 desembolsar. **~lift truck** n empilhadeira f

forlorn /fə'lɔːn/ a abandonado, desolado

form /fɔːm/ n forma f; (document) impresso m, formulário m; Schol classe f • vt/i formar(-se)

formal /'fɔːml/ a formal; ⟨dress⟩ de cerimónia or (P) cerimónia. **~ity** /-'mælətɪ/ n formalidade f

format /'fɔːmæt/ n formato m • vt (pl **formatted**) ⟨disk⟩ formatar

formation /fɔː'meɪʃn/ n formação f

former /'fɔːmə(r)/ a antigo; (first of two) primeiro; **the ~** aquele. **~ly** adv antigamente

formidable /'fɔːmɪdəbl/ a formidável, tremendo

formula /'fɔːmjʊlə/ n (pl **-ae** /-iː/, or **-as**) fórmula f

formulate /'fɔːmjʊleɪt/ vt formular

forsake /fə'seɪk/ vt (pt **forsook**, pp **forsaken**) abandonar

fort /fɔːt/ n Mil forte m

forth /fɔːθ/ adv adiante, para a frente; **and so ~** e assim por diante, etcetera; **go back and ~** andar de trás para diante

forthcoming /fɔːθ'kʌmɪŋ/ a que está para vir, próximo; (communicative) comunicativo, receptivo, (P) recetivo; ⟨book⟩ no prelo

forthright /'fɔːθraɪt/ a franco, direto

fortify /'fɔːtɪfaɪ/ vt fortificar. **~ication** /-ɪ'keɪʃn/ n fortificação f

fortitude /'fɔːtɪtjuːd/ n fortitude f, fortaleza f

fortnight /'fɔːtnaɪt/ n quinze dias mpl, (P) quinzena f. **~ly** a quinzenal • adv de quinze em quinze dias

fortress /'fɔːtrɪs/ n fortaleza f

fortunate /'fɔːtʃənət/ a feliz, afortunado; **be ~** ter sorte. **~ly** adv felizmente

fortune /'fɔːtʃən/ n sorte f; (wealth) fortuna f; **have the good ~ to** ter a sorte de. **~teller** n cartomante mf

forty /'fɔːtɪ/ a & n quarenta m. **~ieth** a & n quadragésimo m

forum /'fɔːrəm/ n fórum m, foro m

forward /'fɔːwəd/ a (in front) dianteiro; (towards the front) para a frente; (advanced) adiantado; (pert) atrevido • n Sport atacante m, (P) avançado m • adv **~(s)** para a frente, para diante; **come ~** apresentar-se; **go ~** avançar • vt ⟨letter⟩ remeter; ⟨goods⟩ expedir; fig (help) favorecer

fossil /'fɒsl/ a & n fóssil m

foster /'fɒstə(r)/ vt fomentar; ⟨child⟩ criar. **~child** n filho m adotivo; **~mother** n mãe f adotiva

fought /fɔːt/ ▶ FIGHT

foul /faʊl/ a (-er, -est) infecto; ⟨language⟩ obsceno; ⟨weather⟩ mau; **~ play** jogo m desleal; (crime) crime m • n Football falta f • vt sujar, emporcalhar. **~mouthed** a de linguagem obscena

found[1] /faʊnd/ ▶ FEEL

found[2] /faʊnd/ vt fundar. **~ation** /-'deɪʃn/ n fundação f; (basis) fundamento m. **~ations** npl (of building) alicerces mpl

founder[1] /'faʊndə(r)/ n fundador m

founder[2] /'faʊndə(r)/ vi afundar-se

foundry /'faʊndrɪ/ n fundição f

fountain /'faʊntɪn/ n fonte f. **~ pen** n caneta-tinteiro f, (P) caneta f de tinta permanente

four /fɔː(r)/ a & n quatro m. **~th** a & n quarto m

fourteen /fɔː'tiːn/ a & n catorze m. **~th** a & n décimo quarto m

fowl /faʊl/ n ave f de capoeira

fox /fɒks/ n raposa f ● vt 🈂 deixar perplexo; enganar; **be ~ed** ficar perplexo

foyer /'fɔɪeɪ/ n foyer m

fraction /'frækʃn/ n fração f; (small bit) bocadinho m, partícula f

fracture /'fræktʃə(r)/ n fratura f ● vt/i fraturar(-se)

fragile /'frædʒaɪl/ a frágil

fragment /'frægmənt/ n fragmento m

fragran|t /'freɪgrənt/ a fragrante, perfumado. **~ce** n fragrância f, perfume m

frail /freɪl/ a (-er, -est) frágil

frame /freɪm/ n Techn (of spectacles) armação f, (of picture) moldura f, (of window) caixilho m; (body) corpo m, (P) estrutura f ● vt colocar a armação em; ‹picture› emoldurar; fig formular; 🈂 incriminar falsamente; tramar; **~ of mind** estado m de espírito

framework /'freɪmwɜːk/ n estrutura f; (context) quadro m, esquema m

France /frɑːns/ n França f

franchise /'fræntʃaɪz/ n Pol direito m de voto; Comm concessão f, franchise f

frank[1] /fræŋk/ a franco

frank[2] /fræŋk/ vt franquear

frantic /'fræntɪk/ a frenético

fraternal /frə'tɜːnl/ a fraternal

fraud /frɔːd/ n fraude f; (person) impostor m. **~ulent** /'frɔːdjʊlənt/ a fraudulento

fraught /frɔːt/ a **~ with** cheio de

fray[1] /freɪ/ n rixa f

fray[2] /freɪ/ vt/i desfiar(-se), puir, esgarçar(-se)

freak /friːk/ n aberração f, anomalia f ● a anormal; **~ of nature** aborto m da natureza. **~ish** a anormal

freckle /'frekl/ n sarda f

free /friː/ a (freer, freest) livre; (gratis) grátis; (lavish) liberal ● vt (pt freed) libertar (from de); (rid) livrar (of de); **~ of charge** grátis, de graça; **a ~ hand** carta f branca. **~lance** a independente, free-lance; **~range** a ‹egg› de galinha criada ao ar livre. **~ly** adv livremente

freedom /'friːdəm/ n liberdade f

freeze /friːz/ vt/i (pt froze, pp frozen) gelar; Culin, Finance congelar(-se) ● n gelo m; Culin, Finance congelamento m. **~r** n congelador m. **~ing** a gélido, glacial; **below ~ing** abaixo de zero

freight /freɪt/ n frete m

French /frentʃ/ a francês; **~ window** porta f envidraçada ● n Lang francês m; **the ~** os franceses. **~man** n francês m; **~woman** n francesa f

frenzy /'frenzɪ/ n frenesi m

frequen|t[1] /'friːkwənt/ a frequente. **~cy** n frequência f. **~tly** adv frequentemente

frequent[2] /frɪ'kwent/ vt frequentar

fresh /freʃ/ a (-er, -est) fresco; (different, additional) novo; 🈂

(*cheeky*) descarado; atrevido. **~ness** *n* frescura *f*

fret /fret/ *vt/i* (*pt* **fretted**) ralar(-se). **~ful** *a* rabugento

friction /'frɪkʃn/ *n* fricção *f*

Friday /'fraɪdɪ/ *n* sexta-feira *f*; **Good ~** Sexta-Feira *f* Santa

fridge /frɪdʒ/ *n* 🄴 geladeira *f*, (P) frigorífico *m*

fried /fraɪd/ ▶ **FRY** ● *a* frito

friend /frend/ *n* amigo *m*. **~ship** *n* amizade *f*

friend|ly /'frendlɪ/ *a* (**-ier, -iest**) amigável, amigo, simpático. **~iness** *n* simpatia *f*, gentileza *f*

fright /fraɪt/ *n* medo *m*, susto *m*; **give sb a ~** pregar um susto em alguém. **~ful** *a* medonho, assustador

frighten /'fraɪtn/ *vt* assustar; **~ off** afugentar. **~ed** *a* assustado; **be ~ed (of)** ter medo (de)

frigid /'frɪdʒɪd/ *a* frígido. **~ity** /-'dʒɪdətɪ/ *n* frigidez *f*, frieza *f*; *Psych* frigidez *f*

frill /frɪl/ *n* babado *m*, (P) folho *m*

fringe /frɪndʒ/ *n* franja *f*; (*of area*) borda *f*; (*of society*) margem *f*; **~ benefits** (*work*) regalias *fpl* extras; **~ theatre** teatro *m* alternativo, teatro *m* de vanguarda

frisk /frɪsk/ *vi* pular, brincar ● *vt* revistar

fritter[1] /'frɪtə(r)/ *n* bolinho *m* frito, (P) frito *m*

fritter[2] /'frɪtə(r)/ *vt* **~ away** desperdiçar

frivol|ous /'frɪvələs/ *a* frívolo. **~ity** /-'vɒlətɪ/ *n* frivolidade *f*

fro /frəʊ/ (= **to and fro**) ▶ **TO**

frock /frɒk/ *n* vestido *m*

frog /frɒg/ *n* rã *f*

frolic /'frɒlɪk/ *vi* (*pt* **frolicked**) brincar, fazer travessuras ● *n* brincadeira *f*, travessura *f*

from /frəm/ emphatic /frɒm/ *prep* de; (*with time, prices etc*) de, a partir de; (*according to*) por, a julgar por

front /frʌnt/ *n* Meteo, Mil, Pol (*of car, train*) frente *f*; (*of shirt*) peitilho *m*; (*of building; also fig*) fachada *f*; (*promenade*) calçada à beira-mar *f* ● *a* da frente; (*first*) primeiro; **in ~ (of)** em frente (de); **~ door** porta *f* da rua; **~-wheel drive** tração *f* dianteira

frontier /'frʌntɪə(r)/ *n* fronteira *f*

frost /frɒst/ *n* gelo *m*, temperatura *f* abaixo de zero; (*on ground, plants etc*) geada *f* ● *vt/i* cobrir(-se) de geada. **~bite** *n* queimadura *f* de frio; **~bitten** *a* queimado pelo frio. **~ed** *a* (*glass*) fosco. **~y** *a* glacial

froth /frɒθ/ *n* espuma *f* ● *vi* espumar, fazer espuma. **~y** *a* espumoso

frown /fraʊn/ *vi* franzir as sobrancelhas ● *n* franzir *m* de sobrancelhas; **~ on** desaprovar

froze, frozen /frəʊz, 'frəʊzn/ ▶ **FREEZE**

froze, frozen /frəʊz, 'frəʊzn/ ▶ **FREEZE**

frugal /'fruːgl/ *a* poupado; (*meal*) frugal

fruit /fruːt/ *n* fruto *m*; (*collectively*) fruta *f*; **~ machine** caça-níqueis *mpl*, (P) máquina *f* de jogo; **~ salad** salada *f* de frutas. **~y** *a* que tem gosto ou cheiro de fruta

fruit|ful /'fruːtfl/ *a* frutífero, produtivo. **~less** *a* infrutífero

fruition /fruː'ɪʃn/ *n* **come to ~** realizar-se

frustrat|e /frʌ'streɪt/ vt frustrar. **~ion** /-ʃn/ n frustração f

fry /fraɪ/ vt/i (pt **fried**) fritar. **~ing pan** n frigideira f

fudge /fʌdʒ/ n Culin doce m de leite, (P) doce m acaramelado ● vt/i **~ (the issue)** lançar a confusão

fuel /'fjuːəl/ n combustível m; (for car) carburante m ● vt (pt **fuelled**) abastecer de combustível; fig atear

fugitive /'fjuːdʒɪtɪv/ a & n fugitivo m

fulfil /fʊl'fɪl/ vt (pt **fulfilled**) cumprir, realizar; ‹condition› satisfazer; **~o.s.** realizar-se. **~ment** n realização f; (of condition) satisfação f

full /fʊl/ a (-er, -est) cheio; ‹meal› completo; ‹price› total, por inteiro; ‹skirt› rodado; **~ moon** lua f cheia; **~ stop** ponto m final; **at ~ speed** a toda velocidade; **to the ~** ao máximo; **be ~ up** Ⓛ (after eating) estar cheio Ⓛ ● adv **in ~** integralmente. **~-scale** a em grande; **~-size** a em tamanho natural; **~-time** a & adv a tempo integral, full-time. **~y** adv completamente

fumble /'fʌmbl/ vt tatear; (in the dark) andar tateando; **~ with** estar atrapalhado com, andar às voltas com

fume /fjuːm/ vi defumar, (P) deitar fumo, fumegar; (with anger) ferver. **~s** npl gases mpl

fun /fʌn/ n divertimento m; **for ~** de brincadeira; **make ~ of** zombar de, fazer troça de. **~fair** n parque m de diversões, (P) feira f de diversões, (P) feira f popular

function /'fʌŋkʃn/ n função f ● vi funcionar. **~al** a funcional

fund /fʌnd/ n fundos mpl ● vt financiar

fundamental /fʌndə'mentl/ a fundamental.

funeral /'fjuːnərəl/ n enterro m, funeral m ● a fúnebre

fungus /'fʌŋɡəs/ n (pl **-gi** /-gaɪ/) fungo m

funnel /'fʌnl/ n funil m; (of ship) chaminé f

funn|y /'fʌnɪ/ a (-ier, -iest) engraçado, cômico; (odd) esquisito. **~ily** adv comicamente; (oddly) estranhamente; **~ily enough** por incrível que pareça

fur /fɜː(r)/ n pelo m; (for clothing) pele f; (in kettle) depósito m, crosta f; **~ coat** casaco m de pele

furious /'fjʊərɪəs/ a furioso

furnace /'fɜːnɪs/ n fornalha f

furnish /'fɜːnɪʃ/ vt mobiliar, (P) mobilar; (supply) prover (with de). **~ings** npl mobiliário m e equipamento m

furniture /'fɜːnɪtʃə(r)/ n mobília f

furry /'fɜːrɪ/ a (-ier, -iest) peludo; ‹toy› de pelúcia, (P) de peluche

furth|er /'fɜːðə(r)/ a & adv mais distante; (additional) adicional, suplementar ● adv mais longe; (more) mais ● vt promover; **~er education** ensino m supletivo, cursos mpl livres, (P) educação f suplementar. **~est** a o mais distante ● adv mais longe

furthermore /fɜːðə'mɔː(r)/ adv além disso

fury /'fjʊərɪ/ n fúria f, furor m

fuse[1] /fjuːz/ vt/i fundir(-se); (P) amalgamar ● n fusível m; **the lights ~d** os fusíveis queimaram

fuse[2] /fjuːz/ n (of bomb) espoleta f

fuselage /'fjuːzəlɑːʒ/ n fuselagem f

fuss /fʌs/ n história(s) f(pl), escarcéu m ● vi preocupar-se com ninharias; **make a ~ of** ligar demasiado para

futile | gape

or (P) a, criar caso com, fazer um espalhafato com. **~y** a exigente, complicado

futile /'fju:taɪl/ a fútil

future /'fju:tʃə(r)/ a & n futuro m; **in ~** no futuro, de agora em diante

futuristic /fju:tʃə'rɪstɪk/ a futurista, futurístico

fuzz /fʌz/ n penugem f; (hair) cabelo m frisado

fuzzy /'fʌzɪ/ a ‹hair› frisado; ‹photo› pouco nítido, desfocado

....

Gg

....

gabble /'gæbl/ vt/i tagarelar, falar, ler muito depressa ● n tagarelice f, algaravia f

gable /'geɪbl/ n empena f, oitão m

gadget /'gædʒɪt/ n pequeno utensílio m; (fitting) dispositivo m; (device) engenhoca f 🔢

Gaelic /'geɪlɪk/ n galês m

gag /gæg/ n mordaça f; (joke) gag m, piada f ● vt (pt gagged) amordaçar

gaiety /'geɪətɪ/ n alegria f

gaily /'geɪlɪ/ adv alegremente

gain /geɪn/ vt ganhar ● vi (of clock) adiantar-se; **~ weight** aumentar de peso; **~ on** (get closer to) aproximar-se de ● n ganho m; (increase) aumento m

gait /geɪt/ n (modo de) andar m

gala /'gɑ:lə/ n gala m; Sport festival m

galaxy /'gæləksɪ/ n galáxia f

gale /geɪl/ n vento m forte

gallant /'gælənt/ a galhardo, valente; (chivalrous) galante, cortês. **~ry** n galhardia f, valentia f; (chivalry) galanteria f, cortesia f

gallery /'gælərɪ/ n galeria f

galley /'gælɪ/ n (pl -eys) galera f; (ship's kitchen) cozinha f

gallon /'gælən/ n galão m = 4,546 litros, Amer = 3.785 litros

gallop /'gæləp/ n galope m ● vi (pt galloped) galopar

gallows /'gæləʊz/ npl forca f

galore /gə'lɔ:(r)/ adv à beça, em abundância

gamble /'gæmbl/ vt/i jogar ● n jogo (de azar) m; fig risco m; **~e on** apostar em. **~er** n jogador m

game /geɪm/ n jogo m; Football desafio m; (animals) caça f ● a bravo; **~ for** pronto para

gamekeeper /'geɪmki:pə(r)/ n guarda-florestal m

gammon /'gæmən/ n presunto m defumado

gang /gæŋ/ n bando m, gang m; (of workmen) turma f, (P) grupo m ● vi **~ up** ligar-se (on contra)

gangling /'gæŋglɪŋ/ a desengonçado

gangrene /'gæŋgri:n/ n gangrena f

gangster /'gæŋstə(r)/ n gângster m, bandido m

gangway /'gæŋweɪ/ n passagem f; (aisle) coxia f; (on ship) portaló m; (from ship to shore) passadiço m

gaol /dʒeɪl/ n & vt = JAIL

gap /gæp/ n abertura f, brecha f; (in time) intervalo m; (deficiency) lacuna f

gape /geɪp/ vi ficar boquiaberto or embasbacado. **~ing** a escancarado

gap year Na Grã-Bretanha, *i* é o período de tempo entre o final dos estudos no ensino secundário e a entrada na universidade. Muitos estudantes dedicam este período a obter experiência laboral relacionada com as suas futuras carreiras profissionais. Outros realizam atividades não-relacionadas com os estudos, e para alguns é uma oportunidade para poupar dinheiro ou viajar.

garage /'gærɑːʒ/ *n* garagem *f*; (*service station*) posto *m* de gasolina, (P) estação *f* de serviço ● *vt* pôr na garagem

garbage /'gɑːbɪdʒ/ *n* lixo *m*; ~ **can** *Amer* lata *f* do lixo, (P) caixote *m* do lixo

garden /'gɑːdn/ *n* jardim *m* ● *vi* jardinar. ~**er** *n* jardineiro *m*. ~**ing** *n* jardinagem *f*

gargle /'gɑːgl/ *vi* gargarejar ● *n* gargarejo *m*

garish /'geərɪʃ/ *a* berrante, espalhafatoso

garland /'gɑːlənd/ *n* grinalda *f*

garlic /'gɑːlɪk/ *n* alho *m*

garment /'gɑːmənt/ *n* peça *f* de vestuário, roupa *f*

garnish /'gɑːnɪʃ/ *vt* enfeitar, guarnecer ● *n* guarnição *f*

garrison /'gærɪsn/ *n* guarnição *f* ● *vt* guarnecer

garrulous /'gærələs/ *a* tagarela

garter /'gɑːtə(r)/ *n* liga *f*

gas /gæs/ *n* (*pl* **gases**) gás *m*; *Med* anestésico *m*; *Amer* 🇺🇸 (*petrol*) gasolina *f* ● *vt* (*pt* **gassed**) asfixiar; *Mil* gasear ● *vi* 🇺🇸 fazer conversa fiada; ~ **fire** aquecedor *m* a gás; ~ **mask** máscara *f* antigás; ~ **meter** medidor *m* or (P) contador *m* do gás

gash /gæʃ/ *n* corte *m*, lanho *m* ● *vt* cortar

gasket /'gæskɪt/ *n* junta *f*

gasoline /'gæsəliːn/ *n* *Amer* gasolina *f*

gasp /gɑːsp/ *vi* arfar, arquejar; *fig* (*with rage, surprise*) ficar sem ar ● *n* arquejo *m*

gastric /'gæstrɪk/ *a* gástrico

gastronomy /gæ'strɒnəmɪ/ *n* gastronomia *f*

gate /geɪt/ *n* portão *m*; (*of wood*) cancela *f*; (*barrier*) barreira *f*; (*airport*) porta *f*

gatecrash /'geɪtkræʃ/ *vt/i* entrar (numa festa) sem convite

gateway /'geɪtweɪ/ *n* (porta de) entrada *f*

gather /'gæðə(r)/ *vt* reunir, juntar; (*pick up, collect*) apanhar; (*amass, pile up*) acumular, juntar; (*conclude*) deduzir; <*cloth*> franzir ● *vi* reunir-se; (*pile up*) acumular-se; ~ **speed** ganhar velocidade. ~**ing** *n* reunião *f*

gaudy /'gɔːdɪ/ *a* (-**ier**, -**iest**) (*bright*) berrante; (*showy*) espalhafatoso

gauge /geɪdʒ/ *n* medida *f* padrão; (*device*) indicador *m*; (*railway*) bitola *f* ● *vt* medir, avaliar

gaunt /gɔːnt/ *a* emagrecido, macilento; (*grim*) lúgubre, desolado

gauze /gɔːz/ *n* gaze *f*

gave /geɪv/ ▶ GIVE

gawky /'gɔːkɪ/ *a* (-**ier**, -**iest**) desajeitado

gay /geɪ/ *a* (-**er**, -**est**) alegre; 🇺🇸 (*homosexual*) homossexual; gay

gaze /geɪz/ *vi* ~ (**at**) olhar fixamente (para) ● *n* contemplação *f*

GB abbr ▶ **GREAT BRITAIN**

gear /gɪə(r)/ n equipamento m; Techn engrenagem f; Auto velocidade f; **in ~** engrenado; **out of ~** em ponto morto ● vt equipar; (adapt) adaptar

gearbox /'gɪəbɒks/ n caixa f de mudança, caixa f de transmissão, (P) caixa f de velocidades

geese /giːs/ ▶ **GOOSE**

gel /dʒel/ n geleia f

gelatine /'dʒelətiːn/ n gelatina f

gem /dʒem/ n gema f, pedra f preciosa

Gemini /'dʒemɪnaɪ/ n Astr Gêmeos mpl, (P) Gémeos mpl

gender /'dʒendə(r)/ n gênero m, (P) género m

gene /dʒiːn/ n gene m

genealogy /dʒiːnɪ'ælədʒɪ/ n genealogia f

general /'dʒenrəl/ a geral; **~ election** eleições fpl legislativas; **in ~** em geral ● n general m. **~ practitioner** n clínico-geral m, (P) médico m de família. **~ly** adv geralmente

generaliz|e /'dʒenrəlaɪz/ vt/i generalizar. **~ation** /-'zeɪʃn/ n generalização f

generate /'dʒenəreɪt/ vt gerar, produzir

generation /dʒenə'reɪʃn/ n geração f

generator /'dʒenəreɪtə(r)/ n gerador m

gener|ous /'dʒenərəs/ a generoso; (plentiful) abundante. **~osity** /-'rɒsətɪ/ n generosidade f

genetic /dʒɪ'netɪk/ a genético. **~s** n genética f

genial /'dʒiːnɪəl/ a agradável

genius /'dʒiːnɪəs/ n (pl-uses) gênio m, (P) génio m

genocide /'dʒenəsaɪd/ n genocídio m

gent /dʒent/ n **the G~s** 🚹 banheiros mpl de homens, (P) lavabos mpl para homens

genteel /dʒen'tiːl/ a elegante, fino, refinado

gentl|e /'dʒentl/ a (er, est) brando, suave. **~eness** n brandura f, suavidade f. **~y** adv brandamente, suavemente

gentleman /'dʒentlmən/ n (pl-men) senhor m; (well-bred) cavalheiro m

genuine /'dʒenjuɪn/ a genuíno, verdadeiro; (belief) sincero

geograph|y /dʒɪ'ɒgrəfɪ/ n geografia f. **~ical** /dʒɪə'græfɪkl/ a geográfico

geolog|y /dʒɪ'ɒlədʒɪ/ n geologia f. **~ical** /dʒɪə'lɒdʒɪkl/ a geológico. **~ist** n geólogo m

geometr|y /dʒɪ'ɒmətrɪ/ n geometria f. **~ic(al)** /dʒɪə'metrɪk(l)/ a geométrico

geranium /dʒə'reɪnɪəm/ n gerânio m

geriatric /dʒerɪ'ætrɪk/ a geriátrico

germ /dʒɜːm/ n germe m, micróbio m

German /'dʒɜːmən/ a & n alemão m, alemã f; Lang alemão m; **G~ measles** rubéola f. **G~ic** /dʒə'mænɪk/ a germânico. **G~y** n Alemanha f

germinate /'dʒɜːmɪneɪt/ vi germinar

gesticulate /dʒe'stɪkjuleɪt/ vi gesticular

gesture /'dʒestʃə(r)/ n gesto m

get /get/ ● *vt* (*pt* **got**, *pp* **got, gotten** US *pres p* **getting**)

••••➤ (*receive*) receber; **we got a letter** recebemos uma carta

••••➤ (*obtain, achieve*) conseguir, obter; **I got a job in São Paulo** consegui um emprego em São Paulo; **he ~s good grades** ele tem boas notas

••••➤ (*buy*) comprar; **~ sb a present** comprar um presente para alguém

••••➤ (*fetch*) ir buscar; **go and ~ a chair** vá buscar uma cadeira

••••➤ (*travel by*) apanhar; **we can ~ the bus** podemos pegar o ônibus

••••➤ (*understand*) perceber; **I don't ~ it** não percebo

••••➤ (*experience*) ter; **~ a surprise** ter uma surpresa; **~ a shock** ter um choque

••••➤ (*illness*) pegar, apanhar; **~ the flu/a cold** pegar uma gripe

••••➤ (*cause to be done*) **~ the TV repaired** mandar arrumar a televisão; **~ one's hair cut** (ir) cortar o cabelo

••••➤ (*ask or persuade*) **~ sb to do sth** fazer com que alguém faça algo; **he got his sister to help him with the homework** ele convenceu a irmã a ajudá-lo no trabalho de casa

● *vi*

••••➤ (*become*) tornar-se, ficar; **he is getting old** está ficando velho; **he got rich** ficou rico

••••➤ (*into state/condition*) **~ married** casar-se; **~ hurt**

ficar ferido; **~ better/worse** melhorar/piorar

••••➤ (*arrive*) chegar; **~ to the airport** chegar ao aeroporto

□ **~ about** ● *vi* (*person*) deslocar-se. **~ along** ● *vi* (*progress*) **how is she getting along?** como ela está progredindo?. **~ along with** ● *vi* dar-se bem com. **~ at** ● *vt* (*have access to*) alcançar; (*criticize*) criticar; (*mean*) querer dizer, insinuar; **what are you getting at?** o que você está insinuando?. **~ away** ● *vi* escapar. **~ back** ● *vi* voltar ● *vt* recuperar. **~ by** ● *vi* safar-se. **~ down** ● *vt/i* descer. **~ in** ● *vi* (*enter*) entrar; ‹*bus, train*› chegar. **~ into** ● *vt* (*dress*) vestir. **~ off** ● *vi* (*from bus, train, horse*) descer ● *vt* (*remove*) remover; ‹*bus, train, horse*› descer de. **~ on** ● *vi* ‹*bus*› subir; (*be on good terms*) **~ on well with sb** dar-se bem com alguém; (*make progress*) **how are you getting on?** como você está indo?. **~ out** ● *vi* sair. **~ over** ● *vt* ‹*illness*› recuperar. **~ round** ● *vt* ‹*rule*› contornar; ‹*person*› convencer. **~ through** ● *vi* (*on the phone*) estabelecer contato. **~ up** ● *vi* levantar-se

getaway /'getweɪ/ *n* fuga *f*
get-up *n* [1] apresentação *f*
ghastly /'gɑːstlɪ/ *a* (-**ier**, -**iest**) horrível; (*pale*) lívido
gherkin /'gɜːkɪn/ *n* pepino *m* pequeno para conservas, cornichão *m*
ghetto /'getəʊ/ *n* (*pl* -**os**) gueto *m*, ghetto *m*
ghost /gəʊst/ *n* fantasma *m*, espectro *m*. **~ly** a fantasmagórico, espectral
giant /'dʒaɪənt/ *a* & *n* gigante *m*

gibberish /'dʒɪbərɪʃ/ n algaravia f, linguagem f incompreensível

giblets /'dʒɪblɪts/ npl miúdos mpl, miudezas fpl

giddy /'gɪdɪ/ a (-ier, -iest) estonteante, vertiginoso; **be** or **feel ~** ter tonturas or vertigens

gift /gɪft/ n presente m, dádiva f; (ability) dom m, dote m. **~wrap** vt (pt -wrapped) fazer um embrulho de presente

gifted /'gɪftɪd/ a dotado

gig /gɪg/ n ▣ show m; sessão f de jazz etc

gigantic /dʒaɪ'gæntɪk/ a gigantesco

giggle /'gɪgl/ vi dar risadinhas nervosas ● n risinho m nervoso

gild /gɪld/ vt dourar

gilt /gɪlt/ a & n dourado m. **~edged** a de toda a confiança

gimmick /'gɪmɪk/ n truque m, artifício m

gin /dʒɪn/ n gin m, genebra f

ginger /'dʒɪndʒə(r)/ n gengibre m ● a louro-avermelhado, ruivo; **~ ale, ~ beer** cerveja f de gengibre, (P) ginger ale m

gingerbread /'dʒɪndʒəbred/ n pão m de gengibre

gingerly /'dʒɪndʒəlɪ/ adv cautelosamente

gipsy /'dʒɪpsɪ/ n = GYPSY

giraffe /dʒɪ'rɑːf/ n girafa f

girder /'gɜːdə(r)/ n trave f, viga f

girl /gɜːl/ n (child) menina f; (young woman) moça f, (P) rapariga f. **~friend** n amiga f; (of boy) namorada f

gist /dʒɪst/ n essencial m

give /gɪv/ vt/i (pt gave, pp given) dar; (bend, yield) ceder; **~ away** dar; (secret) revelar, trair; **~ back** devolver; **~ in** dar-se por vencido, render-se; **~ off** emitir; **~ way** ceder; (traffic) dar prioridade; (collapse) dar de si □ **~ out** vt anunciar ● vi esgotar-se. **~ up** vt/i desistir (de), renunciar (a); **~ o.s. up** entregar-se

given /'gɪvn/ ▶ GIVE a dado; **~ name** nome m de batismo

glacier /'glæsɪə(r)/ n glaciar m, geleira f

glad /glæd/ a contente. **~ly** adv com (todo o) prazer

glamour /'glæmə(r)/ n fascinação f, encanto m, (P) glamour m. **~orize** vt tornar fascinante. **~orous** a fascinante, sedutor, glamoroso

glance /glɑːns/ n relance m, olhar m; **at first ~** à primeira vista ● vi **~ at** dar uma olhada a

gland /glænd/ n glândula f

glar|e /gleə(r)/ vi brilhar intensamente, faiscar ● n luz f crua; fig olhar m feroz; **~e at** olhar ferozmente para. **~ing** a brilhante; (obvious) flagrante

glass /glɑːs/ n vidro m; (vessel, its contents) copo m; (mirror) espelho m; **~es** óculos mpl. **~y** a vítreo

glaze /gleɪz/ vt (door etc) envidraçar; (pottery) vidrar ● n vidrado m

gleam /gliːm/ n raio m de luz frouxa; fig vislumbre m ● vi luzir, brilhar

glee /gliː/ n alegria f

glib /glɪb/ a que tem a palavra fácil, verboso

glide /glaɪd/ vi deslizar; (bird, plane) planar. **~r** /-ə(r)/ n planador m

glimmer /'glɪmə(r)/ n luz f trêmula or (P) trémula, ténue ● vi tremular

glimpse /glɪmps/ n vislumbre m;
catch a ~ of entrever, ver de relance

glint /glɪnt/ n brilho m, reflexo m
● vi brilhar, cintilar

glisten /ˈglɪsn/ vi reluzir

glitter /ˈglɪtə(r)/ vi luzir,
resplandecer ● n esplendor m,
cintilação f

gloat /gləʊt/ vi ~ over ter um
prazer maligno em, exultar com

global /ˈgləʊbl/ a global

globalization
/ˌgləʊbəlaɪˈzeɪʃən, Amer -lɪˈz-/ n
globalização f

globe /gləʊb/ n globo m

gloom /gluːm/ n obscuridade f; fig
tristeza f. ~y a sombrio; (sad) triste;
(pessimistic) pessimista

glorif|y /ˈglɔːrɪfaɪ/ vt glorificar; a
~ied waitress/etc pouco mais que
uma garçonete/etc, (P) empregada-
de-mesa/etc

glorious /ˈglɔːrɪəs/ a glorioso

glory /ˈglɔːrɪ/ n glória f; (beauty)
esplendor m ● vi ~ in orgulhar-se de

gloss /glɒs/ n brilho m ● a brilhante
● vt ~ over minimizar, encobrir. ~y
a brilhante

glossary /ˈglɒsərɪ/ n (pl -ries)
glossário m

glove /glʌv/ n luva f; ~
compartment porta-luvas m

glow /gləʊ/ vi arder; ‹person›
resplandecer ● n brasa f. ~ing a fig
entusiástico

glucose /ˈgluːkəʊs/ n glucose f

glue /gluː/ n cola f ● vt (pres p
gluing) colar

glum /glʌm/ a (glummer,
glummest) sorumbático; (dejected)
abatido

glut /glʌt/ n superabundância f

glutton /ˈglʌtn/ n glutão m. ~ous a
glutão. ~y n gula f

GMO /ˌdʒiːemˈəʊ/ n OGM m,
organismo m geneticamente
modificado

gnash /næʃ/ vt ~ one's teeth
ranger os dentes

gnat /næt/ n mosquito m

gnaw /nɔː/ vt/i roer

---

go /gəʊ/ ● vi (3rd person sing pres.
tense **goes**, pt **went**, pp **gone**)

┈┈▸ ir; **to school/town/the
cinema** ir à escola/à cidade/ao
cinema; ~ **shopping/swimming/
riding** ir às compras/nadar/andar
a cavalo; ~ **for a walk** sair para
um passeio; ~ **for a nap** tirar
uma soneca

┈┈▸ (leave) ir; **I must be ~ing**
tenho de ir

┈┈▸ (vanish) ir-se, desaparecer;
the money's gone o dinheiro
acabou; **my bike's gone** a
minha bicicleta desapareceu; **my
headache is gone** a minha dor
de cabeça desapareceu

┈┈▸ (work, function) funcionar;
is the car ~ing? o carro
funciona?

┈┈▸ (become) ficar; ~ **blind** ficar
cego; ~ **pale/red** ficar pálido/
corado

┈┈▸ (turn out, progress) ir correr;
how's it ~ing? como vai tudo?;
how did the exam ~? como
correu o exame?

┈┈▸ (match) combinar; **the two
colours don't ~ [together]** as
duas cores não combinam

┈┈▸ (in future tenses) **be ~ing
to** ir (+ inf); **it's ~ing to rain** vai

chover; **I'm not ~ing to do it** não vou fazer isso
● n (pl **goes**)
••••➤ (turn) vez f; **it's your ~ é** a sua vez
••••➤ (try) tentativa f; **have a ~ at doing sth** fazer uma tentativa de aco
••••➤ (energy) dinamismo m; **Mary's always got plenty of ~** a Mary sempre foi muito dinâmica
••••➤ (in phrases) **on the ~** em grande atividade; **make a ~ of sth** tornar aco um sucesso.
~ahead n luz f verde ● a dinâmico; **~between** n intermediário
□ **~ across** ● vi ir para diante. **~ away** ● vi ir embora. **~ back** ● vi voltar. **~ back on** ● vi voltar atrás com; (return) voltar. **~ by** ● vi (pass) passar. **~ down** ● vi descer; ‹sun› pôr-se; ‹ship› afundar. **~ for** ● vt ir buscar; (like) gostar de; (attack) atacar. **~ in** ● vi entrar. **~ in for** ● vt ‹exam› apresentar-se a. **~ off** ● vi ir embora; (explode) arrebentar; (sound) soar; (decay) estragar. **~ on** ● vi continuar; (happen) acontecer. **~ out** ● vi sair; ‹light› apagar. **~ over** ● vt (check) verificar, examinar. **~ round** ● vi (be enough) chegar. **~ through** ● vt (check) verificar, examinar. **~ under** ● vi ir abaixo. **~ up** ● vi subir. **~ without** ● vt passar sem

goal /ɡəʊl/ n meta f; (area) baliza f; (score) gol m, (P) golo m. **~post** n trave f

goalkeeper /ˈɡəʊlkiːpə(r)/ n goleiro m, (P) guarda-redes m

goat /ɡəʊt/ n cabra f

gobble /ˈɡɒbl/ vt comer com sofreguidão, devorar

god /ɡɒd/ n deus m. **~daughter** n afilhada f. **~dess** n deusa f. **~father** n padrinho m. **~ly** a devoto. **~mother** n madrinha f. **~son** n afilhado m

God /ɡɒd/ n Deus m

godsend /ˈɡɒdsend/ n achado m, dádiva f do céu

goggles /ˈɡɒɡlz/ npl óculos mpl de proteção

going /ˈɡəʊɪŋ/ n **it is slow/hard ~** é demorado/difícil ● a ‹price, rate› corrente; atual. **~s-on** npl acontecimentos mpl estranhos

gold /ɡəʊld/ n ouro m ● a de/em ouro. **~ mine** n mina f de ouro

golden /ˈɡəʊldən/ a de ouro; (like gold) dourado; (opportunity) único; **~ wedding** bodas fpl de ouro

goldfish /ˈɡəʊldfɪʃ/ n peixe m dourado/vermelho

goldsmith /ˈɡəʊldsmɪθ/ n ourives m inv

golf /ɡɒlf/ n golfe m; **~ club** clube m de golfe, associação f de golfe; (stick) taco m. **~ course** n campo de golfe. **~er** n jogador m de golfe

gone /ɡɒn/ ▶ **GO** a ido, passado; **~ six o'clock** depois das seis

gong /ɡɒŋ/ n gongo m

good /ɡʊd/ a (better, best) bom; **as ~ as** praticamente; **G~ Friday** Sexta-feira f Santa; **~ name** bom nome m ● n bem m; **for ~** para sempre; **it is no ~** não adianta; **it is no ~ shouting/etc** não adianta gritar/etc. **~ afternoon** int boa(s) tarde(s). **~ evening/night** int boa(s) noite(s); **~looking** a bonito; **~ morning** int bom dia

goodbye /ɡʊdˈbaɪ/ int & n adeus m

goodness /'gʊdnɪs/ n bondade f; **my ~!** meu Deus!

goods /gʊdz/ npl Comm mercadorias fpl; **~ train** trem m de carga, (P) comboio m de mercadorias

goodwill /gʊd'wɪl/ n boa vontade f

goose /guːs/ n (pl **geese**) ganso m. **~flesh, ~pimples** ns pele f de galinha

gooseberry /'gʊzbərɪ/ n (fruit) groselha f; (bush) groselheira f

gore[2] /gɔː(r)/ vt perfurar

gorge /gɔːdʒ/ n desfiladeiro m, garganta f ● vt **~ o.s.** empanturrar-se

gorgeous /'gɔːdʒəs/ a magnífico, maravilhoso

gorilla /gə'rɪlə/ n gorila m

gormless /'gɔːmlɪs/ a 🆇 estúpido

gorse /gɔːs/ n giesta f, tojo m, urze f

gory /'gɔːrɪ/ a (-ier, -iest) sangrento

gosh /gɒʃ/ int puxal, (P) carambal

gospel /'gɒspl/ n evangelho m

gossip /'gɒsɪp/ n bisbilhotice f, fofoca f; (person) bisbilhoteiro m, fofoqueiro m ● vi (pt **gossiped**) bisbilhotar

got /gɒt/ ▶ GET; **have ~** ter; **have ~ to do** ter que fazer, (P) ter de fazer

Gothic /'gɒθɪk/ a gótico

gourmet /'gʊəmeɪ/ n gastrônomo m, (P) gastrónomo m, gourmet m

govern /'gʌvn/ vt/i governar. **~ess** n preceptora f. **~or** n governador m; (of school, hospital etc) diretor m

government /'gʌvənmənt/ n governo m

gown /gaʊn/ n vestido m; (of judge, teacher) toga f

GP abbr ▶ GENERAL PRACTITIONER

grab /græb/ vt (pt **grabbed**) agarrar, apanhar

grace /greɪs/ n graça f ● vt honrar; (adorn) ornar; **say ~** dar graças. **~ful** a gracioso

gracious /'greɪʃəs/ a gracioso; (kind) amável, afável

grade /greɪd/ n categoria f; (of goods) classe f, qualidade f; (on scale) grau m; (school mark) nota f ● vt classificar

gradient /'greɪdɪənt/ n gradiente m, declive m

gradual /'grædʒʊəl/ a gradual, progressivo. **~ly** adv gradualmente

graduate[1] /'grædʒʊət/ n diplomado m, graduado m, licenciado m

graduat|**e**[2] /'grædʒʊeɪt/ vt/i formar(-se). **~ion** /-'eɪʃn/ n colação de grau, (P) formatura f

graffiti /grə'fiːtiː/ npl graffiti mpl

graft /grɑːft/ n Med, Bot enxerto m; (work) batalha f ● vt enxertar; (work) batalhar

grain /greɪn/ n grão m; (collectively) cereais mpl; (in wood) veio m; **against the ~** fig contra a maneira de ser

gram /græm/ n grama m

grammar /'græmə(r)/ n gramática f. **~atical** /grə'mætɪkl/ a gramatical

grand /grænd/ a (-er, -est) grandioso, magnífico; ‹duke, master› grão; **~ piano** piano m de cauda

grand|**child** /'græn(d)tʃaɪld/ n (pl **-children**) neto m. **~daughter** n neta f. **~father** n avô m. **~mother** n avó f. **~parents** npl avós mpl. **~son** n neto m

grandeur /'grændʒə(r)/ n grandeza f

grandiose /ˈɡrændɪəʊs/ a grandioso

grandstand /ˈɡrændstænd/ n tribuna f principal

granite /ˈɡrænɪt/ n granito m

grant /ɡrɑːnt/ vt conceder; <a request> ceder a; (admit) admitir (**that** que) ● n subsídio m; Univ bolsa f; **take for ~ed** dar por garantido, contar com

grape /ɡreɪp/ n uva f

grapefruit /ˈɡreɪpfruːt/ n inv grapefruit m, toranja f

graph /ɡrɑːf/ n gráfico m

graphic /ˈɡræfɪk/ a gráfico; fig vívido. **~s** npl Comput gráficos mpl

grapple /ˈɡræpl/ vi **~ with** estar engalinhado com; fig estar às voltas com

grasp /ɡrɑːsp/ vt agarrar; (understand) compreender ● n domínio m; (reach) alcance m; fig (understanding) compreensão f

grasping /ˈɡrɑːspɪŋ/ a ganancioso

grass /ɡrɑːs/ n erva f; (lawn) grama f, (P) relva f; (pasture) pastagem f; ⊠ (informer) delator m ● vt cobrir com grama, (P) relva; ⊠ (betray) delatar; **~ roots** Pol bases fpl. **~y** a coberto de erva

grasshopper /ˈɡrɑːshɒpə(r)/ n gafanhoto m

grate[1] /ɡreɪt/ n (fireplace) lareira f; (frame) grelha f

grate[2] /ɡreɪt/ vt ralar ● vi ranger; **~ one's teeth** ranger os dentes. **~r** /-ə(r)/ n ralador m

grateful /ˈɡreɪtfl/ a grato, agradecido

gratify /ˈɡrætɪfaɪ/ vt (pt **-fied**) contentar, satisfazer. **~ing** a gratificante

gratis /ˈɡreɪtɪs/ a & adv grátis (invar), de graça

gratitude /ˈɡrætɪtjuːd/ n gratidão f, reconhecimento m

gratuitous /ɡrəˈtjuːɪtəs/ a gratuito; (uncalled-for) sem motivo

gratuity /ɡrəˈtjuːətɪ/ n gratificação f, gorjeta f

grave[1] /ɡreɪv/ n cova f, sepultura f, túmulo m

grave[2] /ɡreɪv/ a (-**er, -est**) grave, sério

grave[3] /ɡrɑːv/ a **~ accent** acento m grave

gravel /ˈɡrævl/ n cascalho m miúdo, saibro m

gravestone /ˈɡreɪvstəʊn/ n lápide f, campa f

graveyard /ˈɡreɪvjɑːd/ n cemitério m

gravity /ˈɡrævətɪ/ n gravidade f

gravy /ˈɡreɪvɪ/ n molho (de carne) m

graze[1] /ɡreɪz/ vt/i pastar

graze[2] /ɡreɪz/ vt roçar; (scrape) esfolar ● n esfoladura f, (P) esfoladela f

greas|e /ɡriːs/ n gordura f ● vt engordurar; Culin untar; Mech lubrificar; **~e-proof paper** papel m vegetal. **~y** a gorduroso

great /ɡreɪt/ a (-**er, -est**) grande; ⊡ (splendid) esplêndido. **~-grandfather** n bisavô m; **~-grandmother** n bisavó f. **~ly** adv grandemente, muito. **~ness** n grandeza f

Great Britain /ɡreɪtˈbrɪtən/ n Grã-Bretanha f

Greece /ɡriːs/ n Grécia f

greed | groan

greed /griːd/ n cobiça f, ganância f; (for food) gula f. **~y** a cobiçoso, ganancioso; (for food) guloso

Greek /griːk/ a & n grego m

green /griːn/ a (-er, -est) verde ● n verde m; (grass) gramado m, (P) relvado m; **~s** hortaliças fpl; **~ belt** zona f verde, paisagem f protegida; **~ light** luz f verde. **~ery** n verdura f

> **green card** Nos Estados Unidos, é o documento oficial que qualquer pessoa que não seja cidadão norte-americano deve obter para morar e trabalhar neste país. No Reino Unido, é o documento que se deve obter da companhia de seguros para que a cobertura de uma apólice continue em vigor quando se conduz um veículo no estrangeiro. *i*

greengrocer /'griːnɡrəʊsə(r)/ n quitandeiro m, (P) vendedor m de hortaliças

greenhouse /'griːnhaʊs/ n estufa f; **~ effect** efeito estufa, (P) efeito de estufa

Greenland /'griːnlənd/ n Groenlândia f, (P) Gronelândia f

greet /griːt/ vt acolher. **~ing** n saudação f; (welcome) acolhimento m. **~ings** npl cumprimentos mpl; (Christmas etc) votos mpl, desejos mpl

grenade /ɡrɪ'neɪd/ n granada f

grew /gruː/ ▶ GROW

grey /greɪ/ a (-er, -est) cinzento; ‹hair› grisalho ● n cinzento m

greyhound /'greɪhaʊnd/ n galgo m

grid /ɡrɪd/ n (grating) gradeamento m, grade f; Electr rede f

grief /griːf/ n dor f; **come to ~** acabar mal

grievance /'griːvns/ n razão f de queixa

grieve /griːv/ vt sofrer, afligir ● vi sofrer; **~ for** chorar por

grill /ɡrɪl/ n grelha f; (food) grelhado m; (place) grill m ● vt grelhar; (question) submeter a interrogatório cerrado, apertar com perguntas ● vi grelhar

grille /ɡrɪl/ n grade f; (of car) grelha f

grim /ɡrɪm/ a (grimmer, grimmest) sinistro; (without mercy) implacável

grimace /ɡrɪ'meɪs/ n careta f ● vi fazer careta(s)

grim|e /ɡraɪm/ n sujeira f. **~y** a encardido, sujo

grin /ɡrɪn/ vi (pt grinned) sorrir abertamente, dar um sorriso largo ● n sorriso m aberto

grind /ɡraɪnd/ vt (pt ground) triturar; ‹coffee› moer; (sharpen) amolar, afiar; **~ one's teeth** ranger os dentes; **~ to a halt** parar freando, (P) travar lentamente

grip /ɡrɪp/ vt (pt gripped) agarrar; (interest) prender ● n (of hands) aperto m; (control) controle m, domínio m; **come to ~s with** fazer face a. **~ping** a apaixonante

grisly /'ɡrɪzlɪ/ a (-ier, -iest) macabro, horrível

gristle /'ɡrɪsl/ n cartilagem f

grit /ɡrɪt/ n areia f, grão m de areia; fig (pluck) coragem f, fortaleza f ● vt (pt gritted) ‹road› jogar ou (P) deitar areia em; ‹teeth› cerrar

groan /ɡrəʊn/ vi gemer ● n gemido m

grocer /'grəʊsə(r)/ n dono/a m/f de mercearia. **~ies** npl artigos mpl de mercearia. **~y** n (shop) mercearia f

groggy /'grɒɡɪ/ a (-ier, -iest) grogue, fraco das pernas

groin /ɡrɔɪn/ n virilha f

groom /ɡruːm/ n noivo m; (for horses) moço m de estrebaria ● vt ‹horse› tratar de; fig preparar

groove /ɡruːv/ n ranhura f; (for door, window) calha f; (in record) estria f; fig rotina f

grope /ɡrəʊp/ vi tatear; **~ for** procurar às cegas

gross /ɡrəʊs/ a (-er, -est) (vulgar) grosseiro; (flagrant) flagrante; (of error) crasso; (of weight, figure etc) bruto ● n (pl invar) grosa f. **~ly** adv grosseiramente; (very) extremamente

grotesque /ɡrəʊ'tesk/ a grotesco

grotty /'ɡrɒtɪ/ a 🅰 sórdido

grouch /ɡraʊtʃ/ vi 🅸 ralhar. **~y** a 🅸 rabugento

ground[1] /ɡraʊnd/ n chão m, solo m; (area) terreno m; (reason) razão f, motivo m; **~s** jardins mpl; (of coffee) borra(s) f (pl); (of **~floor** térreo m, (P) rés do chão m ● vt/i Naut encalhar; ‹plane› reter em terra. **~less** a infundado, sem fundamento

ground[2] /ɡraʊnd/ ▶ GRIND

grounding /'ɡraʊndɪŋ/ n bases fpl, conhecimentos mpl básicos

groundsheet /'ɡraʊndʃiːt/ n impermeável m para o chão

groundwork /'ɡraʊndwɜːk/ n trabalhos mpl de base or preliminares

group /ɡruːp/ n grupo m ● vt/i agrupar(-se)

grouse[1] /ɡraʊs/ n (pl invar) galo m silvestre

grouse[2] /ɡraʊs/ vi 🅸 (grumble) resmungar; 🅸 (complain) queixar-se

grovel /'ɡrɒvl/ vi (pt grovelled) humilhar-se; fig rebaixar-se

grow /ɡrəʊ/ vi (pt grew, pp grown) crescer; (become) tornar-se; **~ old** envelhecer; **~ up** crescer, tornar-se adulto ● vt cultivar

growl /ɡraʊl/ vi rosnar ● n rosnadela f

grown /ɡrəʊn/ a **~ man** homem feito. **~up** a adulto ● n pessoa f adulta

growth /ɡrəʊθ/ n crescimento m; (increase) aumento m; Med tumor m

grub /ɡrʌb/ n larva f; 🅰 (food) boia f, rango m, (P) comida f

grubby /'ɡrʌbɪ/ a (-ier, -iest) sujo, porco

grudge /ɡrʌdʒ/ vt dar/reconhecer de má vontade; **~ doing** fazer de má vontade; **~ sb sth** dar algo a alguém de má vontade ● n má vontade f; **have a ~ against** ter ressentimento contra. **grudgingly** adv relutantemente

gruelling /'ɡruːəlɪŋ/ a estafante, extenuante

gruesome /'ɡruːsəm/ a macabro

gruff /ɡrʌf/ a (-er, -est) carrancudo, rude

grumble /'ɡrʌmbl/ vi resmungar (at contra, por)

grumpy /'ɡrʌmpɪ/ a (-ier, -iest) mal-humorado, rabugento

grunt /ɡrʌnt/ vi grunhir ● n grunhido m

guarantee /ɡærən'tiː/ n garantia f ● vt garantir

guard /gɑːd/ vt guardar, proteger ● vi ~ **against** precaver-se contra ● n guarda f; (person) guarda m; (on train) condutor m. ~**ian** n guardião m, defensor m; (of orphan) tutor m

guarded /'gɑːdɪd/ a cauteloso, circunspeto, (P) circunspecto

guerrilla /gə'rɪlə/ n guerrilheiro m; ~ **warfare** guerrilha f, guerra f de guerrilhas

guess /ges/ vt/i adivinhar; (suppose) supor ● n suposição f, conjetura f

guesswork /'geswɜːk/ n suposição f, conjetura(s) f(pl)

guest /gest/ n convidado m; (in hotel) hóspede mf. ~ **house** n pensão f

guidance /'gaɪdns/ n orientação f, direção f, (P) direcção f

guide /gaɪd/ n guia mf ● vt guiar; ~**d missile** míssil m guiado; (remote-control) míssil m teleguiado. ~ **dog** n cão m de cego, cão-guia m; ~**lines** npl diretrizes fpl

Guide /gaɪd/ n Guia f

guidebook /'gaɪdbʊk/ n guia m (turístico)

guilt /gɪlt/ n culpa f. ~**y** a culpado

guinea pig /'gɪnɪpɪg/ n cobaia f, porquinho-da-índia m

guitar /gɪ'tɑː(r)/ n guitarra f, violão m, (P) viola f. ~**ist** n guitarrista mf, tocador m de violão, (P) de viola

gulf /gʌlf/ n golfo m; (hollow) abismo m

gull /gʌl/ n gaivota f

gullible /'gʌləbl/ a crédulo

gully /'gʌlɪ/ n barranco m; (drain) sarjeta f

gulp /gʌlp/ vt engolir, devorar ● vi engolir em seco ● n trago m

gum[1] /gʌm/ n Anat gengiva f

gum[2] /gʌm/ n goma f; (chewing gum) chiclete m; goma f elástica, (P) pastilha f elástica ● vt (pt **gummed**) colar

gun /gʌn/ n (pistol) pistola f; (rifle) espingarda f; (cannon) canhão m ● vt (pt **gunned**) ~ **down** abater a tiro

gunfire /'gʌnfaɪə(r)/ n tiroteio m

gunman /'gʌnmən/ n (pl-**men**) bandido m armado, atirador m

gunpowder /'gʌnpaʊdə(r)/ n pólvora f

gunshot /'gʌnʃɒt/ n tiro m

gurgle /'gɜːgl/ n gorgolejo m ● vi gorgolejar

gush /gʌʃ/ vi jorrar ● n jorro m. ~**ing** a efusivo, derretido

gust /gʌst/ n (of wind) rajada f; (of smoke) nuvem f. ~**y** a ventoso

gusto /'gʌstəʊ/ n gosto m, entusiasmo m

gut /gʌt/ n tripa f; ~**s** (belly) barriga f, (courage) coragem f ● vt (pt **gutted**) estripar; ‹fish› limpar; ‹fire› destruir o interior de

gutter /'gʌtə(r)/ n calha f, canaleta f; (in street) sarjeta f, valeta f

guy /gaɪ/ n (man) cara m, (P) tipo m

guzzle /'gʌzl/ vt/i comer/beber com sofreguidão, encher-se (de)

gym /dʒɪm/ n (gymnasium) ginásio m; (gymnastics) ginástica f

gym|nasium /dʒɪm'neɪzɪəm/ n ginásio m. ~**nast** /'dʒɪmnæst/ n ginasta m. ~**nastics** /-'næstɪks/ npl ginástica f

gynaecolog|y /gaɪnɪ'kɒlədʒɪ/ n ginecologia f. ~**ist** n ginecologista mf

gypsy /'dʒɪpsɪ/ n cigano m

Hh

haberdashery /'hæbədæʃərɪ/ n armarinho m, (P) retrosaria f

habit /'hæbɪt/ n hábito m, costume m; (costume) hábito m; **be in/ get into the ~ of** ter/apanhar o hábito de

habit|able /'hæbɪtəbl/ a habitável. **~ation** /-'teɪʃn/ n habitação f

habitat /'hæbɪtæt/ n habitat m

habitual /hə'bɪtʃʊəl/ a habitual, costumeiro; *<smoker, liar>* inveterado. **~ly** adv habitualmente

hack[1] /hæk/ n (horse) cavalo m de aluguel or (P) aluguer; (writer) escrevinhador m pej. **~er** n Comput micreiro m, hacker m, (P) pirata m informático

hack[2] /hæk/ vt cortar, despedaçar; **~ to pieces** cortar em pedaços

hackneyed /'hæknɪd/ a banal, batido

had /hæd/ ▶ HAVE

haddock /'hædək/ n (invar) hadoque m, eglefim m; **smoked ~** hadoque m fumado

haemorrhage /'hemərɪdʒ/ n hemorragia f

haemorrhoids /'hemərɔɪdz/ npl hemorroidas fpl

haggard /'hægəd/ a desfigurado, com o rosto desfeito, magro e macilento

haggle /'hægl/ vi ~ **(over)** regatear

hail[1] /heɪl/ vt saudar; *<taxi>* fazer sinal para, chamar ● vi ~ **from** vir de

hail[2] /heɪl/ n granizo m, (P) saraiva f, (P) chuva de pedra f ● vi chover

granizo, (P) saraivar

hailstone /'heɪlstəʊn/ n pedra f de granizo

hair /heə(r)/ n (on head) cabelo(s) m(pl); (on body) pêlos mpl; (single strand) cabelo m; (of animal) pêlo m. **~do** n ⊞ penteado m; **~dryer** n secador m de cabelo; **~raising** a horripilante, de pôr os cabelos em pé; **~style** n estilo m de penteado

hairbrush /'heəbrʌʃ/ n escova f para o cabelo

haircut /'heəkʌt/ n corte m de cabelo

hairdresser /'heədresə(r)/ n cabeleireiro m, cabeleireira f

hairpin /'heəpɪn/ n grampo m, (P) gancho m para o cabelo; ~ **bend** curva f fechada, quase em V

hairy /'heərɪ/ a (-ier, -iest) peludo, cabeludo; ⊠ (terrifying) de pôr os cabelos em pé; horripilante

hake /heɪk/ n (pl invar) abrótea f

half /hɑːf/ n (pl halves /hɑːvz/) metade f, meio m; **go halves** dividir as despesas ● a meio; ~ **a dozen** meia dúzia; ~ **an hour** meia hora ● adv ao meio. **~-caste** n mestiço m; **~-hearted** a sem grande entusiasmo; **~-term** n férias fpl no meio do trimestre; **~-time** n meio-tempo m; **~-way** a & adv a meio caminho; **~-wit** n idiota mf

halibut /'hælɪbət/ n (pl invar) halibute m

hall /hɔːl/ n sala f; (entrance) vestíbulo m, entrada f; (mansion) solar m; ~ **of residence** residência f de estudantes

hallmark /'hɔːlmɑːk/ n (on gold etc) marca f do contraste; fig cunho m; selo m

hallo /hə'ləʊ/ *int* & *n* (*greeting, surprise*) olá; (*on phone*) está

Halloween /hæləʊ'iːn/ *n* véspera *f* do Dia de Todos os Santos *or* (P) Dia das Bruxas

hallucination /həluːsɪ'neɪʃn/ *n* alucinação *f*

halo /'heɪləʊ/ *n* (*pl* -oes) halo *m*, auréola *f*

halt /hɔːlt/ *n* parada *f*, (P) paragem *f* ● *vt* deter, fazer parar ● *vi* fazer alto, parar

halve /hɑːv/ *vt* dividir ao meio; ‹*time etc*› reduzir à metade

ham /hæm/ *n* presunto *m*

hamburger /'hæmbɜːgə(r)/ *n* hambúrguer *m*

hammer /'hæmə(r)/ *n* martelo *m* ● *vt/i* martelar; *fig* bater com força

hammock /'hæmək/ *n* rede (de dormir) *f*

hamper[1] /'hæmpə(r)/ *n* cesto *m*, (P) cabaz *m*

hamper[2] /'hæmpə(r)/ *vt* dificultar, atrapalhar

hamster /'hæmstə(r)/ *n* hamster *m*

hand /hænd/ *n* mão *f*, (*of clock*) ponteiro *m*; (*writing*) letra *f*; (*worker*) trabalhador *m*; *Cards* mão *f*; (*measure*) palmo *m*; (**helping**) ~ ajuda *f*, mão *f*; **at** ~ à mão; **on the one** ~... **on the other** ~ por um lado ... por outro; **out of** ~ incontrolável; **to** ~ à mão ● *vt* dar, entregar; ~ **in** *or* **over** entregar; ~ **out** distribuir. ~**baggage** *n* bagagem *f* de mão; ~**out** *n* impresso *m*, folheto *m*; (*money*) esmola *f*, donativo *m*

handbag /'hændbæg/ *n* carteira *f*, bolsa de mão *f*, mala de mão *f*

handbook /'hændbʊk/ *n* manual *m*

handbrake /'hændbreɪk/ *n* freio *m* de mão, (P) travão de mão

handcuffs /'hændkʌfs/ *npl* algemas *fpl*

handful /'hændfʊl/ *n* mão-cheia *f*, punhado *m*; (*a few*) punhado *m*; (*difficult task*) mão de obra *f*; **she's a** ~ 🄸 ela é danada

handicap /'hændɪkæp/ *n* (*in competition*) handicap *m*; (*disadvantage*) desvantagem *f* ● *vt* (*pt* handicapped) prejudicar. ~**ped** *a* deficiente; **mentally** ~**ped** deficiente mental

handicraft /'hændɪkrɑːft/ *n* artesanato *m*, trabalho *m* manual

handiwork /'hændɪwɜːk/ *n* obra *f*, trabalho *m*

handkerchief /'hæŋkətʃɪf/ *n* lenço *m*

handle /'hændl/ *n* (*of door etc*) maçaneta *f*, puxador *m*; (*of cup etc*) asa *f*; (*of implement*) cabo *m*; (*of pan etc*) alça *f*, (P) pega *f* ● *vt* (*touch*) manusear, tocar; (*operate with hands*) manejar; (*deal in*) negociar em; (*deal with*) tratar de; ‹*person*› lidar com; **fly off the** ~ 🄸 perder as estribeiras

handlebar /'hændlbɑː(r)/ *n* guidão *m*, (P) guiador *m*

handmade /'hændmeɪd/ *a* feito à mão

handshake /'hændʃeɪk/ *n* aperto *m* de mão

handsome /'hænsəm/ *a* bonito; *fig* generoso

handwriting /'hændraɪtɪŋ/ *n* letra *f*, caligrafia *f*

handy /'hændɪ/ *a* (-ier, -iest) (*convenient, useful*) útil, prático; ‹*person*› jeitoso; (*near*) à mão

handyman /'hændɪmæn/ n (pl -men) faz-tudo m

hang /hæŋ/ vt (pt hung) pendurar, suspender; ‹head› baixar (pt hanged) ‹criminal› enforcar; ~ **on to** (hold tightly) agarrar-se a; ~ **up** ‹phone› desligar ● vi estar dependurado, pender; ‹criminal› ser enforcado; ~ **about** andar por aí; ~ **back** hesitar; ~ **on** (wait) aguardar; ~ **out** ⊠ (live) morar ● **get the** ~ **of** ⊡ pegar o jeito de, (P) apanhar. ~-**gliding** n asa-delta f; ~**up** n ⊠ complexo m

hangar /'hæŋə(r)/ n hangar m

hanger /'hæŋə(r)/ n (for clothes) cabide m. ~-**on** n parasita mf

hangover /'hæŋəʊvə(r)/ n (from drinking) ressaca f

hanker /'hæŋkə(r)/ vi ~ **after** ansiar por, suspirar por

happen /'hæpən/ vi acontecer, suceder; **he ~s to be out** por acaso ele não está. ~**ing** n acontecimento m

happ|y /'hæpɪ/ a (-ier, -iest) feliz; **be ~y with** estar contente com. ~**y-go-lucky** a despreocupado. ~**ily** adv com satisfação; **she smiled** ~**ily** ela sorriu feliz; (fortunately) felizmente. ~**iness** n felicidade f

harass /'hærəs/ vt amofinar, atormentar, perseguir. ~**ment** n amofinação f, perseguição f; **sexual** ~**ment** assédio m sexual

harbour /'hɑːbə(r)/ n porto m; (shelter) abrigo m ● vt abrigar, dar asilo a; fig (in the mind) ocultar; obrigar

hard /hɑːd/ a (-er, -est) duro; (difficult) difícil; ~-**boiled egg** ovo m cozido; ~ **disk** disco m rígido, (P) duro; ~ **of hearing** meio surdo; ~ **shoulder** acostamento m, (P)

berma f alcatroada; ~ **water** água f dura ● adv muito, intensamente; (look) fixamente; (pull) com força; (think) a fundo, a sério; ~ **by** muito perto; ~ **up** ⊠ sem dinheiro, teso ⊠, liso ⊠. ~**back** n livro m encadernado.

hardboard /'hɑːdbɔːd/ n madeira f compensada, madeira f prensada

harden /'hɑːdn/ vt/i endurecer. ~**ed** a (callous) calejado; (robust) enrijado

hardly /'hɑːdlɪ/ adv mal, dificilmente, a custo; ~ **ever** quase nunca

hardship /'hɑːdʃɪp/ n provação f, adversidade f; (suffering) sofrimento m; (financial) privação f

hardware /'hɑːdweə(r)/ n ferragens fpl; Comput hardware m

hardy /'hɑːdɪ/ a (-ier, -iest) resistente

hare /heə(r)/ n lebre f

harm /hɑːm/ n mal m; **out of ~'s way** a salvo; **there's no ~ in** não há mal em ● vt prejudicar, fazer mal a. ~**ful** a prejudicial, nocivo. ~**less** a inofensivo

harmonica /hɑːˈmɒnɪkə/ n gaita f de boca, (P) beiços

harmon|y /'hɑːmənɪ/ n harmonia f. ~**ious** /-'məʊnɪəs/ a harmonioso. ~**ize** vt/i harmonizar(-se)

harness /'hɑːnɪs/ n arreios mpl ● vt arrear; fig (use) aproveitar; utilizar

harp /hɑːp/ n harpa f ● vi ~ **on** (about) repisar

harpsichord /'hɑːpsɪkɔːd/ n cravo m

harrowing /'hærəʊɪŋ/ a dilacerante, lancinante

harsh /hɑːʃ/ a (-er, -est) duro, severo; ‹texture, voice› áspero;

‹light› cru; ‹colour› gritante;
‹climate› rigoroso. **~ness** n dureza f

harvest /'hɑ:vɪst/ n colheita f, ceifa
f ● vt colher, ceifar

has /hæz/ ▶ **HAVE**

hash /hæʃ/ n picadinho m, carne f
cozida; fig (jumble) bagunça f; **make
a ~ of** fazer uma bagunça de. **~ key**
n tecla f sustenido, (P) tecla f cardinal

hashish /'hæʃiʃ/ n haxixe m

hassle /'hæsl/ n ⊞ (quarrel)
discussão f, ⊞ (struggle) dificuldade
f ● vt ⊞ aborrecer

haste /heɪst/ n pressa f; **make ~**
apressar-se

hasten /'heɪsn/ vt/i apressar(-se)

hast|y /'heɪstɪ/ a (**-ier, -iest**)
apressado; (too quick) precipitado

hat /hæt/ n chapéu m

hatch[1] /hætʃ/ n (for food) postigo m;
Naut escotilha f

hatch[2] /hætʃ/ vt/i chocar; ‹a plot
etc› tramar, urdir

hatchback /'hætʃbæk/ n carro m
de três ou cinco portas

hate /heɪt/ n ódio m ● vt odiar,
detestar. **~ful** a odioso, detestável

hatred /'heɪtrɪd/ n ódio m

haughty /'hɔ:tɪ/ a (**-ier, -iest**)
altivo, soberbo, arrogante

haul /hɔ:l/ vt arrastar, puxar;
‹goods› transportar em camião ● n
(booty) presa f; (fish caught) apanha
f; (distance) percurso m. **~age** n
transporte m de cargas

haunt /hɔ:nt/ vt rondar, frequentar;
‹ghost› assombrar; ‹thought›
obcecar ● n lugar m favorito; **~ed
house** casa f mal-assombrada

have /hæv unstressed həv, əv/
● vt (3 sing pres **has**, pt and pp
had)

····▶ (possess) ter; **I ~ (got) a
car** tenho um carro; **they ~ (got)
problems** eles têm problemas

····▶ (do sth) (have a try) tentar;
~ a bath tomar banho; **~ a meal**
comer uma refeição; **~ a walk**
dar um passeio

····▶ (take, esp. in restaurant,
shop) **I'll ~ the soup** vou querer
a sopa; **I'll ~ the red dress** vou
levar o vestido vermelho

····▶ (receive) receber; **I had
a letter from her** recebi uma
carta dela

····▶ (have sth done) mandar
fazer; **we had the house painted**
mandamos pintar a casa; **~ one's
hair cut** cortar o cabelo

● vaux

····▶ (in perfect tenses) ter;
~ done ter feito; **I ~ seen him**
eu o vi

····▶ (in tag questions) **you've
seen her, ~n't you?** você a viu,
não viu?; **you ~n't seen her,
have you?** você não a viu, viu?

····▶ (in short answers) '**you've
never met him**' -'**yes, I ~**' 'você
nunca o conheceu'- 'sim, conheci'

····▶ (must) **~ to** ter de; **I ~ to
go** tenho de ir; **you don't ~ to
do it** você não tem que fazer isso

□ **have on** ● vt (be wearing)
ter vestido; **~ sb on** gozar com
alguém. **have out** ● vt ‹tooth,
tonsils› extrair; **~ it out with
sb** pôr a coisa em pratos limpos
com alguém

havoc /'hævək/ n estragos mpl; **play
~ with** causar estragos em

hawk[1] /hɔ:k/ n falcão m

hawk[2] /hɔːk/ vt vender de porta em porta. **~er** n vendedor m ambulante

hawthorn /ˈhɔːθɔːn/ n pilriteiro m, estripeiro m

hay /heɪ/ n feno m; **~ fever** febre f do feno

haystack /ˈheɪstæk/ n palheiro m

hazard /ˈhæzəd/ n risco m; **~ warning lights** pisca-alerta m ● vt arriscar. **~ous** a arriscado

haze /heɪz/ n bruma f, neblina f, cerração f

hazel /ˈheɪzl/ n aveleira f. **~nut** n avelã f

hazy /ˈheɪzɪ/ a (-ier, -iest) brumoso, encoberto; fig (vague) vago

he /hiː/ pron ele ● n macho m

head /hed/ n cabeça f; (chief) chefe m; (of beer) espuma f; **~ first** de cabeça; **~s or tails** cara ou coroa?; **~ waiter** chefe m de garçons, (P) empregados de mesa ● a principal ● vt encabeçar, estar à frente de ● vi **~ for** dirigir-se para. **~dress** n toucador m ● n toucado m de frente. **~er** n Football cabeçada f

headache /ˈhedeɪk/ n dor f de cabeça

heading /ˈhedɪŋ/ n cabeçalho m, título m; (subject category) rubrica f

headlamp /ˈhedlæmp/ n farol m

headland /ˈhedlənd/ n promontório m

headlight /ˈhedlaɪt/ n farol m

headline /ˈhedlaɪn/ n título m, cabeçalho m

headlong /ˈhedlɒŋ/ a de cabeça; (rash) precipitado ● adv de cabeça; (rashly) precipitadamente

head|master /hedˈmɑːstə(r)/ n diretor m. **~mistress** n diretora f

headphone /ˈhedfəʊn/ n fone m de cabeça, (P) auscultador m

headquarters /ˈhedkwɔːtəz/ npl sede f; Mil quartel m general

headrest /ˈhedrest/ n apoio m para a cabeça

headroom /ˈhedruːm/ n Auto espaço m para a cabeça; (bridge) limite m de altura, altura f máxima

headstrong /ˈhedstrɒŋ/ a teimoso

headway /ˈhedweɪ/ n progresso m; **make ~** fazer progressos

heady /ˈhedɪ/ a (-ier, -iest) empolgante

health /helθ/ n saúde f; **~ centre** posto m de saúde, (P) centro m de saúde; **~ foods** alimentos mpl naturais. **~y** a saudável, sadio

heap /hiːp/ n monte m, pilha f ● vt amontoar, empilhar; **~s of money** 🆃 dinheiro aos montes 🆃

hear /hɪə(r)/ vt/i (pt **heard** /hɜːd/) ouvir; **~, hear!** apoiado! **~ from** ter notícias de; **~ of or about** ouvir falar de; **I won't ~ of it** nem quero ouvir falar nisso. **~ing** n ouvido m, audição f; Jur audiência f. **~ing-aid** n aparelho m de audição, (P) aparelho m auditivo

hearsay /ˈhɪəseɪ/ n boato m; **it's only ~** é só por ouvir dizer

hearse /hɜːs/ n carro m funerário

heart /hɑːt/ n coração m; **~s** Cards copas fpl; **at ~** no fundo; **by ~** de cor; **~ attack** ataque m de coração; **lose ~** perder a coragem, desanimar. **~beat** n pulsação f, batida f; **~breaking** a de partir o coração; **~broken** a com o coração partido, desfeito; **~to-heart** a com o coração nas mãos

heartburn /'hɑːtbɜːn/ n azia f

hearten /'hɑːtn/ vt animar, encorajar

heartfelt /'hɑːtfelt/ a sincero, sentido

hearth /hɑːθ/ n lareira f

heartless /'hɑːtlɪs/ a insensível, desalmado, cruel

heart|y /'hɑːtɪ/ a (-ier, -iest) caloroso; ‹meal› abundante. ~ily adv calorosamente; ‹eat, laugh› com vontade

heat /hiːt/ n calor m; fig ardor m; (contest) eliminatória f ● vt/i aquecer. ~stroke n insolação f. ~wave n onda f de calor. ~er n aquecedor m. ~ing n aquecimento m

heated /'hiːtɪd/ a fig acalorado; aceso

heathen /'hiːðn/ n pagão m, pagã f

heather /'heðə(r)/ n urze f

heave /hiːv/ vt/i (lift) içar; ‹a sigh› soltar; (retch) ter náuseas; 🅸 (throw) atirar

heaven /'hevn/ n céu m. ~ly a celestial; 🅸 divino

heav|y /'hevɪ/ a (-ier, -iest) pesado; ‹blow, rain› forte; ‹cold, drinker› grande; ‹traffic› intenso. ~ily adv pesadamente; ‹drink, smoke etc› desalmadamente

heavyweight /'hevɪweɪt/ n Boxing peso-pesado m

Hebrew /'hiːbruː/ a hebreu, hebraico ● n Lang hebreu m

heckle /'hekl/ vt interromper, interpelar

hectic /'hektɪk/ a muito agitado, febril

hedge /hedʒ/ n sebe f ● vt cercar ● vi (in answering) usar de evasivas; ~ one's bets fig resguardar-se

hedgehog /'hedʒhɒg/ n ouriço-cacheiro m

heed /hiːd/ vt prestar atenção a, escutar ● n pay ~ to prestar atenção a, dar ouvidos a

heel /hiːl/ n calcanhar m; (of shoe) salto m; 🆇 canalha m

hefty /'heftɪ/ a (-ier, -iest) robusto e corpulento

height /haɪt/ n altura f; (of mountain, plane) altitude f; fig auge m; cúmulo m

heighten /'haɪtn/ vt/i aumentar, elevar(-se)

heir /eə(r)/ n herdeiro m. ~ess n herdeira f

heirloom /'eəluːm/ n peça f de família, (P) relíquia f de família

held /held/ ▶ HOLD¹

helicopter /'helɪkɒptə(r)/ n helicóptero m

hell /hel/ n inferno m; for the ~ of it só por gozo. ~ish a infernal

hello /hə'ləʊ/ int & n = HALLO

helm /helm/ n leme m

helmet /'helmɪt/ n capacete m

help /help/ vt/i ajudar ● n ajuda f; home ~ empregada f, faxineira f, (P) mulher f a dias; ~ o.s. to servir-se de; he cannot ~ laughing ele não pode conter o riso; it can't be ~ed não há remédio. ~er n ajudante mf. ~ful a útil; (serviceable) de grande ajuda. ~less a impotente

helping /'helpɪŋ/ n porção f, dose f

hem /hem/ n bainha f ● vt (pt hemmed) fazer a bainha; ~ in cercar, encurralar

hemisphere /'hemɪsfɪə(r)/ n hemisfério m

hemp /hemp/ n cânhamo m

hen /hen/ n galinha f

hence /hens/ adv (from now) a partir desta altura; (for this reason) daí, por isso; **a week ~** daqui a uma semana. **~forth** adv de agora em diante, doravante

henpecked /'henpekt/ a mandado, (P) dominado pela mulher

her /hɜː(r)/ pron a (a ela); (after prep) ela; **(to) ~** lhe; **I know ~** conheço-a ● a seu(s), sua(s), dela

herald /'herəld/ vt anunciar

heraldry /'herəldrɪ/ n heráldica f

herb /hɜːb/ n erva f culinária ou medicinal

herd /hɜːd/ n manada f; (of pigs) vara f ● vi **~ together** juntar-se em rebanho

here /hɪə(r)/ adv aqui ● int tome; aqui está; **to/from ~** para aqui/daqui

hereafter /hɪərɑːftə(r)/ adv de/para o futuro, daqui em diante ● n **the ~** a vida de além-túmulo, (P) a vida f para além da morte

hereby /hɪəˈbaɪ/ adv Jur pelo presente ato ou decreto, etc

hereditary /hɪˈredɪtrɪ/ a hereditário

here|sy /'herəsɪ/ n heresia f. **~tic** n herege mf. **~tical** /hɪˈretɪkl/ a herético

heritage /'herɪtɪdʒ/ n herança f, patrimônio m, (P) património m

hermit /'hɜːmɪt/ n eremita m

hernia /'hɜːnɪə/ n hérnia f

hero /'hɪərəʊ/ n (pl -oes) herói m

heroic /hɪˈrəʊɪk/ a heroico

heroin /'herəʊɪn/ n heroína f

heroine /'herəʊɪn/ n heroína f

heroism /'herəʊɪzəm/ n heroísmo m

heron /'herən/ n garça f

herring /'herɪŋ/ n arenque m

hers /hɜːz/ poss pron o(s) seu(s), a(s) sua(s), o(s) dela, a(s) dela; **it is ~** é (o) dela or o seu

herself /hɜːˈself/ pron ela mesma/própria; (reflexive) se; **by ~** sozinha; **for ~** para si mesma/própria; **to ~** a/para si mesma/própria; **Mary ~ said so** foi a própria Maria que o disse

hesitant /'hezɪtənt/ a hesitante

hesitat|e /'hezɪteɪt/ vt hesitar. **~ion** /-'teɪʃn/ n hesitação f

heterosexual /hetərəʊ'seksjʊəl/ a & n heterossexual mf

hexagon /'heksəgən/ n hexágono m. **~al** /-'ægənl/ a hexagonal

hey /heɪ/ int eh, olá

heyday /'heɪdeɪ/ n auge m, apogeu m

hi /haɪ/ int olá, viva

hibernat|e /'haɪbəneɪt/ vi hibernar. **~ion** /-'neɪʃn/ n hibernação f

hiccup /'hɪkʌp/ n soluço m ● vi soluçar, estar com soluços

hide[1] /haɪd/ vt/i (pt hid, pp hidden) esconder(-se) (from de). **~-and-seek** n (game) esconde-esconde m, (P) jogo m das escondidas; **~out** n 🖪 esconderijo m

hide[2] /haɪd/ n pele f, couro m

hideous /'hɪdɪəs/ a horrendo, medonho

hiding /'haɪdɪŋ/ n 🖪 (thrashing) sova f; surra f; **go into ~** esconder-se

hierarchy /'haɪərɑːkɪ/ n hierarquia f

hi-fi /haɪˈfaɪ/ a & n (de) alta fidelidade f

high /haɪ/ a (-er, -est) alto; ‹price, number› elevado; ‹voice, pitch› agudo; ~ **chair** cadeira f alta para crianças; ~ **jump** salto m em altura; ~**rise building** edifício m alto, (P) torre f; ~ **school** escola f secundária; **in the** ~ **season** em plena estação; ~ **spot** ponto m culminante; ~ **street** rua f principal; ~ **tide** maré f alta; ~**er education** ensino m superior ● n alta f ● adv alto; **two metres** ~ com dois metros de altura. ~**handed** a autoritário, prepotente; ~**speed** a ultrarápido

highbrow /ˈhaɪbraʊ/ a & n 🔲 intelectual m

highlight /ˈhaɪlaɪt/ n fig ponto m alto ● vt salientar, pôr em relevo, realçar

highly /ˈhaɪlɪ/ adv altamente, extremamente; **speak** ~ **of** falar bem de. ~**strung** a muito sensível, nervoso, tenso

Highness /ˈhaɪnɪs/ n Alteza f

high school Nos Estados Unidos, é o último ciclo de ensino secundário, geralmente frequentado por alunos de idades entre os 14 e os 18 anos. Na Grã-Bretanha, alguns colégios de ensino secundário também se chamam *high schools*.

highway /ˈhaɪweɪ/ n estrada f, rodovia f; **H~ Code** Código m Nacional de Trânsito

hijab /hɪˈdʒɑːb/ n hijab m

hijack /ˈhaɪdʒæk/ vt sequestrar ● n sequestro m. ~**er** n (of plane) pirata (do ar) m

hike /haɪk/ n caminhada no campo f ● vi fazer uma caminhada. ~**r** /-ə(r)/ n excursionista mf, caminhante mf

hilarious /hɪˈleərɪəs/ a divertido, despipilante

hill /hɪl/ n colina f, monte m; ‹slope› ladeira f, subida f. ~**y** a acidentado

hillside /ˈhɪlsaɪd/ n encosta f, vertente f

him /hɪm/ pron o (a ele); (after prep) ele; (to) ~ lhe; **I know** ~ conheço-o

himself /hɪmˈself/ pron ele mesmo/ próprio; (reflexive) se; **by** ~ sozinho; **for** ~ para si mesmo/próprio; **to** ~ a/para si mesmo/próprio; **Peter** ~ **saw it** foi o próprio Pedro que o viu

hind /haɪnd/ a traseiro, posterior

hind|er /ˈhɪndə(r)/ vt empatar, estorvar; (prevent) impedir. ~**rance** n estorvo m

hindsight /ˈhaɪndsaɪt/ n **with** ~ em retrospecto, (P) em retrospetiva

Hindu /hɪnˈduː/ n & a hindu mf. ~**ism** /-ɪzəm/ n hinduísmo m

hinge /hɪndʒ/ n dobradiça f ● vi ~ **on** depender de

hint /hɪnt/ n insinuação f, indireta f; (advice) sugestão f, dica f 🔲 ● vt dar a entender, insinuar ● vi ~ **at** fazer alusão a

hip /hɪp/ n quadril m, anca f

hippie /ˈhɪpɪ/ n hippie mf

hippopotamus /hɪpəˈpɒtəməs/ n (pl -muses) hipopótamo m

hire /ˈhaɪə(r)/ vt alugar; ‹person› contratar ● n aluguel m, (P) aluguer m

his /hɪz/ a seu(s), sua(s), dele ● poss pron o(s) seu(s), a(s) sua(s), o(s) dele, a(s) dele; **it is** ~ é (o) dele o seu

Hispanic /hɪsˈpænɪk/ a hispânico

hiss /hɪs/ n silvo m; (for disapproval) assobio m, vaia f ● vt/i sibilar; (for disapproval) assobiar, vaiar

historian /hɪˈstɔːrɪən/ n historiador m

histor|y /ˈhɪstərɪ/ n história f. **~ic(al)** /hɪˈstɒrɪk(l)/ a histórico

hit /hɪt/ vt (pt hit, pres p hitting) atingir, bater em; (knock against, collide with) chocar com, ir de encontro a; (strike a target) acertar em; (find) descobrir; (affect) atingir; **~ it off** dar-se bem (with com) ● vi **~ on** dar com ● n pancada f; fig (success) sucesso m. **~-and-run** a (driver) que foge depois do desastre; **~-or-miss** a ao acaso

hitch /hɪtʃ/ vt atar, prender; (to a hook) enganchar; **~ up** puxar para cima; **~ a lift, ~hike** viajar de carona or (P) boleia ● n sacão m; (snag) problema m. **~hiker** n o que viaja de carona, boleia

HIV abbr (= human immunodeficiency virus) HIV m, (P) VIH m; **~-positive** soropositivo, (P) seropositivo; **to be ~positive/ negative** ser soropositivo/ soronegativo, (P) ser seropositivo/ seronegativo, ter um resultado positivo/negativo no teste de VIH

hive /haɪv/ n colmeia f ● vt **~ off** separar e tornar independente

hoard /hɔːd/ vt juntar, açambarcar ● n provisão f; (of valuables) tesouro m

hoarding /ˈhɔːdɪŋ/ n tapume m, outdoor m

hoarse /hɔːs/ a (-er, -est) rouco. **~ness** n rouquidão f

hoax /həʊks/ n (malicious) logro m, embuste m; (humorous) trote m ● vt (malicious) enganar, lograr; passar um trote, pregar uma peça em

hob /hɒb/ n placa f de aquecimento (do fogão)

hobble /ˈhɒbl/ vi coxear ● vt pear

hobby /ˈhɒbɪ/ n passatempo m favorito. **~ horse** n fig tópico m favorito

hockey /ˈhɒkɪ/ n hóquei m

hoe /həʊ/ n enxada f ● vt trabalhar com enxada

hog /hɒg/ n porco m; (greedy person) glutão m ● vt (pt hogged) 🄸 açambarcar

hoist /hɔɪst/ vt içar ● n guindaste m, (P) monta-cargas m

hold[1] /həʊld/ vt (pt held) segurar; (contain) levar; (possess) ter, possuir; (occupy) ocupar; (keep, maintain) conservar, manter; (affirm) manter; **~ on to** guardar; (cling to) agarrar-se a; **~ one's breath** suster a respiração; **~ one's tongue** calar-se; **~ the line** não desligar; **~ up** (support) sustentar; (delay) demorar; (rob) assaltar ● vi (of rope etc) aguentar(-se); **~ back** reter; **~ on** 🄸 esperar; **~ out** resistir; **~ with** aguentar ● n (influence) domínio m; **get ~ of** pôr as mãos em; fig apanhar. **~up** n atraso m; Auto engarrafamento m; (robbery) assalto m. **~er** n detentor m; (of post, title etc) titular mf; (for object) suporte m

hold[2] /həʊld/ n (of ship, plane) porão m

holdall /ˈhəʊldɔːl/ n saco m de viagem

holding /ˈhəʊldɪŋ/ n (land) propriedade f; Comm ações fpl, valores mpl, holding m

hole /həʊl/ n buraco m ● vt abrir buraco(s) em, esburacar

holiday /ˈhɒlədeɪ/ n férias fpl; (day off; public) feriado m ● vi passar férias. **~maker** n pessoa f em férias; (in summer) veranista mf, (P) veraneante mf

holiness /ˈhəʊlɪnɪs/ n santidade f

Holland /ˈhɒlənd/ n Holanda f

hollow /ˈhɒləʊ/ a oco, vazio; *fig* falso; <*cheeks*> fundo; <*sound*> surdo ● n (*in the ground*) cavidade f; (*in the hand*) cova f

holly /ˈhɒlɪ/ n azevinho m

holster /ˈhəʊlstə(r)/ n coldre m

holy /ˈhəʊlɪ/ a (**-ier, -iest**) santo, sagrado; <*water*> benta; **H~ Ghost, H~ Spirit** Espírito m Santo

homage /ˈhɒmɪdʒ/ n homenagem f, **pay ~ to** prestar homenagem a

home /həʊm/ n casa f, lar m; (*institution*) lar m, asilo m; (*country*) país m natal ● a caseiro, doméstico; (*of family*) de família; *Pol* nacional, interno; <*football match*> em casa; **H~ Office** Ministério m do Interior; **~ town** cidade f or terra f natal; **~ truth** dura verdade f, verdade(s) f(pl) amarga(s) ● adv (**at**) ~ em casa; **come/go** ~ vir/ir para casa; **make oneself at** ~ não fazer cerimónia or (P) cerimónia. **~made** a caseiro. **~less** a sem casa, desabrigado

homeland /ˈhəʊmlænd/ n pátria f

homely /ˈhəʊmlɪ/ a (**-ier, -iest**) (*simple*) simples; *Amer* (*ugly*) sem graça

homesick /ˈhəʊmsɪk/ **a be ~** ter saudades (de casa)

homework /ˈhəʊmwɜːk/ n trabalho m de casa, dever m de casa

homicide /ˈhɒmɪsaɪd/ n homicídio m; (*person*) homicida mf

homoeopath|y /həʊmɪˈɒpəθɪ/ n homeopatia f. **~ic** a homeopático

homosexual /həʊməˈsekʃʊəl/ a & n homossexual mf

honest /ˈɒnɪst/ a honesto; (*frank*) franco. **~y** n honestidade f

honey /ˈhʌnɪ/ n mel m; 🔲 (*darling*) querido m; querida f; meu bem m

honeycomb /ˈhʌnɪkəʊm/ n favo m de mel

honeymoon /ˈhʌnɪmuːn/ n lua f de mel

honorary /ˈɒnərərɪ/ a honorário

honour /ˈɒnə(r)/ n honra f ● vt honrar. **~able** a honrado, honroso

hood /hʊd/ n capuz m; (*car roof*) capota f, (P) tejadilho m; *Amer* (*bonnet*) capô m, (P) capot m

hoodie /ˈhʊdi/ n moletom m com capuz, (P) sweatshirt f com capuz

hoodwink /ˈhʊdwɪŋk/ vt enganar

hoof /huːf/ n (pl **-fs**) casco m

hook /hʊk/ n gancho m; (*on garment*) colchete m; (*for fishing*) anzol m ● vt enganchar; <*fish*> apanhar, pescar; **off the ~** livre de dificuldades; <*phone*> desligado

hooked /hʊkt/ **a be ~ on** 🔲 ter o vício de, estar viciado em

hookey /ˈhʊki/ n **play ~** *Amer* 🔲 fazer gazeta

hooligan /ˈhuːlɪɡən/ n desordeiro m

hoop /huːp/ n arco m; (*of cask*) cinta f

hooray /huːˈreɪ/ int & n = **HURRAH**

hoot /huːt/ n (*of owl*) pio m de mocho; (*of horn*) buzinada f; (*jeer*) apupo m ● vi (*of owl*) piar; (*of horn*) buzinar; (*jeer*) apupar. **~er** n buzina f; (*of factory*) sirene f

Hoover® /ˈhuːvə(r)/ n aspirador de pó m, (P) aspirador m ● vt passar o aspirador

hop¹ /hɒp/ vi (pt **hopped**) saltar num pé só, (P) pé de coxinho; **~ in** 🔲 subir, saltar 🔲; **~ it** 🔲 pôr-se a andar 🔲; **~ out** 🔲 descer, saltar 🔲 ● n salto m

hop² /hɒp/ n (plant) lúpulo m; **~s** espigas fpl de lúpulo

hope /həʊp/ n esperança f ● vt/i esperar; **~ for** esperar (ter). **~ful** a esperançoso; (promising) promissor; **be ~ful (that)** ter esperança (que), confiar (em que). **~fully** adv esperançosamente; (it is hoped that) é de esperar que. **~less** a desesperado, sem esperança; (incompetent) incapaz

horde /hɔːd/ n horda f

horizon /həˈraɪzn/ n horizonte m

horizontal /hɒrɪˈzɒntl/ a horizontal

hormone /ˈhɔːməʊn/ n hormônio m, (P) hormona f

horn /hɔːn/ n chifre m, corno m; (of car) buzina f, Mus trompa f. **~y** a caloso, calejado

hornet /ˈhɔːnɪt/ n vespão m

horoscope /ˈhɒrəskəʊp/ n horóscopo m

horrible /ˈhɒrəbl/ a horrível, horroroso

horrid /ˈhɒrɪd/ a horrível, horripilante

horrific /həˈrɪfɪk/ a horrífico

horr|or /ˈhɒrə(r)/ n horror m ● a (film etc) de terror. **~ify** vt horrorizar, horripilar

horse /hɔːs/ n cavalo m. **~ chestnut** n castanha-da-Índia f; **~ racing** corrida f de cavalos, hipismo m; **~radish** n rábano m

horseback /ˈhɔːsbæk/ n **on ~** a cavalo

horseplay /ˈhɔːspleɪ/ n brincadeira f grosseira, abrutalhada f

horsepower /ˈhɔːspaʊə(r)/ n cavalo-vapor m

horseshoe /ˈhɔːsfuː/ n ferradura f

horticultur|e /ˈhɔːtɪkʌltʃə(r)/ n horticultura f

hose /həʊz/ n **~(-pipe)** mangueira f ● vt regar com a mangueira

hospice /ˈhɒspɪs/ n hospício m; (for travellers) hospedaria f

hospit|able /həˈspɪtəbl/ a hospitaleiro. **~ality** /-ˈtælətɪ/ n hospitalidade f

hospital /ˈhɒspɪtl/ n hospital m

host¹ /həʊst/ n anfitrião m, dono m da casa. **~ess** n anfitriã f, dona f da casa

host² /həʊst/ n **a ~ of** uma multidão de, um grande número de

host³ /həʊst/ n Relig hóstia f

hostage /ˈhɒstɪdʒ/ n refém m

hostel /ˈhɒstl/ n residência f de estudantes etc, pousada f

hostil|e /ˈhɒstaɪl/ a hostil. **~ity** /hɒˈstɪlətɪ/ n hostilidade f

hot /hɒt/ a (hotter, hottest) quente; Culin picante; **be** or **feel ~** estar com or ter calor; **it is ~** está or faz calor; **~ dog** cachorro-quente m; **~ line** linha direta f esp entre chefes de estado; **~water bottle** saco m de água quente ● vt/i (pt hotted) **~ up** 🇬🇧 aquecer

hotbed /ˈhɒtbed/ n fig foco m

hotel /həʊˈtel/ n hotel m

hound /haʊnd/ n cão m de caça e de corrida, sabujo m ● vt acossar, perseguir

hour /ˈaʊə(r)/ n hora f. **~ly** adv de hora em hora; a de hora em hora; **~ly pay** retribuição f horária; **paid ~ly** pago por hora

house¹ /haʊs/ n (pl **~s** /ˈhaʊzɪz/) casa f, Pol câmara f; **on the ~** por conta da casa. **~warming** n inauguração f da casa

house² /haʊz/ vt alojar; (store) arrecadar, guardar

houseboat /'haʊsbəʊt/ n casa f flutuante

household /'haʊshəʊld/ n família f, agregado m familiar. **~er** n ocupante mf; (owner) proprietário m

housekeep|er /'haʊskiːpə(r)/ n governanta f. **~ing** n (work) tarefas fpl domésticas

housewife /'haʊswaɪf/ n (pl -wives) dona f de casa

housework /'haʊswɜːk/ n tarefas fpl domésticas

housing /'haʊzɪŋ/ n alojamento m; **~ estate** zona f residencial

hovel /'hɒvl/ n casebre m, tugúrio m

hover /'hɒvə(r)/ vi pairar; (linger) deixar-se ficar, demorar-se

hovercraft /'hɒvəkrɑːft/ n (invar) aerobarco m, hovercraft m

how /haʊ/ adv como; **~ long/old is...?** que comprimento/idade tem...?; **~ far?** a que distância?; **~ many?** quantos?; **~ much?** quanto?; **~ often?** com que frequência?; **~ pretty it is** como é lindo; **~ about a walk?** e se fôssemos dar uma volta?; **~ are you?** como vai?; **~ do you do?** muito prazer!; **and ~!** oh se é!

however /haʊ'evə(r)/ adv de qualquer maneira; (though) contudo, no entanto, todavia; **~ small it may be** por menor que seja

howl /haʊl/ n uivo m ● vi uivar

hub /hʌb/ n cubo m da roda; fig centro m. **~cap** n calota f, (P) tampão m da roda

hubbub /'hʌbʌb/ n chinfrim m

huddle /'hʌdl/ vt/i apinhar(-se); **~ together** aconchegar-se

huff /hʌf/ n **in a ~** com raiva, zangado

hug /hʌg/ vt (pt hugged) abraçar, apertar nos braços; (keep close to) chegar-se a ● n abraço m

huge /hjuːdʒ/ a enorme

hull /hʌl/ n (of ship) casco m

hullo /hə'ləʊ/ int & n = HALLO

hum /hʌm/ vt/i (pt hummed) cantar com a boca fechada; (of insect, engine) zumbir ● n zumbido m

human /'hjuːmən/ a humano ● n **~ (being)** ser m humano

humane /hjuː'meɪn/ a humano, compassivo

humanitarian /hjuːmænɪ'teərɪən/ a humanitário

humanity /hjuː'mænətɪ/ n humanidade f

humbl|e /'hʌmbl/ a (-er, -est) humilde ● vt humilhar

humdrum /'hʌmdrʌm/ a monótono, rotineiro

humid /'hjuːmɪd/ a úmido, (P) húmido. **~ity** /-'mɪdətɪ/ n umidade f, (P) humidade f

humiliat|e /hjuː'mɪlɪeɪt/ vt humilhar. **~ion** /-'eɪʃn/ n humilhação f

humility /hjuː'mɪlətɪ/ n humildade f

hum|our /'hjuːmə(r)/ n humor m ● vt fazer a vontade de. **~orous** a humorístico; ‹person› divertido, espirituoso

hump /hʌmp/ n corcova f; (of the back) corcunda f ● vt corcovar, arquear; **the ~** a neura 🔲

hunch¹ /hʌntʃ/ vt curvar; **~ed up** curvado

hunch² /hʌntʃ/ n 🔲 palpite m

hunchback /'hʌntʃbæk/ n corcunda mf

hundred /'hʌndrəd/ a cem ● n centena f, cento m; **~s of** centenas de. **~th** a & n centésimo m

hundredweight /'hʌndrədweɪt/ n quintal m (= 50,8 kg, Amer = 45,36 kg)

hung /hʌŋ/ ▶ HANG

Hungar|y /'hʌŋgərɪ/ n Hungria f. **~ian** /-'geərɪən/ a & n húngaro m

hunger /'hʌŋgə(r)/ n fome f ● vi **~ for** ter fome de; fig desejar vivamente, ansiar por

hungr|y /'hʌŋgrɪ/ a (**-ier, -iest**) esfomeado, faminto; **be ~y** ter fome, estar com fome

hunk /hʌŋk/ n grande naco m

hunt /hʌnt/ vt/i caçar ● n caça f; **~ for** andar à caça de, andar à procura de. **~er** n caçador m. **~ing** n caça f, caçada f

hurdle /'hɜːdl/ n obstáculo m

hurl /hɜːl/ vt arremessar, lançar com força

hurrah, hurray /hʊ'rɑː, hʊ'reɪ/ int & n hurra m, viva m

hurricane /'hʌrɪkən/ n furacão m

hurried /'hʌrɪd/ a apressado. **~ly** adv apressadamente, às pressas

hurry /'hʌrɪ/ vt/i apressar(-se), despachar(-se) ● n pressa f; **be in a ~** estar com or ter pressa; **do sth in a ~** fazer algo à pressa; **~ up!** ande logo, (P) despache-se

hurt /hɜːt/ vt (pt **hurt**) fazer mal a; (injure, offend) magoar, ferir ● vi doer ● a magoado, ferido ● n mal m; ‹feelings› mágoa f. **~ful** a prejudicial; ‹remark etc› que magoa

hurtle /'hɜːtl/ vi despenhar-se; (move rapidly) precipitar-se ● vt arremessar

husband /'hʌzbənd/ n marido m, esposo m

hush /hʌʃ/ vt (fazer) calar; **~ up** abafar, encobrir ● vi calar-se; **~!** silêncio! ● n silêncio m. **~hush** a 🄸 muito em segredo

husky /'hʌskɪ/ a (**-ier, -iest**) (hoarse) rouco, enrouquecido; (burly) corpulento ● n cão m esquimó

hustle /'hʌsl/ vt empurrar, dar encontrões a ● n empurrão m; **~ and bustle** grande movimento m, azáfama f

hut /hʌt/ n cabana f, barraca f de madeira

hutch /hʌtʃ/ n coelheira f

hybrid /'haɪbrɪd/ a & n híbrido m. **~ car** n carro m híbrido

hydraulic /har'drɔːlɪk/ a hidráulico

hydroelectric /haɪdrəʊ'lektrɪk/ a hidrelétrico, (P) hidroeléctrico

hydrogen /'haɪdrədʒən/ n hidrogênio m, (P) hidrogénio m

hygiene /'haɪdʒiːn/ n higiene f

hygienic /har'dʒiːnɪk/ a higiênico, (P) higiénico

hymn /hɪm/ n hino m, cântico m

hyper- /'haɪpə(r)/ pref hiper-

hypermarket /'haɪpəmɑːkɪt/ n hipermercado m

hyphen /'haɪfn/ n hífen m, traço de união m. **~ate** vt hifenizar

hypno|sis /hɪp'nəʊsɪs/ n hipnose f. **~tic** /-'nɒtɪk/ a hipnótico

hypnot|ize /'hɪpnətaɪz/ vt hipnotizar. **~ism** /-ɪzəm/ n hipnotismo m

hypochondriac /haɪpə'kɒndrɪæk/ n hipocondríaco m

hypocrisy /hɪ'pɒkrəsɪ/ n hipocrisia f

hypocrit|e /'hɪpəkrɪt/ n hipócrita mf. **~ical** /-'krɪtɪkl/ a hipócrita

hypodermic /haɪpə'dɜːmɪk/ a hipodérmico ● n seringa f

hypothe|sis /haɪ'pɒθəsɪs/ n (pl **-theses** /-siːz/) hipótese f. **~tical** /-ə'θetɪkl/ a hipotético

hyster|ia /hɪ'stɪərɪə/ n histeria f. **~ical** /hɪ'sterɪkl/ a histérico

I i

I /aɪ/ pron eu

Iberian /aɪ'bɪːrɪən/ a ibérico ● n ibero m

ice /aɪs/ n gelo m; **~ hockey** hóquei m sobre o gelo; **~ lolly** picolé m ● vt/i gelar; ‹cake› cobrir com glacê or (P) glace ● vi **~ up** gelar. **~box** n Amer geladeira f, (P) frigorífico m. **~ (cream)** n sorvete m, (P) gelado m; **~ cube** n cubo m or pedra f de gelo; **~ pack** n saco m de gelo; **~ rink** n rínque m de patinação, (P) patinagem f no gelo; **~ skating** n patinação f, (P) patinagem f no gelo

iceberg /'aɪsbɜːg/ n iceberg m; fig pedaço m de gelo

Iceland /'aɪslənd/ n Islândia f

icicle /'aɪsɪkl/ n pingente m de gelo

icing /'aɪsɪŋ/ n Culin cobertura f de açúcar, glacê m, (P) glace m

icy /'aɪsɪ/ a (**-ier, -iest**) gelado, gélido, glacial; ‹road› com gelo

idea /aɪ'dɪə/ n ideia f

ideal /aɪ'dɪəl/ a & n ideal m. **~ize** vt idealizar. **~ly** adv idealmente

idealis|t /aɪ'dɪəlɪst/ n idealista mf. **~m** /-zəm/ n idealismo m. **~tic** /-'lɪstɪk/ a idealista

identical /aɪ'dentɪkl/ a idêntico

identif|y /aɪ'dentɪfaɪ/ vt identificar ● vi **~y with** identificar-se com. **~ication** /-ɪ'keɪʃn/ n identificação f

identity /aɪ'dentətɪ/ n identidade f; **~ card** carteira f de identidade, (P) bilhete m de identidade

ideolog|y /aɪdɪ'ɒlədʒɪ/ n ideologia f. **~ical** /-ɪə'lɒdʒɪkl/ ideológico

idiom /'ɪdɪəm/ n idioma m; (phrase) expressão f idiomática. **~atic** /-'mætɪk/ a idiomático

idiosyncrasy /ɪdɪə'sɪŋkrəsɪ/ n idiossincrasia f, peculiaridade f

idiot /'ɪdɪət/ n idiota mf. **~ic** /-'ɒtɪk/ a idiota

idl|e /'aɪdl/ a (**-er, -est**) (not active; lazy) ocioso; (unemployed) sem trabalho; (of machines) parado; fig (useless) inútil ● vt/i (of engine) estar em ponto morto. **~eness** n ociosidade f

idol /'aɪdl/ n ídolo m. **~ize** vt idolatrar

idyllic /ɪ'dɪlɪk/ a idílico

i.e. abbr isto é, quer dizer

if /ɪf/ conj se

igloo /'ɪɡluː/ n iglu m

ignite /ɪɡ'naɪt/ vt/i inflamar(-se), acender; (catch fire) pegar fogo; (set fire to) atear fogo a

ignition /ɪɡ'nɪʃn/ n Auto ignição f; **~ (key)** chave f de ignição

ignoran|t /'ɪɡnərənt/ a ignorante; **be ~t of** ignorar. **~ce** n ignorância f

ignore /ɪɡ'nɔː(r)/ vt não fazer caso de, passar por cima de; ‹person in the street etc› fingir não ver

ill /ɪl/ a (*sick*) doente; **~ at ease** pouco à vontade; **~ will** má vontade f, animosidade f ● *adv* mal ● *n* mal m. **~-advised** a pouco aconselhável; **~-bred** a mal-educado; **~-fated** a malfadado; **~-treat** vt maltratar

illegal /ɪˈliːgl/ a ilegal

illegible /ɪˈledʒəbl/ a ilegível

illegitima|te /ɪlɪˈdʒɪtɪmət/ a ilegítimo. **~cy** n ilegitimidade f

illitera|te /ɪˈlɪtərət/ a analfabeto; (*uneducated*) iletrado. **~cy** n analfabetismo m

illness /ˈɪlnɪs/ n doença f

illogical /ɪˈlɒdʒɪkl/ a ilógico

illuminat|e /ɪˈluːmɪneɪt/ vt iluminar; (*explain*) esclarecer. **~ion** /-ˈneɪʃn/ n iluminação f. **~ions** npl luminárias fpl

illusion /ɪˈluːʒn/ n ilusão f

illusory /ɪˈluːsərɪ/ a ilusório

illustrat|e /ˈɪləstreɪt/ vt ilustrar. **~ion** /-ˈstreɪʃn/ n ilustração f

illustrious /ɪˈlʌstrɪəs/ a ilustre

image /ˈɪmɪdʒ/ n imagem f; **(public) ~** imagem f pública

imaginary /ɪˈmædʒɪnərɪ/ a imaginário

imaginat|ion /ɪmædʒɪˈneɪʃn/ n imaginação f. **~ive** /ɪˈmædʒɪnətɪv/ a imaginativo

imagin|e /ɪˈmædʒɪn/ vt imaginar. **~able** a imaginável

imbalance /ɪmˈbæləns/ n desequilíbrio m

imbecile /ˈɪmbəsiːl/ a & n imbecil mf

imitat|e /ˈɪmɪteɪt/ vt imitar. **~ion** /-ˈteɪʃn/ n imitação f

immaculate /ɪˈmækjʊlət/ a imaculado; (*impeccable*) impecável

immaterial /ɪməˈtɪərɪəl/ a (*of no importance*) irrelevante; **that's ~ to me** para mim tanto faz

immature /ɪməˈtjʊə(r)/ a imaturo

immediate /ɪˈmiːdɪət/ a imediato. **~ly** adv imediatamente ● conj logo que, assim que

immense /ɪˈmens/ a imenso

immers|e /ɪˈmɜːs/ vt mergulhar, imergir; **be ~ed in** fig estar imerso em. **~ion** /-ʃn/ n imersão f; **~ion heater** aquecedor m de água elétrico

immigr|ate /ˈɪmɪgreɪt/ vi imigrar. **~ant** n & a imigrante mf, imigrado m. **~ation** /-ˈgreɪʃn/ n imigração f

imminent /ˈɪmɪnənt/ a iminente

immobil|e /ɪˈməʊbaɪl/ a imóvel. **~ize** /-əlaɪz/ vt imobilizar

immoral /ɪˈmɒrəl/ a imoral. **~ity** /ɪməˈrælətɪ/ n imoralidade f

immortal /ɪˈmɔːtl/ a imortal. **~ity** /-ˈtælətɪ/ n imortalidade f. **~ize** vt imortalizar

immun|e /ɪˈmjuːn/ a imune; imunizado (**from** contra). **~ity** n imunidade f

imp /ɪmp/ n diabrete m

impact /ˈɪmpækt/ n impacto m

impair /ɪmˈpeə(r)/ vt deteriorar; (*damage*) prejudicar

impart /ɪmˈpɑːt/ vt comunicar; transmitir (**to** a)

impartial /ɪmˈpɑːʃl/ a imparcial. **~ity** /-ʃɪˈælətɪ/ n imparcialidade f

impassable /ɪmˈpɑːsəbl/ a ‹*road, river*› impraticável, intransitável; ‹*barrier etc*› intransponível

impatien|t /ɪmˈpeɪʃənt/ a impaciente. **~ce** n impaciência f

impeccable /ɪmˈpekəbl/ a impecável

impede /ɪmˈpiːd/ vt impedir, estorvar

impediment /ɪmˈpedɪmənt/ n impedimento m, obstáculo m; **(speech)** ~ defeito (na fala) m

impel /ɪmˈpel/ vt (pt impelled) impelir; forçar (**to do** a fazer)

impending /ɪmˈpendɪŋ/ a iminente

impenetrable /ɪmˈpenɪtrəbl/ a impenetrável

imperative /ɪmˈperətɪv/ a imperativo; <need etc> imperioso ● n imperativo m

imperceptible /ɪmpəˈseptəbl/ a imperceptível, (P) imperceptível

imperfect /ɪmˈpɜːfɪkt/ a imperfeito. ~ion /-əˈfekʃn/ n imperfeição f

imperial /ɪmˈpɪərɪəl/ a imperial; (of measures) legal na GB. ~ism /-lɪzəm/ n imperialismo m

impersonal /ɪmˈpɜːsənl/ a impessoal

impersonate /ɪmˈpɜːsəneɪt/ vt fazer-se passar por; Theat fazer or representar (o papel) de. ~ion /-ˈneɪʃn/ n imitação f

impetuous /ɪmˈpetʃʊəs/ a impetuoso

impetus /ˈɪmpɪtəs/ n ímpeto m

impinge /ɪmˈpɪndʒ/ vi ~ on afetar; (encroach) infringir

implacable /ɪmˈplækəbl/ a implacável

implant /ɪmˈplɑːnt/ vt implantar

implement[1] /ˈɪmplɪmənt/ n instrumento m, utensílio m

implement[2] /ˈɪmplɪment/ vt implementar, executar

implicit /ɪmˈplɪsɪt/ a implícito; (unquestioning) absoluto,

incondicional

implore /ɪmˈplɔː(r)/ vt implorar, suplicar, rogar

imply /ɪmˈplaɪ/ vt implicar; (hint) sugerir, dar a entender, insinuar

impolite /ɪmpəˈlaɪt/ a indelicado, incorreto

import[1] /ɪmˈpɔːt/ vt importar. ~er n importador m

import[2] /ˈɪmpɔːt/ n importação f; (meaning) significado m; (importance) importância f

important /ɪmˈpɔːtnt/ a importante. ~ce n importância f

impos|**e** /ɪmˈpəʊz/ vt impôr; (inflict) infligir ● vi ~ **on** abusar de. ~**ition** /-əˈzɪʃn/ n imposição f; (unfair burden) abuso m

imposing /ɪmˈpəʊzɪŋ/ a imponente

impossib|**le** /ɪmˈpɒsəbl/ a impossível. ~**ility** /-ˈbɪləti/ n impossibilidade f

impostor /ɪmˈpɒstə(r)/ n impostor m

impoten|**t** /ˈɪmpətənt/ a impotente. ~**ce** n impotência f

impoverish /ɪmˈpɒvərɪʃ/ vt empobrecer

impracticable /ɪmˈpræktɪkəbl/ a impraticável

impractical /ɪmˈpræktɪkl/ a pouco prático

imprecise /ɪmprɪˈsaɪs/ a impreciso

impregnate /ˈɪmpregneɪt/ vt impregnar (**with** de)

impresario /ɪmprɪˈsɑːrɪəʊ/ n (pl -os) empresário m

impress /ɪmˈpres/ vt impressionar, causar impressão a; (imprint) imprimir; ~ **sth on sb** inculcar algo em alguém

impression /ɪmˈpreʃn/ n impressão f. **~able** a impressionável. **~ist** n impressionista mf

impressive /ɪmˈpresɪv/ a impressionante, imponente

imprint¹ /ˈɪmprɪnt/ n impressão f, marca f

imprint² /ɪmˈprɪnt/ vt imprimir

imprison /ɪmˈprɪzn/ vt prender, aprisionar. **~ment** n aprisionamento m, prisão f

improbab|le /ɪmˈprɒbəbl/ a improvável

impromptu /ɪmˈprɒmptjuː/ a & adv de improviso ● n impromptu m

improper /ɪmˈprɒpə(r)/ a impróprio; (indecent) indecente, pouco decente; (wrong) incorreto

improve /ɪmˈpruːv/ vt/i melhorar; **~ on** aperfeiçoar. **~ment** n melhoria f; (in house etc) melhoramento m; (in health) melhoras fpl

improvis|e /ˈɪmprəvaɪz/ vt/i improvisar. **~ation** /-ˈzeɪʃn/ n improvisação f

imprudent /ɪmˈpruːdnt/ a imprudente

impuden|t /ˈɪmpjədənt/ a descarado, insolente. **~ce** n descaramento m, insolência f

impulse /ˈɪmpʌls/ n impulso m

impulsive /ɪmˈpʌlsɪv/ a impulsivo

impur|e /ɪmˈpjʊə(r)/ a impuro. **~ity** n impureza f

in /ɪn/ prep em, dentro de; **~ Lisbon/English** em Lisboa/inglês; **~ winter** no inverno; **~ an hour** (at end of, within) numa hora; **~ the rain** na/à chuva; **~ doing ao fazer; ~ the evening** à tardinha; **the best ~** o melhor em ● adv dentro; (at home) em casa; (in fashion) na moda; **we are ~ for** vamos ter ● **in the ~s and**

outs meandros mpl. **~laws** npl 🔒 sogros mpl; **~patient** n doente m internado

inability /ɪnəˈbɪlətɪ/ n incapacidade f (**to do** para fazer)

inaccessible /ɪnækˈsesəbl/ a inacessível

inaccura|te /ɪnˈækjərət/ a inexato. **~cy** n inexatidão f, falta f de rigor

inaction /ɪnˈækʃn/ n inação f

inactiv|e /ɪnˈæktɪv/ a inativo. **~ity** /-ˈtɪvətɪ/ n inação f

inadequa|te /ɪnˈædɪkwət/ a inadequado, impróprio; (insufficient) insuficiente. **~cy** n inadequação f; (insufficiency) insuficiência f

inadvertently /ɪnədˈvɜːtəntlɪ/ adv inadvertidamente; (unintentionally) sem querer, sem ser por mal

inadvisable /ɪnədˈvaɪzəbl/ a desaconselhável, não aconselhável

inane /ɪˈneɪn/ a tolo, oco

inanimate /ɪnˈænɪmət/ a inanimado

inappropriate /ɪnəˈprəʊprɪət/ a impróprio, inadequado

inarticulate /ɪnɑːˈtɪkjʊlət/ a inarticulado; (of person) incapaz de se exprimir claramente

inattentive /ɪnəˈtentɪv/ a desatento

inaugural /ɪˈnɔːgjʊrəl/ a inaugural

inaugurat|e /ɪˈnɔːgjʊreɪt/ vt inaugurar. **~ion** /-ˈreɪʃn/ n inauguração f

inauspicious /ɪnɔːˈspɪʃəs/ a pouco auspicioso

inborn /ɪnˈbɔːn/ a inato

inbox /ˈɪnbɒks/ n caixa f de entrada

inbred /ɪnˈbred/ a inato, congênito, (P) congénito

incalculable /ɪnˈkælkjʊləbl/ a incalculável

incapable /ɪnˈkeɪpəbl/ a incapaz

incendiary /ɪnˈsendɪərɪ/ a incendiário ● n bomba f incendiária

incense[1] /ˈɪnsens/ n incenso m

incense[2] /ɪnˈsens/ vt exasperar, enfurecer

incentive /ɪnˈsentɪv/ n incentivo, estímulo

incessant /ɪnˈsesənt/ a incessante. **~ly** adv incessantemente, sem cessar

incest /ˈɪnsest/ n incesto m. **~uous** /ɪnˈsestjʊəs/ a incestuoso

inch /ɪntʃ/ n polegada f (= 2,54 cm) ● vt/i avançar palmo a palmo or pouco a pouco. **within an ~ of** a um passo de

incidence /ˈɪnsɪdəns/ n incidência f; (rate) percentagem f

incident /ˈɪnsɪdənt/ n incidente m

incidental /ɪnsɪˈdentl/ a incidental, acessório; (casual) acidental; ‹expenses› eventuais; ‹music› de cena, incidental. **~ly** adv incidentalmente; (by the way) a propósito

incinerat|e /ɪnˈsɪnəreɪt/ vt incinerar. **~or** n incinerador m

incision /ɪnˈsɪʒn/ n incisão f

incisive /ɪnˈsaɪsɪv/ a incisivo

incite /ɪnˈsaɪt/ vt incitar, instigar. **~ment** n incitamento m

inclination /ɪnklɪˈneɪʃn/ n inclinação f, tendência f

incline[1] /ɪnˈklaɪn/ vt/i inclinar(-se); **be ~d to** inclinar-se para; (have tendency) ter tendência para

incline[2] /ˈɪnklaɪn/ n inclinação f, declive m

inclu|de /ɪnˈkluːd/ vt incluir; (in letter) enviar junto or em anexo. **~ding** prep inclusive. **~sion** n inclusão f

inclusive /ɪnˈkluːsɪv/ a & adv inclusive; **be ~ of** incluir

incognito /ɪnkɒgˈniːtəʊ/ a & adv incógnito

incoherent /ɪnkəˈhɪərənt/ a incoerente

income /ˈɪnkʌm/ n rendimento m; **~ tax** imposto sobre a renda, (P) imposto sobre o rendimento

incoming /ˈɪnkʌmɪŋ/ a ‹tide› enchente; ‹tenant etc› novo

incomparable /ɪnˈkɒmpərəbl/ a incomparável

incompatible /ɪnkəmˈpætəbl/ a incompatível

incompeten|t /ɪnˈkɒmpɪtənt/ a incompetente. **~ce** n incompetência f

incomplete /ɪnkəmˈpliːt/ a incompleto

incomprehensible /ɪnkɒmprɪˈhensəbl/ a incompreensível

inconceivable /ɪnkənˈsiːvəbl/ a inconcebível

inconclusive /ɪnkənˈkluːsɪv/ a inconcludente

incongruous /ɪnˈkɒŋgrʊəs/ a incongruente; (absurd) absurdo

inconsiderate /ɪnkənˈsɪdərət/ a impensado, inconsiderado; (lacking in regard) pouco atencioso, sem consideração (pelos sentimentos etc de outrem)

inconsisten|t /ɪnkənˈsɪstənt/ a incoerente; (at variance) contraditório; **~t with** incompatível com. **~cy** n incoerência f

inconspicuous /ɪnkənˈspɪkjʊəs/ a que não dá nas vistas, que não chama a atenção

incontinen|t /ɪnˈkɒntɪnənt/ a incontinente. **~ce** n incontinência f

inconvenien|t /ɪnkənˈviːnɪənt/ a inconveniente, incômodo, (P) incómodo. **~ce** n inconveniência f; (drawback) inconveniente m ● vt incomodar

incorporate /ɪnˈkɔːpəreɪt/ vt incorporar; (include) incluir

incorrect /ɪnkəˈrekt/ a incorreto

incorrigible /ɪnˈkɒrɪdʒəbl/ a incorrigível

increas|e¹ /ɪnˈkriːs/ vt/i aumentar. **~ing** a crescente. **~ingly** adv cada vez mais

increase² /ˈɪnkriːs/ n aumento m; **on the ~** aumentando, crescendo, (P) em crescimento, em alta

incredible /ɪnˈkredəbl/ a incrível

incredulous /ɪnˈkredjʊləs/ a incrédulo

incriminat|e /ɪnˈkrɪmɪneɪt/ vt incriminar

incubat|e /ˈɪnkjʊbeɪt/ vt incubar. **~ion** /-ˈbeɪʃn/ n incubação f. **~or** n incubadora f

incur /ɪnˈkɜːr/ vt (pt incurred) ‹displeasure, expense etc› incorrer em; ‹debts› contrair

incurable /ɪnˈkjʊərəbl/ a incurável, que não tem cura

indebted /ɪnˈdetɪd/ a ~ **to sb** em dívida (para) com alguém (**for** por)

indecen|t /ɪnˈdiːsnt/ a indecente. **~t assault** n atentado m contra o pudor. **~cy** n indecência f

indecision /ɪndɪˈsɪʒn/ n indecisão f

indecisive /ɪndɪˈsaɪsɪv/ a inconcludente, não decisivo; (hesitating) indeciso

indeed /ɪnˈdiːd/ adv realmente, deveras, mesmo; (in fact) de fato, (P) facto; **very much ~** muitíssimo

indefinite /ɪnˈdefɪnət/ a indefinido; (time) indeterminado. **~ly** adv indefinidamente

indent /ɪnˈdent/ vt ‹notch› recortar; Typ entrar. **~ation** /-ˈteɪʃn/ n recorte m; Typ entrada f

independen|t /ɪndɪˈpendənt/ a independente. **~ce** n independência f

indescribable /ɪndɪˈskraɪbəbl/ a indescritível

indestructible /ɪndɪˈstrʌktəbl/ a indestrutível

indeterminate /ɪndɪˈtɜːmɪnət/ a indeterminado

index /ˈɪndeks/ n (pl indexes) (in book) índice m; (in library) catálogo m ● vt indexar; **~ card** ficha (de fichário), (P) ficheiro f; **~ finger** index m, (dedo) indicador m. **~-linked** a ligado ao índice de inflação

India /ˈɪndɪə/ n Índia f. **~n** a & n (of India) indiano (m); (American) índio (m)

indicat|e /ˈɪndɪkeɪt/ vt indicar. **~ion** /-ˈkeɪʃn/ n indicação f. **~or** n indicador m; Auto pisca-pisca m; (board) quadro m

indicative /ɪnˈdɪkətɪv/ a & n indicativo m

indict /ɪnˈdaɪt/ vt acusar. **~ment** n acusação f

indifferen|t /ɪnˈdɪfrənt/ a indiferente; (not good) medíocre. **~ce** n indiferença f

indigenous /ɪnˈdɪdʒɪnəs/ a indígena; natural; nativo (**to** de)

indigest|ion /ɪndɪˈdʒestʃən/ n indigestão f. **~ible** /-təbl/ a indigesto

indign|ant /ɪnˈdɪɡnənt/ a
indignado. **~ation** /-ˈneɪʃn/ n
indignação f

indirect /ɪndɪˈrekt/ a indireto. **~ly**
adv indiretamente

indiscr|eet /ɪndɪˈskriːt/ a
indiscreto; (not wary) imprudente.
~etion /-ˈeʃn/ n indiscrição f;
(action, remark etc) deslize m

indiscriminate /ɪndɪˈskrɪmɪnət/
a que tem falta de discernimento;
(random) indiscriminado. **~ly** adv
sem discernimento; (at random)
indiscriminadamente, ao acaso

indispensable /ɪndɪˈspensəbl/ a
indispensável

indispos|ed /ɪndɪˈspəʊzd/ a
indisposto

indisputable /ɪndɪˈspjuːtəbl/ a
indisputável, incontestável

indistinct /ɪndɪˈstɪŋkt/ a indistinto

indistinguishable
/ɪndɪˈstɪŋɡwɪʃəbl/ a indistinguível,
imperceptível; (identical)
indiferenciável

individual /ɪndɪˈvɪdʒʊəl/ a
individual ● n indivíduo m. **~ity**
/-ˈælətɪ/ n individualidade f. **~ly** adv
individualmente

indivisible /ɪndɪˈvɪzəbl/ a
indivisível

indoctrinat|e /ɪnˈdɒktrɪneɪt/ vt
(en)doutrinar

indolen|t /ˈɪndələnt/ a indolente.
~ce n indolência f

indoor /ˈɪndɔː(r)/ a (de) interior,
interno; (under cover) coberto;
<games> de salão. **~s** /ɪnˈdɔːz/ adv
dentro de casa, no interior

induce /ɪnˈdjuːs/ vt induzir, levar;
(cause) causar, provocar

indulge /ɪnˈdʌldʒ/ vt satisfazer;
(spoil) fazer a(s) vontade(s) de ● vi

~ in entregar-se a

indulgen|t /ɪnˈdʌldʒənt/ a
indulgente. **~ce** n (leniency)
indulgência f; (desire) satisfação f

industrial /ɪnˈdʌstrɪəl/ a
industrial; <unrest etc> trabalhista;
<action> reivindicativo; **~ estate**
zona f industrial. **~ist** n industrial m.
~ized a industrializado

industrious /ɪnˈdʌstrɪəs/ a
trabalhador, aplicado

industry /ˈɪndəstrɪ/ n indústria f;
(zeal) aplicação f, diligência f, zelo m

inebriated /ɪˈniːbrɪeɪtɪd/ a
embriagado, ébrio

inedible /ɪˈnedɪbl/ a não
comestível

ineffective /ɪnɪˈfektɪv/ a ineficaz;
<person> ineficiente, incapaz

ineffectual /ɪnɪˈfektʃʊəl/ a
ineficaz, improfícuo

inefficien|t /ɪnɪˈfɪʃnt/ a
ineficiente. **~cy** n ineficiência f

ineligible /ɪnˈelɪdʒəbl/ a
inelegível; (undesirable) indesejável;
be ~ for não ter direito a

inept /ɪˈnept/ a inepto

inequality /ɪnɪˈkwɒlətɪ/ n
desigualdade f

inevitable /ɪnˈevɪtəbl/ a
inevitável, fatal

inexcusable /ɪnɪkˈskjuːzəbl/ a
indesculpável, imperdoável

inexhaustible /ɪnɪɡˈzɔːstəbl/ a
inesgotável, inexaurível

inexpensive /ɪnɪkˈspensɪv/ a
barato, em conta

inexperience /ɪnɪkˈspɪərɪəns/
n inexperiência f, falta f de
experiência. **~d** a inexperiente

inexplicable /ɪnˈeksplɪkəbl/ a
inexplicável

infalli|ble /ɪn'fæləbl/ a infalível

infam|ous /'ɪnfəməs/ a infame.
~**y** n infâmia f

infan|t /'ɪnfənt/ n bebé m, (P) bebé
m; (child) criança f. ~**cy** n infância f;
(babyhood) primeira infância f

infantile /'ɪnfəntaɪl/ a infantil

infantry /'ɪnfəntrɪ/ n infantaria f

infatuat|ed /ɪn'fætʃʊeɪtɪd/ a ~**ed**
with cego ou perdido por. ~**ion**
/-'eɪʃn/ n cegueira f, paixão f

infect /ɪn'fekt/ vt infetar, (P)
infectar; ~ **sb** with contagiar ou
contaminar alguém com. ~**ion** /-ʃn/
n infecção f, (P) infeção f, contágio m.
~**ious** /-ʃəs/ a infeccioso, contagioso

infer /ɪn'fɜː(r)/ vt (pt inferred)
inferir, deduzir. ~**ence** /'ɪnfərəns/ n
inferência f

inferior /ɪn'fɪərɪə(r)/ a inferior;
‹work etc› de qualidade inferior ● n
inferior mf; (in rank) subalterno m.
~**ity** /-'ɒrətɪ/ n inferioridade f

infernal /ɪn'fɜːnl/ a infernal

infertil|e /ɪn'fɜːtaɪl/ a infértil,
estéril. ~**ity** /-ə'tɪlətɪ/ n infertilidade
f, esterilidade f

infest /ɪn'fest/ vt infestar (with de).
~**ation** n infestação f

infidelity /ɪnfɪ'delətɪ/ n
infidelidade f

infiltrat|e /'ɪnfɪltreɪt/ vt/i
infiltrar(-se). ~**ion** /-'treɪʃn/ n
infiltração f

infinite /'ɪnfɪnət/ a & n infinito m.
~**ly** adv infinitamente

infinitive /ɪn'fɪnətɪv/ n infinitivo m

infinity /ɪn'fɪnətɪ/ n infinidade f,
infinito m

infirm /ɪn'fɜːm/ a débil, fraco

inflame /ɪn'fleɪm/ vt inflamar.
~**mable** /-æməbl/ a inflamável.

~**mation** /-ə'meɪʃn/ n inflamação f

inflate /ɪn'fleɪt/ vt ‹balloon etc›
encher de ar; ‹prices› causar
inflação de

inflation /ɪn'fleɪʃn/ n inflação f.
~**ary** a inflacionário

inflection /ɪn'flekʃn/ n inflexão f;
Gram flexão f, desinência f

inflexible /ɪn'fleksəbl/ a inflexível

inflict /ɪn'flɪkt/ vt infligir; impor
(on a)

influence /'ɪnflʊəns/ n influência f
● vt influenciar, influir sobre

influential /ɪnflʊ'enʃl/ a influente

influenza /ɪnflʊ'enzə/ n gripe f

influx /'ɪnflʌks/ n afluência f,
influxo m

inform /ɪn'fɔːm/ vt informar; ~
against ou on denunciar; keep ~**ed**
manter ao corrente ou a par. ~**ant**
n informante mf. ~**er** n delator m,
denunciante mf

informal /ɪn'fɔːml/ a informal;
(simple) simples; sem cerimônia;
(P) cerimónia; (unofficial) oficioso;
(colloquial) familiar; ‹dress› de
passeio, à vontade; ‹dinner,
gathering› íntimo. ~**ity** /-'mælətɪ/
n informalidade f, (simplicity)
simplicidade f, (intimacy) intimidade
f. ~**ly** adv informalmente, sem
cerimônia, (P) cerimónia, à vontade

information /ɪnfə'meɪʃn/
n informação f; (facts, data)
informações fpl; ~ **technology**
tecnologia f de informação

informative /ɪn'fɔːmətɪv/ a
informativo

infrared /ɪnfrə'red/ a
infravermelho

infrequent /ɪn'friːkwənt/ a pouco
frequente. ~**ly** adv raramente

infringe | innings

infringe /ɪnˈfrɪndʒ/ vt infringir; **~ on** transgredir; ‹rights› violar. **~ment** n infração f; ‹rights› violação f

infuriat|e /ɪnˈfjʊərɪeɪt/ vt enfurecer, enraivecer. **~ing** a enfurecedor, de enfurecer, de dar raiva

infus|e /ɪnˈfjuːz/ vt infundir, incutir; ‹herbs, tea› pôr de infusão. **~ion** /-ʒn/ n infusão f

ingen|ious /ɪnˈdʒiːnɪəs/ a engenhoso, bem pensado. **~uity** /-ɪˈnjuːətɪ/ n engenho m, habilidade f, imaginação f

ingenuous /ɪnˈdʒenjʊəs/ a cândido, ingênuo, (P) ingénuo

ingrained /ɪnˈɡreɪnd/ a arraigado, enraizado; ‹dirt› entranhado

ingratiate /ɪnˈɡreɪʃɪeɪt/ vt **~ o.s. with** insinuar-se junto de, cair nas or ganhar as boas graças de

ingratitude /ɪnˈɡrætɪtjuːd/ n ingratidão f

ingredient /ɪnˈɡriːdɪənt/ n ingrediente m

inhabit /ɪnˈhæbɪt/ vt habitar. **~able** a habitável. **~ant** n habitante mf

inhale /ɪnˈheɪl/ vt inalar, aspirar. **~r** /-ə(r)/ n inalador m

inherent /ɪnˈhɪərənt/ a inerente. **~ly** adv inerentemente, em si

inherit /ɪnˈherɪt/ vt herdar (**from** de). **~ance** n herança f

inhibit /ɪnˈhɪbɪt/ vt inibir; (prevent) impedir; **be ~ed** ser (um) inibido. **~ion** /-ˈbɪʃn/ n inibição f

inhospitable /ɪnˈhɒspɪtəbl/ a inóspito; (of person) inospitaleiro, pouco/nada hospitaleiro

inhuman /ɪnˈhjuːmən/ a desumano

inhumane /ɪnhjuːˈmeɪn/ a inumano, cruel

inimitable /ɪˈnɪmɪtəbl/ a inimitável

initial /ɪˈnɪʃl/ a & n inicial f ● vt (pt **initialled**) assinar com as iniciais, rubricar. **~ly** adv inicialmente

initiat|e /ɪˈnɪʃɪeɪt/ vt iniciar (**into** em); ‹scheme› lançar. **~ion** /-ˈeɪʃn/ n iniciação f; (start) início m

initiative /ɪˈnɪʃətɪv/ n iniciativa f

inject /ɪnˈdʒekt/ vt injetar; fig insuflar. **~ion** /-ʃn/ n injeção f

injure /ˈɪndʒə(r)/ vt (harm) fazer mal a, prejudicar, lesar; (hurt) ferir

injury /ˈɪndʒərɪ/ n ferimento m, lesão f; (wrong) mal m

injustice /ɪnˈdʒʌstɪs/ n injustiça f

ink /ɪŋk/ n tinta f

inkling /ˈɪŋklɪŋ/ n ideia f, suspeita f

inlaid /ɪnˈleɪd/ ▶ HIRE

inland /ˈɪnlənd/ a interior ● /ɪnˈlænd/ adv no interior, para o interior; **the I~ Revenue** o Fisco, a Receita Federal

inlay[1] /ɪnˈleɪ/ vt (pt **inlaid**) embutir, incrustar

inlay[2] /ˈɪnleɪ/ n incrustação f, obturação f

inlet /ˈɪnlet/ n braço m de mar, enseada f; Techn admissão f

inmate /ˈɪnmeɪt/ n residente mf; (in hospital) internado m; (in prison) presidiário m

inn /ɪn/ n estalagem f

innate /ɪˈneɪt/ a inato

inner /ˈɪnə(r)/ a interior, interno; fig íntimo; **~ city** centro m da cidade. **~most** a mais profundo, mais íntimo. **~ tube** n câmara f de ar

innings /ˈɪnɪŋz/ n Cricket vez f de bater; Pol período m no poder

innocen|t /'ɪnəsnt/ a & n inocente mf. **~ce** n inocência f

innocuous /ɪ'nɒkjʊəs/ a inócuo, inofensivo

innovat|e /'ɪnəveɪt/ vi inovar. **~ion** /-'veɪʃn/ n inovação f. **~or** n inovador m

innuendo /ɪnjuː'endəʊ/ n (pl -oes) insinuação f, indireta f

innumerable /ɪ'njuːmərəbl/ a inumerável

inoculat|e /ɪ'nɒkjʊleɪt/ vt inocular. **~ion** /-'leɪʃn/ n inoculação f, vacina f

inoffensive /ɪnə'fensɪv/ a inofensivo

inopportune /ɪn'ɒpətjuːn/ a inoportuno

inordinate /ɪ'nɔːdɪnət/ a excessivo, desmedido. **~ly** adv excessivamente, desmedidamente

input /'ɪnpʊt/ n (data) dados mpl; Electr (power) energia f; (computer process) entrada f, dados mpl

inquest /'ɪnkwest/ n inquérito m

inquir|e /ɪn'kwaɪə(r)/ vi informar-se ● vt perguntar, indagar, inquirir; **~e about** procurar informações sobre, indagar; **~e into** inquirir, indagar. **~ing** a (look) interrogativo; (mind) inquisitivo. **~y** n (question) pergunta f; Jur inquérito m; (investigation) investigação f

inquisition /ɪnkwɪ'zɪʃn/ n inquisição f

inquisitive /ɪn'kwɪzɪtɪv/ a curioso, inquisitivo; (prying) intrometido, bisbilhoteiro

insan|e /ɪn'seɪn/ a louco, doido. **~ity** /ɪn'sænətɪ/ n loucura f, demência f

insanitary /ɪn'sænɪtrɪ/ a insalubre, anti-higiênico, (P) anti-higiênico

insatiable /ɪn'seɪʃəbl/ a insaciável

inscri|be /ɪn'skraɪb/ vt inscrever; (book) dedicar. **~ption** /-ɪpʃn/ n inscrição f; (in book) dedicatória f

inscrutable /ɪn'skruːtəbl/ a impenetrável, misterioso

insect /'ɪnsekt/ n inseto m

insecur|e /ɪnsɪ'kjʊə(r)/ a (not firm) inseguro, mal seguro; (unsafe) Psych inseguro. **~ity** n insegurança f, falta f de segurança

insensitive /ɪn'sensətɪv/ a insensível

inseparable /ɪn'seprəbl/ a inseparável

insert[1] /ɪn'sɜːt/ vt inserir; (key) meter, colocar; (add) pôr, inserir. **~ion** /-ʃn/ n inserção f

insert[2] /'ɪnsɜːt/ n coisa f inserida, enxerto m

inside /ɪn'saɪd/ n interior m; **~s** ⚠ tripas fpl ⚠; **~ out** de dentro para fora, do avesso; (thoroughly) por dentro e por fora, a fundo ● a interior, interno ● adv no interior, dentro, por dentro ● prep dentro de; (of time) em menos de

insight /'ɪnsaɪt/ n penetração f, perspicácia f; (glimpse) vislumbre m

insignificant /ɪnsɪg'nɪfɪkənt/ a insignificante

insincer|e /ɪnsɪn'sɪə(r)/ a insincero. **~ity** /-'serətɪ/ n insinceridade f, falta f de sinceridade

insinuat|e /ɪn'sɪnjʊeɪt/ vt insinuar. **~ion** /-'eɪʃn/ n (act) insinuação f; (hint) indireta f, insinuação f

insipid /ɪn'sɪpɪd/ a insípido, sem sabor

insist /ɪn'sɪst/ vt/i **~ (on/that)** insistir (em/em que)

insisten|t /ɪn'sɪstənt/ a insistente. **~ce** n insistência f

insolen|t /'ɪnsələnt/ a insolente. **~ce** n insolência f

insoluble /ɪn'sɒljʊbl/ a insolúvel

insolvent /ɪn'sɒlvənt/ a insolvente

insomnia /ɪn'sɒmnɪə/ n insônia f, (P) insónia f

inspect /ɪn'spekt/ vt inspecionar, examinar; ‹tickets› fiscalizar; ‹passport› controlar; ‹troops› passar revista a. **~ion** /-ʃn/ n inspeção f, exame m; ‹ticket› fiscalização f; ‹troops› revista f. **~or** n inspetor m; (on train) fiscal m

inspir|e /ɪn'spaɪə(r)/ vt inspirar. **~ation** /-ə'reɪʃn/ n inspiração f

instability /ɪnstə'bɪlətɪ/ n instabilidade f

install /ɪn'stɔːl/ vt instalar; ‹heater etc› montar, instalar. **~ation** /-ə'leɪʃn/ n instalação f

instalment /ɪn'stɔːlmənt/ n prestação f; (of serial) episódio m

instance /'ɪnstəns/ n exemplo m, caso m; **for ~** por exemplo; **in the first ~** em primeiro lugar

instant /'ɪnstənt/ a imediato; ‹food› instantâneo ● n instante m. **~ messaging** n mensagem f instantânea. **~ly** adv imediatamente, logo

instantaneous /ɪnstən'teɪnɪəs/ a instantâneo

instead /ɪn'sted/ adv em vez disso, em lugar disso; **~ of** em vez de, em lugar de

instigat|e /'ɪnstɪgeɪt/ vt instigar, incitar. **~ion** /-'geɪʃn/ n instigação f. **~or** n instigador m

instil /ɪn'stɪl/ vt (pt instilled) instilar, insuflar

instinct /'ɪnstɪŋkt/ n instinto m. **~ive** /ɪn'stɪŋktɪv/ a instintivo

institut|e /'ɪnstɪtjuːt/ n instituto m ● vt instituir; ‹legal proceedings› intentar; ‹inquiry› ordenar. **~ion** /-'tjuːʃn/ n instituição f; (school) estabelecimento m de ensino; (hospital) estabelecimento m hospitalar

instruct /ɪn'strʌkt/ vt instruir; (order) mandar, ordenar; ‹a solicitor etc› dar instruções a; **~ sb in sth** ensinar algo a alguém. **~ion** /-ʃn/ n instrução f. **~ions** fpl instruções fpl, modo m de emprego; (orders) ordens fpl. **~ive** a instrutivo. **~or** n instrutor m

instrument /'ɪnstrəmənt/ n instrumento m; **~ panel** painel m de instrumentos

instrumental /ɪnstrʊ'mentl/ a instrumental; **be ~ in** ter um papel decisivo em. **~ist** n instrumentalista mf

insubordinat|e /ɪnsə'bɔːdɪnət/ a insubordinado. **~ion** /-'neɪʃn/ n insubordinação f

insufferable /ɪn'sʌfrəbl/ a intolerável, insuportável

insufficient /ɪnsə'fɪʃnt/ a insuficiente

insular /'ɪnsjʊlə(r)/ a insular; fig (narrow-minded) bitolado, limitado, (P) tacanho

insulat|e /'ɪnsjʊleɪt/ vt isolar; **~ing tape** fita f isolante. **~ion** /-'leɪʃn/ n isolamento m

insulin /'ɪnsjʊlɪn/ n insulina f

insult[1] /ɪn'sʌlt/ vt insultar, injuriar. **~ing** a insultante, injurioso

insult[2] /'ɪnsʌlt/ n insulto m, injúria f

insur|e /ɪn'ʃʊə(r)/ vt segurar, pôr no seguro; Amer ▶ ENSURE. **~ance** n seguro m; **~ance policy** apólice f de seguro

insurmountable /ɪnsə'maʊntəbl/ a insuperável

intact /ɪn'tækt/ a intato, (P) intacto

intake /'ɪnteɪk/ n admissão f; Techn admissão f, entrada f; (of food) ingestão f

intangible /ɪn'tændʒəbl/ a intangível

integral /'ɪntɪɡrəl/ a integral; **be an ~ part of** ser parte integrante de

integrate /'ɪntɪɡreɪt/ vt/i integrar(-se); **~d circuit** circuito m integrado. **~ion** /-'ɡreɪʃn/ n integração f

integrity /ɪn'teɡrəti/ n integridade f

intellect /'ɪntəlekt/ n intelecto m, inteligência f. **~ual** /-'lektʃʊəl/ a & n intelectual mf

intelligent /ɪn'telɪdʒənt/ a inteligente. **~ce** n inteligência f; Mil informações fpl

intelligible /ɪn'telɪdʒəbl/ a inteligível

intend /ɪn'tend/ vt tencionar; (destine) reservar, destinar. **~ed** a intencional, propositado

intense /ɪn'tens/ a intenso; ‹person› emotivo. **~ely** adv intensamente; (very) extremamente. **~ity** n intensidade f

intensify /ɪn'tensɪfaɪ/ vt intensificar. **~ication** /-ɪ'keɪʃn/ n intensificação f

intensive /ɪn'tensɪv/ a intensivo; **~ care** tratamento m intensivo

intent /ɪn'tent/ n intento m, desígnio m, propósito m ● a atento, concentrado; **~ on** absorto em; (intending to) decidido a. **~ly** adv atentamente

intention /ɪn'tenʃn/ n intenção f. **~al** a intencional. **~ally** adv de propósito

inter /ɪn'tɜː(r)/ vt (pt interred) enterrar

inter- /'ɪntə(r)/ pref inter-

interact /ɪntər'ækt/ vi agir uns sobre os outros. **~ion** /-ʃn/ n interação f

intercede /ɪntə'siːd/ vi interceder

intercept /ɪntə'sept/ vt interceptar, (P) intercetar

interchange¹ /ɪntə'tʃeɪndʒ/ vt permutar, trocar. **~able** a permutável

interchange² /'ɪntətʃeɪndʒ/ n permuta f, intercâmbio m; (road junction) trevo m de trânsito, (P) nó m

intercom /'ɪntəkɒm/ n interfone m, (P) intercomunicador m

interconnected /ɪntəkə'nektɪd/ a ‹facts, events etc› ligado

intercourse /'ɪntəkɔːs/ n (sexual) relações fpl sexuais

interest /'ɪntrəst/ n interesse m; (legal share) título m; (in finance) juro(s) m(pl); **rate of ~** taxa f de juros ● vt interessar. **~ed** a interessado; **be ~ed in** interessar-se por. **~ing** a interessante

interface /'ɪntəfeɪs/ n interface f

interfere /ɪntə'fɪə(r)/ vi interferir; intrometer-se (**in** em); (meddle, hinder) interferir (**with** com); (tamper) mexer indevidamente (**with** em). **~ence** n interferência f

interim /'ɪntərɪm/ n **in the ~** nesse/neste ínterim m, (P) interim m ● a interino, provisório

interior /ɪn'tɪərɪə(r)/ a & n interior m

interjection /ɪntə'dʒekʃn/ n interjeição f

interlock /ɪntə'lɒk/ vt/i entrelaçar; ‹pieces of puzzle etc› encaixar(-se); Mech ‹wheels› engrenar, engatar

intermarriage /ɪntə'mærɪdʒ/ n casamento m entre membros de diferentes famílias, raças etc; (between near relations) casamento m consanguíneo. **~y** vi ligar-se por casamento

intermediary /ɪntə'miːdɪərɪ/ a & n intermediário m

intermediate /ɪntə'miːdɪət/ a intermédio, intermediário

interminable /ɪn'tɜːmɪnəbl/ a interminável, infindável

intermission /ɪntə'mɪʃn/ n intervalo m

intermittent /ɪntə'mɪtnt/ a intermitente. **~ly** adv intermitentemente

intern /ɪn'tɜːn/ vt internar. **~ment** n internamento m

internal /ɪn'tɜːnl/ a interno, interior; Amer **the ~ Revenue** a Receita Federal, (P) o Fisco. **~ly** adv internamente, interiormente

international /ɪntə'næʃnəl/ a & n internacional mf

Internet /'ɪntənet/ n Internet f. **~ cafe** n lan house f, (P) cibercafé m

interpret /ɪn'tɜːprɪt/ vt/i interpretar. **~ation** /-'teɪʃn/ n interpretação f. **~er** n intérprete mf

interrogate /ɪn'terəgeɪt/ vt interrogar. **~ion** /-'geɪʃn/ n interrogação f; (by police etc) interrogatório m

interrogative /ɪntə'rɒgətɪv/ a interrogativo ● n (pronoun) pronome m interrogativo

interrupt /ɪntə'rʌpt/ vt interromper. **~ion** /-ʃn/ n interrupção f

intersect /ɪntə'sekt/ vt/i intersetar(-se), (P) intersectar(-se); ‹roads› cruzar-se. **~ion** /-ʃn/ n intersecção f, (P) interseção f; (crossroads) cruzamento m

intersperse /ɪntə'spɜːs/ vt entremear, intercalar; (scatter) espalhar

interval /'ɪntəvl/ n intervalo m; **at ~s** a intervalos

intervene /ɪntə'viːn/ vi (interfere) intervir; (of time) decorrer; (occur) sobrevir, intervir. **~tion** /-'venʃn/ n intervenção f

interview /'ɪntəvjuː/ n entrevista f ● vt entrevistar. **~ee** n entrevistado m. **~er** n entrevistador m

intestine /ɪn'testɪn/ n intestino m. **~al** a intestinal

intimate[1] /'ɪntɪmət/ a íntimo; (detailed) profundo. **~cy** n intimidade f. **~tely** adv intimamente

intimate[2] /'ɪntɪmeɪt/ vt (announce) dar a conhecer, fazer saber; (imply) dar a entender

intimidate /ɪn'tɪmɪdeɪt/ vt intimidar. **~ion** /-'deɪʃn/ n intimidação f

into /'ɪntə emphatic 'ɪntuː/ prep para dentro de; **divide ~ three** dividir em três; **~ pieces** aos/em bocados; **translate ~** traduzir para

intolerable /ɪn'tɒlərəbl/ a intolerável, insuportável

intolerant /ɪn'tɒlərənt/ a intolerante. **~ce** n intolerância f

intonation /ɪntə'neɪʃn/ n entonação f, entoação f, inflexão f

intoxicated /ɪn'tɒksɪkeɪtɪd/ a embriagado, etilizado. **~ion** /-'keɪʃn/ n embriaguez f

intranet /'ɪntrənet/ n rede f corporativa

intransigent /ɪnˈtrænsɪdʒənt/ a intransigente

intransitive /ɪnˈtrænsətɪv/ a ‹verb› intransitivo

intravenous /ɪntrəˈviːnəs/ a intravenoso

intrepid /ɪnˈtrepɪd/ a intrépido, arrojado

intricate /ˈɪntrɪkət/ a intrincado, complexo. ~cy n complexidade f

intrigue /ɪnˈtriːg/ vt intrigar ● n intriga f. ~ing a intrigante, curioso

intrinsic /ɪnˈtrɪnsɪk/ a intrínseco. ~ally /-klɪ/ adv intrinsecamente

introduce /ɪntrəˈdjuːs/ vt ‹programme, question› apresentar; (bring in, insert) introduzir; (initiate) iniciar; ~ sb to sb ‹person› apresentar alguém a alguém

introduction /ɪntrəˈdʌkʃn/ n introdução f; (of/to person) apresentação f. ~ory /-tərɪ/ a introdutório, de introdução; ‹letter, words› de apresentação

introspective /ɪntrəˈspektɪv/ a introspectivo, (P) introspetivo

introvert /ˈɪntrəvɜːt/ n & a introvertido m

intrude /ɪnˈtruːd/ vi intrometer-se, ser a mais. ~r n intruso m. ~sion n intrusão f. ~sive a intruso

intuition /ɪntjuːˈɪʃn/ n intuição f. ~ive /ɪnˈtjuːɪtɪv/ a intuitivo

inundate /ˈɪnʌndeɪt/ vt inundar (with de)

invade /ɪnˈveɪd/ vt invadir. ~r /-ə(r)/ n invasor m

invalid[1] /ˈɪnvəlɪd/ n inválido m

invalid[2] /ɪnˈvælɪd/ a inválido. ~ate vt invalidar

invaluable /ɪnˈvæljʊəbl/ a inestimável

invariable /ɪnˈveərɪəbl/ a invariável. ~y adv invariavelmente

invasion /ɪnˈveɪʒn/ n invasão f

invent /ɪnˈvent/ vt inventar. ~ion n invenção f. ~ive a inventivo. ~or n inventor m

inventory /ˈɪnvəntrɪ/ n inventário m

invert /ɪnˈvɜːt/ vt inverter. ~ted commas npl aspas fpl. ~sion n inversão f

invest /ɪnˈvest/ vt investir; ‹time, effort› dedicar ● vi fazer um investimento; ~ in 1 (buy) gastar dinheiro em. ~ment n investimento m. ~or n investidor m, financiador m

investigate /ɪnˈvestɪgeɪt/ vt investigar. ~ion /-ˈgeɪʃn/ n investigação f; under ~ion em estudo. ~or n investigador m

invidious /ɪnˈvɪdɪəs/ a antipático, odioso

invigorate /ɪnˈvɪgəreɪt/ vt revigorar; (encourage) estimular

invincible /ɪnˈvɪnsəbl/ a invencível

invisible /ɪnˈvɪzəbl/ a invisível

invite /ɪnˈvaɪt/ vt convidar; (bring on) pedir, provocar. ~ation /ɪnvɪˈteɪʃn/ n convite m. ~ing a (tempting) tentador; (pleasant) acolhedor, convidativo

invoice /ˈɪnvɔɪs/ n fatura f ● vt faturar

involuntary /ɪnˈvɒləntrɪ/ a involuntário

involve /ɪnˈvɒlv/ vt implicar, envolver; ~d in implicado em. ~d a (complex) complicado; (at stake) em jogo; (emotionally) envolvido. ~ment n envolvimento m, participação f

invulnerable /ɪnˈvʌlnərəbl/ a invulnerável

inward /ˈɪnwəd/ a interior; ⟨thought etc⟩ íntimo. **~(s)** adv para dentro, para o interior. **~ly** adv interiormente, intimamente

iodine /ˈaɪədiːn/ n iodo m; (antiseptic) tintura f de iodo

IOU /aɪəʊˈjuː/ n, abbr vale m

IQ /aɪˈkjuː/ abbr (= intelligence quotient) QI m, (quociente m de inteligência)

Iran /ɪˈrɑːn/ n Irã m, (P) Irão

Iraq /ɪˈrɑːk/ n Iraque m

irascible /ɪˈræsəbl/ a irascível

irate /aɪˈreɪt/ a irado, enraivecido

Ireland /ˈaɪələnd/ n Irlanda f

iris /ˈaɪərɪs/ n Anat, Bot íris f

Irish /ˈaɪərɪʃ/ a & n (language) irlandês m. **~man** n irlandês m. **~woman** n irlandesa f

iron /ˈaɪən/ n ferro m; (appliance) ferro m de engomar ● a de ferro ● vt passar a ferro; **~ out** fazer desaparecer, fig aplanar, resolver. **~ing** n do the **~ing** passar a roupa. **~ing board** n tábua f de passar roupa, (P) tábua f de engomar

ironic(al) /aɪˈrɒnɪk(l)/ a irônico, (P) irónico

ironmonger /ˈaɪənmʌŋgə(r)/ n ferreiro m, (P) ferrageiro m. **~'s** n (shop) loja f de ferragens

irony /ˈaɪərənɪ/ n ironia f

irrational /ɪˈræʃənl/ a irracional; ⟨person⟩ ilógico, que não raciocina

irreconcilable /ɪrekənˈsaɪləbl/ a irreconciliável

irrefutable /ɪrɪˈfjuːtəbl/ a irrefutável

irregular /ɪˈregjʊlə(r)/ a irregular. **~ity** /-ˈlærətɪ/ n irregularidade f

irrelevant /ɪˈreləvənt/ a irrelevante, que não é pertinente

irreparable /ɪˈrepərəbl/ a irreparável, irremediável

irreplaceable /ɪrɪˈpleɪsəbl/ a insubstituível

irresistible /ɪrɪˈzɪstəbl/ a irresistível

irresolute /ɪˈrezəluːt/ a irresoluto

irrespective /ɪrɪˈspektɪv/ a **~ of** sem levar em conta, independente de

irresponsible /ɪrɪˈspɒnsəbl/ a irresponsável

irreverent /ɪˈrevərənt/ a irreverente

irreversible /ɪrɪˈvɜːsəbl/ a irreversível; ⟨decision⟩ irrevogável

irrigat|e /ˈɪrɪgeɪt/ vt irrigar. **~ion** /-ˈgeɪʃn/ n irrigação f

irritable /ˈɪrɪtəbl/ a irritável, irascível

irritat|e /ˈɪrɪteɪt/ vt irritar. **~ion** /-ˈteɪʃn/ n irritação f

is /ɪz/ ▸ BE

Islam /ˈɪzlɑːm/ n Islã m, (P) Islão. **~ic** /ɪzˈlæmɪk/ a islâmico

island /ˈaɪlənd/ n ilha f; **traffic ~** abrigo m de pedestres, (P) placa f de refúgio

isolat|e /ˈaɪsəleɪt/ vt isolar. **~ion** /-ˈleɪʃn/ n isolamento m

Israel /ˈɪzreɪl/ n Israel m. **~i** /ɪzˈreɪlɪ/ a & n israelense m, (P) israelita mf

issue /ˈɪʃuː/ n questão f; (outcome) resultado m; (of magazine etc) número m; (of stamps, money etc) emissão f; **at ~** em questão; **take ~ with** entrar em discussão com, discutir com ● vt distribuir, dar; ⟨stamps, money etc⟩ emitir; ⟨orders⟩ dar ● vi **~ from** sair de

it /ɪt/ ● *pron*

••••➤ (*subject*) ele, ela; **'Where's the book/chair?' – '~'s in the kitchen'** 'onde está o livro/a cadeira?' – '(ele/ela) está na cozinha'

••••➤ (*object*) o, a; **~'s my book and I want it** o livro é meu e eu quero; **that's my pen, give ~ to me** essa caneta é minha, me dê(!)

••••➤ (*with preposition*) **we talked a lot about ~** falamos muito sobre isso; **Elliott went to ~** o Elliott foi lá

••••➤ (*non-specific*) isto, isso, aquilo; **that's ~** é isso; **take ~** leve isso

••••➤ (*impersonal*) **~ is cold** está frio; **~ is raining** está chovendo; **~ will snow** vai nevar; **~ is the 6th of May today** hoje é seis de maio; **who is ~?** quem é?

italic /ɪˈtælɪk/ *a* itálico. **~s** *npl* itálico *m*

Ital|y /ˈɪtəlɪ/ *n* Itália *f*. **~ian** /ɪˈtæliən/ *a & n* (*person*) Lang italiano *m*

itch /ɪtʃ/ *n* coceira *f*, (*P*) comichão *f*; *fig* (*desire*) desejo *m* ardente ● *vi* coçar, sentir comichão, comichar; **my arm ~es** estou com coceira or (*P*) comichão no braço; **I am ~ing to** estou morto por ▣, (*P*) coceira or (*P*) comichão

item /ˈaɪtəm/ *n* item *m*, artigo *m*; (*on programme*) número *m*; (*on agenda*) ponto *m*; **news ~** notícia *f*. **~ize** /-aɪz/ *vt* discriminar, especificar

itinerant /aɪˈtɪnərənt/ *a* itinerante; ‹*musician, actor*› ambulante

itinerary /aɪˈtɪnərərɪ/ *n* itinerário *m*

its /ɪts/ *a* seu, sua, seus, suas

it's /ɪts/ (= **it is, it has**) ▶ BE, ▶ HAVE

itself /ɪtˈself/ *pron* ele mesmo, ele próprio, ela mesma, ela própria; (*reflexive*) se; (*after prep*) si mesmo, si próprio, si mesma, si própria; **by ~** sozinho, por si

IVF *abbr* (= **in vitro fertilization**) FIV *f*

ivory /ˈaɪvərɪ/ *n* marfim *m*

ivy /ˈaɪvɪ/ *n* hera *f*

> **The Ivy League** O grupo de universidades mais antigas e conceituadas dos Estados Unidos. Situadas no nordeste do país, compõem a *Ivy League* as universidades de Harvard, Yale, Columbia, Cornell, Dartmouth College, Brown, Princeton e Pennsylvania. O termo provém da hera que cresce nos edifícios antigos destas universidades.

Jj

jab /dʒæb/ *vt* (*pt* **jabbed**) espetar ● *n* espetadela *f*; ▣ (*injection*) picada *f*, (*P*) injeção *f*

jabber /ˈdʒæbə(r)/ *vi* tagarelar; (*indistinctly*) falar confusamente ● *n* tagarelice *f*; (*indistinct speech*) algaravia *f*; (*indistinct voices*) algaraviada *f*

jack /dʒæk/ *n* Techn macaco *m*; *Cards* valete *m*; **the Union J~** a bandeira *f* inglesa ● *vt* **~ up** levantar com macaco

jacket /'dʒækɪt/ n casaco (curto) m; (of book) sobrecapa f; (of potato) casca f

jackpot /'dʒækpɒt/ n sorte f grande; **hit the ~** ganhar a sorte grande

Jacuzzi® /dʒə'ku:zi:/ n jacuzzi m, banheira f de hidromassagem

jade /dʒeɪd/ n (stone) jade m

jaded /'dʒeɪdɪd/ a (tired) estafado; (bored) enfastiado

jagged /'dʒægɪd/ a recortado, denteado; (sharp) pontiagudo

jail /dʒeɪl/ n prisão f ● vt prender, colocar na cadeia. **~er** n carcereiro m, (P) guarda mf prisional

jam[1] /dʒæm/ n geleia f, compota f, (P) geleia

jam[2] /dʒæm/ vt/i (pt jammed) (wedge) entalar; (become wedged) entalar-se; (crowd) apinhar(-se); Mech bloquear; Radio provocar interferências em; **~ one's brakes on** ⊡ pôr o pé no freio, (P) no travão subitamente, apertar o freio subitamente ● n (crush) aperto m; (traffic) engarrafamento m; ⊡ (difficulty) apuro m, aperto m. **~-packed** a ⊡ abarrotado (**with** de)

Jamaica /dʒə'meɪkə/ n Jamaica f

jangle /'dʒæŋgl/ n som m estridente ● vi retinir

janitor /'dʒænɪtə(r)/ n porteiro m; (caretaker) zelador m

January /'dʒænjʊərɪ/ n janeiro m

Japan /dʒə'pæn/ n Japão m. **~ese** /dʒæpə'ni:z/ a & n japonês m

jar[1] /dʒɑ:(r)/ n pote m. **jam-~** n frasco m de geleia

jar[2] /dʒɑ:(r)/ vt/i (pt jarred) ressoar; bater ruidosamente (**against** contra); (of colours) destoar; (disagree) discordar (**with** de)

● n (shock) choque m. **~ring** a dissonante

jargon /'dʒɑ:gən/ n jargão m, gíria f profissional

jaundice /'dʒɔ:ndɪs/ n icterícia f

jaunt /dʒɔ:nt/ n (trip) passeata f

jaunty /'dʒɔ:ntɪ/ a (-ier, -iest) (cheerful) alegre, jovial; (sprightly) desenvolto

javelin /'dʒævlɪn/ n dardo m

jaw /dʒɔ:/ n maxilar m, mandíbula f

jazz /dʒæz/ n jazz m ● vt **~ up** animar. **~y** a ⊡ espalhafatoso

jealous /'dʒeləs/ a ciumento; (envious) invejoso. **~y** n ciúme m; (envy) inveja f

jeans /dʒi:nz/ npl (blue-)jeans mpl, calça f de zuarte, (P) calças fpl de ganga

jeep /dʒi:p/ n jipe m

jeer /dʒɪə(r)/ vt/i **~ at** (laugh) fazer troça de; (scorn) escarnecer de; (boo) vaiar ● n (mockery) troça f; (booing) vaia f

jelly /'dʒelɪ/ n gelatina f

jellyfish /'dʒelɪfɪʃ/ n água-viva f

jeopard|y /'dʒepədɪ/ n perigo m. **~ize** vt comprometer, pôr em perigo

jerk /dʒɜ:k/ n solavanco m, (P) safanão m; 🅇 (fool) idiota mf ● vt/i sacudir; (move jerkily) mover (-se) aos solavancos, (P) mover (-se) aos sacões. **~y** a sacudido

jersey /'dʒɜ:zɪ/ n (pl -eys) camisola f, pulôver m, suéter m; (fabric) jérsei m, (P) malha f

jest /dʒest/ n gracejo m, graça f ● vi gracejar, brincar

Jesus /'dʒi:zəs/ n Jesus m

jet[1] /dʒet/ n azeviche m. **~-black** a negro de azeviche

jet[2] /dʒet/ n jato m; (*plane*) (avião a) jato m; **~ lag** cansaço m provocado pela diferença de fuso horário. **~propelled** a de propulsão a jato

jetty /'dʒetɪ/ n (*breakwater*) quebra-mar m; (*landing stage*) desembarcadouro m, cais m

Jew /dʒuː/ n judeu m

jewel /'dʒuːəl/ n joia f. **~ler** n joalheiro m; **~ler's (shop)** joalheria f, (P) joalharia f. **~lery** n joias fpl

Jewish /'dʒuːɪʃ/ a judeu

jib /dʒɪb/ vi (pt jibbed) recusar-se a avançar; (*of a horse*) empacar; **~ at** opor-se a, ter relutância em ● n (*sail*) bujarrona f

jig /dʒɪg/ n jiga f

jiggle /'dʒɪgl/ vt (*rock*) balançar; (*jerk*) sacolejar, (P) sacudir

jigsaw /'dʒɪgsɔː/ n **~(-puzzle)** puzzle m, quebra-cabeça m, (P) quebra-cabeças m

jilt /dʒɪlt/ vt deixar; abandonar; dar um fora em ⧉; (P) mandar passear ⧉

jingle /'dʒɪŋgl/ vt/i tilintar, tinir ● n tilintar m, tinido m; (*advertising etc*) música f de anúncio

jinx /dʒɪŋks/ n ⧉ pessoa ou coisa f azarenta f; *fig* (*spell*) azar m

jitter|s /'dʒɪtəz/ npl **the ~s** ⧉ nervos mpl. **~y** /-ərɪ/ a **be ~y** ⧉ estar nervoso, ter os nervos à flor da pele ⧉

job /dʒɒb/ n trabalho m; (*post*) emprego m; **have a ~ doing** ter dificuldade em fazer; **it is a good ~ that** felizmente que. **~less** a desempregado

jobcentre /'dʒɒbsentə(r)/ n posto m de desemprego, (P) centro m de emprego

jockey /'dʒɒkɪ/ n (pl -eys) jóquei m

jocular /'dʒɒkjʊlə(r)/ a jocoso, galhofeiro, brincalhão

jog /dʒɒg/ vt (pt jogged) dar um leve empurrão em, tocar em; (*memory*) refrescar ● vi *Sport* fazer jogging. **~ging** n jogging m

join /dʒɔɪn/ vt juntar, unir; (*become member*) fazer-se sócio de, entrar para; **~ sb** juntar-se a alguém ● vi (*of roads*) juntar-se, entroncar-se; (*of rivers*) confluir; **~ up** alistar-se ● n junção f, junta ⧉ **~ in** vt/i participar (em)

joiner /'dʒɔɪnə(r)/ n marceneiro m

joint /dʒɔɪnt/ a comum, conjunto; (*effort*) conjunto; **~ author** coautor m ● n junta f, junção f; *Anat* articulação f; *Culin* quarto m; (*roast meat*) carne f assada; ⊠ (*place*) espelunca f. **~ly** adv conjuntamente

jok|e /dʒəʊk/ n piada f, gracejo m ● vi gracejar. **~er** n brincalhão m; *Cards* curinga f de baralho, (P) diabo m. **~ingly** adv na brincadeira

joll|y /'dʒɒlɪ/ a (-ier, -iest) alegre, bem-disposto ● adv ⧉ muito

jolt /dʒəʊlt/ vt sacudir, sacolejar ● vi ir aos solavancos ● n solavanco m; (*shock*) choque m, sobressalto m

jostle /'dʒɒsl/ vt dar um encontrão or encontrões em, empurrar ● vi empurrar, acotovelar-se

jot /dʒɒt/ n (**not a**) ~ nada ● vt (pt jotted) ~ (**down**) apontar, tomar nota de. **~ter** n (*pad*) bloco m de notas

journal /'dʒɜːnl/ n diário m; (*newspaper*) jornal m; (*periodical*) periódico m, revista f. **~ism** n jornalismo m. **~ist** n jornalista mf

journey /'dʒɜːnɪ/ n (pl -eys) viagem f; (*distance*) trajeto m ● vi viajar

jovial /'dʒəuvɪəl/ a jovial

joy /dʒɔɪ/ n alegria f. ~**ride** n passeio m em carro roubado. ~**ful**, ~**ous** adjs alegre

jubil‖ant /'dʒu:bɪlənt/ a cheio de alegria, jubiloso. ~**ation** /-'leɪʃn/ n júbilo m, regozijo m

jubilee /'dʒu:bɪli:/ n jubileu m

Judaism /'dʒu:deɪɪzəm/ n Judaísmo m

judder /'dʒʌdə(r)/ vi trepidar, vibrar ● n trepidação f, vibração f

judge /dʒʌdʒ/ n juiz m ● vt julgar. ~**ment** n (judging) julgamento m, juízo m; (opinion) juízo m; (decision) julgamento m

judic‖iary /dʒu:'dɪʃərɪ/ n magistratura f; (system) judiciário m. ~**ial** a judiciário

judicious /dʒu:'dɪʃəs/ a judicioso

judo /'dʒu:dəu/ n judô m, (P) judo m

jug /dʒʌg/ n (tall) jarro m; (round) botija f. **milk~** n leiteira f

juggle /'dʒʌgl/ vt/i fazer malabarismos (with com). ~**r** /-ə(r)/ n malabarista mf

juice /dʒu:s/ n suco m, (P) sumo m. ~**y** a suculento; 🗊 (story etc) picante

jukebox /'dʒu:kbɒks/ n juke-box m, (P) máquina f de música

July /dʒu:'laɪ/ n julho m

jumble /'dʒʌmbl/ vt misturar ● n mistura f; ~ **sale** venda f de caridade de objetos usados

jumbo /'dʒʌmbəu/ a ~ **jet** (avião) jumbo m

jump /dʒʌmp/ vt/i saltar; (start) sobressaltar(-se); (of prices etc) subir repentinamente; ~ **at** aceitar imediatamente; ~ **the gun** agir prematuramente; ~ **the queue** furar a fila; ~ **to conclusions** tirar conclusões apressadas ● n salto m; (start) sobressalto m; (of prices) alta f

jumper /'dʒʌmpə(r)/ n pulôver m, suéter m, (P) camisola f de lã

jumpy /'dʒʌmpɪ/ a nervoso

junction /'dʒʌŋkʃn/ n junção f; (of roads etc) entroncamento m

June /dʒu:n/ n junho m

jungle /'dʒʌŋgl/ n selva f, floresta f

junior /'dʒu:nɪə(r)/ a júnior; (in age) mais novo (**to** que); (in rank) subalterno; ‹school› primária; ~ **to** (in rank) abaixo de ● n o mais novo m; Sport júnior mf

junk /dʒʌŋk/ n ferro-velho m, velharias fpl; (rubbish) lixo m; ~ **food** comida f sem valor nutritivo, comida f de plástico; ~ **mail** material m impresso, enviado por correio, sem ter sido solicitado; ~ **shop** loja f de ferro-velho, bricabraque m

junkie /'dʒʌŋkɪ/ n 🗙 drogado m

jurisdiction /dʒʊərɪs'dɪkʃn/ n jurisdição f

juror /'dʒʊərə(r)/ n jurado m

jury /'dʒʊərɪ/ n júri m

just /dʒʌst/ a justo ● adv justamente, exatamente; (only) só; ~ **listen!** escuta só! ~ **as** assim como; (with time) assim que; **he has** ~ **left** ele acabou de sair; ~ **as tall** tão exatamente tão alto quanto; ~ **as well that** ainda bem que; ~ **before** um momento antes (de). ~**ly** adv com justiça, justamente

justice /'dʒʌstɪs/ n justiça f; **J~ of the Peace** juiz m de paz

justifiabl‖e /'dʒʌstɪfaɪəbl/ a justificável. ~**y** adv com razão, justificadamente

justif‖y /'dʒʌstɪfaɪ/ vt justificar. ~**ication** /-ɪ'keɪʃn/ n justificação f

jut /dʒʌt/ vi (pt jutted) ~ out fazer saliência, sobressair

juvenile /'dʒuːvənaɪl/ a (youthful) juvenil; (childish) pueril, infantil; (delinquent) jovem; (court) de menores ● n jovem mf

Kk

kaleidoscope /kə'laɪdəskəʊp/ n caleidoscópio m

kangaroo /kæŋɡə'ruː/ n canguru m

karate /kə'rɑːtɪ/ n karatê m, karaté m

kebab /kə'bæb/ n churrasquinho m, espetinho m

keel /kiːl/ n quilha ● vi ~ over virar-se

keen /kiːn/ a (-er, -est) (sharp) agudo; (eager) entusiástico; (of appetite) devorador; (of intelligence) vivo; (of wind) cortante. **~ly** adv vivamente; (eagerly) com entusiasmo. **~ness** n vivacidade f; (enthusiasm) entusiasmo m

keep /kiːp/ (pt kept) vt guardar; ‹family› sustentar; ‹animals› ter, criar; (celebrate) festejar; (conceal) esconder; (delay) demorar; (prevent) impedir (from de); ‹promise› cumprir; ‹shop› ter; ~ in/out impedir de entrar/de sair; ~ up conservar; ~ up (with) acompanhar ● vi manter-se, conservar-se; (remain) ficar; ~ (on) continuar (doing fazendo or (P) a fazer) ● n sustento m; (of castle) torre f de menagem □ ~ back vt (withhold)

reter ● vi manter-se afastado. **~er** n guarda mf

keeping /'kiːpɪŋ/ n guarda f, cuidado m; **in ~ with** em harmonia com, (P) de harmonia com

keepsake /'kiːpseɪk/ n (thing) lembrança f, recordação f

keg /keɡ/ n barril m pequeno

kennel /'kenl/ n casota (de cão) f. **~s** npl canil m

kept /kept/ ▶ KEEP

kerb /kɜːb/ n meio fio m, (P) borda f do passeio

kernel /'kɜːnl/ n (of nut) miolo m

kerosene /'kerəsiːn/ n (paraffin) querosene m, (P) petróleo m; (aviation fuel) gasolina f

ketchup /'ketʃəp/ n molho m de tomate, ketchup m

kettle /'ketl/ n chaleira f

key /kiː/ n chave f; (of piano etc) tecla f; Mus clave f ● a chave ● vt ~ in digitar, bater; **~ed up** tenso. **~ring** n chaveiro m, porta-chaves m invar

keyboard /'kiːbɔːd/ n teclado m

keyhole /'kiːhəʊl/ n buraco m da fechadura

khaki /'kɑːkɪ/ a & n cáqui invar m, (P) caqui invar m

kick /kɪk/ vt/i dar um pontapé or pontapés (a em); ‹ball› chutar (em); (of horse) dar um coice or coices, escoicear; ~ out (fam) pôr na rua; ~ up (fam) ‹fuss, racket› fazer ● n pontapé m; (of gun, horse) coice m; (thrill) excitação f, prazer m. ~-off n chute m inicial, kick-off m

kid /kɪd/ n (goat) cabrito m; (child) garoto m; (leather) pelica f ● vt/i (pt kidded) □ brincar (com)

kidnap /'kɪdnæp/ vt (pt kidnapped) raptar. **~ping** n rapto m

kidney /ˈkɪdnɪ/ n rim m

kill /kɪl/ vt matar; fig (put an end to) acabar com ● n matança f. **~er** n assassino m. **~ing** n matança f, massacre m; (of game) caçada f ● a 🔳 (funny) de morrer de rir; 🔳 (exhausting) de morte

killjoy /ˈkɪldʒɔɪ/ n desmancha-prazeres mf

kilo /ˈkiːləʊ/ n (pl -os) quilo m

kilogram /ˈkɪləgræm/ n quilograma m

kilometre /ˈkɪləmiːtə(r)/ n quilómetro m, (P) quilómetro m

kilowatt /ˈkɪləwɒt/ n quilowatt m

kilt /kɪlt/ n kilt m, saiote m escocês, (P) saia f escocesa

kin /kɪn/ n família f, parentes mpl; **next of ~** os parentes mais próximos

kind¹ /kaɪnd/ n espécie f, gênero m, (P) género m, natureza f; **in ~** em gêneros or (P) géneros; fig (in the same form) na mesma moeda; **~ of** 🔳 (somewhat) de certo modo, um pouco

kind² /kaɪnd/ a (-er, -est) (good) bom; (friendly) gentil, amável. **~-hearted** a bom, bondoso. **~ness** n bondade f

kindergarten /ˈkɪndəɡɑːtn/ n jardim de infância m, (P) infantário m

kindly /ˈkaɪndlɪ/ a (-ier, -iest) benévolo, bondoso ● adv bondosamente, gentilmente, com simpatia; **~ wait** tenha a bondade de esperar

king /kɪŋ/ n rei m. **~-size(d)** a de tamanho grande

kingdom /ˈkɪŋdəm/ n reino m

kingfisher /ˈkɪŋfɪʃə(r)/ n pica-peixe m, martim-pescador m

kink /kɪŋk/ n (in rope) volta f, nó m; fig perversão f. **~y** a 🔳 excêntrico; pervertido; (of hair) encarapinhado

kiosk /ˈkiːɒsk/ n quiosque m; **telephone ~** cabine telefônica, (P) telefónica

kip /kɪp/ n 🔳 sono m ● vi (pt **kipped**) 🔳 dormir

kipper /ˈkɪpə(r)/ n arenque m defumado

kiss /kɪs/ n beijo m ● vt/i beijar(-se)

kit /kɪt/ n equipamento m; (set of tools) ferramenta f; (for assembly) kit m ● vt (pt **kitted**) **~ out** equipar

kitchen /ˈkɪtʃɪn/ n cozinha f; **~ garden** horta f; **~ sink** pia f, (P) lava-louças m

kite /kaɪt/ n (toy) pipa f, (P) papagaio m de papel

kitten /ˈkɪtn/ n gatinho m

kitty /ˈkɪtɪ/ n (fund) fundo m comum, vaquinha f; Cards bolo m

knack /næk/ n jeito m

knapsack /ˈnæpsæk/ n mochila f

knead /niːd/ vt amassar

knee /niː/ n joelho m

kneecap /ˈniːkæp/ n rótula f

kneel /niːl/ vi (pt **knelt**) **~ (down)** ajoelhar(-se)

knelt /nelt/ ▶ KNEEL

knew /njuː/ ▶ KNOW

knickers /ˈnɪkəz/ npl calcinhas (de senhora) fpl

knife /naɪf/ n (pl **knives**) faca f ● vt esfaquear, apunhalar

knight /naɪt/ n cavaleiro m; Chess cavalo m. **~hood** n grau m de cavaleiro

knit /nɪt/ vt (pt **knitted**, or **knit**) tricotar ● vi tricotar, fazer tricô; fig (unite) unir-se; (of bones) soldar-se; **~ one's brow** franzir as sobrancelhas. **~ting** n malha f, tricô m

knitwear /'nɪtweə(r)/ n roupa f de malha, malhas fpl

knob /nɒb/ n (of door) maçaneta f; (of drawer) puxador m; (of radio, TV etc) botão m; (of butter) noz f. **~bly** a nodoso

knock /nɒk/ vt/i bater (em); ☒ (criticize) desancar (em); **~ down** ‹chair, pedestrian› deitar no chão, derrubar; (demolish) jogar or (P) deitar abaixo; ⊤ (reduce) baixar, reduzir; (at auction) adjudicar (**to** a); **~ out** pôr fora de combate, eliminar; (stun) assombrar; **~ over** entornar; **~ up** ‹meal etc› arranjar às pressas ▢ **~ about** vt tratar mal ● vi (wander) andar a esmo. **~ off** vt ⊤ (complete quickly) despachar; ☒ (steal) roubar ● vi ⊤ (stop working; fechar a loja ⊤. **~down** a ‹price› muito baixo; **~kneed** a de pernas de tesoura; **~out** n Boxing nocaute m, KO m. **~er** n aldrava f

knot /nɒt/ n nó m ● vt (pt knotted) atar com nó, dar nó or nós em

knotty /'nɒtɪ/ a (-ier, -iest) nodoso, cheio de nós; (difficult) complicado, espinhoso

know /nəʊ/ vt/i (pt knew, pp known) saber (that que); (person, place) conhecer; **~ about** ‹cars etc› saber sobre, saber de; **~ of** ter conhecimento de, ter ouvido falar de ● n **in the ~** ⊤ por dentro. **~all** n sabe-tudo m ⊤; **~how** n know-how m, conhecimentos mpl técnicos, culturais etc. **~ingly** adv com ar conhecedor; (consciously) conscientemente

knowledge /'nɒlɪdʒ/ n conhecimento m; (learning) saber

m. **~able** a conhecedor, entendido, versado

known /nəʊn/ ▶ KNOW a conhecido

knuckle /'nʌkl/ n nó m dos dedos ● vi **~ under** ceder, submeter-se

Koran /kə'rɑːn/ n Alcorão m, Corão m

Korea /kə'rɪə/ n Coreia f

kosher /'kəʊʃə(r)/ a aprovado pela lei judaica; ⊤ como deve ser

kowtow /kaʊ'taʊ/ vi prostrar-se (**to** diante de); (act obsequiously) bajular

lab /læb/ n ⊤ laboratório m

label /'leɪbl/ n (on bottle etc) rótulo m; (on clothes, luggage) etiqueta f ● vt (pt labelled) rotular; etiquetar, pôr etiqueta em

laboratory /lə'bɒrətrɪ/ n laboratório m

laborious /lə'bɔːrɪəs/ a laborioso, trabalhoso

labour /'leɪbə(r)/ n trabalho m, labuta f; (workers) mão de obra f; **in ~** em trabalho de parto ● vi trabalhar; (try hard) esforçar-se ● vt alongar-se sobre, insistir em. **~ed** a ‹writing› laborioso, sem espontaneidade; ‹breathing, movement› difícil. **~saving** a que poupa trabalho

Labour /'leɪbə(r)/ n (party) Partido m Trabalhista, os trabalhistas ● a trabalhista

labourer /ˈleɪbərə(r)/ n trabalhador m; (on farm) trabalhador m rural

labyrinth /ˈlæbərɪnθ/ n labirinto m

lace /leɪs/ n renda f; (of shoe) cordão m de sapato, (P) atacador m ● vt atar; ‹drink› juntar um pouco (de aguardente, rum etc)

lack /læk/ n falta f ● vt faltar (a), não ter; **be ~ing** faltar; **be ~ing in** carecer de

laconic /ləˈkɒnɪk/ a lacónico, (P) lacónico

lacquer /ˈlækə(r)/ n laca f

lad /læd/ n rapaz m, moço m

ladder /ˈlædə(r)/ n escada f de mão, (P) escadote m; (in stocking) fio m corrido, (P) malha f (caída) ● vi deixar correr um fio, (P) deixar cair uma malha ● vt fazer malhas em

laden /ˈleɪdn/ a carregado (**with** de)

ladle /ˈleɪdl/ n concha (de sopa) f

lady /ˈleɪdɪ/ n senhora f; (title) Lady f; **young ~** jovem f. **~-in-waiting** n dama f de companhia, (P) dama f de honor; **~-like** a senhoril, elegante. **Ladies** n (toilets) toalete m das Senhoras, (P) lavabos m para Senhoras

ladybird /ˈleɪdɪbɜːd/ n joaninha f

lag[1] /læg/ vi (pt **lagged**) atrasar-se, ficar para trás ● n atraso m

lag[2] /læg/ vt (pt **lagged**) ‹pipes etc› revestir com isolante térmico

lager /ˈlɑːgə(r)/ n cerveja f leve e clara; "loura" f 🗙

lagoon /ləˈguːn/ n lagoa f

laid /leɪd/ ▶ LAY[2]

lain /leɪn/ ▶ LIE[2]

lair /leə(r)/ n toca f, covil m

lake /leɪk/ n lago m

lamb /læm/ n cordeiro m, carneiro m; (meat) carneiro m, borrego m

lambswool /ˈlæmzwʊl/ n lã f

lame /leɪm/ a (-er, -est) coxo; fig (unconvincing) fraco

lament /ləˈment/ n lamento m, lamentação f ● vt/i lamentar(-se) (de/por)

laminated /ˈlæmɪneɪtɪd/ a laminado

lamp /læmp/ n lâmpada f

lamp post /ˈlæmppəʊst/ n poste (do candeeiro) (de iluminação pública) m

lampshade /ˈlæmpʃeɪd/ n abajur m, quebra-luz m

lance /lɑːns/ n lança f ● vt lancetar

land /lænd/ n terra f; (country) país m; (plot) terreno m; (property) terras fpl ● a de terra, terrestre; ‹policy etc› agrário ● vt/i desembarcar; Aviat aterrissar, (P) aterrar; (fall) ir parar (**on** em/a); 🗉 (obtain) arranjar; ‹a blow› aplicar, mandar. **~locked** a rodeado de terra

landing /ˈlændɪŋ/ n desembarque m; Aviat aterrissagem f, (P) aterragem f; (top of stairs) patamar m

landlady /ˈlændleɪdɪ/ n (of rented house) senhoria f, proprietária f; (who lets rooms) dona f da casa; (of boarding house) dona f da pensão; (of inn etc) proprietária f, estalajadeira f. **~lord** n (of rented house) senhorio m, proprietário m; (of inn etc) proprietário m, estalajadeiro m

landmark /ˈlændmɑːk/ n (conspicuous feature) ponto m de referência; fig marco m

landscape /ˈlændskeɪp/ n paisagem f ● vt projetar paisagisticamente

landslide /'lændslaɪd/ n desabamento or desmoronamento m de terras m; fig Pol vitória f esmagadora

lane /leɪn/ n senda f, caminho m; (in country) estrada f pequena; (in town) viela f, ruela f; (of road) faixa f, pista f; (of traffic) fila f; Aviat corredor m; Naut rota f

language /'læŋgwɪdʒ/ n língua f; (speech, style) linguagem f; **bad ~** linguagem f grosseira; **~ lab** laboratório m de línguas

languid /'læŋgwɪd/ a lânguido

languish /'læŋgwɪʃ/ vi elanguescer

lank /læŋk/ a (of hair) escorrido, liso

lanky /'læŋkɪ/ a (-ier, -iest) desengonçado, escanifrado

lantern /'læntən/ n lanterna f

lap[1] /læp/ n colo m; Sport volta f completa. **~dog** n cãozinho m de estimação, cão m de colo

lap[2] /læp/ vt **~ up** beber lambendo ● vi marulhar

lapel /lə'pel/ n lapela f

lapse /læps/ vi decair, degenerar-se; (expire) caducar ● n lapso m; Jur prescrição f; **~ into** <thought> mergulhar em; <bad habit> adquirir

latch /lætʃ/ n trinco m

lard /lɑːd/ n banha f de porco

larder /'lɑːdə(r)/ n despensa f

large /lɑːdʒ/ a (-er, -est) grande; **at ~** à solta, em liberdade; **by and ~** em geral. **~ly** adv largamente, em grande parte. **~ness** n grandeza f

lark[1] /lɑːk/ n (bird) cotovia f

lark[2] /lɑːk/ 🆒 pândega f; brincadeira f ● vi **~ about** 🆒 fazer travessuras, brincar

larva /'lɑːvə/ n (pl **-vae** /-viː/) larva f

laryngitis /lærɪn'dʒaɪtɪs/ n laringite f

larynx /'lærɪŋks/ n laringe f

laser /'leɪzə(r)/ n laser m; **~ printer** impressora f a laser

lash /læʃ/ vt chicotear, açoitar; <rain> fustigar ● n chicote m; (stroke) chicotada f; (eyelash) pestana f, cílio m; **~ out** atacar, atirar-se a; 🆒 (spend) esbanjar dinheiro em algo

lasso /læ'suː/ n (pl **-os**) laço m ● vt laçar

last[1] /lɑːst/ a & último; **~ night** ontem à noite, a noite passada; **the ~ straw** a gota d'água ● adv no fim, em último lugar; (most recently) a última vez ● n último m; at (long) **~** por fim, finalmente; **to the ~** até ao fim. **~minute** a de última hora. **~ly** adv finalmente, em último lugar

last[2] /lɑːst/ vt/i durar, continuar. **~ing** a duradouro, durável

late /leɪt/ a (-er, -est) atrasado; (recent) recente; (former) antigo, ex-, anterior; <hour, fruit etc> tardio; (deceased) falecido ● adv tarde; **in ~** july no fim de julho; **of ~** ultimamente; **at the ~st** o mais tardar. **~ness** n atraso m

lately /'leɪtlɪ/ adv nos últimos tempos, ultimamente

latent /'leɪtnt/ a latente

lateral /'lætərəl/ a lateral

lather /'lɑːðə(r)/ n espuma f de sabão ● vt ensaboar ● vi fazer espuma

Latin /'lætɪn/ n Lang latim m ● a latino. **~ America** n América f Latina; **~ American** a & n latino-americano m

latitude /'lætɪtjuːd/ n latitude f

latter /'lætə(r)/ a último, mais recente ● n the **~** este, esta. **~ly** adv recentemente

laudable /'lɔːdəbl/ a louvável

laugh /lɑːf/ vi rir (**at** de); **~ off** disfarçar com uma piada ● n riso m. **~able** a irrisório, ridículo. **~ing stock** n objeto m de troça

laughter /'lɑːftə(r)/ n riso m, risada f

launch[1] /lɔːntʃ/ vt lançar ● n lançamento m; **~ into** lançar-se or meter-se em; **~ing pad** plataforma f de lançamento

launch[2] /lɔːntʃ/ n (boat) lancha f

launder /'lɔːndə(r)/ vt lavar e passar

launderette /lɔːn'dret/ n lavandaria or (P) lavandaria f automática

laundry /'lɔːndrɪ/ n lavanderia f; (clothes) roupa f, (P) lavandaria f; **do the ~** lavar a roupa

laurel /'lɒrəl/ n loureiro m, louro m

lava /'lɑːvə/ n lava f

lavatory /'lævətrɪ/ n privada f, (P) casa de banho f, (room) toalete m, (P) lavabo m

lavender /'lævəndə(r)/ n alfazema f, lavanda f

lavish /'lævɪʃ/ a pródigo; (plentiful) copioso, generoso; (lush) suntuoso, (P) sumptuoso ● vt ser pródigo em, encher de

law /lɔː/ n lei f; (profession, study) direito m; **~ and order** ordem f pública. **~abiding** a cumpridor da lei, respeitador da lei. **~ful** a legal, legítimo. **~fully** adv legalmente, legitimamente. **~less** a sem lei; (act) ilegal; (person) rebelde

law court /lɔːkɔːt/ n tribunal m

lawn /lɔːn/ n gramado m, (P) relvado m. **~ mower** n cortador m de grama, (P) máquina f de cortar a relva

lawsuit /'lɔːsuːt/ n processo m, ação f judicial

lawyer /'lɔːjə(r)/ n advogado m

lax /læks/ a negligente; (discipline) frouxo; (morals) relaxado. **~ity** n negligência f; (of discipline) frouxidão f; (of morals) relaxamento m

laxative /'læksətɪv/ n laxante m, laxativo m

lay[1] /leɪ/ a leigo; **~ opinion** opinião f de um leigo

lay[2] /leɪ/ vt (pt laid) pôr, colocar; (trap) preparar, pôr; (eggs, table, siege) pôr; (plan) fazer; **~ on** (gas, water etc) instalar, ligar; (entertainment etc) organizar; (food) servir; **~ out** (design) traçar, planejar; (spread out) estender, espalhar; (money) gastar ● vi pôr (ovos); **~ aside** pôr de lado; **~ down** pousar; (condition, law, rule) impor; (arms) depor; (one's life) oferecer; (policy) ditar; **~ hold of** agarrar(-se a) □ **~ off** vt (worker) suspender do trabalho ● vi □ parar; desistir. **~ up** vt (store) juntar; (ship, car) pôr fora de serviço

lay[3] /leɪ/ ▶ LIE[2]

layabout /'leɪəbaʊt/ n ⊠ vadio m

lay-by /'leɪbaɪ/ n acostamento m, (P) berma f

layer /leɪə(r)/ n camada f

layman /'leɪmən/ n (pl -men) leigo m

layout /'leɪaʊt/ n disposição f; Typ composição f

laze /leɪz/ vi descansar, vadiar

laz|y /'leɪzɪ/ a (-ier, -iest) preguiçoso. **~iness** n preguiça f. **~ybones** n ⊠ vadio m; vagabundo m

lead[1] /liːd/ vt/i (pt led) conduzir, guiar, levar; (team etc) chefiar, liderar; (life) levar; (choir, band *etc*⟩ dirigir; **~ away** levar; **~ on** *fig* encorajar; **~ the way** ir na frente; **~ up to** conduzir a ● *n* (*distance*) avanço *m*; (*first place*) dianteira *f*; (*clue*) indício *m*, pista *f*; (*leash*) coleira *f*; *Electr* cabo *m*; *Theatr* papel *m* principal; (*example*) exemplo *m*; **in the ~** na frente

lead[2] /led/ *n* chumbo *m*; (*of pencil*) grafite *f*

leader /ˈliːdə(r)/ *n* chefe *m*, líder *m*; (*of country, club, union etc*) dirigente *mf*; *Pol* líder; (*of orchestra*) regente *mf*, maestro *m*; (*in newspaper*) editorial *m*. **~ship** *n* direção *f*, liderança *f*

leading /ˈliːdɪŋ/ *a* principal; **~ article** artigo *m* de fundo, editorial *m*

leaf /liːf/ *n* (*pl* **leaves**) folha *f*; (*flap of table*) aba *f* ● *vi* **~ through** folhear. **~y** *a* frondoso

leaflet /ˈliːflɪt/ *n* prospecto *m*, folheto *m* informativo

league /liːg/ *n* liga *f*; *Sport* campeonato *m* da Liga; **in ~ with** de coligação com, em conluio com

leak /liːk/ *n* (*escape*) fuga *f*; (*hole*) buraco *m* ● *vt/i* ⟨*roof, container*⟩ pingar; *Electr, Gas* ter um escapamento, (*P*) ter uma fuga; *Naut* fazer água; **~ (out)** *fig* divulgar; *fig* divulgar-se. **~y** *a* que tem um vazamento, (*P*) que tem uma fuga

lean[1] /liːn/ *a* (**-er, -est**) magro

lean[2] /liːn/ *vt/i* (*pt* **leaned**, *or* **leant** /lent/) encostar(-se); apoiar-se (*on* em); (*be slanting*) inclinar(-se); **~ back/forward** *or* **over** inclinar-se para trás/para a frente; **~ on** 🔢 pressionar

leaning /ˈliːnɪŋ/ *a* inclinado ● *n* inclinação *f*

leap /liːp/ *vt* (*pt* **leaped** *or* **leapt** /lept/) galgar, saltar por cima de; **~ year** ano *m* bissexto ● *vi* saltar ● *n* salto *m*, pulo *m*. **~frog** *n* eixo-badeixo *m*, (*P*) jogo *m* do eixo

learn /lɜːn/ *vt/i* (*pt* **learned** *or* **learnt**) aprender; (*be told*) vir a saber, ouvir dizer. **~er** *n* principiante *mf*, aprendiz *m*

learn|ed /ˈlɜːnɪd/ *a* erudito. **~ing** *n* saber *m*, erudição *f*

lease /liːs/ *n* arrendamento *m*, aluguel *m*, (*P*) aluguer *m* ● *vt* arrendar, (*P*) alugar

leash /liːʃ/ *n* coleira *f*

least /liːst/ *a* o menor ● *n* o mínimo *m*, o menos *m* ● *adv* o menos; **at ~** pelo menos; **not in the ~** de maneira alguma

leather /ˈleðə(r)/ *n* couro *m*, cabedal *m*

leave /liːv/ *vt/i* (*pt* **left**) deixar; (*depart from*) sair/partir (de), ir-se (de); **be left (over)** restar, sobrar; **~ alone** deixar em paz, não tocar; **~** *vt* omitir ● *n* licença *f*, permissão *f*; **~ of absence** licença *f*; **on ~** *Mil* de licença; **take one's ~** despedir-se (of de)

Leban|on /ˈlebənən/ *n* Líbano *m*

lecherous /ˈletʃərəs/ *a* lascivo

lecture /ˈlektʃə(r)/ *n* conferência *f*; *Univ* aula *f* teórica; *fig* sermão *m* ● *vi* dar uma conferência; *Univ* dar aula(s) ● *vt* pregar um sermão a alguém 🔢. **~r** /-ə(r)/ *n* conferente *mf*, conferencista *mf*; *Univ* professor *m*

led /led/ ▶ **LEAD**[1]

ledge /ledʒ/ *n* rebordo *m*, saliência *f*; (*of window*) peitoril *m*

ledger /ˈledʒə(r)/ *n* livro-mestre *m*, razão *m*

leech /liːtʃ/ *n* sanguessuga *f*

leek /liːk/ n alho-poró m, (P) alho-porro m

leer /lɪə(r)/ vi ~ **(at)** olhar de modo malicioso or manhoso (para) ● n olhar m malicioso or manhoso

leeway /ˈliːweɪ/ n Naut deriva f; fig liberdade f de ação, margem f ⬛

left¹ /left/ ▶ **LEAVE**; ~ **luggage (office)** depósito m de bagagens. ~**overs** npl restos mpl, sobras fpl

left² /left/ a esquerdo; Pol de esquerda ● n esquerda f ● adv à/para a esquerda. ~**-hand** a da esquerda; (position) à esquerda; ~**-handed** a canhoto; ~**-wing** a Pol de esquerda

leg /leg/ n perna f; (of table) pé m, perna f; (of journey) etapa f; **pull sb's** ~ brincar or mexer com alguém; **stretch one's** ~**s** esticar as pernas. ~**room** n espaço m para as pernas

legacy /ˈlegəsɪ/ n legado m

legal /ˈliːgl/ a legal; ⟨affairs etc⟩ jurídico; ~ **adviser** advogado m. ~**ity** /liːˈgælətɪ/ n legalidade f. ~**ly** adv legalmente

legalize /ˈliːgəlaɪz/ vt legalizar

legend /ˈledʒənd/ n lenda f. ~**ary** /ˈledʒəndrɪ/ a lendário

leggings /ˈlegɪŋz/ npl perneiras fpl; (women's) legging m, (P) leggings m

legib|le /ˈledʒəbl/ a legível

legion /ˈliːdʒən/ n legião f

legislat|e /ˈledʒɪsleɪt/ vi legislar. ~**ion** /-ˈleɪʃn/ n legislação f

legislat|ive /ˈledʒɪslətɪv/ a legislativo

legitima|te /lɪˈdʒɪtɪmət/ a legítimo. ~**cy** n legitimidade f

leisure /ˈleʒə(r)/ n lazer m, tempo m livre; **at one's** ~ ao bel prazer, (P) a seu belo prazer; ~ **centre** centro m de lazer. ~**ly** a pausado,

compassado ● adv sem pressa, devagar

lemon /ˈlemən/ n limão m

lemonade /leməˈneɪd/ n limonada f

lend /lend/ vt (pt lent) emprestar; (contribute) dar; ~ **a hand to** (help) ajudar; ~ **itself** to prestar-se a. ~**er** n pessoa f que empresta. ~**ing** n empréstimo m

length /leŋθ/ n comprimento m; (in time) período m; (of cloth) corte m; **at** ~ extensamente; (at last) por fim, finalmente. ~**y** a longo, demorado

lengthen /ˈleŋθən/ vt/i alongar(-se)

lengthways /ˈleŋθweɪz/ adv ao comprido, em comprimento, longitudinalmente

lenien|t /ˈliːnɪənt/ a indulgente, clemente. ~**cy** n indulgência f, clemência f

lens /lenz/ n (of spectacles) lente f; Photo objetiva f

lent /lent/ ▶ **LEND**

Lent /lent/ n Quaresma f

lentil /ˈlentl/ n lentilha f

Leo /ˈliːəʊ/ n Astr Leão m

leopard /ˈlepəd/ n leopardo m

leotard /ˈliːəʊtɑːd/ n collant(s) m(pl), (P) maillot m de ginástica ou dança

leper /ˈlepə(r)/ n leproso m

leprosy /ˈleprəsɪ/ n lepra f

lesbian /ˈlezbɪən/ a lésbico ● n lésbica f

less /les/ a (in number) menor (**than** que) ● n, adv & prep menos; ~ **and** ~ cada vez menos

lessen /ˈlesn/ vt/i diminuir

lesser /ˈlesə(r)/ a menor; **to a** ~ **degree** em menor grau

lesson /'lesn/ n lição f

let /let/ vt (pt let, pres p letting)
deixar, permitir; (lease) alugar,
arrendar; ~ **alone** deixar em paz;
(not to mention) sem falar em, para
não o falar em; ~ **down** baixar;
(deflate) esvaziar; (disappoint)
desapontar; (fail to help) deixar na
mão; ~ **in** deixar entrar; ~ **o.s. in
for** ‹task, trouble› meter-se em;
~ **off** ‹gun› disparar; ‹firework›
soltar, (P) deitar; (excuse) desculpar;
~ **out** deixar sair; ~ **through** deixar
passar; ~ **up** [i] abrandar, diminuir
● v aux ~'s **go** vamos; ~ **him do it**
que o faça ele; ~ **me know** diga-me,
avise-me ● n aluguel m, (P) aluguer
m ● vt/i ~ **go** soltar □ ~ **on** [i] vt
revelar (**that** que) ● vi descoser-se
[i], (P) descair-se [i]. ~**down** n
desapontamento m; ~**up** n [i] pausa
f; trégua f

lethal /'li:θl/ a fatal, mortal

lethargy /'leθədʒɪ/ n letargia f,
apatia f. ~**ic** /lɪ'θɑ:dʒɪk/ a letárgico,
apático

letter /'letə(r)/ n (symbol) letra f;
(message) carta f. ~ **bomb** n carta-
bomba f; ~ **box** n caixa f do correio.
~**ing** n letras fpl

lettuce /'letɪs/ n alface f

leukaemia /lu:'ki:mɪə/ n
leucemia f

level /'levl/ a plano; (on surface)
horizontal; (in height) no mesmo
nível (**with** que) ● n nível m; **on the
~** [i] franco, sincero ● vt (pt levelled)
nivelar; ‹gun, missile› apontar;
‹accusation› dirigir; ~ **crossing**
passagem f de nível. ~**headed** a
equilibrado, sensato

lever /'li:və(r)/ n alavanca f ● vt ~
up levantar com alavanca

leverage /'li:vərɪdʒ/ n influência f

levy /'levɪ/ vt ‹tax› cobrar ● n
imposto m

lewd /lu:d/ a (-er, -est) libidinoso,
obsceno

liability /laɪə'bɪlətɪ/ n
responsabilidade f, [i] (handicap)
desvantagem f; ~**ies** dívidas fpl

liable /'laɪəbl/ a ~ **to do** suscetível
de fazer; ~ **to** ‹illness etc› suscetível
a; ‹fine› sujeito a; ~ **for** responsável
por

liaise /lɪ'eɪz/ vi [i] servir de
intermediário (**between** entre);
fazer a ligação (**with** com)

liaison /lɪ'eɪzn/ n ligação f

liar /'laɪə(r)/ n mentiroso m

libel /'laɪbl/ n difamação f ● vt (pt
libelled) difamar

liberal /'lɪbərəl/ a liberal. ~**ly** adv
liberalmente

Liberal /'lɪbərəl/ a & n liberal mf

liberat|e /'lɪbəreɪt/ vt libertar. ~**ion**
/-'reɪʃn/ n libertação f; (of women)
emancipação f

liberty /'lɪbətɪ/ n liberdade f; **at
~to** livre de; **take ~ies** tomar
liberdades

libido /lɪ'bi:dəʊ/ n (pl -os) libido m

Libra /'li:brə/ n Astr Balança f, Libra

librar|y /'laɪbrərɪ/ n biblioteca f.
~**ian** /-'breərɪən/ n bibliotecário m

> **Library of Congress** A
> biblioteca nacional dos
> Estados Unidos, situada em
> Washington DC. Fundada pelo
> Congresso (Congress), alberga
> mais de 80 milhões de livros em
> 470 línguas, e outros objectos.

Libya /'lɪbɪə/ n Líbia f. ~**n** a & n
líbio m

lice /laɪs/ n ▶ **LOUSE**

483   licence | like

licence /'laɪsns/ n licença f; (for TV) taxa f; (for driving) carteira f, (P) carta f; (behaviour) libertinagem f

license /'laɪsns/ vt dar licença para, autorizar ● n Amer ▶ LICENCE; ~ **plate** placa f do carro, (P) placa f de matrícula, matrícula f

lick /lɪk/ vt lamber; ⊠ (defeat) bater ⊡; dar uma surra em ⊡ ● n lambidela f; **a ~ of paint** uma mão de pintura

lid /lɪd/ n tampa f

lie¹ /laɪ/ n mentira f ● vi (pt lied, pres p lying) mentir; **give the ~ to** desmentir

lie² /laɪ/ vi (pt lay, pp lain, pres p lying) estar deitado; (remain) ficar; (be situated) estar, encontrar-se; (in grave) (on ground) jazer; **~ down** descansar; **~ in, have a ~in** dormir até tarde; **~ low** ⊡ (hide) andar escondido

lieu /luː/ n **in ~** em vez de

lieutenant /lefˈtenənt/ n Army tenente m; Navy 1.º tenente m

life /laɪf/ n (pl lives) vida f; **~ cycle** ciclo m vital; **~ expectancy** probabilidade f de vida, (P) esperança f média de vida; **~ insurance** seguro m de vida. **~guard** n salva-vidas m; **~ jacket** n colete m salva-vidas; **~size(d)** a (de) tamanho natural invar

lifebelt /'laɪfbelt/ n cinto m salva-vidas, (P) boia f de salvação

lifeboat /'laɪfbəʊt/ n barco m salva-vidas

lifeless /'laɪflɪs/ a sem vida

lifelike /'laɪflaɪk/ a natural, real; (of portrait) muito parecido

lifelong /'laɪflɒŋ/ a de toda a vida, perpétuo

lifestyle /'laɪfstaɪl/ n estilo m de vida

lifetime /'laɪftaɪm/ n vida f; **the chance of a ~** uma oportunidade única

lift /lɪft/ vt/i levantar(-se), erguer(-se); ⊡ (steal) roubar; surripiar ⊡; (of fog) levantar, dispersar-se ● n ascensor m, elevador m; **give a ~ to** dar carona, (P) boleia a ⊡. **~-off** n decolagem f, (P) descolagem f

ligament /'lɪgəmənt/ n ligamento m

light¹ /laɪt/ n luz f; (lamp) lâmpada f; (on vehicle) farol m; (spark) lume m ● a claro ● vt (pt lit, or lighted) (ignite) acender; (illuminate) iluminar; **bring to ~** trazer à luz, revelar; **come to ~** vir à luz; **~ up** iluminar(-se), acender(-se)

light² /laɪt/ a & adv (-er, -est) leve. **~headed** a (dizzy) estonteado, tonto; (frivolous) leviano; **~hearted** a alegre, despreocupado. **~ly** adv de leve, levemente, ligeiramente. **~ness** n leveza f

lighten¹ /'laɪtn/ vt/i iluminar(-se); (make brighter) clarear

lighten² /'laɪtn/ vt/i ‹load etc› aligeirar(-se), tornar mais leve

lighter /'laɪtə(r)/ n isqueiro m

lighthouse /'laɪthaʊs/ n farol m

lighting /'laɪtɪŋ/ n iluminação f

lightning /'laɪtnɪŋ/ n relâmpago m; (thunderbolt) raio m ● a muito rápido; like **~** como um relâmpago

lightweight /'laɪtweɪt/ a leve

like¹ /laɪk/ a semelhante (a), parecido (com) ● prep como ● conj ⊡ como ● n igual m, coisa f parecida; **the ~s of you** gente como você(s). **~-minded** a da mesma opinião

like² /laɪk/ vt gostar (de); **I would ~** gostaria (de), queria; **if you ~** se quiser; **would you ~?** gostaria?, queria?. **~able** a simpático

like|ly /ˈlaɪklɪ/ a (**-ier, -iest**) provável ● adv provavelmente; **he is ~ly to come** é provável que ele venha; **not ~ly!** 🄸 nem morto 🄸, nem por sonhos. **~lihood** n probabilidade f

liken /ˈlaɪkən/ vt comparar (**to** com)

likeness /ˈlaɪknɪs/ n semelhança f

likewise /ˈlaɪkwaɪz/ adv também; (*in the same way*) da mesma maneira

liking /ˈlaɪkɪŋ/ n gosto m, inclinação f; (*for person*) afeição f; **take a ~ to** (*thing*) tomar gosto por; (*person*) simpatizar com

lilac /ˈlaɪlək/ n lilás m ● a lilás invar

lily /ˈlɪlɪ/ n lírio m, lis m; **~ of the valley** lírio-do-vale m

limb /lɪm/ n membro m

lime¹ /laɪm/ n cal f

lime² /laɪm/ n (*fruit*) limão m, (P) lima f

lime³ /laɪm/ n **~(-tree)** tília f

limelight /ˈlaɪmlaɪt/ n **be in the ~** estar em evidência

limit /ˈlɪmɪt/ n limite m ● vt limitar. **~ation** /-ˈteɪʃn/ n limitação f. **~ed company** n sociedade f anônima, (P) anónima de responsabilidade limitada

limousine /ˈlɪməziːn/ n limusine f

limp¹ /lɪmp/ vi mancar, coxear ● n **have a ~** coxear

limp² /lɪmp/ a (**-er, -est**) mole, frouxo

line¹ /laɪn/ n linha f; (*string*) fio m; (*rope*) corda f; (*row*) fila f; (*of poem*) verso m; (*wrinkle*) ruga f; (*of business*) ramo m; (*of goods*) linha f. Amer (*queue*) fila f, (P) fila f; **in ~ with** de acordo com ● vt marcar com linhas; <*streets etc*> ladear, enfileirar-se ao longo de; **~d paper** papel m pautado; **~ up** alinhar(-se), enfileirar(-se); (*in queue*) pôr(-se) em fila, (P) fila. **~up** n (*players*) formação f

line² /laɪn/ vt (*garment*) forrar (**with** de)

linear /ˈlɪnɪə(r)/ a linear

linen /ˈlɪnɪn/ n <*sheets etc*> roupa f (branca) de cama; (*material*) linho m

liner /ˈlaɪnə(r)/ n navio m de linha regular, (P) paquete m

linesman /ˈlaɪnzmən/ n Football, Tennis juiz m de linha

linger /ˈlɪŋɡə(r)/ vi demorar-se, deixar-se ficar; (*of smells etc*) persistir

lingerie /ˈlɛ̃ʒərɪ/ n roupa f de baixo/interior (de senhora), lingerie f

linguist /ˈlɪŋɡwɪst/ n linguista mf

linguistic /lɪŋˈɡwɪstɪk/ a linguístico. **~s** n linguística f

lining /ˈlaɪnɪŋ/ n forro m

link /lɪŋk/ n laço m; (*of chain; also fig*) elo m; (*on web page*) link m ● vt unir, ligar; (*relate*) ligar; <*arm*> enfiar; **~ up** (*of roads*) juntar-se (**with** a)

lint /lɪnt/ n Med curativo m de fibra de algodão; (*fluff*) cotão m

lion /ˈlaɪən/ n leão m. **~ess** n leoa f

lip /lɪp/ n lábio m, beiço m; (*edge*) borda f; (*of jug etc*) bico m; **pay ~-service to** fingir pena, admiração etc. **~-read** vt/i entender pelos movimentos dos lábios, ler lábios

lipstick /ˈlɪpstɪk/ n batom m, (P) bâton m

liqueur /lɪˈkjʊə(r)/ n licor m

liquid /'lɪkwɪd/ n & a líquido m. **~ize** vt liquidificar. **~izer** n liquidificador m

liquor /'lɪkə(r)/ n bebida f alcoólica

liquorice /'lɪkərɪs/ n alcaçuz m

Lisbon /'lɪzbən/ n Lisboa f

lisp /lɪsp/ n ceceio m ● vi cecear

list¹ /lɪst/ n lista f ● vt fazer uma lista de; (enter) pôr na lista

list² /lɪst/ vi (of ship) adernar ● n adernamento m

listen /'lɪsn/ vi escutar, prestar atenção; **~ to, ~ in** (to) escutar, pôr-se à escuta. **~er** n ouvinte mf

listless /'lɪstlɪs/ a sem energia, apático

lit /lɪt/ ▶ LIGHT¹

literal /'lɪtərəl/ a literal. **~ly** adv literalmente

litera|te /'lɪtərət/ a alfabetizado. **~cy** n alfabetização f, instrução f

literature /'lɪtrətʃə(r)/ n literatura f; Ⓘ (leaflets etc) folhetos mpl

lithe /laɪð/ a ágil, flexível

litigation /lɪtɪ'geɪʃn/ n litígio m

litre /'liːtə(r)/ n litro m

litter /'lɪtə(r)/ n lixo m; (animals) ninhada f ● vt cobrir de lixo; **~ed with** coberto de. **~ bin** n lata f, (P) caixote m do lixo

little /'lɪtl/ a pequeno; (not much) pouco ● n pouco m ● adv pouco, mal, nem; **a ~** um pouco (de); **he ~ knows** ele mal/nem sabe; **~ by ~** pouco a pouco

live¹ /laɪv/ a vivo; (wire) eletrizado; (broadcast) em direto, ao vivo

live² /lɪv/ vt/i viver; (reside) habitar, morar, viver; **~ down** fazer esquecer; **~ it up** cair na farra; **~ on** viver de; (continue) continuar a viver; **~ up to** mostrar-se à altura de; (fulfil) cumprir

livelihood /'laɪvlɪhʊd/ n modo m de vida

livel|y /'laɪvlɪ/ a (-ier, -iest) vivo, animado. **~iness** n vivacidade f, animação f

liven /'laɪvn/ vt/i **~ up** animar(-se)

liver /'lɪvə(r)/ n fígado m

livestock /'laɪvstɒk/ n gado m

livid /'lɪvɪd/ a lívido; Ⓘ (furious) furioso

living /'lɪvɪŋ/ a vivo ● n vida f; (livelihood) modo m de vida, sustento m; **earn or make a ~** ganhar a vida; **standard of ~** nível m de vida. **~ room** n sala f de estar

lizard /'lɪzəd/ n lagarto m

load /ləʊd/ n carga f; (of lorry, ship) carga f, carregamento m; (weight, strain) peso m; **~s of** montes de ● vt carregar. **~ed** a ‹dice› viciado; Ⓧ (rich) cheio da nota, (P) podre de rico

loaf¹ /ləʊf/ n (pl loaves) pão m

loaf² /ləʊf/ vi vadiar. **~er** n preguiçoso m, vagabundo m

loan /ləʊn/ n empréstimo m ● vt emprestar; **on ~** emprestado

loath /ləʊθ/ a sem vontade de, pouco disposto a, relutante em

loath|e /ləʊð/ vt detestar. **~ing** n repugnância f, aversão f

lobby /'lɒbɪ/ n entrada f, vestíbulo m; Pol lobby m, grupo m de pressão ● vt fazer pressão sobre

lobster /'lɒbstə(r)/ n lagosta f

local /'ləʊkl/ a local; ‹shops etc› do bairro ● n pessoa f do lugar; Ⓘ (pub) taberna f /pub m do bairro; **~ government** administração f municipal. **~ly** adv localmente

locality /ləʊ'kælətɪ/ n localidade f; (position) lugar m

localization /ləʊkəˈlaɪzeɪʃn/ n
localização f

locat|e /ləʊˈkeɪt/ vt localizar;
(situate) situar. **~ion** /-ʃn/ n
localização f. on **~ion** (cinema) em
external, (P) no exterior

lock¹ /lɒk/ n (hair) mecha f de
cabelo

lock² /lɒk/ n (on door etc) fecho m,
fechadura f; (on canal) comporta
f; under **~** and key a sete chaves
● vt/i fechar à chave; Auto ‹wheels›
imobilizar(-se); **~ in** fechar à chave,
encerrar; **~ out** fechar a porta para
deixar na rua, ficar trancado do lado
de fora; **~ up** fechar a casa. **~out**
n lockout m

locker /ˈlɒkə(r)/ n compartimento
m com chave

locket /ˈlɒkɪt/ n medalhão m

locksmith /ˈlɒksmɪθ/ n serralheiro
m, chaveiro m

locomotion /ləʊkəˈməʊʃn/ n
locomoção f

locomotive /ˈləʊkəməʊtɪv/ n
locomotiva f

locum /ˈləʊkəm/ n Med substituto m

locust /ˈləʊkəst/ n gafanhoto m

lodge /lɒdʒ/ n casa f do guarda
numa propriedade; (of porter)
portaria f ● vt alojar; ‹money›
depositar; **~ a complaint**
apresentar uma queixa ● vi
estar alojado (with em casa de);
(become fixed) alojar-se. **~r** /-ə(r)/ n
hóspede mf

lodgings /ˈlɒdʒɪŋz/ n quarto m
mobiliado; (flat) apartamento m

loft /lɒft/ n sótão m

lofty /ˈlɒftɪ/ a (-ier, -iest) elevado;
(haughty) altivo

log /lɒg/ n tronco m, toro m; **sleep
like a ~** dormir como uma pedra

● vt (pt logged) Naut/Aviat lançar
no diário de bordo; **~ off** acabar
de usar, terminar a sessão (de
utilizador); **~ on** iniciar a sessão

loggerheads /ˈlɒgəhedz/ npl at **~**
às turras (with com)

logic /ˈlɒdʒɪk/ a lógico. ● a lógico.
~ally adv logicamente

logistics /ləˈdʒɪstɪks/ n logística f

logo /ˈləʊgəʊ/ n (pl -os) 🔲 emblema
m; logotipo m, (P) logótipo m

loiter /ˈlɔɪtə(r)/ vi andar
vagarosamente; (stand about)
rondar

loll /lɒl/ vi refestelar-se

lollipop /ˈlɒlɪpɒp/ n pirulito m,
(P) chupa-chupa m. **~y** n 🔲 pirulito
m; (P) chupa-chupa m; 🅇 (money)
grana f, pasta f

London /ˈlʌndən/ n Londres

lone /ləʊn/ a solitário. **~r** /-ə(r)/ n
solitário m. **~some** a solitário

lonely /ˈləʊnlɪ/ a (-ier, -iest)
solitário; ‹person› só, solitário

long¹ /lɒŋ/ a (-er, -est) longo,
comprido; **~ face** cara f triste; **~
jump** salto m em distância, (P) em
comprimento; **~playing record**
LP m; **~ wave** ondas fpl longas; so
~! 🔲 até logo! ● adv muito tempo,
longamente; **how ~ is...?** (in size)
qual é o comprimento de...?; **how
~?** (in time) quanto tempo?; **he
will not be ~** ele não vai demorar;
a ~ time muito tempo; **a ~ way**
longe; **as** or **so ~ as** contanto que,
desde que; **~ ago** há muito tempo;
before ~ (future) daqui a pouco,
dentro em pouco; (past) pouco
(tempo) depois; **in the ~ run** no fim
de contas; **~ before** muito (tempo)
antes. **~-distance** a ‹flight› de longa
distância; ‹phone call› interurbano;
~-range a de longo alcance;

⟨*forecast*⟩ a longo prazo; ~**sighted** a que enxerga mal a distância, (P) hipermetrope; ~**standing** a de longa data; ~**suffering** a com paciência exemplar/de santo; ~**term** a a longo prazo; ~**winded** a prolixo

long[2] /lɒŋ/ *vi* ~ **for** ansiar por, ter grande desejo de; ~ **to** desejar. ~**ing** *n* desejo *m* ardente

longevity /lɒnˈdʒevətɪ/ *n* longevidade f, vida f longa

longhand /ˈlɒŋhænd/ *n* escrita f à mão

longitude /ˈlɒndʒɪtjuːd/ *n* longitude f

loo /luː/ *n* 🔲 banheiro *m*, (P) casa f de banho

look /lʊk/ *vt/i* olhar; (*seem*) parecer; ~ **after** tomar conta de, olhar por; ~ **at** olhar para; ~ **down on** desprezar; ~ **for** procurar; ~ **forward to** aguardar com impaciência; ~ **in on** visitar; ~ **into** examinar, investigar; ~ **like** parecer-se com, ter ar de; ~ **on** (*as spectator*) ver, assistir; (*regard as*) considerar; ~ **out** ter cautela; ~ **out for** procurar; (*watch*) estar à espreita de; ~ **round** olhar em redor; ~ **up** ⟨*word*⟩ procurar; (*visit*) ir ver; ~ **up to** respeitar ● *n* olhar *m*; (*appearance*) ar *m*, aspecto *m*; (*good*) ~**s** beleza f. ~**out** *n* Mil posto *m* de observação; (*watcher*) vigia *m*

loom[1] /luːm/ *n* tear *m*

loom[2] /luːm/ *vi* surgir indistintamente; *fig* ameaçar

loony /ˈluːnɪ/ *n & a* 🔲 maluco *m* 🔲; doido *m*

loop /luːp/ *n* laçada f; (*curve*) volta f, arco *m*; Aviat loop *m* ● *vt* dar uma laçada

loophole /ˈluːphəʊl/ *n* (*in rule*) saída f, furo *m*

loose /luːs/ *a* (-er, -est) ⟨*knot etc*⟩ frouxo; ⟨*page etc*⟩ solto; ⟨*clothes*⟩ folgado; (*not packed*) a granel; (*inexact*) vago; ⟨*morals*⟩ dissoluto, imoral; **at a ~ end** sem saber o que fazer, sem ocupação definida; **break ~** soltar-se. ~**ly** *adv* sem apertar; (*roughly*) vagamente

loosen /ˈluːsn/ *vt* (*slacken*) soltar, desapertar; (*untie*) desfazer, desatar

loot /luːt/ *n* saque *m* ● *vt* pilhar, saquear. ~**er** *n* assaltante *mf*, salteador *m*. ~**ing** *n* pilhagem f, saque *m*

lop /lɒp/ *vt* (*pt* lopped) ~ **off** cortar, podar

lopsided /lɒpˈsaɪdɪd/ *a* torto, inclinado para um lado

lord /lɔːd/ *n* senhor *m*; (*title*) lord *m*; **the ~** o Senhor; **the L~'s Prayer** o Pai-Nosso; **(good) L~!** meu Deus!

lorry /ˈlɒrɪ/ *n* caminhão *m*, camião *m*

lose /luːz/ *vt/i* (*pt* lost) perder; **get lost** perder-se; **get lost** 🔲 vai passear! 🔲. ~**r** /-ə(r)/ *n* perdedor *m*

loss /lɒs/ *n* perda f; **be at a ~** estar perplexo; **at a ~ for words** sem saber o que dizer

lost /lɒst/ ▶ LOSE ● *a* perdido; ~ **property** objetos *mpl* perdidos (e achados)

lot[1] /lɒt/ *n* sorte f; (*at auction, land*) lote *m*; **draw ~s** tirar à sorte

lot[2] /lɒt/ *n* **the ~** tudo; (*people*) todos *mpl*; **a ~ (of)**, ~**s (of)** 🔲 uma porção (de), (*P*) montes (de); **quite a ~ (of)** 🔲 uma boa porção (de), (*P*) montes (de) 🔲

lotion /ˈləʊʃn/ *n* loção f

lottery /ˈlɒtərɪ/ *n* loteria f, (P) lotaria f

loud /laʊd/ *a* (-er, -est) alto, barulhento, ruidoso; (*of colours*) berrante ● *adv* alto; **out ~** em voz alta

loudspeaker /laʊd'spiːkə(r)/ *n* alto-falante *m*, (P) altifalante *m*

lounge /laʊndʒ/ *vi* recostar-se preguiçosamente ● *n* sala *f*, salão *m*

louse /laʊs/ *n* (*pl* **lice**) piolho *m*

lousy /'laʊzɪ/ *a* (**-ier, -iest**) piolhento; ⊠ (*very bad*) péssimo

lout /laʊt/ *n* pessoa *f* grosseira, arruaceiro *m*

lovable /'lʌvəbl/ *a* amoroso, adorável

love /lʌv/ *n* amor *m*; *Tennis* zero *m*, nada ● *vt* amar, estar apaixonado por; (*like greatly*) gostar muito de; **in ~** apaixonado (**with** por); **~ affair** aventura *f* amorosa; **she sends you her ~** ela lhe manda lembranças, (P) ela manda-lhe cumprimentos

lovely /'lʌvlɪ/ *a* (**-ier, -iest**) lindo; ⊞ (*delightful*) encantador; delicioso

lover /'lʌvə(r)/ *n* namorado *m*, apaixonado *m*; (*illicit*) amante *m*; (*devotee*) admirador *m*, apreciador *m*

lovesick /'lʌvsɪk/ *a* perdido de amor

loving /'lʌvɪŋ/ *a* amoroso, terno, extremoso

low /laʊ/ *a* (**-er, -est**) baixo ● *adv* baixo ● *n* baixa *f*; (*low pressure*) área de baixa pressão *f*. **~cut** *a* decotado; **~down** *a* baixo, reles ● *n* ⊞ a verdade autêntica, (P) a verdade nua e crua; **~fat** *a* de baixo teor de gordura; **~key** *a fig* moderado; discreto

lower /'laʊə(r)/ *a & adv* ▶ **LOW** ● *vt* baixar; **~ o.s.** (re)baixar-se (**to** a)

lowlands /'laʊləndz/ *npl* planície(s) *f(pl)*

lowly /'laʊlɪ/ *a* (**-ier, -iest**) humilde, modesto

loyal /'lɔɪəl/ *a* leal. **~ly** *adv* lealmente

lozenge /'lozɪndʒ/ *n* (*shape*) losango *m*; (*tablet*) pastilha *f*

lubricate /'luːbrɪkeɪt/ *vt* lubrificar. **~ant** *n* lubrificante *m*. **~ation** /-'keɪʃn/ *n* lubrificação *f*

lucid /'luːsɪd/ *a* lúcido. **~ity** /luː-'sɪdətɪ/ *n* lucidez *f*

luck /lʌk/ *n* sorte *f*; **bad ~** pouca sorte *f*; **for ~** para dar sorte; **good ~!** boa sorte

lucky /'lʌkɪ/ *a* (**-ier, -iest**) sortudo, com sorte; (*event etc*) feliz; (*number etc*) que dá sorte. **~ily** *adv* felizmente

lucrative /'luːkrətɪv/ *a* lucrativo, rentável

ludicrous /'luːdɪkrəs/ *a* ridículo, absurdo

lug /lʌg/ *vt* (*pt* **lugged**) arrastar

luggage /'lʌgɪdʒ/ *n* bagagem *f*. **~ rack** *n* porta-bagagem *m*

lukewarm /'luːkwɔːm/ *a* morno; *fig* sem entusiasmo; indiferente

lull /lʌl/ *vt* (*send to sleep*) embalar; (*suspicions*) acalmar ● *n* calmaria *f*, (P) acalmia *f*

lullaby /'lʌləbaɪ/ *n* canção *f* de embalar

lumbago /lʌm'beɪgəʊ/ *n* lumbago *m*

lumber /'lʌmbə(r)/ *n* trastes *mpl* velhos; (*wood*) madeira *f* cortada ● *vt* **~ sb with** sobrecarregar alguém com

luminous /'luːmɪnəs/ *a* luminoso

lump /lʌmp/ *n* bocado *m*; (*swelling*) caroço *m*; (*in the throat*) nó *m*; (*in liquid*) grumo *m*; (*of sugar*) torrão *m* ● *vt* **~ together** amontoar, juntar indiscriminadamente; **~ sum** quantia *f* total; (*payment*) pagamento *m* feito de uma vez. **~y** *a* grumoso, encaroçado

lunacy /'luːnəsɪ/ *n* loucura *f*

lunar /'luːnə(r)/ *a* lunar

lunatic /'luːnətɪk/ *n* lunático *m*; **~ asylum** manicômio *m*, (P) manicómio *m*

lunch /lʌntʃ/ *n* almoço *m* ● *vi* almoçar. **~time** *n* hora *f* do almoço

luncheon /'lʌntʃən/ *n* (*formal*) almoço *m*; **~ meat** carne *f* enlatada, (P) carnes frias *fpl*; **~ voucher** senha *f* de almoço

lung /lʌŋ/ *n* pulmão *m*

lunge /lʌndʒ/ *n* mergulho *m*, movimento *m* súbito para a frente; (*thrust*) arremetida *f* ● *vi* mergulhar; arremessar-se (**at** para cima de, contra)

lurch[1] /lɜːtʃ/ *n* **leave sb in the ~** deixar alguém em apuros

lurch[2] /lɜːtʃ/ *vi* ir aos ziguezagues, dar guinadas; (*stagger*) cambalear

lure /lʊə(r)/ *vt* atrair, tentar ● *n* chamariz *m*, engodo *m*; **the ~ of the sea** a atração do mar

lurid /'lʊərɪd/ *a* berrante; *fig* (*sensational*) sensacional; *fig* (*shocking*) horrífico

lurk /lɜːk/ *vi* esconder-se à espreita; (*prowl*) rondar; (*be latent*) estar latente

luscious /'lʌʃəs/ *a* apetitoso; (*voluptuous*) desejável

lush /lʌʃ/ *a* viçoso, luxuriante

Lusitanian /lusɪ'teɪnɪən/ *a & n* lusitano *m*

lust /lʌst/ *n* luxúria *f*, sensualidade *f*; *fig* cobiça *f*; desejo *m* ardente ● *vi* **~ after** cobiçar, desejar ardentemente. **~ful** *a* sensual

lustre /'lʌstə(r)/ *n* lustre *m*; *fig* prestígio *m*

lusty /'lʌstɪ/ *a* (**-ier, -iest**) robusto

lute /luːt/ *n* alaúde *m*

Luxemburg /'lʌksəmbɜːg/ *n* Luxemburgo *m*

luxuriant /lʌg'ʒʊərɪənt/ *a* luxuriante

luxurious /lʌg'ʒʊərɪəs/ *a* luxuoso

luxury /'lʌkʃərɪ/ *n* luxo *m* ● *a* de luxo

lying /'laɪŋ/ ▶ LIE[1], LIE[2]

lynch /lɪntʃ/ *vt* linchar

lyric /'lɪrɪk/ *a* lírico. **~s** *npl Mus* letra *f*. **~al** *a* lírico

Mm

MA *abbr* (= Master of Arts) ▶ MASTER

mac /mæk/ *n* 🆃 impermeável *m*; gabardine *f*

macabre /mə'kɑːbrə/ *a* macabro

macaroni /mækə'rəʊnɪ/ *n* macarrão *m*

macaroon /mækə'ruːn/ *n* bolinho *m* seco de amêndoa ralada

machine /mə'ʃiːn/ *n* máquina *f*, legível à máquina *f*, (P) legível por máquina *f* ● *vt* fazer à máquina; (*sewing*) coser à máquina. **~ gun** *n* metralhadora *f*; **~readable** *a* em linguagem de máquina, legível à máquina, (P) legível por máquina

machinery /mə'ʃiːnərɪ/ *n* maquinaria *f*; (*working parts; also fig*) mecanismo *m*

machinist /mə'ʃiːnɪst/ *n* maquinista *m*

macho /'mætʃəʊ/ *a* machista

mackerel /ˈmækrəl/ n (pl invar)
cavala f

mackintosh /ˈmækɪntɒʃ/ n
impermeável m, gabardine f

mad /mæd/ a (**madder, maddest**)
doido, louco; ‹dog› raivoso; 🔲
(angry) furioso 🔲; **~ about** ser doido
por; **like ~** como (um) doido.
~ly adv loucamente; (frantically)
enlouquecidamente. **~ness** n
loucura f

Madagascar /mædəˈɡæskə(r)/ n
Madagáscar m

madam /ˈmædəm/ n senhora f; **no,
~** não senhora

madden /ˈmædn/ vt endoidecer,
enlouquecer; **it's ~ing** é de
enlouquecer

made /meɪd/ ▶ MAKE; **~ to
measure** feito sob medida, (P) à
medida

Madeira /məˈdɪərə/ n Madeira f;
(wine) Madeira m

madman /ˈmædmən/ n (pl -men)
doido m

Mafia /ˈmæfɪə/ n Máfia f

magazine /mæɡəˈziːn/ n revista f,
magazine m; (of gun) carregador m

maggot /ˈmæɡət/ n larva f

magic /ˈmædʒɪk/ n magia f ● a
mágico. **~al** a mágico

magician /məˈdʒɪʃn/ n (conjuror)
mágico m, prestidigitador m;
(wizard) feiticeiro m

magistrate /ˈmædʒɪstreɪt/ n
magistrado m

magnanim|ous /mæɡˈnænɪməs/
a magnânimo. **~ity** /-əˈnɪmətɪ/ n
magnanimidade f

magnet /ˈmæɡnɪt/ n ímã m, (P)
íman m. **~ic** /-ˈnetɪk/ a magnético.

~ism /-ɪzəm/ n magnetismo m

magnificen|t /mæɡˈnɪfɪsnt/ a
magnífico. **~ce** n magnificência f

magnif|y /ˈmæɡnɪfaɪ/ vt aumentar;
‹sound› ampliar, amplificar; **~ying
glass** lupa f. **~ication** /-ɪˈkeɪʃn/ n
aumento m, ampliação f

magnitude /ˈmæɡnɪtjuːd/ n
magnitude f

magpie /ˈmæɡpaɪ/ n pega f

mahogany /məˈhɒɡənɪ/ n
mogno m

maid /meɪd/ n criada f, empregada
f; **old ~** solteirona f

maiden /ˈmeɪdn/ n old use donzela
f ● a ‹aunt› solteira; ‹speech,
voyage› inaugural; **~ name** nome
m de solteira

mail¹ /meɪl/ n correio m; (letters)
correio m, correspondência f ● a
postal ● vt postar, pôr no correio;
(send by mail) mandar pelo correio.
~bag n mala f postal; **~box** n
Amer caixa f do correio; **~ing list**
n lista f de endereços; **~ing
order** n encomenda f por correspondência,
(P) por correio

mail² /meɪl/ n (armour) cota f de
malha

mailman /ˈmeɪlmæn/ n (pl -men)
Amer carteiro m

maim /meɪm/ vt mutilar, aleijar

main¹ /meɪn/ n a principal ● n in
the **~** em geral, essencialmente;
~ road estrada f principal. **~ly** adv
principalmente, sobretudo

main² /meɪn/ n **(water/gas) ~**
cano m de água/gás; **the ~s** Electr a
rede f elétrica

mainland /ˈmeɪnlənd/ n
continente m

mainstay /ˈmeɪnsteɪ/ n fig esteio m

mainstream /'meɪnstriːm/
n tendência f dominante, linha f
principal

maintain /meɪn'teɪn/ vt manter,
sustentar; ‹rights› defender, manter

maintenance /'meɪntənəns/ n
(care, continuation) manutenção f;
(allowance) pensão f

maisonette /meɪzə'net/ n
dúplex m

maize /meɪz/ n milho m

majestic /mə'dʒestɪk/ a majestoso

majesty /'mædʒəstɪ/ n majestade f

major /'meɪdʒə(r)/ a maior; (very
important) de vulto; ~ road estrada
f principal ● n major m ● vi ~ **in** Amer
Univ especializar-se em

majority /mə'dʒɒrətɪ/ n maioria
f; (age) maioridade f ● a a majoritário,
(P) maioritário; **the ~ of people** a
maioria ou a maior parte das pessoas

make /meɪk/ vt/i (pt **made**) fazer;
‹decision› tomar; ‹destination›
chegar a; (cause to) fazer (+ inf)
or (com) que (+ subj); **you ~ me
angry** você me aborrece, (P) tu
aborreces-me; **be made of** ser feito
de; ~ **o.s. at home** estar à vontade;
como em sua casa; ~ **it** chegar;
(succeed) triunfar; **I ~ it two o'clock**
são duas pelo meu relógio; ~ **as
if to** fazer ou fingir que; ~ **believe**
fingir; ~ **do with** arranjar-se com,
contentar-se com; ~ **for** dirigir-se
para; (contribute to) ajudar a; ~ **off**
fugir (with com); ~ **out** avistar,
distinguir; (understand) entender;
‹claim› pretender; ‹a cheque›
passar, emitir; ~ **over** ceder,
transferir ● ~ **on the**
~ ⌧ oportunista ◻ ~ **up** vt fazer,
compor; ‹story› inventar; ‹deficit›
suprir; ~ **up one's mind** decidir-se;
~ **up (one's face)** maquilhar-se, (P)

maquilhar-se ● vi fazer as pazes;
~ **up for** compensar. **~believe**
a fingido ● n fantasia f; ~**up** n
maquilagem f, (P) maquilhagem
f; (of object) composição f; Psych
maneira f de ser, natureza f

maker /'meɪkə(r)/ n fabricante mf

makeshift /'meɪkʃɪft/ n solução f
temporária ● a provisório

making /'meɪkɪŋ/ n **be the ~ of**
fazer, ser a causa do sucesso de;
in the ~ em formação; **he has
the ~s of** ele tem as qualidades
essenciais de

maladjusted /mælə'dʒʌstɪd/ a
desajustado, inadaptado

malaise /mæ'leɪz/ n mal-estar m

malaria /mə'leərɪə/ n malária f

Malay /mə'leɪ/ a & n malaio m. ~**sia**
/-ʒə/ n Malásia f

male /meɪl/ a ‹voice, sex›
masculino; Biol, Techn macho ● n
(human) homem m, indivíduo m do
sexo masculino; (arrival) macho m

malevolen|t /mə'levələnt/ a
malévolo

malfunction /mæl'fʌŋkʃn/
n mau funcionamento m ● vi
funcionar mal

malice /'mælɪs/ n maldade f,
malícia f; **bear sb ~** guardar rancor
a alguém

malicious /mə'lɪʃəs/ a maldoso,
malicioso

malign /mə'laɪn/ vt caluniar,
difamar

malignan|t /mə'lɪɡnənt/ a
‹tumour› maligno; (malevolent)
malévolo

mallet /'mælɪt/ n maço m

malnutrition /mælnjuː'trɪʃn/
n desnutrição f, subalimentação f,
subnutrição f

malpractice /mæl'præktɪs/ n abuso m; (incompetence) incompetência f profissional, negligência f

malt /mɔːlt/ n malte m

Malt|a /'mɔːltə/ n Malta f

maltreat /mæl'triːt/ vt maltratar. **~ment** n mau(s) trato(s) m(pl)

mammal /'mæml/ n mamífero m

mammoth /'mæməθ/ n mamute m ● a gigantesco, colossal

man /mæn/ n (pl **men**) homem m; (in sports team) jogador m; Chess peça f; **~ in the street** o homem m da rua, (P) o cidadão m comum; **~ to man** de homem para homem ● vt (pt **manned**) prover de pessoal; Mil guarnecer; Naut guarnecer, equipar, tripular; (be on duty at) estar de serviço em. **~hour** n hora f de trabalho per capita, homem-hora m; **~hunt** n caça f ao homem; **~made** a artificial

manage /'mænɪdʒ/ vt ‹household› governar; ‹tool› manejar; ‹boat, affair, crowd› manobrar; ‹shop› dirigir, gerir; **I could ~ another drink** até que tomaria mais um drinque ⏺, (P) até tomava mais outra bebida ⏺; **~ to do** conseguir fazer; **managing director** diretor m geral ● vi arranjar-se. **~able** a manejável; (easily controlled) controlável. **~ment** n gerência f, direção f

manager /'mænɪdʒə(r)/ n diretor m; (of bank, shop) gerente m; (of actor) empresário m, representante m; Sport treinador m. **~ess** /-'res/ n diretora f; gerente f. **~ial** /-'dʒɪərɪəl/ a diretivo, administrativo; **~ial staff** gestores mpl

mandate /'mændeɪt/ n mandato m

mandatory /'mændətrɪ/ a obrigatório

mane /meɪn/ n crina f; (of lion) juba f

mango /'mæŋgəʊ/ n (pl **-oes**) manga f

manhandle /'mænhændl/ vt mover à força de braço; (treat roughly) tratar com brutalidade

manhole /'mænhəʊl/ n poço m de inspeção

manhood /'mænhʊd/ n idade f adulta; (quality) virilidade f

mania /'meɪnɪə/ n mania f. **~c** /-ɪæk/ n maníaco m

manicur|e /'mænɪkjʊə(r)/ n manicure f ● vt fazer, arranjar

manifest /'mænɪfest/ a manifesto ● vt manifestar. **~ation** /-'steɪʃn/ n manifestação f

manifesto /mænɪ'festəʊ/ n (pl **-os**) manifesto m

manipulat|e /mə'nɪpjʊleɪt/ vt manipular. **~ion** /-'leɪʃn/ n manipulação f

mankind /mæn'kaɪnd/ n humanidade f, gênero m, (P) género m humano, raça f humana

manly /'mænlɪ/ a viril, másculo

manner /'mænə(r)/ n maneira f, modo m; (attitude) modo(s) m(pl); (kind) espécie f; **~s** maneiras fpl; **bad ~s** má-criação f, falta f de educação; **good ~s** (boa) educação f

mannerism /'mænərɪzm/ n maneirismo m, afetação f

manoeuvre /mə'nuːvə(r)/ n manobra f ● vt/i manobrar

manor /'mænə(r)/ n solar m

manpower /'mænpaʊə(r)/ n mão de obra f

mansion /'mænʃn/ n mansão f

manslaughter /'mænslɔːtə(r)/ n homicídio m involuntário

mantelpiece /'mæntlpiːs/ n (*shelf*) consolo m da lareira, (P) prateleira f da chaminé

manual /'mænjʊəl/ a manual ● n manual m

manufacture /mænjʊ'fæktʃə(r)/ vt fabricar ● n fabrico m, fabricação f. ~r /-ə(r)/ n fabricante mf

manure /mə'njʊə(r)/ n estrume m

manuscript /'mænjʊskrɪpt/ n manuscrito m

many /'menɪ/ a (**more, most**) muitos; ~ **a man/tear**/*etc* muitos homens/muitas lágrimas/*etc*; ~ **of us/them/you** muitos de nós/deles/de vocês; **you may take as ~ as you want** você pode levar quantos quiser; **how ~?** quantos?; **one too** ~ um a mais ● n muitos; (*many people*) muita gente f; **a great ~** muitíssimos

map /mæp/ n mapa m ● vt (*pt* **mapped**) fazer um mapa de, mapear; ~ **out** planear em pormenor; ‹*route*› traçar

maple /'meɪpl/ n bordo m

mar /mɑː(r)/ vt (*pt* **marred**) estragar; ‹*beauty*› desfigurar

marathon /'mærəθən/ n maratona f

marble /'mɑːbl/ n mármore m; (*for game*) bola f de gude, (P) berlinde m

march /mɑːtʃ/ vi marchar ● vt ~ **off** fazer marchar, conduzir à força; **he was ~ed off to prison** levaram-no à força para a prisão ● n marcha f

March /mɑːtʃ/ n março m

mare /meə(r)/ n égua f

margarine /mɑːdʒə'riːn/ n margarina f

margin /'mɑːdʒɪn/ n margem f. ~**al** a marginal; ~**al seat** *Pol* lugar m ganho com pequena maioria. ~**ally** *adv* por uma pequena margem, muito pouco

marigold /'mærɪɡəʊld/ n cravo-de-defunto m, (P) malmequer m

marijuana /mærɪ'wɑːnə/ n maconha f, marijuana f

marina /mə'riːnə/ n marina f

marinade /mærɪ'neɪd/ n marinada f, vinha d'alho, escabeche m ● vt pôr em marinada, (P) pôr em vinha d'alho

marine /mə'riːn/ a marinho; (*of ship, trade etc*) marítimo ● n ‹*shipping*› marinha f; ‹*sailor*› fuzileiro m naval

marital /'mærɪtl/ a marital, conjugal, matrimonial; ~ **status** estado m civil

maritime /'mærɪtaɪm/ a marítimo

mark[1] /mɑːk/ n (*currency*) marco m

mark[2] /mɑːk/ n marca f; (*trace*) marca f, sinal m; (*stain*) mancha f; *School* nota f; (*target*) alvo m; **make one's** ~ ganhar nome ● vt marcar; ‹*exam etc*› marcar, classificar; ~ **out** marcar; ~ **out for** escolher para, designar para; ~ **time** marcar passo. ~**er** n marcador m. ~**ing** n marcas fpl, marcação f

marked /mɑːkt/ a marcado. ~**ly** /-ɪdlɪ/ adv manifestamente, visivelmente

market /'mɑːkɪt/ n mercado m; **on the** ~ à venda; ~ **garden** horta f de legumes para venda; ~ **research** pesquisa f de mercado ● vt vender; (*launch*) comercializar, lançar. ~**place** n mercado m. ~**ing** n marketing m

marksman /'mɑːksmən/ n (*pl* -**men**) atirador m especial

marmalade /'mɑːməleɪd/ n
compota f de laranja, (P) geleia

maroon /məˈruːn/ a & n bordô m,
(P) bordeaux m

marooned /məˈruːnd/ a
abandonado em ilha, costa deserta
etc; fig (stranded) encalhado fig

marquee /mɑːˈkiː/ n barraca or
tenda f grande f; Amer (awning)
toldo m

marriage /'mærɪdʒ/ n casamento
m, matrimônio m, (P) matrimónio
m; ~ **certificate** certidão f de
casamento. ~**able** a casadouro

marrow /'mærəʊ/ n (of bone)
tutano m, medula f; (vegetable)
abóbora f; **chilled to the ~** gelado
até aos ossos

marr|y /'mærɪ/ vt casar(-se) com;
(give or unite in marriage) casar; **get
~ied** casar-se • vi casar-se. **~ied** a
casado; ‹life› de casado, conjugal

Mars /mɑːz/ n Marte m

marsh /mɑːʃ/ n pântano m. ~**y** a
pantanoso

marshal /'mɑːʃl/ n Mil marechal m;
(steward) mestre m de cerimónias,
(P) cerimónias • vt (pt **marshalled**)
dispor em ordem, ordenar; (usher)
conduzir, escoltar

marshmallow /mɑːʃˈmæləʊ/ n
marshmallow m

martial /'mɑːʃl/ a marcial; ~ **law**
lei f marcial

martyr /'mɑːtə(r)/ n mártir mf • vt
martirizar. ~**dom** n martírio m

marvel /'mɑːvl/ n maravilha f,
prodígio m • vi (pt **marvelled**) (feel
wonder) maravilhar-se (at com); (be
astonished) pasmar (at com)

marvellous /'mɑːvələs/ a
maravilhoso

Marxis|t /'mɑːksɪst/ a & n marxista
mf. ~**m** /-zəm/ n marxismo m

marzipan /'mɑːzɪpæn/ n
maçapão m

mascara /mæˈskɑːrə/ n rímel m

mascot /'mæskət/ n mascote f

masculin|e /'mæskjʊlɪn/ a
masculino • n masculino m. ~**ity**
/-'lɪnətɪ/ n masculinidade f

mash /mæʃ/ n (pulp) papa f • vt
esmagar; ~**ed potatoes** purê m or
(P) puré m de batata(s)

mask /mɑːsk/ n máscara f • vt
mascarar

masochis|t /'mæsəkɪst/ n
masoquista mf. ~**m** /-zəm/ n
masoquismo m

mason /'meɪsn/ n maçom m;
(building) pedreiro m. ~**ry** n
maçonaria f, maçom m; (building)
alvenaria f

mass[1] /mæs/ n Relig missa f

mass[2] /mæs/ n massa f; (heap)
montão m; **the ~es** as massas,
grande massa • vt/i aglomerar(-se),
reunir(-se) em massa. ~**produce** vt
produzir em série/massa

massacre /'mæsəkə(r)/ n
massacre m • vt massacrar

massage /'mæsɑːʒ/ n massagem
f • vt massagear, fazer massagens
em, (P) dar massagens a

masseu|r /mæˈsɜː(r)/ n massagista
m. ~**se** /mæˈsɜːz/ n massagista f

massive /'mæsɪv/ a (heavy)
maciço; (huge) enorme

mast /mɑːst/ n mastro m; (for radio
etc) antena f

master /'mɑːstə(r)/ n (in school)
professor m, mestre m; (expert)
mestre m; (boss) patrão m; (owner)
dono m; ~ (boy) menino m; **M~ of
Arts**/etc Licenciado m em Letras/

etc ● *vt* dominar. **~ key** *n* chave-mestra *f*; **~mind** *n* (of *scheme etc*) cérebro *m* ● *vt* planejar, dirigir; **~ stroke** *n* golpe *m* de mestre. **~y** *n* domínio *m* (**over** sobre); (*knowledge*) conhecimento *m*; (*skill*) perícia *f*

masterly /'mɑːstəli/ *a* magistral

masterpiece /'mɑːstəpiːs/ *n* obra-prima *f*

masturbat|e /'mæstəbeɪt/ *vi* masturbar-se. **~ion** /-'beɪʃn/ *n* masturbação *f*

mat /mæt/ *n* tapete *m* pequeno; (*at door*) capacho *m*. (**table**) **~** *n* (of *cloth*) paninho *m* de mesa; (*for hot dishes*) descanso *m* para pratos

match¹ /mætʃ/ *n* fósforo *m*

match² /mætʃ/ *n* (*contest*) competição *f*, torneio *m*; (*game*) partida *f*; (*equal*) par *m*, parceiro *m*, igual *mf*; *fig* (*marriage*) casamento *m*; (*marriage partner*) partido *m* ● *vt/i* (*set against*) contrapor (**against** a); (*equal*) igualar; (*go with*) condizer; (*be alike*) ir com, emparceirar com; **her shoes ~ed her bag** os sapatos dela combinavam com a bolsa. **~ing** *a* condizente, a condizer

matchbox /'mætʃbɒks/ *n* caixa *f* de fósforos

mat|e¹ /meɪt/ *n* companheiro *m*, camarada *mf*; (of *birds, animals*) macho *m*, fêmea *f*; (*assistant*) ajudante *mf* ● *vt/i* acasalar(-se) (**with** com)

mate² /meɪt/ *n* Chess mate *m*, xeque-mate *m*

material /mə'tɪərɪəl/ *n* material *m*; (*fabric*) tecido *m*; (*equipment*) apetrechos *mpl* ● *a* material; (*significant*) importante

materialis|m /mə'tɪərɪəlɪzəm/ *n* materialismo *m*. **~tic** /-'lɪstɪk/ *a* materialista

materialize /mə'tɪərɪəlaɪz/ *vi* realizar-se, concretizar-se; (*appear*) aparecer

maternal /mə'tɜːnl/ *a* maternal

maternity /mə'tɜːnəti/ *n* maternidade *f* ● *a* ‹*clothes*› de grávida; **~ hospital** maternidade *f*; **~ leave** licença *f* de maternidade

mathematic|s /mæθə'mætɪks/ *n* matemática *f*. **~al** *a* matemático. **~ian** /-ə'tɪʃn/ *n* matemático *m*

maths /mæθs/ *n* 🇬🇧 matemática *f*

matinee /'mætɪneɪ/ *n* matinê *f*, (*P*) matinée *f*

matrimon|y /'mætrɪmənɪ/ *n* matrimônio *m*, (*P*) matrimónio *m*

matron /'meɪtrən/ *n* matrona *f*; (*in school*) inspetora *f*; (*former use*) (*senior nursing officer*) enfermeira-chefe *f*

matt /mæt/ *a* fosco, sem brilho, mate

matted /'mætɪd/ *a* emaranhado

matter /'mætə(r)/ *n* (*substance*) matéria *f*; (*affair*) assunto *m*, caso *m*, questão *f*; (*pus*) pus *m*; **as a ~ of fact** na verdade; **no ~ what happens** não importa o que acontecer; **what is the ~?** o que é que há?, (*P*) o que é que se passa?; **what is the ~ with you?** o que é que você tem? ● *vi* importar; **it does not ~** não importa. **~-of-fact** *a* prosaico, terra a terra

mattress /'mætrɪs/ *n* colchão *m*

matur|e /mə'tjʊə(r)/ *a* maduro, amadurecido ● *vt/i* amadurecer; *Comm* vencer-se. **~ity** *n* madureza *f*, maturidade *f*; *Comm* vencimento *m*

maul /mɔːl/ *vt* maltratar, atacar

Mauritius /mə'rɪʃəs/ *n* ilha *f* Maurícia

mausoleum /mɔːsəˈliəm/ n mausoléu m

mauve /məʊv/ a & n lilás m

maxim /ˈmæksɪm/ n máxima f

maxim|um /ˈmæksɪməm/ a & n (pl -ima) máximo m. **~ize** vt aumentar ao máximo, maximizar

---

may /meɪ/ ● vaux (pt might)

••••▸ (possibility) poder; **he ~ come** talvez ele venha; **he ~ have missed his train** ele pode ter perdido o trem; **it ~ rain** talvez chova

••••▸ (permission) **you ~ leave** pode ir; **~ I smoke?** posso fumar?

••••▸ (wish) **~ he be happy** que ele seja feliz; **~ the best man win!** que ganhe o melhor!

••••▸ (in phrases) **I ~ as well go** bem que eu podia ir embora; **we ~ as well give up** bem que podíamos desistir

---

May /meɪ/ n maio m. **M~ Day** n o primeiro de maio

maybe /ˈmeɪbiː/ adv talvez

mayhem /ˈmeɪhɛm/ n (disorder) distúrbios mpl violentos; (havoc) estragos mpl

mayonnaise /meɪəˈneɪz/ n maionese f

mayor /meə(r)/ n prefeito m. **~ess** n prefeita f; (mayor's wife) mulher f do prefeito

maze /meɪz/ n labirinto m

me /miː/ pron me; (after prep) mim; **with ~** comigo; **he knows ~** ele me conhece; **it's ~** sou eu

meadow /ˈmɛdəʊ/ n prado m, campina f

meagre /ˈmiːgə(r)/ a (thin) magro; (scanty) escasso

meal¹ /miːl/ n refeição f

meal² /miːl/ n (grain) farinha f grossa

mean¹ /miːn/ a (-er, -est) mesquinho; (unkind) mau

mean² /miːn/ a médio; **Greenwich ~ time** tempo m médio de Greenwich ● n média f

mean³ /miːn/ vt (pt meant) (intend) tencionar or ter (a) intenção (to de); (signify) querer dizer, significar; (entail) dar em resultado, resultar provavelmente em; (refer to) referir-se a; **be meant for** destinar-se a; **I didn't ~ it** desculpe, foi sem querer; **he ~s what he says** ele está falando sério, (P) ele está a falar a sério

meaning /ˈmiːnɪŋ/ n sentido m, significado m. **~ful** a significativo. **~less** a sem sentido

means /miːnz/ n meio(s) m(pl) ● npl meios mpl pecuniários, recursos mpl; **by ~ of** por meio de, através de; **by all ~** com certeza; **by no ~** de modo nenhum

meant /mɛnt/ ▶ MEAN³

mean|time /ˈmiːntaɪm/ adv (in the) **~time** entretanto. **~while** /-waɪl/ adv entretanto

measles /ˈmiːzlz/ n sarampo m; **German ~** rubéola f

measly /ˈmiːzlɪ/ a 🗵 miserável; ínfimo

measure /ˈmɛʒə(r)/ n medida f ● vt/i medir; **made to ~** feito sob medida; **~ up to** mostrar-se à altura de, (P) à medida. **~d** a medido, calculado. **~ment** n medida f

meat /miːt/ n carne f. **~y** a carnudo; fig (substantial) substancial

mechanic /mɪˈkænɪk/ n mecânico m

mechanic|al /mɪˈkænɪkl/ a
mecânico. **~s** n mecânica f ● npl
mecanismo m

mechan|ism /ˈmekənɪzəm/ n
mecanismo m. **~ize** vt mecanizar

medal /ˈmedl/ n medalha f. **~list** n
condecorado m; **be a gold ~list** ser
medalha de ouro

medallion /mɪˈdælɪən/ n
medalhão m

meddle /ˈmedl/ vi (interfere)
imiscuir-se; intrometer-se (**in** em);
(tinker) mexer (**with** em). **~some** a
intrometido, abelhudo

media /ˈmiːdɪə/ ▶ **MEDIUM** npl;
the ~ a mídia, (P) os media mpl, os
meios de comunicação social or
de massa

mediat|e /ˈmiːdɪeɪt/ vi servir de
intermediário, mediar. **~ion** /-ˈeɪʃn/
n mediação f. **~or** n mediador m,
intermediário m

medical /ˈmedɪkl/ a médico ● n ⚕
(examination) exame m médico

medicat|ed /ˈmedɪkeɪtɪd/
a medicinal. **~ion** /-ˈkeɪʃn/ n
medicamentação f, medicação f

medicinal /mɪˈdɪsɪnl/ a medicinal

medicine /ˈmedsn/ n medicina
f; (substance) remédio m,
medicamento m

medieval /medɪˈiːvl/ a medieval

mediocr|e /miːdɪˈəʊkə(r)/
a medíocre. **~ity** /-ˈɒkrəti/ n
mediocridade f

meditat|e /ˈmedɪteɪt/ vt/i meditar.
~ion /-ˈteɪʃn/ n meditação f

Mediterranean
/medɪtəˈreɪnɪən/ a mediterrâneo
● n the **M~** o Mediterrâneo

medium /ˈmiːdɪəm/ n (pl media)
meio m (pl mediums) (person)
médium mf ● a médio; **~ wave**

Radio onda f média; **the happy ~** o
meio-termo

medley /ˈmedlɪ/ n (pl **-eys**)
miscelânea f

meek /miːk/ a (**-er, -est**) manso,
submisso, sofrido

meet /miːt/ vt (pt **met**) encontrar;
(intentionally) encontrar-se com, ir
ter com; (at station etc) ir esperar,
ir buscar; (make the acquaintance
of) conhecer; (conform with) ir ao
encontro de, satisfazer; ‹opponent,
obligation etc› fazer face a; ‹bill,
expenses› pagar ● vi encontrar-se;
(get acquainted) familiarizar-se; (in
session) reunir-se; **~ with** encontrar;
‹accident, misfortune› sofrer, ter

meeting /ˈmiːtɪŋ/ n reunião f,
encontro m; (between two people)
encontro m. **~ place** n ponto m de
encontro

megalomania
/megæləʊˈmeɪnɪə/ n megalomania
f, mania f de grandeza, (P) das
grandezas

megaphone /ˈmegəfəʊn/ n
megafone m, porta-voz m

melancholy /ˈmelənkɒlɪ/ n
melancolia f ● a melancólico

mellow /ˈmeləʊ/ a (**-er, -est**) ‹fruit,
person› amadurecido, maduro;
‹sound, colour› quente, suave ● vt/i
amadurecer; (soften) suavizar

melodious /mɪˈləʊdɪəs/ a
melodioso

melodrama /ˈmelədrɑːmə/ n
melodrama m. **~tic** /-əˈmætɪk/ a
melodramático

melod|y /ˈmelədɪ/ n melodia f. **~ic**
/mɪˈlɒdɪk/ a melódico

melon /ˈmelən/ n melão m

melt /melt/ vt/i ‹metals› fundir(-se);
‹butter, snow etc› derreter(-se);

(fade away) desvanecer(-se). **~ing pot** n cadinho m

member /'membə(r)/ n membro m; *(of club etc)* sócio m; **M~ of Parliament** deputado m. **~ship** n qualidade f de sócio; *(members)* número m de sócios; *(fee)* cota f; **~ship card** carteira f, *(P)* cartão m de sócio

memento /mɪ'mentəʊ/ n *(pl* -oes) lembrança f, recordação f

memo /'meməʊ/ n *(pl* -os) 🔲 nota f; apontamento m; lembrete m

memoir /'memwɑː(r)/ n *(record, essay)* memória f, memorial m. **~s** npl memórias fpl

memorable /'memərəbl/ a memorável

memorandum /memə'rændəm/ n *(pl* -da, *or* -dums) nota f, lembrete m; *(diplomatic)* memorando m

memorial /mɪ'mɔːrɪəl/ n monumento m comemorativo ● a comemorativo

memorize /'meməraɪz/ vt decorar, memorizar, aprender de cor

memory /'memərɪ/ n memória f; **from ~** de memória, de cor; **in ~ of** em memória de. **~ stick** pente m de memória, *(P)* dispositivo m de memória externa or penf

men /men/ ▶ MAN

menac|e /'menəs/ n ameaça f; *(nuisance)* praga f, chaga f ● vt ameaçar

mend /mend/ vt consertar, reparar; *(darn)* remendar; **~ one's ways** corrigir-se, emendar-se ● n conserto m; *(darn)* remendo m; **on the ~** melhorando

menial /'miːnɪəl/ a humilde

meningitis /menɪn'dʒaɪtɪs/ n meningite f

menopause /'menəpɔːz/ n menopausa f

menstruation /menstrʊ'eɪʃn/ n menstruação f

mental /'mentl/ a mental; ‹hospital› de doentes mentais, psiquiátrico

mentality /men'tælətɪ/ n mentalidade f

mention /'menʃn/ vt mencionar; **don't ~ it!** não tem de quê, de nada ● n menção f

menu /'menjuː/ n *(pl* -us) menu m, *(P)* ementa f

merchandise /'mɜːtʃəndaɪz/ n mercadorias fpl ● vt/i negociar

merchant /'mɜːtʃənt/ n mercador m ● a ‹ship, navy› mercante; **~ bank** banco m comercial

merciful /'mɜːsɪfl/ a misericordioso

merciless /'mɜːsɪlɪs/ a impiedoso, sem dó

mercury /'mɜːkjʊrɪ/ n mercúrio m

mercy /'mɜːsɪ/ n piedade f, misericórdia f; **at the ~ of** à mercê de

mere /mɪə(r)/ a mero, simples. **~ly** adv meramente, simplesmente, apenas

merge /mɜːdʒ/ vt/i fundir(-se), amalgamar(-se); Comm ‹companies› fundir(-se). **~r** /-ə(r)/ n fusão f

meringue /mə'ræŋ/ n merengue m, suspiro m

merit /'merɪt/ n mérito m ● vt *(pt* merited) merecer

mermaid /'mɜːmeɪd/ n sereia f

merriment /'merɪmənt/ n divertimento m, alegria f, folguedo m

merry /'merɪ/ a *(-ier, -iest)* alegre, divertido; **~ Christmas** Feliz Natal.

~go-round n carrossel m; **~making** n festa f, divertimento m

mesh /meʃ/ n malha f

mess /mes/ n (disorder) desordem f, trapalhada f; (trouble) embrulhada f, trapalhada f; (dirt) porcaria f; Mil (place) cantina f, messe f; Mil (food) rancho m; **make a ~ of** estragar • vt **~ up** (make untidy) desarrumar; (make dirty) sujar; (confuse) atrapalhar, estragar • vi **~ about** (behave foolishly) fazer asneiras; **~ about with** (tinker with) entreter-se com, andar às voltas com

message /ˈmesɪdʒ/ n mensagem f; (informal) recado m

messenger /ˈmesɪndʒə(r)/ n mensageiro m

Messiah /mɪˈsaɪə/ n Messias m

messy /ˈmesɪ/ a (-ier, -iest) desarrumado, bagunçado; (dirty) sujo, porco

met /met/ ▶ MEET

metabolism /mɪˈtæbəlɪzm/ n metabolismo m

metal /ˈmetl/ n metal m • a de metal. **~lic** /mɪˈtælɪk/ a metálico; ‹paint, colour› metalizado

metaphor /ˈmetəfə(r)/ n metáfora f. **~ical** /-ˈfɒrɪkl/ a metafórico, (P) metafórico

meteor /ˈmiːtɪə(r)/ n meteoro m

meteorolog|y /miːtɪəˈrɒlədʒɪ/ n meteorologia f. **~ical** /-əˈlɒdʒɪkl/ a meteorológico

meter[1] /ˈmiːtə(r)/ n contador m

meter[2] /ˈmiːtə(r)/ n Amer ▶ METRE

method /ˈmeθəd/ n método m

methodical /mɪˈθɒdɪkl/ a metódico

Methodist /ˈmeθədɪst/ n metodista mf

methylated /ˈmeθɪleɪtɪd/ a **~ spirit** álcool m metílico

meticulous /mɪˈtɪkjʊləs/ a meticuloso

metre /ˈmiːtə(r)/ n metro m

metric /ˈmetrɪk/ a métrico

metropol|is /məˈtrɒpəlɪs/ n metrópole f. **~itan** /metrəˈpɒlɪtən/ a metropolitano

mettle /ˈmetl/ n têmpera f, caráter m; (spirit) brio m

mew /mjuː/ n miado m • vi miar

Mexic|o /ˈmeksɪkəʊ/ n México m. **~an** a & n mexicano m

miaow /miːˈaʊ/ n & vi = MEW

mice /maɪs/ ▶ MOUSE

mickey /ˈmɪkɪ/ n **take the ~ out of** 🗵 fazer troça de, gozar 🆃

micro- /maɪkrəʊ/ pref micro-

microchip /ˈmaɪkrəʊtʃɪp/ n microchip m

microfilm /ˈmaɪkrəʊfɪlm/ n microfilme m

microlight /ˈmaɪkrəʊlaɪt/ n Aviat ultraleve m

microphone /ˈmaɪkrəfəʊn/ n microfone m

microscop|e /ˈmaɪkrəskəʊp/ n microscópio m. **~ic** /-ˈskɒpɪk/ a microscópico

microwave /ˈmaɪkrəʊweɪv/ n micro-onda f; **~ oven** forno m de micro-ondas, (P) micro-ondas m

mid /mɪd/ a meio; **in ~air** no ar, em pleno voo; **in ~March** em meados de março

midday /mɪdˈdeɪ/ n meio-dia m

middle /ˈmɪdl/ a médio, meio; (quality) médio, mediano; **M~ Ages** Idade f Média; **~ class** classe f média; **M~ East** Médio Oriente m; **~ name** segundo nome m • n meio m;

in the ~ of no meio de. **~-aged** a de meia idade; **~-class** a burguês

middleman /'mɪdlmæn/ n (pl -men) intermediário m

midge /mɪdʒ/ n mosquito m

midget /'mɪdʒɪt/ n anão m ● a minúsculo

Midlands /'mɪdləndz/ npl região f do centro da Inglaterra

midnight /'mɪdnaɪt/ n meia-noite f

midriff /'mɪdrɪf/ n diafragma m; (abdomen) ventre m

midst /mɪdst/ n **in the ~ of** no meio de

midsummer /mɪd'sʌmə(r)/ n pleno verão m; (solstice) solstício m do verão

midway /mɪd'weɪ/ adv a meio caminho

midwife /'mɪdwaɪf/ n (pl -wives) parteira f

might[1] /maɪt/ n potência f; (strength) força f. **~y** a poderoso; fig (great) imenso ● adv 🆃 muito

might[2] /maɪt/ ▶ MAY

migraine /'mi:greɪn/ n enxaqueca f

migrant /'maɪgrənt/ a migratório ● n (person) migrante mf, emigrante mf

migrat|e /maɪ'greɪt/ vi migrar. **~ion** /-ʃn/ n migração f

mike /maɪk/ n 🆃 microfone m

mild /maɪld/ a (-er, -est) brando, manso; ‹illness, taste› leve; ‹climate› temperado; ‹weather› ameno. **~ly** adv brandamente, mansamente; **to put it ~ly** para não dizer coisa pior. **~ness** n brandura f

mildew /'mɪldju:/ n bolor m, mofo m; (in plants) míldio m

mile /maɪl/ n milha f (=1,6 km); **~s too big**/etc 🆃 grande demais, (P) demasiado grande. **~age** n (loosely) quilometragem f

milestone /'maɪlstəʊn/ n marco m miliário; fig data f or acontecimento m importante, marco m

militant /'mɪlɪtənt/ a & n militante mf

military /'mɪlɪtrɪ/ a militar

milk /mɪlk/ n leite m ● a (product) lácteo ● vt ordenhar; fig (exploit) explorar. **~shake** n milk-shake m, batido. m. **~y** a (like milk) leitoso; ‹tea etc› com muito leite; **M~y Way** Via f Láctea

milkman /'mɪlkmən/ n (pl -men) leiteiro m

mill /mɪl/ n moinho m; (factory) fábrica f ● vt moer ● vi ~ around aglomerar-se; ‹crowd› apinhar-se. **pepper~** n moedor m de pimenta

millennium /mɪ'lenɪəm/ n (pl -iums, or -ia) milénio m, (P) milénio m

millet /'mɪlɪt/ n painço m, milhete m

milligram /'mɪlɪgræm/ n miligrama m

millilitre /'mɪlɪliːtə(r)/ n mililitro m

millimetre /'mɪlɪmiːtə(r)/ n milímetro m

million /'mɪlɪən/ n milhão m; **a ~ pounds** um milhão de libras. **~aire** /-'neə(r)/ n milionário m

mime /maɪm/ n mímica f; (actor) mímico m ● vt/i exprimir por mímica, mimar

mimic /'mɪmɪk/ vt (pt mimicked) imitar ● n imitador m, parodiante mf

mince /mɪns/ vt picar ● n carne f moída, (P) carne f picada. **~ pie** pastel m recheado com massa de passas, amêndoas, especiarias etc. **~r** n máquina f de moer

mincemeat /'mɪnsmiːt/ n massa f de passas, amêndoas, especiarias etc usada para recheio; **make ~ of** 🇹 arrasar, aniquilar

mind n espírito m, mente f; (*intellect*) intelecto m; (*sanity*) razão f; **to be out of one's ~** estar fora de si; **have a good ~ to** estar disposto a; **make up one's ~** decidir-se; **presence of ~** presença f de espírito; **to my ~** a meu ver ● vt (*look after*) tomar conta de, tratar de; (*heed*) prestar atenção a; (*object to*) importar-se com, incomodar-se com; **do you ~ if I smoke?** você se incomoda or (P) importa-se que eu fume?; **do you ~ helping me?** quer fazer o favor de me ajudar?; **never ~** não se importe, não tem importância; **~ful of** atento a, consciente de. **~less** a insensato

minder /'maɪndə(r)/ n pessoa f que toma conta de crianças mf; (*bodyguard*) guarda-costas m

mine[1] /maɪn/ poss pron o(s) meu(s), a(s) minha(s); **it is ~** é (o) meu or (a) minha

min|e[2] /maɪn/ n mina f ● vt escavar, explorar; (*extract*) extrair; *Mil* minar. **~er** n mineiro m. **~ing** n exploração f mineira ● a mineiro

minefield /'maɪnfiːld/ n campo m minado

mineral /'mɪnərəl/ n mineral m; (*soft drink*) bebida f gasosa; **~ water** água f mineral

minesweeper /'maɪnswiːpə(r)/ n caça-minas m

mingle /'mɪŋgl/ vt/i misturar(-se) (**with** com)

miniature /'mɪnɪtʃə(r)/ n miniatura f ● a miniatural

minibus /'mɪnɪbʌs/ n (*public*) micro-ônibus m, (P) autocarro m

pequeno, miniautocarro m

minim|um /'mɪnɪməm/ a & n (*pl* **-ma**) mínimo m. **~al** a mínimo. **~ize** vt minimizar, dar pouca importância a

miniskirt /'mɪnɪskɜːt/ n minissaia f

minist|er /'mɪnɪstə(r)/ n ministro m; *Relig* pastor m. **~erial** /-'stɪərɪəl/ a ministerial. **~ry** n ministério m

mink /mɪŋk/ n (*fur*) marta f, visão m

minor /'maɪnə(r)/ a & n menor mf

minority /maɪ'nɒrətɪ/ n minoria f ● a minoritário

mint[1] /mɪnt/ n **the M~** a Casa da Moeda; **a ~** uma fortuna; **in ~ condition** em perfeito estado, como novo, impecável ● vt cunhar

mint[2] /mɪnt/ n (*plant*) hortelã f; (*sweet*) pastilha f de hortelã

minus /'maɪnəs/ prep menos; 🇹 (*without*) sem ● n menos m

minute[1] /'mɪnɪt/ n minuto m; **~s** (*of meeting*) ata f

minute[2] /maɪ'njuːt/ a diminuto, minúsculo; (*detailed*) minucioso

mirac|le /'mɪrəkl/ n milagre m. **~ulous** /mɪ'rækjʊləs/ a milagroso, miraculoso

mirage /'mɪrɑːʒ/ n miragem f

mire /maɪə(r)/ n lodo m, lama f

mirror /'mɪrə(r)/ n espelho m; (*in car*) retrovisor m ● vt refletir, espelhar

mirth /mɜːθ/ n alegria f, hilaridade f

misadventure /mɪsəd'ventʃə(r)/ n desgraça f; **death by ~** morte f acidental

misanthropist /mɪs'ænθrəpɪst/ n misantropo m

misapprehension /mɪsæprɪ'henʃn/ n mal-entendido m

misbehav|e /mɪsbɪ'heɪv/ vi
portar-se mal, proceder mal. **~iour**
/-'heɪvɪə(r)/ n mau comportamento
m, má conduta f

miscalculat|e /mɪs'kælkjʊleɪt/
vi calcular mal, enganar-se. **~ion**
/-'leɪʃn/ n erro m de cálculo

miscarr|y /mɪs'kærɪ/ vi abortar
(espontaneamente), ter um
aborto (espontâneo); (fail) falhar,
malograr-se. **~iage** /-ɪdʒ/ n aborto
(espontâneo) m; **~iage of justice**
erro m judiciário

miscellaneous /mɪsə'leɪnɪəs/ a
variado, diverso

mischief /'mɪstʃɪf/ n (of children)
diabrura f, travessura f; (harm)
mal m, dano m; **get into ~** fazer
disparates; **make ~** criar or semear
discórdias

mischievous /'mɪstʃɪvəs/ a
endiabrado, travesso

misconception /mɪskən'sepʃn/
n ideia f errada, (P) ideia f, falso
conceito m

misconduct /mɪs'kɒndʌkt/ n
conduta f imprópria

misconstrue /mɪskən'struː/ vt
interpretar mal

misdemeanour /mɪsdɪ'miːnə(r)/ n delito m

miser /'maɪzə(r)/ n avarento m,
sovina mf. **~ly** a avarento, sovina

miserable /'mɪzrəbl/ a infeliz;
(wretched, mean) desgraçado,
miserável

misery /'mɪzərɪ/ n infelicidade f

misfire /mɪs'faɪə(r)/ vi <plan, gun,
engine> falhar

misfit /'mɪsfɪt/ n inadaptado m

misfortune /mɪs'fɔːtʃən/ n
desgraça f, infelicidade f, pouca
sorte f

misgiving(s) /mɪs'gɪvɪŋ(z)/ n(pl)
dúvida(s) f(pl), receio(s) m(pl)

misguided /mɪs'gaɪdɪd/ a
(mistaken) desencaminhado;
(misled) mal aconselhado, enganado

mishap /'mɪshæp/ n contratempo
m, desastre m

misinform /mɪsɪn'fɔːm/ vt
informar mal

misinterpret /mɪsɪn'tɜːprɪt/ vt
interpretar mal

misjudge /mɪs'dʒʌdʒ/ vt julgar
mal

mislay /mɪs'leɪ/ vt (pt mislaid)
perder, extraviar

mislead /mɪs'liːd/ vt (pt misled)
induzir em erro, enganar. **~ing** a
enganador

mismanage /mɪs'mænɪdʒ/ vt
dirigir mal. **~ment** n má gestão f,
desgoverno m

misnomer /mɪs'nəʊmə(r)/ n
termo m impróprio

misogynist /mɪ'sɒdʒɪnɪst/ n
misógino m

misprint /'mɪsprɪnt/ n erro m
tipográfico

mispronounce /mɪsprə'naʊns/
vt pronunciar mal

misquote /mɪs'kwəʊt/ vt citar
incorretamente

misread /mɪs'riːd/ vt (pt misread
/-'red/) ler or interpretar mal

misrepresent /mɪsreprɪ'zent/ vt
deturpar, desvirtuar

miss /mɪs/ vt/i <chance, bus etc>
perder; <target> errar, falhar; (notice
the loss of) dar pela falta de; (regret
the absence of) sentir a falta de, ter
saudades de; **he ~es her/Portugal**
ele sente a falta or tem saudades
dela/de Portugal/etc; **~ out** omitir;
~ the point não compreender

● falha f; **it was a near ~** foi or escapou por um triz

Miss /mɪs/ n (pl **Misses**) Senhorita f, (P) Menina f

missile /ˈmɪsaɪl/ n míssil m; (object thrown) projétil m

missing /ˈmɪsɪŋ/ a que falta; (lost) perdido; ‹person› desaparecido; **a book with a page ~** um livro com uma página a menos

mission /ˈmɪʃn/ n missão f

missionary /ˈmɪʃənrɪ/ n missionário m

misspell /mɪsˈspel/ vt (pt misspelt or misspelled) escrever mal

mist /mɪst/ n neblina f, névoa f, bruma f, fig névoa f ● vt/i enevoar(-se); ‹window› embaçar(-se)

mistake /mɪˈsteɪk/ n engano m, erro m ● vt (pt mistook, pp mistaken) compreender mal; (choose wrongly) enganar-se em; **~ for** confundir com, tomar por. **~n** /-ən/ a errado; **be ~n** enganar-se. **~nly** /-ənlɪ/ adv por engano

mistletoe /ˈmɪsltəʊ/ n visco m

mistreat /mɪsˈtriːt/ vt maltratar

mistress /ˈmɪstrɪs/ n senhora f, dona f; (teacher) professora f; (lover) amante f

mistrust /mɪsˈtrʌst/ vt desconfiar de, duvidar de ● n desconfiança f

misty /ˈmɪstɪ/ a (-ier, -iest) enevoado, brumoso; ‹window› embaçado; (indistinct) indistinto

misunderstand /mɪsʌndəˈstænd/ vt (pt -stood) compreender mal. **~ing** n mal-entendido m

misuse¹ /mɪsˈjuːz/ vt empregar mal; ‹power etc› abusar de

misuse² /mɪsˈjuːs/ n mau uso m; (abuse) abuso m; (of funds) desvio m

mitten /ˈmɪtn/ n luva f com uma única divisão entre o polegar e os dedos, mitene f

mix /mɪks/ vt/i misturar(-se); **~ with** associar-se com; **~ up** misturar bem; fig (confuse) confundir ● n mistura f. **~up** n trapalhada f, confusão f. **~er** n Culin batedeira f

mixed /mɪkst/ a ‹school etc› misto; (assorted) sortido; **be ~ up** ⚇ estar confuso

mixed-race a ‹couple, marriage› mestiço

mixture /ˈmɪkstʃə(r)/ n mistura f; **cough ~** xarope m para a tosse

MMS abbr (= Multimedia Messaging Service) MMS m

moan /məʊn/ n gemido m ● vi gemer; (complain) queixar-se; lastimar-se (about de)

moat /məʊt/ n fosso m

mob /mɒb/ n multidão f; (tumultuous) turba f; ⚇ (gang) bando m ● vt (pt mobbed) cercar, assediar

mobil∥e /ˈməʊbaɪl/ a móvel; **~e home** caravana f, trailer m; **~e phone** celular m ● n celular m, (P) telemóvel m; **don't forget to switch your ~ off** não se esquece de desligar o celular, (P) não te esqueças de desligar o telemóvel. **~ity** /-ˈbɪlətɪ/ n mobilidade f

mobiliz∥e /ˈməʊbɪlaɪz/ vt/i mobilizar

mock /mɒk/ vt/i zombar de, gozar ● a falso. **~up** n maqueta f

mockery /ˈmɒkərɪ/ n troça f, gozação f, (P) gozo m, (P) um gozo m; **a ~ of** uma gozação de

mode /məʊd/ n modo m; (fashion) moda f

model /ˈmɒdl/ n modelo m ● a modelo; (exemplary) exemplar; (toy) em miniatura ● vt (pt modelled) modelar; ‹clothes› apresentar ● vi ser ou trabalhar como modelo

modem /ˈməʊdem/ n modem m

moderate[1] /ˈmɒdərət/ a & n moderado m. ~ly adv moderadamente; ~ly good sofrível

moderat|e[2] /ˈmɒdəreɪt/ vt/i moderar(-se). ~ion /-ˈreɪʃn/ n moderação f; in ~ion com moderação

modern /ˈmɒdn/ a moderno; ~ languages línguas fpl vivas ou modernas. ~ize vt modernizar

modest /ˈmɒdɪst/ a modesto. ~y n modéstia f

modif|y /ˈmɒdɪfaɪ/ vt modificar. ~ication /-ɪˈkeɪʃn/ n modificação f

module /ˈmɒdjuːl/ n módulo m

moist /mɔɪst/ a (-er, -est) úmido, (P) húmido. ~ure /ˈmɔɪstʃə(r)/ n umidade f, (P) humidade f. ~urizer /-tʃəraɪzə(r)/ n creme m hidratante

moisten /ˈmɔɪsn/ vt/i umedecer, (P) humedecer

mole[1] /məʊl/ n (on skin) sinal m na pele

mole[2] /məʊl/ n (animal) toupeira f

molecule /ˈmɒlɪkjuːl/ n molécula f

molest /məˈlest/ vt meter-se com, molestar

mollycoddle /ˈmɒlɪkɒdl/ vt mimar

molten /ˈməʊltən/ a fundido

moment /ˈməʊmənt/ n momento m

momentar|y /ˈməʊməntrɪ/ a momentâneo. ~ily /ˈməʊməntrəlɪ/

adv momentaneamente

momentous /məˈmentəs/ a grave, importante

momentum /məˈmentəm/ n ímpeto m, velocidade f adquirida

Monaco /ˈmɒnəkəʊ/ n Mônaco m, (P) Mónaco m

monarch /ˈmɒnək/ n monarca mf. ~y n monarquia f

monast|ery /ˈmɒnəstrɪ/ n mosteiro m, convento m. ~ic /məˈnæstɪk/ a monástico

Monday /ˈmʌndɪ/ n segunda-feira f

monetary /ˈmʌnɪtrɪ/ a monetário

money /ˈmʌnɪ/ n dinheiro m; ~ order vale m postal. ~ box n cofre m; ~lender n agiota mf, usurário

mongrel /ˈmʌŋgrəl/ n (cão) vira-lata m, (P) rafeiro m

monitor /ˈmɒnɪtə(r)/ n chefe m de turma; Techn monitor m ● vt controlar; ‹a broadcast› monitorar ou monitorizar (a transmissão)

monk /mʌŋk/ n monge m, frade m

monkey /ˈmʌŋkɪ/ n (pl -eys) macaco m. ~ nut n amendoim m

mono /ˈmɒnəʊ/ n (pl -os) gravação f mono ● a mono invar

monogram /ˈmɒnəgræm/ n monograma m

monologue /ˈmɒnəlɒg/ n monólogo m

monopol|y /məˈnɒpəlɪ/ n monopólio m. ~ize vt monopolizar

monosyllab|le /ˈmɒnəsɪləbl/ n monossílabo m. ~ic /-ˈlæbɪk/ a monossilábico

monotone /ˈmɒnətəʊn/ n tom m uniforme

monoton|ous /məˈnɒtənəs/ a monótono. ~y n monotonia f

monsoon /mɒnˈsuːn/ n monção f

| **monster | most**

monst|er /ˈmɒnstə(r)/ n monstro m. **~rous** a monstruoso

monstrosity /mɒnˈstrɒsəti/ n monstruosidade f

month /mʌnθ/ n mês m

monthly /ˈmʌnθli/ a mensal ● adv mensalmente ● n (periodical) revista f mensal

monument /ˈmɒnjumənt/ n monumento m. **~al** /-ˈmentl/ a monumental

moo /muː/ n mugido m ● vi mugir

mood /muːd/ n humor m, disposição f; **in a good/bad ~** de bom/mau humor. **~y** a de humor instável; (sullen) carrancudo

moon /muːn/ n lua f

moon|light /ˈmuːnlaɪt/ n luar m. **~lit** a iluminado pela lua, enluarado

moonlighting /ˈmuːnlaɪtɪŋ/ n 🆒 segundo emprego m; esp à noite

moor¹ /mʊə(r)/ n charneca f

moor² /mʊə(r)/ vt amarrar, atracar

moose /muːs/ n (pl invar) alce m

moot /muːt/ a discutível ● vt levantar

mop /mɒp/ n esfregão m ● vt (pt mopped) **~ (up)** limpar; **~ of hair** trunfa f

mope /məʊp/ vi estar or andar abatido e triste

moped /ˈməʊped/ n moto f pequena, (P) motorizada f

moral /ˈmɒrəl/ a moral ● n moral f; **~s** moral f, bons costumes mpl

morale /məˈrɑːl/ n moral m

morality /məˈræləti/ n moralidade f

morbid /ˈmɔːbɪd/ a mórbido

more /mɔː(r)/ a & adv mais (**than** (do) que) ● n mais m; **some ~ tea/ pens/etc** mais chá/canetas/etc;

there is no ~ bread não há mais pão; **~ or less** mais ou menos

moreover /mɔːˈrəʊvə(r)/ adv além disso, de mais a mais

morgue /mɔːg/ n morgue f, necrotério m

morning /ˈmɔːnɪŋ/ n manhã f; **in the ~** de manhã

Morocc|o /məˈrɒkəʊ/ n Marrocos m

moron /ˈmɔːrɒn/ n idiota mf

morose /məˈrəʊs/ a taciturno e insociável, carrancudo

morphine /ˈmɔːfiːn/ n morfina f

morsel /ˈmɔːsl/ n bocado (esp de comida) m

mortal /ˈmɔːtl/ a & n mortal mf. **~ity** /mɔːˈtæləti/ n mortalidade f

mortar /ˈmɔːtə(r)/ n argamassa f; (bowl) almofariz m; Mil morteiro m

mortgage /ˈmɔːɡɪdʒ/ n hipoteca f ● vt hipotecar

mortify /ˈmɔːtɪfaɪ/ vt mortificar

mortuary /ˈmɔːtʃərɪ/ n casa f mortuária

mosaic /məʊˈzeɪɪk/ n mosaico m

Moscow /ˈmɒskəʊ/ n Moscou m, (P) Moscovo m

mosque /mɒsk/ n mesquita f

mosquito /məˈskiːtəʊ/ n (pl -oes) mosquito m

moss /mɒs/ n musgo m. **~y** a musgoso

most /məʊst/ a o mais, o maior; (majority) a maioria de, a maior parte de; **for the ~ part** na maior parte, na grande maioria ● n mais m; (majority) a maioria, a maior parte, o máximo ● adv o mais; (very) muito; **at ~** no máximo; **make the ~ of** aproveitar ao máximo,

tirar o melhor partido de. **~ly** adv
sobretudo

motel /məʊ'tel/ n motel m

moth /mɒθ/ n mariposa f, (P)
borboleta f noturna. **(clothes-)~** n
traça f. **~ball** n bola f de naftalina

mother /'mʌðə(r)/ n mãe f;
M~'s Day o Dia da(s) Mãe(s) ● vt
tratar como a um filho. **~hood**
n maternidade f. **~-in-law** n (pl
~s-in-law) sogra f; **~-of-pearl** n
madrepérola f; **~-to-be** n futura mãe
f. **~ly** a maternal

motif /məʊ'tiːf/ n tema m

motion /'məʊʃn/ n movimento m;
(proposal) moção f ● vt/i **~ (to) sb
to** fazer sinal a alguém para. **~less**
a imóvel

motiv|ate /'məʊtɪveɪt/ vt motivar.
~ion /-'veɪʃn/ n motivação f

motive /'məʊtɪv/ n motivo m

motor /'məʊtə(r)/ n motor m; (car)
automóvel m ● a Anat motor; ‹boat›
a motor ● vi ir de automóvel. **~ bike**
🆃 moto f 🆃; **~ car** carro m; **~ cycle**
motocicleta f; **~ cyclist** motociclista
mf; **~ vehicle** veículo m automóvel.
~ing n automobilismo m. **~ized** a
motorizado

motorist /'məʊtərɪst/ n motorista
mf, automobilista mf

motorway /'məʊtəweɪ/ n rodovia
f, (P) autoestrada f

mottled /'mɒtld/ a sarapintado,
pintalgado

motto /'mɒtəʊ/ n (pl **-oes**) divisa
f, lema m

mould[1] /məʊld/ n (container)
forma f, molde m; Culin forma f ● vt
moldar. **~ing** n Archit moldura f

mould[2] /məʊld/ n (fungi) bolor m,
mofo m. **~y** a bolorento

moult /məʊlt/ vi estar na muda

mound /maʊnd/ n monte m
de terra or de pedras; (small hill)
montículo m

mount /maʊnt/ vt/i montar ●
(support) suporte m; (for gem etc)
engaste m; **~ up** aumentar, subir

mountain /'maʊntɪn/ n
montanha f; **~ bike** mountain bike
f, bicicleta f de montanha. **~ous** a
montanhoso

mountaineer /maʊntɪ'nɪə(r)/ n
alpinista mf. **~ing** n alpinismo m

mourn /mɔːn/ vt/i **~ (for)** chorar
(a morte de); **~ (over)** sofrer (por).
~er n pessoa f que acompanha o
enterro. **~ing** n luto m; **in ~ing**
de luto

mournful /'mɔːnfl/ a triste;
(sorrowful) pesaroso

mouse /maʊs/ n (pl **mice**)
camundongo m, (P) rato m. **~mat** n
mousepad m, (P) tapete de rato m

mousetrap /'maʊstræp/ n
ratoeira f

mousse /muːs/ n mousse f

moustache /mə'stɑːʃ/ n bigode m

mouth[1] /maʊθ/ n boca f

mouth[2] /maʊð/ vt/i declamar;
(silently) articular sem som

mouthful /'maʊθfʊl/ n bocado m

mouthpiece /'maʊθpiːs/ n Mus
bocal m, boquilha f; fig (person)
porta-voz mf

mouthwash /'maʊθwɒʃ/ n
líquido m para bochecho

movable /'muːvəbl/ a móvel

move /muːv/ vt/i mover(-se),
mexer(-se), deslocar(-se);
(emotionally) comover; (incite)
convencer, levar a; (act) agir;
(propose) propor; (depart) ir, partir;
(go forward) avançar; **~ (out)**
mudar-se, sair; **~ back** recuar;

~ forward avançar; **~ in** mudar-se para; **~ on!** circulem!; **~ over, please** chegue-se para lá, por favor ● *n* movimento m; (*in game*) jogada f; (*player's turn*) vez f; (*house change*) mudança f; **on the ~** em marcha

movement /'muːvmənt/ n movimento m

movie /'muːvi/ n Amer filme m; **the ~s** o cinema

moving /'muːvɪŋ/ a (*touching*) comovente; (*movable*) móvil; (*in motion*) em movimento

mow /məʊ/ vt (pp mowed, or mown) ceifar; (*lawn*) cortar a grama, (P) relva; **~ down** ceifar. **~er** n (*for lawn*) máquina f de cortar a grama, (P) relva

MP abbr (= Member of Parliament)
▶ MEMBER

MP3 player n MP3 m

Mr /'mɪstə(r)/ n (pl Messrs) Senhor m; **~ Smith** o Sr Smith

Mrs /'mɪsɪz/ n Senhora f; **~ Smith** a Sra Smith; **Mr and ~ Smith** o Sr Smith e a mulher

Ms /mɪz/ n Senhora D. f

much /mʌtʃ/ (more, most) a, adv & n muito m; **very ~** muito, muitíssimo; **you may have as ~ as you need** você pode levar o que precisar; **~ of it** muito or grande parte dele; **so ~ the better/worse** tanto melhor/pior; **how ~?** quanto?; **not ~** não muito; **too ~** demasiado, demais; **he's not ~ of a gardener** não é lá é grande jardineiro

muck /mʌk/ n estrume m; 🔊 (*dirt*) porcaria f ● vi 🔊 **🔊** entreter-se, perder tempo; **~ in** 🔊 ajudar, dar uma mão ● vt **~ up** 🔊 estragar. **~y** a sujo

mucus /'mjuːkəs/ n muco m

mud /mʌd/ n lama f. **~dy** a lamacento, enlameado

muddle /'mʌdl/ vt baralhar, atrapalhar, confundir ● vi **~ through** sair-se bem, desenrascar-se ● n desordem f; (*mix-up*) confusão f, trapalhada f

mudguard /'mʌdɡɑːd/ n para-lama m, (P) para-lamas m

muffle /'mʌfl/ vt abafar; **~ (up)** agasalhar(-se); **~d sounds** sons mpl abafados. **~r** /-ə(r)/ n cachecol m

mug /mʌɡ/ n caneca f; 🔊 (*face*) cara f; 🔊 (*fool*) trouxa mf 🔊 ● vt (pt mugged) assaltar, agredir. **~ger** n assaltante mf. **~ging** n assalto m

muggy /'mʌɡɪ/ a abafado

mule /mjuːl/ n mulo m; (*female*) mula f

mull /mʌl/ vt **~ over** ruminar; fig matutar em

multi- /'mʌltɪ/ pref mult(i)-

multicoloured /'mʌltɪkʌləd/ a multicolor

multinational /mʌltɪ'næʃnəl/ a & n multinacional f

multiple /'mʌltɪpl/ a & n múltiplo m

multipl|y /'mʌltɪplaɪ/ vt/i multiplicar(-se). **~ication** /-ɪ'keɪʃn/ n multiplicação f

multistorey /mʌltɪ'stɔːrɪ/ a (*car park*) em vários níveis, de vários andares

multitude /'mʌltɪtjuːd/ n multidão f

mum¹ /mʌm/ a keep **~** 🔊 ficar calado

mum² /mʌm/ n 🔊 mamãe f 🔊, (P) mamã f 🔊

mumble /'mʌmbl/ vt/i resmungar, resmonear

mummy[1] /ˈmʌmɪ/ n (body) múmia f

mummy[2] /ˈmʌmɪ/ n (esp child's lang) mamãe f, (P) mamã f, mãezinha f 🇬🇧

mumps /mʌmps/ n caxumba f, parotidite f, papeira f

munch /mʌntʃ/ vt mastigar

mundane /mʌnˈdeɪn/ a banal; (worldly) mundano

municipal /mjuːˈnɪsɪpl/ a municipal. **~ity** /-ˈpælətɪ/ n municipalidade f

munitions /mjuːˈnɪʃnz/ npl munições fpl

mural /ˈmjʊərəl/ a & n mural m

murder /ˈmɜːdə(r)/ n assassínio m, assassinato m ● vt assassinar. **~er** n assassino m, assassina f. **~ous** a assassino, sanguinário; (of weapon) mortífero

murky /ˈmɜːkɪ/ a (-ier, -iest) escuro, sombrio

murmur /ˈmɜːmə(r)/ n murmúrio m ● vt/i murmurar

muscle /ˈmʌsl/ n músculo m ● vi **~ in** 🇬🇧 impor-se, intrometer-se

muscular /ˈmʌskjʊlə(r)/ a muscular; (brawny) musculoso

muse /mjuːz/ vi meditar, cismar

museum /mjuːˈzɪəm/ n museu m

mush /mʌʃ/ n papa f de farinha de milho. **~y** a mole; (sentimental) piegas inv

mushroom /ˈmʌʃrʊm/ n cogumelo m ● vi pulular, multiplicar-se com rapidez

music /ˈmjuːzɪk/ n música f. **~al** a musical ● n (show) comédia f musical, musical m. **~al box** n caixa f de música; **~ stand** estante f de música

musician /mjuːˈzɪʃn/ n músico m

musk /mʌsk/ n almíscar m

Muslim /ˈmʊzlɪm/ a & n muçulmano m

mussel /ˈmʌsl/ n mexilhão m

must /mʌst/ v aux dever; **you ~ go** é necessário que você parta; **he ~ be old** ele deve ser velho; **I ~ have done it** eu devo tê-lo feito ● n **be a ~** 🇬🇧 ser imprescindível

mustard /ˈmʌstəd/ n mostarda f

muster /ˈmʌstə(r)/ vt/i juntar(-se), reunir(-se); **pass ~** ser aceitável

musty /ˈmʌstɪ/ a (-ier, -iest) mofado, bolorento

mutation /mjuːˈteɪʃn/ n mutação f

mute /mjuːt/ a & n mudo m

muted /ˈmjuːtɪd/ a (sound) em surdina; (colour) suave

mutilat|e /ˈmjuːtɪleɪt/ vt mutilar. **~ion** /-ˈleɪʃn/ n mutilação f

mutin|y /ˈmjuːtɪnɪ/ n motim m ● vi amotinar-se. **~ous** a amotinado

mutter /ˈmʌtə(r)/ vt/i resmungar

mutton /ˈmʌtn/ n (carne de) carneiro m

mutual /ˈmjuːtʃʊəl/ a mútuo; 🇬🇧 (common) comum. **~ly** adv mutuamente

muzzle /ˈmʌzl/ n focinho m; (device) focinheira f, (P) açaime m; (of gun) boca f ● vt amordaçar; (dog) pôr focinheira(P) açaime em

my /maɪ/ a meu(s), minha(s)

myself /maɪˈself/ pron eu mesmo, eu próprio; (reflexive) me; (after prep) mim (próprio, mesmo); **by ~** sozinho

mysterious /mɪˈstɪərɪəs/ a misterioso

mystery /ˈmɪstərɪ/ n mistério m

mystic /'mɪstɪk/ a & n místico m. **~al** a místico. **~ism** /-sɪzəm/ n misticismo m

mystify /'mɪstɪfaɪ/ vt deixar perplexo

mystique /mɪ'stiːk/ n mística f

myth /mɪθ/ n mito m. **~ical** a mítico

mytholog|y /mɪ'θɒlədʒɪ/ n mitologia f. **~ical** /mɪθə'lɒdʒɪkl/ a mitológico

Nn

nab /næb/ vt (pt nabbed) 🅧 apanhar em flagrante; apanhar com a boca na botija 🅣; pilhar

nag /næg/ vt/i (pt nagged) implicar (com), criticar constantemente; (pester) apoquentar

nail /neɪl/ n prego m; (of finger, toe) unha f; (of polish esmalte m, (P) verniz m para as unhas; **hit the ~ on the head** acertar em cheio; **on the ~** sem demora ● vt pregar. **~ file** n lixa f de unhas

naïve /naɪ'iːv/ a ingênuo, (P) ingénuo

naked /'neɪkɪd/ a nu; **to the ~ eye** a olho nu, à vista desarmada. **~ness** n nudez f

name /neɪm/ n nome m; fig reputação f; fama f ● vt (mention; appoint) nomear; (give a name to) chamar, dar o nome de; ‹a date› marcar; **be ~d after** ter o nome de. **~less** a sem nome, anônimo, (P) anónimo

namely /'neɪmlɪ/ adv a saber

namesake /'neɪmseɪk/ n homônimo m, (P) homónimo m

nanny /'nænɪ/ n ama f, babá f

nap¹ /næp/ n soneca f ● vi (pt napped) dormitar, tirar um cochilo, fazer uma sesta; **catch ~ping** apanhar desprevenido

nap² /næp/ n (of material) felpa f

napkin /'næpkɪn/ n guardanapo m; (for baby) fralda f

nappy /'næpɪ/ n fralda f. **~ rash** n assadura f

narcotic /nɑː'kɒtɪk/ a & n narcótico m

narrat|e /nə'reɪt/ vt narrar. **~ion** /-ʃn/ n narrativa f. **~or** n narrador m

narrative /'nærətɪv/ n narrativa f ● a narrativo

narrow /'nærəʊ/ a (-er, -est) estreito; fig restrito ● vt/i estreitar(-se); (limit) limitar(-se). **~ly** adv (only just) por pouco; (closely, carefully) de perto, com cuidado. **~-minded** a a bitolado, de visão limitada

nasal /'neɪzl/ a nasal

nast|y /'nɑːstɪ/ a (-ier, -iest) (malicious, of weather) mau; (unpleasant) desagradável, intragável; (rude) grosseiro

nation /'neɪʃn/ n nação f. **~wide** a em todo o país, em escala or a nível nacional

national /'næʃnəl/ a nacional ● n natural mf; **~ anthem** hino m nacional. **~ism** n nacionalismo m. **~ize** vt nacionalizar

nationality /næʃə'nælətɪ/ n nacionalidade f

National Trust Fundação britânica cujo objetivo é a conservação de lugares de interesse histórico ou de beleza natural. É financiada por doações e subvenções privadas. É a maior proprietária de terras da Grã-Bretanha. Na Escócia, é um organismo independente chamado *National Trust for Scotland*.

native /'neɪtɪv/ *n* natural *mf*, nativo *m* ● *a* nativo; (country) natal; (inborn) inato; **be a ~ of** ser natural de; **~ language** língua *f* materna; **~ speaker of Portuguese** falante *m* nativo de Português

Nativity /nə'tɪvəti/ *n* **the ~** a Natividade *f*

natter /'nætə(r)/ *vi* fazer conversa fiada, falar à toa, tagarelar

natural /'nætʃrəl/ *a* natural; **~ history** história *f* natural. **~ist** *n* naturalista *mf*. **~ly** *adv* naturalmente; (by nature) por natureza

naturaliz|e /'nætʃrəlaɪz/ *vt/i* naturalizar(-se); (animal, plant) aclimatar(-se). **~ation** /-'zeɪʃn/ *n* naturalização *f*

nature /'neɪtʃə(r)/ *n* natureza *f*; (kind) gênero *m*, (P) género *m*; (of person) índole *f*

naughty /'nɔ:ti/ *a* (-ier, -iest) (child) levado; (indecent) picante

nause|a /'nɔ:sɪə/ *n* náusea *f*. **~ating**, **~ous** *a* nauseabundo, repugnante

nautical /'nɔ:tɪkl/ *a* náutico; **~ mile** milha *f* marítima

naval /'neɪvl/ *a* naval; (officer) de marinha

nave /neɪv/ *n* nave *f*

navel /'neɪvl/ *n* umbigo *m*

navigable /'nævɪɡəbl/ *a* navegável

navigat|e /'nævɪɡeɪt/ *vt* (sea etc) navegar; (ship) pilotar ● *vi* navegar.

~ion /-'ɡeɪʃn/ *n* navegação *f*. **~or** *n* navegador *m*

navy /'neɪvi/ *n* marinha *f* de guerra; **~ (blue)** azul-marinho *m invar*

near /nɪə(r)/ *adv* perto, quase; **~ to** perto de; **draw ~** aproximar(-se) (to de) ● *prep* perto de ● *a* próximo; **N~ East** Oriente *m* Próximo, (P) Próximo Oriente *m* ● *vt* aproximar-se de, chegar-se a. **~ by** *adv* perto, próximo. **~ness** *n* proximidade *f*

nearby /'nɪəbaɪ/ *a* & *adv* próximo, perto

nearly /'nɪəli/ *adv* quase, por pouco; **not ~ as pretty/etc as** longe de ser tão bonita/etc como

neat /ni:t/ *a* (-er, -est) (bem) cuidado; (room) bem arrumado; (spirits) puro, sem gelo. **~ly** *adv* (with care) com cuidado; (cleverly) habilmente. **~ness** *n* aspecto *m* cuidado

necessar|y /'nesəsəri/ *a* necessário. **~ily** *adv* necessariamente

necessitate /nɪ'sesɪteɪt/ *vt* exigir, obrigar a, tornar necessário

necessity /nɪ'sesəti/ *n* necessidade *f*; (thing) coisa *f* indispensável, artigo *m* de primeira necessidade

neck /nek/ *n* pescoço *m*; (of dress) gola *f*; **~ and neck** emparelhados

necklace /'neklɪs/ *n* colar *m*

neckline /'neklaɪn/ *n* decote *m*

nectarine /'nektərɪn/ *n* pêssego *m*

née /neɪ/ *a* em solteira; **Ann Jones ~ Drewe** Ann Jones cujo nome de solteira era Drewe

need /ni:d/ *n* necessidade *f* ● *vt* precisar de, necessitar de; **you ~ not come** não tem de or não precisa (de) vir. **~less** *a* inútil, desnecessário. **~lessly** *adv* inutilmente, sem necessidade

needle /ˈniːdl/ n agulha f ● vt T (*provoke*) provocar

needlework /ˈniːdlwɜːk/ n costura f; (*embroidery*) bordado m

needy /ˈniːdɪ/ a (-**ier, -iest**) necessitado, carenciado, carente

negation /nɪˈɡeɪʃn/ n negação f

negative /ˈneɡətɪv/ a negativo ● n negativa f, negação f; Photo negativo m; **in the** ~ ‹*answer*› na negativa; Gram na forma negativa. ~**ly** adv negativamente

neglect /nɪˈɡlekt/ vt descuidar; ‹*opportunity*› desprezar; ‹*family*› não cuidar de; ‹*duty*› não cumprir; ~ **to** (*omit to*) esquecer-se de ● n falta f de cuidado(s), descuido m; **(state of)** ~ abandono m. ~**ful** a negligente

negligen|t /ˈneɡlɪdʒənt/ a negligente. ~**ce** n negligência f, desleixo m

negligible /ˈneɡlɪdʒəbl/ a insignificante, ínfimo

negotiable /nɪˈɡəʊʃəbl/ a negociável

negotiat|e /nɪˈɡəʊʃɪeɪt/ vt/i negociar; ‹*obstacle*› transpor; ‹*difficulty*› vencer. ~**ion** /-sɪˈeɪʃn/ n negociação f. ~**or** n negociador m

Negro /ˈniːɡrəʊ/ a & n (pl **oes**) negro m, preto m

neigh /neɪ/ n relincho m ● vi relinchar

neighbour /ˈneɪbə(r)/ n vizinho m. ~**hood** n vizinhança f. ~**ing** a vizinho. ~**ly** a de boa vizinhança

neither /ˈnaɪðə(r)/ a & pron nenhum(a) (de dois ou duas), nem um nem outro, nem uma nem outra ● adv tampouco, também não ● conj nem; ~ **big nor small** nem grande

nem pequeno; ~ **am I** nem eu

neocon /ˈniːəʊkɒn/ a & n neoconservador mf

neon /ˈniːɒn/ n néon m

nephew /ˈnevjuː/ n sobrinho m

nerve /nɜːv/ n nervo m; fig (*courage*) coragem f, T (*impudence*) descaramento m, (P) lata f T; **get on sb's nerves** irritar, dar nos nervos de alguém. ~**racking** a de arrasar os nervos, enervante

nervous /ˈnɜːvəs/ a nervoso; **be** or **feel** ~ (*afraid*) ter receio/um certo medo; ~ **breakdown** esgotamento m nervoso. ~**ly** adv nervosamente. ~**ness** n nervosismo m; (*fear*) receio m

nest /nest/ n ninho m ● vi aninhar-se, fazer or ter ninho. ~ **egg** n pé-de-meia m

nestle /ˈnesl/ vi aninhar-se

net[1] /net/ n rede f ● vt (pt **netted**) apanhar na rede. ~**ting** n rede f; **wire** ~**ting** rede f de arame

net[2] /net/ a ‹*weight etc*› líquido

Netherlands /ˈneðələndz/ npl **the** ~ os Países Baixos

nettle /ˈnetl/ n urtiga f

network /ˈnetwɜːk/ n rede f, cadeia f

neuro|sis /njʊəˈrəʊsɪs/ n (pl -**oses** /-siːz/) neurose f. ~**tic** /-ˈrɒtɪk/ a & n neurótico n

neuter /ˈnjuːtə(r)/ a & n neutro m ● vt castrar, capar

neutral /ˈnjuːtrəl/ a neutro; ~ **(gear)** ponto m morto. ~**ity** /-ˈtrælətɪ/ n neutralidade f

never /ˈnevə(r)/ adv nunca; T (*not*) não; **he** ~ **refuses** ele nunca recusa; **I** ~ **saw him** T nunca o vi; ~ **mind** não faz mal, deixe para lá. ~**ending** a interminável

nevertheless /nevəðə'les/ *adv* &
conj contudo, no entanto

new /nju:/ *a* (-er, -est) novo; ~
moon lua *f* nova; ~ **year** ano *m*
novo; **N~ Year's Day** dia *m* de
Ano Novo; **N~ Year's Eve** véspera
f de Ano Novo; **N~ Zealand**
Nova Zelândia *f*; **N~ Zealander**
neozelandês *m*. **~born** *a* recém-
nascido. **~ness** *n* novidade *f*

New Age *n* Nova Era *f*, o
Movimento Nova Era *f*

newcomer /nju:kʌmə(r)/ *n*
recém-chegado *m*

newfangled /nju:'fæŋgld/ *a pej*
moderno

newly /nju:lɪ/ *adv* há pouco,
recentemente. **~weds** *npl* recém-
casados *mpl*

news /nju:z/ *n* notícia(s) *f*(*pl*);
Radio noticiário *m*, notícia(s) *fpl*;
TV telejornal *m*. **~caster**, **~reader**
n locutor *m*; **~flash** *n* notícia *f* de
última hora

newsagent /nju:zeɪdʒənt/ *n*
jornaleiro *m*

newsletter /nju:zletə(r)/ *n*
boletim *m* informativo

newspaper /nju:zpeɪpə(r)/ *n*
jornal *m*

newsreel /nju:zri:l/ *n* atualidades
fpl

newt /nju:t/ *n* tritão *m*

next /nekst/ *a* próximo; (*adjoining*)
pegado, ao lado, contíguo;
(*following*) seguinte ● *adv* a seguir;
~ **to** ao lado de; ~ **to nothing**
quase nada ● *n* seguinte *mf*; ~ **of kin**
parente *m* mais próximo. **~door**
a do lado

nib /nɪb/ *n* bico *m*, (*P*) aparo *m*

nibble /nɪbl/ *vt* mordiscar, dar
dentadinhas em

nice /naɪs/ *a* (-er, -est) agradável,
bom; (*kind*) simpático, gentil;
(*pretty*) bonito; (*respectable*) bem-
educado; correto; (*subtle*) fino,
subtil. **~ly** *adv* agradavelmente;
(*well*) bem

nicety /naɪsətɪ/ *n* sutileza *f*, (*P*)
subtileza *f*

niche /nɪtʃ/ *n* nicho *m*; *fig* bom
lugar *m*

nick /nɪk/ *n* corte *m*, chanfradura
f; ⓧ (*prison*) cadeia *f* ● *vt* dar um
corte em; ⓧ (*steal*) roubar, limpar
①; ⓧ (*arrest*) apanhar; pôr a mão
em ①; **in good** ~ ⓧ em boa forma,
em bom estado; **in the** ~ **of time**
mesmo a tempo

nickel /nɪkl/ *n* níquel *m*; *Amer*
moeda *f* de cinco cêntimos

nickname /nɪkneɪm/ *n* apelido *m*,
(*P*) alcunha *f*; (*short form*) diminutivo
m ● *vt* apelidar de

nicotine /nɪkəti:n/ *n* nicotina *f*

niece /ni:s/ *n* sobrinha *f*

Nigeria /naɪ'dʒɪərɪə/ *n* Nigéria *f*.
~n *a* & *n* nigeriano *m*

night /naɪt/ *n* noite *f*; **at** ~ à/de
noite; **by** ~ de noite ● *a* de noite,
noturno. **~cap** *n* (*drink*) bebida *f*
tomada na hora de deitar; **~club** *n*
boate *f*, (*P*) boîte *f*; **~dress**, **~gown**
ns camisola *f* de dormir, (*P*) camisa
f de noite; **~life** *n* vida *f* noturna;
~ **school** *n* escola *f* noturna; ~ **time**
n noite *f*

nightfall /naɪtfɔ:l/ *n* anoitecer *m*

nightingale /naɪtɪŋgeɪl/ *n*
rouxinol *m*

nightly /naɪtlɪ/ *a* noturno ● *adv* de
noite, à noite, todas as noites

nightmare /'naɪtmeə(r)/ n pesadelo m

nil /nɪl/ n nada m; *Sport* zero m ● a nulo

nimble /'nɪmbl/ a (-er, -est) ágil, ligeiro

nin|e /naɪn/ a & n nove m. **~th** a & n nono m

nineteen /naɪn'tiːn/ a & n dezenove m, (P) dezanove m. **~th** a & n décimo nono m

ninet|y /'naɪntɪ/ a & n noventa m. **~ieth** a & n nonagésimo m

nip /nɪp/ vt/i (pt nipped) apertar, beliscar; ⊤ (rush) ir correndo; ir num pulo ⊤; **~ in the bud** cortar pela raiz ● n aperto m, beliscão m; (drink) gole m, trago m; **a ~ in the air** um frio cortante

nipple /'nɪpl/ n mamilo m

nippy /'nɪpɪ/ a (-ier, -iest) ⊤ (quick) rápido; ⊤ (chilly) cortante

nitrogen /'naɪtrədʒən/ n azoto m, nitrogênio m, (P) nitrogénio m

nitwit /'nɪtwɪt/ n ⊤ imbecil m

no /nəʊ/ a & n nenhum; **~ entry** entrada f proibida; **~ money/time/** etc nenhum dinheiro/tempo/etc; **~ man's land** terra f de ninguém; **~ one** ▶ NOBODY ● adv não; **~ smoking** é proibido fumar; **~ way!** ⊤ de modo nenhum! ● n (pl noes) não m

nob|le /'nəʊbl/ a (-er, -est) nobre. **~ility** /-'bɪlətɪ/ n nobreza f

nobleman /'nəʊblmən/ n (pl -men) nobre m, fidalgo m

nobody /'nəʊbɒdɪ/ pron ninguém ● n nulidade f; **he knows ~** ele não conhece ninguém; **~ is there** não tem ninguém lá, (P) não está lá ninguém

no-brainer /nəʊ'breɪnə(r)/ n trivialidade f

nocturnal /nɒk'tɜːnl/ a noturno

nod /nɒd/ vt/i (pt nodded) **~ (one's head)** acenar (com) a cabeça; **~ (off)** cabecear ● n aceno m com a cabeça (para dizer que sim ou para cumprimentar)

noise /nɔɪz/ n ruído m, barulho m. **~less** a silencioso

nois|y /'nɔɪzɪ/ a (-ier, -iest) ruidoso, barulhento

nomad /'nəʊmæd/ n nômada mf, (P) nómada m. **~ic** /-'mædɪk/ a nômada, (P) nómada

nominal /'nɒmɪnl/ a nominal; <fee, sum> simbólico

nominat|e /'nɒmɪneɪt/ vt (appoint) nomear; (put forward) propor. **~ion** /-'neɪʃn/ n nomeação f

non- /nɒn/ pref não, sem, in-, a-, anti-, des-. **~stick** a não-aderente

nonchalant /'nɒnʃələnt/ a indiferente, desinteressado

non-commissioned /nɒnkə-'mɪʃnd/ a **~ officer** sargento m, cabo m

non-committal /nɒnkə'mɪtl/ a evasivo

nondescript /'nɒndɪskrɪpt/ a insignificante, medíocre, indefinível

none /nʌn/ pron (person) nenhum, ninguém; (thing) nenhum, nada; **~ of us** nenhum de nós; **I have ~** não tenho nenhum; **~ of that!** nada dissol ● adv **~ too** não muito; **he is ~ the happier** nem por isso ele é mais feliz; **~ the less** contudo, no entanto, apesar disso

nonentity /nɒ'nentətɪ/ n nulidade f, zero à m esquerda, João Ninguém m

non-existent /nɒnɪg'zɪstənt/ a
inexistente

nonplussed /nɒn'plʌst/ a
perplexo, pasmado

nonsens|e /'nɒnsns/ n absurdo
m, disparate m. **~ical** /-'sensɪkl/ a
absurdo, disparatado

non-smoker /nɒn'sməʊkə(r)/ n
nãofumante m, (P) nãofumador m

non-stop /nɒn'stɒp/ a
ininterrupto, contínuo; ‹train›
direto; ‹flight› sem escala ● adv
sem parar

noodles /'nuːdlz/ npl talharim m,
(P) macarronete m

nook /nʊk/ n (re)canto m

noon /nuːn/ n meio-dia m

noose /nuːs/ n laço m corrediço

nor /nɔː(r)/ conj & adv nem, também
não; **~ do I** nem eu

norm /nɔːm/ n norma f

normal /'nɔːml/ a & n normal
m; **above/below ~** acima/abaixo
do normal. **~ity** /nɔː'mælətɪ/ n
normalidade f. **~ly** adv normalmente

north /nɔːθ/ n norte m ● a norte,
do norte; (of country, people etc)
setentrional ● adv a, ao/para o
norte; **N~ America** América f do
Norte. **~erly** /'nɔːðəlɪ/ a do norte.
~ward(s) adv para o norte. **N~
American** a & n norte-americano
m; **~east** n nordeste m; **~west** n
noroeste m

northern /'nɔːðən/ a do norte

Norw|ay /'nɔːweɪ/ n Noruega
f. **~egian** /nɔː'wiːdʒən/ a & n
norueguês m

nose /nəʊz/ n nariz m; (of animal)
focinho m ● vi **~ about** farejar; **pay
through the ~** pagar um preço
exorbitante

nosebleed /'nəʊzbliːd/ n
hemorragia f nasal or pelo nariz

nosedive /'nəʊzdaɪv/ n voo m
picado

nostalg|ia /nɒ'stældʒə/ n
nostalgia f. **~ic** a nostálgico

nostril /'nɒstrəl/ n narina f; (of
horse) venta f (usually pl)

nosy /'nəʊzɪ/ a (-ier, -iest) 🅣
bisbilhoteiro

---

not /nɒt/ ● adv

••••➤ não; **~ at all** nada, de
modo nenhum; (reply to thanks)
de nada; **he is ~ at all bored**
ele não está nem um pouco
entediado; **~ yet** ainda não;
I suppose ~ creio que não

---

notable /'nəʊtəbl/ a notável ● n
notabilidade f

notably /'nəʊtəblɪ/ adv
notavelmente; (particularly)
especialmente

notch /nɒtʃ/ n corte m em V ● vt
marcar com cortes; **~ up** ‹score
etc› marcar

note /nəʊt/ n nota f; (banknote)
nota (de banco) f; (short letter)
bilhete m ● vt notar

notebook /'nəʊtbʊk/ n livrinho m
de notas, (P) bloco m de notas

noted /'nəʊtɪd/ a conhecido,
famoso

notepaper /'nəʊtpeɪpə(r)/ n
papel m de carta

noteworthy /'nəʊtwɜːðɪ/ a
notável

nothing /'nʌθɪŋ/ n nada m;
(person) nulidade f, zero m; **he
eats ~** ele não come nada; **~ big**
etc nada (de) grande/etc; **~ else**

nada mais; **~ much** pouca coisa; **for ~** (free) de graça; (in vain) em vão ● adv nada, de modo algum ou nenhum, de maneira alguma ou nenhuma

notice /'nəʊtɪs/ n o anúncio m, notícia f; (in street, on wall) letreiro m; (warning) aviso m; (attention) atenção f; **(advance) ~** pré-aviso m; **at short ~** num prazo curto; **a week's ~** o prazo de uma semana; **hand in one's ~** pedir demissão; **take ~** reparar (of em); **take no ~** não fazer caso (of de) ● vt notar, reparar. **~board** n quadro m para afixar anúncios etc

noticeabl|e /'nəʊtɪsəbl/ a visível. **~y** adv visivelmente

notif|y /'nəʊtɪfaɪ/ vt participar, notificar. **~ication** /-ɪ'keɪʃn/ n participação f, notificação f

notion /'nəʊʃn/ n noção f

notor|ious /nəʊ'tɔːrɪəs/ a notório. **~iety** /-ə'raɪətɪ/ n fama f

notwithstanding /nɒtwɪθ'stændɪŋ/ prep apesar de, não obstante ● adv mesmo assim, ainda assim ● conj embora, conquanto, apesar de (que)

nougat /'nuːgɑː/ n nugá m, torrone m, (P) nogado m

nought /nɔːt/ n zero m

noun /naʊn/ n substantivo m, nome m

nourish /'nʌrɪʃ/ vt alimentar, nutrir. **~ing** a alimentício, nutritivo. **~ment** n alimento m, sustento m

novel /'nɒvl/ n romance m ● a novo, original. **~ist** n romancista mf. **~ty** n novidade f

November /nəʊ'vembə(r)/ n novembro m

novice /'nɒvɪs/ n (beginner) noviço m, novato m; Relig noviço m

now /naʊ/ adv agora; **by ~** a estas horas, por esta altura; **from ~ on** de agora em diante; **~ and again, ~ and then** de vez em quando; **right ~** já ● conj **~ (that)** agora que

nowadays /'naʊədeɪz/ adv hoje em dia, presentemente, atualmente

nowhere /'nəʊweə(r)/ adv (position) em lugar nenhum, em lado nenhum; (direction) a lado nenhum, a parte alguma or nenhuma

nozzle /'nɒzl/ n bico m, bocal m; (of hose) agulheta f

nuance /'njuːɑːns/ n nuance f, matiz m

nuclear /'njuːklɪə(r)/ a nuclear

nucleus /'njuːklɪəs/ n (pl **-lei** /-lɪaɪ/) núcleo m

nud|e /njuːd/ a & n nu m; **in the ~e** nu. **~ity** n nudez f

nudge /nʌdʒ/ vt tocar com o cotovelo, cutucar ● n ligeira cotovelada f, cutucada f

nudis|t /'njuːdɪst/ n nudista mf

nuisance /'njuːsns/ n aborrecimento m; chatice f ⊠; (person) chato m ⊠

null /nʌl/ a nulo; **~ and void** Jur írrito e nulo

numb /nʌm/ a entorpecido, dormente ● vt entorpecer, adormecer

number /'nʌmbə(r)/ n número m; (numeral) algarismo m ● vt numerar; (amount to) ser em número de; (count) contar, incluir. **~ plate** n chapa (do carro) f, (P) matrícula f (do carro)

numeral /'nju:mərəl/ n número m, algarismo m

numerate /'nju:mərət/ a que tem conhecimentos básicos de matemática

numerical /nju:'merɪkl/ a numérico

numerous /'nju:mərəs/ a numeroso

nun /nʌn/ n freira f, religiosa f

nurs|e /nɜːs/ n enfermeira f, enfermeiro m; (nanny) ama(-seca) f, babá f ● vt cuidar de, tratar de; ‹hopes etc› alimentar, acalentar. **~ing** n enfermagem f; **~ing home** clínica f de repouso, (P) lar m de idosos

nursery /'nɜːsərɪ/ n quarto m de crianças; (for plants) viveiro m; **(day) ~ creche** f; **~ rhyme** poema or canção f infantil m; **~ school** jardim m de infância

nurture /'nɜːtʃə(r)/ vt educar

nut /nʌt/ n Bot noz f; Techn porca f de parafuso

nutcrackers /'nʌtkrækəz/ npl quebra-nozes m invar

nutmeg /'nʌtmeg/ n noz-moscada f

nutrient /'nju:trɪənt/ n substância f nutritiva, nutriente m

nutrit|ion /nju:'trɪʃn/ n nutrição f. **~ious** a nutritivo

nutshell /'nʌtʃel/ n casca f de noz; **in a ~** em poucas palavras, em suma

nuzzle /'nʌzl/ vt esfregar com o focinho

nylon /'naɪlɒn/ n nylon m; **~s** meias fpl de nylon

Oo

oak /əʊk/ n carvalho m

OAP abbr (= old-age pensioner) ▶ OLD

oar /ɔː(r)/ n remo m

oasis /əʊ'eɪsɪs/ n (pl oases /-siːz/) oásis m

oath /əʊθ/ n juramento m; (swear word) praga f

oatmeal /'əʊtmiːl/ n farinha f de aveia; (porridge) papa f de aveia

oats /əʊts/ npl aveia f

obedien|t /ə'biːdɪənt/ a obediente. **~ce** n obediência f

obes|e /əʊ'biːs/ a obeso. **~ity** n obesidade f

obey /ə'beɪ/ vt/i obedecer (a)

obituary /ə'bɪtʃʊərɪ/ n necrológio m, (P) necrologia f

object[1] /'ɒbdʒɪkt/ n objeto m; (aim) objetivo m; Gram complemento m

object[2] /əb'dʒekt/ vt/i objetar (que); **~ to** opor-se a, discordar de. **~ion** /-ʃn/ n objeção f

objectionable /əb'dʒekʃnəbl/ a censurável; (unpleasant) desagradável

objectiv|e /əb'dʒektɪv/ a objetivo. **~ity** /-'tɪvətɪ/ n objetividade f

obligation /ɒblɪ'geɪʃn/ n obrigação f; **be under an ~ to sb** dever favores a alguém

obligatory /ə'blɪgətrɪ/ a obrigatório

oblig|e /ə'blaɪdʒ/ vt obrigar; (do a favour) fazer um favor a, obsequiar. **~ed** a obrigado (**to** a); **~ed to** s

em dívida (para) com alguém. **~ing**
a prestável, amável

oblique /əˈbliːk/ a oblíquo

obliterat|e /əˈblɪtəreɪt/
vt obliterar. **~ion** /-ˈreɪʃn/ n
obliteração f

oblivion /əˈblɪvɪən/ n
esquecimento m

oblivious /əˈblɪvɪəs/ a esquecido;
sem consciência (**of/to** de)

oblong /ˈɒblɒŋ/ a oblongo,
alongado ● n retângulo m

obnoxious /əbˈnɒkʃəs/ a ofensivo,
detestável

oboe /ˈəʊbəʊ/ n oboé m

obscen|e /əbˈsiːn/ a obsceno. **~ity**
/-ˈenəti/ n obscenidade f

obscur|e /əbˈskjʊə(r)/ a obscuro
● vt obscurecer; (*conceal*) encobrir.
~ity n obscuridade f

obsequious /əbˈsiːkwɪəs/
a demasiado obsequioso,
subserviente

observan|t /əbˈzɜːvənt/ a
observador. **~ce** n observância f,
cumprimento m

observatory /əbˈzɜːvətrɪ/ n
observatório m

observ|e /əbˈzɜːv/ vt observar.
~ation /ɒbzəˈveɪʃn/ n observação
f; **keep under ~ation** vigiar. **~er** n
observador m

obsess /əbˈses/ vt obcecar. **~ion**
/-ʃn/ n obsessão f. **~ive** a obsessivo

obsessive-compulsive
disorder n transtorno obsessivo-
compulsivo m

obsolete /ˈɒbsəliːt/ a obsoleto,
antiquado

obstacle /ˈɒbstəkl/ n obstáculo m

obstetric|s /əbˈstetrɪks/ n
obstetrícia f. **~ian** /ɒbstɪˈtrɪʃn/ n
obstetra mf

obstina|te /ˈɒbstɪnət/ a
obstinado. **~cy** n obstinação f

obstruct /əbˈstrʌkt/ vt obstruir,
bloquear; (*hinder*) estorvar, obstruir.
~ion /-ʃn/ n obstrução f; (*thing*)
obstáculo m

obtain /əbˈteɪn/ vt obter ● vi
prevalecer, estar em vigor. **~able** a
que se pode obter

obtrusive
/əbˈtruːsɪv/ a importuno; ‹thing›
demasiado em evidência; que
dá muito na(s) vista(s) 🔲

obvious /ˈɒbvɪəs/ a óbvio,
evidente. **~ly** adv obviamente

occasion /əˈkeɪʒn/ n ocasião
f; (*event*) acontecimento m ● vt
ocasionar; **on ~** de vez em quando,
ocasionalmente

occasional /əˈkeɪʒənl/ a
ocasional. **~ly** adv de vez em
quando, ocasionalmente

occult /ɒˈkʌlt/ a oculto

occupation /ɒkjʊˈpeɪʃn/ n
ocupação f. **~al** a profissional;
‹therapy› ocupacional

occup|y /ˈɒkjʊpaɪ/ vt ocupar. **~ant**
~ier ns ocupante mf

occur /əˈkɜː(r)/ vi (*pt* occurred)
ocorrer, acontecer, dar-se; (*arise*)
apresentar-se, aparecer; **~ to sb**
ocorrer a alguém

occurrence /əˈkʌrəns/ n
acontecimento m, ocorrência f

ocean /ˈəʊʃn/ n oceano m

o'clock /əˈklɒk/ adv **it is one ~** é
uma hora; **it is six ~** são seis horas

octagon /ˈɒktəɡən/ n octógono m.
~al /-ˈtæɡənl/ a octogonal

October /ɒkˈtəʊbə(r)/ n outubro m

octopus /ˈɒktəpəs/ n (*pl* -puses)
polvo m

odd /ɒd/ a (-er, -est) estranho, singular; ‹number› ímpar; (left over) de sobra; (not of set) desemparelhado; (occasional) ocasional; ~ **jobs** (paid) biscates *mpl*; (in garden etc) trabalhos *mpl* diversos; **twenty** ~ vinte e tantos. ~**ity** n singularidade f; (thing) curiosidade f. ~**ly** adv de modo estranho

oddment /'ɒdmənt/ n resto m, artigo m avulso

odds /ɒdz/ npl probabilidades *fpl*; (in betting) ganhos *mpl* líquidos; **at** ~ em desacordo; (quarrelling) de mal, brigado; **it makes no** ~ não faz diferença; ~ **and ends** artigos *mpl* avulsos, coisas *fpl* pequenas

odious /'əʊdɪəs/ a odioso

odour /'əʊdə(r)/ n odor m. ~**less** a inodoro

of /əv emphatic ɒv/ ● prep

····➤ de; **a friend** ~ **mine** um amigo meu; **the mother** ~ **the twins** a mãe dos gêmeos; **the fifth** ~ **June** (dia) cinco de junho; **take six** ~ **them** leve seis deles; **the works** ~ **Shakespeare** as obras de Shakespeare; **made** ~ **gold** (feito) de ouro

! the preposition de often contracts with: definite articles o and a to form do, da; demonstrative pronouns este, esse, aquele, isto, isso, aquilo to form deste, desse, daquele, disto, disso, daquilo; personal pronouns ele, ela to form dele, dela.

····➤ (on the part of) da parte de; **it was nice** ~ **him/John** foi simpático da parte dele/da parte do John →For translations of expressions such as **of course**

and **consist of** see entries **course** and **consist**

off /ɒf/ adv embora, fora; (switched off) apagado, desligado; (taken off) tirado, desligado; (cancelled) cancelado; ‹food› estragado; **be well** ~ ser abastado ● prep (fora) de; (distant from) a alguma distância de; **be** ~ (depart) ir-se embora, partir; **be better/worse** ~ estar em melhor/pior situação; **a day** ~ um dia de folga; **20%** ~ redução de 20%; **on the** ~ **chance that** no caso de; ~ **colour** indisposto, adoentado. ~ **licence** n loja f de bebidas alcoólicas; ‹load› vt descarregar; ~**putting** a desconcertante; ~**stage** adv fora de cena; ~**white** a branco-sujo

offal /'ɒfl/ n miudezas *fpl*, fressura f

offence /ə'fens/ n (feeling) ofensa f; (crime) delito m, transgressão f; **give** ~ **to** ofender; **take** ~ ofender-se (at com)

offend /ə'fend/ vt ofender; **be** ~**ed** ofender-se (at com). ~**er** n delinquente m/f

offensive /ə'fensɪv/ a ofensivo; (disgusting) repugnante ● n ofensiva f

offer /'ɒfə(r)/ vt (pt offered) oferecer ● n oferta f; **on** ~ em promoção. ~**ing** n oferenda f

offhand /ɒf'hænd/ a espontâneo; (curt) seco ● adv de improviso, sem pensar

office /'ɒfɪs/ n escritório m; (post) cargo m; (branch) filial f; ~ **hours** horas *fpl* de expediente; **in** ~ no poder; **take** ~ assumir o cargo

officer /'ɒfɪsə(r)/ n oficial m; (policeman) agente m

official /əˈfɪʃl/ *a* oficial ● *n* funcionário *m*. **~ly** *adv* oficialmente

officiate /əˈfɪʃɪeɪt/ *vi* Relig oficiar; **~ as** presidir, exercer as funções de

officious /əˈfɪʃəs/ *a* intrometido

offing /ˈɒfɪŋ/ *n* **in the ~** *fig* em perspectiva

off-licence No Reino Unido, toda e qualquer loja que tenha uma licença para vender bebidas alcoólicas que devem ser consumidas fora do local. Abrem quando os *pubs* estão fechados e também costumam vender bebidas não alcoólicas, tabaco, guloseimas, etc. Muitas vezes alugam copos para festas, etc.

offset /ˈɒfset/ *vt* (*pt* **-set**, *pres p* **-setting**) compensar, contrabalançar

offshoot /ˈɒfʃuːt/ *n* rebento *m*; *fig* efeito *m* secundário

offshore /ˈɒfʃɔː(r)/ *a* ao largo da costa

offside /ɒfˈsaɪd/ *a* & *adv* offside, em impedimento, (P) fora de jogo

offspring /ˈɒfsprɪŋ/ *n* (*pl invar*) descendência f, prole f

often /ˈɒfn/ *adv* muitas vezes, frequentemente; **every so ~** de vez em quando; **how ~?** quantas vezes?

oh /əʊ/ *int* oh, ah

oil /ɔɪl/ *n* óleo *m*; (*petroleum*) petróleo *m*; **~ rig** plataforma f de poço de petróleo; **~ well** poço *m* de petróleo ● *vt* lubrificar. **~ painting** *n* pintura f a óleo. **~y** *a* oleoso; ⟨*food*⟩ gorduroso

oilfield /ˈɔɪlfiːld/ *n* campo *m* petrolífero

ointment /ˈɔɪntmənt/ *n* pomada f

OK /əʊˈkeɪ/ *a* & *adv* 🆗 (está) bem; (está) certo; (está) legal

old /əʊld/ *a* (**-er, -est**) velho; ⟨*person*⟩ velho, idoso; (*former*) antigo; **how ~ is he?** que idade tem ele?; **of ~** (d)antes, antigamente; **~ age** velhice f; **~-age pensioner** reformado *m*, aposentado *m*, pessoa f de terceira idade; **~ boy** antigo aluno *m*; **~ girl** antiga aluna f; **~ maid** solteirona f; **~ man** homem *m* idoso, velho *m*; **~ woman** mulher f idosa, velha f. **~-fashioned** *a* fora de moda

olive /ˈɒlɪv/ *n* azeitona f ● *a* de azeitona; **~ oil** azeite *m*

Olympic /əˈlɪmpɪk/ *a* olímpico; **~ Games** Jogos *mpl* Olímpicos. **~s** *npl* Olimpíadas *fpl*

omelette /ˈɒmlɪt/ *n* omelete f

omen /ˈəʊmən/ *n* agouro *m*

ominous /ˈɒmɪnəs/ *a* agourento

omit /əˈmɪt/ *vt* (*pt* **omitted**) omitir. **~ssion** /-ʃn/ *n* omissão f

on /ɒn/ *prep* sobre, em cima de, de, em; **~ arrival** na chegada, ao chegar; **~ foot** a pé *etc*; **~ doing** ao fazer; **~ time** na hora, dentro do horário; **~ Tuesday** na terça-feira; **~ Tuesdays** às terças-feiras ● *adv* para diante, para a frente; (*switched on*) aceso, ligado; (*tap*) aberto; (*machine*) em funcionamento; (*put on*) posto; (*happening*) em curso; **walk/etc ~** continuar a andar/*etc*; **be ~ at** Film, TV estar levando ou passando, (P) estar a dar; **~ and off** de vez em quando; **~ and ~** sem parar

once /wʌns/ *adv* uma vez; (*formerly*) noutro(s) tempo(s) ● *conj* uma vez que, desde que; **all at ~** de repente; (*simultaneously*) todos ao mesmo tempo; **just this ~** só esta vez; **~ (and) for all** duma vez para sempre; **~ upon a time** era uma vez. **~over** *n* 🔢 vista *f* de olhos

oncoming /'ɒnkʌmɪŋ/ *a* que se aproxima, próximo; **the ~ traffic** o trânsito que vem do sentido oposto, (P) no sentido contrário

one /wʌn/ *a* um(a); (sole) único ● *n* um(a) *mf* ● *pron* um(a) *mf*; (impersonal) se; **~ by** ~ um a um; **a big/red/etc~** um grande/vermelho/etc; **this/that** ~ este/esse; **~ another** um ao outro, uns aos outros. **~sided** *a* parcial; **~way** *a* <street> mão única, (P) via *f* de sentido único; <ticket> simples

oneself /wʌn'self/ *pron* si, si mesmo/próprio; (reflexive) se; **by** ~ sozinho

onion /'ʌniən/ *n* cebola *f*

online /ɒn'laɪn/ *a* conectado *or* (P) ligado (à Internet), online

onlooker /'ɒnlʊkə(r)/ *n* espectador *m*, circunstante *mf*

only /'əʊnlɪ/ *a* único ● *an ~ child* um filho único ● *adv* apenas, só, somente; **he ~ has six** ele só tem seis; **not ~ ... but also** não só ... mas também; **~ too** muito, mais que ● *conj* só que

onset /'ɒnset/ *n* começo *m*; (attack) ataque *m*

onslaught /'ɒnslɔːt/ *n* ataque *m* violento, assalto *m*

onward(s) /'ɒnwəd(z)/ *adv* para a frente/diante

ooze /uːz/ *vt/i* escorrer, verter

opal /'əʊpl/ *n* opala *f*

opaque /əʊ'peɪk/ *a* opaco, tosco

open /'əʊpən/ *a* aberto; <view> aberto, amplo; (free to all) aberto ao público; (attempt) franco; **in**

the ~ air ao ar livre; **keep an ~ house** receber muito, abrir a porta para todos; **~ secret** segredo *m* de polichinelo; **~ sea** mar *m* alto ● *vt/i* abrir(-se); (of shop, play) abrir; **~ on to** dar para; **~ out** *or* **up** abrir(-se). **~-heart** *a* (of surgery) de coração aberto; **~-minded** *a* que tem uma mente aberta; **~-plan** *a* sem divisórias. **~ness** *n* abertura *f*; (frankness) franqueza *f*

opener /'əʊpənə(r)/ *n* (tins) abridor *m* de latas, (P) abre-latas *m invar*; (bottles) saca-rolhas *m invar*

opening /'əʊpənɪŋ/ *n* abertura *f*; (beginning) começo *m*; (opportunity) oportunidade *f*; (job) vaga *f*

openly /'əʊpənlɪ/ *adv* abertamente

Open University A universidade à distância na Grã-Bretanha, fundada em 1969. As aulas são lecionadas por correspondência, através de material impresso, material enviado pela Internet e de programas de televisão emitidos pela BBC. Também há cursos de verão aos quais os alunos devem assistir presencialmente. Não se exige nenhuma qualificação académica para entrar na Open University.   *i*

---

opera /'ɒprə/ *n* ópera *f*. **~ glasses** *npl* binóculo (de teatro) *m*, (P) binóculos *mpl*. **~tic** /ɒpə'rætɪk/ *a* de ópera, operático

operat|e /'ɒpəreɪt/ *vt/i* operar; Techn (pôr a) funcionar; **~e on** Med operar. **~ingtheatre** *n* Med anfiteatro *m*, sala *f* de operações. **~ion** /-'reɪʃn/ *n* operação *f*; **in ~ion** em vigor; Techn em funcionamento. **~ional** /-'reɪʃənl/ *a* operacional.

~or n operador m; (telephonist) telefonista mf

operative /'ɒprətɪv/ a (surgical) operatório; ‹law etc› em vigor

opinion /ə'pɪnɪən/ n opinião f, parecer m; **in my ~** a meu ver. **~ poll** n sondagem (de opinião) f. **~ated** /-eitid/ a dogmático, opinioso

opium /'əʊpɪəm/ n ópio m

Oporto /ə'pɔːtəʊ/ n Porto m

opponent /ə'pəʊnənt/ n adversário m, antagonista mf, oponente mf

opportune /'ɒpətjuːn/ a oportuno

opportunity /ɒpə'tjuːnəti/ n oportunidade f

oppos|**e** /ə'pəʊz/ vt opor-se a; **~ed to** oposto a. **~ing** a oposto

opposite /'ɒpəzɪt/ a & n oposto m, contrário m ● adv em frente ● prep **~ (to)** em frente de/a

opposition /ɒpə'zɪʃn/ n oposição f

oppress /ə'pres/ vt oprimir. **~ion** /-ʃn/ n opressão f. **~ive** a opressivo

opt /ɒpt/ vi **~ for** optar por; **~ out** recusar-se a participar (**of** de); **~ to do** escolher fazer

optical /'ɒptɪkl/ a óptico; **~ illusion** ilusão óptica f

optician /ɒp'tɪʃn/ n oculista mf

optimis|**t** /'ɒptɪmɪst/ n otimista mf. **~m** /-zəm/ n otimismo m. **~tic** /-'mɪstɪk/ a otimista

optimum /'ɒptɪməm/ a & n (pl -ima) ótimo m, (P) óptimo m

option /'ɒpʃn/ n escolha f, opção f; **have no ~ (but)** não ter outro remédio (senão)

optional /'ɒpʃənl/ a opcional, facultativo

opulen|**t** /'ɒpjʊlənt/ a opulento. **~ce** n opulência f

or /ɔː(r)/ conj ou; (with negative) nem; **~ else** senão

oracle /'ɒrəkl/ n oráculo m

oral /'ɔːrəl/ a oral

orange /'ɒrɪndʒ/ n laranja f; (colour) laranja m, cor f de laranja ● a de laranja; (colour) alaranjado, cor de laranja

orator /'ɒrətə(r)/ n orador m. **~y** n oratória f

orbit /'ɔːbɪt/ n órbita f ● vt (pt orbited) gravitar em torno de

orchard /'ɔːtʃəd/ n pomar m

orchestra /'ɔːkɪstrə/ n orquestra f. **~l** /-'kestrəl/ a orquestral

orchestrate /'ɔːkɪstreɪt/ vt orquestrar

orchid /'ɔːkɪd/ n orquídea f

ordain /ɔː'deɪn/ vt decretar; Relig ordenar

ordeal /ɔː'diːl/ n prova f, provação f

order /'ɔːdə(r)/ n ordem f; Comm encomenda f, pedido m ● vt ordenar; ‹goods etc› encomendar; **in ~ that** para que; **in ~ to** para

orderly /'ɔːdəlɪ/ a ordenado, em ordem; (not unruly) ordeiro ● n Mil ordenança f, Med servente m de hospital

ordinary /'ɔːdɪnrɪ/ a normal, ordinário, vulgar; **out of the ~** fora do comum

ordination /ɔːdɪ'neɪʃn/ n Relig ordenação f

ore /ɔː(r)/ n minério m

organ /'ɔːɡən/ n órgão m. **~ist** n organista mf

organic /ɔː'ɡænɪk/ a orgânico

organism /'ɔːɡənɪzəm/ n organismo m

organiz|e /'ɔ:gənaɪz/ vt organizar. **~ation** /-'zeɪʃn/ n organização f. **~er** n organizador m

orgasm /'ɔ:gæzəm/ n orgasmo m

orgy /'ɔ:dʒɪ/ n orgia f

Orient /'ɔ:rɪənt/ n the ~ o Oriente m

orientat|e /'ɔ:rɪənteɪt/ vt orientar. **~ion** /-'teɪʃn/ n orientação f

origin /'ɒrɪdʒɪn/ n origem f

original /ə'rɪdʒənl/ a original; (not copied) original. **~ity** /-'nælətɪ/ n originalidade f. **~ly** adv originalmente; (in the beginning) originariamente

originat|e /ə'rɪdʒəneɪt/ vt/i originar(-se). **~e from** provir de

ornament /'ɔ:nəmənt/ n ornamento m; (object) peça f decorativa. **~al** /-'mentl/ a ornamental

ornate /ɔ:'neɪt/ a florido, floreado

ornitholog|y /ɔ:nɪ'θɒlədʒɪ/ n ornitologia f

orphan /'ɔ:fn/ n órfã(o) f(m) ● vt deixar órfão. **~age** n orfanato m

orthodox /'ɔ:θədɒks/ a ortodoxo

orthopaedic /ɔ:θə'pi:dɪk/ a ortopédico

oscillate /'ɒsɪleɪt/ vi oscilar, vacilar

ostensibl|e /ɒ'stensəbl/ a aparente, pretenso. **~y** adv aparentemente, pretensamente

ostentati|on /ɒsten'teɪʃn/ n ostentação f. **~ous** /-'teɪʃəs/ a ostentoso, ostensivo

osteopath /'ɒstɪəpæθ/ n osteopata mf

ostracize /'ɒstrəsaɪz/ vt pôr de lado, marginalizar

ostrich /'ɒstrɪtʃ/ n avestruz mf

other /'ʌðə(r)/ a, n & pron outro m; (some) **~s** outros; the ~ day no outro dia; the ~ one o outro ● adv ~ than diferente de, senão

otherwise /'ʌðəwaɪz/ adv de outro modo ● conj senão, caso contrário

otter /'ɒtə(r)/ n lontra f

ouch /aʊtʃ/ int ai, ui!

ought /ɔ:t/ v aux (pt ought) dever; **you ~ to stay** você devia ficar; **he ~ to succeed** ele deve vencer; **I ~ to have done it** eu devia tê-lo feito

ounce /aʊns/ n onça f (= 28,35 g)

our /'aʊə(r)/ a o nosso(s), nossa(s)

ours /aʊəz/ poss pron o(s) nosso(s), a(s) nossa(s)

ourselves /aʊə'selvz/ pron nós mesmos/próprios; (reflexive) nos; by ~ sozinhos

oust /aʊst/ vt expulsar, obrigar a sair

out /aʊt/ adv fora; (of light, fire) apagado; (in blossom) aberto, desabrochado, em flor; (of tide) baixo; **be ~** não estar em casa, estar fora (de casa); (wrong) enganar-se; **be ~ to** estar resolvido a; **run**/etc ~ sair correndo or (P) a correr/etc; ~ **of fora de;** (without) sem; ~ **of pity**/etc por pena/etc; **made ~ of** feito de or em; **take ~ of** tirar de; **5 ~ of 6** 5 (de) entre 6; ~ **of date** fora de moda; (not valid) fora do prazo; ~ **of doors** ao ar livre; ~ **of one's mind** doido; ~ **of order** quebrado, (P) avariado; ~ **of place** deslocado; ~ **of the way** afastado. **~and-~** a completo, rematado. **~patient** n doente mf de consulta externa

outboard /'aʊtbɔ:d/ a ~ **motor** motor m de popa

outbox /'aʊtbɒks/ n caixa f de saída

outbreak /ˈaʊtbreɪk/ n (of flu etc) surto m, epidemia f; (of war) deflagração f

outburst /ˈaʊtbɜːst/ n explosão f

outcast /ˈaʊtkɑːst/ n pária m

outcome /ˈaʊtkʌm/ n resultado m

outcry /ˈaʊtkraɪ/ n clamor m; (protest) protesto m

outdated /aʊtˈdeɪtɪd/ a fora da moda, ultrapassado

outdo /aʊtˈduː/ vt (pt -did, pp -done) ultrapassar, superar

outdoor /ˈaʊtdɔː(r)/ a ao ar livre. ~s /-ˈdɔːz/ adv fora de casa, ao ar livre

outer /ˈaʊtə(r)/ a exterior; ~ space espaço (cósmico) m

outfit /ˈaʊtfɪt/ n equipamento m; (clothes) roupa f

outgoing /ˈaʊtɡəʊɪŋ/ a que vai sair; (of minister etc) demissionário; fig sociável. ~s npl despesas fpl

outgrow /aʊtˈɡrəʊ/ vt (pt -grew, pp -grown) crescer mais do que; ‹clothes› já não caber em

outing /ˈaʊtɪŋ/ n saída f, passeio m

outlandish /aʊtˈlændɪʃ/ a exótico, estranho

outlaw /ˈaʊtlɔː/ n fora da lei mf, bandido m ● vt banir, proscrever

outlay /ˈaʊtleɪ/ n despesa(s) f(pl)

outlet /ˈaʊtlet/ n saída f, escoadouro m; (for goods) mercado m, saída f; (for feelings) escape m, vazão m; Electr tomada f

outline /ˈaʊtlaɪn/ n contorno m; (summary) plano m geral, esquema m, esboço m ● vt contornar; (summarize) descrever em linhas gerais

outlive /aʊtˈlɪv/ vt sobreviver a

outlook /ˈaʊtlʊk/ n (view) vista f; (mental attitude) visão f; (future prospects) perspectiva(s) f(pl), (P) perspetiva(s) f(pl)

outlying /ˈaʊtlaɪɪŋ/ a afastado, remoto

outnumber /aʊtˈnʌmbə(r)/ vt ultrapassar em número

outpost /ˈaʊtpəʊst/ n posto m avançado

output /ˈaʊtpʊt/ n rendimento m; (of computer) saída f, output m

outrage /ˈaʊtreɪdʒ/ n atrocidade f, crime m; (scandal) escândalo m ● vt ultrajar

outrageous /aʊtˈreɪdʒəs/ a (shocking) escandaloso; (very cruel) atroz

outright /ˈaʊtraɪt/ adv completamente; (at once) imediatamente; (frankly) abertamente ● a completo; (refusal) claro

outset /ˈaʊtset/ n início m, começo m, princípio m

outside¹ /aʊtˈsaɪd/ n exterior m ● adv (lá) (por) fora ● prep (para) fora de, além de; (in front of) diante de; at the ~ no máximo

outside² /ˈaʊtsaɪd/ a exterior

outsider /aʊtˈsaɪdə(r)/ n estranho m; (in race) cavalo m com poucas probabilidades de vencer, azarão m

outsize /ˈaʊtsaɪz/ a tamanho extra invar

outskirts /ˈaʊtskɜːts/ npl arredores mpl, subúrbios mpl, arrabaldes mpl

outspoken /aʊtˈspəʊkn/ a franco

outstanding /aʊtˈstændɪŋ/ a saliente, proeminente; ‹debt› por saldar; (very good) notável, destacado

outstretched /aʊtˈstretʃt/ a ‹arm› estendido, esticado

outward /ˈaʊtwəd/ a para o exterior; ‹sign etc› exterior; ‹journey› de ida. **~ly** adv exteriormente. **~s** adv para o exterior

outwit /aʊtˈwɪt/ vt (pt -**witted**) ser mais esperto que, enganar

oval /ˈəʊvl/ n & a oval m

> **Oval Office** O Salão Oval
> é o escritório oficial do
> Presidente dos Estados
> Unidos, situado na ala oeste da
> Casa Branca. A forma oval foi
> exigida por George Washington
> para ter contato visual com todos
> os presentes durante as reuniões.
> A princípio, o presidente queria
> que todas as divisões da Casa
> Branca fossem ovais, mas logo
> percebeu que este desenho era
> pouco prático. *(i)*

ovary /ˈəʊvərɪ/ n ovário m

ovation /əʊˈveɪʃn/ n ovação f

oven /ˈʌvn/ n forno m

over /ˈəʊvə(r)/ prep sobre, acima de, por cima de; ‹across› de para o/do outro lado de; ‹during› durante, em; (more than) mais de ● adv por cima; (too) demais, demasiadamente; (ended) acabado; **the film is ~** o filme já acabou; **jump/**etc**~** saltar/etc por cima; **he has some ~** ele tem uns de sobra; **all ~ the country** em/por todo o país; **all ~ the table** por toda a mesa; **~ and above** (besides, in addition to) (para) além de; **~ and ~** repetidas vezes; **~ there** ali, lá, acolá

over- /ˈəʊvə(r)/ pref sobre-, super-; (excessively) demais, demasiado

overall[1] /ˈəʊvərɔːl/ n bata f; **~s** macacão m, (P) fato-macaco m

overall[2] /ˈəʊvərɔːl/ a global; ‹length etc› total ● adv globalmente

overbalance /əʊvəˈbæləns/ vt/i (fazer) perder o equilíbrio

overbearing /əʊvəˈbeərɪŋ/ a autoritário, despótico; (arrogant) arrogante

overboard /ˈəʊvəbɔːd/ adv (pela) borda fora

overcast /əʊvəˈkɑːst/ a encoberto, nublado

overcharge /əʊvəˈtʃɑːdʒ/ vt **~ sb (for)** cobrar demais a alguém (por)

overcoat /ˈəʊvəkəʊt/ n casacão m; (for men) sobretudo m

overcome /əʊvəˈkʌm/ vt (pt -**came**, pp -**come**) superar, vencer; **~ by** sucumbindo a, dominado ou vencido por

overcrowded /əʊvəˈkraʊdɪd/ a apinhado, superlotado; ‹country› superpovoado

overdo /əʊvəˈduː/ vt (pt -**did**, pp -**done**) exagerar, levar longe demais; **~ne** Culin cozinhado demais

overdose /ˈəʊvədəʊs/ n dose f excessiva, (P) overdose f

overdraft /ˈəʊvədrɑːft/ n saldo m negativo

overdraw /əʊvəˈdrɔː/ vt (pt -**drew**, pp -**drawn**) sacar a descoberto, (P) ter a conta a descoberto

overdue /əʊvəˈdjuː/ a em atraso, atrasado; (belated) tardio

overestimate /əʊvərˈestɪmeɪt/ vt sobrestimar, atribuir valor excessivo a

overexpose /əʊvərɪkˈspəʊz/ vt expor demais

overflow[1] /əʊvə'fləʊ/ vt/i
extravasar; transbordar (**with** de)

overflow[2] /'əʊvəfləʊ/ n (outlet)
descarga f; (excess) excesso m

overgrown /əʊvə'grəʊn/ a
que cresceu demais; ‹garden etc›
invadido pela vegetação

overhang /əʊvə'hæŋ/ vt (pt -hung)
estar sobranceiro a, pairar sobre ● vi
projetar-se ● n saliência f

overhaul[1] /əʊvə'hɔːl/ vt fazer uma
revisão em

overhaul[2] /'əʊvəhɔːl/ n revisão f

overhead[1] /əʊvə'hed/ adv em or
por cima, ao or no alto

overhead[2] /'əʊvəhed/ a aéreo. ~s
npl despesas fpl gerais

overhear /əʊvə'hɪə(r)/ vt (pt
-heard) (eavesdrop) ouvir sem
conhecimento do falante; (hear by
chance) ouvir por acaso

overjoyed /əʊvə'dʒɔɪd/ a
radiante, felicíssimo

overlap /əʊvə'læp/ vt/i (pt -lapped)
sobrepor(-se) parcialmente; fig
coincidir

overleaf /əʊvə'liːf/ adv no verso

overload /əʊvə'ləʊd/ vt
sobrecarregar

overlook /əʊvə'lʊk/ vt deixar
passar; (of window) dar para; (of
building) dominar

overnight /əʊvə'naɪt/ adv durante
a noite; fig dum dia para o outro ● a
‹train› da noite; ‹stay, journey, etc›
de noite, noturno; fig súbito

overpass /əʊvə'pɑːs/ n passagem
f superior

overpay /əʊvə'peɪ/ vt (pt -paid)
pagar em excesso

overpower /əʊvə'paʊə(r)/ vt
dominar, subjugar; fig esmagar.
~ing a esmagador; ‹heat›

sufocante, insuportável

overpriced /əʊvə'praɪst/ a
muito caro

overrid|e /əʊvə'raɪd/ vt (pt -rode,
pp -ridden) prevalecer sobre, passar
por cima de. ~ing a primordial,
preponderante; (importance) maior

overripe /'əʊvəraɪp/ a demasiado
maduro

overrule /əʊvə'ruːl/ vt anular,
rejeitar; ‹claim› indeferir

overrun /əʊvə'rʌn/ vt (pt -ran, pp
-run, pres p -running) invadir; ‹a
limit› exceder, ultrapassar

overseas /əʊvə'siːz/ a ultramarino;
(abroad) estrangeiro ● adv no
ultramar, no estrangeiro

oversee /əʊvə'siː/ vt (pt -saw,
pp -seen) supervisionar. ~r
/'əʊvəsɪə(r)/ n capataz m

overshadow /əʊvə'ʃædəʊ/ vt fig
eclipsar; ofuscar

oversight /'əʊvəsaɪt/ n lapso m

oversleep /əʊvə'sliːp/ vi (pt -slept)
acordar tarde, dormir demais

overt /'əʊvɜːt/ a manifesto, claro,
patente

overtake /əʊvə'teɪk/ vt/i (pt -took,
pp -taken) ultrapassar

overthrow /əʊvə'θrəʊ/ vt (pt
-threw, pp -thrown) derrubar, depor
● n /'əʊvəθrəʊ/ Pol derrubada f, (P)
deposição

overtime /'əʊvətaɪm/ n horas
fpl extras

overtones /'əʊvətəʊnz/ npl fig
tom m; implicação f

overture /'əʊvətjʊə(r)/ n
Mus abertura f; fig proposta f;
abordagem f

overturn /əʊvə'tɜːn/ vt/i virar(-se);
‹car, plane› capotar, virar-se

overweight /əʊvəˈweɪt/ a be ~ ter excesso de peso

overwhelm /əʊvəˈwelm/ vt oprimir; (defeat) esmagar; (amaze) assoberbar. **~ing** a esmagador; ‹urge› irresistível

overwork /əʊvəˈwɜːk/ vt/i sobrecarregar(-se) com trabalho ● n excesso m de trabalho

overwrought /əʊvəˈrɔːt/ a muito agitado, superexcitado

ow|e /əʊ/ vt dever. **~ing** a devido; **~ing to** devido a

owl /aʊl/ n coruja f

own[1] /əʊn/ a o próprio; **a house/**etc **of one's ~** uma casa/etc própria; **get one's ~ back** 🔢 ir à forra, (P) desforrar-se; **hold one's ~** aguentar-se; **on one's ~** sozinho

own[2] /əʊn/ vt possuir; **~ up (to)** 🔢 confessar. **~er** n proprietário m, dono m. **~ership** n posse f, propriedade f

ox /ɒks/ n (pl **oxen**) boi m

> **Oxbridge** Termo usado para se referir simultaneamente às universidades mais antigas e prestigiadas do Reino Unido, Oxford e Cambridge, especialmente quando se quer destacar o meio privilegiado com que estão relacionadas. Ultimamente, foram feitos grandes esforços para atrair alunos de todos os meios sociais.

oxygen /ˈɒksɪdʒən/ n oxigênio m, (P) oxigénio m

oyster /ˈɔɪstə(r)/ n ostra f

ozone /ˈəʊzəʊn/ n ozônio m, (P) ozono m; **~ layer** camada f de ozônio, (P) ozono m

Pp

pace /peɪs/ n passo m; fig ritmo m; **keep ~ with** acompanhar, manter-se a par de ● vt percorrer passo a passo ● vi **~ up and down** andar de um lado para o outro

pacemaker /ˈpeɪsmeɪkə(r)/ n Med marca-passo m, (P) pacemaker m

Pacific /pəˈsɪfɪk/ a pacífico ● n **~ (Ocean)** (Oceano) Pacífico m

pacifist /ˈpæsɪfɪst/ n pacifista mf

pacify /ˈpæsɪfaɪ/ vt pacificar, apaziguar

pack /pæk/ n pacote m; Mil mochila f; (of hounds) matilha f; (of lies) porção f; (of cards) baralho m ● vt empacotar; ‹suitcase› fazer; ‹box, room› encher; (press down) atulhar, encher até não caber mais ● vi fazer as malas; **~ into** (cram) apinhar em, comprimir em; **send ~ing** pôr a andar, mandar passear. **~ed** a apinhado; **~ed lunch** merenda f

package /ˈpækɪdʒ/ n pacote m, embrulho m ● vt embalar; **~ deal** pacote m de propostas; **~ holiday** pacote m turístico

packet /ˈpækɪt/ n pacote m; (of cigarettes) maço m

pact /pækt/ n pacto m

pad /pæd/ n (in clothing) chumaço m; (for writing) bloco m de papel; de notas; (for ink) almofada f (de carimbo) f; **(launching) ~** rampa f de lançamento ● vt (pt **padded**) enchumaçar, acolchoar; fig ‹essay etc› encher linguiça, (P) pôr palha em 🔢 **~ding** n chumaço m; fig linguiça f, (P) palha f 🔢

paddle¹ /'pædl/ n remo m de canoa

paddle² /'pædl/ vi chapinhar, molhar os pés; **~ing pool** piscina f de plástico para crianças

paddock /'pædək/ n cercado m; (at racecourse) paddock m

padlock /'pædlɒk/ n cadeado m ● vt fechar com cadeado

paediatrician /piːdɪə'trɪʃn/ n pediatra mf

pagan /'peɪgən/ a & n pagão m, pagã f

page¹ /peɪdʒ/ n (of book etc) página f

page² /peɪdʒ/ vt mandar chamar

pageant /'pædʒənt/ n espetáculo m (histórico); (procession) cortejo m. **~ry** n pompa f

paid /peɪd/ ▶ PAY ● a **put ~ to** 🔲 (end) pôr fim a

pail /peɪl/ n balde m

pain /peɪn/ n dor f; **~s** esforços mpl; **be in ~** sofrer, ter dores; **take ~s to** esforçar-se por ● vt magoar. **~killer** n analgésico m. **~ful** a doloroso; (grievous) (laborious) penoso. **~less** a sem dor, indolor

painstaking /'peɪnzteɪkɪŋ/ a cuidadoso, esmerado, meticuloso

paint /peɪnt/ n tinta f; **~s** (in box) tintas fpl ● vt/i pintar. **~er** n pintor m. **~ing** n pintura f

paintbrush /'peɪntbrʌʃ/ n pincel m

pair /peə(r)/ n par m; **a ~ of scissors** uma tesoura; **a ~ of trousers** um par de calças; **in ~s** aos pares ● vi **~ off** formar pares

Pakistan /pɑːkɪ'stɑːn/ n Paquistão m. **~i** a & n paquistanês m

pal /pæl/ n 🔲 colega mf; amigo m

palace /'pælɪs/ n palácio m

palate /'pælət/ n palato m. **~able** a saboroso, gostoso; fig agradável

palatial /pə'leɪʃl/ a suntuoso, (P) sumptuoso

pale /peɪl/ a (-er, -est) pálido; «colour» claro ● vi empalidecer. **~ness** n palidez f

Palestin|**e** /'pælɪstaɪn/ n Palestina f. **~ian** /-'stɪnɪən/ a & n palestino m, (P) palestiniano

palette /'pælɪt/ n paleta f

palm /pɑːm/ n (of hand) palma f; (tree) palmeira f ● vt **~ off** (on a); **P~ Sunday** Domingo m de Ramos

palpable /'pælpəbl/ a palpável

palpitat|**e** /'pælpɪteɪt/ vi palpitar. **~ion** /-'teɪʃn/ n palpitação f

paltry /'pɔːltrɪ/ a (-ier, -iest) irrisório

pamper /'pæmpə(r)/ vt mimar, paparicar or apaparicar

pamphlet /'pæmflɪt/ n panfleto m, folheto m

pan /pæn/ n panela f; (for frying) frigideira f ● vt (pt panned) 🔲 criticar severamente

panacea /pænə'sɪə/ n panaceia f

panache /pæ'næʃ/ n brio m, estilo m, panache m

pancake /'pænkeɪk/ n crepe m, panqueca f

panda /'pændə/ n panda m

pandemonium /pændɪ'məʊnɪəm/ n pandemônio m, (P) pandemónio m, caos m

pander /'pændə(r)/ vi **~ to** prestar-se a servir, ir ao encontro de, fazer concessões a

pane /peɪn/ n vidraça f

panel /'pænl/ n painel m; (jury) júri m; (speakers) convidados *mpl;* **(instrument)** ~ painel *m* de instrumentos, (P) de bordo. **~ling** *n* apainelamento *m.* **~list** *n* convidado *m* de painel

pang /pæŋ/ *n* pontada *f*, dor *f* aguda e súbita; **~s** (*of hunger*) ataques *mpl* de fome; **~s of conscience** remorsos *mpl*

panic /'pænɪk/ *n* pânico *m* ● *vt/i* (*pt* **panicked**) desorientar(-se), (fazer) entrar em pânico. **~stricken** *a* tomado de pânico

panoram|a /pænə'rɑːmə/ *n* panorama *m.* **~ic** /-'ræmɪk/ *a* panorâmico

pansy /'pænzɪ/ *n* amor-perfeito *m*

pant /pænt/ *vi* ofegar, arquejar

panther /'pænθə(r)/ *n* pantera *f*

panties /'pæntɪz/ *npl* 🄰 calcinhas *fpl*, (P) cuecas *fpl*

pantomime /'pæntəmaɪm/ *n* pantomima *f*

pantry /'pæntrɪ/ *n* despensa *f*

pants /pænts/ *npl* 🄰 (*underwear*) cuecas *fpl*; 🄱 (*trousers*) calças *fpl*

paper /'peɪpə(r)/ *n* papel *m*; (*newspaper*) jornal *m*; (*exam*) prova *f* escrita; (*essay*) comunicação *f*; **on ~** por escrito ● *vt* forrar com papel. **~s** *npl* (*for identification*) documentos *mpl.* **~ clip** *n* clipe *m*

paperback /'peɪpəbæk/ *a & n* ~ **(book)** livro *m* de capa mole

paperweight /'peɪpəweɪt/ *n* pesa-papéis *m invar*, (P) pisa-papéis *m invar*

paperwork /'peɪpəwɜːk/ *n* trabalho *m* de secretária; *pej* papelada *f*

paprika /'pæprɪkə/ *n* páprica *f*, (P) paprica *f*

par /pɑː(r)/ *n* **be below ~** estar abaixo do padrão desejado; **on a ~**

with em igualdade com

parable /'pærəbl/ *n* parábola *f*

parachut|e /'pærəʃuːt/ *n* pára-quedas *m invar* ● *vi* descer de paraquedas. **~ist** *n* paraquedista *mf*

parade /pə'reɪd/ *n Mil* parada *f* militar; (*procession*) procissão *f* ● *vi* desfilar ● *vt* alardear

paradise /'pærədaɪs/ *n* paraíso *m*

paradox /'pærədɒks/ *n* paradoxo *m.* **~ical** /-'dɒksɪkl/ *a* paradoxal

paraffin /'pærəfɪn/ *n* querosene *m*, (P) petróleo *m*

paragon /'pærəgən/ *n* modelo *m* de perfeição

paragraph /'pærəgrɑːf/ *n* parágrafo *m*

parallel /'pærəlel/ *a & n* paralelo *m* ● *vt* (*pt* **paralleled**) comparar(-se) a

paralyse /'pærəlaɪz/ *vt* paralisar

paraly|sis /pə'ræləsɪs/ *n* paralisia *f.* **~tic** /-'lɪtɪk/ *a & n* paralítico *m*

paramedic /pærə'medɪk/ *n* paramédico *m*

parameter /pə'ræmɪtə(r)/ *n* parâmetro *m*

paramount /'pærəmaʊnt/ *a* supremo, primordial

parapet /'pærəpɪt/ *n* parapeito *m*

paraphernalia /pærəfə'neɪlɪə/ *n* equipamento *m*, parafernália *f*; tralha *f* 🄱

paraphrase /'pærəfreɪz/ *n* paráfrase *f* ● *vt* parafrasear

paraplegic /pærə'pliːdʒɪk/ *n* paraplégico *m*

parasite /'pærəsaɪt/ *n* parasita *m*

parasol /'pærəsɒl/ *n* sombrinha *f*, (*on table*) parasol *m*, guarda-sol *m*

parcel /'pɑːsl/ *n* embrulho *m*; (*for post*) encomenda *f*

parch /pɑːtʃ/ vt ressecar; **be ~ed** estar com muita sede

parchment /'pɑːtʃmənt/ n pergaminho m

pardon /'pɑːdn/ n perdão m; Jur perdão m, indulto m; **I beg your ~** perdão, desculpe; **(I beg your) ~?** como? ● vt (pt pardoned) perdoar

parent /'peərənt/ n pai m, mãe f. **~s** npl pais mpl. **~al** /pə'rentl/ a dos pais, paterno, materno

parenthesis /pə'renθəsɪs/ n (pl **-theses** /-siːz/) parêntese m, parêntesis m

parish /'pærɪʃ/ n paróquia f; (municipal) freguesia f. **~ioner** /pə'rɪʃənə(r)/ n paroquiano m

park /pɑːk/ n parque m ● vt estacionar. **~ing** n estacionamento m; **no ~ing** estacionamento proibido. **~ing meter** n parquímetro m

parliament /'pɑːləmənt/ n parlamento m, assembleia f. **~ary** /-'mentrɪ/ a parlamentar

Parliament O Parlamento britânico, o órgão legislativo mais importante, é formado pela Câmara dos Lordes e pela Câmara dos Comuns. A primeira tem de mais de 750 membros, a maioria deles nomeados, com um número de cargos hereditários, algo que está sendo reformado no momento. A Câmara dos Comuns tem de 650 membros eleitos. Ver *Dáil Éireann, Scottish Parliament, Welsh Assembly.*

parochial /pə'rəʊkɪəl/ a paroquial; fig provinciano; tacanho

parody /'pærədɪ/ n paródia f ● vt parodiar

parole /pə'rəʊl/ n **on ~** em liberdade condicional ● vt pôr em liberdade condicional

parquet /'pɑːkeɪ/ n parquê m, parquete m

parrot /'pærət/ n papagaio m

parsley /'pɑːslɪ/ n salsa f

parsnip /'pɑːsnɪp/ n cherovia f, pastinaga f

parson /'pɑːsn/ n pároco m, pastor m

part /pɑːt/ n parte f; (of serial) episódio m; (of machine) peça f; Theat papel m; (side in dispute) partido m; **in ~** em parte; **on the ~ of** da parte de; **~ of speech** categoria f gramatical; **take ~ in** tomar parte em; **these ~s** estas partes ● a parcial ● adv em parte ● vt/i separar(-se) (**from** de). **~time** a & adv a tempo parcial, em part-time

partial /'pɑːʃl/ a (incomplete, biased) parcial; **be ~ to** gostar de. **~ity** /-'ræli/ n parcialidade f; (liking) predileção f (**for** por). **~ly** adv parcialmente

particip|ate /pɑː'tɪsɪpeɪt/ vi participar (**in** em). **~ant** n /-ənt/ participante mf. **~ation** /-'peɪʃn/ n participação f

particle /'pɑːtɪkl/ n partícula f; (of dust) grão m; fig mínimo m

particular /pə'tɪkjʊlə(r)/ a especial, particular; (fussy) exigente; (careful) escrupuloso. **~s** npl pormenores mpl. **in ~** em especial, particularmente. **~ly** adv particularmente

parting /'pɑːtɪŋ/ n separação f; (in hair) risca f ● a de despedida

partisan /pɑːtɪ'zæn/ n partidário m; Mil guerrilheiro m

partition /pɑ:'tɪʃn/ n (of room) tabique m, divisória f; Pol (division) partilha f, divisão f ● vt dividir, repartir; ~ **off** dividir por meio de tabique

partly /'pɑ:tlɪ/ adv em parte

partner /'pɑ:tnə(r)/ n sócio m; Cards, Sport parceiro m; Dancing par m. **~ship** n associação f, parceria f; Comm sociedade f

partridge /'pɑ:trɪdʒ/ n perdiz f

party /'pɑ:tɪ/ n festa f, reunião f; (group) grupo m; Pol partido m; Jur parte f; ~ **line** (telephone) linha f coletiva

pass /pɑ:s/ vt/i (pt passed) passar; (overtake) ultrapassar; ⟨exam⟩ passar; (approve) passar; ⟨law⟩ aprovar; ~ **(by)** passar por; ~ **away** falecer; ~ **out** or **round** distribuir; ~ **out** ⚀ (faint) perder os sentidos, desmaiar; ~ **over** (disregard, overlook) passar por cima de; ~ **up** ⚀ (forgo) deixar perder ● n (permit) Sport passe m; Geog desfiladeiro m, garganta f; (in exam) aprovação f; **make a ~ at** ⚀ atirar-se para or (P) a ⚀

passable /'pɑ:səbl/ a passável; ⟨road⟩ transitável

passage /'pæsɪdʒ/ n passagem f; (voyage) travessia f; (corridor) corredor m, passagem f

passenger /'pæsɪndʒə(r)/ n passageiro m

passer-by /pɑ:sə'baɪ/ n (pl **passers-by**) transeunte mf

passion /'pæʃn/ n paixão f. **~ate** a apaixonado, exaltado

passive /'pæsɪv/ a passivo. ~ **smoking** n fumo m passivo

passport /'pɑ:spɔ:t/ n passaporte m

password /'pɑ:swɜ:d/ n senha f

past /pɑ:st/ a passado; (former) antigo; **these ~ months** estes últimos meses ● n passado m ● prep para além de; (in time) mais de; (in front of) diante de ● adv em frente; **be ~ it** já não ser capaz; **it's five ~ eleven** são onze e cinco

pasta /'pæstə/ n prato m de massa(s)

paste /peɪst/ n cola f; Culin massa(s) f(pl); (dough) massa f; (jewellery) strass m, (P) vidro m ● vt colar

pastel /'pæstl/ n pastel m ● a pastel invar

pasteurize /'pæstʃəraɪz/ vt pasteurizar

pastime /'pɑ:staɪm/ n passatempo m

pastry /'peɪstrɪ/ n massa f (de pastelaria); (tart) pastel m

pasture /'pɑ:stʃə(r)/ n pastagem f

pasty[1] /'pæstɪ/ n empadinha f

pasty[2] /'peɪstɪ/ a pastoso

pat /pæt/ vt (pt patted) (hit gently) dar pancadinhas em; (caress) fazer festinhas a ● n pancadinha f; (caress) festinha f ● adv a propósito; (readily) prontamente ● a preparado, pronto

patch /pætʃ/ n remendo m; (over eye) tapa-olho m; (spot) mancha f; (small area) pedaço m; (of vegetables) canteiro m, (P) leira f; **bad** ~ mau bocado m; **not be a ~ on** não chegar aos pés de ● vt ~ **up** remendar; ~ **up a quarrel** fazer as pazes. **~work** n obra f de retalhos. **~y** a desigual

pâté /'pæteɪ/ n patê m

patent /'peɪtnt/ a & n patente f; ~ **leather** verniz m, polimento m ● vt patentear

paternal /pəˈtɜːnl/ a paternal; ‹relative› paterno

paternity /pəˈtɜːnətɪ/ n paternidade f

path /pɑːθ/ n (pl -s /pɑːðz/) caminho m, trilha f; (in park) aleia f, (P) alameda f; (of rocket) trajetória f

pathetic /pəˈθetɪk/ a patético; ⊤ (contemptible) desgraçado f, desprezível

pathology /pəˈθɒlədʒɪ/ n patologia f. ~ist n patologista mf

patience /ˈpeɪʃns/ n paciência f

patio /ˈpætɪəʊ/ n (pl -os) pátio m

patriot /ˈpætrɪət/ n patriota mf. ~ic /-ˈɒtɪk/ a patriótico. ~ism /-ɪzəm/ n patriotismo m

patrol /pəˈtrəʊl/ n patrulha f ● vt/i patrulhar. ~ car n carro m de patrulha

patron /ˈpeɪtrən/ n (of the arts etc) patrocinador m, mecenas mf; protetor m; (of charity) benfeitor m; (customer) freguês m, cliente mf; ~ saint n padroeiro m, patrono m

patronage /ˈpætrənɪdʒ/ n freguesia f, clientela f; (support) patrocínio m. ~ize vt ser cliente de; (support) patrocinar; (condescend) tratar com ares de superioridade

patter¹ /ˈpætə(r)/ n (of rain) tamborilar m, chuviscar m; ~ of steps som m leve de passos miúdos, corridinha f leve

patter² /ˈpætə(r)/ n (of class, profession) gíria f, jargão m; (chatter) conversa f fiada

pattern /ˈpætn/ n padrão m; (for sewing) molde m; (example) modelo m

paunch /pɔːntʃ/ n pança f

pause /pɔːz/ n pausa f ● vi pausar, fazer (uma) pausa

pave /peɪv/ vt pavimentar; ~e the way preparar o caminho (for para). ~ing stone n paralelepípedo m, laje f

pavement /ˈpeɪvmənt/ n passeio m

pavilion /pəˈvɪlɪən/ n pavilhão m

paw /pɔː/ n pata f ● vt dar patadas em; ‹horse› escarvar; ⊤ ‹person› pôr as patas em cima de

pawn¹ /pɔːn/ n Chess peão m; fig joguete m

pawn² /pɔːn/ vt empenhar; ~shop casa f de penhores, prego m ⊤

pawnbroker /ˈpɔːnbrəʊkə(r)/ n penhorista mf, dono m de casa de penhores, agiota mf

pay /peɪ/ vt/i (pt paid) pagar; ‹interest› render; ‹visit, compliment› fazer; ~ attention prestar atenção; ~ back restituir; ~ for pagar; ~ homage prestar homenagem; ~ in depositar ● n pagamento m; ‹wages› vencimento m, ordenado m, salário m; in the ~ of em pagamento de. ~slip n contracheque m, (P) folha f de pagamento

payable /ˈpeɪəbl/ a pagável

pay as you go n pagamento m de acordo com o uso, (P) pré-pagamento m

payment /ˈpeɪmənt/ n pagamento m; fig (reward) recompensa f

payroll /ˈpeɪrəʊl/ n folha f de pagamentos; be on the ~ fazer parte da folha de pagamentos de uma firma

pea /piː/ n ervilha f

peace /piːs/ n paz f; disturb the ~ perturbar a ordem pública

peaceful /'piːsfl/ a pacífico; (calm) calmo, sereno

peacemaker /'piːsmeɪkə(r)/ n mediador m, pacificador m

peach /piːtʃ/ n pêssego m

peacock /'piːkɒk/ n pavão m

peak /piːk/ n pico m, cume m, cimo m; (of cap) pala f; (maximum) máximo m; **~ hours** horas fpl de ponta; Electr horas fpl de carga máxima; **~ed cap** boné m de pala

peal /piːl/ n (of bells) repique m; (of laughter) gargalhada f, risada f

peanut /'piːnʌt/ n amendoim m; **~s** ▣ (small sum) uma bagatela f

pear /peə(r)/ n pera f

pearl /pɜːl/ n pérola f

peasant /'peznt/ n camponês m, aldeão m

peat /piːt/ n turfa f

pebble /'pebl/ n seixo m, calhau m

peck /pek/ vt/i bicar; (attack) dar bicadas (em) ● n bicada f; ▣ (kiss) beijo m seco or (P) repenicado, beijoca f; **~ing order** hierarquia f, ordem f de importância

peckish /'pekɪʃ/ a **be ~** ▣ ter vontade de comer

peculiar /pɪ'kjuːlɪə(r)/ a bizarro, singular; (special) peculiar (**to** a), característico (**to** de). **~ity** /-'ærətɪ/ n singularidade f; (feature) peculiaridade f

pedal /'pedl/ n pedal m ● vi (pt pedalled) pedalar

pedantic /pɪ'dæntɪk/ a pedante

peddle /'pedl/ vt vender de porta em porta; <drugs> fazer tráfico de

pedestal /'pedɪstl/ n pedestal m

pedestrian /pɪ'destrɪən/ n pedestre mf, (P) peão m ● a pedestre; fig prosaico; **~ crossing** faixa f para

pedestres, (P) passadeira f

pedigree /'pedɪɡriː/ n estirpe f, linhagem f; (of animal) raça f ● a de raça

pedlar /'pedlə(r)/ n vendedor m ambulante

peek /piːk/ vi espreitar ● n espreitadela f

peel /piːl/ n casca f ● vt descascar ● vi <skin> pelar; <paint> escamar-se, descascar; <wallpaper> descolar-se

peep /piːp/ vi espreitar ● n espreitadela f, **~hole** n vigia f; (in door) olho m mágico

peer[1] /pɪə(r)/ vi **~ at/into** (searchingly) perscrutar; (with difficulty) esforçar-se por ver

peer[2] /pɪə(r)/ n (equal, noble) par m

peeved /piːvd/ a ▣ irritado; chateado ▣

peevish /'piːvɪʃ/ a irritável

peg /peɡ/ n cavilha f; (for washing) pregador m de roupa, (P) mola f; (for coats etc) cabide m; (for tent) estaca f ● vt (pt pegged) prender com estacas; **off the ~** prêt-à-porter, (P) pronto-a-vestir m inv

pejorative /pɪ'dʒɒrətɪv/ a pejorativo

pelican /'pelɪkən/ n pelicano m; **~ crossing** passagem f com sinais manobrados pelos pedestres, (P) peões

pellet /'pelɪt/ n bolinha f; (for gun) grão m de chumbo

pelt[1] /pelt/ n pele f

pelt[2] /pelt/ vt bombardear (**with** com) ● vi chover a cântaros; (run fast) correr em disparada or disparado

pelvis /'pelvɪs/ n Anat pélvis m, bacia f

pen[1] /pen/ n (enclosure) cercado m ● vt encurralar. **play-** n cercado m, (P) parque m

pen[2] /pen/ n caneta f ● vt (pt penned) escrever. **~friend** n correspondente mf

penal /'pi:nl/ a penal. **~ize** vt impôr uma penalidade a; Sport penalizar

penalty /'penltɪ/ n pena f; (fine) multa f; Sport penalidade f; **~ kick** pênalti m, (P) penálti f

penance /'penəns/ n penitência f

pence /pens/ ▶ PENNY

pencil /'pensl/ n lápis m ● vt (pt pencilled) escrever or desenhar a lápis. **~ sharpener** n apontador m, (P) apara-lápis m invar or afia-lápis m inv

pendant /'pendənt/ n berloque m

pending /'pendɪŋ/ a pendente ● prep (during) durante; (until) até

pendulum /'pendjʊləm/ n pêndulo m

penetrat|e /'penɪtreɪt/ vt/i penetrar (em). **~ing** a penetrante. **~ion** /-'treɪʃn/ n penetração f

penguin /'peŋgwɪn/ n pinguim m

penicillin /penɪ'sɪlɪn/ n penicilina f

peninsula /pə'nɪnsjʊlə/ n península f

penis /'pi:nɪs/ n pênis m, (P) pénis m

penitentiary /penɪ'tenʃərɪ/ n Amer penitenciária f, cadeia f

penknife /'pennaɪf/ n (pl -knives) canivete m

penniless /'penɪlɪs/ a sem vintém, sem um tostão

penny /'penɪ/ n (pl pennies, or pence) pêni m, (P) péni m; fig centavo m; vintém m

pension /'penʃn/ n pensão f; (in retirement) aposentadoria f,

(P) reforma f ● vt **~ off** reformar, aposentar. **~er** n (old-age) **~er** reformado m

pensive /'pensɪv/ a pensativo

penthouse /'penthaʊs/ n cobertura f, (P) apartamento de luxo (no último andar)

pent-up /'pentʌp/ a reprimido

penultimate /pen'ʌltɪmət/ a penúltimo

people /'pi:pl/ npl pessoas fpl ● n gente f, povo m ● vt povoar; **the Portuguese ~** os portugueses mpl; **~ say** dizem, diz-se

pep /pep/ n vigor m ● vt **~ up** animar; **~ talk** discurso m de encorajamento

pepper /'pepə(r)/ n pimenta f; (vegetable) pimentão m, (P) pimento m ● vt apimentar. **~y** a apimentado, picante

peppermint /'pepəmɪnt/ n hortelã-pimenta f; (sweet) bala f, (P) pastilha f de hortelã-pimenta

per /pɜ:(r)/ prep por; **~ annum** por ano; **~ cent** por cento; **~ kilo**/etc o quilo/etc

perceive /pə'si:v/ vt perceber; (notice) aperceber-se de

percentage /pə'sentɪdʒ/ n percentagem f

perceptible /pə'septəbl/ a perceptível, (P) percetível

percept|ion /pə'sepʃn/ n percepção f, (P) perceção f. **~ive** /-tɪv/ a perceptivo, (P) percetivo, penetrante, perspicaz

perch[1] /pɜ:tʃ/ n poleiro m ● vi empoleirar-se, pousar

perch[2] /pɜ:tʃ/ n (fish) perca f

percolat|e /'pɜ:kəleɪt/ vt/i filtrar(-se), passar. **~or** n máquina f de café com filtro, cafeteira f

percussion /pə'kʌʃn/ n
percussão f

perennial /pə'renɪəl/ a perene;
(plant) perene

perfect[1] /'pɜːfɪkt/ a perfeito. **~ly**
adv perfeitamente

perfect[2] /pə'fekt/ vt aperfeiçoar.
~ion /-ʃn/ n perfeição f. **~ionist** n
perfeccionista mf, (P) perfeccionista
mf

perform /pə'fɔːm/ vt ‹a task›
Mus executar; ‹a function› Theat
desempenhar ● vi representar;
‹function› funcionar. **~ance** n (of
task) Mus execução f; (of function)
Theat desempenho m; (of car)
performance f, comportamento m,
rendimento m; (I (fuss) drama m;
cena f. **~er** n artista mf

perfume /'pɜːfjuːm/ n perfume m

perhaps /pə'hæps/ adv talvez

peril /'perəl/ n perigo m. **~ous** a
perigoso

perimeter /pə'rɪmɪtə(r)/ n
perímetro m

period /'pɪərɪəd/ n período m,
época f; (era) época f; (lesson) hora
f de aula; período m letivo; Med
período m; (full stop) ponto (final)
m ● a (of novel) de costumes; (of
furniture) de estilo. **~ic** /-'ɒdɪk/
a periódico. **~ical** /-'ɒdɪkl/ n
periódico m. **~ically** /-'ɒdɪklɪ/ adv
periodicamente

peripher|y /pə'rɪfərɪ/ n periferia
f. **~al** a periférico; fig marginal; à
margem

perish /'perɪʃ/ vi morrer, perecer;
(rot) estragar-se, deteriorar-se.
~able a (of goods) deteriorável

perjur|e /'pɜːdʒə(r)/ vpr **~ o.s.**
jurar falso, perjurar. **~y** n perjúrio m

perk[1] /pɜːk/ vt/i **~ up** (I)
arrebitar(-se). **~y** a (I) vivo; animado

perk[2] /pɜːk/ n (I) regalia f; extra m

perm /pɜːm/ n permanente f ● vt
have one's hair ~ed fazer uma
permanente

permanen|t /'pɜːmənənt/ a
permanente. **~ce** n permanência f.
~tly adv permanentemente, a título
permanente

permissible /pə'mɪsəbl/ a
permissível, admissível

permission /pə'mɪʃn/ n
permissão f, licença f

permissive /pə'mɪsɪv/ a
permissivo; **~ society** sociedade f
permissiva. **~ness** n permissividade f

permit[1] /pə'mɪt/ vt (pt **permitted**)
permitir; consentir (**sb to** a alguém
que)

permit[2] /'pɜːmɪt/ n licença f; (pass)
passe m

permutation /pɜːmjuː'teɪʃn/ n
permutação f, permuta f

perpendicular
/pɜːpən'dɪkjʊlə(r)/ a & n
perpendicular f

perpetrat|e /'pɜːpɪtreɪt/ vt
perpetrar. **~or** n autor m

perpetual /pə'petʃʊəl/ a perpétuo

perpetuate /pə'petʃʊeɪt/ vt
perpetuar

perplex /pə'pleks/ vt deixar
perplexo. **~ed** a perplexo

persecut|e /'pɜːsɪkjuːt/ vt
perseguir. **~ion** /-'kjuːʃn/ n
perseguição f

persever|e /pɜːsɪ'vɪə(r)/ vi
perseverar. **~ance** n perseverança f

Persian /'pɜːʃn/ a & n Lang persa m

persist /pə'sɪst/ vi persistir
(**in doing** em fazer). **~ence** n

persistência f. **~ent** a persistente; (*obstinate*) teimoso; (*continual*) contínuo, constante. **~ently** adv persistentemente

person /'pɜːsn/ n pessoa f; **in ~** em pessoa

personal /'pɜːsənl/ a pessoal; <*secretary*> particular; **~ stereo** estéreo m pessoal, walkman m. **~ly** adv pessoalmente

personality /pɜːsə'nælətɪ/ n personalidade f; (*on TV*) vedete f, (P) vedeta f

personify /pə'sɒnɪfaɪ/ vt personificar

personnel /pɜːsə'nel/ n pessoal m

perspective /pə'spektɪv/ n perspectiva f, (P) perspetiva f

perspir|e /pə'spaɪə(r)/ vi transpirar. **~ation** /-ə'reɪʃn/ n transpiração f

persua|de /pə'sweɪd/ vt persuadir (**to** a). **~sion** /-'sweɪʒn/ n persuasão f; (*belief*) crença f, convicção f. **~sive** /-'sweɪsɪv/ a persuasivo

pert /pɜːt/ a (*saucy*) atrevido, descarado; (*lively*) vivo

pertinent /'pɜːtɪnənt/ a pertinente

perturb /pə'tɜːb/ vt perturbar, transtornar

Peru /pə'ruː/ n Peru m. **~vian** a & n peruano m

peruse /pə'ruːz/ vt ler com atenção

perva|de /pə'veɪd/ vt espalhar-se por, invadir. **~sive** a penetrante

pervers|e /pə'vɜːs/ a que insiste no erro; (*wicked*) perverso; (*wayward*) caprichoso. **~ity** n obstinação f; (*wickedness*) perversidade f; (*waywardness*) capricho m, birra f

pervert¹ /pə'vɜːt/ vt perverter. **~sion** n perversão f

pervert² /'pɜːvɜːt/ n pervertido m, tarado m

pessimis|t /'pesɪmɪst/ n pessimista mf. **~m** /-zəm/ n pessimismo m. **~tic** /-'mɪstɪk/ a pessimista

pest /pest/ n praga f, inseto m novico; (*animal*) animal m daninho; (*person*) peste f

pester /'pestə(r)/ vt incomodar 🛈

pesticide /'pestɪsaɪd/ n pesticida m

pet /pet/ n animal m de estimação; (*favourite*) preferido m, querido m ● a <*rabbit etc*> de estimação ● vt (*pt* **petted**) acariciar; **~ name** nome m usado em família

petal /'petl/ n pétala f

peter /'piːtə(r)/ vi **~ out** extinguir-se, acabar pouco a pouco, morrer *fig*

petition /pɪ'tɪʃn/ n petição f ● vt requerer

petrify /'petrɪfaɪ/ vt petrificar

petrol /'petrəl/ n gasolina f; **~ pump** bomba f de gasolina; **~ station** posto m de gasolina; **~ tank** tanque m de gasolina

petroleum /pɪ'trəʊlɪəm/ n petróleo m

petticoat /'petɪkəʊt/ n combinação f, anágua f

petty /'petɪ/ a (-**ier, -iest**) pequeno, insignificante; (*mean*) mesquinho; **~ cash** fundo m para pequenas despesas, caixa f pequena

petulan|t /'petjʊlənt/ a petulante, irritável. **~ce** n irritabilidade f

pew /pjuː/ n banco (de igreja) m

phantom /'fæntəm/ n fantasma m

pharmaceutical /fɑːmə'sjuːtɪkl/ a farmacêutico

pharmac|y /ˈfɑːməsɪ/ n farmácia f.
~**ist** n farmacêutico m

phase /feɪz/ n fase f ● vt = in/out
introduzir/retirar progressivamente

PhD abbr of **Doctor of Philosophy** n
doutorado m, (P) doutoramento m

pheasant /ˈfeznt/ n faisão m

phenomen|on /fɪˈnɒmɪnən/ n (pl
-ena) fenómeno m, (P) fenómeno m.
~**al** a fenomenal

philanthrop|ist /fɪˈlænθrəpɪst/
n filantropo m. ~**ic** /-ənˈθrɒpɪk/ a
filantrópico

Philippines /ˈfɪlɪpiːnz/ npl the ~
as Filipinas fpl

philistine /ˈfɪlɪstaɪn/ n filisteu m

philosoph|y /fɪˈlɒsəfɪ/ n filosofia
f. ~**er** n filósofo m. ~**ical** /-əˈsɒfɪkl/
a filosófico

phlegm /flem/ n Med catarro m,
fleuma f

phobia /ˈfəʊbɪə/ n fobia f

phone /fəʊn/ n [1] telefone m; **on
the** ~ no or (P) ao telefone; ~ **book**
lista f telefónica, (P) telefónica;
~ **box** cabine f telefónica or (P)
telefónica; ~ **call** chamada f,
telefonema f ● vt/i [1] telefonar
(para); ~ **back** voltar a telefonar,
ligar de volta. ~**in** n programa de
rádio ou tv com participação dos
ouvintes

phonecard /ˈfəʊnkɑːd/ n cartão m
para uso em telefone público

phonetic /fəˈnetɪk/ a fonético. ~**s**
n fonética f

phoney /ˈfəʊnɪ/ a (-ier, -iest) 🅇
falso; fingido ● n 🅇 (person) fingido
m; 🅇 (thing) falso m, (P) falsificação f

photo /ˈfəʊtəʊ/ n (pl -os) [1] retrato
m; foto f

photocop|y /ˈfəʊtəʊkɒpɪ/ n
fotocópia f ● vt fotocopiar. ~**ier** n

fotocopiadora f

photogenic /fəʊtəʊˈdʒenɪk/ a
fotogénico, (P) fotogénico

photograph /ˈfəʊtəɡrɑːf/ n
fotografia f ● vt fotografar. ~**er**
/fəˈtɒɡrəfə(r)/ n fotógrafo m.
~**ic** /-ˈɡræfɪk/ a fotográfico. ~**y**
/fəˈtɒɡrəfɪ/ n fotografia f

phrase /freɪz/ n expressão f, frase
f; Gram locução f, frase f elíptica
● vt exprimir. ~ **book** n livro m de
expressões idiomáticas

physical /ˈfɪzɪkl/ a físico

physician /fɪˈzɪʃn/ n médico m

physicist /ˈfɪzɪsɪst/ n físico m

physics /ˈfɪzɪks/ n física f

physiology /fɪzɪˈɒlədʒɪ/ n
fisiologia f

physiotherap|y /fɪzɪəʊˈθerəpɪ/ n
fisioterapia f. ~**ist** n fisioterapeuta mf

physique /fɪˈziːk/ n físico m

pian|o /pɪˈænəʊ/ n (pl -os) piano m.
~**ist** /ˈpɪənɪst/ n pianista mf

pick[1] /pɪk/ n (tool) picareta f

pick[2] /pɪk/ vt escolher; ⟨flowers, fruit
etc⟩ colher; ⟨lock⟩ forçar; ⟨teeth⟩
palitar; ~ **a quarrel with** puxar or
(P) pedir uma briga com; ~ **holes in
an argument** descobrir os pontos
fracos dum argumento; ~ **sb's
pocket** bater or (P) roubar a carteira
de alguém; ~ **off** tirar, arrancar; ~
on implicar com; ~ **out** escolher;
(identify) identificar, reconhecer ● n
escolha f; (best) o/a melhor; **take
one's** ~ escolher livremente □ ~ **up**
vt apanhar; ⟨speed⟩ ganhar

pickaxe /ˈpɪkæks/ n picareta f

picket /ˈpɪkɪt/ n piquete m; (single
striker) grevista mf de piquete ● vt (pt
picketed) colocar um piquete em
● vi fazer piquete

pickings /ˈpɪkɪŋz/ npl restos mpl

pickle /ˈpɪkl/ n vinagre m; **~s** picles mpl, (P) pickles mpl; **in a ~** 🔲 numa encrenca 🔲 ● vt conservar em vinagre

pickpocket /ˈpɪkpɒkɪt/ n batedor m de carteiras, (P) carteirista m

picnic /ˈpɪknɪk/ n piquenique m ● vi (pt **picnicked**) piquenicar, (P) fazer um piquenique

picture /ˈpɪktʃə(r)/ n imagem f; (illustration) estampa f, ilustração f; (painting) quadro m, pintura f; (photo) fotografia f, retrato m; (drawing) desenho m; fig descrição f; quadro m; **the ~s** o cinema ● vt imaginar; (describe) pintar, descrever

picturesque /pɪktʃəˈresk/ a pitoresco

pie /paɪ/ n torta f, (P) tarte f; (of meat) empada f

piece /piːs/ n pedaço m, bocado m; (of machine, in game) peça f; (of currency) moeda f; **a ~ of advice/ furniture/**etc um conselho/um móvel/etc; **take to ~s** desmontar ● vt **~ together** juntar, montar

piecemeal /ˈpiːsmiːl/ a aos poucos, pouco a pouco

pier /pɪə(r)/ n molhe m

pierc|e /pɪəs/ vt furar, penetrar. **~ing** a penetrante; (of scream, pain) lancinante

piety /ˈpaɪətɪ/ n piedade f, devoção f

pig /pɪg/ n porco m. **~-headed** a cabeçudo, teimoso

pigeon /ˈpɪdʒɪn/ n pombo m. **~hole** n escaninho m

piggy /ˈpɪgɪ/ a como um porco; **~ bank** cofre m de criança. **~back** adv nas costas, (P) porquinho-mealheiro m

pigment /ˈpɪgmənt/ n pigmento m. **~ation** /-ˈteɪʃn/ n pigmentação f

pigsty /ˈpɪgstaɪ/ n pocilga f, chiqueiro m

pigtail /ˈpɪgteɪl/ n trança f

pilchard /ˈpɪltʃəd/ n peixe m pequeno da família do arenque, sardinha f europeia

pile /paɪl/ n pilha f; (of carpet) pelo m ● vt/i amontoar(-se); empilhar(-se) (**into** em); **a ~ of** 🔲 um monte de 🔲; **~ up** acumular(-se). **~-up** n choque m em cadeia

piles /paɪlz/ npl hemorroidas fpl

pilfer /ˈpɪlfə(r)/ vt furtar

pilgrim /ˈpɪlgrɪm/ n peregrino m, romeiro m. **~age** n peregrinação f, romaria f

pill /pɪl/ n pílula f, comprimido m

pillar /ˈpɪlə(r)/ n pilar m. **~ box** n marco m do correio

pillow /ˈpɪləʊ/ n travesseiro m

pillowcase /ˈpɪləʊkeɪs/ n fronha f

pilot /ˈpaɪlət/ n piloto m ● vt (pt **piloted**) pilotar. **~ light** n piloto m; Electr lâmpada f testemunho; (gas) piloto m

pimple /ˈpɪmpl/ n borbulha f, espinha f

pin /pɪn/ n alfinete m; Techn cavilha f; **have ~s and needles** estar com uma cãibra ● vt (pt **pinned**) pregar or prender com alfinete(s); (hold down) prender, segurar; **~ sb down** fig obrigar alguém a definir-se, apertar (com) alguém fig. **~ up** pregar. **~point** vt localizar com precisão; **~stripe** a de listras finas; **~up** n 🔲 pin-up f

PIN /pɪn/ abbr (= personal identification number) PIN m, (P) código m PIN

pinafore /'pɪnəfɔ:(r)/ n avental m; **~ dress** veste f

pincers /'pɪnsəz/ npl (tool) torquês f, (P) alicate m; Med pinça f; Zool pinça(s) f(pl), tenaz(es) f(pl)

pinch /pɪntʃ/ vt apertar; ⊠ (steal) surripiar ⊞ ● n aperto m; (tweak) beliscão m; (small amount) pitada f; **at a ~** em caso de necessidade

pine¹ /paɪn/ n (tree) pinheiro m; (wood) pinho m

pine² /paɪn/ vi **~ away** definhar, consumir-se; **~ for** suspirar por

pineapple /'paɪnæpl/ n abacaxi m, (P) ananás m

ping-pong /'pɪŋpɒŋ/ n pingue-pongue m

pink /pɪŋk/ a & n rosa m

pinnacle /'pɪnəkl/ n pináculo m

pint /paɪnt/ n quartilho m (= 0,57 l, Amer = 0,47 l)

pioneer /paɪə'nɪə(r)/ n pioneiro m ● vt ser o pioneiro em, preparar o caminho para

pious /'paɪəs/ a piedoso, devoto

pip /pɪp/ n (seed) pevide f

pipe /paɪp/ n cano m, tubo m; (of smoker) cachimbo m ● vt encanar, canalizar; **~ down** calar a boca

pipeline /'paɪplaɪn/ n (for oil) oleoduto m; (for gas) gaseoduto m, (P) gasoduto m; **in the ~** fig encaminhado

piping /'paɪpɪŋ/ n tubagem f; **~ hot** muito quente

pira|te /'paɪərət/ n pirata m. **~cy** n pirataria f

Pisces /'paɪsi:z/ n Astr Peixe m

pistol /'pɪstl/ n pistola f

piston /'pɪstən/ n êmbolo m, pistão m

pit /pɪt/ n (hole) cova f, fosso m; (mine) poço m; (quarry) pedreira f ● vt (pt pitted) picar, esburacar; fig opor; **~ o.s. against** (struggle) medir-se com

pitch¹ /pɪtʃ/ n breu m. **~-black** a escuro como breu

pitch² /pɪtʃ/ vt (throw) lançar; <tent> armar ● vi cair ● n (slope) declive m; (of sound) som m; (of voice) altura f; Sport campo m

pitfall /'pɪtfɔ:l/ n fig cilada f; perigo m inesperado

pith /pɪθ/ n (of orange) parte f branca da casca, mesocarpo m; fig (essential part) cerne m; âmago m

pithy /'pɪθɪ/ a (-ier, -iest) preciso, conciso

piti|ful /'pɪtɪfl/ a lastimoso; (contemptible) miserável. **~less** a impiedoso

pittance /'pɪtns/ n salário m miserável, miséria f

pity /'pɪtɪ/ n dó m, pena f, piedade f; **it's a ~** é uma pena; **take ~ on** ter pena de; **what a ~!** que pena! ● vt compadecer-se de

pivot /'pɪvət/ n eixo m ● vt (pt pivoted) girar em torno de

placard /'plækɑ:d/ n (poster) cartaz m

placate /plə'keɪt/ vt apaziguar, aplacar

place /pleɪs/ n lugar m, sítio m; (house) casa f, (seat, rank etc) lugar m ● vt colocar, pôr; **~ an order** fazer uma encomenda; **at/to my ~** em or na/a minha casa. **~ mat** n pano m de mesa individual

placid /'plæsɪd/ a plácido

plagiar|ize /'pleɪdʒəraɪz/ vt plagiar. **~ism** n plágio m

plague /pleɪg/ n peste f; (of insects) praga f ● vt atormentar, atazanar

plaice /pleɪs/ n (pl invar) solha f

plain /pleɪn/ a (-er, -est) claro; (candid) franco; (simple) simples; (not pretty) sem beleza; (not patterned) liso; **in ~ clothes** à paisana ● adv com franqueza ● n planície f. **~ly** adv claramente; (candidly) francamente

plaintiff /ˈpleɪntɪf/ n queixoso m

plait /plæt/ vt entrançar ● n trança f

plan /plæn/ n plano m, projeto m; (of a house, city etc) plano m, planta f ● vt (pt **planned**) planear, planejar ● vi fazer planos; **~ to do** ter a intenção de fazer

plane[1] /pleɪn/ n (level) plano m; (aeroplane) avião m ● a plano

plane[2] /pleɪn/ n (tool) plaina f ● vt aplainar

planet /ˈplænɪt/ n planeta m

plank /plæŋk/ n prancha f

planning /ˈplænɪŋ/ n planeamento m, planejamento m; **~ permission** permissão f para construir

plant /plɑːnt/ n planta f; Techn aparelhagem f; (factory) fábrica f ● vt plantar; **~ a bomb** colocar uma bomba. **~ation** /-ˈteɪʃn/ n plantação f

plaque /plɑːk/ n placa f; (on teeth) tártaro m, pedra f

plaster /ˈplɑːstə(r)/ n reboco m; (adhesive) esparadrapo m, band-aid m, (P) gesso m; **in ~** engessado; **~ of Paris** gesso m ● vt rebocar; (cover) cobrir (**with** com, de)

plastic /ˈplæstɪk/ a plástico ● n plástica f; **~ surgery** cirurgia f plástica

plate /pleɪt/ n prato m; (in book) gravura f ● vt revestir de metal

plateau /ˈplætəʊ/ n (pl **-eaux** /-əʊz/) planalto m, platô m

platform /ˈplætfɔːm/ n estrado m; (for speaking) tribuna f; Rail plataforma f, cais m; fig programa m de partido político; **~ ticket** bilhete m de gare

platinum /ˈplætɪnəm/ n platina f

platitude /ˈplætɪtjuːd/ n banalidade f, lugar-comum m

platonic /pləˈtɒnɪk/ a platônico, (P) platónico

plausible /ˈplɔːzəbl/ a plausível; (person) convincente

play /pleɪ/ vt/i (for amusement) brincar; ⟨instrument⟩ tocar; ⟨cards, game⟩ jogar; ⟨opponent⟩ jogar contra; ⟨match⟩ disputar; **~ down** minimizar; **~ on** (take advantage of) aproveitar-se de; **~ safe** jogar pelo seguro; **~ up** 🄸 dar problemas (a) ● n jogo m; Theat peça f; (movement) folga f, margem f. **~group** n jardim m de infância

playboy /ˈpleɪbɔɪ/ n playboy m

player /ˈpleɪə(r)/ n jogador m; Theat artista mf; Mus artista mf, executante mf, instrumentista mf

playful /ˈpleɪfl/ a brincalhão m

playground /ˈpleɪɡraʊnd/ n pátio m de recreio

playing /ˈpleɪɪŋ/ n atuação f. **~ card** n carta f de jogar; **~ field** n campo m de jogos

playwright /ˈpleɪraɪt/ n dramaturgo m

plc abbr of (**= public limited company**) SARL

plea /pliː/ n súplica f; (reason) pretexto m, desculpa f; Jur alegação f da defesa

plead /pli:d/ vt/i pleitear; (as
excuse) alegar; ~ **guilty** confessar-se
culpado; ~ **with** implorar a

pleasant /'pleznt/ a agradável

pleas|e /pli:z/ vt/i agradar (a), dar
prazer (a); **they ~e themselves,
they do as they ~e** eles fazem
como bem entendem ● adv por
favor, (P) se faz favor; ~**ed** a
contente; satisfeito (**with** com).
~**ing** a agradável

pleasur|e /'pleʒə(r)/ n prazer m.
~**able** a agradável

pleat /pli:t/ n prega f ● vt preguear

pledge /pledʒ/ n penhor m,
garantia f; fig promessa f ● vt
prometer; (pawn) empenhar

plentiful /'plentɪfl/ a abundante

plenty /'plentɪ/ n abundância f,
fartura f; ~ **(of)** muito (de); (enough)
bastante (de)

pliable /'plaɪəbl/ a flexível

pliers /'plaɪəz/ npl alicate m

plight /plaɪt/ n triste f situação

plinth /plɪnθ/ n plinto m

plod /plɒd/ vi (pt **plodded**)
caminhar lentamente; ⟨work⟩
trabalhar; marrar 🗵

plonk /plɒŋk/ n 🗵 vinho m
ordinário, (P) carrascão m

plot /plɒt/ n complô m, conspiração
f; (of novel and play) trama f; (of land) lote
m ● vt/i (pt **plotted**) conspirar; (mark
out) traçar

plough /plaʊ/ n arado m ● vt/i arar;
~ **back** reinvestir; ~ **into** colidir; ~
through abrir caminho por

ploy /plɔɪ/ n 🗵 estratagema m

pluck /plʌk/ vt apanhar; ⟨bird⟩
depenar; ⟨eyebrows⟩ depilar; Mus
tanger; ~ **up courage** ganhar
coragem ● n coragem f. ~**y** a
corajoso

plug /plʌg/ n tampão m; Electr
tomada f, (P) ficha f ● vt (pt **plugged**)
tapar com tampão; 🗵 (publicize)
fazer grande propaganda de ● vi ~
away 🗵 trabalhar com afinco; ~ **in**
Electr ligar

plum /plʌm/ n ameixa f

plumb /plʌm/ adv exatamente
● vt sondar

plumb|er /'plʌmə(r)/ n bombeiro
m, encanador m, (P) canalizador
m. ~**ing** n encanamento m, (P)
canalização f

plummet /'plʌmɪt/ vi (pt
plummeted) despencar

plump /plʌmp/ a (-er, -est)
rechonchudo, roliço ● vi ~ **for**
optar por

plunder /'plʌndə(r)/ vt pilhar,
saquear ● n pilhagem f, saque m;
(goods) despojo m

plunge /plʌndʒ/ vt/i mergulhar,
atirar(-se), afundar(-se) ● n
mergulho m; **take the ~** fig
decidir-se, dar o salto fig

plural /'plʊərəl/ a plural; ⟨noun⟩ no
plural ● n plural m

plus /plʌs/ prep mais ● a positivo
● n sinal +; fig qualidade f positiva

plush /plʌʃ/ n pelúcia f, peluche
m ● a de pelúcia, de peluche; 🗵
de luxo

ply /plaɪ/ vt (tool) manejar; (trade)
exercer; ~ **sb with drink** encher
alguém de bebidas ● vi ⟨ship, bus⟩
fazer carreira entre dois lugares

plywood /'plaɪwʊd/ n madeira f
compensada, (P) contraplacado m

p.m. /pi:'em/ adv da tarde, da noite

pneumatic /njuː'mætɪk/
a pneumático; ~ **drill** broca f
pneumática

pneumonia /njuːˈməʊnɪə/ n
pneumonia f

poach /pəʊtʃ/ vt/i (steal) caçar或
pescar em propriedade alheia or
ilegalmente; Culin fazer pochê, (P)
escalfar; **~ed eggs** ovos mpl pochês,
(P) ovos mpl escalfados

pocket /ˈpɒkɪt/ n bolso m, algibeira
f ● a de algibeira ● vt meter no
bolso. **~book** n (notebook) livro m
de apontamentos; Amer (handbag)
carteira f; **~ money** (monthly)
mesada f; (weekly) semanada f,
dinheiro m para pequenas despesas

pod /pɒd/ n vagem f

podcast /ˈpɒdkɑːst/ n podcast m

poem /ˈpəʊɪm/ n poema m

poet /ˈpəʊɪt/ n poeta m, poetisa f.
~ic /-ˈetɪk/ a poético

poetry /ˈpəʊɪtrɪ/ n poesia f

poignant /ˈpɔɪnjənt/ a pungente,
doloroso

point /pɔɪnt/ n ponto m; (tip)
ponta f; (decimal point) vírgula f;
(meaning) sentido m, razão m; Electr
tomada f; **~s** Rail agulhas fpl; **on the
~ of** prestes a, quase a; **~ of view**
ponto m de vista; **that is a good ~**
(remark) é uma boa observação; **to
the ~** a propósito; **what is the ~?**
de que adianta? ● vt/i (aim) apontar
(at para); (show) apontar; indicar
(at/to para); **~ out** apontar, fazer
ver. **~blank** a & adv à queima-roupa;
fig categórico

pointed /ˈpɔɪntɪd/ a pontiagudo;
(of remark) intencional, contundente

pointer /ˈpɔɪntə(r)/ n ponteiro m;
🄸 (hint) sugestão f

pointless /ˈpɔɪntlɪs/ a inútil, sem
sentido

poise /pɔɪz/ n equilíbrio m;
(carriage) porte m; fig (self-

possession) presença f; segurança f.
~d a equilibrado; ⟨person⟩ seguro
de si

poison /ˈpɔɪzn/ n veneno m,
peçonha f ● vt envenenar. **blood-
~ing** n envenenamento m do
sangue. **food~ing** n intoxicação f
alimentar. **~ous** a venenoso

poke /pəʊk/ vt/i espetar; (with
elbow) acotovelar; ⟨fire⟩ atiçar ● n
espetadela f; (with elbow) cotovelada
f; **~ about** esgaravatar, remexer,
procurar; **~ fun at** fazer troça/
pouco de; **~ out** ⟨head⟩ enfiar

poker[1] /ˈpəʊkə(r)/ n atiçador m

poker[2] /ˈpəʊkə(r)/ n Cards pôquer
m, (P) póquer m

poky /ˈpəʊkɪ/ a (-ier, -iest)
acanhado, apertado

Poland /ˈpəʊlənd/ n Polônia f, (P)
Polónia f

polar /ˈpəʊlə(r)/ a polar; **~ bear**
urso m branco

pole[1] /pəʊl/ n vara f; (for flag)
mastro m; (post) poste m

pole[2] /pəʊl/ n Geog polo m

Pole /pəʊl/ n polaco m

police /pəˈliːs/ n polícia f; **~ state**
estado m policial; **~ station** distrito
m, delegacia f, (P) esquadra f de
polícia ● vt policiar

police|man /pəˈliːsmən/ n (pl
-men) policial m, (P) polícia m,
guarda m, agente m de polícia.
~woman n (pl -women) polícia f
feminina, (P) mulher-polícia f

policy[1] /ˈpɒlɪsɪ/ n (plan of action)
política f

policy[2] /ˈpɒlɪsɪ/ n (insurance)
apólice f de seguro

polio /ˈpəʊlɪəʊ/ n polio f

polish /ˈpɒlɪʃ/ vt polir, dar lustro
em; ⟨shoes⟩ engraxar; ⟨floor⟩

encerar ● n (for shoes) graxa f; (for floor) cera f; (for nails) esmalte m, (P) verniz m; (shine) polimento m; fig requinte m; ~ **off** acabar (rapidamente); ~ **up** ‹language› aperfeiçoar. **~ed** a requintado, elegante

Polish /ˈpəʊlɪʃ/ a & n polonês m, (P) polaco m

polite /pəˈlaɪt/ a polido, educado, delicado. **~ness** n delicadeza f, cortesia f

political /pəˈlɪtɪkl/ a político

politician /pɒlɪˈtɪʃn/ n político m

politics /ˈpɒlətɪks/ n política f

poll /pəʊl/ n votação f; (survey) sondagem f, pesquisa f; **go to the ~s** votar, ir às urnas ● vt ‹votes› obter. **~ing booth** n cabine f de voto

pollen /ˈpɒlən/ n pólen m

pollut|e /pəˈluːt/ vt poluir. **~ion** /-ʃn/ n poluição f

polo /ˈpəʊləʊ/ n polo m; ~ **neck** gola f rolê

polyester /pɒlɪˈestə/ n poliéster m

polythene /ˈpɒlɪθiːn/ n politeno m. ~ **bag** n saco m de plástico

pomegranate /ˈpɒmɪɡrænɪt/ n romã f

pomp /pɒmp/ n pompa f

pomp|ous /ˈpɒmpəs/ a pomposo. **~osity** /-ˈpɒsətɪ/ n imponência f

pond /pɒnd/ n lagoa f, lago m; (artificial) tanque m, lago m

ponder /ˈpɒndə(r)/ vt/i ponderar; meditar (over sobre)

pony /ˈpəʊnɪ/ n pônei m, (P) pónei m. **~tail** n rabo m de cavalo

poodle /ˈpuːdl/ n caniche m

pool[1] /puːl/ n (puddle) charco m, poça f; (for swimming) piscina f

pool[2] /puːl/ n (fund) fundo m comum; Econ, Comm pool m; (game) forma f de bilhar; **~s** loteca f, (P) totobola m ● vt pôr num fundo comum

poor /pʊə(r)/ a (-er, -est) pobre; (not good) medíocre. **~ly** adv mal ● a doente

pop[1] /pɒp/ n estalido m, ruído m seco ● vt/i (pt **popped**) dar um estalido, estalar; (of cork) saltar; ~ **in/out/off** entrar/sair/ir-se embora; ~ **up** aparecer de repente, saltar

pop[2] /pɒp/ n música f pop ● a pop invar

popcorn /ˈpɒpkɔːn/ n pipoca f

pope /pəʊp/ n papa m

poplar /ˈpɒplə(r)/ n choupo m, álamo m

poppy /ˈpɒpɪ/ n papoula f

popular /ˈpɒpjʊlə(r)/ a popular; (in fashion) em voga, na moda; **be ~ with** ser popular entre. **~ity** /-ˈlærətɪ/ n popularidade f. **~ize** vt popularizar, vulgarizar

populat|e /ˈpɒpjʊleɪt/ vt povoar. **~ion** /-ˈleɪʃn/ n população f

populous /ˈpɒpjʊləs/ a populoso

porcelain /ˈpɔːslɪn/ n porcelana f

porch /pɔːtʃ/ n alpendre m; Amer varanda f

porcupine /ˈpɔːkjʊpaɪn/ n porco-espinho m

pore[1] /pɔː(r)/ n poro m

pore[2] /pɔː(r)/ vi ~ **over** examinar, estudar

pork /pɔːk/ n carne f de porco

pornograph|y /pɔːˈnɒɡrəfɪ/ n pornografia f. **~ic** /-əˈɡræfɪk/ a pornográfico

porridge /ˈpɒrɪdʒ/ n (papa f de) flocos mpl de aveia

port[1] /pɔːt/ n (harbour) porto m

port[2] /pɔːt/ n (wine) (vinho do) Porto m

portable /ˈpɔːtəbl/ a portátil

porter[1] /ˈpɔːtə(r)/ n (carrier) carregador m

porter[2] /ˈpɔːtə(r)/ n (doorkeeper) porteiro m

portfolio /pɔːtˈfəʊliəʊ/ n (pl -os) portfólio m; (case, post) pasta f; (securities) carteira f de investimentos

porthole /ˈpɔːthəʊl/ n vigia f

portion /ˈpɔːʃn/ n (share, helping) porção f; (part) parte f

portrait /ˈpɔːtrɪt/ n retrato m

portray /pɔːˈtreɪ/ vt retratar, pintar; fig descrever. ~al n retrato m

Portug|al /ˈpɔːtjʊgl/ n Portugal m. ~uese /-ˈgiːz/ a & n invar português m

pose /pəʊz/ vt/i (fazer) posar; ‹question› fazer, colocar ● n pose f, postura f; ~ as fazer-se passar por

poser /ˈpəʊzə(r)/ n quebra-cabeças m

posh /pɒʃ/ a 🆇 chique invar

position /pəˈzɪʃn/ n (posição f; (job) lugar m, colocação f; (state) situação f ● vt colocar

positive /ˈpɒzətɪv/ a positivo; (definite) categórico, definitivo; 🆈 (downright) autêntico; she's ~ that ela tem certeza que. ~ly adv positivamente; (absolutely) completamente

possess /pəˈzes/ vt possuir. ~ion /-ʃn/ n posse f; (thing possessed) possessão f

possessive /pəˈzesɪv/ a possessivo

possib|le /ˈpɒsəbl/ a possível. ~ility /-ˈbɪlətɪ/ n possibilidade f

possibly /ˈpɒsəblɪ/ adv possivelmente, talvez; if I ~ can se me for possível; I cannot ~ leave estou impossibilitado de partir

post[1] /pəʊst/ n (pole) poste m ● vt ‹notice› afixar, pregar

post[2] /pəʊst/ n (station, job) posto m ● vt colocar; (appoint) colocar

post[3] /pəʊst/ n (mail) correio m; P~ Office agência f dos correios, (P) estação f dos correios; (corporation) Departamento m dos Correios e Telégrafos, (P) Correios, Telégrafos e Telefones mpl (CTT) ● a postal ● vt mandar pelo correio; keep ~ed manter informado. ~ code n código m postal

post- /pəʊst/ pref pós-

postage /ˈpəʊstɪdʒ/ n porte m

postal /ˈpəʊstl/ a postal; ~ order vale m postal

postcard /ˈpəʊstkɑːd/ n cartão-postal m, (P) (bilhete) postal m

poster /ˈpəʊstə(r)/ n cartaz m

posterity /pɒˈsterətɪ/ n posteridade f

postgraduate /pəʊstˈgrædʒʊet/ n pós-graduado m

posthumous /ˈpɒstjʊməs/ a póstumo. ~ly adv a título póstumo

postman /ˈpəʊstmən/ n (pl -men) carteiro m

postmark /ˈpəʊstmɑːk/ n carimbo m do correio

post-mortem /pəʊstˈmɔːtəm/ n autópsia f

postpone /pəˈspəʊn/ vt adiar. ~ment n adiamento m

postscript /ˈpəʊsskrɪpt/ n post-scriptum m

posture /'pɒstʃə(r)/ n postura f, posição f ● vi posar

post-war /'pəʊstwɔː(r)/ a de após-guerra, (P) do pós-guerra

pot /pɒt/ n pote m; (for cooking) panela f; (for plants) vaso m; ▣ (marijuana) maconha f, (P) marijuana f; **go to ~** ‹business› arruinar, degringolar ▣; ▣ ‹person› estar arruinado or liquidado; **take ~ luck** aceitar o que houver; **take a ~shot** dar um tiro de perto (at em); (at random) dar um tiro a esmo (at em) ● vt (pt potted) **~ (up)** plantar em vaso. **~ belly** n pança f, barriga f

potato /pə'teɪtəʊ/ n (pl -oes) batata f

poten|t /'pəʊtnt/ a potente, poderoso; ‹drink› forte. **~cy** n potência f

potential /pə'tenʃl/ a & n potencial m. **~ly** adv potencialmente

pothol|e /'pɒthəʊl/ n caverna f, caldeirão m; (in road) buraco m

potion /'pəʊʃn/ n poção f

potted /'pɒtɪd/ a (of plant) de vaso; (preserved) de conserva

potter[1] /'pɒtə(r)/ n oleiro m, ceramista mf. **~y** n olaria f, cerâmica f

potter[2] /'pɒtə(r)/ vi entreter-se com isto ou aquilo

potty[1] /'pɒtɪ/ a (-ier, -iest) ▣ doido, pirado ▣; chanfrado ▣

potty[2] /'pɒtɪ/ n -ties f penico m de criança

pouch /paʊtʃ/ n bolsa f; (for tobacco) tabaqueira f

poultry /'pəʊltrɪ/ n aves fpl domésticas, carne f de aves domésticas

pounce /paʊns/ vi atirar-se (on sobre, para cima de) ● n salto m

pound[1] /paʊnd/ n (weight) libra f (= 453 g); (money) libra f

pound[2] /paʊnd/ n (for dogs) canil m municipal; (for cars) parque m de viaturas rebocadas

pound[3] /paʊnd/ vt/i (crush) esmagar, pisar; (of heart) bater com força; (bombard) bombardear; (on piano etc) martelar

pour /pɔː(r)/ vt deitar, derramar ● vi correr; ‹rain› chover torrencialmente; **~ in/out** (of people) afluir/sair em massa; **~ off** or **out** esvaziar, vazar; **~ing rain** chuva f torrencial

pout /paʊt/ vt/i **~ (one's lips)** (sulk) fazer beicinho; (in annoyance) ficar de trombas ● n beicinho m

poverty /'pɒvətɪ/ n pobreza f, miséria f. **~-stricken** a pobre

powder /'paʊdə(r)/ n pó m; (for face) pó de arroz m ● vt polvilhar; ‹face› empoar. **~ room** n toalete m, toucador m. **~y** a como pó

power /'paʊə(r)/ n poder m; Maths, Mech potência f; (energy) energia f; Electr corrente f; **~ cut** corte m de energia, blecaute m, (P) blackout m; **~ station** central f eléctrica; **~ed by** movido a; ‹jet etc› de propulsão. **~ful** a poderoso; Mech potente. **~less** a impotente

practicable /'præktɪkəbl/ a viável

practical /'præktɪkl/ a prático; **~ joke** brincadeira f de mau gosto

practically /'præktɪklɪ/ adv praticamente

practice /'præktɪs/ n prática f; (of law etc) exercício m; Sport treino m; (clients) clientela f; **in ~** (in fact) na prática; (well-trained) em forma; **out of ~** destreinado, sem prática; **put into ~** pôr em prática

practis|e /'præktɪs/ vt/i ‹skill, sport› praticar, exercitar-se em; ‹profession› exercer; (put into practice) pôr em prática. **~ed** a experimentado, experiente. **~ing** a ‹Catholic etc› praticante

practitioner /præk'tɪʃənə(r)/ n praticante mf; **general ~** médico m de clínica geral or de família

pragmatic /præg'mætɪk/ a pragmático

praise /preɪz/ vt louvar, elogiar ● n elogio(s) m(pl), louvor(es) m(pl)

praiseworthy /'preɪzwɜːðɪ/ a louvável, digno de louvor

pram /præm/ n carrinho m de bebê, (P) bebé

prance /prɑːns/ vi (of horse) curvetear, empinar-se; (of person) pavonear-se

prank /præŋk/ n brincadeira f de mau gosto

prawn /prɔːn/ n camarão m grande, (P) gamba f

pray /preɪ/ vi rezar, orar

prayer /preə(r)/ n oração f; **the Lord's P~** o Padre-Nosso. **~ book** n missal m

pre- /priː/ pref pré-

preach /priːtʃ/ vt/i pregar (**at** a). **~er** n pregador m

prearrange /priːə'reɪndʒ/ vt combinar or arranjar de antemão

precarious /prɪ'keərɪəs/ a precário; (of position) instável, inseguro

precaution /prɪ'kɔːʃn/ n precaução f. **~ary** a de precaução

preced|e /prɪ'siːd/ vt preceder. **~ing** a precedente

precedent /'presɪdənt/ n precedente m

precinct /'priːsɪŋkt/ n precinto m; Amer (district) circunscrição f; **(pedestrian) ~** área f de pedestres, (P) zona f para peões

precious /'preʃəs/ a precioso

precipice /'presɪpɪs/ n precipício m

precipitat|e /prɪ'sɪpɪteɪt/ vt precipitar ● a /-ɪtət/ precipitado. **~ion** /-'teɪʃn/ n precipitação f

precis|e /prɪ'saɪs/ a preciso; (careful) meticuloso. **~ely** adv precisamente. **~ion** /-'sɪʒn/ n precisão f

preclude /prɪ'kluːd/ vt evitar, excluir, impedir

precocious /prɪ'kəʊʃəs/ a precoce

preconc|eived /priːkən'siːvd/ a preconcebido. **~eption** /priːkən'sepʃn/ n ideia f preconcebida

precursor /priː'kɜːsə(r)/ n precursor m

predator /'predətə(r)/ n animal m de rapina, predador m. **~y** a predatório

predecessor /'priːdɪsesə(r)/ n predecessor m, antecessor m

predicament /prɪ'dɪkəmənt/ n situação f difícil

predict /prɪ'dɪkt/ vt predizer, prognosticar. **~able** a previsível. **~ion** /-ʃn/ n predição f, (P) previção f, prognóstico m

predictive text messaging n previsão f de texto, (P) escrita f inteligente

predominant /prɪ'dɒmɪnənt/ a predominante, preponderante. **~ly** adv predominantemente, preponderantemente

predominate /prɪ'dɒmɪneɪt/ vi predominar

pre-eminent /priːˈemɪnənt/ a preeminente, superior

pre-empt /priːˈempt/ vt adquirir por preempção. **~ive** a antecipado; Mil preventivo

preen /priːn/ vt alisar; ~ **o.s.** enfeitar-se

prefab /ˈpriːfæb/ n 🔟 casa f pré-fabricada. **~ricated** /-ˈfæbrɪkeɪtɪd/ a pré-fabricada

preface /ˈprefɪs/ n prefácio m

prefect /ˈpriːfekt/ n aluno m autorizado a disciplinar outros; (official) prefeito m

prefer /prɪˈfɜː(r)/ vt (pt **preferred**) preferir. **~able** /ˈprefrəbl/ a preferível

preferen|ce /ˈprefrəns/ n preferência f. **~tial** /-əˈrenʃl/ a preferencial, privilegiado

prefix /ˈpriːfɪks/ n (pl **-ixes**) prefixo m

pregnan|t /ˈpregnənt/ a ‹woman› grávida; ‹animal› prenhe. **~cy** n gravidez f

prehistoric /priːhɪˈstɒrɪk/ a pré-histórico

prejudice /ˈpredʒʊdɪs/ n preconceito m, ideia f preconcebida, prejuízo m; (harm) prejuízo m ● vt influenciar. **~d** a com preconceitos

preliminar|y /prɪˈlɪmɪnərɪ/ a preliminar. **~ies** npl preliminares mpl, preâmbulos mpl

prelude /ˈpreljuːd/ n prelúdio m

premarital /priːˈmærɪtl/ a antes do casamento, pré-marital

premature /ˈpremətjʊə(r)/ a prematuro

premeditated /priːˈmedɪtɪtɪd/ a premeditado

premier /ˈpremɪə(r)/ a primeiro ● n Pol primeiro-ministro m

premises /ˈpremɪsɪz/ npl local m, edifício m; **on the ~** neste estabelecimento, no local

premium /ˈpriːmɪəm/ n prêmio m, (P) prémio m; **at a ~** a peso de ouro

premonition /priːməˈnɪʃn/ n pressentimento m

preoccup|ation /priːɒkjʊˈpeɪʃn/ n preocupação f. **~ied** /-ˈɒkjʊpaɪd/ a preocupado

preparation /prepəˈreɪʃn/ n preparação f; **~s** preparativos mpl

preparatory /prɪˈpærətrɪ/ a preparatório; **~ school** escola f primária particular

prepare /prɪˈpeə(r)/ vt/i preparar(-se) (**for** para); **~d to** pronto a, preparado para

preposition /prepəˈzɪʃn/ n preposição f

preposterous /prɪˈpɒstərəs/ a absurdo, disparatado, ridículo

prerequisite /priːˈrekwɪzɪt/ n condição f prévia

prerogative /prɪˈrɒɡətɪv/ n prerrogativa f

Presbyterian /prezbɪˈtɪərɪən/ a & n presbiteriano m

prescri|be /prɪˈskraɪb/ vt prescrever; Med receitar, prescrever. **~ption** /-ɪpʃn/ n prescrição f; Med receita f

presence /ˈprezns/ n presença f; **~ of mind** presença f de espírito

present[1] /ˈpreznt/ a & n presente mf; **at ~** no momento, presentemente

present[2] /ˈpreznt/ n (gift) presente m, prenda f

present[3] /prɪˈzent/ vt apresentar; ‹film etc› dar; **~ sb with** oferecer a alguém. **~able** a apresentável. **~ation** /preznˈteɪʃn/ n apresentação *f.* **~er** *n* apresentador *m*

presently /'prezntlɪ/ *adv* dentro em pouco, daqui a pouco; *Amer* (*now*) neste momento

preservative /prɪ'zɜ:vətɪv/ *n* preservativo *m*, conservante *m*

preserv|e /prɪ'zɜ:v/ *vt* preservar; (*maintain*) *Culin* conservar ● *n* reserva *f*, *fig* área *f*; terreno *m*; (*jam*) compota *f*. **~ation** /prezə'veɪʃn/ *n* conservação *f*

preside /prɪ'zaɪd/ *vi* presidir (**over** a)

presiden|t /'prezɪdənt/ *n* presidente *mf*. **~cy** *n* presidência *f*. **~tial** /-'denʃl/ *a* presidencial

press /pres/ *vt/i* carregar (**on** em); (*squeeze*) espremer; (*urge*) pressionar; (*iron*) passar a ferro; **be ~ed for** estar apertado com falta de; **~ on** (**with**) continuar (com), prosseguir (com) ● *n* imprensa *f*; *Mech* prensa *f*; (*for wine*) lagar *m*; **~ conference** entrevista *f* coletiva, (*P*) conferência *f* de imprensa

pressing /'presɪŋ/ *a* premente, urgente

pressure /'preʃə(r)/ *n* pressão *f*; **~ group** grupo *m* de pressão ● *vt* fazer pressão sobre. **~ cooker** *n* panela *f* de pressão

pressurize /'preʃəraɪz/ *vt* pressionar, fazer pressão sobre

prestige /pre'sti:ʒ/ *n* prestígio *m*

prestigious /pre'stɪdʒəs/ *a* prestigioso

presumably /prɪ'zju:məblɪ/ *adv* provavelmente, presumivelmente

presum|e /prɪ'zju:m/ *vt* presumir; **~e to** tomar a liberdade de, atrever-se a. **~ption** /-'zʌmpʃn/ *n* presunção *f*

presumptuous /prɪ'zʌmptʃʊəs/ *a* presunçoso

pretence /prɪ'tens/ *n* fingimento *m*; (*claim*) pretensão *f*; (*pretext*) desculpa *f*, pretexto *m*

pretend /prɪ'tend/ *vt/i* fingir (**to do** fazer); **~ to** (*lay claim to*) ter pretensões a, ser pretendente a; (*profess to have*) pretender ter

pretentious /prɪ'tenʃəs/ *a* pretencioso

pretext /'pri:tekst/ *n* pretexto *m*

pretty /'prɪtɪ/ *a* (**-ier, -iest**) bonito, lindo ● *adv* bastante

prevail /prɪ'veɪl/ *vi* prevalecer; **~ on sb** to convencer alguém a. **~ing** *a* dominante

prevalen|t /'prevələnt/ *a* geral, dominante. **~ce** *n* frequência *f*

prevent /prɪ'vent/ *vt* impedir (**from doing** de fazer). **~able** *a* que se pode evitar, evitável. **~ion** /-ʃn/ *n* prevenção *f*. **~ive** *a* preventivo

preview /'pri:vju:/ *n* pré-estreia *f*, (*P*) anteestreia *f*

previous /'pri:vɪəs/ *a* precedente, anterior; **~ to** antes de. **~ly** *adv* antes, anteriormente

pre-war /pri:'wɔ:(r)/ *a* do pré-guerra, (*P*) de antes da guerra

prey /preɪ/ *n* presa *f* ● *vi* **~ on** dar caça a; (*worry*) preocupar, atormentar; **bird of ~** ave *f* de rapina, predador *m*

price /praɪs/ *n* preço *m* ● *vt* marcar o preço de. **~less** *a* inestimável; 🅸 (*amusing*) impagável

prick /prɪk/ *vt* picar, furar ● *n* picada *f*; **~ up one's ears** arrebitar a(s) orelha(s)

prickl|e /'prɪkl/ *n* pico *m*, espinho *m*; (*sensation*) picada *f*. **~y** *a* espinhoso, que pica; ‹*person*› irritável

pride /praɪd/ *n* orgulho *m* ● *vpr* ~ **o.s. on** orgulhar-se de

priest /priːst/ *n* padre *m*, sacerdote *m*. ~**hood** *n* sacerdócio *m*; (*clergy*) clero *m*

prim /prɪm/ *a* (**primmer, primmest**) formal, cheio de nove-horas 🅸;(*prudish*) pudico

primary /ˈpraɪmərɪ/ *a* primário; (*chief, first*) primeiro; ~ **school** escola *f* primária

prime[1] /praɪm/ *a* primeiro, principal; (*first-rate*) de primeira qualidade; **P**~ **Minister** Primeiro-Ministro *m*; ~ **number** número *m* primo

prime[2] /praɪm/ *vt* aprontar, aprestar; (*with facts*) preparar; ‹*surface*› preparar, aparelhar

primeval /praɪˈmiːvl/ *a* primitivo

primitive /ˈprɪmɪtɪv/ *a* primitivo

primrose /ˈprɪmrəʊz/ *n* primavera *f*, prímula *f*

prince /prɪns/ *n* príncipe *m*

princess /prɪnˈses/ *n* princesa *f*

principal /ˈprɪnsəpl/ *a* principal ● *n Schol* diretor *m*. ~**ly** *adv* principalmente

principle /ˈprɪnsəpl/ *n* princípio *m*; **in/on** ~ em/por princípio

print /prɪnt/ *vt* imprimir; (*write*) escrever em letra de imprensa; ~**ed matter** impressos *mpl* ● *n* marca *f*, impressão *f*; (*letters*) letra *f* de imprensa; (*photo*) prova (fotográfica) *f*; (*engraving*) gravura *f*; **out of** ~ esgotado. ~**out** *n* cópia *f* impressa

print|er /ˈprɪntə(r)/ *n* tipógrafo *m*; *Comput* impressora *f*. ~**ing** *n* impressão *f*, tipografia *f*

prior /ˈpraɪə(r)/ *a* anterior, precedente; ~ **to** antes de

priority /praɪˈɒrətɪ/ *n* prioridade *f*

prise /praɪz/ *vt* forçar (com alavanca); ~ **open** arrombar

prison /ˈprɪzn/ *n* prisão *f*. ~**er** *n* prisioneiro *m*

pristine /ˈprɪstiːn/ *a* primitivo; ‹*condition*› perfeito, como novo

privacy /ˈprɪvəsɪ/ *n* privacidade *f*, intimidade *f*; (*solitude*) isolamento *m*

private /ˈpraɪvət/ *a* privado; (*confidential*) confidencial; ‹*lesson, life, house etc*› particular; ‹*ceremony*› íntimo ● *n* soldado *m* raso; **in** ~ em particular; (*of ceremony*) na intimidade. ~**ly** *adv* particularmente; (*inwardly*) no fundo, interiormente

privilege /ˈprɪvəlɪdʒ/ *n* privilégio *m*. ~**d** *a* privilegiado; **be** ~**d to** ter o privilégio de

prize /praɪz/ *n* prêmio *m*, (P) prémio *m* ● *a* premiado; ‹*fool etc*› perfeito ● *vt* ter em grande apreço, apreciar muito. ~**giving** *n* distribuição *f* de prêmios, (P) prémios; ~**winner** *n* premiado *m*, vencedor *m*

pro /prəʊ/ *n* **the** ~**s and cons** os prós e os contras

pro- /prəʊ/ *pref* (*acting for*) pro-; (*favouring*) pró-

probab|le /ˈprɒbəbl/ *a* provável. ~**ility** /-ˈbɪlətɪ/ *n* probabilidade *f*. ~**ly** *adv* provavelmente

probation /prəˈbeɪʃn/ *n* (*testing*) estágio *m*, tirocínio *m*; *Jur* liberdade *f* condicional

probe /prəʊb/ *n Med* sonda *f*; *Fig* (*investigation*) inquérito *m* ● *vt/i* ~ (**into**) sondar, investigar

problem /ˈprɒbləm/ *n* problema *m* ● *a* difícil. ~**atic** /-ˈmætɪk/ *a* problemático

procedure /prəˈsiːdʒə(r)/ n
procedimento m, processo m,
norma f

proceed /prəˈsiːd/ vi prosseguir, ir
para diante, avançar; ~ **to do** passar
a fazer; ~ **with sth** continuar ou
avançar com alguma coisa. **~ing** n
procedimento m

proceedings /prəˈsiːdɪŋz/ npl Jur
processo m; (report) ata f

proceeds /ˈprəʊsiːdz/ npl produto
m, lucro m, proventos mpl

process /ˈprəʊses/ n processo m;
in ~ em curso; **in the ~ of doing**
sendo feito ● vt tratar; Photo revelar

procession /prəˈseʃn/ n procissão
f, cortejo m

procl|aim /prəˈkleɪm/
vt proclamar. **~amation**
/ˌprɒkləˈmeɪʃn/ n proclamação f

procure /prəˈkjʊə(r)/ vt obter

prod /prɒd/ vt/i (pt prodded)
(push) empurrar; (poke) espetar; fig
(urge) incitar ● n espetadela f; fig
incitamento m

prodigy /ˈprɒdɪdʒi/ n prodígio m

produc|e¹ /prəˈdjuːs/ vt/i produzir;
(bring out) tirar, extrair; (show)
apresentar, mostrar; (cause) causar,
provocar; Theat pôr em cena. **~er**
n produtor m. **~tion** /-ˈdʌkʃn/ n
produção f; Theat encenação f

produce² /ˈprɒdjuːs/ n produtos
(agrícolas) mpl

product /ˈprɒdʌkt/ n produto m

productiv|e /prəˈdʌktɪv/ a
produtivo. **~ity** /prɒdʌkˈtɪvəti/ n
produtividade f

profess /prəˈfes/ vt professar; ~ **to
do** alegar fazer

profession /prəˈfeʃn/ n profissão
f. **~al** a profissional; (well done)

de profissional; ‹person› que
exerce uma profissão liberal ● n
profissional mf

professor /prəˈfesə(r)/ n professor
(universitário) m

proficien|t /prəˈfɪʃnt/ a
proficiente, competente. **~cy** n
proficiência f, competência f

profile /ˈprəʊfaɪl/ n perfil m

profit /ˈprɒfɪt/ n proveito m;
(money) lucro m ● vi (pt profited)
~ **by** aproveitar-se de; ~ **from** tirar
proveito de. **~able** a proveitoso; (of
business) lucrativo, rentável

profound /prəˈfaʊnd/ a profundo

profus|e /prəˈfjuːs/ a profuso.
~ion /-ʒn/ n profusão f

program /ˈprəʊɡræm/ n
(computer) ~ programa m ● vt (pt
programmed) programar. **~mer**
n programador m

programme /ˈprəʊɡræm/ n
programa m

progress¹ /ˈprəʊɡres/ n progresso
m; **in ~** em curso, em andamento

progress² /prəˈɡres/ vi progredir.
~ion /-ʃn/ n progressão f

progressive /prəˈɡresɪv/ a
a progressivo; (reforming)
progressista. **~ly** adv
progressivamente

prohibit /prəˈhɪbɪt/ vt proibir
(**sb from doing** alguém de fazer)

project¹ /prəˈdʒekt/ vi projetar
● vi ressaltar, sobressair. **~ion** /-ʃn/
n projeção f; (protruding) saliência
f, ressalto m

project² /ˈprɒdʒekt/ n projeto m

projectile /prəˈdʒektaɪl/ n
projétil m

projector /prəˈdʒektə(r)/ n
projetor m

prolific /prəˈlɪfɪk/ a prolífico

prologue /'prəʊlɒg/ n prólogo m
prolong /prə'lɒŋ/ vt prolongar

> **prom** Nos Estados Unidos, um *prom* é o baile de formatura que se celebra para os estudantes que terminam o *High School*. Em Londres, the *Proms* são uma série de concertos de música clássica aos quais uma grande parte do público assiste de pé. Ocorre no *Royal Albert Hall* no verão, durante oito semanas. Oficialmente, são conhecidos como os *Henry Wood Promenade Concerts*, em memória ao seu fundador. *i*

promenade /prɒmə'nɑːd/ n passeio m ● vt/i passear
prominen|t /'prɒmɪnənt/ a (projecting; important) proeminente; (conspicuous) bem à vista, conspícuo. ~**ce** n proeminência f. ~**tly** adv bem à vista
promiscu|ous /prə'mɪskjʊəs/ a promíscuo, de costumes livres. ~**ity** /prɒmɪs'kjuːətɪ/ n promiscuidade f, liberdade f de costumes
promis|e /'prɒmɪs/ n promessa f ● vt/i prometer. ~**ing** a prometedor, promissor
promot|e /prə'məʊt/ vt promover. ~**ion** /-'məʊʃn/ n promoção f
prompt /prɒmpt/ a pronto, rápido, imediato; (punctual) pontual ● adv em ponto ● vt levar; Theat soprar, servir de ponto para. ~**er** n ponto m. ~**ly** adv prontamente; pontualmente
prone /prəʊn/ a deitado (de bruços); ~ **to** propenso a
pronoun /'prəʊnaʊn/ n pronome m

pron|ounce /prə'naʊns/ vt pronunciar; (declare) declarar. ~**ounced** a pronunciado. ~**ouncement** n declaração f. ~**unciation** /-ʌnsɪ'eɪʃn/ n pronúncia f
proof /pruːf/ n prova f; (of liquor) teor m alcoólico, graduação f ● a ~ **against** à prova de
prop[1] /prɒp/ n suporte m; lit & fig apoio m; esteio m ● vt (pt propped) sustentar, suportar, apoiar; ~ **against** apoiar contra
prop[2] /prɒp/ n ❶ Theat acessório m, (P) adereço m
propaganda /prɒpə'gændə/ n propaganda f
propel /prə'pel/ vt (pt propelled) propulsionar, impelir
propeller /prə'pelə(r)/ n hélice f
proper /'prɒpə(r)/ a correto; (seemly) conveniente; (real) propriamente dito; ❶ (thorough) belo; ~ **noun** substantivo m próprio. ~**ly** adv corretamente; (rightly) com razão, acertadamente; (accurately) propriamente
property /'prɒpətɪ/ n (house) imóvel m; (land, quality) propriedade f; (possessions) bens mpl
prophecy /'prɒfɪsɪ/ n profecia f
prophesy /'prɒfɪsaɪ/ vt/i profetizar; ~ **that** predizer que
prophet /'prɒfɪt/ n profeta m. ~**ic** /prə'fetɪk/ a profético
proportion /prə'pɔːʃn/ n proporção f. ~**al**, ~**ate** adjs proporcional
proposal /prə'pəʊzl/ n proposta f; (of marriage) pedido m de casamento
propos|e /prə'pəʊz/ vt propor ● vi pedir em casamento; ~**e to do**

propor-se fazer. **~ition** /prɒpə-'zɪʃn/ n proposição f; 🔢 (*matter*) caso m; questão f

proprietor /prə'praɪətə(r)/ n proprietário m

propriety /prə'praɪətɪ/ n propriedade f, correção f

prose /prəʊz/ n prosa f

prosecut|e /'prɒsɪkjuːt/ vt Jur processar. **~ion** /-'kjuːʃn/ n Jur acusação f

prospect[1] /'prɒspekt/ n perspectiva f

prospect[2] /prə'spekt/ vt/i pesquisar, prospectar, (P) prospetar

prospective /prə'spektɪv/ a futuro; (*possible*) provável

prosper /'prɒspə(r)/ vi prosperar

prosper|ous /'prɒspərəs/ a próspero. **~ity** /-'sperətɪ/ n prosperidade f

prostitut|e /'prɒstɪtjuːt/ n prostituta f. **~ion** /-'tjuːʃn/ n prostituição f

prostrate /'prɒstreɪt/ a prostrado

protect /prə'tekt/ vt proteger. **~ion** /-ʃn/ n proteção f. **~ive** a protetor. **~or** n protetor m

protégé /'prɒtɪʒeɪ/ n protegido m. **~e** n protegida f

protein /'prəʊtiːn/ n proteína f

protest[1] /'prəʊtest/ n protesto m

protest[2] /prə'test/ vt/i protestar. **~er** n Pol manifestante mf

Protestant /'prɒtɪstənt/ a & n protestante mf

protocol /'prəʊtəkɒl/ n protocolo m

prototype /'prəʊtətaɪp/ n protótipo m

protract /prə'trækt/ vt prolongar, arrastar

protrud|e /prə'truːd/ vi sobressair, sair do alinhamento

proud /praʊd/ a (**er**, **-est**) orgulhoso

prove /pruːv/ vt provar, demonstrar ● vi ~ **(to be) easy/** etc verificar-se ser fácil/etc; ~ **o.s.** dar provas de si. ~**n** /-n/ a provado

proverb /'prɒvɜːb/ n provérbio m. **~ial** /prə'vɜːbɪəl/ a proverbial

provid|e /prə'vaɪd/ vt prover; munir (**sb with sth** alg de alguma coisa) ● vi ~ **for** providenciar para; ⟨person⟩ prover de, cuidar de; (*allow for*) levar em conta; **~ed**, **~ing (that)** desde que, contanto que

providence /'prɒvɪdəns/ n providência f

province /'prɒvɪns/ n província f; fig competência f

provincial /prə'vɪnʃl/ a provincial; (*rustic*) provinciano

provision /prə'vɪʒn/ n provisão f; (*stipulation*) disposição f; **~s** (*food*) provisões fpl

provisional /prə'vɪʒənl/ a provisório. **~ly** adv provisoriamente

proviso /prə'vaɪzəʊ/ n (pl **-os**) condição f

provo|ke /prə'vəʊk/ vt provocar. **~cation** /prɒvə'keɪʃn/ n provocação f. **~cative** /-'vɒkətɪv/ a provocante

prowess /'praʊɪs/ n proeza f, façanha f

prowl /praʊl/ vi rondar ● n **be on the ~** andar à espreita

proximity /prɒk'sɪmətɪ/ n proximidade f

proxy /'prɒksɪ/ n **by ~** por procuração

prude /pruːd/ n puritano m, pudico m

pruden|t /'pru:dnt/ a prudente.
~ce n prudência f

prune[1] /pru:n/ n ameixa f seca

prune[2] /pru:n/ vt podar

pry /prai/ vi bisbilhotar; **~ into**
meter o nariz em, intrometer-se em

psalm /sɑ:m/ n salmo m

pseudo- /'sju:dəʊ/ pref pseudo-

pseudonym /'sju:dənɪm/ n
pseudônimo m, (P) pseudónimo m

psychiatr|y /saɪ'kaɪətrɪ/ n
psiquiatria f. **~ic** /-i'ætrɪk/ a
psiquiátrico. **~ist** n psiquiatra mf

psychic /'saɪkɪk/ a psíquico;
‹person› com capacidade de
telepatia

psychoanalys|e
/saɪkəʊ'ænəlaɪz/ vt psicanalisar. **~t**
/-ɪst/ n psicanalista mf

psychoanalysis
/saɪkəʊə'næləsɪs/ n psicanálise f

psycholog|y /saɪ'kɒlədʒɪ/ n
psicologia f. **~ical** /-ə'lɒdʒɪkl/ a
psicológico. **~ist** n psicólogo m

psychopath /'saɪkəʊpæθ/ n
psicopata mf

pub /pʌb/ n pub m

pub Na Grã-Bretanha, é o
estabelecimento onde se
vende cerveja e outras
bebidas (alcoólicas e não
alcoólicas) para consumo no local.
Pub é a forma abreviada de public
house. Os pubs costumam oferecer
comida e uma série de jogos,
sobretudo dardos, bilhar, etc. O
horário de abertura depende da
licença, sendo o horário normal
das 11 às 23 horas.

puberty /'pju:bətɪ/ n puberdade f

public /'pʌblɪk/ a público;
‹holiday› feriado; **in ~** em público;
~ house pub m; **~ relations**
relações fpl públicas; **~ school** escola
f particular; Amer escola f oficial.
~-spirited a de espírito cívico,
patriótico. **~ly** adv publicamente

publication /pʌblɪ'keɪʃn/ n
publicação f

publicity /pʌ'blɪsətɪ/ n publicidade
f

publicize /'pʌblɪsaɪz/ vt fazer
publicidade de/a

public school Em Inglaterra
e no País de Gales, é um
colégio privado para alunos
entre os 13 e os 18 anos. A maioria
desses colégios são internatos só
para rapazes ou só para raparigas.
Nos Estados Unidos e na Escócia,
o termo refere-se a uma escola
pública.

publish /'pʌblɪʃ/ vt publicar. **~er** n
editor m. **~ing** n publicação f; **~ing
house** editora f

pudding /'pʊdɪŋ/ n pudim m;
(dessert) doce m

puddle /'pʌdl/ n poça f de água,
charco m

puff /pʌf/ n baforada f ● vt/i
lançar baforadas; (breathe hard)
arquejar, ofegar; **~ at** ‹cigar etc›
dar baforadas em; **~ out** (swell)
inchar(-se). **~ pastry** n massa f
folhada

puffy /'pʌfɪ/ a inchado

pull /pʊl/ vt/i puxar; ‹muscle›
distender; **~ a face** fazer uma
careta; **~ one's weight** fig fazer
a sua quota-parte; **~ sb's leg**
brincar com alguém, meter-se
com alguém; **~ away** or **out** Auto

arrancar; **~ down** puxar para baixo; *‹building›* demolir; **~ in** *Auto* encostar(-se); **~ off** tirar; *fig* sair-se bem em, conseguir alcançar; **~ o.s. together** recompor-se, refazer-se; **~ out** partir; *(extract)* arrancar, tirar; **~ through** sair-se bem; **~ up** puxar para cima; *(uproot)* arrancar; *Auto* parar ● *n* puxão *m*; *fig (influence)* influência *f*; empenho *m*; **give a ~** dar um puxão

pullover /ˈpʊləʊvə(r)/ *n* pulôver *m*

pulp /pʌlp/ *n* polpa *f*; *(for paper)* pasta *f* de papel

pulpit /ˈpʊlpɪt/ *n* púlpito *m*

pulsat|e /pʌlˈseɪt/ *vi* pulsar, bater, palpitar. **~ion** /-ˈseɪʃn/ *n* pulsação *f*

pulse /pʌls/ *n* pulso *m*; **feel sb's ~** tirar o pulso de alguém

pummel /ˈpʌml/ *vt* (*pt* **pummelled**) esmurrar

pump[1] /pʌmp/ *n* bomba *f* ● *vt/i* bombear; *‹person›* arrancar or extrair informações de; **~ up** encher com bomba

pump[2] /pʌmp/ *n* *(shoe)* sapato *m*

pumpkin /ˈpʌmpkɪn/ *n* abóbora *f*

pun /pʌn/ *n* trocadilho *m*, jogo *m* de palavras

punch[1] /pʌntʃ/ *vt* esmurrar, dar um murro or soco; *(perforate)* furar, perfurar; *‹a hole›* fazer ● *n* murro *m*, soco *m*; *(device)* furador *m*. **~line** *n* remate *m*; **~up** *n* 🄴 pancadaria *f*

punch[2] /pʌntʃ/ *n* *(drink)* ponche *m*

punctual /ˈpʌŋktʃʊəl/ *a* pontual. **~ity** /-ˈælətɪ/ *n* pontualidade *f*

punctuat|e /ˈpʌŋktʃʊeɪt/ *vt* pontuar. **~ion** /-ˈeɪʃn/ *n* pontuação *f*

puncture /ˈpʌŋktʃə(r)/ *n* *(in tyre)* furo *m* ● *vt/i* furar

pungent /ˈpʌndʒənt/ *a* acre, pungente

punish /ˈpʌnɪʃ/ *vt* punir, castigar. **~able** *a* punível. **~ment** *n* punição *f*, castigo *m*

punt /pʌnt/ *n* *(boat)* chalana *f*

punter /ˈpʌntə(r)/ *n* *(gambler)* jogador *m*; 🄴 *(customer)* freguês *m*, cliente *m*

puny /ˈpjuːnɪ/ *a* (**-ier**, **-iest**) fraco, débil

pup(py) /ˈpʌpɪ/ *n* cachorro *m*, cachorrinho *m*

pupil /ˈpjuːpl/ *n* aluno *m*; *(of eye)* pupila *f*

puppet /ˈpʌpɪt/ *n* *lit* & *fig* fantoche *m*; marionete *f*

purchase /ˈpɜːtʃəs/ *vt* comprar (**from sb** de alguém) ● *n* compra *f*. **~r** /-ə(r)/ *n* comprador *m*

pur|e /pjʊə(r)/ *a* (**-er**, **-est**) puro. **~ely** *adv* puramente. **~ity** *n* pureza *f*

purge /pɜːdʒ/ *vt* purgar; *Pol* sanear ● *n* *Med* purgante *m*; *Pol* saneamento *m*

purif|y /ˈpjʊərɪfaɪ/ *vt* purificar. **~ication** /-ɪˈkeɪʃn/ *n* purificação *f*

puritan /ˈpjʊərɪtən/ *n* puritano *m*. **~ical** /-ˈtænɪkl/ *a* puritano

purple /ˈpɜːpl/ *a* roxo, purpúreo ● *n* roxo *m*, púrpura *f*

purpose /ˈpɜːpəs/ *n* propósito *m*; *(determination)* firmeza *f*; **on ~** de propósito; **to no ~** em vão. **~-built** *a* construído especialmente

purposely /ˈpɜːpəslɪ/ *adv* de propósito, propositadamente

purr /pɜː(r)/ *n* ronrom *m* ● *vi* ronronar

purse /pɜːs/ *n* carteira *f*; *Amer* bolsa *f* ● *vt* franzir

pursue /pəˈsjuː/ *vt* perseguir; *(go on with)* prosseguir; *(engage in)* entregar-se a, dedicar-se a. **~r** /-ə(r)/ *n* perseguidor *m*

pursuit /pəˈsjuːt/ n perseguição f; *fig* atividade f

pus /pʌs/ n pus m

push /pʊʃ/ vt/i empurrar; ⟨button⟩ apertar, premir, carregar; ⟨thrust⟩ enfiar; 🗊 (recommend) insistir; **be ~ed for** ⟨time etc⟩ estar com pouco; **be ~ing thirty/etc** 🗊 estar beirando os or (P) à beira dos trinta/etc; **give the ~ to** 🗙 dar o fora em alguém; **~ sb around** fazer alguém de bobo or (P) de parvo; **~ back** repelir; **~ off** 🗙 dar o fora, (P) mandar embora; **~ on** continuar; **~ up** (lift) levantar; ⟨prices⟩ forçar o aumento de ● n empurrão m; (effort) esforço m; (drive) energia f. **~chair** n carrinho m (de criança); **~over** n canja f 🗊, coisa f fácil; **~up** n Amer flexão f. **~er** n fornecedor m (de droga). **~y** a 🗊 agressivo, furão

put /pʊt/ vt/i (pt put, pres p putting) colocar, pôr; ⟨question⟩ fazer, colocar; **~ the damage at a million** estimar os danos em um milhão; **I'd ~ it at a thousand** eu diria mil; **~ sth tactfully** dizer alguma coisa com tato; **~ across** comunicar; **~ away** guardar; **~ back** repor; (delay) retardar, atrasar; **~ by** pôr de lado; **~ down** pôr em lugar baixo; (write) anotar; (pay) pagar; (suppress) sufocar, reprimir; **~ forward** ⟨plan⟩ submeter; **~ in** (insert) introduzir; (fix) instalar; submeter; **~ in for** fazer um pedido, candidatar-se; **~ off** (postpone) adiar; (disconcert) desanimar; (displease) desagradar; **~ sb off sth** tirar o gosto de alguém por algo; **~ on** ⟨clothes⟩ pôr, vestir; ⟨radio⟩ ligar; ⟨light⟩ acender; ⟨speed, weight⟩ ganhar; ⟨accent⟩ adotar; **~ out** pôr para fora; (stretch) esticar; (extinguish) extinguir, apagar; (disconcert) desconcertar;

(inconvenience) incomodar; **~ up** levantar; ⟨building⟩ erguer, construir; colocar; aumentar; hospedar; oferecer; **~up job** embuste m; **~ up with** suportar, aturar

putty /ˈpʌtɪ/ n massa de vidraceiro f, betume m

puzzl|e /ˈpʌzl/ n puzzle m, quebra-cabeça(s) m ● vt deixar perplexo, intrigar ● vi quebrar a cabeça, ser intrigante. **~ing** a intrigante

pyjamas /pəˈdʒɑːməz/ npl pijama m

pylon /ˈpaɪlən/ n poste m

pyramid /ˈpɪrəmɪd/ n pirâmide f

python /ˈpaɪθn/ n píton m

⋯⋯⋯⋯⋯⋯⋯⋯⋯⋯⋯⋯⋯⋯⋯⋯⋯⋯

Qq

quack¹ /kwæk/ n (of duck) grasnido m ● vi grasnar

quack² /kwæk/ n charlatão m

quadrangle /ˈkwɒdræŋgl/ n quadrângulo m, (of college) pátio m quadrangular

quadruped /ˈkwɒdrʊped/ n quadrúpede m

quadruple /ˈkwɒdrʊpl/ a & n quádruplo m ● /kwɒˈdruːpl/ vt/i quadruplicar. **~ts** /-plɪts/ npl quadrigêmeos mpl, (P) quadrigémeos mpl

quaint /kweɪnt/ a (-er, -est) pitoresco; (whimsical) estranho, bizarro

quake /kweɪk/ vi tremer ● n 🗊 tremor m de terra

qualification /ˌkwɒlɪfɪˈkeɪʃn/ n qualificação f; (accomplishment) habilitação f; (diploma) diploma m; (condition) requisito m, condição f, fig restrição f, reserva f

qualif|y /ˈkwɒlɪfaɪ/ vt qualificar; fig (moderate) atenuar; moderar; fig (limit) pôr ressalvas ou restrições a ● vi fig (be entitled to) ter os requisitos (for para); Sport classificar-se; **he ~ied as a vet** ele formou-se em veterinária. **~ied** a formado; (able) qualificado, habilitado; (moderated) atenuado; (limited) limitado

quality /ˈkwɒlətɪ/ n qualidade f

qualm /kwɑːm/ n escrúpulo m

quandary /ˈkwɒndərɪ/ n dilema m

quantity /ˈkwɒntətɪ/ n quantidade f

quarantine /ˈkwɒrəntiːn/ n quarentena f

quarrel /ˈkwɒrəl/ n zanga f, questão f, discussão f ● vi (pt quarrelled) zangar-se, questionar, discutir. **~some** a conflituoso, brigão

quarry¹ /ˈkwɒrɪ/ n (prey) presa f, caça f

quarry² /ˈkwɒrɪ/ n (excavation) pedreira f

quarter /ˈkwɔːtə(r)/ n quarto m; (of year) trimestre m; Amer (coin) quarto m de dólar; 25 cêntimos mpl; (district) bairro m, quarteirão m; **~s** (lodgings) alojamento m, residência f; Mil quartel m; **from all ~s** de todos os lados; **~ of an hour** quarto m de hora; **(a) ~ past six** seis e quinze; **(a) ~ to seven** quinze para as sete ● vt dividir em quarto; Mil aquartelar. **~final** n Sport quarta f or (P) quartos mpl de final. **~ly** a trimestral ● adv trimestralmente

quartet /kwɔːˈtet/ n quarteto m

quartz /kwɔːts/ n quartzo m ● a ‹watch etc› de quartzo

quash /kwɒʃ/ vt reprimir; Jur revogar

quaver /ˈkweɪvə(r)/ vi tremer, tremular ● n Mus colcheia f

quay /kiː/ n cais m

queasy /ˈkwiːzɪ/ a delicado; **feel ~** estar enjoado

queen /kwiːn/ n rainha f; Cards dama f

queer /kwɪə(r)/ a (-er, -est) estranho; (slightly ill) indisposto; ⊠ (homosexual) bicha; maricas ⊠; (dubious) suspeito ● n ⊠ bicha m; maricas m ⊠

quell /kwel/ vt reprimir, abafar, sufocar

quench /kwentʃ/ vt ‹fire, flame› apagar; ‹thirst› matar, saciar

query /ˈkwɪərɪ/ n questão f ● vt questionar

quest /kwest/ n busca f, procura f; **in ~ of** em demanda de

question /ˈkwestʃən/ n pergunta f, interrogação f; (problem, affair) questão f; **in ~** em questão ou em causa; **out of the ~** fora de toda a questão, (P) fora de questão; **there's no ~ of** nem pensar em; **without ~** sem dúvida; **~ mark** ponto m de interrogação ● vt perguntar, interrogar; (doubt) pôr em dúvida ou em causa. **~able** a discutível

questionnaire /ˌkwestʃəˈneə(r)/ n questionário m

queue /kjuː/ n fila f ● vi (pres p queuing) fazer fila

quibble /ˈkwɪbl/ vi tergiversar, usar de evasivas; (raise petty objections) discutir por coisas insignificantes

quick /kwɪk/ a (**-er, -est**) rápido; **be** ~ despachar-se; **have a** ~ **temper** exaltar-se facilmente ● adv depressa. **~ly** adv rapidamente, depressa. **~ness** n rapidez f

quicken /ˈkwɪkən/ vt/i apressar(-se)

quicksand /ˈkwɪksænd/ n areia f movediça

quid /kwɪd/ n invar ⊠ libra f

quiet /ˈkwaɪət/ a (**-er, -est**) quieto, sossegado, tranquilo ● n quietude f, sossego m, tranquilidade f; **keep** ~ calar-se; **on the** ~ às escondidas, na calada. **~ly** adv sossegadamente, silenciosamente. **~ness** n sossego m, tranquilidade f, calma f

quieten /ˈkwaɪətn/ vt/i sossegar, acalmar(-se)

quilt /kwɪlt/ n coberta f acolchoada; (**continental**) ~ edredão m de penas ● vt acolchoar

quintet /kwɪnˈtet/ n quinteto m

quirk /kwɜːk/ n mania f, singularidade f

quit /kwɪt/ vt (pt **quitted**) deixar ● vi ir-se embora; (resign) demitir-se, desistir; ~ **doing** Amer parar or deixar de fazer

quite /kwaɪt/ adv completamente, absolutamente; (rather) bastante; ~ **(so)!** isso mesmo!, exatamente! ~ **a few** bastante, alguns/algumas; ~ **a lot** bastante

quiver /ˈkwɪvə(r)/ vi tremer, estremecer ● n tremor m, estremecimento m

quiz /kwɪz/ n (pl **quizzes**) teste m; (game) concurso m ● vt (pt **quizzed**) interrogar

quizzical /ˈkwɪzɪkl/ a zombeteiro, (P) gozão m ⊞

quota /ˈkwəʊtə/ n cota f, quota f

quotation /kwəʊˈteɪʃn/ n citação f, (estimate) orçamento m; ~ **marks** aspas fpl

quote /kwəʊt/ vt citar; (estimate) fazer um orçamento ● n ⊞ (passage) citação f, ⊞ (estimate) orçamento m

Rr

rabbi /ˈræbaɪ/ n rabino m

rabbit /ˈræbɪt/ n coelho m

rabid /ˈræbɪd/ a fig fanático; ferrenho; ‹dog› raivoso

rabies /ˈreɪbiːz/ n raiva f

race[1] /reɪs/ n corrida f ● vt ‹horse› fazer correr ● vi correr, dar or fazer uma corrida; (rush) ir em grande or a toda (a) velocidade. **~track** n pista f

race[2] /reɪs/ n (group) raça f ● a racial

racecourse /ˈreɪskɔːs/ n hipódromo m

racehorse /ˈreɪshɔːs/ n cavalo m de corrida

racial /ˈreɪʃl/ a racial

racing /ˈreɪsɪŋ/ n corridas fpl; ~ **car** carro m de corridas

racis|t /ˈreɪsɪst/ a & n racista mf. **~m** /-zəm/ n racismo m

rack[1] /ræk/ n (for luggage) porta-bagagem m, bagageiro m; (for plates) escorredor m de prato ● vt ~ **one's brains** dar tratos à imaginação, (P) dar voltas à cabeça

rack[2] /ræk/ n **go to** ~ **and ruin** arruinar-se; (of buildings etc) cair em ruínas

racket[1] /'rækɪt/ n Sport raquete f, (P) raqueta f

racket[2] /'rækɪt/ n (din) barulheira f; (swindle) roubalheira f, ⊠ (business) negociata f 🗉

racy /'reɪsɪ/ a (-ier, -iest) vivo, vigoroso

radar /'reɪdɑ:(r)/ n radar m ● a de radar

radian|t /'reɪdɪənt/ a radiante. ~ce n brilho m

radiator /'reɪdɪeɪtə(r)/ n radiador m

radical /'rædɪkl/ a & n radical m

radio /'reɪdɪəʊ/ n (pl -os) rádio f; (set) (aparelho de) rádio m; ~ station estação f de rádio, emissora f ● vt transmitir pela rádio

radioactiv|e /reɪdɪəʊ'æktɪv/ a radioativo. ~ity /-'tɪvətɪ/ n radioatividade f

radish /'rædɪʃ/ n rabanete m

radius /'reɪdɪəs/ n (pl -dii /-dɪaɪ/) raio m

raffle /'ræfl/ n rifa f ● vt rifar

raft /rɑ:ft/ n jangada f

rafter /'rɑ:ftə(r)/ n trave f, viga f

rag[1] /ræg/ n farrapo m; (for wiping) trapo m; pej (newspaper) jornaleco m. ~s npl farrapos mpl, andrajos mpl; in ~s maltrapilho

rag[2] /ræg/ vt (pt ragged) zombar de

rage /reɪdʒ/ n raiva f, fúria f ● vi estar furioso; (of storm) rugir; (of battle) estar acesa; **be all the ~** 🗖 fazer furor, estar na moda 🗓

ragged /'rægɪd/ a (clothes, person) esfarrapado, roto; (edge) esfiapado, esgarçado

raid /reɪd/ n Mil ataque m; (by police) batida f; (by criminals) assalto m ● vt fazer um ataque ou uma batida

or um assalto. ~er n atacante m, assaltante m

rail /reɪl/ n (of stairs) corrimão m; (of ship) amurada f; (on balcony) parapeito m; (for train) trilho m, (P) carril m; (for curtain) varão m; **by ~** por estrada, (P) caminho de ferro

railings /'reɪlɪŋz/ npl grade f

railroad /'reɪlrəʊd/ n Amer ▶ RAILWAY

railway /'reɪlweɪ/ n estrada f, (P) caminho m de ferro; ~ line linha f do trem or (P) do comboio; ~ station estação f ferroviária, (P) estação f de caminho de ferro

rain /reɪn/ n chuva f; ~ forest floresta f tropical ● vi chover. ~storm n tempestade f com chuva; ~water n água f da chuva

rainbow /'reɪnbəʊ/ n arco-íris m

raincoat /'reɪnkəʊt/ n impermeável m

raindrop /'reɪndrɒp/ n pingo m de chuva

rainfall /'reɪnfɔ:l/ n precipitação f, pluviosidade f

rainy /'reɪnɪ/ a (-ier, -iest) chuvoso

raise /reɪz/ vt levantar, erguer; (breed) criar; (voice) levantar; (question) fazer, levantar; (price etc) aumentar, subir; (funds) angariar; (loan) obter ● n Amer aumento m

raisin /'reɪzn/ n passa f

rake /reɪk/ n ancinho m ● vt juntar, alisar com ancinho; (search) revolver, remexer; ~ in (money) ganhar a rodos; ~ up desenterrar, ressuscitar

rally /'rælɪ/ vt/i reunir(-se); (reassemble) reagrupar(-se), reorganizar(-se); (health) restabelecer(-se); (strength)

recuperar as forças ● n (*recovery*)
recuperação f; (*meeting*) comício m,
assembleia f; *Auto* rally m, rali m

ram /ræm/ n (*sheep*) carneiro m ● vt
(*pt* rammed) (*beat down*) calcar;
(*push*) meter à força; (*crash into*)
bater contra

rambl|e /ˈræmbl/ n caminhada f,
perambulação f ● vi perambular,
vaguear; ~ **on** divagar. ~**er** n
caminhante mf; (*plant*) trepadeira f.
~**ing** a (*speech*) desconexo

ramp /ræmp/ n rampa f

rampage /ræmˈpeɪdʒ/ vi causar
distúrbios violentos

rampant /ˈræmpənt/ a **be** ~
vicejar, florescer; (*diseases etc*)
grassar

ramshackle /ˈræmʃækl/ a (*car*)
desconjuntado; (*house*) caindo aos
pedaços

ran /ræn/ ▶ RUN

ranch /rɑːntʃ/ n rancho m,
estância f

rancid /ˈrænsɪd/ a rançoso

random /ˈrændəm/ a feito, tirado
etc ao acaso ● n **at** ~ ao acaso, a
esmo, aleatoriamente

randy /ˈrændɪ/ a (-**ier**, -**iest**) lascivo,
sensual

rang /ræŋ/ ▶ RING²

range /reɪndʒ/ n (*distance*) alcance
m; (*scope*) âmbito m; (*variety*) gama
f, variedade f; (*stove*) fogão m; (*of
voice*) registro m, (*P*) registo m;
(*of temperature*) variação f; ~ **of
mountains** cordilheira f, serra f ● vt
dispor, ordenar ● vi estender-se;
(*vary*) variar. ~**r** n guarda-florestal m

rank¹ /ræŋk/ n fila f, fileira f; *Mil*
posto m; (*social position*) classe f,
categoria f; **the** ~ **and file** a massa
f, gente f comum ● vt/i ~ **among**

contar(-se) entre

rank² /ræŋk/ a (-**er**, -**est**) (*plants*)
luxuriante; (*smell*) fétido; (*out-and-
out*) total

ransack /ˈrænsæk/ vt (*search*)
espionar, (*P*) espiar, revistar,
remexer; (*pillage*) pilhar, saquear

ransom /ˈrænsəm/ n resgate m
● vt resgatar; **hold to** ~ prender
como refém

rant /rænt/ vi usar linguagem
bombástica

rap /ræp/ n pancadinha f seca ● vt/i
(*pt* rapped) bater, dar uma pancada
seca em

rape /reɪp/ vt violar, estuprar ● n
violação f, estupro m

rapid /ˈræpɪd/ a rápido. ~**ity**
/rəˈpɪdətɪ/ n rapidez f

rapids /ˈræpɪdz/ npl rápidos mpl

rapist /ˈreɪpɪst/ n violador m,
estuprador m

rapport /ræˈpɔː(r)/ n bom m
relacionamento

raptur|e /ˈræptʃə(r)/ n êxtase m.
~**ous** a extático; (*welcome etc*)
entusiástico

rare¹ /reə(r)/ a (-**er**, -**est**) raro. ~**ely**
adv raramente, raras vezes. ~**ity** n
raridade f

rare² /reə(r)/ a (-**er**, -**est**) *Culin*
malpassado

rarefied /ˈreərɪfaɪd/ a rarefeito;
(*refined*) requintado

rascal /ˈrɑːskl/ n (*dishonest*) patife
m; (*mischievous*) maroto m

rash¹ /ræʃ/ n erupção f cutânea;
irritação f **na pele** 🔲

rash² /ræʃ/ a (-**er**, -**est**)
imprudente, precipitado.
~**ly** adv imprudentemente,
precipitadamente

rasher /'ræʃə(r)/ n fatia f (de presunto ou de bacon)

raspberry /'rɑːzbrɪ/ n framboesa f

rat /ræt/ n rato m, (P) ratazana f; **~ race** fig luta f renhida para vencer na vida, arrivismo m

rate /reɪt/ n (ratio) razão f; (speed) velocidade f; (price) tarifa f; (of exchange) (taxa f de) câmbio m; (of interest) taxa f; ~s (taxes) impostos mpl municipais, taxas fpl; **at this** ~ desse jeito, desse modo; **at any** ~ de qualquer modo, pelo menos; **at the** ~ **of** à razão de ● vt avaliar; fig (consider) considerar

rather /'rɑːðə(r)/ adv (by preference) antes; (fairly) muito, bastante; (a little) um pouco; **I would** ~ **go** preferia ir

rating /'reɪtɪŋ/ n Comm rating m, (P) valor m; (sailor) praça f, marinheiro m; Radio, TV índice m de audiência

ratio /'reɪʃɪəʊ/ n (pl -os) proporção f

ration /'ræʃn/ n ração f ● vt racionar

rational /'ræʃnəl/ a racional; ‹person› sensato, razoável. **~ize** vt racionalizar

rattle /'rætl/ vt/i matraquear; (of door, window) bater; (of bottles) chocalhar; 🔢 agitar; mexer com os nervos de ● n (baby's toy) guizo m, chocalho m; (of football fan) matraca f; (sound) matraquear m, chocalhar m; ~ **off** despejar 🔢

rattlesnake /'rætlsneɪk/ n cobra f cascavel

raucous /'rɔːkəs/ a áspero, rouco

ravage /'rævɪdʒ/ vt devastar, causar estragos a. **~s** npl devastação f, estragos mpl

rave /reɪv/ vi delirar; (in anger) urrar; ~ **about** delirar (de entusiasmo) com

raven /'reɪvn/ n corvo m

ravenous /'rævənəs/ a esfomeado; (greedy) voraz

ravine /rə'viːn/ n ravina f, barranco m

raving /'reɪvɪŋ/ a **~ lunatic** doido m varrido ● adv **~ mad** loucamente

ravish /'rævɪʃ/ vt (rape) violar; (enrapture) arrebatar, encantar. **~ing** a arrebatador, encantador

raw /rɔː/ a (-er, -est) cru; (not processed) bruto; (wound) em carne viva; (weather) frio e úmido, (P) húmido; (immature) inexperiente, verde; **~ deal** tratamento m injusto; **~ material** matéria-prima f

ray /reɪ/ n raio m

razor /'reɪzə(r)/ n navalha f de barba. **~ blade** n lâmina f de barbear

re /riː/ prep a respeito de, em referência a, relativo a

re- /ri/ pref re-

reach /riːtʃ/ vt chegar a atingir; (contact) contatar; (pass) passar; ~ **for** estender a mão para agarrar; ~ **out** estender-se, chegar ● n alcance m; **out of** ~ fora de alcance; **within** ~ **of** ao alcance de; (close to) próximo de

react /rɪ'ækt/ vi reagir

reaction /rɪ'ækʃn/ n reação f. **~ary** a & n reacionário m

reactor /rɪ'æktə(r)/ n reator m

read /riːd/ vt/i (pt read /red/) ler; fig (interpret) interpretar; (study) estudar; (of instrument) marcar, indicar ● n 🔢 leitura f; **~ about** ler um artigo sobre; ~ **out** ler em voz alta. **~able** a agradável or fácil de ler; (legible) legível. **~er** n leitor m; (book) livro m de leitura. **~ing** n leitura f; (of instrument) registro m, (P) registo m

readily /'redɪlɪ/ adv de boa vontade, prontamente; (easily) facilmente

readjust /riːəˈdʒʌst/ vt reajustar, readaptar ● vi readaptar-se, reajustar-se

ready /'redɪ/ a (-ier, -iest) pronto; ~ **money** dinheiro m vivo, (P) pagamento m à vista ● n at the ~ pronto para disparar. ~**made** a pronto; ~**to-wear** a prêt-à-porter, (P) pronto-a-vestir

real /rɪəl/ a real, verdadeiro; (genuine) autêntico; ~ **estate** Amer bens mpl imobiliários ● adv Amer 🔲 realmente

realis|t /'rɪəlɪst/ n realista mf. ~**m** /-zəm/ n realismo m. ~**tic** /-'lɪstɪk/ a realista. ~**tically** /-'lɪstɪkəlɪ/ adv realisticamente

reality /rɪˈælətɪ/ n realidade f. ~ **TV** n reality show m, (P) reality TV f; televisão f de reality shows

realiz|e /'rɪəlaɪz/ vt dar-se conta de, aperceber-se de, perceber; (fulfil; turn into cash) realizar. ~**ation** /-'zeɪʃn/ n consciência f, noção f; (fulfilment) realização f

really /'rɪəlɪ/ adv realmente, na verdade

realm /relm/ n reino m; fig domínio m; esfera f

reap /riːp/ vt (cut) ceifar; (gather) fig colher

reappear /riːəˈpɪə(r)/ vi reaparecer

rear[1] /rɪə(r)/ n traseira f, retaguarda f; **bring up the** ~ ir na retaguarda, fechar a marcha ● a traseiro, de trás, posterior. ~**view mirror** n espelho m retrovisor

rear[2] /rɪə(r)/ vt levantar, erguer; ‹children, cattle› criar; ~ **one's head** levantar a cabeça ● vi (of horse etc)

empinar-se

rearrange /riːəˈreɪndʒ/ vt arranjar doutro modo, reorganizar

reason /'riːzn/ n razão f; **within** ~ razoável ● vt/i raciocinar, argumentar; ~ **with sb** procurar convencer alguém. ~**ing** n raciocínio m

reasonable /'riːznəbl/ a razoável

reassur|e /riːəˈʃʊə(r)/ vt tranquilizar, sossegar. ~**ance** n garantia f. ~**ing** a animador, reconfortante

rebate /'riːbeɪt/ n (refund) reimbolso m; (discount) desconto m, abatimento m

rebel[1] /'rebl/ n rebelde mf

rebel[2] /rɪˈbel/ vi (pt rebelled) rebelar-se, revoltar-se, sublevar-se. ~**lion** n rebelião f, revolta f. ~**lious** a rebelde

rebound[1] /rɪˈbaʊnd/ vi repercutir, ressoar; fig (backfire) recair (on sobre)

rebound[2] /'riːbaʊnd/ n ricochete m

rebuff /rɪˈbʌf/ vt receber mal; repelir 🔲 ● n rejeição f

rebuild /riːˈbɪld/ vt (pt rebuilt) reconstruir

rebuke /rɪˈbjuːk/ vt repreender ● n reprimenda f

recall /rɪˈkɔːl/ vt chamar, mandar regressar; (remember) lembrar-se de ● n (summons) ordem f de regresso

recant /rɪˈkænt/ vi retratar-se

recap /'riːkæp/ vt/i (pt recapped) 🔲 recapitular ● n recapitulação f

recapitulat|e /riːkəˈpɪtjʊleɪt/ vt/i recapitular

reced|e /rɪˈsiːd/ vi recuar, retroceder. **his hair is** ~**ing** ele está ficando or (P) a ficar com entradas.

~ing a ‹forehead, chin› recuado, voltado para dentro

receipt /rɪ'siːt/ n recibo m; (receiving) recepção f, (P) receção; **~s** Comm receitas fpl

receive /rɪ'siːv/ vt receber. **~r** /-ə(r)/ n (of stolen goods) receptador m, (P) recetador m; (of phone) fone m, (P) auscultador m; Radio, TV receptor m, (P) recetor m; **(official)** **~r** síndico m de massa falida

recent /'riːsnt/ a recente. **~ly** adv recentemente

receptacle /rɪ'septəkl/ n recipiente m, receptáculo m, (P) recetáculo m

reception /rɪ'sepʃn/ n recepção f, (P) receção f; (welcome) acolhimento m; (signal) recepção f, (P) receção f (de sinal). **~ist** n recepcionista mf, (P) rececionista mf

receptive /rɪ'septɪv/ a receptivo, (P) recetivo

recess /rɪ'ses/ n recesso m; (of legislature) recesso m; Amer Schol recreio m

recession /rɪ'seʃn/ n recessão f, depressão f (económica)

recharge /riː'tʃɑːdʒ/ vt tornar a carregar, arecarregar

recipe /'resəpɪ/ n Culin receita f

recipient /rɪ'sɪpɪənt/ n recipiente mf; (of letter) destinatário m

reciprocate /rɪ'sɪprəkət/ vt/i reciprocar(-se), retribuir, fazer o mesmo

recital /rɪ'saɪtl/ n (music etc) recital m

recite /rɪ'saɪt/ vt recitar; (list) enumerar

reckless /'reklɪs/ a inconsciente, imprudente, estouvado

reckon /'rekən/ vt/i calcular; (judge) considerar; (think) supor, pensar; **~ on** contar com, depender de; **~ with** contar com, levar em conta

reclaim /rɪ'kleɪm/ vt (demand) reclamar; ‹land› recuperar

recline /rɪ'klaɪn/ vt/i reclinar(-se)

recluse /rɪ'kluːs/ n solitário m, recluso m

recognition /rekəg'nɪʃn/ n reconhecimento m; **beyond ~** irreconhecível; **gain ~** ganhar nome, ser reconhecido

recogniz|e /'rekəgnaɪz/ vt reconhecer. **~able** /'rekəgnaɪzəbl/ a reconhecível

recoil /rɪ'kɔɪl/ vi recuar; ‹gun› dar coice ● n recuo m; ‹gun› coice m; **~ from doing** recusar-se a fazer

recollect /rekə'lekt/ vt recordar-se de. **~ion** /-ʃn/ n recordação f, memória f

recommend /rekə'mend/ vt recomendar. **~ation** /-'deɪʃn/ n recomendação f

recompense /'rekəmpens/ vt recompensar ● n recompensa f

reconcil|e /'rekənsaɪl/ vt ‹people› reconciliar; ‹facts› conciliar; **~ o.s. to** resignar-se a, conformar-se com. **~iation** /-sɪlɪ'eɪʃn/ n reconciliação f

reconnaissance /rɪ'kɒnɪsns/ n reconhecimento m

reconnoitre /rekə'nɔɪtə(r)/ vt/i (pres p **-tring**) Mil reconhecer, fazer um reconhecimento (de)

reconsider /riːkən'sɪdə(r)/ vt reconsiderar

reconstruct /riːkən'strʌkt/ vt reconstruir. **~ion** /-ʃn/ n reconstrução f

record[1] /rɪ'kɔːd/ vt registar; ‹disc, tape etc› gravar; **~ that** referir/

relatar que. **~ing** n (disc, tape etc) gravação f

record² /ˈrekɔːd/ n (register) registro m, (P) registo m; (mention) menção f, nota f; (file) arquivo m; Mus disco m; Sport record(e) m; **have a (criminal) ~** ter cadastro; **off the ~** (unofficial) oficioso; (secret) confidencial ● a record(e) invar. **~ player** n toca-discos m invar, (P) gira-discos m invar

recorder /rɪˈkɔːdə(r)/ n Mus flauta f de ponta; Techn instrumento m registrador, (P) de registo

recount¹ /rɪˈkaʊnt/ vt narrar em pormenor, relatar

recount² /ˈriːkaʊnt/ n Pol nova contagem f

recoup /rɪˈkuːp/ vt compensar; (recover) recuperar

recover /rɪˈkʌvə(r)/ vt recuperar ● vi restabelecer-se. **~y** n recuperação f; (health) recuperação f, restabelecimento m

recreation /rekrɪˈeɪʃn/ n recreação f, recreio m; (pastime) passatempo m. **~al** a recreativo

recruit /rɪˈkruːt/ n recruta m ● vt recrutar. **~ment** n recrutamento m

rectangle /ˈrektæŋgl/ n retângulo m. **~ular** /-ˈtæŋgjʊlə(r)/ a retangular

rectify /ˈrektɪfaɪ/ vt retificar

recuperate /rɪˈkjuːpəreɪt/ vt/i recuperar(-se)

recur /rɪˈkɜː(r)/ vi (pt recurred) repetir-se; (come back) voltar (to a)

recurrent /rɪˈkʌrənt/ a frequente, (P) frequente, repetido, periódico. **~ce** n repetição f

recycle /riːˈsaɪkl/ vt reciclar

red /red/ a (redder, reddest) encarnado, vermelho; (hair) ruivo; **~ carpet** fig recepção f or

(P) receção f solene, tratamento m especial; **R~ Cross** Cruz f Vermelha; **~ herring** fig pista f falsa; **~ light** luz f vermelha; **~ tape** fig papelada f, burocracia f; **~ wine** vinho m tinto ● n encarnado m, vermelho m; **in the ~** em déficit. **~-handed** a em flagrante (delito); com a boca na botija 🄣. **~-hot** a escaldante, incandescente

redden /ˈredn/ vt/i avermelhar(-se); (blush) corar, ruborizar-se

redecorate /riːˈdekəreɪt/ vt decorar/pintar de novo

redeem /rɪˈdiːm/ vt (sins etc) redimir; (sth pawned) tirar do prego 🄣; (voucher etc) resgatar. **~emption** /rɪˈdempʃn/ n resgate m; (of honour) salvação f

redirect /riːdaɪˈrekt/ vt (letter) reendereçar

redness /ˈrednɪs/ n vermelhidão f, cor f vermelha

redo /riːˈduː/ vt (pt -did, pp -done) refazer

redress /rɪˈdres/ vt reparar; (set right) remediar, emendar; **~ the balance** restabelecer o equilíbrio ● n reparação f

reduce /rɪˈdjuːs/ vt reduzir; (temperature etc) baixar. **~tion** /rɪˈdʌkʃn/ n redução f

redundant /rɪˈdʌndənt/ a redundante, supérfluo; (worker) desempregado; **be made ~t** ficar desempregado. **~cy** n demissão f por excesso de pessoal

reed /riːd/ n cara f, junco m; Mus palheta f

reef /riːf/ n recife m

reek /riːk/ n mau cheiro m ● vi cheirar mal, tresandar; **he ~s of wine** ele está com cheiro de or tresanda a vinho

reel /riːl/ n carretel m; (spool) bobina f ● vi cambalear, vacilar ● vt ~ **off** recitar 🔢

refectory /rɪˈfektərɪ/ n refeitório m

refer /rɪˈfɜː(r)/ vt/i (pt referred) ~ **to** referir-se a; (concern) aplicar-se a, dizer respeito a; (consult) consultar; (direct) remeter a/para

referee /refəˈriː/ n árbitro m; (for job) pessoa f que dá referências ● vt (pt refereed) arbitrar

reference /ˈrefrəns/ n referência f; (testimonial) referências fpl; in or with ~ **to** com referência a; ~ **book** livro m de consulta, obra f de referência

referendum /refəˈrendəm/ n (pl -dums, or -da) referendo m, plebiscito m

refill¹ /riːˈfɪl/ vt encher de novo; ‹pen etc› pôr carga nova em

refill² /ˈriːfɪl/ n ‹pen etc› carga f nova, (P) recarga f

refine /rɪˈfaɪn/ vt refinar. ~**d** a refinado; ‹taste, manners etc› requintado. ~**ment** n ‹taste, manners etc› refinamento m, requinte m; Tech refinação f. ~**ry** /-ərɪ/ n refinaria f

reflect /rɪˈflekt/ vt/i refletir (**on/ upon** em). ~**ion** /-ʃn/ n reflexão f; (image) reflexo m. ~**or** n refletor m

reflective /rɪˈflektɪv/ a refletor; (thoughtful) refletido, ponderado

reflex /ˈriːfleks/ a & n reflexo m

reflexive /rɪˈfleksɪv/ a Gram reflexivo, (P) reflexo

reform /rɪˈfɔːm/ vt/i reformar(-se) ● n reforma f. ~**er** n reformador m

refrain¹ /rɪˈfreɪn/ n refrão m, estribilho m

refrain² /rɪˈfreɪn/ vi abster-se (**from** de)

refresh /rɪˈfreʃ/ vt refrescar; (of rest etc) restaurar; ~ **one's memory** avivar or refrescar a memória. ~**ing** a refrescante; (of rest etc) reparador. ~**ments** npl refeição f leve; (drinks) refrescos mpl

refresher /rɪˈfreʃə(r)/ n ~ **course** curso m de reciclagem

refrigerat|e /rɪˈfrɪdʒəreɪt/ vt refrigerar. ~**or** n frigorífico m, refrigerador m, geladeira f

refuel /riːˈfjuːəl/ vt/i (pt refuelled) reabastecer(-se) (de combustível)

refuge /ˈrefjuːdʒ/ n refúgio m, asilo m; **take** ~ refugiar-se

refugee /refjuˈdʒiː/ n refugiado m

refund¹ /rɪˈfʌnd/ vt reembolsar

refund² /ˈriːfʌnd/ n reembolso m

refus|e¹ /rɪˈfjuːz/ vt/i recusar(-se). ~**al** n recusa f; **first** ~**al** preferência f, primeira opção f

refuse² /ˈrefjuːs/ n refugo m, lixo m. ~ **collector** n lixeiro m, (P) homem m do lixo

refute /rɪˈfjuːt/ vt refutar

regain /rɪˈgeɪn/ vt recobrar, recuperar

regal /ˈriːgl/ a real, régio

regard /rɪˈɡɑːd/ vt considerar; (gaze) olhar ● n consideração f, estima f; (gaze) olhar m; ~**s** cumprimentos mpl; (less formally) lembranças fpl, saudades fpl. **as** ~**s** ~**ing** prep no que diz respeito a, quanto a. ~**less** adv apesar de tudo; ~**less of** apesar de

regatta /rɪˈɡætə/ n regata f

regenerate /rɪˈdʒenəreɪt/ vt regenerar

regime /reɪˈʒiːm/ n regime m

regiment /ˈredʒɪmənt/ n regimento m. ~**al** /-ˈmentl/ a de regimento, regimental

region /ˈriːdʒən/ n região f; **in the ~** of por volta de. **~al** a regional

regist|er /ˈredʒɪstə(r)/ n registro m, (P) registo m ● vt (record) anotar; (notice) fixar, registar, prestar atenção a; ‹birth, letter› registrar, (P) registar; ‹vehicle› matricular; ‹emotions etc› exprimir ● vi inscrever-se. **~er office** n registro m, (P) registo m. **~ration** /-ˈstreɪʃn/ n registro m, (P) registo m; (for course) inscrição f, matricula f; **~ration (number)** número m de placa ou de matrícula

registrar /redʒɪˈstrɑː(r)/ n oficial m do registro, (P) registo m civil; Univ secretário m

regret /rɪˈɡret/ n pena f, pesar m; (repentance) remorso m; **I have no ~s** não estou arrependido ● vt (pt regretted) lamentar; sentir (to do fazer); (feel repentance) arrepender-se de, lamentar. **~fully** adv com pena, pesarosamente. **~table** a lamentável. **~tably** adv infelizmente

regular /ˈreɡjʊlə(r)/ a regular; (usual) normal; [T] (thorough) perfeito; verdadeiro; autêntico ● n [T] ‹client› cliente mf habitual. **~ity** /-ˈlærətɪ/ n regularidade f. **~ly** adv regularmente

regulat|e /ˈreɡjʊleɪt/ vt regular. **~ion** /-ˈleɪʃn/ n regulação f, (rule) regulamento m, regra f

rehabilitat|e /riːəˈbɪlɪteɪt/ vt reabilitar. **~ion** /-ˈteɪʃn/ n reabilitação f

rehears|e /rɪˈhɜːs/ vt ensaiar. **~al** n ensaio m; **dress ~al** ensaio m geral

reign /reɪn/ n reinado m ● vi reinar (over em)

reimburse /riːɪmˈbɜːs/ vt reembolsar. **~ment** n reembolso m

rein /reɪn/ n rédea f

reincarnation /riːɪnkɑːˈneɪʃn/ n reencarnação f

reindeer /ˈreɪndɪə(r)/ n invar rena f

reinforce /riːɪnˈfɔːs/ vt reforçar; **~d concrete** concreto m armado, (P) cimento m or betão m armado. **~ment** n reforço m; **~ments** reforços mpl

reinstate /riːɪnˈsteɪt/ vt reintegrar, reintroduzir

reiterate /riːˈɪtəreɪt/ vt reiterar

reject[1] /rɪˈdʒekt/ vt rejeitar. **~ion** /-ʃn/ n rejeição f

reject[2] /ˈriːdʒekt/ n (artigo de) refugo m

rejoic|e /rɪˈdʒɔɪs/ vi regozijar-se (at/over com). **~ing** n regozijo m

rejuvenate /rɪˈdʒuːvəneɪt/ vt rejuvenescer

relapse /rɪˈlæps/ n recaída f ● vi recair

relate /rɪˈleɪt/ vt relatar; (associate) relacionar ● vi **~ to** ter relação com, dizer respeito a; (get on with) entender-se com. **~d** a aparentado; ‹ideas etc› afim, relacionado

relation /rɪˈleɪʃn/ n relação f; (person) parente mf. **~ship** n parentesco m; (link) relação f; (affair) ligação f

relative /ˈrelətɪv/ n parente mf ● a relativo. **~ly** adv relativamente

relax /rɪˈlæks/ vt/i relaxar(-se); fig descontrair(-se). **~ation** /riːlækˈseɪʃn/ n relaxamento m; fig descontração f; (recreation) distração f. **~ing** a relaxante

relay[1] /ˈriːleɪ/ n turma f, (P) turno m; **~ race** corrida f de revezamento, (P) estafetas

relay[2] /rɪˈleɪ/ vt (message) retransmitir

release /rɪ'liːs/ vt libertar, soltar; Mech desengatar, soltar; ‹bomb, film, record› lançar; ‹news› dar, publicar; ‹gas, smoke› soltar, libertar, emitir ● n libertação f; Mech desengate m; (bomb, film, record) lançamento m; (news) publicação f; (gas, smoke) emissão f; **new ~** estreia f

relegate /'relɪgeɪt/ vt relegar

relent /rɪ'lent/ vi ceder. **~less** a implacável, inexorável, inflexível

relevan|t /'reləvənt/ a relevante, pertinente, a propósito. **be ~ to** ter a ver com, dizer respeito a. **~ce** n pertinência f, relevância f

reliab|le /rɪ'laɪəbl/ a de confiança, com que se pode contar; ‹source etc› fidedigno; ‹machine etc› seguro, confiável. **~ility** /-'bɪlətɪ/ n confiabilidade f

reliance /rɪ'laɪəns/ n (dependence) segurança f; (trust) confiança f, fé f (on em)

relic /'relɪk/ n relíquia f. **~s** vestígios mpl, ruínas fpl

relief /rɪ'liːf/ n alívio m; (assistance) auxílio m, assistência f; (outline, design) relevo m; **~ road** estrada f alternativa

relieve /rɪ'liːv/ vt aliviar; (help) socorrer; (take over from) revezar, substituir; Mil render

religion /rɪ'lɪdʒən/ n religião f

religious /rɪ'lɪdʒəs/ a religioso

relinquish /rɪ'lɪŋkwɪʃ/ vt abandonar, renunciar a

relish /'relɪʃ/ n prazer m, gosto m; Culin molho m condimentado ● vt saborear, apreciar, gostar de

relocate /riː'ləʊ'keɪt/ vt/i transferir(-se), mudar(-se)

reluctan|t /rɪ'lʌktənt/ a relutante (**to** em); pouco inclinado (**to** a). **~ce** n relutância f. **~tly** adv a contragosto, relutantemente

rely /rɪ'laɪ/ vi **~ on** contar com; (depend) depender de

remain /rɪ'meɪn/ vi ficar, permanecer. **~s** npl restos mpl; (ruins) ruínas fpl. **~ing** a restante

remainder /rɪ'meɪndə(r)/ n restante m, remanescente m

remand /rɪ'mɑːnd/ vt reconduzir à prisão para detenção provisória ● n **on ~** sob prisão preventiva

remark /rɪ'mɑːk/ n observação f, comentário m ● vt observar, comentar ● vi **~ on** fazer observações or comentários sobre. **~able** a notável

remarry /riː'mærɪ/ vt/i tornar a casar(-se) (com)

remed|y /'remədɪ/ n remédio m ● vt remediar. **~ial** /rɪ'miːdɪəl/ a Med corretivo

rememb|er /rɪ'membə(r)/ vt lembrar-se de, recordar-se de. **~rance** n lembrança f, recordação f

remind /rɪ'maɪnd/ vt (fazer) lembrar (**sb of sth** algo a alguém); **~ sb to do** lembrar a alguém que faça. **~er** n o que serve para fazer lembrar; (note) lembrete m

reminisce /remɪ'nɪs/ vi (re) lembrar (coisas passadas). **~nces** npl reminiscências fpl

reminiscent /remɪ'nɪsnt/ a **~ of** que faz lembrar, evocativo de

remit /rɪ'mɪt/ vt (pt remitted) (money) remeter. **~tance** n remessa (de dinheiro) f

remnant /'remnənt/ n resto m; (trace) vestígio m; (of cloth) retalho m

remorse /rɪˈmɔːs/ n remorsos m.
~ful a arrependido, com remorsos.
~less a implacável

remote /rɪˈməʊt/ a remoto,
distante; ⟨person⟩ distante; ⟨slight⟩
vago, leve; **~ control** comando m à
distância, telecomando m. **~ly** adv
de longe; vagamente

remov|e /rɪˈmuːv/ vt tirar,
remover; ⟨lead away⟩ levar; ⟨dismiss⟩
demitir; ⟨get rid of⟩ eliminar. **~al** n
remoção f; ⟨dismissal⟩ demissão f;
⟨from house⟩ mudança f

remunerat|e /rɪˈmjuːnəreɪt/
vt remunerar. **~ion** /-ˈreɪʃn/ n
remuneração f

rename /riːˈneɪm/ vt rebatizar

render /ˈrendə(r)/ vt retribuir;
⟨services⟩ prestar; Mus interpretar;
⟨translate⟩ traduzir

renegade /ˈrenɪɡeɪd/ n renegado m

renew /rɪˈnjuː/ vt renovar; ⟨resume⟩
retomar. **~able** a renovável.
~al n renovação f; ⟨resumption⟩
reatamento m

renounce /rɪˈnaʊns/ vt renunciar
a; ⟨disown⟩ renegar, repudiar

renovat|e /ˈrenəveɪt/ vt renovar.
~ion /-ˈveɪʃn/ n renovação f

renown /rɪˈnaʊn/ n renome m.
~ed a conceituado, célebre, de
renome

rent /rent/ n aluguel m, (P) aluguer
m, renda f ● vt alugar, arrendar. **~al**
n ⟨charge⟩ aluguel m, (P) aluguer m;
renda f; ⟨act of renting⟩ aluguel m,
(P) aluguer m

renunciation /rɪnʌnsɪˈeɪʃn/ n
renúncia f

reopen /riːˈəʊpən/ vt/i reabrir(-se)

reorganize /riːˈɔːɡənaɪz/ vt/i
reorganizar(-se)

rep /rep/ n 🔢 vendedor m; caixeiro-
viajante m

repair /rɪˈpeə(r)/ vt reparar,
consertar ● n reparo m, conserto
m; **in good ~** em bom estado (de
conservação)

repatriat|e /riːˈpætrɪeɪt/
vt repatriar. **~ion** /-ˈeɪʃn/ n
repatriamento m

repay /riːˈpeɪ/ vt (pt repaid) pagar,
devolver, reembolsar; ⟨reward⟩
recompensar. **~ment** n pagamento
m, reembolso m

repeal /rɪˈpiːl/ vt revogar ● n
revogação f

repeat /rɪˈpiːt/ vt/i repetir(-se)
● n repetição f; ⟨broadcast⟩
retransmissão f. **~edly** adv repetidas
vezes, repetidamente

repel /rɪˈpel/ vt (pt repelled) repelir.
~lent a & n repelente m

repent /rɪˈpent/ vi arrepender-se
(of de). **~ance** n arrependimento m.
~ant a arrependido

repercussion /riːpəˈkʌʃn/ n
repercussão f

repertoire /ˈrepətwɑː(r)/ n
repertório m

repertory /ˈrepətrɪ/ n repertório m

repetit|ion /repɪˈtɪʃn/ n repetição
f. **~ious** /-ˈtɪʃəs/, **~ive** /rɪˈpetətɪv/ a
repetitivo

repetitive strain injury n
lesão f por esforço repetitivo

replace /rɪˈpleɪs/ vt colocar no
mesmo lugar, repor; ⟨take the place
of⟩ substituir. **~ment** n reposição f;
⟨substitution⟩ substituição f; ⟨person⟩
substituto m

replenish /rɪˈplenɪʃ/ vt voltar a
encher, reabastecer; ⟨renew⟩ renovar

replica /ˈreplɪkə/ n réplica f, cópia f,
reprodução f

reply /rɪˈplaɪ/ vt/i responder, replicar ● n resposta f, réplica f

report /rɪˈpɔːt/ vt relatar; (notify) informar; (denounce) denunciar, apresentar queixa de ● vi fazer um relatório; ~ **(on)** ⟨news item⟩ fazer uma reportagem (sobre); ~ **to** (go) apresentar-se a ● n (in newspapers) reportagem f; (of company, doctor) relatório m; Schol boletim m escolar; (sound) detonação f; (rumour) rumores mpl. ~**edly** adv segundo consta. ~**er** n repórter m

repossess /riːpəˈzes/ vt reapossar-se de, retomar

represent /reprɪˈzent/ vt representar. ~**ation** /-ˈteɪʃn/ n representação f

representative /reprɪˈzentətɪv/ a representativo ● n representante mf

repress /rɪˈpres/ vt reprimir. ~**ion** /-ʃn/ n repressão f. ~**ive** a repressor, repressivo

reprieve /rɪˈpriːv/ n suspensão f temporária; (temporary relief) tréguas fpl ● vt suspender temporariamente; fig dar tréguas a

reprimand /ˈreprɪmɑːnd/ vt repreender ● n repreensão f, reprimenda f

reprint /ˈriːprɪnt/ n reimpressão f, reedição f ● vt reimprimir

reproach /rɪˈprəʊtʃ/ vt censurar; repreender (**sb for sth** alguém por algo, algo a alguém) ● n censura f; **above** ~ irrepreensível. ~**ful** a repreensivo, reprovador

reproduc|e /riːprəˈdjuːs/ vt/i reproduzir(-se). ~**tion** /-ˈdʌkʃn/ n reprodução f. ~**tive** /-ˈdʌktɪv/ a reprodutivo, reprodutor

reptile /ˈreptaɪl/ n réptil m

republic /rɪˈpʌblɪk/ n república f. ~**an** a & n republicano m

repugnan|t /rɪˈpʌɡnənt/ a repugnante. ~**ce** n repugnância f

repuls|e /rɪˈpʌls/ vt repelir, repulsar. ~**ion** /-ʃn/ n repulsa f. ~**ive** a repulsivo, repelente, repugnante

reputable /ˈrepjʊtəbl/ a respeitado, honrado; ⟨firm, make etc⟩ de renome, conceituado

reputation /repjʊˈteɪʃn/ n reputação f

repute /rɪˈpjuːt/ n reputação f. ~**d** /-ɪd/ a suposto, putativo; ~**d to be** tido como, tido na conta de. ~**dly** /-ɪdlɪ/ adv segundo consta, com fama de

request /rɪˈkwest/ n pedido m ● vt pedir; solicitar (**of, from** a)

require /rɪˈkwaɪə(r)/ vt requerer. ~**d** a requerido; (needed) necessário, preciso. ~**ment** n fig requisito m; (need) necessidade f; (demand) exigência f

resale /ˈriːseɪl/ n revenda f

rescue /ˈreskjuː/ vt salvar; socorrer (**from** de) ● n salvamento m; (help) socorro m, ajuda f. ~**r** /-ə(r)/ n salvador m

research /rɪˈsɜːtʃ/ n pesquisa f, investigação f ● vt/i pesquisar; fazer investigação (**into** sobre). ~**er** n investigador m

resembl|e /rɪˈzembl/ vt assemelhar-se a, parecer-se com. ~**ance** n semelhança f; similaridade f (**to** com)

resent /rɪˈzent/ vt ressentir(-se de), ficar ressentido com. ~**ful** a ressentido. ~**ment** n ressentimento m

reservation /rezəˈveɪʃn/ n (booking) reserva f; Amer reserva (de índios) f

reserve /rɪˈzɜːv/ vt reservar ● n reserva f; Sport suplente mf; **in** ~ de reserva. **~d** a reservado

reservoir /ˈrezəvwɑː(r)/ n (lake, supply etc) reservatório m; (container) depósito m

reshuffle /riːˈʃʌfl/ vt Pol remodelar ● n Pol reforma (do Ministério) f, remodelação f (ministerial)

reside /rɪˈzaɪd/ vi residir

residen|t /ˈrezɪdənt/ a residente ● n morador m, habitante mf; (foreigner) residente mf; (in hotel) hóspede mf. **~ce** n residência f; (of students) residência f, lar m; **~ce permit** visto m de residência

residential /rezɪˈdenʃl/ a residencial

residue /ˈrezɪdjuː/ n resíduo m

resign /rɪˈzaɪn/ vt (post) demitir-se; ~ **o.s. to** resignar-se a ● vi demitir-se, apresentar a demissão. **~ation** /rezɪɡˈneɪʃn/ n resignação f; (from job) demissão f. **~ed** a resignado

resilien|t /rɪˈzɪlɪənt/ a (springy) elástico; (person) resistente. **~ce** n elasticidade f; (of person) resistência f

resin /ˈrezɪn/ n resina f

resist /rɪˈzɪst/ vt/i resistir (a). **~ance** n resistência f. **~ant** a resistente

resolut|e /ˈrezəluːt/ a resoluto. **~ion** /-ˈluːʃn/ n resolução f

resolve /rɪˈzɒlv/ vt resolver; ~ **to do** resolver fazer ● n resolução f. **~d** a (resolute) resoluto; (decided) resolvido (**to** a)

resonan|t /ˈrezənənt/ a ressonante. **~ce** n ressonância f

resort /rɪˈzɔːt/ vi ~ **to** recorrer a, valer-se de ● n recurso m; (place) estância f, local m turístico; **as a**

last ~ em último recurso; **seaside** ~ praia f, balneário m, (P) estância f balnear

resound /rɪˈzaʊnd/ vi reboar; ressoar (**with** com). **~ing** a ressoante; fig retumbante

resource /rɪˈsɔːs/ n recurso m; **~s** recursos mpl, riquezas fpl. **~ful** a expedito, engenhoso, desembaraçado. **~fulness** n expediente m, engenho m

respect /rɪˈspekt/ n respeito m ● vt respeitar; **with** ~ **to** a respeito de, com respeito a, relativamente a. **~ful** a respeitoso

respectab|le /rɪˈspektəbl/ a respeitável; (passable) passável, aceitável

respective /rɪˈspektɪv/ a respectivo, (P) respetivo. **~ly** adv respectivamente, (P) respetivamente

respiration /respəˈreɪʃn/ n respiração f

respite /ˈrespaɪt/ n pausa f, trégua f, folga f

respond /rɪˈspɒnd/ vi responder (**to** a); (react) reagir (**to** a)

response /rɪˈspɒns/ n resposta f; (reaction) reação f

responsib|le /rɪˈspɒnsəbl/ a responsável; (job) de responsabilidade. **~ility** /-ˈbɪlətɪ/ n responsabilidade f

responsive /rɪˈspɒnsɪv/ a receptivo, (P) recetivo, que reage bem; ~ **to** sensível a

rest¹ /rest/ vt/i descansar, repousar; (lean) apoiar(-se) ● n descanso m, repouso m; (support) suporte m. **~room** n Amer banheiro m, (P) toaletes mpl

rest² /rest/ vi (remain) ficar; **it ~s with him** cabe a ele ● n (remainder) resto m (of de); **the ~ (of the)** (others) os outros

restaurant /'restront/ n restaurante m

restful /'restfl/ a sossegado, repousante, tranquilo

restless /'restlis/ a agitado, desassossegado

restor|e /rɪ'stɔ:(r)/ vt restaurar; (give back) restituir, devolver. **~ation** /restə'reɪʃn/ n restauração f

restrain /rɪ'streɪn/ vt conter, reprimir; **~ o.s.** controlar-se; **~ sb from** impedir alguém de. **~ed** a comedido, reservado. **~t** n controle m; (moderation) moderação f, comedimento m

restrict /rɪ'strɪkt/ vt restringir, limitar. **~ion** /-ʃn/ n restrição f. **~ive** a restritivo

result /rɪ'zʌlt/ n resultado m ● vi resultar (from de); **~ in** resultar em

resum|e /rɪ'zju:m/ vt/i reatar, retomar; ‹work, travel› recomeçar. **~ption** /rɪ'zʌmpʃn/ n reatamento m, retomada f; (of work) recomeço m

résumé /'rezju:meɪ/ n resumo m, (P) CV m

resurgence /rɪ'sɜ:dʒəns/ n reaparecimento m, ressurgimento m

resurrect /rezə'rekt/ vt ressuscitar. **~ion** /-ʃn/ n ressureição f

resuscitat|e /rɪ'sʌsɪteɪt/ vt ressuscitar, reanimar. **~ion** /-'teɪʃn/ n reanimação f

retail /'ri:teɪl/ n retalho m ● a & adv a retalho ● vt/i vender(-se) a retalho. **~er** n retalhista m

retain /rɪ'teɪn/ vt reter; (keep) conservar, guardar

retaliat|e /rɪ'tælɪeɪt/ vi retaliar, exercer represálias, desforrar-se. **~ion** /-'eɪʃn/ n retaliação f, represália f, desforra f

retarded /rɪ'tɑ:dɪd/ a retardado, atrasado

retch /retʃ/ vi fazer esforço para vomitar, estar com ânsias de vômito or (P) vómito

retention /rɪ'tenʃn/ n retenção f

reticen|t /'retɪsnt/ a reticente. **~ce** n reticência f

retina /'retɪnə/ n retina f

retinue /'retɪnju:/ n séquito m, comitiva f

retire /rɪ'taɪə(r)/ vi reformar-se, aposentar-se; (withdraw) retirar-se; (go to bed) ir deitar-se ● vt reformar, aposentar. **~d** a reformado, aposentado. **~ment** n reforma f, aposentadoria f, (P) aposentação f

retiring /rɪ'taɪərɪŋ/ a reservado, retraído

retort /rɪ'tɔ:t/ vt/i retrucar, retorquir ● n réplica f

retrace /ri:'treɪs/ vt **~ one's steps** refazer o mesmo caminho; fig recordar, recapitular

retract /rɪ'trækt/ vt/i retratar(-se), desdizer(-se); ‹wheels› recolher; ‹claws› encolher, recolher

retreat /rɪ'tri:t/ vi retirar-se; Mil retirar, bater em retirada ● n retirada f; (seclusion) retiro m

retrial /ri:'traɪəl/ n novo julgamento

retribution /retrɪ'bju:ʃn/ n castigo (merecido) m; (vengeance) vingança f

retriev|e /rɪ'tri:v/ vt ir buscar; (rescue) salvar; (recover) recuperar; (put right) reparar. **~er** n (dog) perdigueiro m, (P) retriever m

retrograde /'retrəgreɪd/ a
retrógrado ● vt retroceder, recuar

retrospect /'retrəspekt/ n
in ~ retrospetivamente, (P)
retrospetivamente. ~**ive** /-'spektɪv/
a retrospetivo; (of law, payment)
retroativo

return /rɪ'tɜːn/ vi voltar; regressar;
retornar (**to** a) ● vt devolver;
‹compliment, visit› retribuir;
(put back) pôr de volta ● n volta
f, regresso m, retorno m; (profit)
lucro m, rendimento m; (restitution)
devolução f; **in** ~ **for** em troca de; ~
journey viagem f de volta; ~ **match**
Sport desafio m de desforra; ~ **ticket**
bilhete m de ida e volta; **many
happy** ~**s (of the day)** muitos
parabéns

reunion /riː'juːnɪən/ n reunião f

reunite /riːjuː'naɪt/ vt reunir

rev /rev/ n 🇬🇧 Auto rotação f ● vt/i
(pt revved) ~ **(up)** 🇬🇧 Auto acelerar
(o motor)

reveal /rɪ'viːl/ vt revelar; (display)
expor. ~**ing** a revelador

revel /'revl/ vi (pt revelled)
divertir-se; ~ **in** deleitar-se com. ~**ry**
n festas fpl, festejos mpl

revelation /revə'leɪʃn/ n
revelação f

revenge /rɪ'vendʒ/ n vingança f;
Sport desforra f ● vt vingar

revenue /'revənjuː/ n receita f,
rendimento m; **Inland R~** Fisco m

reverberate /rɪ'vɜːbəreɪt/ vi
ecoar, repercutir

revere /rɪ'vɪə(r)/ vt reverenciar,
venerar

reverend /'revərənd/ a reverendo;
R~ Reverendo

reverent /'revərənt/ a reverente.
~**ce** n reverência f, veneração f

reverse /rɪ'vɜːs/ a contrário,
inverso ● n contrário m; (back)
reverso m; (gear) marcha f à ré or (P)
atrás ● vt virar ao contrário; ‹order›
inverter; (turn inside out) virar do
avesso; ‹decision› anular ● vi Auto
fazer marcha à ré or (P) atrás. ~**al**
n inversão f, mudança f em sentido
contrário; (of view etc) mudança f

revert /rɪ'vɜːt/ vi ~ **to** reverter a

review /rɪ'vjuː/ n (inspection;
magazine) revista f; (of a situation)
revisão f; (critique) crítica f ● vt
revistar, passar or (P) fazer revista
em; ‹situation› rever; ‹book, film
etc› fazer a crítica de. ~**er** n crítico m

revis|e /rɪ'vaɪz/ vt rever; (amend)
corrigir. ~**ion** /-ɪʒn/ n revisão f;
(amendment) correção f

reviv|e /rɪ'vaɪv/ vt/i ressuscitar,
reavivar; ‹play› reapresentar;
‹person› reanimar(-se). ~**al** n
reflorescimento m, renascimento m

revoke /rɪ'vəʊk/ vt revogar, anular,
invalidar

revolt /rɪ'vəʊlt/ vt/i revoltar(-se)
● n revolta f.

revolting /rɪ'vəʊltɪŋ/ a
(disgusting) repugnante

revolution /revə'luːʃn/
n revolução f. ~**ary** a
revolucionário m. ~**ize** vt
revolucionar

revolv|e /rɪ'vɒlv/ vi girar; ~**ing
door** porta f giratória

revolver /rɪ'vɒlvə(r)/ n revólver m

revulsion /rɪ'vʌlʃn/ n repugnância
f, repulsa f

reward /rɪ'wɔːd/ n prémio m, (P)
prémio m; (for criminal, for lost
stolen property) recompensa f ● vt
recompensar. ~**ing** a compensador;
‹task etc› gratificante

rewind /riː'waɪnd/ vt (pt **rewound**) rebobinar

rewrite /riː'raɪt/ vt (pt **rewrote**, pp **rewritten**) reescrever

rhetoric /'retərɪk/ n retórica f. **~al** /rɪ'tɒrɪkl/ a retórico; ‹question› retórico

rheumati|c /ruː'mætɪk/ a reumático. **~sm** /'ruːmətɪzm/ n reumatismo m

rhinoceros /raɪ'nɒsərəs/ n (pl -oses) rinoceronte m

rhubarb /'ruːbɑːb/ n ruibarbo m

rhyme /raɪm/ n rima f; (poem) versos mpl ● vt/i (fazer) rimar

rhythm /'rɪðəm/ n ritmo m. **~ic(al)** /'rɪðmɪk(l)/ a rítmico, compassado

rib /rɪb/ n costela f

ribbon /'rɪbən/ n fita f; **in ~s** em tiras

rice /raɪs/ n arroz m

rich /rɪtʃ/ a (-er, -est) rico; ‹food› rico em açúcar e gordura. **~es** npl riquezas fpl. **~ly** adv ricamente

rickety /'rɪkətɪ/ a (shaky) desconjuntado

ricochet /'rɪkəʃeɪ/ n ricochete m ● vi (pt ricocheted /-ʃeɪd/) fazer ricochete, ricochetear

rid /rɪd/ vt (pt rid, pres p ridding) desembaraçar (of de); **get ~ of** desembaraçar-se de, livrar-se de

riddance /'rɪdns/ n good **~!** que alívio!, vai com Deus!

ridden /'rɪdn/ ▶ RIDE

riddle¹ /'rɪdl/ n enigma m; (puzzle) charada f

riddle² /'rɪdl/ vt **~ with** crivar de

ride /raɪd/ vi (pt rode, pp ridden) andar (de bicicleta, a cavalo, de carro) ● vt ‹horse› montar; ‹bicycle› andar de; ‹distance› percorrer ● n

passeio m or volta f (de carro, a cavalo etc); (distance) percurso m. **~r** /-ə(r)/ n cavaleiro m, amazona f; (cyclist) ciclista mf; (in document) aditamento m

ridge /rɪdʒ/ n aresta f; (of hill) cume m

ridicule /'rɪdɪkjuːl/ n ridículo m ● vt ridicularizar

ridiculous /rɪ'dɪkjʊləs/ a ridículo

riding /'raɪdɪŋ/ n equitação f

rife /raɪf/ a **be ~** estar espalhado; (of illness) grassar; **~ with** cheio de

riff-raff /'rɪfræf/ n gentinha f, povinho m, ralé f

rifle /'raɪfl/ n espingarda f ● vt revistar e roubar, saquear

rift /rɪft/ n fenda f, brecha f; fig (dissension) desacordo m; desavença f, desentendimento m

rig¹ /rɪg/ vt (pt rigged) equipar; **~ out** enfarpelar 🔢; **~ up** arranjar ● n (for oil) plataforma f de poço de petróleo

rig² /rɪg/ vt (pt rigged) pej manipular

right /raɪt/ a (correct, moral) certo; correto; (fair) justo; (not left) direito; (suitable) próprio, próprio ● n (entitlement) direito m; (not left) direita f; (not evil) o bem; **~ of way** Auto prioridade f ● vt ‹a wrong› reparar; ‹sth fallen› endireitar ● adv (not left) à direita; (directly) direito; (exactly) mesmo, bem; (completely) completamente; **~ away** logo, imediatamente; **be ~** ‹person› ter razão (**to** em); **be in the ~** ter razão; **on the ~** à direita; **put ~** acertar, corrigir. **~ angle** n ângulo reto m; **~-hand** a à or da direita; **~-handed** a (person) destro; **~-wing** a Pol de direita

righteous /'raɪtʃəs/ a justo, virtuoso

rightful /ˈraɪtfl/ a legítimo

rightly /ˈraɪtlɪ/ adv devidamente, corretamente; (*with reason*) justificadamente

rigid /ˈrɪdʒɪd/ a rígido. **~ity** /rɪˈdʒɪdətɪ/ n rigidez f

rigour /ˈrɪɡə(r)/ n rigor m. **~orous** a rigoroso

rile /raɪl/ vt 🖪 irritar; exasperar

rim /rɪm/ n borda f; (*of wheel*) aro m

rind /raɪnd/ n (*on cheese, fruit*) casca f; (*on bacon*) pele f

ring¹ /rɪŋ/ n (*on finger*) anel m; (*for napkin, key etc*) argola f; (*circle*) roda f, círculo m; *Boxing* ringue m; (*arena*) arena f ● vt rodear, cercar. **~ road** n estrada f periférica or perimetral or (P) circular f

ring² /rɪŋ/ vt/i (*pt* rang, *pp* rung) tocar; (*of words etc*) soar ● n toque m; 🖪 (*phone call*) telefonadela f 🖪; **~ the bell** tocar a campainha; **~ back** telefonar de volta; **~ off** desligar; **~ up** telefonar (a). **~tone** n toque m, (P) tom de toque m

ringleader /ˈrɪŋliːdə(r)/ n cabeça m, cérebro m

rink /rɪŋk/ n rinque m de patinação or (P) patinagem

rinse /rɪns/ vt enxaguar ● n enxaguada f, (P) enxaguadela f; (*hair tint*) enxaguada f, (P) enxaguadela f

riot /ˈraɪət/ n distúrbio m, motim m; (*of colours*) festival m ● vi fazer distúrbios or motins; **run ~** desenfrear-se, descontrolar-se; (*of plants*) crescer em matagal. **~er** n desordeiro m

riotous /ˈraɪətəs/ a desenfreado, turbulento, desordeiro

rip /rɪp/ vt/i (*pt* ripped) rasgar(-se) ● n rasgão m; **~ off** 🖪 (*defraud*) defraudar, enrolar 🖪. **~-off** n 🖪

roubalheira f 🖪

ripe /raɪp/ a (-er, -est) maduro. **~ness** n madureza f, (P) amadurecimento m

ripen /ˈraɪpən/ vt/i amadurecer

ripple /ˈrɪpl/ n ondulação f leve; (*sound*) murmúrio m ● vt/i encrespar(-se), agitar(-se), ondular

rise /raɪz/ vi (*pt* rose, *pp* risen) subir, elevar-se; (*stand up*) erguer-se, levantar-se; (*rebel*) sublevar-se; ‹*sun*› nascer; ‹*curtain, prices*› subir ● n (*increase*) aumento m; (*slope*) subida f, ladeira f; (*origin*) origem f; **give ~ to** originar, causar, dar origem a. **~r** /-ə(r)/ n early **~r** madrugador m

rising /ˈraɪzɪŋ/ n (*revolt*) insurreição f ● a ‹*sun*› nascente

risk /rɪsk/ n risco m ● vt arriscar; **at ~** em risco, em perigo; **at one's own ~** por sua conta e risco; **~ doing** (*venture*) arriscar-se a fazer. **~y** a arriscado

risqué /ˈriːskeɪ/ a picante

rite /raɪt/ n rito m; **last ~s** últimos sacramentos mpl

ritual /ˈrɪtʃʊəl/ a & n ritual m

rival /ˈraɪvl/ n & a rival mf; fig concorrente mf; competidor m ● vt (*pt* rivalled) rivalizar com. **~ry** n rivalidade f

river /ˈrɪvə(r)/ n rio m ● a fluvial

rivet /ˈrɪvɪt/ n rebite m ● vt (*pt* riveted) rebitar; fig prender; cravar. **~ing** a fascinante

road /rəʊd/ n estrada f; (*in town*) rua f; (*small*) fig caminho m; **~ tax** imposto m de circulação. **~block** n barricada f. **~ map** n mapa das estradas; **~ sign** n sinal m, placa f de sinalização; **~works** npl obras fpl (na via)

roadside /ˈrəʊdsaɪd/ n beira f da estrada

roadway /ˈrəʊdweɪ/ n pista f de rolamento, (P) faixa f de rodagem

roadworthy /ˈrəʊdwɜːðɪ/ a em condições de ser utilizado na rua/estrada

roam /rəʊm/ vi errar, andar sem destino ● vt percorrer

roaming /ˈrəʊmɪŋ/ n Telecom roaming m

roar /rɔː(r)/ n berro m, rugido m; (of thunder) ribombo m, troar m; (of sea, wind) bramido m ● vi/t berrar, rugir; (of lion) rugir; (of thunder) ribombar, troar; (of sea, wind) bramir; **with laughter** rir às gargalhadas

roaring /ˈrɔːrɪŋ/ a ‹trade› florescente; ‹success› enorme; ‹fire› com grandes chamas

roast /rəʊst/ vt/i assar ● a & n assado m

rob /rɒb/ vt (pt **robbed**) roubar (**sb of sth** algo de/a alguém); ‹bank› assaltar; (deprive) privar (**of** de). **~ber** n ladrão m. **~bery** n roubo m; (of bank) assalto m

robe /rəʊb/ n veste f comprida e solta; (dressing gown) robe m

robin /ˈrɒbɪn/ n papo-roxo m, (P) pintarroxo m

robot /ˈrəʊbɒt/ n robô m, (P) robot m, autómato m, (P) autómato m

robust /rəʊˈbʌst/ a robusto

rock[1] /rɒk/ n rocha f; (boulder) penhasco m, rochedo m; (sweet) pirulito m, (P) chupa-chupa m comprido; **on the ~s** 🔢 (of marriage) em crise; 🔢 (of drinks) com gelo. **~ bottom** n ponto m mais baixo ● a (of prices) baixíssimo 🔢

rock[2] /rɒk/ vt/i balouçar(-se); (shake) abanar, sacudir; ‹child› embalar ● n

Mus rock m. **~ing chair** n cadeira f de balanço, (P) cadeira f de baloiço; **~ing horse** n cavalo m de balanço, (P) cavalo m de balouço

rocket /ˈrɒkɪt/ n foguete m

rocky /ˈrɒkɪ/ a (-ier, -iest) ‹ground› pedregoso; ‹hill› rochoso; 🔢 (unsteady) instável; 🔢 (shaky) tremido 🔢

rod /rɒd/ n vara f, vareta f; Mech haste f; (for curtains) bastão m, (P) varão m; (for fishing) vara (de pescar) f, (P) cana f de pesca

rode /rəʊd/ ▶ **RIDE**

rodent /ˈrəʊdnt/ n roedor m

rogue /rəʊɡ/ n (dishonest) patife m, velhaco m; (mischievous) brincalhão m

role /rəʊl/ n papel m

roll /rəʊl/ vt/i (fazer) rolar; (into ball or cylinder) enrolar(-se); **be ~ing in money** 🔢 nadar em dinheiro 🔢; **~ over** (turn over) virar-se ao contrário ● n rolo m; (list) rol m, lista f; (bread) pãozinho m; (of ship) balanço m; (of drum) rufar m; (of thunder) ribombo m □ **~ up** vi 🔢 aparecer ● vt ‹sleeves› arregaçar; ‹umbrella› fechar. **~-call** n chamada f; **~ing pin** n rolo m de pastel

roller /ˈrəʊlə(r)/ n cilindro m; (wave) vagalhão m; (for hair) rolo m. **~ blind** n estore m; **~ coaster** n montanha f russa; **~ skate** n patim m de rodas

Roman /ˈrəʊmən/ a & n romano m; **~ numerals** algarismos mpl romanos. **R~ Catholic** a & n católico m

romance /rəʊˈmæns/ n (love affair) romance m, romantismo m

Romania /rʊˈmeɪnɪə/ n Romênia f, (P) Roménia f. **~n** a & n romeno m

romantic /rəʊˈmæntɪk/ a romântico. **~ism** n romantismo *m.* **~ize** *vi* fazer romance ● *vt* romantizar

romp /rɒmp/ *vi* brincar animadamente ● *n* brincadeira *f* animada

roof /ruːf/ *n* (*pl* **roofs**) telhado *m*; (*of car*) teto *m*, (*P*) capota *f*; (*of mouth*) palato *m*, céu *m* da boca; **hit the ~** 🗙 ficar furioso ● *vt* cobrir com telhado. **~-rack** *n* porta-bagagem *m*; **~top** *n* cimo *m* do telhado

rook[1] /rʊk/ *n* (*bird*) gralha *f*

rook[2] /rʊk/ *n* Chess torre *f*

room /ruːm/ *n* quarto *m*, divisão *f*; (*bedroom*) quarto *m* de dormir; (*large hall*) sala *f*; (*space*) espaço *m*, lugar *m*; **~s** (*lodgings*) apartamento *m*, cômodo *m*. **~mate** *n* companheiro *m* de quarto. **~y** *a* espaçoso; ‹*clothes*› amplo, largo

roost /ruːst/ *n* poleiro *m* ● *vi* empoleirar-se. **~er** *n* Amer galo *m*

root[1] /ruːt/ *n* raiz *f*; *fig* origem *f*; **take** ~ criar raízes ● *vt/i* enraizar(-se), radicar(-se); ~ **out** extirpar, erradicar

root[2] /ruːt/ *vi* ~ **about** revolver, remexer; ~ **for** Amer 🗙 torcer por

rope /rəʊp/ *n* corda *f*; **know the ~s** estar por dentro (do assunto) ● *vt* atar; ~ **in** convencer a participar de/em

rose[1] /rəʊz/ *n* rosa *f*; (*nozzle*) ralo *m* (de regador)

rose[2] /rəʊz/ ▶ **RISE**

rosé /ˈrəʊzeɪ/ *n* rosé *m*

roster /ˈrɒstə(r)/ *n* lista (de serviço) *f*, escala (de serviço) *f*

rostrum /ˈrɒstrəm/ *n* tribuna *f*; (*for conductor*) estrado *m*; Sport pódio *m*

rosy /ˈrəʊzɪ/ *a* (**-ier, -iest**) rosado; *fig* risonho

rot /rɒt/ *vt/i* (*pt* **rotted**) apodrecer ● *n* putrefação *f*, podridão *f*; 🗙 (*nonsense*) disparate *m*; asneiras *fpl*

rota /ˈrəʊtə/ *n* escala *f* de serviço

rotary /ˈrəʊtərɪ/ *a* rotativo, giratório

rotat|e /rəʊˈteɪt/ *vt/i* (fazer) girar, (fazer) revolver; (*change round*) alternar. **~ion** /-ʃn/ *n* rotação *f*

rote /rəʊt/ *n* **by ~** de cor, maquinalmente

rotten /ˈrɒtn/ *a* podre; (*corrupt*) corrupto; 🗙 (*bad*) mau; ruim; ~ **eggs** ovos *mpl* podres; **feel ~** (*ill*) não se sentir nada bem

rough /rʌf/ *a* (**-er, -est**) rude; (*to touch*) áspero, rugoso; (*of ground*) acidentado, irregular; (*violent*) violento; (*of sea*) agitado, encapelado; (*of weather*) tempestuoso; (*not perfect*) tosco, rudimentar; (*of estimate etc*) aproximado; ~ **paper** rascunho *m*, borrão *m* ● *n* (*ruffian*) rufia *m*, desordeiro *m* ● *adv* (*live*) ao relento; (*play*) bruto, (*P*) à bruta ● *vt* ~ **it** viver de modo primitivo, não ter onde morar 🗙; ~ **out** fazer um esboço preliminar de. **~ly** *adv* asperamente, rudemente; (*approximately*) aproximadamente. **~ness** *n* rudeza *f*, aspereza *f*; (*violence*) brutalidade *f*

roughage /ˈrʌfɪdʒ/ *n* alimentos *mpl* fibrosos

roulette /ruːˈlet/ *n* roleta *f*

round /raʊnd/ *a* (**-er, -est**) redondo; ~ **trip** viagem *f* de ida e volta ● *n* (*circle*) círculo *m*; (*slice*) fatia *f*; (*postman's*) entrega *f*; (*patrol*) ronda *f*; (*of drinks*) rodada *f*; (*competition*) partida *f*, rodada *f*, (*P*) ronda *f*; Boxing round *m*; (*of talks*) ciclo *m*, série *f*; ~ **of applause**

salva f de palmas ● prep & adv em volta (de); **come ~** (into consciousness) voltar a si; **go** or **come ~ to** (a friend etc) dar um pulo na casa de, passar pela casa de; **~ about** (nearby) por aí; fig mais ou menos; **~ the clock** noite e dia sem parar ● vt arredondar; ‹cape, corner› dobrar, virar; **~ off** terminar; **~ up** (gather) juntar; ‹a figure› arredondar. **~up** n (of cattle) rodeio m; (of suspects) captura f

roundabout /'raʊndəbaʊt/ n carrossel m; (for traffic) rotatória f, (P) rotunda f ● a indireto

rous|e /raʊz/ vt acordar, despertar; **be ~ed** (angry) exaltar-se, inflamar-se, ser provocado; **~ing** a ‹speech› inflamado, exaltado; ‹music› vibrante; ‹cheers› frenético

route /ruːt/ n percurso m, itinerário m; Naut, Aviat rota f

routine /ruː'tiːn/ n rotina f; Theat número m; **daily ~** rotina f diária ● a de rotina, rotineiro

row¹ /raʊ/ n fila f, fileira f; (in knitting) carreira f; **in a ~** (consecutive) seguido em fila or (P) a fio

row² /raʊ/ vt/i remar. **~ing** n remo m. **~ing boat** n barco m a remo

row³ /raʊ/ n 🔲 (noise) barulho m, bagunça f, banzé m 🔲; (🔲) (quarrel) discussão f, briga f ● vi **~ (with)** 🔲 brigar (com), discutir (com)

rowdy /'raʊdɪ/ a (-ier, -iest) desordeiro

royal /'rɔɪəl/ a real

royalty /'rɔɪəltɪ/ n família f real; (payment) direitos (de autor, de patente, etc) mpl

RSI abbr = REPETITIVE STRAIN INJURY

rub /rʌb/ vt/i (pt rubbed) esfregar; (with ointment etc) esfregar,

friccionar ● n esfrega f; (with ointment etc) fricção f; **~ it in** repisar/insistir em; **~ off on** comunicar-se a, transmitir-se a; **~ out** (with rubber) apagar

rubber /'rʌbə(r)/ n borracha f; **~ band** elástico m; **~ stamp** carimbo m

rubbish /'rʌbɪʃ/ n (refuse) lixo m; (nonsense) disparates mpl. **~ dump** n lixeira f

rubble /'rʌbl/ n entulho m

ruby /'ruːbɪ/ n rubi m

rucksack /'rʌksæk/ n mochila f

rudder /'rʌdə(r)/ n leme m

ruddy /'rʌdɪ/ a (-ier, -iest) avermelhado; (of cheeks) corado, vermelho; 🔲 (damned) maldito 🔲

rude /ruːd/ a (-er, -est) mal-educado, malcriado, grosseiro. **~ness** n má-educação f, má-criação f, grosseria f

rudiment /'ruːdɪmənt/ n rudimento m. **~ary** /-'mentrɪ/ a rudimentar

ruffian /'rʌfɪən/ n desordeiro m

ruffle /'rʌfl/ vt ‹feathers› eriçar; ‹hair› despentear; ‹clothes› amarrotar; fig perturbar ● n (frill) franzido m, (P) folho m

rug /rʌg/ n tapete m; (covering) manta f

rugged /'rʌgɪd/ a rude, irregular; ‹coast, landscape› acidentado; ‹character› forte; ‹features› marcado

ruin /'ruːɪn/ n ruína f ● vt arruinar; fig estragar

rule /ruːl/ n regra f; (regulation) regulamento m; Pol governo m; **as a ~** regra geral, por via de regra ● vt governar; (master) dominar; Jur decretar; (decide) decidir ● vi governar; **~ out** excluir; **~d paper** papel *m* pautado. **~r** /-ə(r)/ *n* (sovereign) soberano *m*; (leader) governante *m*; (measure) régua *f*

ruling /'ru:lɪŋ/ a ‹class› dirigente; Pol no poder ● *n* decisão *f*

rum /rʌm/ *n* rum *m*

rumble /'rʌmbl/ vi ribombar, ressoar; (of stomach) roncar ● *n* ribombo *m*, estrondo *m*

rummage /'rʌmɪdʒ/ vt revistar, remexer

rumour /'ru:mə(r)/ *n* boato *m*, rumor *m* ● vt **it is ~ed that** corre o boato de que, consta que

rump /rʌmp/ *n* (of horse etc) garupa *f*; (of fowl) mitra *f*. **~ steak** *n* bife *m* de alcatra

run /rʌn/ vi (pt ran, pp run, pres p running) correr; (flow) correr; (pass) passar; (function) andar, funcionar; (melt) derreter, pingar; ‹bus etc› circular; ‹play› estar em cartaz; ‹colour› desbotar; (in election) candidatar-se (for a); **~ away** fugir; **~ down** descer correndo; **~ out** esgotar-se; ‹lease› expirar; **I ran out of sugar** o açúcar acabou; **~ over** (of vehicle) atropelar; **~ up** deixar acumular ● vt (manage) dirigir, gerir; ‹a risk› correr; ‹a race› participar em; ‹water› deixar correr; ‹a car› ter, manter; **~ across** encontrar por acaso, dar com; **~ down** (of vehicle) atropelar; (belittle) dizer mal de, denigrir; **be ~ down** estar exausto; **~ in** ‹engine› ligar; **~ into** (meet) encontrar por acaso; (hit) bater em, ir de encontro a ● *n* corrida *f*; (excursion) passeio *m*, ida *f*; (rush) corrida *f*, correria *f*; (in cricket) ponto *m*; **be on the ~** estar foragido; **have the ~ of** ter à sua disposição; **in the long ~** a longo prazo; **the ~-up to**

o período que precede □ **~ off** vt ‹copies› tirar; ‹water› deixar correr ● vi fugir. **~-of-the-mill** a vulgar

runaway /'rʌnəweɪ/ *n* fugitivo *m* ● a fugitivo, em fuga; ‹horse› desembestado; ‹vehicle› desarvorado; ‹success› grande

rung[1] /rʌŋ/ *n* (of ladder) degrau *m*

rung[2] /rʌŋ/ ▶ RING[2]

runner /'rʌnə(r)/ *n* (person) corredor *m*; (carpet) passadeira *f*; **~ bean** feijão *m* verde. **~-up** *n* segundo classificado *m*

running /'rʌnɪŋ/ *n* corrida *f*; (functioning) funcionamento *m*; **be in the ~** (competitor) ter probabilidades de êxito ● a consecutivo, seguido; ‹water› corrente; **four days ~** quatro dias seguidos or a fio; **~ commentary** reportagem *f*, comentário *m*

runny /'rʌnɪ/ a derretido

runway /'rʌnweɪ/ *n* pista *f* de decolagem, (P) descolagem

rupture /'rʌptʃə(r)/ *n* ruptura *f*, (P) rutura *f*; Med hérnia *f* ● vt/i romper(-se), rebentar

rural /'rʊərəl/ a rural

ruse /ru:z/ *n* ardil *m*, estratagema *m*, manha *f*

rush[1] /rʌʃ/ *n* (plant) junco *m*

rush[2] /rʌʃ/ vi (move) precipitar-se; (be in a hurry) apressar-se ● vt fazer, mandar etc a toda a pressa; (person) pressionar; Mil tomar de assalto ● *n* tropel *m*; (haste) pressa *f*; **in a ~** a(s) pressa(s); **~ hour** rush *m*, (P) hora *f* de ponta

Russia /'rʌʃə/ *n* Rússia *f*. **~n** a & *n* russo *m*

rust /rʌst/ *n* (on iron, plants) ferrugem *f* ● vt/i enferrujar(-se). **~proof** a inoxidável. **~y** a ferrugento, enferrujado; *fig* enferrujado

rustic /ˈrʌstɪk/ *a* rústico

rustle /ˈrʌsl/ *vt/i* restolhar, (fazer) farfalhar; *Amer* (*steal*) roubar; **~ up** 🔲 ‹*food etc*› arranjar

rut /rʌt/ *n* sulco *m*; *fig* rotina *f*; **in a ~** numa vida rotineira

ruthless /ˈruːθlɪs/ *a* implacável

rye /raɪ/ *n* centeio *m*

....

Ss

....

sabbath /ˈsæbəθ/ *n* (*Jewish*) sábado *m*; (*Christian*) domingo *m*

sabbatical /səˈbætɪkl/ *n Univ* período *m* de licença, licença *f* sabática

sabot|age /ˈsæbətɑːʒ/ *n* sabotagem *f* ● *vt* sabotar. **~eur** /-ˈtɜː(r)/ *n* sabotador *m*

sachet /ˈsæʃeɪ/ *n* saché *m*, saqueta *f*

sack /sæk/ *n* saco *m*, saca *f* ● *vt* 🔲 despedir; **get the ~** 🔲 ser despedido

sacred /ˈseɪkrɪd/ *a* sagrado

sacrifice /ˈsækrɪfaɪs/ *n* sacrifício *m*; *fig* sacrifício *m* ● *vt* sacrificar

sacrileg|e /ˈsækrɪlɪdʒ/ *n* sacrilégio *m*. **~ious** /-ˈlɪdʒəs/ *a* sacrílego

sad /sæd/ *a* (**sadder, saddest**) ‹*person*› triste; ‹*story, news*› triste; **~ly** *adv* tristemente; (*unfortunately*) infelizmente. **~ness** *n* tristeza *f*

sadden /ˈsædn/ *vt* entristecer

saddle /ˈsædl/ *n* sela *f* ● *vt* ‹*horse*› selar; **~ sb with** sobrecarregar alguém com

sadis|m /ˈseɪdɪzəm/ *n* sadismo *m*. **~t** /-ɪst/ *n* sádico *m*. **~tic** /səˈdɪstɪk/ *a* sádico

safe /seɪf/ *a* (**-er, -est**) (*not dangerous*) seguro; (*out of danger*) fora de perigo; (*reliable*) confiável; **~ from** salvo de risco de; **~ and sound** são e salvo; **~ conduct** salvo-conduto *m*; **~ keeping** custódia *f*, (*P*) proteção *f*; **to be on the ~ side** por via das dúvidas ● *n* cofre *m*, caixa-forte *f*. **~ly** *adv* (*arrive etc*) em segurança; (*keep*) seguro

safeguard /ˈseɪfɡɑːd/ *n* salvaguarda *f* ● *vt* salvaguardar

safety /ˈseɪftɪ/ *n* segurança *f*. **~ belt** *n* cinto *m* de segurança; **~ pin** *n* alfinete *m* de fralda, (*P*) alfinete *m* de ama

sag /sæɡ/ *vi* (*pt* **sagged**) afrouxar

saga /ˈsɑːɡə/ *n* saga *f*

sage¹ /seɪdʒ/ *n* (*herb*) salva *f*

sage² /seɪdʒ/ *a* sensato, prudente ● *n* sábio *m*

Sagittarius /sædʒɪˈteərɪəs/ *n Astrol* Sagitário *m*

said /sed/ ▶ SAY

sail /seɪl/ *n* vela *f*; (*trip*) viagem *f* em barco à vela ● *vi* navegar; (*leave*) partir; *Sport* velejar ● *vt* navegar. **~ing** *n* navegação *f* à vela. **~ing boat** *n* barco *m* à vela

sailor /ˈseɪlə(r)/ *n* marinheiro *m*

saint /seɪnt/ *n* santo *m*. **~ly** *a* santo, santificado

sake /seɪk/ *n* **for the ~ of** em consideração a; **for my/your/ his own ~** por mim/por você/por isso

salad /ˈsæləd/ *n* salada *f*. **~ dressing** *n* molho *m* para salada

salary /ˈsælərɪ/ *n* salário *m*

sale /seɪl/ *n* venda *f*; (*at reduced prices*) liquidação *f*; **for ~**

"vende-se"; **on ~** à venda; **~s assistant**, *Amer* **~ clerk** vendedor *m*; **~s department** departamento *m* de vendas

sales|man /ˈseɪlzmən/ *n* (*pl* -**men**) (*in shop*) vendedor *m*; (*traveller*) caixeiro-viajante *m*. **~woman** *n* (*pl* -**women**) (*in shop*) vendedora *f*; (*traveller*) caixeira-viajante *f*

saliva /səˈlaɪvə/ *n* saliva *f*

salmon /ˈsæmən/ *n* (*pl invar*) salmão *m*

saloon /səˈluːn/ *n* (*on ship*) salão *m*; (*bar*) botequim *m*; **~ (car)** sedã *m*

salt /sɔːlt/ *n* sal *m*; **~ water** água *f* salgada, água *f* do mar ● *a* salgado ● *vt* (*season*) salgar; (*cure*) pôr em salmoura. **~ cellar** *n* saleiro *m*. **~y** *a* salgado

salute /səˈluːt/ *n* saudação *f* ● *vt/i* saudar

salvage /ˈsælvɪdʒ/ *n Naut* salvamento *m*; (*of waste*) reciclagem *f* ● *vt* salvar

salvation /sælˈveɪʃn/ *n* salvação *f*

same /seɪm/ *a* (**as** que); **at the ~ time** (*at once*) ao mesmo tempo ● *pron* **the ~** o mesmo ● *adv* **the ~** o mesmo; **all the ~** (*nevertheless*) mesmo assim, apesar de tudo

same-sex *a* ‹*couple, marriage*› do mesmo sexo

sample /ˈsɑːmpl/ *n* amostra *f* ● *vt* experimentar, provar

sanatorium /sænəˈtɔːrɪəm/ *n* (*pl* -**iums**) sanatório *m*

sanctify /ˈsæŋktɪfaɪ/ *vt* santificar

sanctimonious /ˌsæŋktɪˈməʊnɪəs/ *a* santarrão, carola

sanction /ˈsæŋkʃn/ *n* (*approval*) aprovação *f*; (*penalty*) pena *f*, sanção

f ● *vt* sancionar

sanctuary /ˈsæŋktʃʊərɪ/ *n Relig* santuário *m*; (*refuge*) refúgio *m*; (*for animals*) reserva *f*

sand /sænd/ *n* areia *f*; (*beach*) praia *f* ● *vt* (*with sandpaper*) lixar

sandal /ˈsændl/ *n* sandália *f*

sandbank /ˈsændbæŋk/ *n* banco *m* de areia

sandcastle /ˈsændkɑːsl/ *n* castelo *m* de areia

sandpaper /ˈsændpeɪpə(r)/ *n* lixa *f* ● *vt* lixar

sandpit /ˈsændpɪt/ *n* caixa *f* de areia

sandwich /ˈsænwɪdʒ/ *n* sanduíche *m*, (*P*) sandes *f invar* ● *vt* **~ed between** encaixado entre; **~ course** curso *m* profissionalizante envolvendo estudo teórico e estágio em local de trabalho

sandy /ˈsændɪ/ *a* (-**ier, iest**) (*beach*) arenoso; ‹*beach*› arenoso; ‹*hair*› ruivo

sane /seɪn/ *a* (-**er, -est**) (*not mad*) são *m*; (*sensible*) sensato, ajuizado

sang /sæŋ/ ▸ SING

sanitary /ˈsænɪtrɪ/ *a* sanitário; (*system*) sanitário; **~ towel**, *Amer* **~ napkin** toalha *f* absorvente, (*P*) penso *m* higiénico

sanitation /sænɪˈteɪʃn/ *n* condições *fpl* sanitárias, saneamento *m*

sanity /ˈsænɪtɪ/ *n* sanidade *f*

sank /sæŋk/ ▸ SINK

Santa Claus /ˈsæntəklɔːz/ *n* Papai *m* Noel, Pai *m* Natal

sap /sæp/ *n* seiva *f* ● *vt* (*pt* sapped) esgotar, minar

sapphire /ˈsæfaɪə(r)/ *n* safira *f*

sarcas|m /ˈsɑːkæzəm/ *n* sarcasmo *m*. **~tic** /sɑːˈkæstɪk/ *a* sarcástico

sardine /sɑːˈdiːn/ n sardinha f

sash /sæʃ/ n (around waist) cinto m; (over shoulder) faixa f

sat /sæt/ ▶ SIT

satchel /ˈsætʃl/ n sacola f

satellite /ˈsætəlaɪt/ n satélite m; ~ dish antena f de satélite; ~ television televisão f via satélite

satin /ˈsætɪn/ n cetim m

satir|e /ˈsætaɪə(r)/ n sátira f. ~ical /səˈtɪrɪkl/ a satírico. ~ist /ˈsætərɪst/ n satirista mf. ~ize vt satirizar

satisfact|ion /sætɪsˈfækʃn/ n satisfação f. ~ory /-ˈfæktərɪ/ a satisfatório

satisfy /ˈsætɪsfaɪ/ vt satisfazer; (convince) convencer; (fulfil) atender. ~ing a satisfatório

saturat|e /ˈsætʃəreɪt/ vt saturar; fig cansar

Saturday /ˈsætədɪ/ n sábado m

sauce /sɔːs/ n molho m; ▣ (cheek) atrevimento m

saucepan /ˈsɔːspən/ n panela f, (P) caçarola f

saucer /ˈsɔːsə(r)/ n pires m invar

saucy /ˈsɔːsɪ/ a (-ier, -iest) picante

Saudi Arabia /saʊdɪəˈreɪbɪə/ n Arábia f Saudita

sauna /ˈsɔːnə/ n sauna f

saunter /ˈsɔːntə(r)/ vi perambular

sausage /ˈsɒsɪdʒ/ n salsicha f, linguiça f; (pre-cooked) salsicha f

savage /ˈsævɪdʒ/ a (wild) selvagem; (fierce) cruel; (brutal) brutal ● n selvagem m ● vt atacar ferozmente. ~ry n selvageria f, ferocidade f

sav|e /seɪv/ vt (rescue) salvar; (keep) guardar; (collect) colecionar; ‹money› economizar, poupar; ‹time› ganhar; (prevent) evitar; impedir (**from** de) ● n Sport

salvamento m ● prep salvo, exceto. ~er n poupador m. ~ing n economia f, poupança f. ~ings npl economias fpl, poupanças fpl

saviour /ˈseɪvɪə(r)/ n salvador m

savour /ˈseɪvə(r)/ n sabor m ● vt saborear. ~y a (tasty) saboroso; (not sweet) salgado

saw¹ /sɔː/ ▶ SEE¹

saw² /sɔː/ n serra f ● vt (pt sawed, pp sawn or sawed) serrar

sawdust /ˈsɔːdʌst/ n serragem f

saxophone /ˈsæksəfəʊn/ n saxofone m

say /seɪ/ vt/i (pt said /sed/) dizer, falar ● n have a ~ (in sth) ter direito a opinar sobre algo; have one's ~ exprimir sua (a) opinião; I ~! olhe! or escute!. ~ing n ditado m, provérbio m

scab /skæb/ n casca f, crosta f; ▣ (blackleg) fura-greve mf invar

scaffold /ˈskæfəʊld/ n cadafalso m, andaime m. ~ing /-əldɪŋ/ n andaime m

scald /skɔːld/ vt escaldar, queimar ● n escaldadura f, queimadura f

scale¹ /skeɪl/ n (of fish etc) escama f

scale² /skeɪl/ n (ratio, size) escala f; Mus escala f; (of salaries, charges) tabela f; **on a small/large/etc~** numa pequena/grande/etc escala ● vt (climb) escalar; ~ **down** reduzir

scales /skeɪlz/ npl (for weighing) balança f

scallop /ˈskɒləp/ n Culin concha f de vieira; (shape) concha f de vieira

scalp /skælp/ n couro m cabeludo ● vt escalpar

scalpel /ˈskælpl/ n bisturi m

scamper /ˈskæmpə(r)/ vi sair correndo, (P) a correr or à(s) pressa(s)

scampi /'skæmpɪ/ npl camarões mpl fritos

scan /skæn/ vt (pt **scanned**) (intently) perscrutar, esquadrinhar; (quickly) passar os olhos em; Med examinar; (radar) explorar ● n Med exame m

scandal /'skændl/ n (disgrace) escândalo m; (gossip) fofoca f. **~ous** a escandaloso

Scandinavia /skændɪ'nerviə/ n Escandinávia f. **~n** a & n escandinavo m

scanty /'skæntɪ/ a (-ier, -iest) escasso; (clothing) sumário

scapegoat /'skeɪpgəʊt/ n bode m expiatório

scar /skɑː(r)/ n cicatriz f ● vt (pt **scarred**) marcar; fig deixar marcas

scarc|e /skeəs/ a (-er, -est) escasso, raro; **make o.s. ~** [T] sumir, dar o fora [T], (P) desaparecer sem deixar rasto. **~ity** n escassez f. **~ely** adv mal, apenas

scare /skeə(r)/ vt assustar, apavorar; **be ~d** estar com medo (**of** de) ● n pavor m, pânico m; **bomb ~** pânico m causado por suspeita de bomba num local

scarecrow /'skeəkrəʊ/ n espantalho m

scarf /skɑːf/ n (pl **scarves**) (oblong) cachecol m, (square) lenço m de cabelo

scarlet /'skɑːlət/ a escarlate m

scary /'skeərɪ/ a (-ier, -iest) [T] assustador; apavorante

scathing /'skeɪðɪŋ/ a mordaz

scatter /'skætə(r)/ vt (strew) espalhar; (disperse) dispersar ● vi espalhar-se

scavenge /'skævɪndʒ/ vi procurar comida etc no lixo. **~r** /-ə(r)/ n

(person) que procura comida etc no lixo; (animal) que se alimenta de carniça, (P) necrófago

scenario /sɪ'nɑːrɪəʊ/ n (pl **-os**) sinopse f, resumo m detalhado

scene /siːn/ n cena f; (of event) cenário m; (sight) vista f, panorama m; **behind the ~s** nos bastidores; **make a ~** fazer um escândalo

scenery /'siːnərɪ/ n cenário m, paisagem f; Theat cenário m

scenic /'siːnɪk/ a pitoresco, cênico, (P) cénico

scent /sent/ n (perfume) perfume m, fragância f; (trail) rastro m, pista f ● vt (discern) sentir. **~ed** a perfumado, aromático

sceptic /'skeptɪk/ n cético m. **~al** a cético. **~ism** /-sɪzəm/ n ceticismo m

schedule /'ʃedjuːl/ n programa m; (timetable) horário m ● vt marcar, programar; **according to ~** conforme planejado or (P) planeado; **behind ~** atrasado; **on ~** (train) na hora, à hora prevista; (work) em dia

scheme /skiːm/ n esquema m; (plan of work) plano m; (plot) conspiração f, maquinação f ● vi planejar, (P) planear, pej intrigar; maquinar; tramar

schizophreni|a /skɪtsəʊ'friːnɪə/ n esquizofrenia f. **~c** /-'frenɪk/ a esquizofrênico, (P) esquizofrénico

scholar /'skɒlə(r)/ n erudito m, estudioso m, escolar m. **~ly** a erudito. **~ship** n erudição f, saber m; (grant) bolsa f de estudo

school /skuːl/ n escola f; (of university) escola f, faculdade f ● a (age, year, holidays) escolar ● vt ensinar; (train) treinar, adestrar. **~ing** n instrução f; (attendance) escolaridade f

school|boy /'sku:lbɔɪ/ n aluno m. **~girl** n aluna f

school|master /'sku:lmɑ:stə(r)/, **~mistress**, **~teacher** ns professor m, professora f

scien|ce /'saɪəns/ n ciência f; **~ce fiction** ficção f científica. **~tific** /-'tɪfɪk/ a científico

scientist /'saɪəntɪst/ n cientista mf

scissors /'sɪzəz/ npl (pair of) ~ tesoura f

scoff[1] /skɒf/ vi ~ **at** zombar de, (P) troçar de

scoff[2] /skɒf/ vt ⚑ (eat) devorar; tragar

scold /skəʊld/ vt ralhar com

scone /skɒn/ n Culin scone m, bolinho m para o chá

scoop /sku:p/ n (for grain, sugar etc) pá f; (ladle) concha f; (news) furo m ● vt ~ **out** (hollow out) escavar, tirar com concha or pá; **~ up** (lift) apanhar

scoot /sku:t/ vi ⚑ fugir, mandar-se ⚑, (P) pôr-se a milhas ⚑

scooter /'sku:tə(r)/ n (child's) patinete f, (P) trotinete m; (motor cycle) motoreta f, lambreta f

scope /skəʊp/ n âmbito m; fig (opportunity) oportunidade f

scorch /skɔ:tʃ/ vt/i chamuscar(-se), queimar de leve. **~ing** a ⚑ escaldante; abrasador

score /skɔ:(r)/ n Sport contagem f, escore m; Mus partitura f ● vt marcar com corte(s), riscar; (a goal) marcar; Mus orquestrar ● vi marcar pontos; (keep score) fazer a contagem; Football marcar um gol or (P) golo; **a ~ (of)** (twenty) uma vintena (de), vinte; **~s** muitos, dezenas; **on that ~** nesse respeito,

quanto a isso. **~board** n marcador m. **~r** /-ə(r)/ n (score-keeper) marcador m; (of goals) autor m

scorn /skɔ:n/ n desprezo m ● vt desprezar. **~ful** a desdenhoso, escarninho

Scorpio /'skɔ:pɪəʊ/ n Astr Escorpião m

scorpion /'skɔ:pɪən/ n escorpião m

Scot /skɒt/ n, **~tish** a escocês m

Scotch /skɒtʃ/ a escocês ● n uísque m

Scotland /'skɒtlənd/ n Escócia f

Scots /skɒts/ a escocês

> *i*
> **Scottish Parliament** O Parlamento Escocês foi estabelecido em Edimburgo em 1999. Tem competência legislativa e executiva em assuntos internos na Escócia e poderes tributários limitados. Há 129 MSPs (Members of the Scottish Parliament), dos quais 73 são eleitos diretamente e o restante através do sistema de representação proporcional.

scoundrel /'skaʊndrəl/ n patife m, canalha m

scour[1] /'skaʊə(r)/ vt (clean) esfregar, arear. **~er** n esfregão m de palha de aço or de nylon

scour[2] /'skaʊə(r)/ vt (search) percorrer, esquadrinhar

scourge /skɜ:dʒ/ n açoite m; fig flagelo m

scout /skaʊt/ n Mil explorador m ● vi ~ **about (for)** andar à procura de

Scout /skaʊt/ n, (P) escuteiro m

scowl /skaʊl/ n carranca f, ar m carrancudo ● vi fazer um ar carrancudo

scramble /ˈskræmbl/ vi trepar; (crawl) avançar de rastros, rastejar, arrastar-se ● vt ‹eggs› mexer ● n luta f, confusão f

scrap[1] /skræp/ n bocadinho m; ~ **heap** monte m de ferro-velho; ~ **merchant** sucateiro m ● vt (pt scrapped) jogar fora, (P) deitar fora; ‹plan etc› abandonar, pôr de lado. ~s npl restos mpl. ~**book** n álbum m de recortes; ~ **iron** n ferro m velho, sucata f; ~ **paper** n papel m de rascunho. ~**py** a fragmentário

scrap[2] /skræp/ n 🄝 (fight) briga f, pancadaria f 🄝; rixa f

scrape /skreɪp/ vt raspar; (graze) esfolar, arranhar; ~ **through** escapar pela tangente, (P) à tangente or por um triz; ‹exam› passar pela tangente, (P) à tangente; ~ **together** conseguir juntar ● vi (graze, rub) roçar ● n (act of scraping) raspagem f; (mark) raspão m, esfoladura f; fig encrenca f, maus lençóis mpl 🄝

scratch /skrætʃ/ vt/i arranhar(-se); ‹a line› riscar; (to relieve itching) coçar(-se) ● n arranhão m; (line) risco m; (wound with claw, nail) unhada f; **start from** ~ começar do princípio; **up to** ~ à altura, ao nível requerido

scrawl /skrɔːl/ n rabisco m, garrancho m, garatuja f ● vt/i rabiscar, fazer garranchos, garatujar

scrawny /ˈskrɔːnɪ/ a (-ier, -iest) descarnado, ossudo, magricela

scream /skriːm/ vt/i gritar ● n grito m (agudo) m

screech /skriːtʃ/ vi guinchar, gritar; (of brakes) chiar, guinchar ● n guincho m, grito m agudo

screen /skriːn/ n écran m, tela f; (folding) biombo m; fig (protection) manto m; fig capa f fig ● vt resguardar, tapar; ‹film› passar; ‹candidates etc› fazer a triagem de. ~**ing** n Med exame m médico

screw /skruː/ n parafuso m ● vt aparafusar, atarraxar; ~ **up** ‹eyes, face› franzir; 🄝 (ruin) estragar; ~ **up one's courage** cobrar arranjar coragem

screwdriver /ˈskruːdraɪvə(r)/ n chave f de parafusos or de fenda(s)

scribble /ˈskrɪbl/ vt/i rabiscar, garatujar ● n rabisco m, garatuja f

script /skrɪpt/ n escrita f, (of film) roteiro m, (P) guião m. ~**writer** n Film roteirista m, (P) autor m do guião, guionista mf

scroll /skrəʊl/ n rolo (de papel ou pergaminho) m; Archit voluta f ● vt/i Comput passar na tela, (P) no ecrã

scrounge /skraʊndʒ/ vt 🄝 (cadge) filar ‹a›, (P) cravar 🄝 ● vi (beg) parasitar, viver à(s) custa(s) de alguém. ~**r** /-ə(r)/ n parasita mf; filão m 🄝, (P) crava mf 🄝

scrub[1] /skrʌb/ n (land) mato m

scrub[2] /skrʌb/ vt/i (pt scrubbed) esfregar, lavar com escova e sabão; 🄝 (cancel) cancelar ● n esfrega f

scruff /skrʌf/ n **by the** ~ **of the neck** pelo cangote, (P) pelo cachaço

scruffy /ˈskrʌfɪ/ a (-ier, -iest) desmazelado; desleixado

scrum /skrʌm/ n rixa f; Rugby placagem f

scruple /ˈskruːpl/ n escrúpulo m

scrupulous /ˈskruːpjʊləs/ a escrupuloso. ~**ly** adv escrupulosamente; ~**ly clean** impecavelmente limpo

scrutin|y /'skru:tɪnɪ/ n averiguação f, escrutínio m. **~ize** vt examinar em detalhe

scuffle /'skʌfl/ n tumulto m, briga f

sculpt /skʌlpt/ vt/i esculpir. **~or** n escultor m. **~ure** /-tʃə(r)/ n escultura f ● vt/i esculpir

scum /skʌm/ n (on liquid) espuma f, pej (people) gentinha f, escumalha f, ralé f

scurry /'skʌrɪ/ vi dar corridinhas; (hurry) apressar-se; **~ off** escapulir-se

scuttle[1] /'skʌtl/ n ‹bucket, box› balde m para carvão

scuttle[2] /'skʌtl/ vt (ship) afundar abrindo rombos or as torneiras de fundo, afundar voluntariamente

scuttle[3] /'skʌtl/ vi **~ away** or **off** fugir, escapulir-se

sea /si:/ n mar m; **at ~** no alto mar, ao largo; **all at ~** desnorteado; **by ~** por mar ● a do mar, marinho, marítimo; **~ bird** ave f marinha; **~ horse** cavalo-marinho m, hipocampo m; **~ level** nível m do mar; **~ lion** leão-marinho m; **~ shell** concha f; **~ water** água f do mar. **~shore** n litoral m, costa f; (beach) praia f

seafood /'si:fu:d/ n marisco(s) m(pl)

seagull /'si:gʌl/ n gaivota f

seal[1] /si:l/ n (animal) foca f

seal[2] /si:l/ n selo m, sinete m ● vt selar; (with wax) lacrar; **~ off** ‹area› vedar

seam /si:m/ n (in cloth etc) costura f; (of mineral) veio m, filão m. **~less** a sem costura

seaman /'si:mən/ n (pl -men) marinheiro m, marítimo m

seance /'seɪɑːns/ n sessão f espírita

search /sɜːtʃ/ vt/i revistar, dar busca (a); ‹one's heart, conscience

etc› examinar ● n revista f, busca f; (quest) procura f, busca f; (official) inquérito m; **in ~ of** à procura de; **~ for** procurar. **~ party** n equipe f or (P) equipa de busca; **~ warrant** n mandado m de busca. **~ing** a (of look) penetrante; (of test etc) minucioso

searchlight /'sɜːtʃlaɪt/ n holofote m

seasick /'si:sɪk/ a enjoado. **~ness** n enjoo m

seaside /'si:saɪd/ n costa f, praia f, beira-mar f

season /'si:zn/ n (of year) estação f; (proper time) época f; Cricket, Football etc temporada f; **in ~** na época ● vt temperar; ‹wood› secar. **~able** a o próprio da estação. **~al** a sazonal. **~ed** a (of people) experimentado. **~ing** n tempero m. **~ ticket** n (train etc) passe m; (theatre etc) assinatura f

seat /si:t/ n assento m; (place) lugar m; (of bicycle) selim m; (of chair) assento m; (of trousers) fundilho m; **~ of learning** centro m de cultura ● vt sentar; (have seats for) ter lugares sentados para; **be ~ed, take a ~** sentar-se. **~ belt** n cinto m de segurança

seaweed /'si:wi:d/ n alga f marinha

seaworthy /'si:wɜːðɪ/ a navegável, em condições de navegabilidade

seclu|de /sɪ'klu:d/ vt isolar. **~ded** a isolado, retirado. **~sion** /sɪ'klu:ʒn/ n isolamento m

second[1] /'sekənd/ a segundo; **~ thoughts** dúvidas fpl; **on ~ thoughts** pensando melhor ● n segundo m; (in duel) testemunha f; **~ (gear)** Auto segunda (velocidade) *f*; **the ~ of April** dois de Abril; **~s** (*goods*) artigos *mpl* de segunda (categoria) or de refugo ● *adv* (*in race etc*) em segundo lugar ● *vt* secundar. **~best** a escolhido em segundo lugar; **~class** a de segunda classe; **~hand** a de segunda mão ● *n* (*on clock*) ponteiro *m* dos segundos; **~rate** a medíocre, de segunda ordem or categoria. **~ly** *adv* segundo, em segundo lugar

second² /sɪˈkɒnd/ *vt* (*transfer*) destacar (**to** para)

secondary /ˈsekəndrɪ/ *a* secundário; **~ school** escola *f* secundária

secrecy /ˈsiːkrəsɪ/ *n* segredo *m*

secret /ˈsiːkrɪt/ *a* secreto ● *n* segredo *m*; **in ~** em segredo. **~ agent** *n* agente *mf* secreto. **~ly** *adv* em segredo, secretamente

secretary /ˈsekrətrɪ/ *n* secretário *m*, secretária *f*; **S~y of State** ministro *m* de Estado, (*P*) Secretário *m* de Estado; *Amer* ministro *m* dos Negócios Estrangeiros. **~ial** /-ˈteərɪəl/ *a* ‹*work, course etc*› de secretária

secrete /sɪˈkriːt/ *vt* segregar; (*hide*) esconder. **~ion** /-ʃn/ *n* secreção *f*

secretive /ˈsiːkrətɪv/ *a* misterioso, reservado

sect /sekt/ *n* seita *f*. **~arian** /-ˈteərɪən/ *a* sectário

section /ˈsekʃn/ *n* seção *f*; (*of country, community etc*) setor *m*, (*P*) sector *m*; (*district of town*) zona *f*

sector /ˈsektə(r)/ *n* setor *m*

secular /ˈsekjʊlə(r)/ *a* secular, leigo, (*P*) laico; ‹*art, music etc*› profano

secure /sɪˈkjʊə(r)/ *a* seguro, em segurança; ‹*firm*› seguro, sólido; (*in mind*) tranquilo ● *vt* prender

bem or com segurança; (*obtain*) conseguir, arranjar; (*ensure*) assegurar; ‹*windows, doors*› fechar bem. **~ly** *adv* solidamente; (*safely*) em segurança

security /sɪˈkjʊərətɪ/ *n* segurança *f*; (*for loan*) fiança *f*, caução *f*. **~ies** *npl* *Finance* títulos *mpl*

sedate /sɪˈdeɪt/ *a* sereno, comedido ● *vt* *Med* tratar com sedativos

sedation /sɪˈdeɪʃn/ *n* *Med* sedação *f*; **under ~** sob o efeito de sedativos

sedative /ˈsedətɪv/ *n* *Med* sedativo *m*

sediment /ˈsedɪmənt/ *n* sedimento *m*, depósito *m*

seduce /sɪˈdjuːs/ *vt* seduzir

seduction /sɪˈdʌkʃn/ *n* sedução *f*. **~ive** /-tɪv/ *a* sedutor, aliciante

see¹ /siː/ *vt/i* (*pt* **saw**, *pp* **seen**) ver; (*escort*) acompanhar; **~ about** or to tratar de, encarregar-se de; **~ through** ‹*task*› levar a cabo; (*not be deceived by*) não se deixar enganar por; **~ (to it) that** assegurar que, tratar de fazer com que; **~ing that** visto que, uma vez que; **~ you later!** 🔲 até logo! 🔲; **~ off** *vt* (*wave goodbye*) ir e despedir-se de; (*chase*) acompanhar

see² /siː/ *n* sé *f*, bispado *m*

seed /siːd/ *n* semente *f*; *fig* (*origin*) germe(n) *m*; *Tennis* cabeça *f* de série; (*pip*) caroço *m*; **go to ~** produzir sementes; *fig* desmazelar-se 🔲. **~ling** *n* planta *f* brotada a partir da semente

seedy /ˈsiːdɪ/ *a* (**-ier, -iest**) (com um ar) gasto, surrado; (*unwell*) abatido; deprimido; em baixo astral 🔲 or (*P*) em baixo 🔲

seek /siːk/ *vt* (*pt* **sought**) procurar; ‹*help etc*› pedir

seem /siːm/ vi parecer. **~ingly** adv aparentemente, ao que parece

seen /siːn/ ▶ SEE¹

seep /siːp/ vi (ooze) filtrar-se; (trickle) pingar, escorrer, passar

see-saw /ˈsiːsɔː/ n gangorra f, (P) balanço m

seethe /siːð/ vi ~ **with** ⟨anger⟩ ferver de; ⟨people⟩ fervilhar de

segment /ˈsegmənt/ n segmento m; (of orange) gomo m

segregat|e /ˈsegrɪgeɪt/ vt segregar, separar. **~ion** /-ˈgeɪʃn/ n segregação f

seize /siːz/ vt agarrar, (P) deitar a mão a, apanhar; (take possession by force) apoderar-se de; (by law) apreender; confiscar; (P) apresar ● vi ~ **on** ⟨opportunity⟩ aproveitar; ~ **up** ⟨engine etc⟩ grimpar, emperrar; **be ~d with** ⟨fear, illness⟩ ter um ataque de

seizure /ˈsiːʒə(r)/ n Med ataque m, crise f; (law) apreensão f, captura f

seldom /ˈseldəm/ adv raras vezes, raramente, raro

select /sɪˈlekt/ vt escolher, selecionar ● a seleto. **~ion** /-ʃn/ n seleção f; Comm sortido m

selective /sɪˈlektɪv/ a seletivo

self /self/ n (pl **selves**) **the ~** o eu, o ego

self- /self/ pref. **~assurance** n segurança f; **~assured** a seguro de si; **~catering** a em que os hóspedes têm condições de cozinhar; **~centred** a egocêntrico; **~confidence** n autoconfiança f, confiança f em si mesmo; **~confident** a que tem confiança em si mesmo; **~conscious** a inibido, constrangido; **~contained** a independente; **~control** n

autodomínio m; **~controlled** a senhor de si; **~defence** n legítima defesa f; **~employed** a autónomo, independent; **~esteem** n amor m próprio; **~evident** a evidente; **~indulgent** a que não resiste a tentações; (for ease) comodista; **~interest** n interesse m pessoal; **~portrait** n auto-retrato m; **~possessed** a senhor de si; **~respect** n amor m próprio; **~righteous** a que se tem em boa conta; **~sacrifice** n abnegação f, sacrifício m; **~satisfied** a cheio de si; convencido Ⓣ; **~seeking** a egoísta; **~service** a auto-serviço, self-service; **~styled** a pretenso; **~sufficient** a auto-suficiente

self-harm n automutilação f

selfish /ˈselfɪʃ/ a egoísta; ⟨motive⟩ interesseiro. **~ness** n egoísmo m

selfless /ˈselflɪs/ a desinteressado

sell /sel/ vt/i (pt **sold**) vender(-se); **~by date** válido até; **~ off** liquidar; **be sold out** estar esgotado. **~out** n (show) sucesso m; Ⓣ (betrayal) traição f. **~er** n vendedor m

Sellotape® /ˈseləteɪp/ n fita f adesiva, (P) fita-cola f

semen /ˈsiːmən/ n sêmen m, (P) sémen m, esperma m

semester /sɪˈmestə(r)/ n Univ semestre m

semi- /ˈsemɪ/ pref semi-, meio

semibreve /ˈsemɪbriːv/ n Mus semibreve f

semicirc|le /ˈsemɪsɜːkl/ n semicírculo m. **~ular** /-sɜːˈkjʊlə(r)/ a semicircular

semicolon /semɪˈkəʊlən/ n ponto e vírgula m

semi-detached /semɪdɪˈtætʃt/ a ~ **house** casa f geminada

semi-final /semɪˈfaɪnl/ n semifinal f, (P) meia-final f

seminar /ˈsemɪnɑː(r)/ n seminário m

semiquaver /ˈsemɪkweɪvə(r)/ n Mus semicolcheia f

semitone /ˈsemɪtəʊn/ n Mus semítom m

senat|e /ˈsenɪt/ n senado m. ~**or** /-ətə(r)/ n senador m

send /send/ vt/i (pt sent) enviar, mandar; ~ **back** devolver; ~ **for** <person> chamar, mandar vir; <help> pedir; ~ (**away** or **off**) **for** encomendar, mandar vir; ~ **up** 🔲 parodiar. ~**off** n despedida f, bota-fora m. ~**er** n expedidor m, remetente m

senil|e /ˈsiːnaɪl/ a senil. ~**ity** /sɪˈnɪlətɪ/ n senilidade f

senior /ˈsiːnɪə(r)/ a mais velho; mais idoso (**to** do que); (in rank) superior; (in service) mais antigo; (after surname) sênior, (P) sénior; ~ **citizen** pessoa f de idade or da terceira idade, idoso m ● n pessoa f mais velha; Schol finalista mf. ~**ity** /-ˈɒrətɪ/ n (in age) idade f; (in service) antiguidade f

sensation /senˈseɪʃn/ n sensação f. ~**al** a sensacional. ~**alism** n sensacionalismo m

sense /sens/ n sentido m; (wisdom) bom-senso m; (sensation) sensação f; (mental impression) sentimento m; ~**s** (sanity) razão f; **make** ~ fazer sentido; **make** ~ **of** compreender ● vt pressentir. ~**less** a disparatado, sem sentido; Med sem sentidos, inconsciente

sensible /ˈsensəbl/ a sensato, razoável; <clothes> prático

sensitiv|e /ˈsensətɪv/ a sensível (**to** a); (touchy) susceptível. ~**ity** /-ˈtɪvətɪ/ n sensibilidade f

sensory /ˈsensərɪ/ a sensorial

sensual /ˈsenʃʊəl/ a sensual. ~**ity** /-ˈælətɪ/ n sensualidade f

sensuous /ˈsenʃʊəs/ a sensual

sent /sent/ ▶ SEND

sentence /ˈsentəns/ n frase f; Jur (decision) sentença f; (punishment) pena f ● vt ~ **to** condenar a

sentiment /ˈsentɪmənt/ n sentimento m; (opinion) modo m de ver

sentimental /sentɪˈmentl/ a sentimental; <value> valor m estimativo. ~**ity** /-menˈtælətɪ/ n sentimentalidade f, sentimentalismo m or sentimental

sentry /ˈsentrɪ/ n sentinela f

separable /ˈsepərəbl/ a separável

separate[1] /ˈseprət/ a separado, diferente. ~**s** npl (clothes) conjuntos mpl. ~**ly** adv separadamente, em separado

separat|e[2] /ˈsepəreɪt/ vt/i separar(-se). ~**ion** /-ˈreɪʃn/ n separação f

September /sepˈtembə(r)/ n setembro m

septic /ˈseptɪk/ a séptico, (P) sético, infetado

sequel /ˈsiːkwəl/ n resultado m, sequela f; (of novel, film) continuação f

sequence /ˈsiːkwəns/ n sequência f

sequin /ˈsiːkwɪn/ n lantejoula f

serenade /serəˈneɪd/ n serenata f ● vt fazer uma serenata para or (P) a

seren|e /sɪˈriːn/ a sereno. ~**ity** /-ˈenətɪ/ n serenidade f

sergeant /ˈsɑːdʒənt/ n sargento m

serial /ˈsɪərɪəl/ n folhetim m ● a ‹number› de série. **~ize** /-laɪz/ vt publicar em folhetim

series /ˈsɪərɪːz/ n invar série f

serious /ˈsɪərɪəs/ a sério; (very bad, critical) grave, sério. **~ly** adv seriamente, gravemente, a sério; **take ~ly** levar a sério. **~ness** n seriedade f, gravidade f

sermon /ˈsɜːmən/ n sermão m

serpent /ˈsɜːpənt/ n serpente f

servant /ˈsɜːvənt/ n criado m, criada f, empregado m, empregada f

serv|e /sɜːv/ vt/i servir; ‹a sentence› cumprir; Jur (a writ) entregar; Mil servir, prestar serviço; ‹apprenticeship› fazer ● n Tennis saque m, (P) serviço m. **~e as/to** servir de/para; **~e its purpose** servir para o que é 🈁, servir os seus fins; **it ~es you/him** etc **right** é bem feito. **~ing** n (portion) dose f, porção f

server /ˈsɜːvə(r)/ n Comput servidor m

service /ˈsɜːvɪs/ n serviço m; Relig culto m; Tennis saque m, (P) serviço m; (maintenance) revisão f; **~s** Mil forças fpl armadas; **of ~ to** útil a/ para, de utilidade a/para; **~ area** área f de serviço; **~ charge** serviço m; **~ station** posto m de gasolina, (P) posto m de abastecimento ● vt ‹car etc› fazer a revisão de

serviceman /ˈsɜːvɪsmæn/ n (pl -men) militar m

serviette /ˈsɜːvɪˈet/ n guardanapo m

session /ˈseʃn/ n sessão f; Univ ano m acadêmico, (P) académico; Amer Univ semestre m; **in ~** (sitting) em sessão, reunidos

set /set/ vt (pt set, pres p setting) pôr, colocar; (put down) pousar; ‹limit etc› fixar; ‹watch, clock›

regular, acertar; ‹example› dar; ‹exam, task› marcar; (in plaster) engessar; **~ about** or **to** começar a, pôr-se a; **~ fire to** atear fogo a, (P) deitar fogo a; **~ free** pôr em liberdade; **~ off** ‹mechanism› pôr para funcionar, (P) pôr a funcionar; **~ out** (state) expor; (arrange) dispor; **~ sail** partir, içar as velas; **~ square** esquadro m; **~ the table** pôr a mesa; **~ theory** teoria f de conjuntos; **~ up** (establish) fundar, estabelecer ● vi ‹sun› pôr-se; ‹jelly› endurecer, solidificar(-se); **~ in** ‹rain etc› pegar, (P) vir para ficar; **~ off** or **out** partir, começar a viajar ● n (of people) círculo m, roda f; (of books) coleção f; (of tools, chairs etc) jogo m; TV, rádio aparelho m; (hair) mise f; Theat cenário m; Tennis partida f, set m ● a fixo; ‹habit› inveterado; ‹jelly› duro, sólido; ‹book› do programa; ‹meal› a preço fixo; **be ~ on doing** estar decidido a fazer; **~ back** ‹plans etc› atrasar; 🅇 ‹cost› custar. **~-back** n revés m; contratempo m, atraso m 🈁; **~-to** n briga f; **~-up** n (system) sistema m, organização f; (situation) situação f

settee /seˈtiː/ n sofá m

setting /ˈsetɪŋ/ n (framework) quadro m; (of jewel) engaste m; Typ composição f; Mus arranjo m musical

settle /ˈsetl/ vt (arrange) resolver; ‹date› marcar; ‹nerves› acalmar; ‹doubts› esclarecer; ‹new country› colonizar, povoar; ‹bill› pagar ● vi assentar; (in country) estabelecer-se; (in house, chair etc) instalar-se; ‹weather› estabilizar(-se); **~ down** acalmar-se; (become settled) assentar; (sit, rest) instalar-se; **~ for** aceitar; **~ up (with)** fazer contas (com); fig ajustar contas (com). **~r** /-ə(r)/ n colono m, colonizador m

settlement /'setlmənt/ *n*
(*agreement*) acordo *m*; (*payment*)
pagamento *m*; (*colony*) colónia *f*, (P)
colónia *f*; (*colonization*) colonização *f*

seven /'sevn/ *a & n* sete *m*. **~th** *a &*
n sétimo *m*

seventeen /sevn'ti:n/ *a & n*
dezessete *m*, (P) dezassete *m*. **~th**
a & n décimo sétimo *m*

sevent|y /'sevntɪ/ *a & n* setenta *m*.
~ieth *a & n* septuagésimo *m*

sever /'sevə(r)/ *vt* cortar. **~ance**
n corte *m*

several /'sevrəl/ *a & pron* vários,
diversos

sever|e /sɪ'vɪə(r)/ *a* (**-er, -est**)
severo; ‹*pain*› forte, violento;
‹*illness*› grave; ‹*winter*› rigoroso.
~ely *adv* severamente; (*seriously*)
gravemente. **~ity** /sɪ-'verɪtɪ/
n severidade *f*; (*seriousness*)
gravidade *f*

sew /səʊ/ *vt/i* (*pt* **sewed**, *pp* **sewn**
or **sewed**) coser, costurar. **~ing** *n*
costura *f*. **~ing machine** *n* máquina
f de costura

sewage /'sju:ɪdʒ/ *n* efluentes *mpl*
dos esgotos, detritos *mpl*

sewer /'sju:ə(r)/ *n* cano *m* de
esgoto

sewn /səʊn/ ► **sew**

sex /seks/ *n* sexo *m*; **have ~** ter
relações, sexuais ● *a* sexual; **~**
maniac tarado *m* sexual ☐ **~ up**
vt/i tornar mais apelativo. **~y** *a* sexy
invar, que tem sex-appeal

sexist /'seksɪst/ *a & n* sexista *mf*

sexual /'sekʃʊəl/ *a* sexual; **~**
harassment assédio *m* sexual; **~**
intercourse relações *fpl* sexuais.
~ity /-'ælətɪ/ *n* sexualidade *f*

shabb|y /'ʃæbɪ/ *a* (**-ier, -iest**)
(*clothes, object*) gasto, surrado;

(*person*) maltrapilho, mal vestido;
(*mean*) miserável. **~ily** *adv*
miseravelmente

shack /ʃæk/ *n* cabana *f*, barraca *f*

shackles /'ʃæklz/ *npl* grilhões *mpl*,
algemas *fpl*

shade /ʃeɪd/ *n* sombra *f*; (*of colour*)
tom *m*, matiz *m*; (*of opinion*) matiz *m*;
(*for lamp*) abat-jour *m*, quebra-luz *m*;
Amer (*blind*) estore *m*; **a ~ bigger/**
etc ligeiramente maior/*etc*; **in the**
~ à sombra ● *vt* resguardar da luz;
(*darken*) sombrear

shadow /'ʃædəʊ/ *n* sombra *f* ● *vt*
cobrir de sombra; (*follow*) seguir,
vigiar; **S~ Cabinet** gabinete *m*
formado pelo partido da oposição.
~y *a* ensombrado, sombreado; *fig*
vago; indistinto

shady /'ʃeɪdɪ/ *a* (**-ier, -iest**)
sombreiro, (P) que dá sombra;
(*in shade*) à sombra; *fig* (*dubious*)
suspeito; duvidoso

shaft /ʃɑ:ft/ *n* (*of arrow, spear*) haste
f; (*axle*) eixo *m*, veio *m*; (*of mine, lift*)
poço *m*; (*of light*) raio *m*

shaggy /'ʃægɪ/ *a* (**-ier,**
-iest) ‹*beard*› hirsuto; ‹*hair*›
desgrenhado; ‹*animal*› peludo,
felpudo

shake /ʃeɪk/ *vt* (*pt* **shook**, *pp*
shaken) abanar, sacudir; ‹*bottle*›
agitar; ‹*belief, house etc*› abalar
● *vi* estremecer, tremer; **~ hands**
with apertar a mão de; **~ off** (*get*
rid of) sacudir, livrar-se de; **~ one's**
head (*to say no*) fazer que não
com a cabeça; **~ up** agitar ● *n*
(*violent*) abanão *m*, safanão *m*; (*light*)
sacudidela *f*. **~up** *n* (*upheaval*)
reviravolta *f*

shaky /'ʃeɪkɪ/ *a* (**-ier, -iest**) ‹*hand,*
voice› trêmulo, (P) trémulo;
(*unsteady, unsafe*) pouco firme,

inseguro; (*weak*) fraco

shall /ʃæl unstressed ʃəl/ *v aux* **I/we ~ do** (*future*) farei/faremos; **I/you/ he ~ do** (*command*) eu hei-de/tu hás-de/ele há-de fazer

shallot /ʃəˈlɒt/ *n* cebolinha *f*, (*P*) chalota *f*

shallow /ˈʃæləʊ/ *a* (-er, -est) pouco fundo, raso; *fig* superficial

sham /ʃæm/ *n* fingimento *m*; ‹*jewel etc*› imitação *f*; ‹*person*› impostor *m*, fingido *m* ● *a* fingido; (*false*) falso ● *vt* (*pt* **shammed**) fingir

shambles /ˈʃæmblz/ *npl* Ⓣ (*mess*) balbúrdia *f*, trapalhada *f*

shame /ʃeɪm/ *n* vergonha *f*; **it's a ~!** é uma pena; **what a ~!** que pena! ● *vt* (fazer) envergonhar. **~ful** *a* vergonhoso; **~less** *a* sem vergonha, descarado; (*immodest*) despudorado, desavergonhado

shampoo /ʃæmˈpuː/ *n* xampu *m*, (*P*) champô *m*, shampoo *m* ● *vt* lavar com xampu, (*P*) champô or shampoo

shan't /ʃɑːnt/ (= **shall not**) = SHALL

shanty /ˈʃæntɪ/ *n* barraca *f*; **~ town** favela *f*, (*P*) bairro(s) *m(pl)* da lata

shape /ʃeɪp/ *n* forma *f* ● *vt* moldar ● *vi* **~ (up)** andar bem, fazer progressos; **take ~** concretizar-se, avançar. **~less** *a* informe, sem forma; (*of body*) deselegante, disforme

shapely /ˈʃeɪplɪ/ *a* (-ier, -iest) ‹*leg, person*› bem feito, elegante

share /ʃeə(r)/ *n* parte *f*, porção *f*; *Comm* ação *f* ● *vt/i* partilhar (**with com in de**)

shareholder /ˈʃeəhəʊldə(r)/ *n* acionista *mf*

shark /ʃɑːk/ *n* tubarão *m*

sharp /ʃɑːp/ *a* (-er, -est) ‹*knife, pencil etc*› afiado; ‹*pin, point etc*› pontiagudo, aguçado; ‹*words, reply*› áspero; (*of bend*) fechado; (*acute*) agudo; (*sudden*) brusco; (*dishonest*) pouco honesto; (*well-defined*) nítido; (*brisk*) rápido, vigoroso; (*clever*) vivo; **six o'clock ~** seis horas em ponto ● *adv* (*stop*) de repente ● *n Mus* sustenido *m*. **~ly** *adv* (*harshly*) rispidamente; (*suddenly*) de repente

sharpen /ˈʃɑːpən/ *vt* aguçar, ‹*pencil*› fazer a ponta de, (*P*) afiar; ‹*knife etc*› afiar, amolar. **~er** *n* afiadeira *f*, (*for pencil*) apontador *m*, (*P*) apara-lápis *m*, (*P*) afia-lápis *m*

shatter /ˈʃætə(r)/ *vt/i* despedaçar(-se), esmigalhar(-se); ‹*hopes*› destruir(-se); ‹*nerves*› abalar(-se). **~ed** *a* (*upset*) passado; (*exhausted*) estourado Ⓣ

shav|e /ʃeɪv/ *vt/i* barbear(-se), fazer a barba (de) ● *n* **have a ~e** barbear-se; **have a close ~** *fig* escapar por um triz. **~er** *n* aparelho *m* de barbear, (*P*) máquina *f* de barbear. **~ing brush** *n* pincel *m* para a barba; **~ing cream** *n* creme *m* de barbear

shaving /ˈʃeɪvɪŋ/ *n* apara *f*

shawl /ʃɔːl/ *n* xale *m*, (*P*) xaile *m*

she /ʃiː/ *pron* ela ● *n* fêmea *f*

shear /ʃɪə(r)/ *vt* (*pp* **shorn** or **sheared**) ‹*sheep etc*› tosquiar

shears /ʃɪəz/ *npl* tesoura *f* para jardim

sheath /ʃiːθ/ *n* (*pl s* /ʃiːðz/) bainha *f*; (*condom*) preservativo *m*, camisa de Vénus *f*

shed[1] /ʃed/ *n* (*hut*) casinhola *f*, (*for cows*) estábulo *m*

shed[2] /ʃed/ (*pres p* **shedding**) perder, deixar cair; (*spread*) espalhar; (*blood, tears*) deitar, derramar; **~ light on** lançar luz sobre

sheep /ʃiːp/ n (pl invar) carneiro m, ovelha f. **~dog** n cão m de pastor

sheepish /ˈʃiːpɪʃ/ a encabulado

sheepskin /ˈʃiːpskɪn/ n pele f de carneiro; (leather) camurça f

sheer /ʃɪə(r)/ a mero, simples; (steep) íngreme, a pique; ‹fabric› diáfano, transparente ● adv a pique, verticalmente

sheet /ʃiːt/ n lençol m; (of glass, metal) chapa f, placa f; (of paper) folha f

sheikh /ʃeɪk/ n xeque m, sheik m

shelf /ʃelf/ n (pl shelves) prateleira f

shell /ʃel/ n (of egg, nut etc) casca f; (of mollusc) concha f; (of ship, tortoise) casco m; (of building) estrutura f, armação f; (of explosive) cartucho m ● vt descascar; Mil bombardear

shellfish /ˈʃelfɪʃ/ n (pl invar) crustáceo m; (as food) marisco m

shelter /ˈʃeltə(r)/ n abrigo m, refúgio m ● vt abrigar; (protect) proteger; (harbour) dar asilo a ● vi abrigar-se, refugiar-se. **~ed** a ‹life etc› protegido; ‹spot› abrigado

shelve /ʃelv/ vt pôr em prateleiras; (fit with shelves) pôr prateleiras em; fig engavetar; pôr de lado

shelving /ˈʃelvɪŋ/ n (shelves) prateleiras fpl

shepherd /ˈʃepəd/ n pastor m; **~'s pie** empadão m de batata e carne moída ● vt guiar

sheriff /ˈʃerɪf/ n xerife m

sherry /ˈʃerɪ/ n Xerez m

shield /ʃiːld/ n (armour, heraldry) escudo m; (screen) anteparo m ● vt proteger (from contra, de)

shift /ʃɪft/ vt/i mudar de posição, deslocar(-se); (exchange, alter) mudar de ● n mudança f; (workers, work) turno m; **make ~** arranjar-se

shifty /ˈʃɪftɪ/ a (-ier, -iest) velhaco, duvidoso

shimmer /ˈʃɪmə(r)/ vi luzir suavemente ● n luzir m

shin /ʃɪn/ n perna f. **~ bone** n tíbia f, canela f; **~ pad** n Football caneleira f

shin|e /ʃaɪn/ vt/i (pt shone) (fazer) brilhar, (fazer) reluzir; ‹shoes› engraxar; **the sun is ~ing** faz sol ● n lustro m; **~e a torch (on)** iluminar com uma lanterna de mão

shingle /ˈʃɪŋgl/ n (pebbles) seixos mpl

shingles /ˈʃɪŋglz/ npl Med zona f, herpes-zóster f, (P) herpes m

shiny /ˈʃaɪnɪ/ a (-ier, -iest) brilhante; (of coat, trousers) lustroso

ship /ʃɪp/ n barco m, navio m ● vt (pt shipped) transportar; (send) mandar por via marítima; (load) embarcar. **~ment** n (goods) carregamento m; (shipping) embarque m. **~per** n expedidor m. **~ping** n navegação f; (ships) navios mpl

shipbuilding /ˈʃɪpbɪldɪŋ/ n construção f naval

shipshape /ˈʃɪpʃeɪp/ adv & a em (perfeita) ordem, impecável

shipwreck /ˈʃɪprek/ n naufrágio m. **~ed** a naufragado; **be ~ed** naufragar

shipyard /ˈʃɪpjɑːd/ n estaleiro m

shirk /ʃɜːk/ vt fugir a, furtar-se a, (P) baldar-se a ⊠

shirt /ʃɜːt/ n camisa f; (of woman) blusa f; **in ~sleeves** em mangas de camisa

shiver /ˈʃɪvə(r)/ vi arrepiar-se, tiritar ● n arrepio m

shoal /ʃəʊl/ n (of fish) cardume m

shock /ʃɒk/ n choque m, embate m; Electr choque m elétrico; Med choque m ● a a choque m; **absorber** Mech amortecedor m ● vt chocar. **~ing** a chocante; ⊺ (very bad) horrível

shodd|y /ʃɒdi/ a (**-ier, -iest**) mal feito, ordinário, de má qualidade. **~ily** adv mal

shoe /ʃuː/ n sapato m; (footwear) calçado m; (horse) ferradura f, (brake) sapata f, (P) calço (de travão) m; **on a ~string** ⊺ com/por muito pouco dinheiro, na pindaíba ⊺, por uma tuta e meia ⊺ ● vt (pt **shod**, pres p **shoeing**) ⟨horse⟩ ferrar. **~ polish** pomada f, (P) graxa f para sapatos; **~ shop** n sapataria f

shoehorn /ʃuːhɔːn/ n calçadeira f

shoelace /ʃuːleɪs/ n cordão m de sapato, (P) atacador m

shoemaker /ʃuːmeɪkə(r)/ n sapateiro m

shone /ʃɒn/ ▶ SHINE

shoo /ʃuː/ vt enxotar ● int xô

shook /ʃʊk/ ▶ SHAKE

shoot /ʃuːt/ vt (pt **shot**) ⟨gun⟩ disparar; ⟨glance, missile⟩ lançar; (kill) matar a tiro; (wound) ferir a tiro; (execute) executar, fuzilar; (hunt) caçar; (film) filmar, rodar; **~ down** abater (a tiro) ● vi disparar; atirar (at contra, sobre); **~ in/out** (rush) entrar/sair correndo, (P) correr/ surgir abruptamente; **~ up** (spurt) jorrar; (grow quickly) crescer a olhos vistos, dar um pulo; ⟨prices⟩ subir em disparada or (P) disparar ● n Bot rebento m. **~s** n (shots) tiroteio m; **~ing** n carreira f de tiro m; **~ing range** n carreira f de tiro m

shop /ʃɒp/ n loja f; (workshop) oficina f; **~ assistant** empregado m,

caixeiro m, vendedor m; **~ steward** delegado m sindical; **~ window** vitrina f, (P) montra f; **talk ~** falar de coisas profissionais ● vi (pt **shopped**) fazer compras; **~ around** procurar, ver o que há nas lojas. **~ floor** n (workers) trabalhadores mpl; **~soiled** Amer **~worn** adjs enxovalhado. **~per** n comprador m

shopkeeper /ʃɒpkiːpə(r)/ n lojista mf, comerciante mf

shoplift|er /ʃɒplɪftə(r)/ n gatuno m de lojas. **~ing** n furto m or (P) ladrão m de lojas

shopping /ʃɒpɪŋ/ n (goods) compras fpl; **go ~** ir às compras; **~ bag** sacola f or (P) saco m de compras; **~ centre** centro m comercial

shore /ʃɔː(r)/ n (of sea) praia f, costa f, (of lake) margem f

short /ʃɔːt/ a (**-er, -est**) curto; ⟨person⟩ baixo; (brief) breve, curto; (curt) seco, brusco; **be ~ of** (lack) ter falta de; **a ~ time** pouco tempo; **he is called Tom for ~** o diminutivo dele é Tom; **in ~** em suma; **~ circuit** Electr curto-circuito m; **~ cut** atalho m; **~ list** pré-seleção f; **~ story** conto m; **~ wave** Radio onda(s) f(pl) curta(s) ● adv (abruptly) bruscamente, de repente; **cut ~** abreviar; (interrupt) interromper ● n Electr curto-circuito m; (film) curta-metragem f, short m; **~s** (trousers) calção m, (P) calções mpl, short m. **~change** vt (cheat) enganar; **~circuit** vt/i Electr fazer or dar um curto-circuito (em); **~lived** a de pouca duração; **~sighted** a míope; **~tempered** a irritadiço

shortage /ʃɔːtɪdʒ/ n falta f, escassez f

shortbread /ʃɔːtbred/ n shortbread m, biscoito m de massa amanteigada

shortcoming /'ʃɔːtkʌmɪŋ/ n falha f, imperfeição f.

shorten /'ʃɔːtn/ vt/i encurtar(-se), abreviar(-se), diminuir

shorthand /'ʃɔːthænd/ n estenografia f; **~ typist** estenodactilógrafa f, (P) estenodatilógrafa f, (P) estenógrafo m

shortly /'ʃɔːtlɪ/ adv (soon) em breve, dentro em pouco

shot /ʃɒt/ ▸ **SHOOT** n (firing, bullet) tiro m; (person) atirador m; (pellets) chumbo m; (photograph) fotografia f; (injection) injeção f; (in golf, billiards) tacada f; **go like a ~** ir disparado; **have a ~ (at sth)** experimentar (fazer algo). **~gun** n espingarda f, caçadeira f

should /ʃʊd unstressed ʃəd/ v aux **you ~ help me** você devia me ajudar, (P) devias ajudar-me; **I ~ have stayed** devia ter ficado; **I ~ like to** gostaria de or gostava de; **if he ~ come** se ele vier

shoulder /'ʃəʊldə(r)/ n ombro m ● vt ‹responsibility› tomar, assumir; ‹burden› carregar, arcar com. **~ blade** n Anat omoplata f, **~ pad** n enchimento de ombro, ombreira f, (P) chumaço m

shout /ʃaʊt/ n grito m, brado m; (very loud) berro m ● vt/i gritar (at com); (very loudly) berrar (at com). **~ down** fazer calar com gritos. **~ing** n gritaria f, berraria f

shove /ʃʌv/ n empurrão m ● vt/i empurrar; ▪ (put) meter, enfiar; **~ off** ▢ (depart) começar ou pôr-se a andar ▢, dar o fora ▢,(P) cavar ▢

shovel /'ʃʌvl/ n pá f, (machine) escavadora f ● vt (pt shovelled) remover com pá

show /ʃəʊ/ vt (pt showed, pp shown) mostrar; (of dial, needle)

marcar; (put on display) expor; ‹film› dar, passar; **~ in** mandar entrar; **~ out** acompanhar à porta ● vi ver-se, aparecer, estar à vista; **~ up** ser claramente visível, ver-se bem; ▢ (arrive) aparecer ● n mostra f, demonstração f; manifestação f; (ostentation) alarde m, espalhafato m; (exhibition) mostra f, exposição f; Theatre, Cinema espetáculo m, show m; **for ~** para fazer vista, (P) para dar nas vistas; **on ~** exposto, em exposição ▢ **~ off** vt exibir, ostentar ● vi exibir-se, querer fazer figura. **~down** n confrontação f; **~jumping** n concurso m hípico; **~off** n exibicionista mf; **~piece** n peça f digna de se expor. **~ing** n (performance) atuação f, performance f; Cinema exibição f

shower /'ʃaʊə(r)/ n (of rain) aguaceiro m, chuvarada f, (of blows etc) saraivada f; (in bathroom) chuveiro m; ducha f; (P) duche m ● vt **~ with** cumular de, encher de ● vi tomar um banho de chuveiro ou uma ducha, (P) um duche. **~y** a chuvoso

shown /ʃəʊn/ ▸ **SHOW**

showroom /'ʃaʊrʊm/ n espaço m de exposição, show-room m; (for cars) stand m

showy /'ʃəʊɪ/ a (-ier, -iest) vistoso; (too bright) berrante; pej espalhafatoso

shrank /ʃræŋk/ ▸ **SHRINK**

shred /ʃred/ n tira f, retalho m, farrapo m; fig mínimo m; sombra f ● vt (pt shredded) reduzir a tiras, estraçalhar; Culin desfiar. **~der** n trituradora f, (for paper) fragmentadora f, (P) trituradora f

shrewd /ʃruːd/ a (-er, -est) astucioso, fino, perspicaz. **~ness** n astúcia f, perspicácia f

shriek /ʃriːk/ n grito m agudo, guincho m ● vt/i gritar, guinchar

shrill /ʃrɪl/ a estridente, agudo

shrimp /ʃrɪmp/ n camarão m

shrine /ʃraɪn/ n (place) santuário m; (tomb) túmulo m; (casket) relicário m

shrink /ʃrɪŋk/ vt/i (pt shrank, pp shrunk) encolher; (recoil) encolher-se; ~ **from** esquivar-se a, fugir a (+ inf) (de (+ noun), retrair-se de

shrivel /ʃrɪvl/ vt/i (pt shrivelled) encarquilhar(-se)

Shrove /ʃrəʊv/ n ~ **Tuesday** Terça-feira f Gorda or de Carnaval

shrub /ʃrʌb/ n arbusto m. ~**bery** n arbustos mpl

shrug /ʃrʌg/ vt (pt shrugged) ~ **one's shoulders** encolher os ombros; ~ **off** não dar importância a ● n encolher m de ombros

shrunk /ʃrʌŋk/ ▶ SHRINK

shudder /ʃʌdə(r)/ vi arrepiar-se, estremecer, tremer; **I** ~ **to think** tremo só de pensar ● n arrepio m, tremor m, estremecimento m

shuffle /ʃʌfl/ vt ⟨feet⟩ arrastar; ⟨cards⟩ embaralhar, (P) baralhar ● vi arrastar os pés ● n marcha f arrastada (P)

shun /ʃʌn/ vt (pt shunned) evitar, fugir de

shunt /ʃʌnt/ vt/i (train) mudar de linha, manobrar

shut /ʃʌt/ vt (pt shut, pres p shutting) fechar; ~ **in** or **up** trancar ● vi fechar-se; ⟨shop, bank etc⟩ encerrar, fechar; ~ **down** or **up** fechar; ~ **up!** 🔲 cale-se!, cale a boca! □ ~ **up** vi 🔲 (stop talking) calar-se ● vt 🔲 (silence) mandar calar

shutter /ʃʌtə(r)/ n taipais mpl, (P) portada f de madeira; (of laths) persiana f; (in shop) taipais mpl; Photo obturador m

shuttle /ʃʌtl/ n (of spaceship) ônibus m espacial, (P) nave f espacial; ~ **service** (plane) ponte f aérea; (bus) ônibus m, (P) autocarro m

shuttlecock /ʃʌtlkɒk/ n volante m

shy /ʃaɪ/ a (-er, -est) tímido, acanhado, envergonhado ● vi ⟨horse⟩ espantar-se (at com); fig assustar-se (at or away from com). ~**ness** n timidez f, acanhamento m, vergonha f

Sicily /ˈsɪsɪlɪ/ n Sicília f

sick /sɪk/ a doente; ⟨humour⟩ negro; **be** ~ (vomit) vomitar; **be** ~ **of** estar farto de; **feel** ~ estar enjoado. ~**bay** n enfermaria f; ~ **leave** n licença f por doença; ~**room** n quarto m de doente

sicken /ˈsɪkn/ vt (distress) desesperar; (disgust) repugnar ● vi **be** ~**ing for flu** começar a pegar or (P) chocar uma gripe 🔲

sickly /ˈsɪklɪ/ a (-ier, -iest) ⟨person⟩ doentio, achacado; ⟨smell⟩ enjoativo; (pale) pálido

sickness /ˈsɪknɪs/ n doença f, (vomiting) náusea f; vômito m, (P) vómito m

side /saɪd/ n lado m; (of road, river) beira f; (of hill) encosta f; Sport equipe f, (P) equipa f em campo; (extra) nas horas vagas; (secretly) pela calada; ~ **by** ~ lado a lado ● a lateral ● vi ~ **with** tomar o partido de, alinhar com. ~**car** n sidecar m; ~**effect** n efeito m secundário; ~**show** n espetáculo m suplementar;

~step *vt* evitar; **~track** *vt* (fazer) desviar dum propósito

sideboard /ˈsaɪdbɔːd/ *n* aparador *m*

sideburns /ˈsaɪdbɜːnz/ *npl* suíças *fpl*, costeletas *fpl*, (P) patilhas *fpl*

sidelight /ˈsaɪdlaɪt/ *n* Auto luz *f* lateral, (P) farolim *m*

sideline /ˈsaɪdlaɪn/ *n* atividade *f* secundária; Sport linha *f* lateral

sidelong /ˈsaɪdlɒŋ/ *adv* & de lado

sidewalk /ˈsaɪdwɔːk/ *n* Amer passeio *m*

sideways /ˈsaɪdweɪz/ *adv* & a de lado

siding /ˈsaɪdɪŋ/ *n* desvio *m*, ramal *m*

siege /siːdʒ/ *n* cerco *m*

siesta /sɪˈestə/ *n* sesta *f*

sieve /sɪv/ *n* peneira *f*; (for liquids) coador *m* ● *vt* peneirar; ‹liquids› passar, coar

sift /sɪft/ *vt* peneirar; (sprinkle) polvilhar; **~ through** examinar minuciosamente, esquadrinhar

sigh /saɪ/ *n* suspiro *m* ● *vt/i* suspirar

sight /saɪt/ *n* vista *f*; (scene) cena *f*; (on gun) mira *f* ● *vt* avistar, ver, divisar; **at** or **on ~** à vista; **catch ~ of** avistar; **in ~** à vista, visível; **lose ~ of** perder de vista; **out of ~** longe dos olhos, longe da vista

sightsee|ing /ˈsaɪtsiːɪŋ/ *n* visita *f*, turismo *m*; **go ~ing** visitar lugares turísticos. **~r** /-ə(r)/ *n* turista *mf*

sign /saɪn/ *n* sinal *m*; (symbol) signo *m* ● *vt* (in writing) assinar ● *vi* (make a sign) fazer sinal; **~ on** or **up** ‹workers› assinar contrato. **~ language** *n* mímica *f*, linguagem *f* gestual

signal /ˈsɪɡnəl/ *n* sinal *m* ● *vi* (pt signalled) fazer signal ● *vt* comunicar (por sinais); ‹person›

fazer sinal para

signature /ˈsɪɡnətʃə(r)/ *n* assinatura *f*; **~ tune** indicativo *m* musical

significan|t /sɪɡˈnɪfɪkənt/ *a* importante; (meaningful) significativo. **~ce** *n* importância *f*; (meaning) significado *m*

signify /ˈsɪɡnɪfaɪ/ *vt* significar

signpost /ˈsaɪnpəʊst/ *n* poste *m* de sinalização ● *vt* sinalizar

silence /ˈsaɪləns/ *n* silêncio *m* ● *vt* silenciar, calar

silent /ˈsaɪlənt/ *a* silencioso; (not speaking) calado; ‹film› mudo. **~ly** *adv* silenciosamente

silhouette /sɪluˈet/ *n* silhueta *f* ● *vt* **be ~d against** estar em silhueta contra

silicon /ˈsɪlɪkən/ *n* silicone *m*; **~ chip** circuito *m* integrado

silk /sɪlk/ *n* seda *f*. **~en, ~y** *adjs* sedoso

sill /sɪl/ *n* (of window) parapeito *m*; (of door) soleira *f*, limiar *m*

sill|y /ˈsɪlɪ/ *a* (-ier, -iest) tolo, idiota. **~iness** *n* tolice *f*, idiotice *f*

silt /sɪlt/ *n* aluvião *m*, sedimento *m*

silver /ˈsɪlvə(r)/ *n* prata *f*; (silverware) prataria *f*, pratas *fpl* ● *a* de prata; **~ paper** papel *m* prateado; **~ wedding** bodas *fpl* de prata

silversmith /ˈsɪlvəsmɪθ/ *n* ourives *m*

silverware /ˈsɪlvəweə(r)/ *n* prataria *f*, pratas *fpl*

SIM card /ˈsɪm kɑːd/ *n* SIM *m*, (P) cartão SIM

similar /ˈsɪmɪlə(r)/ *a* **~ (to)** semelhante (a), parecido (com). **~ity** /-əˈlærətɪ/ *n* semelhança *f*

simmer /ˈsɪmə(r)/ *vt/i* cozinhar em fogo brando; fig (smoulder) ferver;

fremir; **~ down** acalmar(-se)

simpl|e /ˈsɪmpl/ a (**-er, -est**)
simples. **~e-minded** a simples;
(*feeble-minded*) pobre de espírito,
tolo. **~icity** /-ˈplɪsətɪ/ n simplicidade
f. **~y** adv simplesmente; (*absolutely*)
absolutamente, simplesmente

simpleton /ˈsɪmpltən/ n
simplório m

simplif|y /ˈsɪmplɪfaɪ/ vt simplificar.
~ication /-ɪˈkeɪʃn/ n simplificação f

simulat|e /ˈsɪmjʊleɪt/ vt simular,
imitar. **~ion** /-ˈleɪʃn/ n simulação f,
imitação f

simultaneous /sɪmlˈteɪnɪəs/ a
simultâneo, concomitante. **~ly** adv
simultaneamente

sin /sɪn/ n pecado m ● vi (pt **sinned**)
pecar

---

since /sɪns/ ● prep

····▸ desde; **I haven't seen him
~ Monday** não o vejo desde
segunda-feira; **I have been
waiting ~ yesterday** estou
esperando desde ontem; **she
had been living in Lisbon ~
1985** ela estava vivendo em
Lisboa desde 1985

● adv

····▸ desde então; **he hasn't
been seen ~** ninguém o viu
desde então

● conj

····▸ (*in time expressions*) desde
que; **~ she's been working here**
desde que ela trabalha aqui

····▸ (*because*) como, visto que;
~ he was ill, he couldn't go
como estava doente, não pôde ir

---

sincer|e /sɪnˈsɪə(r)/ a sincero. **~ely**
adv sinceramente. **~ity** /-ˈserətɪ/ n

sinceridade f

sinful /ˈsɪnfl/ a (*wicked*)
pecaminoso; (*shocking*) escandaloso

sing /sɪŋ/ vt/i (pt **sang**, pp **sung**)
cantar. **~er** n cantor m

singe /sɪndʒ/ vt (pres p **singeing**)
chamuscar

single /ˈsɪŋgl/ a único, só;
(*unmarried*) solteiro; <bed> de
solteiro; <room> individual; <ticket>
de ida, simples; **in ~ file** em fila
indiana; **~ parent** pai m solteiro,
mãe f solteira ● n (*ticket*) bilhete m
de ida ou simples; (*record*) disco m
de 45 r.p.m.; **~s** Tennis singulares
mpl ● vt **~ out** escolher. **~-handed**
a sem ajuda, sozinho; **~-minded** a
decidido, aferrado à sua ideia, (P)
determinado, tenaz. **singly** adv um
a um, um por um

singular /ˈsɪŋgjʊlə(r)/ n singular
m ● a (*uncommon*) Gramm singular;
(*noun*) no singular

sinister /ˈsɪnɪstə(r)/ a sinistro

sink /sɪŋk/ vt (pt **sank**, pp **sunk**)
<ship> afundar, ir a pique; (*well*) abrir;
(*invest money*) empatar; (*lose money*)
enterrar ● vi afundar-se; (*of ground*)
ceder; (*of voice*) baixar; **~ in** fig ficar
gravado, entrar 🄸; **~ or swim** ou vai
ou racha 🄸 ● n pia f, (P) lava-louça m

sinner /ˈsɪnə(r)/ n pecador m

sip /sɪp/ n gole m ● vt (pt **sipped**)
beberucar, beber aos golinhos

siphon /ˈsaɪfn/ n sifão m ● vt **~ off**
extrair por meio de sifão

sir /sɜː(r)/ n senhor m; (*title*) Sir m;
Dear S~ Exmo Senhor; **excuse me, ~**
desculpe, senhor; **no, ~** não, senhor

siren /ˈsaɪərən/ n sereia f, sirene f

sister /ˈsɪstə(r)/ n irmã f; (*nun*) irmã
f, freira f; (*nurse*) enfermeira-chefe f;
~-in-law cunhada f

sit /sɪt/ vt/i (pt **sat**, pres p **sitting**) sentar(-se); ~ **for an exam** fazer um exame, prestar uma prova; be ~**ting** estar sentado; ~ **around** não fazer nada; ~ **down** sentar-se; ~ **up** endireitar-se na cadeira; (not go to bed) passar a noite acordado. ~**ting** n reunião f, sessão f; (in restaurant) serviço m. ~**ting room** n sala f de estar

site /saɪt/ n local m; (building) terreno m para construção, lote m ● vt localizar, situar

situat|e /'sɪtʃʊeɪt/ vt situar. be ~**ed** estar situado. ~**ion** /-'eɪʃn/ n (position, condition) situação f; (job) emprego m, colocação f

six /sɪks/ a & n seis m. ~**th** a & n sexto m

sixteen /sɪk'stiːn/ a & n dezesseis m, (P) dezasseis m. ~**th** a & n décimo sexto m

sixt|y /'sɪkstɪ/ a & n sessenta m. ~**ieth** a & n sexagésimo m

size /saɪz/ n tamanho m; (of person, garment etc) tamanho m, medida f, (P) número m; (of shoes) número m; (extent) grandeza f ● vt ~ **up** calcular o tamanho de; ⟨↑⟩ (judge) formar um juízo sobre, avaliar. ~**able** a bastante grande, considerável

sizzle /'sɪzl/ vi chiar, rechinar

skate¹ /skeɪt/ n (pl invar) (fish) (ar) raia f

skat|e² /skeɪt/ n patim m ● vi patinar. ~**er** n patinador m. ~**ing** n patinação f, (P) patinagem f. ~**ing rink** n rinque m de patinação or (P) patinagem f

skateboard /'skeɪtbɔːd/ n skate m

skelet|on /'skelɪtən/ n esqueleto m; (framework) armação f, ~**on crew** or **staff** pessoal m reduzido;

~**on key** chave f mestra. ~**al** a esquelético

sketch /sketʃ/ n esboço m, croqui(s) m; Theat sketch m, peça f curta e humorística; (outline) ideia f or (P) ideia f geral, esboço m ● vt esboçar, delinear ● vi fazer esboços. ~**book** n caderno m de desenho

sketchy /'sketʃɪ/ a (-ier, -iest) incompleto, esboçado

skewer /'skjʊə(r)/ n espeto m

ski /skiː/ n (pl -s) esqui m ● vi (pt **ski'd**, or **skied**, pres p **skiing**) esquiar; (go skiing) fazer esqui. ~**er** n esquiador m. ~**ing** n esqui m

skid /skɪd/ vi (pt **skidded**) derrapar, patinar ● n derrapagem f

skilful /'skɪlfl/ a hábil, habilidoso

skill /skɪl/ n habilidade f, jeito m; (craft) arte f; ~**s** aptidões fpl. ~**ed** a hábil, habilidoso; (worker) especializado

skim /skɪm/ vt (pt **skimmed**) tirar a espuma de; (milk) desnatar, tirar a nata de; (pass or glide over) deslizar sobre, roçar ● vi ~ **through** ler por alto, passar os olhos por; ~**med milk** leite m desnatado

skimp /skɪmp/ vt (use too little) poupar em ● vi ser poupado

skimpy /'skɪmpɪ/ a (-ier, -iest) ⟨clothes⟩ sumário, mínimo; ⟨meal⟩ escasso; racionado fig

skin /skɪn/ n (of person, animal) pele f; (of fruit) casca f ● vt (pt **skinned**) ⟨animal⟩ esfolar, tirar a pele de; ⟨fruit⟩ descascar

skinny /'skɪnɪ/ a (-ier, -iest) magricela, escanzelado

skint /skɪnt/ a 🅰 sem dinheiro; na última lona 🅰,(P) nas lonas 🅰

skip¹ /skɪp/ vi (pt **skipped**) saltar, pular; (jump about) saltitar; (with *rope*) pular corda, (P) saltar à corda ● *vt* ‹*page*› saltar; ‹*class*› faltar a ● *n* salto m. **~ping rope** n corda f de pular or (P) de saltar

skip² /skɪp/ n (*container*) container m or (P) contentor m grande para entulho

skipper /'skɪpə(r)/ n capitão m

skirmish /'skɜːmɪʃ/ n escaramuça f

skirt /skɜːt/ n saia f ● *vt* contornar, ladear. **~ing board** n rodapé m

skittle /'skɪtl/ n pino m. **~s** npl boliche m, (P) jogo m da laranjinha

skive /skaɪv/ vi ★ eximir-se de um dever; evitar trabalhar, (P) furtar-se ao trabalho ★

skull /skʌl/ n caveira f, crânio m

skunk /skʌŋk/ n (*animal*) gambá m, (P) doninha f

sky /skaɪ/ n céu m. **~-blue** a & n azul-celeste m

skylight /'skaɪlaɪt/ n clarabóia f

skyscraper /'skaɪskreɪpə(r)/ n arranha-céus m invar

slab /slæb/ n (of *marble*) placa f; (of *paving stone*) laje f; (of *metal*) chapa f; (of *cake*) fatia f grossa

slack /slæk/ a (-er, -est) ‹*rope*› bambo, frouxo; ‹*person*› descuidado, negligente; ‹*business*› parado, fraco; ‹*period, season*› morto ● *n* the **~** (in *rope*) a parte bamba ● *vt/i* ‹*be lazy*› estar com preguiça; fazer cera *fig*

slacken /'slækən/ *vt/i* ‹*speed, activity etc*› afrouxar, abrandar

slain /sleɪn/ ▶ **SLAY**

slam /slæm/ *vt* (pt **slammed**) bater violentamente com; (*throw*) atirar; ★ (*criticize*) criticar; malhar ● *vi* ‹*door etc*› bater violentamente ● *n* (*noise*) bater m, pancada f

slander /'slɑːndə(r)/ n calúnia f, difamação f ● *vt* caluniar, difamar. **~ous** a calunioso, difamatório

slang /slæŋ/ n calão m, gíria f. **~y** a de calão

slant /slɑːnt/ *vt/i* inclinar(-se); ‹*news*› apresentar de forma tendenciosa ● *n* inclinação f; (*bias*) tendência f; (*point of view*) ângulo m; **be ~ing** ser/estar inclinado or em declive

slap /slæp/ *vt* (pt **slapped**) (*strike*) bater, dar uma palmada em; (on *face*) esbofetear, dar uma bofetada em; (put *forcefully*) atirar com ● *n* palmada f, bofetada f ● *adv* em cheio. **~-up** a ★ (*excellent*) excelente

slapdash /'slæpdæʃ/ a descuidado; (*impetuous*) precipitado

slapstick /'slæpstɪk/ n farsa f com palhaçadas

slash /slæʃ/ *vt* (*cut*) retalhar, dar golpes em; (*sever*) cortar; ‹*a garment*› golpear; *fig* (*reduce*) reduzir drasticamente; fazer um corte radical em ● *n* corte m, golpe m

slat /slæt/ n (in *blind*) ripa f, (P) lâmina f

slate /sleɪt/ n ardósia f ● *vt* ★ (*criticize*) criticar severamente

slaughter /'slɔːtə(r)/ *vt* chacinar, massacrar; ‹*animals*› abater ● *n* chacina f, massacre m, mortandade f; (*animals*) abate m

slaughterhouse /'slɔːtəhaʊs/ n matadouro m

slave /sleɪv/ n escravo m ● *vi* mourejar, trabalhar como um escravo. **~-driver** n *fig* o que obriga os outros a trabalharem como escravos; condutor m de escravos. **~ry** /-əri/ n escravatura f

slay /sleɪ/ vt (pt **slew**, pp **slain**) matar

sleazy /'sliːzɪ/ a (**-ier**, **-iest**) ⊞ esquálido; sórdido

sledge /sledʒ/ n trenó m. **~hammer** n martelo m de forja, marreta f

sleek /sliːk/ a (**-er**, **-est**) liso, macio e lustroso

sleep /sliːp/ n sono m ● vi (pt **slept**) dormir ● vt ter lugar para, alojar; **go to ~** ir dormir, adormecer; **put to ~** (kill) mandar matar; **~ around** ser promíscuo. **~er** n aquele que dorme; Rail (beam) dormente m; (berth) couchette f. **~ing bag** n saco m de dormir, (P) saco-cama m. **~less** a insone; (night) em claro, insone. **~walker** n sonâmbulo m

sleepy /'sliːpɪ/ a (**-ier**, **-iest**) sonolento; **be ~y** ter ou estar com sono

sleet /sliːt/ n geada f miúda ● vi cair geada miúda

sleeve /sliːv/ n manga f; (of record) capa f; **up one's ~** de reserva, escondido, (P) na manga. **~less** a sem mangas

sleigh /sleɪ/ n trenó m

sleight /slaɪt/ n **~ of hand** prestidigitação f, passe m de mágica

slender /'slendə(r)/ a esguio, esbelto; fig (scanty) escasso

slept /slept/ ▶ **SLEEP**

sleuth /sluːθ/ n ⊞ detetive m

slew¹ /sluː/ vi (turn) virar-se

slew² /sluː/ ▶ **SLAY**

slice /slaɪs/ n fatia f ● vt cortar em fatias; Golf, Tennis cortar

slick /slɪk/ a (slippery) escorregadio; (cunning) astuto, habilidoso; (unctuous) melífluo ● n (oil) ~ mancha f de óleo, (P) derrame m de petróleo

slide /slaɪd/ vt/i (pt **slid**) escorregar, deslizar ● n escorregadela f, escorregão m; (in playground) escorrega m; (for hair) prendedor m, (P) travessa f; Photo diapositivo m, slide m. **~ing** a ‹door, panel› corrediço, de correr; **~ing scale** escala f móvel

slight /slaɪt/ a (**-er**, **-est**) (slender, frail) delgado, franzino; (inconsiderable) leve, ligeiro; **not in the ~est** em absoluto ● vt desconsiderar, desfeitear ● n desconsideração f, desfeita f. **the ~est** a o/a menor. **~ly** adv ligeiramente, um pouco

slim /slɪm/ a (**slimmer**, **slimmest**) magro, esbelto; ‹chance› pequeno, remoto ● vi (pt **slimmed**) emagrecer

slime /slaɪm/ n lodo m. **~y** a lodoso; (slippery) escorregadio; fig (servile) servil; bajulador

sling /slɪŋ/ n (weapon) funda f; (for arm) tipoia f ● vt (pt **slung**) atirar, lançar

slip /slɪp/ vt/i (pt **slipped**) escorregar; (move quietly) mover-se de mansinho; **~ away** esgueirar-se; **~ by** passar sem se dar conta, passar despercebido; **~ into** (go) entrar de mansinho, enfiar-se em; ‹clothes› enfiar; **~ped disc** disco m deslocado; **~ sb's mind** passar pela cabeça de alguém; **~ up** ⊞ cometer uma gafe ● n escorregadela f, escorregão m; (mistake) engano m, lapso m; (petticoat) combinação f; (of paper) tira f de papel; **give the ~ to** livrar-se de, escapar(-se) de; **~ of the tongue** lapso m. **~ road** n acesso m a autoestrada; **~-up** n ⊞ gafe f

slipper /'slɪpə(r)/ n chinelo m

slippery /'slɪpərɪ/ a escorregadio; fig ‹person› que não é de confiança; sem escrúpulos

slipshod /'slɪpʃɒd/ a ‹person› desleixado, desmazelado; ‹work› feito sem cuidado, desleixado

slit /slɪt/ n fenda f; (cut) corte m; (tear) rasgão m ● vt (pt **slit**, pres p **slitting**) fender; (cut) fazer um corte em, cortar

slither /'slɪðə(r)/ vi escorregar, resvalar

sliver /'slɪvə(r)/ n (of cheese etc) fatia f; (splinter) lasca f

slog /slɒg/ vt (pt **slogged**) (hit) bater com força ● vi (walk) caminhar com passos pesados e firmes; (work) trabalhar duro ● n (work) trabalheira f; (walk, effort) estafa f

slogan /'sləʊgən/ n slogan m, lema m, palavra f de ordem

slop /slɒp/ vt/i (pt **slopped**) transbordar, entornar. ~s npl (dirty water) água(s) f(pl) suja(s); (liquid refuse) despejos mpl

slop|e /sləʊp/ vt/i inclinar(-se), formar declive ● n (of mountain) encosta f; (of street) rampa f, ladeira f. ~ing a inclinado, em declive

sloppy /'slɒpɪ/ a (-ier, -iest) ‹ground› molhado, com poças de água; ‹food› aguado; ‹clothes› desleixado; ‹work› descuidado; feito de qualquer jeito or maneira 🄸; ‹person› desmazelado; (maudlin) piegas

slosh /slɒʃ/ vt entornar; 🄸 (splash) esparrinhar, (P) salpicar; 🗴 (hit) bater em; dar (uma) sova em ● vi chapinhar

slot /slɒt/ n ranhura f; (in timetable) horário m; TV espaço m; Aviat slot m ● vt/i (pt **slotted**) enfiar(-se), meter(-se), encaixar(-se). ~

machine n (for stamps, tickets etc) distribuidor m automático; (for gambling) caça-níqueis m, (P) slot machine f

slouch /slaʊtʃ/ vi (stand, move) andar com as costas curvadas; (sit) sentar-se em má postura

slovenly /'slʌvnlɪ/ a desmazelado, desleixado

slow /sləʊ/ a (-er, -est) lento, vagaroso ● adv devagar, lentamente ● vt/i ~ (up or down) diminuir a velocidade, afrouxar; Auto desacelerar; **be** ~ ‹clock etc› atrasar-se, estar atrasado; **in** ~ **motion** em câmara lenta. ~**ly** adv devagar, lentamente, vagarosamente

slow|coach /'sləʊkəʊtʃ/, ~**poke** Amer ns lesma m/f; pastelão m fig

sludge /slʌdʒ/ n lama f, lodo m

slug /slʌg/ n lesma f

sluggish /'slʌgɪʃ/ a (slow) lento, moroso; (lazy) indolente, preguiçoso

sluice /sluːs/ n (gate) comporta f; (channel) canal m ● vt lavar com jorros de água

slum /slʌm/ n favela f, (P) bairro m da lata; (building) cortiço m

slumber /'slʌmbə(r)/ n sono m ● vi dormir

slump /slʌmp/ n (in prices) baixa f, descida f; (in demand) quebra f na procura; Econ depressão f ● vi (fall limply) cair, afundar-se; (of price) baixar bruscamente

slung /slʌŋ/ ▶ SLING

slur /slɜː(r)/ vt/i (pt **slurred**) (speech) pronunciar indistintamente, mastigar ● n (in speech) som m indistinto; (discredit) nódoa f, estigma m

slush /slʌʃ/ n (snow) neve f meio
derretida; **~ fund** Comm fundo m
para subornos, (P) saco m azul. **~y**
a ‹road› coberto de neve derretida,
lamacento

slut /slʌt/ n (dirty woman) porca f,
desmazelada f; (immoral woman)
desavergonhada f, (P) galdéria f

sly /slaɪ/ a (**slyer, slyest**) (crafty)
manhoso; (secretive) sonso,
subreptício ● n **on the ~** na calada

smack¹ /smæk/ n palmada f,
(on face) bofetada f ● vt dar uma
palmada em or uma tapa em; (on the
face) esbofetear, dar uma bofetada
em ● adv 🄯 em cheio; direto

smack² /smæk/ vi **~ of sth** cheirar
a algo

small /smɔːl/ a (**-er, -est**) pequeno;
~ change trocado m, dinheiro m
miúdo; **~ talk** conversa f fiada,
bate-papo m ● n **~ of the back** zona
f dos rins ● adv (cut etc) em pedaços
pequenos, aos bocadinhos

smallpox /ˈsmɔːlpɒks/ n varíola f

smarmy /ˈsmɑːmɪ/ a (**-ier, -iest**) 🄯
bajulador; puxa-saco 🄯, (P) lambe-
botas mf inv

smart /smɑːt/ a (**-er, -est**)
elegante; (clever) esperto, vivo;
(brisk) rápido ● vi (sting) arder, picar

smarten /ˈsmɑːtn/ vt/i **~ (up)**
arranjar(-se), dar um ar mais
cuidado a; **~ (o.s.) up** embelezar-se,
arrumar-se, (P) pôr-se elegante/
bonito; (tidy) arranjar-se

smash /smæʃ/ vt/i (to pieces)
despedaçar(-se); espatifar(-se)
🄯 ; ‹a record› quebrar, (P) partir;
‹opponent› esmagar; (ruin) (fazer)
falir; (of vehicle) espatifar(-se) ● n
(noise) estrondo m; (blow) pancada
f forte, golpe m; (collision) colisão f;
Tennis smash m

smashing /ˈsmæʃɪŋ/ a 🄯
formidável; estupendo 🄯

smattering /ˈsmætərɪŋ/ n
leves noções fpl, conhecimento m
superficial

smear /smɪə(r)/ vt (stain; discredit)
manchar; (coat) untar, besuntar ● n
mancha f, nódoa f; Med esfregaço m

smell /smel/ n cheiro m, odor m;
(sense) cheiro m; olfato m ● vt/i (pt
smelt, or **smelled**) **~ (of)** cheirar (a).
~y a mal-cheiroso

smelt¹ /smelt/ ▶ SMELL

smelt² /smelt/ vt (ore) fundir

smile /smaɪl/ n sorriso m ● vi sorrir

smirk /smɜːk/ n sorriso m falso or
afetado

smock /smɒk/ n guarda-pó m

smog /smɒg/ n mistura f de
nevoeiro e fumaça, smog m

smoke /sməʊk/ n fumo m, fumaça
f ● vt fumar; ‹bacon etc› fumar,
defumar ● vi fumar, fumegar.
~screen n lit & fig cortina f de
fumaça or (P) de fumo. **~less** a
‹fuel› sem fumo. **~r** /-ə(r)/ n
(person) fumante mf, (P) fumador
m. **smoky** a ‹air› enfumaçado,
fumacento, fumoso

smooth /smuːð/ a (**-er, -est**)
liso; (soft) macio; (movement)
regular, suave; (manners) lisonjeiro,
conciliador, suave ● vt alisar; **~ out**
fig aplanar, remover

smother /ˈsmʌðə(r)/ vt (stifle)
abafar, sufocar; (cover, overwhelm)
cobrir (with de); (suppress) abafar,
reprimir

smoulder /ˈsməʊldə(r)/ vi lit & fig
arder; abrasar-se

SMS abbr (= Short Message or
Messaging Service) mensagem
f de texto

smudge /smʌdʒ/ n mancha f, borrão m ● vt/i sujar(-se), manchar(-se), borrar(-se)

smug /smʌg/ a (**smugger**, **smuggest**) presunçoso; convencido ▣

smuggl|e /'smʌgl/ vt contrabandear, fazer contrabando de. **~er** n contrabandista mf. **~ing** n contrabando m

smut /smʌt/ n fuligem f. **~ty** a cheio de fuligem; ▣ (obscene) indecente; sujo ▣

snack /snæk/ n refeição f ligeira. **~ bar** n lanchonete f, (P) snack(-bar) m

snag /snæg/ n (obstacle) obstáculo m; (drawback) problema m, contra m, contratempo m; (in cloth) rasgão m; (in stocking) fio m puxado, (P) malha f

snail /sneɪl/ n caracol m; **at a ~'s pace** em passo de tartaruga or (P) caracol

snake /sneɪk/ n serpente f, cobra f

snap /snæp/ vt/i (pt **snapped**) (whip, fingers) (fazer) estalar; (break) estalar(-se), partir(-se) com um estalo, rebentar; (say) dizer irritadamente ● n estalo m; (photo) instantâneo m, (P) instantânea f; Amer (fastener) mola f ● a súbito, repentino; **~ at** (bite) abocanhar, tentar morder; (speak angrily) retrucar or (P) retorquir asperamente; **~ up** (buy) comprar rapidamente

snappy /'snæpɪ/ a (**-ier**, **-iest**) ▣ vivo; animado; **make it ~** ▣ vai rápido!, apresse-se! ▣

snapshot /'snæpʃɒt/ n instantâneo m, (P) fotografia f) instantânea f

snare /sneə(r)/ n laço m, cilada f, armadilha f

snarl /snɑːl/ vi rosnar ● n rosnadela f

snatch /snætʃ/ vt (grab) agarrar, apanhar; (steal) roubar; **~ from sb** arrancar de/a alguém ● n (theft) roubo m; (bit) bocado m, pedaço m

sneak /sniːk/ vi (slink) esgueirar-se furtivamente; ▣ (tell tales) fazer queixa(s); delatar ● vt ▣ (steal) rapinar ▣ ● n ▣ dedo-duro m; queixinhas mf ▣. **~ing** a secreto. **~y** a sonso

sneer /snɪə(r)/ n sorriso m de desdém ● vi sorrir desdenhosamente

sneeze /sniːz/ n espirro m ● vi espirrar

snide /snaɪd/ a ▣ sarcástico

sniff /snɪf/ vi fungar ● vt/i **~ (at)** (smell) cheirar; (dog) farejar; **~ at** fig (in contempt) desprezar ● n fungadela f

snigger /'snɪgə(r)/ n riso m abafado ● vi rir dissimuladamente

snip /snɪp/ vt (pt **snipped**) cortar com tesoura ● n pedaço m, retalho m; ▣ (bargain) pechincha f

snipe /snaɪp/ vi dar tiros de emboscada. **~r** /-ə(r)/ n franco-atirador m

snivel /'snɪvl/ vi (pt **snivelled**) choramingar, lamuriar-se

snob /snɒb/ n esnobe mf, (P) snob mf. **~bery** n esnobismo m, (P) snobismo m. **~bish** a esnobe, (P) snob

snog /snɒg/ Brit vt/i (pres p etc. **-gg-**) ▣ beijar apaixonadamente or ▣ longa troca de carícias e beijos f

snooker /'snuːkə(r)/ n snooker m, sinuca f

snoop /snuːp/ vi ▣ bisbilhotar; meter o nariz em toda a parte; **~ on** espiar, espionar

snooty | socialist

602

snooty /'snu:tɪ/ a (-ier, -iest) ▣ convencido; arrogante

snooze /snu:z/ n ▣ soneca f ▣ ● vi ▣ tirar or (P) fazer uma soneca

snore /snɔ:(r)/ n ronco m ● vi roncar, (P) ressonar

snorkel /'snɔ:kl/ n tubo m de respiração, snorkel m

snort /snɔ:t/ n resfôlego m, bufido m ● vi resfolegar, bufar

snout /snaʊt/ n focinho m

snow /snəʊ/ n neve f ● vi nevar; **be ~ed under** fig (be overwhelmed) estar sobrecarregado de fig. **~board** n snowboard m; **~drift** n banco m de neve; **~plough** n limpa-neve m. **~y** a nevado, coberto de neve

snowball /'snəʊbɔ:l/ n bola f de neve ● vi atirar bolas de neve (em); fig acumular-se; ir num crescendo; aumentar rapidamente

snowdrop /'snəʊdrɒp/ n Bot fura-neve m

snowfall /'snəʊfɔ:l/ n nevada f, (P) nevão m

snowflake /'snəʊfleɪk/ n floco m de neve

snowman /'snəʊmæn/ n (pl -men) boneco m de neve

snub /snʌb/ vt (pt snubbed) desdenhar, tratar com desdém ● n desdém m

snuffle /'snʌfl/ vi fungar

snug /snʌg/ a (snugger, snuggest) (cosy) aconchegado; (close-fitting) justo

snuggle /'snʌgl/ vt/i (nestle) aninhar-se, aconchegar-se; (cuddle) aconchegar

so /səʊ/ adv tão, de tal modo; (thus) assim, deste modo ● conj por isso, portanto, por consequinte; **~ am I** eu também; **~ does he** ele

também; **that is ~** é isso; **I think ~** acho que sim; **five or ~** uns cinco; **~ as to** de modo a; **~ far** até agora, até aqui; **~ long!** até já! ▣; **~ many** tantos; **~ much** tanto; **~ that** para que, de modo que; **~-and-** fulano m. **~-called** a pretenso, soi-disant, chamado; **~-so** a & adv assim assim, mais ou menos

soak /səʊk/ vt/i molhar(-se), ensopar(-se), encharcar(-se); **leave to ~** pôr de molho; **~ through** repassar □ **~ in**, **~ up** vt absorver, embeber. **~ing** a ensopado, encharcado

soap /səʊp/ n sabão. m; (toilet) ~ sabonete m vt ensaborar; **~ opera** Radio novela f radiofônica, (P) radiofónica; TV telenovela f; **~ flakes** flocos mpl de sabão; **~ powder** sabão m em pó. **~y** a ensaboado

soar /sɔ:(r)/ vi voar alto; (go high) elevar-se; (hover) pairar

sob /sɒb/ n soluço m ● vi (pt sobbed) soluçar

sober /'səʊbə(r)/ a (not drunk, calm, of colour) sóbrio; (serious) sério, grave ● vt/i **~ up** (fazer) ficar sóbrio ▣, (fazer) curar a bebedeira ▣

soccer /'sɒkə(r)/ n ▣ futebol m

sociable /'səʊʃəbl/ a sociável

social /'səʊʃl/ a social; (sociable) sociável; ‹gathering, life› de sociedade; **~ security** previdência f social, (P) segurança f social; (for old age) pensão f, (P) reforma f; **~ worker** assistente mf social ● n reunião f social. **~ media** n mídia m social, (P) meios mpl de comunicação social; **~ networking site** n rede f social. **~ly** adv socialmente; (meet) em sociedade

socialis|t /'səʊʃəlɪst/ n socialista mf. **~m** /-zəm/ n socialismo m

socialize /'səʊʃəlaɪz/ vi socializar(-se), reunir-se em sociedade; ~ **with** frequentar, conviver com

society /sə'saɪətɪ/ n sociedade f

sociolog|y /səʊsɪ'ɒlədʒɪ/ n sociologia f. ~**ist** n sociólogo m

sock[1] /sɒk/ n meia f curta; (men's) meia f (curta), (P) peúga f; (women's) soquete f

sock[2] /sɒk/ vt ✗ (hit) esmurrar; dar um murro em 🆃

socket /'sɒkɪt/ n cavidade f; (for lamp) suporte m; Electr tomada f; (of tooth) alvéolo m

soda /'səʊdə/ n soda f; (baking) ~ Culin bicarbonato m de soda; ~(-**water**) água f gasosa, soda f limonada, (P) água f gaseificada

sodden /'sɒdn/ a ensopado, empapado

sodium /'səʊdɪəm/ n sódio m

sofa /'səʊfə/ n sofá m

soft /sɒft/ a (-**er**, -**est**) (not hard, feeble) mole; (not rough, not firm) macio; (gentle, not loud, not bright) suave; (tender-hearted) sensível; ‹fruit› sem caroço; ‹wood› de coníferas; ‹drink› não-alcoólico; ~ **spot** fig fraco m. ~**ness** n moleza f; (to touch) maciez f; (gentleness) suavidade f, brandura f

soften /'sɒfn/ vt/i amaciar, amolecer; (tone down, lessen) abrandar

software /'sɒftweə(r)/ n software m

soggy /'sɒgɪ/ a (-**ier**, -**iest**) ensopado, empapado

soil[1] /sɔɪl/ n solo m, terra f

soil[2] /sɔɪl/ vt/i sujar(-se). ~**ed** a sujo

solace /'sɒlɪs/ n consolo m; (relief) alívio m

solar /'səʊlə(r)/ a solar

sold /səʊld/ ▶ SELL a ~ **out** esgotado

soldier /'səʊldʒə(r)/ n soldado m ● vi ~ **on** 🆃 perseverar com afinco, batalhar 🆃

sole[1] /səʊl/ n (of foot) planta f, sola f do pé; (of shoe) sola f

sole[2] /səʊl/ n (fish) solha f

sole[3] /səʊl/ a único. ~**ly** adv unicamente

solemn /'sɒləm/ a solene

solicit /sə'lɪsɪt/ vt (seek) solicitar ● vi (of prostitute) aproximar-se de homens na rua, angariar clientes

solicitor /sə'lɪsɪtə(r)/ n advogado m

solicitous /sə'lɪsɪtəs/ a solícito

solid /'sɒlɪd/ a sólido; (not hollow) maciço, cheio, compacto; ‹gold etc› maciço; ‹meal› substancial ● n sólido m; ~**s** (food) alimentos mpl sólidos

solidarity /sɒlɪ'dærətɪ/ n solidariedade f

solidify /sə'lɪdɪfaɪ/ vt/i solidificar(-se)

solitary /'sɒlɪtrɪ/ a solitário, só; (only one) um único; ~ **confinement** prisão f celular, solitária f

solitude /'sɒlɪtjuːd/ n solidão f

solo /'səʊləʊ/ n (pl **os**) solo m ● a solo; ~ **flight** voo m (a) solo. ~**ist** n solista m

soluble /'sɒljʊbl/ a solúvel

solution /sə'luːʃn/ n solução f

solv|e /sɒlv/ vt resolver, solucionar. ~**able** a resolúvel, solúvel

solvent /'sɒlvənt/ a (dis)solvente; Comm solvente ● n (dis)solvente m

sombre /'sɒmbə(r)/ a sombrio

some /sʌm/ ● a

••••▸ (*unspecified number*) uns, umas; **he ate ~ olives** ele comeu umas azeitonas; **have ~ more vegetables** coma mais uns vegetais; (*unspecified amount*) algum(a); **there's still ~ milk in the fridge** ainda há algum leite no congelador; **I need to buy ~ bread** preciso comprar pão; **would you like ~ coffee?** quer café?

••••▸ (*certain, not all*) alguns, algumas; **~ people say...** algumas pessoas dizem...; **I like ~ modern writers** gosto de alguns escritores modernos

••••▸ (*indefinite*) um(a)... qualquer, uns... quaisquer, umas... quaisquer; **~ man came to the house** um homem entrou na casa; **there must be ~ mistake** deve haver um erro qualquer; **for ~ reason** por algum motivo; **~ day next week** algum dia da semana que vem

••••▸ (*considerable amount*) **we've known each other for ~ time** nos conhecemos há algum tempo

● *pron*

••••▸ (*part of an amount*) um pouco; **would you like ~?** quer um pouco?; **if you want sugar, I'll give you** se quiser açúcar, lhe dou um pouco

••••▸ (*a number of*) alguns, algumas; **here are ~ of our suggestions** aqui estão algumas das nossas sugestões; **~ are mine, but ~ aren't** alguns são meus, mas os outros não

● *adv*

••••▸ (*approximately*) uns, umas; **~ thirty people attended the funeral** umas trinta pessoas estiveram no funeral

somebody /'sʌmbədi/ *pron* alguém ● *n* **be a ~** ser alguém

somehow /'sʌmhaʊ/ *adv* (*in some way*) de algum modo, de alguma maneira; (*for some reason*) por alguma razão

someone /'sʌmwʌn/ *pron & n* = SOMEBODY

somersault /'sʌməsɔːlt/ *n* cambalhota *f*; (*in the air*) salto *m* mortal ● *vi* dar uma cambalhota/um salto mortal

something /'sʌmθɪŋ/ *pron & n* uma/alguma/qualquer coisa *f*, algo; **~ good/**etc uma coisa boa/etc, qualquer coisa de bom/etc; **~ like** um pouco como

sometime /'sʌmtaɪm/ *adv* a certa altura, um dia ● *a* (*former*) antigo; **~ last summer** a certa altura no verão passado; **I'll go ~** hei-de ir um dia

sometimes /'sʌmtaɪmz/ *adv* às vezes, de vez em quando

somewhat /'sʌmwɒt/ *adv* um pouco, um tanto (ou quanto)

somewhere /'sʌmweə(r)/ *adv* (*position*) em algum lugar; (*direction*) para algum lugar

son /sʌn/ *n* filho *m*. **~-in-law** *n* (*pl* **~s-in-law**) genro *m*

sonata /sə'nɑːtə/ *n* Mus sonata *f*

song /sɒŋ/ *n* canção *f*

soon /suːn/ *adv* (**-er, -est**) em breve, dentro em pouco, daqui a pouco; (*early*) cedo; **as ~ as possible** o mais rápido possível; **I would ~er stay** preferia ficar; **~ after** pouco depois;

~er or later mais cedo ou mais tarde

soot /sʊt/ n fuligem f

sooth|e /suːð/ vt acalmar, suavizar;
‹pain› aliviar. **~ing** a ‹remedy›
calmante, suavizante; ‹words› (re)
confortante

sophisticated /səˈfɪstɪkeɪtɪd/ a
sofisticado, refinado, requintado;
‹machine etc› sofisticado

sopping /ˈsɒpɪŋ/ a encharcado,
ensopado

soppy /ˈsɒpɪ/ a (-ier, -iest) 🔲
(sentimental) piegas; 🔲 (silly) bobo,
(P) tonto

soprano /səˈprɑːnəʊ/ n (pl ~s) & a
soprano mf

sorbet /ˈsɔːbeɪ/ n (water ice) sorvete
m feito sem leite

sorcerer /ˈsɔːsərə(r)/ n feiticeiro m

sordid /ˈsɔːdɪd/ a sórdido

sore /sɔː(r)/ a (-er, -est) dolorido;
(vexed) aborrecido (at, with com)
● n ferida f; **have a ~ throat** ter a
garganta inflamada, ter dores de
garganta

sorely /ˈsɔːlɪ/ adv fortemente,
seriamente

sorry /ˈsɒrɪ/ a (-ier, -iest) (state, sight
etc) triste; **be ~ to/that** (regretful)
sentir muito/que, lamentar que; **be
~ for** (repentant) ter pena de,
estar arrependido de; **feel ~ for** ter
pena de; **~!** desculpe, perdão!

sort /sɔːt/ n gênero m, (P) género
m, espécie f, qualidade f; **of ~s** 🔲
uma espécie de 🔲 pej; **out of ~s**
indisposto ● vt separar por grupos;
(tidy) arrumar; **~ out** ‹problem›
resolver; (arrange, separate) separar,
distribuir

soufflé /ˈsuːfleɪ/ n Culin suflê m,
(P) soufflé m

sought /sɔːt/ ▶ SEEK

soul /səʊl/ n alma f; **the life and ~
of** fig a alma f de fig

soulful /ˈsəʊlfl/ a emotivo,
expressivo, cheio de sentimento

sound[1] /saʊnd/ n som m, barulho
m, ruído m; **~ barrier** barreira f
de/do som ● vt/i soar; (seem) dar
a impressão de; parecer (as if
que); **~ a horn** tocar uma buzina,
buzinar; **~ like** parecer ser, soar
como. **~proof** a à prova de som ● vt
fazer o isolamento sonoro de, isolar;
~track n (of film) trilha f sonora, (P)
banda f sonora

sound[2] /saʊnd/ a (-er, -est)
(healthy) saudável, sadio; (sensible)
sensato, acertado; (secure) firme,
sólido; **~ asleep** profundamente
adormecido. **~ly** adv solidamente

sound[3] /saʊnd/ vt (test) sondar;
Med (views) auscultar

soup /suːp/ n sopa f

sour /ˈsaʊə(r)/ a (-er, -est) azedo
● vt/i azedar, envinagrar

source /sɔːs/ n fonte f; (of river)
nascente f

south /saʊθ/ n sul m ● a sul, do sul;
(of country, people etc) meridional;
S~ Africa/America África/América
do Sul f ● adv a, ao/para (o) sul. **S~
African/American** a & n sul-africano/
sul-americano m; **~east** n sudeste
m; **~ward** a do sudeste m. **~erly**
/ˈsʌðəlɪ/ a do sul, meridional.
~ward(s) adv para (o) sul

southern /ˈsʌðən/ a do sul,
meridional, austral

souvenir /suːvəˈnɪə(r)/ n
recordação f, lembrança f

sovereign /ˈsɒvrɪn/ n & a soberano
m. **~ty** n soberania f

Soviet /ˈsəʊvɪət/ a soviético; **the ~
Union** a União Soviética

sow[1] /səʊ/ vt (pt sowed, pp sowed or sown) semear

sow[2] /saʊ/ n Zool porca f

soy /sɔɪ/ n ~ sauce molho m de soja

soya /'sɔɪə/ n soja f; ~bean semente f de soja

spa /spɑː/ n termas fpl

space /speɪs/ n espaço m; (room) lugar m; (period) espaço m, período m ● a <research etc> espacial ● vt ~ out espaçar

space|craft /'speɪskrɑːft/ n (pl invar) ~ship n nave f espacial

spacious /'speɪʃəs/ a espaçoso

spade /speɪd/ n (gardener's) pá f de ferro; (child's) pá f; ~s Cards espadas fpl

spaghetti /spə'getɪ/ n espaguete m, (P) esparguete m

Spain /speɪn/ n Espanha f

spam /spæm/ n Spam® Culin marca barata de carne de porco enlatada; Comput spam m ● vt (pres p etc. -mm-) enviar spam

span[1] /spæn/ n (of arch) vão m; (of wings) envergadura f; (of time) espaço m, duração f; (measure) palmo m ● vt (pt spanned) (extend across) transpor; (measure) medir em palmos; (in time) abarcar, abranger, estender-se por

span[2] /spæn/ ▶ SPIN

Spaniard /'spænɪəd/ n espanhol m

Spanish /'spænɪʃ/ a espanhol ● n Lang espanhol m

spank /spæŋk/ vt dar palmadas or chineladas em. ~ing n (with hand) palmada f; (with slipper) chinelada f

spanner /'spænə(r)/ n (tool) chave f de porcas; (adjustable) chave f inglesa

spar /spɑː(r)/ vi (pt sparred) jogar boxe, esp para treino; fig (argue) discutir

spare /speə(r)/ vt (not hurt; use with restraint) poupar; (afford to give) dispensar, ceder; **have an hour to** ~ dispor de uma hora; **have no time to** ~ não ter tempo a perder ● a (in reserve) de reserva, de sobra; <tyre> sobressalente; <bed> extra; <room> de hóspedes ● n (part) sobressalente m; ~ **time** horas fpl vagas, tempo m livre

sparing /'speərɪŋ/ a poupado; **be** ~ **of** poupar em, ser poupado com. ~ly adv frugalmente

spark /spɑːk/ n centelha f, faísca f ● vt lançar faíscas; ~ **off** (initiate) desencadear, provocar

sparkle /'spɑːkl/ vi cintilar, brilhar ● n brilho m, cintilação f

sparkling /'spɑːklɪŋ/ a <wine> espumante

sparrow /'spærəʊ/ n pardal m

sparse /spɑːs/ a esparso; <hair> ralo. ~ly adv <furnished etc> escassamente

spasm /'spæzəm/ n (of muscle) espasmo m; (of coughing, anger etc) ataque m, acesso m

spasmodic /spæz'mɒdɪk/ a espasmódico; (at irregular intervals) intermitente

spastic /'spæstɪk/ n deficiente mf motor

spat /spæt/ ▶ SPIT[1]

spate /speɪt/ n (in river) enxurrada f, cheia f; **a** ~ **of** <letters etc> uma avalanche de

spatter /'spætə(r)/ vt salpicar (with de, com)

spawn /spɔːn/ n ovas fpl ● vi desovar ● vt gerar em quantidade

speak /spiːk/ *vt/i* (*pt* **spoke**, *pp* **spoken**) falar (**to/with sb about sth** com alguém de/sobre alg coisa); (*say*) dizer; ~ **out/up** falar abertamente; (*louder*) falar mais alto; ~ **one's mind** dizer o que se pensa; **so to** ~ por assim dizer; **English/Portuguese spoken** fala-se inglês/português

speaker /'spiːkə(r)/ *n* (*in public*) orador *m*; (*loudspeaker*) alto-falante *m*; (*of a language*) pessoa *f* de língua nativa, falante *mf* nativo/a de uma língua

spear /spɪə(r)/ *n* lança *f*

spearhead /'spɪəhed/ *n* ponta *f* de lança ● *vt* (*lead*) estar à frente de, encabeçar

special /'speʃl/ *a* especial. ~**ity** /-ɪ'ælətɪ/ *n* especialidade *f*. ~**ly** *adv* especialmente. ~**ty** *n* especialidade *f*

specialist /'speʃəlɪst/ *n* especialista *mf*

specialize /'speʃəlaɪz/ *vi* especializar-se (**in** em). ~**d** *a* especializado

species /'spiːʃiːz/ *n* (*pl invar*) espécie *f*

specific /spə'sɪfɪk/ *a* específico. ~**ally** *adv* especificamente, explicitamente

specif|**y** /'spesɪfaɪ/ *vt* especificar. ~**ication** /-ɪ'keɪʃn/ *n* especificação *f*. ~**ications** *npl* (*of work etc*) caderno *m* de encargos

specimen /'spesɪmɪn/ *n* espécime(n) *m*, amostra *f*

speck /spek/ *n* (*stain*) mancha *f* pequena; (*dot*) pontinho *m*, pinta *f*; (*particle*) grão *m*

speckled /'spekld/ *a* salpicado, manchado

specs /speks/ *npl* 🄸 óculos *mpl*

spectacle /'spektəkl/ *n* espetáculo *m*; (**pair of**) ~**s** (**par** *m* de) óculos *mpl*

spectacular /spek'tækjʊlə(r)/ *a* espetacular

spectator /spek'teɪtə(r)/ *n* espectador *m*

spectrum /'spektrəm/ *n* (*pl* -**tra**) espectro *m*; (*of ideas etc*) faixa *f*, gama *f*, leque *m*

speculat|**e** /'spekjʊlert/ *vi* especular; fazer especulações or conjecturas; (*P*) conjectura *f*; *Comm* especular; fazer especulação (**in** em). ~**ion** /-'leɪʃn/ *n* especulação *f*, conjectura *f*; *Comm* especulação *f*. ~**or** *n* especulador *m*

speech /spiːtʃ/ *n* (*faculty*) fala *f*; (*diction*) elocução *f*; (*dialect*) falar *m*; (*address*) discurso *m*. ~**less** *a* mudo; sem fala, (*P*) sem palavras (**with** com, de)

speed /spiːd/ *n* velocidade *f*, rapidez *f* ● *vt/i* (*pt* **sped**, **move**) (*send*) despedir, mandar; (*drive too fast*) ultrapassar o limite de velocidade; (*drive too fast*) ultrapassar o limite de velocidade; ~ **camera** radar *m*; ~ **limit** limite *m* de velocidade; ~ **up** acelerar(-se). ~ **dating** *n*: forma rápida de conhecer vários possíveis namorados, através de conversas breves; ~ **dial** *n* discagem *f* rápida, (*P*) marcação *f* rápida. ~**ing** *n* excesso *m* de velocidade

speedometer /spiː'dɒmɪtə(r)/ *n* velocímetro *m*

speed|**y** /'spiːdɪ/ *a* (-**ier**, -**iest**) rápido; (*prompt*) pronto. ~**ily** *adv* rapidamente; (*promptly*) prontamente

spell[1] /spel/ *n* (*magic*) sortilégio *m*

spell[2] /spel/ *vt/i* (*pt* **spelled**, *or* **spelt**) escrever; *fig* (*mean*) significar; ter como resultado; ~ **out** soletrar; *fig* (*explain*) explicar claramente. ~**ing** n ortografia f

spell³ /spel/ n (*short period*) período m curto, breve espaço m de tempo; (*turn*) turno m

spend /spend/ vt (*pt* **spent**) ‹*money, energy*› gastar (**on** em); ‹*time, holiday*› passar

spendthrift /ˈspendθrɪft/ n perdulário m, esbanjador m

spent /spent/ ▶ SPEND a (*used*) gasto

sperm /spɜːm/ n (*pl* ~**s** or ~) (*semen*) esperma m, sêmen m, (P) sémen m; (*cell*) espermatozóide m

spew /spjuː/ vt/i vomitar, lançar

sphere /sfɪə(r)/ n esfera f

spic|e /spaɪs/ n especiaria f, condimento m; fig picante m ● vt condimentar. ~**y** a condimentado; fig picante

spider /ˈspaɪdə(r)/ n aranha f

spik|e /spaɪk/ n (*of metal etc*) bico m, espigão m, ponta f. ~**y** a guarnecido de bicos ou pontas, pontiagudo

spill /spɪl/ vt/i (*pt* **spilled**, or **spilt**) derramar(-se), entornar(-se), espalhar(-se); ~ **over** transbordar, extravasar

spin /spɪn/ vt/i (*pt* **spun**, *pres p* **spinning**) ‹*wool, cotton*› fiar; ‹*web*› tecer; ‹*turn*› (fazer) girar, (fazer) rodopiar; ~ **out** ‹*money, story*› fazer durar; ‹*time*› (fazer) parar ● n volta f; Aviat parafuso m; **go for a** ~ dar uma volta ou um giro or (P) um passeio. ~ **drier** n centrifugadora f para a roupa, secadora f, (P) máquina f de secar (a roupa); ~**off** n bônus m, (P) bónus m inesperado; (*by-product*) derivado m

spinach /ˈspɪnɪdʒ/ n (*plant*) espinafre m; (*as food*) espinafres mpl

spindl|e /ˈspɪndl/ n roca f, fuso m; Mech eixo m. ~**y** a alto e magro; (*of plant*) espigado

spine /spaɪn/ n espinha f, coluna f vertebral; (*prickle*) espinho m, pico m; (*of book*) lombada f

spineless /ˈspaɪnlɪs/ a fig (*cowardly*) covarde; sem fibra fig

spinster /ˈspɪnstə(r)/ n solteira f; pej solteirona f

spiral /ˈspaɪərəl/ a (em) espiral; (*staircase*) em caracol ● n espiral f ● vi (*pt* **spiralled**) subir em espiral

spire /ˈspaɪə(r)/ n agulha f, flecha f

spirit /ˈspɪrɪt/ n espírito m; (*boldness*) coragem f, brio m; ~**s** (*morale*) moral m, (*drink*) bebidas fpl alcoólicas; **in high** ~**s** alegre ● vt ~ **away** dar sumiço em, arrebatar

spirited /ˈspɪrɪtɪd/ a fogoso; ‹*attack, defence*› vigoroso, enérgico

spiritual /ˈspɪrɪtʃʊəl/ a espiritual

spiritualism /ˈspɪrɪtʃʊəlɪzəm/ n espiritismo m

spit¹ /spɪt/ vt/i (*pt* **spat**, or **spit**, *pres p* **spitting**) cuspir; (*of rain*) chuviscar; (*of cat*) bufar ● n cuspe m, (P) cuspo m; **the** ~**ting image of** o retrato vivo de, a cara chapada de 🔲

spit² /spɪt/ n (*for meat*) espeto m; (*of land*) restinga f, (P) língua f de terra

spite /spaɪt/ n má vontade f, despeito m, rancor m ● vt aborrecer, mortificar. **in** ~ **of** a despeito de, apesar de. ~**ful** a rancoroso, maldoso

splash /splæʃ/ vt salpicar, respingar ● vi esparrinhar, salpicar, esparramar(-se); ~ (**about**) chapinhar ● n (*act, mark*) salpico m; (*sound*) chape m; (*of colour*) mancha f; **make**

a ~ (*striking display*) fazer um vistão, causar furor

splendid /ˈsplendɪd/ a esplêndido, magnífico; (*excellent*) estupendo ⬚; ótimo

splendour /ˈsplendə(r)/ n esplendor m

splint /splɪnt/ n Med tala f

splinter /ˈsplɪntə(r)/ n lasca f, estilhaço m; (*under the skin*) farpa f, lasca f ● vi estilhaçar-se, lascar-se; **~ group** grupo m dissidente

split /splɪt/ vt/i (*pt* **split**, *pres p* **splitting**) rachar, fender(-se); (*divide, share*) dividir; (*tear*) romper(-se) ● n racha f, fenda f; (*share*) quinhão m, parte f; Pol cisão f ● **~ on** (*inform on*) denunciar; **~ one's sides** rebentar de riso, (P) desmanchar-se a rir; **~ up** (*of couple*) separar-se; **a ~ second** uma fração de segundo; **~ting headache** dor f de cabeça forte

splurge /splɜːdʒ/ n ⬚ espalhafato m; estardalhaço m ● vi ⬚ (*spend*) gastar os tubos, (P) gastar à doida ⬚

splutter /ˈsplʌtə(r)/ vi falar cuspindo; ‹*engine*› cuspir; ‹*fat*› crepitar

spoil /spɔɪl/ vt (*pt* **spoilt** *or* **spoiled**) estragar; (*pamper*) mimar ● n **~(s)** (*plunder*) despojo(s) m(pl), espólios mpl. **~sport** n desmancha-prazeres mf invar. **~t** a (*pampered*) mimado, estragado com mimos

spoke[1] /spəʊk/ n raio m

spoke[2] **spoken** /spəʊk, ˈspəʊkən/ ▶ SPEAK

spokes|man /ˈspəʊksmən/ n (*pl* -men); **~woman** n (*pl*-women) porta-voz mf

sponge /spʌndʒ/ n esponja f ● vt (*clean*) lavar com esponja; (*wipe*)

limpar com esponja ● vi **~ on** ⬚ (*cadge*) viver à(s) custa(s) de. **~ bag** n bolsa f de toalete; **~ cake** n pão de ló m. **~r** /-ə(r)/ n ⬚ parasita mf ⬚

sponsor /ˈspɒnsə(r)/ n patrocinador m; (*for membership*) (sócio) proponente m ● vt patrocinar; (*for membership*) propor. **~ship** n patrocínio m

spontaneous /spɒnˈteɪnɪəs/ a espontâneo

spoof /spuːf/ n ⬚ paródia f

spooky /ˈspuːkɪ/ a (-ier, -lest) ⬚ fantasmagórico; que dá arrepios

spool /spuːl/ n (*of sewing machine*) bobina f; (*for thread, line*) carretel m, (P) carrinho m

spoon /spuːn/ n colher f. **~feed** vt (*pt* -fed) alimentar de colher; *fig* (*help*) dar na bandeja para *fig*, (P) dar de bandeja a *fig*. **~ful** n colherada f

sporadic /spəˈrædɪk/ a esporádico, acidental

sport /spɔːt/ n esporte m, (P) desporto m; **(good) ~** 🗙 (*person*) gente f fina, (P) bom tipo m, (P) tipo m fixe ⬚. **~s car/coat** carro m /casaco m esporte or (P) de desporto ● vt (*display*) exibir, ostentar. **~y** a ⬚ esportivo; (P) desportivo

sporting /ˈspɔːtɪŋ/ a esportivo, (P) desportivo; **a ~ chance** uma certa possibilidade de sucesso, uma boa chance

sports|man /ˈspɔːtsmən/ n (*pl* -men); **~woman** n (*pl* women) desportista mf. **~manship** n (*spirit*) espírito m esportivo, (P) desportivo; (*activity*) esportismo m, (P) desportismo m

spot /spɒt/ n (*mark, stain*) mancha f; (*in pattern*) pinta f, bola f; (*drop*) gota f; (*place*) lugar m, ponto m;

(*pimple*) borbulha f, espinha f; TV spot m televisivo; **a ~ of** 🔢 um pouco de; **be in a ~** 🔢 estar numa encrenca 🔢, (P) estar metido numa alhada 🔢; **on the ~** no local; (*there and then*) ali mesmo, logo ali ● vt (*pt* **spotted**) manchar; 🔢 (*detect*) descobrir; detectar 🔢; **~ check** inspeção f de surpresa; (*of cars*) fiscalização f de surpresa; **~ on a** 🔢 certo, exacto. **~ted** a manchado; (*with dots*) de pintas, de bolas; (*animal*) malhado; **~ty** a (*with pimples*) com borbulhas

spotless /'spɒtlɪs/ a impecável, imaculado

spotlight /'spɒtlaɪt/ n foco m; Cine, Theat refletor m, holofote m

spouse /spaʊz/ n cônjuge mf, esposo m

spout /spaʊt/ n (*of vessel*) bico m; (*of liquid*) esguicho m, jorro m; (*pipe*) cano m ● vi jorrar, esguichar; **up the ~** 🗵 (*ruined*) liquidado 🗵 (P) acabado

sprain /spreɪn/ n entorse f, mau jeito m ● vt torcer, dar um mau jeito a

sprang /spræŋ/ ▶ **SPRING**

sprawl /sprɔːl/ vi (*sit*) estirar-se, esparramar-se; (*fall*) estatelar-se; ‹*town*› estender-se, espraiar-se

spray¹ /spreɪ/ n (*of flowers*) raminho m, ramalhete m

spray² /spreɪ/ n (*water*) borrifo m, salpico m; (*from sea*) borrifo m de espuma; (*device*) bomba f, aerossol m; (*for perfume*) vaporizador m, atomizador m ● vt aspergir, borrifar, pulverizar; (*with insecticide*) pulverizar

spread /spred/ vt/i (*pt* **spread**) (*extend, stretch*) estender(-se); ‹*news, fear, illness etc*› alastrar(-se),

espalhar(-se), propagar(-se); ‹*butter etc*› passar, (P) barrar; ‹*wings*› abrir ● n (*expanse*) expansão f, extensão f; (*spreading*) propagação f; (*paste*) pasta f para passar no pão, (P) para barrar no pão; 🔢 (*meal*) banquete m. **~sheet** n Comput folha f de cálculo

spree /spriː/ n **go on a ~** 🔢 cair na farra, (P) ir para a farra

sprightly /'spraɪtlɪ/ a (**-ier, -iest**) vivo, animado

spring /sprɪŋ/ vi (*pt* **sprang**, *pp* **sprung**) (*arise*) nascer; (*jump*) saltar, pular; **~ up** surgir ● vt (*produce suddenly*) sair-se com; (*a surprise*) fazer (**on sb** a alguém); **~ from** vir de, originar-se de, provir de ● n salto m, pulo m; (*device*) mola f; (*season*) primavera f; (*of water*) fonte f, nascente f; **~ onion** cebolinha f. **~clean** vt fazer limpeza geral

springboard /'sprɪŋbɔːd/ n trampolim m

springtime /'sprɪŋtaɪm/ n primavera f

springy /'sprɪŋɪ/ a (**-ier, -iest**) elástico

sprinkle /'sprɪŋkl/ vt (*with liquid*) borrifar, salpicar; (*with salt, flour*) polvilhar (**with** de); **~ sand** /etc espalhar areia/etc. **~r** /-ə(r)/ n (*in garden*) regador m; (*for fires*) sprinkler m

sprinkling /'sprɪŋklɪŋ/ n (*amount*) pequena quantidade f; (*number*) pequeno número m

sprint /sprɪnt/ n Sport corrida f de pequena distância, sprint m ● vi correr em sprint or a toda a velocidade; Sport correr

sprout /spraʊt/ vt/i brotar, germinar; (*put forth*) deitar ● n (*on plant etc*) broto m; (**Brussels**) **~s**

couves *f* de Bruxelas

sprung /sprʌŋ/ ▶ SPRING *a*
‹*mattress etc*› de molas

spry /spraɪ/ *a* (spryer, spryest)
vivo, ativo; (*nimble*) ágil

spud /spʌd/ *n* 🄧 batata *f*

spun /spʌn/ ▶ SPIN

spur /spɜ:(r)/ *n* (*of rider*) espora *f*;
fig (*stimulus*) aguilhão *m*; *fig* espora
f fig ● *vt* (*pt* **spurred**) esporear, picar
com esporas; (*incite*) aguilhoar,
esporear; **on the ~ of the moment**
impulsivamente, no calor do
momento

spurn /spɜ:n/ *vt* desdenhar,
desprezar, rejeitar

spurt /spɜ:t/ *vi* jorrar, esguichar; *fig*
(*accelerate*) acelerar subitamente;
dar um arranco súbito ● *n* jorro
m, esguicho *m*; (*of energy, speed*)
arranco *m*, arrancada *f*, surto *m*

spy /spaɪ/ *n* espião *m* ● *vt* (*make
out*) avistar, descortinar ● *vi* ~ (**on**)
espiar, espionar; ~ **out** descobrir.
~**ing** *n* espionagem *f*

squabble /'skwɒbl/ *vi* discutir,
brigar ● *n* briga *f*, disputa *f*

squad /skwɒd/ *n* Mil pelotão *m*;
(*team*) equipe *f*, (P) equipa *f*; **firing ~**
pelotão *m* de fuzilamento; **flying ~**
brigada *f* móvel

squadron /'skwɒdrən/ *n* Mil
esquadrão *m*; Aviat esquadrilha *f*;
Naut esquadra *f*

squal|id /'skwɒlɪd/ *a* esquálido,
sórdido. ~**or** *n* sordidez *f*

squall /skwɔ:l/ *n* borrasca *f*

squander /'skwɒndə(r)/ *vt*
desperdiçar

square /skweə(r)/ *n* quadrado *m*,
(*in town*) largo *m*, praça *f*, (*T-square*)
régua-tê *f*; (*set square*) esquadro *m*;
go back to ~ one recomeçar tudo
do princípio, voltar à estaca zero
● *a* (*of shape*) quadrado; ‹*metre,
mile etc*› quadrado; (*honest*) direito,
honesto; (*of meal*) abundante,
substancial; **(all) ~** (*quits*) quite(s);
~ **brackets** parênteses *mpl* retos
● *vt* Math elevar ao quadrado;
(*settle*) acertar; ~ **up to** enfrentar
● *vi* (*agree*) concordar. ~**ly** *adv*
diretamente; (*fairly*) honestamente

squash /skwɒʃ/ *vt* (*crush*) esmagar;
(*squeeze*) espremer; (*crowd*)
comprimir, apertar ● *n* (*game*)
squash *m*; Amer (*marrow*) abóbora
f; **lemon ~** limonada *f*; **orange ~**
laranjada *f*. ~**y** *a* mole

squat /skwɒt/ *vi* (*pt* **squatted**)
acocorar-se, agachar-se; (*be a
squatter*) ser ocupante ilegal
● *a* (*dumpy*) atarracado. ~**ter** *n*
ocupante *mf* ilegal de casa vazia,
posseiro *m*

squawk /skwɔ:k/ *n* grasnido *m*,
crocito *m* ● *vi* grasnar, crocitar

squeak /skwi:k/ *n* guincho *m*, chio
m; (*of door, shoes etc*) rangido *m* ● *vi*
guinchar, chiar; (*of door, shoes etc*)
ranger. ~**y** *a* ‹*shoe etc*› que range;
‹*voice*› esganiçado

squeal /skwi:l/ *vi* dar gritos
agudos, guinchar ● *n* grito *m* agudo,
guincho *m*; ~ (**on**) 🄧 (*inform on*)
delatar, (P) denunciar

squeamish /'skwi:mɪʃ/ *a*
(*nauseated*) que enjoa à toa,
impressionável, delicado

squeeze /skwi:z/ *vt* ‹*lemon, sponge
etc*› espremer; ‹*hand, arm*› apertar;
(*extract*) arrancar, extorquir (**from**
de) ● *vi* (*force one's way*) passar à
força, meter-se por ● *n* aperto *m*,
apertão *m*; (*hug*) abraço *m*; Comm
restrições *fpl* de crédito

squid /skwɪd/ *n* lula *f*

squiggle /'skwɪgl/ n rabisco m, floreado m

squint /skwɪnt/ vi ser estrábico or vesgo; (with half-shut eyes) franzir os olhos, (P) semicerrar os olhos ● n Med estrabismo m

squirm /skwɜ:m/ vi (re)torcer-se, contorcer-se

squirrel /'skwɪrəl/ n esquilo m

squirt /skwɜ:t/ vt/i esguichar ● n esguicho m

stab /stæb/ vt (pt stabbed) apunhalar; (knife) esfaquear ● n punhalada f, (with knife) facada f, (of pain) pontada f, T (attempt) tentativa f

stabilize /'steɪbəlaɪz/ vt estabilizar

stab|le[1] /'steɪbl/ a (-er, -est) estável. ~ility /stə'bɪləti/ n estabilidade f

stable[2] /'steɪbl/ n cavalariça f, estrebaria f

stack /stæk/ n pilha f, montão m; (of hay etc) meda f ● vt ~ (up) empilhar, amontoar

stadium /'steɪdɪəm/ n estádio m

staff /stɑ:f/ n pessoal m; (in school) professores mpl; Mil estado-maior m; (stick) bordão m, cajado m; (pl staves) Mus pauta f ● vt prover de pessoal

stag /stæg/ n veado (macho) m, cervo m. ~ party n T reunião f masculina; (before wedding) despedida f de solteiro

stage /steɪdʒ/ n Theat palco m; (phase) fase f, ponto m; (platform in hall) estrado m; **go on the** ~ seguir a carreira teatral, ir para teatro T; ~ **door** entrada f dos artistas ● vt encenar, pôr em cena; fig (organize) organizar. ~**fright** n nervosismo m, medo m do palco

stagger /'stægə(r)/ vi vacilar, cambalear ● vt (shock) atordoar, chocar; (holidays etc) escalonar. ~**ing** a atordoador, chocante

stagnant /'stægnənt/ a estagnado, parado

stagnat|e /stæg'neɪt/ vi estagnar. ~ion f escadaria f

stain /steɪn/ vt manchar, pôr nódoa em; (colour) tingir, dar cor a ● n mancha f, nódoa f; (colouring) corante m; ~**ed glass window** vitral m; ~**less steel** aço m inoxidável

stair /steə(r)/ n degrau m; ~**s** escada(s) f(pl)

stair|case /'steəkeɪs/, ~**way** /-weɪ/ ns escada(s) f(pl), escadaria f

stake /steɪk/ n (post) estaca f, poste m; (wager) parada f, aposta f; **at** ~ em jogo; **have a** ~ **in** ter interesse em ● vt (area) demarcar, delimitar; (wager) jogar, apostar; ~ **a claim to** reivindicar

stale /steɪl/ a (-er, -est) estragado, velho; (bread) duro, mofado; (smell) rançoso; (air) viciado; (news) velho

stalemate /'steɪlmeɪt/ n (chess) empate m; fig (deadlock) impasse m; beco sem saída m

stalk[1] /stɔ:k/ n (of plant) caule m

stalk[2] /stɔ:k/ vi andar com um ar empertigado ● vt (prey) perseguir furtivamente, tocaiar

stall /stɔ:l/ n (in stable) baia f; (in market) banca f, barraca f; ~**s** Theat poltronas fpl de orquestra; Cinema plateia f ● vt/i Auto enguiçar, (P) ir abaixo; ~ **(for time)** ganhar tempo, empatar

stalwart /'stɔ:lwət/ a forte, rijo; (supporter) fiel

stamina /'stæmɪnə/ n resistência f

stammer /'stæmə(r)/ vt/i gaguejar ● n gagueira f, (P) gaguez f

stamp /stæmp/ vt/i — (**one's foot**) bater com o pé (no chão), pisar com força ● vt estampar; ‹letter› estampilhar, selar; (with rubber stamp) carimbar; ~ **out** ‹fire, rebellion etc› esmagar; ‹disease› erradicar ● n estampa f; (for postage) selo m; fig (mark) cunho m; **rubber** ~ carimbo m. ~ **collecting** n filatelia f

stampede /stæm'piːd/ n (scattering) debandada f; (of horses, cattle etc) debandada f; fig (rush) corrida f ● vt/i (fazer) debandar; ‹horses, cattle etc› tresmalhar

stance /stæns/ n posição f, postura f

stand /stænd/ vi (pt stood) estar em pé; (keep upright position) ficar em pé; (rise) levantar-se; (be situated) encontrar-se, ficar, situar-se; Pol candidatar-se (for por); ~ **back** recuar; ~ **by** or **around** estar parado sem fazer nada; ~ **by** (be ready) estar a postos; ‹promise, person› manter-se fiel a; ~ **down** desistir, retirar-se; ~ **out** (be conspicuous) sobressair; ~ **still** estar/ficar imóvel; ~ **still!** não se mexa!, fique, quieto!; ~ **to reason** ser lógico; ~ **up** levantar-se, pôr-se em or de pé ● vt pôr (de pé), colocar; (tolerate) suportar, aguentar; ~ **a chance** ter uma possibilidade; ~ **for** representar, simbolizar; 🇬🇧 (tolerate) aturar; ~ **in for** substituir; ~ **up to** enfrentar ● n posição f, (support) apoio m; Mil resistência f; (at fair) stand m, pavilhão m; (in street) quiosque m; (for spectators) arquibancada f, (P) bancada f; Amer (witness box) banco m das testemunhas. ~**by** a (for emergency) de reserva; ‹ticket›

de stand-by, (P) de reserva ● n (at airport) stand-by m; **on ~by** Mil de prontidão; Med de plantão; ~**in** n substituto m, suplente mf; ~**offish** a 🇬🇧 (aloof) reservado, distante

standard /'stændəd/ n norma f, padrão m; (level) nível m; (flag) estandarte m, bandeira f; ~**s** (morals) princípios mpl; ~ **of living** padrão m de vida, (P) nível de vida ● a regulamentar; (average) standard, normal; ~ **lamp** candeeiro m de pé

standardize /'stændədaɪz/ vt padronizar

standing /'stændɪŋ/ a em pé, de pé invar, ‹army, committee etc› permanente ● n posição f; (reputation) prestígio m; (duration) duração f; ~ **order** (at bank) ordem f permanente, (P) autorização f de pagamento por transferência bancária

standpoint /'stændpɔɪnt/ n ponto m de vista

standstill /'stændstɪl/ n paralisação f; **at a ~** parado, paralisado; **bring/come to a ~** (fazer) parar, paralisar(-se), imobilizar(-se)

stank /stæŋk/ ▶ STINK

staple[1] /'steɪpl/ n (for paper) grampo m, (P) agrafo m ● vt ‹paper› grampear, (P) agrafar. ~**r** /-ə(r)/ n grampeador m, (P) agrafador m

staple[2] /'steɪpl/ a principal, básico ● n Comm artigo m básico

star /stɑː(r)/ n estrela f; (cinema) estrela f, vedete f, (P) vedeta f; (celebrity) celebridade f ● vt (pt starred) (of film) ter no papel principal, (P) ter como ator principal ● vi ~ **in** ser a vedete or (P) vedeta, ter o papel principal em. ~**dom** n celebridade f, estrelato m

starch /stɑːtʃ/ n amido m, fécula f; (for clothes) goma f ● vt pôr em goma, engomar. ~y a (of food) farináceo, feculento; fig (of person) rígido; formal

stare /steə(r)/ vi ~ at olhar fixamente ● n olhar m fixo

stark /stɑːk/ a (-er, -est) (desolate) árido, desolado; (severe) austero, severo; (utter) completo, rematado; ‹fact etc› brutal ● adv completamente; ~ **naked** nu em pelo, (P) em pelota (P)

starling /ˈstɑːlɪŋ/ n estorninho m

starry /ˈstɑːrɪ/ a estrelado. ~-eyed a [T] sonhador; idealista

start /stɑːt/ vt/i começar; ‹machine› ligar, pôr em andamento; ‹fashion etc› lançar; (leave) partir; (cause) causar, provocar; (jump) sobressaltar-se, estremecer; (of car) arrancar, partir ● n começo m, início m; (of race) largada f, partida f; (lead) avanço m; (jump) sobressalto m, estremecimento m; **by fits and ~s** aos arrancos, intermitentemente; **for a ~** para começar; **give sb a ~** sobressaltar alguém, pregar um susto a alguém; ~ **to do** começar a or pôr-se a fazer. ~er n Auto arranque m; (competitor) corredor m; Culin entrada f. ~ing point n ponto de partida

startl|e /ˈstɑːtl/ vt (make jump) sobressaltar, pregar um susto a; (shock) alarmar, chocar. ~ing a alarmante; (surprising) surpreendente

starv|e /stɑːv/ vi (suffer) passar fome; (die) morrer de fome; **be ~ing** [T] (very hungry) ter muita fome, (P) estar esfomeado, morrer de fome [T] ● vt fazer passar fome a; (deprive) privar. ~ation /-ˈveɪʃn/ n fome f

stash /stæʃ/ vt [X] guardar; esconder; enfurnar [T]

state /steɪt/ n estado m, condição f; (pomp) pompa f, gala f; Pol Estado m; **in a ~** muito abalado ● a de Estado, do Estado; ‹school› público; ‹visit etc› oficial ● vt afirmar (**that** que); ‹views› exprimir; (fix) marcar, fixar

stately /ˈsteɪtlɪ/ a (-ier, -iest) majestoso; ~ **home** solar m, palácio m

statement /ˈsteɪtmənt/ n declaração f; (of account) extrato m de conta

> ***i***
> **state school** Na Grã-Bretanha, é um colégio federal de educação gratuita, financiado direta ou indiretamente pelo governo. Inclui educação primária e secundária, colégios especializados, comprehensive schools, etc.

statesman /ˈsteɪtsmən/ n (pl -men) homem m de estado, estadista m

static /ˈstætɪk/ a estático ● n Radio, TV estática f, interferência f

station /ˈsteɪʃn/ n (position) posto m; (rail, bus, radio) estação f; (rank) condição f, posição f social ● vt colocar; ~ed at or in Mil estacionado em. ~ **wagon** n perua f, (P) carrinha f

stationary /ˈsteɪʃnrɪ/ a estacionário, parado, imóvel; ‹vehicle› estacionado, parado

stationer /ˈsteɪʃənə(r)/ n dono de papelaria; ~'s **shop** papelaria f. ~y n artigos mpl de papelaria; (writing paper) papel m de carta

statistic /stəˈtɪstɪk/ n dado m estatístico. ~s n (as a science) estatística f. ~al a estatístico

statue /'stætju:/ n estátua f

stature /'stætʃə(r)/ n estatura f

status /'steɪtəs/ n (pl -uses) situação f, posição f, categoria f; (prestige) prestígio m, importância f, status m; ~ **quo** status quo m; ~ **symbol** símbolo m de status

statut|e /'stætju:t/ n estatuto m, lei f. ~**ory** /-ʊtri/ a estatutário, regulamentar; ‹holiday› legal

staunch /stɔːntʃ/ a (-er, -est) ‹friend› fiel, leal

stave /steɪv/ n Mus pauta f ● vt ~ **off** (keep off) conjurar, evitar; (delay) adiar

stay /steɪ/ vi estar, ficar, permanecer; (dwell temporarily) ficar, alojar-se, hospedar-se; (spend time) demorar-se; ~ **behind** ficar para trás; ~ **in** ficar em casa; ~ **put** 🔲 não se mexer; ~ **up** (late) deitar-se tarde, ficar acordado até tarde ● vt ‹hunger› enganar ● n estada f, visita f, permanência f. ~**ing power** n resistência f

steadfast /'stedfɑːst/ a firme, constante

stead|y /'stedi/ a (-ier, -iest) (stable) estável, firme, seguro; (regular) regular, constante; ‹hand, voice› firme ● vt firmar, fixar, estabilizar; (calm) acalmar; **go ~y with** 🔲 namorar, ter uma relação estável com. ~**ily** adv firmemente, (regularly) regularmente, de modo constante

steak /steɪk/ n bife m

steal /stiːl/ vt/i (pt stole, pp stolen) roubar (**from sb** de alguém); ~ **away/in**/etc sair/entrar/etc furtivamente, esgueirar-se; ~ **the show** pôr os outros na sombra, roubar a atenção de todos

stealth /stelθ/ n **by** ~ furtivamente, na calada, às escondidas. ~**y** a furtivo

steam /stiːm/ n vapor m de água; (on window) condensação f; ~ **iron** ferro m a vapor ● vt (cook) cozinhar a vapor ● vi soltar vapor, fumegar; (move) avançar; ~ **up** ‹window› embaciar. ~ **engine** n máquina f a vapor; (locomotive) locomotiva f a vapor. ~**y** a (heat) úmido, (P) húmido

steamer /'stiːmə(r)/ n (ship) (barco a) vapor m; Culin utensílio m para cozinhar a vapor

steel /stiːl/ n aço m; ~ **industry** siderurgia f ● a de aço ● vpr ~ **o.s.** endurecer-se, fortalecer-se

steep[1] /stiːp/ vt (soak) mergulhar, pôr de molho; (permeate) passar, impregnar; ~**ed in** fig ‹vice, misery etc› mergulhado em; fig ‹knowledge, wisdom etc› impregnado de, repassado de

steep[2] /stiːp/ a (-er, -est) íngreme, escarpado; 🔲 exagerado; exorbitante; ‹slope› subir a pique; ‹price› disparar

steeple /'stiːpl/ n campanário m, torre f

steeplechase /'stiːpltʃeɪs/ n (race) corrida f de obstáculos

steer /stɪə(r)/ vt/i guiar, conduzir, dirigir; ‹ship› governar, (P) comandar; fig guiar; orientar; ~ **clear of** evitar passar perto de. ~**ing** n Auto direção f. ~**ing wheel** n Auto volante m

stem[1] /stem/ n caule m, haste f; (of glass) pé m; (of pipe) boquilha f; (of word) radical m ● vi (pt stemmed) ~ **from** provir de, vir de

stem[2] /stem/ vt (pt stemmed) (check) conter; (stop) estancar

stem cell n célula-tronco f, célula f estaminal

stench /stentʃ/ n mau cheiro m, fedor m

stencil /stensl/ n estênsil m, (P) stencil ● vt (pt stencilled) <document> policopiar

step /step/ vi (pt stepped) ir andar; ~ **down** (resign) demitir-se; ~ **in** (intervene) intervir ● vt ~ **up** aumentar ● n passo m, passada f; (of stair, train) degrau m; (action) medida f, passo m; ~**s** (ladder) escada f; **in** ~ no mesmo passo, a passo certo; fig em conformidade (with com). ~**ladder** n escada f portátil; ~**ping stone** n fig (means to an end) ponte f; trampolim m

step brother /stepbrʌðə(r)/ n meio-irmão m. ~**daughter** n nora f, (P) enteada f. ~**father** n padrasto m. ~**mother** n madrasta f. ~**sister** n meia-irmã f. ~**son** n genro m, (P) enteado m

stereo /steriəʊ/ n (pl -os) estéreo m; (record player etc) equipamento or sistema m estéreo m ● a estéreo invar. ~**phonic** /-ə'fɒnɪk/ a estereofônico, (P) estereofónico

stereotype /steriətaip/ n estereótipo m

sterile /sterail/ a estéril

steriliz|e /sterəlaiz/ vt esterilizar. ~**ation** /-'zeiʃn/ n esterilização f

sterling /stɜːlɪŋ/ n libra f esterlina ● a esterlino; (silver) de lei; fig excelente; de (primeira) qualidade

stern¹ /stɜːn/ a (-er, -est) severo

stern² /stɜːn/ n (of ship) popa f, ré f

stethoscope /steθəskəʊp/ n estetoscópio m

stew /stjuː/ vt/i estufar, guisar; (fruit) cozer ● n ensopado m; ~**ed** fruit compota f

steward /stjʊəd/ n (of club etc) econômo m, (P) ecónomo m; administrador m; (on ship etc) camareiro m (de bordo), (P) comissário m (de bordo). ~**ess** /-'des/ n aeromoça f; (P) assistente f de bordo

stick¹ /stɪk/ n pau m; (for walking) bengala f; (of celery) talo m

stick² /stɪk/ vt (pt stuck) <glue> colar; (thrust) cravar, espetar; 🔲 (put) enfiar, meter; 🔲 (endure) aguentar, aturar, suportar; **be stuck with sb/sth** 🔲 não conseguir descartar-se or livrar-se de alguém/ algo 🔲; ~ **to** <promise> ser fiel a ● vi (pt stuck) <adhere> colar, aderir; (remain) ficar enfiado or metido; (be jammed) emperrar, ficar engatado; **in one's mind** ficar na memória; ~ **up for** 🔲 tomar o partido de, defender ● ~ **out** vt <head> esticar, pôr de fora; <tongue etc> mostrar ● vi (protrude) sobressair. ~**up** n 🔲 assalto à mão armada m; ~**ing plaster** n esparadrapo m, (P) adesivo m

sticker /stɪkə(r)/ n adesivo m, etiqueta f (adesiva)

sticky /stɪkɪ/ a (-ier, -iest) pegajoso; <label, tape> adesivo; <weather> abafado, mormacento

stiff /stɪf/ a (-er, -est) teso, hirto, rígido; <limb, joint> (hard) duro; (unbending) inflexível; <price> elevado; puxado 🔲; <penalty> severo; <drink> forte; <manner> reservado, formal; **be bored/ scared** ~ 🔲 estar muito aborrecido/ com muito medo, 🔲 estar morto de aborrecimento/medo; ~ **neck** torcicolo m. ~**ness** n rigidez f

stiffen /'stɪfn/ vt/i (harden)
endurecer; <limb, joint> emperrar

stifle /'staɪfl/ vt/i abafar, sufocar.
~ing a sufocante

stigma /'stɪgmə/ n estigma m.
~tize vt estigmatizar

stiletto /stɪ'letəʊ/ n (pl -os) estilete
m. **~ heel** n salto m alto fino

still[1] /stɪl/ a imóvel, quieto; (quiet)
sossegado; **~ life** natureza f morta
● n silêncio m, sossego m ● adv
ainda; (nevertheless) apesar disso,
apesar de tudo; **keep ~!** fique
quieto!, não se mexa!

still[2] /stɪl/ n (apparatus) alambique m

stillborn /'stɪlbɔːn/ a natimorto,
(P) nado-morto

stilted /'stɪltɪd/ a afetado, (P)
afetado

stilts /stɪlts/ npl pernas fpl de pau,
(P) andas fpl

stimulate /'stɪmjʊleɪt/ vt
estimular. **~ant** n estimulante
m. **~ating** a estimulante. **~ation**
/-'leɪʃn/ n estimulação f

stimulus /'stɪmjʊləs/ n (pl -li /-laɪ/)
(spur) estímulo m

sting /stɪŋ/ n picada f; (organ)
ferrão m ● vt (pt stung) picar ● vi
picar, arder

stingy /'stɪndʒɪ/ a (-ier, -iest) pão-
duro m; sovina (with com)

stink /stɪŋk/ n fedor m, catinga
f, mau cheiro m ● vi (pt stank or
stunk, pp stunk) **~ (of)** cheirar (a),
tresandar (a) ● vt **~ out** <room etc>
empestar. **~ing** a malcheiroso; **~ing
rich** 🅭 podre de rico 🅸

stint /stɪnt/ vi **~ on** poupar em,
apertar em ● n (work) tarefa f, parte
f, quinhão m

stipulate /'stɪpjʊleɪt/ vt estipular.
~ion /-'leɪʃn/ n condição f,

estipulação f

stir /stɜː(r)/ vt/i (pt stirred) (move)
mexer(-se), mover(-se); (excite)
excitar; <a liquid> mexer; **~ up**
<trouble etc> provocar, fomentar ● n
agitação f, rebuliço m

stirrup /'stɪrəp/ n estribo m

stitch /stɪtʃ/ n (in sewing) Med
ponto m; (in knitting) malha f, ponto
m; (pain) pontada f; **in ~es** 🅸 às
gargalhadas 🅸 ● vt coser

stock /stɒk/ n Comm estoque
m, (P) stock m, provisão f; Finance
valores mpl, fundos mpl; (family)
família f, estirpe f; Culin caldo m;
(flower) goivo m; **in ~** em estoque;
out of ~ esgotado; **take ~** fig fazer
um balanço; **~ market** Bolsa (de
Valores) f; (de Valores) ● a (goods)
corrente, comum; (hackneyed)
estereotipado ● vt <shop etc>
abastecer, fornecer; (sell) vender ● vi
~ up with abastecer-se de. **~ cube**
n cubo m de caldo; **~taking** n Comm
inventário m

stockbroker /'stɒkbrəʊkə(r)/ n
corretor m da Bolsa

stocking /'stɒkɪŋ/ n meia f

stockist /'stɒkɪst/ n armazenista m

stockpile /'stɒkpaɪl/ n reservas fpl
● vt acumular reservas de, estocar

stocky /'stɒkɪ/ a (-ier, -iest)
atarracado

stoic /'stəʊɪk/ n estoico m.

stoke /stəʊk/ vt <boiler, fire>
alimentar, carregar

stole[1] /stəʊl/ n (garment) estola f

stole[2], **stolen** /stəʊl, stəʊlən/
▶ STEAL

stomach /'stʌmək/ n estômago
m; (abdomen) barriga f, ventre m ● vt
(put up with) aturar. **~ ache** n dor f

de estômago; (*abdomen*) dores *fpl* de barriga

stone /stəʊn/ *n* pedra *f*; (*pebble*) seixo *m*; (*in fruit*) caroço *m*; (*weight*) 6,348 kg; *Med* cálculo *m*, pedra *f* ● *vt* apedrejar; <*fruit*> tirar o caroço de; **within a ~e's throw (of)** muito perto (de). **~e-cold** *a* gelado. **~e-deaf** totalmente surdo. **~ed** *a* 🗙 (*drunk*) bebão *m* 🗙, (*P*) bêbado *m* 🗙; 🗙 (*drugged*) drogado, (*P*) pedrado 🗙. **~y** *a* pedregoso.

stood /stʊd/ ▶ **STAND**

stool /stuːl/ *n* banco *m*, tamborete *m*

stoop /stuːp/ *vi* (*bend*) curvar-se, baixar-se; (*condescend*) condescender, dignar-se; **~ to sth** rebaixar-se a (fazer) algo ● *n* **walk with a ~** andar curvado

stop /stɒp/ *vt/i* (*pt* **stopped**) parar; (*prevent*) impedir (**from** de); <*hole, leak etc*> tapar, vedar; <*pain, noise etc*> parar; 🗙 (*stay*) ficar; **~ it!** acabe logo com isso!, (*P*) para com isso! ● *n* (*of bus*) parada *f*, (*P*) paragem *f*; (*full stop*) ponto *m* final; **put a ~ to** pôr fim a. **~watch** *n* cronômetro *m*, (*P*) cronómetro *m*

stopgap /stɒpgæp/ *n* substituto *m* provisório; tapa-buracos *mpl* 🗙 ● *a* temporário

stoppage /stɒpɪdʒ/ *n* parada *f*, (*P*) paragem *f*; (*of work*) paralização *f* de trabalho; (*of pay*) suspensão *f*

stopper /stɒpə(r)/ *n* rolha *f*, tampa *f*

storage /stɔːrɪdʒ/ *n* (*of goods, food etc*) armazenagem *f*, armazenamento *m*; **in cold ~** no frigorífico

store /stɔː(r)/ *n* reserva *f*, provisão *f*; (*warehouse*) armazém *m*, entreposto *m*; (*shop*) grande armazém *m*; *Amer* loja *f*; (*in computer*) memória

f; **be in ~** estar guardado; **have in ~ for** reservar para; **set ~ by** dar valor a ● *vt* (*for future*) pôr de reserva, juntar, fazer provisão de; (*in warehouse*) armazenar. **~room** *n* depósito *m*, almorifado *m*, (*P*) armazém *m*

storey /stɔːrɪ/ *n* (*pl* **-eys**) andar *m*

stork /stɔːk/ *n* cegonha *f*

storm /stɔːm/ *n* tempestade *f*; **a ~ in a teacup** uma tempestade num copo de água ● *vt* tomar de assalto ● *vi* enfurecer-se. **~y** *a* tempestuoso

story /stɔːrɪ/ *n* estória *f*, (*P*) história *f*; (*in press*) artigo *m*, matéria *f*; *Amer* (*storey*) andar *m*; 🗙 (*lie*) cascata *f*, (*P*) peta *f*

stout /staʊt/ *a* (**-er, -est**) (*fat*) gordo, corpulento; (*strong, thick*) resistente, sólido, grosso; (*brave*) resoluto ● *n* cerveja *f* preta forte

stove /stəʊv/ *n* (*for cooking*) fogão (de cozinha) *m*

stow /stəʊ/ *vt* **~ (away)** (*put away*) guardar, arrumar; (*hide*) esconder ● *vi* **~ away** viajar clandestinamente

stowaway /stəʊəweɪ/ *n* passageiro *m* clandestino

straggle /strægl/ *vi* (*lag behind*) desgarrar-se, ficar para trás; (*spread*) estender-se desordenadamente. **~r** /-ə(r)/ *n* retardatário *m*

straight /streɪt/ *a* (**-er, -est**) direito; (*tidy*) em ordem; (*frank*) franco; direto; (*of hair*) liso; (*of drink*) puro; **keep a ~ face** não se desmanchar, manter um ar sério ● *adv* (*in straight line*) reto; (*directly*) direito; direto; diretamente; **~ ahead** or **on** (*sempre*) em frente; **~ away** logo, imediatamente; **go ~** viver honestamente ● *n* linha *f* reta

straighten /streɪtn/ *vt* endireitar; (*tidy*) arrumar, pôr em ordem

straightforward /streɪtˈfɔːwəd/ a franco, sincero; (easy) simples

strain[1] /streɪn/ n (breed) raça f; (streak) tendência f, veia f

strain[2] /streɪn/ vt (rope) esticar, puxar; (tire) cansar; (filter) filtrar, passar; ‹vegetables, tea etc› coar; Med distender, torcer; fig forçar; pôr à prova ● vi esforçar-se ● n tensão f; fig (effort) esforço m; Med distensão f; ~s (music) melodias fpl; ~ one's ears apurar o ouvido. ~ed a forçado; ‹relations› tenso. ~er n coador m, (P) passador m

strait /streɪt/ n estreito m; ~s estreito m; fig apuros mpl, dificuldades fpl. ~laced a severo, puritano

strand /strænd/ n (thread) fio m; (lock of hair) mecha f, madeixa f

stranded /ˈstrændɪd/ a (person) em dificuldades, deixado para trás, abandonado

strange /streɪndʒ/ a (-er, -est) estranho. ~ly adv estranhamente

stranger /ˈstreɪndʒə(r)/ n estranho m, desconhecido m

strangle /ˈstræŋgl/ vt estrangular, sufocar

strap /stræp/ n (of leather etc) correia f; (of dress) alça f; (of watch) pulseira f com correia ● vt (pt strapped) prender com correia

strapping /ˈstræpɪŋ/ a robusto, grande

strata ▶ STRATUM

strategic /strəˈtiːdʒɪk/ a estratégico; (of weapons) estratégico de longo alcance

strategy /ˈstrætədʒɪ/ n estratégia f

stratum /ˈstrɑːtəm/ n (pl strata) estrato m, camada f

straw /strɔː/ n palha f; (for drinking) canudo m, (P) palhinha f; **the last ~** a última gota f

strawberry /ˈstrɔːbrɪ/ n (fruit) morango m; (plant) morangueiro m

stray /streɪ/ vi (deviate from path etc) extraviar-se; desencaminhar-se; afastar-se (from de); (lose one's way) perder-se; (wander) vagar, (P) vaguear, errar ● a perdido, extraviado; (isolated) isolado, raro, esporádico ● n animal m perdido ou vadio

streak /striːk/ n risca f, lista f; (strain) veia f; (period) período m; ~ of lightning relâmpago m ● vt listrar, riscar ● vi ir como um raio

stream /striːm/ n riacho m, córrego m, regato m; (current) corrente f; fig (flow) jorro m; torrente f; Schol nível m, grupo m ● vi correr; (of banner, hair) flutuar; (sweat) escorrer, pingar

streamer /ˈstriːmə(r)/ n (of paper) serpentina f; (flag) flâmula f, bandeirola f

streamline /ˈstriːmlaɪn/ vt dar forma aerodinâmica a; fig racionalizar. ~d a ‹shape› aerodinâmico

street /striːt/ n rua f; **the man in the ~** fig o homem da rua, (P) o cidadão m comum; ~ lamp poste m de iluminação

streetcar /ˈstriːtkɑː(r)/ n Amer bonde m, (P) (carro m) elétrico m

strength /streŋθ/ n força f; (of wall) solidez f; (of fabric etc) resistência f; **on the ~ of** à base de, em virtude de

strengthen /ˈstreŋθn/ vt fortificar, fortalecer, reforçar

strenuous /ˈstrenjʊəs/ a enérgico; (arduous) árduo; estrênuo, (P) estrénuo; (*tiring*) fatigante, esgotante

stress /stres/ *n* acento *m*; (*pressure*) pressão *f*, tensão *f*; Med stress *m*, (*P*) (e)stresse(*s*) *m* ● *vt* acentuar, sublinhar; (*sound*) acentuar. **~ful** *a* estressante, (*P*) (e)stressant(*e*)

stretch /stretʃ/ *vt* (*pull taut*) esticar; ‹*arm, leg, neck*› estender, esticar; ‹*clothes*› alargar; ‹*truth*› forçar, torcer ● *vi* estender-se; (*after sleep etc*) espreguiçar-se; (*of clothes*) alargar-se; **~ one's legs** esticar as pernas ● *n* extensão *f*, trecho *m*; (*period*) período *m*; (*of road*) troço *m*; **at a ~** sem parar ● *a* (*of fabric*) com elasticidade

stretcher /stretʃə(r)/ *n* maca *f*, padiola *f*

strew /stru:/ *vt* (*pt* strewed, *pp* strewed *or* strewn) (*scatter*) espalhar; (*cover*) juncar, cobrir

strict /strɪkt/ *a* (-er, -est) estrito, rigoroso. **~ly** *adv* estritamente; **~ly speaking** a rigor, (*P*) em rigor

stride /straɪd/ *vi* (*pt* strode, *pp* stridden) caminhar a passos largos ● *n* passada *f*; **make great ~s** *fig* fazer grandes progressos; **take sth in one's ~** fazer algo sem problemas

strident /straɪdnt/ *a* estridente

strife /straɪf/ *n* conflito *m*, dissensão *f*, luta *f*

strike /straɪk/ *vt* (*pt* struck) bater (em); ‹*blow*› dar; ‹*match*› riscar, acender; ‹*gold etc*› descobrir; (*of clock*) soar, dar, bater (horas); (*of lightning*) atingir ● *vi* fazer greve; (*attack*) atacar; **~ a bargain** fechar negócio; **~ off** *or* **out** riscar; **~ up** *Mus* começar a tocar; ‹*friendship*› travar ● *n* (*of workers*) greve *f*; *Mil* ataque *m*; (*find*) descoberta *f*; **on ~** em greve

striker /straɪkə(r)/ *n* grevista *mf*

striking /straɪkɪŋ/ *a* notável, impressionante; (*attractive*) atraente

string /strɪŋ/ *n* corda *f*, fio *m*; (*of violin, racket etc*) corda *f*; (*of pearls*) fio *m*; (*of onions, garlic*) réstia *f*; (*of lies etc*) série *f*; (*row*) fila *f*; **pull ~s** usar pistolão, (*P*) puxar os cordelinhos ● *vt* (*pt* strung) (*thread*) enfiar; **~ out** espaçar-se. **~ed** *a* ‹*instrument*› de cordas. **~y** *a* filamentoso, fibroso; ‹*meat*› com nervos

stringent /strɪndʒənt/ *a* rigoroso, estrito

strip[1] /strɪp/ *vt/i* (*pt* stripped) (*undress*) despir(-se); ‹*machine*› desmontar; (*deprive*) despojar, privar. **~per** *n* artista *mf* de strip-tease; (*solvent*) removedor *m*, (*P*) decapante *m*

strip[2] /strɪp/ *n* tira *f*; (*of land*) faixa *f*; **comic ~** história *f* em quadrinhos, (*P*) banda *f* desenhada; **~ light** tubo *m* de luz fluorescente

stripe /straɪp/ *n* risca *f*, lista *f*, barra *f*. **~d** *a* listrado, com listras

strive /straɪv/ *vi* (*pt* strove, *pp* striven) esforçar-se (**to** por)

strode /strəʊd/ ▸ STRIDE

stroke[1] /strəʊk/ *n* golpe *m*; (*of pen*) penada *f*, (*P*) traço *m*; (*in swimming*) braçada *f*; (*in rowing*) remada *f*; Med ataque *m*, congestão *f*; **~ of genius** rasgo *m* de genialidade or de génio; **~ of luck** golpe *m* de sorte

stroke[2] /strəʊk/ *vt* (*with hand*) acariciar, fazer festas em

stroll /strəʊl/ *vi* passear, dar uma volta; **~ in/etc** entrar/*etc* tranquilamente ● *n* volta *f*, (*P*) passeio *m*

strong /strɒŋ/ a (-er, -est) forte; ‹shoes, fabric etc› resistente; **be a hundred/**etc~ ser em número de cem/etc; ~ **language** linguagem f grosseira, palavrões mpl. ~**room** n casa-forte f. ~**ly** adv (greatly) fortemente, grandemente; (with energy) com força; (deeply) profundamente

stronghold /strɒŋhəʊld/ n fortaleza f, fig baluarte m; bastião m ▶ STRIVE

strove /strəʊv/ ▶ STRIVE

struck /strʌk/ ▶ STRIKE ● a ~ **on** ⊠ apaixonado por, (P) apanhado por ⊠

structur|e /strʌktʃə(r)/ n estrutura f, (of building etc) edifício m, construção f. ~**al** a estrutural, de estrutura, de construção

struggle /strʌgl/ vi (to get free) debater-se; (contend) lutar; (strive) esforçar-se (**to, for** por); ~ **to one's feet** levantar-se a custo ● n luta f; (effort) esforço m; **have a ~ to** ter dificuldade em

strum /strʌm/ vt (pt **strummed**) ‹banjo etc› dedilhar

strung /strʌŋ/ ▶ STRING

strut /strʌt/ n (support) suporte m, escora f ● vi (pt **strutted**) (walk) pavonear-se

stub /stʌb/ n (of pencil, cigarette) ponta f; (of tree) cepo m, toco m; (counterfoil) talão m, canhoto m ● vt (pt **stubbed**) ~ **one's toe** dar uma topada; ~ **out** esmagar

stubble /stʌbl/ n (on chin) barba f por fazer; (of crop) restolho m

stubborn /stʌbən/ a teimoso, obstinado. ~**ness** n teimosia f, obstinação f

stubby /stʌbɪ/ a (-ier, -iest) ‹finger› curto e grosso; ‹person›

atarracado

stuck /stʌk/ ▶ STICK² a emperrado. ~**up** a ⊡ (snobbish) convencido; esnobe, (P) snob

stud¹ /stʌd/ n tacha f; (for collar) botão m de colarinho ● vt (pt **studded**) enfeitar com tachas; ~**ded with** salpicado de

stud² /stʌd/ n (horses) haras m, (P) coudelaria. ~ (**farm**) n coudelaria f; ~ (**horse**) n garanhão m

student /stjuːdnt/ n Univ estudante mf, aluno m; Schol aluno m ● a ‹life, residence› universitário

studio /stjuːdɪəʊ/ n (pl -os) estúdio m; ~ **flat** estúdio m

studious /stjuːdɪəs/ a ‹person› estudioso; (deliberate) estudado

study /stʌdɪ/ n estudo m; (office) escritório m ● vt/i estudar

stuff /stʌf/ n substância f, matéria f; ⊠ (things) coisa(s) f ● vt encher; ‹animal› empalhar; (cram) apinhar, encher ao máximo; Culin rechear; (block up) entupir; (put) enfiar, meter. ~**ing** n enchimento m; Culin recheio m

stuffy /stʌfɪ/ a (-ier, -iest) abafado, mal arejado; (dull) enfadonho

stumbl|e /stʌmbl/ vi tropeçar; ~ **across** or **on** dar com, encontrar por acaso, topar com. ~**ing block** n obstáculo m

stump /stʌmp/ n (of tree) cepo m, toco m; (of limb) coto m; (of pencil, cigar) ponta f

stumped /stʌmpt/ a ⊡ (baffled) atrapalhado; perplexo

stun /stʌn/ vt (pt **stunned**) aturdir, estontear

stung /stʌŋ/ ▶ STING

stunk /stʌŋk/ ▶ STINK

stunning /ˈstʌnɪŋ/ a atordoador; 🄵 (delightful) fantástico; sensacional

stunt[1] /stʌnt/ vt <growth> atrofiar. **~ed** a atrofiado

stunt[2] /stʌnt/ n (feat) façanha f, proeza f; (trick) truque m; Aviat acrobacia f aérea. **~ man** n dublê m, (P) duplo m

stupefy /ˈstjuːpɪfaɪ/ vt estupefazer, (P) estupefear, espantar

stupendous /stjuːˈpendəs/ a estupendo, assombroso, prodigioso

stupid /ˈstjuːpɪd/ a estúpido, obtuso. **~ity** /-ˈpɪdəti/ n estupidez f. **~ly** adv estupidamente

stupor /ˈstjuːpə(r)/ n estupor m, torpor m

sturdy /ˈstɜːdɪ/ a (-ier, -iest) robusto, vigoroso, forte

stutter /ˈstʌtə(r)/ vi gaguejar ● n gagueira f, (P) gaguez f

sty /staɪ/ n (pigsty) pocilga f, chiqueiro m

styl|e /staɪl/ n estilo m; (fashion) moda f; (kind) gênero m, (P) género m; (pattern) feitio m, modelo m; in **~e** (live) em grande estilo; (do things) com classe ● vt (design) desenhar, criar; **~e sb's hair** fazer um penteado em or (P) a alguém. **~ist** n (of hair) cabeleireiro m

stylish /ˈstaɪlɪʃ/ a elegante, na moda

suave /swɑːv/ a polido, de fala mansa, (P) melifluo

subconscious /sʌbˈkɒnʃəs/ a & n subconsciente m

subcontract /sʌbkənˈtrækt/ vt dar de subempreitada, (P) subcontratar

subdivide /sʌbdɪˈvaɪd/ vt subdividir

subdue /səbˈdjuː/ vt <enemy, feeling> dominar, subjugar; <sound, voice> abrandar. **~d** a (weak) submisso; (quiet) recolhido; <light> velado

subject[1] /ˈsʌbdʒɪkt/ a <state etc> dominado; **~ to** sujeito a ● n assunto m; Schol, Univ disciplina f, matéria f; (citizen) súdito m, (P) súbdito m. **~ matter** n conteúdo m, tema m, assunto m

subject[2] /səbˈdʒekt/ vt submeter

subjective /səbˈdʒektɪv/ a subjetivo

subjunctive /səbˈdʒʌŋktɪv/ a & n subjuntivo m, (P) conjuntivo m

sublime /səˈblaɪm/ a sublime

submarine /sʌbməˈriːn/ n submarino m

submerge /səbˈmɜːdʒ/ vt submergir, mergulhar ● vi submergir, mergulhar

submissive /səbˈmɪsɪv/ a submisso

submi|t /səbˈmɪt/ vt/i (pt **submitted**) submeter(-se) (**to** a); Jur (argue) alegar. **~ssion** /-ˈmɪʃn/ n submissão f

subnormal /sʌbˈnɔːml/ a subnormal; <temperature> abaixo do normal

subordinate[1] /səˈbɔːdɪnət/ a subordinado, subalterno; Gram subordinado ● n subordinado m, subalterno m

subordinate[2] /səˈbɔːdɪneɪt/ vt subordinar (**to** a)

subscribe /səbˈskraɪb/ vt/i subscrever, contribuir (**to** para); **~ to** <theory, opinion> subscrever, aceitar; <newspaper> assinar. **~r** /-ə(r)/ n subscritor m, assinante m

subscription /səbˈskrɪpʃn/
n subscrição f; (to newspaper)
assinatura f

subsequent /ˈsʌbsɪkwənt/ a
subsequente, posterior. **~ly** adv
subsequentemente, a seguir,
posteriormente

subservient /səbˈsɜːvɪənt/ a
servil, subserviente

subside /səbˈsaɪd/ vi ‹flood, noise
etc› baixar; ‹land› ceder, afundar;
‹wind, storm, excitement› abrandar,
acalmar. **~nce** /-əns/ n (of land)
afundamento m

subsidiary /səbˈsɪdɪərɪ/ a
subsidiário ● n Comm filial f,
sucursal f

subsid|y /ˈsʌbsədɪ/ n subsídio
m, subvenção f. **~ize** /-ɪdaɪz/ vt
subsidiar, subvencionar

subsist /səbˈsɪst/ vi subsistir; **~ on**
viver de. **~ence** n subsistência f;
~ence allowance ajudas fpl de custo

substance /ˈsʌbstəns/ n
substância f

substandard /sʌbˈstændəd/ a de
qualidade inferior

substantial
/səbˈstænʃl/ a substancial. **~ly** adv
substancialmente

substitut|e /ˈsʌbstɪtjuːt/ n
(person) substituto m; suplente mf
(for de); (thing) substituto m (for
de) ● vt substituir (for por). **~ion**
/-ˈtjuːʃn/ n substituição f

subtitle /ˈsʌbtaɪtl/ n subtítulo m,
(P) legenda f

subtle /ˈsʌtl/ a (-er, -est) sutil, (P)
subtil. **~ty** n sutileza f, (P) subtileza f

subtotal /ˈsʌbtəʊtl/ n soma f parcial

subtract /səbˈtrækt/ vt subtrair,
diminuir. **~ion** /-kʃn/ n subtração f,
diminuição f

suburb /ˈsʌbɜːb/ n subúrbio m,
arredores mpl. **~an** /səˈbɜːbən/
a dos subúrbios, suburbano. **~ia**
/səˈbɜːbɪə/ n pej os arredores, os
subúrbios

subver|t /səbˈvɜːt/ vt subverter.
~sion /-ʃn/ n subversão f. **~sive**
/-sɪv/ a subversivo

subway /ˈsʌbweɪ/ n passagem f
subterrânea; Amer (underground)
metropolitano m, (P) metro m

succeed /səkˈsiːd/ vi ser bem-
sucedido, ter êxito; **~ in doing
sth** conseguir fazer algo ● vt
(follow) suceder a. **~ing** a seguinte,
sucessivo

success /səkˈses/ n sucesso m,
êxito m

succession /səkˈseʃn/ n sucessão
f; (series) série f; **in ~** seguidos,
consecutivos

successive /səkˈsesɪv/ a sucessivo,
consecutivo

successor /səkˈsesə(r)/ n
sucessor m

succinct /səkˈsɪŋkt/ a sucinto

succulent /ˈsʌkjʊlənt/ a suculento

succumb /səˈkʌm/ vi sucumbir

---

such /sʌtʃ/ a

••••▶ (of that kind) tal,
semelhante, assim; **~ a book**
um tal livro; **~ a person** uma tal
pessoa; **~ people** essas pessoas;
there is no ~ thing uma coisa
assim não existe

••••▶ (so much) tanto; **I've got
~ a headache!** tenho uma dor
de cabeça tão grande!; **it was ~
fun!** foi tão divertido!

● adv

••••▶ tão; **~ a big house** uma
casa tão grande; **he has ~ lovely**

blue eyes ele tem uns olhos azuis tão bonitos; **~ a long time** tanto tempo

••••▶ (in phrases) **as ~:** the new job is not a promotion **as ~:** o novo emprego não é bem uma promoção; **there is no garden as ~** não existe um jardim no real sentido da palavra; **in ~ a way that** de tal maneira que; **~ as** tal como; **wild flowers ~ as** primroses are becoming rare as flores selvagens, tais como as prímulas, estão ficando raras; **~ as?** por exemplo?; **~ is: ~ is** life assim é a vida

such-and-such /ʌ on ~-and-~ **day** in july em tais e tais dias de julho

suck /sʌk/ vt chupar; <breast> mamar; **~ in** or **up** (absorb) absorver, aspirar; (engulf) tragar; **~ up to** puxar o saco a 🔢; **~ one's thumb** chuchar no dedo. **~er** n 🔳 (greenhorn) trouxa mf 🔢; Bot broto m

suction /'sʌkʃn/ n sucção f

sudden /'sʌdn/ a súbito, repentino; **all of a ~** de repente, de súbito. **~ly** adv subitamente, repentinamente

sue /su:/ vt (pres p suing) processar

suede /sweɪd/ n camurça f

suet /'su:ɪt/ n sebo m

suffer /'sʌfə(r)/ vt/i sofrer; (tolerate) tolerar, suportar. **~er** n sofredor m, o que sofre; (patient) doente mf, vítima f. **~ing** n sofrimento m

suffice /sə'faɪs/ vi bastar, chegar, ser suficiente

sufficien|t /sə'fɪʃnt/ a suficiente, bastante

suffocat|e /'sʌfəkeɪt/ vt/i sufocar. **~ion** /-'keɪʃn/ n sufocação f, asfixia f

sugar /'ʃʊɡə(r)/ n açúcar m; **brown ~** açúcar m preto, (P) açúcar m amarelo ● vt adoçar, pôr açúcar em. **~ lump** n torrão m de açúcar, (P) quadradinho m de açúcar. **~y** a açucarado; fig (too sweet) delicodoce, (P) adocicado

suggest /sə'dʒest/ vt sugerir. **~ion** /-tʃn/ n sugestão f. **~ive** a sugestivo; (improper) brejeiro, picante; **be ~ive of** sugerir, fazer lembrar

suicid|e /'su:ɪsaɪd/ n suicídio m; **commit ~e** suicidar-se. **~ attack** n ataque m suicida; **~ bomber** n terrorista mf suicida, (P) bombista mf suicida. **~al** /-'saɪdl/ a suicida

suit /su:t/ n terno m, (P) fato m; (woman's) costume m, (P) fato m de saia e casaco; Cards naipe m; **follow ~** fig seguir o exemplo ● vt convir a; (of garment, style) ficar bem em or (P) a; (adapt) adaptar. **~able** a conveniente; apropriado (**for** para). **~ably** adv convenientemente. **~ed** a **be ~ed to** ser feito para, servir para; **be well ~ed** (matched) combinar-se bem; (of people) ser o ideal

suitcase /'su:tkeɪs/ n mala f (de viagem)

suite /swi:t/ n (of rooms; mus) suíte f, (P) suite f; (of furniture) mobília f

suitor /'su:tə(r)/ n pretendente m

sulk /sʌlk/ vi amuar, ficar emburrado. **~y** a amuado, emburrado 🔢

sullen /'sʌlən/ a carrancudo

sulphur /'sʌlfə(r)/ n enxofre m

sultana /sʌl'tɑːnə/ n (fruit) passa f branca, (P) sultana f

sultry /'sʌltrɪ/ a (-ier, -iest) abafado, opressivo; fig sensual

sum /sʌm/ n soma f; (amount of money) soma f, quantia f, importância f; (*in arithmetic*) conta f ● vt (*pt* **summed**) somar; **~ up** recapitular, resumir; (*assess*) avaliar, medir

summar|y /'sʌməri/ n sumário m, resumo m ● a sumário. **~ize** vt resumir

summer /'sʌmə(r)/ n verão m, estio m ● a de verão, veranil. **~ time** n verão m, época f de verão. **~y** a estival, próprio de verão, veranil

summer camp Nos Estados Unidos, é o acampamento de verão, considerado um aspecto importante na vida de muitas crianças. Praticam-se atividades ao ar livre em ambiente natural, como natação, montanhismo, sobrevivência ao ar livre. Nesses acampamentos, milhares de estudantes trabalham como supervisores.

summit /'sʌmɪt/ n cume m, cimo m; **~ conference** Pol conferência f de cúpula, (P) (reunião f de) cimeira

summon /'sʌmən/ vt mandar chamar; (*to meeting*) convocar; **~ up** <*strength, courage etc*> chamar a si, fazer apelo a

summons /'sʌmənz/ n Jur citação f, intimação f ● vt citar, intimar

sumptuous /'sʌmptʃʊəs/ a suntuoso, (P) sumptuoso, luxuoso

sun /sʌn/ n sol m ● vt (*pt* **sunned**) **~ o.s.** aquecer-se ao sol. **~glasses** npl óculos mpl de sol. **~roof** n teto m solar; **~tan** n bronzeado m. **~tanned** a bronzeado. **~tan oil** n óleo m de bronzear

sunbathe /'sʌnbeɪð/ vi tomar um banho de sol

sunburn /'sʌnbɜːn/ n queimadura f solar. **~t** a queimado pelo sol

Sunday /'sʌndɪ/ n domingo m; **~ school** catecismo m, (P) catequese f

sundr|y /'sʌndrɪ/ a vários, diversos; **all and ~y** todo o mundo, todo e cada um. **~ies** npl artigos mpl diversos

sunflower /'sʌnflaʊə(r)/ n girassol m

sung /sʌŋ/ ▶ SING

sunk /sʌŋk/ ▶ SINK

sunken /'sʌŋkən/ a <*ship etc*> afundado; <*eyes*> fundo

sunlight /'sʌnlaɪt/ n luz f do sol, sol m

sunny /'sʌnɪ/ a (-ier, -iest) <*room, day etc*> ensolarado

sunrise /'sʌnraɪz/ n nascer m do sol

sunset /'sʌnset/ n pôr m do sol

sunshade /'sʌnʃeɪd/ n (*awning*) toldo m; (*parasol*) para-sol m, (P) guarda-sol m

sunshine /'sʌnʃaɪn/ n sol m, luz f do sol

sunstroke /'sʌnstrəʊk/ n Med insolação f

super /'suːpə(r)/ a 🄸 (*excellent*) formidável

superb /suːˈpɜːb/ a soberbo, esplêndido

superficial /suːpəˈfɪʃl/ a superficial

superfluous /suːˈpɜːflʊəs/ a supérfluo

superhuman /suːpəˈhjuːmən/ a sobre-humano

superimpose /suːpərɪmˈpəʊz/ vt sobrepor (**on** a)

superintendent /suːpərɪnˈtendənt/ n

superintendente *m*; (*of police*) comissário *m*, chefe *m* de polícia

superior /suːˈpɪərɪə(r)/ *a & n* superior *m*. **~ity** /-ˈɒrətɪ/ *n* superioridade *f*

superlative /suːˈpɜːlətɪv/ *a* supremo, superlativo ● *n Gram* superlativo *m*

supermarket /ˈsuːpəmɑːkɪt/ *n* supermercado *m*

supernatural /suːpəˈnætʃrəl/ *a* sobrenatural

superpower /ˈsuːpəpaʊə(r)/ *n* superpotência *f*

supersede /suːpəˈsiːd/ *vt* suplantar, substituir

superstiti|on /suːpəˈstɪʃn/ *n* superstição *f*. **~ous** /-ˈstɪʃəs/ *a* supersticioso

superstore /ˈsuːpəstɔː(r)/ *n* hipermercado *m*

supervis|e /ˈsuːpəvaɪz/ *vt* supervisar, fiscalizar, supervisionar. **~ion** /-ˈvɪʒn/ *n* supervisão *f*. **~or** *n* supervisor *m*; (*shop*) chefe *mf* de seção *m* or (*P*) secção (*firm*) chefe *mf* de serviço

supper /ˈsʌpə(r)/ *n* jantar *m*; (*late at night*) ceia *f*

supple /ˈsʌpl/ *a* flexível, maleável

supplement[1] /ˈsʌplɪmənt/ *n* suplemento *m*. **~ary** /-ˈmentrɪ/ *a* suplementar

supplement[2] /ˈsʌplɪment/ *vt* suplementar

supplier /səˈplaɪə(r)/ *n* fornecedor *m*

suppl|y /səˈplaɪ/ *vt* suprir, prover; *Comm* fornecer, abastecer ● *n* provisão *f*; (*of goods, gas etc*) fornecimento *m*, abastecimento *m* ● *a* ‹*teacher*› substituto; **~ies** (*food*)

víveres *mpl*; *Mil* suprimentos *mpl*; **~y and demand** oferta e procura

support /səˈpɔːt/ *vt* (*hold up, endure*) suportar, aguentar; (*provide for*) sustentar, suster; (*back*) apoiar, patrocinar; *Sport* torcer por ● *n* apoio *m*; *Techn* suporte *m*. **~er** *n* partidário *m*; *Sport* torcedor *m*, (*P*) adepto *m*

suppos|e /səˈpəʊz/ *vt/i* supor; **~e that** supondo que, na hipótese de que; **he's ~ed to do** ele deve fazer; (*believed to*) consta que ele faz. **~ed** *a* suposto. **~edly** /-ɪdlɪ/ *adv* segundo dizem; (*probably*) supostamente, em princípio. **~ing** *conj* se. **~ition** /sʌpəˈzɪʃn/ *n* suposição *f*

suppress /səˈpres/ *vt* (*put an end to*) suprimir; (*restrain*) conter, reprimir; (*stifle*) abafar, sufocar; *Psych* recalcar. **~ion** /-ʃn/ *n* supressão *f*; (*restraint*) repressão *f*; *Psych* recalque *m*, (*P*) recalcamento *m*

suprem|e /suːˈpriːm/ *a* supremo. **~acy** /-eməsɪ/ *n* supremacia *f*

surcharge /ˈsɜːtʃɑːdʒ/ *n* sobretaxa *f*; (*on stamp*) sobrecarga *f*

sure /ʃʊə(r)/ *a* (**-er, -est**), seguro, certo ● *adv* 🇺🇸 (*certainly*) deveras; não há dúvida que; de certeza; **be ~ about** or of ter a certeza de; **be ~ to** (*not fail*) não deixar de; **he is ~ to find out** ele vai descobrir com certeza; **make ~** assegurar. **~ly** *adv* com certeza, certamente

surf /sɜːf/ *n* ressaca *f*, rebentação *f*. **~er** *n* surfista *mf*. **~ing** *n* surfe *m*, (*P*) surf *m*, jacaré-na-praia *m*

surface /ˈsɜːfɪs/ *n* superfície *f* ● *a* superficial ● *vt/i* revestir; (*rise, become known*) emergir; **~ mail** via *f* marítima

surfboard /'sɜːfbɔːd/ n prancha f de surfe, (P) surf

surge /sɜːdʒ/ vi ‹waves› ondular, encapelar-se; (move forward) avançar ● n (wave) onda f, vaga f; (motion) arremetida f

surgeon /'sɜːdʒən/ n cirurgião m

surg|ery /'sɜːdʒərɪ/ n cirurgia f; (office) consultório m; (session) consulta f; (consulting hours) horas fpl de consulta. **~ical** a cirúrgico

surly /'sɜːlɪ/ a (-ier, -iest) carrancudo, trombudo

surmise /sə'maɪz/ vt imaginar, supor, calcular ● n conjetura f; hipótese f

surmount /sə'maʊnt/ vt sobrepujar, vencer, (P) superar

surname /'sɜːneɪm/ n sobrenome m, (P) apelido m

surpass /sə'pɑːs/ vt superar, ultrapassar, exceder

surplus /'sɜːpləs/ n excedente m, excesso m; Finance saldo m positivo ● a excedente, em excesso

surpris|e /sə'praɪz/ n surpresa f ● vt surpreender. **~ed** a surpreendido; admirado (at com). **~ing** a surpreendente. **~ingly** adv surpreendentemente

surrender /sə'rendə(r)/ vi render-se ● vt (hand over) Mil entregar ● n Mil rendição f; (of rights) renúncia f

surrogate /'sʌrəgeɪt/ n delegado m; **~ mother** mãe f de aluguel, (P) aluguer

surround /sə'raʊnd/ vt rodear, cercar; Mil etc cercar. **~ing** a circundante, vizinho. **~ings** npl arredores mpl, (P) redondezas fpl; (setting) meio m, ambiente m

surveillance /sɜː'veɪləns/ n vigilância f

survey¹ /sə'veɪ/ vt ‹landscape etc› observar; (review) passar em revista; (inquire about) pesquisar; ‹land› fazer o levantamento de; ‹building› vistoriar; inspecionar. **~or** n (of buildings) fiscal m; (of land) agrimensor m

survey² /'sɜːveɪ/ n (inspection) vistoria f, inspeção f; (general view) panorâmica f; (inquiry) pesquisa f

survival /sə'vaɪvl/ n sobrevivência f; (relic) relíquia f, vestígio m

surviv|e /sə'vaɪv/ vt/i sobreviver (a). **~or** n sobrevivente mf

susceptib|le /sə'septəbl/ a (prone) susceptível (to a); (sensitive, impressionable) susceptível, sensível

suspect¹ /sə'spekt/ vt suspeitar; (doubt, distrust) desconfiar de, suspeitar de

suspect² /'sʌspekt/ a & n suspeito m

suspen|d /sə'spend/ vt (hang, stop) suspender; (from duty etc) suspender; **~ded sentence** suspensão f de pena. **~sion** n suspensão f; **~sion bridge** ponte f suspensa or pênsil

suspender /sə'spendə(r)/ n (presilha f de) liga f; **~s** Amer (braces) suspensórios mpl. **~ belt** n cinta-liga f, (P) cinta f de ligas, (P) cinto m de ligas

suspense /sə'spens/ n ansiedade f, incerteza f; (in book etc) suspense m, tensão f

suspicion /sə'spɪʃn/ n suspeita f; (distrust) desconfiança f; (trace) vestígio m, (P) traço m

suspicious /sə'spɪʃəs/ a desconfiado; (causing suspicion) suspeito; **be ~ of** desconfiar de

sustain /sə'steɪn/ vt (support) suster, sustentar; (suffer) sofrer; (keep up) sustentar; Jur (uphold) sancionar; ‹interest, effort› manter; **~ed effort** esforço m contínuo

sustenance /'sʌstɪnəns/ n (food) alimento m, sustento m

SUV abbr (= sport utility vehicle) carro m esporte, (P) veículo m utilitário desportivo

swagger /'swægə(r)/ vi pavonear-se, andar com arrogância

swallow[1] /'swɒləʊ/ vt/i engolir; **~ up** (absorb, engulf) devorar, tragar

swallow[2] /'swɒləʊ/ n (bird) andorinha f

swam /swæm/ ▶ SWIM

swamp /swɒmp/ n pântano m, brejo m ● vt (flood, overwhelm) inundar, submergir

swan /swɒn/ n cisne m

swank /swæŋk/ vi 🅱 (show off) gabar-se, mostrar-se 🅱

swap /swɒp/ vt/i (pt swapped) 🅱 trocar (for por) ● n 🅱 troca f

swarm /swɔːm/ n (of insects, people) enxame m ● vi formigar; **~ into** or **round** invadir

swarthy /'swɔːðɪ/ a (-ier, -iest) moreno, trigueiro

swat /swɒt/ vt (pt swatted) ‹fly etc› esmagar, esborrachar

sway /sweɪ/ vt/i oscilar, balançar(-se); (influence) mover, influenciar ● n oscilação f, balanceio m; (rule) domínio m, poder m

swear /sweə(r)/ vt/i (pt swore, pp sworn) jurar; (curse) praguejar; rogar pragas (at/a contra); **~ by** jurar por; 🅱 (recommend) ter grande fé em. **~ word** n palavrão m

sweat /swet/ n suor m ● vi suar. **~y** a suado

sweater /'swetə(r)/ n suéter m, (P) camisola f

sweatshirt /'swetʃɜːt/ n suéter m or (P) camisola f de malha or algodão

Swed|e /swiːd/ n sueco m. **~en** n Suécia f. **~ish** a & n sueco m

sweep /swiːp/ vt/i (pt swept) varrer; (go majestically) avançar majestosamente; (carry away) arrastar; ‹chimney› limpar ● n (with broom) varredela f; (curve) curva f; (movement) gesto m largo; (chimney)**~** limpa-chaminés m. **~ing** a ‹gesture› largo; ‹action› de grande alcance; **~ing statement** generalização f fácil

sweet /swiːt/ a (-er, -est) doce; 🅱 (charming) doce; gracinha, (P) encanto; 🅱 (pleasant) agradável ● n doce m; **~ corn** milho m; **~ pea** ervilha-de-cheiro f; **~ shop** confeitaria f; **have a ~ tooth** gostar de doce, (P) ser guloso. **~ness** n doçura f

sweeten /'swiːtn/ vt adoçar; fig (mitigate) suavizar. **~er** n (for tea, coffee) adoçante m; 🅱 (bribe) agrado m, (P) suborno m

sweetheart /'swiːthɑːt/ n namorado m, namorada f; (term of endearment) querido m, querida f, amor m

swell /swel/ vt/i (pt swelled, pp swollen, or swelled) (expand) inchar; (increase) aumentar ● n (of sea) ondulação f ● a 🅱 (excellent) excelente; 🅱 (smart) chique. **~ing** n Med inchação f, inchaço m

swelter /'sweltə(r)/ vi fazer um calor abrasador; (person) abafar (com calor)

swept /swept/ ▸ SWEEP

swerve /swɜːv/ vi desviar-se, dar uma guinada

swift /swɪft/ a (-er,, -est) rápido, veloz

swig /swɪg/ vt (pt swigged) 🔲 (drink) emborcar 🔲; beber em longos tragos ● n 🔲 trago m; gole m

swim /swɪm/ vi (pt swam, pp swum, pres p swimming) nadar; ‹room, head› rodar ● vt atravessar a nado; (distance) nadar ● n banho m. **~mer** n nadador m. **~ming** n natação f. **~ming bath, ~ming pool** ns piscina f. **~ming cap** n touca f de banho or (P) de natação; **~ming costume, ~suit** ns maiô m, (P) fato m de banho; **~ming trunks** npl calção m or (P) calções mpl de banho

swindle /'swɪndl/ vt trapacear, fraudar, (P) vigarizar ● vt vigarice f. **~r** /-ə(r)/ n vigarista mf

swine /swaɪn/ npl (pigs) porcos mpl ● n (pl invar) 🔲 (person) animal m; canalha m 🔲. **~ flu** n gripe f suína

swing /swɪŋ/ vt/i (pt swung) balançar(-se); (turn round) girar ● n (seat) balanço m; (of opinion) reviravolta f; Mus swing m; (rhythm) ritmo m; **in full ~** no máximo, em plena atividade; **~ round** (of person) virar-se

swipe /swaɪp/ vt 🔲 (hit) bater em; dar uma pancada em; 🔲 (steal) afanar 🔲; roubar ● n 🔲 (hit) pancada f; **~ card** cartão m magnético

swirl /swɜːl/ vi rodopiar, redemoinhar ● n turbilhão m, redemoinho m

swish /swɪʃ/ vt/i sibilar, zunir, (fazer) cortar o ar; (with brushing sound) roçar ● a 🔲 chique, fino

Swiss /swɪs/ a & n suíço m

switch /swɪtʃ/ n interruptor m; (change) mudança f ● vt (transfer) transferir; (exchange) trocar ● vi desviar-se; **~ off** desligar

switchboard /'swɪtʃbɔːd/ n (telephone) PBX m, mesa f telefônica or (P) telefónica

Switzerland /'swɪtsələnd/ n Suíça f

swivel /'swɪvl/ vt/i (pt swivelled) (fazer) girar; **~ chair** cadeira f giratória

swollen /'swəʊlən/ ▸ SWELL a inchado

swoop /swuːp/ vi ‹bird› lançar-se; cair (down on sobre); ‹police› dar uma batida policial, (P) fazer uma rusga

sword /sɔːd/ n espada f

swore /swɔː(r)/ ▸ SWEAR

sworn /swɔːn/ ▸ SWEAR a ‹enemy› jurado, declarado; ‹ally› fiel

swot /swɒt/ vt/i (pt swotted) 🔲 (study) estudar muito, (P) marrar ⊠ ● n 🔲 estudante m muito aplicado, (P) marrão m ⊠

swum /swʌm/ ▸ SWIM

swung /swʌŋ/ ▸ SWING

syllable /'sɪləbl/ n sílaba f

syllabus /'sɪləbəs/ n (pl -uses) programa m

symbol /'sɪmbl/ n símbolo m. **~ic(al)** /-'bɒlɪk(l)/ a simbólico. **~ism** n simbolismo m

symbolize /'sɪmbəlaɪz/ vt simbolizar

symmetr|y /'sɪmətrɪ/ n simetria f. **~ical** /sɪ'metrɪkl/ a simétrico

sympathize /'sɪmpəθaɪz/ vi **~ with** ter pena de, condoer-se de; fig

compartilhar os sentimentos de. **~r**
n simpatizante *mf*

sympath|y /'sɪmpəθɪ/ *n* (*pity*)
pena *f*, compaixão *f*; (*solidarity*)
solidariedade *f*; (*condolences*)
pêsames *mpl*, condolências *fpl*; **be in
~y with** estar de acordo com. **~etic**
/-'θetɪk/ *a* compreensivo, simpático;
(*likeable*) simpático; (*showing pity*)
compassivo

symphon|y /'sɪmfənɪ/ *n* sinfonia *f*
● *a* sinfônico; (*P*) sinfónico

symptom /'sɪmptəm/ *n* sintoma *m*

synagogue /'sɪnəgɒg/ *n*
sinagoga *f*

synchronize /'sɪŋkrənaɪz/ *vt*
sincronizar

syndrome /'sɪndrəʊm/ *n Med*
síndrome *f*, (*P*) síndroma *f*

synonym /'sɪnənɪm/ *n*
sinônimo *m*, (*P*) sinónimo *m*. **~ous**
/sɪ'nɒnɪməs/ *a* sinônimo; (*P*)
sinónimo (**with** de)

synopsis /sɪ'nɒpsɪs/ *n* (*pl* **-opses**
/-siːz/) sinopse *f*, resumo *m*

synthesis /'sɪnθəsɪs/ *n* (*pl* **-theses**
/-siːz/) síntese *f*

synthetic /sɪn'θetɪk/ *a* sintético

Syria /'sɪrɪə/ *n* Síria *f*

syringe /sɪ'rɪndʒ/ *n* seringa *f* ● *vt*
seringar, injetar

syrup /'sɪrəp/ *n* (*liquid*) xarope *m*;
(*treacle*) calda *f* de açúcar. **~y** *a fig*
melado; enjoativo

system /'sɪstəm/ *n* sistema *m*;
(*body*) organismo *m*; (*order*) método
m. **~atic** /sɪstə'mætɪk/ *a* sistemático

Tt

tab /tæb/ *n* (*flap*) lingueta *f*; (*for
fastening, hanging*) aba *f*; (*label*)
etiqueta *f*; (*loop*) argola *f*; *Amer* 🇺🇸
(*bill*) conta *f*; **keep ~s on** 🇺🇸 vigiar

table /'teɪbl/ *n* mesa *f*; (*list*) tabela *f*,
lista *f*; **at ~** à mesa; **lay** or **set the ~**
pôr a mesa; **turn the ~s** inverter as
posições; **~ tennis** pingue-pongue
m; **~ of contents** índice *m* (*das
matérias*) ● *vt* (*submit*) apresentar;
(*postpone*) adiar. **~cloth** *n* toalha
de mesa *f*

tablespoon /'teɪblspuːn/ *n* colher
f grande de sopa

tablet /'tæblɪt/ *n* (*of stone*) lápide *f*,
placa *f*; (*drug*) comprimido *m*

tabloid /'tæblɔɪd/ *n* tablóide *m*;
~ journalism *pej* jornalismo *m*
sensacionalista, imprensa *f* marrom

taboo /tə'buː/ *n & a* tabu *m*

taciturn /'tæsɪtɜːn/ *a* taciturno

tack /tæk/ *n* (*nail*) tacha *f*; (*stitch*)
ponto *m* de alinhavo; *Naut* amura
f; *fig* (*course of action*) rumo *m* ● *vt*
(*nail*) pregar com tachas; (*stitch*)
alinhavar ● *vi Naut* bordejar; **~ on**
(*add*) acrescentar, juntar

tackle /'tækl/ *n* equipamento *m*,
apetrechos *mpl*; *Sport* placagem *f* ● *vt*
<*problem etc*> atacar; *Sport* placar;
<*a thief etc*> agarrar-se a

tacky /'tækɪ/ *a* (**-ier, -iest**)
peganhento, pegajoso

tact /tækt/ *n* tato *m*. **~ful** *a* cheio de
tato, diplomático. **~fully** *adv* com
tato. **~less** *a* sem tato

tactic /'tæktɪk/ n (*expedient*) tática f. **~s** n(pl) (*procedure*) tática f. **~al** a tático

tadpole /'tædpəʊl/ n girino m

tag /tæg/ n (*label*) etiqueta f; (*on shoelace*) agulheta f; (*phrase*) chavão m, clichê m ● vi (pt **tagged**) etiquetar; (*add*) juntar ● vi ~ **along** ⚹ andar atrás, seguir

tail /teɪl/ n cauda f, rabo m; (*of shirt*) fralda f; **~s!** (*tossing coin*) coroa! ● vt (*follow*) seguir, vigiar ● vi ~ **away** or **off** diminuir, baixar. **~back** n (*traffic*) fila f, (P) bicha f; **~ light** n Auto farolete m traseiro, (P) farolim m traseiro

tailor /'teɪlə(r)/ n alfaiate m ● vt ‹*garment*› fazer; fig (*adapt*) adaptar. **~-made** a feito sob medida, (P) por medida; **~-made for** fig feito para, talhado para

take /teɪk/ vt/i (pt **took**, pp **taken**) (*get hold of*) agarrar em, pegar em; (*capture*) tomar; ‹*a seat, a drink, train, bus etc*› tomar; (*carry*) levar (**to** a, para); (*contain, escort*) levar; (*tolerate*) suportar, aguentar; ‹*choice, exam*› fazer; ‹*photo*› tirar; (*require*) exigir; **be ~n by** or **with** ficar encantado com; **be ~n ill** adoecer; **it ~s time** to leva tempo para; ~ **after** parecer-se a; ~ **away** levar; ~ **away from** tirar de alguém/de algo; ~ **back** aceitar de volta; (*return*) devolver; (*accompany*) acompanhar; (*statement*) retirar, retratar; ~ **down** ‹*object*› tirar para baixo; ‹*notes*› tirar, tomar; ~ **in** ‹*garment*› meter para dentro; (*include*) incluir; (*cheat*) enganar, levar ⚹; (*grasp*) compreender; (*receive*) receber; ~ **it that** supor que; ~ **on** ‹*task*› encarregar-se de; ‹*staff*› admitir, contratar; ~ **out** tirar; (*on an outing*) levar para sair;

~ **part** participar or tomar parte (**in** em); ~ **place** ocorrer, suceder; ~ **sides** tomar partido; ~ **sides with** tomar o partido de; ~ **to** gostar de, simpatizar com; ‹*activity*› tomar gosto por, entregar-se a; ~ **up** ‹*object*› apanhar, pegar em; ‹*hobby*› dedicar-se a; (*occupy*) ocupar, tomar □ ~ **off** vt (*remove*) tirar; (*mimic*) imitar, macaquear ● vi Aviat decolar, levantar voo, (P) descolar. ~ **over** vt tomar conta de, assumir a direção de ● vi tomar o poder; ~ **over from** (*relieve*) render, substituir; (*succeed*) suceder a. **~-away** n (*meal*) comida f para levar, take-away m; (*shop*) loja f que só vende comida para ser consumida em outro lugar; **~-off** n imitação f; Aviat decolagem f, (P) descolagem f; **~-over** n Pol tomada f de poder; Comm take-over m

takings /'teɪkɪŋz/ npl receita f

talcum /'tælkəm/ n talco m; ~ **powder** pó m (de) talco

tale /teɪl/ n conto m, história f

talent /'tælənt/ n talento m. **~ed** a talentoso, bem dotado

talk /tɔːk/ vt/i falar; (*chat*) conversar; ~ **into doing** convencer a fazer; ~ **nonsense** dizer disparates; ~ **over** discutir; ~ **shop** falar de assuntos profissionais; ~ **to o.s.** falar sozinho, falar com os seus botões ● n conversa f; (*mode of speech*) fala f; (*lecture*) palestra f; **small** ~ conversa f banal; **there's** ~ **of** fala-se de

talkative /'tɔːkətɪv/ a falador, conversador, tagarela

tall /tɔːl/ a (**-er, -est**) alto; ~ **story** ⚹ história f do arco-da-velha

tally /'tælɪ/ vi corresponder (**with** a); conferir (**with** com)

tame /teɪm/ a (-er, -est) manso; (*domesticated*) domesticado; (*dull*) insípido ● vt amansar, domesticar

tamper /'tæmpə(r)/ vi ~ **with** mexer indevidamente em; (*text*) alterar

tampon /'tæmpən/ n Med tampão m; (*sanitary towel*) toalha f higiênica, (P) tampão m

tan /tæn/ vt/i (*pt* tanned) queimar, bronzear; (*hide*) curtir ● n bronzeado m ● a castanho amarelado

tandem /'tændəm/ n (*bicycle*) tandem m; **in** ~ em tandem, um atrás do outro

tang /tæŋ/ n (*taste*) sabor m or gosto m característico m; (*smell*) cheiro m característico

tangerine /tændʒə'ri:n/ n tangerina f

tangible /'tændʒəbl/ a tangível

tangle /'tæŋgl/ vt emaranhar, enredar; **become** ~d emaranhar-se, enredar-se ● n emaranhado m

tank /tæŋk/ n tanque m, reservatório m; (*for petrol*) tanque m, (P) depósito m; (*for fish*) aquário m; Mil tanque m

tanker /'tæŋkə(r)/ n carro-tanque m, camião-cisterna m; (*ship*) petroleiro m

tantaliz|e /'tæntəlaɪz/ vt atormentar, tantalizar. ~**ing** a tentador

tantamount /'tæntəmaʊnt/ a be ~ **to** equivaler a

tantrum /'tæntrəm/ n chilique m, ataque m de mau gênio, (P) génio, birra f

tap¹ /tæp/ n (*for water etc*) torneira f; **on** ~ 🔲 (*available*) disponível ● vt (*pt* tapped) ⟨*resources*⟩ explorar;

⟨*telephone*⟩ grampear 🔲, pôr escutas in or colocar sob escuta

tap² /tæp/ vt/i (*pt* tapped) bater levemente. ~ **dance** n sapateado m

tape /teɪp/ n (*for dressmaking*) fita f; (*sticky*) fita f adesiva, (P) fita-cola f, (**magnetic**) ~ fita (magnética) f ● vt (*tie*) atar, prender; (*stick*) colar; (*record*) gravar. ~ **measure** n fita f métrica; ~ **recorder** n gravador m

taper /'teɪpə(r)/ n vela f comprida e fina ● vt/i ~ (**off**) estreitar(-se), afilar(-se). ~**ed** ~**ing** adjs ⟨*fingers etc*⟩ afilado; ⟨*trousers*⟩ afunilado

tapestry /'tæpɪstrɪ/ n tapeçaria f

tar /tɑ:(r)/ n alcatrão m ● vt (*pt* tarred) alcatroar

target /'tɑ:gɪt/ n alvo m ● vt ter como alvo

tariff /'tærɪf/ n tarifa f; (*on import*) direitos mpl aduaneiros

Tarmac® /'tɑ:mæk/ n macadame (alcatroado) m, (P) asfalto m; (*runway*) pista f

tarnish /'tɑ:nɪʃ/ vt/i (fazer) perder o brilho; (*stain*) manchar

tarpaulin /tɑ:'pɔ:lɪn/ n lona f impermeável (alcatroada or (P) asfaltada or encerada)

tart¹ /tɑ:t/ a (-er, -est) ácido; fig (*cutting*) mordaz; azedo

tart² /tɑ:t/ n Culin torta f de fruta, (P) tarte f; 🔲 (*prostitute*) prostituta f; mulher f da vida 🔲 ● vt ~ **up** 🔲 embonecar(-se)

tartan /'tɑ:tn/ n tecido m escocês ● a escocês

task /tɑ:sk/ n tarefa f, trabalho m; **take to** ~ repreender, censurar. ~ **force** n Mil força-tarefa f, (P) unidade f especial

tassel /'tæsl/ n borla f

633 | **taste | teaspoon**

taste /teɪst/ n gosto m; fig (sample) amostra f; **have a ~ of** (experience) provar ● vt (eat, enjoy) saborear; (try) provar; (perceive taste of) sentir o gosto de ● vi **~ of** or **like** ter o sabor de, saber a. **~ful** a de bom gosto. **~less** a insípido, insosso; fig (not in good taste) sem gosto; fig (in bad taste) de mau gosto

tasty /ˈteɪstɪ/ a (-ier, -iest) saboroso, gostoso

tat /tæt/ ▶ TIT²

tatter|s /ˈtætəz/ npl farrapos mpl. **~ed** /-əd/ a esfarrapado

tattoo /təˈtuː/ vt tatuar ● n tatuagem f

tatty /ˈtætɪ/ a (-ier, -iest) 🗓 enxovalhado; em mau estado

taught /tɔːt/ ▶ TEACH

taunt /tɔːnt/ vt escarnecer de, zombar de ● n escárnio m

Taurus /ˈtɔːrəs/ n Astr Touro m

taut /tɔːt/ a esticado, retesado; fig (of nerves) tenso

tawdry /ˈtɔːdrɪ/ a (-ier, -iest) espalhafatoso e ordinário

tax /tæks/ n taxa f, imposto m; (on income) imposto m de renda, (P) sobre o rendimento; **~ relief** isenção f de imposto; **~ return** declaração f do imposto de renda, (P) sobre o rendimento; **~ year** ano m fiscal ● vt taxar, lançar impostos sobre; tributar; fig (put to test) pôr à prova. **~-free** a isento de imposto. **~able** a tributável, passível de imposto. **~ation** /-ˈeɪʃn/ n impostos mpl, tributação f. **~ing** a penoso, difícil

taxi /ˈtæksɪ/ n (pl -is) táxi m; **~ rank**, **~ stand** ponto m de táxis, (P) praça f de táxis ● vi (pt taxied, pres p taxiing) Aviat rolar na pista, taxiar.

~cab n táxi m; **~driver** n motorista mf de táxi

taxpayer /ˈtækspeɪə(r)/ n contribuinte mf

tea /tiː/ n chá m; (meal) high ~ refeição f leve à noite. **~bag** n saquinho m de chá; **~ break** n intervalo m para o chá; **~ leaf** n folha f de chá; **~ shop** n salão m or casa f de chá; **~time** n hora f do chá; **~ towel** n pano m de prato

teach /tiːtʃ/ vt (pt taught) ensinar, dar aulas de, lecionar (sb sth alg coisa a alguém) ● vi ensinar, ser professor. **~er** n professor m. **~ing** n ensino m; (doctrines) ensinamento(s) m(pl) ● a pedagógico, de ensino; ‹staff› docente

teacup /ˈtiːkʌp/ n xícara f de chá, (P) chávena f

teak /tiːk/ n teca f

team /tiːm/ n equipe f, (P) equipa f; (of oxen) junta f; (of horses) parelha f ● vi **~ up** juntar-se, associar-se (with a). **~work** n trabalho m de equipe, (P) equipa

teapot /ˈtiːpɒt/ n bule m

tear¹ /teə(r)/ vt/i (pt tore, pp torn) rasgar(-se); (snatch) arrancar, puxar; (rush) lançar-se, ir numa correria; fig dividir ● n rasgão m; **~ o.s. away** arrancar-se (from de)

tear² /tɪə(r)/ n lágrima f. **~ gas** n gases mpl lacrimogênios, (P) gás m lacrimogénio

tearful /ˈtɪəfl/ a lacrimoso, choroso. **~ly** adv choroso, com (as) lágrimas nos olhos

tease /tiːz/ vt implicar; (make fun of) caçoar de, (P) fazer troça de

teaspoon /ˈtiːspuːn/ n colher f de chá

teat /tiːt/ n (of bottle) bico m; (of animal) teta f

technical /ˈteknɪkl/ a técnico. **~ity** /-ˈkælətɪ/ n questão f de ordem técnica. **~ly** adv tecnicamente

technician /tekˈnɪʃn/ n técnico m

technique /tekˈniːk/ n técnica f

technolog|y /tekˈnɒlədʒɪ/ n tecnologia f. **~ical** /-əˈlɒdʒɪkl/ a tecnológico

teddy /ˈtedɪ/ a **~ (bear)** ursinho m de pelúcia, (P) peluche

tedious /ˈtiːdɪəs/ a maçante

tedium /ˈtiːdɪəm/ n tédio m

tee /tiː/ n Golf tee m

teem¹ /tiːm/ vi **~ (with)** (swarm) pulular (de), fervilhar (de), abundar (em)

teem² /tiːm/ vi **~ (with rain)** chover torrencialmente

teenage /ˈtiːneɪdʒ/ a juvenil, de/para adolescente. **~r** /-ə(r)/ n jovem mf, adolescente mf

teens /tiːnz/ npl **in one's ~** na adolescência, entre os 13 e os 19 anos

teeter /ˈtiːtə(r)/ vi cambalear

teeth /tiːθ/ ▶ TOOTH

teeth|e /tiːð/ vi começar a ter dentes; **~ing troubles** fig problemas mpl iniciais

teetotaller /tiːˈtəʊtlə(r)/ n abstêmio m, (P) abstémio m

telecommunications /ˌtelɪkəmjuːnɪˈkeɪʃnz/ npl telecomunicações fpl

telegram /ˈtelɪɡræm/ n telegrama m

telepath|y /tɪˈlepəθɪ/ n telepatia f

telephone /ˈtelɪfəʊn/ n telefone m ● vt ‹person› telefonar a; ‹message› telefonar ● vi telefonar; **~ book**

lista f telefônica, (P) telefónica; **~ box, ~ booth** cabine f telefónica, (P) telefónica; **~ call** chamada f; **~ directory** lista f telefônica, (P) telefónica, guia m telefônico; **~ number** número m de telefone

telephoto /telɪˈfəʊtəʊ/ n **~ lens** teleobjetiva f

telescop|e /ˈtelɪskəʊp/ n telescópio m ● vt/i encaixar(-se). **~ic** /-ˈskɒpɪk/ a telescópico

televise /ˈtelɪvaɪz/ vt televisionar, transmitir pela televisão

television /ˈtelɪvɪʒn/ n televisão f; **~ set** aparelho m de televisão, televisor m

teleworking /ˈtelɪwɜːkɪŋ/ n teletrabalho m

tell /tel/ vt (pt told) dizer (sb sth alg coisa a alguém); ‹story› contar; (distinguish) distinguir, diferençar, diferenciar; **I told you so** bem lhe disse; **~ off** 🔢 (scold) ralhar com, dar uma bronca em; **~ tales** mexericar, fofocar ● vi (know) ver-se, saber; **~ of** falar de; **~ on** (have effect on) afetar; 🔢 (inform on) fazer queixa de 🔢. **~tale** n mexeriqueiro m, fofoqueiro m ● a (revealing) revelador

telly /ˈtelɪ/ n 🔢 TV f 🔢

temp /temp/ n 🔢 empregado m temporário

temper /ˈtempə(r)/ n humor m, disposição f; (anger) mau humor m ● vt temperar; **keep/lose one's ~** manter a calma/perder a calma or a cabeça, zangar-se

temperament /ˈtemprəmənt/ n temperamento m. **~al** /-ˈmentl/ a caprichoso

temperate /ˈtempərət/ a moderado, comedido; ‹climate› temperado

temperature /'temprətʃə(r)/ n
temperatura f; **have a ~** estar com
or ter febre

tempestuous /tem'pestʃʊəs/ a
tempestuoso

template /'templ(e)ɪt/ n molde m

temple[1] /'templ/ n templo m

temple[2] /'templ/ n Anat têmpora
f, fonte f

tempo /'tempəʊ/ n (pl **-os**) Mus
tempo m; (pace) ritmo m

temporar|y /'temprərɪ/ a
temporário, provisório

tempt /tempt/ vt tentar; **~ sb to
do** tentar alguém a fazer, dar a
alguém vontade de fazer. **~ation**
/-'teɪʃn/ n tentação f. **~ing** a
tentador

ten /ten/ a & n dez m

tenac|ious /tɪ'neɪʃəs/ a tenaz. **~ity**
/-æsətɪ/ n tenacidade f

tenant /'tenənt/ n inquilino m,
locatário m

tend[1] /tend/ vt tomar conta de,
cuidar de

tend[2] /tend/ vi **~ to** (be apt to)
tender a, ter tendência para

tendency /'tendənsɪ/ n tendência f

tender[1] /'tendə(r)/ a (soft, delicate)
terno; (sore, painful) sensível,
dolorido; (loving) terno, meigo.
~-hearted a compassivo. **~ly** adv
(lovingly) ternamente, meigamente;
(delicately) delicadamente. **~ness** n
(love) ternura f, meiguice f

tender[2] /'tendə(r)/ vt <money>
oferecer; <apologies, resignation>
apresentar ● vi **~ (for)** apresentar
orçamento (para) ● n Comm
orçamento m; **legal ~** (money)
moeda f corrente

tendon /'tendən/ n tendão m

tenement /'tenəmənt/ n prédio
m de apartamentos de renda
moderada; Amer (slum) prédio m
pobre

tennis /'tenɪs/ n tênis m, (P) ténis m;
~ court quadra f de tênis, (P) court
m de ténis

tenor /'tenə(r)/ n (meaning) teor m;
Mus tenor m

tense[1] /tens/ n Gram tempo m

tense[2] /tens/ a (**-er, -est**) tenso ● vt
<muscles> retesar

tension /'tenʃn/ n tensão f

tent /tent/ n tenda f, barraca f

tentative /'tentətɪv/ a provisório;
(hesitant) hesitante

tenterhooks /'tentəhʊks/ npl **on
~** em suspense

tenth /tenθ/ a & n décimo m

tenuous /'tenjʊəs/ a tênue, (P)
ténue

tepid /'tepɪd/ a tépido, morno

term /tɜːm/ n (word) termo m;
(limit) prazo m, termo m; Schol
etc período m, trimestre m; Amer
semestre m; (of imprisonment)
(duração de) pena f; **~ of office**
Pol mandato m; **come to ~s with**
chegar a um acordo com; (become
resigned to) resignar-se a; **~s**
(conditions) condições fpl; **on good/
bad ~s** de boas/más relações;
not on speaking ~s de relações
cortadas ● vt designar, denominar,
chamar

terminal /'tɜːmɪnl/ a terminal,
final; <illness> fatal, mortal, terminal
● n (oil, computer) terminal m; Rail
estação f terminal; Electr borne m;
(air) ~ terminal m (de avião)

terminat|e /'tɜːmɪneɪt/ vt
terminar, pôr termo a ● vi terminar.

terminology | thankless

~ion /-'neɪʃn/ n término m, (P) terminação f, termo m

terminology /tɜːmɪ'nɒlədʒɪ/ n terminologia f

terminus /'tɜːmɪnəs/ n (pl -ni /-naɪ/) (rail, coach) estação f terminal

terrace /'terəs/ n terraço m; (in cultivation) socalco m; (houses) casas fpl em fileira contínua, lance m de casas; **the ~s** Sport arquibancada f, (P) bancada f (principal); **~d house** casa f ladeada por outras casas

terrain /te'reɪn/ n terreno m

terrib|le /'terəbl/ a terrível. **~y** adv terrivelmente; ◻ (very) extremamente; espantosamente

terrific /tə'rɪfɪk/ a terrífico, tremendo; ◻ (excellent; great) tremendo, fantástico. **~ally** adv ◻ (very) tremendamente; ◻ (very well) lindamente; maravilhosamente

terrif|y /'terɪfaɪ/ vt aterrar, aterrorizar; be **~ied** of ter pavor de

territorial /terɪ'tɔːrɪəl/ a territorial

territory /'terɪtərɪ/ n território m

terror /'terə(r)/ n terror m, pavor m

terrorism /'terərɪzəm/ n terrorismo m

terroris|t /'terərɪst/ n terrorista mf. **~m** /-zəm/ n terrorismo m

terrorize /'terəraɪz/ vt aterrorizar, aterrar

terse /tɜːs/ a conciso, lapidar; (curt) lacónico, (P) lacónico

test /test/ n teste m, exame m, prova f; Schol prova f, teste m; (of goods) controle m; (of machine etc) ensaio m; (of strength) prova f; **put to the ~** pôr à prova; **~ match** jogo m internacional ● vt examinar; (check) controlar; (try) ensaiar; ‹pupil› interrogar, (P) examinar. **~ tube** n

proveta f; **~-tube baby** bebê m de proveta, (P) bebé-proveta mf

testament /'testəmənt/ n testamento m; **Old/New T~** Antigo/ Novo Testamento m

testicle /'testɪkl/ n testículo m

testify /'testɪfaɪ/ vt/i testificar, testemunhar, depor

testimonial /testɪ'məʊnɪəl/ n carta f de recomendação

testimony /'testɪmənɪ/ n testemunho m

tetanus /'tetənəs/ n tétano m

tether /'teðə(r)/ vt prender com corda ● n **be at the end of one's ~** estar nas últimas

text /tekst/ n texto m; **~ message** mensagem f escrita or (P) sms m ● vt enviar uma mensagem de texto a

textbook /'tekstbʊk/ n compêndio m, manual m, livro m de texto

textile /'tekstaɪl/ n & a têxtil m

texture /'tekstʃə(r)/ n (of fabric) textura f; (of paper) grão m

Thai /taɪ/ a & n tailandês m. **~land** n Tailândia f

Thames /temz/ n Tâmisa f

than /ðæn unstressed ðən/ conj que, do que; (with numbers) de; **more/less ~ ten** mais/menos de dez

thank /θæŋk/ vt agradecer; **~ you!** obrigado! **~s!** ◻ obrigado. **~s** npl agradecimentos mpl; **~s to** graças a; **T~sgiving (Day)** Amer Dia m de Ação de Graças

thankful /'θæŋkfl/ a grato; agradecido; reconhecido (for por). **~ly** adv com gratidão; (happily) felizmente

thankless /'θæŋklɪs/ a ingrato

that /ðæt *unstressed* ðət/ ● *a*

····▸ (*nearer*) esse/essa; **I want ~ drink** quero essa bebida; **give me ~ one** me dê esse; (*further away*) aquele/aquela; **~ drink over there** aquela bebida lá

● *pron*

····▸ esse/essa; (*indefinite*) isso; **what's ~ on your shirt?** o que é isso na sua camiseta?; (*further away*) aquele/aquela; (*indefinite*) aquilo; **who's ~?** quem é?; **~'s Peter over there** aquele ali é o Peter; **those are my parents** aqueles são os meus pais; **what's ~ over there on the hill?** o que é aquilo lá na montanha?

● *rel pron*

····▸ que; **where's the letter ~ came yesterday?** onde está a carta que veio ontem?; **the man ~ stole the car** o homem que roubou o carro

❗ With a preposition, use *o qual, a qual* when referring to objects: **the chair that I was sitting on** *a cadeira na qual eu estava sentada*

❗ With a preposition, use *quem* when referring to people: **the people that I've talked about** *as pessoas de quem falei*; **the girls that I was talking to** *as meninas com quem eu estava falando* (*referring to time*) em que; **the year ~ he died** o ano em que ele morreu; **the day ~ we went to the beach** o dia em que fomos para a praia

● *adv*

····▸ tão, tanto assim; **he's not ~ stupid** ele não é assim tão

estúpido; **it isn't ~ cold** não está assim tanto frio

● *conj*

····▸ que; **I don't think ~ he'll come** não me parece que ele venha; **we know ~ you're right** sabemos que você tem razão

····▸ (*in phrases*) **~ is (to say)** isto é; **~'s right** é isso mesmo; **like ~** assim; **don't be like ~!** não seja assim!

thatch /θætʃ/ *n* colmo *m*. **~ed** *a* de colmo; **~ed cottage** casa *f* com telhado de colmo

thaw /θɔː/ *vt/i* derreter(-se), degelar; ‹*food*› descongelar ● *n* degelo *m*, derretimento *m*

the *before vowel* /ðɪ *before consonant* ðə *stressed* ðiː/ ● *definite article*

····▸ o, a; (*pl* os, as; **~ dog** o cão; **~ tree** a árvore; **go to ~ dentist** ir ao dentista; **in ~ garden** no jardim

❗ When the articles *o* and *a* follow the prepositions *a, de,* and *em,* they often contract to form *ao, à, do, da* and *no, na.* (+ *adjective to form noun*) **~ blind** os cegos; **~ unemployed** os desempregados; **~ impossible** o impossível; (+ *nationality*) **~ French** os franceses; **~ Portuguese** os portugueses; (*per*) **paid by ~ hour** pago por hora; **sold by ~ dozen** vendido por dúzia

● *adv*

····▸ **~ more...~ more...** quanto mais...tanto mais...

theatre /ˈθɪətə(r)/ *n* teatro *m*
theatrical /θɪˈætrɪkl/ *a* teatral
theft /θeft/ *n* roubo *m*

their /ðeə(r)/ a deles, delas, seu

theirs /ðeaz/ poss pron o(s) seu(s), a(s) sua(s), o(s) deles, a(s) delas; **it is ~** é (o) deles/delas or o seu

them /ðem unstressed ðəm/ pron os, as; (after prep) eles, elas; **(to) ~** lhes

theme /θiːm/ n tema m; **~ park** parque m temático

themselves /ðəm'selvz/ pron eles mesmos/próprios, elas mesmas/ próprias; (reflexive) se; (after prep) si (mesmos, próprios); **by ~** sozinhos; **with ~** consigo

then /ðen/ adv (at that time) então, nessa altura; (next) depois, em seguida; (in that case) então, nesse caso; (therefore) então, portanto, por conseguinte

theolog|y /θɪ'ɒlədʒɪ/ n teologia f. **~ian** /θɪə'ləʊdʒən/ n teólogo m

theor|y /'θɪərɪ/ n teoria f. **~etical** /-'retɪkl/ a teórico

therapeutic /θerə'pjuːtɪk/ a terapêutico

therap|y /'θerəpɪ/ n terapia f. **~ist** n terapeuta mf

there /ðeə(r)/ adv aí, ali, lá; (over there) lá, acolá ● int (triumphant) pronto, aí está; (consoling) então, vamos lá; **he goes ~** ele vai aí or lá; **~ he goes** aí vai ele; **~ is, ~ are** há; **~ you are** (giving) toma; **~ and then** logo ali. **~abouts** adv por aí. **~by** adv desse modo

therefore /'ðeəfɔː(r)/ adv por isso, portanto, por conseguinte

thermal /'θɜːml/ a térmico

thermometer /θə'mɒmɪtə(r)/ n termômetro m, (P) termómetro m

Thermos® /'θɜːməs/ n garrafa f térmica, (P) termo m

thermostat /'θɜːməstæt/ n termostato m

thesaurus /θɪ'sɔːrəs/ n (pl **-ri** /-raɪ/) dicionário m de sinónimos, (P) sinónimos

these /ðiːz/ ▶ THIS

thesis /'θiːsɪs/ n (pl **theses** /-siːz/) tese f

they /ðeɪ/ pron eles, elas; **~ say (that)...** diz-se or dizem que

thick /θɪk/ a (-er, -est) espesso, grosso; ⊞ (stupid) estúpido ● adv = THICKLY ● **in the ~ of** no meio de. **~skinned** a insensível. **~ly** adv espessamente; (spread) em camada espessa. **~ness** n espessura f, grossura f

thicken /'θɪkən/ vt/i engrossar, espessar(-se); **the plot ~s** o enredo complica-se

thief /θiːf/ n (pl **thieves** /θiːvz/) ladrão m, gatuno m

thigh /θaɪ/ n coxa f

thimble /'θɪmbl/ n dedal m

thin /θɪn/ a (thinner, thinnest) (slender) estreito, fino, delgado; (lean, not plump) magro; (sparse) ralo, escasso; (flimsy) leve, fino; <soup> aguado; <hair> ralo ● adv = THINLY ● vt/i (pt thinned) (of liquid) diluir(-se); (of fog etc) dissipar(-se); (of hair) rarear; **~ out** (in quantity) diminuir, reduzir; <seedlings etc> desbastar. **~ly** adv (sparsely) esparsamente. **~ness** n (of board, wire etc) finura f; (of person) magreza f

thing /θɪŋ/ n coisa f; **~s** (belongings) pertences mpl; **the best ~ is** to o melhor é; **for one ~** em primeiro lugar; **just the ~** exatamente o que era preciso; **poor ~** coitado

think /θɪŋk/ vt/i (pt thought) pensar (about, of em); (carefully) refletir (about, of em, sobre); **I ~ so** eu acho que sim; **~ better of it**

(*change one's mind*) pensar melhor; ~ **nothing of** achar natural; ~ **of** (*hold opinion of*) pensar de, achar de; ~ **over** pensar bem em; ~ **up** inventar. ~ **tank** n comissão f de peritos

third /θɜːd/ a o terceiro; T~ **World** Terceiro Mundo m; ~**party insurance** seguro m contra terceiros ● n terceiro m; (*fraction*) terço m. ~**rate** a inferior, medíocre. ~**ly** adv em terceiro lugar

thirst /θɜːst/ n sede f. ~**y** a sequioso, sedento; **be** ~**y** estar com or ter sede

thirteen /θɜːˈtiːn/ a & n treze m. ~**th** a & n décimo terceiro m

thirt|y /ˈθɜːtɪ/ a & n trinta m. ~**ieth** a & n trigésimo m

this /ðɪs/ (*pl* **these**) ● a

····▸ este, esta; **I don't like** ~ **car** não gosto deste carro; ~ **morning** esta manhã; ~ **Wednesday** esta quarta-feira; ~ **one** este, esta; **these ones** estes, estas; **I'll have** ~ **one, please** quero este, por favor

● pron

····▸ este, esta; (*indefinite*) isto; **what's** ~? o que é isto?; **what are these?** o que são (estes/ estas)?; ~ **is the kitchen** esta é a cozinha; **after** ~ depois disto

● adv

····▸ ~ **far** tão longe; **I didn't think we would get** ~ **far** nunca pensei que chegássemos tão longe; ~ **high** desta altura; **it's about** ~ **high** é mais ou menos desta altura

····▸ (*in phrases*) **like** ~ assim, desta forma; **do it like** ~ faça assim; ~ **and that** isto e aquilo;

'what did you talk about?'– **'oh,** ~ **and that'** 'de que falaram?'– 'oh, disto e daquilo'

thistle /ˈθɪsl/ n cardo m

thorn /θɔːn/ n espinho m, pico m. ~**y** a espinhoso; *fig* bicudo; espinhoso

thorough /ˈθʌrə/ a consciencioso; (*deep*) completo, profundo; <*cleaning, washing*> a fundo. ~**ly** adv <*clean, study etc*> completo, a fundo; (*very*) perfeitamente, muito bem

thoroughbred /ˈθʌrəbred/ n <*horse etc*> puro-sangue m invar

those /ðəʊz/ ▶ **THAT**

though /ðəʊ/ *conj* se bem que, embora, conquanto ● adv ⚀ contudo; no entanto

thought /θɔːt/ ▶ **THINK** ● n pensamento m; ideia f; **on second** ~**s** pensando bem

thoughtful /ˈθɔːtfl/ a pensativo; (*considerate*) atencioso, solícito. ~**ly** adv pensativamente; (*considerately*) com consideração, atenciosamente

thoughtless /ˈθɔːtlɪs/ a irrefletido; (*inconsiderate*) pouco atencioso. ~**ly** adv sem pensar; (*inconsiderately*) sem consideração

thousand /ˈθaʊznd/ a & n mil m; ~**s of** milhares de. ~**th** a & n milésimo m

thrash /θræʃ/ vt surrar, espancar; (*defeat*) dar uma surra or sova em; ~ **about** debater-se; ~ **out** debater a fundo, discutir bem

thread /θred/ n fio m; (*for sewing*) linha f de coser; (*of screw*) rosca f ● vt enfiar; ~ **one's way** abrir caminho, furar

threadbare /ˈθredbeə(r)/ a puído, surrado

threat /θret/ n ameaça f

threaten /'θretn/ vt/i ameaçar

three /θri:/ a & n três m

thresh /θreʃ/ vt ‹corn etc› malhar, debulhar

threshold /'θreʃəʊld/ n limiar m, soleira f; fig limiar m

threw /θru:/ ▶ THROW

thrift /θrɪft/ n economia f, poupança f. ~y a econômico, (P) económico, poupado

thrill /θrɪl/ n arrepio m de emoção, frêmito m, (P) frémito m ● vt excitar(-se), emocionar(-se), (fazer) vibrar; **be ~ed** estar/ficar encantado. ~ing a excitante, emocionante

thriller /'θrɪlə(r)/ n livro ou filme de suspense m

thriv|e /θraɪv/ vi (pt **thrived** or **throve**, pp **thrived** or **thriven**) prosperar, florescer; (grow strong) dar-se bem (on com). ~ing a próspero

throat /θrəʊt/ n garganta f; **have a sore ~** ter dores de garganta

throb /θrɒb/ vi (pt **throbbed**) ‹wound, head› latejar; ‹heart› palpitar, bater; ‹engine› also fig vibrar, trepidar ● n (of pain) latejo m, espasmo m; (of heart) palpitação f, batida f; (of engine) vibração f, trepidação f

throes /θrəʊz/ npl **in the ~ of** fig às voltas com, no meio de

throne /θrəʊn/ n trono m

throttle /'θrɒtl/ n Auto válvula-borboleta f, estrangulador m, acelerador de mão ● vt estrangular

through /θru:/ prep através de, por; (during) durante; (by means of way of, out of) por; (by reason of) por, por causa de ● adv através;

(entirely) completamente, até o fim; **be ~** ter acabado (**with** com); Telephone estar ligado; **come** or **go ~** (cross, pierce) atravessar; **get** ‹exam› passar; **be wet ~** estar ensopado or encharcado ● a ‹train, traffic etc› direto

throughout /θru:'aʊt/ prep durante, por todo; **~ the country** por todo o país (afora); **~ the day** durante todo a dia, pelo dia afora ● adv completamente, (place) por toda a parte; (time) durante todo o tempo

throw /θrəʊ/ vt (pt **threw**, pp **thrown**) atirar, jogar, lançar; Ⓘ (baffle) desconcertar; **~ a party** Ⓘ dar uma festa; **~ away** jogar fora, (P) deitar fora; **~ off** (get rid of) livrar-se de; **~ out** ‹person› expulsar; (reject) rejeitar; **~ over** (desert) abandonar, deixar; **~ up** ‹one's arms› levantar; (resign from) abandonar; Ⓘ (vomit) vomitar ● n lançamento m; (of dice) lance m

thrush /θrʌʃ/ n (bird) tordo m

thrust /θrʌst/ vt (pt **thrust**) arremeter, empurrar, impelir ● n empurrão m, arremetida f; **~ into** (put) enfiar em, mergulhar em; **~ upon** (force on) impor a

thud /θʌd/ n som m surdo, baque m

thug /θʌg/ n bandido m, facínora m, malfeitor m

thumb /θʌm/ n polegar m; **under sb's ~** completamente dominado por alguém ● vt ‹book› manusear; **~ a lift** pedir carona, (P) boleia

thumbtack /'θʌmtæk/ n Amer percevejo m

thump /θʌmp/ vt/i bater (em), dar pancadas (em); (with fists) dar murros (em); ‹piano› martelar (em); (of heart) bater com força (em) pancada f; (thud) baque m

thunder /'θʌndə(r)/ n trovão m, trovoada f; (loud noise) estrondo m ● vi (weather, person) trovejar; ~ **past** passar como um raio. **~y** a (weather) tempestuoso

thunderbolt /'θʌndəbəʊlt/ n raio m e ribombo m de trovão; fig raio m fulminante fig

thunderstorm /'θʌndəstɔːm/ n tempestade f com trovoadas, temporal m

Thursday /'θɜːzdɪ/ n quinta-feira f

thus /ðʌs/ adv assim, desta maneira; ~ **far** até aqui

thwart /θwɔːt/ vt frustrar, contrariar

thyme /taɪm/ n tomilho m

tick¹ /tɪk/ n (sound) tique-taque m; (mark) sinal m; 𝗜 (moment) instantinho m ● vt ~ (**off**) marcar com sinal; ~ **off** 𝗜 (scold) dar uma bronca em 𝗜 (P) ralhar com; ~ **over** (engine, factory) funcionar em marcha lenta, (P) em 'ralenti'

tick² /tɪk/ n (insect) carrapato m

ticket /'tɪkɪt/ n bilhete m; (label) etiqueta f; (for traffic offence) aviso m de multa. ~ **collector** n (railway) guarda m; ~ **office** n bilheteira f

tickle /'tɪkl/ vt fazer cócegas; fig (amuse) divertir ● n cócegas fpl, comichão m

ticklish /'tɪklɪʃ/ a coceguento, sensível a cócegas; fig delicado; melindroso

tidal /'taɪdl/ a de marés, que tem marés; ~ **wave** onda f gigantesca; fig onda f de sentimento popular, vaga f de fundo

tide /taɪd/ n maré f; (of events) marcha f, curso m; **high** ~ maré f

cheia, preia-mar f; **low** ~ maré f baixa, baixa-mar f ● vt ~ **over** (help temporarily) aguentar

tid|y /'taɪdɪ/ a (-ier, -iest) ‹room› arrumado; ‹appearance, work› asseado, cuidado; (methodical) bem ordenado; 𝗜 ‹amount› belo 𝗜 ● vt arrumar, arranjar. **~iness** n arrumação f, ordem f

tie /taɪ/ vt (pres p tying) atar, amarrar, prender; (link) ligar, vincular; ‹a knot› dar, fazer ● vi Sport empatar ● n fio m, cordel m; (necktie) gravata f; (link) laço m, vínculo m; Sport empate m; ~ **in with** estar ligado com, relacionar-se com; ~ **up** amarrar, atar; ‹animal› prender; ‹money› imobilizar; (occupy) ocupar

tier /tɪə(r)/ n cada fila f, camada f, prateleira f etc colocada em cima de outra; (in stadium) bancada f; (of cake) andar m; (of society) camada f

tiger /'taɪgə(r)/ n tigre m

tight /taɪt/ a (-er, -est) ‹clothes› apertado, justo; ‹rope› esticado, tenso; ‹control› rigoroso; ‹knot, schedule, lid› apertado; 𝗜 (drunk) embriagado 𝗜; **be in a ~ corner** fig estar em apuros or num aperto, (P) estar entalado 𝗜 ● adv = **TIGHTLY**. **~ly** adv bem; (squeeze) com força

tighten /'taɪtn/ vt/i ‹rope› esticar; ‹bolt, control› apertar; ~ **up on** apertar o cinto

tightrope /'taɪtrəʊp/ n corda (de acrobacias) f; ~ **walker** funâmbulo m

tights /taɪts/ npl collants mpl, meias-colant fpl

tile /taɪl/ n (on wall, floor) ladrilho m, azulejo m; (on roof) telha f ● vt ladrilhar, pôr azulejos em; (roof) telhar, cobrir com telhas

till¹ /tɪl/ vt ‹land› cultivar

till² /tɪl/ *prep & conj* = UNTIL

till³ /tɪl/ *n* caixa (registadora) *f*

tilt /tɪlt/ *vt/i* inclinar(-se), pender ● *n* (*slope*) inclinação *f*; **(at) full ~ a** toda a velocidade

timber /'tɪmbə(r)/ *n* madeira (de construção) *f*; (*trees*) árvores *fpl*

time /taɪm/ *n* tempo *m*; (*moment*) momento *m*; (*epoch*) época *f*, tempo *m*; (*by clock*) horas *fpl*; (*occasion*) vez *f*; (*rhythm*) compasso *m*; **~s** (*multiplying*) vezes *fpl*; **at ~s** às vezes; **for the ~ being** por agora, por enquanto; **from ~ to ~** de vez em quando; **have a good ~** divertir-se; **have no ~ for** não ter paciência para; **in no ~** num instante; **in ~ a** tempo; (*eventually*) com o tempo; **in two days' ~** daqui a dois dias; **on ~** na hora, (*P*) a horas; **take your ~** não se apresse; **what's the ~?** que horas são?; **~ bomb** bomba-relógio *f*; **~ off** tempo *m* livre; **~ zone** fuso *m* horário ● *vt* escolher a hora para; (*measure*) marcar o tempo de; *Sport* cronometrar; (*regulate*) acertar. **~ limit** *n* prazo *m*

timeless /'taɪmlɪs/ *a* intemporal; (*unending*) eterno

timely /'taɪmlɪ/ *a* oportuno

timer /'taɪmə(r)/ *n* Techn relógio *m*; (*with sand*) ampulheta *f*

timetable /'taɪmteɪbl/ *n* horário *m*

timid /'tɪmɪd/ *a* tímido; (*fearful*) assustadiço, medroso

timing /'taɪmɪŋ/ *n* (*measuring*) cronometragem *f*; (*of artist*) ritmo *m*; (*moment*) cálculo *m* do tempo, timing *m*; **good/bad ~** (*moment*) momento *m* bem/mal escolhido

tin /tɪn/ *n* estanho *m*; (*container*) lata *f*; **~ foil** papel *m* de alumínio; **~ plate** lata *f*, folha(-de-Flandes) *f* ● *vt* (*pt* tinned) estanhar; ‹*food*› enlatar;

~ned foods conservas *fpl*. **~ opener** *n* abridor *m* de latas, (*P*) abre-latas *m*. **~ny** *a* ‹*sound*› metálico

tinge /tɪndʒ/ *vt* **~ (with)** tingir (de); *fig* dar um toque (de) ● *n* tom *m*, matiz *m*; *fig* toque *m*

tingle /'tɪŋgl/ *vi* (*sting*) arder; (*prickle*) picar ● *n* ardor *m*; (*prickle*) picadela *f*

tinker /'tɪŋkə(r)/ *n* latoeiro *m* ambulante ● *vi* **~ (with)** mexer (em), tentar consertar

tinkle /'tɪŋkl/ *n* tinido *m*, tilintar *m* ● *vt/i* tilintar

tinsel /'tɪnsl/ *n* fio *m* prateado/ dourado, enfeites *mpl* metálicos de Natal; *fig* falso brilho *m*; ouropel *m*

tint /tɪnt/ *n* tom *m*, matiz *m*; (*for hair*) tintura *f*, tinta *f* ● *vt* tingir, colorir

tiny /'taɪnɪ/ *a* (-ier, -iest) minúsculo, pequenino

tip¹ /tɪp/ *n* ponta *f*; **(have sth) on the ~ of one's tongue** ter algo na ponta da língua

tip² /tɪp/ *vt/i* (*pt* tipped) (*tilt*) inclinar(-se); (*overturn*) virar(-se); (*pour*) colocar, (*P*) deitar; (*empty*) despejar(-se); **~ off** avisar, prevenir ● *n* (*money*) gorjeta *f*; (*advice*) sugestão *f*; dica *f* 🄸; (*for rubbish*) lixeira *f*. **~-off** *n* (*warning*) aviso *m*; (*information*) informação *f*

tipsy /'tɪpsɪ/ *a* ligeiramente embriagado, alegre, tocado 🄸

tiptoe /'tɪptəʊ/ *n* **on ~** na ponta dos pés

tire¹ /'taɪə(r)/ *vt/i* cansar(-se) (*of* de). **~eless** *a* incansável, infatigável. **~ing** *a* fatigante, cansativo

tire² /'taɪə(r)/ *n* Amer pneu *m*

tired /'taɪəd/ *a* cansado, fatigado; **~ of** (*sick of*) farto de; **~ out** morto de cansaço

tiresome /'taɪəsəm/ a maçador; aborrecido; chato ⊠

tissue /'tɪʃuː/ n tecido m; (handkerchief) lenço m de papel. **~ paper** n papel m de seda

tit[1] /tɪt/ n (bird) chapim m, canário-da-terra m

tit[2] /tɪt/ a give ~ **for tat** pagar na mesma moeda

titbit /'tɪtbɪt/ n petisco m

title /'taɪtl/ n título m

---

to /tuː/ unstressed tə/ ● prep

••••> (direction) a; **go ~ the beach** ir para a praia; **go ~ the dentist** ir ao dentista; **go ~ a party** ir a uma festa; **go ~ Portugal** (for a short time) ir a Portugal; (for good) ir para Portugal; **go ~ bed** ir para a cama; **go ~ school/university** ir para a escola/faculdade

! The preposition a often contracts with the definite articles o and a to form ao and à.

••••> (up to) até; **go ~ the end of the street** ir até ao fim da rua; **~ this day** até hoje; **from Monday ~ Friday** de segunda a sexta

••••> (expressing indirect object) **give sth ~ sb** dar algo para alguém; **give the book ~ her** dá-lhe o livro para ela; **give it ~ me** me dá isso

••••> (attitude) para (com); **she was nice ~ him** ela foi simpática para com ele

••••> (in telling time) para; **it's ten ~ six** são dez para as seis

••••> (expressing duration) **it lasts three ~ four hours** dura entre três a quatro horas

● infinitive particle

••••> (forming infinitive) ~ **eat** comer

! In an infinitive to is not translated: **to sing** cantar; **to go** ir (purpose) para; **I set out ~ buy food** saí para ir buscar comida

••••> (after be + adjectives) de; **easy/difficult ~ read** ser fácil/difícil de ler; **it's easy ~ forget** é fácil esquecer

••••> (in phrases) **go ~ and fro** andar de um lado para o outro.

~do n [!](fuss) agitação f; **he made a great ~do about being left off the guest list** causou muita agitação por ter sido excluído da lista de convidados; **~be** adj **her husband-~be** o seu futuro marido →For verbal expressions using the infinitive to such as **to tell sb to do sth** and **to help sb to do sth** see entries **tell** and **help**

---

toad /təʊd/ n sapo m

toady /'təʊdɪ/ n lambe-botas 🄸 mf, puxa-saco 🄸 m ● vi puxar saco 🄸 bajular, ser um(a) lambe-botas

toast /təʊst/ n fatia f de pão torrado, torrada f; (drink) brinde m, saúde f ● vt (bread) torrar; (drink to) brindar, beber à saúde de. **~er** n torradeira f

tobacco /tə'bækəʊ/ n tabaco m

toboggan /tə'bɒgən/ n tobogã m

today /tə'deɪ/ n & adv hoje m

toddler /'tɒdlə(r)/ n criança f que está aprendendo a andar or (P) a aprender a andar

toe /təʊ/ n dedo m do pé; (of shoe, stocking) biqueira f; **on one's ~s** alerta, vigilante ● vt **~ the line** andar na linha. **~nail** n unha f do dedo do pé

TOEFL – Test of English as a Foreign Language Exame *i* que se faz para se candidatar a qualquer universidade americana e que certifica o domínio do inglês dos estudantes que falam outros idiomas como língua materna.

toffee /'tɒfɪ/ n puxa-puxa m, (P) caramelo m. **~ apple** n maçã f caramelizada

together /tə'geðə(r)/ adv junto, juntamente, juntos; (at the same time) ao mesmo tempo; **~ with** juntamente com. **~ness** n camaradagem f, companheirismo m

toil /tɔɪl/ vi labutar ● n labuta f, labor m

toilet /'tɔɪlɪt/ n banheiro m, (P) casa f de banho; (grooming) toalete f; **~ water** água-de-colônia f, (P) água-de-colónia. **~ paper** n papel m higiênico or (P) higiénico; **~ roll** n rolo m de papel higiênico, (P) higiénico

toiletries /'tɔɪlɪtrɪz/ npl artigos mpl de toalete

token /'təʊkən/ n sinal m, prova f; (voucher) cheque m; (coin) ficha f ● a simbólico

told /təʊld/ ▶ TELL ● a **all ~** (all in all) ao todo

tolerable /'tɒlərəbl/ a tolerável; (not bad) sofrível, razoável

toleran|t /'tɒlərənt/ a tolerante (of para com). **~ce** n tolerância f

tolerate /'tɒləreɪt/ vt tolerar

toll¹ /təʊl/ n pedágio m, (P) portagem f; **death ~** número m de mortos; **take its ~** (of age) fazer sentir o seu peso

toll² /təʊl/ vt/i (of bell) dobrar

tomato /tə'mɑːtəʊ/ n (pl -oes) tomate m

tomb /tuːm/ n túmulo m, sepultura f

tomboy /'tɒmbɔɪ/ n menina f levada (e masculinizada), (P) maria-rapaz f

tombstone /'tuːmstəʊn/ n lápide f, pedra f tumular

tomorrow /tə'mɒrəʊ/ n & adv amanhã m; **~ morning/night** amanhã de manhã/à noite

ton /tʌn/ n tonelada f (= 1016 kg); **(metric) ~** tonelada f (= 1000 kg); **~s of** 🄵 montes de 🄵, (P) carradas de 🄵

tone /təʊn/ n tom m; (of radio, telephone etc) sinal m; (colour) tom m, tonalidade f; Med tonicidade f ● vt **~ down** atenuar ● vi **~ in** combinar-se, harmonizar-se (with com); **~ up** ⟨muscles⟩ tonificar. **~deaf** a sem ouvido musical

tongs /tɒŋz/ n tenaz f; (for sugar) pinça f; (for hair) pinça f

tongue /tʌŋ/ n língua f. **~-in-cheek** a & adv sem ser a sério, com ironia, a brincar. **~-tied** a calado. **~-twister** n trava-língua m

tonic /'tɒnɪk/ n Med tônico m, (P) tónico m; Mus tônica f, (P) tónica f ● a tônico, (P) tónico

tonight /tə'naɪt/ adv & n hoje à noite, logo à noite, esta noite f

tonne /tʌn/ n (metric) tonelada f

tonsil /'tɒnsl/ n amígdala f

tonsillitis /tɒnsɪ'laɪtɪs/ n amigdalite f

too /tuː/ adv demasiado, demais; (also) também, igualmente; 🔟 (very) muito

took /tʊk/ ▶ TAKE

tool /tuːl/ n (carpenter's, plumber's etc) ferramenta f; (gardener's) utensílio m; fig (person) joguete m. **~bag** n saco m de ferramenta(s)

toot /tuːt/ n toque m de buzina ● vt/i **~ (the horn)** buzinar

tooth /tuːθ/ n (pl teeth) dente m. **~less** a desdentado

toothache /ˈtuːθeɪk/ n dor f de dentes

toothbrush /ˈtuːθbrʌʃ/ n escova f de dentes

toothpaste /ˈtuːθpeɪst/ n pasta f de dentes, dentifrício m, (P) dentífrico

toothpick /ˈtuːθpɪk/ n palito m

top¹ /tɒp/ n (highest point; upper part) alto m, cima m, topo m; (of hill; also fig) cume m; (upper surface) cimo m, topo m; (surface of table) tampo m; (lid) tampa f; (of bottle) rolha f; (of list) cabeça f; **from ~ to bottom** de alto a baixo; **on ~ of** em cima de; fig além de; **on ~ of that** ainda por cima ● a <shelf etc> de cima, superior; (in rank) primeiro; (best) melhor; (distinguished) eminente; (maximum) máximo; **~ gear** Auto a velocidade mais alta; **~ hat** chapéu m alto; **~ secret** ultrassecreto ● vt (pt topped) (exceed) ultrapassar, ir acima de; **~ up** encher; (mobiles) recarregar; **~ped with** coberto de. **~heavy** a mais pesado na parte de cima

top² /tɒp/ n (toy) pião m; **sleep like a ~** dormir como uma pedra

topic /ˈtɒpɪk/ n tópico m, assunto m

topical /ˈtɒpɪkl/ a da atualidade, corrente

topless /ˈtɒplɪs/ a com o peito nu, topless

topple /ˈtɒpl/ vt/i (fazer) desabar, (fazer) tombar, (fazer) cair

top-up card n cartão m pré-pago

top-up fees npl: contribuição complementar às mensalidades da universidade, para fins de matrícula; (P) contribuição suplementar acrescida às propinas da universidade

torch /tɔːtʃ/ n (electric) lanterna f elétrica; (flaming) archote m, facho f

tore /tɔː(r)/ ▶ TEAR¹

torment¹ /ˈtɔːment/ n tormento m

torment² /tɔːˈment/ vt atormentar, torturar; (annoy) aborrecer, chatear

torn /tɔːn/ ▶ TEAR¹

tornado /tɔːˈneɪdəʊ/ n (pl -oes) tornado m

torpedo /tɔːˈpiːdəʊ/ n (pl -oes) torpedo m ● vt torpedear

torrent /ˈtɒrənt/ n torrente f. **~ial** /təˈrenʃl/ a torrencial

torso /ˈtɔːsəʊ/ n (pl -os) torso m

tortoise /ˈtɔːtəs/ n tartaruga f

tortoiseshell /ˈtɔːtəʃel/ n (for ornaments etc) tartaruga f

tortuous /ˈtɔːtʃʊəs/ a (of path etc) que dá muitas voltas, sinuoso; fig tortuoso; retorcido

torture /ˈtɔːtʃə(r)/ n tortura f, suplício m ● vt torturar

Tory /ˈtɔːrɪ/ a & n 🔟 conservador m

toss /tɒs/ vt atirar, jogar, (P) deitar; (shake) agitar, sacudir ● vi agitar-se, debater-se; **~ a coin**, **~ up** tirar cara ou coroa

tot[1] /tɒt/ n criancinha f; ⊞ (glass) copinho m

tot[2] /tɒt/ vt/i (pt totted) ~ **up** ⊞ somar

total /ˈtəʊtl/ a & n total m ● vt (pt **totalled**) (find total of) totalizar; (amount to) elevar-se a, montar a. ~**ity** /-ˈtæləti/ n totalidade f. ~**ly** adv totalmente

totalitarian /təʊtælɪˈteəriən/ a totalitário

totter /ˈtɒtə(r)/ vi cambalear, andar aos tombos; (of tower etc) oscilar

touch /tʌtʃ/ vt/i tocar; (of ends, gardens etc) tocar-se; (tamper with) mexer em; (affect) comover; ~ **down** Aviat aterrissar, (P) aterrar; ~ **off** disparar; (cause) dar início a, desencadear; ~ **on** (mention) tocar em; ~ **up** retocar ● n (sense) tato m; (contact) toque m; (of colour) toque m, retoque m; a ~ **of** (small amount) um pouco de; **get in** ~ **with** entrar em contato, (P) contacto com; **lose** ~ perder contato, (P) contacto. ~**and-go** a (risky) arriscado; (uncertain) duvidoso, incerto; ~**line** n linha f lateral

touching /ˈtʌtʃɪŋ/ a comovente, comovedor

touchy /ˈtʌtʃi/ a melindroso, suscetível, que se ofende facilmente

tough /tʌf/ a (-er, -est) (hard, difficult; relentless) duro; (strong) forte, resistente ● n ~ (**guy**) valentão m, durão m ⊞; ~ **luck!** ⊞ pouca sorte!, que azar!

toughen /ˈtʌfn/ vt/i (person) endurecer; (strengthen) reforçar

tour /tʊə(r)/ n viagem f; (visit) visita f; (by team etc) tournée f; **on** ~ em tournée ● vt visitar

tourism /ˈtʊərɪzəm/ n turismo m

tourist /ˈtʊərɪst/ n turista mf ● a turístico; ~ **office** agência f de turismo

tournament /ˈtʊənəmənt/ n torneio m

tousle /ˈtaʊzl/ vt despentear, esguedelhar

tout /taʊt/ vi angariar clientes (**for** para) ● vt (try to sell) tentar revender ● n (hotel etc) angariador m; (ticket) cambista m, (P) revendedor m

tow /təʊ/ vt rebocar; ~ **away** ‹vehicle› rebocar ● n reboque m; **on** ~ a reboque. ~**path** n caminho m de sirga; ~ **rope** n cabo m de reboque

toward(s) /təˈwɔːd(z)/ prep para, em direção a, na direção de; (of attitude) para com; (time) por volta de

towel /ˈtaʊəl/ n toalha f; (tea towel) pano m de prato ● vt (pt **towelled**) esfregar com a toalha. ~ **rail** n toalheiro m. ~**ling** n atoalhado m, (P) pano m turco

tower /ˈtaʊə(r)/ n torre f; ~ **block** prédio m alto ● vi ~ **above** dominar. ~**ing** a muito alto; fig (of rage etc) violento

town /taʊn/ n cidade f; **go to** ~ ⊞ perder a cabeça ⊞; ~ **council** município m; ~ **hall** câmara f municipal; ~ **planning** urbanização f

toxic /ˈtɒksɪk/ a tóxico

toy /tɔɪ/ n brinquedo m ● vi ~ **with** ‹object› brincar com; ‹idea› considerar, cogitar

trace /treɪs/ n traço m, rastro m, sinal m; (small quantity) traço m, vestígio m ● vt seguir ou encontrar a pista de; (draw) traçar; (with tracing paper) decalcar

track /træk/ n (of person etc) rastro m, pista f; (racetrack, of tape) pista

f; (*record*) faixa f; (*path*) trilho m,
carreiro m; *Rail* via f ● vt seguir a
pista or a trajetória de; **keep ~ of**
manter-se em contato com; (*keep
oneself informed*) seguir; **~ down**
(*find*) encontrar, descobrir; (*hunt*)
seguir a pista de; **~ suit** conjunto m
de jogging, (P) fato m de treino

tractor /'træktə(r)/ n trator m

trade /treɪd/ n comércio m; (*job*)
ofício m, profissão f; (*swap*) troca
f; **~ mark** marca f de fábrica; **~
union** sindicato m ● vt/i comerciar
(em), negociar (em); **~ on** (*exploit*)
tirar partido de, abusar de ● vt
(*swap*) trocar; **~ in** ‹*used article*›
trocar. **~r** /-ə(r)/ n negociante mf,
comerciante mf

tradesman /'treɪdzmən/ n (*pl
-men*) comerciante m

trading /'treɪdɪŋ/ n comércio m;
~ estate zona f industrial

tradition /trə'dɪʃn/ n tradição f.
~al a tradicional

traffic /'træfɪk/ n (*trade*) tráfego
m, tráfico m; (*on road*) trânsito
m, tráfego m; *Aviat* tráfego m; **~
circle** *Amer* giratória f, (P) rotunda
f; **~ island** ilha f de pedestres,
(P) refúgio m para peões; **~ jam**
engarrafamento m; **~ warden**
guarda mf or (P) polícia mf de trânsito
● vi (*pt* **trafficked**) traficar (**in** em).
~ lights npl sinal m luminoso, (P)
semáforo m. **~ker** n traficante mf

tragedy /'trædʒədɪ/ n tragédia f.

tragic /'trædʒɪk/ a trágico

trail /treɪl/ vt/i arrastar(-se), rastejar;
(*of plant, on ground*) rastejar; (*of
plant, over wall*) trepar; (*track*) seguir
● n (*of powder, smoke etc*) esteira f;
rastro m, (P) rasto m; (*track*) pista f;
(*beaten path*) trilho m

trailer /'treɪlə(r)/ n reboque
m; *Amer* (*caravan*) reboque m;
caravana f, trailer m; (*film*) trailer m,
apresentação f de filme

train /treɪn/ n *Rail* trem m, (P)
comboio m; (*procession*) fila f; (*of
dress*) cauda f; (*retinue*) comitiva
f ● vt (*instruct, develop*) educar,
formar, treinar; ‹*plant*› guiar;
‹*sportsman, animal*› treinar; ‹*aim*›
assestar, apontar ● vi estudar,
treinar-se. **~ed** a (*skilled*) qualificado;
‹*doctor etc*› diplomado. **~er** n *Sport*
treinador m; (*shoe*) tênis m, (P) ténis
m. **~ing** n treino m

trainee /treɪ'niː/ n estagiário m

trait /treɪ(t)/ n traço m,
característica f

traitor /'treɪtə(r)/ n traidor m

tram /træm/ n bonde m, (P) (carro)
elétrico m

tramp /træmp/ vi marchar (com
passo pesado) ● vt percorrer,
palmilhar ● n som m de passos
pesados; (*vagrant*) vagabundo
m, andarilho m; (*hike*) longa
caminhada f

trample /'træmpl/ vt/i **~ (on)** pisar
com força; *fig* menosprezar

trampoline /'træmpəliːn/ n (*lona
f usada como*) trampolim m

trance /trɑːns/ n (*hypnotic*) transe
m; (*ecstasy*) êxtase m, arrebatamento
m; *Med* estupor m

tranquil /'træŋkwɪl/ a tranquilo,
sossegado. **~lity** /-'kwɪlətɪ/ n
tranquilidade f, sossego m

tranquillizer /'træŋkwɪlaɪzə(r)/ n
(*drug*) tranquilizante m, calmante m

transact /træn'zækt/ vt ‹*business*›
fazer; efetuar. **~ion** /-kʃn/ n
transação f

transcend /træn'send/ vt
transcender

transcri|be /træn'skraɪb/ vt
transcrever. **~pt, ~ption** /-ɪpʃn/ ns
transcrição f

transfer[1] /træns'fɜ:(r)/ vt (pt
transferred) transferir; ‹power,
property› transmitir; **~ the charges**
(telephone) ligar a cobrar ● vi
mudar(-se), ser transferido; (change
planes etc) fazer transferência

transfer[2] /'trænsfɜ:(r)/ n
transferência f; (of power,
property) transmissão f; (image)
decalcomania f

transform /træns'fɔ:m/ vt
transformar. **~ation** /-ə'meɪʃn/
n transformação f. **~er** n Electr
transformador m

transfusion /træns'fju:ʒn/ n (of
blood) transfusão f

transient /'trænzɪənt/ a
transitório, transiente, efêmero, (P)
efémero, passageiro

transistor /træn'zɪstə(r)/ n (device,
radio) transístor m

transit /'trænsɪt/ n trânsito m; **in ~**
em trânsito

transition /træn'zɪʃn/ n transição
f. **~al** a transitório

transitive /'trænsətɪv/ a transitivo

transitory /'trænsɪtərɪ/ a
transitório

translat|e /trænz'leɪt/ vt traduzir.
~ion /-ʃn/ n tradução f. **~or** n
tradutor m

transmi|t /trænz'mɪt/ vt (pt
transmitted) transmitir. **~ssion** n
transmissão f. **~tter** n transmissor m

transparen|t /træns'pærənt/ a
transparente. **~cy** n transparência f;
Photo diapositivo m

transpire /træn'spaɪə(r)/ vi ‹secret
etc› transpirar, vir a saber-se;
(happen) suceder, acontecer

transplant[1] /træns'plɑ:nt/ vt
transplantar

transplant[2] /'trænsplɑ:nt/ n Med
transplantação f, (P) transplante m

transport[1] /træn'spɔ:t/ vt (carry,
delight) transportar. **~ation** /-'teɪʃn/
n transporte m

transport[2] /'trænspɔ:t/ n (of
goods, delight etc) transporte m

transpose /træn'spəʊz/ vt
transpor

transvestite /trænz'vestaɪt/ n
travesti mf

trap /træp/ n armadilha f, ratoeira
f, cilada f ● vt (pt **trapped**) apanhar
na armadilha; (cut off) prender,
bloquear

trapdoor /træp'dɔ:(r)/ n alçapão m

trapeze /trə'pi:z/ n trapézio m

trash /træʃ/ n (worthless stuff)
porcaria f; (refuse) lixo m; (nonsense)
disparates mpl. **~ can** n Amer lata f
do lixo, (P) caixote m do lixo. **~y** a
que não vale nada, porcaria

trauma /'trɔ:mə/ n trauma m,
traumatismo m. **~tic** /-'mætɪk/ a
traumático

travel /'trævl/ vi (pt **travelled**)
viajar; (of vehicle, bullet, sound)
ir ● vt percorrer ● n viagem f; **~
agent** agente mf de viagem. **~ler** n
viajante mf; **~ler's cheque** cheque
m de viagem

travesty /'trævəstɪ/ n paródia f,
caricatura f

trawler /'trɔ:lə(r)/ n traineira f, (P)
arrastão m

tray /treɪ/ n tabuleiro m, bandeja f

treacherous /'tretʃərəs/ a
traiçoeiro

treachery /'tretʃərɪ/ n traição f, perfídia f, deslealdade f

treacle /'triːkl/ n melaço m

tread /tred/ vt/i (pt trod, pp trodden) (step) pisar; (walk) andar, caminhar; (walk along) seguir; ~ sth into ‹carpet› esmigalhar or pisar algo sobre/em ● n passo m, maneira f de andar; (of tyre) trilho m

treason /'triːzn/ n traição f

treasure /'treʒə(r)/ n tesouro m ● vt ter o maior apreço por; (store) guardar bem guardado. ~r n tesoureiro m

treasury /'treʒərɪ/ n (building) tesouraria f; (department) Ministério m das Finanças or da Fazenda; fig tesouro m

treat /triːt/ vt/i tratar; ~ sb to sth convidar alguém para algo ● n (pleasure) prazer m, regalo m; (present) mimo m, gentileza f

treatment /'triːtmənt/ n tratamento m

treaty /'triːtɪ/ n (pact) tratado m

treble /'trebl/ a triplo ● vt/i triplicar ● n Mus (voice) soprano m

tree /triː/ n árvore f

trek /trek/ n viagem f penosa; (walk) caminhada f ● vi (pt trekked) viajar penosamente; (walk) caminhar

trellis /'trelɪs/ n grade f para trepadeiras, treliça f

tremble /'trembl/ vi tremer

tremendous /trɪ'mendəs/ a (fearful, huge) tremendo; (excellent) fantástico; formidável

tremor /'tremə(r)/ n tremor m, estremecimento m; (earth) ~ abalo (sísmico) m, tremor m de terra

trench /trentʃ/ n fossa f, vala f; Mil trincheira f

trend /trend/ n tendência f; (fashion) moda f. ~y a na (última) moda, (P) na berra

trepidation /trepɪ'deɪʃn/ n (fear) receio m, apreensão f

trespass /'trespas/ vi entrar ilegalmente (on em); no ~ing entrada f proibida. ~er n intruso m

trial /'traɪəl/ n jur julgamento m, processo m; (test) ensaio m, experiência f, prova f; (ordeal) provação f; on ~ em julgamento; and error tentativas fpl, (P) tentativa f e erro

triangle /'traɪæŋgl/ n triângulo m. ~ular /-'æŋgjʊlə(r)/ a triangular

tribe /traɪb/ n tribo f. ~al a tribal

tribunal /traɪ'bjuːnl/ n tribunal m

tributary /'trɪbjʊtərɪ/ n afluente m, tributário m

tribute /'trɪbjuːt/ n tributo m; pay ~ to prestar homenagem a, render tributo a

trick /trɪk/ n truque m; (prank) partida f; (habit) jeito m ● vt enganar; do the ~ (work) dar resultado

trickle /'trɪkl/ vi pingar, gotejar, escorrer ● n fio m de água etc; fig (small number) punhado m

tricky /'trɪkɪ/ a (crafty) manhoso; ‹problem› delicado, complicado

tricycle /'traɪsɪkl/ n triciclo m

trifle /'traɪfl/ n ninharia f, bagatela f; (sweet) sobremesa f feita de pão-de-ló, frutas e creme ● vi ~ with brincar com; a ~ um pouquinho

trifling /'traɪflɪŋ/ a insignificante

trigger /'trɪgə(r)/ n (of gun) gatilho m ● vt ~ (off) (initiate) desencadear, despoletar

trim /trɪm/ a (trimmer, trimmest) bem arranjado, bem cuidado; ‹figure› elegante, esbelto ● vt (*pt* trimmed) (*cut*) aparar; ‹sails› orientar, marear; (*ornament*) enfeitar; guarnecer (**with** com) ● *n* (*cut*) aparadela *f*, corte *m* leve; (*decoration*) enfeite *m*; (*on car*) acabamento(s) *m(pl)*, estofado *m*; **in ~** em ordem; (*fit*) em boa forma. **~ming(s)** *n* (*dress*) enfeite *m*; *Culin* guarnição *f*, acompanhamento *m*

trinket /'trɪŋkɪt/ *n* bugiganga *f*; (*jewel*) bijuteria *f*, berloque *m*

trio /'triːəʊ/ *n* (*pl* -os) trio *m*

trip /trɪp/ *vi* (*pt* tripped) (*stumble*) tropeçar, dar um passo em falso; (*go or dance lightly*) andar/dançar com passos leves ● *vt* **~ (up)** fazer tropeçar, passar uma rasteira a ● *n* (*journey*) viagem *f*, (*outing*) passeio *m*, excursão *f*; (*stumble*) tropeção *m*, passo *m* em falso

tripe /traɪp/ *n* (*food*) dobrada *f*, tripas *fpl*; 🎦 (*nonsense*) disparates *mpl*

triple /'trɪpl/ *a* triplo, tríplice ● *vt/i* triplicar. **~ts** /-plɪts/ *npl* trigêmeos *mpl*, (*P*) trigémeos *mpl*

triplicate /'trɪplɪkət/ *n* **in ~** em triplicado

tripod /'traɪpɒd/ *n* tripé *m*

trite /traɪt/ *a* banal, corriqueiro

triumph /'traɪəmf/ *n* triunfo *m* ● *vi* triunfar (**over** sobre); (*exult*) exultar, rejubilar(-se). **~ant** /-'ʌmfənt/ *a* triunfante

trivial /'trɪvɪəl/ *a* insignificante

trod, trodden /trɒd, 'trɒdn/
▶ TREAD

trolley /'trɒlɪ/ *n* carrinho *m*; (**tea-**)**~** carrinho *m* de chá

trombone /trɒm'bəʊn/ *n* *Mus* trombone *m*

troop /truːp/ *n* bando *m*, grupo *m*; **~s** *Mil* tropas *fpl*; **~ing the colour** a

saudação da bandeira ● *vi* **~ in/out** entrar/sair em bando or grupo

trophy /'trəʊfɪ/ *n* troféu *m*

tropic /'trɒpɪk/ *n* trópico *m*; **~s** trópicos *mpl*. **~al** *a* tropical

trot /trɒt/ *n* trote *m*; **on the ~** 🎦 a seguir, a fio ● *vi* (*pt* trotted) trotar; (*of person*) correr em passos curtos, ir num or a trote 🎦; **~ out** 🎦 (*produce*) exibir; 🎦 (*state*) desfiar

trouble /'trʌbl/ *n* (*difficulty*) dificuldade(s) *f(pl)*, problema(s) *m(pl)*; (*distress*) desgosto(s) *m(pl)*, aborrecimento(s) *m(pl)*; (*pains, effort*) cuidado *m*, trabalho *m*, maçada *f*, (*inconvenience*) transtorno *m*; incômodo *m*, (*P*) incómodo *m*; *Med* doença *f*; **~(s)** (*unrest*) agitação *f*, conflito(s) *m(pl)*; **be in ~** estar em apuros, estar em dificuldades; **get into ~** meter-se em encrenca/ apuros; **it is not worth the ~** não vale a pena ● *vt/i* (*bother*) incomodar(-se), (*P*) maçar(-se); (*worry*) preocupar(-se); (*agitate*) perturbar. **~maker** *n* desordeiro *m*, provocador *m*; **~shooter** *n* mediador *m*, negociador *m*. **~d** *a* agitado, perturbado; (*of sleep*) agitado; (*of water*) turvo

troublesome /'trʌblsəm/ *a* problemático, importuno, (*P*) maçador

trough /trɒf/ *n* (*drinking*) bebedouro *m*; (*feeding*) comedouro *m*; **~ (of low pressure)** depressão *f*, linha *f* de baixa pressão

trounce /traʊns/ *vt* (*defeat*) esmagar; (*thrash*) espancar

troupe /truːp/ *n* *Theat* companhia *f*, troupe *f*

trousers /'traʊzəz/ *npl* calça *f*, (*P*) calças *fpl*; **short ~** calções *mpl*

trousseau /'truːsəʊ/ n (pl -s /-əʊz/) (of bride) enxoval m de noiva

trout /traʊt/ n (pl invar) truta f

trowel /'traʊəl/ n (garden) colher f de jardineiro; (for mortar) trolha f

truan|t /'truːənt/ n absenteísta mf, (P) absentista mf; Schol gazeteiro m; **play ~t** fazer gazeta. **~cy** n absenteísmo m, (P) absentismo m

truce /truːs/ n trégua(s) f(pl), armistício m

truck /trʌk/ n (lorry) caminhão m, (P) camião m; (barrow) carro m de bagageiro; (wagon) vagão m aberto. **~ driver** n motorista mf de caminhão, (P) camionista mf

trudge /trʌdʒ/ vi caminhar com dificuldade, caminhar a custo, arrastar-se

true /truː/ a (-er, -est) verdadeiro; (accurate) exato; (faithful) fiel; **come ~** (happen) realizar-se, concretizar-se; **it is ~** é verdade

truffle /'trʌfl/ n trufa f

truly /'truːlɪ/ adv verdadeiramente; (faithfully) fielmente; (truthfully) sinceramente

trump /trʌmp/ n trunfo m; **~ card** carta f de trunfo; ① (valuable resource) trunfo m ● vt jogar trunfo, trunfar; **~ up** forjar, inventar

trumpet /'trʌmpɪt/ n trombeta f

truncheon /'trʌntʃən/ n cassetete m

trunk /trʌŋk/ n (of tree, body) tronco m; (of elephant) tromba f; (box) mala f grande; Amer Auto mala f; **~s** (for swimming) calção m or calções mpl de banho. **~ call** n chamada f interurbana; **~ road** n estrada f nacional

trust /trʌst/ n confiança f; (association) truste m; ① trust m;

consórcio m; (foundation) fundação f; (responsibility) responsabilidade f; Jur fideicomisso m; **in ~** em fideicomisso; **on ~** (without proof) sem verificação prévia; (on credit) a crédito, (P) à confiança ● vt (rely on) ter confiança em, confiar em; (hope) esperar; **~ sb with sth** confiar alguma coisa a alguém ● vi **~ in** or **to** confiar em. **~ed** ‹friend etc› de confiança, seguro. **~ful**, **~ing** adjs confiante. **~y** a fiel

trustee /trʌs'tiː/ n administrador m; Jur fideicomissário m

trustworthy /'trʌstwɜːðɪ/ a (digno) de confiança

truth /truːθ/ n (pl -s /truːðz/) verdade f. **~ful** a ‹account etc› verídico; ‹person› verdadeiro, que fala verdade

try /traɪ/ vt/i (pt tried) tentar, experimentar; (be a strain on) cansar, pôr à prova; Jur julgar; **~ for** ‹post, scholarship› candidatar-se a; ‹record› tentar alcançar. **~ on** ‹clothes› provar; **~ out** experimentar; **~ to do** tentar fazer ● n (attempt) tentativa f, experiência f; ‹Rugby› ensaio m. **~ing** a difícil

T-shirt /'tiːʃɜːt/ n T-shirt f, camiseta f de algodão de mangas curtas

tub /tʌb/ n selha f; ① (bath) tina f; banheira f

tuba /'tjuːbə/ n Mus tuba f

tubby /'tʌbɪ/ a (-ier, -iest) baixote e gorducho

tub|e /'tjuːb/ n tubo m; ① (railway) metrô m, (P) metro m; **inner ~e** câmara f de ar. **~ing** n tubos mpl, tubagem f

tuberculosis /tjuːbɜːkjʊ'ləʊsɪs/ n tuberculose f

tubular /'tjuːbjʊlə(r)/ a tubular

tuck /tʌk/ n (fold) prega f cosida; (for shortening or ornament) refego m ● vt/i fazer pregas; (put) guardar, meter, enfiar; (hide) esconder; **~ in** or **into** 🔢 (eat) atacar; **~ in** <shirt> meter as fraldas para dentro; <blanket> prender em; **~** <person> cobrir bem, aconchegar. **~ shop** n Schol loja f de balas, (P) pastelaria f (junto à escola)

Tuesday /'tjuːzdɪ/ n terça-feira f

tuft /tʌft/ n tufo m

tug /tʌɡ/ vt/i (pt tugged) puxar com força; <vessel> rebocar ● n (boat) rebocador m; (pull) puxão m; **~ of war** disputa f cabo-de-guerra

tuition /tjuː'ɪʃn/ n ensino m

tulip /'tjuːlɪp/ n tulipa f

tumble /'tʌmbl/ vi tombar, baquear, dar um trambolhão ● n tombo m, trambolhão m. **~ drier** n máquina f de secar (roupa)

tumbledown /'tʌmbldaun/ a em ruínas

tumbler /'tʌmblə(r)/ n copo m

tummy /'tʌmɪ/ n 🔢 (stomach) estômago m; 🔢 (abdomen) barriga f. **~ ache** n 🔢 dor f de barriga/de estômago

tumour /'tjuːmə(r)/ n tumor m

tumult /'tjuːmʌlt/ n tumulto m. **~uous** /-'mʌltjʊəs/ a tumultuado, barulhento, agitado

tuna /'tjuːnə/ n (pl invar) atum m

tune /tjuːn/ n melodia f ● vt <engine> regular, (P) afinar; <piano etc> afinar ● vi **~ in (to)** Radio, TV ligar (em), (P) sintonizar; **~ up** afinar; **be in ~/out of ~** <instrument> estar afinado/ desafinado; <singer> cantar afinado/ desafinado. **~ful** a melodioso, harmonioso. **~r** n afinador m; Radio

sintonizador m

tunnel /'tʌnl/ n túnel m ● vi (pt tunnelled) abrir um túnel (**into** em)

turban /'tɜːbən/ n turbante m

turbine /'tɜːbaɪn/ n turbina f

turbulen|t /'tɜːbjʊlənt/ a turbulento. **~ce** n turbulência f

turf /tɜːf/ n (pl turfs or turves) gramado m, (P) relva f, relvado m; **the ~** (racing) turfe m, hipismo m; **~ accountant** corretor m de apostas ● vt **~ out** 🔢 jogar fora, (P) deitar fora

Turk /tɜːk/ n turco m. **~ey** n Turquia f. **~ish** a turco m ● n Lang turco m

turkey /'tɜːkɪ/ n peru m

turmoil /'tɜːmɔɪl/ n agitação f, confusão f, desordem f; **in ~** em ebulição

turn /tɜːn/ vt/i virar(-se), voltar(-se), girar; (change) transformar(-se) (**into** em); (become) ficar, tornar-se; <corner> virar, dobrar; <page> virar, voltar; **~ against** virar-se or voltar-se contra; **~ down** recusar; (fold) dobrar para baixo; (reduce) baixar; **~ in** (hand in) entregar; 🔢 (go to bed) deitar-se; **~ off** <light etc> apagar; <tap> fechar; <road> virar (para rua transversal); **~ on** <light etc> acender, ligar; <tap> abrir; **~ round** virar-se, voltar-se ● n volta f; (in road) curva f; (of mind, events) mudança f; (occasion, opportunity) vez f; (attack) ataque m; crise f; 🔢 (shock) susto m; **do a good ~** prestar (um) serviço; **in ~** por sua vez, sucessivamente; **speak out of ~** dizer o que não se deve, cometer uma indiscrição; **take ~** revezar-se; **~ of the century** virada f or (P) viragem f do século □ **~ away** vi virar-se or voltar-se para o outro lado ● vt (avert) desviar; (reject) recusar:

(send back) mandar embora. **~ back**
vi *(return)* devolver; *‹vehicle›* dar
meia volta, voltar para trás ● vt
(fold) dobrar para trás. **~ out** vt
‹light› apagar; *(empty)* esvaziar,
despejar; *‹pocket›* virar do avesso;
(produce) produzir ● vi *(transpire)* vir
a saber-se, descobrir-se; ▢ *(come)*
aparecer. **~ up** vi aparecer, chegar;
(be found) aparecer ● vt *(find)*
desenterrar; *(increase)* aumentar;
‹collar› levantar. **~out** n assistência
f; **~up** n *(of trousers)* dobra f

turning /ˈtɜːnɪŋ/ n rua f
transversal; *(corner)* esquina f.
~ point n momento m decisivo

turnip /ˈtɜːnɪp/ n nabo m

turnover /ˈtɜːnəʊvə(r)/ n *(pie,
tart)* pastel m, empada f; *(money)*
faturamento m, (P) facturação f; *(of
staff)* rotatividade f

turnpike /ˈtɜːnpaɪk/ n Amer
auto-estrada f com pedágio, (P)
portagem

turnstile /ˈtɜːnstaɪl/ n *(gate)*
torniquete m, borboleta f

turntable /ˈtɜːnteɪbl/ n *(for record)*
prato m do toca-disco, (P) gira-
discos; *(record player)* toca-disco m,
(P) gira-discos m

turquoise /ˈtɜːkwɔɪz/ a turquesa
invar

turret /ˈtʌrɪt/ n torreão m, torrinha f

turtle /ˈtɜːtl/ n tartaruga-do-mar f.
~neck a de gola alta

tusk /tʌsk/ n *(tooth)* presa f;
(elephant's) defesa f, dente m

tutor /ˈtjuːtə(r)/ n professor
m particular; *Univ* professor m
universitário

tutorial /tjuːˈtɔːrɪəl/ n *Univ*
seminário m

TV /tiːˈviː/ n tevê f, (P) TV

tweet /twiːt/ n pio m, pipilo m
● vi pipilar

tweezers /ˈtwiːzəz/ npl pinça f

twelve /twelv/ a & n doze m;
~ (o'clock) doze horas. **~fth** a & n
décimo segundo m; **T~fth Night**
véspera f de Reis

twenty /ˈtwentɪ/ a & n vinte m.
~ieth a & n vigésimo m

twice /twaɪs/ adv duas vezes

twiddle /ˈtwɪdl/ vt/i **~ (with)**
(fiddle with) torcer, brincar (com);
~ one's thumbs girar os polegares,
não ter nada para fazer

twig /twɪg/ n galho m, graveto m

twilight /ˈtwaɪlaɪt/ n crepúsculo m
● a crepuscular

twin /twɪn/ n & a gêmeo m, (P)
gémeo m ● vt *(pt twinned)* *(pair)*
emparelhar, emparceirar; **~ beds**
par m de camas de solteiro

twine /twaɪn/ n guita f, cordel m
● vt/i *(weave together)* entrançar;
(wind) enroscar(-se)

twinge /twɪndʒ/ n dor f aguda e
súbita, pontada f; fig pontada f, (P)
ferroada f

twinkle /ˈtwɪŋkl/ vi cintilar, brilhar
● n cintilação f, brilho m

twirl /twɜːl/ vt/i *(fazer)* girar;
‹moustache› torcer

twist /twɪst/ vt torcer; *(weave
together)* entrançar; *(roll)* enrolar;
(distort) torcer, deturpar; **~ sb's
arm** fig forçar alguém ● vi *‹rope
etc›* torcer-se, enrolar-se; *‹road›*
dar voltas or curvas, serpentear
● n *(act of twisting)* torcedura f, (P)
torcedela f; *(of rope)* nó m; *(of events)*
reviravolta f

twit /twɪt/ n ▢ idiota mf

twitch /twɪtʃ/ vt/i contrair(-se) ● n (tic) tique m; (jerk) puxão m

two /tu:/ a & n dois m; **in** or **of ~ minds** indeciso; **put ~ and ~ together** tirar conclusões. **~-faced** a de duas caras, hipócrita; **~-piece** n (garment) duas-peças m invar; (P) fato m de duas peças; **~-seater** n (car) carro m de dois lugares; **~-way** a (of road) mão dupla

twosome /'tu:səm/ n par m

tycoon /taɪ'ku:n/ n magnata m

tying /'taɪɪŋ/ ▶ TIE

type /taɪp/ n (example, print) tipo m; (kind) tipo m; género m, (P) género m; ⊞ (person) cara m, (P) tipo m ⊞ ● vt/i (write) bater à máquina, datilografar; (P) dactilografar

typescript /'taɪpskrɪpt/ n texto m datilografado, (P) dactilografado

typewrit|**er** /'taɪpraɪtə(r)/ n máquina f de escrever. **~ten** /-ɪtn/ a batido à máquina, datilografado, (P) dactilografado

typhoid /'taɪfɔɪd/ n ~ (fever) febre f tifóide

typhoon /taɪ'fu:n/ n tufão m

typical /'tɪpɪkl/ a típico. **~ly** adv tipicamente

typify /'tɪpɪfaɪ/ vt ser o (protó)tipo de, tipificar, symbolizar

typing /'taɪpɪŋ/ n datilografia f, (P) dactilografia f

typist /'taɪpɪst/ n datilógrafo m, (P) dactilógrafo m

tyrann|**y** /'tɪrənɪ/ n tirania f. **~ical** /tɪ'rænɪkl/ a tirânico

tyrant /'taɪərənt/ n tirano m

tyre /'taɪə(r)/ n pneu m

Uu

ubiquitous /ju:'bɪkwɪtəs/ a ubíquo, omnipresente

UFO /'ju:fəʊ/ n OVNI m

ugl|**y** /'ʌglɪ/ a (-**ier**, -**iest**) feio. **~iness** n feiura f, (P) fealdade f

UK abbr ▶ UNITED KINGDOM

ulcer /'ʌlsə(r)/ n úlcera f

ulterior /ʌl'tɪərɪə(r)/ a ulterior; **~ motive** razão f inconfessada, segundas intenções fpl

ultimate /'ʌltɪmət/ a último, derradeiro; (definitive) definitivo; (maximum) supremo; (basic) fundamental. **~ly** adv finalmente

ultimatum /ʌltɪ'meɪtəm/ n (pl -ums) ultimato m

ultra- /'ʌltrə/ pref ultra-, super-

ultraviolet /ʌltrə'vaɪələt/ a ultravioleta

umbilical /ʌm'bɪlɪkl/ a ~ **cord** cordão m umbilical

umbrella /ʌm'brelə/ n guarda-chuva m

umpire /'ʌmpaɪə(r)/ n Sport árbitro m ● vt arbitrar

umpteen /'ʌmpti:n/ a 🔀 sem conta; montes de ⊞; **for the ~th time** 🔀 pela centésima or enésima vez

UN abbr (= United Nations) ONU f

un- /ʌn/ pref não, pouco

unable /ʌn'eɪbl/ a **be ~ to do** ser incapaz de/não poder fazer

unabridged /ʌnə'brɪdʒd/ a ⟨text⟩ integral

unacceptable /ˌʌnəkˈseptəbl/ a
inaceitável, inadmissível

unaccompanied
/ˌʌnəˈkʌmpənid/ a só,
desacompanhado

unaccountable /ˌʌnəˈkaʊntəbl/
a ⟨strange⟩ inexplicável; ⟨not
responsible⟩ que não tem que dar
contas a alguém or que não pode
ser responsabilizado

unaccustomed /ˌʌnəˈkʌstəmd/
a desacostumado; **~ to** não
acostumado or não habituado a

unadulterated /ˌʌnəˈdʌltəreitid/
a ⟨pure, sheer⟩ puro

unaided /ʌnˈeidid/ a sem ajuda,
sozinho, por si só

unanim|ous /juːˈnænɪməs/
a unânime. **~ously** adv
unanimemente, por unanimidade

unarmed /ʌnˈɑːmd/ a desarmado,
indefeso

unashamed /ˌʌnəˈʃeimd/ a
desavergonhado, sem vergonha.
~ly /-idli/ adv sem vergonha

unassuming /ˌʌnəˈsjuːmɪŋ/ a
modesto, despretencioso

unattached /ˌʌnəˈtætʃt/ a
⟨person⟩ livre

unattainable /ˌʌnəˈteinəbl/ a
inacessível

unattended /ˌʌnəˈtendid/ a
⟨person⟩ desacompanhado; ⟨car,
luggage⟩ abandonado

unattractive /ˌʌnəˈtræktɪv/ a sem
atrativos; ⟨offer⟩ de pouco interesse,
pouco apetecível

unauthorized /ʌnˈɔːθəraizd/ a
não-autorizado, sem licença

unavoidabl|e /ˌʌnəˈvɔidəbl/ a
inevitável. **~y** adv inevitavelmente

unaware /ˌʌnəˈweə(r)/ a **be
~ of** desconhecer, ignorar, não

ter consciência de. **~s** /-eəz/ adv
(unexpectedly) inesperadamente;
catch sb ~s apanhar alguém
desprevenido or de surpresa

unbalanced /ʌnˈbælənst/ a
⟨mind, person⟩ desequilibrado or
instável

unbearable /ʌnˈbeərəbl/ a
insuportável

unbeat|able /ʌnˈbiːtəbl/ a
imbatível. **~en** a não vencido,
invicto; (unsurpassed) insuperado

unbelievable /ˌʌnbɪˈliːvəbl/ a
inacreditável, incrível

unbiased /ʌnˈbaiəst/ a imparcial

unblock /ʌnˈblɒk/ vt desbloquear,
desobstruir; ⟨pipe⟩ desentupir

unbreakable /ʌnˈbreikəbl/ a
inquebrável

unbroken /ʌnˈbrəʊkən/ a
(intact) intato, inteiro; (continuous)
ininterrupto

unburden /ʌnˈbɜːdn/ vpr **~ o.s.**
(open one's heart) desabafar (**to**
com)

unbutton /ʌnˈbʌtn/ vt desabotoar

uncalled-for /ʌnˈkɔːldfɔː(r)/ a
injustificável, gratuito

uncanny /ʌnˈkæni/ a (**-ier, -iest**)
estranho, misterioso

unceasing /ʌnˈsiːsɪŋ/ a incessante

uncertain /ʌnˈsɜːtn/ a incerto;
be ~ whether não saber ao certo
se, estar indeciso quanto a. **~ty** n
incerteza f

unchang|ed /ʌnˈtʃeindʒd/ a
inalterado, sem modificação. **~ing** a
inalterável, imutável

uncivilized /ʌnˈsɪvilaizd/ a não
civilizado, bárbaro

uncle /ˈʌŋkl/ n tio m

uncomfortable /ʌnˈkʌmfətəbl/
a ⟨thing⟩ desconfortável; incômodo,

(P) incómodo; (*unpleasant*) desagradável; **feel** or **be** ~ (*uneasy*) sentir-se or estar pouco à vontade

uncommon /ʌnˈkɒmən/ a pouco vulgar, invulgar, fora do comum. **~ly** adv invulgarmente, excepcionalmente

uncompromising /ʌnˈkɒmprəmaɪzɪŋ/ a intransigente

unconcerned /ʌnkənˈsɜːnd/ a (*indifferent*) indiferente (**by** a)

unconditional /ʌnkənˈdɪʃənl/ a incondicional

unconscious /ʌnˈkɒnʃəs/ a inconsciente (**of** de). **~ly** adv inconscientemente

unconventional /ʌnkənˈvenʃənl/ a não convencional, fora do comum

uncooperative /ʌnkəʊˈɒpərətɪv/ a <*person*> pouco cooperativo; do contra Ⅱ

uncork /ʌnˈkɔːk/ vt desarrolhar, tirar a rolha de

uncouth /ʌnˈkuːθ/ a rude, grosseiro

uncover /ʌnˈkʌvə(r)/ vt descobrir, revelar

undecided /ʌndɪˈsaɪdɪd/ a (*irresolute*) indeciso; (*not settled*) por decidir, pendente

undeniable /ʌndɪˈnaɪəbl/ a inegável, incontestável

under /ˈʌndə(r)/ prep debaixo de, sob; (*less than*) com menos de; (*according to*) conforme, segundo; ~ **age** menor de idade; ~ **way** em preparo, (P) em preparação ● adv por baixo, debaixo

under- /ˈʌndə(r)/ pref sub-

undercarriage /ˈʌndəkærɪdʒ/ n *Aviat* trem m de aterrissagem or (P) de aterragem

underclothes /ˈʌndəkləʊðz/ npl
▶ **UNDERWEAR**

undercoat /ˈʌndəkəʊt/ n (*of paint*) primeira mão f, (P) primeira demão f

undercover /ʌndəˈkʌvə(r)/ a <*agent, operation*> secreto

undercurrent /ˈʌndəkʌrənt/ n corrente f subterrânea; fig filão m; fig tendência f oculta

undercut /ʌndəˈkʌt/ vt (pt **undercut**, pres p **undercutting**) *Comm* vender a preços mais baixos do que a concorrência

underdeveloped /ʌndədɪˈveləpt/ a atrofiado; <*country*> em vias de desenvolvimento

underdog /ˈʌndədɒg/ n desprotegido m; o mais fraco

underdone /ˈʌndədʌn/ a (*of meat*) mal passado

underestimate /ʌndərˈestɪmeɪt/ vt subestimar, não dar o devido valor a

underfed /ʌndəˈfed/ a subalimentado, subnutrido

underfoot /ʌndəˈfʊt/ adv debaixo dos pés; (*on the ground*) no chão

undergo /ʌndəˈgəʊ/ vt (pt **-went**, pp **-gone**) (*be subjected to*) sofrer; (*treatment*) ser submetido a

undergraduate /ʌndəˈgrædʒʊət/ n estudante mf universitário

underground[1] /ˈʌndəˈgraʊnd/ adv debaixo da terra; fig (*secretly*) clandestinamente

underground[2] /ˈʌndəgraʊnd/ a subterrâneo; fig (*secret*) clandestino ● n *Rail* metro(politano) m, (P) metro m

undergrowth /ˈʌndəɡrəʊθ/ n mato m

underhand /ˈʌndəhænd/ a (deceitful) sonso, dissimulado

under|lie /ʌndəˈlaɪ/ vt (pt -lay, pp -lain, pres p -lying) estar por baixo de. ~lying a subjacente

underline /ʌndəˈlaɪn/ vt sublinhar, ressaltar

undermine /ʌndəˈmaɪn/ vt minar, solapar

underneath /ʌndəˈniːθ/ prep sob, debaixo de, por baixo de ● adv abaixo, em baixo, por baixo

underpaid /ʌndəˈpeɪd/ a mal pago

underpants /ˈʌndəpænts/ npl (man's) cuecas fpl

underpass /ˈʌndəpɑːs/ n (for cars, people) passagem f inferior

underprivileged /ʌndəˈprɪvɪlɪdʒd/ a desfavorecido

underrate /ʌndəˈreɪt/ vt subestimar, depreciar

underside /ˈʌndəsaɪd/ n lado m inferior, base f

underskirt /ˈʌndəskɜːt/ n anágua f

understand /ʌndəˈstænd/ vt/i (pt -stood) compreender, entender. ~able a compreensível. ~ing a compreensivo ● n compreensão f, ‹agreement› acordo m, entendimento m

understatement /ˈʌndəsteɪtmənt/ n versão f atenuada da verdade, litotes f, eufemismo m

understudy /ˈʌndəstʌdɪ/ n substituto m

undertak|e /ʌndəˈteɪk/ vt (pt -took, pp -taken) empreender; ‹responsibility› assumir; ~e to

encarregar-se de. ~ing n (task) empreendimento m; (promise) compromisso m

undertaker /ˈʌndəteɪkə(r)/ n agente m funerário; papa-defuntos m 🄸, (P) coveiro m

undertone /ˈʌndətəʊn/ n in an ~ a meia voz ou em surdina

undervalue /ʌndəˈvæljuː/ vt avaliar por baixo, subestimar

underwater /ʌndəˈwɔːtə(r)/ a submarino ● adv debaixo de água

underwear /ˈʌndəweə(r)/ n roupa f interior or de baixo

underweight /ˈʌndəweɪt/ a be ~ estar com o peso abaixo do normal, ter peso a menos

underwent /ʌndəˈwent/ ▶UNDERGO

underworld /ˈʌndəwɜːld/ n (of crime) submundo m, (P) bas-fonds mpl

underwriter /ˈʌndəraɪtə(r)/ n segurador m, subscritor m; (marine) underwriter m, segurador m

undeserved /ʌndɪˈzɜːvd/ a imerecido, injusto

undesirable /ʌndɪˈzaɪərəbl/ a indesejável, inconveniente

undies /ˈʌndɪz/ npl 🄸 roupa f de baixo or interior

undignified /ʌnˈdɪɡnɪfaɪd/ a pouco digno, sem dignidade

undisputed /ʌndɪˈspjuːtɪd/ a incontestado

undo /ʌnˈduː/ vt (pt -did, pp -done /dʌn/) desfazer; ‹knot› desfazer, desatar; ‹coat, button› abrir; leave ~ne não fazer, deixar por fazer. ~ing n desgraça f, ruína f

undoubted /ʌnˈdaʊtɪd/ a indubitável. ~ly adv indubitavelmente

undress /ʌnˈdres/ vt/i despir(-se);
get ~ed despir-se

undu|e /ʌnˈdjuː/ a excessivo,
indevido. **~ly** adv excessivamente,
indevidamente

undying /ʌnˈdaɪɪŋ/ a eterno,
perene

unearth /ʌnˈɜːθ/ vt desenterrar;
fig descobrir

unearthly /ʌnˈɜːθlɪ/ a
sobrenatural, misterioso; **~ hour** 🔢
hora f absurda or inconveniente

uneasy /ʌnˈiːzɪ/ a (ill at ease) pouco
à vontade; (worried) preocupado

uneconomic /ʌnˌiːkəˈnɒmɪk/ a
antieconômico

uneducated /ʌnˈedʒʊkeɪtɪd/ a
‹person› inculto, sem instrução

unemploy|ed /ʌnɪmˈplɔɪd/
a desempregado. **~ment** n
desemprego m; **~ment benefit**
auxílio-desemprego m, (P) subsídio
m de desemprego

unending /ʌnˈendɪŋ/ a
interminável, sem fim

unequal /ʌnˈiːkwəl/ a desigual.
~led a sem igual, inigualável

unequivocal /ʌnɪˈkwɪvəkl/ a
inequívoco, claro

uneven /ʌnˈiːvn/ a desigual,
irregular

unexpected /ʌnɪkˈspektɪd/ a
inesperado. **~ly** a inesperadamente

unfair /ʌnˈfeə(r)/ a injusto (to
com). **~ness** n injustiça f

unfaithful /ʌnˈfeɪθfl/ a infiel

unfamiliar /ʌnfəˈmɪlɪə(r)/ a
estranho, desconhecido; **be ~ with**
desconhecer, não conhecer, não
estar familiarizado com

unfashionable /ʌnˈfæʃənəbl/ a
fora de moda

unfasten /ʌnˈfɑːsn/ vt ‹knot›
desatar, soltar; ‹button› abrir

unfavourable /ʌnˈfeɪvərəbl/ a
desfavorável

unfeeling /ʌnˈfiːlɪŋ/ a insensível

unfit /ʌnˈfɪt/ a sem preparo físico,
(P) preparação física, fora de forma;
(unsuitable) impróprio (for para)

unfold /ʌnˈfəʊld/ vt desdobrar;
(expose) expor, revelar ● vi
desenrolar-se

unforeseen /ʌnfɔːˈsiːn/ a
imprevisto, inesperado

unforgettable /ʌnfəˈgetəbl/ a
inesquecível

unforgivable /ʌnfəˈgɪvəbl/ a
imperdoável, indesculpável

unfortunate /ʌnˈfɔːtʃənət/
a (unlucky) infeliz; (regrettable)
lamentável; **it was very ~ that** foi
uma pena/lamentável que. **~ly** adv
infelizmente

unfounded /ʌnˈfaʊndɪd/ a
‹rumour etc› infundado, sem
fundamento

unfriendly /ʌnˈfrendlɪ/ a pouco
amável, antipático, frio

unfurnished /ʌnˈfɜːnɪʃt/ a sem
mobília

ungainly /ʌnˈgeɪnlɪ/ a
desajeitado, deselegante

ungrateful /ʌnˈgreɪtfl/ a ingrato

unhappy /ʌnˈhæpɪ/ a (-ier,
-iest) infeliz, triste; (not pleased)
descontente; pouco contente
(with com). **~iness** n infelicidade
f, tristeza f

unharmed /ʌnˈhɑːmd/ a
incólume, são e salvo, ileso

unhealthy /ʌnˈhelθɪ/ a (-ier, -iest)
‹climate etc› doentio, insalubre;
‹person› adoentado, com pouca
saúde

unholy /ʌnˈhəʊlɪ/ a (**-ier, -iest**) ‹person, act etc› ímpio; **⊡** (great) incrível; espantoso

unhurt /ʌnˈhɜːt/ a ileso, incólume

unicorn /ˈjuːnɪkɔːn/ n unicórnio m

uniform /ˈjuːnɪfɔːm/ n uniforme m ● a uniforme, sempre igual. **~ity** /-ˈfɔːmətɪ/ n uniformidade f. **~ly** adv uniformemente

unif|y /ˈjuːnɪfaɪ/ vt unificar. **~ication** /-ɪˈkeɪʃn/ n unificação f

unilateral /juːnɪˈlætrəl/ a unilateral

unimaginable /ʌnɪˈmædʒɪnəbl/ a inimaginável

unimportant /ʌnɪmˈpɔːtnt/ a sem importância, insignificante

uninhabited /ʌnɪnˈhæbɪtɪd/ a desabitado

unintentional /ʌnɪnˈtenʃənl/ a involuntário, não propositado

uninterest|ed /ʌnˈɪntrəstɪd/ a desinteressado (**in** em), indiferente (**in** a). **~ing** a desinteressante, sem interesse

union /ˈjuːnɪən/ n união f; (trade union) sindicato m; **U~ Jack** bandeira f britânica. **~ist** n sindicalista mf; Pol unionista mf

unique /juːˈniːk/ a único, sem igual

unisex /ˈjuːnɪseks/ a unissexo

unison /ˈjuːnɪsn/ n **in ~** em uníssono

unit /ˈjuːnɪt/ n unidade f; (of furniture) peça f, unidade f, (P) módulo m

unite /juːˈnaɪt/ vt/i unir(-se). **U~d Kingdom** n Reino m Unido; **U~d Nations (Organization)** n Organização f das Nações Unidas; **U~d States (of America)** Estados mpl Unidos (da América)

unity /ˈjuːnətɪ/ n unidade f; fig (harmony) união f

universal /juːnɪˈvɜːsl/ a universal

universe /ˈjuːnɪvɜːs/ n universo m

university /juːnɪˈvɜːsətɪ/ n universidade f ● a universitário; ‹student, teacher› universitário, da universidade

unjust /ʌnˈdʒʌst/ a injusto

unkempt /ʌnˈkempt/ a desmazelado, desleixado; (of hair) despenteado, desgrenhado

unkind /ʌnˈkaɪnd/ a desagradável, duro

unknowingly /ʌnˈnəʊɪŋlɪ/ adv sem saber, inconscientemente

unknown /ʌnˈnəʊn/ a desconhecido ● n **the ~** o desconhecido

unleaded /ʌnˈledɪd/ a sem chumbo

unless /ʌnˈles/ conj a não ser que, a menos que, salvo se, se não

unlike /ʌnˈlaɪk/ a diferente ● prep ao contrário de

unlikely /ʌnˈlaɪklɪ/ a improvável

unlimited /ʌnˈlɪmɪtɪd/ a ilimitado

unload /ʌnˈləʊd/ vt descarregar

unlock /ʌnˈlɒk/ vt abrir (com chave), (P) destrancar

unluck|y /ʌnˈlʌkɪ/ a (**-ier, -iest**) infeliz, sem sorte; ‹number› que dá azar; **be ~y** ter pouca sorte, ter azar. **~ily** adv infelizmente

unmarried /ʌnˈmærɪd/ a solteiro, celibatário

unmask /ʌnˈmɑːsk/ vt desmascarar

unmistakable /ʌnmɪsˈteɪkəbl/ a ‹voice etc› inconfundível; (clear) claro, inequívoco

unnatural /ʌnˈnætʃrəl/ a que não é natural; (*wicked*) desnaturado

unnecessary /ʌnˈnesəserɪ/ a desnecessário; (*superfluous*) supérfluo, dispensável

unnerve /ʌnˈnɜːv/ vt desencorajar, desmoralizar, intimidar

unnoticed /ʌnˈnəʊtɪst/ a **go ~** passar despercebido

unobtrusive /ʌnəbˈtruːsɪv/ a discreto

unofficial /ʌnəˈfɪʃl/ a oficioso, que não é oficial; <*strike*> ilegal, não autorizado

unorthodox /ʌnˈɔːθədɒks/ a pouco ortodoxo, não ortodoxo

unpack /ʌnˈpæk/ vt <*suitcase etc*> desfazer; <*contents*> desembalar, desempacotar ● vi desfazer a mala

unpaid /ʌnˈpeɪd/ a não remunerado; <*bill*> a pagar, por pagar

unpalatable /ʌnˈpælətəbl/ a <*food, fact etc*> desagradável, intragável

unparalleled /ʌnˈpærəleld/ a sem paralelo or comparação, incomparável

unpleasant /ʌnˈpleznt/ a desagradável (**to** com); <*person*> antipático

unplug /ʌnˈplʌɡ/ vt (*pt* -plugged) *Electr* desligar a tomada, (*P*) tirar or desligar a ficha da tomada

unpopular /ʌnˈpɒpjʊlə(r)/ a impopular

unprecedented /ʌnˈpresɪdentɪd/ a sem precedentes, inaudito, nunca visto

unpredictable /ʌnprəˈdɪktəbl/ a imprevisível

unprepared /ʌnprɪˈpeəd/ a sem preparação, improvisado; <*person*> desprevenido

unpretentious /ʌnprɪˈtenʃəs/ a despretencioso, sem pretensões

unprincipled /ʌnˈprɪnsəpld/ a sem princípios, sem escrúpulos

unprofessional /ʌnprəˈfeʃnl/ a <*work*> de amador; <*conduct*> sem consciência profissional, pouco profissional

unprofitable /ʌnˈprɒfɪtəbl/ a não lucrativo

unqualified /ʌnˈkwɒlɪfaɪd/ a sem habilitações; <*success etc*> total, absoluto; **be ~ to** não estar habilitado or ter qualificações para

unquestionable /ʌnˈkwestʃənəbl/ a incontestável, indiscutível, inquestionável

unravel /ʌnˈrævl/ vt (*pt* unravelled) desenredar, desemaranhar; <*knitting*> desmanchar

unreal /ʌnˈrɪəl/ a irreal

unreasonable /ʌnˈriːznəbl/ a pouco razoável, disparatado; (*excessive*) excessivo

unrecognizable /ʌnˈrekəɡnaɪzəbl/ a irreconhecível

unrelated /ʌnrɪˈleɪtɪd/ a <*facts*> desconexo; sem relação (**to** com); <*people*> não aparentado (**to** com)

unreliable /ʌnrɪˈlaɪəbl/ a que não é de confiança

unrest /ʌnˈrest/ n agitação f, distúrbios mpl

unrivalled /ʌnˈraɪvld/ a sem igual, incomparável

unroll /ʌnˈrəʊl/ vt desenrolar

unruly /ʌnˈruːlɪ/ a indisciplinado, turbulento

unsafe /ʌnˈseɪf/ a (*dangerous*) que não é seguro, perigoso; <*person*> em perigo

661

unsatisfactory | unusual

unsatisfactory /ˌʌnsætɪsˈfæktərɪ/
a insatisfatório, pouco satisfatório

unsavoury /ʌnˈseɪvərɪ/ a
desagradável, repugnante

unscathed /ʌnˈskeɪðd/ a ileso,
incólume

unscrew /ʌnˈskruː/ vt desenroscar,
desaparafusar

unscrupulous /ʌnˈskruːpjʊləs/ a
sem escrúpulos, pouco escrupuloso,
sem consciência

unseemly /ʌnˈsiːmlɪ/ a
inconveniente, indecoroso,
impróprio

unsettle /ʌnˈsetl/ vt perturbar,
agitar. ~d a perturbado; ‹weather›
instável, variável; ‹bill› não saldado,
por pagar

unshakeable /ʌnˈʃeɪkəbl/ a
‹person, belief etc› inabalável

unshaven /ʌnˈʃeɪvn/ a com a
barba por fazer, por barbear

unsightly /ʌnˈsaɪtlɪ/ a feio

unskilled /ʌnˈskɪld/ a
inexperiente; ‹work, worker› não
especializado; ‹labour› mão-de-
obra f não especializada

unsociable /ʌnˈsəʊʃəbl/ a
insociável, misantropo

unsophisticated
/ˌʌnsəˈfɪstɪkeɪtɪd/ a simples, natural

unsound /ʌnˈsaʊnd/ a pouco
sólido; of ~ mind Jur que não está
em plena posse das suas faculdades
mentais

unspeakable /ʌnˈspiːkəbl/ a
indescritível; (bad) inqualificável

unstable /ʌnˈsteɪbl/ a instável

unsteady /ʌnˈstedɪ/ a ‹step›
vacilante, incerto; ‹ladder› instável;
‹hand› pouco firme

unstuck /ʌnˈstʌk/ a (not stuck)
descolado; come ~ 🆃 (fail) falhar

unsubscribe /ˌʌnsəbˈskraɪb/
vi descadastrar-se, (P) anular uma
inscrição/subscrição

unsuccessful /ˌʌnsəkˈsesfl/ a
‹candidate› malsucedido; ‹attempt›
malogrado, fracassado; be ~ não
ter êxito

unsuit|able /ʌnˈs(j)uːtəbl/ a
impróprio; pouco apropriado;
inadequado (for para)

unsure /ʌnˈʃʊə(r)/ a incerto

unsuspecting /ˌʌnsəˈspektɪŋ/
a sem desconfiar de nada,
insuspeitado

untangle /ʌnˈtæŋgl/ vt
desemaranhar, desenredar,
desembaraçar

unthinkable /ʌnˈθɪŋkəbl/ a
impensável, inconcebível

untid|y /ʌnˈtaɪdɪ/ a (-ier, -iest)
‹room, desk etc› desarrumado;
‹appearance› desleixado,
desmazelado; ‹hair› despenteado.
~iness n desordem f; (of
appearance) desmazelo m

untie /ʌnˈtaɪ/ vt ‹knot, parcel›
desatar, desfazer; ‹person›
desamarrar

until /ənˈtɪl/ prep até. not ~ não
antes de ● conj até que

untimely /ʌnˈtaɪmlɪ/ a
inoportuno, intempestivo; ‹death›
prematuro

untold /ʌnˈtəʊld/ a incalculável

untoward /ˌʌntəˈwɔːd/ a
inconveniente, desagradável

untrue /ʌnˈtruː/ a falso

unused¹ /ʌnˈjuːzd/ a (new) novo,
por usar; (not in use) não utilizado

unused² /ʌnˈjuːst/ a ~ to não
habituado a, não acostumado a

unusual /ʌnˈjuːʒʊəl/ a insólito,
fora do comum

unveil /ʌnˈveɪl/ vt descobrir, revelar; ‹statue, portrait etc› desvelar

unwanted /ʌnˈwɒntɪd/ a (useless) que já não serve; ‹child› indesejado

unwelcome /ʌnˈwelkəm/ a desagradável; ‹guest› indesejável

unwell /ʌnˈwel/ a indisposto

unwieldy /ʌnˈwiːldɪ/ a difícil de manejar, pouco jeitoso

unwilling /ʌnˈwɪlɪŋ/ a relutante (**to** em), pouco disposto (**to** a)

unwind /ʌnˈwaɪnd/ vt/i (pt unwound /ʌnˈwaʊnd/) desenrolar(-se); 🗉 (relax) descontrair(-se)

unwise /ʌnˈwaɪz/ a imprudente, insensato

unwittingly /ʌnˈwɪtɪŋlɪ/ adv sem querer

unworthy /ʌnˈwɜːðɪ/ a indigno

unwrap /ʌnˈræp/ vt (pt unwrapped) desembrulhar, abrir, desfazer

unwritten /ʌnˈrɪtn/ a ‹agreement› verbal, tácito

up /ʌp/ adv (to higher place) cima, para cima, para o alto; (in higher place) em cima, no alto; (out of bed) acordado, de pé, (P) a pé; (up and dressed) pronto; (finished) acabado; ‹sun› alto; **be ~ against** enfrentar; **be ~ in** 🗉 saber; **be ~ to** (do) estar fazendo, (P) estar a fazer; (plot) estar tramando, (P) estar a tramar; ‹task› estar à altura de; **come** or **go ~** subir; **feel ~ to doing** (able) sentir-se capaz de fazer; **it is ~ to you** depende só de você, (P) de ti; **walk ~ and down** andar dum lado para o outro or para a frente e para trás ● prep no cimo de, em cima de, no alto de; **~ the street/**

river/ etc pela rua/pelo rio/etc acima ● vt (pt upped) (increase) aumentar ● npl **have ~s and downs** fig ter (os seus) altos e baixos. **~-and-coming** a prometedor; **~market** a requintado, fino

upbringing /ˈʌpbrɪŋɪŋ/ n educação f

update /ʌpˈdeɪt/ vt atualizar

upheaval /ʌpˈhiːvl/ n pandemônio m, (P) pandemónio m, revolução f fig; (social, political) convulsão f

uphill /ˈʌphɪl/ a ladeira acima, ascendente; fig (difficult) árduo ● adv /ʌpˈhɪl/ **go ~** subir

uphold /ʌpˈhəʊld/ vt (pt upheld) sustentar, manter, apoiar, defender

upholster /ʌpˈhəʊlstə(r)/ vt estofar. **~y** n estofados mpl, (P) estofo(s) m(pl)

upkeep /ˈʌpkiːp/ n manutenção f

upon /əˈpɒn/ prep sobre

upper /ˈʌpə(r)/ a superior ● n (of shoe) gáspea f; **have the ~ hand** estar por cima or em vantagem, estar em posição de superioridade; **~ class** classe f alta

upright /ˈʌpraɪt/ a vertical; (honourable) honesto, honrado, (P) reto

uprising /ˈʌpraɪzɪŋ/ n insurreição f, sublevação f, levantamento m

uproar /ˈʌprɔː(r)/ n tumulto m, alvoroço m

uproot /ʌpˈruːt/ vt desenraizar; fig erradicar; desarraigar

upset[1] /ʌpˈset/ vt (pt upset, pres upsetting) (overturn) entornar, virar; ‹plan› contrariar, transtornar; ‹stomach› desarranjar, (P) indispor; ‹person› contrariar, transtornar, incomodar ● a aborrecido

upset[2] /ˈʌpset/ n transtorno m; (of stomach) indisposição f; (distress) choque m

upshot /ˈʌpʃɒt/ n resultado m

upside-down /ʌpsaɪdˈdaʊn/ adv lit & fig ao contrário; de pernas para o ar, (P) de pantanas 🄸

upstairs /ʌpˈsteəz/ adv (at/to) em/para cima, no/para o andar de cima ● /ˈʌpsteəz/ a (flat etc) de cima, do andar de cima

upstart /ˈʌpstɑːt/ n arrivista mf

upstream /ʌpˈstriːm/ adv rio acima, contra a corrente

uptake /ˈʌpteɪk/ n **be quick on the ~** pegar, (P) apanhar rapidamente as coisas; fig ser de compreensão rápida, ser vivo

up-to-date /ʌptəˈdeɪt/ a moderno, atualizado

upturn /ˈʌptɜːn/ n melhoria f

upward /ˈʌpwəd/ a ascendente, voltado para cima. **~s** adv para cima

uranium /jʊˈreɪnɪəm/ n urânio m

urban /ˈɜːbən/ a urbano

urge /ɜːdʒ/ vt aconselhar vivamente (to a); **~ on** (impel) incitar (a) ● n (strong desire) grande vontade f

urgen|t /ˈɜːdʒənt/ a urgente; **be ~t** urgir, ser insistente. **~cy** n urgência f

urinal /jʊəˈraɪnl/ n urinol m

urin|e /ˈjʊərɪn/ n urina f. **~ate** vi urinar

urn /ɜːn/ n urna f; (for tea, coffee) espécie f de samovar

us /ʌs unstressed əs/ pron nos; (after preps) nós; **with ~** connosco; **he knows ~** ele nos conhece, (P) ele conhece-nos

US abbr (= United States) ► UNITE

USA abbr (= United States of America) ► UNITE

usable /ˈjuːzəbl/ a utilizável

usage /ˈjuːzɪdʒ/ n uso m

USB abbr (= universal serial bus) USB. **~ key** n pen drive m, (P) pen m; **~ port** porta f USB

USB port /juːesbiːˈpɔːt/ n porto m USB, (P) entrada f USB

use[1] /juːz/ vt usar, utilizar, servir-se de; (exploit) servir-se de; (consume) gastar, usar, consumir; **~ up** esgotar, consumir. **~r** /-ə(r)/ n usuário m, (P) utente mf. **~r-friendly** a fácil de usar

use[2] /juːs/ n uso m, emprego m; **in ~** em uso; **it is no ~ shouting/**etc não serve de nada ou não adianta gritar/etc; **make ~ of** servir-se de; **of ~** útil

used[1] /juːzd/ a (second-hand) usado

used[2] /juːst/ pt **he ~ to sing** ele costumava or ele tinha por costume or hábito cantar ● a **~ to singing** acostumado a or habituado a cantar

use|ful /ˈjuːsfl/ a útil. **~less** a inútil; ‹person› incompetente

username /ˈjuːzəneɪm/ n nome m de usuário, (P) nome m de utilizador

usher /ˈʌʃə(r)/ n lanterninha m, (P) arrumador m ● vt **~ in** mandar or fazer entrar. **~ette** n vaga-lume f, (P) arrumadora f

USSR abbr URSS

usual /ˈjuːʒʊəl/ a usual, habitual, normal; **as ~** como de costume, como habitualmente; **at the ~ time** na hora de costume, (P) à(s) hora(s) de costume. **~ly** adv habitualmente, normalmente

utensil /juːˈtensl/ n utensílio m

uterus /ˈjuːtərəs/ n útero m

utilitarian /juːtɪlɪˈteərɪən/ a utilitário

utility /juːˈtɪlətɪ/ n utilidade f; **(public) ~** serviço m público;

~ **room** área f de serviço (para as máquinas de lavar a roupa e a louça)

utilize /ˈjuːtɪlaɪz/ vt utilizar

utmost /ˈʌtməʊst/ a (furthest, most intense) extremo; **the ~ care/** etc (greatest) o maior cuidado/etc ● **do one's ~** fazer todo o possível or tudo, fazer tudo ao alcance de alguém

utter¹ /ˈʌtə(r)/ a completo, absoluto. **~ly** adv completamente

utter² /ˈʌtə(r)/ vt proferir; ‹sigh, shout› dar

U-turn /ˈjuːtɜːn/ n retorno m, (P) inversão f de marcha fig, reviravolta f

Vv

vacan|t /ˈveɪkənt/ a ‹post, room, look› vago; ‹mind› vazio; ‹seat, space, time› desocupado, livre. **~cy** n (post) vaga f; (room in hotel) vago m

vacate /vəˈkeɪt/ vt vagar, deixar vago

vacation /vəˈkeɪʃn/ n férias fpl

vaccinat|e /ˈvæksɪneɪt/ vt vacinar. **~ion** /-ˈneɪʃn/ n vacinação f

vaccine /ˈvæksiːn/ n vacina f

vacuum /ˈvækjʊəm/ n (pl -cuums, or -cua) vácuo m, vazio m. ~ **cleaner** n aspirador m (de pó)

vagina /vəˈdʒaɪnə/ n vagina f

vagrant /ˈveɪɡrənt/ n vadio m, vagabundo m

vague /veɪɡ/ a (-er, -est) vago; (outline) impreciso; **be ~ about** ser vago acerca de, não precisar. **~ly** adv vagamente

vain /veɪn/ a (-er, -est) (conceited) vaidoso; (useless) vão, inútil; (fruitless) infrutífero; **in ~** em vão. **~ly** adv em vão

valentine /ˈvæləntaɪn/ n (card) cartão m do dia de São Valentim or dia dos Namorados

valiant /ˈvæliənt/ a corajoso, valente

valid /ˈvælɪd/ a válido. **~ity** /vəˈlɪdətɪ/ n validade f

validate /ˈvælɪdeɪt/ vt validar, confirmar, ratificar

valley /ˈvælɪ/ n vale m

valuable /ˈvæljʊəbl/ a (object) valioso, de valor; ‹help, time etc› precioso. **~s** npl objetos mpl de valor

valuation /væljʊˈeɪʃn/ n avaliação f

value /ˈvæljuː/ n valor m ● vt avaliar; (cherish) dar valor a. ~ **added tax** imposto m de valor adicional, (P) acrescentado

valve /vælv/ n Anat, Techn (of car tyre) válvula f; (of bicycle tyre) pipo m; (of radio) lâmpada f, válvula f

vampire /ˈvæmpaɪə(r)/ n vampiro m

van /væn/ n (large) caminhão m; (small) camionete f, comercial m, (P) carrinha f (comercial); ‹milkman's, baker's etc› camionete f; Rail bagageiro m, (P) furgão m

vandal /ˈvændl/ n vândalo m. **~ism** /-əlɪzəm/ n vandalismo m

vandalize /ˈvændəlaɪz/ vt destruir, estragar, vandalizar

vanilla /vəˈnɪlə/ n baunilha f

vanish /ˈvænɪʃ/ vi desaparecer, sumir-se, desvanecer-se

vanity /ˈvænətɪ/ n vaidade f. ~ **case** n bolsa f de maquilagem, (P) de maquilhagem

vantage point /'vɑ:ntɪdʒpɔɪnt/ n (bom) ponto m de observação

vapour /'veɪpə(r)/ n vapor m; (mist) bruma f

vari|able /'veərɪəbl/ a variável. ~ation /-'eɪʃn/ n variação f. ~ed /-ɪd/ a variado

variance /'veərɪəns/ n at ~ em desacordo (with com)

variant /'veərɪənt/ a diverso, diferente ● n variante f

varicose /'værɪkəʊs/ a ~ veins varizes fpl

variety /və'raɪətɪ/ n variedade f; (entertainment) variedades fpl

various /'veərɪəs/ a vários, diversos, variados

varnish /'vɑ:nɪʃ/ n verniz m ● vt envernizar; ‹nails› pintar

vary /'veərɪ/ vt/i variar

vase /vɑ:z/ n vaso m, jarra f

vast /vɑ:st/ a vasto, imenso. ~ly adv imensamente, infinitamente

vat /væt/ n tonel m, dorna f, cuba f

VAT /vi:eɪ'ti:, væt/ abbr ICM m; (P) IVA m

vault[1] /vɔ:lt/ n (roof) abóbada f; (in bank) casa-forte f; (tomb) cripta f; (cellar) adega f

vault[2] /vɔ:lt/ vt/i saltar ● n salto m

VDU abbr ▶ VISUAL DISPLAY UNIT

veal /vi:l/ n (meat) vitela f

veer /vɪə(r)/ vi virar, mudar de direção

vegan /'vi:gən/ a & n vegetariano m estrito, (P) vegano

vegetable /'vedʒɪtəbl/ n hortaliça f, legume m ● a vegetal

vegetarian /vedʒɪ'teərɪən/ a & n vegetariano m

vegetation /vedʒɪ'teɪʃn/ n vegetação f

vehement /'vi:əmənt/ a veemente. ~ly adv veementemente

vehicle /'vi:ɪkl/ n veículo m

veil /veɪl/ n véu m ● vt velar, cobrir com véu; fig esconder; disfarçar

vein /veɪn/ n (in body; mood) veia f; (in rock) veio m, filão m; (of leaf) nervura f

velocity /vɪ'lɒsɪtɪ/ n velocidade f

velvet /'velvɪt/ n veludo m

vendetta /ven'detə/ n vendeta f

vending machine /'vendɪŋməʃi:n/ n vendedora f automática, (P) máquina f de distribuição, automática

vendor /'vendə(r)/ n vendedor m; street~ vendedor m ambulante

veneer /və'nɪə(r)/ n folheado m; fig fachada f; máscara f

venerable /'venərəbl/ a venerável

Venezuela /venɪz'weɪlə/ n Venezuela f. ~n a & n venezuelano m

vengeance /'vendʒəns/ n vingança f; with a ~ furiosamente, em excesso, com mais força do que se pretende

venison /'venɪzn/ n carne f de veado

venom /'venəm/ n veneno m. ~ous /'venəməs/ a venenoso

vent[1] /vent/ n (in coat) abertura f

vent[2] /vent/ n (hole) orifício m, abertura f; (for air) respiradouro m ● vt (anger) descarregar (on para o em cima de); give ~ to fig desabafar, dar vazão a

ventilat|e /'ventɪleɪt/ vt ventilar. ~ion /-'leɪʃn/ n ventilação f. ~or n ventilador m

ventriloquist /ven'trɪləkwɪst/ n ventríloquo m

venture /'ventʃə(r)/ n empreendimento m arriscado, aventura f ● vt/i arriscar(-se)

venue /'venjuː/ n o porto m de encontro

veranda /və'rændə/ n varanda f

verb /vɜːb/ n verbo m

verbal /'vɜːbl/ a verbal; (literal) literal

verbose /vɜː'bəʊs/ a palavroso, prolixo

verdict /'vɜːdɪkt/ n veredito m; (opinion) opinião f

verge /vɜːdʒ/ n beira f, borda f; on the ~ of doing prestes a fazer ● vi ~ on estar à beira de

verify /'verɪfaɪ/ vt verificar

vermin /'vɜːmɪn/ n animais mpl nocivos, verme m; (lice, fleas etc) parasitas mpl

vermouth /'vɜːməθ/ n vermute m

vernacular /və'nækjʊlə(r)/ n vernáculo m; (dialect) dialeto m

versatil|e /'vɜːsətaɪl/ a versátil; ‹tools› que serve para vários fins, multiuso. ~ity /-'tɪlətɪ/ n versatilidade f

verse /vɜːs/ n (poetry) verso m, poesia f; (stanza) estrofe f; (of Bible) versículo m

version /'vɜːʃn/ n versão f

versus /'vɜːsəs/ prep contra

vertical /'vɜːtɪkl/ a vertical. ~ly adv verticalmente

vertigo /'vɜːtɪgəʊ/ n vertigem f

verve /vɜːv/ n verve f, vivacidade f

very /'verɪ/ adv muito; the ~ first/best/etc (emph) o primeiro/melhor/etc de todos; ~ much muito; ~ well muito bem ● a (actual) mesmo, próprio; (exact) preciso; exato; at the ~ end mesmo or precisamente

no fim; the ~ day/etc o próprio or o mesmo dia/etc

vessel /'vesl/ n vaso m, recipiente m

vest[1] /vest/ n corpete m, (P) camisola f interior; Amer (waistcoat) colete m

vest[2] /vest/ vt conferir (in a); ~ed interests interesses mpl

vestige /'vestɪdʒ/ n vestígio m

vestry /'vestrɪ/ n sacristia f

vet /vet/ n 1 veterinário m ● vt (pt vetted) ‹candidate etc› examinar atentamente, estudar

veteran /'vetərən/ n veterano m; (war) ~ veterano m de guerra

veterinary /'vetərɪnərɪ/ a veterinário a. ~ surgeon n veterinário m

veto /'viːtəʊ/ n (pl -oes) veto m; (right) direito m de veto ● vt vetar, opor o veto a

vex /veks/ vt aborrecer, irritar, contrariar; ~ed question questão f muito debatida, assunto m controverso

via /'vaɪə/ prep por, via

viab|le /'vaɪəbl/ a viável. ~ility /-'bɪlətɪ/ n viabilidade f

viaduct /'vaɪədʌkt/ n viaduto m

vibrant /'vaɪbrənt/ a vibrante

vibrat|e /vaɪ'breɪt/ vt/i (fazer) vibrar. ~ion /-ʃn/ n vibração f

vicar /'vɪkə(r)/ n (Anglican) pastor m; (Catholic) vigário m, pároco m. ~age n presbitério m, (P) vicariato m

vice[1] /vaɪs/ n (depravity) vício m

vice[2] /vaɪs/ n Techn torno m

vice- /vaɪs/ pref vice-. ~chairman n vice-presidente m; ~chancellor n vice-chanceler m; Univ reitor m; ~president n vice-presidente mf

vice versa /ˌvaɪsɪˈvɜːsə/ adv
vice-versa

vicinity /vɪˈsɪnətɪ/ n vizinhança f,
cercania f (s) fpl, arredores mpl; **in the
~ of** nos arredores de

vicious /ˈvɪʃəs/ a (spiteful) mau,
maldoso; (violent) brutal, feroz;
~ circle círculo m vicioso. **~ly**
adv maldosamente; (violently)
brutalmente, ferozmente

victim /ˈvɪktɪm/ n vítima f

victimiz|e /ˈvɪktɪmaɪz/ vt
perseguir. **~ation** /-ˈzeɪʃn/ n
perseguição f

victor /ˈvɪktə(r)/ n vencedor m

victor|y /ˈvɪktərɪ/ n vitória f. **~ious**
/-ˈtɔːrɪəs/ a vitorioso

video /ˈvɪdɪəʊ/ a vídeo ● n (pl -os)
🔲 vídeo ● vt (record) gravar em
vídeo; **~ cassette** videocassete m,
(P) cassete f de vídeo; **~ recorder**
(gravador m de) vídeo m, (P) câmara
f de vídeo

vie /vaɪ/ vi (pres p **vying**) rivalizar;
competir (**with** com)

view /vjuː/ n vista f ● vt ver;
(examine) examinar; (consider)
considerar, ver; ⟨a house⟩ visitar,
ver; **in my ~** a meu ver, na minha
opinião; **in ~ of** em vista de; **on ~**
em exposição, à mostra; (open to
the public) aberto ao público; **with a
~ to** com a intenção de, com o fim
de. **~er** n TV telespectador m; (for
slides) visor m

viewfinder /ˈvjuːfaɪndə(r)/ n
visor m

viewpoint /ˈvjuːpɔɪnt/ n ponto
m de vista

vigil /ˈvɪdʒɪl/ n vigília f; (over corpse)
velório m; Relig vigília f

vigilan|t /ˈvɪdʒɪlənt/ a vigilante.
~ce n vigilância f. **~te** /vɪdʒɪˈlæntɪ/
n vigilante m

vig|our /ˈvɪgə(r)/ n vigor m. **~orous**
/ˈvɪgərəs/ a vigoroso

vile /vaɪl/ a (base) infame, vil; 🔲
(bad) horroroso; péssimo

vilify /ˈvɪlɪfaɪ/ vt difamar

villa /ˈvɪlə/ n vivenda f, vila f;
(country residence) casa f de campo

village /ˈvɪlɪdʒ/ n aldeia f, povoado
m. **~r** n aldeão m, aldeã f

villain /ˈvɪlən/ n patife m, mau-
caráter m

vindicat|e /ˈvɪndɪkeɪt/ vt
vindicar, justificar. **~ion** /-ˈkeɪʃn/ n
justificação f

vindictive /vɪnˈdɪktɪv/ a vingativo

vine /vaɪn/ n (plant) vinha f

vinegar /ˈvɪnɪgə(r)/ n vinagre m

vineyard /ˈvɪnjəd/ n vinha f,
vinhedo m

vintage /ˈvɪntɪdʒ/ n (year)
ano m da colheita de qualidade
excepcional, ano m vintage ● a
⟨wine⟩ de colheita excepcional e
de um determinado ano; ⟨car⟩ de
museu 🔲; fabricado entre 1917
e 1930

viola /vɪˈəʊlə/ n Mus viola f, violeta f

violat|e /ˈvaɪəleɪt/ vt violar. **~ion**
/-ˈleɪʃn/ n violação f

violen|t /ˈvaɪələnt/ a violento. **~ce**
n violência f. **~tly** adv violentamente,
com violência

violet /ˈvaɪələt/ n Bot violeta f;
(colour) violeta m ● a violeta

violin /vaɪəˈlɪn/ n violino m. **~ist** n
violinista mf

VIP /viːaɪˈpiː/ abbr (= **very
important person**) VIP m,
personalidade f importante

viper /ˈvaɪpə(r)/ n víbora f

virgin /'vɜ:dʒɪn/ a & n virgem f. **~ity** /və'dʒɪnɪtɪ/ n virgindade f

Virgo /'vɜ:gəʊ/ n Astr Virgem f

viril|e /'vɪraɪl/ a viril, varonil. **~ity** /vɪ'rɪlətɪ/ n virilidade f

virtual /'vɜ:tʃʊəl/ a verdadeiro, que é na prática (embora não em teoria); **a ~ failure**/etc praticamente um fracasso/etc. **~ly** adv praticamente

virtue /'vɜ:tʃu:/ n (goodness, chastity) virtude f; (merit) mérito m; **by** or **in ~ of** por or em virtude de

virtuos|o /vɜ:tʃʊ'əʊsəʊ/ n (pl **-si** /-si:/) virtuoso m

virtuous /'vɜ:tʃʊəs/ a virtuoso

virus /'vaɪərəs/ n (pl **-es**) vírus m; ▣ (disease) virose f

visa /'vi:zə/ n visto m

vise /vaɪs/ n Amer (vice) torno m

visib|le /'vɪzəbl/ a visível. **~ility** /-'bɪlətɪ/ n visibilidade f. **~ly** adv visivelmente

vision /'vɪʒn/ n (dream, insight) visão f; (seeing, sight) vista f, visão a

visionary /'vɪʒənərɪ/ a visionário; (plan, scheme etc) fantasista, quimérico ● n visionário m

visit /'vɪzɪt/ vt (pt **visited**) (person) visitar, fazer uma visita a; (place) visitar ● vi estar de visita ● n (tour, call) visita f; (stay) estada f, visita f. **~or** n visitante mf; (guest) visita f

visor /'vaɪzə(r)/ n viseira f; (in vehicle) visor m

vista /'vɪstə/ n vista f, panorama m

visual /'vɪʒʊəl/ a visual. **~ display unit** n terminal m de vídeo. **~ly** adv visualmente

visualize /'vɪʒʊəlaɪz/ vt visualizar; (foresee) imaginar, prever

vital /'vaɪtl/ a vital. **~ statistics** npl estatísticas fpl demográficas; ▣ (of woman) medidas fpl

vitality /vaɪ'tælətɪ/ n vitalidade f

vitamin /'vɪtəmɪn/ n vitamina f

vivac|ious /vɪ'veɪʃəs/ a cheio de vida, vivo, animado. **~ity** /-'væsətɪ/ n vivacidade f, animação f

vivid /'vɪvɪd/ a vívido; (imagination) vivo. **~ly** adv vividamente

vixen /'vɪksn/ n raposa f fêmea

vocabulary /və'kæbjʊlərɪ/ n vocabulário m

vocal /'vəʊkl/ a vocal; fig (person) eloquente; **~ cords** cordas fpl vocais. **~ist** n vocalista mf

vocation /və'keɪʃn/ n vocação f; (trade) profissão f. **~al** a vocacional, profissional

vociferous /və'sɪfərəs/ a vociferante

vodka /'vɒdkə/ n vodka m

vogue /vəʊg/ n voga f, moda f, popularidade f; **in ~** em voga, na moda

voice /vɔɪs/ n voz f ● vt (express) exprimir. **~mail** n (system) correio m de voz, (P) caixa f de correio de voz ;(message) mensagem f de voz

void /vɔɪd/ a vazio; Jur nulo, sem validade ● n vácuo m, vazio m; **make ~** anular, invalidar; **~ of** sem, destituído de

volatile /'vɒlətaɪl/ a (substance) volátil; fig (changeable) instável, volúvel

volcan|o /vɒl'keɪnəʊ/ n (pl **-oes**) vulcão m. **~ic** /-ænɪk/ a vulcânico

volition /və'lɪʃn/ n of one's own **~** de sua própria vontade

volley /'vɒlɪ/ n (of blows etc) saraivada f; (of gunfire) salva f; Tennis voleio m. **~ball** n voleibol m, vôlei m, (P) vôlei m

volt /vəʊlt/ n volt m. **~age** n voltagem f

voluble /ˈvɒljʊbl/ a falante, loquaz

volume /ˈvɒljuːm/ n (book, sound) volume m; (capacity) capacidade f

voluntar|y /ˈvɒləntərɪ/ a voluntário; (unpaid) não remunerado. **~ily** /-trəlɪ/ adv voluntariamente

volunteer /vɒlənˈtɪə(r)/ n voluntário m ● vi oferecer-se or voluntariar-se (**to do** para fazer); Fld alistar-se como voluntário ● vt oferecer espontaneamente

voluptuous /vəˈlʌptʃʊəs/ a voluptuoso, sensual

vomit /ˈvɒmɪt/ vt/i (pt vomited) vomitar ● n vômito m, (P) vómito m

voodoo /ˈvuːduː/ n vodu m, (P) vudu m

voraci|ous /vəˈreɪʃəs/ a voraz. **~ty** /vəˈræsɪtɪ/ n voracidade f

vot|e /vəʊt/ n voto m; (right) direito m de voto ● vt/i votar. **~er** n eleitor m

vouch /vaʊtʃ/ vi **~ for** responder por, garantir

voucher /ˈvaʊtʃə(r)/ n (for meal, transport) vale m; (receipt) comprovante m

vow /vaʊ/ n voto m ● vt (loyalty etc) jurar (**to** a); **~ to do** jurar fazer

vowel /ˈvaʊəl/ n vogal f

voyage /ˈvɔɪdʒ/ n viagem (por mar) f. **~r** /-ə(r)/ n viajante m

vulgar /ˈvʌlɡə(r)/ a ordinário, grosseiro; (in common use) vulgar. **~ity** /-ˈɡærətɪ/ n (behaviour) grosseria f, vulgaridade f

vulnerab|le /ˈvʌlnərəbl/ a vulnerável. **~ility** /-ˈbɪlətɪ/ n vulnerabilidade f

vulture /ˈvʌltʃə(r)/ n urubu m, (P) abutre m

vying /ˈvaɪɪŋ/ ▶ VIE

Ww

wad /wɒd/ n bucha f, tampão m; (bundle) maço m, rolo m

wadding /ˈwɒdɪŋ/ n enchimento m

waddle /ˈwɒdl/ vi bambolear-se, rebolar-se, gingar

wade /weɪd/ vi **~ through** fig avançar a custo por; ‹mud, water› patinhar em

wafer /ˈweɪfə(r)/ n (biscuit) bolacha f de baunilha; Relig hóstia f

waffle[1] /ˈwɒfl/ n [] (talk) lenga-lenga f; papo m; conversa f; [] (writing) lenga-lenga f ● vi [] escrever muito sem dizer nada de importante

waffle[2] /ˈwɒfl/ n Culin waffle m

waft /wɒft/ vi flutuar ● vt espalhar, levar suavemente

wag /wæɡ/ vt/i (pt wagged) abanar, agitar, sacudir

wage[1] /weɪdʒ/ vt ‹campaign, war› travar

wage[2] /weɪdʒ/ n **~(s)** (weekly, daily) salário m, ordenado m. **~ earner** n trabalhador m assalariado; **~ freeze** n congelamento m de salários

wager /ˈweɪdʒə(r)/ n (bet) aposta f ● vt apostar (**that** que)

waggle /ˈwæɡl/ vt/i abanar, agitar, sacudir

wagon /ˈwæɡən/ n (horse-drawn) carroça f; Rail vagão m de mercadorias

waif /weɪf/ n criança f abandonada

wail /weɪl/ vi lamentar-se, gemer lamentosamente ● n lamentação f, gemido m lamentoso

waist /weɪst/ n cintura f. **~line** n cintura f

waistcoat /ˈweɪskəʊt/ n colete m

wait /weɪt/ vt/i esperar; **~ for** esperar; **~ on** servir; **keep sb ~ing** fazer alguém esperar ● n espera f; **lie in ~ (for)** estar escondido à espera (de), armar uma emboscada (para). **~ing list** n lista f de espera; **~ing room** n sala f de espera

wait|er /ˈweɪtə(r)/ n garçon m, (P) empregado m (de mesa). **~ress** n garçonete f, (P) empregada f (de mesa)

waive /weɪv/ vt renunciar a, desistir de

wake[1] /weɪk/ vt/i (pt woke, pp woken) **~ (up)** acordar, despertar ● n (before burial) velório m

wake[2] /weɪk/ n (ship) esteira (de espuma) f; **in the ~ of** (following) atrás de, na sequência de

Wales /weɪlz/ n País m de Gales

walk /wɔːk/ vi andar, caminhar; (not ride) ir a pé; (stroll) passear; **~ out** (go away) sair; (on strike) fazer greve; **~ out on** abandonar ● vt ‹streets› andar por, percorrer; ‹distance› andar, fazer a pé, percorrer; ‹dog› (levar para/a) passear ● n (stroll) passeio m, volta f; (excursion) caminhada f; (gait) passo m, maneira f de andar; (pace) passo m; (path) caminho m; **it's a 5-minute ~** são 5 minutos a pé; **~ of life** meio m, condição f social. **~over** n vitória f fácil

walker /ˈwɔːkə(r)/ n caminhante mf

walkie-talkie /wɔːkɪˈtɔːkɪ/ n walkie-talkie m

walking /ˈwɔːkɪŋ/ n andar (a pé) m, marcha (a pé) f ● a Ⓘ ‹dictionary› vivo. **~ stick** n bengala f

wall /wɔːl/ n parede f; (around land) muro m; (of castle, town; also fig) muralha f; (of stomach etc) parede(s) f(pl); **go to the ~** sucumbir, falir; ‹firm› ir à falência ● vt ‹city› fortificar; ‹property› murar; **up the ~** Ⓘ fora de si

wallet /ˈwɒlɪt/ n carteira f

wallflower /ˈwɔːlflaʊə(r)/ n Bot goivo m; **be a ~** fig tomar chá de cadeira, (P) esperar sentado

wallop /ˈwɒləp/ vt (pt walloped) Ⓧ espancar Ⓘ ● n Ⓧ pancada f forte

wallow /ˈwɒləʊ/ vi (in mud) chafurdar; fig regozijar-se

wallpaper /ˈwɔːlpeɪpə(r)/ n papel m de parede ● vt forrar com papel de parede

Wall Street Rua, em Manhattan, Nova Iorque, onde se encontram a Bolsa de Valores e as sedes de muitas instituições financeiras. Quando se fala de *Wall Street*, muitas vezes se está falando dessas instituições.

walnut /ˈwɔːlnʌt/ n (nut) noz f; (tree) nogueira f

waltz /wɔːls/ n valsa f ● vi valsar

wand /wɒnd/ n (magic) varinha f mágica or de condão

wander /ˈwɒndə(r)/ vi andar ao acaso, vagar, errar; ‹river› serpentear; ‹mind, speech› divagar; (stray) extraviar-se. **~er** n vagabundo m, andarilho m. **~ing** a errante

wane /weɪn/ *vi* diminuir; (*decline*) declinar ● *on the* ~ em declínio; ‹*moon*› no quarto minguante

wangle /ˈwæŋgl/ *vt* 🇪 conseguir algo através de pistolão 🇵 (P) conseguir algo através de persuasão ou manipulação

want /wɒnt/ *vt* querer (**to do** fazer); (*need*) precisar (de); (*ask for*) exigir, requerer; **I ~ you to go** eu quero que você vá/que tu vás ● *vi* **~ for** ter falta de ● *n* (*need*) necessidade f, precisão f; (*desire*) desejo m; (*lack*) falta f, carência f; **for ~ of** por falta de. **~ed** *a* ‹*criminal*› procurado pela polícia; (*in ad*) precisa(m)-se

WAP /wæp/ *a* WAP

war /wɔː(r)/ *n* guerra f; **at ~** em guerra; **on the ~path** em pé de guerra

warble /ˈwɔːbl/ *vt/i* gorjear

ward /wɔːd/ *n* (*in hospital*) enfermaria f; *Jur* (*minor*) pupilo m; *Pol* círculo m eleitoral ● *vt* **~ off** ‹*a blow*› aparar; ‹*anger*› desviar; ‹*danger*› prevenir, evitar

warden /ˈwɔːdn/ *n* (*of institution*) diretor m; (*of park*) guarda m

warder /ˈwɔːdə(r)/ *n* guarda (de prisão) m, carcereiro m

wardrobe /ˈwɔːdrəʊb/ *n* (*place*) armário m; guarda-roupa m, (P) guarda-fato m, (P) roupeiro m; (*clothes*) guarda-roupa m

warehouse /ˈweəhaʊs/ *n* (*pl* **-s** /-haʊzɪz/) armazém m, depósito m de mercadorias

wares /weəz/ *npl* (*goods*) mercadorias fpl, artigos mpl

warfare /ˈwɔːfeə(r)/ *n* guerra f

warlike /ˈwɔːlaɪk/ *a* marcial, guerreiro; (*bellicose*) belicoso

warm /wɔːm/ *a* (**-er, -est**) quente; (*hearty*) caloroso, cordial; **be** *or* **feel ~** estar com *or* ter *or* sentir calor ● *vt/i* **~ (up)** aquecer(-se). **~hearted** *a* afetuoso, com calor humano. **~ly** *adv* (*heartily*) calorosamente; **wrap up ~ly** agasalhar-se bem. **~th** *n* calor m

warn /wɔːn/ *vt* avisar, prevenir; **~ sb off sth** (*advise against*) pôr alguém de prevenção *or* de pé atrás com algo; (*forbid*) proibir algo a alguém. **~ing** *n* aviso m; **~ing light** lâmpada f de advertência; **without ~ing** sem aviso, sem prevenir

warp /wɔːp/ *vt/i* ‹*wood etc*› empenar; *fig* (*pervert*) torcer; deformar; desvirtuar. **~ed** *a fig* deturpado; pervertido

warrant /ˈwɒrənt/ *n* autorização f; (*for arrest*) mandato (de captura) m; *Comm* título m de crédito, warrant m ● *vt* justificar; (*guarantee*) garantir

warranty /ˈwɒrənti/ *n* garantia f

warrior /ˈwɒrɪə(r)/ *n* guerreiro m

warship /ˈwɔːʃɪp/ *n* navio m de guerra

wart /wɔːt/ *n* verruga f

wartime /ˈwɔːtaɪm/ *n* **in ~** em tempo de guerra

wary /ˈweərɪ/ *a* (**-ier, -iest**) cauteloso, prudente

was /wɒz unstressed wəz/ ▶ BE

wash /wɒʃ/ *vt/i* lavar(-se); (*flow over*) molhar, inundar; **~ one's hands of** lavar as mãos de; **~ out** ‹*cup etc*› lavar; ‹*stain*› tirar lavando; **~ up** lavar a louça; *Amer* (*wash oneself*) lavar-se ● *n* lavagem f; (*dirty clothes*) roupa f para lavar; (*of ship*) esteira f; (*of paint*) fina camada f de tinta; **have a ~** lavar-se. **~basin** *n* pia f, (P) lavatório m; **~cloth** *Amer* (*facecloth*) toalha f de rosto;

~out n ⊠ fiasco m; **~room** n Amer
banheiro m, (P) casa f de banho.
~able a lavável. **~ing** n (dirty) roupa
f suja; (clean) roupa f lavada. **~ing
machine** n máquina f de lavar roupa;
~ing powder n detergente m em
pó; **~ing-up** n lavagem f da louça

washed-out /wɒʃt'aut/ a (faded)
desbotado; (exhausted) exausto

washer /'wɒʃə(r)/ n (machine)
máquina f de lavar roupa, louça f;
(ring) anilha f

wasp /wɒsp/ n vespa f

waste /weist/ vt desperdiçar,
esbanjar; ‹time› perder ● vi **~ away**
consumir-se ● a (useless) inútil;
‹materials› de refugo; **~ paper**
papéis mpl velhos ou usados;
~paper basket cesto m de papéis
● n desperdício m, perda f; (of
time) perda f; (rubbish) lixo m; **lay ~**
assolar, devastar; **~ (land)** (desolate)
região f desolada, ermo m; (unused)
(terreno) baldio m; **~disposal unit**
triturador m de lixo

wasteful /'weistfl/ a dispendioso;
‹person› esbanjador, gastador,
perdulário

watch /wɒtʃ/ vt/i ver bem, olhar
com atenção, observar; ‹game, TV›
ver; (guard, spy on) vigiar; (be careful
about) tomar or ter cuidado com;
~ out (look out) estar à espreita (for
de); (take care) acautelar-se ● n vigia
f, vigilância f; Naut quarto m; (for
telling time) relógio m. **~dog** n cão
m de guarda; **~tower** n torre f de
observação. **~ful** a atento, vigilante

watchmaker /'wɒtʃmeikə(r)/ n
relojoeiro m

watchman /'wɒtʃmən/ n (pl
-men) (of building) guarda m;
(night-)**~** guarda-noturno m

water /'wɔːtə(r)/ n água f; **~ polo**
polo m aquático ● vt regar; **~ down**
juntar água a, diluir; ‹milk, wine›
aguar, batizar ⊞; fig (tone down)
suavizar ● vi (of eyes) lacrimejar,
chorar. **~ closet** n WC m, banheiro
m, (P) lavabos mpl; **~colour** n
aquarela f; **~melon** n melancia f;
~ pistol n pistola f de água; **~ polo**
n polo m aquático; **~skiing** n esqui
m aquático

watercress /'wɔːtəkres/ n
agrião m

waterfall /'wɔːtəfɔːl/ n queda f de
água, cascata f

watering can /'wɔːtəriŋkæn/ n
regador m

waterlogged /'wɔːtəlɒgd/
a saturado de água; ‹land›
empapado, alagado; ‹vessel›
inundado, alagado

waterproof /'wɔːtəpruːf/ a
impermeável; ‹watch› à prova
de água

watershed /'wɔːtəʃed/ n fig
momento m decisivo; (in affairs)
ponto m crítico

watertight /'wɔːtətait/ a à prova
de água, hermético; fig ‹argument
etc› inequívoco; irrefutável

waterway /'wɔːtəwei/ n via f
navegável

watery /'wɔːtəri/ a ‹colour› pálido;
‹eyes› lacrimoso; ‹soup› aguado;
‹tea› fraco

watt /wɒt/ n watt m

wave /weiv/ n onda f; (in hair)
Radio onda f; (sign) aceno m ● vt
acenar com; ‹sword› brandir; ‹hair›
ondular; **~e goodbye** dizer adeus
● vi acenar (com a mão); ‹hair etc›
ondular; ‹flag› tremular. **~length**
n comprimento m de onda. **~y** a
ondulado

waver /'weɪvə(r)/ *vi* vacilar; (*hesitate*) hesitar

wax[1] /wæks/ *n* cera *f* ● *vt* encerar; ‹*car*› polir

wax[2] /wæks/ *vi* (*of moon*) aumentar, crescer

waxwork /'wækswɜːk/ *n* (*dummy*) figura *f* de cera. ~**s** *npl* (*exhibition*) museu *m* de figuras de cera

way /weɪ/ *n* (*road, path*) caminho *m*, estrada *f*, rua *f* (**to** para); (*distance*) percurso *m*; (*direction*) (P) direção *f*; (*manner*) modo *m*, maneira *f*; (*means*) meios *mpl*; (*respect*) respeito *m*; ~**s** (*habits*) costumes *mpl*; **be in the** ~ atrapalhar; **be on one's or the** ~ estar a caminho; **by the** ~ a propósito; **by** ~ **of** por, via, através; **get one's own** ~ conseguir o que quer; **give** ~ (*yield*) ceder; (*collapse*) desabar; *Auto* dar a preferência *or* (P) a prioridade; **in a** ~ de certo modo; **make one's** ~ ir; **that** ~ dessa maneira; **this** ~ desta maneira; **in** entrada *f*; ~ **out** saída *f* ● *adv* 🄸 consideravelmente; de longe. ~**out** *a* 🄸 excêntrico

waylay /weɪ'leɪ/ *vt* (*pt* **-laid**) (*assail*) armar uma cilada para; (*stop*) interceptar, (P) intercetar

wayward /'weɪwəd/ *a* (*wilful*) teimoso; (*perverse*) caprichoso, difícil

WC /dʌb(ə)ljuːˈsiː/ *n* WC *m*, banheiro *m*, (P) casa *f* de banho

we /wiː/ *pron* nós

weak /wiːk/ *a* (**-er, -est**) fraco; (*delicate*) frágil. ~**en** *vt/i* enfraquecer; (*give way*) fraquejar. ~**ness** *n* fraqueza *f*; (*fault*) ponto *m* fraco; **a** ~**ness for** (*liking*) um fraco por

weakling /'wiːklɪŋ/ *n* fraco *m*

wealth /welθ/ *n* riqueza *f*; (*riches, resources*) riquezas *fpl*; (*quantity*) abundância *f*

wealthy /'welθɪ/ *a* (**-ier, -iest**) rico

wean /wiːn/ *vt* ‹*baby*› desmamar; (*from habit etc*) desabituar

weapon /'wepən/ *n* arma *f*

wear /weə(r)/ *vt* (*pt* **wore**, *pp* **worn**) (*have on*) usar, trazer; (*put on*) pôr; (*expression*) ter; (*damage*) gastar; ~ **black/red/**etc vestir-se de preto/vermelho/etc; ~ **down** gastar; ‹*person*› extenuar; ~ **off** passar; ~ **on** ‹*time*› passar lentamente; ~ **out** gastar; ‹*tire*› esgotar ● *vi* (*last*) durar; (*become old, damaged etc*) gastar-se ● *n* (*use*) uso *m*; (*deterioration*) gasto *m*, uso *m*; (*endurance*) resistência *f*; (*clothing*) roupa *f*; ~ **and tear** desgaste *m*

wear|y /'wɪərɪ/ *a* (**-ier, -iest**) fatigado, cansado; (*tiring*) fatigante, cansativo ● *vi* ~**y of** cansar-se de

weasel /'wiːzl/ *n* doninha *f*

weather /'weðə(r)/ *n* tempo *m*; **under the** ~ 🄸 (*ill*) indisposto, achacado ● *a* meteorológico ● *vt* (*survive*) aguentar, resistir a. ~**-beaten** *a* curtido pelo tempo; ~ **forecast** *n* boletim *m* meteorológico

weave[1] /wiːv/ *vt* (*pt* **wove**, *pp* **woven**) ‹*cloth etc*› tecer; ‹*plot*› urdir, criar ● *n* (*style*) tipo *m* de tecido. ~**er** /-ə(r)/ *n* tecelão *m*, tecelã *f*

weave[2] /wiːv/ *vi* (*move*) serpear; (*through traffic, obstacles*) ziguezaguear

web /web/ *n* (*of spider*) teia *f*; (*fabric*) tecido *m*; *Comput* web *m*, rede *f*; (*on foot*) membrana *f* interdigital. ~**bed** *a* ‹*foot*› palmado. ~**footed** *a* palmípede; ~**log** blog *m*, (P) blogue *m*; **to keep/write a** ~**log** ter um blog *or* (P) blogue; ~ **page** *n* página *f* web; ~**site** *n* site *m*, síto *m*

wed /wed/ vt/i (pt **wedded**) casar(-se)

wedding /'wedɪŋ/ n casamento m. **~ cake** n bolo m de noiva; **~ ring** n aliança (de casamento) f

wedge /wedʒ/ n calço m, cunha f; (cake) fatia f; (of lemon) quarto m; (under wheel etc) calço m, cunha f ● vt calçar; (push) meter or enfiar à força; (pack in) entalar

Wednesday /'wenzdɪ/ n quarta-feira f

weed /wi:d/ n erva f daninha ● vt/i arrancar as ervas, capinar; **~ out** suprimir, arrancar. **~killer** n herbicida m. **~y** a fig ‹person› fraco

week /wi:k/ n semana f; **a ~ today/tomorrow** de hoje/de amanhã a oito dias. **~ly** a semanal ● a & n (periodical) (jornal) semanário m ● adv semanalmente, todas as semanas

weekday /'wi:kdeɪ/ n dia m de semana

weekend /'wi:kend/ n fim m de semana

weep /wi:p/ vt/i (pt **wept**) chorar (for sb por alguém); **~ing willow** n (salgueiro-)chorão m

weigh /weɪ/ vt/i pesar; **~ anchor** levantar âncora or ferro, zarpar; **~ down** (weight) sobrecarregar; (bend) envergar; fig acabrunhar; **~ up** I (examine) pesar

weight /weɪt/ n peso m; **lose ~** emagrecer; **put on ~** engordar. **~lifter** n halterofilista m; **~lifting** n halterofilia f. **~y** a pesado; ‹subject etc› de peso; (influential) influente

weir /wɪə(r)/ n represa f, açude m

weird /wɪəd/ a (-er, -est) misterioso; (strange) estranho, bizarro

welcom|e /'welkəm/ a agradável; (timely) oportuno; **~e to do** livre para fazer ● int bem-vindo! ● n acolhimento m ● vt acolher, receber; (as greeting) dar as boas vindas a; **be ~e** ser bem-vindo; **you're ~e!** (after thank you) não tem de quê!, de nada!. **~ing** a acolhedor

weld /weld/ vt soldar ● n solda f. **~er** n soldador m

welfare /'welfeə(r)/ n bem-estar m; (aid) assistência f, previdência f social; **W~ State** Estado-Providência m

well[1] /wel/ n (for water, oil) poço m; (of stairs) vão m; (of lift) poço m

well[2] /wel/ adv (**better**, **best**) bem; **we may as ~ go** é melhor irmos andando; **as ~ as** tão bem como; (in addition) assim como; **be ~** (healthy) ir or passar bem; **do ~** (succeed) sair-se bem, ser bem-sucedido; **very ~** muito bem; **~ done!** bravo!, muito bem! ● a bem invar ● int bem!. **~-behaved** a bem-comportado, educado; **~-being** n bem-estar m; **~-done** a (of meat) bem passado; **~-dressed** a bem-vestido; **~-heeled** a I (wealthy) rico; **~-informed** a versado, bem informado; **~-known** a (bem-)conhecido; **~-meaning** a bem-intencionado; **~-off** a rico, próspero; **~-read** a instruído; **~-spoken** a bem-falante; **~-timed** a oportuno; **~-to-do** a rico; **~-wisher** n admirador m, simpatizante mf

wellington /'welɪŋtən/ n (boot) bota f alta de borracha

Welsh /welʃ/ a galês ● n Lang galês m

Welsh Assembly A Assembleia Nacional de Gales começou a funcionar em Cardiff, em 1999. Embora a

Assembleia não tenha poderes para criar impostos, ela passou a ter poderes legislativos depois de um referendo em 2011. É formada por 60 membros ou AMs (*Assembly Members*); 40 são eleitos diretamente e os restantes, das listas regionais, através do sistema de representação proporcional.

went /went/ ▸ GO

wept /wept/ ▸ WEEP

were /wɜː(r)/ unstressed wə(r)/ ▸ BE

west /west/ n oeste m; **the W~** Pol o Oeste, o Ocidente ● a ocidental, do oeste; **the W~ Indies** as Antilhas ● adv a oeste, para oeste. **~erly** a ocidental, oeste. **~ward(s)** adv para oeste

western /'westən/ a ocidental, do oeste; Pol ocidental ● n (film) filme m de cowboys, bangue-bangue m

westernize /'westənaɪz/ vt ocidentalizar

wet /wet/ a (**wetter, wettest**) molhado; (of weather) chuvoso, de chuva; 🅸 ⟨person⟩ fraco; **get ~** molhar-se; **~ blanket** 🅸 desmancha-prazeres mf invar 🅸; **~ paint** pintado de fresco; **~ suit** roupa f de mergulho ● vt (wetted) molhar

whack /wæk/ vt 🅸 bater em ● n 🅸 pancada f. **~ed** a 🅸 morto de cansaço; rebentado 🅸

whale /weɪl/ n baleia f

wharf /wɔːf/ n (pl **wharfs**) cais m

what /wɒt/ ● pron

••••▸ (in questions) o que; **~ is it?** o que é?; **~ do you want?** o que você quer?; **~ is your name?** como você se chama?; **~ is your favourite?** qual é o seu favorito?;

~ happened? o que aconteceu?; **~?** (say that again) o quê?/como?

••••▸ (introducing clause) o que; I **don't know ~ he wants** não sei o que ele quer; **tell me ~ happened** conte-me o que aconteceu; I **don't agree with ~ you're saying** não concordo com o que diz; **do ~ I tell you** faça o que lhe digo

••••▸ (with prepositions) que; **~ are you thinking about?** em que você está pensando?; **~'s it for?** para o que é isso?

••••▸ (in phrases) **~ about me/ him?** e eu/ele?; **~ about a cup of coffee?** que tal uma xícara de café?; **~ if the train is late?** e se o trem se atrasar?; **~ for?** para quê?; **so ~?** e depois?

● a

••••▸ (in questions) qual; **~ train did you catch?** qual foi o trem que você pegou?; **~ time is it?** que horas são?; **~ colour is it?** que cor é essa?; **~ shoes should I wear?** que sapatos eu uso?; **~ time does it start?** a que horas começa?

••••▸ (in exclamations) que; **~ an idea!** que ideia!; **~ luck!** que sorte!; **~ a huge house!** que casa enorme!

whatever /wɒt'evə(r)/ a *~ book/ etc* qualquer livro/etc que seja ● pron (no matter what) qualquer que seja; (anything that) o que quer que, tudo o que; **~ happens** aconteça o que acontecer; **do ~ you like** faça o que quiser; **nothing ~** absolutamente nada

whatsoever /wɒtsəʊ'evə(r)/ a & pron = WHATEVER

wheat /wi:t/ n trigo m

wheel /wi:l/ n roda f; **at the ~** (of vehicle) ao volante; (helm) ao leme ● vt empurrar ● vi rodar, rolar

wheelbarrow /'wi:lbærəʊ/ n carrinho m de mão

wheelchair /'wi:ltʃeə(r)/ n cadeira f de rodas

when /wen/ adv, conj & pron quando; **the day/moment ~** o dia/momento em que

whenever /wen'evə(r)/ conj & adv (at whatever time) quando quer que, quando; (every time that) (de) cada vez que, sempre que

where /weə(r)/ adv, conj & pron onde, aonde; (in which place) em que, onde; (whereas) enquanto que, ao passo que; **~ is he going?** aonde é que ele vai?. **~abouts** adv onde ● n paradeiro m. **~by** adv pelo que. **~upon** adv após o que, depois do que

whereas /weər'æz/ conj enquanto que, ao passo que

wherever /weər'evə(r)/ conj & adv onde quer que; **~ can it be?** onde pode estar?

whether /'weðə(r)/ conj se; **not know ~** não saber se; **~ I go or not** caso eu vá ou não

which /wɪtʃ/ ● a

····▸ (in questions) que, qual; **~ book do you need?** de que/qual livro precisa?; **~ bag is yours?** qual das malas é a sua?; **~ way is the bank/hospital/supermarket?** como se vai para o banco/hospital/supermercado?

● pron

····▸ (in questions) qual; **~ is yours?** qual é o seu/a sua?; **there**

are three peaches, **~ do you want?** há três pêssegos, qual você quer?; **~ is the biggest?** qual é a maior?

····▸ (relative) que, o qual/a qual; (pl) os quais/as quais; **the book ~ is on the table** o livro que está em cima da mesa; **she made a serious mistake, ~ was unusual for her** ela fez um erro grave, o que era incomum para ela; **her work about ~ I know nothing** o trabalho dela, do qual nada sei; **the play ~ I took part in** a peça da qual eu participei

! Note that if o qual or a qual are preceded by the prepositions em or de, they often contract with them to form no qual, na qual, do qual, da qual.

whichever /wɪtʃ'evə(r)/ a **~ book/etc** qualquer livro/etc que seja; **take ~ book you wish** leve o livro que quiser ● pron qualquer, quaisquer

whiff /wɪf/ n (of fresh air) sopro m, lufada f; (smell) baforada f

while /waɪl/ n (espaço de) tempo m, momento m; **once in a ~** de vez em quando ● conj (when) enquanto; (while) embora; (whereas) enquanto que ● vt **~ away** ‹time› passar

whim /wɪm/ n capricho m

whimper /'wɪmpə(r)/ vi gemer; ‹baby› choramingar ● n gemido m; (baby) choro m

whimsical /'wɪmzɪkl/ a ‹person› caprichoso; (odd) bizarro

whine /waɪn/ vi lamuriar-se, queixar-se; ‹dog› ganir ● n lamúria f, queixume m; (dog) ganido m

whip /wɪp/ n chicote m ● vt (pt whipped) chicotear; Culin bater;

~ up excitar; (*cause*) provocar; 🔲 ‹*meal*› preparar rapidamente; **~ped cream** creme *m* chantilly ● *vi* (*move*) ir a toda a pressa. **~round** *n* 🔲 coleta *f*; vaquinha *f*

whirl /wɜːl/ *vt/i* (fazer) rodopiar, girar ● *n* rodopio *m*

whirlpool /ˈwɜːlpuːl/ *n* redemoinho *m*

whirlwind /ˈwɜːlwɪnd/ *n* redemoinho *m* de vento, turbilhão *m*

whirr /wɜː(r)/ *vi* zunir, zumbir

whisk /wɪsk/ *vt/i* (*snatch*) levar/tirar bruscamente; Culin bater; ‹*flies*› sacudir ● *n* Culin batedeira *f*; **~ away** (*brush away*) sacudir

whisker /ˈwɪskə(r)/ *n* fio *m* de barba. **~s** *npl* (*of animal*) bigode *m*; (*beard*) barba *f*; (*sideboards*) suíças *fpl*

whisky /ˈwɪskɪ/ *n* uísque *m*

whisper /ˈwɪspə(r)/ *vt/i* sussurrar, murmurar; (*of stream, leaves*) sussurrar ● *n* sussurro *m*, murmúrio *m*; **in a ~** baixinho, em voz baixa

whistle /ˈwɪsl/ *n* assobio *m*; (*instrument*) apito *m* ● *vt/i* assobiar; (*with instrument*) apitar

white /waɪt/ *a* (**-er, -est**) branco, alvo; (*pale*) pálido; **go ~** (*turn pale*) empalidecer; (*of hair*) branquear, embranquecer; **~ coffee** café *m* com leite; **~collar worker** empregado *m* de escritório; **~ elephant** *fig* trambolho *m*, elefante *m* branco; **~ lie** mentirinha *f* ● *n* (*colour; of eyes; person*) branco *m*; (*of egg*) clara (de ovo) *f*. **~ness** *n* brancura *f*

whiten /ˈwaɪtn/ *vt/i* branquear

Whitsun /ˈwɪtsn/ *n* Pentecostes *m*

whizz /wɪz/ *vi* (*pt* **whizzed**) (*through air*) zunir, sibilar; (*rush*) passar a toda a velocidade. **~kid** *n* 🔲 prodígio *m*

who /huː/ *interr pron* quem ● *rel pron* que, o(a) qual, os(as) quais

whoever /huːˈevə(r)/ *pron* (*no matter who*) quem quer que, seja quem for; (*the one who*) aquele que

whole /həʊl/ *a* inteiro, todo; (*not broken*) intacto; **the ~ house**/*etc* toda a casa/*etc* ● *n* totalidade *f*; (*unit*) todo *m*; **as a ~** no conjunto, como um todo; **on the ~** de um modo geral. **~hearted** *a* de todo o coração; ‹*person*› dedicado; **~heartedly** *adv* sem reservas, sinceramente

wholefood /ˈhəʊlfuːd/ *n* comida *f* integral

wholemeal /ˈhəʊlmiːl/ *a* **~ bread** pão *m* integral

wholesale /ˈhəʊlseɪl/ *n* venda *f* por grosso ou por atacado ● *a* ‹*firm*› por grosso, por atacado; *fig* sistemático; em massa ● *adv* (*in large quantities*) por atacado; *fig* em massa; em grande escala. **~r** /-ə(r)/ *n* grossista *mf*, atacadista *mf*

wholesome /ˈhəʊlsəm/ *a* sadio, saudável

wholewheat /ˈhəʊlwiːt/ *a* **= WHOLEMEAL**

wholly /ˈhəʊlɪ/ *adv* inteiramente, completamente

whom /huːm/ *interr pron* quem ● *rel pron* (*that*) que; (*after prep*) quem, que, o qual

whore /hɔː(r)/ *n* prostituta *f*

whose /huːz/ *rel pron* & *a* cujo, de quem ● *interr pron* de quem; **~ hat is this?, ~ is this hat?** de quem é este chapéu?; **~ son are you?** de quem é que o senhor é filho?

why /waɪ/ *adv* porque, por que motivo, por que razão, porquê; **she doesn't know ~ he's here** ela não sabe porque or por que motivo ele está aqui; **she doesn't know ~** ela não sabe porquê; **do you know ~?** você sabe porquê? ● *int* (*protest*) ora, ora essa; (*discovery*) oh; **~ yes/** *etc* ah, sim

wick /wɪk/ *n* torcida *f*, mecha *f*, pavio *m*

wicked /ˈwɪkɪd/ *a* mau, malvado; (*mischievous, spiteful*) maldoso

wicker /ˈwɪkə(r)/ *n* verga *f*, vime *m*

wicket /ˈwɪkɪt/ *n* Cricket arco *m*

wide /waɪd/ *a* (-**er, -est**) largo; (*extensive*) vasto, grande, extenso; **two metres ~** com dois metros de largura ● *adv* longe; (*fully*) completamente; **open ~** <*door, window*> abrir(-se) de par em par, escancarar(-se); <*mouth*> abrir bem; **~ awake** (bem) desperto, (bem) acordado; **far and ~** por toda a parte. **~ly** *adv* largamente; (*travel, spread*) muito; (*generally*) geralmente; (*extremely*) extremamente

widen /ˈwaɪdn/ *vt/i* alargar(-se)

widespread /ˈwaɪdspred/ *a* muito espalhado, difundido, generalizado

widow /ˈwɪdəʊ/ *n* viúva *f*. **~ed** *a* <*man*> viúvo; <*woman*> viúva; **be ~ed** enviuvar, ficar viúvo or viúva. **~er** *n* viúvo *m*

width /wɪdθ/ *n* largura *f*

wield /wiːld/ *vt* <*axe etc*> manejar; *fig* <*power*> exercer

wife /waɪf/ *n* (*pl* **wives**) mulher *f*, esposa *f*

wi-fi, Wi-Fi®, wifi /ˈwaɪfaɪ/ *n* wi-fi *m*

wig /wɪg/ *n* cabeleira (postiça) *f*; (*judge's etc*) peruca *f*

wiggle /ˈwɪgl/ *vt/i* remexer(-se), retorcer(-se), mexer(-se) dum lado para outro

wild /waɪld/ *a* (-**er, -est**) selvagem; (*of plant*) silvestre; (*mad*) louco; (*enraged*) furioso, violento; **~-goose chase** falsa pista *f*, tentativa *f* inútil, (*P*) caça *f* aos gambozinos ● *adv* a esmo; (*without control*) à solta. **~s** *npl* regiões *fpl* selvagens. **~ly** *adv* violentamente; (*madly*) loucamente

wilderness /ˈwɪldənɪs/ *n* deserto *m*

wildlife /ˈwaɪldlaɪf/ *n* animais *mpl* selvagens

wilful /ˈwɪlfl/ *a* <*person*> voluntarioso; (*act*) intencional, propositado

will[1] /wɪl/ *v aux* **you ~** sing/**he ~ do**/*etc* tu cantarás or tu vais cantar/ ele fará or ele vai fazer/*etc*; (*1st person: future: expressing will or intention*) **I ~** sing/**he ~ do**/*etc* eu cantarei or eu vou cantar/nós faremos or nós vamos fazer/*etc*; **~ you have a cup of coffee?** quer tomar um cafezinho?; **~ you shut the door?** quer fazer o favor de fechar a porta?

will[2] /wɪl/ *n* vontade *f*; (*document*) testamento *m*; **at ~** à vontade, quando or como se quiser ● *vt* (*wish*) querer; (*bequeath*) deixar em testamento. **~power** *n* força *f* de vontade

willing /ˈwɪlɪŋ/ *a* pronto, de boa vontade; **~ to** disposto a. **~ly** *adv* (*with pleasure*) de boa vontade, de bom grado; (*not forced*) voluntariamente. **~ness** *n* boa vontade *f*, disposição *f* (**to do** em para fazer)

willow /ˈwɪləʊ/ *n* salgueiro *m*

willy-nilly /wɪlɪˈnɪlɪ/ *adv* de bom ou de mau grado, quer queira ou não

wilt /wɪlt/ vi murchar, definhar

wily /ˈwaɪlɪ/ a (**-ier, -iest**) manhoso, matreiro

win /wɪn/ vt/i (pt **won**, pres p **winning**) ganhar ● n vitória f. □ ~ **over** vt convencer, conquistar

winc|e /wɪns/ vi estremecer, contrair-se

winch /wɪntʃ/ n guincho m ● vt içar com guincho

wind[1] /wɪnd/ n vento m; (breath) fôlego m; (flatulence) gases mpl; **get ~ of** fig ouvir rumor de; **put the ~ up** assustar; **in the ~** no ar; ~ **farm** central f eólica; ~ **instrument** Mus instrumento m de sopro. **~swept** a varrido pelo vento

wind[2] /waɪnd/ vt/i (pt **wound**) enrolar(-se); (wrap) envolver, pôr em volta; (of path, river) serpentear; ~ (**up**) ‹clock etc› dar corda em/a; ~ **up** (end) terminar, acabar; fig ‹speech etc› concluir; ‹firm› liquidar; **he'll ~ up in jail** ele vai acabar na cadeia

windfall /ˈwɪndfɔːl/ n fruta f caída; fig (money) sorte f grande

windmill /ˈwɪndmɪl/ n moinho m de vento

window /ˈwɪndəʊ/ n janela f; (of shop) vitrine f, (P) montra f; (counter) guichê m, (P) guichet m; **go ~shopping** ir ver vitrines/montras. ~ **box** n jardineira f; (P) floreira f; ~ **cleaner** n limpador m de janelas; **~pane** n vidro m, vidraça f; ~ **sill** n peitoril m

windpipe /ˈwɪndpaɪp/ n traqueia f

windscreen /ˈwɪndskriːn/ n para-brisa m, (P) para-brisas m invar. ~ **wiper** /-waɪpə(r)/ n limpador m de para-brisa, (P) limpa m para-brisas

windshield /ˈwɪndʃiːld/ n Amer = WINDSCREEN

windsurf|er /ˈwɪndsɜːfə(r)/ n surfista mf, (P) praticante mf de windsurf. **~ing** n surfe m, (P) windsurf f

windy /ˈwɪndɪ/ a (**-ier, -iest**) ventoso; **it is very ~** está ventando muito, (P) está muito vento

wine /waɪn/ n vinho m; ~ **bar** bar m para degustação de vinhos; ~ **waiter** garçon m, (P) empregado m de vinhos. ~ **cellar** n adega f, cave f; ~ **list** n lista f de vinhos; ~ **tasting** prova f or degustação f de vinhos

wine glass /ˈwaɪnɡlɑːs/ n copo m de vinho; (with stem) cálice m

wing /wɪŋ/ n asa f; Mil flanco m; Archit ala f; Auto para-lamas m invar, (P) guarda-lamas m invar; **~s** Theat bastidores mpl; **under sb's ~** debaixo das asas de alguém

wink /wɪŋk/ vi piscar o olho; ‹light, star› cintilar, piscar ● n piscadela f; **not sleep a ~** não pregar olho

winner /ˈwɪnə(r)/ n vencedor m

winning /ˈwɪnɪŋ/ a vencedor, vitorioso; (number) premiado; (smile) encantador, atraente. **~s** npl ganhos mpl

winter /ˈwɪntə(r)/ n inverno m ● vi hibernar. **~ry** a de inverno, invernoso; ‹smile› glacial

wipe /waɪp/ vt limpar; (dry) enxugar, limpar ● n limpadela f; ~ **off** limpar; ~ **out** (destroy) aniquilar, limpar 🗆; (cancel) cancelar; ~ **up** enxugar

wir|e /ˈwaɪə(r)/ n arame m; 🗆 (telegram) telegrama m; (**electric**) **~e** fio elétrico m ● vt ‹a house› montar a instalação elétrica em; 🗆 (telegraph) telegrafar. **~ing** n Electr instalação f elétrica

wireless /'waɪəlɪs/ n rádio f; (set) rádio m

wisdom /'wɪzdəm/ n sagacidade f, sabedoria f; (common sense) bom senso m, sensatez f; **~ tooth** dente m (do) siso

wise /waɪz/ a (-er, -est) ‹person› sábio, avisado, sensato; ‹look› entendedor; **~ guy** 🇬🇧 sabichão m, 🇬🇧 sabe-tudo m 🇬🇧; **none the ~r** sem entender nada

wisecrack /'waɪzkræk/ n 🇬🇧 (boa) piada f

wish /wɪʃ/ n (desire, aspiration) desejo m, vontade f; (request) pedido m; (greeting) desejo m, voto m; **I have no ~ to go** não tenho nenhum desejo or nenhuma vontade de ir; **with best ~es** (formal) (in letter) com os melhores cumprimentos, com saudações cordiais; (on greeting card) com desejos or votos (for de) ● vt (desire, bid) desejar; (want) apetecer; ter vontade de; desejar (to do fazer); **~ sb well** desejar felicidades a alguém; **I don't ~ to go** não me apetece ir, não tenho vontade de ir, não desejo ir; **I ~ he'd leave** eu gostaria que ele partisse, quem dera que ele partisse ● vi **~ for** desejar

wishful /'wɪʃfl/ a **~ thinking** sonhar acordado, impossível de concretizar

wishy-washy /'wɪʃɪwɒʃɪ/ a sem expressão, fraco, inexpressivo

wistful /'wɪstfl/ a melancólico, saudoso

wit /wɪt/ n inteligência f; (humour) presença f de espírito, humor m; (person) senso m or (P) sentido m de humor; **be at one's ~'s** or **~s' end** não saber o que fazer; **keep one's ~s about one** estar alerta; **live by** one's **~s** ganhar a vida de maneira suspeita; **scared out of one's ~s** apavorado

witch /wɪtʃ/ n feiticeira f, bruxa f. **~craft** n feitiçaria f, bruxaria f, magia f

with /wɪð/ prep com; (having) de; (because of) de; (at the house of) em casa de; **the man ~ the beard** o homem de barbas; **fill**/etc**~** encher/ etc de; **laughing/shaking**/etc **~** a rir/a tremer/etc de; **I'm not ~ you** 🇬🇧 não estou compreendendo-o, (P) não te estou a compreender

withdraw /wɪð'drɔː/ vt/i (pt **withdrew**, pp **withdrawn**) retirar(-se); ‹money› tirar. **~al** n retirada f; Med estado m de privação. **~n** a ‹person› retraído, fechado

wither /'wɪðə(r)/ vt/i murchar, secar. **~ed** a ‹person› mirrado. **~ing** a fig (scornful) desdenhoso

withhold /wɪð'həʊld/ vt (pt **withheld**) negar, recusar; (retain) reter; (conceal, not tell) esconder (from de)

within /wɪ'ðɪn/ prep & adv dentro (de), por dentro (de); (in distances) a menos de; **~ a month** (before) dentro de um mês; **~ sight** à vista

without /wɪ'ðaʊt/ prep sem; **~ fail** sem falta; **go ~ saying** não ser preciso dizer

withstand /wɪð'stænd/ vt (pt **withstood**) resistir a, opor-se a

witness /'wɪtnɪs/ n testemunha f; (evidence) testemunho m ● vt testemunhar, presenciar; ‹document› assinar como testemunha; **bear ~ to** testemunhar, dar testemunho de. **~ box** n banco m das testemunhas

witticism /'wɪtɪsɪzəm/ n dito m espirituoso

witty /'wɪtɪ/ a (-ier,, -iest)
espirituoso

wives /waɪvz/ ▶ WIFE

wizard /'wɪzəd/ n feiticeiro m; fig
(genius) gênio m, (P) génio m

wizened /'wɪznd/ a encarquilhado

wobbl|e /'wɒbl/ vi (of jelly, voice,
hand) tremer; (stagger) cambalear,
vacilar; (of table, chair) balançar. **~y**
a (trembling) trêmulo, (P) trémulo;
(staggering) cambaleante, vacilante;
‹table, chair› pouco firme

woe /wəʊ/ n dor f, infortúnio m

woke, woken /wəʊk, 'wəʊkən/
▶ WAKE¹

wolf /wʊlf/ n (pl wolves /wʊlvz/)
lobo m; **cry ~** dar alarme falso, (P)
falso alarme ● vt ‹food› devorar.
~ whistle n assobio m de admiração

woman /'wʊmən/ n (pl women)
mulher f. **~ly** a feminino

womb /wu:m/ n seio m, ventre m;
Med útero m; fig seio m

women /'wɪmɪn/ ▶ WOMAN; **~'s
movement** movimento m feminista

won /wʌn/ ▶ WIN

wonder /'wʌndə(r)/ n admiração f;
(thing) maravilha f ● vt perguntar-se
a si mesmo (**if** se) ● vi admirar-se
(**at** de, com), ficar admirado (**at**
de, com); espantar-se (**at** de, com);
(reflect) pensar (**about** em); **it is no
~** não admira (**that** que)

wonderful
/'wʌndəfl/ a maravilhoso. **~ly** adv
maravilhosamente; **it works ~ly**
funciona às mil maravilhas

won't /wəʊnt/ (= will not) = WILL¹

wood /wʊd/ n madeira f, pau m,
(for burning) lenha f. **~(s)** n (area)
bosque m, mata f, floresta f. **~ed**
a arborizado. **~en** a de ou em
madeira, de pau; fig (stiff) rígido; fig

(inexpressive) inexpressivo; de pau

woodcut /'wʊdkʌt/ n gravura f
em madeira

woodland /'wʊdlənd/ n região f
arborizada, bosque m, mata f

woodpecker /'wʊdpekə(r)/ n
(bird) pica-pau m

woodwind /'wʊdwɪnd/ n Mus
instrumentos mpl de sopro de
madeira

woodwork /'wʊdwɜːk/ n
(of building) madeiramento m;
(carpentry) carpintaria f

woodworm /'wʊdwɜːm/ n
caruncho m

wool /wʊl/ n lã f. **~len** a de lã.
~lens npl roupas fpl de lã. **~ly** a de
lã; (vague) confuso ● n [] (garment)
roupa f de lã

word /wɜːd/ n palavra f; (news)
notícia f(pl); (promise) palavra
f ● vt exprimir, formular; **by ~ of
mouth** de viva voz, por via oral;
have a ~ with dizer duas palavras
a; **in other ~s** em outras palavras,
(P) por outras palavras. **~ processor**
n processador m de texto(s). **~ing** n
termos mpl, redação f. **~y** a prolixo

wore /wɔː(r)/ ▶ WEAR

work /wɜːk/ n trabalho m; (product,
book etc) obra f; (building etc) obras
fpl; **at ~** no trabalho; **out of ~**
desempregado ● vt/i (of person)
trabalhar; Techn (fazer) funcionar,
(fazer) andar; (of drug etc) agir,
fazer efeito; ‹farm, mine› explorar;
‹land› lavrar; **~ sb** (make work) fazer
alguém trabalhar; **~ in** introduzir,
inserir; **~ loose** soltar-se; **~ off**
(get rid of) descarregar; **~ed up**
‹person› enervado, transtornado,
agitado. **~ out** vt (solve) resolver;
(calculate) calcular; (devise) planejar,
(P) planear ● vi (succeed) resultar;

Sport treinar-se; **~ up** *vt* criar ● *vi* (*to climax*) ir num crescendo; **~s** *npl Techn* mecanismo *m*; (*factory*) fábrica *f*

workable /'wɜːkəbl/ *a* viável, praticável

workaholic /wɜːkə'hɒlɪk/ *n* **be a ~** 🔢 trabalhar como um possesso, 🔢 ser viciado em trabalho

worker /'wɜːkə(r)/ *n* trabalhador *m*, trabalhadora *f*; (*factory*) operário *m*

working /'wɜːkɪŋ/ *a* (*day, clothes, hypothesis, lunch etc*) de trabalho; **the ~ class(es)** a classe operária, a(s) class(es) trabalhadora(s), o proletariado; **~ mother** mãe *f* que trabalha; **~ party** comissão *f* consultiva, de estudo *etc*; **in ~ order** em condições de funcionamento. **~class** *a* operário, trabalhador. **~s** *npl* mecanismo *m*

workman /'wɜːkmən/ *n* (*pl* **-men**) trabalhador *m*; (*factory*) operário *m*. **~ship** *n* trabalho *m*, execução *f*, mão-de-obra *f*; (*skill*) arte *f*, habilidade *f*

workshop /'wɜːkʃɒp/ *n* oficina *f*, (*P*) workshop *m*

world /wɜːld/ *n* mundo *m*; **a ~ of** muito(s), grande quantidade de, um mundo de ● *a* mundial. **~wide** *a* mundial, universal

worldly /'wɜːldlɪ/ *a* terreno; (*devoted to the affairs of life*) mundano; **~ goods** bens *mpl* materiais. **~wise** *a* com experiência do mundo

worm /wɜːm/ *n* verme *m*; (*earthworm*) minhoca *f* ● *vt* **~ one's way into** insinuar-se, introduzir-se, enfiar-se

worn /wɔːn/ *a* usado. **~out** *a* ‹*thing*› completamente gasto; ‹*person*› esgotado

worry /'wʌrɪ/ *vt/i* preocupar(-se); **don't ~** fique descansado, não se preocupe ● *n* preocupação *f*. **~ied** *a* preocupado. **~ying** *a* preocupante, inquietante

worse /wɜːs/ *a* & *adv* pior ● *n* pior *m*; **get ~** piorar; **from bad to ~** de mal a pior; **~ luck** pouca sorte, pena

worsen /'wɜːsn/ *vt/i* piorar

worship /'wɜːʃɪp/ *n* (*reverence*) reverência *f*, veneração *f*; (*religious*) culto *m*; **Your/His W~** Vossa/Sua Excelência *f* ● *vt* (*pt* **worshipped**) adorar, venerar ● *vi* fazer as suas devoções, praticar o culto

worst /wɜːst/ *a* & *n* (**the**) **~** (*o/a*) pior *mf*; **if the ~ comes to the ~** se o pior acontecer, na pior das hipóteses; **do one's ~** fazer todo o mal que se quiser; **get the ~ of it** ficar a perder; **the ~ (thing) that** o pior que ● *adv* pior

worth /wɜːθ/ *a* **be ~** valer; (*deserving*) merecer ● *n* valor *m*, mérito *m*; **ten pounds ~ of** dez libras de; **it's ~ it, it's ~ while** vale a pena; **it's not ~ my while** não vale a pena; **it's ~ waiting/***etc* a pena esperar/*etc*; **for all one's ~** 🔢 dando tudo por tudo. **~less** *a* sem valor

worthwhile /wɜːθ'waɪl/ *a* que vale a pena; ‹*cause*› louvável, meritório

worthy /'wɜːðɪ/ *a* (**-ier, -iest**) (*deserving*) digno; merecedor (**of** de); (*laudable*) meritório, louvável ● *n* (*person*) pessoa *f* ilustre

would /wʊd/ *unstressed* wəd/ *v aux* **he ~ do/you ~ sing**/*etc* (*conditional tense*) ele faria/você cantaria/*etc*; **he ~ have done** ele teria feito; **she ~ come every day** (*used to*) ela vinha ou costumava vir aqui todos os dias;

~ **you please come here?** chegue aqui por favor; ~ **you like some tea?** você quer um chá?; **he ~n't go** (*refused to*) ele não queria ir; **~be author/doctor**/*etc* aspirante a autor/médico/*etc*

wound¹ /wuːnd/ *n* ferida *f* ● *vt* ferir; **the ~ed** os feridos *mpl*

wound² /waʊnd/ ▶ **WIND**²

wove, woven /wəʊv, ˈwəʊvn/ ▶ **WEAVE**²

wrangle /ˈræŋgl/ *vi* disputar, discutir, brigar ● *n* disputa *f*, discussão *f*, briga *f*

wrap /ræp/ *vt* (*pt* **wrapped**) ~ **(up)** embrulhar (**in** em); (*in cotton wool, mystery etc*) envolver (**in** em); **~ped up in** (*engrossed*) absorto em, mergulhado em ● *vi* ~ **up** (*dress warmly*) abrigar-se bem, agasalhar-se bem ● *n* xaile *m*. **~per** *n* (*of sweet*) papel *m*; (*of book*) capa *f* de papel. **~ping** *n* embalagem *f*

wrath /rɒθ/ *n* ira *f*

wreath /riːθ/ *n* (*pl* **-s** /-ðz/) (*of flowers, leaves*) coroa *f*, grinalda *f*

wreck /rek/ *n* (*sinking*) naufrágio *m*; (*ship*) navio *m* naufragado; (*remains*) destroços *mpl* de navio; (*vehicle*) veículo *m* destroçado; **be a nervous ~** estar com os nervos arrasados ● *vt* destruir; (*ship*) fazer naufragar, afundar; *fig* (*hope*) acabar. **~age** *n* (*pieces*) destroços *mpl*

wren /ren/ *n* (*bird*) carriça *f*

wrench /rentʃ/ *vt* (*pull*) puxar; (*twist*) torcer; (*snatch*) arrancar (**from** a) ● *n* (*pull*) puxão *m*; (*of ankle, wrist*) torcedura *f*; (*tool*) chave *f* inglesa; *fig* dor *f* de separação

wrestl|e /ˈresl/ *vi* lutar; debater-se (**with** com or contra). **~er** *n* lutador *m*. **~ing** *n* luta *f*

wretch /retʃ/ *n* desgraçado *m*, miserável *mf*; (*rascal*) miserável *mf*

wretched /ˈretʃɪd/ *a* (*pitiful, poor*) miserável; (*bad*) horrível, desgraçado

wriggle /ˈrɪgl/ *vt/i* remexer(-se), contorcer-se

wring /rɪŋ/ *vt* (*pt* **wrung**) (*twist; clothes*) torcer; ~ **out of** (*obtain from*) arrancar a; **~ing wet** encharcado; (*of person*) encharcado até aos ossos

wrinkle /ˈrɪŋkl/ *n* (*on skin*) ruga *f*; (*crease*) prega *f* ● *vt/i* enrugar(-se)

wrist /rɪst/ *n* pulso *m*. **~watch** *n* relógio *m* de pulso

write /raɪt/ *vt/i* (*pt* **wrote**, *pp* **written**) escrever; ~ **back** responder; ~ **down** escrever, tomar nota de; ~ **off** (*debt*) dar por liquidado; (*vehicle*) destinar à sucata; ~ **out** (*in full*) escrever por extenso; ~ **up** (*from notes*) redigir. **~-off** *n* perda *f* total; **~up** *n* relato *m*; (*review*) crítica *f*

writer /ˈraɪtə(r)/ *n* escritor *m*, autor *m*

writhe /raɪð/ *vi* contorcer(-se)

writing /ˈraɪtɪŋ/ *n* escrita *f*; **~(s)** (*works*) escritos *mpl*, obras *fpl*; **in ~** por escrito. **~ paper** *n* papel *m* de carta

written /ˈrɪtn/ ▶ **WRITE**

wrong /rɒŋ/ *a* (*incorrect, mistaken*) mal, errado; (*unfair*) injusto; (*wicked*) mau; (*amiss*) que não está bem; **Mus** (*note*) falso; (*clock*) que não está certo; **what's ~?** qual é o problema?; **what's ~ with it?** (*amiss*) o que é que não está bem?; (*morally*) que mal há nisso?, que mal tem? ● *adv* mal; **go ~** (*err*) desencaminhar-se, correr mal; (*fail*) ir mal; (*vehicle*) quebrar ● *n* mal m; (*injustice*) injustiça f; **he's in the ~** (*his fault*) ele não tem razão ● vt (*be unfair to*) ser injusto com; (*do a wrong to*) fazer mal a. **~ly** adv mal; (*blame etc*) sem razão, injustamente

wrongful /'rɒŋfl/ a injusto, ilegal

wrote /rəʊt/ ▶ **WRITE**

wrung /rʌŋ/ ▶ **WRING**

wry /raɪ/ a (**wryer, wryest**) torto; ‹*smile*› forçado; **~ face** careta f

. . . .

Xmas /'krɪsməs/ n ▶ **CHRISTMAS**

X-ray /'eksreɪ/ n raio X m; (*photograph*) radiografia f ● vt radiografar; **have an ~** tirar uma radiografia

xylophone /'zaɪləfəʊn/ n xilofone m

. . . .

yacht /jɒt/ n iate m. **~ing** n iatismo m, andar m de iate; (*racing*) regata f de iate

yank /jæŋk/ vt 🗓 puxar bruscamente ● n 🗓 puxão m

Yank /jæŋk/ n 🗓 ianque mf

yap /jæp/ vi (pt **yapped**) latir

yard¹ /jɑːd/ n (*measure*) jarda f (=0,9144 m)

yard² /jɑːd/ n (*of house*) pátio m; Amer (*garden*) jardim m; (*for storage*) depósito m

yardstick /'jɑːdstɪk/ n jarda f, fig bitola f; craveira f

yarn /jɑːn/ n (*thread*) fio m; 🗓 (*tale*) longa f história

yawn /jɔːn/ vi bocejar; (*be wide open*) abrir-se, escancarar-se ● n bocejo m

year /jɪə(r)/ n ano m; **school/tax ~** ano m escolar/fiscal; **be ten ~s old/** etc ter dez/etc anos de idade. **~book** n anuário m. **~ly** a anual ● adv anualmente

yearn /jɜːn/ vi **~ for, to** desejar, ansiar por, suspirar por. **~ing** n desejo m; anseio m (**for** de)

yeast /jiːst/ n levedura f

yell /jel/ vt/i gritar, berrar ● n grito m, berro m

yellow /'jeləʊ/ a amarelo; 🗓 (*cowardly*) covarde; poltrão ● n amarelo m

yelp /jelp/ n (*of dog etc*) ganido m ● vi ganir

yes /jes/ n & adv sim m. **~man** n 🗓 lambe-botas m invar; puxa-saco m

yesterday /'jestədɪ/ n & adv ontem m; **~ morning/afternoon/evening** ontem de manhã/à tarde/à noite; **the day before ~** anteontem; **~ week** há oito dias, há uma semana

yet /jet/ adv ainda; (*already*) já; **as ~** até agora, por enquanto; **his best book ~** o seu melhor livro até agora ● conj contudo, no entanto

Yiddish /'jɪdɪʃ/ n ídiche m, (P) iídiche m

yield /jiːld/ vt (*produce*) produzir, dar; ‹*profit*› render; (*surrender*) entregar ● vi (*give way*) ceder or dar prioridade ● *n* produção *f*; *Comm* rendimento *m*

yoga /'jəʊgə/ *n* ioga *f*

yoghurt /'jɒgət/ *n* iogurte *m*

yoke /jəʊk/ *n* jugo *m*, canga *f*; (*of garment*) pala *f* ● *vt* jungir; (*unite*) unir, ligar

yolk /jəʊk/ *n* gema (de ovo) *f*

yonder /'jɒndə(r)/ *adv* acolá, além

you /juː/ *pron* (*familiar*) tu, você; *pl* vocês; (*polite*) vós, o(s) senhor(es), a(s) senhora(s); (*object*) te, lhe; *pl* vocês; (*polite*) o(s), a(s), lhes, vós, o(s) senhor(es), a(s) senhora(s); (*after prep*) ti, si, você; *pl* vocês; (*polite*) vós, o senhor, a senhora; *pl* os senhores, as senhoras; (*indefinite*) se; (*after prep*) si, você; **with ~** (*familiar*) contigo, consigo, com você; *pl* com vocês; (*polite*) com o senhor/a senhora; *pl* convosco, com os senhores/as senhoras; **I know ~** (*familiar*) eu te conheço, (*P*) eu conheço-te, eu o/a conheço, (*P*) eu conheço-o/-a, eu os/as conheço, (*P*) eu conheço-os/-as; (*polite*) eu vos conheço, (*P*) eu conheço-vos, conheço o senhor/a senhora; *pl* conheço os senhores/as senhoras; **~ can see the sea** você pode ver o mar, (*P*) tu podes ver o mar

young /jʌŋ/ *a* (**-er, -est**) jovem, novo, moço ● *n* ‹*people*› jovens *mpl*, a juventude *f*, a mocidade *f*; (*of animals*) crias *fpl*, filhotes *mpl*

youngster /'jʌŋstə(r)/ *n* jovem *mf*, moço *m*, rapaz *m*

your /jɔː(r)/ *a* (*familiar*) teu, tua, seu, sua; *pl* teus, tuas, seus, suas; (*polite*) vosso, vossa, do senhor, da senhora; *pl* vossos, vossas, dos senhores, das senhoras

yours /jɔːz/ *poss pron* (*familiar*) o teu, a tua, o seu, a sua; *pl* os teus, as tuas, os seus, as suas; (*polite*) o vosso, a vossa, o/a do senhor, o/a da senhora; *pl* os vossos, as vossas, os/as do(s) senhor(es), os/as da(s) senhora(s); **a book of ~** um livro seu; **~ sincerely/faithfully** atenciosamente, com os cumprimentos de

yourself /jɔː'self/ (*pl* **-selves**) *pron* (*familiar*) tu mesmo/a, você mesmo/a; *pl* vocês mesmos/as; (*polite*) vós mesmo/a, o senhor mesmo, a senhora mesma; *pl* vós mesmos/as, os senhores mesmos, as senhoras mesmas; (*reflexive*) (*familiar*) te; a ti mesmo/a; se; a si mesmo/a; *pl* a vocês mesmos/as; (*polite*) ao senhor mesmo, à senhora mesma; *pl* aos senhores mesmos, às senhoras mesmas; (*after prep: familiar*) ti mesmo/a, si mesmo/a, você mesmo/a; *pl* vocês mesmos/as; (*after prep: polite*) vós mesmo/a, o senhor mesmo, a senhora mesma; *pl* vós mesmos/as, os senhores mesmos, as senhoras mesmas; **with ~** (*familiar*) contigo mesmo/a, consigo mesmo/a, com você; *pl* com vocês; (*polite*) convosco, com o senhor, com a senhora; *pl* com os senhores, com as senhoras; **by ~** sozinho

youth /juːθ/ *n* (*pl* **-s** /-ðz/) mocidade *f*, juventude *f*; (*young man*) jovem *m*, moço *m*; **~ club** centro *m* de jovens; **~ hostel** albergue *m* da juventude. **~ful** *a* juvenil, jovem

yo-yo® /'jəʊjəʊ/ *n* (*pl* **-os**) ioiô *m*

Yugoslav /'juːgəslɑːv/ *a & n* iugoslavo *m*, (*P*) jugoslavo *m*. **~ia** /-'slɑːvɪə/ *n* Iugoslávia *f*, (*P*) Jugoslávia *f*

Zz

zany /'zeɪnɪ/ a **-ier, -iest** tolo, bobo, pateta

zeal /ziːl/ n zelo m

zealous /'zeləs/ a zeloso

zebra /'zebrə, 'ziːbrə/ n zebra f; ~ **crossing** faixa f para pedestres, (P) passagem f para peões, passadeira f

zenith /'zenɪθ/ n zênite m, (P) zénite m, auge m

zero /'zɪərəʊ/ n (pl -os) zero m; ~ **hour** a hora H; **below** ~ abaixo de zero

zest /zest/ n (gusto) entusiasmo m; fig (spice) sabor m especial; (lemon or orange peel) casca f de limão/laranja ralada

zigzag /'zɪgzæg/ n ziguezague m ● a & adv em ziguezague ● vi (pt **zigzagged**) ziguezaguear

zinc /zɪŋk/ n zinco m

zip /zɪp/ n (vigour) energia f, alma f; ~ **(fastener)** fecho m ecler ● vt (pt **zipped**) fechar o fecho ecler de ● vi ir a toda a velocidade. **Z~ code** n Amer CEP de endereçamento postal m, (P) código m postal

zipper /'zɪpə(r)/ n (= zip(-fastener)) ▸ ZIP

zodiac /'zəʊdɪæk/ n zodíaco m

zombie /'zɒmbɪ/ n zumbi m; 🇧 zumbi m, (P) autómato m, zombie m

zone /zəʊn/ n zona f

zoolog|y /zəʊ'ɒlədʒɪ/ n zoologia f. ~**ical** /-ə'lɒdʒɪkl/ a zoológico. ~**ist** n zoólogo m

zoom /zuːm/ vi (rush) sair roando; ~ **off** or **past** passar zunindo; ~ **lens** zum m, zoom m

zucchini /zuː'kiːnɪ/ n (pl invar) Amer courgette f

Portuguese verbs

Portuguese verbs can be divided into three categories: regular verbs, those with spelling peculiarities determined by their sound and irregular verbs.

Regular verbs:

in -ar (e.g. comprar)

Present: compr|o, ~as, ~a, ~amos, ~ais, ~am
Future: comprar|ei, ~ás, ~á, ~emos, ~eis, ~ão
Imperfect: compr|ava, ~avas, ~ava, ~ávamos, ~áveis, ~avam
Preterite: compr|ei, ~aste, ~ou, ~amos (P: ~ámos), ~astes, ~aram
Pluperfect: compr|ara, ~aras, ~ara, ~áramos, ~áreis, ~aram
Present subjunctive: compr|e, ~es, ~e, ~emos, ~eis, ~em
Imperfect subjunctive: compr|asse, ~asses, ~asse, ~ássemos, ~ásseis, ~assem
Future subjunctive: compr|ar, ~ares, ~ar, ~armos, ~ardes, ~arem
Conditional: comprar|ia, ~ias, ~ia, ~íamos, ~íeis, ~iam
Personal infinitive: comprar, ~es, ~, ~mos, ~des, ~em
Present participle: comprando
Past participle: comprado
Imperative: compra, comprai

in -er (e.g. bater)

Present: bat|o, ~es, ~e, ~emos, ~eis, ~em
Future: bater|ei, ~ás, ~á, ~emos, ~eis, ~ão
Imperfect: bat|ia, ~ias, ~ia, ~íamos, ~íeis, ~iam

Preterite: bat|i, ~este, ~eu, ~emos, ~estes, ~eram
Pluperfect: bat|era, ~eras, ~era, ~êramos, ~êreis, ~eram
Present subjunctive: bat|a, ~as, ~a, ~amos, ~ais, ~am
Imperfect subjunctive: bat|esse, ~esses, ~esse, ~êssemos, ~êsseis, ~essem
Future subjunctive: bat|er, ~eres, ~er, ~ermos, ~erdes, ~erem
Conditional: bater|ia, ~ias, ~ia, ~íamos, ~íeis, ~iam
Personal infinitive: bater, ~es, ~, ~mos, ~des, ~em
Present participle: batendo
Past participle: batido
Imperative: bate, batei

in -ir (e.g. admitir)

Present: admit|o, ~es, ~e, ~imos, ~is, ~em
Future: admitir|ei, ~ás, ~á, ~emos, ~eis, ~ão
Imperfect: admit|ia, ~ias, ~ia, ~íamos, ~íeis, ~iam
Preterite: admit|i, ~iste, ~iu, ~imos, ~istes, ~iram
Pluperfect: admit|ira, ~iras, ~ira, ~íramos, ~íreis, ~iram
Present subjunctive: admit|a, ~as, ~a, ~amos, ~ais, ~am
Imperfect subjunctive: admit|isse, ~isses, ~isse, ~íssemos, ~ísseis, ~issem
Future subjunctive: admit|ir, ~ires, ~ir, ~irmos, ~irdes, ~irem
Conditional: admitir|ia, ~ias, ~ia, ~íamos, ~íeis, ~iam
Personal infinitive: admitir, ~es, ~, ~mos, ~des, ~em

Present participle: admitindo
Past participle: admitido
Imperative: admite, admiti

Regular verbs with spelling changes:

-ar verbs:

in -car (e.g. **ficar**)

Preterite: fiquei, ficaste, ficou, ficamos (P: ficámos), ficastes, ficaram
Present subjunctive: fique, fiques, fique, fiquemos, fiqueis, fiquem

in -çar (e.g. **abraçar**)

Preterite: abracei, abraçaste, abraçou, abraçamos (P: abraçámos), abraçastes, abraçaram
Present subjunctive: abrace, abraces, abrace, abracemos, abraceis, abracem

in -ear (e.g. **passear**)

Present: passeio, passeias, passeia, passeamos, passeais, passeiam
Present subjunctive: passeie, passeies, passeie, passeemos, passeeis, passeiem
Imperative: passeia, passeai

in -gar (e.g. **apagar**)

Preterite: apaguei, apagaste, apagou, apagamos (P: apagámos), apagastes, apagaram
Present subjunctive: apague, apagues, apague, apaguemos, apagueis, apaguem

in -oar (e.g. **voar**)

Present: voo, voas, voa, voamos, voais, voam

averiguar

Preterite: averiguei, averiguaste, averiguou, averiguamos (P: averiguámos), averiguastes, averiguaram
Present subjunctive: averigue, averigues, averigue, averiguemos, averigueis, averiguem

enxaguar

Present: enxaguo, enxaguas, enxagua, enxaguamos, enxaguais, enxaguam
Preterite: enxaguei, enxaguaste, enxaguou, enxaguamos (P: enxaguámos), enxaguastes, enxaguaram
Present subjunctive: enxágue, enxagues, enxague, enxaguemos, enxagueis, enxaguem
Similarly: aguar, desaguar

saudar

Present: saúdo, saúdas, saúda, saudamos, saudais, saúdam
Present subjunctive: saúde, saúdes, saúde, saudemos, saudeis, saúdem
Imperative: saúda, saudai

-er verbs:

in -cer (e.g. **tecer**)

Present: teço, teces, tece, tecemos, teceis, tecem
Present subjunctive: teça, teças, teça, teçamos, teçais, teçam

in -ger (e.g. **proteger**)

Present: protejo, proteges, protege, protegemos, protegeis, protegem
Present subjunctive: proteja, protejas, proteja, protejamos, protejais, protejam

in -**guer** (e.g. **erguer**)

Present: ergo, ergues, ergue, erguemos, ergueis, erguem
Present subjunctive: erga, ergas, erga, ergamos, ergais, ergam

in -**oer** (e.g. **roer**)

Present: roo, róis, rói, roemos, roeis, roem
Imperfect: roía, roías, roía, roíamos, roíeis, roíam
Preterite: roí, roeste, roeu, roemos, roestes, roeram
Past participle: roído
Imperative: rói, roei

-**ir** verbs:

in -**ir** with -**e**- in stem (e.g. **vestir**)

Present: visto, vestes, veste, vestimos, vestis, vestem
Present subjunctive: vista, vistas, vista, vistamos, vistais, vistam
Similarly: mentir, preferir, refletir, repetir, seguir, sentir, servir

in -**ir** with -**o**- in stem (e.g. **dormir**)

Present: durmo, dormes, dorme, dormimos, dormis, dormem
Present subjunctive: durma, durmas, durma, durmamos, durmais, durmam
Similarly: cobrir, descobrir, tossir

in -**ir** with -**u**- in stem (e.g. **subir**)

Present: subo, sobes, sobe, subimos, subis, sobem
Similarly: consumir, cuspir, fugir, sacudir, sumir

in -**air** (e.g. **sair**)

Present: saio, sais, sai, saímos, saís, saem
Imperfect: saía, saías, saía, saíamos, saíeis, saíam

Preterite: saí, saíste, saiu, saímos, saístes, saíram
Pluperfect: saíra, saíras, saíra, saíramos, saíreis, saíram
Present subjunctive: saia, saias, saia, saiamos, saiais, saiam
Imperfect subjunctive: saísse, saísses, saísse, saíssemos, saísseis, saíssem
Future subjunctive: sair, saíres, sair, sairmos, sairdes, saírem
Personal infinitive: sair, saíres, sair, sairmos, sairdes, saírem
Present participle: saindo
Past participle: saído
Imperative: sai, saí

in -**gir** (e.g. **dirigir**)

Present: dirijo, diriges, dirige, dirigimos, dirigis, dirigem
Present subjunctive: dirija, dirijas, dirija, dirijamos, dirijais, dirijam

in -**guir** (e.g. **distinguir**)

Present: distingo, distingues, distingue, distinguimos, distinguis, distinguem
Present subjunctive: distinga, distingas, distinga, distingamos, distingais, distingam

in -**uir** (e.g. **atribuir**)

Present: atribuo, atribuis, atribui, atribuímos, atribuís, atribuem
Imperfect: atribuía, atribuías, atribuía, atribuíamos, atribuíeis, atribuíam
Preterite: atribuí, atribuíste, atribuiu, atribuímos, atribuístes, atribuíram
Pluperfect: atribuíra, atribuíras, atribuíra, atribuíramos, atribuíreis, atribuíram
Present subjunctive: atribua, atribuas, atribua, atribuamos, atribuais, atribuam
Imperfect subjunctive: atribuísse, atribuísses, atribuísse,

atribuíssemos, atribuísseis,
atribuíssem
Future subjunctive: atribuir, atribuíres,
atribuir, atribuirmos, atribuirdes,
atribuírem
Personal infinitive: atribuir, atribuíres,
atribuir, atribuirmos, atribuirdes,
atribuírem
Present participle: atribuindo
Past participle: atribuído
Imperative: atribui, atribuí

proibir

Present: proíbo, proíbes, proíbe,
proibimos, proibis, proíbem
Present subjunctive: proíba, proíbas,
proíba, proibamos, proibais,
proíbam
Imperative: proíbe, proibi
Similarly: coibir

reunir

Present: reúno, reúnes, reúne,
reunimos, reunis, reúnem
Present subjunctive: reúna, reúnas,
reúna, reunamos, reunais, reúnam
Imperative: reúne, reuni

in **-struir** (e.g. **construir**) – like **atribuir**
except:

Present: construo, constróis/construis,
constrói/construi, construímos,
construís, constroem/construem
Imperative: constrói/construi, construí

in **-duzir** (e.g. **produzir**)

Present: produzo, produzes, produz,
produzimos, produzis, produzem
Imperative: produz(e), produzi
Similarly: luzir, reluzir

Irregular verbs

caber

Present: caibo, cabes, cabe, cabemos,
cabeis, cabem
Preterite: coube, coubeste, coube,
coubemos, coubestes, couberam
Pluperfect: coubera, couberas,
coubera, coubéramos, coubéreis,
couberam
Present subjunctive: caiba, caibas, caiba,
caibamos, caibais, caibam
Imperfect subjunctive: coubesse,
coubesses, coubesse, coubéssemos,
coubésseis, coubessem
Future subjunctive: couber, couberes,
couber, coubermos, couberdes,
couberem

dar

Present: dou, dás, dá, damos, dais, dão
Preterite: dei, deste, deu, demos,
destes, deram
Pluperfect: dera, deras, dera, déramos,
déreis, deram
Present subjunctive: dê, dês, dê, demos,
deis, deem
Imperfect subjunctive: desse, desses,
desse, déssemos, désseis, dessem
Future subjunctive: der, deres, der,
dermos, derdes, derem
Imperative: dá, dai

dizer

Present: digo, dizes, diz, dizemos,
dizeis, dizem
Future: direi, dirás, dirá, diremos,
direis, dirão
Preterite: disse, disseste, disse,
dissemos, dissestes, disseram
Pluperfect: dissera, disseras, dissera,
disséramos, disséreis, disseram
Present subjunctive: diga, digas, diga,
digamos, digais, digam

Imperfect subjunctive: dissesse, dissesses, dissesse, disséssemos, dissésseis, dissessem

Future subjunctive: disser, disseres, disser, dissermos, disserdes, disserem

Conditional: diria, dirias, diria, diríamos, diríeis, diriam

Present participle: dizendo

Past participle: dito

Imperative: diz, dizei

estar

Present: estou, estás, está, estamos, estais, estão

Preterite: estive, estiveste, esteve, estivemos, estivestes, estiveram

Pluperfect: estivera, estiveras, estivera, estivéramos, estivéreis, estiveram

Present subjunctive: esteja, estejas, esteja, estejamos, estejais, estejam

Imperfect subjunctive: estivesse, estivesses, estivesse, estivéssemos, estivésseis, estivessem

Future subjunctive: estiver, estiveres, estiver, estivermos, estiverdes, estiverem

Imperative: está, estai

fazer

Present: faço, fazes, faz, fazemos, fazeis, fazem

Future: farei, farás, fará, faremos, fareis, farão

Preterite: fiz, fizeste, fez, fizemos, fizestes, fizeram

Pluperfect: fizera, fizeras, fizera, fizéramos, fizéreis, fizeram

Present subjunctive: faça, faças, faça, façamos, façais, façam

Imperfect subjunctive: fizesse, fizesses, fizesse, fizéssemos, fizésseis, fizessem

Future subjunctive: fizer, fizeres, fizer, fizermos, fizerdes, fizerem

Conditional: faria, farias, faria, faríamos, faríeis, fariam

Present participle: fazendo

Past participle: feito

Imperative: faz(e), fazei

frigir

Present: frijo, freges, frege, frigimos, frigis, fregem

Present subjunctive: frija, frijas, frija, frijamos, frijais, frijam

Imperative: frege, frigi

haver

Present: hei, hás, há, hemos/havemos, haveis/heis, hão

Preterite: houve, houveste, houve, houvemos, houvestes, houveram

Pluperfect: houvera, houveras, houvera, houvéramos, houvéreis, houveram

Present subjunctive: haja, hajas, haja, hajamos, hajais, hajam

Imperfect subjunctive: houvesse, houvesses, houvesse, houvéssemos, houvésseis, houvessem

Future subjunctive: houver, houveres, houver, houvermos, houverdes, houverem

Imperative: há, havei

ir

Present: vou, vais, vai, vamos, ides, vão

Imperfect: ia, ias, ia, íamos, íeis, iam

Preterite: fui, foste, foi, fomos, fostes, foram

Pluperfect: fora, foras, fora, fôramos, fôreis, foram

Present subjunctive: vá, vás, vá, vamos, vades, vão

Imperfect subjunctive: fosse, fosses, fosse, fôssemos, fôsseis, fossem

Future subjunctive: for, fores, for, formos, fordes, forem

Present participle: indo
Past participle: ido
Imperative: vai, ide

ler

Present: leio, lês, lê, lemos, ledes, leem
Imperfect: lia, lias, lia, líamos, líeis, liam
Preterite: li, leste, leu, lemos, lestes, leram
Pluperfect: lera, leras, lera, lêramos, lêreis, leram
Present subjunctive: leia, leias, leia, leiamos, leiais, leiam
Imperfect subjunctive: lesse, lesses, lesse, lêssemos, lêsseis, lessem
Future subjunctive: ler, leres, ler, lermos, lerdes, lerem
Present participle: lendo
Past participle: lido
Imperative: lê, lede
Similarly: crer

odiar

Present: odeio, odeias, odeia, odiamos, odiais, odeiam
Present subjunctive: odeie, odeies, odeie, odiemos, odieis, odeiem
Imperative: odeia, odiai
Similarly: incendiar

ouvir

Present: ouço (P also: oiço), ouves, ouve, ouvimos, ouvis, ouvem
Present subjunctive: ouça, ouças, ouça, ouçamos, ouçais, ouçam (P also: oiça, oiças, oiça, oiçamos, oiçais, oiçam)

pedir

Present: peço, pedes, pede, pedimos, pedis, pedem
Present subjunctive: peça, peças, peça, peçamos, peçais, peçam
Similarly: despedir, impedir, medir

perder

Present: perco, perdes, perde, perdemos, perdeis, perdem
Present subjunctive: perca, percas, perca, percamos, percais, percam

poder

Present: posso, podes, pode, podemos, podeis, podem
Preterite: pude, pudeste, pôde, pudemos, pudestes, puderam
Pluperfect: pudera, puderas, pudera, pudéramos, pudéreis, puderam
Present subjunctive: possa, possas, possa, possamos, possais, possam
Imperfect subjunctive: pudesse, pudesses, pudesse, pudéssemos, pudésseis, pudessem
Future subjunctive: puder, puderes, puder, pudermos, puderdes, puderem

polir

Present: pulo, pules, pule, polimos, polis, pulem
Present subjunctive: pula, pulas, pula, pulamos, pulais, pulam
Imperative: pule, poli

pôr

Present: ponho, pões, põe, pomos, pondes, põem
Future: porei, porás, porá, poremos, poreis, porão
Imperfect: punha, punhas, punha, púnhamos, púnheis, punham
Preterite: pus, puseste, pôs, pusemos, pusestes, puseram
Pluperfect: pusera, puseras, pusera, puséramos, puséreis, puseram
Present subjunctive: ponha, ponhas, ponha, ponhamos, ponhais, ponham
Imperfect subjunctive: pusesse, pusesses, pusesse, puséssemos,

pusésseis, pusessem

Future subjunctive: puser, puseres, puser, pusermos, puserdes, puserem

Conditional: poria, porias, poria, poríamos, poríeis, poriam

Present participle: pondo

Past participle: posto

Imperative: põe, ponde

Similarly: compor, depor, dispor, opor, supor etc

prover

Present: provejo, provês, provê, provemos, provedes, proveem

Present subjunctive: proveja, provejas, proveja, provejamos, provejais, provejam

Imperative: provê, provede

querer

Present: quero, queres, quer, queremos, quereis, querem

Preterite: quis, quiseste, quis, quisemos, quisestes, quiseram

Pluperfect: quisera, quiseras, quisera, quiséramos, quiséreis, quiseram

Present subjunctive: queira, queiras, queira, queiramos, queirais, queiram

Imperfect subjunctive: quisesse, quisesses, quisesse, quiséssemos, quisésseis, quisessem

Future subjunctive: quiser, quiseres, quiser, quisermos, quiserdes, quiserem

Imperative: quer, querei

requerer

Present: requeiro, requeres, requer, requeremos, requereis, requerem

Present subjunctive: requeira, requeiras, requeira, requeiramos, requeirais, requeiram

Imperative: requer, requerei

rir

Present: rio, ris, ri, rimos, rides, riem

Present subjunctive: ria, rias, ria, riamos, riais, riam

Imperative: ri, ride

Similarly: sorrir

saber

Present: sei, sabes, sabe, sabemos, sabeis, sabem

Preterite: soube, soubeste, soube, soubemos, soubestes, souberam

Pluperfect: soubera, souberas, soubera, soubéramos, soubéreis, souberam

Present subjunctive: saiba, saibas, saiba, saibamos, saibais, saibam

Imperfect subjunctive: soubesse, soubesses, soubesse, soubéssemos, soubésseis, soubessem

Future subjunctive: souber, souberes, souber, soubermos, souberdes, souberem

Imperative: sabe, sabei

ser

Present: sou, és, é, somos, sois, são

Imperfect: era, eras, era, éramos, éreis, eram

Preterite: fui, foste, foi, fomos, fostes, foram

Pluperfect: fora, foras, fora, fôramos, fôreis, foram

Present subjunctive: seja, sejas, seja, sejamos, sejais, sejam

Imperfect subjunctive: fosse, fosses, fosse, fôssemos, fôsseis, fossem

Future subjunctive: for, fores, for, formos, fordes, forem

Present participle: sendo

Past participle: sido

Imperative: sê, sede

ter

Present: tenho, tens, tem, temos, tendes, têm

Imperfect: tinha, tinhas, tinha, tínhamos, tínheis, tinham
Preterite: tive, tiveste, teve, tivemos, tivestes, tiveram
Pluperfect: tivera, tiveras, tivera, tivéramos, tivéreis, tiveram
Present subjunctive: tenha, tenhas, tenha, tenhamos, tenhais, tenham
Imperfect subjunctive: tivesse, tivesses, tivesse, tivéssemos, tivésseis, tivessem
Future subjunctive: tiver, tiveres, tiver, tivermos, tiverdes, tiverem
Present participle: tendo
Past participle: tido
Imperative: tem, tende

trazer

Present: trago, trazes, traz, trazemos, trazeis, trazem
Future: trarei, trarás, trará, traremos, trareis, trarão
Preterite: trouxe, trouxeste, trouxe, trouxemos, trouxestes, trouxeram
Pluperfect: trouxera, trouxeras, trouxera, trouxéramos, trouxéreis, trouxeram
Present subjunctive: traga, tragas, traga, tragamos, tragais, tragam
Imperfect subjunctive: trouxesse, trouxesses, trouxesse, trouxéssemos, trouxésseis, trouxessem
Future subjunctive: trouxer, trouxeres, trouxer, trouxermos, trouxerdes, trouxerem
Conditional: traria, trarias, traria, traríamos, traríeis, trariam
Imperative: traze, trazei

valer

Present: valho, vales, vale, valemos, valeis, valem
Present subjunctive: valha, valhas, valha, valhamos, valhais, valham

ver

Present: vejo, vês, vê, vemos, vedes, veem
Imperfect: via, vias, via, víamos, víeis, viam
Preterite: vi, viste, viu, vimos, vistes, viram
Pluperfect: vira, viras, vira, víramos, víreis, viram
Present subjunctive: veja, vejas, veja, vejamos, vejais, vejam
Imperfect subjunctive: visse, visses, visse, víssemos, vísseis, vissem
Future subjunctive: vir, vires, vir, virmos, virdes, virem
Present participle: vendo
Past participle: visto
Imperative: vê, vede

vir

Present: venho, vens, vem, vimos, vindes, vêm
Imperfect: vinha, vinhas, vinha, vínhamos, vínheis, vinham
Preterite: vim, vieste, veio, viemos, viestes, vieram
Pluperfect: viera, vieras, viera, viéramos, viéreis, vieram
Present subjunctive: venha, venhas, venha, venhamos, venhais, venham
Imperfect subjunctive: viesse, viesses, viesse, viéssemos, viésseis, viessem
Future subjunctive: vier, vieres, vier, viermos, vierdes, vierem
Present participle: vindo
Past participle: vindo
Imperative: vem, vinde

Verbos irregulares ingleses

Infinitivo	Pretérito	Particípio passado	Infinitivo	Pretérito	Particípio passado
be	was	been	**drive**	drove	driven
bear	bore	borne	**eat**	ate	eaten
beat	beat	beaten	**fall**	fell	fallen
become	became	become	**feed**	fed	fed
begin	began	begun	**feel**	felt	felt
bend	bent	bent	**fight**	fought	fought
bet	bet, betted	bet, betted	**find**	found	found
			flee	fled	fled
bid	bade, bid	bidden, bid	**fly**	flew	flown
bind	bound	bound	**freeze**	froze	frozen
bite	bit	bitten	**get**	got	got, gotten US
bleed	bled	bled	**give**	gave	given
blow	blew	blown	**go**	went	gone
break	broke	broken	**grow**	grew	grown
breed	bred	bred	**hang**	hung, hanged	hung, hanged
bring	brought	brought			
build	built	built	**have**	had	had
burn	burnt, burned	burnt, burned	**hear**	heard	heard
			hide	hid	hidden
burst	burst	burst	**hit**	hit	hit
buy	bought	bought	**hold**	held	held
catch	caught	caught	**hurt**	hurt	hurt
choose	chose	chosen	**keep**	kept	kept
cling	clung	clung	**kneel**	knelt	knelt
come	came	come	**know**	knew	known
cost	cost, costed (vt)	cost, costed	**lay**	laid	laid
			lead	led	led
cut	cut	cut	**lean**	leaned, leant	leaned, leant
deal	dealt	dealt			
dig	dug	dug	**learn**	learnt, learned	learnt, learned
do	did	done			
draw	drew	drawn	**leave**	left	left
dream	dreamt, dreamed	dreamt, dreamed	**lend**	lent	lent
			let	let	let
drink	drank	drunk	**lie**	lay	lain

Infinitivo	Pretérito	Particípio passado	Infinitivo	Pretérito	Particípio passado
lose	lost	lost	**spend**	spent	spent
make	made	made	**spit**	spat	spat
mean	meant	meant	**spoil**	spoilt,	spoilt,
meet	met	met		spoiled	spoiled
pay	paid	paid	**spread**	spread	spread
put	put	put	**spring**	sprang	sprung
read	read	read	**stand**	stood	stood
ride	rode	ridden	**steal**	stole	stolen
ring	rang	rung	**stick**	stuck	stuck
rise	rose	risen	**sting**	stung	stung
run	ran	run	**stride**	strode	stridden
say	said	said	**strike**	struck	struck
see	saw	seen	**swear**	swore	sworn
seek	sought	sought	**sweep**	swept	swept
sell	sold	sold	**swell**	swelled	swollen,
send	sent	sent			swelled
set	set	set			
sew	sewed	sewn, sewed	**swim**	swam	swum
shake	shook	shaken	**swing**	swung	swung
shine	shone	shone	**take**	took	taken
shoe	shod	shod	**teach**	taught	taught
shoot	shot	shot	**tear**	tore	torn
show	showed	shown	**tell**	told	told
shut	shut	shut	**think**	thought	thought
sing	sang	sung	**throw**	threw	thrown
sink	sank	sunk	**thrust**	thrust	thrust
sit	sat	sat	**tread**	trod	trodden
sleep	slept	slept	**under-**	**under-**	understood
sling	slung	slung	**stand**	stood	
smell	smelt,	smelt,	**wake**	woke	woken
	smelled	smelled	**wear**	wore	worn
speak	spoke	spoken	**win**	won	won
spell	spelled,	spelled,	**write**	wrote	written
	spelt	spelt			